Arabic Morphology and Phonology

Arabic Morphology and Phonology

Based on the Marāḥ al-arwāḥ
by Aḥmad b. ʿAī b. Masʿūd

By

Joyce Åkesson

BRILL

LEIDEN | BOSTON

This paperback was originally published in hardback under ISBN 90 04 12028 9 in the series *Studies in Semitic Languages and Linguistics*, volume 35, 2001.

Library of Congress Cataloging-in-Publication Data

Ibn Mas'ud, Ahmad ibn 'Ali, 13th cent.
[Marāḥ al-arwāh. English & Arabic]
Arabic morphology and phonology : based on the Marāḥ al-arwāh by Aḥmad b. 'Aī b. Mas'ūd / presented with an introduction, Arabic edition, English translation and commentary by Joyce Åkesson.
p. cm. — (Studies in Semitic languages and linguistics, ISSN 0081-8461 ; v. 35)
Includes bibliographical references and indexes.
ISBN 9004120289 (alk. paper)
1. Arabic language—Morphology—Early works to 1800. 2. Arabic language—Verb—Early works to 1800. 3. Arabic language—Morphology. 4. Arabic language—Verb.. I. Åkesson, Joyce. II. Title. III. series.

PJ6131 .I23613 2000
492.7'5—dc21 00-050729
CIP

ISBN 978-90-04-34694-9 (paperback, 2017)
ISBN 978-90-04-34757-1 (e-book)
ISBN 90 04 12028 9 (hardback, 2001)

This book is printed on acid-free paper and produced in a sustainable manner.

CONTENTS

Preface IX

PART ONE

I. Introduction
§ 1 The Background: Works on Morphology 3
§ 2 Aḥmad b ʿAlī b Masʿūd 7
§ 3 The Commentaries 9
§ 4 The Manuscripts of the *Marāḥ* 13
§ 5 The Printed texts of the *Marāḥ* 14
§ 6 The Principles of Edition 15
§ 7 Topics in works dealing with morphology 24
§ 8 A general Introduction to the *Marāḥ* 27

II. Arabic Text, Translation and Commentary
II.1 Arabic Text: المقدّمة 38
II.1 Translation: Introduction 39
II.1.1 Commentary: Introduction 40
II.2 Arabic Text: الباب الأوّل في لصحيح 48
II.2 Translation: The 1st Chapter is about the Strong Verb 49
§ 1 فصل في الماضي 54
§ 1 The perfect 55
§ 2 فصل في المستقبل 66
§ 2 The imperfect 67
§ 3 فصل في الأمر والنهي 72
§ 3 The imperative and the prohibition 73
§ 4 فصل في اسم الفاعل 80
§ 4 The active participle 81
§ 5 فصل في اسم المفعول 86
§ 5 The passive participle 87
§ 6 فصل في اسم الزمان والمكان 88
§ 6 The nouns of time and place 89
§ 7 فصل في اسم الآلة 90
§ 7 The noun of instrument 91
II.2.1 Commentary: The Strong Verb 92

Part Two

II.3 Arabic Text: الباب الثاني في المضاعف. 194
II.3 Translation: The 2nd Chapter is about the Doubled Verb 195
II.3.1 Commentary: The Doubled Verb 204

II.4 Arabic Text: الباب الثالث في المهموز 240
II.4 Translation: The 3rd Chapter is about the Hamzated Verb 241
II.4.1 Commentary: The Hamzated Verb 250

II.5 Arabic Text: الباب الرابع في المثال 270
II.5 Translation: The 4th Chapter is about the Verb with Weak 1st Radical 271
II.5.1 Commentary: The Verb with Weak 1st Radical 274

II.6 Arabic Text: الباب الخامس في الأجوف. 282
II.6 Translation: The 5th Chapter is about the Verb with Weak 2nd Radical 283
II.6.1 Commentary: The Verb with Weak 2nd Radical 296

II.7 Arabic Text: الباب السادس في الناقص 326
II.7 Translation: The 6th Chapter is about the Verb with Weak 3rd Radical 327
II.7.1 Commentary: The Verb with Weak 3rd Radical 336

II.8 Arabic Text: الباب السابع في اللفيف. 372
II.8 Translation: The 7th Chapter is about the Verb that is doubly Weak 373
II.8.1 Commentary: The Verb that is doubly Weak 376

III. Bibliographical references 380
III.1 Primary sources 380
§ 1 Manuscripts used 380
§ 2 Printed texts used 380
§ 3 Literature 380
III.2 Secondary sources 386

IV. Abbreviations 393
§ 1 Abbreviations of terms 393
§ 2 Abbreviations of titles 393

V. Indices 395
§ 1 Index of Qur'anic quotations in the *Marāḥ* 395
§ 2 Index of verse quotations in the *Marāḥ* 396
§ 3 Index of names in the *Marāḥ* 397
§ 4 Index of examples in the *Marāḥ* 398
§ 5 Index of Qur'anic quotations in the Introduction and Commentary 407
§ 6 Index of Qur'anic readers in the Introduction and Commentary 410
§ 7 Index of verse quotations in the Commentary 411
§ 8 Index of poets in the Commentary 414

§ 9 Index of peoples, tribes, leaders, celebrities, schools, places, languages and deities in the Introduction and Commentary 415

§ 10 Index of authors and titles in the Introduction and Commentary 418

§ 11 Glossary and subject-index of the Commentary 426

PREFACE

Writing this book has been a very thrilling and rewarding experience. This is partly due to my passion for the field of Arabic morpho-phonology which made me venture into and even beyond its various disciplines, and to the support that I have received from different persons.

This study comes after my book, Ibn Masʿūd, *Marāḥ I,* which deals with the strong verb, that has been published some ten years ago. After it I embarked on preparing the second part of the work, which is a study of the doubled, the hamzated and the weak verbs. The more I studied books in this field, the more I realized that the collected results of my research could, when properly systematized, represent a sort of "comprehensive" study of the Arabic morphophonology with its two main topics: on the one hand a presentation of the morphological forms, and on the other, a study of the phonological rules and theories that led to their making. This incited me in presenting together in this work the strong verb, the doubled, the hamzated and the weak verbs. The above mentioned Part I studied in this volume embodies many substantial additions, and can therefore be considered as an altogether different work from the earlier published book. Furthermore, references are made to the published book in those parts that have been studied more in detail there. The entire present study presented here grew to become more than just an Edition, Introduction, Translation and Commentary of Ibn Maʿūd's *Marāh.* It is both a convenient introduction to a specific Arabic text in morpho-phonology of the 13th century A.D.,—and even before this period—, and to the field of morpho-phonology in general with its basics and intricacies; and since no other Arabic text in morpho-phonology has been published in modern times with an English translation and a comprehensive commentary, it is my hope that it will be of use for the readers.

Ibn Maʿūd's *Marāh* can be regarded as the fruit of some six centuries of studies in morphophonology. At the time of Ibn Masʿūd's living, as I established it to be sometime between the 2nd half of the 7th/13th and the beginning of the 8th/14th century, Arabic grammar has reached its climax through a succession of distinguished and original Arab grammarians.

The *Marāḥ,* which we have have here between our hands, is concise but still comprehensive, and so demands for its understanding a vast literature. During these years of intensive research I was impelled to use various linguistic works, such as lexicons, grammars compiled by both Arabs and Arabists, works on Arabic morphology, syntax, linguistic principles and theories, debates between the grammatical "schools", sessions between different Arabic grammarians, qurʾanical readings, poetry, and many other topics. I have as well interested myself in a few well-known works on the comparative grammar of the Semitic languages. References to them are integrated whenever I felt them to be relevant. My ambition has been constantly to integrate as many works as possible relating to this field, my belief being that it is necessary to consult many sources to become familiar with the subject, and my contention that the matters treated by these eminent researchers all merit our respectful interest and attention.

The *Marāḥ* is divided into seven chapters. The first one focuses on the study of the strong verb, the second one on the doubled, the third one on the hamzated, the fourth one on the verb with weak 1st radical, the fifth one on the verb with weak 2nd radical, the sixth one on the verb with 3rd weak radical and the seventh one on the verb that is doubly weak. Each of these chapters presents as well the *maṣdar* of the characteristic class of verb and its nine derivatives specified to be: the perfect, the imperfect, the imperative and the prohibition, the active participle, the passive participle and the nouns of time, place and instrument.

The present volume covers five main parts: the Introduction, the Arabic Edition accompanied with the English Translation and the Commentary, and the Indices.

As previously indicated in my first book's preface, the present Edition has been restricted to the oldest manuscripts of the Bibliothèque Nationale and to two printed texts from the University of Cairo. MS A is the basic manuscript of my Edition. Editing principles have been kept simple with only some adopted conventions necessary to present a correct Arabic text. Whenever I remarked by comparing with the other MSS and two prints, that trifling slips of the pen occurred in MS A, such as grammatical errors, errors of spelling, missing or misplaced added words affecting the context's correctness or its sense, I corrected these errors, supplied the missing word or elided the misplaced added one directly in my Arabic text. I have pointed to the deficiency in the Apparatus and referred to the source or sources of the adapted variant or variants. The original page numbers of the MS A are included in the margin. Poetical lines are presented between double guillemets "" and Qur'anic verses between brackets (). I have also furnished the Arabic section with comprehensive indices.

The English Translation alongside the Arabic text and the translations of the Arabic extracts in the Introduction and Commentary do not aim to be more literal than the original ones. They may seem unidiomatic for some because of a desire to stay as close as possible to the Arabic texts. I have, in cases of enumerations, and in order to clarify for the reader, divided the long texts into sections and in many instances I have numbered them. I have tried to use short sentences, and I have added explanations between straight brackets [] whenever I judged them as being necessary for the understanding of the context. The attribution to the different qur'anical suras and the indication of the different morphological forms are included as well by me between straight brackets.

Each word or passage in the Translation that is commented on in the Commentary is followed by a number between brackets.

The Commentary is arranged by numbered sections, most of which consist of one or more paragraphs. The numbering refers to the English Translation, separates different topics from each other, facilitates cross-reference, and hopefully, gives a certain order and structure to the work. The sub-paragraphs are introduced by letters. They contain mostly additional material connected in some manner with the basic topics.

When dealing in the Commentary with so many autorities, some of whom necessarily influenced Ibn Masʿūd, it became essential in the Introduction to provide the reader with a general background that introduces them and their works briefly, and that touches on some general questions, such as a few essential themes found in works of morphology, which I consider as important for the study of the *Marāḥ* in particular and for other works of this character in general.

The Commentary does what it can do to clarify most of the issues emerging in the *Marāh* and inspired by it, by integrating in some details the opinions of important researchers chosen before and after the compilation. It is necessary to specify that I do not discuss all the opinions concerning a special topic, but that I usually select the one or ones which I consider as the most representative. If for instance one of the well-known exploiters of the Arabic inheritance: Zamaḫšarī, Ibn Yaʿīš, Ibn Mālik, Badraddīn, Howell or Wright is referred to for a topic, this does not imply usually that this authority is its inventor, but that he/she has been chosen for explaining best an issue that is existent in the *Marāh* or that is inspired by it. Naturally, the older the grammarian is the more original the theory is, and philologists such as Sībawaihī, Ibn Fāris, al-Zağğāğī and Ibn Ğinnī can be considered mostly as founders. It is also important to mention that if many linguists are referred to, this does not mean that they all treated the question in the same manner. Some developed this special topic more than others by shedding new lights on it, whereas others summarized and introduced new topics demanding further inquiries, which I also tried mostly to integrate in the study.

Ibn Masʿūd's presentation of the morphological forms is concise and his examples are limited to the most important ones. This makes me believe that his book's function was at first meant to be pedagogical and that the group to which he adressed himself to was the majority. In such cases I have felt impelled to develop a little more the study of the forms by referring to other grammarians who have dealt with them more exhaustively. I have as well supplied paradigms whenever I felt it to be appropriate. Likewise, whenever I felt that important definitions, rules and processes were required, and that other controversies were involved, I have tried to present them, and in most cases, also develop them as clearly as possible. Important themes such as the arguments of the Basrans and the Kufans concerning the question of the origin of the derivation of the *maṣdar* or the verb, the reasons of the declension or the undeclinability of the noun, verb and particle in Arabic, the reasons why a certain vowel is chosen to mark a specific form, the controversies concerning the *ʾafʿal* of superiority in the forms indicative of colours, subjects relating to syntax and to some linguistic theories, a few discussions raised in some of the grammarians' sessions, are only some examples of the topics which are presented and discussed in this work. I have as well and as frequently as possible, integrated quotations from various Arabic sources, ancient as well as modern, which I have as well translated. Quotations from Western sources are not neglected either. The intention with this material is to provide general background information in the field of morpho-phonology, to present a lively picture of the linguistic thinking, and to enable the reader to study these passages in their contexts, verify the advanced statements and hopefully, be stimulated for further investigations.

Qur'anical quotations in the English sections are inserted between brackets and are attributed to the suras and verses of *The Holy Qurʾān* edited by Yusuf Ali.

Verses of poetry are identified by reference to some of their various sources. It is my hope that they bring out, beside the linguistic feature for which they have been chosen, some of the poets' special topics, interests, experiences and spiritual aspirations, so as to provide the reader with insight into the Arabic culture.

The English section has as well been rounded off with extensive indices, which facilitate the use of the book. Most of the discussed matters in the Translation and in the Commentary are mentioned and referred to by their paragraph's numbering in the section Glossary and subject-index of the Commentary. Numbers followed by letters there refer only to the subparagraphs found in the Commentary. They contain mostly additional material connected in some manner with the basic topics. I trust that this index will be of use in practice since it contains most of the topics that are treated in the field of morpho-phonology and should enable the reader to find readily those themes dealing with the topics that interest him. The Arabic examples used in the *Marāḥ*, the Qurʾanic quotations, verses of poetry, grammarians, tribes, Qurʾanic readers, peoples, schools, places, languages, dialects, referred to in the *Marāḥ* or in my Introduction and Commentary, or in both, are enclosed in separate indices.

I am indebted to the personnel of the Bibliothèque Nationale, Paris, who have facilitated my labour in every respect during the summers of 1986 and 1987 when I was studying the Manuscripts of the *Marāh* preserved there. I am as well grateful to the University of Cairo who went to the trouble of sending me the copies of some printed texts of the *Marāh*.

I have as well appreciated the criticisms and comments of distinguished authorities, some who have helped me by writing constructive reviews of my previous book.

I would like to offer my appreciation and gratitude to Professor Gösta Vitestam of the Department of Middle East Languages at Lund University. It is he who has directed my attention to both Ibn Masʿūd's *Marāh* and to Dunqūze's *Šarḥ al-marāḥ*, and who has kindly initiated the project of studying the fascinating field of Arabic morpho-phonology some seventeen years ago. He has helped me and encouraged me at various stages of my research with his enthusiasm, kindness, sensitivity, witty remarks and suggestions.

I am very thankful to the late Prof. Tryggve Kronholm, Department of Asian and African Languages of the University of Uppsala, for many inspiring and valuable discussions.

I owe much gratitude to Prof. Kees Versteegh, Nijmegen University, who kindly read two versions of this work, and offered me his invaluable insights, suggestions, criticism and references to important literature. I thank him very much as well for his willingness in including the work in the series Studies in Semitic Languages and Linguistics.

I extend my heartfelt thanks to Mrs Trudy Kamperveen, Editor of the Middle East and Islamic Studies and Mr. Jan Fehrmann, Editor of the Islamic and Asian Studies Department of E.J. Brill, for their untiring cooperation.

Last but not least, my family and friends deserves my deepest gratitude. They have all shared my dreams and encouraged me with their affectionate support. My parents, Mounir Hakim and Irene Egeland, have always stressed the value of education and different cultures. My brother, James Hakim, and his family and my parents in-law, Carl-Eric and Ellen Åkesson, have always been encouraging and enthusiastic. My husband, Ph. D. Anders Åkesson, and our son, Filip, have been very caring, helpful and understanding. It is to them that I dedicate this book.

Needless to say, the errors, oversights and infelicities are entirely my own.

Lund, August 2000

PART ONE

I. INTRODUCTION

§ 1. The Background: Works on Morphology

The study of الصرف "morphology" independently from النحو "syntax" occurred before the *Marāḥ al-arwāḥ,* even if it was not very common, as most of the grammarians considered the *Kitāb* of Sībawaihī (d. 177/793),[1] which embraced both fields while still distinguishing them from each other, a model which they followed in their works.

The study of morphology alone seems to have been introduced in Kūfa by the Kufan grammarian Abū l-Ḥasan Aḥmad[2] who wrote the *Kitāb al-taṣrīf.* It was then treated by ʿAlī b. al-Ḥasan al-Aḥmar (d. 194/809)[3] in his book *al-Taṣrīf,*[4] by al-Farrāʾ (d. 207/822)[5] in his book with the same title,[6] and by al-Aḫfaš al-Awsaṭ (d. 215/830 or 225/839)[7] in his book with the same title as well.[8] It was further developed by the Basran grammarians Abū ʿUmar al-Ǧarmī (d. 225/839)[9] who wrote the *Kitāb al-abniya wa l-taṣrīf,* Abū ʿUṯmān al-Māzinī (d. 249/862)[10]

---

[1] Sībawaihi, ʿAmr b. ʿUṯmān b. Qanbar, see Suyūṭī, *Buġya II,* 229-230, Zubaidī, *Ṭabaqāt* 66-72, Brockelmann, *GAL I,* 99-100, *S I,* 160, Sezgin, *Geschichte IX,* 51-63. He was the pupil of al-Ḫalīl. His work *al-Kitāb* can be considered as one of the first monuments in Arabic prose (Troupeau, *Lexique* 8). Concerning him, Roman, *Étude* 43 remarks:

> "Sībawaihi, apparaît, dans le livre qu'il a signé, comme l'observateur le plus fin des faits de langue et comme l'inventeur admirable d'une organisation de ces faits organisés par lui dans la mesure où sa critériologie autorisait une systématisation des faits observés...".

For an idea of the citations referring to ancient grammarians in *al-Kitāb* see Troupeau, *Grammairiens* 309-311; for an idea of the formation of the Arabic grammatical terminology see Troupeau, *Lexique* 12 sqq., Versteegh, *Grammar* 2-9; for discussions concerning some defective constructions see Yāqūt, *Tarākīb* 77-110.

[2] According to Ibn al-Nadīm, *Fihrist* 66, he was a pupil of al-Ruʾāsī (Muḥammad b. al-Ḥasan b. Abī Sāra, the teacher of al-Kisāʾī and of al-Farrāʾ, see for him Suyūṭī, *Buġya I,* 82-83, Sezgin, *Geschichte IX,* 125-126) and studied well the teachings of the famous Kufan grammarian al-Kisāʾī.

[3] ʿAlī b. al-Ḥasan, he was also named Ibn al-Mubārak and was known as al-Aḥmar the šaiḫ of the Arabic language and the friend of al-Kisāʾī. Beside his work in morphology, he wrote *Tafattun al-bulaġāʾ.* For him see Suyūṭī, *Buġya II,* 158-159, Sezgin, *Geschichte VIII,* 118-119. He is not to be mixed up with Ḫalaf al-Aḥmar d. 180/796.

[4] Cf. Qifṭī, *Inbāh IV,* 104, Suyūṭī, *Buġya II,* 159.

[5] Al-Farrāʾ, Yaḥyā b. Ziyād, see Suyūṭī, *Buġya II,* 333, Ibn al-Anbārī, *Nuzha* 134, Yāqūt, *Muʿǧam XX,* 9, Zubaidī, *Ṭabaqāt* 131-133, Brockelmann, *GAL I,* 118, *S I,* 178-179, Sezgin, *Geschichte VIII,* 123-125, *IX,* 131-134. He studied under both al-Kisāʾī and Yūnus. He wrote *Maʿānī l-qurʾān, al-Luġāt, al-Maṣādir fī l-qurʾān, al-Ǧamʿ wa l-taṯniya fī l-qurʾān, al-Nawādir, al-Maqṣūr wa l-mamdūd, Faʿala wa-afʿala, al-Muḏakkar wa l-muʾannaṯ* and other works.

[6] The book is referred to by Sezgin, *Geschichte IX,* 133. A reference to it is given in a discussion concerning the reading of بِمُصْرِخِيَّ in the sur. 14: 22 (وَمَا أَنْتُمْ بِمُصْرِخِيَّ) "Nor can ye listen to mine [cries]". Ḥamza chose to vowel its 2nd *y* with a kasra, i.e. بِمُصْرِخِيِّ while the remaining readers vowelled it with a fatḥa. It is on this occasion that Abū ʿAlī said: "Al-Farrāʾ said in his book *al-Taṣrīf...* " (cf. Baġdādī, *Ḫizāna II,* 259, Hindāwī, *Manāhiǧ* 66).

[7] Al-Aḫfaš al-Awsaṭ, Saʿīd b. Masʿada, see Sīrāfī, *Aḫbār* 50-52, Suyūṭī, *Buġya I,* 590-591, Zubaidī, *Ṭabaqāt* 72-74, Ibn al-Anbārī, *Nuzha* 185, Qifṭī, *Inbāh II,* 36, Brockelmann, *GAL I,* 104-105, *S I,* 165, Sezgin, *Geschichte VIII,* 80, *IX,* 68-69. He wrote *Maʿānī l-qurʾān, al-Maqāyīs fī l-naḥw, al-Ištiqāq, al-Masāʾil* and other works.

[8] The book is referred to by Qifṭī, *Inbāh II,* 42, Hindāwī, *Manāhiǧ* 66-67, Sezgin, *Geschichte IX,* 69.

[9] Abū ʿUmar al-Ǧarmī, Ṣāliḥ b. Isḥāq, see Sīrāfī, *Aḫbār* 72-74, Suyūṭī, *Buġya II,* 8-9, Zubaidī, *Ṭabaqāt* 74-75, Brockelmann, *GAL I,* 108, Sezgin, *Geschichte IX,* 72-73. He studied grammar under al-Aḫfaš and Yūnus and the lexicon under al-Aṣmaʿī. Beside his work mentioned in morphology, he wrote *al-Tanbīh, Kitāb al-ʿArūḍ, Muḫtaṣar fī l-naḥw, Ġarīb Sībawaihi* and other works.

[10] Al-Māzinī, Abū ʿUṯmān Bakr b. Muḥammad b. Baqīya, see Suyūṭī, *Buġya I,* 463-466, Yāqūt, *Muʿǧam VII,*

who wrote the *Kitāb al-taṣrīf,* al-Mubarrad (d. 285/898)[11] who wrote *al-taṣrīf*[12] or *al-taṣārīf*[13] al-Rummānī (d. 384/994)[14] who wrote the *Kitāb al-taṣrīf,*[15] and later, the Baghdadian grammarians Abū ʿAlī l-Fārisī (d. 377/987)[16] who wrote *al-Takmila*[17] and Ibn Ǧinnī (d. 393/1002)[18] who wrote the *Muḫtaṣar al-taṣrīf al-mulūkī,*[19] *al-Munṣif fī šarḥ taṣrīf al-Māzinī* and the *Sirr ṣināʿat al-iʿrāb.*

A new discipline was now established, and among the well-known grammarians treating the subject of morphology before Aḥmad b. ʿAlī b. Masʿūd who was active during the 2nd half of the 7th/13th century or the beginning of the 8th/14th century, the following ones can be mentioned: al-Muʾaddib (who lived during the 4th century/10th century)[20] who wrote the *Daqāʾiq*

107, Baġdādī, *Tārīḫ VII,* 93-94, Luġawī, *Marātib* 126-129, Qifṭī, *Inbāh I,* 246-256, Sīrāfī, *Aḫbār* 74-85, Ibn Ǧinnī, *Munṣif III,* 313-343, Zubaidī, *Ṭabaqāt* 87-93, Brockelmann, *GAL I,* 108, *S I,* 168, Sezgin, *Geschichte VIII,* 92, *IX,* 75-76. He studied under al-Aḫfaš. Beside his work mentioned in morphology, he wrote *ʿIlal al-naḥw, Tafāsīr kitāb Sībawaihi, al-Alif wa l-lām* and other works. It can be mentioned that he admired greatly the *Kitāb* of Sībawaihi. According to Sīrāfī, *Aḫbār* 50, he is mentioned as having said:

"مَن أراد أن يعمل كبيرا في النحو بعد كتاب سيبويه فليستحي."

"Let him be ashamed, he who wanted to achieve something great in grammar after Sıbawaihi!".

[11] Al-Mubarrad, Muḥammad b. Yazīd, see Sīrāfī, *Aḫbār* 96-108, Suyūṭī, *Buġya I,* 269-271, Zubaidī, *Ṭabaqāt* 101-110, Ibn al-Anbārī, *Nuzha* 279, Brockelmann, *GAL I,* 109-110, *S I,* 168-169, Sezgin, *Geschichte VIII,* 98, *IX,* 78-80, Bernards, *Traditions* 19-37. He studied under al-Māzinī and al-Siǧistānī. He put Sībawaihi on a pedestal with his works *Kitāb al-madḫal ilā Sībawaihi, Kitāb maʿnā kitāb Sībawaihi* and *Kitāb al-radd ʿalā Sībawaihi.* Alike al-Māzinī and other grammarians, he admired the *Kitāb* of Sībawaihi. According to Sīrāfī, *Aḫbār* 50 and Suyūṭī, *Buġya II,* 229, he used to say to the one who wanted to study it: ! هل ركبت البحر "Have you traversed the sea!". Concerning his own book *Kitāb al-radd ʿalā Sībawaihi,* Bernards, *Ǧarmī* 40 mentions that he brought forward 130 grammatical issues on which he disagreed with Sībawaihi. However, he is reported by Ibn Ǧinnī, *Ḫaṣāʾiṣ I,* 206 as having changed his mind when he grew older and wiser as what was transmitted by his close friend Ibn al-Sarrāǧ. For discussions concerning al-Mubarrad's role in the transmission of *al-Kitāb* see Versteegh, *Grammar* 13-14, Bernards, *Traditions* 90-93. Al-Mubarrad wrote as well *Maʿānī l-qurʾān, al-Kāmil, al-Muqtaḍab, al-Maqṣūr wa l-mamdūd, al-Ištiqāq, Iʿrāb al-qurʾān, Šarḥ šawāhid al-kitāb* and other works.

[12] Cf. Qifṭī, *Inbāh III,* 252.

[13] Cf. Ibn Ḫair, *Fihrist* 312.

[14] Al-Rummānī, ʿAlī b. ʿĪsā b. ʿAlī b. ʿAbdallāh, see Suyūṭī, *Buġya II,* 180-181, Brockelmann, *G I,* 113, *S I,* 175, Sezgin, *Geschichte IX,* 111-113. He studied under al-Zaǧǧāǧ and Ibn al-Sarrāǧ. He wrote *al-Tafsīr, Šarḥ uṣūl Ibn al-Sarrāǧ, Šarḥ Sībawaihi, Šarḥ muḫtaṣar al-Ǧarmī, Šarḥ al-alif wa l-lām li-l-Māzinī, Šarḥ al-Muqtaḍab, Šarḥ al-ṣifāt, Maʿānī l-ḥurūf* and other works.

[15] It is referred to by Sezgin, *Geschichte IX,* 112.

[16] Abū ʿAlī l-Fārisī, al-Ḥasan b. Aḥmad b. ʿAbd al-Ġaffār, see Baġdādī, *Tārīḫ VII,* 275-276, Qifṭī, *Inbāh I,* 273-275, Suyūṭī, *Buġya I,* 496-498, Ibn Ǧinnī, *Munṣif III,* 344-346, Brockelmann, *S I,* 175, Sezgin, *Geschichte VIII,* 109-110, *IX,* 101-110. He studied under al-Zaǧǧāǧ and Ibn al-Sarrāǧ. Among his brilliant pupils, Ibn Ǧinnī and ʿAlī b. ʿĪsā al-Rabaʿī can be mentioned. He wrote *Abyāt al-iʿrāb, Taʿlīqa ʿalā kitāb Sībawaihi, al-Maqṣūr wa l-mamdūd* and other works.

[17] Cf. Qifṭī, *Inbāh I,* 274, 387, Suyūṭī, *Buġya I,* 496.

[18] Ibn Ǧinnī, Abū l-Fatḥ ʿUṯmān, see Baġdādī, *Tārīḫ XI,* 311-312, Suyūṭī, *Buġya II,* 132, Yāqūt, *Muʿǧam XII,* 81-115, Ibn al-ʿImād, *Šaḏarāt II,* 140-141, Ibn Tiġribirdī, *Nuǧūm IV,* 205, Ibn Ǧinnī, *Munṣif III,* 347-350, Brockelmann, *GAL I,* 131, *S I,* 191-193, Méhiri, *Théories* 19-86, Sezgin, *Geschichte IX,* 173-182. He studied under Abū ʿAlī al-Fārisī. Beside these mentioned works, he wrote *al-Ḫaṣāʾiṣ fī l-naḥw, Šarḥ al-maqṣūr wa l-mamdūd, al-Lumaʿ fī l-naḥw, al-Muḏakkar wa l-muʾannaṯ, Maḥāsin al-ʿarabīya* and other works.

[19] It was edited and translated into Latin by G. Hoberg in Ibn Ǧinnī, *de Flexione.* An Arabic edition by M. Saʿīd b. Muṣṭafa al-Naʿsān, Cairo 1913, exists as well (cf. Sezgin, *Geschichte IX,* 178).

[20] We do not know anything about al-Qāsim b. Muḥammad b. Saʿīd al-Muʾaddib except that he is the author of this important work in morphology, that he was one of the learned of the 4th century, and that he was the pupil of al-Haiṯam b. Kulaib al-Šāšī (d. 330) in the provins of al-Šāš (see the introduction written by the editors of his work Muʾaddib, *Taṣrīf* 8).

al-taṣrīf,[21] al-Maidānī (d. 518/1124)[22] who wrote the *Nuzhat al-ṭarf fī ʿilm al-ṣarf,*[23] Ibn Yaʿīš (d. 642/1245)[24] who wrote the *Šarḥ al-mulūkī,* Ibn al-Ḥāǧib (d. 646/1249)[25] who wrote the *Šāfiya,* al-Zanǧānī (d. 654/1256-57)[26] who wrote the *Kitāb al-ʿIzzī,*[27] Ibn ʿUṣfūr (d. 669/1270)[28] who wrote *al-Mumtiʿ fī l-taṣrīf,* Ibn Mālik (d. 672/1273)[29] who wrote the *Lāmīyat al-afʿāl,*[30] Ibn Mālik's son, Badr al-Dīn (d. 686/1286)[31] who wrote the *Lāmīya's* commentary[32] and al-Astarābāḏī (d. 686/1286)[33] who wrote the *Šarḥ šāfiyat Ibn Ḥāǧib.*

The *Marāḥ* usually forms a part of the compilation *Maǧmūʿ al-mutūn "A Compilation of Linguistic Texts".* It is usually followed by the *ʿIzzī* compiled by al-Zanǧānī, the *Maqṣūd* compiled possibly by the Imām Abū Ḥanīfa,[34] and both the *Bināʾ* and the *Amṯila* compiled by anonymous writers.[35]

Four works in morphology written by Baghdadian grammarians are known to have been edited with a translation, namely the *Kitāb al-taṣrīf al-mulūkī* compiled by Ibn Ǧinni, the *Kitāb*

---

[21] For a discussion concerning the subjects treated in this book and some comments concerning its importance see Muʾaddib, *Taṣrīf* 4-7.

[22] Maidānī, Aḥmad b. Muḥammad b. Aḥmad, see Suyūṭī, *Buġya I,* 356-357, Brockelmann, *S I,* 506-507. He studied under al-Wāḥidī. Beside his work mentioned in morphology, he wrote *al-Amṯāl, al-Maṣādir* and other works.

[23] The work is also mentioned in the introduction to Ibn Ǧinnī, *de Flexione* 3.

[24] Ibn Yaʿīš, Yaʿīš b. ʿAlī b. Yaʿīš b. Muḥammad, see Suyūṭī, *Buġya II,* 351-352, Brockelmann, *S II,* 521. He studied grammar under Fityān al-Ḥalabī and Abū l-ʿAbbās al-Baizūrīy and questions of Arabic under al-Kindī.

[25] Ibn al-Ḥāǧib, ʿUṯmān b. ʿUmar b. Abū Bakr b. Yūnus Ǧamāl al-Dīn Abū ʿAmr, see Suyūṭī, *Buġya II,* 134-135, Brockelmann, *S I,* 531-539. He studied under al-Qāsim al-Šāṭibī and Muḥammad al-Ġaznawī. Beside his work mentioned in morphology, he wrote *al-Kāfiya* (upon syntax), *al-Amālī fī l-naḥw* and other works.

[26] Al-Zanǧānī, ʿAbd al-Wahhāb b. Ibrāhīm, see Suyūṭī, *Buġya II,* 122, Brockelmann, *S I,* 497-498. Beside his work mentioned in morphology, he wrote *Šarḥ al-hādī, Matn al-hādī* and other works.

[27] The *ʿIzzī* is one of the first grammatical works known in Europe. It was translated into Latin and edited in Rome by J. Bapt. Raymundus in 1610. It was commented on by ʿUmar al-Taftāzānī in a book named *Šarḥ al-ʿIzzī* (cf. Derenbourg 97, Flügel 179).

[28] Ibn ʿUṣfūr, ʿAlī b. Muʾmin, see Suyūṭī, *Buġya II,* 210, Brockelmann, *S I,* 546-547. He studied under Abū ʿAlī al-Šalawbīn, one of the learned ones in al-Andalus, and Abū l-Ḥasan al-Dabbāǧ. Beside his work mentioned in morphology, he wrote *al-Azhār, Īḍāḥ al-mušakkal, Šarḥ al-īḍāḥ li-Abī ʿAlī l-Fārisī, Šurūḥ al-ǧumal li-l-Zaǧǧāǧī :al-Kabīr, al-Awsaṭ* and *al-Ṣaġīr, Šarḥ kitāb Sībawaihi, al-Ḍarāʾir, al-Miftāḥ, al-Hilāl* and other works.

[29] Ibn Mālik, Muḥammad b. ʿAbd Allāh b. ʿAbd Allāh, see Suyūṭī, *Buġya I,* 130-137, Brockelmann, *S I,* 521-527. He studied under al-Saḫāwīy and al-Ḥasan b. al-Ṣabbāḥ and others. Ibn Yaʿīš was his pupil. Beside his work mentioned in morphology, he wrote *al-Fawāʾid fī l-naḥw, al-Kāfiya al-šāfiya* [its summary being *al-Alfiya]* and other works.

[30] The work is composed in verses which render it obscure. It was translated by Goguyer into French in the same volume containing the *Alfīya.*

[31] Badr al-Dīn, Muḥammad b. Muḥammad b. ʿAbd Allāh, see Suyūṭī, *Buġya I,* 225, Brockelmann, *S I,* 527. He studied under his father Ibn Mālik. Beside his work mentioned in morphology, he wrote *al-Miṣbāḥ fī ḫtiṣār al-miftāḥ fī l-maʿānī, Šarḥ al-mulḥa, Šarḥ al-ḥāǧibīya, Šarḥ alfīya* (a commentary on his father's *Alfīya)* and *Šarḥ al-kāfiya* (a commentary on his father's *Kāfiya)* and other works.

[32] Ibn Mālik, *Lāmīya* followed by Badraddīn's commentary, was translated into German by Kellgren and edited both with the Arabic text and Kellgren's translation by Volck.

[33] Al-Astarābāḏī, al-Raḍī, see Suyūṭī, *Buġya I,* 567-568. He wrote also a commentary on *al-Kāfiya.*

[34] This is the usual assumption. Derenbourg 97 referring to Zenker, *Bibliotheca Orientalis I,* no 138, mentions that the author is named "l'imām Yousuf le Ḥanéfite". A tract of a manuscript mentioned by Brill, *Manuscripts* 82 (181), fol. 124b-146b, contains a commentary in Turkish of this work ascribed to Abū Ḥanīfa. Flügel 180 mentions also the eventuality that Zain al-Dīn Muḥammad b. al-Ḥasan al-Tabrīzī could be the writer.

[35] Flügel 180 mentions that both works were commented on together in a book by Ḥamīd al-Kaffawī, and that there exists also another commentary of them both named *Asās al-bināʾ.* Another commentary of this work exists in a tract of a manuscript mentioned by Brill, *Manuscripts* 82 (181), fol. 20b-121a, named *Muršid al-ġināʾ šarḥ amṯilat al-bināʾ.* The *Bināʾ al-afʿāl* is not written by al-Dunqūzī as stated there.

al-ʿizzī compiled by al-Zanǧānī, the *Lāmīyat al-afʿāl* compiled by Ibn Mālik and the *Lāmīya's* commentary compiled by Ibn Mālik's son, Badr al-Dīn.

Troupeau mentions two editions relating to this period, namely the *Kitāb al-taṣrīf al-mulūkī* compiled by Ibn Ǧinni and the *Kitāb al-ʿizzī* compiled by al-Zanǧānī.[36] Beside these a few editions without corresponding translations exist, namely *al-Takmila*[37] compiled by Abū ʿAlī l-Fārisī, both *al-Munṣif* and the *Sirr ṣināʿat al-iʿrāb* compiled by Ibn Ǧinnī, the *Daqāʾiq al-taṣrīf* compiled by al-Muʾaddib, the *Šarḥ al-mulūkī* compiled by Ibn Yaʿīš, *al-Mumtiʿ* compiled by Ibn ʿUṣfūr and the *Šarḥ šāfīyat Ibn Ḥāǧib* compiled by al-Astarābādī.

A few well-known books dealing with some special morpho-phonological topics are *al-Qalb wa-l-ibdāl* by Ibn al-Sikkīt (d. 244/858),[38] the *Kitāb al-maqṣūr wa-l-mamdūd ʿalā ḥurūf al-muʿǧam* by Ibn Wallād (d. 332/943),[39] the *ʿIlal al-taṯniya*[40] and *al-Muqtaḍab fī ism al-mafʿūl al-muʿtall al-ʿayn*[41] by Ibn Ǧinnī and the *Kitāb al-afʿāl* by Saraqusṭī (d. after 400/1010).[42]

---

36 Troupeau, *Grammaire* 403.

37 This treatise was edited by Kāẓim al-Marǧān and published by the Cairo University 1972.

38 Ibn al-Sikkīt, Yaʿqūb b. Isḥāq, see Suyūṭī, *Buġya II,* 349, Brockelmann, *G I,* 120-121, *S I,* 180-181, Sezgin, *Geschichte VIII,* 129-136, *IX,* 137-138. He studied under both the Basrans and the Kufans grammarians, such as al-Farrāʾ, Abū ʿAmr al-Šabyāni and al-Aṯram. He wrote many books in grammar. He was the tutor of the children of al-Mutawakkil, who caused him to be trampled to death by the Turkish bodyguard because he refused to say that his two pupils, al-Mutawakkil's sons, were dearer to him than the two sainted youths, Ḥasan and al-Ḥusain, the sons of ʿAlī. Instead, Ibn al-Sikkīt declared that Qanbar, ʿAlī's servant, was better than him and both his sons.

39 Ibn Wallād, Aḥmad b. Muḥammad, see Suyūṭī, *Buġya I,* 386, Brockelmann, *S I,* 201, Sezgin, *Geschichte IX,* 206-207. He was the pupil of al-Zaǧǧāǧ.

40 It was edited by Ṣ. al-Tamīmī and R. ʿAbd al-Tawwāb, Cairo 1992.

41 It was edited by E. Probster, Leipzig 1904 under the title of *al-Muġtaṣab,* and by W. F. al-Kīlānī, Cairo 1343/1924. It is a study of the passive participle that is derived from verbs with 2nd weak radical. It was commented on by al-Ġarnāṭī (d. 528) (cf. Méhiri, *Théories* 71).

42 Saraqusṭī, Abū ʿUṯmān Saʿīd b. Muḥammad al-Maʿāfirī, see Suyūṭī, *Buġya I,* 589, Saraqusṭī, *Afʿāl* 11-20. He studied under Abū Bakr b. al-Qawṭīya, whose book *al-Afʿāl,* he enlarged. He died as a victim of a battle. For a description of the subjects of the book see Saraqusṭī, *Afʿāl* 24-28.
Other books with the same title are the *Kitāb al-afʿāl* by Abū Bakr b. al-Qawṭīya, printed in Leiden 1894 and in Cairo 1371/1952, and the *Kitāb al-afʿāl* by Ibn al-Qaṭṭāʿ, printed in Ḥaidar Abād 1361 A.H.

§ 2. Aḥmad b. ʿAlī b. Masʿūd

We do not know anything about Šams al-Milla wa-l-Dīn Abū l-Faḍā'il[1] Aḥmad b. ʿAlī b. Masʿūd, except that he wrote the *Marāḥ al-arwāḥ* in morphology, which according to Suyūṭī is a مختصر وجيز مشهور بأيدي الناس "famous concise book at the disposal of the people", but of whose author's identity لم أقف له على ترجمة "I did not find any biography".[2] Ḥağğī Ḫalīfa also mentioned him and presented some of his commentators, but he did not mention anything else about his life.[3]

He did not escape the attention of de Sacy who refers to him by writing: "Ahmed, fils d'Ali, fils de Masoud, dans son Traité du tasrif ou de la conjugaison intitulé مُراح الأرْواح compte 15 lettres permutables...[4] Furthermore, concerning the quadriliteral verbs, he refers to him by writing: "Ahmed, fils d'Ali, fils de Masoud, dans le مُراح الأرْواح, ne reconnaît que six formes des verbes quadrilitères...".[5]

He was not neglected either by Hoberg who used a printed text of the 13th century of the *Marāḥ al-arwāḥ* from the *Mağmūʿ al-mutūn* as a source of references in his commentary to Ibn Ginnī, *de Flexione.*

He was as well referred to as صاحب المراح "the writer of the *Marāḥ*" by the archbishop and grammarian Germānos Farḥāt[6] of the eighteenth century in his book *Baḥṯ al-maṭālib,*[7] and by his commentator Saʿīd al-Dīn al-Ḫūrī l-Šartūnī of the same book. It is concerning the definition of the derivation that Farḥāt refers to Ibn Masʿūd by quoting from the *Marāḥ* in the following manner:

"الاشتقاق... ما قاله صاحب المراح وهو أن تجد بين اللفظين تناسباً في اللفظ والمعنى".

> The derivation... is what the author of the *Marāḥ* said concerning it, that you find a reciprocal relation between the two words, both in pronunciation and in meaning".[8]

Quotations from the *Marāḥ* written by al-Šartūnī in the notes are also found in Farḥāt, *Baḥṯ*[9] suggesting that the *Marāḥ* has been studied and appreciated by both these authors.

---

1 Cf. Ahlwardt nr. 6809.

2 Suyūṭī, *Buġya I*, 347.

3 Cf. Ḥağğī Ḫalīfa, *Kašf II,* 1651.

4 De Sacy, *I,* 33. The consonants of substitution are presented in the Arabic text fols. 33b-34b l. 5.

5 De Sacy, *I,* 126 in the note. The reference is to the Arabic text fols. 4a-4b ll. 5-6 and see my notes in the commentary (41).

6 He was born in Aleppo 1670 A.D., was an archbishop there in 1725 and died 1732 (cf. the note 1 of al-Šartūnī to Farḥāt, *Baḥṯ* 3).

7 I am thankful to Abu Haidar, *Reviews of Books* 442, who drew my attention to this fact. The book that I had the privilege to study is at the Library of Uppsala, and was formally given as a gift from the Jesuite missionaries of Beirut (Syria) to His Majesty, Oscar the Second, king of Sweden and Norway. *Baḥṯ al-maṭālib* was often printed in the Orient, and was as well commented on. Among its commentaries, I can mention *Miṣbāḥ al-ṭālib fī baḥṯ al-maṭālib,* which is an edition of *Baḥṯ al-maṭālib* containing in the notes the commentary of Buṭrus al-Bustānī (d. 1883), Beirut 1854, and another shorter grammar written by him, *Miftāḥ al-miṣbāḥ fī l-ṣarf wa-l-naḥw li-l-madāris,* 1st edition, Beirut 1862, 2nd edition 1867. Nāṣīf al-Yāziğī gave his own summary to the work, namely *Faṣl al-ḫiṭāb fī uṣūl luġat al-iʿrāb,* 1st edition, Beirut 1836, 2nd edition 1866 (cf. Fleisch, *Traité I,* 45). These commentaries were used by Wright, as stated by him in his preface to the second edition, p. V.

8 Farḥāt, *Baḥṯ* 13, Bustānī, *Miṣbāḥ* 7. The passage is found in the Arabic text fols. 2a-3a ll. 8-9.

9 See Farḥāt, *Baḥṯ* 16, 58, 59.

Ibn Masʿūd lived probably before the beginning of the 8th/14th century because the first commentator whom we know about, namely Ḥasan Pāša b. ʿAlāʾ al-Dīn al-Aswad al-Niksārī died in 827/1424.[10]

Suyūṭī distinguishes between Aḥmad b. ʿAlī b. Masʿūd, the writer of the *Marāh,* and Aḥmad b. ʿAlī b. Masʿūd b. ʿAbd Allāh, known as Ibn Saqqāʾ. The latter was learned in grammar, was a pupil of both al-Ḫaššāb and Abū l-Waqt and died in 613/1216-7.[11]

We are a bit perplexed however, by a statement made by al-Baġdādī,[12] attributing a commentary of the *Marāḥ,* namely *Fatḥ al-fattāḥ fī šarḥ al-marāḥ* or *Fatḥ al-fattāḥ bi-qūt al-arwāḥ*—known to us to be commented on by Tāǧ al-Dīn ʿAbd al-Wahhāb b. Ibrāhīm b. Maḥmūd b. ʿAlī b. Muḥammad al-ʿUrḍī al-Ḥalabī al-Šāfiʿī (d. 967/1559)[13]—as commented on by Tāǧ al-Dīn ʿAbd al-Wahhāb b. Ibrāhīm b. ʿAbd al-Wahhāb al-Zanǧānī (d. 654/1256-57),[14] the author of the *ʿIzzī.* This error can be explained by the similarity of both names.

The thought that al-Zanǧānī known to us as the author of *Šarḥ al-hādī, Matn al-hādī* and *al-ʿIzzī* of the 7th/13th century, could be a commentator of the *Marāḥ al-arwāḥ* as well, written many years after him, is rather confusing.

Of course, we can assume that Aḥmad b. ʿAlī b. Masʿūd lived during the beginning of the 7th/13th century, that he and Aḥmad b. ʿAlī b. Masʿūd b. ʿAbd Allāh, known as Ibn Saqqāʾ, are one and the same, and that both Tāǧ al-Dīn ʿAbd al-Wahhāb b. Ibrāhīm al-Šāfiʿī and Tāǧ al-Dīn ʿAbd al-Wahhāb b. Ibrāhīm b. ʿAbd al-Wahhāb al-Zanǧānī wrote two different commentaries to which they gave the same title.

This would have been possible if other biographers had pointed out that fact, or if we had found out that some of the manuscripts of the *Marāḥ* were from the 7th/13th century, i.e. before or during al-Zanǧānī's lifetime, but this is not the case.[15]

---

[10] Cf. Baġdādī, *Hadīya I,* 287.

[11] Cf. Suyūṭī, *Buġya I,* 347, Ṣafadī, *Wāfī VII,* 210 nr. 3159.

[12] Baġdādī, *Hadīya I,* 638.

[13] Cf. Ḥāǧǧī Ḫalīfa, *Kašf II,* 1651, Brockelmann, *S II,* 14, Dār al-kutub al-miṣrīya II, 65 (163), my introduction to Ibn Masʿūd, *I,* 12.

[14] He is mentioned in my introduction pp. 5–6.

[15] For a general discussion concerning Ibn Masʿūd see Sellheim, *Handschriften* 56-58.

§ 3. The Commentaries

The many commentaries which have been written[1] bear witness to the importance of the *Marāḥ al-arwāḥ* and its popularity among its readers. These are some of them:

– Ḥasan Pāšā b. ʿAlāʾa l-Dīn al-Aswad al-Niksārī's commentary *al-Mifrāḥ* (800/ 1397)[2] *"The One who rejoices whenever Fortune renders him happy"*. Baġdādī specifies that Ḥasan Pāšā b. ʿAlāʾa l-Dīn ʿAlī l-Aswad al-Rūmī l-Ḥanafī settled in Brussa and died in 827 [/1424).[3]

It starts with:

"بِسْمِ الله الرَّحمنِ آلرَّحيم وبه نَسْتَعِين الحمد لله الذي صرَّف أفكار قلوبِنا الى الصراط المستقيم ونوَّرها بنور الهدى الى الدّين القويم".

"In the name of God, Most Gracious, Most Merciful. He on Whom we turn for help. Praise be to God Who directed our hearts' thoughts towards the straight way and Who enlightened them with the guidance's light towards the true religion".[4]

Nīksārī writes praising the *Marāh:*

"فإنَّ الكتاب المسمى بمراح الأرواح في التصريف للإمام... أفضل المتأخرين كاشف أسرار المتقدّمين ابي الفضل أحمد بن علي بن مسعود... كتاب جليل القدر عظيم الشأن ظاهر الخطر بأمر البرهان مستجمع لفوايد شريفة ومحتوٍ لزوايد لطيفة".

"It is so that the book given the title مراح الأرواح in morphology, [written] by the Imām,... the best among the later authors who reveals the secrets of the earlier authors, Abū l-Faḍl Aḥmad b. ʿAlī Ibn Masʿūd..., is of great value and importance. Its significance is revealed by its methods of demonstration, by its collection of distinguished results and by its intellectually refined material".[5]

Ḥāǧǧī Ḫalīfa notes that the commentary mediates between conciseness and lengthiness, containing some useful lessons.[6]

– Yūsuf b. ʿAbd-al-Malik b. Baḫšāyiše's commentary written around 839, entitled *Rāḥ al-arwāḥ*[7] *"The Hand of the Souls"*.

– ʿAbd al-Mahdī l-Ḥanafī's commentary.[8] According to Ḥāǧǧī Ḫalīfa, his name was Badr al-Dīn Maḥmūd b. Aḥmad al-ʿAinī l-Ḥanafī, and he died in 855 [/1451]. He named his commentary *Mallāḥ al-arwāḥ "The Sailor of the Souls"*. It was one of his first works, compiled when he was 19 years old.[9]

---

[1] It can be noted that most of these commentaries are manuscripts or unedited printed texts found in different libraries.

[2] He is mentioned by Brockelmann, *GAL II,* 21, *S II,* 14. A manuscript is found in Münch. 758, Vienna I, 187, 204, Br. Mus. Or. 5814 (DL 49), Manch. 739, Bodl. II, 419, Pet. 153, etc. I also possess a manuscript, Niksārī, *Mifrāh,* which I used in my commentary. Its main part was written in the 18th century. It consists of 62 fols with 21 lines to the page, and measures 208 X 134 mm.

[3] Baġdādī, *Hadīya I,* 287.

[4] Niksārī, *Mifrāḥ,* fol. 2a ll. 1-3.

[5] Niksārī, *Mifrāḥ,* fol. 2a ll. 7-11.

[6] Ḥāǧǧī Ḫalīfa, *Kašf II,* 1651.

[7] Cf. Brockelmann, *S II,* 14. A manuscript is found in Dam. Z. 65, 13, Alger 27, Cairo II, 85. The date which is given is incorrect 939/1435. It is corrected in *GAL II,* 21 as 839/1435.

[8] Cf. Brockelmann, *S II,* 14. In *GAL II,* 21, he is named ʿAbdul Mahdí Hanafiya and is said to be mentioned in Dehli Fárúqí Press, 1883.

[9] Ḥāǧǧī Ḫalīfa, *Kašf II,* 1651.

– *Šarḥ al-marāḥ,*[10] written by Šams al-Dīn A. Dunqūz,[11] whom Ḥāǧǧī Ḫalīfa states as being called Aḥmad and being known as Dīkqūz.[12] His full name is Šams al-Dīn Aḥmad b. ʿAbdallah al-Rūmī l-Ḥanafī, and he lived around 860 [/1456] in Brussa.[13]

It starts with:

"اللهمَ يا مُصرِّف القلوب صرِّف قلوبنا نحو رضائك وصلِّ على من أُوتي جوامع الكلم من بين أنبيائك":

"O God, You who dispose freely over our hearts, direct our hearts[14] to Your approval, and pray upon the One to Whom the universal language has come to among your prophets".

Ḥāǧǧī Ḫalīfa writes that it is a useful commentary which was taken into consideration.[15]

– A commentary on the commentary of Šams al-Dīn A. Dunqūz written by an anonymous scholar.[16]

It starts with:

"الحمد لله الذي أفاض الخير والجود على كلّ من اتّصف بصفة الوجود".

"Praise be to God who poured forth welfare and generosity on each one who has distinguished himself with the quality of living".

– Ibn Kamāl Pāšā's (d. 940/1533) commentary *al-Falāḥ*[17] *"The Success"*. It has also been translated into Turkish and named *Rayḥān al-arwāḥ "the Sweet Odour of the Souls"*.[18] Two other commentators have also given this title to their commentaries of the *Marāḥ,* namely ʿAlī b. Safar[19] and Muḥammad Ḥāmid al-Ālūsī.[20]

It starts with:

[10] Cf. Brockelmann, *GAL II,* 21, *S II,* 14, Dār al-kutub al-miṣrīya II, 63 (13), Brill, *Manuscripts* 76 (166), (167). I also possess a manuscript which I have used in my commentary, namely Dunqūz, *Šarḥ,* that was written by the copyist Muṣṭafā b. Muḥammad at the beginning of Ǧumāda II 1003/March 1585. It consists of 99 fols with 19 lines to the page, and measures 206 X 139 mm. A manuscript is also found in Berl. 6814 (anon.), Vienna 203, Krafft 755, Bol. 328/30, Paris 4185/6 etc. It has also been printed with *al-Falāḥ* in its margin (see Ibn Kamāl Pāšā, *Falāḥ* in the bibliography; and for other printed texts see Dār al-kutub al-miṣrīya II, 63 (138, 139, 260)).

[11] For an interesting etymological study of the word see Sellheim, *Handschriften II,* 58-59 in the note.

[12] Ḥāǧǧī Ḫalīfa, *Kašf II,* 1651. In the *Šarḥ al-Marāḥ B,* he is referred to as *al-mawlā* "the master" Fāḍil al-Ḥiqaq known as Dunqūz. I am very thankful to Prof. Gösta Vitestam, Department of Middle East languages, Lund, who drew my attention to this manuscript and who had the great kindness to let me study it during many years.

[13] Cf. Baġdādī, *Hadīya I,* 131, Kaḥḥāla, *Muʿǧam I,* 220, Brockelmann, *S II,* 14, Ḥāǧǧī Ḫalīfa, *Kašf II,*1651, Sellheim, *Handschriften II,* 58. Two manuscripts referred to as nr. 10/ Mūnīr Walī and nr. 327/ Ǧaʿfar Walī respectively, are at the University of Alexandria (cf. Zaydān, *Maḫṭūṭāt II,* par. 806 and 807 p. 67). The manuscripts are wrongly attributed to Ḥasan b. ʿAlāʾ al-Dīn al-Aswad.

[14] Compare sur. 9: 127 (صَرَفَ ٱللَّهُ قُلُوبَهُم) "God hath turned their hearts".

[15] Ḥāǧǧī Ḫalīfa, *Kašf II,* 1651.

[16] Cf. Dār al-kutub al-miṣrīya II, 62 (20).

[17] Cf. Brockelmann, *S II,* 14. A manuscript is found in Berl. 6813 (cf. Ahlwardt), Pet. AMK 941, Egypt (cf. Dār al-kutub al-miṣrīya II, 65 (39, 138, 139 and 272)). A tract of the wok is found in a manuscript mentioned by Brill, *Manuscripts* 81 (180), fols 12b-101b. I have used a printed text, Ibn Kamāl Pāšā, *Falāḥ,* in my commentary.

[18] Ḥāǧǧī Ḫalīfa, *Kašf II,* 1651.

[19] Cf. Brockelmann, *S II,* 14.

[20] Sellheim, *Handschriften II,* 58 discusses the possibility that he could be the copyist of a manuscript instead.

"نحمدُكَ يا من بيده الخير والجود وبقدرته تصريف كلّ موجود وفُحص الإنسان منه بخاصة أمر السجود فمن أطاعه فصحيح سالم مسعود ومن عصاه فمعتلّ ناقص مردود".

"We praise You Who have at hand power and generosity and Who is capable of changing everything in existence. You by Whom man is tested through his prostration. The one who obeys Him is healthy, strong and happy, and the one who disobeys him is sick, imperfect and denied".[21]

Ibn Kamāl Pāšā writes praising the *Marāḥ:*

"لما رأيتُ المختصر في الصرف الذي صنّفه الفاضل المحقّق والعالم المدقّق علاّمة الورى شمس الملّة والدين أحمد بن علي بن مسعود جعلهم الله قريناً لنبيّه في مقام محمود مع صغر حجمه ووجازة نظمه مشتملاً على غرر الفرائد ودرر الفوائد محتوياً على دقائق الأسرار العربيّة ونكات العلوم الأدبيّة... فأردتُ أن أشرحه شرحاً يُزيل صعابه ويُخرج من قشره لبابه".

"When I saw the abridged study in morphology that the eminent researcher and the accurate scholar, the most erudite of all men, Šams al-Milla wa l-Dīn Aḥmad b. ʿAlī Ibn Masʿūd,—may God join him to his prophet in a praised abode—has compiled, in spite of its small size and the conciseness of its structure, comprising the finest of precious pearls and the most useful of lessons, containing the intricacies of the Arabic secrets and the witty remarks of the literary learnings... I desired to devise a commentary upon it which would eliminate its difficulties and which would bring out the quintessence from its cover".[22]

– ʿAbd al-Raḥīm Ḫalīl's commentary which is a summary of Dunqūz's commentary and which starts with:

"الحمدُ لله الذي أطلعنا على كتابه بالعلوم العربيّة والتصريف".

"Praise be to God who revealed to us His book with the Arabic learnings, and the morphology, etc.".[23]

– Tāǧ al-Dīn ʿAbd al-Wahhāb's commentary *Fatḥ al-fattāḥ fī šarḥ al-marāḥ*[24] *"the Opening of the Gates of Profit in the Commentary of the Marāḥ al-arwāḥ"* or *Fatḥ al-fattāḥ bi-qūt al-arwāḥ (fī šarḥ al-marāḥ) "The Opening of the Gates of Profit through the Nourishment of the Souls (in the Commentary of the Marāḥ)"*. His full name is Tāǧ al-Dīn ʿAbd al-Wahhāb b. Ibrāhīm b. Māḥmūd b. ʿAlī b. Muḥammad al-ʿUrḍī l-Ḥalabī l-Šāfiʿī and he died in 967/1559.

It starts with:

"الحمد لله الذي صرّفنا أحسن تصريف".

"Praise be to God who has changed us for the best".

– Muṣṭafā b. Šaʿbān's commentary. He was known as Surūrī and died in 969/1561.[25]

---

[21] Ibn Kamāl Pāšā, *Falāḥ* 1 ll. 1-2.

[22] Ibn Kamāl Pāšā, *Falāḥ* 2 ll. 4-18.

[23] Cf. Ḥāǧǧī Ḫalīfa, *Kašf II,* 1651, Dār al-kutub al-miṣrīya II, 63 (36). Brockelmann, *GAL II,* 21 names the commentator as ʿAbd al-Raḥmān b. Ḫalīl Rūmī. A manuscript is found in Krafft 54. Another manuscript referred to as nr 8/ Mūnīr Walī is found at the University of Alexandria (cf. Zaydān, *Maḫṭūṭāt II,* par. 805. pp. 66-67).

[24] Cf. Ḥāǧǧī Ḫalīfa, *Kašf II,* 1651, Brockelmann, *S II,* 14, Dār al-kutub al-miṣrīya II, 65 (163).

[25] Cf. Ḥāǧǧī Ḫalīfa, *Kašf II,* 1651.

– Muṣnafak's extensive commentary, which is found in the library of Abū l-Fatḥ in his mosque and which starts with:

"الحمد لله المتقدَس من الإدغام".

"Praise be to God who is holy and not incorporated".[26]

– M. b. A. b. Hilāl's commentary.[27]
– H. ʿA. Fāse's commentary.[28]
– Sanān al-Dīn Yūsuf's commentary *Rawwāḥ al-arwāḥ* "The Promptness of the Souls". He was known as Qirra Sanān and was also the author of *al-Ḍamāʾir "The Pronouns"*. He was one of the learned men in the Ottoman state.[29]
It starts with:

"الحمد لله الذي أرسل رسوله إلينا باللغة الفصيحة وزيَن ما يدلُ على كلامه القديم بالنكتة البليغة":

"Praise be to God who has sent to us his prophet with the perspicuous tongue and who has embellished all that is suggestive of His old language with an eloquent witticism".

– *Al-Iṣbāḥ ʿalā marāḥ al-arwāḥ "The Entering upon Morning on the Marāḥ al-arwāḥ"* by an anonymous author.[30]
– A commentary by an anonymous author.[31]
– Another commentary by an anonymous author.[32]
It starts with:

"قال العبد المفتقر الى الله الودود وإنما اختار الإفتقار لأنَ المقام مقام الإستعانة في التأليف وإظهار العبر والإحتياج":

"Thus speaks the slave in need of the Friendly God, and he chose poverty because the situation in the compilation is to ask for help, to give a good example and to show one's need".

---

26 Ibid.
27 Cf. Brockelmann, *S II,* 14, Ḥāǧǧī Ḫalīfa, *Kašf II,* 1651. A manuscript is found in Pet. AMK 941.
28 Cf. Brockelmann, *S II,* 14. A manuscript is found in Qar. 1219.
29 Cf. Ḥāǧǧī Ḫalīfa, *Kašf II,* 1651, Dār al-kutub al-miṣrīya II, 63 (14).
30 Cf. Dār al-kutub al-miṣrīya II, (192).
31 Cf. Brockelmann, *GAL II,* 21. A manuscript is found in Pet. 154, Krafft 55, etc.
32 Cf. *A Catalogue of the Arabic Manuscripts in the Salar Jang Collection,* ed. M. Nizamuddin VI, India, 102 (2611).

§ 4. The Manuscripts of the *Marāḥ*

The manuscripts are referred to in many catalogues, among which:
- Ahlwardt VI, 179-180 nr. 6805-6806.
- Atsiz, nr. 181.
- Azhar IV, 94-96.
- Dār al-kutub al-miṣrīya II, 67-68 nr. 36, 47, 78, 79, 80, 83, 84, 85, 87, 197, 208, 214.
- Derenbourg, 97-99 nr. 163-166.
- Ǧubūrī III, 381 nr. 5801.
- Flügel, 178-184 nr. 189-198.
- Levi Della Vida V, 337.
- Mingana IV, 284-285 nr. 1524-1526 and 1531-1532.
- Šibīn al-Kūm[1] 33, 2; 51,1.
- de Slane, nr. 4166-4187 and 7106.[2]
- Steiner I, 240-241 nr. 3874-3875 .
- Ṭalas, 193 nr. 2657.
- Taškent, 406; 3795 .
- Topkapı, nr. 7971, 1; 7972, 2; 7973, 1; 7978, 1; 7979, 1.
- University of Cairo, nr. 16394, 16408, 16429, 16540.
- Yale, nr. 4-5.

---

[1] Cf. RIMA II, 267 and 270.

[2] Only the MSS 4166/74 are mentioned by Brockelmann, *S II,* 14.

§ 5. The Printed texts of the *Marāḥ*

The *Marāḥ* has been printed both independently and as included with other works in the *Maǧmūʿ al-mutūn.* It has been printed as an independent work in Cawnpore 1885, Dehli 1887, Lahore 1887,[1] Būlāq 1240/1824, 1244/1828, 1247/1831, 1249/1833, 1257/1841, Ind. 1267/1851, Delhi 1293/1875, Lahore 1906 and Istanbul 1286/1861, 1291/1873.[2]

It has been printed with other works in Istanbul 1233/1817, Bulāq 1244/1828,[3] 1262/1846, 1276/1860, 1280/1864, 1282/1866 and Cairo 1299/1881, 1305/1887, 1309/1891, 1321/1904, 1344/1927.[4] The Dār al-kutub al-miṣrīya refers to the above-mentioned Būlāq printed texts of the *Maǧmūʿa,* i.e. 1244/1828 (65 and 81), 1262/1846 (45), 1268/1852 (59),[5] 1280/1864 (53) and 1282/1866 (55 and 56)[6] and to the following: the printed text of al-Astāna printing house 1254/1838 (82), 1278/1862 (57), the printed text of the printing house al-Šarqīya, Cairo 1298/1880 (95 and 104), the printed text of the Wahbīya printing house, Cairo 1299/1881 (90 and 103) and the printed text of the printing house al-Maymanīya, Cairo 1309/1891 (142 and 143).[7]

To these may be added the printed text of the Printing house al-ʿUṯmānīya 1304/1886 found at the Library of Cairo University[8] and the printed text of Būlāq 1841 found at the Library of Tübingen University.[9]

---

1 Brockelmann, *GAL II,* 21.

2 Ibid, *S II,* 14.

3 Ibid, *GAL II,* 21.

4 Ibid, *S II,* 14.

5 See Ibn Masʿūd, *Print U.*

6 See Ibn Masʿūd, *Print K.*

7 Dār al-kutub al-miṣrīya II, 67-68.

8 See Ibn Masʿūd, *Print L.*

9 See Ibn Masʿūd, *Print T.*

§ 6. The Principles of Edition

For the edition of this extract I have chosen the oldest manuscripts of the Bibliothèque Nationale and two prints from Cairo University.[1] It can be stressed that the variant readings between the manuscripts are few, and that the printed texts are mostly copies of each other with only small variations.[2] It is important for the reader to note that they are mostly found in libraries and are almost impossible to find in circulation.

A (= ا) *Bibliothèque Nationale, Paris 4166.* Fol. 1a gives us the name of an ancient owner of the manuscript, namely Muḥammad b. Tamǧar al-Kirsānī. It also has the stamp of the Bibliothecæ Regia. De Slane describes it as follows:[3]

> "Papier. 73 feuillets. Hauteur, 19 centimètres; largeur, 13 centimètres et demi. 13 lignes par page".

The *Marāḥ al-arwāḥ* is the first part of this codex which consists of four works that constitute the *Maǧmūʿ al-mutūn.* It ends on fol. 36 and is followed by *al-ʿIzzī fī-l-taṣrīf* which ends on fol. 49, *al-Maqṣūd* which ends on fol. 66 and *al-Amṯila al-muḫtalifa* which ends on fol. 72. All four works are written in nasḫī script.

The text in fol. 72b finishes with the following postscript revealing the name of the copyist:

"تمَّ الكتاب بعون الله الملك الوهَّاب على يد العبد الضعيف محمَّد بن يحيى بن يوسف الأرُنيقي غفر الله له ولوالديه ولأجداده ولجميع المؤمنين والمؤمنات والمسلمين والمسلمات الأحياء منهم والأموات في يوم ضحوة الجمعة الخامس عشرين مُحرَّم الحرام في سلك شهور سنة سبع وأربعين وتسعمائة من الهجرة النبويَّة المصطفويَّة الحمد لله على التمام وللرسول أفضل السلام وعلى آله وصحبه الكرام".

> "The book was completed with God's assistance, the Giver, at the hand of the weak slave Muḥammad b. Yaḥya b. Yūsuf al-Arunīqī, may God watch over him, his parents, his ancestors, all the believers,—men and women—, the Muslims,—men and women, the dead among them and the living,—on the forenoon of Friday the 25th of Muḥarram al-Ḥarām among the course of the months in the year 947 [/1540] of the chosen Hiǧra of the Prophet, praise be to God for His perfection and the best greeting to the Messenger, his honourable family and his followers".

After this postscript follow four verses of poetry in Turkish.

The handwriting is neat. Many glosses commenting on the *Marāḥ* occur between the lines and in the margins, representing in an artistic and graceful manner, trees, flowers, jugs, columns and other objects. The text is rarely vowelled but is on the whole reliable and does not contain many corrupt readings.

One of the features of this text is the hyphenation of some words in the left margin, mostly after the conjunction *wa,* e.g. و– اشتقاق[4] for واشتقاق, و– خمسة[5] for وخمسة, و– يجزم[6] for ويجزم but also elsewhere, e.g. با– داة[7] for باداة and واو– لاهم[8] for واولاهم.

---

[1] For the plates see Ibn Masʿūd, *Marāḥ I,* XIV-XXII.

[2] As an example, it can be noted that Ibn Masʿūd, *Print T,* is almost a copy of *Print L, Print U* and *Print Y.*

[3] De Slane, 671.

[4] MS A, fol. 2a ll. 2-3.

[5] Ibid, fol. 4b ll.1-2.

[6] Ibid, fol. 12b ll. 8-9.

[7] Ibid, fol. 7b ll. 12-13.

[8] Ibid, fol. 15a ll. 11-12.

The *tā᾽ marbūṭa* occurs in some cases instead of the *tā᾽ maftūḥa,* e.g. ومسعاة for ومسعات,[9] which is also noticed in the MSS BCDI, and الإخبارة for الإخبارات,[10] the accusative instead of the nominative, e.g. وإثني as in the MSS BI for وإثنا,[11] the masc. instead of the fem, e.g. ستا as in MSS BCDEG for ستة,[12] وحذف for وحذفت,[13] يصير for تصير,[14] and the fem. instead of the masc., e.g. ترتقي for يرتقي.[15] A few corrupt readings occur as well, e.g. وغلابط for وعلابط[16] as in the MSS EI and the print L, رو for روا,[17] and سنتان for ثنتان.[18]

B (= ب) *Bibliothèque Nationale, Paris, 4167.* The *Marāḥ* is the first work and is followed by the *'Izzī* on fol. 52, *al-Maqṣūd* on fol. 72 and *al-Amṯila al-muḫtalifa* on fol. 96. De Slane describes it thus:[19]

"Papier. 105 feuillets. Hauteur, 18 centimètres et demi; largeur, 11 centimètres. 11 lignes par page".

The *Marāḥ* has the following colophon in fol. 52 revealing the name of the copyist and the date and place where it was written:

"تمّ بعون الله الملك الوهّاب في سنة ٩٦٦ ، كتبه الفقير يوسف بن عبد الله ، دار محروسة قسطنطينيّة:"

"It was completed with the assistance of God, the Giver in the year 966 [/1559]. The needy Yūsuf b. ʿAbdallāh wrote it in Dār Maḥrūsa, Constantinople".

The manuscript ends in the following way:

"تمّ بعون الله وحسن توفيقه أمين يا رب العالمين".

"It was accomplished with the assistance of God and the good fortune granted by Him, Amen, O Lord over both worlds".

The handwriting is clear, and all the three works were written in nasḫī script by the same copyist. It does not have many glosses between the lines or in the margins.

The *alif mamdūda* occurs in some cases instead of the *alif maqṣūra,* e.g. ارعوا for إرعوى,[20] وقلسا for وقلسى,[21] the *ḏ* instead of the *z,* e.g. ذلذل ذلذالاً for زلزل زلزالاً,[22] and the *tā marbūṭa* instead of the *tā᾽ mamdūda,* e.g. زيدة for زيدت.[23] Corrupt readings indicating mechanical copy-

[9] Ibid, fols. 3a-4a l. 6, the note below.
[10] Ibid, fols. 5a-5b l. 10, the note below.
[11] Ibid, fols. 4a-4b l. 1, the note below.
[12] Ibid, fols. 5b-7a l. 18, the note below.
[13] Ibid, text fols. 14a-15a l. 3, the note below.
[14] Ibid, fols. 20a-21a l. 8, the note below.
[15] Ibid, fols. 3a-4a l. 3, the note below.
[16] Ibid, fols. 5a-5b l. 6, the note below.
[17] Ibid, fols. 24a-24b l. 3, the note below.
[18] Ibid, fols. 33b-34b l. 18, the note below.
[19] De Slane, 671.
[20] The Arabic text fols. 4a-4b l. 3, the note below.
[21] Ibid l. 5, the note below.
[22] Ibid, fols. 3a-4a l. 9, the note below.
[23] Ibid, fols. 4b-5a l. 8, the note below.

ing and a poor knowledge of the Arabic language occur, e.g. كدده تكادو instead of كدت تكاد,[24] لأصل instead of لأجل,[25] الزعالة instead of الذَّعَالت[26] as in the MS I, and عمير for عَمْبر.[27] The use of Form VII of the verb instead of the passive voice of Form I, e.g. وينجزم for ويجزم, which is common with MSS DGHI and the Print L,[28] as well as the use of one form of the *maṣdar* instead of MS A's form, e.g. Form III مشابهة for Form V تشبّها, which is common with MSS DGH and the Print L,[29] as well as additions, e.g. والإختصار after للايجاز,[30] which is common with MS C, والكسر أفصح after زلزالا,[31] which is common with MS E, اي قارب after المحسنين,[32] which is common with MSS CG, indicates that it belongs to a different source.

C (= جـ) *Bibliothèque Nationale, Paris, 4168.* The *Marāḥ* is followed by the *'Izzī* on fol. 38 and *al-Maqṣūd* on fol. 65. De Slane describes it as follows:[33]

> "Papier. 81 feuillets. Hauteur, 19 centimètres; largeur, 14 centimètres. Écritures diverses du XVIe siècle".

The text is richly commented on. The name of the copyist is not revealed, nor is the date of the copy. It ends in the following way:

"تمّت تماما بعون الملك المثال".

"It was completed wholly with the assistance of the Ideal King".

In some cases, the *tā' maftūḥa* occurs instead of the *tā' marbūṭa*, e.g. علامت for علامة,[34] باداة for باداة,[35] and the *ṡ* replaces the *ṯ* e.g. وكشرتهن instead of وكثرتهن.[36] It has also some additions, e.g. after مهدوي occurs وهو اسم مفعول في الهداية,[37] after يلتبس occurs بالمفرد,[38] after أفْعَلُ occurs نحو أحمر,[39] and after اخْشَيْنَ occurs فقلبت الياء الاولى ألفا لتحركها وانفتاح ما قبلها ونظيره اخشيين بيائين.[40] Corrupt readings occur, e.g. ودرية for ودِرَايَة.[41]

D (= د) *Bibliothèque Nationale, Paris, 4169.* The *Marāḥ* is followed on fol. 38 by the *'Izzī* and on fol. 54 by *al-Maqsūd.* De Slane describes it thus:[42]

---

24 Ibid, fols. 3a-4a l. 17, the note below.
25 Ibid, fols. 4b-5a l. 9, the note below.
26 Ibid, fols. 34b-35a l. 3, the note below.
27 Ibid, fols. 35a-35b l. 4, the note below.
28 Ibid, fols. 12a-13a l. 9, the note below.
29 Ibid, fols. 13a-13b l. 9, the note below.
30 Ibid, fols. 5a-5b l. 10, the note below.
31 Ibid, fols. 3a-4a l. 9, the note below.
32 Ibid, fols. 15a-16a l. 8, the note below.
33 De Slane, 671.
34 The Arabic text fols. 14a-15a l. 3, the note below.
35 Ibid, fols. 7b-8b l. 2, the note below.
36 Ibid, fols. 3a-4a l. 12, the note below.
37 Ibid, fols. 7b-8b l. 9, the note below.
38 Ibid l. 17, the note below.
39 Ibid, fols. 14a-15a l. 14, the note below.
40 Ibid, fols. 24a-24b l. 2, the note below.
41 Ibid, fols. 3a-4a l. 5, the note below.
42 De Slane, 671.

"Papier. 69 feuillets. Hauteur, 20 centimètres et demi; largeur, 12 centimètres et demi. 13 lignes par page. Ms. du XVIe siècle".

The manuscript contains only a few glosses. The handwriting is neat and the script is nasḫī. Neither the name of the copyist nor the date of the copy is revealed. The manuscript, which curiously enough also introduces the book of Cultic Purity, ends in the following way:

"تمَ الكتاب بعون الله الملك الوهَاب كتاب الطهارة قال الله تعالى يا أيُها الذين آمنوا إذا قمتم الى الصلاة فاغسلوا وجوهكم وأيديكم الى المرافق وامسحوا بروؤسكم وأرجلكم الى الكعبين ففرض الطهارة غسل الأعضاء ومسح الرأس والمرفقين".

"The book was accomplished with the assistance of God, the Giving King. *The Book of Cultic Purity*. God, the Sublime, said: O You who believe, if you rise to pray, wash your faces and hands until the elbows and rub your heads and legs until the ankles as the duty of the cultic purity is the washing of the members and the rubbing of the head and the elbows".

The *tā᾽maftūḥa* can in some cases occur instead of the *tā᾽marbūṭa,* e.g. لمساوات for لمساواة,[43] which is common with MSS GI, and the *tā᾽marbūṭa* can occur instead of the *tā᾽maftūḥa,* e.g. وعدة for وَعَدَت.[44] Additions are noticed, e.g. after فَعِل occurs بكسر العين,[45] which is common with MS I and the print K, after اطَّرَب occurs لزيادة صفة الضاد,[46] which is common with MS I, after يرى occurs في سقوط الهمزة,[47] after الياء occurs لإزالة توالي الكسرات[48] etc.

E (= هـ) *Bibliothèque Nationale, Paris, 4170.* The *Marāḥ* is the first work and is followed on fol. 46 by the *ʿIzzī,* on fol. 64 by *al-Maqṣūd,* on fol. 82 by *Binā᾽al-afʿāl,* on fol. 93 by *al-Amṯila al-muḫtalifa* and on fol. 107 by a prayer written in Turkish and which is recited at funerals. De Slane describes it as follows:[49]

"Papier. 107 feuillets. Hauteur, 19 centimètres et demi; largeur, 13 centimètres et demi. 13 lignes par page. Ms. du XVIe siècle".

The text is nearly devoid of glosses.The handwriting is clumsy.
The *Marāḥ* ends in the following way on fol. 46:

"تمَ الكتاب بعون الله الملك الوهَاب وحسن التوفيق".

"The book was ended with the assistance of God, the Giving King, and the good fortune".

The manuscript ends in the following way:

"تمَ الكتاب بعون الله الملك الوهَاب... صليَ على محمَد وعلى آل محمَد كما صلَيت على إبراهيم وعلى آل إبراهيم إنَك حميد مجيد اللهمَ بارك على محمَد وعلى آل محمَد كما باركت على إبراهيم وعلى آل إبراهيم".

[43] The Arabic text fols. 20a-21a l. 4, the note below.
[44] Ibid, fols. 26a-26b l. 3, the note below.
[45] Ibid, fols. 14a-15a l. 12, the note below.
[46] Ibid, fols. 20a-21a l. 3, the note below.
[47] Ibid, fols. 23a-24a l. 9, the note below.
[48] Ibid, fols. 32a-32b l. 16, the note below.
[49] De Slane, 671.

> "The book was accomplished with the assistance of God, the Giving King... May You pray on Muḥammad and on Muḥammad's family as You have prayed on Abraham and Abraham's family, You are praiseworthy and glorious, O God, bless Muḥammad and Muḥammad's family as You have blessed Abraham and Abraham's family".

Hyphenation occurs inconsistently at the left margin, e.g. و-نعم[50] instead of ونعم, الاشتقا-ق[51] instead of الإشتقاق, الفا- عل[52] instead of الفاعل etc.

Additions could imply the involvement of the copyist or the contamination of another tradition; e.g. after وزلزالاً occurs والكسر أفصح,[53] which is in accordance with MS B's reading, after الثلاثيَ occurs لأن الياء كسرتان والميم فاعطي الفرع للفرع والأصل للأصل,[54] after الكسرات occurs كسرة فيصير توالي الكسرات,[55] and after سِياط occurs أصله سِواط.[56] In some cases the alif is omitted in the 3rd person of the masc. pl. of the perfect, e.g. قالو instead of قالوا,[57] ضربو instead of ضربوا,[58] رمو instead of رموا,[59] دعو instead of دَعَوْا[60] which is common with MSS ACEI, etc. The first element of an *iḍāfa* construction can occur as made definite, e.g. الاصل الاشتقاق[61] instead of أصل الاشتقاق. In some cases, the *tāʾ maftūḥa* occurs instead of the *tāʾ marbūṭa,* e.g. ورحمت for ورحمة[62] and the *š* instead of the *s,* e.g. ونشَابة for ونسَابة.[63]

G (= ز) *Bibliothèque Nationale, Paris, 4172.* The *Marāḥ* is followed by the *ʿIzzī* on fol. 60 and the *Maqṣūd* on fol. 85. De Slane describes it in the following way:[64]

> "Papier. 111 feuillets. Hauteur, 18 centimètres; largeur, 12 centimètres et demi. 11 lignes par page. Ms. du XVIe siècle".

No collation is included in the manuscript. The handwriting is clear. It is dependent on the MSS BDGE, as it contains some of their variants, e.g. ووقوعه for وفي وقوعه,[65] اربع حركات instead of الحركات[66] etc. In some cases, the *tāʾ maftūḥa* occurs instead of the *tāʾ marbūṭa,* e.g. لكثرت for لكثرة.[67] A few additions occur, e.g. instead of كالمُدْهنِ والمُدُقَ we read نحو المدق والمكحلة

---

[50] MS E, fol. 3a ll. 8-9.
[51] Ibid, fol. 4b ll. 11-12.
[52] Ibid, fol. 8a ll. 1-2.
[53] Ibid, fols. 3a-4a l. 9, the note below.
[54] Ibid, fols. 10b-11a l. 3, the note below.
[55] Ibid, fols. 16b-17a l. 7, the note below.
[56] Ibid, fols. 16b-17a l. 7, the note below.
[57] Ibid, fols. 2a-3a l. 16, the note below.
[58] Ibid, fols. 4b-5a l. 9, the note below.
[59] Ibid, the note below.
[60] Ibid, fols. 27b-28a l. 10, the note below.
[61] Ibid, fols. 2a-3a ll. 4-5, the note below.
[62] Ibid, fols. 3a-4a l. 3.
[63] Ibid, fols. 15a-16a l. 12, the note below.
[64] De Slane, 671.
[65] The Arabic text fols. 9b-10b l. 4, the note below.
[66] Ibid, fols. 10b-11a l. 15, the note below.
[67] Ibid l. 4, the note below.

والمحرضة[68] and after أَيْنُقٌ occurs على وزن أعفل بعد القلب.[69]

H (= ح) *Bibliothèque Nationale, Paris, 4173.* The *Marāḥ* is followed by the *ʿIzzī* on fol. 38, *al-Maqṣūd* on fol. 53, *Binā' al-afʿāl* on fol. 69 and *al-Amṯila al-muḫtalifa* on fol. 79. De Slane describes it in the following way:[70]

"Papier. 92 feuillets. Hauteur, 21 centimètres; largeur, 12 centimètres. 15 lignes par page".

The name of the copyist is not revealed. The *Marāḥ* ends in the following way on fol. 38a:

"تمّ الكتاب بعون الله الوهّاب سنة ١٠٣٢".

"The book was accomplished with the assistance of God, the Giver, in the year 1033 [/1624]".

The manuscript ends as follows:

"تمّ الكتاب بعون الله الملك الوهّاب سنة ١٠٣٢ الحمد لله على الإتمام والصلوة والسلام على سيّد الأنام وعلى آله وأصحابه الأكرام".

"The book was accomplished with the assistance of God, the Giver, in the year 1033 (/1624). Praised be God for the completion and the prayer and the greeting for the Master of mankind, his honourable family and followers".

A short vowel can occur lengthened, e.g. للدالاة for للدلالة,[71] the *t* occurs instead of the *s*, e.g. وكثره for وكسر,[72] and the *š* instead of the *t*, e.g. للكشرة for لكثرته.[73] A few additions can occur, e.g. after اطـرب occurs من الطاء الضاد صوت مدة لمزيادة[74] after المجتلبة occurs لانعدام الاحتياج اليها,[75] and after الصحيح occurs في احتمال الحركات.[76] Some corrupt readings occur, e.g. يضربين instead of تضربين,[77] واقيس instead of وأقيس,[78] الصحح instead of الصحيح,[79] etc.

I (= ط) *Bibliothèque Nationale, Paris, 4174.* The *Marāḥ* is followed by the *ʿIzzī* on fol. 38, *al-Maqṣūd* on fol. 52, *Binā' al-afʿāl* on fol. 66 and *al-Amṯila al-muḫtalifa* on fol. 74. De Slane decribes it in the following manner:[80]

"Papier. 87 feuillets. Hauteur, 21 centimètres; largeur, 13 centimètres. 13 lignes par page. Ms. du XVIIe siècle".

The *Marāḥ* ends in the following way:

"تمّ الكتاب بعون الله الملك العلاّم قد وقع الفراغ من هذه النسخة الشريفة في آخر

[68] Ibid, fols. 17a-17b l. 6, the note below.
[69] Ibid, fols. 30b-31b l. 4, the note below.
[70] De Slane, 672.
[71] The Arabic text fols. 10b-11a l. 8, the note below.
[72] Ibid, fols. 11b-12a l. 13, the note below.
[73] Ibid l. 11, the note below.
[74] Ibid, fols. 20a-21a l. 1, the note below.
[75] Ibid l. 14, the note below.
[76] Ibid, fols. 21a-22a l. 4, the note below.
[77] Ibid, fols. 11a-11b l. 5, the note below.
[78] Ibid, fols. 22a-23a l. 4, the note below.
[79] Ibid, fols. 25b-26a l. 2, the note below.
[80] De Slane, 672.

جمادي كتبه الفقير المذنب المحتاج الى رحمة الله تعالى مراد بن نصوح غفر الله له ولوالديه وأحسن إليهما وإليه".

"The book was accomplished with the assistance of God, the Omniscient. This honourable transcript was completed in the end of Ǧumādī. The guilty in need of God's mercy, Murād b. Naṣūḥ, wrote it. May God forgive him and his parents and do well to them both and to him".

In some cases the *ẓ* occurs instead of the *ḍ*, e.g. بالظمَة instead of بالضمَة,[81] the *ḍ* instead of the *ẓ*, e.g. ونضيره instead of ونظيره,[82] the *ẓ* instead of the *ḏ*, e.g. والشواظ instead of والشواذ,[83] the *s* instead of the *ṯ*, e.g. لكسرة for لكثرة,[84] the *tāʾ maftūḥa* instead of the *tāʾ marbūṭa*, e.g. علامت for علامة,[85] بمنزلت for بمنزلة[86] and the *alif mamdūda* instead of the *alif maqṣūra*, e.g. جرا for جرى.[87] Corrupt readings also occur, e.g. الحقيقة instead of الخفيفة,[88] اشملل instead of شملل[89] etc. Additions suggesting the involvement of the copyist or the contamination from another tradition exist, e.g. after أنا حروف occurs لأنه على تقدير زيادة الألف يلتبس بالتثنية وعلى تقدير زيادة النون يلتبس بجمع المؤنث[90] after يَضْرِبُ occurs يضربان يضربون,[91] after الألف occurs فرقا بينه وبين الماضي,[92] after أيْنُق occurs على وزن افعل بعد القلب,[93] etc.

The following prints have been used in this edition:

K (= ک), *the print of the printing house al-Ḫaidawīya,* 1282/1865. It does not contain any vowel and is almost an exact copy of the *Print U,* and the *Print Y.* The name of the man who printed it is not revealed. It offers only very few glosses in the margins. Corrupt readings also occur, e.g. فيتعيَن بعد for وبالعين,[94] ايتسر for ايسْرَ[95] which is common with the print L.[96] Additions occur as well, e.g. after زائدة one can read والزيادة في التغيير اولى,[97] after حَمُقَ occurs بضم العين,[98] etc.

L (= ل), *the print of the printing house al-ʿUṯmānīya,* 1304/1886. It has been printed by ʿAbd

---

[81] The Arabic text fols. 13a-13b l. 7, the note below, fols. 33b-34b l. 12, the note below.
[82] Ibid, fols. 11b-12a l. 9, the note below.
[83] Ibid, fols. 3a-4a l. 14, the note below. For discussions concerning the case of the *ḍ* that occurs instead of the *ẓ* and the *ẓ* instead of the *ḍ* in Middle Arabic see Knutsson, *Studies* 106.
[84] The Arabic text fols. 4b-5a l. 6, the note below.
[85] Ibid, fols. 12a-13a l. 13, the note below.
[86] Ibid, fols. 5b-7a l. 6, fols. 30a-30b l. 8, the notes below.
[87] Ibid, fols. 3a-4a l. 2, the note below.
[88] Ibid, fols. 13a-13b l. 11, the note below.
[89] Ibid, fols. 4a-4b l. 5, the note below.
[90] Ibid, fols. 5b-7a l. 13, the note below.
[91] Ibid, fols. 9b-10b l. 2, the note below.
[92] Ibid, fols. 14a-15a l. 4, the note below.
[93] Ibid, fols. 30b-31b l. 2, the note below.
[94] Ibid, fols. 9b-10b l. 6, the note below.
[95] Ibid, fols. 22a-23a l. 12, the note below.
[96] Ibid, fols. 33b-34b l. 4, the note below.
[97] Ibid, fols. 10b-11a l. 8, the note below.
[98] Ibid, fols. 14a-15a l. 11, the note below.

al-Qādir Rāšid known as Ḫulūṣī Zādah who, as he himself states it, served as a corrector at the Printing house al-ʿUṯmānīya 1304 [/1886].[99] It is nearly a copy of the print K with only some variances, which I showed in my Apparatus. It contains a few quotations copied from al-Niksārī's commentary *al-Mifrāḥ,* Dunqūze's *Šarḥ al-marāḥ* and Ibn Kamāl Pāšā's *al-Falāḥ* and a few vowels given to some words. Unfortunately, many defective vowellings occur, e.g, وخنق وصغر[100] instead of وخَنق وصغر,[101] والنُعوت[102] instead of والنَعوت,[103] وفُروقَة[104] instead of وفَرَوقَة,[105] عَدَوَة[106] instead of عَدُوَة,[107] which render it unreliable. I have not inserted these variances in my Apparatus.

It is not stated in the print which is the basic manuscript that was used. I believe that it is a later manuscript than the MS A. The additions that reveal an attempt to explain for the reader, e.g. هي ياء for الياء,[108] المفعول الأوَل instead of الأوَل,[109] can imply that it belongs to a later tradition. The additions of التحقيقية after الكسرة and التقديرية after الضمة[110] seem to be typical of the prints.

I chose the MS A as my basic manuscript because it is the oldest one among the MSS mentioned by Brockelmann,[111] because of its relatively good language and because of its lack of additions of the kind that I observed in the other MSS and both prints,—a fact which makes me believe that it is closer to the original redaction. For example, MS E has after زائدة: والزايد اولى بالتغيير, MS I has والزايد بالتغيير اولى, the print K has والزيادة في التغيير اولى,[112] MS B and the print K have after واو هو: ويحذف[113] etc.

It is unrealistic to believe that it is possible to establish the author's original text exactly without possessing it. The subsequent manuscripts and prints offer small variances which are dependent on the copyists' linguistic backgrounds, their involvement in the study and other factors. By variances, I mean in this case correct words or expressions and even reversed order of words. As examples of correct words or expressions I mention the use of يصير in the MSS BCDEG instead of يكون in the MS A,[114] يجوز in the MSS BCI and both the prints KL instead of يجيء in the MS A,[115] واخشوشن in the MSS BDEGI and the prints KL instead of واعشوشب in the MS A,[116] يلزم الثقل in the MSS DEGI for يثقل in the MS A,[117] the use of one form of a verb

[99] L, 143.
[100] Ibid, 4 l. 4.
[101] The Arabic text fols. 3a-4a l. 4.
[102] L, 4 l. 19.
[103] The Arabic text fols. 3a-4a l. 16.
[104] L, 18 l. 10.
[105] The Arabic text fols. 15a-16a l. 12.
[106] L, 18 l. 10.
[107] The Arabic text fols. 15a-16a l. 14.
[108] Ibid, fols. 7b-8b l. 2.
[109] Ibid l. 6.
[110] Ibid, fols. 4b-5a ll. 10-11.
[111] Brockelmann, *S II,* 14.
[112] The Arabic text fols. 10b-11a l. 8, the note below.
[113] Ibid, fols. 7a-7b l. 13, the note below.
[114] Ibid, fols. 7b-8b l. 5, the note below.
[115] Ibid, fols. 20a-21a l. 13, the note below.
[116] Ibid, fols. 4a-4b l. 2, the note below.
[117] Ibid, fols. 14a-15a l. 6, the note below.

instead of another, e.g. وينجزم in the MSS BGHI instead of ويجزم in the MS A,[118] يحتمل in the MSS CDHI and the print L instead of يتحمّل in the MS A,[119] the use of one form of a *maṣdar* instead of another, e.g. ولانعدام in the MSS BCDEGI and the prints KL instead of ولعدم in the MS A,[120] مشابهة in the MSS BDGH, تشبيها in the MSS CE, instead of تشبّها in the MS A.[121] As some examples of reversed order of words I can mention وأعجف وأسمر in the MSS CDE and the prints KL instead of وأسمر وأعجف in MS A,[122] ويفضل وينظر ويرطم in the MSS BDEGI for وينَضَل ويَلَطم وينظُر in the MS A with as well the variant ويفضل chosen among them instead of وينَضَل,[123] and القيلولة والغيبوبة in the MSS BDH and the print L for الغيبوبة والقيلولة in the MS A.[124]

I do not believe either that the remaining manuscripts and prints found in the different libraries all over the world would have contributed much to the constitution of the text. Adopting the MS A as my basic manuscript means that I followed its readings when they were correct, but did not hesitate to correct the ones which break the laws of classical Arabic grammar, or to suply the missing words which are important for understanding the context. In doing so I based my judgement on the other MSS and the prints. I did not neglect to report most of these variances in the Apparatus, except for the cases of hyphenation and corrupt *shadda, madda,* and hamza, which I did not insert but adjusted directly in the edition. The hamza usually occurs on the line when it should be on the alif, e.g. ءاكرم.[125] A *madda* sometimes occurs over the alif, e.g. اليآء, الفآء, the *y* is written inside the words instead of the *hamza ʿalā kursī al-yāʾ,* e.g. الزوايد instead of الزوائد. I changed these variations in accordance with accepted practice. The alif is elided in ثلثة[126] which is typical of this period, and I have kept it this way. I have indicated the original fol. numbers of the MS A in the margin and I have presented the poetical lines between double guillemets "" and the Qur'anic verses between brackets (). The addition of والله أعلم is unique in MS A[127] implying the involvement of the copyist. I have as well added a fair number of vowels, mostly to all the morphological forms and examples, and in other instances as well, to facilitate the reading of the text.

---

[118] Ibid, fols. 12a-13a l. 9, the note below.
[119] Ibid, fols. 22a-23a l. 6, the note below.
[120] Ibid, fols. 3a-4a l. 13, the note below.
[121] Ibid, fols. 13a-13b l. 9, the note below.
[122] Ibid, fols. 14a-15a l. 10, the note below.
[123] Ibid, fols. 20a-21a l. 11, the note below.
[124] Ibid, fols. 26b-27b l. 16, the note below.
[125] Ibid, fols. 12a-13a l. 6, the note below.
[126] Ibid, fols. 2a-3a l. 8, fols. 5b-7a l. 17, l. 18, fols. 24b-25b l. 1.
[127] Ibid, fols. 11a-11b l. 7, the note below.

§ 7. Topics in works dealing with morphology

As was already mentioned, the first well-known treatise that deals with syntax and morphology is Sībawaihi's *al-Kitāb*. The subject of morphology is found in the major part of the second volume. The main morpho-phonological topics that Sībawaihi presents are the forms of nouns, adjectives and verbs in the groundform and in the augmented forms, the phonological change(s) due to the unsoundness of a weak consonant in forms that have a weak consonant or more, the substitution of the consonants, the addition of an augment to a form, the linguistic analogy between one form and another and the assimilation of one consonant to another.[1] These themes can be considered as classical for many works in morphology that follow it.

The phonological procedures that are carried out in a word are specifically recognized by Ibn Ǧinnī in his *Muḫtaṣar al-taṣrīf al-mulūkī*[2] as: زيادة بدل حذف تغيير بحركة او سكون ادغام "Addition, substitution, elision, change by giving a vowel or a sukūn and assimilation".[3] Ibn Ǧinnī's study in this particular work is based on these vital points and is a presentation of the specific forms affected by them.

It is with his commentary on al-Māzinī's study *al-Munṣif*,[4] namely *al-Munṣif fī šarḥ taṣrīf al-Māzinī*,[5] that the study of morpho-phonology developed in particular. This book's importance resides in the fact that it was compiled by this brilliant linguist, well-known for his ability in integrating theories in his analyses, commenting on the early work in morpho-phonology of the Basran grammarian, al-Māzinī. It does not only give a picture of the study of morpho-phonology when it was still new after the period of Sībawaihi, but also of how it was treated by a later grammarian during a period that witnesses more than a century and a half of theoretical activities. Concerning it, Guillaume remarks:

> "Il suffit en effet de lire quelques pages du MUN *[Munṣif]* pour se rendre compte à quel point l'analyse de IG [Ibn Ǧinnī] est plus riche [que celle de al-Māzinī], et intègre des problématiques et des démarches nouvelles, qui, au-delà de son apport personnel, au demeurant non négligeable, représentent le fruit de plus d'un siècle d'activité théorique intense".[6]

Its chapters' titles reveal to us most of the topics which are usually studied in this field. It can be observed generally that the book deals with the base forms of the nouns and verbs, the augmented forms by an augment or more, the linguistic analogy between one strong form and another, the forms with 1st radical *y* or *w*, the forms with 2nd radical *y* or *w*, the forms in which the *w* is changed into a *y*, the forms with 3rd radical hamza in verbs with 2nd radical *y* or *w*, the forms with 3rd radical *y* or *w*, the forms in which the *y* is changed into a *w*, the forms with 2nd and 3rd radical yā's, the forms with 2nd and 3rd radical wāws, the linguistic analogy between one weak form and another, and forms in which the infixed *t* of Form VIII is changed into another consonant. Again we notice that the main points that are stressed by Sībawaihi regarding morphology are taken into consideration, with the exception of the assimilation of a consonant to another that pertains to the doubled verb.

In his *Sirr Ṣināʿat al-iʿrāb*,[7] Ibn Ǧinnī takes up the twenty-nine consonants of the Arabic

---

[1] Cf. Hindāwī, *Manāhiǧ* 41.

[2] For a short description of the work see Méhiri, *Théories* 71.

[3] Ibn Ǧinnī, *de Flexione* 8.

[4] Al-Māzinī's work was never found alone.

[5] For a short description of the work see Méhiri, *Théories* 74-75.

[6] Guillaume, *Morphonologie* 224.

[7] For a discussion concerning the title *Ṣināʿat al-iʿrāb*, which may confuse the reader because of the word *iʿrāb* in it, by making him possibly believe that Ibn Ǧinnī has treated syntax and not morphology in this work,—which is not the case -, see Hindāwī, *Manāhiǧ* 70-73 and Hindāwī's introduction to Ibn Ǧinnī, *Sirr I*, 24-25. The conclusion that Hindāwī, *Manāhiǧ* 73 reaches, is that Ibn Ǧinnī with the title of his book, intended to treat the formation of the

alphabet which he studies at the level of phonetics, phonology and morphology. Each section treats a consonant regarding its originality in the base form, its addition, its elision, its substitution and its unsoundness,—if it is a weak consonant—, in many different forms.[8]

The *Šāfiya* is a new and shorter version of the morphological part of Zamaḫšarī's (d. 538/ 1143-4)[9] *Mufaṣṣal.*[10]

The part of the *Mufaṣṣal* that deals with morphology presents the following topics: the pronouns, the *maṣdar,* the active and passive participles, the assimilated adjective, the elative, the nouns of time and place, the noun of instrument, the groundform and the derived forms of the triliteral and quadriliteral nouns, the quinquiliteral nouns, the perfect, the imperfect and the imperative, the groundfrom and the derived forms of both the triliteral and quadriliteral verbs, the energetic, the alleviation of the hamza, the augments in nouns and verbs, the substitution of the consonants, the unsoundness of a weak consonant and the assimilation of a consonant to another. These classical morphological themes, with the exception of the groundform and the derived forms of the triliteral and of the quadriliteral and quinquiliteral nouns, are as well dealt with by Ibn Masʿūd in a more concise manner and in a differently structured work, but with an interest in explaining the reasons of each linguistic phenomenon which does not occur frequently in the *Mufaṣṣal.*

A study of the *ʿIzzī,* which follows the *Marāḥ* in the compilation *Maǧmūʿ al-mutūn "A Compilation of Linguistic Texts",* can give us a glimpse of its general plan. Al-Zanǧānī deals in it with the groundform and the derived forms of the triliteral and quadriliteral verbs, the perfect, the imperfect and the imperative, both the energetic nūns, the doubled verb, the weak verbs: the verbs with 1st radical *w* or *y,* those with 2nd radical *w* or *y,* those with 3rd radical *w* or *y,* the verbs that are doubly weak and the hamzated verbs. He integrates at the end of his work the active and passive participles and the noun of instrument. He does not study the substitution of the consonants as Ibn Masʿūd does, nor does he treat the assimilation and the unsoundness of a weak consonant as exhaustively as him.

A question which might be of interest is why the *ʿIzzī* follows the *Marāḥ* in spite of the fact that al-Zanǧānī lived before Ibn Masʿūd. The answer would be, according to my opinion, that the *Marāḥ* is larger than the *ʿIzzī* and that it was more popular for the readers because of its pedagogical character. Differently from the *Izzī,* it contains references to some important grammarians, to both the Basran and the Kufan grammarians, to qur'anical citations, to verses of poetry, and to some dialectal variants. Another important factor which is worth having in mind, is Ibn Masʿūd's method of presenting the morphological data and of explaining the reasons of each phonological procedure. Both works can therefore be separated from each other regarding the different methods that have been adopted. Al-Zanǧānī's descriptive method is more similar to al-Zamaḫšarī's in his part of the *Mufaṣṣal* that treats morphology.

As for the *Maqṣūd* which occurs usually after the *ʿIzzī* in the same compilation, it is a sort of summary of it. The *Bināʾ* which occurs after it deals only and generally with the forms of verbs.

In Ibn Masʿūd, *MS J,* the *Šāfiya* of Ibn al-Ḥāǧib replaces the *ʿIzzī,* which means that it has

---

words regarding the phonological procedures that affect them. It is these same words that bring forth the syntactical rules when they are combined in sentences.

[8] For a description of the work see Méhiri, *Théories* 76-78, Hindāwī's introduction to Ibn Ǧinnī, *Sirr* 17-19.

[9] Al-Zamaḫšarī, Maḥmūd b. ʿUmar, see Suyūṭī, *Buġya II,* 279-280, Darwīš, *Maʿāǧim* 128 sqq., Qifṭī, *Inbāh III,* 265-272, Ibn Ḫallikān, *Dictionary III,* 321-328, Brockelmann, *S I,* 507-513. He studied grammar under Abū l-Ḥasan ʿAlī b. al-Muẓaffar al-Nīsābūrī and Abū Muḍar al-Iṣbahānī. He wrote *al-Mufaṣṣal, al-Kaššāf fī l-tafsīr, al-Fāʾiq fī ġarīb al-ḥadīṯ, al-Maqāmāt, Šarḥ abyāt al-kitāb, Asās al-balāġa* and other works.

[10] Cf. Fleish, *Esquisse* 16. *Al-Mufaṣṣal* which deals with both syntax and morphology, forms the basis of C. Caspari's *Grammatica Arabica* of 1848 that Wright, *Grammar* is based on. It is commented on by Ibn Yaʿīš, *Šarḥ al-Mufaṣṣal* which forms the basis of Howell's *Grammar of the Classical Arabic Language.*

also been a part of some of the works of the *Maǧmūʿ al-mutūn.* Deeply influenced by al-Zamaḫšarī, it is not surprising that Ibn al-Ḥāǧib has also commented on the *Mufaṣṣal* in a *Šarḥ,* which he called *al-Īḍāḥ.*[11] It is also interesting to observe that one of the commentators of the *Šarḥ al-šāfiya,*[12] namely al-Ǧārburdīy (d. 746/1345),[13] copied al-Zanǧānī extensively.[14]

Summarizing this short discussion it can be said that Sībawaihi was among the first who formulated the morphological themes. Ibn Ǧinnī elucidated many issues by integrating the methodological questions relating to both morphology and phonology. A trend has been established that has been followed and developed by many grammarians, among them Ibn Masʿūd.

It is hence possible in many works to distinguish between two different approaches, one that is mainly concerned in presenting the morphological data and another one which integrates as well the theoretical speculations.

---

[11] Cf. Suyūṭī, *Buġya II,* 135.

[12] Ten commentaries of *al-Šāfiya* exist (cf. Fleish, *Esquisse* 16).

[13] Al-Ǧārburdīy, Aḥmad b. al-Ḥasan Faḫr al-Din, see Suyūṭī, *Buġya I,* 303. Beside his mentioned work, he wrote *Šarḥ al-kaššāf* and other works.

[14] Cf. Suyūṭī, *Buġya II,* 122.

§ 8. A general Introduction to the *Marāḥ*

Having taken into account the works on morphology compiled before the *Marāḥ* and some of the main morpho-phonological topics treated in some of them, the following observations can shed light on the general background which helped develop Ibn Masʿūd's method in dealing with the subject of morpho-phonology. The obstacles which stand in the way of examining the author's private background is that we do not know anything about his life, his teachers and his pupils. In spite of the fact that his work has been commented on, little as well is known about his commentators and their commentaries which are preserved mostly in manuscript forms and are housing in different Libraries in the world. Perhaps some future investigations shall answer some puzzling questions concerning our author, his commentators and their private circles.

As Ibn Masʿūd indicates in his introduction,[1] the *Marāḥ* is divided into seven chapters: the strong verb, the doubled verb, the hamzated verb, the verb with 1st radical *w* or *y*, the verb with 2nd radical *w* or *y*, the verb with 3rd radical *w* or *y*, and the verb that is doubly weak. Each chapter deals with its characteristic class of verb, its *maṣdar* and the nine subordinates derived from it: the perfect, the imperfect, the imperative and the prohibition, the active participle, the passive participle, the nouns of time and place and the noun of instrument. A work of this nature studies the procedure(s) of *al-taṣrīf* that affect(s) a certain form.

It should be borne in mind when studying such a late work that many of the morpho-phonological themes that are taken up have been treated in earlier studies. This does not mean however that the methods adopted by our writer are the same as those of his predecessors. If we are looking for an original contribution, it is in the techniques employed by Ibn Masʿūd in presenting and looking for the reasons that lay behind the phonological procedures,—whether they relate to the development of a form from a base form, as e.g. قَالَ from قَوَلَ "to say", a verb with 2nd *w* radical, or to the generation of a form from another as e.g the active participle "hitting" ضَارِبٌ from the verb in the perfect ضَرَبَ "to hit" -, that we may find it.

Here *qiyās* "analogy" plays a vital role. By it is meant this intellectual ability of explaining the "order of things" with the intention of proving that everything falls within the language's well-established system. The methods adapted are to compare the various issues with other ones already met and investigated, and by doing so being able to discover a certain pattern[2] or more, in order to put together the common facts and to isolate the deviant ones. This process of reasoning relies on rules, causes[3] and principles, such which leads to the integration of logic into grammar.[4] As Guillaume writes concerning grammar and the integration of principles in it:

> "La grammaire, en effet, n'est pour les GA [grammairiens arabes] qu'un ensemble de principes explicites visant à reproduire une capacité intuitive et comme innée des anciens Arabes: celle de produire un nombre infini d'énoncés grammaticalement corrects".[5]

---

[1] Cf. the Arabic text fols. 1b-2a.

[2] Cf. Bohas/Guillaume/Kouloughli, *Linguistic* 23.

[3] One of the early works that deals with the grammatical causes is *al-Īḍāḥ fī ʿilal al-naḥw* by al-Zaǧǧāǧī (d. 339) (al-Zaǧǧāǧī, ʿAbd al-Raḥmān b. Isḥāq, see Suyūṭī, *Buġya II*, 77, Zubaidī, *Ṭabaqāt* 119, Ibn al-Anbārī, *Nuzha* 379, Qifṭī, *Inbāh II*, 160-161, Ibn al-ʿImād, *Šaḏarāt II*, 357, Brockelmann, *GAL I*, 112, *S I*, 170-171, Versteegh, *Zaǧǧāǧī* 2-6. He studied under al-Zaǧǧāǧ. He wrote as well *al-Ǧumal, al-Kāfī, Šarḥ kitāb al-alif wa-l-lām li-l-Māzinī, al-Lāmāt, al-Amālī* and other books). The book treats the causes of the grammatical facts by citing the Kufans' opinions with the terms used by the Basrans (cf. Zaǧǧāǧī, *Īḍāḥ* 78). The science is introduced by Ḍaif in his preface to this work as فلسفة العلل النحوية "the philosophy of the grammatical causes" implying the infiltration of logic into grammar (for discussions see Versteegh, *Zaǧǧāǧī* 45-46). The work is translated and commented on by Versteegh, *Zaǧǧāǧī*.

[4] For discussions concerning the possible influence of Stoic logic see Versteegh, *Elements*.

[5] Guillaume, *Morphonologie* 240.

There is a difference of meaning between the *qiyās* in the earliest period and the one that occurs in later Arabic grammar. Concerning its original meaning Versteegh remarks:

> "... Originally *qiyās* was the rule by which words are derived from other words, and which divides words into various classes, each with its own rule... The verb *qāsa* means "to formulate, to set up a rule which governs certain groups or classes of words".[6]

Concerning both its meanings he remarks:

> "In later Arabic grammar, the *qiyās* became an instrument to set up linguistic arguments, which were always based on similarities between words and parts of speech, but in the earliest period the *qiyās* was an instrument of language production: with its help the grammarians could produce new forms, that were not attested in the language of the Beduin. It could even be used to correct existing forms, if they did not conform to the genius of the Arabic language, which is the real sense of the *qiyās al-ʿArabiyya*".[7]

Qiyās in later Arabic grammar is the fruit of the scientific spirit nourished by the translations from the Greek, which developed mostly during the 3th century of the Hiǧra[8] and onwards. It is this interest in Greek philosophy that drove hundreds of pupils at the beginning of this period into listening daily to Abū Bišr Mattā b. Yūnus (d. 338/940), the translator of *Posterior Analytics,* explaining the *Organon* of Aristotle.[9]

In the field of grammar, these Arab grammarians who were well-acquainted with philosophy and religion,[10] became challenged by new methods of dealing with theories, and found themselves obliged to explain old themes, which did not create any problem before in a new satisfying manner.[11] Concerning this change of attitude in presenting their discipline Guillaume remarks:

> "Il semble en effet qu'à cette époque bien des choses qui allaient de soi pour les anciens grammairiens commencent à faire problème, et que même le statut privilégié dont jouissait leur discipline dans l'ancienne organisation du savoir sont remis en cause par l'introduction de problématiques et de démarches nouvelles. Il y a là comme un "défi" qui oblige les GA (grammairiens arabes) à expliciter une bonne partie des fondements théoriques de leur pratique, à énoncer les conditions auxquelles leurs analyses sont recevables et à démontrer qu'elles y satisfont".[12]

The importance of analogy is attested by many of the Arabic grammarians. Ibn al-Anbārī writes:

> "إعلم أنَ إنكار القياس في النحو لا يتحقَق ، لأنَ النحو كلّه قياس... فمن أنكر القياس فقد أنكر النحو".
>
> "Know that the denial of the analogy in grammar cannot be possible because grammar is all based on analogy... And the one who denied analogy also denied grammar".[13]

---

[6] Versteegh, *Qiyās.*

[7] Versteegh, *Grammar* 37.

[8] Endress's edition of twelve extracts from the Institution Theologica, translated from works on Greek philosophy by Arabs of the 3rd century: *Proclus Arabus,* gives us an idea of how well the Arabs were acquainted with the Greek philosophy.

[9] Cf. Arnaldez, *Sciences* 366. Among one of the recent works concerning the Arabic translations of the *Organon,* the work of ʿAbd al-Raḥman al-Badawī, of which three volumes have been published in Cairo 1948, can be referred to (for discussions see Walzer, *Translations;* for discussions concerning the translation of Aristotle's work into Arabic see Peters, *Aristotle* 57-67, for discussions concerning the existence of a well-defined Arabic philosophy see Madkūr, *Falsafa* 1-27).

[10] Cf. Weiss, *Subject* 605 note 1, Vollers, *Review of Nöldeke* 126-127, Kopf, *Influences* 46-50.

[11] For discussions see Versteegh, *Zaǧǧāǧī* 45.

[12] Guillaume, *Morphonologie* 233.

[13] Ibn al-Anbārī, *Lumaʿ* 44. It is also quoted by Ḥassān, *Uṣūl* 168 and referred to by Versteegh, *Elements* 111 in his notes.

Also Abū ʿAlī l-Fārisī is known to have said to Ibn Ǧinnī:

"أخطئ في خمسين مسألة في اللغة ولا أخطئ في واحدة من القياس".

"I might commit errors in fifty linguistic questions, but I do not co mmit any error in any question concerning analogy".[14]

Ibn Ǧinnī also affirms that any grammarian of great competence can present theories contrary to those of the Kufans and of the Basrans by using the analogy.[15]

By applying the methods of *qiyās,* Ibn Masʿūd is enabled to compare a word's pattern in which a phonological procedure is carried out, e.g. an assimilation, a substitution, an elision or a change that is caused by an unsound weak consonant, etc., to a so-called أصل[16] "an underlying form", or to another word's pattern, or also to compare a part of speech to another, e.g the imperfect verb to the active participle, etc.,[17] and by doing so, revealing some important rules and principles, which leads to a better understanding of the investigated data. For instance among the many examples that Ibn Masʿūd presents in his study, he takes up احْمَرَّ "to be red" underlyingly احْمَرَرَ that is formed according to the stem IX افْعَلَّ underlyingly افْعَلَلَ, in which both last consonants of the base forms are assimilated because they are identical. By reading the example ارْعَوَى "to abstain", which is a 3rd radical *w* verb, he could observe from the word's pattern that it is formed according to افْعَلَلَ, and by comparing it with احْمَرَرَ, he could conclude that no assimilation of one weak consonant to the other is carried out in it resulting in ارْعَوَّ or ارْعَيَّ, on the basis that the *w* and the *y* are not identical weak consonants, and by being so, prohibit the assimilation.[18] The treatment of a given issue can be complex because it can depend on numerous rules that touch other points of the question, among which many are connected to other issues. For instance, by explaining why no morpho-phonological procedure is carried out in قَوْلٌ "a saying", Ibn Masʿūd contrasts the vowelless weak consonant preceded by a fatḥa in it with the vowelless weak consonant preceded by a kasra in مِوْزَانٌ in which a phonological change is carried out by changing the *w* into a *y* resulting in مِيزَانٌ "balance", and with the vowelless weak consonant preceded by a ḍamma in يُيْسِرُ in which a phonological change is carried out by changing the *y* into a *w* resulting in يُوسِرُ "is well off".[19] The difference that is highlighted in the sequences of these three examples is the vowel preceding the vowelless weak consonant, a fatḥa in the first case, a kasra in the second, and a ḍamma in the third. The deduced rule is that the fatḥa is light when it precedes a light vowelless weak consonant,

---

[14] Ibn Ǧinnī, *Ḫaṣāʾiṣ II,* 88.

[15] Ibn Ǧinnī, *Ḫaṣāʾiṣ I,* 189. This is possible as long as what is reported does not contradict the foundations of the language, as putting the object in the nominative, the subject in the genitive and the second element of the *iḍāfa* in the nominative, as mentioned by Ibn Ǧinnī, *Ḫaṣāʾiṣ I,* 387.

[16] أصل is interpreted by Bohas, *Aspects* 205, especially note 7, as "abstract representation" or "underlying representation". The use of the term "underlying form" does not mean that it has occurred historically before the current form (for discussions see Ibn Ǧinnī, *Ḫaṣāʾiṣ I,* 256-257, Guillaume, *Morphonologie* 222-241, *Aspects* 342-358, Mokhlis, *Taṣrīf* 43-45).

[17] Cf. the Arabic text fols. 4b-5a, fols. 9b-10b and my notes (43), (47), (93), (122).

[18] Cf. the Arabic text fols. 4a-4b and my notes (40).

[19] Cf. the Arabic text fols. 26b-27b.

which is the reason why no phonological change is carried out in قَوْلٌ, by contrast to the other cases in which the vowels are considered as heavy.

By looking for the reasons of most of the morpho-phonological phenomena, e.g. the choice of an augment or more, the elision of a consonant or of a vowel, the transfer of a vowel or of a consonant, the assimilation, the change carried out due to an unsound weak consonant, the substitution, the inflection or uninflectedness of a word, etc., Ibn Masʿūd is able to draw his conclusions by supporting his theories on principles and causes that have been established before him. Like many of those grammarians well-acquainted with logic[20] who precede him, he adheres to the idea that everything in the Arabic language must have an explanation.[21] His intention is to show that there exists in the field of morpho-phonology a perfect system of logical principles and causes which can be discovered by an intuitive soul.[22]

Most of the judgements in presenting general linguistic theories are made according to the principles of what is necessary, forbidden, liked, disliked, weak or possible. One of the general principles is that what is not considered in the Classical language cannot be used in the analogy.[23] Consequently, he writes that the pattern فَوْعَلٌ does not exist in "their language",[24] by which he means according to both the Basran and Kufan grammarians,—and even also before their time, as the Arabic language is considered to have been talked correctly by the Ancients,[25]—which implies that no word can analogically be formed according to it.

The following are some of the causes[26] and principles that Ibn Masʿūd relied on in his arguments, which determine for instance the choice of a vowel or of a vowellessness, the elision or the addition of an augment, the dislike of certain combinations, the commensurability to a certain form or the declension or the undeclinability of a certain part of speech:

– The cause of resemblance between two parts of speech, as e.g. the resemblance of the

---

[20] The difference between logic and Arabic grammar has been treated by some, e.g. Aḥmad b. al-Ṭayyib al-Saraḫsī, the pupil of al-Kindī (cf. Abed, *Logic* XIV) and Yaḥya b. ʿAdī (cf. Elamrani-Jamal, *Ibn ʿAdī* 1-15). For discussions concerning the grammarians' conception of grammar and logic see Versteegh, *Elements* 123-127; for discussions concerning the debate between the grammarians and the logicians see Abed, *Logic* XIV sqq.

[21] This is also stressed by Ibn Ǧinnī, *Ḫaṣāʾiṣ I*, 53-54.

[22] Guillaume, *Principes* 17 writes concerning this insight that those interested in the reasons of linguistic facts have:

"Une intuition: que le désordre *apparent* des faits linguistiques recouvre un ordre secret, caché—*merveilleux*".

Or as he writes in *Système* citing Antoine Meillet:

"Chaque langue forme un système où tout se tient et a un plan d'une merveilleuse rigueur".

[23] Cf. Ibn al-Anbārī, *Inṣāf* Q. 94, 273, particularly ll. 9-11.

[24] Cf. the Arabic text fols. 16b-17a.

[25] According to Zaǧǧāǧī, *Īḍāḥ* 65-66 who refers to al-Ḫalīl's saying, the grammarian's task is similar to the one of a wise man who penetrates a monument that is remarkably built and who tries to imagine how the architect has built it. For each thing that this man discovers in the building, he wonders: Somehow, this was constructed because of this reason or that other. It is possible that this monument's wise architect has built this special construction for the same reason that the man who penetrated the monument mentions, as well as it is possible that he did it for a completely other reason. The grammar is then a reconstruction adapted to the natural temperament of the Ancient idealized desert Arabs. Referring to them Bohas, *Aspects* 209 writes:

"Ces Arabes étaient bien sûr, ceux de l'époque ancienne, seuls détenteurs de la langue arabe, locuteurs par excellence et les seuls dont l'usage linguistique soit recevable, selon toute la tradition des grammairiens arabes".

For a more detailed discussion concerning this subject see Fück, *ʿArabīya* ch. 9, Bohas, *Aspects* 214-215, Guillaume, *Morphonologie* 240-241, Versteegh, *Zaǧǧāǧī* 31-32.

[26] Zaǧǧāǧī, *Īḍāḥ* 64-65 presents three sorts of grammatical causes: the علل تعليميّة "educational causes", the علل قياسيّة "causes accordant with analogy", and the علل جدليّة نظريّة "theoretical causes proposed as a basis for discussion" (for discussions see Bohas, *Aspects* 210-214, ʿĪd, *Uṣūl* 137-138, Versteegh, *Zaǧǧāǧī* 90-91).

imperfect to the active participle which is a noun, which is why the imperfect is made declinable as the noun.[27]

The resemblance of the *li*– of indirect command prefixed to the jussive, e.g. لِيَضْرِبْ "let him hit!" to the preposition *li*– prefixed to the noun in the genitive, which is the reason why it is given a kasra, as the jussive in verbs corresponds to the genitive in nouns.[28]

The resemblance of an example which is formed according to a certain form to an example commensurable to the same form. Examples are فَخْذٌ "thigh" and فَهْوَ which are formed according to فَعْلٌ. فَخْذٌ is underlyingly فَخِذٌ commensurable to فَعِلٌ, and فَهْوَ "and so he" is underlyingly فَهُوَ commensurable to فَعُلٌ. The similarity between both these examples is the *f* vowelled by a fatḥa and the resemblance between both the forms فَعِلٌ and فَعُلٌ. The vowel of the *ḫ* that follows the vowelled *f* in فَخِذٌ is elided resulting in فَخْذٌ on the analogy of the elision of the vowel of the *h* that follows the conjunction, the *fa-*, in فَهُوَ resulting in فَهْوَ. In accordance with this rule, the *li*– of indirect command following both the conjunctions, the *wa*– and the *fa-,* is made vowelless, e.g. وَلْيَضْرِبْ "and let him hit!" said instead of وَلِيَضْرِبْ and فَلْيَضْرِبْ "and so let him hit!" said instead of فَلِيَضْرِبْ.[29]

The resemblance in meaning between two words can be the reason of an existent similarity between both their patterns. An example is مِسْكِينَةٌ "poor", which takes the *tāʾ marbūṭa* in spite of its being on the pattern مِفْعِيلٌ that does not have a separate form for the fem., because it is compared with its synonym فَقِيرَةٌ "poor".[30]

The contrary may also apply, i.e. the fact that two words have opposite meanings can be the cause that a similarity exits between both their patterns. Examples are عَدُوَّةٌ "enemy (fem.)", which takes the *tāʾ marbūṭa,* in spite of the fact that it should not be suffixed to the pattern فَعُولٌ that has the meaning of the active participle, because it is compared with its opposite صَدِيقَةٌ "female friend",[31] and المَوَتَانُ "much death" to which the ending *-ānu* is suffixed to, because it is compared with its opposite الحَيَوَانُ "much life".[32]

– The cause of differenciating between two linguistic phenomena to avoid ambiguity, as suffixing the *alif mamdūda* after the agent pronoun *ū* that marks the 3rd person of the masc. pl. of the perfect, e.g. رَضُوا "they were satisfied", to differenciate this *w* from the *w* of the conjunction that occurs between two verbs, e.g. حَضَرَ وَتَكَلَّمَ زَيْدٌ "Zaid came and talked", which could have been read حَضَرُوتَكَلَّمَ "they were present, he talked" if this *ā* did not occur.[33]

The infixed *ī* is made to precede the *n* in the ending *-īna* of the 2nd person of the fem. of the

[27] Cf. the Arabic text fols. 4b-5a, fols. 9b-10b and my notes (43), (47), (93), (122).
[28] Cf. the Arabic text fols. 11b-12a, and my notes (107), (108).
[29] Cf. the Arabic text fols. 11b-12a and my notes (109), (110).
[30] Cf. the Arabic text fols. 15a-16a and my notes (151).
[31] Cf. the Arabic text fols. 15a-16a and my notes (152).
[32] Cf. the Arabic text fols. 27b-28a and my notes (271), (271 b).
[33] Cf. the Arabic text fols. 4b-5a and my notes (50).

sing., e.g. تَضْرِبِينَ "you hit, fem. sing.", to differenciate this form from the pl. form تَضْرِبْنَ "you hit, fem. pl.".[34]

The suffixed pronoun of the nominative of the 1st person of the pl. of the perfect is a *n* followed by an *ā*, namely the *-nā*, .g. ضَرَبْنَا "we hit" to differenciate this *n* from the *n* of the fem. of the 3rd person of the pl. vowelled by a fatḥa, namely the *-na*, e.g. ضَرَبْنَ "they hit, fem. pl.".[35]

– The cause of treating equally two patterns, as giving the common gender to the pattern فَعِيلٌ that has the meaning of the passive participle مَفْعُولٌ, e.g. قَتِيلٌ which means مَقْتُولٌ or مَقْتُولَةٌ "murdered" for both the masc. and fem. sing., and to فَعُولٌ that has the meaning of the active participle فَاعِلٌ, e.g. صَبُورٌ which means صَابِرٌ or صَابِرَةٌ "patient" for both the masc. and fem. sing., so that both these patterns are treated equally.[36]

– The cause of priority,[37] as giving the sukūn to the immediately consonant following a prefix, e.g. يَضْرِبُ "he hits", or preceding a suffix, e.g. ضَرَبْنَ "they hit, fem. pl.", in order to prevent the disliked succession of four vowels, because this consonant is prior in its position to be given the sukūn than any other consonant.[38]

The suffixed pronouns of the nominative of both the 1st and 2nd persons are not suppressed but manifested, e.g. ضَرَبْتُ "I hit", ضَرَبْتَ "you hit /masc. sing.", ضَرَبْنَا "we hit", etc., because it is prior to maintain them due to the strength of these persons,[39] in relation to the 3rd persons of the sing., e.g. ضَرَبَ "he hit" and ضَرَبَتْ "she hit".

– The cause of heaviness,[40] which justifies the elision of a consonant, as e.g. the elision of the weak consonant *w* in يَعِدُ "he promises" underlyingly يَوْعِدُ, because of its occurrence between a *y* and a kasra,[41] which implies a heaviness which is disliked; and the elision of the *ā* in هُدَبِدٌ "very thick milk" underlyingly هُدَابِدٌ, عُلَبِطٌ "a lot of sheep, also a fat man" underlyingly عُلَابِطٌ,[42] and مِخْيَطٌ "a needle" underlyingly مِخْيَاطٌ,[43] because of the dislike that the Arabs have for long words.[44] Ibn Ǧinnī remarks that each time you have difficulty in explaining [a linguis-

---

[34] Cf. the Arabic text fols. 7b-8b.

[35] Cf. ibid, fols. 5b-7a.

[36] Cf. ibid, fols. 15a-16a.

[37] The term أولى mentioned by Ibn Masʿūd to characterize priority occurs in the Arabic text fols. 8b-9b, fols. 10b-11a, fols. 14a-15a, fols. 15a-16a and 31 a. It occurs 81 times in Sībawaihi's *Kitāb* according to Troupeau, *Lexique* 222. One of its synonyms أقْيَسُ together with the term قِيَاس occurs 187 times according to him, cf. ibid, 179 and the other one أَجْدَرُ occurs 50 times according to him, cf. ibid, 54-55. For a discussion of this cause or the *a fortiori* argument in *fiqh*, *nahw* and *kalām* see Gwynne, *A fortiori* 165-177.

[38] Cf. the Arabic text fols. 10b-11a.

[39] Cf. ibid, fols. 8b-9b.

[40] For a discussion concerning the terms lighter-heavier with interesting references see Owens, *Foundations* 202-203.

[41] Cf. the Arabic text fols. 2a-3a, fols. 26a-26b.

[42] Cf. ibid, fols. 5a-5b and my notes (56).

[43] Cf. the Arabic text fols. 5a-5b and my notes (57).

[44] This dislike is also expressed by Ḫalīl, *ʿAyn II*, 248, whose introduction is translated by Haywood, *Lexicography* 29:

tic fact], search [for the reasons of its particularity] in the field of the lightness and heaviness of the pronunciation.[45] In the light of this rule, the assimilation is justified, e.g. اِحْمَارّ "to be very red" and اِحْمَرَّ "to be red" underlyingly اِحْمَارَرَ and اِحْمَرَرَ[46] respectively.

– The cause of compensating for what is lost, as in عَدَّ الأَمْرِ which is said instead of عِدَّةَ الأَمْرِ in which الأَمْرِ that is the second element of the *iḍāfa* construction, is a compensation for the elided *tāʾ marbūṭa* of عَدَّ,[47] that is the first element of the *iḍāfa* construction, and in الإِقَامَةُ and الإِسْتِقَامَةُ in which the *tāʾ marbūṭa* is a compensation for the elision of the vowel of the 2nd weak radical *w* of the verb that is changed into an *ā*.[48]

– By principle the verbs should be undeclinable.[49]
– By principle the marker of invariability should be the sukūn.[50]
– By principle, the declension pertains to nouns.[51]
– Two markers of the fem. are not to be combined, e.g. مُسْلِمَاتٌ underlyingly مُسْلِمَتَاتٌ.[52] According to this rule the suffix *-t* marker of the 3rd person of the fem. sing. of the perfect, e.g. ضَرَبَتْ "she hit", is elided in the 3rd person of the fem. of the pl., e.g. ضَرَبْنَ "they hit /fem. pl.", which did not become ضَرَبَتْنَ.[53]

– Two vowelless consonants are not to be combined.[54] This is why the suffixed *t* of the fem. is vowelled by a fatḥa in the dual, namely *-t(a)ā*, as it precedes the vowelless *ā*, in e.g. ضَرَبَتَا "they both hit /fem. dual",[55] and why the vowelless *alif maqṣūra* of حُبْلَى "pregnant" is changed into a *y* vowelled by a fatḥa in the plural حُبْلَيَاتٌ.[56]

– The combination of two unsound weak consonants is forbidden.[57] In accordance with this principle the 2nd radical *w* of the base form طَوَيَ "to fold" that is vowelled by a fatḥa and preceded by one, is not changed into an *ā*,—and thus remains sound—, to prevent such a

---

"The Arabs have no root with more than five letters, whether noun or verb. So whatever letters you find in noun or verb in excess of five must be addition to the root, not part of the original form of the word".

This remark said by al-Ḫalīl is also mentioned by Muʾaddib, *Taṣrīf* 184, 396.

[45] Ibn Ǧinnī, *Ḫaṣāʾiṣ I*, 78.
[46] Cf. the Arabic text fols. 4a-4b.
[47] Cf. ibid, fols. 25b-26a-fols. 26a-26b and my notes (248).
[48] Cf. the Arabic text fols. 26a-26b and my notes (249).
[49] Cf. the Arabic text fols. 13a-13b, fols. 4b-5a and my notes (43), (44).
[50] Cf. my notes (45).
[51] Cf. the Arabic text fols. 4b-5a and my notes (43), (44).
[52] Cf. the Arabic text fols. 5a-5b.
[53] Cf. ibid.
[54] Cf. the Arabic text fols. 5b-7a, 13a-13b, 21a, 21a-22a, 22a-23a, 23a-24a, 26b-27b, 28a-29a, 29a-30a, 30a-30b, 30b-31b, 32a-32b, 35a-35b. The principle is also mentioned by Ibn al-Anbārī, *Inṣāf* Q. 96, 283 l. 9. Ibn Ǧinnī, *Ḫaṣāʾiṣ I*, 90, *II*, 497 remarks that a cluster of vowelless consonants may occur in Persian. Furthermore, he notes 493 sqq. that in some examples and in the pause this cluster can occur (for discussions concerning the cluster see my notes (229)).
[55] Cf. the Arabic text fols. 5a-5b.
[56] Cf. ibid.
[57] Cf. the Arabic text fols. 27b-28a. This rule is also mentioned by e.g. Ibn al-Anbārī, *Inṣāf* Q. 112, 329.

combination, as it is taken into account that the verb's 3rd radical *y* is changed into an *alif maqṣūra* resulting in طوى.[58]

– It is impossible to start with a vowelless consonant.[59] Ibn Ǧinnī writes that the case [of those who pretend that one can start with a vowelless consonant] is similar to the case of the sophists who doubt of evident things and those whose mind is deficient.[60]

– The frequency of usage of a word can be the reason of the elision of a consonant in its structure, e.g. بسم الله written instead of بِاسْمِ الله "in the name of God".[61]

– The heaviness implied by a sequence of two vowels, two consonants, or a consonant and a vowel of which the combination is disliked, should be avoided. Thus no noun of the pattern فُعِلٌ occurs because of the dislike of combining the ḍamma and the kasra. As an exception to this rule, Ibn Masʿūd mentions وُعِلٌ "a mountain goat" and دُئِلٌ "a jackal".[62] Not only the combination of the kasra and the ḍamma following each other in a word is disliked, but also the combination of the *y* and the *w* which therefore do not occur as 2nd and 3rd radical.[63] By analogy with the disliked فُعِلٌ, the kasra that precedes the ḍamma in فِعُلٌ is forbidden.[64] An exception to this rule is the anomalous rare noun حِبُكٌ that is according to this form.[65] A combination of kasras is as well disliked. This is why the 2nd radical *m* is vowelled by a fatḥa in the name of place الْمَرْمَى "a place of throwing or shooting arrows" that is said instead of الْمَرْمِي with the last *y* considered as two kasras. The pattern becomes commensurable to مَفْعَلٌ instead of مَفْعِلٌ to avoid this combination, and so breaks the rule that requires that رَمَى يَرْمِي is according to the conjugation فَعَلَ يَفْعِلُ of which the noun of place should principally be according to مَفْعِلٌ.[66]

– A vowelless consonant that occurs between two vowelled consonants is not taken into account, because the vowelless consonant is not considered as a firm separative between them both.[67] This is why the *w* of قِنْوَةٌ "sheep or goats taken for oneself" is changed into a *y*, i.e. قِنْيَةٌ on account of the kasra of the *q* that precedes it by two consonants of which the 2nd has a sukūn,[68] and why the connective hamza of the imperative in اُكْتُبْ is given a ḍamma instead of the kasra on account of the ḍamma of the 2nd radical of the verb that follows it by two consonants of which the 2nd has a sukūn.[69]

– The elision of what has no meaning in a word in relation to what has, is prior.[70] This is why

---

[58] Cf. the Arabic text fols. 36b-37a.

[59] Cf. ibid, fols. 10b-11a and my notes (102). This rule is also mentioned by e.g. Ibn al-Anbārī, *Inṣāf* Q. 105, 306 l. 5.

[60] Ibn Ǧinnī, *Munṣif I*, 53. However, he notes in *Ḫaṣāʾiṣ I*, 91 that his teacher Abū ʿAlī did not seem to express a dislike that words in Persian can begin with a vowelless consonant.

[61] Cf. the Arabic text fols. 12a-13a.

[62] Cf. ibid, fols. 13b-14a, 26a-26b

[63] Cf. Ibn Ǧinnī, *Ḫaṣāʾiṣ I*, 255-256.

[64] Cf. the Arabic text fols. 26a-26b, Ibn Ǧinnī, *Munṣif I*, 20.

[65] Cf. my notes (133).

[66] Cf. the Arabic text fols. 16b-17a.

[67] Cf. ibid, fols. 11b-12a, 30a-30b. This principle is also mentioned by e.g. Ibn al-Anbārī, *Inṣāf* Q. 118, 343.

[68] Cf. the Arabic text fols. 12 a-12b and my notes (113).

[69] Cf. the Arabic text fols. 11b-12a, 12a-13a and my notes (111), (112).

[70] Cf. the Arabic text fols. 10b-11a and my notes (101).

the marker is not to be elided.[71] Examples that can be mentioned are verbs of Form V تَتَفَعَّلُ and VI تَتَفَاعَلُ that occur in the imperfect of the 2nd person of the fem. and the 3rd person of the masc. sing. with one of the tā's elided, whether it is the imperfect prefix *ta* or the infix *ta* of reflexivity, namely تَفَعَّلُ and تَفَاعَلُ respectively, depending on which *t* is viewed as less prior than the other.[72]

– Four consecutive vowelled consonants cannot be combined together, which is the reason why a vowelless consonant is meant to break their combination. By analogy to this rule, the *ḍ* in يَضْرِبُ "he hits", which is the immediate consonant after the prefix, is given a sukūn. This means also that the immediate consonant before a suffix is given a sukūn, e.g. ضَرَبْتَ and ضَرَبْنَ.[73] As what concerns هُدَبِدٌ and عُلَبِطٌ in which the four vowels follow each other, they are the alleviated forms of هُدَابِدٌ and عُلَابِطٌ. As for the four vowels following each other in ضَرَبَكَ "he hit you", they are accepted because the verb and its suffixed pronoun of the accusative, the *-ka,* are regarded as two separated words in spite of their occurrence as one word.[74]

– No noun occurs with a *w* at its end that is preceded by a consonant vowelled with a *ḍamma* unless the pronoun هُوَ,[75] which is counted to pertain to the same category as the noun, if one considers that the parts of the speech are three: noun, verb and particle.[76] This is the reason why the plural of the noun دَلْو "bucket" is made أَدْلٌ to avoid the occurrence of the *w* at the end of the word.[77] However, the *w* can be found at the end of the verb, e.g. يَدْعُو "he invites".

– The *m* has the characteristic of only being suffixed to the noun, and more specifically to the pronoun, which is counted to pertain to the same category as the noun.[78]

The author of the *Marāḥ* does not only present many of the morphological patterns and explain the reasons of most of the phonological procedures concerning them, but he also wants to justify the facts, and sometimes his explanation goes beyond the field of grammar. He writes for instance that the *t* is made a marker of the fem. in ضَرَبَتْ "she hit", because the *t* originates from the second point of articulation, in the same manner as the female species is second in the creation after the male.[79]

---

71 Cf. the Arabic text fols. 5b-7a, 10b-11a, 30b-31b and my notes (101).
72 Cf. my notes (101).
73 Cf. the Arabic text fols. 10b-11a.
74 Cf. ibid, fols. 5a-5b and my notes (55).
75 Cf. the Arabic text fols. 5b-7a and my notes (63).
76 Cf. my notes (10 b).
77 Cf. the Arabic text fols. 5b-7a and my notes (64).
78 Cf. the Arabic text fols. 5b-7a and my notes (62).
79 Cf. the Arabic text fols. 4b-5a and my notes (52).

II. ARABIC TEXT, TRANSLATION AND COMMENTARY

II.1. Arabic Text: المقدّمة

بسم الله الرحمن الرحيم

* ١ ب قال المفتقر الى الله الودود، أحمد بن عليَ بن مسعود، غفر الله له ولوالديه، وأحسن إليهما وإليه: إعلم أنَ الصرف أمَ العلوم والنحو أبوها، ويقوي في الدرايات داروها، ويطغي في الروايات عاروها، فجمعت فيه كتاباً موسوماً بمراح الأرواح، وهو للصبيَ جناح النجاح وراح رحراح، وفي معيدته حين راح مثل تفَاح او راح، وبالله أعتصم عمَا يصمَ وأستعين، وهو نعم المولى ونعم المعين.

* ٢ آ إعلم أسعدك الله أنَ الصرَاف يحتاج في معرفة الأوزان* الى سبعة أبواب الصحيح والمضاعف والمهموز والمثال والأجوف والناقص واللفيف واشتقاق تسعة أشياء من كلَ مصدر وهي الماضي والمستقبل والأمر والنهي واسم الفاعل والمفعول والزمان والمكان والآلة فكسرته على سبعة أبواب

Fols. 1b-2a

٣ الصرف: التصريف ا/ الدرايات: الدريات ا/ ٤ عاروها: عارها ب/ ٦ يصمَ: يعصم ب/ ٧ إعلم... الله: — ز/ ٧ الله: + في الدارين هـ/ ٩ وهي: فهي جـ ط/ والمفعول: واسم المفعول لـ/ ٩–١ والزمان والمكان: والمكان والزمان ب هـ ط/

II.1. Translation: Introduction

In the name of God, Most Gracious, Most Merciful

[Fol. 1 b] Thus speaks Aḥmad b. ʿAlī b. Masʿūd,(1) a man in need of the friendly God,(2) may He forgive him and his parents their sins and do good to them both and to him:

"Know that morphology is the mother and syntax the father of sciences,(3) and those who comprehend it [sc. her: i.e. the mother, morphology] become stronger in the sciences, and those who are devoid of it go astray in the traditions.(4) So I compiled on this subject a book entitled مراح الأرواح *"The Place of Rest of the Spirits",*(5) and it is for the boy the wing of success(5) and a wide palm, and in his "abdomen"(7) when he finds rest, like apples or wine.(8) And by God, I seek protection from what is distressing and I turn to Him for help, and He is [sur. 8: 40] "the Best to protect" and to help.(9)

Know then, may God make you happy, that in order to know the morphological patterns **[Fol. 2 a]**, the grammarian needs seven classes [of verbs]: الصحيح "the Strong Verb", المضاعف "the Doubled Verb", المهموز "the Hamzated Verb", المثال "the Verb with Weak 1st Radical", الأجوف "the Verb with Weak 2nd Radical", الناقص "the Verb with Weak 3rd Radical" and اللفيف "the Verb that is doubly Weak"; and the derivation of nine patterns from each infinite noun [which are the following]: الماضي "the perfect", المستقبل "the imperfect", الأمر "the imperative", النهي "the prohibition", اسم الفاعل والمفعول "the active and passive participle" and الزمان والمكان والآلة "the [nouns of] time, place and instrument".(10)

This is why I divided it [sc. the book] into seven chapters.

II.1.1. COMMENTARY

Introduction

(1) For discussions concerning Ibn Masʿūd see the Introduction pp. 7-8.

(2) الفقير الى الله and المفتقر are epithets that a man often writes before his name (for discussions see my notes to Ibn Masʿūd, *I,* 40). Furthermore some consider that poverty in this earth can be rewarded by paradise after death (cf. Ǧawzīya, *Arwāḥ* 111-112).

(3) Both terms الصرف and التصريف have been used to designate "morphology". The *Marāḥ al-arwāḥ* has also been considered as a book in التصريف. For instance Ibn Masʿūd, *MS A,* fol. 1b has التصريف instead of الصرف (cf. the Arabic text fols. 1b-2a in the notes). Suyūṭī, *Muzhir I,* 347 mentions Aḥmad b. ʿAlī Ibn Masʿūd as the author of the *Marāḥ* in التصريف. More specifically, *al-ṣarf* is the study of the structure of the words, whereas *al-taṣrīf* (for the main definitions see Hindāwī, *Manāhiğ* 15-16; for the definitions according to Sībawaihi, al-Rummānī, Ibn Ǧinnī and al-Sīrāfī (d. 368/979) see Hindāwī, *Manāhiğ* 16-20; for a detailed discussion with interesting references see Fleisch, *Taṣrīf,* Owens, *Foundations* 98 sqq., Bohas, *Étude* 15-21, Bohas/Guillaume/Kouloughli, *Linguistic* 73 sqq.) is the study of the processes that lead to their making. There are two main parts referred to by *al-taṣrīf* (cf. Ibn ʿUṣfūr, *I,* 31-32; for discussions see Bohas/Guillaume/Kouloughli, *Linguistic* 76-80). The first one relates to the derivation of the forms from a root, and for this reason it is associated with اشْتقاق "derivation" (for discussions concerning the derivation see Suyūṭī, *Muzhir I,* 200-207, Bohas, *Étude* 174-178; for a distinction of four sorts see Owens, *Foundations* 106-108), and more specifically with الإشْتقَاقُ الصَّغيرُ "the little derivation" (cf. (14); for the derivatives see (10)). Zabīdī, *Tāğ XXIV,* 20 notes:

"والتصريف في الكلام اشْتِقاق بَعْضِه من بَعْض".

"*Al-taṣrīf* in the language is the derivation of some of them [sc. the words] from each other".

Owens, *Foundations* 98 remarks:

> "The core of Arabic morphology revolves around the concepts of *taṣrīf,* which can be broadly translated as 'morphology' and in some contexts as 'derivation', and to a lesser degree *ʾishtiqāq* 'derivation'".

There is then a close relationship between *al-taṣrīf* and the derivation (for discussions see Hindāwī, *Manāhiğ* 48 sqq.). According to the procedures of *al-taṣrif* and of the derivation, one single word is enabled to circulate freely from one form to another so that it obtains this specific form's meaning (cf. Ibn Ǧinnī, *Munṣif I,* 3-4). For instance ضَرَبَ can be made commensurable to جَعْفَرٌ so that it becomes ضَرْبَبٌ, to قَمَطْرٌ so that it becomes ضِرَبٌّ, to دِرْهَمٌ so that it becomes ضِرْبَبٌ, to عَلِمَ so that it becomes ضَرِبَ, or to ظَرُفَ so that it becomes ضَرُبَ. According to the procedures of the derivation, the root is taken into consideration, and from

it different forms are derived. For instance, from the *maṣdar* الضَّرْبُ, the perfect ضَرَبَ, the imperfect يَضْرِبُ, the active participle ضَارِبٌ, etc., are derived.
The second part of *al-taṣrif* relates to the study of the phonological change/(s) that is/(are) carried out in the base form of a word in order to make it circulate to another form, without however changing its meaning (cf. Ibn ʿUṣfūr, *I,* 33-34). Some examples are the phonological changes that are carried out for instance in some weak verbs, e.g. قَوَلَ that becomes قَالَ "to say" (cf. (266)), بَيَعَ that becomes بَاعَ "to sell", and اِوْتَعَدَ that becomes اِتَّعَدَ "to promise" (cf. (198)). Concerning both sorts of *taṣrīf,* it can be noted generally that the main phonological procedures that are carried out in a word are recognized as the addition of an augment or more, the substitution of one consonant for another, the elision of a consonant or of a vowel, a vowel's change and the assimilation of one consonant to another. As Ibn Ǧinnī, *de Flexione* 8 writes:

"فمعنى التصريف هو ما أريناك من التلعّب بالحروف الاصول لما يراد فيها من المعاني المفادة منها... فليعلم انّ التصريف ينقسم الى خمسة اضرب زيادة بدل حذف تغيير بحركة او سكون ادغام".

"The meaning of *al-taṣrīf* is what we have showed you concerning the "circulation" of radicals in order to obtain the meanings gained by them [sc. the range of forms]. Let it be known than, that *al-taṣrīf* is divided into five classes: addition, substitution, elision, a vowel's change, sukūn and assimilation".

Ibn Yaʿīš, *Mulūkī* 95 writes:

"لم يكن بد من لفظ خاص يدلّ على ذلك المعنى بعينه. فلهذا وجب التصريف واختلاف الأبنية بالزيادة والنقص والتغيير ونحو ذلك ليدلّ كلّ لفظ على المعنى المراد".

"It was necessary to have a special word which would indicate this special characteristic meaning. This is why *al-taṣrīf* was necessary and the variations of forms [which occur] by addition, elision, change and so on, so that each word would refer to the intended meaning".

الصرف can be defined as التصريف, but it is more specifically the study of the morphemes (cf. Bašar, *Dirāsāt* 221, Ḥassān, *Luġa* 153), which is the smallest meaningful entity in a word. It can be a prefix as the *-mu* that marks the active participle of Form IV, e.g. مُكْرِم "honouring" or its passive participle, e.g. مُكْرَمٌ, an infix as the *ā* that marks the active participle of the groundform فاعِلٌ, or a suffix, e.g. the ending *-āni* that marks the dual of the masc. sing. of the nominative, the ending *-ūna* that marks the pl. of the nominative, the ending *-ātu* that marks the fem. pl. of the nominative, etc. (for other examples of morphemes see Astarābāḏī, *Šarḥ al-kāfiya I,* 5; for further discussions see Hindāwī, *Manāhiǧ* 20 sqq.). Carter, *Širbīnī* 343-344: 17.1 (1) distinguishes between two sets of terminology:

"the morphological set *ṣarf-taṣrīf-taṣarruf* ('process of being conjugated'), and the cognate series *ṣarf-mutaṣarrif-munṣarif,* denoting the syntactic freedom of the fully inflected noun...".

The fully inflected noun and imperfect verb are submitted to the اِعْرابُ (for discussions concerning the declinable imperfect see (122)). The term can mean as well the complete vowelling of the form (for discussions see ʿUkbarī, *Masāʾil* 102-105, Fleisch, *Iʿrāb* 1250, Owens, *Foundations* 40). The formal *iʿrāb* is different from the syntactical *iʿrāb,* as the latter is mainly concerned with the ending of the declinable word in accordance with its operator's rule (cf. my notes (43)). Carter, *Širbīnī* 37: 2. 15 (1) distinguishes between both its meanings with the following words:

> "*Iʿrāb* may be understood in two different ways, (a) as a process of change in word endings (thus 'abstract'), or (b) as a set of morphemes (thus 'formal')".

Concerning this conception of morphology as as a generative system Owens, *Foundations* 122 remarks:

> "There is no doubt that the morphological system was regarded as a generative system, one which not only accounted for all existing morphological patterns, but also allowed the speakers to apply the rule to create new patterns as they needed them".

b) النحو "syntax" (for definitions see Ismāʿīl, *Tadrīs* 201-202, Sayyid, *Kāfī I,* 2) is the science of knowing the changing or the invariable state of the forms' ending in the sentence (cf. Ibn Ǧinnī, *Munṣif I,* 4), so that the meaning of the sentence is understood. The word's ending can be مُعْرَبٌ "declinable, variable", which has to do with the word's position or the operator's operation on it in the sentence, or مَبْنِيّ "undeclinable, invariable" (for discussions concerning إِعْرَابٌ and بِنَاءٌ see (43)). النحو is compared by Ibn Masʿūd to the father who corrects the children. Both morphology and syntax constitute together the science of grammar. Its knowledge enables the person to express himself with coherence and to understand what is told or written (cf. Zaǧǧāǧī, *Īḍaḥ* 95-96, Ibn Ḫaldūn, *Muqaddima III,* 320, Versteegh, *Elements* 130, *Zaǧǧāǧī* 164; for discussions concerning the profit of the study of grammar and its connection to logic see Versteegh, *Elements* 123-127). It can be added that the ability of learning a science requires as well a certain love towards it. The love of the Arabic language is expressed by many writers (e.g. Ibn Fāris, *Ṣāḥibī* 40-46, Zubaidī, *Ṭabaqāt* 11, al-Ṯaʿālibī (d. 429/1037) in the *Fiqh al-luġa wa-sirr al-ʿarabīya* translated by Loucel, *Origine* 65-66)). As well, for some persons, grammar, beside other sciences, is studied "with the aim of seeing the greatness of the Creator" (cf. Riad's commentary 68 to Ibn Ḥazm, *Aḫlāq* 15 l. 15). Furthermore, the term النحو can as well mean generally grammar. According to the tradition it is believed that the first (cf. Mubārak, *Naḥw* 10-37) to have written about grammar was Abū l-Aswad al-Duʾalī, Ẓālim b. ʿAmr (d. 69/688) (for him see Sīrāfī, *Aḫbār* 13-20, Zubaidī, *Ṭabaqāt* 13 sqq., Ibn Ḫallikān, *Dictionary I,* 662, Luġawī, *Marātib* 24, Qifṭī, *Inbāh I,* 4 sqq., Suyūṭī, *Buġya II,* 22-23; for some discussions referring to him as the one who divided with his studies grammar and lexicography see Haywood, *Lexicography* 11-17). The question is however disputed, as some believed that the first who wrote about grammar was ʿAbd Allāh b. Abī Isḥāq (cf. Pellat, *Milieu* 130, Talmon, *Who* 128-145), whereas others believed that it was Naṣr b. ʿĀṣim (d. 89/708) (cf. Sīrāfī, *Aḫbār* 20, Zubaidī, *Ṭabaqāt* 27), or ʿAbd al-Raḥmān b. Hurmuz (d. 117/735) (cf. Sīrāfī, *Aḫbār* 21-22), or both Yaḥyā b. Yaʿmar (d. 129/747) and ʿAṭāʾ b. Abī l-Aswad al-Duʾalī (cf. Qifṭī, *Inbāh I,* 380-381). For further discussions see Versteegh, *Grammar* 160 sqq.

(4) The importance of morphology (for discussions see Ibn Fāris, *Ṣāḥibī* 191) and its usefulness in the acquisition of sciences (cf. Massignon, *Opera I,* Presses Universitaires de France, 205) is stressed upon by Ibn Masʿūd. By doing so, he specifies the subject of his study.

(5) مراح "the place of rest" is the noun of place of رَاحَ, one of whose meanings is ارْتَاحَ "to find rest, recreation, to be pleased". Both the *maṣdars* رَاحٌ and رَوْحٌ can mean ارتياحٌ "rest" (cf. Ibn Manẓūr, *III,* 1767, Zābidī, *Tāǧ IV,* 418). رَوْحٌ occurs in the sur. 56: 89: (فَرَوْحٌ وَرَيْحَانٌ) "(There is for him) Rest and Satisfaction". Ibn Manẓūr, *III,* 1766 and Zabīdī, *Tāǧ VI,* 426 link one of its meanings to the gladness and happiness deriving from the truth, used so by ʿAli. It is also interesting to compare the meanings that are associated with the word راحة (for discussions with references to other works see Riad's commentary p. 63 to Ibn Ḥazm, *Aḫlāq* 9) in Arabic and in some of the other Semitic languages. According to Ibn Fāris, *Maqāyīs II,* 454, the three consonants, the *r, w* and *ḥ* combined together (روح) point to سَعَةٌ "wideness or power", فُسْحَةٌ "ampleness, extensive possibilities, or holidays" and اطِّرادٌ "continuity". Leslau, *Soqotri* 395 mentions that Soqotri *raḥ* "to be at rest" corresponds to Šauri *šerīḥ* "to relax", Daṯīna راح, Arabic استروح "to relax", Hebrew רוה *råwaḥ* "to be large", Syriac ܪܘܚ *rewaḥ* and South Arabic *hrwḥt* "enlargement, magnification". Ibn Masʿūd means that the place of rest of الأرواح "the spirits, the intellectuals, or the higher beings" is acquired through higher knowledge and contemplation (see my introduction to Ibn Masʿūd, *I,* 28). According to Ibn Kamāl Pāša, *Falāḥ* 4, مراح is derived from الرَّوح. As for the reason why Ibn Masʿūd gave his book the title مراح الأرواح, Ibn Kamāl Pāšā 4 ll. 34-35 writes:

"المراح اسم مكان من الرَّوح بفتح الراء من الإستراحة والأرواح جمع روح وهي النفس الناطقة فمعناه في الأصل موضع راحة النفوس الناطقة وإنما سُمّي به لأنَّ النفس الناطقة لما كانت طالبة للكمالات العلميّة وهي لا تُحصل إلاّ بآلاتها تألّمت واضطربت الى أن تجد تلك الآلة كالمرضى تألّمت الى أن تجد دواء شافياً ولما كان هذا الكتاب مُشتملاً على ما هي آلة لتلك العلوم تتلذّذ به النفوس وتصير راحة".

"The مراح is a noun of place from الرَّوح "the refreshment" with the vowelling of the *r* by a fatḥa, from الإستراحة "the rest, recreation" , and الأرواح "the souls, spirits" is the pl. of روح, which is the rational eloquent soul. Its meaning is then originally the place of rest of the rational eloquent souls. It [sc. the book] was somehow given this title, because when the rational soul aspires for scientific perfections,—and they can only be obtained with its tools—, it suffered and grieved until it found this tool, like the sick men suffer until they find a curing medecine. So this book comprises the specific tool for the acquistion of these learnings that the souls take delight in and thus become harmonious".

Furthermore, according to the Qurʾān and to the Arabic philosophy, there is a difference in meaning between الروح "the spirit" and النفس "the soul". The Spirit is God's, which he breathed into Adam, and by doing so elevated his status as sur. 15: 29 says: (فَإذَا سَوَّيْتُهُ وَنَفَخْتُ فِيهِ مِنْ رُوحِي فَقَعُوا لَهُ سَاجِدِينَ) "When I have fashioned him (in due proportion) and breathed into him of My spirit, fall ye down in obeisance unto him". As for the soul, it is the carnal soul as referred to by sur. 12: 53 (وَمَا أُبَرِّئُ نَفْسِي إنَّ ٱلنَّفْسَ لأَمَّارَةٌ بِالسُّوءِ) "Nor do I absolve my own self (of blame): the (human) soul is certainly prone to evil". It can however achieve full rest and satisfaction as sur. 89: 27-28 says: (يا أيها ٱلنَّفْسُ ٱلْمُطْمَئِنَّةُ ٱرْجِعِي إِلَى رَبِّكِ رَاضِيَةً مَرْضِيَّةً) "(To the righteous soul will be said:) "O (thou) soul, in (complete) rest and satisfaction! Come back thou to thy Lord,—well pleased (thyself), and well-pleasing unto Him!".

(6) جناح النجاح are the first words that are used to rhyme with the rhyming title مراح الأرواح and with the words that follow them, i.e. راح رحراح "a wide palm" and تفاح او راح "apples or wine". As for the concept of الجناح "wing" that is associated with knowledge, Ibn Manẓūr, *I,* 697 referring to the Ḥadīṯ, mentions that the Angels lay down their wings for the person who pursues knowledge, so that they shall be a ground for him when he walks and as a sign of humiliation to glorify his claim. This lowering of the wings of the Angels refers to the sur. 2: 34 when God by His grace taught Adam the nature of things: (وإذا قُلْنَا لِلْمَلَائِكَةِ ٱسْجُدُوا لِآدَمَ فَسَجَدُوا) "And behold, We said to the Angels 'Bow down to Adam:' and they bowed down", or when He breathed into Him of His spirit as sur. 15: 29 says (for it see (5)). Adam and mankind are synonymous here. This general idea of humiliation associated with the lowering of the wings, is pointed out as well in sur. 15: 58 (وَٱخْفِضْ جَنَاحَكَ لِلْمُؤْمِنِينَ) "But lower thy wing (in gentleness) to the Believers", sur. 17: 24 (وَٱخْفِضْ لَهُمَا جَنَاحَ ٱلذُّلِّ مِنَ ٱلرَّحْمَةِ) "And, out of kindness lower to them the wing of humility" and in sur. 26: 215 (وَٱخْفِضْ جَنَاحَكَ لِمَنِ ٱتَّبَعَكَ مِنَ ٱلْمُؤْمِنِينَ) "And lower thy wing to the Believers who follow thee". النجاح "the success", which is the person's strive after growth, is an important factor that contributes to his happiness and to future success and increasing growth (for this theme see Ismāʿīl, *Tadrīs* 68; for the qualities required for acquiring success in different fields see Ǧawzīya, *Fawāʾid* 246-247).

(7) The word معيدته "abdomen" is used by Ibn Masʿūd as a metaphor instead of "intellect", which he is referring to. Each is the nourishment's place: the intellect is the place of the nourishment of the soul as the stomach is the place of the nourishment of the body.

(8) According to Ibn Masʿūd, the importance of this book to the reader equalizes the importance of apples or wine to the body and soul (cf. my notes to Ibn Masʿūd, *I,* 42). It is possible that this comparison reveals a certain inclination towards Sufism. It can be mentioned that the word تُفَّاحة "apple" pointing to its benificiency, has been used by Ibn al-Naḥḥās (d. 338/950) (Aḥmad b. Muḥammad, see for him Suyūṭī, *Buġya I,* 362) in the title of his work dealing with syntax, *al-Tuffāḥa fī l-naḥw "The Apple in Syntax"* (for its description see Omar, *Studies* 243-244). Wine is considered by the Ṣūfī as being able to cure the sick and to bring back the dead to life. A poet, quoted by Baldick, *Islam* 135, writes:

> "And if an enchanter (the Sufi teacher) had traced the letters of the wine's name on the forehead of one possessed the sign would have cured him".

Ibn al-Fāriḍ, quoted by Baldick, *Islam* 135, writes:

"And if they had sprinkled some of that wine on the dust of a dead man's tomb
His spirit would have returned to him and his body would have come back to life".

Furthermore wine refers to the ecstasy felt by the Sufi through his union with God as a cupbearer (cf. Ibn al-Fāriḍ, *Poems* 39-40, Baldick, *Islam* 82). It can be linked with reality and spiritual truth (cf. Ḥāfiẓ, *Dīwān* 98, Baldick, *Islam* 100), it has overnatural powers (cf. Ḫayyām, *Rubai'āt* XLIII), guides the disciple on the right Path and prevents him from going astray through the miraculous grace of the spiritual "friends", who can be physically absent or dead teachers (cf. Baldick, *Islam* 100).

(9) Ibn Masʿūd relies here with humility on God so that He helps him fullfill his task. This is an echo of the sur. 22: 78 (وَٱعْتَصِمُوا بِٱللَّهِ هُوَ مَوْلَاكُمْ فَنِعْمَ ٱلْمَوْلَىٰ وَنِعْمَ ٱلنَّصِيرُ) " And hold fast to God! He is your Protector—The best to protect and the best to help!". Compare also *Širbīnī's* words in Carter, *Širbīnī* 4: فإنه أكرم مسؤول وأعزّ مأمول "for He is the most bountiful of those to whom prayers are addressed, and the mightiest on whom all our hopes rest".

(10) It was common for the grammarians to explain the grammatical rules after the verb اعْلَمْ يا فَتى "Know o young man!" (cf. Ḥassan, *Uṣūl* 27). The pedagogical spirit seems to have started being manifest in al-Farrā's period who directs himself in *Maʿānī* I, 17 to المبتدىء للتعليم "the beginner in the instruction". After him, it is al-Aḫfaš who tested his pupils with deliberate errors inserted in forged verses for the purpose of teaching them the language (cf. Baġdādī, *Ḫizāna* II, 300).
According to the Basrans, the derivatives (for discussions concerning the derivation see (3), (14)) are: the perfect, the imperfect, the imperative, the active and passive participles, the assimilated adjective, the elative, the nouns of time, place and instrument; and the *maṣdar* is considered as the origin of the derivation by them. However according to the Kufans, the *maṣdar* is included among the derivatives whereas the perfect is excluded, as they consider the verb to be the origin of the derivatives (cf. ʿAbd al-Raḥīm, *Ṣarf* 79). This debate between the Basrans and Kufans concerning which of the *maṣdar* or the perfect is the origin of the derivation, is discussed by Ibn Masʿūd in the present Arabic text fols. 2a-3a, 3a-4a and in my notes (12)-(21). The *maṣdar* is not always included among the derived nouns, because of, as Carter, *Širbīnī* 373 in his notes 19:33 (1) remarks, "its disputed status as the source of all verbal paradigms". Ibn Masʿūd who follows the Basrans, presents nine derivatives of the *maṣdar*. The same derivatives are presented by Bustānī, *Miṣbāḥ* 19, the editor and commentator of Farḥāt, *Baḥt*. Suyūṭī, *Ašbāh* II, 288, who refers to the *Taḏkara* of Ibn al-Ṣāʾiġ, presents as well nine derivatives of the *maṣdar*, but some of them being different than those that are mentioned by Ibn Masʿūd, namely: the verb, the active participle, مبالغة اسم الفاعل "[the forms of] the active participle denoting intensification" which he named مِثَالٌ, namely: the patterns مِفْعَالٌ ,فَعِلٌ ,فَعِيلٌ, فَعُولٌ and فَعَّالٌ, the passive participle, the elative, the assimilated adjective, the noun of the *maṣdar*, the noun of instrument, and the nouns of time and place which he counts as one. Abū Ḥanīfa, *Maqṣūd* 3 refers to six derivatives of the *maṣdar*, namely: the perfect, the imperfect, the imperative, the prohibition and the active and passive participles. Rāġihī, *Taṭbīq* 75-89 refers to six nouns derived from verbs, namely: the comparative noun, the active and passive participles, the nouns of time, place and instrument and اسم مُبالغة "the noun which expresses intensiveness". Zamaḫšarī, 96, commented on by Ibn Yaʾīš, *VI*, 43, presents eight derivatives of nouns connected with verbs, comprising: the

maṣdar, the active participle, the passive participle, the assimilated adjective, the elative, the nouns of time and place and the noun of instrument. With his division of forms that are derived from the *maṣdar,* Ibn Masʿūd intends to make the reader believe that the verbs are derived from the *maṣdar,* which is the opinion of the Basrans, and that he sides with them (for discussions see my notes (12)-(21)). As for the assimilated adjective and the noun of superiority referred to by Zamaḫšarī, Ibn Masʿūd presents them within the chapter of the active participle (see the Arabic text fols. 14a-15a, 15a-16a).

b) As remarked, the division of the forms presented here by Ibn Masʿūd, includes only the category of the noun and the verb. The *maṣdar,* the active and passive participle, the adjective, the nouns of time, place and instrument and the pronoun pertain to the noun category, wheras the verb tenses, namely the perfect, the imperfect, the imperative and the prohibition, pertain to the verb category. As noticed, the particle, which is the third category of speech according to the Arabic grammatical tradition, is not treated by him in this study, as it is not included among the categories of words that are derived from the verb or the *maṣdar.* This division of the language into three main categories: اسمٌ "noun", فعْلٌ "verb" and حرْفٌ "particle" has been transmitted by Sībawaihi, *I,* 1 (cf. Rundgren, *Einfluß* 129, Versteegh, *Elements* 39, Owens, *Foundations* 125). Zaǧǧāǧī, *Iḍāḥ* 41-45 presents a critique to this tripartite divi sion, which he then however defends. This division seems to have been borrowed from the Greeks (for discussions considering the Greek influence see Merx, *Historia* 137-153, *Origine* 13-26, Weiss, *Nationalgrammatik* 349-390, Versteegh, *Grammar* 22-23, *Elements* 38-89, *Education,* Fischer, *Origin* LIII, 1962-1963, 1-21, LIV, 1963-1964, 132-160; for opinions considering the Arabic linguists to be free from Greek influence see Massignon, *Réflexions* 6, Weiss, *Nationalgrammatik* 349, Carter, *Origines,* Troupeau, *Lexique* 13, *Origine* 125-138, *Logique* 246, Badawī, *Aristotles* 126-127, Sezgin, *Geschichte* 9 sqq.).

II.2. Arabic Text: الباب الأوّل في الصحيح

الصحيح هو الذي ليس في مقابلة الفاء والعين واللام حرف علّة وتضعيف وهمزة نحو ضَرَبَ، واختصّ الفاء والعين واللام للوزن حتّى يكون فيه من حروف الشفّة والوسط والحلق شيء. فقولنا الضَّرْبُ مصدر يتولّد منه الأشياء التسعة، وهو أصل في الإشتقاق عند البصريّين لأنّ مفهومه واحد ومفهوم الفعل متعدّد لدلالته على الحدث
والزمان* والواحد قبل المتعدّد. وإذا كان أصلاً للأفعال يكون أصلاً لمتعلّقاتها او لأنّه اسم * ٢ ب
والإسم مستغن عن الفعل وأيضاً يُقال له مصدر لأنّ هذه الأشياء تصدر عنه. الإشتقاق أن تجد بين اللفظين تناسباً في اللفظ والمعنى وهو على ثلثة أنواع: صغير وهو أن يكون بينهما تناسب في الحروف والترتيب نحو ضَرَبَ من الضَّرْبِ، وكبير وهو أن يكون بينهما تناسب في اللفظ دون الترتيب نحو جَبَذَ من الجَذْبِ، وأكبر وهو أن يكون بينهما تناسب في المخرج نحو نَعَقَ من النَّهْقِ والمراد من الإشتقاق المذكور ههنا اشتقاق صغير. قال الكوفيّون ينبغي أن يكون الفعل أصلاً لأنّ إعلاله مدار لإعلال المصدر وجوداً وعدماً. أمّا وجوداً ففي يَعِدُ عِدَةً وقَامَ قِيَاماً، وأمّا عدماً ففي يَوْجَلُ
وَجَلاً وَقَاوَمَ* قِوَاماً ومداريّته تدلّ على إصالته وأيضاً يؤكّد الفعل به نحو ضَرَبْتُ ضَرْباً * ٣ آ
وهو بمنزلة ضَرَبْتُ ضَرَبْتُ والمؤكّد أصل دون المؤكّد، ويُقال له مصدر لكونه مصدوراً عن الفعل كما قالوا له مَشْرَبٌ عَذْبٌ وَمَرْكَبٌ فَارِهٌ أي مَشْرُوبٌ وَمَرْكُوبٌ. قلنا في جوابهم إعلال المصدر للمشاكلة لا للمداريّة كحذف الواو في تَعِدُ والهمزة في تُكْرِمُ

Fols. 2a-3a

٢ حرف.. وهمزة: من حروف العلّة والهمزة والتضعيف جـ/ وتضعيف وهمزة: وهمزة وتضعيف ب: والهمزة والتضعيف د/ ٣ ضرب: يضرب د/ ٤–٥ أصل... الإشتقاق: الأصل الإشتقاق هـ/ ٧ مستغن: + في الإفادة د/ الأشياء: + المذكورة ك/ ٨ الاشتقاق: والاشتقاق جـ ل/ على: — د/ ثلثة: ثلاثة ل/ ٩ تناسب: تناسبا ب جـ حـ ط/ ١١ نعق: شعق ب/ المذكور: المذكورة حـ/ ههنا: — ب هـ ط/ ١٢ عدة: عدّة ب/ ١٤ ومداريته: ومدار ليته ب/ إصالته: الإصالة جـ/ به: بالمصدر ب/ ١٥ بمنزلة: بمنزلت جـ/ مصدر: المصدر ب/ ١٦ قالوا: قالو هـ/ له: — ب جـ د ز حـ ط/

II.2. Translation: The 1st Chapter is about the Strong Verb[11]

The strong verb is the one in which neither the *f* [sc. the 1st radical] nor the *'* [sc. the 2nd radical] and nor the *l* [sc. the 3rd radical] is a weak consonant, a doubled consonant or a hamza, e.g. ضَرَبَ "he hit". The *f*, the *'* and the *l* were chosen for the pattern [sc. فَعَلَ], so that there would be a labial, a medial and a guttural consonant in its structure. As for our saying الضَّرْبُ "the hitting", it is then an infinite noun from which the nine patterns originate. It is the origin of the derivation according to the Basrans because its meaning is one, whereas the meaning of the verb which is indicative of the accident and the time **[Fol. 2 b]** is various, and because the one is prior to the numerous.[12] And if it is the origin of the derivation of the verb, it is also the origin of the derivation of their derivatives, or because it is a noun and the noun can do without the verb.[13] It is also stated as *maṣdar* "a source of derivation" because these patterns are derived from it. The derivation is that you find a reciprocal relation between two words, both in pronunciation and in meaning, and it is of three kinds:

1– small, meaning that there should be a reciprocal relation between them both in the consonants and in the order, e.g. ضَرَبَ "he hit" from الضَّرْبُ "the hitting".

2– big, meaning there should be a reciprocal relation between them in the pronunciation but not the order, e.g. جَبَذَ "to attract" from الجَذْبُ "the attraction".

3– bigger, meaning that there should be a reciprocal relation between them both in the point of articulation, e.g. نَعَقَ "to croak" from النَّهْقُ "the bray".[14]

It is the small derivation that is meant when taking up the question of the derivation here. The Kufans said that the verb ought to be the origin of the derivation, because the existence of an unsound weak consonant in its structure is the crucial factor for the existence of an unsound weak consonant in the *maṣdar*, and when [the factor is] non-existent, of its non-existence [in the *maṣdar*].[15] When existent, as in e.g. يَعِدُ عِدَةً "to promise" and قَامَ "to stand up" قِيَاماً, and when non-existent, as in e.g. يَوْجَلُ وَجَلاً "to be afraid" and قَاوَمَ "to resist" قِوَاماً **[Fol. 3 a]**.[16] The fact that it is the crucial factor indicates that it is the origin as well, as the verb is also emphasized by it, e.g. ضَرَبْتُ ضَرْباً "I hit a hitting", which is of the same rank as ضَرَبْتُ ضَرَبْتُ "I hit I hit"; and the emphasized is the origin and not the emphasizer.[17] It is also named *maṣdar* since it is issued from the verb, as they applied [for their theory] the example مَشْرَبٌ عَذْبٌ "a fresh drink" and مَرْكَبٌ فَارِهٌ "a quick mount" by which they meant مَشْرُوبٌ "a drink" and مَرْكُوبٌ "a mount" [as passive participles].[18] We [sc. the Basrans] answered them and said that the change due to an unsound weak consonant that is carried out in the *maṣdar* is for the purpose of analogy and does not point to the crucial factor, as the elision of the *w* in تَعِدُ "you promise" and the hamza in تُكْرِمُ "you honour".[19]

والمؤكَّديَة لا تدلُّ على الإصالة في الإشتقاق بل في الإعراب كما في جاءَني زَيْدٌ زَيْدٌ
وقولهم مَشْرَبٌ عَذْبٌ ومَرْكَبٌ فارهٌ من باب جَرَى النهْرُ وسَالَ الميزاب. ومصدر الثلاثيَ
كثير وعند سيبويه يرتقي الى اثنين وثلثين باباً نحو قَتْلٍ وفسْقٍ وشُغْلٍ ورَحْمَةٍ ونشْدَةَ
وكُدْرَةٍ ودَعْوَى وذكْرَى وبُشْرَى وليَانٍ وحرْمَانٍ وغُفْرَانٍ ونَزَوَانٍ وطَلَبٍ وخَنَقٍ وصغَرٍ
وهُدًى* وغَلَبةٍ وسَرِقَةٍ وذَهابٍ وصرافٍ وسؤالٍ وزَهادَةٍ ودرَايَةٍ ودُخُولٍ وقَبُولٍ ووَجيف * ٣ ب
وصُهُوبَةٍ ومَدْخَلٍ ومَرْجِعٍ ومَسْعَاةٍ ومَحْمدَةَ. ويجيء على وزن اسمِ الفاعل والمفعول نحو
قُمْتُ قائماً ونحو قوله تعالى (بأَيِّكُمُ ٱلْمَفْتُونُ) ويجيء للمبالغة نحو التَّهْدَارِ والتَّلْعَاب
والْحِثِّيثَى والدِّلِّيلَى. ومصدر غير الثلاثيَ يجيء على سنن واحد إلاَ في كَلَّمَ يجيء كلاّماً
وفي قَاتَلَ قتَالاً وقيتَالاً وفي تَحَمَّلَ تحمَّالاً وفي زَلْزَلَ زِلْزَالاً. الأفعال التي تشتقَ من
المصدر خمسة وثلثون باباً: ستَة منها للثلاثيَ المجرَد نحو ضَرَبَ يَضْرِبُ وقَتَلَ يَقْتُلُ
وعَلِمَ يَعْلَمُ وفَتَحَ يَفْتَحُ وكَرُمَ يَكْرُمُ وحَسِبَ يَحْسِبُ. وتسمَى الثلاثة الأولى دعائم الأبواب
لاختلاف حركاتهنَ في عين الماضي والمستقبل وكثرتهنَ وفَتَحَ يَفْتَحُ لا يدخل في
الدعائم لانعدام اختلاف الحركات ولعدمِ مجيئته بغير حرف* الحلق وأمَا ركَنَ يَرْكَنُ * ٤ آ
وأَبَى يَأْبَى فمن اللغات المتداخلة والشواذ. وأمَا بَقَى يَبْقَى وفَنَى يَفْنَى وقَلَى يَقْلَى فلغات
طيَ وقد فرُوا من الكسرة الى الفتحة وكَرُمَ يَكْرُمُ لا يدخل في الدعائم لأنَه لا يجيء إلا
من الطبائع والنعوت وحَسِبَ يَحْسِبُ لا يدخل في الدعائم لقلَته. وقد جاء
فَعُلَ يَفْعَلُ على لغة من قال كُدْتَ تَكَادُ وهي شاذة كفَضِلَ يَفْضُلُ ودِمْتَ تَدُومُ

Fols. 3a-4a

١ كما: + قالوا ل/ ٢ جرى: جرا ط/ ٣ يرتقي: ترتقي ا ج د ط/ وثلثين: وثلاثين ل/ ورحمة: ورحمت ه/ ٤ وبشرى وليان: وليَان وبشرى ط/ ونزوان: وزادان ه/ وطلب وخنق: وخنق وطلب ب/ ٥ وهدى: وهدا ج/ ودراية: وديراية ب: ودرية ج/ ٦ ومسعاة: ومسعات ا ب ج د ط/ اسم: اسمي ل/ ٧ التهدار: التهذاب ا/ ٨ والحثيثي: والخثي ب: والدليلي ز/ والدليلي: الدليل د: والحثَيثي ز/ ٩ زلزل زلزالا: ذلذل ذلذالا ب/ زلزالا: + والكسر أفصح ب: والكسر أفصح لأنَه أصل ه/ ١٠ المصدر: + وهي ب ه ط ل/ وثلثون : وثلاثون ل/ منها: — د/ المجرَد: — د/ ١١ وتسمَى: ويسمى ا: وسمي ب/ ١٢ عين: — ا د/ وكثرتهنَ: وكثرتهن ج/ ١٣ الدعائم: دعائم الأبواب د/ ولعدم: ولانعدام ب ج د ه ز ط ك ل/ ١٤ وأبَى: واباي ط/ اللغات: اللغة ب ط/ والشواذ: والشواظ ط/ ١٥ قد: وقد ا/ يدخل: تدخل د/ ١٦ وحسب: وكذلك حسب ل/ يدخل: تدخل د/ لقلَته: + استعمالا ل/ ١٧ يفعل: + بالفتح ط/ كدت تكاد: كدَده تكادو ب/

The emphasized word does not indicate that it is the origin of the etymological derivation, but of the declension, as in جاءني زيدٌ زيدٌ "Zaidun , Zaidun came to me".[20] As for their saying مَشْرَبٌ عَذْبٌ "a fresh drinking place" and مَرْكَبٌ فارِهٌ "a quick place of travelling" [regarded as nouns of place by us], they belong to the same chapter as the river streams and the drain flows.[21] The *maṣdar* of the triliteral is formed upon many patterns, and according to Sībawaihī, it amounts to thirty-two, namely: قَتْلٌ "killing", فِسْقٌ "profligacy", شُغْلٌ "occupying", رَحْمَةٌ "having mercy", نِشْدَةٌ "seeking", كُدْرَةٌ "being turbid", دَعْوى "praying", ذِكْرى "remembering", بُشْرى "announcing happy news", لَيّانٌ "softening", حِرْمانٌ "refusing", غُفْرانٌ "forgiving", نَزَوانٌ "escaping", طَلَبٌ "demanding", خَنِقٌ "strangling", صِغَرٌ "being small", هُدًى "guiding" **[Fol. 3 b]**, غَلَبَةٌ "overcoming", سَرِقَةٌ "stealing", ذَهابٌ "going away", صِرافٌ "being in heat", سُؤالٌ "requesting", زَهادَةٌ "abstinence", دِرايَةٌ "knowing", دُخولٌ "entering", قَبولٌ "accepting", وَجيفٌ "beating of the heart", صُهوبَةٌ "being reddish", مَدْخَلٌ "entering", مَرْجِعٌ "retreating", مَسْعاةٌ "endeavouring" and مَحْمَدَةٌ "praising".[22] It is formed upon the pattern of the active participle and of the passive participle, e.g. قُمْتُ قائمًا "I rose, I stood up",[23] and in the words of the Allmighty [sur. 68: 6] (بأيِّكم المَفْتونُ) "Which of you is afflicted with madness".[24] It is used to express energy or intensification, e.g. التَّهْدارُ "much fermentation", التِّلْعابُ "intensive sporting", الحِثِّيثَى "much incitement" and الدِّلِّيلَى "much guidance".[25] The *maṣdar* of the forms beyond the groundform of the triliteral follows an invariable rule,[26] except in كَلَّمَ "to talk to" of which the *maṣdar* is كلامٌ "a talk", in قاتَلَ "to fight against" of which the *maṣdar* is قتالٌ and قيتالٌ "a fight, a battle", in تَحَمَّلَ "to burden oneself" of which the *maṣdar* is تِحِمّالٌ "a burden" and in زَلْزَلَ "to shake" of which the *maṣdar* is زِلْزالٌ "a concussion, convulsion, an earthquake".[27]

The verbs which are derived from the *maṣdar* fall into thirty-five forms:[28]

– Six of them belong to the groundform of the triliteral verb, e.g. ضَرَبَ يَضْرِبُ "to hit", قَتَلَ يَقْتُلُ "to kill", عَلِمَ يَعْلَمُ "to know",[29] فَتَحَ يَفْتَحُ "to open", كَرُمَ يَكْرُمُ "to be generous" and حَسِبَ يَحْسِبُ "to assume".The first three are named the pillars of the conjugations because of the variation of the vowels of their 2nd radical in the perfect and in the imperfect, and because of their numerousness. فَتَحَ يَفْتَحُ "to open" is not included among the pillars due to the lack of variation [of the medial vowel], and because it only occurs with a guttural consonant **[Fol. 4 a]**.[30] رَكَنَ يَرْكَنُ "to lean"[31] and أَبَى يَأبَى "to refuse"[32] belong to the dialectal varieties which intruded and to the anomalies. As for بَقَى يَبْقَى "to stay", فَنَى يَفْنَى "to pass away" and قَلَى يَقْلَى "to fry", they belong to the dialect of the Ṭayyīs who escaped form the kasra and applied the fatḥa.[33] كَرُمَ يَكْرُمُ "to be generous" is not included among the pillars either because it only occurs among the verbs which are descriptive of a state or of a quality.[34] So is حَسِبَ يَحْسِبُ "to assume"[35] [not included] because of the rarity of its use. فَعِلَ يَفْعَلُ occur in accordance with the dialect of those who said كُدْتَ تَكادُ "to be about to do",[36] which is anomalous as فَضِلَ يَفْضُلُ "to remain"[37] and دِمْتَ تَدومُ "to persevere".[38]

واثنا عشر لمنشعبة الثلاثيّ نحو أكْرَمَ وقَطّعَ وقَاتَلَ وتَفَضّلَ وتَضَارَبَ وانْصَرَفَ واحْتَقَرَ واسْتَخْرَجَ واعْشَوْشَبَ واجْلَوّذَ واحْمَارّ واحْمَرّ أصلهما احْمَارَرَ واحْمَرَرَ فأُدغمتا للجنسيّة ويدلّ عليه ارْعَوَى وهو ناقص من باب افْعَلّ ولا يُدغم لانعدام الجنسيّة وواحد للرباعيّ المجرّد نحو دَحْرَجَ وثلثة لمنشعبة الرباعيّ نحو احْرَنْجَمَ واقْشَعَرّ وتَدَحْرَجَ وستّة للملحق دَحْرَجَ* ٤ ب نحو شَمْلَلَ وحَوْقَلَ وبَيْطَرَ وجَهْوَرَ وقَلْنَسَ وقَلْسَى وخمسة للملحق تَدَحْرَجَ نحو تَجَلْبَبَ وتَجَوْرَبَ وتَشَيْطَنَ وتَرَهْوَكَ وتَمَسْكَنَ واثنان للملحق احْرَنْجَمَ نحو اقْعَنْسَسَ واسْلَنْقَى ومصداق الإلحاقِ اتّحاد المصدرين.

Fols. 4a-4b

١ واثنا: واثني ا ب ط/ وقطّع: — حـ/ وانصرف: — حـ/ ٢ واعشوشب: واخشوشن ب د ه ز ط ك ل/ واحمارّ واحمرّ: واحمرّ واحمارّ ب د/ احمارر واحمرر: احمرر واحمارر ب د/ فادغمتا: وادغمتا ب/ ٣ ويدلّ: وتدلّ د ط/ ارعوى: ارعوا ب/ ناقص: لفيف ز/ لانعدام: لعدم د/ ٤ المجرّد: — د/ وثلثة: وثلاثة ل/ احرنجم... وتدحرج: تدحرج واحرنجم واقشعرّ ب جـ ك ل: وتدحرج واقشعرّ واحرنجم ز/ ٥ شَمْلَلَ: اشملل ط/ وقلنس وقلسى: وقلسا وقلنسا ب/ ٦ وترهوك وتمسكن: وتمسكن وترهوك جـ/ ٧ واسلنقى: واسليقى ب/ الإلحاق: الحاق ا/

– Twelve of them belong to the derived forms of the triliteral verbs, e.g. [Form IV] أَكْرَمَ "to honour", [Form II] قَطَّعَ "to cut", [Form III] قَاتَلَ "to fight", [Form V] تَفَضَّلَ "to deign", [Form VI] تَضَارَبَ "to strike", [Form VII] اِنْصَرَفَ "to depart", [Form VIII] اِحْتَقَرَ "to despise", [Form X] اِسْتَخْرَجَ "to remove", [Form XII] اِعْشَوْشَبَ "to cover with luxuriant herbage", [Form XIII] اِجْلَوَّذَ "to last long", [Form XI] اِحْمَارَّ "to be very red" and [Form IX] اِحْمَرَّ "to be red"(39) underlyingly اِحْمَارَرَ and اِحْمَرَرَ in which both of them [sc. the rā'ʾs] are assimilated because they were of the same kind. -اِرْعَوَى "to abstain", which is a verb with weak 3rd radical formed according to the pattern اِفْعَلَّ, proves this [sc. the theory of assimilation concerning two identical consonants], as no assimilation is carried out in it because of the lack of similarity [of the weak consonants].(40)

– One belongs to the groundform of the quadriliteral, e.g. [Form I] دَحْرَجَ "to roll".

– Three belong to the derived patterns of the quadriliteral, e.g. [Form III] اِحْرَنْجَمَ "to gather together in a mass", [Form IV] اِقْشَعَرَّ "to shudder with horror" and [Form II] تَدَحْرَجَ "to roll along".

– Six belong to the patterns which are coordinated by an augment to **[Fol. 4 b]** [Form I of the quadriliteral] دَحْرَجَ "to roll", e.g. شَمْلَلَ "to gather ripe dates and also to be active or nimble", حَوْقَلَ "to say لا حَوْلَ ولا قُوَّةَ إلاّ بالله "there is no power and no strength save in God", بَيْطَرَ "to practise the veterinary art or farriery", جَهْوَرَ "to utter one's speech in a loud voice", قَلْنَسَ and قَلْسَى "to put on a cap called قَلَنْسُوَة".

– Five belong to the patterns which are coordinated by more than one augment to [Form II of the quadriliteral] تَدَحْرَجَ, e.g. تَجَلْبَبَ "to put on a جِلْبَاب", تَجَوْرَبَ "to put on a جَوْرَاب, a sock", تَشَيْطَنَ "to act like a devil", تَرَهْوَكَ "to show a feebleness in one's walk" and تَمَسْكَنَ "to become poor".

– Two belong to the patterns which are coordinated by more than one augment to [Form III of the quadriliteral] اِحْرَنْجَمَ, e.g. اِقْعَنْسَسَ "to have a hump in front" and اِسْلَنْقَى "to lay on one's back".

The criterion of the coordination by an augment or more [to a specific pattern of a verb] is the identical structure between the patterns of both [their] *maṣdars*.(41)

§ 1. فصل في الماضي

وهو يجيء على أربعة عشر وجهاً نحو ضَرَبَ الى ضَرَبْنَا. وإنّما بُني الماضي لفوات موجب الإعراب فيه وعلى الحركة لمشابهته بالإسم في وقوعه صفة للنكرة نحو مَرَرْتُ بِرَجُلٍ ضَرَبَ وَضَارِبٍ وعلى الفتح لأنّه أخ السكون لأنَ الفتح جزء الألف والألف أخ السكون ولم يُعرب لأنَ اسم الفاعل لم يأخذ منه العمل بخلاف المستقبل لأنَ اسم الفاعل أخذ منه العمل فأُعطي الإعراب له عوضاً عنه أو لكثرة مشابهته له يعني يُعرب المضارع لكثرة مشابهته باسم الفاعل وبُني الماضي على الحركة لقلَة مشابهته له* وبُني الأمر *٥ آ
على السكون لعدم مشابهته له. زيدت الألف والواو والنون في آخره حتَى يدللن على هُمَا وهُمُوا وهُنَ، وضَمّ الباء في ضَرَبُوا لأجل الواو بخلاف رَمَوا لأنَ الميم ليست بما قبلها وضُمّ في رَضُوا وإن لم يكن الضاد ما قبلها حتَى لا يلزم الخروج من الكسرة التحقيقيَة الى الضمَة التقديريَة. وكُتب الألف في ضَرَبُوا للفرق بين واو الجمع وواو العطف في مثل حَضَرَ وتَكَلّمَ زَيْدٌ وقيل للفرق بين واو الجمع وواو الواحد في مثل لم يَدْعُوا ولم يَدْعُو. جُعلت التاء علامة للمؤنَث في مثل ضَرَبَتْ لأنَ التاء من المخرج الثاني والمؤنَث أيضاً ثان في التخليق، وهذه التاء ليست بضمير كما يجيء. وأُسكنت الباء في مثل

Fols. 4b-5a

٢ وهو يجيء: ويجيء ب/ ٣ موجب: + الإعلال ا/ لمشابهته: لمشابهة ب/ بالاسم: للاسم ل/ ٤ وضارب: او ضارب ل/ أخ(1): أخو ل/ الفتحة: الفتح ل/ جزء: جزءو ب ج/ ٤–٥ والألف... السكون: — ا د: والألف لازم السكون ب/ ٤ أخ: أخو ل/ ٥ يعرب: + الماضي ح/ ٦ فأُعطي: واعطي ه/ عنه: — ا/ لكثرة: لكسرة ب ط/ ٧ باسم: لاسم ل/ باسم الفاعل: له ب ج د ه/ ٧–٨ وبني... له: — ز/ ٨ زيدت: زيدة ب: وزيدت ل/ في آخره: — ا/ يدللن: يدلَ ب/ ٩ وهموا: وهمو ط ل/ ضربوا: ضربو ه/ لأجل: لأصل ب/ بخلاف: وبخلاف ه/ رموا: رمو ه/ ١٠ التحقيقيَة ك ل: — ا ب ج د ه ز ح ط/ ١١ التقديريَة ك ل: — ا ب ج د ه ز ح ط/ وكتب: كتبت د/ الألف: + بعد واو الجمع ه/ في: + مثل ل/ واو... العطف: واو العطف وواو الجمع ب د ه/ ١٢–١٣ لم... يدعو: لم يدعو ولم يدعوا ب ج د ه ز ط ل/ ١٢ مثل: — د/ ١٤ كما: لما د/ يجيء: + من بعد ب: سيجيء ل/

§ 1. The perfect

It falls into fourteen patterns from ضَرَبَ "he hit" to ضَرَبْنا "we hit".(42) The only reason the perfect was made undeclinable was because it lacks the factor that would make it declinable;(43) and with a vowel [given as its marker of invariabilty], because of its resemblance to the noun when it occurs as an epithet that modifies an indefinite noun, e.g. مَرَرْتُ بِرَجُلٍ ضَرَبَ وَضارِبٌ "I passed a man who was hitting".(44) And with the fatḥa [as its marker], because it is the brother of the sukūn, as the fatḥa is a part of the alif and the alif is the brother of the sukūn.(45) It was not made declinable, because the active participle [in the sense of the past] did not acquire from it [sc. the perfect] the ability to operate, by contrast to the imperfect, as the active participle acquired its ability to operate from it [sc. the imperfect].(46) So the declension was given to it [sc. the imperfect] instead of it [sc. the perfect], or because of its great resemblance to it [sc. the active participle],(47) i.e. that the imperfect was made declinable because of its great resemblance to the active participle, the perfect was made undeclinable with a vowel [sc. the fatḥa] because of its small degree of resemblance to it, **[Fol. 5 a]** and the imperative was made undeclinable with the sukūn because of its lack of resemblance to it.(48)

The *ā* [in e.g. ضَرَبا], the *w* [in e.g. ضَرَبُوا] and the *n* [in e.g. ضَرَبْنَ] are suffixed [to the form] to be suggestive of هُما "they both /dual", هُموا "they /masc. pl." and هُنَّ "they /fem. pl.". The *b* is vowelled by a ḍamma in ضَرَبُوا "they hit /masc. pl." for the sake of the *w*, by contrast to [the *m* vowelled by a fatḥa in] رَمَوا "they threw /masc. pl.", because the *m* is not the immediate consonant preceding it [sc. the *w]*. However, it [sc. the consonant preceding the *w]* is vowelled by a ḍamma in رَضُوا "they consented /masc. pl.", in spite of the fact that the *ḍ* is not the immediate consonant preceding it, so that it will not be necessary to incline from the underlying kasra [of the base form رَضِيُوا] to the adventitious ḍamma [of رَضُوا].(49)

The *ā* is suffixed in ضَرَبُوا "they hit /masc. pl." to differentiate between the *w* of the pl. and the *w* of the conjunction, as in e.g. حَضَرَ وتَكَلَّمَ زَيْدٌ "Zaid was present and talked" [which can also be read as حَضَرُوتَكَلَّمَ "they were present, he talked"];(50) and it is said to differentiate between the *w* of the pl. and the *w* of the sing., e.g. لَمْ يَدْعوا "they did not call /masc. pl. (jussive)" and لَمْ يَدْعو "he did not call (jussive, used defectively in a dialectal variant)".(51)

The *t* was made a marker of the fem. in ضَرَبَتْ "she hit" because the *t* originates from the second point of articulation,(52) and the female species is also second in the creation. This *t* is not a pronoun as it will be discussed.

The *b* was made vowelless in

ضَرَبْنَ وضَرَبْتُ ـَ حتَى لا يجتمع أربع حركات متواليات فيما هو كالكلمة الواحدة ومن ثمَ لا يجوز العطف على الضمير المرفوع المتَصل بغير التأكيد لا يُقال ضَرَبْتُ وزَيْدٌ بل يُقال ضَرَبْتُ أنا وزَيْدٌ بخلاف ضَرَبَتَا لأنَ التاء فيه في حكم السكون ومن ثمَ تسقط الألف في رَمَتَا لكون الحركة* [* ٥ ب] عارضة إلاَ في لغة رديَة إذ يقول أهلها رَمَاتَا وبخلاف مثل ضَرَبَكَ لأنَه ليس كالكلمة الواحدة لأنَ ضميره منصوب وبخلاف هُدَبِدٍ وعُلَبِطٍ لأنَ أصلهما هُدَابِدٌ وعُلَابِطٌ ثمَ قُصرا للتخفيف كما في مِخْيَطٍ أصله مِخْيَاطٌ وحُذفت التاء في مثل ضَرَبْنَ لأنَ أصله ضَرَبَتْنَ حتَى لا يجتمع علامتا التأنيث كما في مُسْلِمَاتٍ وإن لم يكونا من جنس واحد لثقل الفعل بخلاف حُبْلَيَاتٍ لعدم الجنسيَة ولعدم الثقل في الإسم. وسُوَي بين تثنيتي المخاطب والمخاطبة وبين الإخبارات أيضا لقلة الإستعمال في التثنية. ووضع الضمائر للإيجاز وعدم الإلتباس في الإخبارات. زيدت الميم في ضَرَبْتُمَا حتَى لا يلتبس بألف الإشباع في مثل قول الشاعر:

أخُوكَ أخُو مُكَاشَرَةٍ وَضِحْكٍ وَحَيَاكَ آلْإلَه فكَيْفَ أنْتَا

وخُصَت الميم للزيادة في ضَرَبْتُمَا لأنَ تحته أنْتُمَا مُضمر فأُدخل الميم في أنْتُمَا لقرب الميم الى

Fols. 5a-5b

١ ضربن وضربت : ضربت وضربن حـ/ حتَى... الواحدة: — ا/ متواليات: — د/ ٢ الضمير... المتَصل: ضميره ا د/ ٣ تسقط: يسقط ط/ ٤ الحركة: حركته ز/ يقول: تقول جـ/ مثل: — ا د/ عارضة: عارضا ب جـ د: عارضيَة هـ/ اذ: — جـ د هـ حـ ل/ وبخلاف: + مثل د/ ٥ ضمير: —ا د/ وعلبط: وغلبط ا هـ ط ل/ ٦ وعلابط: وغلابط ا هـ ط ل/ أصله: أصلها ل/ ٧ مثل: — ا/ يكونا: تكونا ل/ ٨ ولعدم... الإسم: — ا د: وأعدم الثقل في الإسم ك/ ٩ أيضا: — ب جـ د هـ حـ ك ل/ ١٠ للإيجاز: + والإختصار ب جـ/ الإخبارات: الاخباراة ا/ زيدت: وزيدت ل/ ١١ بألف الإشباع: بالألف للإشباع ب/ ١٢ مُكاشرة: مكاسراة هـ/ فكيف: وكيف ز/ ١٢ وخصَت: واختصَت ط/ للزيادة: — ب جـ د هـ ز ل/ فادخل: وادخلت ب جـ د هـ ز ل: وادخل ط/ الميم: —ك/ الى: من ل/

ضَرَبْنَ "they hit /fem. pl." and ضَرَبْتُ "/1 sing.", "/2 masc. sing." and "/2 fem. sing.", so that four consecutive vowels would not be combined together, [because the vowelled agent suffix is considered] as if belonging to the same word. However, it is impossible to couple to the pronoun [of the nominative] without emphasizing it. It is not allowed to say ضَرَبْتُ وزَيْدٌ "I hit and Zaid", but it is said ضَرَبْتُ أنا وزَيْدٌ "I and Zaid hit".(53) It [sc. the vowellessness of the *b* in ضَرَبْنَ] is contrasted to [its vowelling in] ضَرَبَتَا "they both hit /fem. dual" [that implies the combination of four consecutive vowels], because the *t* [which becomes vowelled in it] is ruled by the sukūn [of the vowelless *ā]*. However, the alif *[maqṣūra]* is dropped in رَمَتَا "they threw /fem.dual", because the vowel is adventitious, except in a defective dialect **[Fol. 5 b]** whose people say رَماتا.(54) It is also contrasted to [its vowelling in] ضَرَبَكَ "he hit you /masc. sing." [in which four consecutive vowels are combined], because it [sc. ضَرَبَكَ] is not considered as one single word as its pronoun is in the accusative.(55) It is also contrasted to [the combination of four consecutive vowels in] هُدَبِدٌ "very thick milk" and عُلَبِطٌ "a lot of sheep, also a fat man" underlyingly هُدابِدٌ and عُلابِطٌ, which are both shortened for the sake of alleviation,(56) as in مِخْيَطٌ "a needle" underlyingly مِخْياطٌ.(57) The *t* was elided in the example of ضَرَبْنَ "they hit /fem. pl." underlyingly ضَرَبَتْنَ, so that two markers of the fem. will not be combined together, as in مُسْلِماتٌ [underlyingly مُسْلِمَتاتٌ] "muslim women", in spite of the fact that they [sc. the *t* and the *n* of ضَرَبَتْنَ] are not of the same kind, [but the elision is carried out] because of the heaviness [implied by both their combination] in the verb,(58) contrarily to حُبْلَيَاتٌ "pregnant women" because they [sc. the two markers of the fem.] are not of the same kind and [the elision of one marker is not carried out] because the heaviness does not take place in the noun.(59) The duals of the 2nd person of the masc. and of the fem. [of ضَرَبَ : ضَرَبْتُما] were made homonym, as well as one form was made sufficient for the 1st person of the sing. [sc. ضَرَبْتُ "I hit] and of the pl. [sc. ضَرَبْنا "we hit"], because the dual is rarely used.

The pronouns are suffixed for the sake of abbreviation and so that there will not be any risk of mixing up the persons together.

The *m* is infixed in ضَرَبْتُما "you both hit /masc. and fem. dual" so that it will not be mixed up with the sing. form [sc. ضَرَبْتَ] in which the alif of saturation can be suffixed [i.e. ضَرَبْتا], as the case which occurs in the saying of the poet:

"أخوكَ أخُو مُكاشَرَةٍ وضِحْكٍ وحَيَّاكَ الإلَه فكَيفَ أنْتا".

"Your brother is the brother of cheerfulness and laughter
And may God preserve your life, in what condition are you in?".(60)

The *m* is specifically chosen to be infixed in ضَرَبْتُما "you both hit /masc. and fem. dual" because أنْتُما "you both /masc. and fem. dual" is suppressed in its form. The *m* is infixed in أنْتُما because of the proximity of the *m* to

التاء في المخرج* [٦ آ] الشفويَ وقيل تبعا لهُما وضمَت التاء لأنَها ضمير الفاعل وفُتحت التاء في الواحد خوفاً من الإلتباس بالمتكلَم ولا التباس في التثنية وقيل إتباعاً للميم لأنَ الميم شفويَة فجعلوا حركة التاء من جنسها وهو الضمَ الشفويَ زيدت الميم في ضَرَبْتُم حتَى يُطَرد بتثنيته وضمير الجمع فيه محذوف وهو الواو لأنَ أصله ضَرَبْتُمُوا فحُذفت الواو لأنَ الميم بمنزلة الإسم ولا يوجد في آخر الإسم واو ما قبلها مضموم إلاَ هُوَ ومن ثمَ يُقَال في جمع دَلْوٍ أدْلٍ أصله أدْلُوٌ بخلاف ضَرَبُوا لأنَ باءه ليس بمنزلة الإسم وبخلاف ضَرَبْتُمُوهُ لأنَ الواو خرج من الطرف* [٦ ب] بسبب الضمير كما في العَظَايَة. وشُدَد النون في ضَرَبْتُنَ دون ضَرَبْنَ لأنَ أصله ضَرَبْتُمْنَ فأُدغم الميم في النون لقرب الميم من النون ومن ثمَ تُبدل الميم من النون في مثل عَمْبَرٍ أصله عَنْبَر وقيل أصله ضَرَبْتُنَ فأُريد أن يكون ما قبل النون ساكناً ليُطَرد بجميع نونات النساء ولا يُمكن إسكان تاء المخاطبة لاجتماع الساكنين ولا يُمكن حذفها لأنَها علامة والعلامة لا تُحذف فأُدخل النون لقرب النون من النون ثمَ أُدغم فصار ضَرَبْتُنَ. زيدت التاء في ضَرَبْتُ لأنَ تحته أنا مُضمر ولا يُمكن الزيادة من حروف أنا للإلتباس فاختير التاء لوجوده في أخواته. زيدت النون في ضَرَبْنَا لأنَ تحته نَحْنُ مضمر ثمَ زيدت الألف حتَى لا يُلتبس بضَرَبْنَ فصار ضَرَبْنا وقيل تحته إنَنا مضمر.

وتدخل المضمرات في الماضي وأخواته وهي ترتقي الى ستَين نوعاً إلاَ أنَها في الأصل ثلاثة مرفوع ومنصوب ومجرور ثمَ* [٧ آ] يصير كلَ واحد منها اثنين نظراً الى اتَصاله وانفصاله، فاضرب الإثنين في الثلثة حتَى يصير ستَة ثمَ أخرج المجرور المنفصل حتَى لا

Fols. 5b-7a

١ الشفويَ: — جـ ز ل/ لهما: + لما يجيء ا د/ التاء: + في ضربتما ب جـ د ط ك ل/ لأنَها: لأنَه د/ التاء: — د ل/ ٢ بالمتكلَم: — د/ ولا التباس: والالتباس ا/ ٣ زيدت: وزيدة ب: وزيدت ك ل/ ٤ الواو: — ا/ ٦ ليس: ليست د ك ل/ بمنزلة: بمنزلت ط/ ٧ نون: النون في ل/ ٩ الميم... النون: — ا/ عمبر: + لأن د/ ١٠ المخاطبة: الخطاب د/ ١٢ فصار ضربتنَ: — ا/ وزيدت: زيدت د/ ١٣ حروف أنا: حروفه ا: + لأنه على تقدير زيادة الألف يلتبس بالتثنية وعلى تقدير زيادة النون يلتبس بجمع المؤنث ط/ للالتباس: للالباس د/ زيدت: وزيدت ل/ ١٤ فصار ضربنا — ا د/ ١٦ وتدخل: تدخل ل/ ١٧ ثلثة: ثلاثة ل/ ١٨ الثلثة: الثلاثة ل/ ستة: ستا ا ب جـ د هـ ز/

the *t* in the point of articulation originating from the region of the lips,(61) **[Fol. 6 a]** and it is said in accordance with هُما "they both /masc. and fem. dual". The *t* is vowelled by a ḍamma [in ضَرَبْتُما] because it is the pronoun of the subject. It is vowelled by a fatḥa in the [2nd person of the] masc. sing. from fear of mixing it up [with the 1st person]. Such a confusion is not implied by the dual, and it is said [that it is vowelled by a ḍamma] for the sake of analogy with the *m*, because the *m* is labial. This is why they [sc. the grammarians] vowelled the *t* according to [a vowel of] its kind, which is the labial ḍamma. The *m* is suffixed in ضَرَبْتُمْ "you hit /masc. pl.", so that it is analogous to its [sc. the verb's *m* of the] dual [sc. ضَرَبْتُما]. The pronoun of the pl., which is the *ū*, was elided in it, as it is underlyingly ضَرَبْتُمُوا, because the *m* is a noun suffix;(62) and hence there is no noun that ends up with a *w* that is preceded by a consonant vowelled by a ḍamma except هُوَ "he".(63) On account of that, the pl. of دَلْوٌ "a bucket" is said to be أَدْلٍ underlyingly أَدْلُوٌ.(64) It [sc. the case of ضَرَبْتُمُوا] is contrasted to [the case of] ضَرَبُوا "they hit / masc. pl." [in which the *w* at the extremity is preceded by a ḍamma], because its [sc. ضَرَبُوا 's] *b* is not a noun suffix, and it is contrasted to [the case of] ضَرَبْتُمُوهُ "you hit him /masc. pl.", in which the *w* left its position at the extremity of the word **[Fol. 6 b]** because of the object pronoun,(65) similarly to the case of العَظَايَةُ "a certain reptile" [in which the *y* left its position at the extremity of the word because of the *tā᾽ marbūṭa]*.(66) The *n* of ضَرَبْتُنَّ "you hit /fem. pl." is doubled and not [the *n]* of ضَرَبْنَ "they hit /fem. pl.", because it is underlyingly ضَرَبْتُمْنَ, in which the *m* is assimilated to the *n* on account of the proximity of the *m* to the *n*,(67) – and hence the *m* is substituted for the *n* in e.g. عَمْبَرٌ "a storehouse" underlyingly عَنْبَرٌ -.(68) And it is said [by some] that its base form is ضَرَبْتُنَ, and the intention was that the consonant preceding the *n* should be vowelless so that it would be followed by the *n* of the fem. pl., but it was impossible to make the *t* of the 2nd person of the fem. vowelless as this would imply the cluster of two vowelless consonants, as well as it was impossible to elide it because it is a marker [of the 2nd person], and the marker should not to be elided, so the *n* was infixed because of the proximity of the *n* to the *n*, and then it was assimilated to it so that it became ضَرَبْتُنَّ.(69) The *t* is suffixed in ضَرَبْتُ "I hit", because أنا "I" is suppressed in its form. It was impossible to suffix any of أنا 's consonants from fear of confusion.(70) So the *t* was chosen because it occurs in its cognates. The *n* is infixed in ضَرَبْنا "we hit" because نَحْنُ "we" is suppressed in its form, and then the *ā* is suffixed so that it will not be mixed up with ضَرَبْنَ "they hit /fem. pl.", and it was said that إنّا "we" is suppressed in its form.

The pronouns enter the perfect and its cognates and develop up to sixty forms,(71) which however are underlyingly three: those which are in the nominative, those which are in the accusative and those which are in the genitive. Then **[Fol. 7 a]** each one of them becomes two regarding its being suffixed and separate. So multiply the two by three so that you get six, and then extract the separate pronoun of the genitive, so that it will not

يلزم تقديم المجرور على الجار فبقي لك خمسة مرفوع متّصل ومنفصل ومنصوب
متّصل ومنفصل ومجرور متّصل ثمّ انظر إلى المرفوع المتّصل وهو يحتمل
ثمانية عشر وجها في العقل ستّة في الغائب مع الغائبة وستّة في المخاطب مع المخاطبة
وستّة في الحكاية واكتفي بخمسة في الغائب والغائبة باشتراك التثنية لقلّة استعمالها
وكذلك في المخاطب والمخاطبة وفي الحكاية بلفظين لأنّ المتكلّم يرى في أكثر
الأحوال أو يعلم بالصوت أنّه مذكّر أو مؤنّث فبقي لك اثنا عشر نوعاً، وإذا صار قسم
واحد من تلك القسمة اثني عشر نوعاً فيصير كلّ واحد منها مثل ذلك فيحصل لك
بضرب الخمسة في اثني عشر ستّون* نوعاً، إثنا عشر للمرفوع المتّصل نحو ضَرَبَ الى * ٧ ب
ضَرَبْنَا، واثنا عشر للمرفوع المنفصل نحو هو ضَرَبَ الى نَحْنُ ضَرَبْنَا. والأصل في هُوَ أن
يُقال هُوَ هُوا هُوُوا ولكن جُعل الواو ميماً في الجمع لاتّحاد مخرجهما ولكراهيَة اجتماع
الواوين في الطرف فصار هُمُوا ثمّ حُذف الواو كما مرّ في ضَرَبْتُمُوا وحمُلت التثنية عليه
وقيل حتّى تقع الفتحة على الميم القويّ، وأُدخل الميم في أنتما كما مرّ في ضَرَبْتُمَا وحُمل
الجمع عليه، ولا يُحذف واو هُوَ لقلّة حروفه من القدر الصالح ويُحذف إذا تُعانق بشيء
آخر لحصول كثرة الحروف بالمعانقة مع وقوع الواو على الطرف ويُبقى الهاء مضموماً على
حاله نحو لَهُ ويُكسر الهاء إذا كان ما قبله مكسوراً أو ياء ساكنة حتّى لا يلزم الخروج

Fols. 7a-7b

١ الجار: الجاري ب: + ولا يقال زيد ب جـ/ فبقي: فيبقى ب/ ومنفصل: ومرفوع منفصل ل/ ٢ ومنفصل: ومنصوب منفصل ل/ وهو يحتمل: وهي تحتمل حـ/ ٢ وجها: نوعا د ل/ ستّة: ستا ب جـ د هـ ز/ الغائب... الغائبة: الغيبة ب د ز/ وستّة: وستا ب د هـ ز/ ٤ ستّة: وستا د/ الغائب والغائبة: الغيبة ب د ز/ باشتراك: باشترك هـ/ ٥ وفي: واكتفي في ل/ ٦ فبقي: فيبقى هـ/ اثنا: اثني ١ ب ط/ ٧ القسمة: الأقسام ب/ نوعا: - د/ ٨ اثنا: اثني ا جـ حـ: فاثني هـ: واثنين ط/ ٩ واثنا: واثني ا هـ/ للمرفوع: - ز/ للمرفوع المنفصل: للمنفصل د/ ١٠ ولكراهيَة: ولكراهة د/ ولكراهيَة اجتماع: واجتماع ا/ ١١ في الطرف: - ا: في اللفظ ز/ ضربتموا: ضربتمو ز ك/ وحملت: وحمل د/ ١٢ تقع: يقع ا د/ ١٣ يحذف: تحذف ب جـ حـ ك ل/ ويحذف: + واو هو ب ك: وحذفت هـ: وتحذف ل/ ١٤ ويبقى: وتبقي ب هـ ط: وبقي جـ د/ مضموماً: مضمومة ب هـ حـ ط/ ١٥ حاله: حالها ب هـ حـ ط/ ما: - ا/

be necessary to let the element governed by the operator of the genitive precede the operator of the genitive, [e.g. زَيْد بـ instead of بِزَيْدٍ "by Zaid" or كَ بـ instead of بِكَ "by you"], and so five are left for you:

– The suffixed and separate pronoun of the nominative.

– The suffixed and separate pronoun of the accusative.

– The suffixed pronoun of the genitive.

Then direct your attention to the suffixed pronoun of the nominative, which implies eighteen patterns in the mind:

– Six for the 3rd person of the masc. and the fem.

– Six for the 2nd person of the masc. and the fem.

– Six for the 1st persons.

Five were made sufficient for the 3rd person of the masc. and the fem. with the homonymy of the dual,[(72)] because it is so rarely used. This is also the case of the 2nd person of the masc. and fem. Two were made sufficient for the 1st persons [of the sing. and pl.],[(73)] because in most cases the 1st person sees or knowns by his voice if he is a male or a female.[(74)] So there are twelve patterns left for you.

And if one single part of this division implies twelve patterns, then each of the others implies the same, and by multiplying the five patterns by twelve you obtain sixty **[Fol. 7 b]**:

1– Twelve for the suffixed pronoun of the nominative from ضَرَبَ "he hit" to ضَرَبْنَا "we hit".[(75)]

2– Twelve for the separate pronoun of the nominative from هُوَ ضَرَبَ "he hit" to نَحْنُ ضَرَبْنَا "we hit".[(76)] The base forms of هُوَ "he"[(77)] are said to be هُوَ "he /sing.", هُوا "they both /masc. dual" and هُوُوا "they /masc.pl." with the *w* changed into a *m* in the pl. on account of the oneness of both their points of articulation and because of the dislike of combining two wāws at the extremity of the word, so it became هُمُوا, and then the *w* was elided as has been mentioned concerning the case of ضَرَبْتُمُوا "you hit /masc. pl.". Then the dual was ascribed to it, and it was said so that the *m,* which is a strong consonant, becomes vowelled by a fatḥa.[(78)]

The *m* is infixed in أنتُما "you /masc. dual" as was mentioned concerning the case of ضَرَبْتُمَا "you hit /masc. dual", and then the pl. was ascribed to it.[(79)]

The *w* of هُوَ should not be elided because of its small number of consonants in proportion to the proper number determining a word. It is however elided if it is suffixed to another word, because of the large number of consonants obtained through the suffixation together with the occurrence of the *w* at the extremity of the word. The *h* remains unchanged vowelled by a ḍamma, e.g. لَهُ "to him". It is vowelled by a kasra if the consonant preceding it is vowelled by a kasra or if it is a vowelless *y,* so that it will not be necessary to deviate

من الكسرة الى الضمَة نحو غلامه وفيه ويُجعل ياء هيَ ألفاً كما يُجعل الياء في يا غُلاَمي فيُقال يا غُلاَمَا وفي يا بَادِيَةُ يا بَادَاةُ ويُجعل ياء هي ميماً في التثنية حتَى لا تقع الفتحة على الياء الضعيفة* (٨ آ) مع ضعفها وشدَد نون هُنَ كما مرَ في ضَرَبْتُنَ، واثنا عشر للمنصوب المتَصل نحو ضَرَبَهُ الى ضَرَبَنَا ولا يجوز فيه اجتماع ضميرَي الفاعل والمفعول في مثل ضَرَبْتَكَ وضَرَبْتُنِي حتَى لا يكون الشخص الواحد فاعلاً ومفعولاً في حالة واحدة إلاَ في أفعال القلوب نحو عَلِمْتَكَ فَاضِلاً وعَلِمْتُنِي فاضلاً لأنَ المفعول الأوَل ليس بمفعول في الحقيقة ولهذا قيل في تقديره عَلِمْتَ فَضْلَكَ وعَلِمْتُ فَضْلِي، واثنا عشر للمنصوب لمنفصل نحو إيَاهُ ضَرَبَ الى إيَانا ضَرَبْنا، واثنا عشر للمجرور المتَصل نحو ضاربه الى ضَارِبِنا، وفي مثل ضَارِبُويَ جُعل الواو ياءً ثمَ أُدغم كما في مَهْدِيَ أصله مَهْدُويَ. والمرفوع المتَصل يستتر في خمسة مواضع في الغائب نحو ضَرَبَ ويَضْرِبُ ولِيَضْرِبْ ولا يَضْرِبُ وفي الغائبة نحو ضَرَبَتْ وتَضْرِبُ ولِتَضْرِبْ ولا تَضْرِبُ وفي المخاطب الذي في غير* (٨ ب) الماضي نحو تَضْرِبُ واضْرِبْ ولا تَضْرِبُ، وياء تَضْرِبِينَ علامة الخطاب وفاعله مستتر عند الأخفش وعند العامة هي ضمير بارز للفاعل كواو يَضْرِبُونَ، عُيِّنَ الياء في تَضْرِبِينَ لمجيئه في هَذِي أَمَةُ الله للتأنيث ولم يُزد في تَضْرِبِينَ من حروف أنت للإلتباس بالتثنية في زيادة الألف واجتماع النونين في زيادة النون وتكرار التاءين في زيادة التاء وأُبرز الياء في تَضْرِبِينَ للفرق بينه وبين جمعه ولم يُفرق بحركة ما قبل النون حتَى لا يلتبس بالنون الثقيلة في الصورة ولا يُحذف النون حتَى لا يلتبس بالمذكَر وفي المضارع للمتكلَم نحو أَضْرِبُ ونَضْرِبُ وفي الصفة نحو ضَارِبٍ وضَارِبَانِ وضَارِبُونَ الى آخره.

Fols. 7b-8b

١ ويجعل: وتجعل ل/ يجعل: تجعل ل/ الياء: — د ل/ ٢ يا: فيقال يا ل/ باداة: بادات ج/ ويجعل: وتجعل ل/ ياء هي: الياء ا: — د/ تقع: يقع ا د/ ٣ الضعيفة: الضعيف د/ واثنا: واثني ا ج/ ٥ يكون: يصير ب ج د ه ز ل/ ٦ المفعول: — ا/ ٧ علمت... فضلي: علمت فضلي وعلمت فضلك د/ ٧ و ٨ واثنا: واثني ا/ ٩ ضاربوي: ضاربيَ د/ ادغم: ادغمت ا/ مهدويَ: + وهو اسم مفعول في الهداية ج/ ١٢ عيّن: وعيّن د ل/ ١٤ لمجيئه: لمجيئته ا/ أنت: + للتأنيث ا/ للالتباس: للالباس د/ ١٥ التاءين: التاء ل/ ١٦ وابرز: وابرزت ا: وابراز د/ في تضربين: —ا د/ جمعه: + وهو تضربن ز/ ١٧ يلتبس: + بالمفرد ج/ ١٨ نحو: — ا/ وضاربان... الى آخره: ضاربان ضاربون ا/

from the kasra to the ḍamma, e.g. غُلامه "his boy" and فيه "in him".(80) The *y* of هيَ "she" is changed into an *ā* [in ـها "her"] in the same manner as it is changed [into one] in يا غُلامي "Oh my boy!", which is said يا غُلاما, and in يا باديَة "Oh, desert!" [which is said] يا باداة.(81) The *y* [of هيَ "she"] is changed into a *m* in the dual [ـهُما "them /dual"] so that the weak fatḥa does not have to vowel the weak *y* [i.e. ـهيا] **[Fol. 8 a]**. The *n* of ـهُنَّ "them /fem. pl." is doubled as was mentioned concerning ضَرَبْتُنَّ "you hit /fem. pl.". 3– Twelve for the suffixed pronoun of the accusative from ضَرَبَهُ "he hit him" to ضَرَبَنا "he hit us".(82) It is impossible to combine both the agent and the object pronouns [of the same person], e.g. ضَرَبْتَكَ "you hit you" [corrupt], and ضَرَبْتُنِي "I hit I" [corrupt], so that the one only person does not become an agent and an object at the same time, except in the verbs of heart, e.g. عَلِمْتَكَ فاضلاً "you knew yourself being eminent" and عَلِمْتُنِي فاضلاً "I knew myself being eminent", because the first [sc. the object pronoun] is not the real object,(83) and this is why it is said by implication عَلِمْتَ فَضْلَكَ "you knew your eminence" and عَلِمْتُ فَضْلِي "I knew my eminence". 4– Twelve are for the separate pronoun of the accusative from إيّاهُ ضَرَبَ "he hit him" to إيّانا ضَرَبْنا "we hit ourselves".(84) 5– Twelve are for the suffixed pronoun of the genitive from ضاربُهُ "the one who is hitting him" to ضاربُنا "the one who is hitting us".(85) In the example ضاربُوي "the ones who are hitting me", the *w* is changed into a *y*, and is then assimilated to it [i.e. ضاربيَّ],(86) as in مَهْدِيّ "rightly guided, Mahdi" underlyingly مَهْدُوي. The suffixed agent pronoun is latent in five cases: 1– In the 3rd person of the masc. sing., e.g. ضَرَبَ "he hit (perfect)", يَضْرِبُ "he hits (imperfect)", لِيَضْرِبْ "let him hit (imperative)" and لا يَضْرِبُ "he shall not hit (prohibition)". 2– In the 3rd person of the fem. sing., e.g. ضَرَبَتْ "she hit (perfect)", تَضْرِبُ "she hits (imperfect)", لِتَضْرِبْ "let her hit (imperative)" and لا تَضْرِبُ "she shall not hit (prohibition)". 3– In the 2nd person of the masc. sing. in other **[Fol. 8 b]** than the perfect, e.g. تَضْرِبُ "you hit (imperfect)", اِضْرِبْ "hit! (imperative)" and لا تَضْرِبُ "you shall not hit (prohibition)". The *y* of تَضْرِبِينَ "you hit /fem. sing." is the marker of the 2nd person of the fem. sing. Its subject is latent according to al-Aḫfaš, although it is the prominent pronoun of the subject according to the majority,(87) as the *ū* of يَضْرِبونَ "they hit". The *y* was chosen in تَضْرِبِينَ (88) because of its occurrence in [هذي in] هذي أمَةُ الله "this is God's maid-servant", in which it marks the fem.(89) None of the consonants of أنتِ are infixed [instead of it] in تَضْرِبِينَ from fear of mixing it up with the dual by infixing the *ā*, of combining both the nūns by infixing the *n* and of repeating both the tāʾs by infixing the *t*. So the *y* was made prominent in تَضْرِبِينَ to differentiate between it and its pl. [sc. تَضْرِبْنَ "you hit /fem. pl."]. No distinction [between تَضْرِبِينَ and تَضْرِبْنَ] was made by means of vowelling what precedes the *n* so that it will not be mixed up with the doubled *n* in the representation [i.e. تَضْرِبْنَّ]. The *n* is not elided either so that it [sc. the form] will not be mixed up with the 2nd person of the masc. sing. [sc. تَضْرِبُ]. 4)– In the 1st persons of the imperfect, e.g. أضْرِبُ "I hit" and نَضْرِبُ "we hit". 5)– In the epithet, e.g. ضارِبٌ "hitting /masc. sing.", ضارِبان "/masc. dual" and ضارِبون "/masc. pl.", etc.

واستتر في المرفوع دون المنصوب والمجرور لأنّه بمنزلة جزء الفعل، واستتر في الغائب
* ٩ آ والغائبة دون التثنية والجمع لأنَّ الإستتار خفيف فإعطاء* الخفيف للمفرد السابق أولى
دون المتكلّم والمخاطب اللذَين في الماضي لأنَّ الإستتار قرينة ضعيفة والإبراز قرينة قويّة،
فإعطاء الإبراز القويَّ للمتكلّم القويَّ والمخاطب القويَّ أولى، واستُتر في مخاطب
المستقبل ومتكلّمه للفرق وقيل يستتر في هذه المواضع دون غيرها لوجود الدليل فيها
وهو عدم الإبراز في مثل ضَرَبَ والتاء في مثل ضَرَبَتْ والياء في مثل يَضْرِبُ والتاء في
مثل تَضْرِبُ والهمزة في مثل أضْرِبُ والنون في مثل نَضْرِبُ وهي حروف ليست بأسماء
والصفة في مثل ضَارِبٍ وضَارِبَانِ وضَارِبُونَ ولا يجوز أن يكون التاء في ضَرَبَتْ ضميراً كتاء
ضَرَبْتُ لوجود عدم حذفها بالفاعل الظاهر نحو ضَرَبَتْ هِنْدٌ ولا يجوز أن يكون ألف
* ٩ ب ضاربانِ ضميراً لأنّه يتغيّر في حالة النصب والجرّ والضمير لا يتغيّر كألف يَضْرِبان*
والإستتارُ واجب في مثل افْعَلْ وتَفْعَلُ وأفْعَلُ ونَفْعَلُ لدلالة الصيغة عليه وقُبِحَ افْعَلْ
زَيْدٌ وتَفْعَلُ زَيْدٌ وأفْعَلُ زَيْدٌ ونَفْعَلُ زَيْدُون.

Fols. 8b-9b

٢ فإعطاء: واعطاء ب جـ د ز ط: فاعطاه حـ/ ٢ اللذين: الذين ا: الذي حـ/ ٤ القويَّ: — حـ/ مخاطب: المخاطب ا/ ٥ بينهما: — د ل/ فيها: — ا/ ٧ ليست: ليس جـ/ ٨ وضاربان وضاربون: ضاربان ضاربون ا/ التاء في: تاء ب جـ د هـ ز حـ ط ك ل/ ٩ لوجود: بوجود ب/ بالفاعل الظاهر: بالفاعلة الظاهرة ا د/ ١٠ حالة: حال د/ ١١ والإستتار: الاستتار جـ ز/ عليه: + وعدم الاستعمال ك/ ١٢ وأفعل... زيدون: — ب/

It [sc. the pronoun] was made latent in the nominative and not in the accusative and the genitive because it holds a position as being a part of the verb.

It was made latent in the 3rd person of the masc. and of the fem. sing. and not in the dual and in the pl. because the latency is light. So giving **[Fol. 9 a]** the light latency to the antecedent which is in the sing., is more prior than giving it to the 1st and to the 2nd persons of the perfect, because the latency is a weak evidence [of the subject] and the prominence is a strong evidence of it. So giving the strong prominence to the strong 1st person and to the strong 2nd person is prior. It was made latent in the 2nd person of the masc. sing. and the 1st person [of the sing. and pl.] of the imperfect for the purpose of making a distinction [between the perfect and the imperfect]. It was said that it was made latent in these cases and not in others, because of the existence of the evidence in them, namely: the latency, in e.g. ضَرَبَ "he hit", the *t* in e.g. ضَرَبَتْ "she hit", the *y*, in e.g. يَضْرِبُ "he hits", the *t*, in e.g. تَضْرِبُ "you hit /masc. sing.", "she hit /fem. sing.", the hamza, in e.g. أَضْرِبُ "I hit" and the *n*, in e.g. نَضْرِبُ "we hit", – and they [sc. the imperfect prefixes] are prefixes and not nouns [sc. agent pronouns] -, and in the epithets, e.g. ضارِبٌ "/masc. sing.", ضارِبانِ "/masc. dual" and ضارِبونَ "/masc. pl.".(90)

It is impossible that the *t* in ضَرَبَتْ "she hit" is a pronoun as the *t* in ضَرَبْتُ "I hit", "/2 masc. sing." and "/2 fem. sing.", because it is not elided by the manifested subject, e.g. ضَرَبَتْ هِنْدٌ "Hind hit".

It is also impossible that the *ā* in ضارِبانِ "hitting /masc. dual (active participle)" is a pronoun, because it varies in the case of the accusative and the genitive, and the pronoun does not vary as the *ā* of يَضْرِبانِ "they both hit /masc. dual".

[Fol. 9 b] The latency is obligatory in اِفْعَلْ "do! /masc. sing. (imperative)", تَفْعَلُ "/2 masc. sing. (imperfect)", أَفْعَلُ "/1 sing." and نَفْعَلُ "/1 pl." because of the indication of the [verb's] form to it [sc. the latent subject].

As for اِفْعَلْ زَيْدٌ "Zaid do! (imperative)", تَفْعَلُ زَيْدٌ "You Zaid do", أَفْعَلُ زَيْدٌ "I Zaid do" and نَفْعَلُ زَيْدونَ "we Zaids do", they are disliked.

§ 2. فصل في المستقبل

وهو أيضاً يجيء على أربعة عشر وجهاً نحو يَضْرِبُ الى آخره ويُقال له مستقبل لوجود معنى الإستقبال في معناه ويُقال له أيضاً مضارع لأنّه مشابه بضَارِب في الحركات والسكنات وفي وقوعه صفة للنكرة وفي دخول لام الإبتداء نحو إنَ زَيْداً لَقَائِمٌ وليَقُومُ وباسم الجنس في العموم والخصوص يعني أنَ اسم الجنس يختصَ بلام العهد كما يختصَ يَضْرِبُ بِسَوْفَ أو بالسين وبالعين في الإشتراك بين الحال والإستقبال. زيدت على الماضي من حروف أتين حتّي يصير مستقبلاً لأنَ الماضي بتقدير النقصان منه يصير أقلَ من القدر الصالح وزيدت في الأوّل دون الآخر لأنَ في الآخر يلتبس بالماضي واشتقَ من الماضي* [١٠ آ] لأنَ الماضي يدلَ على الثبات بخلاف المستقبل وزيدت في المستقبل دون الماضي لأنَ المزيد عليه بعد المجرّد والمستقبل بعد زمان الماضي فأُعطي السابق للسابق واللاحق للاحق. وعُيِّنت الألف للمتكلّم وحده لأنَ الألف من أقصى الحلق وهو مبدأ المخارج، والمتكلّم هو الذي يبدأ الكلام وقيل للموافقة بينه وبين أنا وعُيِّنت الواو للمخاطب لكونه من منتهى المخارج، والمخاطب هو الذي ينتهي الكلام به ثمَ قُلبت الواو تاء حتّى لا يجتمع الواوات في مثل وَوَوْجَلُ في العطف، ومن ثمَ قيل الأوّل من كلَ كلمة لا يصلح لزيادة الواو وحُكم أنَ واو وَرَنْتَلٍ أصل. وعُيِّنت الياء للغائب لأنَ الياء من وسط الفم، والغائب هو الذي في وسط الكلام بين المتكلّم والمخاطب. وعُيِّنت النون للمتكلّم إذا كان معه غيره لتعيّنها لذلك في ضَرَبْنَا. وقيل زيدت النون* [١٠ ب] لأنّه لم يبق من حروف

Fols. 9b-10b

٢ يضرب: + يضربان يضربون ط/ ٣ له: + أيضا ل/ ٤ وفي وقوعه: ووقوعه ب د ه ز ك ل/ ٥ اسم الجنس: — د/ يختصَ: يتخصَص ل/ العهد: + نحو الرجل ج/ ٦ يختصَ: يتخصَص ل/ وبالعين في: فيتعين بعد ك/ ٧ زيدت: وزيدت ك ل/ من: — ب د ه ز ل/ أتين: + او ناتي ب/ الماضي: — د/ منه: — ا د/ ٨ لأنَ: لأنه ل/ ٩ لأنَ الماضي: لأنَه د ل/ بخلاف المستقبل: — ب ج د ه ز ح ل/ ١١ وحده: — د/ ١٢ الكلام: + به ا د/ ١٤ مثل: نحو ل/ ١٥ لزيادة: بزيادة ا/ وحكم: وحكي د ه ط: وحكمى ح: ولهذا حكي ك/ ١٧ الذي: + يكون د ل/ الكلام... المتكلّم: كلام المتكلّم د/

§ 2. The imperfect(91)

It also falls into fourteen patterns from يَضْرِب "he hits" etc.(92) It is named مُسْتَقْبَل "future" because of the existence of the meaning of the future in it. It is also named مُضارِع "[the pattern] which is similar" because:

– It is commensurable with ضارِب "hitting" [sc. the active participle] in its vowels and in its sukūn.

– It occurs as the epithet of the undefined noun.

– It admits the inceptive *l*, e.g. إنّ زَيْداً لقائم ولَيقوم "certainly Zaid is standing and stands".

– It is similar to the generic noun in being general and particular, i.e. that the generic noun is distinguished by the article that is used to denote previous knowledge as يَضْرِب is distinguished by *sawfa* and by the *s* [which concern the future].

– The حال "the denotative of state" [e.g. ضارِب "hitting"] and the imperfect يَضْرِب "he hits" are specifically similar in meaning.(93)

The consonants of أتين(94) are prefixed to the perfect so that it becomes an imperfect, because if the perfect is decreased it will be less than the proper number [determining a word]. They are prefixed rather than suffixed, because if they were suffixed, it [sc. the imperfect] would be mixed up with the perfect. It is derived from the perfect **[Fol. 10 a]** because the perfect denotes stability by contrast to the future.(95) The prefixation occurs in the imperfect and not in the perfect, because the word which is augmented by prefixes comes after the word which is unaugmented, and the future comes after the perfect tense. So the antecedent [sc. the suffixation] is given to the antecedent [sc. the perfect] and the following [sc. the prefixation] to the following [sc. the imperfect]. The alif [sc. the *ʾ]* was chosen [as a prefix] for the 1st person alone, because the alif originates from the farthest part of the throat, which is the starting point of the points of articulation, just as the 1st person is the one who starts the conversation. It was also said because of the agreement between it and أنا "I". The *w* was chosen [in the base form as a prefix] for the 2nd person, as it is the ultimate of all the points of articulation, and the 2nd person is the one by whom the conversation ends. Then the *w* was changed into a *t* to avoid the combination of many wāws, as in ووَوْجَل "and you are afraid" [instead of the correct وتَوْجَل] in the case of the syndesis. Hence, it was said that it is incorrect to prefix a *w* to the word. So the *w* of وَرَنْتَل "a calamity" is deemed as a radical.(96) The *y* was chosen [as a prefix] for the 3rd persons [masc. sing. and pl., fem. pl. and the duals], because the *y* originates from the middle of the mouth, just as the 3rd person stands in the middle of the conversation between the 1st and the 2nd person.(97) The *n* was chosen [as a prefix] for the 1st person of the pl. because it was also chosen in ضَرَبْنا "we hit". It was also said that the *n* was prefixed **[Fol. 10 b]** because there were no

العلَة شيء وهو قريب من حروف العلَة في خروجها عن هواء الخيشوم. وفُتحت هذه الحروف للخفَة إلاَ في الرباعيَ وهو فَعْلَلَ وأفْعَلَ وفَعَلَ وفَاعَلَ لأنَ هذه الأربعة رباعيَة والرباعيُ فرع الثلاثيَ والضمَ أيضاً فرع للفتح وقيل لقلَة استعمالهنَ ويُفتح ما وراءهنَ لكثرة حروفهنَ. وأمَا يُهَرِيقُ فأصله يُرِيقُ وهو من الرباعيَ فزيدت الهاء على خلاف القياس. وتُكسر حروف المضارعة في بعض اللغات إذا كان ماضيه مكسور العين أو مكسور الهمزة حتَى تدلَ على كسرة الماضي نحو يعْلَمُ وتعْلَمُ وإعْلَمُ ونعْلَمُ ويسْتَنْصِرُ وتسْتَنْصِرُ واسْتَنْصِرُ ونسْتَنْصِرُ. وفي بعض اللغات لا يُكسر الياء لثقل الكسرة على الياء، وعُيِّنَت حروف المضارعة للدلالة على كسرة العين في الماضي لأنَها زائدة وقيل لأنَه يُلزم بكسر الفاء توالي الحركات وبكسر* (١١ آ) العين يلزم الإلتباس بين يَفْعَلُ ويَفْعِلُ وبكسر اللام يُلزم إبطال الإعراب. وتُحذف التاء الثانية في مثل تَتَقَلَدُ وتَتَبَاعَدُ وتَتَبَخْتَرُ لاجتماع الحرفين من جنس واحد وعدم إمكان الإدغام، وعُيِّنَت التاء الثانية للحذف لأنَ الأولى علامة والعلامة لا تُحذف. وأُسكنت الفاء في يَضْرِبُ فراراً عن توالي الحركات وعُيِّنَت الفاء للسكون لأنَ توالي الحركات لزم من الياء فإسكان الحرف الذي هو قريب منه يكون أولى، ومن ثمَ عُيِّنَت الباء في ضَرَبْنَ للإسكان لأنَه قريب من النون الذي لزم منه توالي الحركات. وسوِي بين المخاطب والغائبة في المستقبل لاستوائهما في الماضي نحو نَصَرْتَ وَنَصَرَتْ ولكن لا يُسكن في غائبة المستقبل لضرورة الإبتداء بالساكن ولا يُضم

Fols. 10b-11a

٢ وأفعل... وفاعل: وفاعل وأفعل وفعَل ل/ ٣ الثلاثي: + فاعطي الفرع للفرع والأصل للأصل ه/ للفتح: الفتح ل/ ٤ لكثرة: لكثرت ز/ ٥ وتكسر: ويكسر د/ اللغات: اللغة ا ل/ ٦ تدلَ: يدل د/ نحو: مثاله ل/ ٧ اللغات: اللغة ا ل/ يكسر: تكسر ب ج ه ز ح ط ك ل/ ٨ للدلالة: لدلالة ب: للدالالة ح/ زائدة: + والزائد اولى بالتغيير ه: والزايد بالتغيير اولى ط: والزيادة في التغيير اولى ك/ ٩ الإلتباس: الالباس د/ ١١ التاء: − ج د ح ط ك/ للحذف: − ج د ح ط ك/ الأولى: الاول د ه ز/ ١٢ الفاء: الضاد ل/ يضرب: مثل يضرب د/ عن: من ل/ ١٣ الفاء: الضاد ج ز ك ل/ من: + زيادة ك/ الحرف: حرف ل/ الحرف... قريب: الفاء التي يكون قريبا د/ ١٤ يكون: −د/ ١٥ الحركات: اربع حركات ب د ه ز: اربعة حركات ج: اربع الحركات ط/ المستقبل: + مثل تضرب ج ل/ ١٦ نصرت ونصرت: ضربت وضربت ل/

weak consonants left over [to be chosen], and because it is close to the weak consonants which are issued from the inside of the nose. These prefixes were vowelled by a fatḥa for the sake of lightness, except in the measures whose structure is formed of four consonants [in which the prefixes are vowelled by a ḍamma], which are: [Form I of the quadriliteral] فَعْلَلَ, [Form IV of the groundform of the triliteral] أَفْعَلَ, [Form II of the groundform of the triliteral] فَعَّلَ and [Form III of the groundform of the triliteral] فَاعَلَ, because these four are constituted of four consonants, and they are derived from measures constituted of three consonants, just as the ḍamma is also derived from the fatḥa. It is said [that they are vowelled by a ḍamma] on account of the rarity of their use, and they are vowelled by a fatḥa [in the measures] beyond them [i.e. those formed of five and six consonants], because of their large number of consonants. As for يُهَرِيقُ "he spills", its base form is يُرِيقُ, which is formed of four consonants in which the *h* is infixed [before the 1st radical] in opposition to the analogy.(98) The imperfect prefixes are vowelled by a kasra in some dialects, if the 2nd radical or the [prefixed] hamza of its perfect is vowelled by a kasra, so that the kasra is indicative of the kasra [of the 2nd radical or of the hamza] of the perfect, e.g. يِعْلَمُ "he knows", تِعْلَمُ "/2 masc. sing." and "/3 fem. sing.", اِعْلَمُ "/1 sing.", نِعْلَمُ "/1 pl.", يِسْتَنْصِرُ "he asks for assistance", تِسْتَنْصِرُ "/2masc. sing." and "3 fem. sing.", اِسْتَنْصِرُ "/1 sing." and نِسْتَنْصِرُ "1 pl.".(99) In some dialects, the *y* is not given a kasra because of the heaviness of the kasra vowelling the *y*.(100) The imperfect prefixes are chosen to give indication of the kasra of the 2nd radical of the perfect, because they are prefixed.
It is said that vowelling the 1st radical with the kasra would necessarily imply the [disliked] succession of the [four] vowels, vowelling the 2nd radical with the kasra **[Fol. 11 a]** would necessarily imply mixing up [the forms] يَفْعَلُ and يَفْعِلُ, and vowelling the 3rd radical with the kasra would necessarily cancel the declension. The 2nd *t* was elided in تَتَقَلَّدُ "you assume / masc. sing." and "/3 fem. sing.", تَتَبَاعَدُ "you leave /masc. sing." and "3 fem. sing." and تَتَبَخْتَرُ "you perfume yourself /masc. sing." and "3 fem. sing.", on account of the combination of two consonants of the same kind and the impossibility of assimilating one to the other. The 2nd *t* was chosen to be elided because the 1st one is a marker, and the marker is not to be elided.(101)
The 1st radical was made vowelless in يَضْرِبُ "he hits" to avoid the [disliked] succession of the [four] vowels. The 1st radical was chosen to be vowelless because the succession of the vowels was caused by the [imperfect prefix] *y*, so it became prior to give a sukūn to the consonant that is next to it. Hence the *b* in ضَرَبْنَ "they hit /fem. pl." was chosen to be vowelless because it was next to the *n* which caused the succession of the vowels. The 2nd person of the masc. and the 3rd person of the fem. sing. were made homonymous in the imperfect tense [e.g. تَضْرِبُ "you or she hits] because of their homonymy in [the representation in] the perfect, e.g. نَصَرْتَ, نَصَرَتْ "you or she saved /masc. sing.". However, it [sc. the *t*] was not made vowelless in the 3rd person of the fem. of the imperfect because it was the initial consonant.(102)
It was not vowelled by a ḍamma

* ١١ ب حتَى لا يلتبس بالمجهول في نحو تُمْدَحُ ولا يُكسر حتَى لا يُلتبس* بلغة تِعْلَمُ. فإن قيل يُلزم الإلتباس أيضاً بالفتحة، قلنا في الفتحة موافقة بينها وبين اخواتها مع خفَة الفتحة. وأُدخل في آخر المستقبل نون علامة للرفع لأنَ آخر الفعل صار باتَصال ضمير الفاعل بمنزلة وسط الكلمة إلاَ نون يَضْرِبْنَ وهي علامة التأنيث كما في فَعَلْنَ ومن ثمَ يُقال يَضْرِبْنَ بالياء حتَى لا يجتمع علامتا التأنيث، والياء في تَضْرِبينَ ضمير الفاعل كما مرَ. وإذا أُدخل لم على المستقبل ينقل معناه الى الماضي لأنَه مشابه بكلمة الشرط في النقل والله أعلم.

Fols. 11a-11b

١ نحو: – ا د/ يكسر: تكسر جـ ز/ ٢ الالتباس: الالباس د/ بالفتحة: في الفتحة ب/ قلنا: + اذ ل/ أخواتها: أخواته جـ/ ٣ الفتحة: الفتح جـ/ ٤ وهي: وهو هـ/ في: + الماضي نحو ك/ ٥ يضربن: – ا د/ علامتا: علامت حـ/ التأنيث: تأنيث ط/ تضربين: يضربين حـ/ ٦ وإذا: + قيل ا/ لم... المستقبل: على المستقبل لم هـ/ ينقل: ينتقل ا د/ مشابه: + في العمل ب: مشابهة في العمل هـ/ بكلمة: لكلمة ل/ ٦–٧ في النقل: – جـ د هـ/ ٧ والله أعلم: – ب جـ د هـ ز حـ ط ك ل/

so that it would not be mixed up with the passive voice, as e.g. تُمْدَحُ "you are praised /masc. sing." and "3 fem. sing.", and it was not vowelled by a kasra so that it would not be confused **[Fol. 11 b]** with the dialectal تِعْلَمُ "you know /masc. sing.".(103) If it is said that the fatḥa also implied confusion, we answer that there was a similarity between it [sc. the fatḥa of the *t]* and its cognates(104) together with the fact that the fatḥa is light.

The *n* was suffixed to the imperfect [in the 2nd person of the fem. sing. تَضْرِبِينَ] as a marker of the indicative, because the pronoun of the subject [sc. the *ī]* that is attached to the final radical of the verb holds the position of the middle of the word. It is different from the *n* of يَضْرِبْنَ "they hit /fem. pl." which is the marker of the fem. as in فَعَلْنَ "they did /fem. pl.". Hence it is said [يَضْرِبْنَ] with the [imperfect prefix] *y* [and not the *t]* so that two markers of the fem. [sc. the *t* and the *n]* will not be combined together. The *ī* in تَضْرِبِينَ "you hit /fem. sing." is the pronoun of the subject as was mentioned above.

If لَمْ "not/ (jussive particle)" is prefixed to the imperfect, it will transfer its meaning into the past, because it is similar to the conditional word [إِنْ "if"] in [the particularity] of transferring, —and God knows best—.

§ 3. فصل في الأمر والنهي

الأمر صيغة يُطلب بها الفعل عن الفاعل نحو لِيَضْرِبْ الى آخره واِضْرِبْ الى آخره وهو مشتقٌ من المضارع لمناسبة بينهما في الإستقباليَة. زيدت اللام في الغائب لأنَها من وسط المخارج والغايب في وسط كلام المتكلّم والمخاطب وأيضاً من حروف الزوائد وهي التي يشتملها قول الشاعر:

* ١٢ آ
هَوِيتُ السَمانَ فَشَيَّبْنَنِي   وقد كُنْتُ قِدْماً هَوِيتُ* السَمانَ.

أي حروف هَوِيتُ السَمانَ، ولم يُزد من حروف العلَة حتَى لا يجتمع حرفا علَة، وكُسرت اللام لأنَها مشابهة باللام الجارة لأنَ الجزم في الأفعال بمنزلة الجرّ في الأسماء، وأُسكنت اللام بالواو والفاء نحو وَلْيَضْرِبْ فَلْيَضْرِبْ كما أُسكنت الخاء في فَخْذٍ ونظيره بالواو وَهْوَ بسكون الهاء وفي الفاء فَهْوَ وحُذف حرف الإستقبال في المخاطب للفرق بينه وبين مخاطب المضارع، وعُيّن الحذف في المخاطب لكثرة استعماله، ومن ثمَ لا تُحذف مع اللام في مجهوله نحو لِتُضْرَبْ لقلّة استعماله. واجتلبت همزة الوصل بعد حذف حرف المضارعة إذا كان ما بعده ساكناً للإفتتاح، وكُسرت الهمزة لأنَ الكسرة أصل في تحريك همزات

Fols. 11b-12a

٢ عن: من ل/ ليضرب: + ليضربا ليضربوا ط/ واضرب... آخره: – ا د/ ٣ الإستقباليّة: المستقبل ط/ زيدت: وزيدت ل/ في : + امر ل/ ٤ والغايب ... والمخاطب: ا's margin: – د ل/ ٥ وهي: وحروف الزوايد هي د/ يشتملها: يشملها ل/ ٦ وقد: فقد ل/ ٧ أي: او ل/ علّة: العلة ا/ وكسرت: وكسرة ا/ ٨ باللام: بلام ا د ل/ الجارة: + في الصورة نحو لزيد ب: + نحو لزيد ه/ بمنزلة الجرَ: كالجر ه/ ٩ اللام: – ا د/ وليضرب فليضرب: فلتضرب ط/ اسكنت: اسكن ا د/ فخذ: + وكبد ط/ ونظيره: ونضيره ط/ بالواو: في الواو ل/ ١٠ وفي... فهو: – د ل/ وحذف : وحذفت ا د/ للفرق: + ولم يزد من حروف العلة حتى لا يجتمع حرف علة ب/ ١٠–١١ بينه... المضارع: – ا د/ ١١ وعيّن: وعينت ا/ لكثرة استعماله: لكثرته ا: للكثرة د: للكشرة ح/ ١٢ مجهوله: مجهول ل/ نحو: اعني يقال ب ج د ح ط/ همزة الوصل: الهمزة ا د/ ١٢ للإفتتاح: + بالإبتداء ب/ وكسرت: وكثره ب ح: وكسرة ز/ تحريك: – ا د/ همزات الوصل: الساكن ح/

§ 3. The imperative[105] and the prohibition

The imperative is a mood through which the action is ordered from the subject, e.g. لِيَضْرِبْ "let him hit" etc. and اِضْرِبْ "hit! /2 masc. sing." etc. It is derived from the imperfect because of a similarity between them both in indicating future time.

The *li*– [of command] was prefixed to the 3rd person of the sing., because it originates from one of the middle points of articulation, and the 3rd person stands in the middle of the conversation between the 1st and the 2nd person. It is also one of the additional consonants which are included in the poet's saying:

"هَوِيتُ السِمانَ فَشَيَّبْنَنِي   وقد كُنْتُ قِدْماً هَوِيتُ السِمانَ".

"I loved the plump women, and they turned me hoary, when I had of old loved **[Fol. 12 a]** the plump women".[106]

– meaning the consonants of هَوِيتُ السمان -.

None of the weak consonants were prefixed to it to avoid the combination of two weak consonants. The *l* [of the imperative] was vowelled by a kasra because it resembles the preposition,[107] as the jussive mood in the verbs corresponds to the genitive case in the nouns.[108] The *li*– was made vowelless by [the conjunctions] the *wa*– and the *fa*-, e.g. وَلْيَضْرِبْ "and let him hit!" and فَلْيَضْرِبْ "then let him hit", just as the *ḫ* was made vowelless in فَخْذٌ "thigh".[109] Its counterpart with the *wa*– is وَهْوَ "and he" with the vowellessness of the *h* and with the *fa*– فَهْوَ "and so he".[110]

The imperfect prefix was elided in the 2nd persons of the masc. and fem. sing. and pl. [in the imperative] to differentiate them from the 2nd persons of the masc. and fem. sing. and pl. of the imperfect. The elision was chosen for the 2nd persons because of the frequency of their use. Hence, it is not elided with the *li*– in its passive voice, e.g. لِتُضْرَبْ "may you be hit!" because it is so rarely used.

The connective hamza was prefixed after the elision of the imperfect prefix that is followed by a vowelless consonant, to begin the word. It was vowelled by a kasra because the kasra is principal in vowelling the connective hamza.[111]

الـوصـل. ولم يُكسـر في مثـل أُكْتُـبْ لأنَ بتقـديـر الكسـرة يُلـزم الخـروج مـن الكسـرة الى الضمَة ولا اعتبار للكاف الساكن لأنَ الحرف الساكن لا يكون حاجزاً حصيناً عندهم، ومن
ثمَ يُجعل واو قِنْوَة ياءً* فيُقال قِنْيَةٌ وقيل يُضمَ للإتّباع. وفُتح ألف أيْمُنٍ مع كونه * ١٢ ب
للوصل لأنَه جمع يَمين وألفه للقطع ثمَ جُعل للوصل لكثرته. وفُتح ألف التعريف لكثرته أيضاً. وفُتح ألف أكْرِمْ لأنَه ليس من ألف الأمر بل ألف قطع محذوف من تُؤَكْرِمُ حُذفت الهمزة لاجتماع الهمزتين في أأكْرِمُ، ولا تُحذف ألف الوصل في الخطَ حتَى لا يلتبس الأمر من باب عَلِمَ بأمر عَلَمَ. فإن قيل يُعلم بالإعجام قلنا الإعجام يُترك كثيراً ومن‌ثمَ فرَقوا بين عُمَر وعَمْرو بالواو، وحُذفت في بِسْمِ الله لكثرة استعماله ولا تُحذف في اقْرَأ باسم رَبِّكَ لقلَة استعماله. ويُجزم آخره في الغائب باللام إجماعاً لأنَ اللام مشابهة بكلمة الشرط في النقل. وكذلك المخاطب مجزوم عند الكوفيين لأنَ أصل اضْرِبْ لِتَضْرِبْ عندهم، ومن ثمَ قرأ النبيُ عليه السلام (فبذلك فَلْتَفْرَحُوا)، فحُذفت اللام لكثرة الاستعمال ثمَ حُذفت علامة الإستقبال للفرق بينه وبين مضارع المخاطب فبقي الضاد
ساكناً* فاجتلبت همزة الوصل ووُضعت موضع علامة الإستقبال فأُعطي له أثر علامة * ١٣ آ
الإستقبال كما أُعطي لفاء رُبَ عمل رُبَ في مثل قول الشاعر:

Fols. 12a-13a

١ يكسر: + ويضمَ ب: تكسر د ل/ لأنَ: لأنَه ل/ ٢ لأنَ... الساكن: – ب/ الحرف: حرف ج ط: – ح/ ٣ يجعل: جعل ب ط/ فيقال: ويقال د ل/ يضم: تضمَ د ل/ ٤ لكثرته: لكثرة الإستعمال ج/ ٥ ألف قطع: الألف القطع ب/ ٦ تؤكرم: تواكرم د: ياءكرم ه/ حذفت الهمزة: –ا د/ أأكرم: ءاكرم ا ح: اءكرم ج د ل/ تحذف: يحذف ب د ح/ ٧ باب: – ز ح ل/ يترك: تترك ا ل/ ٨ وحذفت: وحذف ب د/ استعماله: الاستعمال د ح: + لأن أصله باسم الله ه/ تحذف: يحذف د/ ٩ باسم: بسم ل/ ويجزم: وينجزم ب د ز ح ط ل/ آخره: آخر الأمر ب: أمر الآخر ج: الأمر د/ في الغائب: l's margin ا: – د/ الغائب: + اذا كان ا/ ١٠ بكلمة: لكلمة ل/ النقل: + لأن حروف الشرط ينقل الماضي الى المستقبل واللام ينقل الاستقبال الى الأمر ط/ مجزوم: – د ل/ ١١ عليه السلام: صلىَ الله عليه وسلَم ل/ فحذفت: فحذف د/ ١٢ الإستعمال: استعماله ه ز ط ل/ حذفت: حذف ب د ز/ مضارع المخاطب: المضارع ا د/ ١٣ فاجتلبت: واجتلبت ج د ح ل/ فاعطي: واعطي ب ج د ه ز ط/ علامة: علامت ط/ ١٤ مثل: – د/

It was not vowelled by a kasra in اُكْتُبْ "write!", because if the kasra was chosen, it would be necessary to deviate from the kasra to the ḍamma [of the 2nd radical]. The vowelless *k* is not taken into account because the vowelless consonant is not considered as an impassable separative by them.(112) – On account of that, the *w* of قِنْوَة "sheep or goats taken for oneself / not for sale, acquisition" was changed into a *y,* **[Fol. 12 b]** and it was said قِنْيَة -,(113) and it is stated that it [sc. the connective hamza] was vowelled by a ḍamma for the purpose of analogy.

The alif of أَيْمُن "oaths" was vowelled by a fatḥa in spite of the fact that it is connective, because it is the pl. of يَمِين in which the alif is the disjunctive alif that is then made connective because of the frequency of its use.(114)

The alif of the definite article *[ʾal-]* was also vowelled by a fatḥa because of the frequency of its use as well.(115)

The alif of [Form IV] أَكْرِمْ "honour!" was vowelled by a fatḥa because it is not the [prefix] hamza of the imperative, but a disjunctive alif from تُؤَكْرِمُ "you honour /masc. sing.", which was elided on account of the combination of the two hamzas in أُأَكْرِمُ "I honour".(116)

The connective hamza was not elided in the writing, so that the imperative of the groundform عَلِمَ "he knew" [sc. اِعْلَمْ] will not be mixed up with the imperative of [Form II] عَلَّمَ "he taught" [sc. عَلِّمْ]. If it was said that it could be recognized by the dots, we would answer that the dots are often omitted. Thereupon, they differentiated between عُمَرُ "ᶜOmar" and عَمْرٌو "ᶜAmr" by adding the *w.*(117)

It was elided in بِسْمِ الله "in the name of God" because of the frequency of its use. It was not elided in إِقْرَأْ بِاسْمِ رَبِّكَ "recite in the name of your God" because it was so rarely used.(118)

The 3rd person of the masc. sing. of the imperative is put in the jussive mood by means of the *li–* according to a common consensus, because the *li–* is similar to the conditional word [sc. إِنْ "if"] in the [particularity of] transferring.

In the same manner, the 2nd persons [of the masc. and fem. sing. and pl.] are put in the jussive mood according to the Kufans, because they consider the origin of اِضْرِبْ "hit!" to be لِتَضْرِبْ "may you hit".(119) Hence the prophet, may God grant him salvation, recited [sur. 10: 59] (فَبِذَلِكَ فَلْتَفْرَحُوا) "– In that, may you rejoice".(120) The *li–* [in لِتَضْرِبْ] was elided because of the frequency of its use. Then the imperfect prefix was elided to differentiate it [sc. the imperative] from the 2nd persons of the imperfect. The *ḍ* remained vowelless, **[Fol. 13 a]** and the connective hamza was chosen and prefixed instead of the imperfect prefix, and the influence of the marker of the future was given to it, just as the action of رُبَّ was given to the [conjunction] *fa–* before رُبَّ "many", as in the poet's saying:

"فَمَثْلِكِ حُبْلَى قد طَرَقْتُ ومُرْضِعٍ فَأَلْهَيْتُها عن ذي تَمائِمَ مُحْوِلِ".

وعند البصريّين فهو مبني لأنّ الأصل في الأفعال البناء وإنّما أُعرب المضارع لمشابهة بينه وبين الإسم ولم تبق المشابهة بينه وبين الأمر بحذف حرف المضارعة ومن ثمّ قيل فَلْتَفْرَحُوا معرب بالإجماع لوجود علّة الإعراب وهي حرف المضارعة. وزيدت في آخر الأمر نونا التأكيد لتأكيد معنى الطلب نحو لِيَضْرِبَنَّ لِيَضْرِبانِّ لِيَضْرِبُنَّ لِتَضْرِبَنَّ لِتَضْرِبانِّ لِيَضْرِبْنانِّ وكذا اضْرِبَنَّ الى آخره، وفُتح الباء في لِيَضْرِبَنَّ فراراً عن اجتماع الساكنين وفُتح النون للخفّة وحُذف واو لِيَضْرِبُوا اكتفاءً بالضمّة وياء اضْرِبي اكتفاءً بالكسرة ولم يُحذف ألف التثنية اكتفاءً بالفتحة حتّى لا يلتبس بالواحد، وكُسرت النون الثقيلة بعد
ألف التثنية تشبّها بنون* التثنية، وحُذفت النون التي تدلّ على الرفع في مثل هل * ١٣ ب
يَضْرِبانِّ لأنّ ما قبل النون الثقيلة يصير مبنياً وأُدخل الألف الفاصلة في مثل لِيَضْرِبْنانِّ فراراً من اجتماع النونات. وحكم الخفيفة مثل حكم الثقيلة إلاّ أنّها لا تدخل بعد الألفين لاجتماع الساكنين في غير حدّه وعند يونس تدخل قياساً على الثقيلة. وكلاهما يدخلان على الفعل في سبع مواضع لوجود معنى الطلب فيها الأمر كما مرّ والنهي نحو لا تَضْرِبَنَّ والاستفهام نحو هل تَضْرِبَنَّ والتمنّي نحو لَيْتَكَ تَضْرِبَنَّ والعرض نحو ألا تَضْرِبَنَّ والقسم

Fols. 13a-13b

٢ فهو: — د ل/ ٣ الإسم... وبين: — ح/ تبق: يبق ا د/ بينه... الأمر: بين الأمر والإسم ه ز ط/ الأمر: الاسم ب: + والاسم ح/ حرف: — د/ المضارعة: + بني على السكون ج/ قيل: + قوله تعالى ب ه: + قوله د ز: + في قوله تعالى ط/ ٤ وزيدت: وزيد ا ب د ه ز ح/ ٥ نونا التأكيد: نونان د/ معنى: — ا د/ نحو: في د/ ليضربانّ... لتضربنّ: — ا/ ٦ ليضربنان: لتضربنان ل/ ليضربنان... آخره: — ا/ وكذا: + في د/ اضربنّ: + اضربان ه/ عن: من ل/ ٧ بالضمّة: بالظمة ط/ ٨ اكتفاء بالفتحة: — ا د/ وكسرت: وكسر د ل/ النون: نون د/ ٩ تشبّها: مشابهة ب د ز ح ل: تشبيها ج ه/ وحذفت: وحذف ا د/ التي: + هي ب ج ه ز ك ل/ ١٠ مثل: —ا د/ ١١ الخفيفة: الحقيقة ط/ مثل حكم: كحكم ك ل/ تدخل: يدخل ا/ بعد: بين ل/ ١٢ في: على ل/ وكلاهما يدخلان: وكلتاهما تدخلان ل/ ١٢ على الفعل: — ب ج د ه ز ط ك ل/ سبع: سبعة ا د/ نحو: — ا/ ١٤ نحو... تضربنّ: — ب/

"فَمِثْلِكِ حُبْلَى قد طَرَقْتُ ومُرْضِعٍ   فألْهَيْتُها عن ذي تمائم مُحْوِلِ"

"And many a pregnant woman suckling her baby such as you I have come to by night and I diverted her from her squint-eyed child with an amulet".(121)

According to the Basrans, it [sc. the imperfect] is undeclinable(122) because verbs are by principle undeclinable.(123) But somehow, the imperfect was made declinable because of a similarity between it and the noun. Such a resemblance did not remain between it [sc. the noun] and the imperative after the elision of the imperfect prefix.(124) Thereupon, it was said that فَلْتَفْرحوا is declinable according to a common consensus because of the existence of the cause of the declension, which is the imperfect prefix.

Both the energetic nūns are suffixed to the verb of command to intensify the order, e.g. لِيَضْرِبَنّ "may he hit!", لِيَضْرِبانّ "/3 masc. dual", لِيَضْرِبُنّ "/3 masc. pl.", لِتَضْرِبَنّ "/3 fem. sing.", لِتَضْرِبانّ "/3 fem. dual", لِيَضْرِبْنانّ "/3 fem. pl." and similarly اضْرِبَنّ "hit! /2 masc. sing. (imperative En. I.)" etc.(125)

The *b* is vowelled by a fatḥa in لِيَضْرِبَنّ to avoid the cluster of two vowelless consonants and the *n* is vowelled by a fatḥa for the sake of alleviation.

The *ū* of لِيَضْرِبوا "let them hit!" [resulting in لِيَضْرِبُنّ] is elided with the sufficiency of the ḍamma. The *ī* of اضْرِبي "hit /2nd person of the fem." [resulting in اضْرِبِنّ] is elided with the sufficiency of the kasra. The *ā* of the dual is not elided with the sufficiency of the fatḥa so that there would not be any confusion with the sing. The doubled *n* is vowelled by a kasra after the alif of the dual because of its resemblance to the *n* **[Fol. 13 b]** of the dual.(126) The *n* which marks the indicative is elided in هل يَضْرِبانّ because what precedes the doubled *n* becomes invariable.(127)

The separating *ā* is infixed in لِيَضْرِبْنانّ "let them hit! /fem. pl." to avoid the combination of the nūns.(128)

The predicament of the single *n* is the same as the predicament of the double *n*, except that it is not suffixed after both alifs [sc. the alif of the 2nd persons of the masc. and fem. dual of the imperative En. II resulting in اضْرِبانْ and the alif infixed in the 2nd fem. pl. of the imperative En. II resulting in اضْرِبْنانْ], to avoid the cluster of two vowelless consonants at the extremity.(129) But according to Yūnus [and to the Kufans], it is suffixed on the analogy of the doubled one.(130) Both of them [sc. the energetic nūns] are suffixed to the verb in seven cases because they contain the meaning of the order:

– The imperative, as was mentioned.
– The prohibition, e.g. لا تَضْرِبَنّ "do not hit!".
– The interrogation, e.g. هل تَضْرِبَنّ "will you hit?".
– The optative, e.g. ليتك تَضْرِبَنّ "I wish you would hit".
– The request, e.g. ألا تَضْرِبَنّ "are you not going to hit?".
– The oath,

نحو والله لأضْربَنَ والنفي قليلاً لمشابهته بالنهي نحو لا تَضْربَنَ والنهي مثل الأمر في جميع الوجوه إلاَ أنَه معرب بالإجماع. ويجيء المجهول من الأشياء المذكورة من الماضي نحو ضُربَ الى آخره ومن المستقبل نحو يُضْرَبُ الى آخره. والغرض من وضعه امَا لخساسة الفاعل أو لعظمته أو لشهرته او لجهالته أو للخوف منه أو عليه واختصَ بصيغة فُعلَ في الماضي لأنَ* معناه غير معقول وهو إسناد الفعل الى المفعول فجُعلت * ١٤ آ صيغته أيضاً غير معقولة وهي فُعلَ ومن ثمَ لا يجيء على هذه الصيغة كلمة في الأسماء إلاَ وُعلٌ ودُئلٌ. وفي المستقبل على يُفْعَلُ لأنَ هذه الصيغة غير معقولة أيضاً لأنَها مثل فُعْلَلٍ في الحركات والسكنات ولا يجيء عليه كلمة أيضاً. ويجيء في الزوائد من الثلاثيَ المجرَد بضمَ الأوَل وكسر ما قبل الآخر في الماضي نحو أُكْرمَ وبضمَ الأوَل وفتح ما قبل الآخر في المستقبل تبعاً للثلاثيَ إلاَ في سبعة أبواب ويُضمَ أوَل المتحرَك مع ضمَ الأوَل وكسر ما قبل الآخر وهي تُفُعَلَ وتُفُوعلَ وأُفْتُعلَ وأُنْفُعلَ وأُفْعُنْللَ وأُسْتُفْعلَ وأُفْعُوعلَ وضُمَ الفاء في الأولين حتَى لا يلتبسا بمضارعي فَعَلَ وفاعَلَ وضُمَ أوَل المتحرَك منه في الخمسة الباقية حتَى لا يلتبس بالأمر في الوقف يعني إذا قلتَ وٱفْتَعلْ بفتح التاء في المجهول في الوقف بوصل الهمزة وٱفْتَعلْ في الأمر يُلزم الإلتباس فضُمَ التاء لإزالته فقسَ الباقي عليه.

Fols. 13b-14a

١ لمشابهته: مشابهة ب جـ د هـ ز حـ ط ك ل: + في الصورة د/ ٢ بالإجماع: بالاجتماع ب د/ ٣ ضرب: + زيد ل: ضُربا ضُربوا ط/ يضرب: + زيد ل/ ٤ او(3)... عليه: — ا: او لخوف له ب: او لخوفه او لجهله د: او خوفا عليه او لجهالته جـ: او خوفا له او خوفا عليه حـ: او خوفا عليه او جهلا له هـ/ ٥ فجعلت: فجعل د ل/ ٦ معقولة: معقول ا د/ كلمة... الأسماء: في الأسماء كلمة د/ ٧ هذه: — ا/ غير... لأنَها: — ا د/ ٩ المجرَد: — د/ نحو أكرم: — ا د/ ١٠ ويضمَ... يضم: بضمَ أوَل متحرَك منه د/ ١٠–١١ وبضمَ... الآخر: ا's margin: فإنَ المجهول فيها يجيء بضم اوَل المتحرَك منه مع ضم الأوَل وكسر ما قبل الآخر ك: فإنَ أوَل المتحرَك يُضمَ مع ضمَ الأوَل ويكسر ما قبل الآخر ل/ أوَل: — ا: الأوَل ل/ ١١ وكسر: ويكسر ل/ وافعنلل: وافعلَ ا: وافْعُوَل د/ ١٢ يلتبسا: يلتبس ل/ ١٣ منه: — ا د/ ١٤ بفتح التاء: — ا: + في الماضي ك/ الإلتباس: اللبس د/ ١٥ الباقي عليه: عليه الباقي د/

e.g. والله لا تَضْرِبَنَّ "by God, do not hit!".(131)

– The negation is rarely used because of its resemblance to the prohibition, e.g. لا تَضْرِبَنَّ "do not hit!", and the prohibition is similar to the imperative in all respects, except that it is declinable according to a common consensus.

The passive voice of the patterns mentioned occurs in the perfect, e.g. ضُرِبَ "he was hit" etc., and in the imperfect, e.g. يُضْرَبُ "he is being hit" etc. The purpose of using it is either to express the baseness of the subject, its sublimity, celebrity, anonymity, the dread from it or the fearing for it.(132)

It is specified with the pattern فُعِلَ in the perfect because **[Fol. 14 a]** its meaning, which is the reference of the verb to the object is not rational. This is why its pattern which is فُعِلَ, was also made irrational. Hence no noun occurs according to this pattern except وُعِلٌ "a mountain goat" and دُئِلٌ "a jackal".(133)

It occurs in the imperfect according to يُفْعَلُ because this pattern is as well irrational as it is similar to فُعْلَلٌ in the vowels and in the sukūn, and there is no noun that occurs according to this pattern.

It occurs in the derived patterns of the triliteral verbs in the perfect by vowelling the 1st consonant by a ḍamma and the consonant before the last one by a kasra, e.g [Form IV] أُكْرِمَ "to be honoured", and in the imperfect, by giving the 1st mobile consonant a ḍamma and the consonant preceding the last one a fatḥa in conformability with the triliteral, except in seven forms in which the 1st prefixed consonant and the vowelled consonant are given a ḍamma and the consonant preceding the last one is given a kasra, namely:

1– [Form V] تُفُعِّلَ.

2– [Form VI] تُفُوعِلَ.

3– [Form VIII] اُفْتُعِلَ.

4– [Form VII] اُنْفُعِلَ.

5– [Form XIV of the triliteral or Form III of the quadriliteral] اُفْعُنْلِلَ.

6– [Form X] اُسْتُفْعِلَ.

7– [Form XII] اُفْعُوعِلَ.(134)

The 1st radical was vowelled by a ḍamma in the first two forms so that they would not be mixed up with the imperfect of [Form II] فَعَّلَ [sc. تُفَعِّلُ] and of [Form III] فَاعَلَ [sc. تُفَوْعِلُ in the pause] respectively. The 1st mobile consonant was vowelled by a ḍamma in the five remaining forms, so that there would be not be any confusion with the imperative in the pause, i.e. if you say [concerning Form VIII] وَآفْتَعِلْ by vowelling the *t* with a fatḥa instead in the passive voice in the pause by connecting the hamza and وَآفْتَعِلْ in the imperative, they were necessarily mixed up, so the *t* was vowelled by a ḍamma to avoid the confusion, and the remaining [forms] were made commensurable to it.(135)

§ 4. فصل في اسم الفاعل

* ١٤ ب وهو اسم مشتقّ* من المضارع لمن قام به الفعل بمعنى الحدوث واشتقّ منه لمناسبتهما في الوقوع صفة للنكرة وغيره. وصيغته من الثلاثيّ على وزن فاعِلٍ وحُذفت علامة الإستقبال من يَضْرِبُ فأُدخل الألف لخفّته بين الفاء والعين لأنّ في الأوّل يصير مشابهاً بالمتكلّم وكُسر عينه لأنّ بتقدير النصب يصير مشابهاً بماضي المفاعلة وبتقدير الضمّ يلزم الثقل وبتقدير الكسر أيضاً يلزم الإلتباس بأمر باب المُفاعَلَة ولكن أُبقي مع ذلك للضرورة وقيل اختيار الإلتباس بالأمر أولى لأنّ الأمر مشتقّ من المستقبل والفاعل مشابه به. وتجيء الصفة المشبَّهة على هذه الأبنية نحو فَرِقٍ وشَكْسٍ وصُلْبٍ ومِلْحٍ وجُنُبٍ وحَسَنٍ وخَشِنٍ وشُجَاعٍ وجَبَانٍ وعَطْشَانٍ وأحْوَلَ وهو مختصّ بباب فَعِلَ ألاّ ستّة أبواب تجيء من باب فَعُلَ نحو أحْمَقَ وأخْرَقَ وآدَمَ وأرْعَنَ وأسْمَرَ وأعْجَفَ. وزاد الأصمعي الأعْجَمَ*

* ١٥ آ وقال الفرّاء الأحْمَقُ من حَمِقَ وهو لغة في حَمُقَ وكذلك يجيء خَرِقَ وسَمِرَ وعَجِفَ أعني فَعِلَ لغة فيهنّ. ويجيء أفْعَلُ لتفضيل الفاعل من الثلاثيّ غير مزيد فيه ممّا ليس بلون ولا عيب ولا يجيء من المزيد فيه لعدم إمكان محافظة جميع حروفها في أفْعَلَ ولا يجيء من لون ولا عيب لأنّ فيهما يجيء أفْعَلُ للصفة فيلزم الإلتباس ولا يجيء أفْعَلُ

Fols. 14a-15a

٢ بمعنى: على معنى د/ ٣ وحذفت: وحذف ا/ علامة: علامت جـ/ ٤ فادخل: وادخل ب ز ك ل/ الألف: + فرقا بينه وبين الماضي ط/ لخفَته: لخفَتها ل/ لأنَ: لأنه ل/ ٥ بالمتكلَم: للمتكلَم ل: + وفي الآخر يصير مشابها بتثنية الماضي حـ/ وكسر: وكسرت ل/ لأنَ: لأنه ل/ النصب: الفتح ل/ بماضي: لماضي ل/ ٦ يلزم الثقل: يثقل د هـ ز ط ل/ ٧ مشتقَ: مأخوذ ك/ ٧–٨ والفاعل... به: مشتق من المستقبل هـ/ ٨ وتجيء: ويجيء ا د/ الصفة: صفة ا/ المشبَهة: المشابهة ل/ وملح: وصلح ل/ ٩ وشجاع وجبان: وجبان وشجاع ب جـ د هـ ز ل/ أبواب: — ا د/ ١٠ تجيء: يجيء ا د/ باب: — د ك ل/ وأسمر وأعجف: وأعجف وأسمر جـ د هـ ك ل/ ١١ وقال: قال د/ الأحمق: أحمق ا د/ حَمِقَ: + بكسر العين ك/ حَمُقَ: + بضم العين ك/ ١٢ فَعِلَ: + بكسر العين د ط ك/ الثلاثيَ: ثلاثي د/ ١٤ يجيء : — ا د/ أفعل[1]: + نحو أحمر جـ/ أفعل[2]: — ا/

§ 4. The active participle[136]

It is a noun which is derived **[Fol. 14 b]** from the imperfect denoting the subject, whereby the accident caused by its verb exists. It is derived from it [sc. the imperfect] because of the similarity that exists between them both in occurring as the epithet of the indefinite noun and for other reasons [which have been mentioned].[137]

Its pattern [of the groundform of] the triliteral is according to فاعِلٌ with the imperfect prefix elided from يَضْرِبُ "he hits" and the *ā* infixed because of its lightness between the 1st and the 2nd radical. The reason why it was not prefixed is that it would resemble the 1st person of the sing. [of the imperfect].

The 2nd radical was vowelled by a kasra because:

– If it was vowelled by the marker of the accusative [sc. the fatḥa] it would resemble the perfect of the pattern [of the *maṣdar* of Form III] مُفاعَلَةٌ [sc. فاعَلَ] .

– If it was vowelled by a ḍamma the heaviness would be unavoidable.

– If it was vowelled by a kasra it would be mixed up with the imperative of the pattern [of the *maṣdar* of Form III] مُفاعَلَةٌ [sc. فاعِلْ], but it was retained in spite of that, because it was necessary. It was said that the choice [of the pattern] which could cause a confusion with the imperative is prior, because the imperative is derived from the imperfect, and the active participle is similar to it [in its derivation].

The assimilated epithet occurs according to these patterns, e.g. فَرِقٌ "fearful", شَكِسٌ "perverse, stubborn", صُلْبٌ "hard, rigid", مَلِحٌ "witty", جُنُبٌ "polluted", حَسَنٌ "handsome", خَشِنٌ "rough", شُجاعٌ "courageous", جَبانٌ "coward", عَطْشانٌ "thirsty", أَحْوَلُ "squinting", which pertain to the conjugation فَعِلَ, with the exception of six which occur derived from the conjugation فَعُلَ, e.g. أَحْمَقُ "foolish", أَخْرَقُ "unskillful, clumsy", آدَمُ "brown", أَرْعَنُ "careless, silly", أَسْمَرُ "brown" and أَعْجَفُ "lean, meagre". Al-Aṣmaʿī added الأَعْجَمُ "non-Arab, dumb, speechless", **[Fol. 15 a]** and al-Farrāʾ said that أَحْمَقُ is from حَمِقَ which is a dialectal variant of حَمُقَ. In the same manner خَرِقَ "to be unskillful", سَمِرَ "to be brown" and عَجِفَ "to be lean" occur, which I mean are formed according to فَعِلَ as a dialectal variant.[138]

The أَفْعَلُ that expresses the superiority [or excess] of the active participle[139] is formed from the groundform of the triliteral, and not from its derived forms or from verbal adjectives that denote colors or deformities.

It is not formed from the derived patterns because of the impossibility of maintaining all of its consonants within the pattern أَفْعَلُ.

It is not formed from verbal adjectives that denote colors[140] or deformities because in them أَفْعَلُ denotes the epithet, and so the confusion would be unavoidable.

It is not formed

لتفضيل المفعول حتّى لا يلتبس بتفضيل الفاعل فإن قيل لم لا يُجعل على العكس حتّى لا يلزم الإلتباس قلنا جعله للفاعل أولى لأنّ الفاعل مقصود والمفعول فضلة في الكلام وأيضاً يُمكن التعميم في الفاعل دون المفعول ونحو أشْغَلَ من ذات النَحيَيْنِ لتفضيل المفعول وهو أعْطاهُمْ وأوْلاهُمْ من الزوائد وأحْمَقَ من هَبَنَقَة من العيوب شاذ. ويجيء
الفاعلُ على فَعيلٍ نحو نَصيرٍ ويستوي فيه المذكَر* والمؤنّث إذا كان بمعنى المفعول نحو * ١٥ ب
قَتيلٍ وجَريحٍ فرقاً بين الفاعل والمفعول إلاّ إذا جُعلت الكلمة من عداد الأسماء نحو ذَبيحَة ولَقيطَة وقد شُبّه به ما هو بمعنى الفَاعِلِ نحو قوله تعالى (إنَ رَحْمَةَ اللّه قَريبُ من المُحْسنين). ويجيء على فَعُولٍ للمبالغة نحو مَنُوعٍ ويستوي فيه المذكَر والمؤنّث إذا كان بمعنى فَاعِلٍ نحو امْرأةٍ صَبورٍ ورَجُلٍ صَبُورٍ ويُقال في فَعُولٍ بمعنى المفعول نحو نَاقَة حَلُوبَة وأُعطي الإستواء في فَعيلٍ للمفعول وفي فَعُولٍ للفاعل طلباً للعدل بينهما. ويجيء للمبالغة نحو صَبَّارٍ وسَيْفٍ مِجْذَمٍ وهو مُشترك بين الآلة والمبالغة للفاعل وفِسّيقٍ وكُبّارٍ وطُوّالٍ وعلاّمَة ونَسّابَة وراوِيَة وفَرُوقَة وضُحَكَة وضُحْكَة ومِجْذامَة ومِسْقَامٍ ومِعْطيرٍ ويستوي المذكَر والمؤنّث في التسعة الأخيرة لقلّتهن. وأمّا قولهم مِسْكينَةٌ فمحمول على فَقيرَة كما قالوا هيَ عَدُوَةُ اللّه وإن لم يدخل الهاء في فَعُولٍ الذي للفَاعِلِ حملاً له على صَديقَة
لأنّه نقيضه. وصيغته من غير الثلاثي المجرّد* على صيغة المستقبل بميم مضمومة وكسر ما * ١٦ آ

Fols. 15a-16a

٢ مقصود: + في الكلام ه ز ح ط/ ٤ أعْطاهُمْ وأوْلاهُمْ: اعطي هم واولى هم ط/ وأوْلاهُمْ:– ج/ المفعول: المفعل ل/ ٤–٥ ويجيء الفاعل: فصل اسم الفاعل يجيء ح/ ٥ على: + وزن ه/ المفعول: مفعول ك ل/ ٦ قتيل وجريح: رجل قتيل وامرأة قتيل ب/ ٧ يشبّه: شبّه ل/ الفاعل: فاعل ب ج ل/ رَحْمَةَ: رحمت ب ط ك/ ٨ المحسنين: + اي قارب ب ج ز/ على: – ا د/ ٩ ورجل صبور: – د/ ويقال... ناقة: ناقة ا/ فعول بمعنى: – د/ ١٠ واعطي: فاعطي ج د ه ل/ ١١ والمبالغة للفاعل: وبين مبالغة الفاعل ب د ك ل: وبين المبالغة اسم الفاعل ط/ ١٢ وعلاّمَة: وعلامت ج/ ونسّابة: ونشابة ه/ وفَرُوقة وضُحَكَة: وضحكة وفروقة ه/ وضُحْكَة: – ج ح ط: وضحك ل/ ومِجْذَامَة: ومجزامة ج ه/ ومِجْذَامَة... ومِعْطير: ومسقام ومجزام ومعطير ط/ ١٣ التسعة: السبعة ب/ وأمّا: اما د/ فمحمول: فمحمولة د ط: فهي محمولة ب/ ١٤ يدخل: تدخل ل/ الهاء: التاء ج ه/ حملا: + له ل/ ١٥ لأنّه نقيضه: – ب ه/ المجرّد: – ب ج د ه ز ح ط ل/

to denote the superiority of the مَفْعُول "passive participle", so that it will not be mixed up with the superiority of the فَاعِل "active participle". If it is asked why the situation was not reversed in order to avoid the confusion, we answer that granting [the superiority] to the subject is prior because it is it which is intended, and the object is of secondary importance in the sentence. It is also possible to universalize the subject and not the object. However, the examples أَشْغَلُ مِن ذاتِ النَحيَيْن "more preoccupied than the owner of the two butter jars"[141] denoting the superiority of the passive participle, هُو أَعْطاهُم وأَوْلاهُم "he is the one among them who gives more freely and bestows more liberally" [denoting the superiority] of the derived forms [sc. Form IV],[142] and أَحْمَق مِن هَبَنَّقَة "more stupid than Habannaqa"[143] denoting [the superiority of one of] the deformities, are anomalous. The active participle occurs according to the pattern فَعيل e.g. نَصير "helper". The masc. and the fem. become of common gender in it [Fol. 15 b] if it had the meaning of the passive participle, e.g. قَتيل "murdered" and جَريح "wounded" to differentiate [فَعيل with the meaning of] the active participle from [the one with the meaning of] the passive participle,[144] except if the word is counted among the nouns, e.g. ذَبيحَة "a female victim" and لَقيطَة "a female foundling".[145] It [sc. the pattern] with the meaning of the active participle was formed according to it [sc. فَعيل] in the words of the Allmighty [sur. 7: 54] (إنَّ رَحْمَةَ اللهِ قَريبٌ مِنَ المُحْسِنين) "Verily God's mercy is nigh unto them who do well".[146] It occurs according to فَعول to denote intensification, e.g. مَنوع "one who is offering great resistance".[147] The masc. and the fem. become of common gender if it has the meaning of the active participle, e.g. إمرأةٌ صَبورٌ "a patient woman" and رَجُلٌ صَبورٌ "a patient man",[148] but it is said concerning فَعول denoting the passive participle, e.g ناقَةٌ حَلوبَةٌ "a she-camel for milking". The common gender was given to فَعيل that has the meaning of the passive participle and to فَعول that has the meaning of the active participle, so that they are both treated equally. It also occurs to denote intensity, e.g. صَبّار "having an intense degree of patience", سَيْفٌ مِجْذَمٌ "a sword which cuts off quickly" which is common to the instrumental noun and to the pattern that denotes the intensification of the active participle,[149] فِسّيق "very sinful", كُبّار "very large", طُوَال "very tall", عَلّامَة "very learned", نَسّابَة "a great genealogist", راوية "one who hands down poems or historical facts by oral tradition", فَروقَة "very timid", ضُحَكَة "prone to laughter", ضُحْكَة "very ridiculous", مِجْذامَة "a man who quickly cuts the tie of affection", مِسْقام "often diseased" and مِعْطير "one who uses much perfume".[150] The masc. and the fem. were made common in the last nine patterns because they are so rarely used. As for their saying مِسْكينَة "poor /fem. sing.", it is sylleptic to فَقيرَة "poor".[151] [Fol. 16 a] Likewise they said هي عَدُوَّةُ الله "she is God's enemy", in spite of the fact that the h [sc. the t marbūṭa] is not to be suffixed to the pattern فَعول with the meaning of the active participle, on the analogy of صَديقَة "female friend", because it is its opposite in meaning.[152] Its pattern in the forms beyond the groundform of the triliteral is according to the pattern of the imperfect with the m vowelled by a ḍamma and the consonant before the last one vowelled by a kasra,[153]

قبل الآخر نحو مُكْرِمٍ فاختير الميم لتعذّر حرف العلّة وقرب الميم من الواو في كونها
شفويّة وضُمّ الميم للفرق بينه وبين الموضع ونحو مُسْهَبٍ للفاعل على صيغة المفعول من
أسْهَبَ ويَافعٍ من أيْفَعَ شاذ. وبُني ما قبل تاء التأنيث على الحركة في نحو ضَارِبَة لأنّه ٣
صار بمنزلة وسط الكلمة كما في نون التأكيد وياء النسبة وعلى الفتح للخفّة.

Fol. 16a

١ فاختير: واختير هـ/ حرف: حروف ب جـ د هـ/ في كونها: لكونهما هـ/ كونها: كونه ا/ ٢ شفويّة: بشفويّة ب: بشفويين ط/ على... المفعول: – ا/ ٣ وبني: ويبنى هـ ط/ الحركة: الفتحة جـ: الفتح ط/ ٤ الفتح: الفتحة ب ط/ للخفّة: للفتحة حـ/

e.g. مُكْرِمٌ "a man who treats you with respect". The *m* was chosen because of the impossibility of prefixing any of the weak consonants and because of the proximity of the *m* to the *w* in being formed by the lips. The *m* was vowelled by a ḍamma to differentiate it [sc. the active participle] from the noun of place [sc. the pattern مَفْعَلٌ].

As for مُسْهَبٌ "loquacious in his speech" from [Form IV] أَسْهَبَ "to prolong in the speech" as a pattern of the active participle that has the form of the passive participle, and يافِعٌ "a grown-up boy" from [Form IV] أَيْفَعَ "to grow up", they are anomalous.(154)

The consonant preceding the *t* that marks the fem. is given a marker of invariability which is a vowel, e.g. ضارِبَةٌ "hitting /fem. sing.", because it becomes holding the position of the middle of the word, as the case of [the consonant preceding] the energetic *n*(155) and the *y* of the relative noun or adjective.(156) Its vowel is the fatḥa because of its lightness.

§ 5. فصل في اسم المفعول

وهو اسم مشتقَ من يُفْعَلُ لمن وقع عليه الفعل. وصيغته من الثلاثيَ على وزن مَفْعُولٍ نحو مَضْرُوبٍ وهو مشتقَ من يُضْرَبُ لمناسبة بينهما. فأُدخل الميم مقام الزائد لتعذَر حرف العلَة فصار مُضْرَبٌ ثمَ فُتح الميم حتَى لا يلتبس بمفعول باب الإفعال فصار مَضْرَبٌ ثمَ ضُمَ الراء حتَى لا يلتبس بالموضع فصار مَضْرُبٌ ثمَ أُشبعت الضمَة* ١٦ب لانعدام مَفْعُلٍ في كلامهم بغير التاء فصار مَضْرُوب. وغيَر مفعول الثلاثيَ دون مفعول سائر الأفعال والموضع حتَى يصير مشابهاً في التغيير باسم الفاعل أعني غُيِّر الفاعل من يَفْعَلُ ويَفْعُلُ الى فَاعِلٍ والقياس فَاعَلٌ وفَاعُلٌ فغُيِّر المفعول أيضاً لمؤاخاة بينهما. وصيغته من غير الثلاثيَ على صيغة الفاعل بفتح ما قبل الآخر نحو مُسْتَخْرَجٍ.

Fols. 16a-16b

٣ مضروب: مضروف حـ/ فادخل: وادخل د حـ/ ٤ حرف: حروف ب جـ هـ/ ٤–٥ ثمَ... مضرب: s margin؟/ ٥ فصار مضرُب: s margin؟/ أُشبعت: اشبع ا/ لانعدام: لعدم ب/ ٦ التاء: + احتراز من مكرمة جـ د هـ: احتراز عن مكرم ط/ فصار: مافصار حـ/ ٨ فغيَر: وغيَر ب جـ د/ لمؤاخاة: لمؤاخات ا: للمواخاة ز: لمواخان حـ/ وصيغته: فصيغته ز/ ٩ صيغة: وزن هـ/ الفاعل: اسم الفاعل د ل/

§ 5. The passive participle(157)

It is a noun which is derived from [the passive voice] يُفْعَلُ denoting the one [or thing] on whom or on which the act falls upon.

Its pattern in [the groundform of] the triliteral is according to the pattern مَفْعولٌ, e.g. مَضْروبٌ "he is hit /masc. sing.". It is derived from يُضْرَبُ "he is hit" because of a similarity between them both. The *m* was prefixed instead of the prefixed consonant [of the imperfect] because of the impossibility of prefixing a weak consonant, so it became مُضْرَبٌ. Then the *m* was vowelled by a fatḥa so that it would not be mixed up with the passive participle of the pattern [of the *maṣdar* of Form IV] افعالٌ [sc. مُفْعَلٌ], so it became مَضْرَبٌ. Then the *r* was vowelled by a ḍamma so that it would not be mixed up with the noun of place so it became مَضْرُبٌ. Then the ḍamma was lengthened **[Fol. 16 b]** because the pattern مَفْعُلٌ does not exist in their [sc. the Arabs'] language without a *t* so it became مَضْروبٌ.

The modification [of the structure in relation to the root] concerns the pattern of the passive participle of the [groundform of the] triliteral, and not the patterns of the remaining verb forms or the noun of place, so that it would be similar in the modification to the active participle [of the triliteral]. I mean that the active participle of يَفْعِلُ and يَفْعُلُ was modified to become فاعِلٌ, in spite of the fact that the analogy would have required فاعَلٌ and فاعُلٌ, so the pattern of the passive participle was also modified because of a similarity between them both.

Its pattern in the forms beyond the groundform of the triliteral is according to the pattern of the active participle, but with the consonant preceding the last one vowelled by a fatḥa, e.g. مُسْتَخْرَجٌ "extracted from".(158)

§ 6. فصل في اسم الزمان والمكان

إسم المكان هو اسم مشتقّ من يَفْعَلُ لمكان وقع فيه الفعل فزيدت الميم كما في المفعول لمناسبة بينهما وكونهما محليَن لوقوع الفعل ولم يُزد الواو حتّى لا يُلتبس به وصيغته من باب يَفْعَلُ مَفْعَلٌ كالمَذْهَب إلاّ من المثال فإنّه بكسر العين فيه نحو المَوْعِد والمَوْجِل حتّى لا يُظن أنّ وزنه فَوْعَلٌ مثل جَوْرَبٍ لأنّه اسم ليس من اسم المكان والزمان ولا يُظنّ في الكسر لأنّ فَوْعِلاً لا يوجد في كلامهم. وصيغته من باب* يَفْعِلُ مَفْعِلٌ (* ١٧ آ) إلاّ من الناقص فإنّه بفتح العين فيه نحو الْمَرْمَى فراراً عن توالي الكسرات ولا يُبنى من يَفْعُلُ مَفْعُلٌ لثقل الضمّة فقُسم موضعه بين مَفْعِلٍ ومَفْعَلٍ وأُعطي للمَفْعِلِ أحد عشر اسماً نحو الْمَنْسِك والْمَجْزِر والْمَنْبِت والْمَطْلِع والْمَشْرِق والْمَغْرِب والْمَفْرِق والْمَسْقِط والْمَسْكِن والْمَرْفِق والْمَسْجِد والباقي للمَفْعَلِ لخفّة الفتحة. واسم الزمان مثل المكان نحو مَقْتَلِ الحُسَيْنِ.

Fols. 16b-17a

١ اسم: اسمي ك ل/ ٢ هو: – د ل/ فيه الفعل: الفعل فيه ب/ فزيدت: زيدت ز/ ٣ وكونهما... الفعل: – ب ج د ه ز ط ك ل/ يزد: تزد د ل/ ٤–٥ الموعد والموجل: الموجل د: موعد وموجل ل/ ٥–٦ لأنّه... والزمان: – ا: لأنه اسم ليس من الزمان والمكان ب ج ه: لأنه ليس من الزمان والمكان ز: لأنه ليس من اسم المكان والزمان ه: لأنه ليس باسم زمان ولا مكان ك/ المكان والزمان: مكان ولا زمان د/ ٦ فوعلا: فوعل ل/ وصيغته من: ومن ا د/ من: في ل/ يفعل: يفعيل حـ/ مفعل: + كالمجلس جـ/ ٧ عن: من ل/ الكسرات: + لأن الياء كسرتان والميم كسرة فيصير توالي الكسرات ه: + وعلى الميم كسرة فيصير توالي الكسرات ز: + والميم كسرة واحدة فيصير توالي الكسرات ط/ ٨ وأعطي: فاعطي ك ل/ للمفعل: + بكسر العين ز/ ٩–١٠ والمنبت... والمسجد: والمطلع والمنبت والمشرق والمغرب والمفرق والمسقط والمسكن والمحشر والمسجد ط/ والمسقط... والمسكن: والمسكن والمسقط ب/ والمسقط... والمرفق: والمرفق والمسقط والمسكن ك ل/ والمسقط... والمسجد: والمسجد والمسقط والمسكن والمرفق حـ/ ١٠ والمرفق: والمفرق ا/ والمرفق والمسجد: والمسجد والمرفق د/ ١١ نحو... الحسين: – ب ج/

§ 6. The nouns of time and place(159)

The noun of place is a noun derived from يَفْعَلُ denoting the place with respect to the occurrence of the act therein.

The *m* was prefixed [instead of the imperfect prefix] as in the passive participle because of a similarity between them both in being the recipients of the occurrence of the verb therein.

The *w* was not infixed [as in the passive participle] so that it would not be mixed up with it.

Its pattern of the conjugation يَفْعَلُ is مَفْعَلٌ, e.g. اَلْمَذْهَبُ "the place of departure", except in the verb with 1st weak radical, as its 2nd radical is vowelled by a kasra , e.g. اَلْمَوْعِدُ "the place of a promise or an appointment" and اَلْمَوْجِلُ "the place that is dreaded",(160) so that it would not be believed that its pattern is فَوْعَلٌ, e.g. جَوْرَبٌ "a sock or stocking",(161) which is neither a noun of place or time. It is not accepted with a kasra either because فَوْعِلٌ does not exist in their [sc. the Arabs'] language.

Its pattern of the conjugation **[Fol. 17 a]** يَفْعِلُ is مَفْعِلٌ, except in the verb with 3rd weak radical, as its 2nd radical is vowelled by a fatḥa, e.g. اَلْمَرْمَى "a place of throwing or shooting arrows",(162) to avoid the combination of the kasras.

The pattern مَفْعُلٌ is not to be formed of يَفْعُلُ because of the heaviness of the ḍamma.

So the noun of place was divided between the patterns مَفْعَلٌ and مَفْعِلٌ, and the following eleven nouns were given to the pattern مَفْعِلٌ : اَلْمَنْسِكُ "the place where a sacrifice is offered during a religious festival", اَلْمَجْزِرُ "the place where animals are slaughtered, slaughterhouse", اَلْمَنْبِتُ "the place where a plant grows", اَلْمَطْلِعُ "the place of ascent or rising", اَلْمَشْرِقُ "the place where the sun rises, the east", اَلْمَغْرِبُ "the place where the sun sets, the west", اَلْمَفْرِقُ "the place of division, the crown of the head", اَلْمَسْقِطُ "the place where anything falls", اَلْمَسْكِنُ "the place where one dwells, habitation", اَلْمَرْفِقُ "the place on which one rests, the elbow", and اَلْمَسْجِدُ "the place of prostration in prayer, a mosque".(163)

The remaining patterns occur formed upon the pattern مَفْعَلٌ because of the lightness of the fatḥa.

The noun of time is similar to the noun of place, e.g. مَقْتَلُ الْحُسَيْنِ "the time or place of the killing of Ḥusain".

§ 7. فصل في اسم الآلة

وهو اسم مشتقَ من يَفْعَلُ للآلة وصيغته مِفْعَلٌ. ومن ثمَ قال الصرفيَون المَفْعَلُ للموضع والمِفْعَلُ للآلة والفَعْلَةُ للمرَة والفِعْلَةُ للحالة. وكسرت الميم للفرق بينه وبين الموضع ويجيء على وزن مِفْعَالٍ نحو مِقْرَاضٍ ومِفْتَاحٍ. ويجيء مضموم العين والميم نحو المُسْعُطِ والمُنْخُلِ، قال سيبويه هذان من عداد الأسماء يعني أنَ المُسْعُطَ والمُنْخُلَ اسم لهذا الوعاء* وليس بآلة وكذلك أخواته كالمُدْهُنِ والمُدُقِ.

* ١٧ ب

Fols. 17a-17b

٣ للموضع: + ويجيء على وزن مفعلة كمكسحة ز/ وكسرت: وكسرة ا/ ٤ ويجيء: + مفعل ط/ مقراض: مقراص ل/ ٥ المسعط: المسقط ب حـ ط/ سيبويه: + رحمة الله عليه جـ/ أنَ: – ا/ ٦ اسم: + مختصَ ط/ أخواته: الأخوات حـ/ كالمُدْهُنِ والمُدُقَ: – ا د: نحو المدق والمكحلة والمحرضة ز/

§ 7. The noun of instrument[164]

It is a noun which is derived from يَفْعَلُ denoting the instrument, and its pattern is مِفْعَلٌ.

Hence, the grammarians said that الْمَفْعَلُ is for the noun of place, الْمِفْعَلُ for the noun of instrument, الْفَعْلَةُ for the noun that expresses the doing of an action once[165] and الْفِعْلَةُ for the noun of kind.[166]

The *m* was vowelled by a kasra to differentiate it from the noun of place.

It occurs formed upon the pattern مِفْعَالٌ, e.g. مِقْرَاضٌ "a pair of scissors" and مِفْتَاحٌ "a key".[167]

It occurs with the 2nd radical and the *m* vowelled by a ḍamma, e.g. مُسْعُطٌ "an instrument for introducing medicine into the nose" and مُنْخُلٌ "a sieve". Sībawaihī said that both these nouns are counted among the nouns [which are not derived], i.e. that مُسْعُطٌ and مُنْخُلٌ are respectively the names of these recipients **[Fol. 17 b]** and not nouns of instrument, and so are their cognates, e.g. مُدْهُنٌ "a thing [or pot or vase] in which oil, flash or phial was put" and مُدُقَ "a thing with which one bruises, brays or pounds".[168]

II.2.1. COMMENTARY

The Strong Verb

(11) For a general study of الصحيح "the Strong Verb" see Mu'addib, *Taṣrīf* 147-184, Ibn Ya'īš, *Mulūkī* 38-45, Zanǧānī, *'Izzī* 2-6, Farḥāt, *Baḥt* 16-51, 'Abd al-Ḥamīd, *Taṣrīf* 607-608, de Sacy, 149-225, Wright, 52-68, Blachère, 38 sqq., Bakkūš, *Taṣrīf* 84-97, 'Abd al-Raḥīm, *Ṣarf* 18-21. For a comparative study with corresponding forms in some of the other Semitic languages see Brockelmann, *Grundriss* 504 sqq., Wright, *Comparative Grammar* 161-226.

(12) This is an important question that Ibn Mas'ūd discusses by referring to the Basrans' (for a detailed presentation of these grammarians and their works see Brockelmann, *S I,* 158-177, *GAL I,* 96-116, Flügel, *Schulen* 26-114, Sezgin, *Geschichte IX,* 28-115) and the Kufans' (for a detailed presentation of these grammarians and their works see Brockelmann, *S I,* 177-184, *GAL I,* 117-124, Flügel, *Schulen* 117-180, Sezgin, *Geschichte IX,* 116-150) debate.

According to the Arabic grammatical tradition, the Basran "school" has been established by al-Mubarrad in Baġdād with his work *Ṭabaqāt al-naḥwīyīn al-baṣrīyīn* (cf. Ibn al-Nadīm, *Fihrist* 59). Facing al-Mubarrad in Baġdād, was his rival, the Kufan Ṯa'lab (d. 291/904) (Ṯa'lab, Aḥmad b. Yaḥyā b. Yasār al-Šaybānī, see Suyūṭī, *Buġya I,* 396-398, Zubaidī, *Ṭabaqāt* 155, Ibn al-Anbārī, *Nuzha* 293, Yāqūt, *Mu'ǧam V,* 102-146, Qifṭī, *Inbāh I,* 138, Brockelmann, *GAL I,* 121-122, *S I,* 181-182, Sezgin, *Geschichte VIII,* 141-147, *IX,* 140-142), who was a follower of al-Kisā'ī (d. 183/799) (al-Kisā'ī, 'Alī b. Ḥamza b. 'Abd Allāh see Suyūṭī, *Buġya II,* 162-164, Brockelmann, *GAL I,* 117-118, *S I,* 177-178, Sezgin, *Geschichte VIII,* 117, *IX,* 127-131) and al-Farrā'. It was Ṯa'lab with his *Kitāb iḫtilāf al-naḥwīyīn* (which is not preserved), who paved the way for the genre of grammatical debates between the schools (cf. Fleisch, *Esquisse* 10). The historical reality of both these schools has been however challenged (for discussions see Versteegh, *Elements* chapter 5, *Zayd Ibn 'Alī's commentary* 9-11, Bernards, *Traditions* 93-98, Owens, *Foundations* 9, *Theory* 2-3, Talmon, *'Ayn* 278-280). What is agreed upon is that the Basrans and the Kufans are known to have adopted two different attitudes towards the Arabic language (for a discussion concerning their methods see Fleisch, *Traité* 7-11). The Basrans are known to be normative and orthodox wheras the Kufans are known to be descriptive and heterodox (cf. Suyuṭī, *Iqtirāḥ* 100, Weil in his introduction to Ibn al-Anbārī, *Inṣāf* 47, Carter, *Širbīnī* 195 note 9.4 (3), *Ṣarf* 299-304). This does not mean however that the Kufans neglected the grammatical analogy (cf. Versteegh, *Elements* 111). It is thanks to them that many of the interesting linguistic features that deviate from Classical Arabic have been presented, discussed and preserved (cf. Blau, *Judaeo-Arabic* 9 note 4). Concerning the grammatical terminology, the Basran terminology is more known than the Kufan one. Carter, *Ṣarf,* Maḫzūmī, *Madrasa,* especially 303-316, Troupeau, *Lexique* 15-16, Rāǧiḥī, *Farrā',* Versteegh, *Grammar* 9-16 have contributed in revealing some of its obscurities. Concerning some well-known studies (for a detailed presentation see Sezgin, *IX,* 23-24) that deal with the debates of both these "schools", the three following works can be mentioned: the *Īḍāḥ* by al-Zaǧǧāǧī, the *Inṣāf* by Ibn al-Anbārī (d. 577/1181) (Ibn al-Anbārī, Abū l-Barakāt Kamāl al-Dīn 'Abd al-Raḥmān b. Muḥammad b. 'Ubaid Allāh, see Suyūṭī, *Buġya II,* 86-88, Brockelmann, *S I,* 494-495) and the *Masā'il* by al-'Ukbarī (d. 616/1218) (al-'Ukbarī, 'Abd Allāh b. al-Ḥusain b. 'Abd Allāh b. al-Ḥusain, see Suyūṭī, *Buġya II,* 38-40, Brockelmann, *S I,* 495-496). The *Masā'il* resembles the *Inṣāf* in character, but presents only some of the debates.

Baġdād became the center for the successors of the Basran grammarian Mubarrad and the Kufan grammarian Ṯa'lab. Some of these grammarians mixed the doctrines of both the "schools" in their teachings (for a discussion concerning the opposition of both the "schools" and their "fusion" see Fleisch, *Traité* 11-15; for a presentation of the grammarians belonging to the Baghdadian "school" and their works see Brockelmann, *S I,* 184-195, *GAL I,* 124-132, Flügel, *Schulen* 183 sqq., Sezgin, *Geschichte IX,*.151-187), whereas others showed a preference for the Basran methods which finally became victorious.

According to Mu'addib, *Taṣrīf* 44, the *maṣdar* "verbal noun" has been termed as so by Ḫalīl b. Aḥmad. A special definition of the *maṣdar* is presented by Sībawaihi, *I,* 11, namely اسم الحدث "the noun of the action", or اسم الحدث والحدثان "the noun of both the action and the accident (of the agent)". Zamaḫšarī, 16 writes:

"هو المَصْدَرُ سُمِّي بذلك لأنَّ الفعلَ يصدُرُ عنه ويسمِّيه سيبويه الحَدَثَ والحَدَثانَ...
وينقسم الى مُبْهَم نحو ضربتُ ضَرْبًا والى موقّت نحو ضربتُ ضَرْبَةً وضربتَيْنِ."

> "It is the *maṣdar;* it was named so because the verb is derived from it, and Sībawaihi named it the noun indicative of the accident or (of) both the accident and the action... And it is divided into vague e.g. ضَرَبْتُ ضَرْباً "I hit a hitting" and having a limited extent in space or time, e.g. ضَرَبْتُ ضَرْبَةً وَضَرْبَتَيْنِ "I hit one hitting and two".

The debate between the Basrans and Kufans that is presented by Ibn Mas'ūd, concerns the *maṣdar* and the verb. The *maṣdar* is considered as being the origin of derivation according to the Basrans (for an introduction to their opinions see Zaǧǧāǧī, *Īḍāḥ* 56, Ibn Ǧinnī, *Munṣif I,* 65, *Ḫaṣā'iṣ I,* 113, 119, 121, Ibn al-Anbārī, *Inṣāf* Q. 28, 102-107, *Asrār* 69, 71, 176), whereas the verb is considered as being the origin of the derivation according to the Kufans (for an introduction to their opinions see Ibn al-Anbārī, *Inṣāf* Q. 28, 102-109, Qīrawānī, *Mušakkil* fol. 15; for a study of the debate between both schools see Zaǧǧāǧī, *Īḍāḥ* 56-63, Zamaḫšarī, 16-18, Ibn al-Anbārī, *Inṣāf* Q. 28, 102-107, 'Ukbarī, *Masā'il* 68-76, Ibn Ya'īš, *I,* 110 sqq., de Sacy, *I,* 278-280, Lane, *II,* 1662, Bohas, *Étude* 129-148). The Basrans tend to deal with the *maṣdar* and the verb as logicians whereas the Kufans tend to deal with them as philologists (cf. de Sacy, *I,* 280, my notes (13b)). As remarked below, many of the arguments presented by the Basrans offer some similarities with the ones that are used in other fields than the one of pure grammar. This occurs easily when such serious notions as أصل "origin" and فرْع "derivative" are involved. As Arkoun, *Logocentrisme* 10 remarks:

> "Aṣl: source, racine, origine, fondement, signale au départ la différence inauguratrice à laquelle il faut sans cesse revenir pour vérifier la légitimité de toute initiative humaine et du discours qui l'exprime. Mais l'esprit s'éloigne de la différence à mesure qu'il s'engage dans la recherche d'une cohérence logique".

The main idea emphasized here by Ibn Mas'ūd, is the Basrans' concept of the *maṣdar's* oneness contra the verb's plurality. What is meant by these notions is that the *maṣdar* does not distinguish between the tenses because it points to an unlimited time, it has only one pattern, e.g. الضربُ "the hitting" and القتلُ "the killing" and points only to الحدثُ "the happening". As for the verb it is divided into three tenses: ماضي "perfect", حاضر "present" or فعل في الحال "a verb referring to present time" (for discussions concerning it see Zaǧǧāǧī, *Īḍāḥ* 86-88, Ibn Ya'īš, *VII,* 4) and مستقبل "imperfect". It points to a fixed time, has many patterns and points to two things: the happening and the time. According to Ibn al-Anbārī, *Inṣāf* Q. 28, 103, the *maṣdar's* reference to an unlimited time characterizes it as المُطْلَقُ "the absolute" whereas the verb's reference to a limited time characterizes it as المُقَيَّدُ "the limited". The Basrans' logical conclusion is that just as the absolute is the origin of the limited and the number one is the origin of the number two, the *maṣdar* is the origin of derivation of the verb (for these arguments see Ibn al-Anbārī, *Inṣāf* Q. 28, 103-104, my notes to Ibn Masʿūd, *I,* 43-44).

b) Each *maṣdar* is a noun whereas each noun is not a *maṣdar.* The *maṣdar* is named specifically as اسم الحدث "the noun of the action", or اسم الحدث والحدثان "the noun of both the action and the accident [of the agent]" by Sībawaihi, *I,* 11 as it was mentioned.

It is interesting to remark that the Basrans' conception of the *maṣdar's* superiority in relation to the verb, resembles their conception of the noun's superiority in relation to the verb and to the particle. The superiority of the noun seems according to some (e.g. Ibn Ǧinnī, *Ḫaṣā'iṣ I,* 41-42) to have been determined by the sur. 2: 31 (وَعَلَّمَ آدَمَ الْأَسْمَاءَ كُلَّهَا) "And He taught Adam the nature of all things", [literally: the names, or nouns of things]". This incited Ibn Ǧinnī, *Ḫaṣā'iṣ I,* 41-42 to write:

"فإن قيل: فاللغة فيها أسماء، وأفعال، وحروف، وليس يجوز أن يكون المعلَّم من ذلك الأسماء دون غيرها: مما ليس بأسماء، فكيف خصّ الأسماء وحدها؟
قيل: اعتمد ذلك من حيث كانت الأسماء أقوى القُبُل الثلاثة، ولا بدّ لكل كلام مفيد من الاسم، وقد تستغنى الجملة المستقلّة عن كل واحد من الحرف والفعل".

> "If it was said: the langage comprises nouns, verbs and particles, and it is impossible to learn about the nouns without the other categories. Why then, did He [sc. God in this sur.] give importance to the nouns only?
> One would answer: this determination is due to the fact that the nouns are the strongest among the three [categories]. Each statement that means something is in need of a noun, and an independent proposition can manage without both the particle and the verb".

Already in the dispute presented by Ibn al-Anbārī, *Inṣāf* Q. 1, 1-6 and ʿUkbarī, *Masā'il* 54-62 concerning the morphological derivation of الإسمُ (for discussions concerning this word in the Semitic languages see Rundgren, *Bildungen* 152-155), the Basrans claimed that it is derived from السُّمُوّ "the highness, exaltedness" (for their opinions see Ibn Ǧinnī, *Tafsīr* 184, Maʿarrī, *Risāla* 133, Ibn Sīda, *Muḫaṣṣaṣ XVII,* 134, Ibn al-Šağarī, *Amālī II,* 66), whereas the Kufans claimed that it is derived from الوَسمُ "the sign" (for their opinions see Maʿarrī, *Risāla* 133). The Kufans were mostly interested in the etymology of the word, whereas the Basrans stressed on the superiority of the noun, which according to their definition elevates itself above the named one, and is indicative of what is beneath. They added also that it was superior in rank in relation to the verb and to the particle. Their argument (for it see Versteegh, *Zağğāğī* 137-138) is that in nominal sentences the noun can be used as a مُبْتَدَأ "topic" or a خَبَر "predicate", whereas the verb can only be used as a predicate, and is for this reason dependent on the agent (cf. (13)), and the particle cannot be used for any of these purposes.

(13) The Basrans' argument referred to by Ibn Masʿūd, is the independence of the *maṣdar* as a noun contra the dependence of the verb on its agent in the sentence (cf. Ibn al-Anbārī, *Inṣāf* 103, Weiss, *Subject* 615, *Speech* 28-36, my notes (12 b)). Nouns are independent as they can occur in nominal sentences without any verb and can function as topics or predicates. Furthermore two nouns combined together can form a complete sentence with one of them being a topic and the other one a predicate (cf. Versteegh, *Zağğāğī* 137). If verbs are to occur in such sentences, they can only function as predicates to the nouns, and not as topics. In both verbal or nominal sentences, no verb can exist without that it refers to an agent, manifested or suppressed. In some cases the subject of a verb could be a latent pronoun,—and it should be kept in mind that according to most of the Arab grammarians the pronoun belongs to the same category as the noun, as the categories are three: noun, verb and particle (cf. (10 b), (63)) -, but this does not mean that the verb is deprived of a subject (for some remarks concerning the relations between the verb and its agents see Retsö, *Sentences* 72). Weiss, *Subject* 617 writes:

> "The verb carried within itself the demand for completion into a sentence, the noun did not; hence the verb could function only as a predicate-expression, whereas the noun was syntactically versatile".

Rundgren, *Representation* 112 points to the dependence of the verb with these words:

> "From another point of view I would like to repeat the fact that it is never the 'verb' in itself that 'indicates', simply because the 'verb' is only an entity by abstraction. The verb can never as such be a 'component of a sentence', only as a predicate phrase *qatala* can have this function, or, more correctly, the function of being an immediate constituent of a texteme".

b) Concerning both the main ideas of the *maṣdar's* oneness and independence contra the verb's plurality and dependence (see further Versteegh, *Elements* 130 sqq. for his particular comments concerning this question), I find it appropriate in this context to interject the following comments that refer to the fields of philosophy and theology, as it is interesting to notice that the Basrans are using some of the arguments of the philosophers and theologians to prove their views. In both these fields, the ideas concerning oneness contra plurality can be associated with the Oneness of God Who is at rest (for it see Abū Rīda, *Rasā'il I,* 153), as opposed to the plurality of the stages in the person's life (cf. Ġazālī, *Tabernacle* 57-58), before that he reaches a state of oneness with God (cf. Grunebaum, *Islam* in his 1st page to *L'idéal humain* 243-282), or as opposed to the plurality of God's Signs (cf. Hallaq, *Ibn Taymīya* 59). God is independent (for discussions see ibid 51, Ibn Sīna, *Šifā'* 65 sqq, Lawkarī, *Ḥaqq* 181-183, Heer, *Existence* 227), self-subsisting, whereas the created is not (cf. Ġazālī, *Tabernacle* 52). Each man and each created object refer to God with some of their qualities (cf. Hallaq, *Ibn Taymīya* 59-60, Ibn Taymīya, *Ǧahd* 189), which prove that they derive from Him. The unlimited time linked to the *maṣdar* (cf. (12)) can be associated with the concept of God Who does not enter in temporality and is Eternal (cf. Ǧāmī, *Naqd* 103). God is as well referred to as *al-qadīm* "the Eternal" by Abū l-Huḏail (d. 227/842 or 235/850), one of the founders of the Muʿtazilite's doctrines in Vitestam's introduction to Dārimī, *Radd* 32. This epithet is also used by Ibn Ǧinnī, *Ḫaṣā'iṣ I,* 45, Suyūṭī, *Muzhir I,* 9 and Ibn Sīda, *Muḫaṣṣaṣ* 5. In the Qur'ān, God is identified with Time by the pagans. Sur. 45: 24 has: (نَمُوتُ وَنَحْيَا وَمَا يُهْلِكُنَا إِلاَّ ٱلدَّهْرُ) "We shall die and we live, and nothing but Time can destroy us" (cf. Wensinck, *Concordance II,* 155). In the same manner, God's language, the Qur'ān, is considered as being untouched by time (cf. Roman, *Expression* 11, *Origine* 14, in particular the notes, *Étude I,* 38).

(14) For the little derivation or minor etymology see Suyūṭī, *Muzhir I,* 202 204, Weiss, *Subject* 618-619, *Waḍʿ* 353-354, Ṣubḥī, *Fiqh* 173-186, for the big derivation see Ṣubḥī, *Fiqh* 186-209 and many of the examples mentioned by Bohas, *Matrices* 95-141, and for the biggest derivation see Ibn Ǧinnī, *Ḫaṣā'iṣ II,* 133-139, Ṣubḥī, *Fiqh* 210-242. An early work that treats the subject of the big derivation is Ibn Fāris, *Maqāyīs* (for some remarks concerning it see Haywood, *Lexicography* 101-102). For the three sorts of derivation see Ibn Mālik, *La Alfīya* in the "Lexique" 290, Lane, *II,* 1577, Bustānī, *Muḥīṭ* 495, Bohas, *Étude* 174 in the notes; for a brief differenciation between the minor an the major etymology see Weiss, *Waḍʿ* 353; for the derivatives see (10).

b) The phenomenon of the transposition of the consonants in a word (for discussions concerning some cases see (291), (292), (293), (294); for its occurrence in some modern Arabic dialects see ʿAbd al-Tawwāb, *Taṭawwur* 58-60; for a developed study of the metathesis in some of the Semitic languages see Brockelmann, *Grundriss* 267-278), that distinguishes it from another word, is usually associated with the big derivation. In his باب القلب "the chapter on the transposition", Ibn Fāris, *Ṣāḥibī* 202 discusses the customary procedures that the Arabs have of transposing the consonants, e.g. جَذَبَ and جَبَذَ "to attract" (cf. Suyūṭī, *Muzhir I,* 282 sqq., the notes of Barth to Ṯaʿlab, *Faṣīḥ* 28-29). There exists however a difference of opinion concerning both جَذَبَ and جَبَذَ, the Kufans considering the shifting of the consonants to be a phenomenon of transposition whereas the Basrans considering the two different words as pertaining to two different dialectal variants (cf. ʿAbd al-Tawwāb, *Taṭawwur* 60). Ibn Manẓūr, *I,* 573 and Lane, *I,* 373 precise that جَبَذَ belongs to the dialect of Tamīm.

c) An allusion to the biggest derivation is made by Ibn Fāris, *Ṣāḥibī* 201-202 within باب أجناس الكلام في الاتّفاق والافْتراق "the chapter of the conformity and distinction of word categories" in which he also treats اختلاف اللّفظ والمَعْنَى "the distinction between both words and meanings", اخْتلاف اللّفظ واتّفاق المعنى "the distinction between both words and the conformity of their meanings", اتّفاق اللّفظ واخْتلاف المعنى "the conformity of both words and the distinction of their meanings", اتفاق اللّفظ وتَضادُ المعنى "the conformity of both words and the opposition of their meanings (i.e. opposites, enantiosema)" (for Arabic works dealing with opposites see Ibn al-Anbārī, *Aḍdād,* Quṭrub, *Aḍdād* 241-284, 385-461, 493-544, Hafftner, *Aḍdād,* for studies undertaken by Orientalists see Redslob, *Wörter,* Cohen, *Études* 80-104, *Aḍdād,* Giese, *Aḍdād,* for a discussion of such words with references to some of the other Semitic languages see Nöldeke, *Neue Beiträge* 67-101) and تقارب اللّفظين والمعْنيين "the conformity of both words and meanings", which refers to the biggest derivation. As examples Ibn Fāris takes up الحَزْمُ "the firmness" and الحَزْنُ "the hard ground"... الخَضْمُ "the act of munching, which is with the whole mouth" and القَضْمُ "the act of gnawing, which is with the extremity of the teeth" (for examples see (340 c), (368), (374), and for further examples see many of those mentioned by Bohas, *Matrices* 144-152). Ibn Ǧinnī, *Ḫaṣāʾiṣ II,* 157-158 studies as well the meaning of the consonants *q* and *ḫ* in الخَضْمُ and القَضْمُ (cf. Ṣubḥī, *Fiqh* 143).

(15) One of the Kufans' arguments is introduced here. It pertains to the field of phonology and stresses the idea of the dependence of the *maṣdar* on the verb regarding the unsoundness or the soundness of the weak consonant in its structure. If a phonological change due to the unsoundness of the weak consonant is carried out in the verb, then a phonological change is carried out as well in the *maṣdar.* If the weak consonant remains sound in the verb it remains as well sound in the *maṣdar.*

(16) It is the phonological change that is carried out in a verb due to the unsoundness of the weak consonant in it or the lack of change due to the soundness of the weak consonant in it, that determines according to the Kufans, whether the weak consonant of its *maṣdar* is unsound or sound. This dependency of the *maṣdar* on the verb is the reason why the Kufans chose to consider the verb as entitled to be the origin of the *maṣdar* (for their arguments see Ibn al-

Anbārī, *Inṣāf* 102, my notes to Ibn Masʿūd, *I,* 45-46; for a refutation against this opinion see (19)). An example of a verb with the 1st radical *w* unsound is يَعِدُ "he promises" in the imperfect, underlyingly يَوْعِدُ, in which the *w* is elided (cf. (244)), which determines that its *maṣdar* is عِدَةٌ "a promise" underlyingly وِعْدٌ with the *w* that is elided as well (for this elision see (247), Sībawaihi, *II,* 81, Wright, *II,* 118, Lane, *II,* 2952), and with the *tāʾ marbūṭa* suffixed in it as a compensation for this elision. Another example is قَامَ underlyingly قَوَمَ in which the *w* is changed into an *ā*, whose *maṣdar* is قِيَامٌ in which a phonological change due to the unsound weak consonant is carried out to accord with the phonological change that is carried out in its verb, as it is underlyingly قِوَامٌ in which the *w* is changed into a *y*. Some examples of verbs in which the weak consonant is sound are يَوْجَلُ (cf. Sībawaihi, *II,* 266, Zamaḫšarī, 178) and قَاوَمَ, both of which retain their 2nd radical *w*. It is this soundness of the weak consonant in the verb that leads consequently according to the Kufans, to its soundness in the *maṣdar'*s structure, i.e. وَجَلٌ and قِوَامٌ respectively.

(17) According to the Kufans who refer to the phrase ضَرَبْتُ ضَرْباً "I hit a hitting", the *maṣdar* ضَرْباً emphasizes the verb ضَرَبْتُ (for a refutation of this argument see (20)). The *maṣdar* is the مُؤَكِّد "emphasizer" and the verb is the مُؤَكَّد "emphasized", and they say that it is appropriate that the emphasized is the origin of the emphasizer. This argument has been deduced by Abū Bakr Muḥammad b. al-Qāsim b. al-Anbārī (d. 328/939), one of Taʿlab's pupils and one of the best Kufan grammarians (for him see Qifṭī, *Inbāh III,* 201, Suyūṭī, *Buġya I,* 212-214, Sezgin, *Geschichte VIII,* 151-154, *IX,* 144-147). Another argument proposed by the Kufans that refers to the field of syntax which can be added here, is that the verb is the regent and governs the *maṣdar,* which is a noun, in the accusative (for discussions see Zaǧǧāǧī, *Īḍāḥ* 61, Ibn al-Anbārī, *Inṣāf* 102, ʿUkbarī, *Masāʾil* 74, Suyūṭī, *Ašbāh I,* 130, my notes to Ibn Masʿūd, *I,* 46-47). It has then a power over the noun and is so endowed to be its origin. In the phrase ضَرَبْتُ ضَرْباً, ضَرْباً is put in the accusative by the verb ضَرَبْتُ.

(18) According to the Basrans, the literary meaning of the word *maṣdar* is the place of issuance of the verb (for their argument see (21)). They take up the example مَصْدَرُ الإِبِلِ "the place of issuance of the camels" and consider the place of issuance as entitled to be the origin of the derivation of the action, which is the issuance of the camels. Hence the noun of place that is traditionally seen as derived from the verb, is in this case the place of derivation of the verb. The Kufans object against this argument as they regard the meaning of the pattern مَصْدَرٌ as being similar to the meaning of the pattern of the past participle مَصْدُورٌ, which is a derivative of the verb (cf. Ibn al-Anbārī, *Inṣāf* 103). In order to defend their opinion they take up the examples مَرْكَبٌ—which is a noun of place according to the Basrans, "a quick place of riding" -, that they themselves consider as the past participle مَرْكُوبٌ "anything which is ridden, a mount", and مَشْرَبٌ—which is a place of drinking according to the Basrans -, that they consider as the

past participle مَشْروبٌ "a drink". The example مَشْرَبٌ in the meaning of the past participle مَشْروبٌ "a drink" that is used to defend the Kufans' theory, occurs in a verse said by Nuṣaib, cited by Zağğāğī, *Īḍāḥ* 62:

"وقد عادَ عذْبُ الماءِ بَحْراً فزادني على ظمئي أن أبحر المشرَبُ العَذْبُ".

"Again the freshness of the water had become sea, and my thirst augmented that the fresh drink became salty".

Another variant is cited by Ibn Manẓūr, *I,* 215:

"وقد عادَ ماءُ الأرضِ بحراً فزادني الى مرضي أنْ أبْحرَ المشربُ العذبُ"

"Again the water of the earth became sea, and my sickness augmented that the fresh drink became salty".

(19) The Basrans' arguments against the Kufans' theories which pertain to the field of phonology are presented here. The Kufans believe that it is the dependency of the sound or the unsound weak consonant in the *maṣdar* on the sound or the unsound weak consonant in the verb, that makes the verb fit to be the origin of derivation of the *maṣdar* (for their opinion see (16)). According to the Basrans, the phonological change of the unsound weak consonant that is carried out in the *maṣdar,* which is on the analogy of the one that is carried out in the verb, is only due to avoid a certain heaviness in its structure (for their arguments see Ibn al-Anbārī, *Inṣāf* 105). According to them, this does not point to the origin or to the derivative. In order to defend their theory, they take up the example يَعِدُ "he promises" underlyingly يَوْعِدُ, in which the *w* is elided because it occurs between the *y* and the kasra, which causes a heaviness in the structure. The *w* is also elided from تَعِدُ "/2 masc. sing." and "/3 fem. sing." underlyingly تَوْعِدُ, in spite of the fact that it does not occur between the *y* and the kasra, so that it is similar in its form to يَعِدُ. Another example is أُكْرِمُ underlyingly أُأَكْرِمُ "I honour", in which one of both hamzas is elided because of the heaviness of both their combination. It is also elided from تُكْرِمُ "/2 masc. sing." and "/3 fem. sing." underlyingly تُؤَكْرِمُ, in spite of the fact that two hamzas are not combined in them, by analogy to أُكْرِمُ (compare the case of the imperative of Form IV أَكْرِمْ "honour!" discussed in my notes (116)). This does not mean that the 3rd person يَعِدُ or the 1st person أُأَكْرِمُ is the base form of the remaining persons. Furthermore another Basran argument that can be added here against the Kufan one, is that there exist verbs in which the weak consonant is unsound whereas the weak consonant of their *maṣdars* is sound. An example is وَعَدَ "to promise" that loses its 1st radical *w* in the imperfect يَعِدُ, but that has also the *maṣdar* وَعْدٌ with the 1st radical *w* retained, and وَزَنَ "to balance" that loses its 1st radical *w* in the imperfect يَزِنُ, but that has the *maṣdar* وَزْنٌ with the 1st radical *w* retained (cf. Zağğāğī, *Īḍāḥ* 60, ʿUkbarī, *Masāʾil* 75). This means that the soundness or unsoundness of a weak consonant in the verb is not a necessary condition for the soundness or the unsoundness of a weak consonant in the *maṣdar.*

(20) The Basrans' arguments against the Kufans' who regard the *maṣdar* as the emphasizer of the verb (for it see (17)) are presented here (cf. Ibn al-Anbārī, *Inṣāf* 105-106, my notes to Ibn Masʿūd, *I*, 46-47). According to the Basrans, the emphasized word is not the origin of derivation of the other word, but can be considered as the origin of its declension, as in جَاءَنِي زَيْدٌ زَيْدٌ "Zaidun, Zaidun came to me", in which the first Zaidun can only be the origin of the second one regarding the aspect of the declension, and the second Zaydun is not derived from it. Furthermore, in an example as ضَرَبْتُ ضَرْباً, it is the written *maṣdar* that is emphasized, and not the information and the time that the verb encompasses. In other words, the verb ضَرَبْتُ is not emphasized by the *maṣdar* ضَرْباً. Thus ضَرَبْتُ ضَرْباً cannot be compared to the example ضَرَبْتُ أَحْدَثْتُ "I hit, I hit", in which the second verb emphasizes the first one, but rather to أَحْدَثْتُ ضَرْباً ضَرْباً "I let happen a hitting, a hitting", in which the second *maṣdar* emphasizes the first one.

b) Nouns, verbs and particles can be emphasized (for a general definition of مُؤَكَّد and مُؤَكِّد with examples see Reckendorf, *Syntax* 68-69; for a general study of the emphasis see Howell, *I*, fasc. I, 389-394, Carter, *Širbīnī* 294-298). A case that concerns the emphasis of a noun that can be presented, is أَخَاكَ أَخَاكَ, that occurs in the following verse said by Miskīn al-Dārimī, cited by Sībawaihi, *I*, 108, Širbīnī, *Šarḥ* 42, Šinqīṭī, *Durar I*, 146, Carter, *Širbīnī* 296, Howell, *I*, fasc. I, 158:

"أَخَاكَ أَخَاكَ إِنَّ مَنْ لَا أَخَا لَهُ   كَسَاعٍ إِلَى الهَيْجَا بِغَيْرِ سِلَاحٍ".

"[Cleave to] your brother, your brother; verily he who has no brother is like one running to the fray without a weapon".

c) Some cases concerning the emphasis of verbs that can be presented, are أَتَاكَ أَتَاكَ and اَحْبِسْ اَحْبِسْ, that occur in the following verse said by an unknown poet, cited by Širbīnī, *Šarḥ* 42, Šinqīṭī, *Durar II*, 145, 158, Carter, *Širbīnī* 296, Howell, *I*, fasc. I, 392:

"فَأَيْنَ إِلَى أَيْنَ النَّجَاءُ بِبَغْلَتِي   أَتَاكَ أَتَاكَ اللَّاحِقُونَ اَحْبِسْ اَحْبِسْ".

"Where, to where are you hurrying with my mule? The pursuers have come to you, have come to you. Stop! Stop!".

d) A case concerning the emphasis of a particle that can be presented, is لَا لَا, that occurs in the following verse said by Ǧamīl, cited by Širbīnī, *Šarḥ* 42, Šinqīṭī, *Durar II*, 159, Carter, *Širbīnī* 298, Howell, *I*, fasc. I, 392:

"لَا لَا أَبُوحُ بِحُبِّ بَثْنَةَ إِنَّهَا   أَخَذَتْ عَلَيَّ مَوَاثِقاً وَعُهُوداً".

"I will not, not reveal the love of Baṭna [sc. Buṭaina] for she has taken against me covenants and oaths".

(21) This is the Basrans' last argument against the Kufans' theory (for it see (18)) concerning the *maṣdar* which according to them refers to the passive participle and not to the noun of place (see my notes to Ibn Masʿūd, *I*, 48-50). The *maṣdar* is considered by the Basrans as the noun of place from which the action issues (cf. Ibn al-Anbārī, *Inṣāf* 107; see further for the particular questions and views Zaǧǧāǧī, *Īḍāḥ* 61-62 who takes up a discussion between himself and Abū Bakr b. al-Anbārī and the interpretation of the text by Versteegh, *Zaǧǧāǧī* 78-79). The example مَرْكَبٌ فارهٌ refers to the place of riding by them and مَشْرَبٌ عذبٌ to the place of drinking; and the quickness الفَراهة and the freshness العُذوبَة were attributed metaphorically to these nouns of place respectively, because of a proximity in the meaning between them, in the same manner as it is said in the sur. 2: 25, 61: 12, 64: 9, 65: 11, etc. تَجري من تَحْتِها الأنهارُ "Beneath which rivers flow", and the river does not flow but the water flows in it.

(22) This sentence is quoted from Zamaḫšarī, 96-97. The patterns that are presented are 1) فَعْلٌ, 2) فِعْل, 3) فُعْل, 4) فَعْلَة, 5) فِعْلَة, 6) فُعْلَة, 7) فَعْلى, 8) فِعْلى, 9) فُعْلى, 10) فَعْلانُ, 11) فِعْلان, 12) فُعْلان, 13) فَعَلان, 14) فَعَلٌ, 15) فِعَل, 16) فُعَل, 17) فَعَلَة, 18) فِعَلَة, 19) فَعَالٌ, 20) فِعال, 21) فُعال, 22) فَعالَة, 23) فِعالَة, 24) فُعُولٌ, 25) فَعُول, 26) فَعِيل, 27) فُعُولَة, 28) مَفْعَلٌ, 29) مَفْعِل, 30) مَفْعَلَة, 31) مَفْعِلَة, 32) مَفْعُلَة. Two other patterns that can be added are فُعَالَةٌ, e.g. بُغَايَةٌ "seeking" and فَعالِيَةٌ, e.g. كَرَاهِيَةٌ "disliking" (cf. Ibn Kamāl Pāšā, *Falāḥ* 13). For a general study of the *maṣdar* in Arabic and in some of the other Semitic languages see Wright, *Comparative Grammar* 195-196.

b) Some other patterns that include as well other classes than the strong verb (for a study see Wright, *I,* 111-112 who mentions fourty-four forms, Howell, *I,* fasc. IV 1516-1517 who mentions fourty-six forms and Ibn Mālik, *Lāmīya* verse 62-70 who mentions fourty-nine forms), are فُعْلَلٌ as سُودَدٌ "being lord", فَعَلُوتٌ as جَبَرُوتٌ "being haughty", تَفْعَلٌ as تُدْرَأ "ability to repel foes", فَيْعَلُولَةٌ as كَيْنُونَةٌ "being", فَعْلُولَةٌ as صَيْرُورَةٌ "becoming", فُعَلْنِيَةٌ as بُلَنْهِيَةٌ "ease", فَعِيلَةٌ as شَبِيبَةٌ "becoming adolescent", فَاعُولَةٌ as ضَارُورَةٌ "affliction", تَفْعَلَةٌ as تَهْلُكَةٌ "perishing", مَفَاعِلَةٌ as مَسَائِيَةٌ "displeasing" and فُعْلَةٌ and فُعْلَى as غُلْبَةٌ and غُلْبَى "overcoming".

c) As for some of these patterns' indications with other examples as well:

The measure فَعْلٌ is from transitive verbs of the forms فَعَلَ and فَعِلَ, e.g. ضَرَبَ "to hit": ضَرْبٌ and قَتَلَ "to kill": قَتْلٌ. The transitive verbs refer to the doing of an action that falls on something or someone contrarily to the intransitive verbs (cf. Mubarrad, *Muqtaḍab IV,* 299, Ibn Yaʿīš, *VII,* 62; for a general study of the transitive and intransitive verbs see Zamaḫšarī, 115-116, Ibn Yaʿīš, *VII,* 62-69, Howell, *II-III,* 96-119; for rendering intransitive verbs transitive and transitive verbs intransitive see Abū Ḥanīfa, *Maqṣūd* 8). For instance in the examples ضَرَبْتَ زيدا "you hit Zaid" and كَلَّمتَ عمرا "you talked to ʿAmr" that comprehend the transitive verbs ضَرَبْتَ and كَلَّمتَ, the action of the hitting fell upon Zaid and the action of the talking was made to reach ʿAmr (cf. Mubarrad, *Muqtaḍab IV,* 299). In the examples of the intransitive verbs قامَ "he rose" and ذَهَبَ "he went", it is not asked on whom القِيامُ "the action of rising" and on whom الذَهابُ "the action of going" fell (cf. Ibn Yaʿīš, *VII,* 62). A distinctive feature that exists bewteen the transitive and intransitive verbs is according to Muʾaddib, *Taṣrīf* 148, that the pronoun of the accusative is fit to be suffixed to the transitive verb, e.g. ضربتُه "I hit him" and شتمتُه "I scolded him" whereas it is not fit to be suffixed to the intransitive verbs, e.g. قمتُ "I got up" and قعدتُ "I sat down".

– The measure فُعْلَةٌ is from the intransitive verbs of the form فَعِلَ, when indicative of colors, e.g. سمر "to be tawny": سُمْرَةٌ. It can also be indicative of defects, e.g. نُفْخَةٌ "inflation of the belly", and أُدْرَةٌ "scrotal hernia".

– فَعْلانٌ is anomalous, e.g. لوى "delayed payment", لَيَانٌ. An example formed according to this measure is شَنْآنٌ "hatred" (cf. Ibn Manẓūr, *IV,* 2335), which is also allowable with the fatḥa of the 2nd radical as it has been read by some in the sur. 5: 3 (وَلَا يَجْرِمَنَّكُمْ شَنَآنُ قَوْمٍ) "And let not the hatred of some people in (once) shutting you out". فَعَلانٌ is indicative of violent motion, e.g. جَالَ "to go round about": جَوَلَانٌ, and نَزَا "to leap": نَزَوَانٌ.

– The measure فَعَلٌ is from the intransitive verbs of the form فَعِلَ, e.g. مَرِضَ "to be sick": مَرَضٌ, and فَرِحَ "to be glad": فَرَحٌ.

– The examples formed according to the form فُعَلٌ are هُدًى "guiding" and سُرًى "journeying by night". هُدًى has been treated both as a masc. noun and as a fem. (compare the *maṣdar* ضَرْبٌ used as fem. or masc. in the examples presented by Wright, *II,* 181 أَوْجَعَتْنِي ضَرْبُكَ and أَوْجَعَنِي ضَرْبُكَ "your striking caused me pain" and see further for examples Fischer, *Infinitive* 839-859, my notes (296 c)). It occurs in the following verse recited by Ibn Barrīy to Yazīd b. Ḫaḏḏāq, cited by Ibn Manẓūr, *IV,* 2850, *VI,* 4638 and Fischer, *Infinitive* 854, in which the verb يُعْدِي that follows it, occurs as a 3rd person of the masc. sing. by Ibn Manẓūr, *IV,* 2850 and Fischer, *Infinitive* 854, and as a 3rd person of the fem. sing. by Ibn Manẓūr, *VI,* 2850:

"وَلَقَدْ أَضَاءَ لَكَ الطَّرِيقُ وَأَنْهَجَتْ   سُبُلُ الْمَكَارِمِ وَالْهُدَى يُعْدِي".

> "And verily, the Path has been illuminated for you, and the accesses to the noble deeds have been made clear, as the [sc. your] leadership has helped [you on the way]."

– The measures فَعَالٌ, e.g. جَمَالٌ "being comely", فُعُولَةٌ, e.g. مُلُوحَةٌ "salty", فَعَالَةٌ, e.g. كَرَامَةٌ "generosity" and فُعْلٌ, e.g. حُسْنٌ "beauty", are from the form فَعُلَ which is indicative of a state or descriptive of a quality (for this form see (34)).

– The measure فِعَالٌ is indicative of:

a)–sound, but not as frequently as فُعَالٌ and فَعِيلٌ, e.g. عِرَارٌ "crying of the he-ostrich".

b)–the time of the accident being close, e.g. حِصَادٌ "season for reaping".

c)–refusal, e.g. أَبَى "to refuse", إِبَاءٌ ; and أَبَقَ "to run away", إِبَاقٌ.

– The measure فُعَالٌ (for a study see Diem, *Fuʿāl* 43-68) is usually indicative of:

a)–ailment, e.g. سَعَلَ "to cough": سُعَالٌ.

b)–sound, e.g. صَرَخَ "to scream": صُرَاخٌ.

In some cases, both فُعَالٌ and فَعِيلٌ are used for sound, e.g. صَرِيخٌ and صُرَاخٌ from صَرَخَ "to scream", and نَبِيحٌ and نُبَاحٌ from نَبَحَ "to bark".

– The measure فِعَالَةٌ is from the transitive or intransitive verbs of the form فَعَلَ, when indicative of a craft or an office, e.g. كَتَبَ "to write": كِتَابَةٌ.

– The measure فُعُولٌ (for a linguistic study with statistical results see Malā'ika, *Fu'ūl* 3-30) is from the intransitive verbs of the form فَعَلَ, e.g. رَكَعَ "to bow": رُكُوعٌ and دَخَلَ "to enter": دُخُولٌ.

– As for the measure فَعُولٌ, the only example formed according to it according to al-Aṣma'ī, referred to by Mu'addib, *Taṣrīf* 51, is قَبُول "accepting".

– ذِكْرَى formed according to the measure فِعْلَى occurs in the sur. 51: 55 (وَذَكِّرْ فَإِنَّ ٱلذِّكْرَى تَنْفَعُ ٱلْمُؤْمِنِينَ) "But teach (thy Message): For teaching benefits the Believers". It also occurs in the following verse said by Ǧamīl, *Dīwān* 159, cited by Mu'addib, *Taṣrīf* 53:

"فيَا قَلْبُ دَعْ ذِكْرَى بُثَيْنَةَ إِنَّهَا   وَإِنْ كُنْتَ تَهْوَاهَا تَضَنُّ وَتَبْخَلُ".

"O heart, give up remembering Buṯaina! For even if you do love her, she is enervated and will not grant you [anything]".

For a detailed presentation of the measures see Sībawaihi, *II,* 224-264, Zaǧǧāǧī, *Ǧumal* 354-358, Mu'addib, *Taṣrīf* 44-58, Ibn Ya'īš, *VI,* 43-47, Ibn Mālik, *Lāmīya* 244-247, Volck/Kellgren, *Ibn Mālik* 16-20, Howell, *I,* fasc. IV, 1516-1529, Vernier, *I,* 156-162, Wright, *II,* 110-114, Fleisch, *Traité I,* 349 sqq.

(23) The example قائما that is formed according to the pattern of the ac ive participle فَاعِلٌ, replaces the *maṣdar* قياما that is formed according to فِعَالٌ, and has its meaning. قُمْ قائما said instead of قُمْ قياماً occurs in the following verse cited by Ibn Fāris, *Ṣāḥibī* 237 who discusses the active participle as a substitute for the *maṣdar:*

"قُمْ قائماً قُمْ قائماً   لَقِيتَ عَبْداً نائما".

"Get up! Get up! You met a sleeping slave!".

The active participle occurs also instead of the *maṣdar* in the following verse said by Bišr b. Abī Ḫāzim praising Aus b. Ḥāriṯa b. La'm al-Ṭā'ī, cited by Zamaḫšarī, 97, Ibn Ya'īš, *VI,* 51, Howell, *I,* fasc. IV, 1557, Fleischer, *Beiträge III,* 331, in which كافي occurs anomalously in the nominative instead of the accusative كافيا, the *y* being made vowelless by poetic licence, in the meaning of كفاية:

"كَفَى بِٱلنَّأْيِ مِنْ أَسْمَاءَ كَافِي   وَلَيْسَ لِحُبِّهَا إِذْ طَالَ شَافِي".

"Sufficient indeed [for me as a trial] is the distance from Asmā'; and there is no healer for the love of her, since it has lasted long".

Compare with the nominative كافي used instead of the accusative كافيا mentioned above another case in which the *y* is elided for the sake of poetic licence in the following verse said by Maǧnūn b. 'Āmir, cited by Ibn Ya'īš, *VI,* 51 and Ibn Hišām, *Muġnī I,* 289, in which واشٍ is treated defectively as a noun in the nominative used instead of the accusative واشياً:

"ولَوْ أنّ واشٍ باليَمامة دارُهُ   ودَاري بأعْلى حَضْرَمَوْتَ اهْتَدَى ليا".

"If a slanderer has his house in Yamāma and my house was in the highest place of Ḥaḍramawt, he would find his way to me".

The same phenomenon occurs in the following verse said by al-Farazdaq, cited by Ibn Fāris, *Ḏamm* 20 (with مُجَلَّفا written by Ibn Fāris who corrects the wrong مُجَلَّفُ and criticizes al-Farazdaq's use of the nominative instead of the accusative), Frayḥa, *Tabsīṭ* 16 and Abū Ḥaidar, *Dual* 40, both mentioning al-Farazdaq's intentional use of the nominative مُجَلَّفُ instead of the accusative مُجَلَّفا:

"وَعَضُّ زَمَانٍ يا آبْنَ مرْوانَ لَمْ يَدَعْ   مِنَ ٱلمالِ إلاّ مُسْحَتاً أو مُجَلَّفُ".

"And a biting time, O Ibn Marwān, which has left all wealth either depleted or badly ravaged".

b) The *maṣdar* can occur on the measure of فاعِلَةٌ (for a study see Ibn Fāris, *Ṣāḥibī* 237, Zamaḫšarī, 97, Ibn Yaʿīš, *VI,* 50-52) as in the sur. 69: 8 (فَهَلْ تَرَى لَهُمْ مِنْ باقِيَةٍ) "Then seest thou any of them left surviving?", in which باقِيَةٍ has the meaning of بَقاءٌ, in the sur. 56: 2 (لَيْسَ لِوَقْعَتِها كاذِبَةٌ) "Then will no (soul) entertain falsehood", in which كاذِبَةٌ has the meaning of كَذِبٌ and in the sur. 69: 4 (فَأَمّا ثَمُودُ فَأُهْلِكُوا بالطّاغِيَةِ) "But the Thamūd,—they were destroyed by a terrible storm of thunder and lightning!", in which بالطّاغِيَةِ has the meaning of بالْطُّغْيانِ.

(24) The example المَفْتُونُ that is formed according to the pattern of the passive participle مَفْعُولٌ replaces the *maṣdar* الفِتْنَةُ that is formed according to the pattern فِعْلَةٌ, and has its meaning. The sur. is also cited by Ibn Fāris, *Ṣāḥibī* 237, Zamaḫšarī, 98, Ibn Yaʿīš, *VI,* 53. The passive participle occurs also instead of the *maṣdar* in the following verse said by an unknown poet, cited by Howell, *I,* fasc. IV, 1551, in which مَعْقُولا occurs instead of عَقْلاً:

"لَمْ يَتْرُكُوا لِعِظامِهِ لَحْماً لا لِفُؤادِهِ مَعْقُولا".

"They have not left flesh to his bones, nor understanding to his mind".

b) The pattern of the *maṣdar* can occur instead of the pattern of the passive participle, and has its meaning (for some cases of the active and passive partiple occurring instead of the *maṣdar* and vice versa see Wright, *II,* 132-133), as in the sur. 31: 11 (هَذا خَلْقُ ٱللهِ) "Such is the Creation of God", in which خَلْقُ occurs instead of مَخْلُوقُ the "created".

c) The *maṣdar* of the derived patterns of the triliteral occurs formed according to the pattern of the passive participle of the specific form, which is also applicable to the passive participle and to the nouns of time and place. This pattern is found in these following examples, just to mention a few:

– In the following verse said by Umayya b. Abī al-Ṣalt, cited by Sībawaihi, *II,* 267, Muʾaddib, *Taṣrīf* 125, Zamaḫšarī, 98, Ibn Yaʿīš, *VI,* 50, 53, Ibn Manẓūr, *VI,* 4206, Howell, *I,* fasc. IV, 1552, in which مُمْسانا occurs instead of الإمْساءُ and مُصْبَحنا instead of الإصْباحُ:

"الْحَمْدُ لله مُمْسَانَا وَمُصْبِحَنَا   بِالْخَيْرِ صَبَّحَنَا رَبِّي وَمَسَّانَا".

"Praise be to God at our entering upon the evening, and at our entering upon the morning! May my Lord make us pass the morning, and make us pass the evening, in weal".

– In the following one said by a man of the Banū Māzin, cited by Zamaḫšarī, 98, Ibn Yaʿīš, *VI*, 53, Howell, *I*, fasc. IV, 1552, in which الْمُجَرَّب occurs instead of التَجْرِبَة:

"وَعِلْمُ بَيَانِ ٱلْمَرْءِ عِنْدَ ٱلْمُجَرَّبِ".

"The knowledge of the quality of the man is acquired on the occasion of experience".

– In the following one said by ʿAlqama b. ʿAbada, cited by Zamaḫšarī, 98, Ibn Yaʿīš, *VI*, 54, Ahlwardt, *Divans* 107, Freytag, *Hamasae* 346, Howell, *I*, fasc. IV, 1552, in which الْمُنَدَّى occurs instead of التَّنْدِيَة:

"فَإِنَّ ٱلْمُنَدَّى رِحْلَةٌ فَرَكُوبُ".

"Then verily the feeding between two drinkings is a starting and riding".

– In the following one said by Ruʾba b. al-ʿAǧǧāǧ, cited by Sībawaihi, *II*, 268, Zamaḫšarī, 98, Ibn Yaʿīš, *VI*, 54, Howell, *I*, fasc. IV, 1553, in which الْمَوْقَى occurs instead of التَّوْقِيَة:

"إِنَّ ٱلْمَوْقَى مِثْلَ مَا وُقِيتُ".

"Verily the preservation shall be like my having been preserved".

– In the following one said by Zaid al-Ḫail al-Ṭāʾī, cited by Sībawaihi, *II*, 268, Zamaḫšarī, 98, Ibn Yaʿīš, *VI*, 55, Freytag, *Hamasae* 84, Fleischer, *Beiträge III*, 339, Howell, *I*, fasc. IV, 1553, in which مُقَاتَلًا occurs instead of قِتَالًا:

"أُقَاتِلُ حَتَّى لَا أَرَى لِي مُقَاتَلًا".

"I fight until I see not for me any fighting".

– In the following one said by an unknown poet, cited by Zamaḫšarī, 98, Ibn Yaʿīš, *VI*, 55, Howell, *I*, fasc. IV, 1553, in which مُصَلْصَلِه occurs instead of صَلْصَلَتِه:

"كَأَنَّ صَوْتَ ٱلصَّنَا فِي مُصَلْصَلِهْ".

"As though the sound of the cymbal were in his [sc. the horse's] neighing".

– In the sur. 23: 29 (أَنْزِلْنِي مُنْزَلًا مُبَارَكًا) "Enable me to disembark with thy blessing" mentioned by Ibn Muǧāhid, *Sabʿa* 445, that is read with مَنْزِلًا instead of مُنْزَلًا by ʿĀṣim;—the sur. 11: 41 (بِٱسْمِ الله مُجْرَاهَا وَمُرْسَاهَا) "In the name of God whether it move or be at rest" read so by the majority, and that is cited with the following two variants (بِٱسْمِ الله مُجْرِيهَا وَمُرْسِيهَا) and (بِٱسْمِ الله مَجْرِيهَا وَمُرْسِيهَا) (cf. Muʾaddib, *Taṣrīf* 125);—and the sur. 26: 227 (أَيَّ مُنْقَلَبٍ يَنْقَلِبُونَ) "What vicissitudes their affairs will take!".

d) The pattern of the passive participle of what exceeds three consonants occurs formed according to the pattern of a noun of time, as مُدْخَل and مُخْرَج of the sur. 17: 80 (رَبِّ أَدْخِلْنِي مُدْخَلَ صِدْقٍ وَأَخْرِجْنِي مُخْرَجَ صِدْقٍ) "My Lord! Let my entry be by the Gate of Truth and Honour, and likewise my exit by the Gate of Truth and Honour" (cf. Penrice, *Dictionary* 41, 47), and of a *maṣdar*, as مُمَزَّق of the sur. 34: 19 (وَمَزَّقْنَاهُمْ كُلَّ مُمَزَّقٍ) "And we dispersed them all in scattered fragments". For discussions and references see further Nöldeke, *Grammatik* 16-17.

e) The *maṣdar* can occur instead of the imperative, and has its meaning, as in the sur. 30: 17 (فَسُبْحَانَ اللهِ حِينَ تُمْسُونَ وَحِينَ تُصْبِحُونَ) "So (give) glory to God when ye reach eventide and when ye rise in the morning", in which فَسُبْحَانَ occurs instead of فَسَبِّحُوا and in the sur. 47: 4 (فَإِذَا لَقِيتُمُ ٱلَّذِينَ كَفَرُوا فَضَرْبَ ٱلرِّقَابِ) "Therefore when ye meet the Unbelievers (in fight), smite at their necks", in which فَضَرْبَ occurs instead of فَٱضْرِبُوا (cf. Muʾaddib, *Taṣrīf* 105-107).

f) The *maṣdar* can occur instead of the adjective, as in رَجُلٌ دَنَفٌ "a seriously ill man" in which دَنَفٌ occurs instead of دَنِفٌ, in قَوْمٌ رِضًا "pleasant people" in which رِضًا occurs instead of مَرْضِيُّونَ and in رَجُلٌ عَدْلٌ "a just man" in which عَدْلٌ occurs instead of عَادِلٌ (cf. Ibn Ǧinnī, *Ḫaṣāʾiṣ III*, 259).

g) The active participle can occur instead of the passive participle, and has its meaning, as عَاصِم of the sur. 11: 43 (لَا عَاصِمَ ٱلْيَوْمَ مِنْ أَمْرِ ٱللهِ) "This day nothing can save from the Command of God", has the meaning of مَعْصُوم, رَاضِيَة of the sur. 69: 21 (فَهُوَ فِي عِيشَةٍ رَاضِيَةٍ) "And he will be in a life of Bliss", has the meaning of مَرْضِيٌّ بِهَا, and آمِنًا of the sur. 29: 67 (جَعَلْنَ حَرَمًا آمِنًا) "We have made a Sanctuary secure", has the meaning of مَأْمُونًا فِيهِ (cf. Ṯaʿālibī, *Fiqh* 215).

h) The passive participle can occur instead of the active participle and has its meaning, as مَأْتِيًّا in the sur. 19: 61 (إِنَّهُ كَانَ وَعْدُهُ مَأْتِيًّا) "For his promise must (necessarily) come to pass), has the meaning of آتِيًا (cf. ibid).

(25) The examples تَهْذَارٌ and تَلْعَابٌ are Form I *maṣdars* that are formed according to the measure تَفْعَالٌ, which denotes multiplication and intensification, i.e. much هَدْرٌ "fermenting" and لَعِبٌ "sporting" (for a study of these measures see Sībawaihi, *II*, 261, Zamaḫšarī, 98, Ibn Yaʿīš, *VI*, 55-56, Howell, *I*, fasc. IV, 1559-1563, Volck/Kellgren, *Ibn Mālik* 22, Wright, *II*, 116-117). The pattern تِفْعَالٌ with the *t* given the kasra does not denote intensification, and the two examples that are known to be formed according to it are تِبْيَانٌ "explanation" and تِلْقَاءٌ "meeting". تِبْيَانٌ occurs in the sur. 16: 89 (وَنَزَّلْنَا عَلَيْكَ ٱلْكِتَابَ تِبْيَانًا لِكُلِّ شَيْءٍ) "And We have sent down to thee the Book explaining all things". تِلْقَاءٌ occurs in the meaning of لُقْيَانٌ "meeting" in the following verse said by al-Rāʿī, cited by Howell, *I*, fasc. IV, 1561:

"أَمَّلْتُ خَيْرَكَ هَلْ تَأْتِي مَوَاعِدُهُ   فَٱلْيَوْمَ قَصَّرَ عَنْ تِلْقَائِكَ ٱلْأَمَلُ".

"I have hoped for your bounty. Will its promises come? For today hope has fallen short of meeting you".

Both تِشْرابٌ and تَشْرابٌ "drinking" that are formed according to تِفْعالٌ and تَفْعالٌ, have also been heard. Some read defectively تِشْرابِي instead of تَشْرابِي from the following verse said by Ṭarafa, cited by Howell, *I*, fasc. IV, 1561:

"وَمَا زَالَ تَشْرابِي ٱلْخُمُورَ وَلَذَّتِي وَبَيْعِي وَإِنْفَاقِي طَرِيفِي وَمُتْلَدِي".

"And my tippling wines ceased not, and my pleasure, and my selling and my expending my property new and old".

Both حِثِّيثَى (see Ibn Manẓūr, *II*, 773, Lane, *I*, 512) and دِلِّيلَى (see Ibn Manẓūr, *II*, 1414, Lane, *I*, 901) are Form I *maṣdars* formed upon the measure فِعِّيلَى, which also denotes multiplication and intensification. Other examples are قِتِّيتَى "much mischief-making", هِجِّيرَى "much evil-speaking" and خِلِّيفَى "being much engrossed with the business of the *Ḫilāfa*" (cf. Daqr, *Muʿǧam* 57, my notes (270 b)). The last example occurs in the saying said by ʿUmar in the tradition لَوْلَا ٱلْخِلِّيفَى لَأَذَّنْتُ "Had I not been much engrossed with the business of the *Ḫilāfa*, I would chant the call to prayer". فِعِّيلَى can as well be formed from Form VI تَفَاعَلَ, e.g. رِمِّيَّا (cf. Ibn Wallād, *Maqṣūr* 56) from Form VI تَرَامٍ, in the example كَانَ بَيْنَهُمْ رِمِّيَّا "there was between them much shooting one at another".

(26) The *maṣdars'* patterns of the derived forms of the groundform of the triliteral and quadriliteral (for a study see Ibn Mālik, *Lāmīya* 246-249, Volck/Kellgren, *Ibn Mālik* 20-23, Howell, *I*, fasc. IV, 1529-1545, Wright, *II*, 115-118) are analogous with their verbs (cf. Zamaḫšarī, 97). The reason of this resemblance in forms, is that these verbs' forms follow special patterns, and do not vary as the forms of the groundform of the triliteral in which the vowel of the 2nd radical in many cases alternate in the perfect and in the imperfect (cf. Ibn Yaʿīš, *VI*, 47). The order of the *maṣdars'* derived patterns of the triliteral and quadriliteral which follow the specific forms of verbs, is presented in the following manner by Zamaḫšarī, 97: أَفْعَلَ إفْعالٌ, افْتَعَلَ افْتِعال, انْفَعَلَ انْفِعال, اسْتَفْعَلَ اسْتِفْعال, افْعَلَّ افْعِلال, افْعالَّ افْعِيلال, افْعَوَّلَ افْعِوّال, افْعَوْعَلَ افْعِيعال, افْعَنْلَلَ افْعِنْلال, تَفاعَلَ تَفاعُل and تَفَعْلَلَ افْعِلّال.

b) The well-known patterns of the derived forms of the *maṣdar* of the triliteral with their numbering are according to Western grammars:

Form II: تَفْعِيلٌ, تَفْعِلَةٌ, تَفْعُلَةٌ, تَفْعَالٌ, تِفْعَالٌ, فِعَّالٌ, فِعِّيلَى and فِعِّيلَاءُ.

Form III: مُفَاعَلَةٌ, فِعَالٌ, فِيعَالٌ and فِعَالٌ.

Form IV: إفْعَالٌ.

Form V: تَفَعُّلٌ and تِفِعَّالٌ.

Form VI: تَفَاعُلٌ, تَفَاعَلٌ, and تَفَاعِلٌ.

Form VII: انْفِعَالٌ.

Form VIII: افْتِعَالٌ and فِعَّالٌ.

Form IX: افعلالٌ.

Form X: استفعالٌ.

Form XI: افعيلالٌ.

Form XII: افعيعالٌ.

Form XIII: افعوالٌ.

Form XIV: افعنلالٌ.

Form XV: افعنلاء.

c) The well-known patterns of the *maṣdar* of the groundform and derived patterns of the quadriliteral with their numbering are:

Form I: فَعلَلَةٌ, فِعلالٌ, and فَعلالٌ.

Form II: تَفَعلُلٌ.

Form III: افعنلالٌ.

Form IV: افعلالٌ.

(27) The examples of the *maṣdar* of the derived patterns of the triliteral and groundform of the quadriliteral which are introduced here (cf. Zamaḫšarī, 97, Ibn Yaʿīš, *VI,* 47-50), are those that are not analogous with their verbs. كِلَّامٌ is formed according to the pattern of the *maṣdar* of Form II فِعَّالٌ with the 1st radical vowelled by a kasra and the 2nd radical doubled. The pattern occurs by the Yemenites (cf. Rabin, 37), and is curent in Daṯīna (cf. Landberg, *Dathina* 536). An example that can be added is كِذَّابٌ which occurs in the sur. 78: 28 (وكَذَّبُوا بآياتنا كِذَّابًا) "But they (impudently) treated our signs as false". The alleviated form occurs in the sur. 78: 35 (لا يَسْمَعُونَ فيها لَغْوًا ولا كِذَابًا) "No Vanity shall they hear therein, nor Untruth". According to Ibn Manẓūr, *V,* 3841, al-Farrāʾ said that ʿAlī b. Abī Ṭālib alleviated the form in both these surs., i.e. said كِذابٌ, whereas ʿAṣim and the inhabitants of al-Madīna said كِذَّابٌ, which is a correct Yemenite dialectal variant. The alleviated form occurs in the following verse said by an unknown poet, cited by Howell, *I,* fasc. IV, 1534:

"فَصَدَقْتُهَا وكَذَبْتُهَا وَٱلْمَرْءُ يَنْفَعُهُ كِذَابُهُ".

"Then I spoke truth to her, and then I lied to her: and man is profited by his lying".

قِتَالٌ with the *q* vowelled by a kasra and the 2nd radical lightened, is formed according to the *maṣdar* of Form III فِعَالٌ, and قِيتَالٌ with the infixation of the *ī* is formed according to the *maṣdar* of Form III فِيعَالٌ. تِحِمَّالٌ is formed according to the pattern of Form V تِفِعَّالٌ. Another example that can be added is تِمِلَّاقٌ "affection", which occurs in the following verse said by an unknown poet, cited by Zamaḫšarī, 97, Ibn Yaʿīš, *VI,* 47, *IX,* 157, *Mulūkī* 194, Volck/Kellgren, *Ibn Mālik* 21, Freytag, *Hamasae* 551, Ḫuḍarī, *Ḥāšiya II,* 38, Howell, *I,* fasc. IV, 1538:

"ثَلاثَةُ أَحْبَابٍ فَحُبٌّ عَلاقَةٌ وَحُبٌّ تِمِلَّاقٌ وَحُبٌّ هُوَ ٱلْقَتْلُ".

"There are three loves; for there is a love that is attachment, and a love that is affection, and a love that is murder".

زَلْزَالٌ is formed according to the Form of the quadriliteral فَعْلَالٌ (for the form see (177 b)).

(28) The conjugations of the groundform of the triliteral verbs and its derived forms are at first presented, and then are followed by the groundform of the quadriliteral and its derived forms (see (29)-(41)). For some well-known definitions of the verb see (12 b). For the debate concerning the verb as being the origin of the derivation according to the Kufans and the *maṣdar* as being the origin of derivation according to the Basrans see (12)-(21).

(29) The verbs' conjugations of Form I can be termed as "verbal stems", "modifications" (cf. Leemhuis, *Stems* 1), "stirps" (cf. Diakonoff, *Semito-Hamitic* 97) or "forms" (cf. Goshen-Gottstein, *System* 70 note 1). ضَرَبَ يَضْرِبُ is formed according to the conjugation فَعَلَ يَفْعِلُ, قَتَلَ يَقْتُلُ is formed according to the conjugation فَعَلَ يَفْعُلُ and عَلِمَ يَعْلَمُ is formed according to the conjugation فَعِلَ يَفْعَلُ (for a study of the forms see Wright, *II,* 30, 57-59, Vernier, *I,* 129-134). Concerning the form فَعَلَ (for discussions see Bakkūš, *Taṣrīf* 87-94, Bohas, *Étude* 53-60), it may be remarked that whenever the Quraišīs vowel the 2nd radical of verbs in the perfect with a fatḥa, e.g. زَهَدَ "to abstain" and حَقَدَ "to harbor feelings of hatred", the Banū Tamīm vowel it with a kasra, i.e. زَهِدَ and حَقِدَ (cf. Ṣubḥī, *Fiqh* 82). The imperfect of فَعَلَ with fatḥa of the 2nd radical can become يَفْعِلُ or يَفْعُلُ, e.g. ضَرَبَ يَضْرِبُ "to hit" and قَتَلَ يَقْتُلُ "to kill". Verbs of the form يَفْعُلُ with the ḍamma are more numerous than those of the form يَفْعِلُ with the kasra: 802 / 516, and in the Qur'ān 102 / 88 (cf. Bakkūš, *Taṣrīf* 91). Verbs of the conjugation فَعَلَ يَفْعُلُ (for discussions concerning its use see ʿAbd al-Raḥīm, *Ṣarf* 63-64) denote generally superiority, e.g. شَعَرَهُ يَشْعُرُهُ "he excelled him in composing poetry". This form is referred to as فَعَلَ ٱلدَّالُ عَلَى ٱلْغَلَبَةِ (cf. Wright, *II,* 58), or is specified for المبالغة "the superiority" (cf. Astarābāḏī, *Šarḥ al-šāfiya I,* 70; for a study of this form see Roman, *Étude II,* 985-992).

فَعِلَ (for discussions see Bakkūš, *Taṣrīf* 85-87, Bohas, *Étude* 60; for discussions concerning its use see ʿAbd al-Raḥīm, *Ṣarf* 65-66) with the kasra of the 2nd radical in the perfect and its fatḥa in the imperfect, namely يَفْعَلُ, can denote: 1– a temporary state or condition, e.g. غَضِبَ "to be angry" and فَرِحَ "to be happy", 2– refer to physical activities or needs, e.g. رَكِبَ "to ride" and شَرِبَ "to drink", or 3– is indicative of the subject's submission to the verb without any participation of his will, e.g. تَبِعَ "to follow" and خَسِرَ "to loose". In most of the cases it becomes يَفْعَلُ, except for some anomalies mentioned below. The Banū Tamīm vowel the 2nd radical of the verb in the imperfect with a fatḥa showing a preference for the form فَعِلَ يَفْعَلُ, e.g. يَفْرَغُ فَرَاغًا "he is finished with" whereas the Quraišīs vowel it with a ḍamma showing a preference for the form فَعَلَ يَفْعُلُ, i.e. يَفْرُغُ فُرُوغًا (cf. Ṣubḥī, *Fiqh* 82, Anīs, *Lahǧāt* 88). There exist some anomalies concerning the form فَعِلَ (for the dialectal variant known as the تَلْتَلَة see my notes

(99)). Sībawaihi, *II,* 279 mentions some cases of verbs in which the 2nd radical is made vowelless in the perfect and the 1st radical is given a kasra, e.g. لَعْبَ for لَعِبَ "to play", نِعْمَ for نَعِمَ "to lead a life of ease", بِنْسَ for بَنِسَ "to be miserable" (for a detailed study concerning نِعْمَ and بِنْسَ see Nöldeke, *Neue Beiträge* 217-229; it can be mentioned that they are considered as two nouns by the Kufans, whereas they are considered as two undeclinable verbs in the perfect by the Basrans, for their debate see Ibn al-Anbārī, *Inṣāf* Q. 14, 47-57) and شِهْدَ for شَهِدَ "to witness". شِهْدَ occurs instead of شَهِدَ in the following verse said by al-Aḫtal, *Dīwān* 64, cited by Sībawaihi, *II,* 279, Muʾaddib, *Taṣrīf* 207 (with شَهْدَ mentioned by Muʾaddib instead), Åkesson, *Elision* 23:

"اذا غَابَ عنَّا غابَ عنَّا فُراتُنا   وإن شِهْدَ أجْدَى فَضْلُه وجَداوِلُهْ".

"If he withdrew from us then the sweet water has withdrawn, and if he was present then his graciousness was of use and so were his curriculums".

An anomaly concerning the form فِعْل from فَعِلَ that can be mentioned, is that its 2nd vowelless radical is given a kasra resulting in فِعِل. This peculiarity pertains to the dialect of the Banū Huḏail. An example mentioned by Sībawaihi, *II,* 457 and Nöldeke, *Neue Beiträge* 217 [with القوم "the people" instead of الحَيّ by him] is نِعِمَ "to lead a life of ease", which occurs in the following verse said by Ṭarafa:

" نِعِمَ الساعُونَ في الحَيّ الشُّطُرْ".

"So wonderful you take care of the remoted quarter!".

The Banū Tamīm and the Banū Huḏail give the same anomalous kasra to the 1st radical when it is followed by a kasra in adjectives and nouns, e.g. لِئيمٌ instead of لَئيمٌ "ignoble", نِحيفٌ instead of نَحيفٌ "skinny" and رِغيفٌ instead of رَغيفٌ "flat loaf of bread" (cf. Ibn Sīda, *Muḫaṣṣaṣ* XIV, 213, my notes (174)). According to Ibn Ǧinnī, *Ḫaṣāʾiṣ II,* 143, this inclination of a vowel to the vowel of a guttural consonant pertains to الإدغام الأصغر "the partial assimilation" (for it see (174)).

b) A question worth taking up in this context is why the conjugation فَعِلَ with the kasra given to the 2nd radical in the perfect becomes يَفْعَلُ with the fatḥa of the 2nd radical in the imperfect, and why the conjugation فَعَلَ with the fatḥa given to the 2nd radical in the perfect becomes يَفْعِلُ with the kasra of the 2nd radical in the imperfect. According to the theories presented by Ibn Ǧinnī, *Munṣif I,* 187, the vowel of the 2nd radical of the imperfect must differ from the vowel of the perfect, as each tense is opposite to the other. So the imperfect of فَعِلَ is formed according to يَفْعَلُ and the imperfect of فَعَلَ is in most of the cases formed according to يَفْعِلُ. There is as well according to him, a certain harmony in the sounds between the fatḥa and the fatḥa in two different words of an example, e.g. مَرَرْتُ بعُمَرَ "I passed by ʿUmar" and ضَرَبْتُ عُمَرَ "I hit ʿUmar", and in the inclination of the kasra to the fatḥa and the fatḥa to the kasra in, e.g. الهندات ضَرَبْتُ "I hit the Hinds" and مَرَرْتُ بالهندات "I passed by the Hinds".

(30) فَتَحَ يَفْتَحُ is formed according to فَعَلَ يَفْعَلُ. As a rule it can be said that when the 2nd or 3rd radical of the verb is a guttural consonant, namely a hamza, *h*, *ʿ*, *ḥ*, *ġ* or *ḫ*, the 2nd radical of the imperfect is vowelled by a fatḥa (cf. Sībawaihi, *II*, 270-272). According to Ibn Ǧinnī, *Ḫaṣā'iṣ II*, 143, the fatḥa that is chosen, which is made to accord with the fatḥa of the 2nd or 3rd guttural consonant, pertains to الإدغام الأصغر "the partial assimilation" (for discussions concerning it see (174)).

b) Some anomalies occur that do not follow the rule, e.g. قَعَدَ يَقْعُدُ "to sit", دَخَلَ يَدْخُلُ "to enter" with the 2nd radical of the imperfect given the ḍamma, and رَجَعَ يَرْجِعُ "to return" with it given the kasra. Furthermore, verbs of this conjugation could have the 2nd radical of the imperfect given the fatḥa or the kasra, e.g. نَعَقَ يَنْعَقُ or يَنْعِقُ "to croak", or the fatḥa or the ḍamma, e.g. سَلَخَ يَسْلَخُ or يَسْلُخُ "to flay", or even one of all three vowels, e.g. رَجَحَ يَرْجَحُ or يَرْجِحُ or يَرْجُحُ "to incline (of a scale of a balance) (cf. Wright, *II*, 58; for further discussions see Wright, *II*, 57-58, Aro, *Vokalisierung* 56-57, Fleisch, *Traité II*, 258-260).

(31) رَكَنَ يَرْكَنُ is formed according to فَعَلَ يَفْعَلُ. It is anomalous as it follows the rule of verbs having a guttural consonant as their 2nd or 3rd radical (cf. (30)), while not having any itself. It could be a combination of two forms (cf. Wright, *II*, 58) or of two dialectal varieties (cf. Lane, *I*, 1148).

(32) أَبَى يَأْبَى, a verb with 3rd *y* radical, is formed according to فَعَلَ يَفْعَلُ. It is anomalous as it follows the rule of verbs that have a guttural consonant as their 2nd or 3rd radical (cf. (30)), when it is its 1st radical that has one. Sībawaihi, *II*, 273 notes that they compared يَأْبَى "he refuses" with يَقْرَأُ "he reads". This verb can present anomalous forms, namely: يِئْبَى and يِيبَى (cf. Wright, *II*, 93). The formation تِئْبَى with the imperfect prefix vowelled by a kasra that is meant to conform with the kasra of the 2nd radical of the perfect أَبِيَ, pertains to the dialectal variant known as the تَلْتَلَةٌ (for discussions see Sībawaihi, *II*, 275-277, my notes (99)). تِئْبَى is said by most of the Arabs except the Ḥiğāzīs (cf. Volck/Kellgren, *Ibn Mālik* 11). The تَلْتَلَةٌ does not usually apply to the 3rd person of the masc. sing. of the imperfect, because of the dislike that the Arabs have for the *y* being combined with a kasra, which they find heavy (cf. Fleisch, *Traité I*, 137-138). However the case of يِئْبَى occurs which is anomalous. This verb with a hamza as its 1st radical is formed according to يِيجَلُ "he is afraid", a verb with 1st weak radical on the basis of its integration within the conjugation فَعِلَ and having a *y* that follows the imperfect prefixed *y* (cf. Sībawaihi, *II*, 276)

(33) All the three verbs بَقِيَ, فَنِيَ and قَلِيَ are with 3rd *y* radical and are formed according to فَعِلَ. The *y*, which is preceded by a kasra in them, is usually changed into an *alif maqṣūra* by the

Ṭayyīs, i.e. بَقَى, فَنَى and قَلَى (cf. Ibn Manẓūr, *I,* 331, Rabin, 196-197, Åkesson, *Conversion* 28-29).

(34) كَرُمَ يَكْرُمُ is formed according to فَعُلَ يَفْعُلُ. This conjugation denotes the quality and is intransitive (for a study see Sībawaihi, *II,* 272, Wright, *II,* 59, Vernier, *I,* 134, Bakkūš, *Taṣrīf* 84, Åkesson, *Verb and Infinitive* 38-39, ʿAbd al-Raḥīm, *Ṣarf* 67, Bohas, *Étude* 60-62, Guillaume, *Aspects* 383-391). The form فَعُلَ is indicative of a lasting state whereas the form فَعِلَ is indicative of a momentary one (cf. de Sacy, *I,* 145; for a study concerning both forms see Fleisch, *Traité II,* 249-257).

b) A question worth taking up in this context is why the heavy ḍamma, and not the fatḥa or the kasra, is chosen to vowel the 2nd radical of the conjugation فَعُلَ. According to a theory presented by Ibn Ğinnī, *Munṣif I,* 189, verbs of this conjugation are intransitive, and intransitive verbs occur less frequently than transitive verbs, which implies that the intransitive is heavier than the transitive. By analogy, the heavy ḍamma is chosen for the heavy intransitive verb, so that what is heavy occurs less in the language than what is light, and the light fatḥa or kasra is chosen for the 2nd radical فَعَلَ or فَعِلَ because the transitive verbs are frequently used.

(35) حَسِبَ يَحْسِبُ is formed according to فَعِلَ يَفْعِلُ (for a study see Ibn ʿUṣfūr, *I,* 176-177, Howell, *II-III,* 253, Wright, *II,* 58, ʿAbd al-Raḥīm, *Ṣarf* 67). Vollers, *Volkssprache* 129, referring to Baiḍāwī, notes that Ibn ʿAmir, Ḥamza and ʿĀṣim read يَحْسَبُ instead of يَحْسِبُ from all the sur. of the Qurʾān. Chouémi, *Verbe* 65 points to the fact that some dialectal particularities occur with verbs of this form which have been preserved in the Qurʾān. Furthermore, references to this form in some of the other Semitic languages are given.

(36) كُدْتَ تَكَادُ is a verb with 2nd radical *w.* Its base form is كَوُدْتَ تَكْوَدُ, and it is formed according to فَعُلَ يَفْعَلُ. In the perfect كَوُدْتَ, the *w* is changed into an *ā,* i.e. كَادْتَ, which causes a cluster of two vowelless consonants, the *ā* and the *d.* So the *ā* is elided and the *k* is vowelled by a ḍamma to notify of the elided *w,* i.e. كُدْتَ. In the imperfect تَكْوَدُ, the fatḥa is shifted from the *w* to the *k,* i.e. تَكَوْدُ, and then the vowelless *w* is changed into the *ā* due to the influence of the fatḥa preceding it, i.e. تَكَادُ. Concerning this particular change that is carried out in the base forms كَوُدْتَ تَكْوَدُ resulting in كُدْتَ تَكَادُ, Niksārī, *Mifrāḥ* fol. 5b ll. 21-23 writes:

"لأنّ أصلهما كَوُدْتَ تَكْوَدُ فأُعلَ الأوّل بقلب الواو ألفا ثم اجتمع ساكنان فحُذف الألف ثم ضُمَّ الكاف ليدلّ على الواو المحذوفة والثاني بنقل الحركة من الواو الى ما قبلها ثمّ بقلبها ألفا فصار تَكَادُ."

"As both their [sc. كُدْتَ and تَكَادُ 's] base forms are كَوُدْتَ تَكْوَدُ. Then a change due to the unsound weak consonant is carried out in the first one [i.e. كَوُدْتَ] by changing the *w* into an *ā,* which caused the cluster of two vowelless consonants [i.e. كَادْتَ]. So the *ā* was elided and the *k* was vowelled by a ḍamma to notify of the elided *w* [i.e. كُدْتَ]. And [a change is carried out] in the second one [i.e. تَكْوَدُ], by shifting the vowel from the *w* to the consonant preceding it [i.e. تَكَوْدُ], and then changing it [sc. the *w]* into an *ā*, so that it became تَكَادُ".

كُدْتَ تَكَادُ is mentioned by Sībawaihi, *II,* 240 as a dialectal variant by some Arabs (cf. Ibn Ǧinnī, *Munṣif I,* 189). Ibn Manẓūr, *V,* 3952 precises that it is the dialectal variant of the Banū ʿAdīy (cf. Saraqusṭī, *Afʿāl II,* 193 in the notes). The most usual form used by the majority of the Arabs is however كِدْتَ with the *k* vowelled by a kasra as remarked by Saraqusṭī, *Afʿāl II,* 193. It occurs in the following verse said probably by Ṣābiʾ, *Ġurar* 321:

"أما ٱشْتَقْتَ يا مَوْلَايَ حينَ فَقَدْتَني فَقَدْ كِدْتُ مِنْ شَوْقِي إليكَ أطيرُ".

"Were you not filled with longing when you lost me, my lord? I almost flew towards you so much I yearned for you!".

(37) فَضَلَ يَفْضَلُ should have occurred formed according to فَعَلَ يَفْعُلُ (for discussions concerning the conjugation see (29)), but it occurs anomalously as though it is formed according to فَعِلَ يَفْعَلُ. Concerning it, Sībawaihi, *II,* 240 remarks that it is an anomaly, and that فَضِلَ يَفْضَلُ would have followed more the analogy. However, Niksārī, *Mifrāḥ* fol. 6a ll. 3-6, who refers to Ibn Ḥāğib's saying, means that by him it is not an anomaly. He writes:

"إنَّ المفهوم من كلام المصنف أنَّ فضِلَ يَفْضُلُ شاذ إلاَّ أنه عند ابن الحاجب رحمه الله ليس شاذ بل من باب التداخل وذلك لأنَّ العرب يقولون فَضَلَ يَفْضُلُ بالفتح في الماضي والضمّ في الغابر وفضِلَ يَفْضَلُ بالكسر في الماضي والفتح في الغابر فأُخذ الماضي من الثاني والمضارع من الأوّل فقيل فضِلَ يَفْضُلُ".

"It is understood from the saying of the writer [sc. Ibn Masʿūd] that فَضِلَ يَفْضُلُ "to remain" is anomalous. However, according to Ibn al-Ḥāğib, may God have mercy upon him, it is not anomalous, but is subjected to the intrusion of dialectal variants. This is so because the Arabs say فَضَلَ يَفْضُلُ with the fatḥa [of the 2nd radical] in the perfect and with its ḍamma in the imperfect, and فَضِلَ يَفْضَلُ with the kasra [of the 2nd radical] in the perfect and with its fatḥa in the imperfect. So the perfect is taken from the second example [sc. فَضِلَ], and the imperfect from the first one [sc. يَفْضُلُ], and it is said فَضِلَ يَفْضُلُ".

فَضِلَ occurs in the following verse said by ʿĪsā b. ʿUmar to Abū l-Aswad, cited by Ibn Ǧinnī, *Munṣif I,* 256:

"ذَكَرْتُ ٱبْنَ عَبَّاسٍ بِبابِ ٱبْنِ عامِرٍ وما مَرَّ مِنْ عَيْشِي ذَكَرْتُ وَمَا فَضِلَ".

"I remembered Ibn ʿAbbās at the door of Ibn ʿĀmir. And I remembered all that passed of my life and what remained [of it]".

Other anomalous examples are حَضِرَ يَحْضُرُ "to be present" and نَعِمَ يَنْعَمُ and يَنْعُمُ "to be affluent" (cf. Wright, *II,* 58-59). As a counterpart of فَضِلَ يَفْضُلُ, Ibn Duraid, *Ištiqāq* 64 takes up only حَضِرَ يَحْضُرُ "to attend".

(38) The base form of دمْتَ تدوم, a verb with 2nd radical *w,* is دومْتَ تَدْوُمُ formed according to the measure فعل يفْعُلَ (for discussions see Ibn Ǧinnī, *Munṣif I,* 256). Concerning it Ibn Manẓūr, *II,* 1457 writes:

"قال أبو الْحسَن: في هذه الْكلمَةُ نظرٌ، ذهَبَ أهْلُ اللغَة في قَوْلهمْ دمْتَ تَدُومُ إلى أنها نادرةٌ كمتَ تَموتُ، وفضل يفْضُلُ، وحضر يحْضُرُ، وذهَبَ أبو بكْر إلى أنها مُتركّبَةٌ فقال: دُمْتَ تدُومُ كقُلْتَ تقُولُ، ودمْتَ تَدامُ كخفْتَ تخافُ، ثمّ تَركّبَت اللّغتان فظَنَ قَوْمٌ أنْ تَدُومُ على دمْتَ، وتَدامُ على دُمْتَ".

"Abū l-Ḥasan said: "There is a speculation concerning this word. The linguists believed that دمْتَ تَدُومُ is rare as متَ تَمُوتُ "to dye", فضل يفْضُلُ "to remain" and حضر يحْضُرُ "to attend". Abū Bakr believed that it is a combination [of two forms]. He said: دُمْتَ تَدُومُ is according to قُلْتَ تقُولُ "to say", and دمْتَ تَدامُ is according to خفْتَ تخافُ "to be afraid". Then both dialectal variants were combined together, and some people believed that تَدُومُ is formed according to دمْتَ, and تَدامُ is formed according to دُمْتَ".

Concerning the variant يدَامُ, it occurs in the following verse said by an unknown poet, cited by Ibn Ǧinnī, *Ḫaṣāʾiṣ I,*380, Ibn Manẓūr, *II,* 1457, Guillaume, *Aspects* 400:

"يا ميَ لا غرْوَ ولا مَلاما   في الْحبَ إنَ الحبَ لنْ يدَاما".

"O Mayya, there is no wonder and no reproach in love,—as verily love is not to last!—".

Concerning متَ تموتُ, there exists another dialectal variant known to be of the Ṭayyīs, namely متَ تَماتُ (cf. Vollers, *Volkssprache* 191), which occurs in the following verse said by an unknown poet, cited by Ibn Manẓūr, *VI,* 4295, Howell, *II-III,* 254:

"بُنَيّتي سَيّدَةَ الْبَنَاتِ   عَيْشِي ولَا نَأمَنُ أنْ تَمَاتِي".

"My little daughter, princess of daughters, you are my life, and we do not feel safe from fear that you should die".

متَ can also be said مُتَ (for discussions see Rabin, 114-115, Vollers, *Volkssprache* 141-142). The readings of متَ / مُتَ in the sur. 2: 157, sur. 19: 23, sur. 19: 66 are inconsistent. The tendency of the upholders of the Ḥiǧāzī tradition seem to be مُتَ, but not in all cases.

(39) The presentation of the order of the derived forms of the triliteral verb differs between Arabic and the Western grammars. For instance concerning the Arabs' presentation, Zanǧānī, *ʿIzzī* 2-3 presents at first the perfect that is formed of four consonants: 1– أفْعَلَ, e.g. أكرَمَ "to honour", 2– فَعّلَ, e.g. فرّحَ "to gladden" and 3– فاعَلَ, e.g. قاتَلَ "to fight". He then proceeds with the perfect that is formed of five consonants: 1– تَفَعّلَ, e.g. تَكَسّرَ "to break", 2– تَفاعَلَ,

e.g. تَبَاعَدَ "to become distant", 3- اِنْفَعَلَ, e.g. اِنْقَطَعَ "to disrupt", 4- اِفْتَعَلَ, e.g. اِجْتَمَعَ "to assemble" and 5- اِفْعَلَّ, e.g. اِحْمَرَّ "to be red". He concudes his presentation with the perfect that is formed of six consonants: 1- اِسْتَفْعَلَ, e.g. اِسْتَخْرَجَ "to remove", 2- اِفْعَالَّ, e.g. اِحْمَارَّ "to be very red", 3- اِفْعَوْعَلَ, e.g. اِعْشَوْشَبَ "to be covered with luxuriant herbage", 4- اِفْعَنْلَلَ e.g. اِقْعَنْسَسَ "to have a hump in front", 5- اِفْعَنْلَى, e.g. اِسْلَنْقَى "to lay on one's back", and 6- اِفْعَوَّلَ, e.g. اِجْلَوَّذَ "to last long".

b) Ibn Masʿūd enumerates the derived forms of the triliteral verb as twelve, although the well-known are fourteen. The two more anomalous forms which are not mentioned by him are the following: Form XIV: اِفْعَنْلَلَ, e.g. اِسْحَنْكَكَ "to be dark" and Form XV اِفْعَنْلَى, e.g. اِحْبَنْطَى "to be swollen or filled with rage". This is a presentation of them with their numbering and their various meanings according to Western grammars. Some of the paradigms of the verbs are presented in both the perfect and the imperfect:

(2): Form II: فَعَّلَ, e.g. قَطَّعَ "to cut" (for a study of this form with its corresponding forms in some of the other Semitic languages see Wright, *Comparative Grammar* 198-202). In the Semitic languages Form II can be designated by the symbol D that refers to the doubled 2nd radical (cf. Ungnad, *Bezeichnung*).

Its paradigm in the perfect, active, is the following:

	sing.	dual	pl.
1st	قَطَّعْتُ		قَطَّعْنَا
2nd masc.	قَطَّعْتَ	قَطَّعْتُمَا	قَطَّعْتُمْ
2nd fem.	قَطَّعْتِ	قَطَّعْتُمَا	قَطَّعْتُنَّ
3rd masc.	قَطَّعَ	قَطَّعَا	قَطَّعُوا
3rd fem.	قَطَّعَتْ	قَطَّعَتَا	قَطَّعْنَ

Its paradigm in the imperfect of the indicative, active, is the following:

	sing.	dual	pl.
1st	أُقَطِّعُ		نُقَطِّعُ
2nd masc.	تُقَطِّعُ	تُقَطِّعَانِ	تُقَطِّعُونَ
2nd fem.	تُقَطِّعِينَ	تُقَطِّعَانِ	تُقَطِّعْنَ
3rd masc.	يُقَطِّعُ	يُقَطِّعَانِ	يُقَطِّعُونَ
3rd fem.	تُقَطِّعُ	تُقَطِّعَانِ	يُقَطِّعْنَ

The meaning of Form II:
– It intensifies the meaning of the root.
– It can be similar to the groundform, e.g. زِلْتُهُ and زَيَّلْتُهُ "I separated it" (cf. Zamaḫšarī, 129, Howell, *II-III*, 271). It can also have its meaning or the meaning of Form V, e.g. بَدَّلَ, بَدَلَ and تَبَدَّلَ "to exchange". Some verbs are also intransitive (cf. Blachère, 51). For some examples found in the dialects see Marçais, *Dialecte* 91, Cantineau, *Dialecte* 147.

– It makes causative transitive verbs, e.g. عَلِمَ "to know" in the groundform, عَلَّمَ "to teach".

– It indicates the time when a thing is done, e.g. صَبَّحْنَا مَسَّيْنَا وَسَحَّرْنَا "we went to find him in the morning, in the evening and at dawn" (cf. Sībawaihi, *II*, 251).

– It has an estimative meaning, e.g. صَدَقَ "to believe" in the groundform, صَدَّقَ "to consider as sincere", and كَذَبَ "to lie" in the groundform, كَذَّبَ "to consider as a liar".

– It makes someone or something do a thing, e.g. كَتَّبَ "to make someone write".

– It is derived from nouns and expresses their meanings, e.g. خُبْزٌ "bread", خَبَّزَ "to bake bread" (cf. Vernier, *I*, 138).

– It expresses the negation of the idea existing in the groundform, e.g. فَزِعَ "to fear", فَزَّعَ "to deliver from fear" (cf. Vernier, *I*, 138).

– It expresses a blessing, e.g. سَقَّيْتُهُ ورَعَّيْتُهُ " I said to him: سَقْياً ورَعْياً "May God preserve you and give you rain" (cf. Sībawaihi, *II*, 249, Howell, *II-III*, 271, Vernier, *I*, 138).

– It denotes a movement from one place to another, e.g. شَرَّقَ "to go to the Orient", غَرَّبَ "to go to the Occident" (cf. Vernier, *I*, 137) and كَوَّفَ "to go to al-Kūfa" (cf. Howell, *II-III*, 271).

– It denotes becoming its root, e.g. عَجَّزَتِ ٱلْمَرْأَةُ "the woman became a عَجُوزٌ "an old woman" (cf. Howell, *II-III*, 271).

(3): Form III فَاعَلَ, e.g. قَاتَلَ "to fight" (for a study of this form with its corresponding forms in some of the other Semitic languages see Wright, *Comparative Grammar* 202-204).

Its paradigm in the perfect, active, is the following:

	sing.	dual	pl.
1st	قَاتَلْتُ		قَاتَلْنَا
2nd masc.	قَاتَلْتَ	قَاتَلْتُمَا	قَاتَلْتُمْ
2nd fem.	قَاتَلْتِ	قَاتَلْتُمَا	قَاتَلْتُنَّ
3rd masc.	قَاتَلَ	قَاتَلَا	قَاتَلُوا
3rd fem.	قَاتَلَتْ	قَاتَلَتَا	قَاتَلْنَ

Its paradigm in the imperfect of the indicative, active, is the following:

	sing.	dual	pl.
1st	أُقَاتِلُ		نُقَاتِلُ
2nd masc.	تُقَاتِلُ	تُقَاتِلَانِ	تُقَاتِلُونَ
2nd fem.	تُقَاتِلِينَ	تُقَاتِلَانِ	تُقَاتِلْنَ
3rd masc.	يُقَاتِلُ	يُقَاتِلَانِ	يُقَاتِلُونَ
3rd fem.	تُقَاتِلُ	تُقَاتِلَانِ	يُقَاتِلْنَ

The meaning of Form III:

– It denotes the idea of reciprocity, e.g. ضَارَبْتُهُ "I hit him and he hit me" (cf. Sībawaihi, *II*, 253).

– It denotes the idea of rivality, e.g. شَرُفَ "to be high-ranking" in the groundform, شَارَفَ "to vie for precedence in honor or nobility" (cf. Vernier, *I*, 139).

– It denotes enduring the action of the groundform, e.g. قَسا "to be harsh" and قاسى "to suffer" (cf. Vernier, *I,* 139).

– It comprehends the meaning of the prepositions, e.g. جَالَسَ السُّلْطَانَ and جَلَسَ عِنْدَ السُّلطان "he sat near the sultan" (cf. Vernier, *I,* 138-139).

– It can be similar to the groundform, e.g. سفر and سافر "to go forth to journey" (cf. Zamaḫšarī, 129, Howell, *II-III,* 272).

– It can be similar to Form II فعَّل, e.g. ضاعفْتُ "I doubled [the thing]", like ضعَّفْتُه (cf. Zamaḫšarī, 129, Howell, *II-III,* 273).

– It can be similar to Form IV أفْعل, e.g. راعنا سَمْعَك "make your ear to be possessed of mindfulness for us", like أرْعِنا (cf. Howell, *II-III,* 272).

(4): Form IV أفْعل, e.g. أكْرَم "to honour" (for a study of the Semitic causative conjugation see Retsö, *Diathesis* 49-138). In the Semitic languages Form IV can be deignated by the symbol C (causative) and by the symbol H that refers to the hamza in Arabic, and to the prefix, etc. in the other Semitic languages (cf. Ungnad, *Bezeichnung).*

Its paradigm in the perfect, active, is the following:

	sing.	dual	pl.
1st	أكْرَمْتُ		أكْرَمْنَا
2nd masc.	أكْرَمْتَ	أكْرَمْتُمَا	أكْرَمْتُمْ
2nd fem.	أكْرَمْتِ	أكْرَمْتُمَا	أكْرَمْتُنَّ
3rd masc.	أكْرَمَ	أكْرَمَا	أكْرَمُوا
3rd fem.	أكْرَمَتْ	أكْرَمَتَا	أكْرَمْنَ

Its paradigm in the imperfect of the indicative, active, is the following:

	sing.	dual	pl.
1st	أُكْرِمُ		نُكْرِمُ
2nd masc.	تُكْرِمُ	تُكْرِمَانِ	تُكْرِمُونَ
2nd fem.	تُكْرِمِينَ	تُكْرِمَانِ	تُكْرِمْنَ
3rd masc.	يُكْرِمُ	يُكْرِمَانِ	يُكْرِمُونَ
3rd fem.	تُكْرِمُ	تُكْرِمَانِ	يُكْرِمْنَ

The meaning of Form IV.

– It can be similar to the groundform, e.g. شَغَلْتُهُ and أشْغَلْتُهُ "I busied him" (cf. Zamaḫšarī, 129, Howell, *II-III,* 268). For a general presentation of some verbs of Form I and IV in Arabic with their different meanings see Ṯaʿlab, *Faṣīḥ* 11-14 بابُ فَعَلْتُ وأفْعَلْتُ باختلاف المعنى For a list of manuscripts and books treating the subject see Saraqusṭī, *Afʿāl I,* 8-9. The independent works that he mentions are: the *Kitāb faʿaltu wa-afʿaltu* by al-Aṣmaʿī, of which the manuscript 2/28 exists in Cairo, the *Kitāb faʿaltu wa-afʿaltu* by Abū ʿUbaid, of which the manuscript 3/281 exists in Cairo, the *Kitāb faʿaltu wa-afʿaltu* by Abū Ḥātim al-Siǧistānī, of which many manuscripts exist in Cairo and the *Kitāb faʿaltu wa-afʿaltu* by Abū Isḥāq al-Zaǧǧāǧ, which was printed in Cairo 1368 A.H. For a detailed presentation of such verbs in both these forms with different meanings in which the 1st radical is: the hamza see Saraqusṭī, *Afʿāl I,* 67-82, the *b, IV,*

70-100, the *t, III*, 354-363, the *ṭ, III*, 613-621, the *ğ, II*, 253-280, the *ḥ, I*, 336-377, the *ḫ, I*, 440-473, the *d, III*, 294-311, the *ḏ, III*, 589-596, the *r, III*, 18-61, the *z, III*, 443-457, the *s, III*, 500-532, the *š, II*, 330-363, the *ṣ, III*, 383-403, the *ḍ, II*, 208-222, the *ṭ, III*, 249-262, the *ẓ, III*, 579-583, the *ʿ, I*, 204-254, the *ġ, II*, 7-24, the *f, IV*, 8-37, the *q, II*, 55-95, the *k, II*, 146-165, the *l, II*, 417-442, the *m, IV*, 144-172, the *n, III*, 128-177, the *h, I*, 131-144, the *w, IV*, 227-253 and the *y, IV*, 295-297. For a presentation of a list of verbs of both these forms with identical meaning see Retsö, *Diathesis* 223-235, and for a presentation of such verbs in which the 1st radical is a: hamza see Saraqusṭī, *Afʿāl I*, 65-67, *b, IV*, 65-70, *t, III*, 353-354, *ṭ, III*, 612-613, *ğ, II*, 244-253, *ḥ, I*, 327-336, *ḫ, I*, 434-440, *d, III*, 289-294, *ḏ, III*, 588-589, *r, III*, 1-18, *z, III*, 438-443, *s, III*, 492-499, *š, II*, 323-330, *ṣ, III*, 376-383, *ḍ, II*, 205-207, *ṭ, III*, 247-249, *ẓ, III*, 579, *ʿ, I*, 195-204, *ġ, II*, 1-6, *f, IV*, 8-37, *q, II*, 50-55, *k, II*, 141-146, *l, II*, 410-416, *m, IV*, 137-144, *n, III*, 116-128, *h, I*, 128-131, *w, IV*, 219-227 and *y, IV*, 294-295. For a presentation of verbs in the groundform and in the causative forms in Geʿez, Syriac and Biblical Hebrew with identical meaning see Retsö, *Diathesis* 206-214.

– It can be similar to Form II فَعَّلَ, as it signifies to make someone do something or supposes an action or a state, e.g. أَكْتَبَ، كَتَبَ "to make someone write" and أَكْذَبَ، كَذَبَ "to accuse someone of being a liar". For a study of the agreement and differenciation in meaning of both Form II and Form IV in Arabic see Leemhuis, *Stems* 8 sqq., and for this study in Hebrew see 16-17. For a comparison between Form IV in Arabic with the one in some the Semitic languages see Roman, *Étude* 925, Rosenthal, *Aramaic* & 99, 157, 166.

– It can be formed from nouns, e.g. أَقْفَرَ "to become a desert" from قَفْرٌ "desert", أَرَابَ "to incur suspicion" from رَيْبٌ "suspicion" (cf. Sībawaihi, *II*, 250, Howell, *II-III*, 272, Vernier, *I*, 140).

– It denotes entering a place or time, e.g. أَنْجَدَ "to enter Nağd", أَجْبَلَ "to enter the mountain" and أَصْبَحَ "to enter upon the morning" (cf. Howell, *II-III*, 267, Vernier, *I*, 140).

– It denotes moving from one place to another, e.g. أَحْجَزَ "he went to al-Ḥiğāz" and أَغْرَبَ "he went to the Occident" (cf. Vernier, *I*, 140-141).

– It denotes finding a quality in the object, e.g. أَحْمَدْتُهُ "I found him such as to be praised" (cf. Zamaḫšarī, 128, Howell, *II-III*, 268).

– It denotes exposing (for discussions see Larcher, *'Afʿala* 7 sqq.), e.g. أَقْتَلْتُهُ "I exposed him to slaughter" and أَبَعْتُهُ "I exposed him to sale" (cf. Zamaḫšarī, 128, Howell, *II-III*, 267).

– It denotes depriving, e.g. أَشْكَيْتُهُ "I removed his complaint" (cf. Zamaḫšarī, 129, Howell, *II-III*, 268).

– It denotes negating the groundform, e.g. شَفَى "to be cured" and أَشْفَى "not to be cured" (cf. Vernier, *I*, 140).

(5): Form V تَفَعَّلَ, e.g. تَفَضَّلَ "to deign".

Its paradigm in the perfect, active, is the following:

	sing.	dual	pl.
1st	تَفَضَّلْتُ		تَفَضَّلْنَا
2nd masc.	تَفَضَّلْتَ	تَفَضَّلْتُمَا	تَفَضَّلْتُمْ
2nd fem.	تَفَضَّلْتِ	تَفَضَّلْتُمَا	تَفَضَّلْتُنَّ

	3rd masc.	تَفَضَّلَ	تَفَضَّلَا	تَفَضَّلُوا
	3rd fem.	تَفَضَّلَتْ	تَفَضَّلَتَا	تَفَضَّلْنَ

Its paradigm in the imperfect of the indicative, active, is the following:

	sing.	dual	pl.
1st	أَتَفَضَّلُ		نَتَفَضَّلُ
2nd masc.	تَتَفَضَّلُ	تَتَفَضَّلَانِ	تَتَفَضَّلُونَ
2nd fem.	تَتَفَضَّلِينَ	تَتَفَضَّلَانِ	تَتَفَضَّلْنَ
3rd masc.	يَتَفَضَّلُ	يَتَفَضَّلَانِ	يَتَفَضَّلُونَ
3rd fem.	تَتَفَضَّلُ	تَتَفَضَّلَانِ	يَتَفَضَّلْنَ

The meaning of Form V:

– It is the reflexive to Form II فَعَّلَ, e.g. كَسَّرْتُهُ فَتَكَسَّرَ "I broke it in pieces and it broke in pieces" (cf. Zamaḫšarī, 127, Howell, *II-III*, 261).

– It denotes affecting, e.g. تَشَجَّعَ "he encouraged himself", or endeavouring to acquire, e.g. تَحَلَّمَ "he endeavoured to acquire forbearance" (cf. Sībawaihi, *II,* 255, Zamaḫšarī, 127, Howell, *II-III,* 261-262).

– It is similar to Form X اِسْتَفْعَلَ, with its two meanings of believing and requiring, e.g. تَكَبَّرَ "he believed himself to be great" and تَبَيَّنَهُ "he sought the settlement and manifestation of it" (cf. Zamaḫšarī, 127-128, Howell, *II-III,* 262).

– It denotes a repeated action that occurs progressively in time, e.g. تَجَرَّعَهُ "he swallowed it in successive gulps" (cf. Zamaḫšarī, 127, Howell, *II-III,* 263).

– It denotes taking for oneself, e.g. تَدَيَّرْتُ المكانَ "I took the place for an abode" and تَوَسَّدْتُ التُّرابَ "I took the dust for a pillow" (cf. Zamaḫšarī, 128, Howell, *II-III,* 263).

– It denotes associating with a religion, a sect, a nation or a tribe, e.g. تَنَصَّرَ "to become a Christian", تَهَوَّدَ "to become a Jew", تَقَيَّسَ "to associate with the Qaisī tribe", تَعَرَّبَ "to become an Arab" and تَشَأَّمَ "to become a Syrian" (cf. Vernier, *I,* 143).

– It denotes abstaining from the action of the groundform, e.g. تَهَجَّدَ "to stay awake at night" and تَحَوَّبَ "to abstain from sin" (cf. Zamaḫšarī, 128, Vernier, *I,* 143).

(6): Form VI تَفَاعَلَ, e.g. تَضَارَبَ "to strike" (for a study of this form with its corresponding forms in some of the other Semitic languages see Wright, *Comparative Grammar* 212-214).

Its paradigm in the perfect, active, is the following:

	sing.	dual	pl.
1st	تَضَارَبْتُ		تَضَارَبْنَا
2nd masc.	تَضَارَبْتَ	تَضَارَبْتُمَا	تَضَارَبْتُمْ
2nd fem.	تَضَارَبْتِ	تَضَارَبْتُمَا	تَضَارَبْتُنَّ
3rd masc.	تَضَارَبَ	تَضَارَبَا	تَضَارَبُوا

3rd fem.	تَضَارَبَتْ	تَضَارَبَتَا	تَضَارَبْنَ

Its paradigm in the imperfect of the indicative, active, is the following:

	sing.	dual	pl.
1st	أَتَضَارَبُ		نَتَضَارَبُ
2nd masc.	تَتَضَارَبُ	تَتَضَارَبَانِ	تَتَضَارَبُونَ
2nd fem.	تَتَضَارَبِينَ	تَتَضَارَبَانِ	تَتَضَارَبْنَ
3rd masc.	يَتَضَارَبُ	يَتَضَارَبَانِ	يَتَضَارَبُونَ
3rd fem.	تَتَضَارَبُ	تَتَضَارَبَانِ	يَتَضَارَبْنَ

The meaning of Form VI:

– It denotes an action done by two and more, e.g. تَضَارَبَا "they both fought together" and تَضَارَبُوا "they fought together" (cf. Zamaḫšarī, 128, Howell, *II-III,* 265).

– It is similar to the groundform, e.g. تَوَانَيْتُ "I flagged in the matter" (cf. Zamaḫšarī, 128, Howell, *II-III,* 264).

– It is the reflexive of Form II فَعَّلَ, e.g. عَظَّمْتُهُ فَتَعَاظَمَ "I glorified him and he was glorified" (cf. Vernier, *I,* 143).

– It is the reflexive of Form III فَاعَلَ, e.g. بَاعَدْتُهُ فَتَبَاعَدَ "I made him to remove to a distance, and he removed to it" (cf. Zamaḫšarī, 128, Howell, *II-III,* 265).

– It is similar to Form VIII اِفْتَعَلَ, e.g. تَضَارَبُوا and اِضْطَرَبُوا "they hit each other", and تَقَاتَلُوا and اِقْتَتَلُوا "they killed each other" (cf. Sībawaihi, *II,* 254).

– It denotes stimulating an action or a state, e.g. تَجَاهَلْتُ "I feigned to be ignorant" (cf. Zamaḫšarī, 128, Howell, *II-III,* 264).

(7): Form VII اِنْفَعَلَ, e.g. اِنْصَرَفَ "to depart" (for a study of this form with its corresponding forms in some of the other Semitic languages see Wright, *Comparative Grammar* 215-218).

Its paradigm in the perfect, active, is the following:

	sing.	dual	pl.
1st	اِنْصَرَفْتُ		اِنْصَرَفْنَا
2nd masc.	اِنْصَرَفْتَ	اِنْصَرَفْتُمَا	اِنْصَرَفْتُمْ
2nd fem.	اِنْصَرَفْتِ	اِنْصَرَفْتُمَا	اِنْصَرَفْتُنَّ
3rd masc.	اِنْصَرَفَ	اِنْصَرَفَا	اِنْصَرَفُوا
3rd fem.	اِنْصَرَفَتْ	اِنْصَرَفَتَا	اِنْصَرَفْنَ

Its paradigm in the imperfect of the indicative, active, is the following:

	sing.	dual	pl.
1st	أَنْصَرِفُ		نَنْصَرِفُ
2nd masc.	تَنْصَرِفُ	تَنْصَرِفَانِ	تَنْصَرِفُونَ
2nd fem.	تَنْصَرِفِينَ	تَنْصَرِفَانِ	تَنْصَرِفْنَ

3rd masc.	يَنْصَرِفُ	يَنْصَرِفَانِ	يَنْصَرِفُونَ
3rd fem.	تَنْصَرِفُ	تَنْصَرِفَانِ	يَنْصَرِفْنَ

The meaning of Form VII:

– It is the passive of the groundform فَعَلَ, e.g. كَسَرْتُهُ فَانْكَسَرَ "I broke it and it broke" (cf. Sībawaihi, *II*, 252, Zamaḫšarī, 129, Howell, *II-III*, 273).

(8) Form VIII اِفْتَعَلَ, e.g. اِحْتَقَرَ "to despise". When it is compared to some of the other forms of the derived verbs, as Form IV أَفْعَلَ, Form V تَفَعَّلَ, Form VII اِنْفَعَلَ and Form X اِسْتَفْعَلَ, it is the only form in which the augment occurs after the 1st radical. Furthermore in some of the other Semitic languages as in Hebrew, e.g. *hitpaqqéd* that corresponds to اِفْتَقَدَ "to miss" (cf. ʿAbd al-Raḥīm, *Ṣarf* 39) and in the Aramaic reflexive (cf. Wright, *II*, 42), the *t* precedes the 1st radical (for a possible explanation of the actual form see Wright, *Comparative Grammar* 208). This is why its base form may be اِتْفَعَلَ, and then the *t* and the 1st radical *f* changed place together (cf. ʿAbd al-Raḥīm, *Ṣarf* 39, ʿAbdat, *ʾAbḥāṯ* 136-137).

Its paradigm in the perfect, active, is the following:

	sing.	dual	pl.
1st	اِحْتَقَرْتُ		اِحْتَقَرْنَا
2nd masc.	اِحْتَقَرْتَ	اِحْتَقَرْتُمَا	اِحْتَقَرْتُمْ
2nd fem.	اِحْتَقَرْتِ	اِحْتَقَرْتُمَا	اِحْتَقَرْتُنَّ
3rd masc.	اِحْتَقَرَ	اِحْتَقَرَا	اِحْتَقَرُوا
3rd fem.	اِحْتَقَرَتْ	اِحْتَقَرَتَا	اِحْتَقَرْنَ

Its paradigm in the imperfect of the indicative, active, is the following:

	sing.	dual	pl.
1st	أَحْتَقِرُ		نَحْتَقِرُ
2nd masc.	تَحْتَقِرُ	تَحْتَقِرَانِ	تَحْتَقِرُونَ
2nd fem.	تَحْتَقِرِينَ	تَحْتَقِرَانِ	تَحْتَقِرْنَ
3rd masc.	يَحْتَقِرُ	يَحْتَقِرَانِ	يَحْتَقِرُونَ
3rd fem.	تَحْتَقِرُ	تَحْتَقِرَانِ	يَحْتَقِرْنَ

The meaning of Form VIII:

– It is similar to the groundform, e.g. كَسَبَ and اِكْتَسَبَ "to obtain" (cf. Zamaḫšarī, 129, Howell, *II-III*, 276, Vernier, *I*, 145).

– It is the reflexive of the groundform, e.g. سَمِعَ "to hear" and اِسْتَمَعَ "to listen to" and جَمَعَ "to collect" and اِجْتَمَعَ "to collect themselves".

– It is similar to Form VI تَفَاعَلَ, e.g. تَقَاتَلُوا and "they killed each other" and اِقْتَتَلُوا and تَجَاوَرُوا and اِجْتَوَرُوا "they became mutual neighbours" (cf. Sībawaihi, *II*, 254).

– It is similar to Form VII اِنْفَعَلَ, e.g. غَمَمْتُهُ فَاغْتَمَّ وَانْغَمَّ "I grieved him and he grieved" (cf. Sībawaihi, *II*, 252, Zamaḫšarī, 129, Howell, *II-III*, 274).

– It denotes making for oneself, e.g. اِشْتَوَى "to roast meat" (cf. Sībawaihi, *II*, 256, Zamaḫšarī, 129, Howell, *II-III*, 275).

(9): Form IX اِفْعَلَّ, e.g. اِحْمَرَّ "to be red".

Its paradigm in the perfect, active, is the following:

	sing.	dual	pl.
1st	اِحْمَرَرْتُ		اِحْمَرَرْنَا
2nd masc.	اِحْمَرَرْتَ	اِحْمَرَرْتُمَا	اِحْمَرَرْتُمْ
2nd fem.	اِحْمَرَرْتِ	اِحْمَرَرْتُمَا	اِحْمَرَرْتُنَّ
3rd masc.	اِحْمَرَّ	اِحْمَرَّا	اِحْمَرُّوا
3rd fem.	اِحْمَرَّتْ	اِحْمَرَّتَا	اِحْمَرَرْنَ

Its paradigm in the imperfect of the indicative, active, is the following:

	sing.	dual	pl.
1st	أَحْمَرُّ		نَحْمَرُّ
2nd masc.	تَحْمَرُّ	تَحْمَرَّانِ	تَحْمَرُّونَ
2nd fem.	تَحْمَرِّينَ	تَحْمَرَّانِ	تَحْمَرِرْنَ
3rd masc.	يَحْمَرُّ	يَحْمَرَّانِ	يَحْمَرُّونَ
3rd fem.	تَحْمَرُّ	تَحْمَرَّانِ	يَحْمَرِرْنَ

The meaning of Form IX:
– It is used for permanent colours or defects.

(10): Form X اِسْتَفْعَلَ, e.g. اِسْتَخْرَجَ "to extract" (for a study of this form with its corresponding forms in some of the other Semitic languages see Wright, *Comparative Grammar* 214-215).

Its paradigm in the perfect, active, is the following:

	sing.	dual	pl.
1st	اِسْتَخْرَجْتُ		اِسْتَخْرَجْنَا
2nd masc.	اِسْتَخْرَجْتَ	اِسْتَخْرَجْتُمَا	اِسْتَخْرَجْتُمْ
2nd fem.	اِسْتَخْرَجْتِ	اِسْتَخْرَجْتُمَا	اِسْتَخْرَجْتُنَّ
3rd masc.	اِسْتَخْرَجَ	اِسْتَخْرَجَا	اِسْتَخْرَجُوا
3rd fem.	اِسْتَخْرَجَتْ	اِسْتَخْرَجَتَا	اِسْتَخْرَجْنَ

Its paradigm in the imperfect of the indicative, active, is the following:

	sing.	dual	pl.
1st	أَسْتَخْرِجُ		نَسْتَخْرِجُ
2nd masc.	تَسْتَخْرِجُ	تَسْتَخْرِجَانِ	تَسْتَخْرِجُونَ
2nd fem.	تَسْتَخْرِجِينَ	تَسْتَخْرِجَانِ	تَسْتَخْرِجُونَ
3rd masc.	يَسْتَخْرِجُ	يَسْتَخْرِجَانِ	يَسْتَخْرِجُونَ
3rd fem.	تَسْتَخْرِجُ	تَسْتَخْرِجَانِ	يَسْتَخْرِجْنَ

The meaning of Form X:

– It is similar to the groundform, e.g. قَرَّ and اِسْتَقَرَّ "to rest" (cf. Zamaḫšarī, 130, Howell, *II-III*, 277).

– It denotes the request of the act, e.g. اِسْتَعْمَلَهُ "he required his working" (cf. Sībawaihi, *II*, 255, Zamaḫšarī, 130, Howell, *II-III*, 277).

– It denotes becoming transmuted, e.g. اِسْتَحْجَرَ الطِّينُ "the clay became stone" (cf. Zamaḫšarī, 130, Howell, *II-III*, 277).

– It denotes finding someone to be of a certain quality, e.g. اِسْتَعْظَمْتُهُ "I found him to be grand" (cf. Zamaḫšarī, 130, Howell, *II-III*, 278).

– It denotes appointing someone for a position, e.g. اِسْتَوْزَرَ "to appoint one as a minister" (cf. Vernier, *I*, 146).

(11) Form XI: اِفْعَالَّ, e.g. اِحْمَارَّ "to be very red".
The meaning of Form XI:

– It intensifies Form IX اِفْعَلَّ.

(12) Form XII: اِفْعَوْعَلَ, e.g اِخْشَوْشَنَ "to become very harsh".
The meaning of Form XII:
– It denotes intensity.

(13) Form XIII: اِفْعَوَّلَ, e.g. اِجْلَوَّذَ "to last long".
The two more anomalous forms which are not mentioned by Ibn Masʿūd are the following:

(14) Form XIV: اِفْعَنْلَلَ, e.g. اِسْحَنْكَكَ "to be dark".

(15) Form XV اِفْعَنْلَى e.g. اِحْبَنْطَى "to be swollen or filled with rage" (cf. Wright, *II*, 46-47). ʿAbd al-Ḥamīd, *Taṣrīf* 599 mentions thirty-seven forms of triliteral verbs that include the groundform, the augmented, and the مُلْحَق "coordinated to the quadriliteral by an augment or more" (for it see (41)). A larger list comprising fourty-three forms, excluding the groundform, is presented by Howell, *II-III*, 254-257. For a presentation and study of the triliteral verbs' forms see Zamaḫšarī, 126-130, Zanǧānī, *ʿIzzī* 2-3, Vernier, *I*, 125-150, Howell, *II-III*, 245-279, Wright, *II*, 29-47, Blachère, 38-73, Roman, *Étude II*, 917-947, Fischer, *Grammatik* 87-89, Fleisch, *Traité II*, 227-340.

(40) The reason of the assimilation of the *r* to the *r* in both the base forms اِحْمَارَرَ and اِحْمَرَرَ resulting in اِحْمَارَّ and اِحْمَرَّ respectively, is the combination of two vowelled identical consonants. No assimilation of the *w* to the *alif maqṣūra* is carried out in اِرْعَوَى in spite of the verb's formation,– as with the case of اِحْمَرَّ,–on the pattern of اِفْعَلَّ, on the account that both these weak consonants are not of the same kind. Hence اِرْعَوَى is not said اِرْعَوَّ by the Arabs (cf. Wright, *II*, 43, 91). It can be interesting to remark that the question concerning the measure of اِرْعَوَى occupied Ibn al-Ḫayyāṭ (d. 320/932) (Muḥammad b. Aḥmad b. Manṣūr Abū Bakr, see Zubaidī, *Ṭabaqāt* 75, Yāqūt, Muʿǧam *XVII*, 141, Suyūṭī, *Muzhir I*, 48, Sezgin, *Geschichte IX*,.163-164. He was well acquainted with both the Basrans' and the Kufans' methods and was one of al-Zaǧǧāǧī's teachers. He wrote *Maʿānī l-qurʾān, al-Naḥw l-kabīr, al-Muqniʿ fī l-naḥw* and other works), referred to by Suyūṭī, *Ašbāh III*, 210-211 who writes:

"قال أبو بكر محمد بن أحمد بن منصور المعروف بابن الخياط ، وهو من شيوخ أبي القاسم الزجاجي ، ومن أصحاب أبي العباس أحمد بن يحيى : أقمت سنين أسأل عن وزن ارْعَوَى فلم أجد مَنْ يعرفه ، ووزنه له فرع وأصل ، فأصله أن يكون افْعَلَّ مثل احْمَرَّ كأنّه ارْعَوَّ ، وكرهوا أن يقولوا ذلك ، لأن الواو المشددة لم تقع في آخر الماضي ولا المضارع ، ولو نطقوا بارْعَوَّ ثم استعملوه مع التاء لوجب إظهار الواوين ، كما أنهم إذا ردّوا احْمَرَّ إلى التاء قالوا : احمَرَرْتُ وأظهروا المدغم ، فلم يقولوا ارْعَوَوْتُ فيجمعوا بين الواوين كما لم يقولوا قَوَوْتُ ، فقلبوا الواو الثانية منه ، ولا ريب أنَّ إحدى الواوين زائدة ، كما لا ريب في أنَّ إحدى الراءين في احمررت زائدة ، قال : فإنْ قيل فما الحاصل في وزن ارْعوى؟ قال : فجائز أن يقول : افْعَلل ، قال : ولو قال قائل : افْعَلى لكان وجهاً ، والأول أقيس".

"Abū Bakr Muḥammad b. Aḥmad b. Manṣūr, known as Ibn al-Ḫayyāṭ, who is one of the teachers of Abū l-Qāsim al-Zağğāğī and one of the friends of Abū l-ʿAbbās Aḥmad b. Yaḥyā [Ṯaʿlab], said: "I spent years inquiring about the measure of ارْعَوَى without finding anyone who knew it. It is so that its measure has a derivative and a base form. Its base form is that it should be formed according to افْعَلَّ as احْمَرَّ, as if it was ارْعَوَّ, but they disliked to say it so, because the doubled *w* does not occur as the last weak consonant neither in the perfect nor in the imperfect. And if they said ارْعَوَّ and then suffixed the [agent] *t* to it, then it would have been necessary to separate both the wāws, in the same manner as when they suffixed the *t* to احْمَرَّ and said احمَرَرْتُ "I became red" and dissoluted. But they did not say ارْعَوَوْتُ with the combination of both wāws in the same manner as they did not say قَوَوْتُ "I became strong", so they changed the 2nd *w* in it into another [weak] consonant. There is no doubt that one of both the wāws is additional, as well as there is no doubt that one of both the rāʾs in احمَرَرْتُ is additional". He said: "And if it was asked what happened with the measure ارْعَوَى?". He answered: "It is possible that it is on the measure of افْعَلَل. He said: "And if a sayer said it is on the measure افْعَلَى, it would also have been a possibility, but the first follows better the analogy".

As for its paradigm: Its perfect, active is ارْعَوَى. Its imperfect is يَرْعَوِي. Its imperative is ارْعَوِ. Its active participle is مُرْعَوٍ. Its *maṣdar* is ارْعِوَاءٌ. Its perfect, passive is أُرْعُوِيَ. Its imperfect is يُرْعَوَى. Its passive participle is مُرْعَوًى.

(41) Quadriliteral verbs (for a general presentation see Zamaḫšarī, 130, Vernier, *I,* 150-154, Howell, *II-III,* 280-282, Wright, *II,* 47-49, Blachère, 73-76, Roman, *Étude II,* 982-983, Fischer, *Grammatik* 89-90, Fleisch, *Traité II,* 427-463) can: 1– be formed from foreign words of more than three consonants, e.g. تَسَرْوَلَ "to put on سَرَاوِيلُ 'trousers or drawers'" from the Persian شَلْوَارْ, 2– be combinations of well-known syllables in common expressions, e.g. بَسْمَلَ "to say بِسْمِ ٱللّٰه 'in the name of God'" (see below), 3– be a repeated biliteral root (for discussions see

Bohas, *Structure* 39-44) expressing a sound or a movement, e.g. زَلْزَلَ "to shake", 4– be a developed triliteral verb through the insertion of a 4th consonant or more (cf. Wright, *II,* 47-48, de Sacy, *I,* 125, 126-128 note 1, Roman, *Étude II,* 982-983 and my presentation below), e.g. زَحْلَفَ "to roll along" from زَحَفَ "to advance slowly" .

Ibn Masʿūd presents the groundform of the quadriliteral and its well-known three derived forms. A fourth one that is more anomalous exists as well. An introduction to them with their numbering and their general meanings is here presented:

(1) Form I: فَعْلَلَ e.g. دَحْرَجَ "to roll". The form is similar to the groundform of the triliteral فَعَلَ. As for the derived forms, they are:

(2) Form II: تَفَعْلَلَ e.g. تَدَحْرَجَ "to roll along". The form is the passive of the groundform of the quadriliteral فَعْلَلَ .

(3) Form III: افْعَنْلَلَ e.g. احْرَنْجَمَ "to gather together in a mass".

(4) Form IV افْعَلَلَّ e.g. اقْشَعَرَّ "to shudder with horror". The form denotes intensity.

(5) Form V: افْعَلَلَّ e.g. اهْرَمَّعَ "to be fast in the race" (cf. Vernier, *I,* 153). It denotes intensity. The development of the triliteral verb into being of four, five, or six consonants, is what Ibn Masʿūd, who follows the traditional grammarians, names for مُلْحَق "coordinated to another pattern by the addition of an augment or more to its root" (cf. ʿAbd al-Ḥamīd, *Taṣrīf* 599, Fleisch, *Traité II,* 464, Fleisch, *Taṣrīf,* Bohas, *Étude* 100-116, Mokhlis, *Taṣrīf* 90-92). The verb which is coordinated to another pattern of verb by an augment or more, has a *maṣdar* which is of the same structure as this verb's *maṣdar.* An example is the triliteral verb جَلَبَ "to bring about", which by the duplication of its 3rd radical *b* becomes جَلْبَبَ "to clothe with a garment" coordinated to Form I of the quadriliteral دَحْرَجَ, of which the *maṣdar* جَلْبَبَةٌ is of the same structure as دَحْرَجَةٌ. Some of the different forms of quadrilterals that a triliteral verb can be coordinated to are the following:

– مُلْحَق دَحْرَجَ coordinated to Form I of the quadriliteral فَعْلَلَ, e.g. دَحْرَجَ by the addition of an augment (cf. ʿAbd al-Ḥamīd, *Taṣrīf* 598).

– ملحق تَدَحْرَجَ coordinated to Form II of the quadriliteral تَفَعْلَلَ, e.g. تَدَحْرَجَ by the addition of more than one augment (cf. Suyūṭī, *Muzhir II,* 27).

– ملحق احْرَنْجَمَ coordinated to Form III of the quadriliteral افْعَنْلَلَ, e.g. احْرَنْجَمَ by the addition of more than one augment (cf. Suyūṭī, *Muzhir II,* 27).

De Sacy, *I,* 125 writes referring to الْمُلْحَقَاتُ بِالرُّبَاعِي:

> "Je ne crois pas devoir faire une classe particulière de certains verbes nommés par les grammairiens arabes الْمُلْحَقَاتُ بِالرُّبَاعِي, c'est à dire *attachés à la suite du verbe quadrilitère,* ou pour m'exprimer d'une manière plus concise, *quasi-quadrilitères.* Ce sont des verbes de quatre lettres, formés de racines trilitères, soit par le redoublement de la dernière lettre, comme شَمْلَلَ et جَلْبَبَ, dérivés des racines شَمَلَ et جَلَبَ, soit par l'insertion entre les radicales d'un و ou d'un ى ; tels sont les verbes

حَوْقَلَ, دَهْوَرَ, بَيْطَرَ, جَزْيَلَ et سَلْقَى, formés des racines trilitères حَقَلَ, دَهَرَ, بَطَرَ, جَزَلَ et سَلَقَ. Quelques grammairiens comprennent aussi sous cette dénomination les verbes qui deviennent quadrilitères par l'insertion d'un ن, comme جَنْدَلَ et قَلْنَسَ, qu'ils dérivent des racines جَدَلَ et قَلَسَ".

The presentation of these coordinated forms relate only to the groundform of the quadriliteral, and not to all the forms as one would expect with the generalization اَلْمُلْحَقَاتُ بِالرُّبَاعِيِّ. De Sacy does not discuss here the forms that are coordinated to Form II or Form III of the quadriliteral. But it is also possible that only verbs of four consonants are considered as quadriliteral by some grammarians, and not those others consisting of more consonants as those of the derived forms of the quadriliteral. This discussion is taken up *en passant* in his note 1 to pp. 126-128:

> "Car plusieurs autre lettres que le و, le ى, et le ن semblent être entrées comme lettres accessoires ou formatives dans des racines trilitères, pour donner naissance à des verbes ou à des noms de quatre, de cinq et de six lettres..." [to which he gives some examples, but he concludes his analysis with these words]: "... mais toutes ces observations ne pourraient conduire qu'à des hypothèses étymologiques tout à fait étrangères à la grammaire".

The example of verbs that are coordinated by an augment or more to Form I of the quadriliteral presented by Ibn Masʿūd are not however, complete. In fact, de Sacy, *I,* 126 in the note remarks:

> "Ahmed, fils d'Ali, fils de Masoud, dans le مَرَاحُ ٱلْأَرْوَاحِ, ne reconnaît que six formes des verbes quadrilitères, qu'il appelle مُلْحَقُ دَحْرَجَ, et voici les exemples qu'il en donne شَمْلَلَ, حَوْقَلَ, بَيْطَرَ, جَهْوَرَ, قَلْنَشَ [which should have been قَلْنَسَ] et قَلْسَى [which should have been قَلْسَى]".

Abū Ḥanīfa, *Maqṣūd* 2 reckognizes also six forms that are coordinated to the groundform of the quadriliteral only, but instead of فَعْنَلَ, e.g. قَلْنَسَ, he has the form فَيْعَلَ, e.g. عَثْيَرَ "to stumble". The forms that are coordinated by an augment to the groundform of the quadriliteral vary from one grammarian to another (e.g. Ibn ʿUṣfūr, *I,* 167 sqq., ʿAbd al-Ḥamīd, *Taṣrīf* 598-599, Suyūṭī, *Muzhir II,* 27-28, Howell, *II-III,* 257-258). De Sacy, *I,* 126 in the note discusses some variations between the grammarians including among them Ibn Masʿūd whom he names. One of them to whom he refers to, Lumsden, M., *A Grammar of the Arabic language* 149-150, presents seven forms that are coordinated to the groundform of the quadriliteral, but adds according to de Sacy: "qu'on pourrait beaucoup en augmenter le nombre". Ibn Masʿūd refers with his examples to six forms that are co-ordinated to Form I of the quadriliteral دَحْرَجَ according to فَعْلَلَ, without mentioning the forms. The forms are presented here with a discussion:

(1) فَعْلَلَ with the two last radicals identical, e.g. شَمْلَلَ.

(2) فَوْعَلَ with the infixed *w* after the 1st radical, e.g. حَوْقَلَ. The verb is usually a combination of syllables in the frequently used expression لَا حَوْلَ وَلَا قُوَّةَ إِلَّا بِاللهِ "there is no power and no strength save in God". It means however to grow old in the following verse said by Ru'ba, cited by Ibn Ǧinnī, *Munṣif I,* 39, *III,* 7, Ibn Yaʿīš, *VII,* 155, *Mulūkī* 66, Ibn Manẓūr, *II,* 947, Howell, *I,* fasc. IV, 1541:

"يَا قَوْمِ قَدْ حَوْقَلْتُ أَوْ دَنَوْتُ   وَبَعْدَ حِيقَالِ ٱلرِّجَالِ ٱلْمَوْتُ".

"O my people, I have grown old and impotent, or have come near to it; and after men's growing old and impotent is death".

Other examples that are similar to حَوْقَلَ in being a combination of syllables in well-known expressions, but which are formed according to فَعْلَلَ and not to فَوْعَلَ, are:

– بَسْمَلَ "to say باسم الله "in the name of God", جَعْفَدَ "to say جُعِلْتُ فداك "may I become your ransom!".

– حَسْبَلَ "to say حَسْبِيَ ٱللّٰهُ "God is sufficient for me".

– حَمْدَلَ "to say الحَمْدُ لله "praise belongs to God".

– دَمْعَزَ "to say أَدامَ ٱللّٰهُ عِزَّكَ "may God make your strength last".

– سَبْحَلَ "to say سُبْحانَ ٱللّٰهِ "God be praised".

– سَمْعَلَ "to say سَلامٌ عَلَيْكَ "peace be with you!".

– طَلْبَقَ "to say أَطالَ ٱللّٰهُ بَقاكَ "may God make your life last!".

– مَشْأَلَ "to say ما شاءَ ٱللّٰهُ "whatever God intend".

– فَذْلَكَ "to cast up an account, saying فَذَلِكَ كَذا وكَذا "this then is so and so much".

– حَيْعَلَ "to say حَيِّ على ٱلصَّلاة "Come to the prayer!", which occurs in the following verse said by an unknow poet, cited by Ibn Manẓūr, *VI,* 4693:

"إلى أَنْ دَعَا دَاعِي الصَّبَاحِ فَحَيْعَلا".

"Until the caller for prayer in the morning said: "So come to prayer!".

The *maṣdar* is حَيْعَلَةٌ, and it occurs in the following verse said by unknown poet, cited by Ṯaʿālibī, *Fiqh* 253, Muʾaddib, *Taṣrīf* 398, Ibn Manẓūr, *VI,* 4693, Ṣubḥī, *Fiqh* 244:

"أَقُولُ لَهَا وَدَمْعُ العَيْنِ جَارٍ   أَلَمْ تُحْزِنْكِ حَيْعَلَةُ المُنَادِي".

"I say to her while the tears of the eyes are shedding: "Doesn't the caller's invitation for prayer make you sad?".

(3) فَيْعَلَ with the infixed *y* after the 1st radical (for examples of thirty-six verbs formed according to both the forms فَوْعَلَ and فَيْعَلَ see Fleisch, *Verbes* 84-88).

(4) فَعْوَلَ with the infixed *w* after the 2nd radical, e.g. جَهْوَرَ.

(5) فَعْنَلَ with the infixed *n* after the 2nd radical, e.g. قَلْنَسَ.

(6) فَعْلَى with the suffixed *alif maqṣūra* after the 3rd radical, e.g. قَلْسَى.

ʿAbd al-Ḥamīd, *Taṣrīf* 599 adds فَنْعَلَ and فَعْيَلَ and Howell, *II-III,* 257 has فَنْعَلَ, فَعَّالَ, فَعْمَلَ, and فَعْلَنَ. The following derived forms of the triliteral, which form patterns coordinated to the groundform of the quadriliteral فَعْلَلَ, are added below. It is worth noting concerning this presentation, that not all these forms are considered by the grammarians to be coordinated to the quadriliteral's pattern, but are formed according to it:

A– the following forms with prefix:

(7) the *t:* تَفْعَلَ, e.g. تَرْمَسَ "to absent oneself from battle" from رَمَسَ "to conceal" (cf. Volck/ Kellgren, *Ibn Mālik* 10, Suyūṭī, *Muzhir II,* 27, Howell, *II-III,* 255).

(8) the *s:* سَفْعَلَ, e.g. سَنْبَسَ "to hasten" from نَبَسَ (cf. Suyūṭī, *Muzhir II,* 27, Volck/ Kellgren, *Ibn Mālik* 9, Howell, *II-III,* 255, Wright, *II,* 47).

(9) the ʿ: عَفْعَلَ, e.g. زَهْزَقَ "to laugh much" i.e. أَهْزَقَ (cf. al-Ḫalīl in his introduction to the *Kitāb al-ʿayn* translated by Haywood, *Lexicography* 32, Volck/Kellgren, *Ibn Mālik* 9, Ibn Manẓūr, *III,* 1878, Howell, *II-III,* 254, Wright, *II,* 48).

(10) the *h:* هَفْعَلَ, e.g. هَلْقَمَ "to swallow" (cf. Suyūṭī, *Muzhir II,* 27, Howell, *II-III,* 255).

(11) the *m:* مَفْعَلَ, e.g. مَرْحَبَ "to welcome" (cf. Suyūṭī, *Muzhir II,* 27).

(12) the *n:* نَفْعَلَ, e.g. نَرْجَسَ "to be dirty" (cf. Suyūṭī, *Muzhir II,* 27).

(13) the *y:* يَفْعَلَ, e.g. يَرْنَأَ "to dye red with henna" (cf. Suyūṭī, *Muzhir II,* 27).
B– the following forms with infix after the 1st radical:

(14) The ʿ: فَعْعَلَ, e.g. ثَعْجَرَ "to shed blood or something else" (cf. Fleisch, *Traité II,* 441; for more examples concerning this particular form see 441-442).

(15) the *m:* فَمْعَلَ (cf. Suyūṭī, *Muzhir II,* 27), e.g. زَمْلَقَ "to eject (the stallion) its semen before insertion" (cf. Volck/Kellgren, *Ibn Mālik* 10, Howell, *II-III,* 255).

(16) the *n:* فَنْعَلَ (cf. Volck/Kellgren, *Ibn Mālik* 10, Suyūṭī, *Muzhir II,* 27, ʿAbd al-Ḥamīd, *Taṣrīf* 599), e.g. دَنْقَعَ الرَّجُلُ "the man became poor and clave to the earth" (cf. Ibn ʿUṣfūr, *I,* 171, Howell, *II-III,* 257).

(17) the *h:* فَهْعَلَ (cf. Suyūṭī, *Muzhir II,* 27), e.g. رَهْمَسَ "to conceal" from رَمَسَ (cf. Volck/ Kellgren, *Ibn Mālik* 9, Howell, *II-III,* 255; for more examples concerning this particular form see Fleisch, *Traité II,* 440-441).
C– the following forms with infix after the 2nd radical:

(18) the ʾ: فَعْأَلَ, e.g. بَرْأَلَ الدِّيكُ "the cock ruffled the feathers of his neck" (cf. Howell, *II-III,* 257).

(19) the *t:* فَعْتَلَ, e.g. كَلْتَبَ "to act with slyness" (cf. Volck/Kellgren, *Ibn Mālik* 10, Howell, *II-III,* 255).

(20) the ʿ: فَعْعَلَ, e.g. خَبْعَلَ "to walk slowly because of a disturbance" (cf. Fleisch, *Traité II,* 442. For more examples concerning this particular form see 442-443).

(21) the 1st radical: فَعْفَلَ, e.g. زَهْزَقَ in the meaning of أَزْهَقَ "to destroy" (cf. Suyūṭī, *Muzhir II,* 27). However, according to Ibn Manẓūr, *III,* 1878 and others already mentioned, زَهْزَقَ is in the meaning of أَهْزَقَ "to laugh boisterously, which classifies it under عَفْعَلَ mentioned above.

(22) the *m:* فَعْمَلَ, e.g. جَلْمَطَ "to shave (one's head)" from جَلَطَ (cf. Howell, *II-III,* 255, Wright, *II,* 47).

(23) the *y:* فَعْيَلَ (cf. Suyūṭī, *Muzhir II,* 27, ʿAbd al-Ḥamīd, *Taṣrīf* 599), e.g. عَذْيَطَ "(a man) stooled in coition" (cf. Volck/Kellgren, *Ibn Mālik* 9, Howell, *II-III,* 255).
D– the following forms with suffix:

(24) the *r:* فَعْلَرَ, e.g. شَمْخَرَ "to be proud" from شَمَخَ "to be high" (cf. Fleisch, *Traité II,* 444).

(25) the *s:* فَعْلَسَ, e.g. خَلْبَسَ "to seduce and take away" from خَلَبَ "to delude" (cf. Volck/Kellgren, *Ibn Mālik* 9, Suyūṭī, *Muzhir II*, 27, Howell, *II-III*, 254, Wright, *II*, 47, Fleisch, *Traité II*, 444).

(26) the *l:* فَعْلَلَ, e.g. شَمْعَلَ "to spread itself" from شَمَعَ "to be scattered" (cf. Wright, *II*, 47, Fleisch, *Traité II*, 443; for more examples see Fleisch, *Traité II*, 443).

(27) the *m:* فَعْلَمَ, e.g. غَلْصَمَ "cut his epiglottis" from غَلَصَ (cf. Volck/Kellgren, *Ibn Mālik* 10, Suyūṭī, *Muzhir II*, 27, Howell, *II-III*, 255; for more examples concerning this particular form see Fleisch, *Traité II*, 443-444).

(28) the *n:* فَعْلَنَ, e.g. قَطْرَنَ "to smear (the camel) with pitch" from قَطَرَ (cf. Suyūṭī, *Muzhir II*, 27, Volck/Kellgren, *Ibn Mālik* 9, Howell, *II-III*, 255, Wright, *II*, 48).

Ibn Masʿūd refers with his examples to five forms that are formed according to Form II of the quadriliteral تَدَحْرَجَ according to تَفَعْلَلَ, without mentioning them. They are the following:

(1) تَفَعْلَلَ with the prefixed *t* and the two last radicals identical, e.g. تَجَلْبَبَ.

(2) تَفَوْعَلَ with the prefixed *t* and the infixed *w* after the 1st radical, e.g. تَجَوْرَبَ.

(3) تَفَيْعَلَ with the prefixed *t* and the infixed *y* after the 1st radical, e.g. تَشَيْطَنَ.

(4) تَفَعْوَلَ with the prefixed *t* and the infixed *w* after the 2nd radical, e.g. تَرَهْوَكَ.

(5) تَمَفْعَلَ with the prefixed *t* and the infixed *m* before the 1st radical, e.g. تَمَسْكَنَ.

The following forms may be added:

A– The following form with infix after the 1st radical:

(6) the *h:* تَفَهْعَلَ, e.g. تَرَهْشَفَ "to suck" from رَشَفَ (cf. Volck/Kellgren, *Ibn Mālik* 9, Howell, *II-III*, 255).

B– The following forms with infix after the 2nd radical:

(7) the *n:* تَفَعْنَلَ, e.g. تَقَلْنَسَ "to put on oneself a cap" (cf. Ibn ʿUṣfūr, *I*, 168, Suyūṭī, *Muzhir II*, 27).

(8) the *y:* تَفَعْيَلَ, e.g. تَرَهْيَأَ "(the clouds) moved, and were prepared for the rain" (cf. Ibn Manẓūr, *III*, 1748, ʿAbd al-Ḥamīd, *Taṣrīf* 599).

C– The following forms with suffix:

(9) the *t:* تَفَعْلَتَ, e.g. تَعَفْرَتَ "to act as a devil" (cf. Suyūṭī, *Muzhir II*, 27, Wright, *II*, 48).

(10) the *l:* تَفَعْلَلَ, e.g. تَشَمْعَلَ "to disperse itself" from شَمَعَ (for discussions see Fleisch, *Traité II*, 443).

(11) the *alif maqṣūra:* تَفَعْلَى (cf. Suyūṭī, *Muzhir II*, 27, ʿAbd al-Ḥamīd, *Taṣrīf* 599), e.g. تَسَلْقَى "to be thrown down upon one's back" from سَلْقَى (cf. Volck/Kellgren, *Ibn Mālik* 10, Howell, *II-III*, 255).

Ibn Masʿūd refers with his examples to two forms that are formed according to Form III of the quadriliteral اِحْرَنْجَمَ according to اِفْعَنْلَلَ, without mentioning them. They are the following:

(1) اِفْعَنْلَسَ with the prefixation of the hamza, the infixation of the *n* after the 2nd radical and the suffixation of the *s*, e.g. اِقْعَنْسَسَ.

(2) اِفْعَنْلَى with the prefixation of the hamza, the infixation of the *n* after the 2nd radical and the

suffixation of the *alif maqṣūra*, e.g. اسْلَنْقى. Another example that can be mentioned formed according to this measure is احْرَنْبَى (cf. Saraqusṭī, *Afʿāl I*, 432), which means according to Abū 'Utmān "laying on the back and lifting up one's legs". It can also mean according to al-Aṣmaʿī "to prepare oneself for anger and evil".
To these the following forms may be added:
A– The following form with infix after the 1st radical:

(3) the *w:* افْوَنْعَلَ, e.g. احْوَنْصَلَ "to bend its neck and stuck out its crop (the bird)" (cf. Suyūṭī, *Muzhir II,* 27, Volck/Kellgren, *Ibn Mālik* 9, Howell, *II-III,* 256, Wright, *II,* 49).
B– The following forms:

(4) the doubled *m* after the 2nd radical: افْعَمَّلَ, e.g. ادْلَمَّسَ "to be dark (the night)" (cf. Volck/Kellgren, *Ibn Mālik* 10, Howell, *II-III,* 256).

(5) the *w* after the 2nd radical and the two last consonants being identical: افْعَوْلَلَ, e.g. اعْثَوْجَجَ "to be bulky" from اعْثَوْثَجَ (cf. Volck/Kellgren, *Ibn Mālik* 10, Suyūṭī, *Muzhir II,* 27, Howell, *II-III,* 256).
C– The following form with suffix after the 3rd radical:

(6) the hamza: افْعَنْلأ, e.g. احْبَنْطَأ "to be big-bellied" from حَبِطَ (cf. Suyūṭī, *Muzhir II,* 28, Howell, *II-III,* 256).

Ibn Masʿūd does not refer to any measure formed according to Form IV of the quadriliteral اقْشَعَرَّ that is according to افْعَلَلَّ, with the prefixation of the hamza and the doubling of the last radical. The following forms can be mentioned:
A– The following forms with infix after the 1st radical:

(2) the *l:* افْلَعَلَّ (cf. Suyūṭī, *Muzhir II,* 28), e.g. اسْلَهَمَّ "to be agitated (the body) and altered" from سَهُمَ (cf. Volck/Kellgren, *Ibn Mālik* 9, Howell, *II-III,* 256).

(3) the *w:* افْوَعَلَّ, e.g. اكْوَألَّ "to be short and stunted" (cf. Ibn ʿUṣfūr, *I,* 172, Volck/Kellgren, *Ibn Mālik* 9, Howell, *II-III,* 256).
B– The following form with infix after the 2nd radical:

(4) the hamza: افْعَالَّ (cf. Suyūṭī, *Muzhir II,* 28), e.g. اجْفَاظَّ "to be on the brink of death" (cf. Volck/Kellgren, *Ibn Mālik* 9, Ibn Manẓūr, *I,* 641, Howell, *II-III,* 256).

(42) The paradigm of a strong verb of Form I, e.g. ضَرَبَ "to hit", in the perfect, active, is the following:

	sing.	dual	pl.
1st	ضَرَبْتُ		ضَرَبْنَا
2nd masc.	ضَرَبْتَ	ضَرَبْتُمَا	ضَرَبْتُمْ
2nd fem.	ضَرَبْتِ	ضَرَبْتُمَا	ضَرَبْتُنَّ
3rd masc.	ضَرَبَ	ضَرَبَا	ضَرَبُوا
3rd fem.	ضَرَبَتْ	ضَرَبَتَا	ضَرَبْنَ

For a general study of الماضي "the perfect" see Muʾaddib, *Taṣrīf* 15-27, Zamaḫšarī, 108, Ibn

Yaʿīš, *VII,* 4-6, Howell, *II-III,* 4-7, Wright, *III,* 1-18. The perfect is considered as being divided into three kinds by Mu'addib, *Taṣrīf* 17: نص "literally", by which he means that the form is the perfect's form and the meaning is the past, ممثّل "representative of", by which he means that the form is the perfect's form whereas the meaning is the future (for discussions see my notes (44 b)), and راهن "permanent, lasting", as in the sur. 33: 27 that he presents p. 19 (وكان اللّهُ على كُلِّ شَيْءٍ قديراً) "And God has power over all things", i.e. He has had power in the past, He has power today and power after today as well. Perhaps these special terms have been used by other Kufans. I myself was unable to find them by any one else than by al-Mu'addib. For a study of the perfect in Arabic and in some of the other Semitic languages see Wright, *Comparative Grammar* 165-179.

(43) بناءٌ "uninflectedness, undeclinability, invariability" (for definitions see de Sacy, *I,* 395, Lane, *I,* 260) and اعْرابٌ "inflection, declension" (for discussions concerning both these terms see Sībawaihi, *I,* 1 sqq., Ibn Fāris, *Ṣāḥibī* 77-78, Ibn Ǧinnī, *Ḫaṣā'iṣ I,* 35 sqq., *Lumaʿ* 1-2, de Sacy, *I,* 394-395, Bohas/Guillaume/Kouloughli, *Linguistic* 53-55; for an interesting study from the perspective of the dialectal variations existing between the tribes, together with Sībawaihi's attempt to present them in a neat theory see Baalbaki, *Iʿrāb* 17-33; for discussions concerning how long ago the inflectedness has been existent in the bedouins' living speech see Fleisch, *Traité I,* 281-282, Blau, *Judaeo-Arabic* 2-3)) pertain mostly to the field of النحو "syntax" (for it see (3 b)). However اعْرابٌ can as well refer to the formal *iʿrāb,* which is the complete vowelling of the word (for discussions see (3)). بناءٌ implies that the word's ending is invariable, whereas اعْراب implies that the ending's state varies in accordance with the operator governing it. Nouns are by principle declinable, except for some which are undeclinable (for the reasons why a noun can be undeclinable see Zamaḫšarī, 9-10, Ibn Yaʿīš, *I,* 58-71, Zabīdī, *Tāǧ XXIV,* 21-22). The perfect verb is undeclinable whereas the imperfect is declinable. All particles are undeclinable. Concerning the declinable noun, the case inflections are الرَّفْعُ "the nominative", النَّصْبُ "the accusative" and الْجَرُّ "the genitive". Concerning the declinable imperfect verb, the mode inflections are الرَّفْعُ "the indicative", النَّصْبُ "the subjunctive" and الجَزْمُ "the jussive". The question concerning which of the three parts of speech (for a discussion concerning them see (10 b)): the noun, verb or particle, is entitled to be declinable or undeclinable, has been a debated subject by many Arab grammarians (e.g. Zaǧǧāǧī, *Īḍāḥ* 77-82; for discussions see Versteegh, *Zaǧǧāǧī* 127-128). The declension has been given principally to the nouns whereas the undeclinability has been given to the verbs,—with the exception of the imperfect (for discussions see (47), (122)),—and to the particle. Zaǧǧāǧī, *Īḍāḥ* 77 presents the Basrans' opinion concerning this question with these words:

"قال الخليل وسيبويه وجميع البصريين: المستحق للإعراب من الكلام الأسماء، والمستحق للبناء الأفعال والحروف. هذا هو الأصل... فكل اسم رأيته مُعْرَباً فهو على أصله، وكل اسم رأيته غير معرب فهو خارج عن أصله، وكل فعل رأيته مبنيًا فهو على أصله، وكل فعل رأيته معرباً فقد خرج عن أصله، والحروف كلها مبنية على أصولها".

"Al-Ḫalīl, Sībawaihiand all the Basrans said: "What deserved the declension in the language are the nouns and what deserved the undeclinability are the verbs and the particles. This is the principle... So each noun you find declinable follows its basic principle, and each noun you find undeclinable has deviated from it. Each verb you find undeclinable follows its basic principle, and each verb you find declinable has deviated from it, and all the particles are basically undeclinable".

The reason why the declension is given to the nouns, with the exception of some, is to make it possible in the sentence to separate the subject from the object (cf. Ibn Ǧinnī, *Ḫaṣā'iṣ I,* 35), the operator from the governed noun, etc. (cf. de Sacy, *I,* 395 and *Anthologie* 186 in the commentary), whereas the undeclinability is given to the verbs and particles as they are not divided into such categories (cf. Zağǧāǧī, *Ǧumal* 260). Ibn Ǧinnī, *Ḫaṣā'iṣ I,* 35 writes:

"ألا ترى أنك إذا سمعت أكرم سعيد أباه وشكر سعيدا أبوه ، علمت برفع أحدهما ونصب الآخر الفاعل من المفعول ، ولو كان الكلام شَرْجا واحدا لآستبهم أحدهما من صاحبه":

"Don't you notice that if you hear: أَكْرَمَ سعيدٌ أباهُ "Sa'īd honoured his father" and شَكَرَ سعيدا أبوه "his father thanked Sa'īd", you know by the fact that one [noun] is in the nominative and the other in the accusative, who is the subject and who is the object. If all the nouns had the same declinable ending, then they both [sc. the nominative and accusative cases] would be confused".

It is possible to state that the perfect, imperative and particles are undeclinable because of a lack of resemblance to the noun, whereas the imperfect is declinable because of its resemblance to the noun. The reason of the perfect's undeclinability is as insinuated by Ibn Mas'ūd with his words, that: "it lacked the factor that would have made it declinable", by which he meant that it does not resemble the noun completely (cf. (44)).

b) A question noteworthy to be taken up here is why the marker of the declension occurs at the end of the word, and not at its beginning or its middle (for discussions see Zağǧāǧī, *Īḍāḥ* 76, 'Ukbarī, *Masā'il* 95-98, Suyūṭī, *Ašbāh I,* 83, Versteegh, *Zağǧāǧī* 118-120). One reason presented by Zağǧāǧī, *Īḍāḥ* 76, is that as the noun is formed according to different forms in which the middle radical can be vowelless or vowelled by different vowels, e.g. فَعْلٌ, فِعْلٌ, فُعْلٌ, فَعَلٌ, فَعِلٌ etc., the marker of the declension could not occur at the middle of the word, as the listener would not be able to know if it is a marker of declension or undeclinability. According to Quṭrub's (d. 210/825) (Muḥammad b. al-Mustanīr Abū 'Alī, see Suyūṭī, *Buġya I,* 242-243, Brockelman. *GAL I,* 101-102, *S I,* 161, Sezgin, *Geschichte VIII,*.61-67, *IX,* 64-65) opinion, the marker of the declension could only occur at the end of the word, so that the measures would not all be mixed up together, or so that two vowelless consonants would not be combined together, or so that the word would not begin with a vowelless consonant (cf. 'Ukbarī, *Masā'il* 95-96). 'Ukbarī, *Masā'il* 95-96 refers to his opinion in this manner:

"وقال قُطْرُب: إنما جُعل أخيراً لتعذر جعله وسطاً ، إذ لو كان وسطاً لاختلطت الأبنية ، وربما أفضى إلى الجمع بين ساكنين ، أو الإبتداء بالساكن ، وكل ذلك خطأ لا يوجد مثله فيما إذا جعل أخيراً":

"And Quṭrub said: "Somehow it [sc. the marker of the declension] was made to occur at the end of the word, because of the impossibility of its occurrence at its middle. If this was to occur, then the measures would unavoidably be confused, and this would possibly lead to the cluster of two vowelless consonants or to beginning the word with a vowelless consonant. And all of that is erroneous, and can only be avoided if it occurs at the end of the word".

These theories are propounded almost in the same manner by al-Mubarrad to whom Abū Isḥāq al-Zağāğ (d. 311/923) (Ibrāhīm b. al-Sirrī b. Sahl, see Zubaidī, *Ṭabaqāt* 121, Suyūṭī, *Buġya* 411-413. He was the pupil of al-Mubarrad and the teacher of al-Zağāğī. He wrote *Maʿānī l-Qurʾān, al-Ištiqāq, Faʿaltu wa-faʿaltu* (mentioned in 39 b), *Muḫtaṣar al-naḥw* and other works] refers to (cf. Zağğāğī, *Īḍāḥ* 76).

c) Another interesting discussion concerns which is original, the marker of the declension or undeclinability (for discussions see ʿUkbarī, *Masāʾil* 106-109, Suyūṭī, *Ašbāh I,* 163). One argument is that the declension is original, as it makes the meaning of the sentence understandable by indicating who/which is the subject and who/which is the object, whereas the undeclinability does not, as its markers are of no help to explain the sentence's meaning (cf. ʿUkbarī, *Masāʾil* 107). Those who believe that the undeclinability is original refer to the argument that the markers of the undeclinability are fixed whereas the markers of the declension are circulating, and as the fixed is original in relation to the circulating, the markers of the undeclinability are original in relation to the markers of the declension (cf. ʿUkbarī, *Masāʾil* 108). The answer to this argument is that the notion of the derivative and of the origin is not determined regarding what is fixed or what is circulating, but regarding the usefulness of clarifying the sentence's meaning, which is why the marker of the declension is original in importance (cf. ʿUkbarī, *Masāʾil* 108-109).

(44) The reason why the perfect is undeclinable and why its marker of undeclinability is a vowel, is that the perfect is partly similar to the noun. Its vowelling separates it from the undeclinable imperative, which does not present any similarity with the noun, and which for this reason is given a marker that does not exist in the noun, namely the sukūn (for discussions see Ibn Yaʿīš, *VII,* 4-5, my notes (48)). This similarity of the perfect to the noun is noticed in the fact that like the noun, it can function as a modifier, صِفَة (for discussions concerning this term see Owens, *Foundations* 154-156), to the indefinite noun. This is remarked in the sentence مَرَرْتُ بِرَجُلٍ ضَرَبَ وَضَارِبٍ, in which both the perfect ضَرَبَ and the active participle of the noun ضَارِبٍ have the same function (cf. Ibn Yaʿīš, *VII,* 4). It can as well in the same manner as the active participle, function as a خَبَرٌ "predicate" in a nominal sentence. An example is زَيْدٌ قَامَ "Zaid was getting up", in which the perfect قَامَ is a predicate to the topic زَيْدٌ in the same manner as the active participle قَائِمٌ is a predicate to the same topic in the sentence زَيْدٌ قَائِمٌ (cf. ibid). It can as well have the same meaning as the imperfect, which is considered to be the form that is similar to the declinable noun, and thus can replace it. For instance in a sentence as إِنْ قُمْتَ قُمْتُ "If you rise, I shall rise", the perfects قُمْتَ قُمْتُ that occur after the conditional إِنْ, can be used instead of the imperfect forms تَقُمْ أَقُمْ after the same conditional, i.e. إِنْ تَقُمْ أَقُمْ (cf. ibid, my notes to Ibn Masʿūd, *I,* 54-55 and see further for examples (44 b)). The reasons why the perfect and the imperative are undeclinable and the imperfect is declinable are presented by Ibn Yaʿīš, *VII,* 4-5 in the following manner:

"وقال وهو مبني على الفتح وللسائل أن يسأل فيقول ثم لم بني الفعل الماضي على الفتح فالجواب أنَ أصل الأفعال كلّها أن تكون ساكنة الآخر وذلك من قبل أنَ العلَة التي من أجلها وجب إعراب الإسماء غير موجودة فيها لأنَ العلَة الموجبة لإعراب الأسماء الفصل بين فاعلها ومفعولها وليس ذلك في الأفعال إلاَ أنَ الأفعال انقسمت ثلاثة أقسام

قسم ضارع الأسماء مضارعة تامة فاستحقّ به أن يكون معربا وهو الفعل المضارع الذي في أوّله الزوائد الأربع... والضرب الثاني من الأفعال ما ضارع الأسماء مضارعة ناقصة وهو الفعل الماضي: والضرب الثالث ما لم يضارع الأسماء بوجه من الوجوه وهو فعل الأمر... الذي ليس في أوّله حرف المضارعة الذي لم يضارع الإسم البتَة فبقي على أصله ومقتضى القياس فيه السكون وتوسّط حال الماضي فنقص عن درجة الفعل المضارع وزاد على فعل الأمر لأنَ فيه بعض ما في المضارع وذلك أنَه يقع موقع الإسم فيكون خبرا نحو قولك زيد قام فيقع موقع قائم ويكون صفة نحو مررت برجل قام فيقع موقع مررت برجل قائم وقد وقع أيضا موضع الفعل المضارع في الجزاء نحو قولك إن قمت قمت والمراد إن تقم أقم فلمّا كان فيه ما ذكرنا من المضارعة للأسماء والأفعال المضارعة ميز بالحركة على فعل الأمر":

"And he [sc. Zamaḫšarī, 108] said that it [sc. the perfect] is undeclinable and vowelled by a fatḥa, such which incites the questioner to ask why the perfect verb is given the fatḥa as its marker of invariability. The answer is that by principle, all the [tenses of] verbs should have had a sukūn as their marker of invariability, because the reason which made it necessary to make the nouns declinable is not existent concerning them. As for the reason of the nouns' declinability, it is is to distinguish between their subjects and their objects, and this is not to be found as what concerns the verbs.

However, the verbs are divided into three categories: One category which ضَارَعَ "was similar" to the nouns completely, and which therefore deserved to be declinable, and it is the imperfect, which has at its beginning [one of] the four prefixes... The second category among the verbs is what is partly similar to the nouns, which is the perfect. The third category among the verbs is what did not at all resemble the nouns, which is the imperative verb... It did not have at its beginning any imperfect prefix and did not in any way resemble the noun, which is why it remained according to its base form, and the analogy necessitated for it a sukūn... The state of the perfect is in between [these categories]. It is lower than the level of the imperfect and higher than the [level of] the imperative, as it has some of the imperfect's properties, namely: It occurs instead of the noun and is a خَبَرٌ "predicate", as you say زيد قامَ "Zaid was getting up", in which it [قامَ] is used instead of قائمٌ. It is a صفةٌ "epithet", e.g. مَرَرْتُ بِرَجُلٍ قامَ "I passed by a man getting up", which occurs instead of مَرَرْتُ بِرَجُلٍ قائم ... It also occurs instead of the imperfect in the conditional sentence, e.g. إنْ قُمْتَ قُمْتُ "If you rise, I shall rise", and the intended is إنْ تَقُمْ أقُمْ. Since it possesses the similarities that we mentioned with the nouns and with the imperfect, it was distinguished with a vowel from the imperative".

b) It is not only the perfect's resemblance to the noun which makes it suitable to be given a vowel as its marker of undeclinability, but its resemblance as well to the imperfect. As it is this resemblance which is one of the reasons that its marker is the fatḥa, I find it here of interest to present some cases in which the perfect replaces the imperfect. The meaning can be the present or the future. Some examples referring to the present are: كُنْتَ "you were" used in the meaning of أنْتَ "you are" according to Ibn Fāris, Ṣāḥibī 236, in e.g. the sur. 27: 27 (قَالَ سَنَنْظُرُ أَصَدَقْتَ أَمْ كُنْتَ مِنَ ٱلْكَاذِبِينَ) "(Solomon) said: "Soon shall we see whether thou hast told the truth or lied!" and the sur. 2: 143 (وَمَا جَعَلْنَا ٱلْقِبْلَةَ ٱلَّتِي كُنْتَ عَلَيْهَا) "And We appointed the Qibla to which thou wast used", كُنْتُمْ "you were" used in the meaning of أَنْتُمْ "you are" in the sur. 3: 110 (كُنْتُمْ خَيْرَ أُمَّةٍ) "Ye are the best of Peoples" and أَتَى used in the meaning of يَأْتِي according to Ibn Fāris, *Ṣāḥibī* 219 and Muʾaddib, *Taṣrīf* 17 in the sur. 16: 1 (أَتَى أَمْرُ ٱللَّهِ) "(Inevitable) cometh (to pass) the Command of God". Both al-Ḫalīl and Sībawaihi remark concerning the sur. 30: 51 (وَلَئِنْ أَرْسَلْنَا رِيحاً فَرَأَوْهُ مُصْفَرّاً لَظَلُّوا مِنْ بَعْدِهِ يَكْفُرُونَ) "And if We (but) send a Wind from which they see (their tilth) turn yellow,—behold, they become, thereafter, ungrateful (Unbelievers)!", that لَظَلُّوا occurs in the meaning of لَيَظَلُّنَّ (cf. Makkī, *Mušakkal* 484, ʿAbd al-Qādir, *ʾAṯar* 60). Some examples that refer to the future are according to Muʾaddib, *Taṣrīf* 17-18 found in the sur. 35: 9 (وَٱللَّهُ ٱلَّذِي أَرْسَلَ ٱلرِّيَاحَ فَتُثِيرُ سَحَاباً فَسُقْنَاهُ) "It is God Who sends forth the Winds, so that they raise up the Clouds and We drive them", in which فَسُقْنَاهُ occurs instead of فَنَسُوقُهُ, the sur. 5: 119 (وَإِذْ قَالَ ٱللَّهُ يَا عِيسَى ٱبْنَ مَرْيَمَ) "And behold! God will say: "O Jesus the son of Mary!", in which قَالَ occurs instead of يَقُولُ and the sur. 7: 50 (وَنَادَى أَصْحَابُ ٱلنَّارِ أَصْحَابَ ٱلْجَنَّةِ) "The Companions of the Fire will call to the Companions of the Garden", in which وَنَادَى occurs instead of وَيُنَادِي. Likewise, Ibn al-Anbārī referred to by Ibn Manẓūr, *I*, 49, remarks that the perfect has the meaning of the future in both the sur. 22: 25 (إِنَّ ٱلَّذِينَ كَفَرُوا وَيَصُدُّونَ عَنْ سَبِيلِ ٱللَّهِ) "As to those who have rejected (God), and would keep back (men) from the Way of God", in which كَفَرُوا occurs instead of يَكْفُرُونَ, and the sur. 5: 37 (إِلَّا ٱلَّذِينَ تَابُوا مِنْ قَبْلِ أَنْ تَقْدِرُوا عَلَيْهِمْ) "Except for those who repent before they fall into your power", in which تَابُوا occurs instead of يَتُوبُونَ. Farrāʾ, *Maʿānī I*, 243-244 believes that in the sur. 3: 156 (يَا أَيُّهَا ٱلَّذِينَ آمَنُوا لَا تَكُونُوا كَٱلَّذِينَ كَفَرُوا وَقَالُوا لِإِخْوَانِهِمْ إِذَا ضَرَبُوا فِي ٱلْأَرْضِ...) "O ye who believe! Be not like the Unbelievers, who say of their brethren, when they are travelling through the earth...", إِذَا ضَرَبُوا is used in the meaning of the future. The proof of this argument is that if it referred to a past time, then إِذْ would have been used, and not إِذَا which is specially made to precede the imperfect and indicates future time (for discussions concerning إِذْ that determines the past and إِذَا the future see Ibn Manẓūr, *I*, 49-50; for a general presentation of examples with إِذْ see Cantarino, *Syntax III*, 284-290 and with إِذَا see Wright, *III*, 9-11, Cantarino, *Syntax III*, 291-306). Likewise, when the conditional particle إِذَا is made to precede a definite noun, the meaning of the verb that is said in the past tense is the future, as in the sur. 81: 1-2 (إِذَا ٱلشَّمْسُ كُوِّرَتْ وَإِذَا ٱلنُّجُومُ ٱنْكَدَرَتْ) "When the sun (with its spacious light) is folded up; when the stars fall, losing their lustre" (cf. Wright, *III*, 9-10). In spite of the fact that إِذْ, which determines the past occurs in the sur. 6: 93 (وَلَوْ تَرَى إِذِ ٱلظَّالِمُونَ فِي غَمَرَاتِ ٱلْمَوْتِ) "If thou couldst but see how the wicked (do fare) in the flood of confusion at death!", its meaning is that of إِذَا that determines the future, as al-Laiṯ referred to by Ibn Manẓūr, *I*, 49 remarks, because this situation did not occur yet. It is not only after the conditional particle إذا that the perfect can have the meaning of the present or future (cf. Šādilī, *ʿAnāṣir* 19-20), but also after لَوْ (for examples see Cantarino, *Syntax III*, 320-326), حَتَّى (for examples see Wright, *III*, 13-14, Cantarino, *Syntax III*, 84-97), the adverbial relatives لمّا (for examples see Wright, *III*, 17, Cantarino, *Syntax III*, 177 sqq.) and رُبّما (for examples see Cantarino, *Syntax III*, 225-227).

(45) Similar to the term أخ "brother" chosen by Ibn Masʿūd that indicates the close relationship between the vowel and the weak consonant, is the term ابنة "daughter" (cf. Carter, *Širbīnī* 47: 3.1 (2)). Concerning such a term Carter remarks in his notes 47: 3.1 (2) that it is:

> "an extremely common anthropomorphism. That the short vowels *a, i, u* are homorganic with the consonants *ʾ, y, w* has been an axiom of Arabic phonology from the first".

Ibn Masʿūd states that the fatḥa is the brother of the sukūn, by which he means that it is closest to it regarding the lightness of the pronunciation. For this reason it is appropriate to be given as a marker of invariability to the undeclinable perfect. Principally, the perfect, like all other tenses of verbs, should have had a vowelless invariable ending. However, as it is partly similar to the noun (for the arguments see (43)), it was given a vowel. This vowel could not be the ḍamma, because the ḍamma was given to the imperfect that is totally similar to the noun (cf. (47), (93)). It could not either be the kasra because the kasra is forbidden to mark the verbs' endings in the same manner as the sukūn is forbidden to mark the nouns' endings (for discussions why the verbs cannot have a genitive and the nouns a jussive see Zağğāğī, *Īḍāḥ* 107 sqq., Versteegh, *Zağğāğī*, 182 sqq.), so it was given the fatḥa as the fatḥa is somewhere in between the sukūn of the undeclinable verb, i.e. the imperative that is not at all similar to the noun (cf. (48)) and the ḍamma of the declinable imperfect (cf. Ibn Yaʿīš, *VII*, 5, my notes to Ibn Masʿūd, *I*, 55-56). Another reason that can be added proposed by Ibn Yaʿīš, *VII*, 5 concerning why the perfect's ending cannot be given the ḍamma, is that some Arabs used the ḍamma instead of the *ū* to mark the pl., e.g. قامُ said instead of قاموا "they rose /masc. pl.". Another example is كانُ said instead of كانوا in the following verse said by an anonymous poet, cited by Muʾaddib, *Taṣrīf* 15, Ibn Yaʿīš, *VII*, 5, Ibn Ḫālawaihi, *Qirāʾāt I*, 352, Ibn al-Anbārī, *Inṣāf* Q. 72, 222, (Q. 56, 169 with الشفاة instead of الأساة), Afandī, *Tanzīl* 353, Nöldeke, *Beiträge* 17, Howell, *I*, fasc. II, 517 with وَلو instead of فَلو:

" فَلَو أنَّ ٱلأطبا كانُ حَوْلِي وكانَ مَعَ ٱلأطبَاءِ الأُساةُ ".

"O, if the physicians had been around me and the surgeons were with the physicians!".

Other examples with the ḍamma replacing the suffixed pronoun of the nominative, the *ū*, presented by Muʾaddib, *Taṣrīf* 296 are لم يَذْهَبُ إخْوَتُكَ "your brothers did not go" said by some Arabs with لم يَذْهَبُ instead of لم يَذْهَبُوا. Some read as well the sur. 53: 31 as (لِيَجْزِيَ ٱلَّذِينَ أساءُ) "So that He rewards those who do Evil" with أساءُ instead of أساءوا. The same phenomenon occurs in the following verse said by an unknown poet recited by al-Kisāʾī, in which طارُ occurs instead of طاروا:

"مَتَى أَقُولُ خَلَتْ عَنْ أَهْلِهَا آلدَّارُ   كَأَنَّهُم بِجَنَاحَيْ طَائِرٍ طَارُ".

"When I say that the house was emptied from its kinsfolk, as though they flew away on a bird's wings".

Ibn Manẓūr, *I*, 697 presents the last verse with كَأَنَّا instead of كَأَنَّهُم, and according to him the verse is recited by al-Farrāʾ. Zamaḫšarī, *Kaššāf II*, 25 mentions concerning the sur. 23: 1 (قَدْ أَفْلَحَ ٱلْمُؤْمِنُونَ) "The Believers must (Eventualy) win through,—", that according to the reading of Ṭalḥa b. Muṣarraf, أَفْلَحُ occurs with the ḍamma given to the last radical marking the pl., similarly to كَانُ in فَلَوْ أَنَّ ٱلْأَطِبَّا كَانُ حَوْلِي (cf. Afandī, *Tanzīl* 353 who quotes also Zamaḫšarī; compare the elision of the *ū* of the pl. of the 3rd person of the masc. pl. of the perfect with the 3rd radical made vowelless in صَنَعْ said instead of صَنَعُوا "they did" which occurs in the verse mentioned in (307 d)). Another theory propounded by Muʾaddib, *Taṣrīf* 16-17 concerning why the perfect' final radical is vowelled by a fatḥa, is that because the perfect's action is completed and done with, it is deemed as weak. For this reason it is given the weakest of the three vowels, which is the fatḥa. The proof of the fatḥa's weakness according to him, is that the Arabs do not elide it from any form, contrarily to the ḍamma and the kasra (for this elision see (109); for a study of the anomalous elision and addition of a vowel see Åkesson, *Elision* 21 sqq.). An exception to this rule is the example قَطْعَ that occurs instead of قَطَعَ which is considered by Muʾaddib as belonging to an unknown dialectal variant that is not to be taken into consideration, in the following verse (cf. Muʾaddib, *Taṣrīf* 17, Åkesson, *Elision* 25):

"قَطْعَ عَمْرو سَاعِدَىْ وَهَبْ".

"'Amr has cut off both Wahab's arms".

The rare elision of the fatḥa of the 2nd radical occurs as well in a case of a verb of Form VII, e.g. اِنْطْلَقَ said instead of اِنْطَلَقَ "to take off" (cf. Sībawaihī, *II*, 278, Åkesson, *Elision* 23).

(46) The resemblance that exists between the perfect and the active participle form of the noun, اِسْمُ ٱلْفَاعِلِ, is that the active participle refers to past time when it is used as the first element of an *ʾiḍāfa* construction, as in e.g. انا قاتِلُ غُلامِكَ "I am the killer of your servant", in which the active participle قاتِلُ that is put in the nominative before the noun in the genitive غُلامِكَ, reveals that the action of the killing is completed, in the same manner as قَتَلْتُ does in the sentence انا قَتَلْتُ غُلامَكَ "I have killed your servant". The difference between the perfect and the active participle is that the active participle that occurs as a first element of an *ʾiḍāfa* construction, and thus refers to a completed action in the past, is unable to govern the noun after it in the accusative as the perfect does. As remarked in the sentence انا قاتِلُ غُلامِكَ, the active participle قاتِلُ does not operate on غُلامِكَ by putting it in the accusative, i.e. غُلامَكَ, as the perfect does in the sentence انا قَتَلْتُ غُلامَكَ. It is this difference that Ibn Masʿūd refers to when he writes that "the active participle [in the sense of the past] did not acquire from it [sc. the perfect] the ability to operate". This is one of the reasons why the perfect, which does not resemble the active participle completely, is made undeclinable. The active participle loses its resemblance in meaning with the perfect and becomes similar to the imperfect in its reference to future time when it is used as a subject that governs the noun after it in the accusative, as in e.g. اَنَا قَاتِلٌ غُلَامَكَ "I am going to kill your servant", which has the same meaning as أَنَا سَأَقْتُلُ غُلَامَكَ or أَنَا أَقْتُلُ غُلَامَكَ. It is this similarity of the imperfect to the active participle that is referred to by Ibn Masʿūd with these words: "by contrast to the imperfect, as the active participle [in the sense of the future] acquired its ability to operate" (see further for a study Howell, *I,* fasc. IV, 1631-1637, Reckendorf, *Syntax* 174-175). The active participle in the sense of the future that operates as a verb on the noun by putting it in the accusative, is also termed by the Kufans as "the permansive verb" (cf. (46 b)). An amusing story which illustrates for us an example of an active participle that has the sense of the past and so is unable to govern the noun in the accusative, and an example of one that has the sense of the future and so is able to do so, is narrated by Suyūṭī, *Ašbāh III,* 535-536. It reports a dialogue told by al-Marzubānī, who in his turn has heard it from someone else, between the grammarian al-Kisāʾī and the judge Abū Yūsuf in the presence of Hārūn al-Rašīd (193/809). It praises also the importance of syntax:

"اجتمعت وابو يوسف القاضي عند هارون الرشيد، فجعل ابو يوسف يَذُمُّ النحو ويقول: ما النحو! فقلت وأردت ان أُعَلِّمَه فضل النحو: ما تقول في رجل قال لرجل: انا قاتلٌ غلامكَ، وقال له آخر: انا قاتلٌ غلامكَ، ايهما كنت تأخذ به؟ قال آخُذُهما جميعاً، فقال له هارون: أخطأتَ، وكان له عِلْمٌ بالعربيَّة، فاسْتَحْيَى، وقال: كيف ذلك؟ فقال: الذي يُؤخذ بقَتْل الغلام هو الذي قال: انا قاتلُ غلامكَ بالاضافة، لانه فعل ماض. فأما الذي قال: انا قاتلٌ غلامكَ بلا اضافة فانه لا يُؤخذ، لأنَّه مُسْتَقْبَل، لم يَكُن بَعْدُ":

"I [sc. al-Kisāʾī] met with the judge Abū Yūsuf by Hārūn al-Rašīd, and Abū Yūsuf started dispraising syntax by saying: "What is syntax!". So I said to him with the intention of teaching him the importance of syntax: "What would you say about a man who said to another: انا قاتلُ غلامكَ "I am the killer of your servant" and the other said to him: انا قاتلٌ غلامكَ "I am going to kill your servant", whom of the two would you arrest?". He said: "I would arrest them both". So Hārūn who had a good knowledge of Arabic, said to him: "You are wrong". So he got embarassed and said: "In which manner?". He answered: "The one who is to be arrested for the killing of the servant is the one who said: انا قاتلُ غلامكَ by using an *iḍāfa* construction, because it [sc. the active participle in it] refers to an action in the past. As for the one who said: انا قاتلٌ غلامكَ without using an *iḍāfa* construction, he is not to be arrested because it [sc. the active participle] refers to [an action in] the future, which did not yet occur".

It can be mentioned in this context that the active participle بَاسِطٌ of the sur. 18: 18 (وكَلْبُهُم بَاسِطٌ ذِرَاعَيْهِ بِالْوَصِيدِ) "Their dog streching forth his two fore-legs on the threshold", that is made to govern the noun after it in the accusative, refers to the past by some (cf. Ibn Ǧinnī, *Muḥtasib II,* 327), and more particularly by al-Kisāʾī (cf. Ibn Hišām, *Masālik* 217), and by Hišām and Abū Ǧaʿfar (cf. the notes to ibid), whereas it is considered as having the meaning of the present time by the majority (cf. Ibn Hišām, *Masālik* 217, Suyūṭī, *Ašbāh I,* 385, Howell, *I,* fasc. IV, 1633).

b) The Kufans name the active participle for الفعل الدائم "the permansive verb" (the term is also mentioned in (93), (174 b); for discussions including some references to some modern researchers who accept it and others who refuse it see Rāǧiḥī, *Farrā*ʾ 115-138) when it operates on the noun following it, and sometimes as well for الفعل "verb". When it does not operate, they include it among the noun categories and name it as الإسم "the noun" (cf. Rāǧiḥī, *Farrā*ʾ 115). The use of the term الفعل الدائم is criticized by the Basrans (for the controversy between both schools see Versteegh, *Zaǧǧāǧī* 146). The notion of a derived noun, i.e. the active participle, as being considered as a verb is totally rejected by the logicians (for discussions see Farābī, *Šarḥ* 42, Abed, *Logic* 130-136). Some allusions to the controversies are referred to by Zaǧǧāǧī, *Maǧālis* 318 in the session between Abū l-ʿAbbās Aḥmad b. Yaḥyā [Ṯaʿlab] and Abū l-Ḥasan Muḥammad b. Kaisān:

"حدثني بعض أصحابنا قال: أخبرنا أبو الحسن بن كيسان قال: قال لي أبو العباس: كيف تقول مررت برجل قائم أبوه؟ فأجبته بخفض قائم ورفع الأب. فقال لي: بأي شيء ترفعه؟ فقلت بقائم. فقال: أو ليس هو عندكم اسماً وتعيبوننا بتسميته فعلا دائماً؟ فقلت: لفظه لفظ الأسماء، وإذا وقع موقع الفعل المضارع وأدى معناه عمل عمله، لأنه قد يعمل عمل الفعل ما ليس بفعل إذا ضارعه".

"Some of our friends said to me: "Abū l-Ḥasan b. Kīsān reported to us, he said: "Abū l-ʿAbbās said to me: "How do you say مَرَرْتُ برَجُلٍ قائمٍ أبوهُ "I passed by a man whose father is standing?". I answered him: "by putting قائمٍ "standing" in the genitive and الأبُ "the father" in the nominative. So he asked me: "By what do you govern it in the nominative?". I answered: "By قائمٍ "standing". So he said: "Is it not a noun according to you and you reproach us of naming it for فعل دائم "a permansive verb?". He said: "Its form is a nominal form, and if it occurred in the position of the imperfect verb and led to its meaning, it governed similarly to it, because words which are not verbs govern as verbs when they become similar to them".

In the session between the Kufan Abū l-ʿAbbās Ṯaʿlab and the Basran Abū l-ʿAbbās al-Mubarrad, Zaǧǧāǧī, *Maǧālis* 349 writes:

"قال ثعلب: كلّمت ذات يوم محمد بن يزيد البصري فقال: كان الفرّاء يناقض، يقول قائم فعل، وهو اسم لدخول التنوين عليه. فإن كان فعلاً لم يكن اسماً، وإن كان اسماً فلا ينبغي أن تسمّيه فعلاً.

فقلت: الفرّاء يقول قائم فعل دائم لفظه لفظ الأسماء لدخول دلائل الأسماء عليه، ومعناه معنى الفعل لأنّه يَنصب فيقال قائم قياما، وضاربٌ زيداً، فالجهة التي هو فيها اسمٌ ليس هو فيها فعلاً، والجهة التي هو فيها فعل ليس هو فيها اسماً. فأنت لم نصبتَ به وهو عندك اسم؟ فقال: لمضارعته يَفْعَلُ".

"Ṯaʿlab said: "I talked one day with Muḥammad b. Yazīd al-Baṣrī [sc. al-Mubarrad], and he said: "Al-Farrāʾ was contradicting himself by saying that [the active participle] قائم "standing" is a verb while it is a noun, as it admits the nunation. So if it is a verb it cannot be a noun, and if it is a noun then you ought not name it a verb".

So I said: "Al-Farrāʾ said that قائم "standing" is a فعل دائم "permansive verb", whose form is a nominal form as it admits the marking signs that are characteristic for the nouns, and whose meaning is the verb's meaning as it governs in the accusative, as it is said قائمٌ قياما "he is standing a standing" and ضاربٌ زيداً "the one who is hitting Zaid". So according to the aspect in which it is a noun it is not a verb, and according to the aspect in which it is a verb it is not a noun. How about yourself, why did you make it govern in the accusative while you consider it as a noun?". He said: "Because of its similarity to [the imperfect] يَفْعَلُ".

The main arguments against considering the active participle as a permansive verb (for them see Sīrāfī, *Šarḥ I,* fol. 493, quoted by al-Mubārak, the editor of Zaǧǧāǧī, *Īḍāḥ* in his notes 86) are the following: The active participle is a noun, and examples such as قائمٌ, ضاربٌ and their likes, are affected by factors that affect the nouns only and not the verbs. They are declinable as the nouns are, by being put in the nominative, accusative and genitive, they accept the nunation and the definite article, and they can occur as an element of an *iḍāfa* construction. The operating function of the active participle on the noun that follows it which is similar to the verb, is not a sufficient reason to name the active participle a verb, as this would mean that each term that operates in the same manner as another one can be named by the other's name, which is unacceptable. Examples to that are the conjunction إنَّ "that" and its sisters, عشرين "twenty" and its likes, and in some cases the *maṣdar,* all which could have been named verbs as they put the noun that follows them in the accusative as the verb does. In the same manner, nouns that put the nouns following them in the genitive could have been named prepositions, as the prepositions are specifically reckognized to put the nouns following them in the genitive. If the meaning of the active participle in a phrase as زيد ضاربٌ عمراً "Zaid is hitting 'Amr" relates to the meaning of the imperfect in زيد يَضْرِبُ عمراً "Zaid is hitting 'Amr", then it is also possible to make the imperfect relate to the active participle and to name the imperfect a noun. According to Maḫzūmī to whom Rāǧiḥī, *Farrā'* 136 refers, the permansive verb that al-Farrā' considered as being the active participle, corresponds to the stative in the Akkadian language (cf. Ungnad-Matouš, *Des Akkadischen* 64-65, Rowton, *Permansive* 233-303).

(47) One of the reasons why the imperfect is declinable is its resemblance to the active participle form of the noun, اسمُ الفاعل, which is a noun (cf. (46), (93)). The phonological form of the imperfect يَضْرِبُ and of the active participle ضاربٌ are commensurable regarding the vowelling or the vowellessness of both these forms' respective consonants (cf. Owens, *Foundations* 208).

(48) The imperative is undeclinable according to the Basrans (for their opinion see Ibn Ǧinnī, *Ḫaṣā'iṣ III,* 83, *Tamām* 15, Suyūṭī, *Ašbāh II,* 353-354). Its last radical is given the sukūn, which is a marker that is not given to the noun,—except in the pause which is a special case –, because its does not offer any similarity nor in meaning and nor in form, with the noun (cf. Ibn Ya'īš, *VII,* 4, my notes to Ibn Mas'ūd, *I,* 55). However according to the Kufans the imperative is underlyingly declinable rather than undeclinable, and the loss of the last vowel is a process which is similar to the case of the declinable imperfect that is put in the jussive mood when it follows the *li–* of the imperative, e.g. لِيَفْعَلْ "let him do" (cf. my notes (119), (120), (184); for the Kufans' opinion see Farrā', *Ma'ānī I,* 491, Ṯa'lab, *Maǧālis II,* 456, Ibn al-Anbārī, *Qaṣā'id* 38; for the debate see Ibn al-Anbārī, *Inṣāf* Q. 72, 214-224, *Asrār* 125-126, Zamaḫšarī, 114-115, 'Ukbarī, *Masā'il* 114-119, Ibn Ya'īš, *VII,* 61-62).

(49) The 3rd weak radical is elided in the weak verbs to which the pronoun of the agent of the masc. pl., the *ū*, is suffixed to, e.g. رَمَوْا underlyingly رَمَيُوا (cf. (303)), and رَضُوا underlyingly رَضِيُوا (see further (275), (303)). In رَمَيُوا, the sequence ـَيُو becomes ـَوْ, namely رَمَوْا. In رَضِيُوا, the sequence ـِيُو, becomes ـُو, namely رَضُوا (for discussions see Wright, *II*, 89).

(50) Different opinions concern the reason of the occurrence of the separating alif, *the élif otiosum,* after the suffixation of the agent pronoun of the 3rd person of the masc. pl. to a verb in the perfect, e.g. حَضَرُوا "they came". It is also named ألف الوقاية *"the guarding alif"* (cf. Wright, *I*, 11). According to al-Farrā''s theory, this alif is suffixed after the *w* that marks the pl. so that it is possible to differentiate between the *w* which is a radical in verbs with 3rd weak radical and the *w* that marks the pl. As an example of a verb in the sing. that ends with a *w* radical, يَدْعُو "he calls" can be mentioned and as an example of a verb in the jussive that ends with the suffixed pronoun of the nominative of the masc. pl., the *ū,* preceding the alif, لم يدْعوا "they did not call" can be mentioned. Had it not been for the alif, both the singular and the pl. of the verb would be mixed together. As for al-Aḫfaš, he believes that it was suffixed so that the *w* of the pl. is not confused with the *w* of the conjunction *wa* (cf. ʿAbd al-Tawwāb's note on Rāzī, in Ḫalīl b. Aḥmad ..., *Ḥurūf* 135). The example حَضَرُوتَكَلَّمَ mentioned by Ibn Masʿūd refers to the opinion of al-Aḫfaš. If an alif did not ocur after the *w*, it could be read as حَضَرَوتَكَلَّمَ "He came and talked" or حَضَرُوتَكَلَّمَ "they came, he talked", which would cause an inevitable confusion. Wright, *I*, 11 and Mu'addib, *Taṣrīf* 21 adhere to this opinion without referring to al-Aḫfaš. See further Ṣūlī, *Adab* 246, Fleisch, *Traité II,* 116-117 note 2.

b) Different additional alifs (seventeen sorts are presented by Ṯaʿālibī, *Fiqh* 226-227 and fourty by Fairūzābādī, *Baṣā'ir II,* 9-11) can be mentioned in this context (for them see Rāzī, in Ḫalīl b. Aḥmad ..., *Ḥurūf* 134-135):

– ألف الوصل "the connective alif" (for it see (111), (111 b), (114), (115), (118)).

– ألف القطع "the disjunctive alif" (for it see (114), (115), (116)).

– ألف الإستفهام "the alif of interrogation", e.g. أزَيْدٌ عندك؟ "is Zaid by you?".

– ألف النداء "the vocative alif", e.g. أزيدُ أقْبِلْ "O Zaid approach!" (for it see Wright, *II*, 294).

– ألف الأصل "the alif radical", e.g. هذا أسدٌ "this is a lion".

– ألف البدل "the substituted alif", e.g. هذا أحدٌ underlyingly هذا وَحَدٌ "this is someone" (for the substitution of the hamza for the *w* see (235), (290), (291), (292), (316) (317), (318), (318 b), (319), (321), (322), (323), (327 c)).

– ألف التفضيل "the alif prefixed to the comparative and superlative forms", e.g. زيد أفضل من عمرو "Zaid is better than ʿAmr" (for the elative see (139)-(143 c)).

– ألف المنقلبة "the alif changed from another consonant", e.g. قال underlyingly قَوَلَ "he said" (for the substitution of the alif for the *w* see (36), (38), (211), (265), (266), (270), (276), (278), (279), (284), for the *y* see (33), (54), (81), (265), (270), (285), (303), (304) and for the hamza see (217), (218), (220), (237), (327 b), (369)).

– ألف الضمير "the alif which is the suffixed pronoun of the dual of the nominative", e.g. ضَرَبَا "they both hit".

– ألف الندبة "the alif of lamentation", e.g. وازيداه "alas for Zaid!" (cf. Zaǧǧāǧī, Ǧumal 190, Wright, II, 295).

– الألف المقصورة "the alif that can be abbreviated" (cf. Wright, I, 11, Daqr, Muʿǧam 55-57; and for examples see (269), (269 b)).

– الألف الممدودة "the lenghtened alif" (cf. Wright, I, 11, 24-25, Daqr, Muʿǧam 57).

– ألف الإلحاق "the appended alif, which gives the word the form of a quadriliteral or quinqueliteral" (cf. Wright, II, 152).

(51) Concerning لم يَدْعو "he did not call", the jussive should have been applied resulting in the elision of the *w*, and لم يَدعُ should have been said. Ibn Masʿūd refers here to an anomalous case in which the jussive is not taken into consideration in a specific dialectal variant, and the indicative is chosen instead. This phenomenon occurs in the following verse said by Abū ʿAmr b. ʿAlāʾ al-Māzinī to the poet al-Farazdaq, who has at first insulted him and then apologized for having done so. In it, لم تَهْجُو with the defective maintainance of the *w* occurs instead of لم تَهجُ with its elision, in the same manner as لم يَدعو mentioned by Ibn Masʿūd occurs instead of لم يَدعُ. The verse is cited by Farrāʾ, Maʿānī I, 162, II, 188, Ibn Ǧinnī, Sirr II, 630, Munṣif II, 115, Zamaḫšarī, 184, Ibn al-Anbārī, Inṣāf Q. 2, 10, Ibn Yaʿīš, X, 104, 105, Ibn ʿUṣfūr, Ḍarāʾir 45, Ibn al-Šaǧarī, Amālī I, 85, Baġdādī, Šarḥ 406, Howell, IV, fasc. I, 1576, Freytag, Hamasae 78, Košut, Streitfragen 309, 344, Wright, IV, 389:

"هَجَوْتَ زَبَانَ ثُمَّ جِئْتَ مُعْتَذِراً   مِنْ هَجْوِ زَبَانَ لَمْ تَهْجُو وَلَمْ تَدَعْ".

"You did satirize Zabbān: then you came, apologizing for satirizing Zabbān: you did not satirize [him], nor did you leave [him] alone".

ʿAbd Yaġūṯ b. Waqqāṣ al-Ḥāriṯī has لم تَرى used anomalously as an indicative instead of the jussive لم تَرَ in the following verse which he said when he was imprisoned. It is cited by Ibn Ǧinnī, Sirr I, 76, Muʾaddib, Taṣrīf 398, Zamaḫšarī, 185, Afandī, Tanzīl 564, Ibn Yaʿīš, X, 107, Ibn Hišām, Muġnī I, 277, Ǧāmiʿ 15, Ḫuḍarī, Ḥāšiya 62, Tibrīzī, Iḫtiyārāt 771, Ibn Manẓūr, IV, 2325, Howell, IV, fasc. I, 1577, Freytag, Darstellung 505:

"وَتَضْحَكُ مِنِّي شَيْخَةٌ عَبْشَمِيَّةٌ   كَأَنْ لَمْ تَرَى قَبْلِي أَسِيراً يَمَانِيَا".

"And an ʿAbšamī old dame laughs at me, as though she had not seen a Yamānī captive before me".

Zamaḫšarī, Kaššāf II, 547 cites the last part of the verse in his commentary to sur. 20: 77 (لا تَخَافُ دَرَكاً ولا تَخْشَى) "Without fear of being overtaken (by Pharaoh) and without (any other) fear", (i.e. do not be afraid of being overtaken (by Pharaoh) and do not be scared), in which the weak last radical of the verb لا تَخْشَى is retained, in spite of its being a negative imperative. Furthermore, he writes that لا تَخَافُ has been read as لا تخف by some.

An unknown poet has لَا أَنْسَاهُ for لَا أَنْسَهُ in the following verse cited by Zamaḫšarī, 185, Ibn Yaʿīš, *X,* 107, Howell, *IV,* fasc. I, 1577, Wright, *IV,* 389:

"مَا أَنْسَ لَا أَنْسَاهُ آخِرَ عِيشَتِي   مَا لَاحَ بِٱلْمَعْزَاءِ رَيْعُ سَرَابِ".

"Whatever I forgot, I shall not forget him to the end of my life, so long as there appears on the rugged ground a quivering of mirage".

Ru'ba b. al-ʿAǧǧāǧ has وَلَا تَرَضَّاهَا for وَلَا تَرَضَّهَا in the following verse cited by Ibn Ǧinnī, *Sirr I,* 78, *Ḫaṣā'iṣ I,* 307, *Munṣif II,* 78, 115, Zamaḫšarī, 185, Ibn al-Anbārī, *Inṣāf* Q. 2, 10, Ibn Yaʿīš, *I,* 106, *X,* 107, Suyūṭī, *Ašbāh I,* 431, Baġdādī, *Ḫizāna III,* 534, *Šarḥ* 409, Howell, *IV,* fasc. I, 1577, Freytag, *Hamasae* 803, Košūt, *Streitfragen* 310, 344:

"إِذَ ٱلْعَجُوزُ غَضِبَتْ فَطَلِّقِ   وَلَا تَرَضَّاهَا وَلَا تَمَلَّقِ".

"When the old woman is angry, then divorce [her]; and seek not to pacify her, nor coax [her]".

For discussions concerning such cases see Ibn Ǧinnī, *Munṣif II,* 114-116, Zamaḫšarī, 184-185, Ibn Yaʿīš, *X,* 104-107, Nöldeke, *Grammatik* 11, Howell, *IV,* fasc. I, 1576-1577, Wright, *IV,* 389.

b) As anomalous as the use of the indicative instead of the jussive is the use of the indicative instead of the subjunctive, which occurs in the reading of Ibn Muḥaiṣin of the sur. 2: 233 (لِمَنْ أَرَادَ أَنْ يُتِمُّ ٱلرَّضَاعَةَ) "If the father desires to complete the term" with أَنْ يُتِمُّ instead of أَنْ يُتِمَّ (cf. Ibn Hišām, *Muġnī I,* 30). It has also been read so by Ibn Muǧāhid (cf. the notes to Ibn Ǧinnī, *Munṣif I,* 446). This phenomenon occurs also in the following verse said by an unknown poet, cited by Ṯaʿlab, *Maǧālis* 322, Ibn Ǧinnī, *Sirr II,* 549, *Ḫaṣā'iṣ I,* 390, *Munṣif I,* 278, Ibn Yaʿīš, *VII,* 9 in the notes, 15, Ibn Hišām, *Muġnī I,* 30, Baġdādī, *Ḫizāna III,* 559, Ibn ʿUṣfūr, *Ḍarā'ir* 163, Suyūṭī, *Ašbāh I,* 296, Howell, *II-III,* 593, in which أَنْ تَقْرَآنِ occurs instead of أَنْ تَقْرَآ:

"أَنْ تَقْرَآنِ عَلَى أَسْمَاءَ وَيْحَكُمَا   مِنِّي ٱلسَّلَامَ وَأَنْ لَا تُشْعِرَا أَحَدَا".

"That you two should pronounce over Asmā' [mercy be upon you two!] from me is the greeting, and that you do not let anyone know".

c) Another anomaly is the occurrence of the subjunctive after the suppressed subjunctival أَنْ, as in the following verse said by Maisūn bint Baḥdal, the wife of Muʿāwiya b. Abī Sufyān and the mother of his son Yazīd, whose longing for the desert and her poetry caused Muʿāwiya to divorce her, in which وَتَقَرَّ occurs instead of وَأَنْ تَقَرَّ. It is cited by Sībawaihi, *I,* 379, Zaǧǧāǧī, *Ǧumal* 199, Ibn Yaʿīš, *VII,* 25, Ibn ʿAqīl, *II,* 358, Šinqīṭī, *Durar II,* 110, Suyūṭī, *Šarḥ* 224, Širbīnī, *Šarḥ* 6, Howell, *II-III,* 52, Barrānī, *Maṭālib* 89, Bustānī, *Miṣbāḥ* in the notes 354, Carter, *Širbīnī* 110:

"وَلُبْسُ عَبَاءَةٍ وَتَقَرَّ عَيْنِي   أَحَبُّ إِلَيَّ مِنْ لُبْسِ ٱلشُّفُوفِ".

"And the wearing of a woolen garment and [that] my eyes be cool [from tears] are dearer to me than the wearing of the finest garments".

d) Another anomaly is the use of the jussive after the subjunctival أنْ, which occurs in the verse said by Imru'u l-Qais in which أنْ يأتنا occurs instead of أنْ يأتينا (cf. Nöldeke, *Grammatik* 1). It is cited by Ibn Hišām, *Muġnī I,* 30, Howell, *II-III,* 592, Šādilī, *ʿAnāṣir* 40:

"إذا ما غدَوْنا قال وِلْدانُ أهْلنا   تعالَوْا إلى أنْ يأتنا ٱلصَيْدُ نحْطِبِ".

"Whenever we go forth in the morning, the lads of our people say: 'Come, until the hunting come to us we will gather firewood [to roast it']".

The same phenomenon occurs in the following verse said by Ǧamīl, cited by Ibn Hišām, Muġnī *I,* 30, Åkesson, *Elision* 27, Howell, *II-III,* 592, in which أنْ تعلَمْ occurs instead of أنْ تعلَمَ:

"أحاذِرُ أنْ تعلَمْ بها فتردَّها   فتترُكَها ثقلاً عليَّ كما هيا".

"I fear that she would know it (sc. my want], and would reject it, and leave it to be a burden upon me, as it already is".

The use of the jussive after أنْ is adapted in the dialectal variant of some tribes, as the Banū Ṣabāḥ from Ḍabba (cf. Sādilī, *ʿAnāṣir* 40). The verb takes the jussive also after لنْ as well in this dialect (cf. Ibn Mālik, *Šawāhid* 160). The indicative has also been used after أنْ and its sisters (cf. Suyūṭī, *Hamʿ II,* 3). For further discussions concerning the confusion betwen the moods see Howell, *II-III,* 592-594, Wright, *IV,* 389, Baalbaki, *Iʿrāb* 18.

e) The jussive occurs anomalously instead of the indicative in the sur. 11: 105 (يوْمَ يأتِ) "The day it arrives", in which يأتِ occurs instead of يأتي. The elision of the *y* and the maintainance of the kasra is frequent in the dialect of Huḏail (cf. Zamaḫšarī, *Kaššāf II,* 293, Ibn Manẓūr, *I,* 22; see further for discussions Rabin, 89, Nöldeke, *Grammatik* 11). The jussive occurs anomalously with the pronoun of the accusative suffixed, e.g. يتْبَعْهُمْ which is said instead of يتْبَعُهُمْ "he follows them" (cf. Vollers, *Volkssprache* 143). Another example is يتْبعْهُمُوا which is read in this manner from the sur. 26: 224 instead of يتبَعُهُمُوا and يتبعُهُمُوا "Follow them" (cf. ibid 128, referring to Baiḍāwī). The jussive or the subjunctive with the elision of the *n* of the indicative from a verb that occurs in the 2nd person of the fem sing. of the imperfect, replaces anomalously the indicative in the following verse said by an anonymous poet, cited by Carter, *Širbīnī* 82, Šinqīṭī, *Durar I,* 27, in which تدْلُكي occurs instead of تدْلُكين:

"أبيتُ أبْكي وتَبيتي تدْلُكي   وجْهَك بٱلعَنْبَر وٱلمِسْك ٱلذكيّ".

"I pass the night weeping, and you spend the night rubbing your face with amber and pure musk".

f) The subjunctive occurs anomalously after the apocopative لمْ in the reading of Abū Ǧaʿfar al-Manṣūr of the sur. 94: 1 (ألمْ نشْرَحَ لك صدْرَك) for (ألمْ نشْرَحْ لك صدْرَك) "Have We not expanded thee thy breast?-" (cf. Šādilī, *ʿAnāṣir* 218). Comparable to it is the occurrence of the subjunctive after the apocopative لمّا in the reading of Ibn Waṯṯāb and al-Naḫfī of the sur. 3: 142 (ولمّا يعلَمَ ٱللهُ ٱلّذين جاهَدُوا منْكُمْ) instead of (ولمّا يعلَمِ ٱللهُ ٱلّذين جاهَدُوا منْكُمْ) "Without God testing those of you who fought hard (in His Cause)" (cf. Šāḏilī, *ʿAnāṣir* 219; for discussions concerning this dialectal variant that occurs by some Arabs see Baalbaki, *Iʿrāb* 18).

(52) The *t* suffix that is attached to the root in the 3rd person of the fem. sing. of the perfect, e.g. ضَرَبَتْ "she hit", originates according to Ibn Masʿūd, from the second point of articulation. As the *t* is a dental consonant, it detains a position between a laryngeal and a labial. On this basis, it and other dentals come after laryngeals, and so originate from the second point of articulation (cf. Smyth, *Reviews of Books* 712). Other sorts of *t* exist (cf. Rāzī, in Ḫalīl b. Aḥmad ..., *Ḥurūf* 150), which can be mentioned in this context. It can: 1– be prefixed as a *t* prefix in the imperfect, e.g. تَفْعَلُ "you are doing", 2– be suffixed as a *tāʾ ṭawīla* in the noun, e.g. عَنْكَبوتٌ "a spider", 3– be suffixed as a *tāʾ marbūṭa* marking the fem. sing., e.g. الضارِبَةُ "the one who is hitting /fem.sing." and القائمَةُ "the one who is rising" (for discussions concerning the origin of the *t* of the fem. as a suffix and its occurrence as a *tāʾ marbūṭa* or *ṭawīla* with interesting references to some other researchers' opinions see Fleisch, *Traité I,* 312-314), 4– be substituted for the *s* (for this substitution see (194), (329), (333), (334)), 5– be substituted for the *w* (for this substitution see (96), (198), (247), (330), (331), 6– strengthen the idea of intensiveness: التاء لتأكيد المبالغة "the *t* meant to strengthen the idea of intensiveness" (see Rāḍī, *Naẓarīya* 257-258, Wright, *II,* 139-140, my notes (150), (274)), and 7– be التاء للتخصيص "the *t* of particularization" applied to the اسم الوحدة "the noun of individuality". For a study of the *t's* occurrence in some of the Semitic languages see Brockelmann, *Grundriss* 383-388, 405-410.

(53) In spite of the fact that the suffixed pronoun of the nominative is considered to be at one with its verb, it is not allowed to conjoin another agent to it by a conjunction without emphasizing the suffixed pronoun by an independent pronoun (cf. Ibn Ǧinnī, *Lumaʿ* 39). The suffixed pronoun of the agent can be manifest as the *-tu* of ضَرَبْتُ in e.g. ضَرَبْتُ أنا وزَيْدٌ "I hit, I and Zaid" or suppressed as in قُمْ in e.g. قُمْ أنْتَ وزَيْدٌ "get up, you and Zaid". The reason of this emphasis of the suffixed agent, whether manifested or suppressed, is to differentiate such types of sentences from those coupling betweeen two actions, e.g. ضَرَبْتُ وجَلَسْتُ "I hit and I sat". An example that can be presented with such a coupling that occurs after a verb in which the pronoun of the agent is suffixed is found in the sur. 21: 54 (قالَ لَقَدْ كُنْتُمْ أَنْتُمْ وآباؤُكُمْ فى ضَلالٍ مُبينٍ) "He said, "Indeed ye have been in manifest Error -ye and your fathers", in which كُنْتُمْ أَنْتُمْ وآباؤُكُمْ is said instead of كُنْتُمْ وآباؤُكُمْ and an example in which the pronoun is suppressed is found in the sur. 2: 35 (وقُلْنا يا آدَمُ اسْكُنْ أَنْتَ وزَوْجُكَ الْجَنَّةَ) "We said: "O Adam! dwell thou and thy wife in the Garden;" in which اسْكُنْ أَنْتَ وزَوْجُكَ is said instead of اسْكُنْ وزَوْجُكَ (see further for a study Mubarrad, *Kāmil I,* 321-322, Zamaḫšarī, 50, Ibn Yaʿīš, *III,* 76-77, Ibn ʿAqīl, *II,* 236-238, Howell, *I,* fasc. I, 492-498, Reckendorf, *Syntax* 332). This is in accordance with the teachings of the Basrans. As far as the Kufans are concerned, they accept this connection without having to emphasize the antecedent (for the debate see Ibn al-Anbārī, *Inṣāf* Q. 66, 196-198, for discussions see ʿAbd al-ʿAzīz, *Fuṣḥā* 229-231). The coupling with the separate emphasizing pronoun did not occur anomalously for the sake of metric exigency in the following verse said by ʿUmar b. Abī Rabīʿa, cited by Sībawaihi, *I,* 342, Mubarrad, *Kāmil I,* 322, Ibn Ǧinnī, *Ḫaṣāʾiṣ II,* 386, Zamaḫšarī, 50, Ibn Yaʿīš, *III,* 76, Ibn al-Anbārī, *Inṣāf* Q. 66, 197, Ibn ʿAqīl, *II,* 238, Alee,

Wasīṭ 113, Howell, *I,* fasc. I, 494, ʿAbd al-ʿAzīz, *Fuṣḥā* 229 in which إذْ أَقْبَلَتْ وَزُهْرٌ was said instead of إذْ أَقْبَلَتْ هِيَ وَزُهْرٌ:

"قُلْتُ إذْ أَقْبَلَتْ وَزُهْرٌ تَهَادَى   كَنِعَاجِ ٱلْفَلَا تَعَسَّفْنَ رَمْلَا".

"I said, when she and fair-faced [women] approached: They walk with an elegant swinging of the body in their gait, like the wild cows of the deserts when they have wandered at random in a tract of sand".

b) According to the Basrans, if a noun is coupled by a conjunction to a pronoun in the genitive suffixed to a preposition preceding it, it must be preceded by an emphasizing preposition, e.g. مررتُ بكَ وبزَيد "I passed by you and by Zaid", which is said instead of مررتُ بكَ وزَيد as well as it must be put in the genitive. The Kufans however believed that it is possible to couple after the suffixed pronoun of the genitive without a preposition, i.e. مررتُ بكَ وزيد "I passed by you and Zaid". For their debate see Ibn al-Anbārī, *Inṣāf* Q. 65, 192-196. Ibn Ǧinnī, *Ḫaṣāʾiṣ I,* 102-103 accepts this coupling without a preposition, but with the noun being put in the accusative, namely: مررتُ بكَ وزيدا. In line with the Kufans teaching, the accusative وَٱلْأَرْحَامَ of the sur. 4: 1 (وَٱتَّقُوا ٱللَّهَ ٱلَّذِي تَسَاءَلُونَ بِهِ وَٱلْأَرْحَامَ) "Reverence God, through Whom ye demand your mutual (rights), and (reverence) the wombs (that bore you)", was read instead by the Kufan Ḥamza as وَٱلْأَرْحَامِ as a noun in the genitive (cf. Zamaḫšarī, 51, de Sacy, *Anthologie* [Ḥarīrī, *Durra*] 44). Ibn Yaʿīš, *III,* 78 mentions that this reading was considered as weak by most of the grammarians. Concerning وَٱلْأَرْحَامِ of this sur., the Kufan grammarian al-Farrāʾ showed a preference to the Basrans' theory, which forbade the coupling after the suffixed pronoun without a preposition, and preferred to read it وَبِٱلْأَرْحَامِ. Ibn Ḫālawaihi does not however consider Ḥamza's reading as weak (for discussions see Ibn Ḫālawaihi, *Qirāʾāt I,* 127-129, Rāǧiḥī, *Farrāʾ* 43). Another example in which the conjoining with the emphasizing preposition did not occur for the sake of metric exigency is فَما بكَ والأَيَّامِ which is said instead of فَما بكَ وَبِٱلْأَيَّامِ (cf. Zamaḫšarī, *Kaššāf I,* 493), that occurs in the following verse cited by Sībawaihi, *I,* 344, Ibn al-Sarrāǧ, *Uṣūl II,* 119, Ibn Yaʿīš, *III,* 78, 79, Ibn al-Anbārī, *Inṣāf* Q. 65, 192, Ibn ʿAqīl, *II,* 240, Baġdādī, *Ḫizāna II,* 338, Howell, *I,* fasc. I, 498:

"فَالْيَوْمَ قَرَّبْتَ تَهْجُونا وتَشْتِمُنا   فاذْهَبْ فَما بكَ والأَيَّامِ مِنْ عَجَبِ".

"And today, you approached us satirizing and reviling us: so go away, for there is not any wonder at you and the days!".

(54) The base form of رَمَتَا is رَمَيَتَا in which the *y* vowelled by a fatḥa is changed into an *ā* due to the influence of the fatḥa preceding it, so that it became رَمَاتَا. The reason why the *ā* is elided in رَمَاتَا is that it precedes the suffixed *t* that marks the fem. sing. of the 3rd person in رَمَتْ, which is underlyingly vowelless, but which is given accidently the fatḥa in the dual to prevent the cluster of two vowelless consonants, the vowelless *t* and the vowelless *ā* of the dual following it, i.e. رَمَتَا is said instead of رَمَتْا. As the underlying sukūn of the suffix *t* of the 3rd person of the sing. is still taken into consideration, the *ā* (which is underlyingly a *y* radical vowelled by a fatḥa before its being changed) is elided from رَمَاتَا, as it is assumed theoretically that there is a cluster of two vowelless consonants, the vowelless *ā* of the changed *y* radical and the vowelless suffixed *t* of the fem. (cf. (304); compare the discussion which is almost similar concerning دَعَتَا underlyingly دَعَوَتَا in (289)). Some people whose dialectal variant is defective maintain however the *ā* of the changed *y* radical and say رَمَاتَا (cf. Zamaḫšarī 154, Ibn Yaʿīš, *IX,* 27-29, Wright, *II,* 89, Åkesson, *Conversion* 28) in consideration of its formal vowel.

(55) The case of the perfect verb in which the 3rd radical is made vowelless when the pronoun of the nominative is suffixed to it, e.g. ضَرَبْنَ "they hit, /fem. pl." and ضَرَبْتُ "I hit", "you hit, /masc. sing." and "you hit /fem. sing." is contrasted to the case of the perfect verb in which the 3rd radical is given a fatḥa when the pronoun of the accusative is suffixed to it, e.g. ضَرَبَكَ "he hit you.", thus allowing the disliked combination of four vowelled consonants (for the principle that four vowelled consonants cannot follow each other in one word see Zaǧǧāǧī, *Īḍāḥ* 75, Ibn Ǧinnī, *Sirr I,* 220-221, Ḥassān, *Uṣūl* 228). In spite of the fact that the attached pronouns of the nominative and the accusative are suffixed to the verb, the suffixed pronoun of the nominative is considered by the Arab grammarians as one with its verb, whereas the pronoun of the accusative is regarded as another word separated from it (cf. Bohas, *Étude* 93). The verb is in need of an agent, manifest or suppressed (for discussions see (12 b), (13)), which is why it is considered as one with its pronoun of the agent, whereas it can manage without an object, which is the reason why it and its pronoun of the object are considered as two separate words (cf. Ibn Ǧinnī, *Sirr I,* 221).

(56) هُدَبِدٌ is underlyingly هُدَابِدٌ and عُلَبِطٌ is underlyingly عُلَابِطٌ formed according to فُعَالِلٌ, both having their *ā* elided. The disliked succession of the four vowels occurs in both these abbreviated forms (cf. Sībawaihi, *II,* 366). A similar case with the four consecutive vowels occurring in one word is found in عَرَتُنٌ "a plant used in dyeing" formed according to فَعَلُلٌ underlyingly عَرَنْتُنٌ, in which the *n* is elided (cf. Ibn Manẓūr, *IV,* 2869), and جَنَدِلٌ "stones" formed according to فَعَلِلٌ underlyingly جَنَادِلُ in which a contraction is carried out (cf. Ibn Manẓūr, *I,* 699; for discussions see Ibn Ǧinnī, *Ḫaṣā ʾiṣ III,* 114, Ibn Yaʿīš, *VI,* 136)).

(57) The base form of مُخْيِطٌ is مِخْيَاطٌ in which the *ā* is elided (cf. my notes (278), Zamaḫšarī, 182, Ibn Yaʿīš, *X,* 86) for the sake of alleviation.

(58) A parallel is drawn between the elision of one of the two markers of the fem. in both the examples: the *t* in the verb ضَرَبْنَ underlyingly ضَرَبَتْنَ with the *t* marking the fem. sing. and the *-na* marking the fem. pl. combined together, and the *t* of the noun مُسْلِمَاتٌ underlyingly مُسْلِمَتَاتٌ with the *t* marking the fem sing. and the *t* of the ending *-ātu* of the fem. pl. combined together. The reason of eliding one of both tāʾs of the fem. in مُسْلِمَاتٌ is the heaviness implied by the combination of two consonants of the same kind together (cf. Ibn Ǧinnī, *Ḫaṣā ʾiṣ III,* 235, Ibn al-Anbārī, *Inṣāf* Q. 4, 20). In spite of the fact that the two markers of the fem. are not identical in the verb ضَرَبَتْنَ, one of them, i.e. the *t,* is elided because there is a heaviness implied by this combination when it takes place in the verb (compare the case of تَضْرِبِينَ in which the *y* was chosen as an affix, and not the *t* to avoid the combination of two identical markers of the fem.

(88) and the case of يَضْرِبْنَ in which the *y* was chosen as a prefix and not the *t* to avoid the combination of two markers of the fem.(97)), contrarily to if it was to occur in the noun (see e.g. the case of حُبْلَيَات discussed in (59)), as verbs are considered as heavier than nouns. This theory concerning the heaviness and lightness is well-known in the Arabic grammatical tradition (cf. Sībawaihi, *I,* 5; e.g. Zağğāğī, *Īḍāḥ* 100-101 has reserved a chapter for the reasons of the heaviness of the verb and the lightness of the noun). The main argument why the verb is considered as heavier than the noun is that it cannot manage without an agent, whether this agent is a noun or a pronoun and whether it is manifest or suppressed, and that it implies with its form both the event and the agent. As for the noun it can do without a verb, can function as a topic or predicate in a nominal sentence, and does not with its form refer to the accident (for discussions see (12 b), (13), Baalbaki, *Hierarchy* 15, Versteegh, *Zağğāğī* 177-181, Guillaume, *Cause* 242-243).

(59) The *alif maqṣūra* that marks the fem. in حُبْلَى is allowed to be combined with the *t* that marks the fem. pl. of the ending *-ātun* after this alif's change into a *y*, i.e. حُبْلَيَات (cf. Zamaḫšarī, 79, Ibn Yaʿīš, *V,* 61-62, Wright, *II,* 192, 197), because both the *y* and the *t* are different consonants. The *alif maqṣūra*'s change into a *y* vowelled by a fatḥa occurs necessarily to avoid the cluster of two vowelless consonants, the vowelless *alif maqṣūra* and the vowelless *ā* of the fem. pl. ending *-ātun,* i.e. حُبْلىاتٌ or حُبْلاتٌ becomes حُبْلَيَاتٌ. There is no heaviness implied by the combination of both these markers of the fem. when it takes place in the noun contrarily to if it is to occur in the verb (see e.g. the case of يَضْرِبْنَ that occurs instead of تَضْرِبْنَ (58)), as the theory referred to here is that nouns are lighter than verbs (for discussions see (58)).

(60) The poetical special language offers peculiarities that are not found in other styles of writing (for a discussion concerning some possible peculiarities occurring in some well-known verses see Ibn al-Sarrāğ, *Uṣūl III,* 435 sqq., Rāḍī, *Naẓarīya* 295 sqq.; for a discussion criticizing the poets' usages see Ibn Fāris, *Ḏamm,* edited, introduced, translated and discussed by Sanni, *Ibn Fāris* 11-20; for a discussion criticizing the grammarians' control over the language of poets and the reciters of the Qurʾān see Ṣubḥi, *Fiqh* 131-134; for a general study concerning works dealing with speech errors in Arabic, both in reading and writing, and also those that are made in understanding the Qurʾān see Anwar, *Fathers;* for a short list referring to the famous poets of the Banū Tamīm and of the Huḏailīs see Ṣubḥi, *Fiqh* 66). Al-Ḫalīl is said to have admitted that the poets are given possibilities which are not permitted to others than them (cf. Ḥāzim al-Qarṭāğannī, *Minhāğ* 143-144). According to al-Aḫfaš, the poets are obliged to use certain words for the sake of metric exigency, which makes them accustomed to these expressions and constructions in their language (cf. Anīs, *Asrār* 323). Ibn Ğinnī, *Ḫaṣāʾiṣ II,* 392-393 alludes to the poet's desire of adventurous experimentation. The metre of the verse cited by Ibn Masʿūd is *wāfir.* The poet is unknown. The same verse occurs in Ibn al-Anbārī, *Inṣāf* Q. 96, 284 and the same explanation mentioned by Ibn Masʿūd is presented. أنتا with the fatḥa of أَنْتَ lenghtened into an *ā* occurs as a pronoun of the masc. sing. of the 2nd person instead of the normal أَنْتَ. If the form for the dual أنتما with the infixation of the *m* did not exist, both the sing. and the dual would be confused. The *ā* suffixed to أَنْتَ resulting in أنتا is named ألف الوصل والصلة "the alif suffixed after a final short vowel" (cf. Ibn al-Anbārī, *Inṣāf* Q. 96, 284). Concerning the normal structure of أَنْتَ, the Basrans believed that أَنْ is the pronoun and that the تَ is a suffix that specifies the 2nd person (cf. Carter, *Širbīnī* 256 and the notes 257). Another verse reminiscent of the one cited by Ibn Masʿūd regarding the theme is cited by Ibn Manẓūr, *V*, 3881:

"إنَّ مِنَ الإخوانِ إخْوانَ كِشْرَةٍ   وإخْوانَ كَيْفَ الحالُ والبالُ كُلُّهُ".

"Some brothers keep on laughing and joking and some brothers are in another state of mind".

Zamaḫšarī, *Asās* 545 has instead:

"وإنَّ مِنَ الإخوانِ إخْوانَ كِشْرَةٍ   وإخوانَ حيَّاكَ الإلٰهُ ومرحبا".

"And some brothers keep on laughing and joking and some brothers greet you with a "may God preserve your life!" and welcome you"].

Another example concerning أنتا that marks the sing. with the suffixation of this particular alif occurs in the following verse said by Sālim b. Dāra, cited by Muʾaddib, *Taṣrīf* 25, Ibn Yaʿīš, *I*, 127, 130, Baġdādī, *Ḫizāna I*, 289, Ibn al-Anbārī, *Inṣāf* Q. 45, 144, Q. 96, 284:

"يَا مُرَّ يَا آبْنَ وَاقِعٍ يَا أنْتَا   أنْتَ آلَّذِي طَلَّقْتَ عَامًا جُعْتَا".

"O Murr, O Ibn Wāqiʿ, O you! it is you who divorced [your wife] in a year when you were hungry!".

A variant of the verse is believed to be by al-Aḥwaṣ (cf. Howell, *I*, Fasc. I 47A, Daqr, *Muʿǧam* 393), but it is probably by Sālim b. Dāra al-Ġaṭafānī mentioned above (cf. Qālī, *Nawādir* 455). It is also cited by Ibn Ǧinnī, *Sirr I*, 359, in the notes of the commentator al-Šartūnī of Farḥāt, *Baḥṯ* 241, Daqr, *Muʿǧam* 393:

"يَا أبْجَرَ بْنَ أبْجَرَ يَا أنْتَا   أنْتَ آلَّذِي طَلَّقْتَ عَامَ جُعْتَا".

"O Abǧar Ibn Abǧar, O you! it is you who divorced [your wife] in a year when you were hungry!".

b) It is usual that in poetry, the *ā*, the *w* or the *y* that lengthens the fatḥa, ḍamma or kasra is suffixed to the word at the ends of verses. This lenghtening of the vowels is appropriate for the repetition and the reiteration of sound, and marks a difference between poetry and prose (cf. Ibn Yaʿīš, *IX*, 78). This occurs in the following verse said by Imruʾu l-Qais, cited by Sībawaihi, *II*, 325, Ibn Ǧinnī, *Munṣif I*, 224, Ibn Yaʿīš, *IX*, 78, Howell, *IV*, fasc. I, 791, in which وَمَنْزِلِي occurs instead of وَمَنْزِلِ:

"قِفَا نَبْكِ مِنْ ذِكْرَى حَبِيبٍ وَمَنْزِلِي".

"Tarry you two: we will weep at the remembrance of a beloved and a place of alighting".

The verse is also cited by Howell, *I*, fasc. I, 351, with وَمَنْزِلِ instead. A linguistic feature worth to be mentioned is the use of the dual to the verb قفا (for a discussion why the dual might have been chosen see Abū Ḥaidar, *Dual* 40-48, Åkesson, *Conversion* in the notes to 29-30). The lengthening of the vowel occurs as well in the following verse said by Ibn Ḥilliza al-Yaškūrī, cited by Howell, *IV*, fasc. I, 791, in which أسْمَاءُو occurs instead of أسْمَاءُ, and الثَّوَاءُو instead of الثَّوَاءُ:

"آذَنَتْنَا بِبَيْنِهَا أسْمَاءُو   رُبَّ ثَاوٍ يُمَلُّ مِنْهُ آلثَّوَاءُو".

"[The beloved] Asmāʾ has announced to us her intention of departing. Many a sojourner [there is], of whose sojourning one is wearied!".

See further for a study Sībawaihi, *II*, 325-326, Ibn Ǧinnī, *Munṣif I*, 224, Ibn Yaʿīš, *IX*, 78, Howell, *IV*, fasc. I, 791 sqq.

(61) The points of articulation of the *m* and the *t* are close to each other. The *t* is formed by the tip of the tongue and the roots of the two upper central incissors and the *m* is formed between the lips (see my notes (188)).

(62) Besides being an infix in a pronoun, e.g. أَنْتُمَا "you two", or a suffix in it, e.g. أَنْتُم "you /masc. pl.", the *m* can be a prefix in a noun (for discussions see Fleisch, *Traité I*, 422-434), e.g. مَوْعِدٌ "a place of a promise or an appointment" or a suffix in it (for discussions see ibid, 465-467), e.g. ابْنُم meaning الإِبْن "the son" in which it marks intensification (cf. Zaǧǧāǧī, *Maǧālis* 134). It is not to be prefixed, infixed or suffixed directly to the verbs (cf. Ibn Yaʿīš, *Mulūkī* 150). In the cases of the 2nd persons of the masc. and fem. dual and the masc. pl. of the perfect, e.g. ضَرَبْتُمَا "you hit /masc. and fem. dual" and ضَرَبْتُم "you hit /masc. pl.", the *m* is a part of the suffixed pronouns تُمَا and تُم. For a study of the *m*'s occurrence in some of the Semitic languages see Brockelmann, *Grundriss* 396.

b) In some anomalous cases of verbs the *m* can be prefixed or infixed (for examples see Ibn Ǧinnī, *Sirr I*, 432-433). These forms are تَمَفْعَل and مَفْعَل. Examples formed according to تَمَفْعَل are تَمَسْكَنَ الرَّجُلُ "the man became poor", تَمَدْرَعَ "he wore a loose outer garment of wool with sleeves, slit in front", تَمَنْدَلَ "to clean oneself with a handkerchief", تَمَنْطَقَ "to tighten one's belt", تَمَسْلَمَ الرَّجُلُ "the man named himself Muslim" and تَمَوْلَى "to behave arrogantly". Examples formed according to مَفْعَل are مَرْحَبَك اللهُ ومَسْهَلَك "may God welcome you and make the place smooth, plain, or not rugged for you", [مَسْهَلَك is from the expression أَهْلاً وسَهْلاً, from أَتَيْتَ قَوْماً أَهْلاً وَمَوْضِعاً سَهْلاً "Thou hast come to a people who are like kinsfolk, and to a place that is smooth, plain, or not rugged" (cf. Lane, *I*, 1453)], and مَخْرَقَ الرَّجُلُ "the man was profuse in liberality, bounty, or munificence".

(63) The pronoun is considered by many Arab grammarians as belonging to the same category as the noun, as generally the parts of speech are three: the noun, verb and particle (cf. Sībawaihi, *I*, 1). This tripartite division of the language seems to be an influence from the Greeks (see my notes (10 b)). The point at issue here is that there is no noun ending with a *w* preceded by a ḍamma (cf. Ibn Ǧinnī, *de Flexione* 42-43, Ibn Yaʿīš, *X*, 104) except the pronoun هُوَ. The verbs however can end with a *w* preceded by a ḍamma without this combination being deemed heavy, e.g. يَغْزُو "he assaults" and يَدْعُو "he calls".

(64) The reason why the pl. of دَلْو with 3rd weak radical is formed according to the pattern فَعْلٌ, namely أَدْلٍ (cf. Ibn Ǧinnī, *de Flexione* 43, Zamaḫšarī, 185, Ibn Yaʿīš, *X*, 107-108, Ibn Mālik, *Alfīya* 147, Goguyer's commentary to verse 617, Lane, *I*, 909, Wright, *II*, 209) and not on the pattern أَفْعُلٌ, namely أَدْلُو, is to avoid having it ending with a *w* preceded by a ḍamma, which is disliked by the Arabs.

(65) The underlying *ū* in ضَرَبْتُمُوهُ is maintained between the pronoun of the nominative of the 2nd person of the masc. pl., *-tum,* and the pronoun of the accusative of the 3rd person of the sing. , *-hu,* and thus is not longer at the extremity of the word, which is the reason why it is not elided. The base form of ضَرَبْتُمْ is ضَرَبْتُمُوا, and the suffixed pronoun of the accusative, the *-hu,* is also another reason why the verb is brought back to its base form (cf. Ibn Yaʿīš, *III,* 95). The principle that the pronouns bring back the words to their base form can be considered a rule (cf. Sībawaihi, *I,* 341-342). The suffixed pronoun of the pl. of the 2nd person of the masc. pl., the *ū,* can be elided according to Yūnus referred to by Sībawaihi, *I,* 342, who accepts instead of the examples أعْطَيْتُكُمُوهُ and أعْطَيْتُكُمُوهَا, أعْطَيْتُكُمْهُ and أعْطَيْتُكُمْهَا. Ibn Ǧinnī, *Sirr I,* 103 considers the saying of Yūnus of أعْطَيْتُكُمْهُ to be an anomaly. It can be added as well that it is not only the suffixed pronouns, but as well the dual endings (cf. Suyūṭī, *Ašbāh I,* 203-204; for a general discussion concerning the dual suffix *-āni* marking the nominative see Carter, *Širbīnī* 59: 3.43 (1); for examples concerning the dual of the three cases see 91-93: 4.5 (1)) and the diminutive (cf. Suyūṭī, *Ašbāh I,* 218, (363)) that bring back the word to its base form (for discussions see Rāḍī, *Naẓarīya* 192-193).

(66) The suffixation of the *tāʾ marbūṭa* in العَظاءَةُ is the reason why the hamza, which is not longer at the extremity of the word, is changed into the *y* resulting in العَظايَةُ (cf. Ibn Yaʿīš, *X,* 109; for discussions see Ibn Ǧinnī, *Munṣif II,* 128-129).

(67) The theory that is presented by Ibn Masʿūd concerning ضَرَبْتُنَّ, is that its base form is ضَرَبْتُمْنَ. The *m* is assimilated to the *n* as their points of articulation are close to each other: the *m* originates between the lips and the *n* from the upper part of the nose (cf. (188)). Another theory presented by Ibn Yaʿīš, *III,* 87 concerning the doubling of the *n* in ضَرَبْتُنَّ is that two nūns should arise as compared to the *m* and the *ū* of the masc. pl., i.e. ضَرَبْتُمُوا (cf. my notes to Ibn Masʿūd, *I,* 61).

(68) The base form of عَمْبَرٌ is عَنْبَرٌ (cf. Sībawaihi, *II,* 342, Ibn Ǧinnī, *de Flexione* 26, Zamaḫšarī, 174-175, Ibn Yaʿīš, *X,* 33-36, Bohas, *Étude* 229-232, my notes (365)). The substitution of the *m* for the *n* is necessary when it occurs vowelless before the *b* because of the heaviness implied by the combination of the soft and nasal *n* and the rigid *b.* Another example is شَمْبَاءُ "having sharp canine teeth" said instead of شَنْبَاءُ.

(69) According to this theory, the base form of ضَرَبْتُنَّ with the doubling of the *-nna,* is ضَرَبْتُنَ with the alleviation of the *-na* that marks the fem. pl. The *-tu* preceding the *-na* that marks the fem. pl. in ضَرَبْتُنَ should have been vowelless, i.e. ضَرَبْتْنَ, similarly to the consonant preceding the *n* that marks the fem. pl. of the 3rd person of the fem. ضَرَبْنَ "they hit". However the *-tu* of the addressed 2nd person of the pl. could not be vowelless, i.e. ضَرَبْتْنَ, as this would imply a cluster of two vowelless consonants, the *b* and the *t.* So it was necessary to vowel it, and the vowel that was chosen was a ḍamma, namely ضَرَبْتُنَّ. Moreover, in order to avoid mixing it up with the 1st person of the sing. ضَرَبْتُ, it was necessary to infix an augment after the *-tu*. If one is to speculate which among the usal infixes and suffixes, namely the *m, y, ā,* and *ū,* is the appropriate augment that is to be infixed, it could not be the *m* because the form does not refer to the dual or to the masc. pl. of the 2nd person. It could not be the *ā* or the *y* either, on account of the ḍamma of the *t* that forbids it, nor could it be the *w* to avoid that the marker of the masc. pl., i.e. the *ū,* would be combined with the marker of the fem. pl., i.e. the *-na,* so the *n* was chosen to be infixed, and was then assimilated to the *n* of the fem. pl. (cf. my notes to Ibn Masʿūd, *I,* 61-62).

(70) The reason why the attached pronoun *-tu* was chosen to be suffixed to the base form of the perfect فَعَلْ, e.g. ضَرَبْ in the perfect of the 1st person of the sing. resulting in ضَرَبْتُ, and why none of the *ʾa,* the *n* or the *ā* of أنا, or of the weak consonants, the *w* or the *y,* was suffixed instead, is that if the *ā* was suffixed it would be confused with the 3rd person of the masc. dual ضَرَبا, if the *n* was suffixed it would be confused with the 3rd person of the fem. pl. ضَرَبْنَ, if the *w* was suffixed it would be confused with the 3rd person of the masc. pl. ضَرَبُوا, and if the *y* was suffixed it would be impossible to vowel it with the marker of the nominative, i.e. the ḍamma, because of the heaviness implied by this combination (cf. my notes to Ibn Masʿūd, *I,* 62).

(71) Sixty sorts of pronouns and the same distribution presented by Ibn Masʿūd are as well mentioned by Carter, *Širbīnī* 194. As for this manner of referring to determined numbers, Carter, 195 remarks in his notes:

> "The urge to calculate total combinations of elements is a relatively late phenomenon in grammar... The motive is clear: not only is enumeration a useful aide-mémoire, it also establishes the limits of the material to be taught (i.e. what is 'Arabic' and what is not). In origin it may be connected with the propositional calculus in the scholastic processing of the *Organon* which the Arabs inherited from Greek".

(72) The dual of the 3rd person of the masc. of e.g. ضَرَبَ is ضَرَبا and of the fem. sing. ضَرَبَتا. The *ā* alone is the pronoun in both these duals, because in the case of the fem. the *t* is the marker of the fem. and not a pronoun. This is the homonymy of both the dual of the fem. and masc. meant by Ibn Masʿūd regarding the suffixation of the *ā* to the basic form of the perfect. The dualizations of both the 3rd person of the masc. and fem. sing. are Proto-Semitic (cf. Moscati, *Grammar* 141).

(73) Two expressions are given to the 1st persons: أنا "I" and نَحْنُ "we" (for نَحْنُ see (74)), because "of the rarity of ambiguity in the 1st persons" (cf. Howell, *I,* fasc. II, 513-514). Concerning the reason why no form for the dual has been chosen for the 1st person of the sing. أنا, differently from the 2nd person أنْتَ which has the dual أنْتُما, Ibn Manẓūr, *I,* 160 presents the following theory:

"فإنْ قِيلَ: لِمَ ثَنَّوْا أنْتَ فقالوا أنْتُما ولَمْ يُثَنُّوا أنا؟ قِيلَ: لَمَّا لَمْ تَجُزْ أنا وأنا لِرَجُلٍ

آخَرَ لَمْ يُثَنُّوا ، وأمّا أَنتَ فَثَنَّوْهُ بأَنْتُما لأنّكَ تُجيزُ أَنْ تَقولَ لِرَجُلٍ أَنْتَ وَأَنتَ لآخَرَ مَعَه ، فَلِذلِكَ ثُنِّيَ":

"And if it is asked: "Why did they give a dual form to أَنْتَ as they said أَنْتُما, and they did not give a dual form to أنا?". It is answered: "When it was not possible to say أنا وأنا "I and I" [with the latter أنا] referring to another man, they did not form a dual [for it]. As what concerns أَنْتَ, they gave it the dual form أَنْتُما, because it is possible for you to say to a man أَنْتَ وأَنْتَ "you and you" [with the latter] referring to another one with him. For this reason it was given a dual form".

b) A debate concerning the structure of أنا "I" was raised between the Basrans and the Kufans, the Basrans considering the *ʾa* and the *n* as being the pronoun, and the *ā* as being suffixed after the *n* to make the fatḥa plain, whereas the Kufans consider the *ā* as belonging to the pronoun's structure (for discussions see Ibn Yaʿīš, *III,* 93-94, Howell, *I,* fasc. II, 520-522, Carter, *Širbīnī* 256).

c) There exist four dialectal variants concerning أَنَ, namely أَنَ, أنا, آنَ, أَنْ, and أنه (for أنه see my notes (345), (373)) according to Quṭrub (cf. Ibn Manẓūr, *I,* 160). Ibn Ḫālawaihi, *Qirāʾāt I,* 92 mentions these four: آنَا, أَنَا, أَنْ and أَنَه. The usual أنا occurs in the following verse said by ʿUdail according to Ibn Manẓūr, *I,* 160, but it is probably said according to my opinion by Ḥumaid b. Ḥuraiṯ b. Baḥdal al-Kalbī (cf. the notes to Muʾaddib, *Taṣrīf* 538, the notes to Ibn Ǧinnī, *Munṣif I,* 356, the notes to Ibn Yaʿīš, *III,* 93). It is also cited by Ibn Ǧinnī, *Munṣif I,* 10, Howell, *I,* fasc. II, 521:

"أنَا سَيْفُ ٱلْعَشِيرَةِ فَاعْرِفُونِي حُمَيداً قَدْ تَذَرَّيْتُ ٱلسَّنَامَا".

"I am the sword of the paternal kinsfolk; therefore know me praiseworthy, having mounted upon the summit".

آنَ which is of the dialectal variant of Quḍāʿa, occurs in the following verse said by ʿAdīy, cited by Ibn Manẓūr, *I,* 160:

"يا لَيْتَ شِعْرِي! آنَ ذُو عَجَّةٍ مَتَى أَرَى شَرْباً حَوَالَى أَصِيصْ؟".

"I wish I knew! I am the one who is yelling. When do I see water around a flowerpot?".

It may be noted when comparing the independent personal pronoun of Akkadian, Ugaritic, Hebrew, Syriac, Arabic and Ethiopic, that the 1st and 2nd persons of the sing. and pl. belong to the same system *-an* plus suffixes (cf. Moscati, *Grammar* 102).

(74) One form is sufficient for the separate pronoun of the 1st person of the pl. نَحْنُ (for discussions concerning its structure see Fleisch, *Traité II,* 10-11). The 1st person of the pl. can refer to himself/herself and to another or to others, e.g. نحنُ خارِجانِ "we are both going out" and نحنُ خارِجونَ "we are going out /masc. pl.". According to Ibn Yaʿīš, *III,* 94, the 1st person is aware of himself (or herself) by his senses, and he is talking about himself and others. As he cannot be confused with another, there is no need to have separate forms for the dual (for the question of the dual to the 1st persons in Semitic see Wagner, *Dualis* 229-233), the fem. and the masc. The same theory applies as well for the 1st person of the sing. أَنَا (cf. (73)).

b) Different theories exist as for why the 2nd *n* of نَحْنُ is vowelled by a ḍamma (for them see Ibn Yaʿīš, *III*, 94). According to Abū Isḥaq al-Zaǧǧāǧ, the ḍamma is chosen because نَحْنُ marks the pl., and the ḍamma is close in its nature to the *ū* that marks the pl. in verbs, e.g. قَامُوا "they got up", and in nouns, e.g. الزَّيْدُونَ "the Zaids". According to Abū l-ʿAbbās al-Mubarrad, نَحْنُ was compared and made commensurable to قَبْلُ "before" and بَعْدُ "after" that are used before the sing., the dual and the pl. According to Abū l-Ḥasan al-Aḫfaš al-Ṣaġīr, نَحْنُ is the agent pronoun, which is the reason why the *n* should be given the vowel of the nominative, i.e. the ḍamma. According to Quṭrub the base form of نَحْنُ is نَحُنْ with the 2nd radical vowelled by the ḍamma, which was then shifted to the 3rd radical *n* (for this theory see also Zaǧǧāǧī, *Maǧālis* 136-137). According to Muʾaddib, *Taṣrīf* 206-207, the ḍamma, which is the strongest of vowels, was chosen because نَحْنُ reveals strength as it comprehends two meanings, the one of the dual and the one of the pl., e.g. نَحْنُ ضَرَبْنَا زَيْداً can be used for the dual, i.e. "we have both hit Zaid" and for the pl., i.e. "we have hit Zaid".

(75) The paradigm of the attached pronouns of the nominative is the following:—It can be noted that the 3rd person of the masc. and fem. sing. is latent, and that the suffix of the 3rd person of the fem. sing., the ـَتْ , is a marker of the feminine form and not a pronoun–:

	sing.	dual	pl.
1st	ـْتُ		ـْنَا
2nd masc.	ـْتَ	ـْتُمَا	ـْتُمْ
2nd fem.	ـْتِ	ـْتُمَا	ـْتُنَّ
3rd masc.	—	ـَا	ـُوا
3rd fem.	ـَتْ	ـَتَا	ـْنَ

For the paradigm of the verb ضَرَبَ "to hit" in the perfect, active see (42).

b) Some questions worth taking up are why the *t* of the suffixed pronoun of the nominative of the dual is given a ḍamma, e.g. ضَرَبْتُمَا "you both hit", a fatḥa in the 2nd person of the masc. sing., e.g. ضَرَبْتَ, and a kasra in the 2nd person of the fem. sing., e.g. ضَرَبْتِ. The main ideas presented below by Niksārī, are that the ḍamma of the *t* in ضَرَبْتُمَا marks the nominative because the suffixed pronoun is the pronoun of the agent, and the ḍamma is the agent's vowel. Furthermore there is no risk of confusing this form with the 1st person ضَرَبْتُ because of the infixation of the *m* followed by an *ā*. The fatḥa was chosen to mark the masc. sing. in ضَرَبْتَ and the kasra was chosen to mark the fem. sing. in ضَرَبْتِ, because the masc. form is considered as a base form in relation to the fem. For this reason the light fatḥa was chosen for it and the heavy kasra was chosen for the fem. Niksārī, *Mifrāḥ* fol. 7a ll. 19-fol. 12 ll. 1-5 writes:

"إنَما ضُمَت التاء في ضَرَبْتُمَا لأنَ التاء ضمير الفاعل وعلامته الرفع ولا فرق بين الرفع والضم في اللفظ. وأمَا فتحة التاء في الواحد فللخوف من الإلباس لأنَها لو ضُمَت يلزم الإلتباس بنفس المتكلَم الواحد ولو كُسرت يلزم الإلتباس بالمخاطبة. فإن قيل لمَ عُيَن الفتحة في المخاطب والكسرة في المخاطبة إذ انَه لو عُكس بأن يكون الكسرة في المخاطب والفتحة في المخاطبة يرتفع الإلباس أيضا. قلنا الفتحة أولى للمخاطب والكسرة أولى للمخاطبة لأنَ المذكَر أصل والمؤنث فرع والفتحة خفيفة والكسرة ثقيلة وإعطاء الخفيف للأصل أولى من العكس. ولا يلزم ذلك الإلتباس في التثنية بسبب ضمَة التاء فلهذا ضُمَت التاء فيها".

"The reason why the *t* was vowelled by a ḍamma in ضَرَبْتُمَا "you both hit /dual" is that the *-tu* is the agent pronoun, and its vowel is the nominative's vowel, and there is no difference between the nominative and the ḍamma in the meaning. As for the fatḥa of the *-ta* that marks the 2nd person of the masc. sing. [in e.g. ضَرَبْتَ], it was given to avoid the confusion, because if it was given a ḍamma the confusion would be unavoidable with the 1st person of the sing. [i.e. ضَرَبْتُ], and if it was given a kasra it would be necessarily confused with the 2nd person of the fem. sing. [i.e. ضَرَبْتِ]. And if it is asked: "Why was the fatḥa chosen to mark the 2nd person of the masc. sing. [i.e. ضَرَبْتَ] and the kasra [chosen to mark] the 2nd person of the fem. sing. [i.e. ضَرَبْتِ], and not vice versa by chosing the kasra to mark the 2nd person of the masc. sing. [i.e. ضَرَبْتِ] and the fatḥa to mark the 2nd person of the fem. sing. [i.e. ضَرَبْتَ)], which would as well eliminate the possibility of confusing [the forms together]?". We answer: "The fatḥa is prior [to be chosen] to mark the 2nd person of the masc. sing. and the kasra is prior to mark the 2nd person of the fem. sing, because the masc. sing. is the base form and the fem. sing. is the derivative, and the fatḥa is light and the kasra is heavy, and so giving the light vowel to the base form is more prior than doing the contrary. Such a confusion [with other forms] cannot occur in the dual because of the ḍamma of the *-tu,* and this is why the ḍamma was given to the *t* in it".

(76) The twelve forms of the separate pronoun of the nominative are the following comprising two identical forms in the dual:

	sing.	dual	pl.
1st	أنَا		نَحْنُ
2nd masc.	أنْتَ	أنْتُمَا	أنْتُمْ
2nd fem.	أنْتِ	أنْتُمَا	أنْتُنَّ
3rd masc.	هُوَ	هُمَا	هُمْ
3rd fem.	هِيَ	هُمَا	هُنَّ

b) Some interesting questions worth taking up in this context are why the *t* in أنتَ is given a fatḥa in the masc. sing., a kasra in the fem. sing. أَنْتِ, and a ḍamma in the dual أَنْتُمَا (for the theories presented here see Zağğāğī, *Mağālis* 136: the session between Muḥammad b. Aḥmad b. Kaisān with Abū l-ʿAbbās Muḥammad b. Yazīd al-Mubarrad). According to some the *t* was given the fatḥa in أَنْتَ "you" marking the masc. sing. and the kasra in أَنْتِ marking the fem. sing., to differenciate between both these 2nd persons. The *t* marking the dual form followed by the *mā* ending, was vowelled by a ḍamma in أَنْتُمَا "you two", because it is known that this vowel does not mark neither the masc. nor the fem. sing., so it became specific for the dual. According to others the *t* of the dual was vowelled by a ḍamma to differenciate it from the *t* of the sing., whose vowel varies from a fatḥa if it marks the masc. sing. to a kasra if it marks the fem. sing.

(77) A debate between the Kufans and Basrans was raised concerning the structure of هُوَ (for it see Zağğāğī, *Mağālis* 137, Ibn Yaʿīš, *III,* 96-97, Ibn al-Anbārī, *Inṣāf* Q. 96, 282-285, Howell, *I,* fasc. II, 522 sqq., Carter, *Širbīnī* 256). According to the Kufans, the pronoun is the *h* alone, as they consider the lengthening element, the *w,* as strengthening the word. Their main argument is that the *w* is dropped in the dual هُمَا and in the pl. هُمْ. As for the Basrans, they consider both the *h* and the *w* to form its underlying structure. It may be noted when comparing the independent personal pronouns of the 3rd persons in Akkadian, Ugaritic, Hebrew, Syriac, Arabic and Ethiopic, that their structures relate to the demonstratives (cf. Moscati, *Grammar* 102).

b) The *w* of the pronoun هُوَ is elided for the sake of metric exigency in the following verse said by ʿUğair al-Salūlī Ğāhilīy, cited by Ibn Ğinnī, *Ḫaṣāʾiṣ I,* 69, Ḥarīrī, *Šarḥ* 214, Ibn al-Sarrāğ, *Uṣūl III,* 460, Ibn al-Anbārī, *Inṣāf* Q. 96, 282, Baġdādī, *Ḫizāna II,* 396, Ibn Manẓūr, *VI,* 4596, Howell, *I,* fasc. II, 523, in which فَبَيْنَاهُ is said instead of فَبَيْنَا هُوَ:

"فَبَيْنَاهُ يَشْرِي رَحْلَهُ قَالَ قَائِلٌ: لِمَنْ جَمَلٌ رِخْوُ ٱلْمِلَاطِ نَجِيبُ".

"Then, while he was selling his camel-saddle, a sayer said: "Who has a he-camel soft in the side of the hump, well-bred?".

c) The *y* of the pronoun هِيَ is elided for the sake of metric exigency in the following verse said by Ibn al-ʿAbbās, cited by Sībawaihi, *I,* 8, Ibn Fāris, *Ḏamm* 19 Ibn Ğinnī, *Ḫaṣāʾiṣ I,* 89, Ḥarīrī, *Šarḥ* 215, Ibn al-Sarrāğ, *Uṣūl III,* 461, Muʾaddib, *Taṣrīf* 539, Ibn al-Anbārī, *Inṣāf* Q. 96, 282, 284, Ibn Manẓūr, *VI,* 4596, Howell, *I,* fasc. IV, 1559, in which إِذْهِ is said instead of إِذْ هِيَ:

"هَلْ تَعْرِفُ ٱلدَّارَ عَلَى تِبْرَاكَا دَارٌ لِسُعْدَى إِذْهِ مِنْ هَوَاكَا".

"Do you know the dwelling on Tibrāk? It was a dwelling of Suʿdā when she was one of your beloved".

d) As for some anomalies concerning the stuctures of هُوَ and هِيَ, the Banū Asad make vowelless the *w* and *y* and say هُوْ and هِيْ (cf. Ibn Manẓūr, *VI,* 4597). Some of the Arabs (Ibn Manẓūr, *VI,* 4597), among them the Hamdan, double the *w* and *y,* and say instead هُوَّ and هِيَّ (cf. Rabin, 71)

(78) According to the theory presented here, the masc. pl. base form of هو is هُوَوا, of which the 1st *w* is changed into a *m* because of the heaviness implied by the combination of both the wāws, so the form became هُمُوا. Then the 2nd *w* and the *ā* were elided resulting in هم. In the dual, the *ā* was suffixed, the dual's base form being هُوا according to him, so it became هُما. Another theory concerning هُما with the affixation of the *m* is propounded by Ibn Ya'īš, *III,* 97 who considers its base form to be هوما, and not as Ibn Mas'ūd هُوا (cf. my notes to Ibn Mas'ūd, *I,* 63). Concerning the pronouns هُما and هُم, some believed that هُ is the pronoun while others believed that all the consonants form these pronouns' structure (cf. Carter, *Širbīnī* 256).

(79) The base forms of the duals and pl. of أَنْتَ and أَنْتِ are deprived of the *m,* i.e. أَنْتا "/2 masc. and fem. dual", أَنْتوا "/2 masc. pl." and أَنْتُنّ "/2 fem. pl." with the alleviation of the *n*. These forms with the affixation of the *m* become أَنْتُما, أَنْتُموا and أَنْتُمْنَ (cf. my notes to Ibn Mas'ūd, *I,* 63).

(80) The ḍamma is given to the suffixed pronoun of the genitive of the 3rd person of the masc. sing., the *h,* if the vowel preceding it is a fatḥa, e.g. لَهُ "to him/it". The kasra is given to it if it is preceded by the kasra, e.g. بِهِ "by him/it" or by a vowelless *y* لَدَيْهِ "he/it has" (for discussions see Sībawaihi, *II,* 320-322 in his chapter treating the *h* which is the attached pronoun vowelled by the kasra). For the paradigm of the suffixed pronouns of the genitive see (85).

b) Anomalies can occur. Al-Kisā'ī's mentions that in the dialect of Quḍā'a بِهْ occurs instead of بِهِ, e.g. مَرَرْتُ بِهْ "I passed by him" and لَهْ ocurs instead of لَهُ, e.g. المالُ لَهْ "the money is his" (cf. Ibn Ǧinnī, *Ḫaṣā'is I,* 390, *II,* 10). Sībawaihi, *II,* 321 mentions that the Ḥiğāzīs say بِهُو instead of بِهِ, e.g. مَرَرْتُ بِهُو قَبْلُ "I passed by him before" and لَدَيْهُو instead of لَدَيْهِ, e.g. لَدَيْهُو مالٌ "he has money" (for further examples see Rabin, 99).

(81) When the vocative (for its study see Zamaḫšarī, 18-23, Ibn Ya'īš, *I,* 127, *II,* 2-17, Howell, *I,* fasc. I, 160 sqq., Wright, *III,* 85-94, Carter, *Širbīnī* 418-432, Daqr, *Mu'ğam* 392-399) يا precedes a noun in which the pronoun of the genitive of the 1st person of the sing., the *ī,* is suffixed to, e.g. غلامي, its *ī* can be changed into an *ā* in the Ṭayyīs' dialectal variant, and consequently the consonant before it, i.e. the *m,* is vowelled by a fatḥa, i.e. يا غلاما (cf. Ibn Ǧinnī, *Luma'* 45, Vernier, *I,* 382-383, Åkesson, *Conversion* 29-30). Other allowable dialectal variants that can be added here are: 1– the final *ī* can be elided with the consonant preceding it being vowelled by a kasra: i.e. يا غلامِ, 2– maintained, i.e. يا غلامي, 3– elided with the consonant preceding it being vowelled by a ḍamma, i.e. يا غلامُ and 4– the *ā* can be elided with the sufficiency of the fatḥa preceding it, i.e. يا غلامَ (cf. Ibn Ya'īš, *II,* 10-11, Howell, *I,* fasc. I, 176-177). If the vocative precedes a word in which the *y* is a radical and is preceded by a kasra, e.g.

بادِيَةٌ, it is changed into an *ā,* i.e. يا باداةُ instead of يا بادِيَةُ (cf. Ibn Yaʿīš, *II,* 11, Åkesson, *Conversion* 30).

b) In other cases than with the vocative, the *y* of a word is changed into the *ā* by the Banū l-Ḥāriṯ b. Kaʿb when it is vowelless and preceded by a consonant given the fatḥa, e.g. عَلَيْهَا "upon her" that becomes عَلَاهَا, إِلَيْكَ "for you" that becomes إِلَاكَ and لَدَيْكَ "for you" that becomes لَدَاكَ (cf. Rabin, 67-68). This occurs as well in some nouns in the dual in the accusative and genitive cases, of which the ending ـَيْنِ some Arabs change into ـَانِ (cf. Ibn Ǧinnī, *Taṯniya* 57-58, Ibn Ḫālawaihi, *Laysa* 333, Ibn ʿAqīl, *Musāʿid* 40, Åkesson, *Conversion* 30-31). Ibn Ǧinnī, *Taṯniya* 57-58 refers to this dialectal variant by presenting the examples ضَرَبْتُ الزيدانِ "I hit both Zaids" in which الزيدانِ occurs instead of الزَيْدَيْنِ and مَرَرْتُ بِالزَيْدَانِ "I passed by both Zaids" in which بِالزَيْدَانِ occurs instead of بِالزَيْدَيْنِ.

(82) The twelve forms of the attached pronoun of the accusative are the following comprising two identical forms for the dual:

	sing.	dual	pl.
1st	ـنِي		ـنَا
2nd masc.	ـكَ	ـكُمَا	ـكُمْ
2nd fem.	ـكِ	ـكُمَا	ـكُنَّ
3rd masc.	ـهُ	ـهُمَا	ـهُمْ
3rd fem.	ـهَا	ـهُمَا	ـهُنَّ

b) Concerning the 2nd person of the fem. sing., the *-ki,* in the dialectal variant known as الكَسْكَسَةُ, the Banū Bakr add the *s* after it, e.g. أَعْطَيْتُكِسْ "I gave you" (cf. Mubarrad, *Kāmil II,* 224) said instead of أَعْطَيْتُكِ in pause, or even substitute the *s* for it. As for the Rabīʿa and the Banū Asad, they add the *š* after it in their own dialectal variant known as الكَشْكَشَةُ, e.g. رَأَيْتُكِشْ said instead of رَأَيْتُكِ "I saw you" and بِكِشْ said instead of بِكِ "in you" (for further examples and references see Vollers, *Volkssprache* 11-12, Brockelmann, *Grundriss* 206; for a discussion why the *-ki* is affected by the *kaškaša* and not the agent pronoun, the *-ti* see Watson, *Kaškaša* 66-79). The Arabs did not always differenciate between الكَسْكَسَةُ and الكَشْكَشَةُ, as they named both phenomenas for either of these terms (cf. Cantineau, *Cours* 118). Furthermore both the *-ki* and the 2nd person of the masc. sing., the *-ka,* have been replaced by the *š,* which pertains to another dialectal variant known as الشَنْشَنَةُ that is peculiar to the dialect of the Yemenites and the inhabitants of Šiḥr in Hadramaut, e.g. لَبَّيْشِ said instead of لَبَّيْكِ "at your service" (for discussions see Rabin, 49-50). The Banū Tamīm change the *-ki* into a *-š* in pause, e.g. دارِشْ said intead of دارِكْ in جَعَلَ اللهُ لَكِ البَرَكَةَ في دارِشْ "May God bless you in your home" (cf. Mubarrad, *Kāmil II,* 223). This substitution can occur as well in context, e.g. the sur. 19: 24

(جَعَلَ رَبُّكِ تَحْتَكِ سَرِيًّا) "Hath provided a rivulet beneath thee" that has been read by some as (جَعَلَ رَبُّشِ تَحْتَشِ سَرِيًّا) (cf. Cantineau, *Cours* 84, *Études* 65).

(83) It is impossible to combine both the suffixed agent and object pronouns that refer to the same person in the verb, except in some mental verbs (for them see Zamaḫšarī, 117-118, Ibn Yaʿīš, *VII,* 77 sqq., Howell, *II-III,* 133-165, Wright, *III,* 48 sqq., Blachère, 264-265, Daqr, *Muʿǧam* 213). In most cases, except in the examples cited below, the mental verb is followed by a حَالٌ "circumstantial accusative" or by a verb that expresses the state or the condition of the suffixed object in connection with the act. The reason why this combination is accepted is that the suffixed object pronoun is not the real object of the verb. Examples that can be added to the ones presented here are عَلِمْتُنِي مُنْطَلِقًا "I knew myself going away", وَجَدْتَكَ فَعَلْتَ كَذَا "you found yourself doing this" and رَآهُ عَظِيمًا "he considered himself great" (cf. Zamaḫšarī, 118). The combination without a following circumstantial accusative or a verb is accepted however in the verbs عَدِمَ "to loose" and فَقَدَ "to mislay", e.g. عَدِمْتُنِي "I lost myself" and فَقَدْتُنِي "I mislaid myself" (cf. Ibn Maḍāʾ, *Radd* 107 in the notes, Ibn Yaʿīš, *VII,* 88-89). A verse said by Ǧirān al-ʿAwd, cited by Zamaḫšarī, 118, Ibn Yaʿīš, *VII,* 88-89, Howell, *II-III,* 166, has عَدِمْتُنِي with the combination of both the agent and object pronouns:

"لَقَدْ كَانَ لِى عَنْ ضَرَّتَيْنِ عَدِمْتُنِى وَعَمَّا أُلاقِى مِنْهُمَا مُتَزَحْزَحُ".

"Indeed I have got from two rival wives—may I loose myself! [i.e. may I perish!]—and from that [trouble] which I undergo from them both a place of retreat!".

(84) The twelve forms of the separate pronoun of the accusative are the following, comprising two identical forms for the dual:

	sing.	dual	pl.
1st	إِيَّايَ		إِيَّانَا
2nd masc.	إِيَّاكَ	إِيَّاكُمَا	إِيَّاكُمْ
2nd fem.	إِيَّاكِ	إِيَّاكُمَا	إِيَّاكُنَّ
3rd masc.	إِيَّاهُ	إِيَّاهُمَا	إِيَّاهُمْ
3rd fem.	إِيَّاهَا	إِيَّاهُمَا	إِيَّاهُنَّ

b) Different opinions concern the forms' structure (for discussions see Ibn Ǧinnī, *Sirr I,* 312-313, Ibn al-Anbārī, *Inṣāf* Q. 98, 288-292, Zamaḫšarī, *Kaššāf I,* 60-61, Ibn Yaʿīš, *III,* 98 sqq.; for a discussion concerning the origin of the particle إِيَّا see Bravmann, *Studies* 182-185). According to the teachings of the Kufans, the *-ka* in إِيَّاكَ, the *-hu* in إِيَّاهُ and the *-ya* in إِيَّايَ are the pronouns of the accusative, and إِيَّا is a lengthening element that strengthens the word. Some believed also that the whole word is the pronoun. As for the Basrans they considered إِيَّا to be the pronoun and the *-ka, -hu* and *-ya* to be suffixes which are entitled to invariability.

(85) The twelve forms of the attached pronoun of the genitive are the following, comprising two identical forms for the dual:

	sing.	dual	pl.
1st	ـِي		ـنَا
2nd masc.	ـكَ	ـكُمَا	ـكُمْ
2nd fem.	ـكِ	ـكُمَا	ـكُنَّ
3rd masc.	ـهُ	ـهُمَا	ـهُمْ
3rd fem.	ـهَا	ـهُمَا	ـهُنَّ

(86) When the suffixed pronoun of the genitive of the 1st person of the sing. is attached to a word that ends with the diphtong *-(u)ū*, e.g. ضَارِبُوي "the ones who are hitting me" in the nominative case from the sound pl. ضَارِبُونَ of ضَارِبٌ, or the diphtong *-(i)ī*, e.g. ضَارِبِيي in the accusative and genitive from the sound pl. ضَارِبِينَ, the *w* is changed into a *y* in the first example, and is then assimilated to it resulting in ضَارِبِيَّ, and the *y* in the second example is assimilated to the 2nd *y* resulting in ضَارِبِيَّ. It can be added that the same phenomenon occurs if the word ends with the diphtong *-aw* or *-ay*, e.g. مُصْطَفَيَّ "my elect" for both مُصْطَفَوْيَ in the nominative case from مُصْطَفَوْنَ, and مُصْطَفَيْيَ in the accusative and genitive from مُصْطَفَيْنَ, which are the sound pls. of مُصْطَفًى. For a study see Sībawaihi, *II,* 104, Wright, *II,* 252-253, Vernier, *I,* 340, 381.

(87) The reason for al-Aḫfaš to state that the infixed *ī* in تَضْرِبِينَ is not a pronoun but a marker of the feminine form and that the pronoun is latent, is that both the 2nd person of the masc. and 3rd person of the fem. sing. of the imperfect in e.g. تَضْرِبُ, are common and lack a prominent pronoun. It is then for the sake of analogy that al-Aḫfaš insisted in having the sings. of the imperfect as treated uniformly (cf. Howell, *I,* fasc. II, 519, Šāḏilī, *ʿAnāṣir* 30).

(88) The reason why the *y* was chosen as an infix in تَضْرِبِينَ and not the *t,* is that the prefixed *t* of the addressed 2nd person prohibited this infixation, as this would imply a disliked repetition of two tāʾs if تَضْرِبْتِنَ is said. This dislike of combining two markers of the fem. in the verb is noticed in the case of the perfect of the 3rd person of the fem. pl. ضَرَبْنَ underlyingly ضَرَبَتْنَ (for discussions see (58)) and in the case of the imperfect of the 3rd person of the fem. pl. يَضْرِبْنَ in which the *y* was chosen as a prefix and not the *t* (for discussions see (97)).

(89) The *h* that marks the fem. sing. in the demonstratif pronoun هٰذِهِ is substituted for the *y* of the base form هٰذِي (cf. Rāzī, in Ḫalīl b. Aḥmad ..., *Ḥurūf* 154, Sībawaihi, *II,* 341, Ibn Ǧinnī, *Sirr II,* 556, Zamaḫšarī, 176, Ibn Yaʿīš, *III,* 131, *X,* 44-45, Suyūṭī, *Ašbāh I,* 404, my notes (346)). This implies that there exists a closeness between the *h* and the *y* in marking the the feminine form and justifies why the *y* was chosen as an infix that marks the fem. in تَضْرِبِينَ.

Blachère, 202 mentions the forms of the demonstratif pronoun هَذِي and هَذِه, but does not discuss the phenomenon of substitution.

b) There exist different dialectal variants concerning هَذِه (for them see Howell, *IV*, fasc. I, 1363-1364). The Banū Tamīm say هَذِهْ for هَذِه in the pause, and هَذِهِي when they continue. Qais and the people of al-Ḥiǧāz make pause and context alike and say هَذِهْ or هَذِه. Sībawaihi, *II*, 322 mentions that he has heard the phrase هَذِه أَمَةُ الله said by one who was confident of his Arabic among the Arabs as هَذِهْ أَمَةُ الله, with the *h* rendered vowelless.

(90) The well-know cases of the latency of the suffixed agent pronoun (for discussions see Howell, *I*, fasc. II, 544, Ibn Maḍāʾ, *Radd* 90-93, Bustānī, *Miṣbāḥ* 23, Daqr, *Muʿǧam* 217-218) concern the 3rd person of the masc. and fem. sing. of the perfect, the 1st persons of the sing. and pl., the 2nd person of the masc. sing. or the 3rd person of the fem. sing. and the 3rd person of the masc. sing. of the imperfect, the 2nd person of the masc. sing. of the imperative and all the epithets, verbal nouns and adverbs.

(91) For a study of المُضارِع "the imperfect" see Muʾaddib, *Taṣrīf* 28-43, Zamaḫšarī, 108-114, Ibn Yaʿīš, *VII*, 6-58, Howell, *II-III*, 8 sqq., Wright, *III*, 18 sqq.. The imperfect is considered as being divided into two sorts by Muʾaddib, *Taṣrīf* 28: نص "literally", which means that the tense stands for what the imperfect stands for, namely the present or the future, e.g. يَضْرِبُ زَيْدٌ غَداً عمراً "Zaid shall hit ʿAmr tomorrow", and مُمَثَّل "representative of", which means that the form is the imperfect's form but that the meaning is intended for the past tense (for a discussion concerning this subject see (93 c)). As I remarked about al-Muʾaddib's terminology concerning the division of the perfect into three sorts (see (42)), it is possible that he was the only one to use this terminology concerning the division of the imperfect into two sorts, or that it has been used by other Kufans. I myself was unable to find it by any one else than him. For a study of the imperfect in Arabic and in some of the other Semitic languages see Wright, *Comparative Grammar* 179-188.

(92) The imperfect has three moods: the indicative, subjunctive and jussive. The strong verb of Form I ضَرَبَ becomes يَضْرِبُ in the imperfect of the indicative, active. Its paradigm is the following:

	sing.	dual	pl.
1st	أَضْرِبُ		نَضْرِبُ
2nd masc.	تَضْرِبُ	تَضْرِبَانِ	تَضْرِبُونَ
2nd fem.	تَضْرِبِينَ	تَضْرِبَانِ	تَضْرِبْنَ
3rd masc.	يَضْرِبُ	يَضْرِبَانِ	يَضْرِبُونَ
3rd fem.	تَضْرِبُ	تَضْرِبَانِ	يَضْرِبْنَ

Concerning the ending *-ūna* that marks the masc. pl. and *-āni* that marks the dual of the imperfect of the indicative, it can be remarked that they are the same as those that mark the sound pl. and the dual respectively of nouns occurring in the nominative, e.g. مُعَلَّمُونَ "teachers", مُعَلَّمَانِ

"two teachers". The reason why they were chosen to be attached to the imperfect is the similarity between the imperfect and the noun (for it see (93)). Another question of interest here is why the *ā* was chosen to mark the dual and the *ū* chosen to mark the sound masc. pl. in nouns occurring in the nominative. According to Ibn Ǧinnī, *Taṯniya* 70-72, the dual is more frequently used than the masc. sound pl., because not all nouns can have a masc. sound pl. Some have a broken pl. and others have a fem. pl. with the ending *-āt.* So the light *ā* was chosen for the frequently used dual and the heavy *ū* for the rarely used pl., so that what is deemed as heavy becomes rarely used and what is deemed as light becomes frequently used in the language. According to Abū ʿAlī referred to by Ibn Ǧinnī, *Taṯniya* 72, the pl. is stronger than the dual as it refers to different numbers whereas the dual refers only to two. For this reason the *w,* which is stronger than the *ā,* was chosen to mark the pl. that is stronger than the dual (for discussions see Zaǧǧāǧī, *Īḍāḥ* 121-129, Versteegh, *Zaǧǧāǧī* 216-230). Concerning the *-na* of the indicative of the 2nd person of the fem. sing. in the ending *-īna* (for the reasons of the choice of the *y* see (88), (89)), e.g. تَضْرِبِينَ, it can be remarked that it offers a similarity with the *-na* of the ending *-īna* in nouns that occur in the masc. sound pl. of the accusative, e.g. رَأَيْتُ الطَّالِبِينَ "I saw the demanding persons" and of the genitive, e.g. عِنْدَ الطَّالِبِينَ "by the demanding persons", which is probably the reason why it was as well vowelled by a fatḥa (cf. Muʾaddib, *Taṣrīf* 34). This is why Muʾaddib, *Taṣrīf* 35 states that the *n* of آمِينَ "Amen" was as well vowelled by a fatḥa because of its similarity with the *-na* of the ending *-īna* in the sound masc. pl. of nouns. The *n* of the imperfect of the indicative of the dual of 2nd person of the masc. and fem. e.g. تَضْرِبَانِ, of the 3rd person of the masc. يَضْرِبَانِ and of the 3rd person of the fem. تَضْرِبَانِ that follows the *ā,* is given the kasra because of a similarity between it and the *n* of the ending *-āni* of the dual vowelled by a kasra in nouns occurring in the dual of the nominative, e.g. طَالِبَانِ "two students". According to al-Kisāʾī's theory referred to by Muʾaddib, *Taṣrīf* 29-30, the *n* was vowelled by a kasra, because when two vowelless consonants of which the 1st one is the weak consonant *ā,* are combined in one word it is of common usage that the 2nd consonant is vowelled by a kasra. Examples are دَرَاكِ "attain you! (an imperative verbal noun meaning أَدْرِكْ)", قَطَامِ "Qaṭāmi, name of a woman" (for it see Ibn Manẓūr, *V,* 3682) and حَذَامِ "Ḥazāmi, name of a woman" (for it see Ibn Manẓūr, *II,* 813). Another theory mentioned by Muʾaddib, *Taṣrīf* 30 is that the *n* of the dual of the ending *-āni* is given a kasra to differenciate it from the *n* of the pl. of the ending *-ūna* given a fatḥa. The *n* of the dual has been given anomalous vowels in nouns (cf. Rabin, 67, Muʾaddib, *Taṣrīf* 197, Ibn Ǧinnī, *Taṯniya* 87, Ibn ʿAqīl, *Musāʿid* 40, Ibn Yaʿīš, *IV,* 143). An example with the *n* given anomalously a fatḥa in a verb is recorded in (أتعدَانَنِي) read so by Abū ʿAmr of the sur. 46: 17 instead of (أتعدَانِنِي) "Do you hold out the promise to me" (cf. Ibn Ḫālawaihi, *Qirāʾāt II,* 318). Furthermore the *n* of the 2nd and 3rd persons of the masc. pl. that follows the *w* in e.g. تَضْرِبُونَ and يَضْرِبُونَ offers a similarity with the *n* vowelled by a fatḥa that follows the *ū* in nouns of the masc. sound pl. of the nominative, e.g. الزَّيْدُونَ "the Zaids". According to Abū ʿAlī's theory reported by Muḥammad b. al-Mustanīr Quṭrub referred to by Muʾaddib, *Taṣrīf* 30, the reason of vowelling the *n* in nouns of the masc. sound pl. of the nominative with the lightest of vowels, the fatḥa, is to lighten its combination with the heaviest weak consonant among the weak consonants marking the declension, which is the *w.*

The paradigm of Form I ضَرَبَ in the subjunctive, active, is the following:

	sing.	dual	pl.
1st	أَضْرِبَ		نَضْرِبَ
2nd masc.	تَضْرِبَ	تَضْرِبَا	تَضْرِبُوا
2nd fem.	تَضْرِبِي	تَضْرِبَا	تَضْرِبْنَ
3rd masc.	يَضْرِبَ	يَضْرِبَا	يَضْرِبُوا
3rd fem.	تَضْرِبَ	تَضْرِبَا	يَضْرِبْنَ

For a general study of the subjunctive see Mu'addib, *Taṣrīf* 35-41, Zamaḫšarī, 109-112, Ibn Yaʿīš, *VII,* 15-40, Howell, *II-III,* 20-54b, Wright, *III,* 22, 24-34. A question worth taking up is why the fatḥa was chosen to mark the subjunctive. According to some theories mentioned by Ibn Yaʿīš, *VII,* 15, the subjunctival أنْ resembles the conjunction أنَّ that puts the noun following it in the accusative. The resemblance between both these words is not only in their shapes, but the verb in the subjunctive after أنْ together with it can be replaced by the verb's *maṣdar,* which is put in the accusative by the verb preceding it. As the accusative in nouns corresponds to the subjunctive in verbs, the verb after أنْ is put in the subjunctive mood. Furthermore the subjunctivals لَنْ, إذَنْ and كَيْ are brought into relation with أنْ. Mu'addib, *Taṣrīf* 40 presents the following examples: أقومُ لتقومَ معي "I shall get up so that you get up with me" which can mean كَيْ تَقومَ "so that you get up", and أحبُّ أنْ تقومَ "I like you to get up". The verb after أنْ has the meaning of the *maṣdar,* and the sentence can be likened to: أحبُّ قيامَك "I like your getting up" with قيامَك put in the accusative by the verb أحبُّ. Another example is يُعْجِبُني أنْ تجلسَ "I like you to sit down" which can be replaced by the sentence يُعْجِبُني جُلُوسُكَ "I like your sitting down".

The paradigm of Form I ضَرَبَ in the jussive, active, is the following:

	sing.	dual	pl.
1st	أَضْرِبْ		نَضْرِبْ
2nd masc.	تَضْرِبْ	تَضْرِبَا	تَضْرِبُوا
2nd fem.	تَضْرِبِي	تَضْرِبَا	تَضْرِبْنَ
3rd masc.	يَضْرِبْ	يَضْرِبَا	يَضْرِبُوا
3rd fem.	تَضْرِبْ	تَضْرِبَا	يَضْرِبْنَ

For a general study of the jussive see Mu'addib, *Taṣrīf* 41-43, Zamaḫšarī, 112-114, Ibn Yaʿīš, *VII,* 40-58, Howell, *II-III,* 55-88, Wright, *III,* 22-24, 35-41. A question worth taking up is why was the sukūn chosen to mark the jussive mood. One theory mentioned by Ibn Yaʿīš, *VII,* 41, is that the apocopatives لَمْ "not" and لمّا "not yet" transfer the verb that is in the present tense to the past tense. As the verb is transferred to a limit in time which is not possible to be applied to the noun, it took an inflectional marker that is not existent in the noun, which is the sukūn. To the question why the subjunctivals أنْ "that" and لنْ "shall not", which transfer the verbs to the future tense and put them in the subjunctive mood, do not put them instead in the jussive mood by giving them a sukūn marker, Ibn Yaʿīš answers that they resemble the heavy conjunction أنَّ,

so they operated in the same manner as it. According to Quṭrub's theory (cf. Mu'addib, *Taṣrīf* 42), the jussive that has the sukūn marker is applied to the heavy verb, because the sukūn is lighter than the vowel, and the light noun does not need to become more alleviated by the light sukūn. According to Abū Ǧaʿfar al-Ruʾāsī (cf. ibid), the apocopatives operate on the verb by putting it in the jussive mood because they can only be prefixed to the verb and not to the noun, moreover, they indicate an action that occurs in the past with a form of a verb that is specific for the present or for a coming action. Hence it is impossible to say لَمْ عبد الله يخرج instead of لم يَخْرُجْ عبد الله "ʿAbd Allāh did not go out". So when they were combined uniquely with the verbs, they operated on them by putting them in the jussive mood which is particular for the verbs. According to the theory of Abū Muḥammad ʿAbd Allah b. Muslim (cf. ibid), the verb in the jussive mood to which لَمْ is prefixed to, is transferred to the past time, whereas it is transferred to the future time when the subjunctival لَنْ is prefixed to it. In order to differenciate between both these moods, the verb in the jussive received a sukūn marker whereas it received a fatḥa marker in the subjunctive.

(93) The main arguments according to the Arabic grammatical tradition which prove that the imperfect is similar to the noun (for them see Ibn Yaʿīš, *VII,* 6; my notes (46), (47), are presented here. The imperfect's form is commensurable to the active participle's form. For instance the form يَضْرِبُ "he hits" is commensurable to the form of the active participle ضارِبٌ, as each of its consonants corresponds in its mobility or vowellessness to the state of the consonant of the other form (cf. (47)). Just like the active participle, the imperfect can occur as a modifier, صِفَةٌ, of an indefinite noun. In a sentence as هذا رَجُلٌ يَضْرِبُ "this is a hitting man", the imperfect that follows the indefinite noun functions as a modifier, and corresponds in its meaning to the modifier in the example هذا رَجُلٌ ضارِبٌ (cf. Owens, *Foundations* 208). The inceptive *la–* which is specific to be prefixed to nouns which it emphasizes, e.g. إنَّ زيداً لقائمٌ "verily Zaid is getting up", can be prefixed to the imperfect, i.e. إنَّ زيداً ليَقومُ, and the meaning is the same. This particular *la-* cannot be made to precede the perfect, i.e. إنَّ زيداً لَقامَ with the very same specific meaning that this affirmative *la–* introduces. The imperfect can be general, by which it is meant that is vague, because it can be valid for the tenses of the present and future (cf. Ibn Ḫālawaihi, *Iʿrāb* 4), e.g. يَضْرِبُ can mean "he hits, he is hitting *or* he shall hit". It is this vagueness that is considered as similar to the vagueness of the indefinite noun, e.g. رأيْتُ رَجُلاً "I saw a man", in which رَجُلاً "a man" refers to an indefinite man. The prefixation of the *s* or *sawfa* (for discussions concerning their etymology see Rundgren, *Bildungen* 122-123) to the imperfect specifies its meaning by making it refer to a special tense which is the future, e.g. زيد سيَضْرِبُ (for discussions with examples see Reckendorf, *Syntax* 13-14, Šāḏilī, *ʿAnāṣir* 24-26) and سوفَ يَضْرِبُ "Zaid will hit", in the same manner as the prefixation of the definite article to the indefinite noun renders it definite (for the question concerning which is prior the indefinite noun or the definite one see Ṣaymarī, *Tabṣira* 97-98), e.g. رأيتُ الرَّجُلَ "I saw the man". The imperfect functions as a حال "denotative of state", in e.g. زيد يَضْرِبُ, and corresponds in its function and meaning to the active participle, in e.g. زيد ضاربٌ "Zaid is hitting". The Kufans name the active participle which operates like the verb as الفعل الدائم "the permansive verb" (for discussions see (46 b)), which is a term that is criticised by the Basrans. Another important resemblance of the imperfect to the noun that can be added, is its dual and pl. suffixes, respectively -*āni* and -*ūna* (for discussions see (92)), which are particular to be suffixed to the noun (for a detailed discussion see Maḫzūmī, *Naḥw* 136-137). The declension of the imperfect is specified with الرفع "the indicative mood" that corresponds to the nominative case of the nouns, النصب "the subjunctive mood" (for the reasons why the fatḥa was chosen see (92)) that corresponds to the accusative case of the nouns and الجزم "the jussive mood" (for the reasons why the sukūn was chosen see (92)) that corresponds to the genitive case of the nouns. It can be mentioned that a debate arose between the Basrans and the Kufans concerning the reasons of vowelling the imperfect's final consonant with a ḍamma. The Kufans believed that the imperfect prefixes imposed on it the indicative mood, and when the particles which govern the verb in the subjunctive and jussive mood were made to precede it, the subjunctive and the jussive moods were imposed on it. Otherwise it had to be inflected with the رفع, i.e. the vowel *u* of the nominative (for discussions see Ibn al-Anbārī, *Inṣāf* Q. 74, 226-228, *Asrār* 13-14, Ibn Yaʿīš, *VII*, 12-13).

b) Not only the active participle ضاربٌ as mentioned in e.g. زيد ضاربٌ can replace the imperfect يَضْرِبُ in زيد يَضْرِبُ "Zaid is hitting", but also both these passive participles مَجْموعٌ and مَشْهودٌ which occur in the sur. 11: 103 (ذَٰلِكَ يَوْمٌ مَجْمُوعٌ لَهُ ٱلنَّاسُ وَذَٰلِكَ يَوْمٌ مَشْهُودٌ) "That is a Day for which mankind will be gathered together: that will be a Day of Testimony" (cf. Zarkašī, *Burhān III*, 376).

c) The imperfect resembles the perfect in some cases as it can occur with the meaning of the past. This is indicated by Ibn Fāris, *Ṣāḥibī* 219, who refers to a verse which is said to have been said by Šamr b. ʿAmr al-Ḥanafī, in which أَمُرُّ has the meaning of مَرَرْتُ:

"وَلَقَدْ أمرُّ عَلَى ٱللَّئِيمِ يَسُبُّنِي   فَمَضَيْتُ عَنْهُ وَقُلْتُ لَا يَعْنِينِي".

"At times I have passed by the evil one who insulted me, but I moved away from him and said: 'It does not matter to me'".

Ibn Ǧinnī, *Ḫaṣāʾiṣ III*, 330, 332, the commentator to Zamaḫšarī, *Kaššāf I*, 70, Ibn Hišām, *Muġnī I*, 102, Suyūṭī, *Ašbāh II*, 103, 600, Ibn Manẓūr, *I*, 508, Daqr, *Muʿǧam* 124, Rāḍī, *Naẓarīya* 314 have فَمَضَيْتُ ثُمَّتَ قُلْتُ لَا يَعْنِينِي "but I moved away, and then I said: 'It does not matter to me'". Zamaḫšarī, *Kaššāf I*, 70 mentions that there is no reference to a special time in the sur. 1: 7 (صِرَاطَ ٱلَّذِينَ أَنْعَمْتَ عَلَيْهِمْ) "The way of those on whom Thou hast bestowed Thy Grace", in the same manner as there is no indication of time in وَلَقَدْ أمرُّ عَلَى ٱللَّئِيمِ يَسُبُّنِي. Other examples concerning the imperfect having the meaning of the perfect occur in the sur. 2: 91 (فَلِمَ تَقْتُلُونَ أَنْبِيَاءَ اللهِ مِنْ قَبْلُ؟) "Why then have ye slain the prophets of God in times gone by" in which تَقْتُلُونَ has the meaning of قَتَلْتُمْ (cf. Ibn Fāris, *Ṣāḥibī* 220, Rāǧiḥī, *Farrāʾ* 61), in the sur. 2: 102 (وَاتَّبَعُوا مَا تَتْلُو ٱلشَّيَاطِينُ) "They followed what the evil ones gave out (falsely)" in which تَتْلُو has the meaning of تَلَتْ, and in the sur. 5: 20 (وَقَالَتِ ٱلْيَهُودُ وَٱلنَّصَارَىٰ نَحْنُ أَبْنَاءُ ٱللهِ

(وأحبّاؤُه قُلْ فلِمَ يُعذِّبُكم ؟) "Both the Jews and the Christians say: "We are sons of God, and his Beloved. Say: "Why then doth He punish you for your sins?", in which فلم يُعذِّبُكم has the meaning of فلم عذّب أباءكم "Why did He punish your fathers?" (cf. Ibn Fāris, *Ṣāḥibī* 220; for other examples see Cantarino, *Syntax I,* 65-66, Šāḏilī, *'Anāṣir* 26-27).

d) The imperfect is used to indicate present time when it occurs after the affirmative *la-,* as in the sur. 12: 13 (إنّي ليَحْزُنُني أنْ تَذْهَبُوا به) "Really it saddens me that ye should take him away", and the negative ما as in the sur. 31: 34 (وما تَدْرِي نَفْسٌ ماذا تَكْسِبُ غداً) "Nor does any one know what it is that he will earn on the morrow". It also denotes the present in independent and general statements, in dependent positions and to express something that occurs habitually (for discussions with examples see Cantarino, *Syntax I,* 63-64, Šāḏilī, *'Anāṣir* 23-24).

e) The imperfect denotes the future when the *s* or *sawfa* is prefixed to it (cf. (93)). Other cases are when it determines an action that is contrasted with a present or past situation, in questions, after an imperative and in simple statements projected into the future that have the meaning of an imperative (for discussions with examples see Cantarino, *Syntax I,* 66-67).

(94) The four prefixes of the imperfect can be combined in different mnemonic words (cf. Ibn Mālik, *Lāmīya* 238, Volck/Kellgren, *Ibn Mālik* 10, Raymundus, *Tasriphi* 17, Wright, *II,* 56): e.g. أتين, أنيْتُ or نأتي.

(95) The past is stable in relation to the present or the future because the accident in the past is accomplished and cannot be changed whereas present or future actions can be changed.

(96) According to Ibn Mas'ūd's original theory, the imperfect prefix of the 2nd person is underlyingly a *w,* which is substituted by the *t* (for other cases of the substitution of the *w* by the *t* see (52), (198), (247), (330), (331)). The reason of this substitution is to avoid the possible combination of three wāws in the case of the syndesis when a verb is with 1st radical *w,* e.g. ووَوْجَلُ "and you are afraid" said instead of the correct وتَوْجَلُ. Dunqūz, *Šarḥ* fol. 33a ll. 16-17 remarks concerning this combination of the wāws:

"وهو مستكره لأنه يشبه بنباح الكلب".

"It is disliked because it could be compared to the barking of the dog".

The reason of the choice of the original *w* is according to Ibn Mas'ūd, that it is the ultimate of the points of articulation, just as the 2nd person that is addressed by the 1st person is the one by whom the conversation ends. If one considers that the consonants' points of articulation originate from between the farthest part of the throat to the lips, then Ibn Mas'ūd's theory can be justified as to why the vowelled alif or the hamza that originates from the farthest part of the throat and is a laryngal, is chosen as an imperfect prefix for the 1st person of the sing., and why the *w,* which originates more exactly from between the lips and is a labial (for the consonants see (188)), is chosen originally for the 2nd person.

In ورَنْتَل "a calamity" (cf. Ibn Ǧinnī, *Ḫaṣā'iṣ I,* 140, 212, Zamaḫšarī, 170, Ibn Ya'īš, *IX,* 150, Ibn Manẓūr, *VI,* 4820), the *w* is not a prefix but a radical, as the pattern is فعَنْلَلُ.

(97) الغائب "the 3rd person" here in which the imperfect prefix is a *y,* refers to the masc. sing., the masc. pl., the fem. pl. and the duals. According to Ibn Mas'ūd's original theory, the *y* was chosen as an imperfect prefix because it originates from the middle of the mouth, just as the third person stands in the middle of the conversation between the first and the second person. The *y* originates more exactly from the middle of the tongue and the middle part of the upper palate (for the consonants see (188)). The reasons why the *t* was chosen as an imperfect prefix, and not the *y* for the 3rd person of the fem. sing., الغائبة, e.g. تَضْرِبُ "she hits, fem. sing." and not يَضْرِبُ, is on the one hand to avoid confusing it with the masc. sing. يَضْرِبُ, and on the other, to conform this *t* with the *t* which is chosen as a suffix that marks the fem. sing. in the perfect (cf. Wright, *Comparative Grammar* 184), i.e. ضَرَبَتْ "she hit". The *y* and not the *t*, was chosen however as an imperfect prefix for the 3rd person of the fem. pl., i.e. يَضْرِبْنَ and not تَضْرِبْنَ (compare with the forbidden form تَفْعَلْنَ that occurs instead of the correct one يَضْرِبْنَ referred to by تَضْرِبْنَ, the accepted form in Hebrew תִּקְטֹלְנָה cf. ibid, 185), to avoid the combination of two markers of the fem.: the *t* prefix and the *n* suffix if the *t* was to be chosen instead (compare the case of ضَرَبْنَ underlyingly ضَرَبَتْنَ discussed in (58) and the case of تَضْرِبِينَ discussed in (88)). An exception to this rule is the anomalous reading تَتَفَطَّرْنَ of the sur. 42: 5 which has been recorded instead of the correct form يَتَفَطَّرْنَ "Rent asunder" (cf. Wright, *II,* 56, *Comparative Grammar* 185). The prefixation of the *t* in this example is due probably to a false analogy with the 3rd person of the fem. sing. The *y* occurs very rarely as a prefix to nouns in Arabic and in some of the other Semitic languages (for examples see Wright, *Comparative Grammar* 182, Cohen, *Études* 34). It occurs in some nouns of animals, e.g. يَرْخُومٌ "male vulture", يَعْبُوبٌ "horse", of plants, e.g. يَعْضِيدٌ "a kind of plant", and in a few adjectives, e.g. يَخْضِيرٌ "green". These nominal forms could have derived from verbs in the 3rd person of the masc. sing. of the imperfect with some modifications (for examples and discussions see Cohen, *Études* 34).

(98) يُهَرِيقُ "he spills" seems to be formed of five consonants, and according to the rule should have had its imperfect prefix given a fatḥa. However it is underlyingly Form IV يُرِيقُ in which the *h* is anomalously infixed (for discussions see (212); compare it with הֵרִיק in Hebrew). Furthermore it can be mentioned concerning this verb that in its Form I أَرَقْتُ "I spilled", a kind of alleviation of the hamza being its inceptive consonant can be remarked by its change into a *h*, i.e. هَرَقْتُ (for discussions see (343)). It is possible that the *h* is infixed in Form IV because of an analogy with this substituted *h*.

(99) Dialectal variants (for a presentation see Suyūṭī, *Muẓhir I,* 133-136, Karmalī, *Luġāt* 529-536, Riḍā, *Luġa* 114-115, Köfler, *Dialekte* 47-49, Rabin) are generally divided into an Eastern group centered on the Persian Gulf under Tamīm and a Western one under Ḥiǧāz (cf. Blau, *Judaeo-Arabic* 1, Rabin, 11). The allusion made here by Ibn Masʿūd is to the dialectal variant known as the تَلْتَلَةُ (for discussions see Sībawaihi, *II,* 275-277, Fleisch, *Traité I,* 137; and see the example يِنبِي discussed in my notes (32)). The تَلْتَلَةُ بَهْرَاءَ is peculiar to the inhabitants of Bahrāʾ who pronounce the imperfect prefix vowelled by a kasra, e.g. تِفْعَلُ "you do" to conform it with the kasra of the 2nd radical of the perfect of Form I فَعِلَ. The same particularity occurs in the dialect of Qais, and is named تَضَجُّع قَيْس. Also Tamīm (for a detailed study of this dialectal variant and its particularities see Ṣubḥī, *Fiqh* 72-105), Rabīʿa and most of the Arabs, except the Ḥiğāzis, give a kasra to the imperfect prefix of all the persons, except the 3rd person of the masc. sing., a phenomenon which however seems to occur in the Quḍāʿa dialects (cf. (100)). The forms of the verbs presented here in which the imperfect prefix is vowelled by the kasra in this dialect, is Form I formed according to the conjugation فَعِلَ يَفْعَلُ, e.g. عَلِمَ يَعْلَمُ "to know" in which the kasra gives notice of the kasra of the 2nd radical *l* of the perfect عَلِمَ, i.e. اِعْلَمُ "I know", تِعْلَمُ "/2 masc. and 3 fem. sing. (imperfect)", يِعْلَمُ "/3 masc. sing" and نِعْلَمُ "/1st pl.", Form X اِسْتَفْعَلَ يِسْتَفْعِلُ, e.g. يِسْتَنْصِرُ "he asks for assistance" with a kasra given to the imperfect prefix whose perfect is اِسْتَنْصَرَ, so that the kasra gives notice of the hamza's kasra of the perfect. Furthermore it can be added that the imperfect prefix is given a kasra in Form V تَفَعَّلَ يِتَفَعَّلُ, e.g. تِتَكَلَّمُ "you talk or she talks", in Form VII اِنْفَعَلَ يِنْفَعِلُ, e.g. تِنْطَلِقُ "you dash along or she dashes along" and in Form II of the quadriliteral تَفَعْلَلَ يِتَفَعْلَلُ, e.g. تِتَدَحْرَجُ "you roll along, or she rolls along" (cf. Volck/Kellgren, *Ibn Mālik* 11).

(100) The dialectal variants alluded by Ibn Masʿūd are probably those of Qais, Tamīm, Asad, Rabīʿa and most of the Arabs who give the imperfect prefix a kasra, except when it concerns the 3rd person of the masc. sing. (cf. Rabin, 61), on account of the heaviness of the combination of the *y* and the kasra. An anomalous verb with this vowelling occurs however (see the example of يِبْقَى discussed in my notes (32)). The vowelling of the *y* imperfect prefix of the 3rd person of the masc. sing. with a kasra takes place in the Quḍāʿa dialects, in Hebrew, Western Aramaic and Ugaritic (cf. Rabin, 61).

(101) According to a general principle, the marker should not be elided (cf. Ḥassān, *Uṣūl* 142, my introduction pp. 34-35). In verbs of Form V تَتَفَعَّلُ and VI تَتَفَاعَلُ that occur in the 2nd person of the fem. and the 3rd person of the masc. sing. of the imperfect, e.g. تَتَقَلَّدُ "you assume /masc. sing." and "/3 fem. sing." and تَتَبَاعَدُ "you move away or she moves away", two tā's are combined together. The 1st one is the imperfect prefix and the 2nd one is the marker of reflexivity. The repetition of the tā's is considered as heavy by some who prefer to elide one of them for the sake of alleviation (for a study of this particular elision see Howell, *IV,* fasc. II, 1822-1828, de Sacy, *I,* 221, Wright, *II,* 65, Vernier, *I,* 346, my notes (207)). Thus تَتَقَلَّدُ becomes تَقَلَّدُ after the elision and تَتَبَاعَدُ becomes تَبَاعَدُ. Ibn Masʿūd, who follows the theory of Sībawaihi, *II,* 475-476 and that of the Basrans, believes that the 2nd *t* that marks the reflexivity is more fit to be elided, because the 1st one is more important as it is the prefix marking the imperfect. The Kufans however believe that it is the 1st *t* that should be elided because the 2nd one marks the reflexivity whereas the 1st one is prefixed, and its elision is easier (for the debate see Ibn al-Anbārī, *Inṣāf* Q. 93, 269-271; for the assimilation of the *t* that marks the reflexivity to the 1st radical see (207)).

(102) The imperfect prefix *t* of the 3rd person of the fem. sing., e.g. تَضْرِبُ "she hits", is not rendered vowelless contrarily to the suffixed *t* of the feminine form of the perfect, e.g. ضَرَبَتْ "she hit", because of the principle that it is impossible to begin with a vowelless consonant.

(103) The dialectal variant referred to by the example تِعْلَم is the *taltala* (for discussions concerning it see (99)).

(104) The imperfect prefix *t* is given the fatḥa on the analogy that the other imperfect prefixes of the imperfect, the hamza of the 1st person of the sing., the *n* of the 1st person of the pl. and the *y* of the 3rd persons are given the same vowel.

(105) For a study of الأمر "the imperative" see Mu'addib, *Taṣrīf* 99-121, Zamaḫšarī, 114-115, Ibn Ya'īš, *VII,* 58-62, Howell, *II-III,* 88-96, Wright, *II,* 61-62, Blachère, 46-47, Beeston, *Language* 84. For a study of the imperative in Arabic and in some of the Semitic languages see Wright, *Comparative Grammar* 188-191.

The paradigm of Form I ضَرَبَ in the imperative is the following:

	sing.	dual	pl.
2nd masc.	اِضْرِبْ	اِضْرِبَا	اِضْرِبُوا
2nd fem.	اِضْرِبِي	اِضْرِبَا	اِضْرِبْنَ

b) Twenty-three meanings of the imperative in the Qur'ān are distinguished from each other by Mu'addib, *Taṣrīf* 118-121, namely:

1– وُجُوب "duty or obligation", as in the sur. 2: 43 (وَأَقِيمُوا ٱلصَّلَاةَ وَآتُوا ٱلزَّكَاةَ) "And be steadfast in prayer; practise regular charity".

2– وعيد "promising", as in the sur. 41: 40 (اِعْمَلُوا مَا شِئْتُمْ) "Do what ye will".

3– اِعْتِبَار "consideration", as in the sur. 27: 69 (قُلْ سِيرُوا فِي ٱلْأَرْضِ فَٱنْظُرُوا) "Say: "Go ye through the earth and see".

4– تَرغِيب "invitation or incitement", as in the sur. 62: 10 (وَٱبْتَغُوا مِنْ فَضْلِ اللهِ وَاذْكُرُوا ٱللهَ كَثِيرًا) "And seek of the Bounty of God: and celebrate the Praises of God often".

5– اِبَانَة "elucidating, explaining", as in the sur. 10: 101 (قُلِ ٱنْظُرُوا مَاذَا فِي ٱلسَّمَاوَاتِ وَٱلْأَرْضِ) "Say: "Behold all that is in the heavens and on earth".

6– اِبَاحَة "permission, authorization", as in the sur. 5: 3 (وَإِذَا حَلَلْتُمْ فَٱصْطَادُوا) "But when ye are clear of the Sacred Precincts and of pilgrim garb, ye may hunt".

7– مُهَدِّد "treatening", as in the sur. 9: 64 (قُلِ ٱسْتَهْزِءُوا) "Say: "Mock ye!".

8– تَنْبِيه "warning, awakening, rousing", as in the sur. 6: 47 (قُلْ أَرَأَيْتَكُمْ إِنْ أَتَاكُمْ عَذَابُ ٱللهِ بَغْتَةً أَوْ جَهْرَةً) "Say: "Think ye, if the Punishment of God comes to you, whether suddenly or openly".

9– أدب "politeness, good manners", as in the sur. 24: 61 (فَإِذَا دَخَلْتُمْ بُيُوتًا فَسَلِّمُوا عَلَىٰ أَنْفُسِكُمْ) "But if ye enter houses, salute each other".

10– اِنْتِهَار "reprimand, rejection", as in the sur. 6: 91 (قُلْ مَنْ أَنْزَلَ ٱلْكِتَابَ ٱلَّذِي جَاءَ بِهِ مُوسَىٰ نُورًا) "Say: "Who then sent down the Book which Moses brought?—a light".

11– شَهَادَة "testimony, statement", as in the sur. 5: 9 (كُونُوا قَوَّامِينَ لِلَّهِ شُهَدَاءَ بِالْقِسْطِ) "Stand out firmly for God, as witnesses to fair dealing".

12– لُطْف "mildness, gentleness", as in the sur. 17: 93 (قُلْ سُبْحَانَ رَبِّي هَلْ كُنْتُ الاَّ بَشَرًا رَسُولًا) "Say: "Glory to my Lord! Am I aught but a man,—an apostle?".

13– تَخْوِيف "intimidation", as in the sur. 2: 94 (فَتَمَنَّوُا ٱلْمَوْتَ إِنْ كُنْتُمْ صَادِقِينَ) "Then seek ye for death, if ye are sincere".

14– مَسْخ "transmutation, transformation, metamorphosis", as in the sur. 7: 166 (قُلْنَا لَهُمْ كُونُوا قِرَدَةً خَاسِئِينَ) "We said to them: "Be ye apes, despised and rejected".

15– تَحْذِير "cautioning", as in the sur. 4: 71 (يَا أَيُّهَا الَّذِينَ آمَنُوا خُذُوا حِذْرَكُمْ) "O ye who believe! Take your precautions".

16– تَكْوِين "bringing forth, shaping, creating", as in the sur. 16: 40 (إِنَّمَا قَوْلُنَا لِشَيْءٍ إِذَا أَرَدْنَاهُ أَنْ نَقُولَ لَهُ كُنْ فَيَكُونُ) "For to anything which We have willed, We but say the Word, "Be", and it is".

17– اِبْتِهَال "supplication, prayer", as in the sur. 3: 61 (فَقُلْ تَعَالَوْا نَدْعُ أَبْنَاءَنَا وَأَبْنَاءَكُمْ وَنِسَاءَنَا وَنِسَاءَكُمْ وَأَنْفُسَنَا وَأَنْفُسَكُمْ ثُمَّ نَبْتَهِلْ) "Say: "Come! let us gather together,—our sons and your sons, our women and your women, ourselves and yourselves: then let us earnestly pray".

18– اِسْتِبْسَال "death, defiance", as in the sur. 9: 83 (فَٱقْعُدُوا مَعَ ٱلْخَالِفِينَ) "Then sit ye (now) with those who lag behind".

19– اِسْتِغْفَار "asking for forgiveness", as in the sur. 71: 10 (اِسْتَغْفِرُوا رَبَّكُمْ إِنَّهُ كَانَ غَفَّارًا) "Ask forgiveness from your Lord; for he is Oft-Forgiving".

20– تَعَوُّذ "seeking the protection", as in the sur. 23: 97 (وَقُلْ رَبِّ أَعُوذُ بِكَ مِنْ هَمَزَاتِ ٱلشَّيَاطِينِ) "And say "O my Lord! I seek refuge with Thee from the suggestions of the Evil Ones".

21– تَوْبِيخ "reproach, rebuke", as in the sur. 2: 93 (قُلْ بِئْسَ مَا يَأْمُرُكُمْ بِهِ إِيمَانُكُمْ) "Say: "Vile indeed are the behests of your Faith".

22– إِزْعَاج "disturbance", as in the sur. 17: 64 (وَٱسْتَفْزِزْ مَنِ ٱسْتَطَعْتَ مِنْهُمْ) "Lead to destruction those whom thou canst among them".

23– دُعَاء "invocation, call, prayer", as in the sur. 40: 60 (اُدْعُونِي أَسْتَجِبْ لَكُمْ) "Call on Me; I will answer your (Prayer)".

(106) The metre is *Mutaqārib*. The verse is said by al-Māzinī and is cited by Ibn Ǧinnī, *de Flexione* 9, *Munṣif I,* 98, Ḥarīrī, *Šarḥ* 173, Ibn Yaʿīš, *IX,* 141, *Mulūkī* 100, Howell, *IV,* fasc. I, 1096. Ibn Ǧinnī, *de Flexione* 8-9 and Ibn Yaʿīš, *IX,* 141 mention that Abū l-ʿAbbās [Mubarrad] asked Abū ʿUṯmān [Māzinī] about the additional consonants, and so he recited the following verse to him. Other phrases containing the augments (for them see Zamaḫšarī, 170, Ibn Manẓūr, *III,* 1898, Lane, *I,* 1275-1276) are اليوم تنساه "today you forget it" (cf. my commentary to Ibn Masʿūd, *I,* 66), أتاه سليمان "Sulaimān came to him" and سألتمونيها "you (/masc. pl.) have asked me about them". For a study of the addition of the augments to the forms see Ibn Ǧinnī, *de Flexione* 8-19, Muʾaddib, *Taṣrīf* 368-377, Ibn ʿUṣfūr, *I,* 201-294, Zamaḫšarī, 170-172, Ibn Yaʿīš, *IX,* 141-158, *Mulūkī* 100-212, Howell, *I,* fasc. IV, 1770-1813, *IV,* fasc. I, 1091-1181.

For a detailed study including among these consonants the *b,* the *f,* and the *k* which are not mentioned among the augments mentioned above, beginning with: 1– the hamza see Ibn Ğinnī, *Sirr I,* 107-118, 2– the *b,* 133-143, 3– the *t,* 157-167, 4– the *f,* 260-264, 5– the *k,* 291-292, 6– the *l,* 321-409, 7– the *m,* 426-433, 8– the *n* including the nunation see *Sirr II,* 444-518, 9– the *h,* 563-571, 10– the *w,* 594-650, 11– the *ā,* 687-727 and 12– the *y,* 767-769.

(107) The *li–* of the imperative is given a kasra because of its resemblance to the *li–* that is the preposition, e.g. لِيَضْرِبْ "let him hit!". Ibn Ğinnī, *Sirr I,* 390 remarks, referring to the saying of al-Farrāʾ, that some vowel the *–l* of the imperative anomalously with a fatḥa, e.g. لَيَقُمْ زَيْدٌ "let Zaid get up!".

(108) The jussive mood in the verbs corresponds to the genitive case in the nouns (cf. Sībawaihi, *I,* 4). Nouns cannot be put in the jussive mood in the same manner as verbs cannot be put in the genitive case (cf. Carter, *Širbīnī* 40, 42; for discussions concerning why the verbs cannot occur in the genitive case see Zağğāğī, *Īḍāḥ* 107 sqq.).

(109) فَخْذٌ "thigh" underlyingly فَخِذٌ occurs with the elision of the kasra of the 2nd radical (cf. Åkesson, *Elision* 21). Sībawaihi, *II,* 277 mentions that the elision of the kasra occurs in the dialectal variant of Bakr b. Wāʾil and of a lot of the people of the Banū Tamīm. The elision of the unstressed ḍamma occurs as well, e.g. رَجْلٌ for رَجُلٌ "the man", and of the fatḥa, e.g. حَصْبُ from the sur. 21: 98 read in this manner by Ibn Katīr, Abū ʿAmr, Ibn ʿĀmir and Yaʿqūb instead of حَصَبُ "fuel" (cf. Vollers, *Volkssprache* 97, Åkesson, *Elision* 25). The elision of the kasra occurs as well in an active participle of Form VIII, e.g. مُنْتَفْخًا said instead of مُنْتَفِخًا "to be swollen" (cf. Sībawaihī, *II,* 278, Åkesson, *Elision* 22). The Bakr b. Wāʾil and the Banū Tamīm elide the kasra as well from the 2nd radical in the perfect in some verbs of Form I in the active voice, e.g. عَلْمَ said instead of عَلِمَ "he knew". Another example is ضَجْرَ used instead of ضَجِرَ, which occurs in the following verse said by Aḫṭal, *Dīwān* 217 satirizing Kaʿb b. Ğuʾail, cited by Muʾaddib, *Taṣrīf* 16, Ibn Ğinnī, *Munṣif I,* 21, Ibn Yaʿīš, *Mulūkī* 31, Ibn Manẓūr, *IV,* 2554, Ibn al-Anbārī, *Inṣāf* Q. 14, 56, Howell, *II-III,* 245-246, Åkesson, *Elision* 22:

"فَإِنْ أَهْجُهُ يَضْجَرْ كَمَا ضَجْرَ بَازِلٌ   مِنَ آلْأُدْمِ دَبْرَتْ صَفْحَتَاهُ وَغَارِبُهْ".

> "And if I satirize him, he will groan as groans a youthful he-camel of the intensely white [ones], whose two sides and the top of whose hump have been galled".

Compare in Ethopic the special form of the intransitive verbs with the elision of the kasra from the 2nd radical, e.g. *gabra* said instead of *gabĭra* "to do" and *mĕḥra* said instead of *maḥĭra* "to have pity upon" (cf. Wright, *II,* 98).

The elision of the kasra of the 2nd radical occurs as well in the passive voice, e.g. قُصْدَ for قُصِدَ "was saved, economized", which occurs in the example لَمْ يُحْرَمْ مَنْ قُصْدَ لَهُ "he was not to be deprived, he for whom it has been economized" (cf. Sībawaihi, *II,* 277-279). Another example of a verb in the passive voice is عُصْرَ for عُصِرَ "was pressed out", mentioned by Sībawaihi, *II,* 278, which occurs in the following verse said by Abū l-Nağm, *Dīwān* 103, cited by Muʾaddib, *Taṣrīf* 17, Ibn Ğinnī, *Munṣif I,* 24, *II,* 124, Ibn al-Anbārī, *Inṣāf* Q. 14, 57, Ibn Manẓūr, *IV,* 2971, Åkesson, *Elision* 22:

"لو عُصْرَ منه البانُ والمسكُ آنْعَصَرَ".

"If [the moist of] the ben tree and the musk were pressed out from it (sc. a young girl's hair], it was pressed".

For the elision of the fatḥa of the 2nd radical of a verb in the groundform and in the derived form see (45).

(110) There exists a similarity between the hā's of both the separate pronouns of the 3rd person of the masc. sing. هُوَ and fem. sing. هِيَ made vowelless after the conjunctions *wa–* and *fa–* and the intensifying particle *la–,* i.e. وَهْوَ "and he", فَهْوَ "and so he", and لَهْوَ "indeed he", and وَهْيَ, فَهْيَ and لَهْيَ, and the *li–* of the 3rd person of the imperative or indirect command (for its study see Wright, *III,* 35-36, Beeston, *Language* 84) made vowelless after the *fa–* and the *wa-*, e.g. فَلْيَنْظُرْ "then let him see" and وَلْيَضْرِبْ "and let him hit" (cf. Sībawaihi, *II,* 298, Åkesson, *Elision* 25).

b) The *li–* of the imperative is anomalously made vowelless after ثُمَّ "then" in the reading of al-Kisā'ī of both the sur. 22: 15 (ثُمَّ لْيَقْطَعْ) "And cut (himself) off" and the sur. 22: 29 (ثُمَّ لْيَقْضُوا تَفَثَهُمْ) "Then let them complete the rites prescribed for them" said instead of (ثُمَّ لِيَقْطَعْ) and (ثُمَّ لِيَقْضُوا تَفَثَهُمْ) (cf. Ibn Ǧinnī, *Sirr I,* 335). It is also the readings of ʿĀṣim and Ḥamza (cf. Ibn Muǧāhid, *Sabʿa* 434-435, Hindāwī, *Manāhiǧ* 111-112, Åkesson, *Elision* 21-22). The reading of sur. 22:15 with this elision carried out, is also attributed to the Kufans by Ibn Ǧinnī, *Ḫaṣā'iṣ II,* 330, and is found ugly by him.

c) the *li–* of the imperative is anomalously elided (for examples see Wright, *III,* 35-36) for the sake of metric exigency in the following verse said by ʿUmrān b. Ḥaṭṭān, cited by Fārisī, *Masā'il* 469, Ibn Ǧinnī, *Sirr I,* 390, Ibn Yaʿīš, *VII,* 6, *IX,* 24, in which وَيُسْمِعْكَ occurs instead of وَلْيُسْمِعْكَ:

"فَتَضْحِي صَرِيعاً ما تُجِيبُ لِدَعْوَةٍ وَلَا تُسْمِعُ الدَّاعِي وَيُسْمِعْكَ مَن دَعَا".

"And you became crazy not listening to any prayer, nor did you let the implorer be heard. And may God let you hear the one who implored!".

(111) According to the Basrans the connective hamza is by principle given the kasra. The Kufans believe however that the connective hamza should follow in its vowel the vowel of the 2nd radical of the verb (for the debate see Ibn al-Anbārī, *Inṣāf* Q. 107, 309-312 and cf. Bohas, *Étude* 95-105). According to others, the connective prefixed hamza should by principle have been vowelless because it is a prefix, and it is prior to consider a prefix as being vowelless than vowelled (cf. Ibn al-Anbārī, *Inṣāf* Q. 107, 310). However, as it is impossible to begin a word with a vowelless consonant, Ibn Masʿūd remarks that the kasra is given to it, as by principle the kasra is given to the vowelless consonant. It can be added that Ibn Ǧinnī, *Sirr I,* 116 referring to Quṭrub's saying, mentions that the hamza is given a kasra anomalously instead of the ḍamma which is meant to agree with the 2nd radical's vowel, in اِقْتُلْ "kill!" said instead of اُقْتُلْ. Likewise, he discusses among some examples, أُغْزِي "attack! / fem. sing." whose hamza is given a ḍamma in spite of the fact that the 2nd radical is given a kasra, and اِرْمُوا whose hamza is given a kasra in spite of the fact that the 2nd radical is given a ḍamma. As for the reason of giving it such a vowel, he points out that the base form of أَغْزِي is أَغْزُوِي, and of اِرْمُوا, اِرْمِيُوا (cf. also Ibn Ǧinnī, *Munṣif I*, 54-55). So the hamza is given a vowel in both these last examples, which in its nature reveals the elided weak consonant of the base form. In أَغْزِي, the ḍamma points out to the elided *w* of أَغْزُوِي, and in اِرْمُوا the kasra points out to the elided *y* of اِرْمِيُوا.

b) The connective alif (for a general study see Wright, *I*, 19-24) can occur at the beginning of some nouns, e.g. هٰذَا ٱبْنُكَ "this is your son". In both nouns and verbs it takes the *waṣla* when it does not begin the sentence. This alif which is existent in Arabic, is in some cases not existent in some of the other Semitic languages. Some examples are: اِبْنُ and בַּן "son", اِسْتُ and שֵׁת "backside", اِسْمٌ and שֵׁם, שֻׁםֿ "noun", اُقْتُلْ and קְטֹל "kill!", اِنْقَتَلَ and נִקְטַל "to be killed" (for discussions see Barth, *Nominalbildung* 681, 694-695, *Grammatik* 7-10, 21).

(112) The vowelless consonant that occurs between two vowelled ones is not a sufficient separative between two vowels or between two weak consonants whose combination is disliked, to prevent the change of one into the other (for discussions see (113), (290)). This is a principle which is taken into consideration (cf. Ḥassān, *Uṣūl* 217, my Introduction p. 34).

(113) قِنْيَةٌ is mentioned in (257). The *w* of the base form قِنْوَةٌ is changed into a *y* (cf. Ibn Ǧinnī, *Ḫaṣā'iṣ I*, 93, Ibn Manẓūr, *V*, 3759), on account of the influence of the kasra of the *q*. In spite of the fact that the *n* separates both the *qi* and the *wa*, its sukūn renders it too weak to stop the influence of the kasra preceding the *w* by two consonants, which is the reason why the *w* is changed into the *y* in order to agree with the kasra. In some cases, the Ḥiǧāzī dialect has a *y* and kasra against Eastern *w* and ḍamma, e.g. قِنْيَةٌ and مِصْحَفٌ "a codex" against قِنْوَةٌ and مُصْحَفٌ by the people of Tamīm (cf. Rabin, 101). As verbs, قَنَيْتُ and قَنَوْتُ "I took the cattle to milk it" are considered as pertaining to two dialectal variants (cf. Ibn Manẓūr, *V*, 3759 who refers to the Kufans). According to Ibn Ǧinnī, *Ḫaṣā'iṣ III*, 59, the best of both these dialectal variants is قَنَوْتُ.

(114) A curiosity that can be noted is that Ibn Masʿūd uses the Kufan term الف instead of the Basran term همزة (cf. Rāǧiḥī, *Farrā'* 79, for examples of other terms see 79, 139-143, Maḫzūmī, *Madrasa* 306-316, Versteegh, *Grammar* 12). Al-Farrā', and so also the Kufans, used specifically the term alif for همزة القطع "the disjunctive hamza" and الألف الخفيفة "the light alif" for همزة الوصل "the connective hamza" (for discussions see Rāǧiḥī, *Farrā'* 79 sqq.). The hamza of أَيْمُنْ is underlyingly a disjunctive hamza, which became considered as connective, because it is softened after the prepositions مَعَ "with" and مِنْ "from" that becomes مِنَ when combined with it, and the assertative particle *la-*, e.g. لَأَيْمُنُ ٱللّٰهِ "by the oaths of God", in which it becomes a *waṣla*, or لَيْمُنُ ٱللّٰهِ in which it is elided (cf. Sībawaihi, *II*, 296-297, Ibn Ǧinnī, *Munṣif I*, 61, Zaǧǧāǧī, *Ǧumal* 85-86, 257-259, Wright, *I*, 20, Vernier, *I*, 105-106). The reason of its weakening is the frequency of its use. It can be added that a debate was raised between the Kufans and the Basrans about الأَيْمُن "oath", the Kufans judging it as being the pl. of يَمِين "the right hand, an oath, power" and the Basrans judging it as being a noun in the sing. derived from اليُمْن "prosperity, good fortune" (cf. Ibn al-Anbārī, *Inṣāf* Q. 59, 176-178, Goguyer's notes to verse 941 of Ibn Mālik, *Alfīya* 213).

لَيْمُن occurs in the following verse said by Nuṣaib, *Dīwān* 94, cited by Ibn Ǧinnī, *Sirr I,* 106, 115, *Munṣif I,* 58, Ibn al-Sarrāǧ, *Uṣūl I,* 434, Zamaḫšarī, *Asās* 714, Ibn Hišām, *Muġnī I,* 101, Ibn Manẓūr, *VI,* 4969, Howell, *IV,* fasc. I, 878, Daqr, *Muʿǧam* 81:

'فقالَ فريقُ القومِ لمّا نَشَدتُهُم نَعَمْ وفريقٌ لَيْمُنُ اللهِ ما ندري".

> "Then a group of the people said: "yes" when I seeked them, and another group said: "By the oaths of God, we do not know".

b) Ibn Ǧinnī, *Sirr I,* 106 cites another variant of this above-mentioned line with أاذا إذْ نحوتهم "is this him?, if I went toward them" instead of لمّا نَشَدتُهُم. The variant أاذا is the result of the substitution of the hamza for the *h* of أهَذا, i.e. أذا, together with the insertion of the *ā* between it and the interrogative أ, i.e. أاذا (for the substitution of the hamza for the *h* see (115 b), (235), (325); for the insertion of the *ā* between two vowelled hamzas see (233)).

(115) According to al-Ḫalīl, the definite article (for different interpretations concerning it see Ibn ʿAqīl, *I,* 178) is the hamza and *l–* together, and the hamza is considered as disjunctive by him, because it is not vowelled by a kasra. As for Sībawaihi, the article is the *l–* only, and the hamza is connective (cf. ibid, 177, Ḥarīrī, *Šarḥ* 14, my notes to Ibn Masʿūd, *I,* 67). The dispute is also mentioned by Barrānī, *Maṭālib* 104, Carter, *Širbīnī* 264-267. Concerning al-Ḫalīl's and Sībawaihi's different opinions regarding this question, Ullendorff, *Article* 633 remarks:

> "Khalīl's opinion is somewhat more consistent insofar as he considers exclusively the graphic picture, while Sībawaihi takes some account also of pronunciation—though without being able to rid himself of the compelling impact of the spelling pattern".

According to Wright, *II,* 269, the article is formed of the demonstrative consonant, the *l-,* and the prosthetic alif is prefixed to lighten the pronunciation. He remarks however, that some grammarians regard the alif as integrated in the article's structure. The article *ʾal–* is connected with the idea of عَهْدِيَّةٌ "previous knowledge" and functions as جِنْسِيَّةٌ "generic". Ibn Hišām, *Muġnī I,* 49-50 distinguishes between three different types respectively (for discussions see Gully, *Semantics* 146-148; for the assimilation of the *l–* of *al–* to the solar consonants see (176); for the article *ʾam* substituted for *ʾal–* in some dialectals variant see (364); for the insertion of the interrogative hamza *ʾa–* to the definite article and the lengthening of the alif into a *madda* see (229), (233 b)).

b) Other functions of *ʾal–* apart from being the definite article are:

– the relative *ʾal–* which is prefixed to a noun, as in the sentence مِنَ آلقَوْمِ الرَّسُولُ آللهِ مِنْهُمْ which is said instead of مِنَ آلقَوْمِ الّذِينَ رَسُولُ آللهِ مِنْهُمْ "the people of whom is the Apostle of God" (cf. Wright, *Comparative Grammar* 117).

– prefixed to the imperfect, as in the following verse said by al-Farazdaq addressed to one of the Banū ʿUḏra, cited by Carter, *Širbīnī* 22, Šinqīṭī, *Durar I,* 61, Howell, *I,* fasc. II, 596, in which ٱلتُّرْضَى occurs instead of ٱلَّذِي تُرْضَى [the first half-verse is cited by de Sacy, *I,* 449]:

"مَا أَنْتَ بِٱلْحَكَمِ ٱلتُّرْضَى حُكُومَتُهُ   وَلَا ٱلْأَصِيلِ وَلَا ذِي ٱلرَّأْيِ وَٱلْجَدَلِ".

"You are not the judge whose judgement is approved, nor the man of pure lineage, nor the possessor of sound opinion and skill in argument".

– prefixed to an adverb, as in the following verse said by an anonymous author, cited by Ibn Hišām, *Muġnī I,* 49, Howell, *I,* fasc. II, 596, in which ٱلْمَعَهْ occurs instead of ٱلَّذِي مَعَهْ [the first half-verse is cited by de Sacy, *I,* 450]:

"مَنْ لَا يَزَالُ شَاكِرًا عَلَى ٱلْمَعَهْ   فَهْوَ حَرٍ بِعِيشَةٍ ذَاتِ سَعَهْ".

"The one who does not cease to be thankful [to God] for what is with him is worthy of a life endowed with plenty".

– the interrogative أَلْ which occurs instead of هَلْ, prefixed to a verb in the perfect, e.g. أَلْ فَعَلْتَ said instead of هَلْ فَعَلْتَ "have you done?" (cf. Carter, *Širbīnī* 22, who refers to Quṭrub's report) occurring with the substitution of the hamza of *ʾal–* for the *h* of هَلْ (for further discussions concerning the substitution of the hamza for the *h* in other examples than with *ʾal* see (114 b), (325)).

(116) The reason why the prefixed hamza in the imperative of Form IV أَكْرِمْ is given a fatḥa, is to avoid confusing it with the hamza of Form I اِكْرِمْ "honour! /masc. sing." formed according to اِفْعِلْ in which the prefixed hamza is given a kasra. The base form of the imperfect Form IV يُكْرِمُ "/3 masc. sing." is يُؤَكْرِمُ, of تُكْرِمُ "/2 masc. sing." and "/3 fem. sing." تُؤَكْرِمُ, etc., with the infixed hamza of Form IV elided, on the analogy of its elision in أُأَكْرِمُ "/1st person sing.", in which the combination of two hamzas is disliked, resulting in أُكْرِمُ "/1 sing." (cf. Bohas, *Étude* 208-209, my notes (19)). The conclusion that is to be drawn is that the prefixed hamza in the imperative أَكْرِمْ is in reality the disjunctive hamza vowelled by a fatḥa of the Form IV of the perfect أَفْعَلَ, which is existent in the base form of the imperfect تُؤَكْرِمُ before its elision resulting in تُكْرِمُ. It can be added that the passive يُؤَكْرَمَا with the anomalous retention of the hamza occurs in the following verse said by an unknown poet, cited by Ibn Ǧinnī, *Munṣif I,* 37, Ibn al-Anbārī, *Inṣāf* Q. 1, 4, Q. 28, 105, Q. 112, 328, Fleisch, *Traité II,* 281 in the note:

" فَإِنَّهُ أَهْلٌ لِأَنْ يُؤَكْرَمَا".

"Because he deserves to be honoured".

According to Kurylowicz, *Apophonie* & 96 and 73 note 3, the hamza in the imperfect *yuqtalu* never existed. This is contradictory to the example يُؤَكْرَمَا cited above. For a discussion against Kurylowicz's opinion see Fleisch, *Traité II,* 280-281 in the note.

(117) Both names عُمَر and عَمْرو have the same three radicals, but have different vowels, namely عُمَر "'Umar" and عَمْرو "'Amr" (cf. Wright, *I,* 12). عُمَرُ is the nominative and عُمَرَ is the accusative and genitive whereas عَمْرو is triptotic. The addition of the *w* to these three radicals distinguishes عَمْرو "'Amr" from عُمَر "'Umar", and does not affect the sound of the tanwīn. Hence عَمْرٌو "'Amrun" is said in the nominative whereas the accusative is عَمْرًا and the genitive is عَمْرٍو.

(118) The connective hamza is elided in باسْم الله, which is said بِسْم الله "In the name of God" when it commences a sentence and is not followed by a verb (cf. Wright, *I,* 23, Vernier, *I,* 109, Bustānī, *Muḥīṭ* 431, Penrice, *Dictionary* 72). Compare בשם האלהים (cf. Wright, *I,* 23). This elision occurs in the expression بِسْم الله الرحمن الرحيم because of the frequence of use. The Arabs' usage of abbreviating words which are frequently used, is also reported by al-Farrā᾽ (for discussions see Rāǧiḥī, *Farrā᾽* 28). باسْم is not abbreviated in the sur. 56: 74 (فَسَبِّحْ بِٱسْمِ رَبِّكَ ٱلْعَظِيمِ) "Then celebrate with praise the name of thy Lord, the Supreme!", as it is not frequently used.

(119) The Kufans believed that the imperative is declinable, and that the loss of the last vowel is a process which is similar to the case of the declinable imperfect that is put in the jussive mood when it follows the *li–* of the imperative (cf. (48); for discussions see the example فَلْتَفْرَحوا in (120) and the imperative أُمْدُدْ that is underlyingly لِتَمْدُدْ in (184)).

(120) For a general study concerning the qur᾽anical readings by the Kufans see Hindāwī, *Manāhiǧ* 104-107, by the Basrans see 107-118 and by the learned in morphology see 118-143. The example فَلْتَفْرَحوا of this sur. as a 2nd person of the masc. pl. is mentioned by Zaǧǧāǧī, *Ǧumal* 216, Ibn Ya'īš, *Mulūkī* 348, Ibn al-Anbārī, *Inṣāf* Q. 72, 214. It is read in this manner instead of the usual 3rd person of the masc. pl. فَلْيَفْرَحوا found in the Qur'ān. According to Mu᾽addib, *Taṣrīf* 111, it is the reading of al-Ḥasan al-Baṣrī, whereas according to al-Farrā᾽'s saying as reported by Rāǧiḥī, *Farrā᾽* 49, it is the reading of Zaid b. Ṯābit. The point of taking up this example in this context is that the Kufans only recognize the imperative as a part of the declinable imperfect, as it is originally by them an imperfect preceded by the *li–* of command (for discussions see Ḥadīṯī, *Nuḥāt* 84, my notes (48), (119)).

(121) There exist sixteen dialectal variants concerning رُبَّ (cf. Ibn Hišām, *Muġnī I,* 138). Eight interpretations of it exist, all of them having the meaning of either plurality and frequency or littleness and rarity (cf. Suyūṭī, *Hawāmi' II,* 25). The Kufans believe that رُبَّ is a noun whereas the Basrans believe that it is a particle (for their debate see Ibn al-Anbārī, *Inṣāf* Q. 121, 354-355). In examples in which the conjunction, the *wa–* or the *fa-,* precedes a noun in the genitive that is assumed to be preceded by an elided رُبَّ (for a study of some examples see Reckendorf, *Syntax* 330; for a detailed study of رُبَّ maintained or elided in many examples see Howell, *II-III,* 348-356), e.g. فمِثْلِكِ underlyingly فرُبَّ مِثْلِكِ "for many as you", the Kufans and the Basran grammarian al-Mubarrad believed that the conjunction preceding the elided رُبَّ governs by itself the indefinite noun in the genitive. As for the Basrans, they believed that it is not the *wa–* of رُبَّ that governs, but the virtual رُبَّ (cf. my notes to Ibn Mas'ūd, *I,* 68-69; see for this debate Ibn al-Anbārī, *Inṣāf* Q. 55, 165-167). As for the verse (for two other versions see my notes to Ibn Mas'ūd, *I,* 69), the metre is *ṭawīl* and the poet is Imru'u l-Qais. It is cited by Ḥarīrī, *Šarḥ* 12, 66, Ibn Hišām, *Muġnī I,* 136, *Masālik* 73, Ibn Manẓūr, *III,* 1660, Naḥḥās, *Commentar* 14-15, Bustānī, *Muḥīṭ* 338, Daqr, *Mu'ğam* 195. Another variant is also cited by Ibn al-Anbārī, *Inṣāf* Q. 55, 166, in which مِثْلِكِ is governed in the genitive without a conjunction and without رُبَّ preceding it:

"مِثْلِكِ أوْ خَيْرٍ تَرَكْتُ رَذِيَّةٍ   تُقَلِّبُ عَيْنَيْهَا إذَا طَارَ طَائِرُ".

"Many a weakened and frightened [camel] as you or even better than you I have left, agitating its eyes if a bird flew!".

Other examples with رُبَّ governing in spite of its elision are found in these verses, just to mention a few:

– In the following said by Imru'u l-Qais cited by Ṯa'ālibī, *Fiqh* 257, Ibn Hišām, *Muġnī II,* 361, *Masālik* 75, Howell, *II-III,* 355, Daqr, *Mu'ğam* 195, Sayyid, *Kāfī I,* 308, Ḥasan, *Baḥṯ* 83, in which وَلَيْلٍ occurs instead of وَرُبَّ لَيْلٍ:

"وَلَيْلٍ كَمَوْجِ البَحْرِ أرْخَى سُدُولَهُ   عَلَيَّ بِأنْوَاعِ الهُمُومِ لِيَبْتَلِي".

"And many a night like the wave of the sea, that let down its curtains upon me with various worries to try [me!]".

– in the following said by Nahšal b. Ḥarrī, cited by Ibn al-Ğawzī, *Kanz* 40 translated and commented on by Vitestam p. 63, in which وَيَوْمٍ occurs instead of وَرُبَّ يَوْمٍ:

"وَيَوْمٍ كَأنَّ ٱلْمُصْطَلِينَ بِحَرِّهِ   وَإنْ لَمْ يَكُنْ نَاراً قِيَامٌ عَلَى ٱلْجَمْرِ".

"For how many a day did it not seem as if those who were baked in its heat, were lying—even if it was not a real fire—on glowing embers".

– in the following said by Ru'ba Ibn al 'Ağğāg, cited by Daqr, *Mu'ğam* 195, in which وَبَلَدٍ occurs instead of وَرُبَّ بَلَدٍ:

"بَلْ بَلَدٍ مِلْءُ الفِجَاجِ قَتَمُهْ   لا يُشْتَرَى كَتَّانُهُ وَجُهْرُمُهْ".

"But many a city whose road between two mountains is filled with dust, from where nor its linen nor its Ğuhrumīs [sc. inhabitants from a village in Fāris] can be bought!".

– in the following said by Ğamīl, *Dīwān* 118, cited by Ibn Ğinnī, *Sirr I,* 133, *Ḫaṣā'iṣ I,* 285, *III,* 150, Ibn al-Anbārī, *Inṣāf* Q. 55, 166, Ibn Hišām, *Muġnī I,* 121, *Masālik* 77, Suyūṭī, *Ašbāh I,* 588, Ibn Manẓūr, *I,* 665, Howell, *II-III,* 352, Daqr, *Mu'ğam* 195, in which رَسْمِ دَارٍ occurs with both the conjunction, the *wa-*, and رُبَّ elided instead of وَرُبَّ رَسْمِ دَارٍ, which is rare:

"رَسْمِ دَارٍ وَقَفْتُ فِي طَلَلِهْ   كِدْتُ أقْضِي الحَيَاةَ مِنْ جَلَلِهْ".

"Many a vestige of a dwelling, in the ruins whereof I stood, for the sake of which I almost ended life!".

(122) According to the Basrans, the perfect, imperfect and imperative are originally undeclinable, as by principle verbs are undeclinable. The imperfect became however declinable because of its similarity to the noun (cf. (46), (47), (93)). The opinion of the Kufans concerning this declinability differs slightly from the Basrans. They agreed with the Basrans that the imperfect should be declinable, but believed that its declinability is original. By introducing this idea, they opposed the rule that the declinability is principal for the nouns, and assumed that it can as well apply to the verbs as in the case of the imperfect. Their main argument is that the imperfect could refer to different tenses, as the future or a continuous time in the sentences. As well as the use of the three moods, the indicative, subjunctive or jussive, imposes on it different significations. This flexibility similar to the noun's flexibility is according to them the reason of its original declinability. For a study of these arguments see Zaǧǧāǧī, *Īḍāḥ* 80-82, Ibn al-Anbārī, *Inṣāf* Q. 73, 224-225, ʿUkbarī, *Masāʾil* 83-85, Ibn Yaʿīš, *VII,* 12-14.

(123) Verbs are by principle undeclinable (cf. Ḥassān, *Uṣūl* 220). This is the opinion of the Basrans that Ibn Masʿūd is referring here to, which is that the perfect, imperfect and imperative are originally undeclinable. The Kufans believe however that the imperfect is originally declinable (cf. 122), and that the imperative was declinable before that it became undeclinable (cf. (48), (119), (120)).

(124) For the reasons of the imperfect's declinability see (46), (47), (93).

(125) For the corroborative *n* see Sībawaihi, *II,* 152 sqq., Zamaḫšarī, 155, Ibn Yaʿīš, *IX,* 37-45, Ibn ʿAqīl, *II,* 308-319, Farḥāt, *Baḥṯ* 39, Howell, *II-III,* 706-718, Wright, *II,* 61, Vernier, *I,* 32, Daqr, *Muʿǧam* 412-416. For discussions concerning nasal-based energic verbal suffixes in some of the Semitic languages see Testen, *Suffixes* 293-311. The Energetic comprehends the category of the imperfect, Energetic I and II, and the imperative, Energetic I and II.

The paradigm of ضرب in the imperfect, active, Energetic I, is the following:

	sing.	dual	pl.
1st	أَضْرِبَنَّ		نَضْرِبَنَّ
2nd masc.	تَضْرِبَنَّ	تَضْرِبَانِّ	تَضْرِبُنَّ
2nd fem.	تَضْرِبِنَّ	تَضْرِبَانِّ	تَضْرِبْنَانِّ
3rd masc.	يَضْرِبَنَّ	يَضْرِبَانِّ	يَضْرِبُنَّ
3rd fem.	تَضْرِبَنَّ	تَضْرِبَانِّ	يَضْرِبْنَانِّ

Its paradigm in the imperfect, active, Energetic II, is the following:

	sing.	dual	pl.
1st	أَضْرِبَنْ		نَضْرِبَنْ
2nd masc.	تَضْرِبَنْ	...	تَضْرِبُنْ
2nd fem.	تَضْرِبِنْ	...	
3rd masc.	يَضْرِبَنْ	...	يَضْرِبُنْ
3rd fem.	تَضْرِبَنْ	...	

Its paradigm in the imperative, active, Energetic I, is the following:

	sing.	dual	pl.
2nd masc.	اضْرِبَنَّ	اضْرِبَانِّ	اضْرِبُنَّ
2nd fem.	اضْرِبِنَّ	اضْرِبَانِّ	اضْرِبْنَانِّ

Its paradigm in the imperative, active, Energetic II, is the following:

	sing.	dual	pl.
2nd masc.	اضْرِبَنْ	...	اضْرِبُنْ
2nd fem.	اضْرِبِنْ	...	...

b) The single *n* is suppressed when a vowelless consonant occurs after it in order to avoid the cluster of two vowelless consonants. This is noticed in لَا تُهِينَ, which occurs instead of لَا تُهِينَنْ that precedes a word starting with the definite article, and thus implying a cluster of two vowelless consonants, in the following verse said by al-Aḍbaṭ b. Quraiʿ al-Saʿdī, cited by Zamaḫšarī, 156, Ibn Yaʿīš, *IX,* 43, 44, Ibn ʿAqīl, *II,* 316, Alee, *Wasīṭ* 227 sq., Ibn Manẓūr, *V,* 3751, Howell, *II-III,* 442, 717, Daqr, *Muʿǧam* 416:

"لَا تُهِينَ ٱلْفَقِيرَ عَلَّكَ أَنْ تَرْ كَعَ يَوْماً وَٱلدَّهْرُ قَدْ رَفَعَهْ".

"Do not despise the poor: maybe that you may be low one day, when fortune has raised him".

c) The single *n* is elided anomalously in, e.g. اضْرِبَ which occurs instead of اضْرِبَنْ for the sake of metric exigency, in the following verse said by Ṭarafa, cited by Ibn Ǧinnī, *Ḫaṣāʾiṣ I,* 126, Ibn Yaʿīš, *IX,* 44, Ibn ʿAqīl, *II,* 317 in the notes, Ibn Manẓūr, *V,* 3751, Howell, *II-III,* 717-718:

"اضْرِبَ عَنْكَ ٱلْهُمُومَ طَارِقَهَا ضَرْبَكَ بِٱلسَّيْفِ قَوْنَسَ ٱلْفَرَسِ".

"Do surely strike away the worries from you, their comer by night, like your striking with the sword the crest of the horse".

d) The doubled *n* is elided anomalously in the following verse said by ʿAbd Allāh b. Rawāḥa al-Anṣārī, cited by Suyūṭī, *Šarḥ* 315, Howell, *II-III,* 716-717, in which لَنَأْتِيهَا occurs intead of لَنَأْتِيَنَّهَا:

"فَلَا وَأَبِي لَنَأْتِيهَا جَمِيعاً وَلَوْ كَانَتْ بِهَا عَرَبٌ وَرُومُ".

"Then no, by my father, verily we will undertake it [sc. the warlike expedition], all together, even though Arabs and Greeks".

e) The doubled *n* is not to be suffixed to the perfect, but this occurs anomalously in دَامِنَّ in the following verse said by an unknown poet, mentioned by al-Šartūnī, the commentator of Farḥāt, *Baḥṯ* 38 in the notes, Howell, *II-III,* 710:

"دَامِنَّ سَعْدُكِ لَوْ رَحِمْتِ مُتَيَّماً لَوْلَاكِ لَمْ يَكُ لِلصَّبَابَةِ جَانِحَا".

"Everlasting may your good fortune be if you take pity upon a thrall that, if it were not for you, would not be inclined to fondness!".

f) The doubled *n* is not to be suffixed to the active participle, but this occurs anomalously in أقائلن which is an active participle preceded by the alif of interrogation, in the following verse said by Ruʾba, mentioned by Suyūṭī, *Šarḥ* 257, Šinqīṭī, *Durar II,* 101, Howell, *II-III,* 715:

"أَرَيْتَ إِنْ جَاءَتْ بِهِ أُمْلُودَا مُرَجَّلاً وَيَلْبَسُ ٱلْبُرُودَا
أَقَائِلُنَّ أَحْضِرُوا ٱلشُّهُودَا".

"Tell me, if she brings him delicate, combed, and wearing striped garments, will you indeed say: 'Present the witnesses'?".

This suffixation of the *n* to the active participle in the following verse is probably caused by the resemblance of the active participle to the imperfect (for discussions concerning this similarity see (46), (47), (93)).

g) The doubled *n* can be anomalously alleviated and replaced by a single *n.* Both the sur. 6: 80 (أَتُحَاجُّونِّي) "(Come) ye to dispute with me" and the sur. 15: 54 (فَبِمَ تُبَشِّرُونِّ) "Of what, then, is your good news?", were read by Nāfiʿ with the alleviated *n,* i.e. (أَتُحَاجُّونِي) and (فَبِمَ تُبَشِّرُونِ) (cf. the notes to Ibn al-Sarrāǧ, *Uṣūl II,* 201).

(126) Different from the cases in which the agent suffixes, the *ū* marking the pl. in both the 2nd person of the masc. pl. in e.g. تَضْرِبُونَ and the 3rd person of the masc. pl. in e.g. يَضْرِبُونَ, and the *ī* marking the fem. in the 2nd person of the fem. sing. in e.g. تَضْرِبِينَ are elided, with the ḍamma of the *b* being indicative of the *ū* in both تَضْرِبُنَّ and يَضْرِبُنَّ, and its kasra being indicative of the -*ī* in تَضْرِبِنَّ, the *ā* of the agent marking the dual, i.e. the dual of the 2nd person of the masc. and fem., in e.g. تَضْرِبَانِّ and the dual of the 3rd person of the masc. in e.g. يَضْرِبَانِّ and of the fem. in e.g. تَضْرِبَانِّ, is maintained, to prevent any confusion with the sing. forms. These forms are namely the 2nd person of the masc. sing. تَضْرِبَنَّ, the 2nd person of the fem. sing. تَضْرِبِنَّ, the 3rd person of the masc. sing. يَضْرِبَنَّ and the 3rd person of the fem. sing. تَضْرِبَنَّ. Another reason why the *ā* is not elided is, according to Ibn ʿAqīl, *II,* 314, its lightness.

b) The reason why the doubled *n* is vowelled by a kasra in the duals is because of its resemblance to the -*ni* of the declinable forms, i.e. the -*ni* of the dual of nouns, e.g. رَجُلَانِ "two men", and the -*ni* of the imperfect of the indicative of verbs, e.g. يَضْرِبَانِ "they both hit /masc. dual". It is this *n's* occurrence after the infixed *ā* which made it similar to the -*ni* of the dual occurring after the infixed *ā* (cf. Sībawaihi, *II,* 160).

(127) يَضْرِبَانِّ "/3 masc. dual" is underlyingly يَضْرِبَانِنَّ, in which the 1st *n,* which is the -*na* of the indicative marking the declension, is elided as it is combined with the doubled *n* that is invariable. The reason of this elision is to avoid the combination of a declinable marker with an undeclinable one.

(128) The *ā* is inserted before the double *n* in لِيَضْرِبْنَانِّ "let them hit! /fem. pl." that is said instead of لِيَضْرِبْنَنَّ, to avoid the combination of the -*na* that marks the fem., namely in لِيَضْرِبْنَ,

with the doubled *n* (cf. Sībawaihi, *II,* 160, Ibn ʿAqīl, *II,* 316).

(129) Both the alifs referred to by Ibn Masʿūd concerning the examples اضْرِبانْ "/2nd masc. and fem. dual (imperative En. II)" and اضْرِبْنانْ "/2nd fem. pl. (imperative En. II)"), are the *ā* of the dual in the first example, and the *ā* which is infixed before the single *n* in the 2nd person of the fem. pl. in the second example (compare it with the *ā* that is infixed before the doubled *n* in (128)). As discussed in (130), these forms with the vowelless single *n* suffixed to them are not accepted by any grammarian because of the implied cluster of two vowelless consonants, the vowelless *n* and the vowelless *ā,* except by Yūnus.

(130) Yūnus, b. Ḥabīb al-Ḍabbīy al-Walāʾ al-Baṣrī Abū ʿAbd al-Raḥmān, influenced both al-Kisāʾī and al-Farrāʾ. He died 182/798. About him see Sīrāfī, *Aḫbār* 33-38, Suyūṭī, *Buġya II,* 365, Brockelmann, *GAL I,* 97-98, Sezgin, *Geschichte VIII,* 57-58, *IX* 49-51. This anomalous suffixation of the single *n* on the analogy of the doubled one (cf. (129)) seems to have only been accepted by him (cf. Sībawaihi, *II,* 160, Ibn al-Sarrāğ, *Uṣūl II,* 203, Ibn Ğinnī, *Ḫaṣāʾiṣ I,* 92, Ibn al-Anbārī, *Inṣāf* Q. 94, 271-277, Zamaḫšarī, 155, Ibn Yaʿīš, *IX,* 37-38, Ibn ʿAqīl, *II,* 315-316).

(131) For the cases of the occurrence of the doubled and the single *n* see Sībawaihi, *II,* 152 sqq., Vernier, *I,* 40-42. For the paradigms of the Energetic I and II see (125).

(132) For a study of المجهول "the passive voice" see Zamaḫšarī, 116-117, Ibn Yaʿīš, *VII,* 69-73, Howell, *II-III,* 120-132, Cantarino, *Syntax I,* 52-58, Carter, *Širbīnī* 170-187, Retsö, *Passive* 21 sqq. A question worth taking up in this context is why the ḍamma was chosen to vowel the 1st radical of the form فُعِلَ. According to Muʾaddib, *Taṣrīf* 206-207, the ḍamma, which is the strongest of vowels, was given to it because the passive voice reveals strength by referring to both the agent and the object.

The paradigm of a strong verb of Form I, e.g. ضَرَبَ in the active voice that becomes ضُرِبَ in the perfect, passive, is the following:

	sing.	dual	pl.
1st	ضُرِبْتُ		ضُرِبْنَا
2nd masc.	ضُرِبْتَ	ضُرِبْتُمَا	ضُرِبْتُمْ
2nd fem.	ضُرِبْتِ	ضُرِبْتُمَا	ضُرِبْتُنَّ
3rd masc.	ضُرِبَ	ضُرِبَا	ضُرِبُوا
3rd fem.	ضُرِبَتْ	ضُرِبَتَا	ضُرِبْنَ

Its paradigm in the imperfect of the indicative, passive, is the following:

	sing.	dual	pl.
1st	أُضْرَبُ		نُضْرَبُ
2nd masc.	تُضْرَبُ	تُضْرَبَانِ	تُضْرَبُونَ
2nd fem.	تُضْرَبِينَ	تُضْرَبَانِ	تُضْرَبْنَ
3rd masc.	يُضْرَبُ	يُضْرَبَانِ	يُضْرَبُونَ

3rd fem. تُضْرَبُ تُضْرَبَانِ يُضْرَبْنَ

For a study of the form *yuqtal* as a passive marker in Biblical Hebrew, Ugaritic and Byblos see Retsö, *Diathesis* 32-48. For a study of it and of the derived forms in Arabic and in some of the other Semitic languages see Wright, *Comparative Grammar* 222-226.

(133) Both وُعِلٌ and دُئِلٌ (for the latter see Ibn Manẓūr, *II,* 131, Nöldeke, *Beiträge* 78-79 who has interesting references to other works, Lane, *I,* 840, my notes (253)) are among the rare nouns formed upon the pattern فُعِلٌ with the 1st radical vowelled by a ḍamma and the 2nd one vowelled by a kasra, which offers a disliked combination (cf. Ibn Manẓūr, *VI,* 4875, my notes to Ibn Masʿūd, *I,* 70). Another rare noun is حِبُكٌ formed upon the measure فِعُلٌ with the 1st radical vowelled by a kasra followed by the 2nd one vowelled by a ḍamma (cf. Lane, *I,* 503). According to al-Aḫfaš referred to by Ibn Manẓūr, *II,* 1312 and Bustānī, *Muḥīṭ* 266, Abū l-Aswad al-Duʾalī was referred to as دُئِلٌ (for discussions concerning different spellings of the name see Sīrāfī, *Aḫbār* 13-14, Flügel, *Schulen* 19-20). دُئِلٌ is also used as a name for a tribe of Kināna (Ibn Manẓūr, *II,* 1313). It occurs as well in the following verse (for some references see Nöldeke, *Beiträge* 78-79) said by Kaʿb b. Mālik al-Anṣārī describing the army of Abū Sufyān, when he made a raid upon al-Madīna. It is cited by Ibn Ǧinnī, *Munṣif I,* 20, Ibn Yaʿīš, *Mulūkī* 24, Sīrāfī, *Aḫbār* 14, Ibn Duraid, *Ištiqāq* 170, Ibn Manẓūr, *II,* 1312, Howell, *I,* fasc. IV, 1767-1768:

"جَاؤوا بِجَيْشٍ لَوْ قِيسَ مُعْرَسُهُمْ مَا كَانَ إِلاَّ كَمُعْرَسِ ٱلدُّئِلِ".

"They brought an army such that, if its halting-ground were measured, it would be only like the halting ground of the weasel".

Another variant than دُئِلٌ that can be mentioned for the sake of curiosity is الدَّأَلَى, which is the gait of the wolf. It occurs in the following verse, which according to Ibn Manẓūr, *II,* 1312, Sībawaihi recited when he was referring to what the Arabs have mentioned among the tales said by the animals. It concerns a lizard talking to its son, and is cited by Ibn Wallād, *Maqṣūr* 47, Ibn Manẓūr, *II,* 1312:

"أَهَدَمُوا بَيْتَكَ لا أَبَا لَكَا وَأَنَا أَمْشِي الدَّأَلَى حَوَالَكَا ؟".

"Did they destroy your home—then you do not have any father—, while I am walking the gait of the wolf around you?".

(134) The paradigms of the derived forms of some of the verbs that are cited as examples only (in the active voice) by Ibn Masʿūd in the Arabic text fols. 4a-4b, in the perfect and imperfect of the indicative, passive, are the following: ,

Form II فَعَّلَ, e.g. قَطَّعَ "to cut" becomes قُطِّعَ in the perfect, passive and يُقَطَّعُ in the imperfect of the indicative, passive. Form III فَاعَلَ, e.g. قَاتَلَ "to fight" becomes قُوتِلَ in the perfect, passive and يُقَاتَلُ in the imperfect of the indicative, passive. Form IV أَفْعَلَ, e.g. أَكْرَمَ "to honour" becomes أُكْرِمَ in the perfect, passive and يُكْرَمُ in the imperfect of the indicative, passive. Form V تَفَعَّلَ becomes تُفُعِّلَ in the perfect, passive and يُتَفَعَّلُ in the imperfect of the indicative, passive (it can be noted as well that the active form تَفَعَّلَ can be used as a passive, for its

paradigm and meaning see (39 b)). Form VI تَفاعَلَ becomes تُفُوعِلَ in the perfect, passive and يُتَفاعَلُ in the imperfect of the indicative, passive. Form VII اِنْفَعَلَ becomes اُنْفُعِلَ in the perfect, passive and يُنْفَعَلُ in the imperfect of the indicative, passive (it can be noted as well that the active form اِنْفَعَلَ can be used as a passive, for its paradigm and meaning see (39 b)). Form VIII اِفْتَعَلَ, e.g. اِحْتَقَرَ "to despise" becomes اُحْتُقِرَ in the perfect, passive and يُحْتَقَرُ in the imperfect of the indicative, passive (it can be noted as well that the active form اِفْتَعَلَ can be used as a passive, for its paradigm and meaning see (39 b)). Form IX اِفْعَلَّ has usually no passive. Form X اِسْتَفْعَلَ, e.g. اِسْتَخْرَجَ "to extract" becomes اُسْتُخْرِجَ in the perfect, passive and يُسْتَخْرَجُ in the imperfect of the indicative, passive.
Retsö, *Passive* 29 presents five different passive forms for the transitive Form I *qatal– yaqtul-*, namely: 1– *qutil– yuqtal-*, 2– *ʾinqatal– yanqatil-*, 3– *ʾunqutil– yunqatal-*, 4– *ʾiqtatal yaqtatil–* and 5– *ʾuqtutil– yuqtatal-*. He presents p. 30 three passive forms from the intensive-factive Form II *qattal– yuqattil-,*namely: 1– *quttil– yuqattal-,* 2– *taqattal– yataqattal–* and 3– *tuquttil-yutaqattal-*. The forms added by Ibn Masʿūd are: Form VI تُفُوعِلَ, Form X اُسْتُفْعِلَ, Form XII اُفْعُوعِلَ and Form XIV of the triliteral or Form III of the quadriliteral اُفْعُنْلِلَ. Those that are not mentioned by him are the active forms that have the meaning of the passive, namely: Form V تَفَعَّلَ يَتَفَعَّلُ, Form VII اِنْفَعَلَ يَنْفَعِلُ and Form VIII اِفْتَعَلَ يَفْتَعِلُ. For a general discussion of the derived forms of the triliteral in Arabic and in some of the other Semitic languages see Wright, *Comparative Grammar* 223-226.

(135) The 1st radical is given a ḍamma together with the characteristic *t* that marks the reflexivity in Form V and VI of the passive voice, i.e. تُفُعِّلَ and تُفُوعِلَ. The prosthetic alif and the 1st radical are given the ḍamma in Form VII, i.e. اُنْفُعِلَ and the prosthetic alif and the infixed *t* are given the ḍamma in both Form VIII, i.e. اُفْتُعِلَ and Form X اُسْتُفْعِلَ. Cf. Wright, *II,* 64.

(136) For a study of اسم الفاعل "the active participle" see Zamaḫšarī, 99-101, Ibn Yaʿīš, *VI,* 68-80, Wright, *II,* 131-132, Howell, *I,* fasc. IV, 1606-1650, Bohas, *Étude* 148-152. For a general study of it in Arabic and in some of the other Semitic languages see Wright, *Comparative Grammar* 196-197. For its being named الفعل الدائم "the permansive verb" by the Kufans see (46 b)).

(137) For the similarity between the active participle and the imperfect see (46), (47), (93).

(138) The assimilated adjective, الصفة المشبهة (for a detailed presentation see Zamaḫšarī, 101, Ibn Yaʿīš, *VI,* 81 sqq., de Sacy, *I,* 320-321, Wright, *II,* 133 sqq., Vernier, *I,* 211-212, ʿAbd al-Raḥīm, *Ṣarf* 88-92, Bohas, *Étude* 155-157) is derived from Form I of the triliteral verb. It is formed according to these principal measures: 1– فَعْلٌ, 2– فَعَلٌ, 3– فَعِلٌ, 4– فَعُلٌ, 5– فِعْلٌ, 6– فُعْلٌ, 7– فُعُلٌ, 8– فُعَلٌ, 9– فَعَالٌ, 10– فُعَالٌ, 11– فَعِيلٌ, 12– فَعُولٌ, 13– فَعْلَانٌ, 14– فِعْلَانٌ, 15– فُعْلَانٌ and

16– أَفْعَلُ. For a study of أَفْعَلُ with interesting references see Fischer, *Farb–* 5-15. It may be noted concerning the alif prefix in this form that it has been used in some old words in Semitic to designate different parts of the body (cf. Retsö, *Diathesis* 84). This could explain why it has been chosen for the أَفْعَلُ of defects and deformities (cf. ibid). Zabīdī, *Tāğ XXIV,* 124 mentions the formation of أَفْعَلُ from فَعَلَ يَفْعُلُ according to the examples cited by Ibn Mas'ūd, together with the example that is referred to by him as having been said by al-Farrā'. For أَحْمَقُ see Fischer, *Farb–* 138, for أَسْمَرُ see 36-44, for آدَمُ see 340-343, Kronholm, *Ephrem* 54 note 23, and for أَعْجَمُ see Fischer, *Farb–* 112-113. As for the two dialectal variants فَعِلَ and فَعُلَ from which the assimilated adjectives derive, Sībawaihi, *II,* 233-234 mentions that some Arabs say أَدُمَ and أَدِمَ for أَدَمَ "to be brown". Astarābādī, *Šarḥ al-šāfiya I,* 71 referring to Ibn al-Ḥāğib, mentions that both dialectal variants فَعِلَ and فَعُلَ are applied for سَمِرَ, أَدِمَ "to be brown", عَجِفَ "to be lean", حَمِقَ "to be foolish", خَرِقَ "to be unskillful", عَجِمَ "to be dumb" and رَعِنَ "to be silly".
For al-Aṣma'ī, 'Abd al-Malik b. Quraib (d. 216/831) see Sīrāfī, *Aḫbār* 58-67, Suyūṭī, *Buġya II,* 112-113, Zubaidī, *Ṭabaqāt* 183-192, Luġawī, *Marātib* 46-65, Brockelmann, *GAL I,* 104, *S I,* 163-165, Sezgin, *Geschichte VIII,* 71-76, *IX,* 66-67.

(139) For a study of the elative, the أَفْعَلُ of superiority, see Wehr, *Elativ* (1952) 565-621, Fischer, *Farb–* 142 sqq., Fleisch, *Traité I,* 409-417, Wright, *II,* 140-143, Blachère, 97-98, Cantarino, *Syntax II,* 467-486, Daqr, *Mu'ğam* 11-20, Bohas, *Étude* 157-158. The elative أَفْعَلُ resembles the Form IV أَفْعَلَ, and there could be a slight similarity in meaning between them both in a few cases of verbs of Form IV that denote finding a quality in the object. An example is "I أَكْبَرْتُ زَيْدًا Zayd is greater than his friend" and Form IV of the verb زَيْدٌ أَكْبَرُ مِنْ صَدِيقِهِ is made Zayd great". The first زَيْدٌ أَكْبَرُ مِنْ صَدِيقِهِ can suggest that Zayd has become greater than his friend because I made him so by being impressed by him, and the latter أَكْبَرْتُ زَيْدًا, that I was so impressed by Zayd's greatness that I made him greater than his friend. Perhaps this connection between both forms explain why the *h* is as well prefixed in Hebrew elatives and the *š* in Akkadian. However Wehr, *Elativ* 37 does not find any connection between both these forms. A common origin is as well assumed between the pattern أَفْعَلُ that denotes colours or defects and the elative أَفْعَلُ with reservations by Fischer, *Farb–* 6, 64, 142. It may be added that a debate (for it see Ibn al-Anbārī, *Inṣāf* Q. 15, 57-68) was raised between the Kufans and Basrans concerning the classification of أَفْعَلَ in a *ta'ağğub* phrase of the type ما أَحْسَنَ زَيْدًا "How wonderful Zayd is!", the Kufans regarding أَفْعَلَ as a noun and the Basrans regarding it as a verb. For discussions concerning the alif prefix in nouns and verbs that denote the intensive, expressive and affective see Løkkegaard, *'Ašrē hā-'īš* 264-266.

(140) The elative is not to be formed on the pattern specific for colours. The Kufans however allow the أَفْعَلُ of superiority to be formed of the colors بَيَاضٌ "whiteness" and سَوَادٌ "blackness", e.g. أَبْيَضُ مِنْ "whiter than" and أَسْوَدُ مِنْ "blacker than" (for أَبْيَضُ and أَسْوَدُ see Fischer, *Farb–* 243-249, 273-277) whereas the Basrans do not allow it (for their debate see Ibn al-Anbārī, *Inṣāf* Q. 16, 68-70). أَبْيَض is used to denote superiority in the following verse said by Ru'ba b. al-ʿAǧǧāǧ and cited by Ibn al-Anbārī, *Inṣāf* Q. 16, 68, Ibn Yaʿīš, *VI,* 93, Ibn Manẓūr, *I,* 397, Bustānī, *Muḥīṭ* 63, 439, Howell, *I,* fasc. IV, 1700, Lane, *I,* 283:

"جَارِيَةٌ فِي دِرْعِهَا ٱلْفَضْفَاضِ   أَبْيَضُ مِنْ أُخْتِ بَنِي إِبَاضِ".

"A maid in her wide shift whiter than the sister of the Banū Ibāḍ".

(It can be noted that Howell writes أَبَاض). Nöldeke, *Grammatik* 16 mentions a part of the verse and discusses on pp. 16-17 other cases of anomaly of the elative.

Another verse said by an unknown poet, cited by Ibn al-Anbārī, *Inṣāf* Q. 16, 70, Howell, *I,* fasc. IV, 1701, has also أَبْيَضُ مِنْ, but it does not denote superiority in this case, but refers to a thing,—in this case a sword,—which is white. And مِن is used in the meaning of كَائِنٌ مِن "of" in it:

"وَأَبْيَضُ مِنْ مَاءِ ٱلْحَدِيدِ كَأَنَّهُ   شِهَابٌ بَدَا وَٱللَّيْلُ دَاجٍ عَسَاكِرُهُ".

"And a white [sword], of water of iron, [flashing] as though it were a shooting-star that appeared when the shades of night were dark".

أَسْوَدُ is used to denote superiority in the following verse said by al-Mutanabbī and cited by de Sacy, *Anthologie* [Ḥarīrī, *Durra]* 34, Howell, *I,* fasc. IV, 1700, Bustānī, *Muḥīṭ* 439:

"إِبْعَدْ بَعِدْتَ بَيَاضاً لَا بَيَاضَ لَهُ   لَأَنْتَ أَسْوَدُ فِي عَيْنِي مِنَ الظُّلَمِ".

"Begone [i.e. may you perish!], whiteness that hast no lustre. Assuredly you are blacker in my eye than darkness itself".

(141) The elative أَشْغَلُ in the proverb أَشْغَلُ مِنْ ذَاتِ النِّحْيَيْنِ (cf. Zamaḫšarī, 102, Freytag, *Proverbia* 687, Lane, *I,* 1567, Bustānī, *Muḥīṭ* 471) is formed anomalously as an elative of the pattern of the passive participle مَشْغُولٌ. The proverb is connected with a woman from Banū Taim Allāh b. Ṯallaba who came to the market of ʿUkāẓ to sell two jars of butter, and who was so busied by them when she was carrying them that she was assaulted by Ḫawaṭ b. Ǧubair al-Anṣarī without being able to defend herself (cf. Bustānī, *Muḥīṭ* 471).

(142) The elatives أَعْطَى and أَوْلَى in both the examples أَعْطَاهُمْ and أَوْلَاهُمْ are formed anomalously from Form IV أَعْطَى "to give" and أَوْلَى "to entrust". Other examples of the elative formed from the derived form occur in the sur. 2: 282 (ذَلِكُمْ أَقْسَطُ عِنْدَ ٱللّٰهِ وَأَقْوَمُ لِلشَّهَادَةِ) "It is juster in the sight of God, more suitable as evidence, and more convenient to prevent doubts among yourselves", in which أَقْسَطُ is formed from Form IV أَقْسَطَ "to act justly" and أَقْوَمُ from Form IV أَقَامَ "to make right". Likewise, أَخْوَفُ "more dreadful" is formed anomalously from

Form IV أَخْوَفَ "to scare", in this saying of Suḥaim b. Waṯīl, cited by Sībawaihi, *I*, 199, Ğarğāwī, *Šarḥ* 167, Howell, *I*, fasc. IV, 1736:

"مَرَرْتُ بِوَادِي ٱلسِّبَاعِ وَلَا أَرَى كَوَادِي ٱلسِّبَاعِ حِينَ يُظْلِمُ وَادِيَا
أَقَلَّ بِهِ رَكْبٌ أَتَوْهُ تَئِيَّةً وَأَخْوَفَ إِلَّا مَا وَقَى ٱللهُ سَارِيَا".

"I passed by the vale of Wild Beasts; and I do not know any vale like the vale of Wild Beasts, when it grows dark, wherein riders that have come to it tarry less [then they do in it], and more dreadful save so long as God guards a wayfarer".

(143) أَحْمَقُ "stupid" is an adjective formed according to the form أَفْعَلُ specific for defects. In the proverb أَحْمَقُ مِن هَبَنَّقَة (cf. Zamaḫšarī, 102, Freytag, *Proverbia II*, 392), it is used anomalously as an elative, i.e. "more stupid". The proverb is connected with the story of Yazīd b. Ṯarwān al-Qaisī who had around his neck a necklace of sea-shells and coloured pearls to remind him of whom he was if he lost his way. One day when his brother has stolen it from him when he was asleep, he did not know more who he was and believed that his brother was Yazīd (cf. Bustānī, *Muḥīṭ* 195).

b) Other proverbs with the anomalous formations of the elative occur (for a detailed presentation and discussion of some cases of anomalies see Sībawaihi, *II*, 268-269, Zamaḫšarī, 102, Ibn Yaʿīš, *VI*, 91-95, de Sacy, *Anthologie* [Ḥarīrī, *Durra]* 33-34, 51-52, Vernier, *I*, 229-231, Wright, *II*, 141-143), as formed from:

– a substantive, e.g. أَلَصُّ مِنْ شِظَاظ "more of a robber than Šiẓāẓ" from لِصّ (cf. Howell, *I*, fasc. IV, 1702) and آبَلُ مِنْ حُنَيْفِ الْحَنَاتِمِ "more skilled in good management of camels than Ḥunaif al-Ḥanātim" from the active participle آبِلٌ (cf. Howell, *I*, fasc. IV, 1702, Vernier, *I*, 230, Fleisch, *Traité I*, 414).

– the passive voice of a verb, e.g. هُوَ أَزْهَى مِنْ دِيك "he is more self conceited than a cock" (cf. Zamaḫšarī, 102, Howell, *I*, fasc. IV, 1703, Vernier, *I*, 230) from زُهِيَ.

c) Some words can be formed on the pattern of the elative without referring to excess being so used as epithets, as the use of أَهْوَنُ "easier" in the meaning of "easy" in the sur. 30: 27 (وَهُوَ ٱلَّذِي يَبْدَؤُ ٱلْخَلْقَ ثُمَّ يُعِيدُهُ وَهُوَ أَهْوَنُ عَلَيْهِ) "It is He Who begins (the process of) creation; then repeats it; and for Him it is most easy" that has been interpreted as well as "... and it is easy to Him" (cf. Howell, *I*, fasc. IV, 1720), and أَطْوَل "taller", which occurs in the meaning of "tall" according to Vernier, *I*, 231, in the following verse said by al-Farazdaq, cited by Zamaḫšarī, 103, Ğarğāwī, *Šarḥ* 164, Howell, *I*, fasc. IV, 1718:

"إِنَّ ٱلَّذِي سَمَكَ ٱلسَّمَاءَ بَنَى لَنَا بَيْتًا دَعَائِمُهُ أَعَزُّ وَأَطْوَلُ".

"Verily, He that raised the heaven has built for us a house, whose pillars are mighty and tall".

However, according to Howell, *I*, fasc. IV, 1718, the meaning of أَعَزُّ وَأَطْوَلُ refers to the elative "taller": i.e. أَعَزُّ مِنْ دَعَائِمِ كُلِّ بَيْتٍ وَأَطْوَلُ مِنْهَا "mightier than the pillars of every house and taller than they" with a suppression occurring anomalously.

(144) The example قَتِيلٌ formed according to the pattern فَعِيلٌ in the meaning of the passive participle مَفْعُولٌ taken as an adjective: مَقْتُولٌ "killed /masc." and مَقْتُولَةٌ "/fem." and the example جَرِيحٌ in the meaning of مَجْرُوحٌ "hurt /masc." and مَجْرُوحَةٌ "/fem.", do not, according to the rule, have a separate form for the fem. (cf. Zamaḫšarī, 83, Ibn Yaʿīš, V, 102, de Sacy, I, 351-352, Wright, II, 186, Vernier, I, 368-369, Blachère, 114-116).

(145) When the adjective according to the pattern فَعِيلٌ in the meaning of the passive participle مَفْعُولٌ is taken as a substantive, it has a separate form for the fem. (cf. Vernier, I, 370, Wright, II, 186). Another example that can be added is رَأَيْتُ قَتِيلَةَ ٱلْحَرُورِيَة "I saw (the woman) whom the Ḥarūrīs had murdered" (cf. Wright, II, 186).

(146) This sur. is also cited by Zamaḫšarī, 83, Ibn Yaʿīš, V, 102, Wright, II, 186. قَرِيبٌ which is formed according to the pattern فَعِيلٌ in the sur. إِنَّ رَحْمَةَ ٱللهِ قَرِيبٌ مِنَ ٱلْمُحْسِنِينَ has the meaning of the active participle فَاعِلٌ. The rule would have required that the fem. قَرِيبَةٌ is used in accordance with the substantive رَحْمَةٌ that is in the fem. It is however anomalously taken as an adjective that has the meaning of the passive participle (for them see (144)), which is why it does not have a separate form for the fem.

(147) The adjectives of the form فَعُولٌ can instead of denoting a high degree of their subject's quality indicate an act done with frequency or violence (cf. Wright, II, 136). It denotes intensiveness when it is formed from a transitive triliteral verb, e.g. غَفُورٌ "much forgiving" from غَفَرَ "to forgive", and it is an assimilated adjective when it is formed from an intransitive verb, mostly from فَعُلَ, e.g. طَهُورٌ "pure" from طَهُرَ "to be pure" (cf. ʿAbd al-ʿAzīz, Fuṣḥā 149). As an example of the pattern فَعُولٌ, هَيُوجٌ "to be able to arise to lust" can be mentioned, which occurs in the following verse said by al-Rāʿī, cited by Sībawaihi, I, 46, Ibn ʿAqīl, II, 113, Ǧarǧāwī, Šarḥ 150, Howell, I, fasc. IV, 1616 (only the 2nd verse is cited by Ibn Manẓūr, VI, 4733. It can be noted that it governs as a verb the substantive إِخْوَانَ in the accusative):

"عَشِيَةَ سُعْدَى لَوْ تَرَاءَتْ لِرَاهِبٍ بِدُومَةَ تَجْرُ دُونَهُ وَحَجِيجُ
قَلَى دِينَهُ وَٱهْتَاجَ لِلشَّوْقِ إِنَّهَا عَلَى ٱلشَّوْقِ إِخْوَانَ ٱلْعَزَاءِ هَيُوجُ".

"On an evening such that, if Suʿda had shown herself to an anchorite at Dūma, below whom were traders and pilgrims, he would have hated his religion, and been roused to lust. Verily she is wont to rouse the brothers of ascetism to lust".

For a discussion concerning the occurrence of فَعُولٌ as a *maṣdar* see ʿAbd al-ʿAzīz, *Fuṣḥā* 149-150. This pattern as a noun in the meaning of مَفْعُولٌ is used mostly for medicaments (for a list see ibid, 147-149).

(148) When an adjective is on the pattern فَعُولٌ in the meaning of the active participle فَاعِلٌ,

it does not have a separate form for the fem., e.g. صَبُورٌ for both the masc. and fem. in the meaning of صابِرٌ "patient /masc." and صابِرةٌ /fem." (cf. Wright, *II,* 185, Fleisch, *Traité I,* 337). An anomalous case, namely عَدُوَّةٌ occurs however (see (152)).

(149) The form فَعَّالٌ denotes intensification, e.g. زَيْدٌ نَحَّارُ الْجَزُورِ "Zaid is a great slaughterer of the fatted beast" (cf. Howell, *I,* fasc. IV, 1614). مِفْعَلٌ refers to one that is an apparatus and instrument for the act, e.g. مِحْرَبٌ "warlike" and that مِفْعالٌ refers to one that is accustomed to the act, e.g. إمرأة مِذْكارٌ and مِئْناثٌ "a woman accustomed to give birth to male and female" (cf. Howell, *I,* fasc. IV, 1622).

b) The forms مِفْعَلٌ, مِفْعالٌ, and مِفْعِيلٌ were underlyinglly nouns of instrument, but became afterwards intensive adjectives (cf. Wright, *II,* 186, Fleisch, *Traité I,* 337). They do not have a separate form for the fem. (for discussions see ʿAbd al-ʿAzīz, *Fuṣḥā* 166-168). An anomalous case, namely مِسْكِينَةٌ occurs (see (151)).

(150) The adjectives presented by Ibn Masʿūd are formed according to patterns that denote intensiveness (for a detailed presentation of such forms with examples see Wright, *II,* 137-140, Vernier, *I,* 213-214, Blachère, 90-91). These patterns without the suffixation of the *tāʾ marbūṭa* are:

1– فِعِّيلٌ as فِسِّيقٌ "very sinful, wicked" and شِرِّيبٌ "addicted to wine".

2– فُعَّالٌ as كُبَّارٌ "very large" and طُوَّالٌ "very tall".

To these may be added:

3– فَعُّولٌ as فَرُّوقٌ "timid" and قَيُّومٌ "everlasting".

4– فُعُّولٌ as قُدُّوسٌ "most holy".

5– فُعَلٌ as قُلَبٌ "shifting".

6– فاعُولٌ as فارُوقٌ "timid".

Among the forms mentioned in (149), i.e. مِفْعَلٌ, مِفْعالٌ, and مِفْعِيلٌ, Ibn Masʿūd takes up:

7– مِفْعالٌ as مِسْقامٌ "often diseased".

8– مِفْعِيلٌ as مِعْطِيرٌ "one who uses much perfume".

To these may be added:

9– مِفْعَلٌ as مِزْحَمٌ "pressing much".

As for the adjectives with the suffixation of the *tāʾ marbūṭa* (for التاء المبالغة لتأكيد "the *t* meant to strenghten the idea of intensiveness" see my notes (52), (274)), Ibn Masʿūd mentions the following:

10– فَعَّالَةٌ from فَعَّالٌ as عَلَّامَةٌ "very learned" and نَسَّابَةٌ "a great genealogist".

11– فاعِلَةٌ from فاعِلٌ as راوِيَةٌ "one who hands down poems or historical facts by oral tradition".

12– فَعُّولَةٌ from فَعُّولٌ as فَرُّوقَةٌ "very timid".

13– فُعَلَةٌ from فُعَلٌ as ضُحَكَةٌ "prone to laughter".

14– فُعْلَةٌ from فُعَلٌ as ضُحْكَةٌ "very ridiculous".

15– مِفْعَالَةٌ from مِفْعَالٌ as مِجْذَامَةٌ "a man who quickly cuts the tie of affection".
To these may be added:

16– فَاعُولَةٌ from فَاعُولٌ as فَارُوقَةٌ "very timid".
These patterns are common for both the masc. and fem. sing.

(151) The form مِفْعِيلٌ (for it see (149), (150)) designates intensiveness, and does not have a separate form for the fem. However anomalously مِسْكِينَةٌ, which is on this pattern is in the fem. This occurs because it is compared to its contrary فَقِيرَةٌ "poor" (for a discussion concerning words formed to accord with their contraries see Suyūṭī, *Ašbāh I,* 420-426) that is formed according to the pattern فَعِيلٌ (cf. Sībawaihi, *II,* 218, Ibn Manẓūr, *III,* 2056, Lane, *I,* 1395, Vernier, *I,* 373-374).

(152) The form فَعُولٌ in the meaning of the active participle فَاعِلٌ does not have a separate form for the fem. (for it see (148)). However anomalously عَدُوَّةٌ, which is on this pattern is in the fem. In this case it has been compared to its contrary صَدِيقَةٌ "friend /fem" which is on the pattern فَعِيلٌ (cf. Suyūṭī, *Ašbāh I,* 422, Ibn Manẓūr, *IV,* 2848, Lane, *II,* 1980, Vernier, *I,* 369).

b) The masc. sing. عَدُوٌّ alike its opposite صَدِيقٌ can occur to mark the pl. (see further for other examples (296, b)). As an example, عَدُوٌّ occurs in the sur. 4: 101 (إِنَّ ٱلْكَافِرِينَ كَانُوا لَكُمْ عَدُوًّا مُبِينًا) "For the Unbelievers are unto you open enemies". Both the singulars عَدُوٌّ and صَدِيقٌ applied for the pl., are combined in the following verse said by an unknown poet, cited by Afandī, *Šarḥ* 206, Howell, *I,* fasc. III, 967:

"وَقَوْمٍ عَلَيَّ ذَوِي مِئْرَةٍ   أَرَاهُمْ عَدُوًّا وَكَانُوا صَدِيقَا".

"And many a people full of hostility against me I thought them to be enemies, when they were friends".

(153) The active participle of the derived forms of the triliteral verb is formed according to the form of the imperfect by replacing the imperfect prefix with the *-m* vowelled by a ḍamma and by having the 2nd radical vowelled by a kasra (for examples see Vernier, *I,* 38, Wright, *I,* 300-301). Some of the derived forms of the triliteral of the active participle of the verbs mentioned in the Arabic text fols. 4a-4b that can be presented here are:

Form II يُقَطِّعُ: مُقَطِّعٌ, Form III يُقَاتِلُ: مُقَاتِلٌ, Form IV يُكْرِمُ: مُكْرِمٌ, Form V يَتَفَضَّلُ: مُتَفَضِّلٌ, Form VI يَتَضَارَبُ: مُتَضَارِبٌ, Form VII يَنْصَرِفُ: مُنْصَرِفٌ, Form VIII يَحْتَقِرُ: مُحْتَقِرٌ and Form X يَسْتَخْرِجُ: مُسْتَخْرِجٌ.

As for the groundform and some of the derived forms of the quadriliteral verb, the following examples may be presented:

Form I يُدَحْرِجُ: مُدَحْرِجٌ, Form II يَتَدَحْرَجُ: مُتَدَحْرِجٌ, Form III يَحْرَنْجِمُ: مُحْرَنْجِمٌ and Form IV يَقْشَعِرُّ: مُقْشَعِرٌّ.

(154) Form IV مُسْهَبٌ (cf. Ibn Manẓūr, *III,* 2131, Lane, *I,* 1450) from the verb of Form IV أَسْهَبَ, is the form that is intended for the active participle. It is formed anomalously according to Form IV of the passive participle مُفْعَلٌ, and not according to Form IV of the active participle مُفْعِلٌ. As for يافعٌ "a grown-up boy" it is the only active participle of the verb of Form IV أَيْفَعَ, which is anomalously formed according to the form of the active participle of the verb of Form I: فاعِلٌ (cf. Ibn Manẓūr, *VI,* 4963, Vernier, *I,* 169).

(155) For the corroborative *n* see (125).

(156) النِسبةُ "the relative noun or adjective" (for a study see Zamaḫšarī, 89-93, Ibn Yaʿīš, *V,* 141-157, Wright, *II,* 149-151, Blachère, 99-101, Fleisch, *Traité I,* 434-450, Fischer, *Grammatik* 65-66) is formed by adding the ending *-iyyu* to the word from which it is derived. It indicates that a person or thing is connected with it in respect of origin, family, sect, trade, character, etc., e.g. دِمَشْقِيٌّ "born or living in دِمَشْقُ "Damascus", شَمْسِيٌّ "solar" from شَمْسٌ "the sun" and عَقْلِيٌّ "intellectual" from عَقْلٌ "the intellect".

(157) For a study of اسم المفعول "the passive participle" see Zamaḫšarī, 101, Ibn Yaʿīš, *VI,* 80-81, Wright, *II,* 131-132, Howell, *I,* fasc. IV, 1651-1661, Bohas, *Étude* 152-154. For a general study of it in Arabic and in some of the other Semitic languages see Wright, *Comparative Grammar* 197-198.

(158) The passive participle's derived forms of the triliteral, as well as Form I of the quadriliteral and its derived forms are formed according to the imperfect's form by replacing the imperfect prefix vowelled by the ḍamma by the *-m* and having the 2nd radical vowelled by a fatḥa. Some examples are Form II رَكَّبَ يُرَكِّبُ "to compose": مُرَكَّبٌ "composed", Form IV أَكْرَمَ يُكْرِمُ "to honour": مُكْرَمٌ "honoured" and Form I of the quadriliteral دَحْرَجَ يُدَحْرِجُ "to roll": مُدَحْرَجٌ "rolled", etc. (cf. Wright, *II,* 300-301, Vernier, *I,* 166-167). Some of the derived forms of the triliteral of the passive participle that can be presented here of the verbs mentioned in the Arabic text fols. 4a-4b are:

Form II يُقَطِّعُ: مُقَطَّعٌ, Form III يُقَاتِلُ: مُقَاتَلٌ, Form IV يُكْرِمُ: مُكْرَمٌ, Form V يَتَفَضَّلُ: مُتَفَضَّلٌ, Form VI يَتَضَارَبُ: مُتَضَارَبٌ, Form VII يَنْصَرِفُ: مُنْصَرَفٌ, Form VIII يَحْتَقِرُ: مُحْتَقَرٌ and Form X يَسْتَخْرِجُ: مُسْتَخْرَجٌ.

As for the groundform and some of the derived forms of the quadriliteral verb mentioned by him, the following examples may be presented:

Form I يُدَحْرِجُ: مُدَحْرَجٌ, Form II يَتَدَحْرَجُ: مُتَدَحْرَجٌ, Form III يَحْرَنْجِمُ: مُحْرَنْجَمٌ and Form IV يَقْشَعِرُّ: مُقْشَعَرٌّ.

(159) For a study of اسم الزمان والمكان "the nouns of time and place" see Zamaḫšarī, 103-104, Zanǧānī, *ʿIzzī* 13, Ibn Yaʿīš, *VI,* 107-111, Farḥāt, *Baḥṯ* 49-50, Wright, *II,* 124-130, Howell, *I,* fasc. IV, 1744-1755, Fleisch, *Traité I,* 429-432, Fischer, *Grammatik* 45-46, Bohas, *Étude* 158-159.

(160) The form مَفْعِلٌ as a noun of place of verbs with 1st radical *w* (for a study see Sībawaihi, *II,* 266, de Sacy, *I,* 303, Wright, *II,* 126-127, Vernier, *I,* 189) retains the 1st radical and has its 2nd radical invariably vowelled by a kasra, e.g. مَوْعِدٌ "the time or place of a promise or appointment" from وَعَدَ "to promise" whose imperfect is يَعِدُ, and مَوْجِلٌ "a place that is dreaded" from وَجِلَ "to be afraid" whose imperfect is يَوْجَلُ.

(161) جَوْرَبٌ is an arabicized word from the Persian كَوْرَبٌ or كُورَبٌ underlyingly كَوْرْ پَا or پَا كُورْ "tomb of the foot" (cf. Lane, *I,* 403).

(162) The form مَفْعَلٌ as a noun of place of verbs with 3rd radical *y* (for a study see Zamaḫšarī, 104, Wright, *II,* 127-128, Vernier, *I,* 188) has always its 2nd radical vowelled by a fatḥa whatever the vowel of the imperfect is, e.g. اَلْمَرْمَى "a place of throwing or shooting arrows" from رَمَى "to throw" whose imperfect is يَرْمِي, مَطْوًى "a fold" from طَوَى "to fold" whose imperfect is يَطْوِي and مَرْعًى "pasture-ground" from رَعَى whose imperfect is يَرْعَى.

(163) Another noun of place formed according to مَفْعِلٌ (for a presentation of examples see Zamaḫšarī, 104, Wright, *II,* 125-126, Vernier, *I,* 189, Blachère, 95), which is not mentioned by Ibn Masʿūd, is اَلْمَنْخِرُ "the place where the breath passes through the nose". Both مَنْسِكٌ and مَنْسَكٌ with the *s* vowelled by a kasra or a fatḥa have been read of the sur. 22: 67 جَعَلْنَا مَنْسَكًا "Have We appointed rites and ceremonies" (cf. Mu'addib, *Taṣrīf* 124, Ibn Manẓūr, *VI,* 4412). مَطْلِعٌ with a kasra is said to be of the dialect of Tamīm and مَطْلَعٌ with a fatḥa is said to be of the dialect of the Ḥiğāzis (cf. Sībawaihi, *II,* 264, Volck/Kellgren: *Ibn Mālik* 24, Ibn Manẓūr, *VI,* 2689; for a general presentation of some words occurring in two dialectal variants with different vowels given to one of their consonants or with other phonetic changes affecting them see Ṯaʿlab, *Faṣīḥ* 41-43). In the sur. 97: 5 حَتَّى مَطْلِعِ ٱلْفَجْرِ "Until the rise of Morn!", مَطْلِع means طُلُوع. The reading with the kasra is al-Kisā'ī's, by which he meant the noun of place (cf. Ibn Ḫālawaihi, *Qirā'āt II,* 510, Ibn Muğāhid, *Sabʿa* 693).

(164) For a study of اسم الآلة "the noun of instrument" see Zamaḫšarī, 104-105, Ibn Yaʿīš, *VI,* 111-112, Farḥāt, *Baḥṯ* 51-52, Wright, *II,* 130-131, Howell, *I,* fasc. IV, 1756-1759, Fleisch, *Traité I,* 428-429, Blachère, 97, Fischer, *Grammatik* 46-47, Bohas, *Étude* 159-161.

(165) The form فَعْلَةٌ refers to nouns that express the doing of an action مَرَّة "once" (for a study with examples see Zamaḫšarī, 98, Ibn Yaʿīš, *VI,* 56-57, Zanğānī, *ʿIzzī* 13-14, Farḥāt, *Baḥṯ* 51, Volck/Kellgren, *Ibn Mālik* 20, Wright, *II,* 122-123, Fleisch, *Traité I,* 332-334, Vernier, *I,* 184-186). It is formed by adding the *tā' marbūṭa* to the *maṣdar.* فَعْلٌ is chosen for the groundform of the triliteral, تَفْعِيلٌ to Form II and فَعْلَالٌ to Form I of the quadriliteral.

(166) The form فِعْلَةٌ refer to الحالة "the noun of kind". It points out to the manner of doing what is intended by the verb. Examples are جِلْسَةٌ "way of sitting" and رِكْبَةٌ "way of riding". For a presentation with examples Zamaḫšarī, 98, Farḥāt, *Baḥṯ* 51, Wright, *II,* 123-124, Vernier, *I,* 187.

(167) For a study of the instrumental noun formed according to the measure مِفْعَالٌ with examples see Sībawaihi, *II,* 267, Zamaḫšarī, 104-105, Wright, *II,* 130. Instrumental nouns are also formed on the measure of مِفْعَلٌ or مِفْعَلَةٌ. Hence, the nouns مِجْرَفَةٌ, مِحَسَّةٌ and مِقْرَعَةٌ combined together formed upon the measure مِفْعَلَةٌ occur in a verse said by al-Farazdaq in an elegy on a groom, cited by Howell, *I,* fasc. IV, 1757:

"لِيَبْكِ أَبَا ٱلْخَنْسَاءِ بَغْلٌ وَبَغْلَةٌ   وَمِخْلَاةُ سَوْءٍ قَدْ أُضِيعَ شَعِيرُهَا
وَمِجْرَفَةٌ مَطْرُوحَةٌ وَمِحَسَّةٌ   وَمِقْرَعَةٌ صَفْرَاءُ بَالٍ سُيُورُهَا".

"Let a he-mule, and a she-mule, and a nose-bag of evil, whose barley has been wasted, and a rejected broom, and a curry comb, and a yellow whip whose thongs are worn out, bewail Abū l-Ḫansā".

(168) The passage referred here in which Sībawaihi discusses the nouns of recipients, is found in Sībawaihi, *II,* 265. For الْمُسْعُطُ and الْمُنْخُلُ formed according to the pattern مُفْعُلٌ see Zamaḫšarī, 105, Ibn Mālik, *Lāmīya* 254, Volck/Kellgren, *Ibn Mālik* 26-27, Raymundus, *Tasriphi* 114-115, Wright, *II,* 131, Vernier, *I,* 192, Fleisch, *Traité I,* 429. Other examples exist, as الْمُدُقّ (cf. Sībawaihi, *II,* 265, Lane, *I,* 807), الْمُنْصُلُ "the sword" (cf. Ibn Manẓūr, *VI,* 4447), and الْمُدْهُنُ (cf. Sībawaihi, *II,* 265). According to the rule, الْمُدْهُنُ should have been الْمِدْهَنُ, or it was so underlyingly (cf. Ibn Manẓūr, *II,* 1446, Lane, *I,* 927). Instrumental nouns of the measure مُفْعُلَةٌ and مُفْعَلَةٌ exist as well, but they are said to be anomalous, e.g. الْمُكْحُلَةُ "a thing in which there is a preparation of pulverized antimony used for darkening the edges of the eyelids" (cf. Sībawaihi, *II,* 265) and الْمُحْرُضَةُ "a vessel made of wood, or of brass" (cf. Ibn Manẓūr, *II,* 837, Lane, *I,* 549.

PART TWO

II.3. Arabic Text: الباب الثاني في المضاعف

ويُقال له الأصمَ لشدَته ولا يُقال له صحيح لصيرورة أحد حرفيه حرف علَة في نحو تَقَضَى البازي. وهو يجيء من ثلثة أبواب نحو سَرَ يَسُرُ وفَرَ يَفِرُ وعَضَ يَعَضُ ولا يجيء من باب فَعُلَ يَفْعُلُ إلاَ قليلاً نحو حَبَ يَحُبُ فهو حَبيب ولَبَ يَلُبُ فهو لَبيبٌ. وإذا اجتمع فيه حرفان من جنس واحد أو متقاربان في المخرج يُدغم الأوَل في الثاني لثقل المكرَر نحو مَدَ الى آخره ونحو ﴿أخْرَج شَطأه﴾ وقالَت طَائفَةٌ. الإدغام إلباث الحرف في مخرجه مقدار إلباث الحرفين كذا نُقل عن جار الله العلاَمة وقيل إسكان الأوَل وإدراجه في الثاني. والمُدغم والمُدغم فيه حرفان في اللفظ وحرف واحد في الكتابة نحو مدَ أو حرفان في اللفظ والكتابة كالرَحْمن. اجتماع الحرفين على ثلثة أضرب الأوَل أن يكونا متحركين يجب فيه الإدغام نحو مَدَ إلاَ في الإلحاقيَات نحو قَرْدَد حتَى لا* * ١٨ آ يبطل الإلحاق والأوزان التي تُلزم الإلتباس فيها مثل صَكَك وسُرُر وجُدَد وطَلَل ومَدَد حتَى لا يلتبس بصَكَ وسُرَ وجُدَ وطَلَ ومدَ. ولا يلتبس في مثل رَدَ وفَرَ وعَضَ لأنَ رَدَ يُعلم من يَرُدُ أنَ أصله رَدَدَ لأنَ المضاعف لا يجيء من فَعَلَ يَفْعُلُ وفَرَ أيضاً يُعلم من يَفِرُ أنَ أصله فَرَرَ لأنَ المضاعف لا يجيء من فَعَلَ يَفْعِلُ وعَضَ أيضاً يُعلم من يَعَضُ أنَ أصله عَضِضَ لأنَ المضاعف لا يجيء من فَعَلَ يَفْعَلُ. ولا يُدغم حَيِيَ في بعض اللغات حتَى لا يقع الضمَ على الياء في يَحَيُ وقيل الياء الأخيرة غير لازمة لأنَها تسقط تارةً نحو حَيُوا وتُقلب تارةً ألفاً نحو يَحيى. والثاني أن يكون الأوَل

Fols. 17b-18a

٢ ثلثة: ثلاثة ل/ ٤ يَفْعُلُ: + بضم العين فيهما د/ حبَ: + أصله حبب ج/ يحبَ: – ا د/ يلبَ: – ا د/ ٦ الى آخره: –ا: مداً مدَوا ط/ ونحو أخرج: وأخرج د/ الحرف: + الواحد د/ ٩ نحو مدَ: كمدَ ل/ نحو... والكتابة: – د/ واجتماع: اجتماع ا/ ثلثة: ثلاثة ل/ ١٠ متحركين: + في الكلمة د/ نحو مدَ: –ا ب ج ز/ ١١ تلزم: يلزم ا د: + فيها ل/ فيها: – د ل/ مثل: نحو ل/ ١٢ ومدَ: –ا د/ ١٣ أنَ: لأنَ ا/ يَفْعُلُ: + بضم العين فيهما د ط/ ١٤ أنَ... فرَرَ: – ا د/ يَفْعِلُ: + بكسر العين فيهما د/ ١٥ أنَ... عَضِضَ: – ا د/ يَفْعَلُ: + بفتح العين فيهما د/ ١٦ يقع الضم: تقع الضمة ل/ الياء: + الضعيف ح ط/ ١٧ تسقط: يسقط د/ ألفاً: – ا د/

II.3. Translation: The 2nd Chapter is about the Doubled Verb[169]

It is named الأصمّ "the solid verb" because of the doubling [of the consonants] in it. It is not named strong, because one of its both consonants can [in some cases] be changed into a weak consonant, e.g. تَقَضَّىَ البازي "the hawk flew down swiftly".[170] It falls into three conjugations, e.g.: 1– سَرَّ يَسُرُّ "to gladden", 2– فَرَّ يَفِرُّ "to escape" and 3– عَضَّ يَعَضُّ "to bite". The conjugation فَعُلَ يَفْعُلُ does not occur unless rarely, e.g. حَبَّ يَحُبُّ "to love" and he is حَبِيبٌ "dear" and 4– لَبَّ يَلُبُّ "to become possessed by understanding" and he is لَبِيبٌ "a person of understanding".[171] If two consonants of the same kind or close to each other in the point of articulation are combined, the 1st one is assimilated to the 2nd one because of the heaviness of the repeated consonant, e.g. مَدَّ "to stretch" etc.,[172], e.g. [sur. 48: 29] (أَخْرَجَ شَطْأَهُ) "Which sends forth its blade" and قَالَت طَائِفَةٌ "a sect said".[173] The assimilation can either be carried out [from one consonant] to a consonant that remains in its own point of articulation or between two [identical] consonants that remain in their own point of articulation.[174] This is what was transmitted by "the neighbour of God, the most learned of men" [sc. Zamaḫšarī].[175] It was said that it is assimilating the 1st vowelless consonant to the 2nd one [which is vowelled]. The consonant that can be assimilated [to another] and the consonant to which it is assimilated to can be two consonants in the pronunciation and one consonant in the writing, e.g. مَدَّ or two consonants in the pronunciation and in the writing as e.g. الرَّحْمَنُ "the Merciful".[176] The combination of two consonants falls into three categories:

1– the first is that both consonants are vowelled. In this case the assimilation is necessary, e.g. مَدَّ [underlyingly مَدَدَ], except in the coordinatives, e.g. قَرْدَدٌ "elevated ground", so that the formation would not **[Fol. 18 a]** be excluded [from coordination to فَعْلَلٌ],[177] and in the patterns which would cause confusion [between a paradigm and another], e.g. صَكَكٌ "the colliding of the knees in running", سُرُرٌ "bedsteads", جُدَدٌ "the stripes that are on the back of the ass", طَلَلٌ "the remains of a dwelling or house" and مَدَدٌ "assistance", so that they would not be mixed up with صَكٌّ "a written acknowledgement of a debt", سُرٌّ "the navel-string of a child", جُدٌّ "a part of the river near the land", طَلٌّ "weak rain" and مَدٌّ "extension".[178] There is no risk of confusion that can arise concerning e.g. رَدَّ "to drive back", فَرَّ "to escape" and عَضَّ "to bite",[179] because it is known from يَرُدُّ that رَدَّ is underlyingly رَدَدَ, as the doubled verb does not occur according to the conjugation فَعُلَ يَفْعُلُ, from يَفِرُّ that فَرَّ is underlyingly فَرَرَ as the doubled verb does not occur according to the conjugation فَعِلَ يَفْعِلُ and from يَعَضُّ that عَضَّ is underlyingly عَضِضَ as the doubled verb does not occur according to the conjugation فَعَلَ يَفْعَلُ. In some dialectal variants the assimilation is not carried out in حَيِيَ "to live", so that the ḍamma does not have to vowel the y in يَحْيِي "he lives". It was said that the last y is not necessary, because it is dropped sometimes, e.g. حَيُوا "/3 masc. pl." and it is changed into an alif [maqṣūra] sometimes, e.g. يَحْيَى.[180] 2– The second is that the 1st consonant

ساكناً يجب فيه الإدغام ضرورة نحو مَدّ على وزن فَعْلٍ. والثالث أن يكون الثاني
ساكناً والإدغام فيه ممتنع لعدم شرط الإدغام وهو تحرُّك الثاني وقيل لا بدّ من تسكين
الأوَّل فيجتمع ساكنان فتفرُّ من ورطة وتقع في ورطة* أخرى وقيل لوجود الخفّة بالساكن * ١٨ ب
مع عدم شرط الإدغام، ولكن جوّزوا الحذف في بعض المواضع نظراً الى اجتماع
المتجانسين نحو ظَلْتَ كما جوّزوا القلب في نحو تَقَضّى البازي وعليه قراءة من قرأ
(وقَرْنَ في بُيُوتِكُنَّ) من القَرار أصله اقْرِرْنَ فحُذفت الراء الأولى فنُقلت حركتها الى
القاف ثمّ حُذفت الهمزة لعدم الإحتياج إليها فصار قِرْنَ وقيل من وَقَرَ يَقِرُ وقاراً وإذا
قُرِىء قَرْنَ بفتح القاف يكون من أقَرُّ بالمكان وهو لغة في أقِرُّ فيكون أصله اقْرَرْنَ
فنُقلت حركة الراء الى القاف فصار قَرْنَ. هذا إذا كان سكونه لازماً وإذا كان
عارضاً يجوز الإدغام وعدمه نحو أُمْدُدْ ومُدَّ بفتح الدال ومُدِّ بالكسر لأنّ الكسر
أصل في تحريك الساكن ومُدُّ بالضمّ للإتباع، ومن ثمّ لا يجوز فِرُّ بضمّ الراء لعدم
الإتباع ولا يجوز الإدغام في أُمْدُدْنَ لأنّ السكون الثاني لازم وتقول بالنون* الثقيلة * ١٩ آ
أُمْدُدَنَّ أُمْدُدانِّ أُمْدُدُنَّ أُمْدُدِنَّ أُمْدُدانِّ أُمْدُدْنانِّ وبالخفيفة أُمْدُدَنْ أُمْدُدُنْ أُمْدُدِنْ
اسم الفاعل مادّ والمفعول مَمدود واسم الزمان والمكان مَمَدّ والآلة مِمَدّ والمجهول مُدَّ
يُمَدُّ ويجوز الإدغام إذا وقع قبل تاء الإفتعال حرف من حروف أتَثَدْذَزٍ سَشَصٍ ضَطٍ
ظَوِيَ نحو اتَّخَذَ وهو شاذ ونحو اتَّجَرَ ونحو اثّارَ ويجوز فيه اتّأرَ بالتاء لأنّ التاء

Fols. 18a-19a

٢ ساكناً: ساكنة ا/ فيه ممتنع: ممتنع فيه ل/ تسكين: + الأوّل ب ه ز ح ط/ ٣ فيجتمع: فاجتمع ا/ وتقع... أخرى: وتقع في أخرى ب ج د ه ز ك: فتقع في أخرى ل/ ٦ فنقلت: فنقل د/ ٨ بفتح القاف: –ا د: بالفتح ه/ بالمكان: + بفتح القاف ب ج د ه ط/ ٩ فنقلت: فنقل ا ده ز/ حركة: –ا: فتح ب د: فتحة ج ه ز ط/ ١٠ عارضاً: غير لازم د/ الدال: + للخفة ج د ه ح ط ك/ ١١ يجوز: يجيء د/ بضمّ الراء: بالضم ا/ ١٢ السكون: سكون د/ ١٤ ماد: مادّان مادّون ب/ ممدود: + ممدودان ممدودون ب/ والآلة: واسم الآلة د/ الى آخره: – ل/ ١٥ حرف من: – د/ ١٦ بالتاء: –ا: من الثاء د/

is vowelless, and in this case the assimilation is necessary, e.g. مدّ "an extension", which is according to the pattern فَعْل.

3– The 3rd is that the 2nd consonant is vowelless. In this case the assimilation is forbidden as the condition of the assimilation which is the vowelling of the 2nd consonant, is absent. Then it was said that it was necessary to render vowelless the 1st consonant, but this would lead to the combination of two vowelless consonants, so you would escape from one difficult situation and fall into another **[Fol. 18 b]**. It was also said [that it is forbidden] because of the existence of the lightness due to the [2nd] vowelless consonant together with the absence of the condition of the assimilation, [which is the vowelling of the 2nd consonant]. However, the elision [of one of the identical consonants] is made possible by them in some cases on account of the combination of two identical consonants, e.g. ظَلْتَ "you continued all day /masc. sing.",(181) as is also the change into a weak consonant, e.g. تَقَضَّى البازي "the hawk flew down swiftly".(182) Accordingly [with the elision], some recited [sur. 33: 33] (وقِرْنَ في بُيُوتِكُنَّ) "And stay quietly in Your houses": [وقِرْنَ is] from القَرار "a state of settledness". Its base form is اقْرِرْنَ "stay! /2 fem. pl. of the imperative", in which the 1st *r* is elided and its vowel is shifted to the *q,* and then the prosthetic alif is elided because it is not longer needed, so it became قِرْنَ. It was also said that it is from وَقَرَ يَقِرُ وقارًا "to sit quiet". [Some held that] if قَرْنَ is read [with the *q* vowelled by the fatha], it would be from أقَرُ "I rest or remain (in the place)", which is a dialectal variant of أقِرُ, so its base form would be اقْرَرْنَ with the vowel of the *r* shifted to the *q,* so that it became قَرْنَ.(183) This is the case if the sukūn [of the 2nd consonant] is obligatory. However, if it is accidental, the assimilation is sometimes possibly carried out and sometimes not, e.g. اُمْدُدْ "stretch! /masc. sing. of the imperative", مُدَّ with the vowelling of the *d* by a fatha [to alleviate], مُدِّ by the kasra because the kasra is principal in vowelling the vowelless consonant and مُدُّ(184) by the damma for the purpose of analogy [with the vowel of the 1st radical]. On account of that [sc. that the damma in مُدُّ is given for the purpose of analogy], it is impossible to say فِرُّ "flee! /masc. sing. of the imperative" with the vowelling of the *r* by a damma because of the lack of analogy [with the vowel of the 1st radical]. The assimilation is made impossible in اُمْدُدْنَ "stretch! /fem. pl. of the imperative" because the sukūn of the 2nd [consonant among two identical consonants] is obligatory.(185)

You say with the energetic *n* **[Fol. 19 a]**: اُمْدُدَنَّ "/2 masc. sing. (imperative En. 1)", اُمْدُدانِّ "/2 dual", اُمْدُدُنَّ "/2 masc. pl.", اُمْدُدِنَّ "/2 fem. sing.", اُمْدُدانِّ "/2 dual", اُمْدُدْنانِّ "/2 fem. pl.". With the single *n:* اُمْدُدَنْ "/2 masc. sing. (imperative En. II)", اُمْدُدِنْ "/2 fem. sing." and اُمْدُدُنْ "/2 masc. pl.". The active participle is مادّ, the passive participle مَمْدود, the nouns of time and place مَمَدّ, the noun of instrument مِمَدّ and the passive voice مُدَّ يُمَدُّ, etc.(186) The assimilation is possibly carried out if one of the consonants of أتثذدز سَشَص ضط ظوى precedes the [infixed] *t* of [Form VIII] افْتِعال, e.g. 1– اتَّخَذَ "to take" which is an anomaly, 2– اتَّجَرَ "to trade", and 3– اثّأرَ "to get one's revenge", possibly said اتَّأرَ with the *t,*(187) because the *t*

والثاء من المهموسة وحروفها سَتَشْحَثُكَ خَصْفَة فيكونان من جنس واحد نظراً الى المهموسيَة فيجوز لك الإدغام بجعل التاء ثاءً والثاء تاءً ونحو ادّانَ لا يجوز فيه غير إدغام الدّال في الدال لأنّه إذا جُعلت التاء دالاً لبعده من الدال في المهموسيَة ولقرب الدال من التاء في المخرج يُلزم حينئذ حرفان من جنسٍ واحد فيُدغم ونحو اذّكَرَ يجوز فيه ادّكَرَ واذْدكَرَ لأنَ الدال من المجهوريَة فجُعلت التاء دالاً

* ١٩ ب كما في ادّانَ فيجوز* لك الإدغام نظراً الى اتّحادهما في المجهوريّة بجعل الدال ذالاً والذال دالاً والبيان نظراً الى عدم اتّحادهما في الذات ونحو ازّانَ مثل اذّكَرَ ولكن لا يجوز فيه الإدغام بجعل الزاء دالاً لأنَ الزاء أعظم من الدال في امتداد الصوت فيصير حينئذ كوضع القصعة الكبيرة في الصغيرة او لأنّه يوازي بادّانَ ونحو اسَّمَعَ يجوز فيه الإدغام لأنَ السين والتاء من المهموسيّة ولا يجوز فيه الإدغام بجعل السين تاءً لعظم السين في امتداد الصوت ويجوز البيان لعدم الجنسيّة في الذات ونحو اشّبَهَ مثل اسَّمَعَ ونحو اصّبَرَ يجوز فيه اصْطَبَرَ لأنَ الصاد من المستعلية المطبقة وحروفها صَطْ ضَظْ خَغَق ، الأربعة الأولى مستعلية مطبقة والثلاثة الأخيرة مستعلية فقط والتاء من المنخفضة فجُعل التاء طاءً لمباعدة بينهما في الإستعلائيّة وقرب التاء

* ٢٠ آ من الطاء في المخرج فصار اصْطَبَرَ* كما في ستّ أصله سُدُسٌ فجُعل السين والدال تاءً لقرب السين من التاء في المهموسيّة والتاء من الدال في المخرج ثمَ أُدغم فصار ستّ ثمّ يجوز لك الإدغام بجعل الطاء صاداً نظراً الى اتّحادهما في الإستعلائيّة نحو اصّبَرَ ولا يجوز لك الإدغام فيه بجعل الصاد طاءً لعظم الصاد أعني لا يُقال اطّبَرَ ويجوز البيان لعدم الجنسيّة في الذات ونحو اضّرَبَ مثل

Fols. 19a-20a

٤ الدال... التاء: التاء من الدال ا/ المخرج: المهموسيّة ب هـ ز حـ/ يلزم: فيلزم ا/ فيدغم: فتدغم جـ/ ٥ المجهوريّة: المجهورة ل/ فجُعلت: فجعل د ز ط ك ل/ ٦–٧ الدال... دالاً: الذال دالا والدال ذالا ا/ ٨ الزاء(1+2): الزاي ل/ ٩ في: + القصعة د/ لأنّه: لأن ا/ اسّمع: استمع ب/ ١٠ المهموسيّة: المهموسة ك ل/ فيه: –ا ب د ز حـ/ ١٢ صط ضظ: صططظض ب هـ حـ/ والثلثة: والثلاثة ز ط ك ل/ ١٤ في الاستعلائيّة: –ا ب د ز حـ ط ك/ ١٦ والتاء: + قريب هـ/ أُدغم: ادغمت ا/ ١٧ الى اتّحادهما: لاتحادهما د/ ١٨ فيه: –ل/ ١٩ البيان: + نحو اصطبر حـ/ ونحو: ويجوز ا/

and the *ṯ* are among the voiceless consonants, which are comprised in سَتَشْحَثُكَ خَصْفَةُ "Ḫaṣfah shall press you in the matter".(188) So both are of the same sort on account of their being among the voiceless consonants. You can therefore assimilate by changing the *t* into a *ṯ* and the *ṯ* into a *t*. As for 4– اِدّان "to buy upon credit", only the doubling of the *d* is possible in it. As for the reason of this, it is that when the [infixed] *t*, which is among the voiceless consonants, is changed into the *d* in spite of its distance to it in this respect, it is done so on account of the proximity of the *d* to it in the point of articulation, such which causes necessarily the combination of two identical consonants, so that one is assimilated to the other.(189) As for 5– اِذْكَر "to remember", both اِدَّكَر and اِذْدَكَر are possible to be used instead, because the *d* [and the *ḏ]* are among the voiced consonants. Thus the *t* is changed into the *d* as in اِدّان, and then you can possibly **[Fol. 19 b]** assimilate on account of both their conformity in being among the voiced consonants, by changing the *d* into the *ḏ* and the *ḏ* into the *d*. It is possible as well to dissolve as they both [sc. the *d* and the *ḏ]* disagree in the essence.(190) As for 6– اِزّان "to be ornamented", it is similar to اِذْكَر. It is however impossible to assimilate in it by changing the *z* into the *d* because of the excellency of sibilance of the *z* in comparison to the *d*. Hence it [sc. the procedure] would be as if placing the large bowl over the little one, or [on the other hand, if the *z* is assimilated to the *d]* there would be a confusion with اِدّان.(191) As for 7– اِسَّمَع "to listen", the assimilation is possibly carried out in it because the *s* and the *t* are among the voiceless consonants. It is impossible however to assimilate by changing the *s* into the *t* because of the excellency of sibilance of the *s*. It is possible as well not to assimilate [in اِسْتَمَع], because they both [sc. the *s* and the *t]* disagree in the essence. As for 8– اِشَّبَه "to liken" it is similar to اِسَّمَع [regarding the assimilation]. As for 9– اِصَّبَر "to acquire patience", it is possible to use اِصْطَبَر instead of it,(192) because the *ṣ* is among the elevated covered consonants which are صْطَ ضَظ خَغَق. The four 1st ones are elevated and covered and the three last ones are only elevated.(193) The *t* is among the depressed consonants, but it is changed into the *ṭ* which is among the elevated consonants, in spite of the distance between them both in this respect, because of the proximity of the *t* to the *ṭ* in the point of articulation, so it became اِصْطَبَر **[Fol. 20 a]**, similarly to سِتّ "six" underlyingly سُدْس, in which the *s* and the *d* are changed into the *t* because of the homogeneity of the *s* and the *t* in being among the voiceless consonants and because of the proximity of the *t* to the *d* in the point of articulation, and then an assimilation is carried out so that it became سِتّ.(194) So it is possible for you to assimilate [in اِصْطَبَر] by changing the *ṭ* into the *ṣ* on account of both their conformity in being among the elevated consonants, i.e. اِصَّبَر. It is not possible for you however to assimilate by changing the *ṣ* into the *ṭ* because of the excellency of sibilance of the *ṣ*. I mean that it is impossible to say اِطَّبَر. It is possible as well not to assimilate because of their [sc. the *ṭ* and the *ṣ's]* lack of similarity in the essence. As for 10– اِضَّرَب "to be in a state of agitation",(195) it is similar to

اصَبَرَ أعني يجوز اضَرَبَ واضْطَرَبَ ولا يجوز اطَرَبَ ونحو اطَّلَبَ لا يجوز فيه غير الإدغام لاجتماع الحرفين من جنس واحد بعد قلب تاء الإفتعال طاءً لقرب التاء من الطاء في المخرج ونحو اظَّلَمَ يجوز فيه الإدغام بجعل الطاء ظاءً والظاء طاءً لمساواة بينهما في العظم ويجوز البيان لعدم الجنسيّة في الذات مثل اظَّلَمَ واطَّلَمَ واظْطَلَمَ ونحو اتَّعَدَ فجُعل الواو تاء لأنه إن لم يُجعل تاء يصير ياء لكسرة* ما * ٢٠ ب قبلها فيُلزم حينئذ كون الفعل مرّة يائياً نحو ايتَعَدَ ومرّةً واوياً نحو يَوْتَعدُ لعدم موجب القلب او يُلزم توالي الكسرات ونحو اتَّسَرَ فجُعل الياء تاء فراراً عن توالي الكسرات ولم يُدغم في مثل ايتَكَلَ لأنَ الياء ليست بلازمة يعني تصير همزة إذا جعلته ثلاثياً نحو أكَلَ، ومن ثمّ لا يُدغم حَيِيَ في بعض اللغات وإدغام اتّخَذَ شاذ. ويجوز الإدغام إذا وقع بعد تاء الإفتعال من حروف تَدْذُز سَصَضْطَظ نحو يَقَتّلُ ويَبَدّلُ ويَعَذّرُ ويَنَزّعُ ويَبَسّمُ ويَخَصّمُ ويَنَضّلُ ويَلَطّمُ ويَنَظّرُ ولكن لا يجوز في إدغامهنَ إلاّ الإدغام بجعل التاء مثل العين لضعف استدعاء المؤخّر. وعند بعض الصرفيين لا يجيء هذا الإدغام في الماضي حتّى لا يلتبس بماضي التفعيل لأنَ عندهم تُنقل حركة التاء الى ما قبلها وتُحذف الهمزة المجتلبة، وعند بعضهم يجيء بكسر الفاء نحو خِصّمَ لأنَ عندهم كسر الفاء لالتقاء* الساكنين، وعند بعضهم * ٢١ آ يجيء بالمجتلبة نحو اِخِصّمَ نظراً الى سكون أصله ويجوز في مستقبله كسر الفاء

Fols. 20a-21a

١ يجوز: + في ا/ اطَرب: + لزيادة صفة الضاد د ط: + لزيادة مدّة صوت الضاد من الطاء ﺣ/ غير: الا د ﺣ/ ٤ لمساواة: لمساوات د ز ط/ ٦–٧ لعدم... القلب ا's margin: – د ل/ ٨ ايتكل: + أصله اتّكل ز/ تصير: يصير ا/ ٩ نحو أكل: – ا ب ﺣ/ اللغات: اللغة ا/ ١١ ويَبَسّمُ: – ا/ ويَنَضّلُ: ويتفضّل ﺣ/ ويَنَضّلُ... ويَنَظّرُ: ويفضّل وينظّر ويرطّم ب د ﻫ ز ط/ ١٢ لضعف... المؤخّر: + اي لضعف استدعاء الحروف التي بعد تاء الإفتعال ا's margin/ ١٣ يجيء: يجوز ب ﺟ ط ك ل/ ١٤ الهمزة: همزة ا: – د/ المجتلبة: + لانعدام الاحتياج اليها ﺣ/ ١٥ كسر: يكسر ا/

اصْبِرْ. I mean that both اضْرَبْ and اضْطَرَبْ are possible, but not اطْرَبْ. As for 11– اطْلَبْ "to seek", there is no other way than to assimilate in it, because of the combination of two identical consonants [sc. the ṭā's] after the change of the infixed *t* of افْتِعَال into the *ṭ*, on account of the proximity of the *t* to the *ṭ* in the point of articulation.[196] As for 12– اظَّلَمَ "to take upon oneself the bearing of the wrong", the assimilation is possibly carried out in it by changing the *ṭ* into the *ẓ* and the *ẓ* into the *ṭ* on account of the similarity between them both in being among the emphatic consonants. It is possible as well to dissolve because of their lack of similarity in the essence, i.e. اظَّلَمَ [with the change of the *ṭ* into the *ẓ*], اطَّلَمَ [with the change of the *ẓ* into the *ṭ*] and اظْطَلَمَ [with the dissolution].[197] As for 13– اتَّعَدَ "to accept a promise", the *w* [of اِوْتَعَدَ] is changed into the *t*, because if this did not occur, it would have to be changed into the *y* due to [the influence of] the kasra **[Fol. 20 b]** of the consonant preceding it. Hence the verb would necessarily seem to be at one time as though having a *y* radical, i.e. ايتَعَدَ, and at another as though having a *w* radical, i.e. يُوتَعَدُ because of the impossibility of changing the [weak] consonant into another, or the succession of the kasras will be unavoidable.[198] As for 14– اتَّسَرَ "to play at hazard", the *y* [of اِيتَسَرَ] is assimilated to the *t* to avoid the succession of the kasras.[199] The assimilation is not carried out in ايتَكَلَ "to eat, devour", because the *y* is not necessary, i.e. that it becomes a hamza if you bring it back to the groundform, i.e. أَكَلَ.[200] On account of that [i.e. because the *y* is not necessary], the assimilation is not carried out in حَيِيَ "to live" in some dialects.[201] As for the assimilation that is carried out in اتَّخَذَ "to take for oneself", it is anomalous.[202]

The assimilation is possibly carried out if one of the consonants of تَدْذُرْ سَصَضْطَظ follows the [infixed] *t* of Form VIII افْتِعَال, e.g. 1– يَقْتَلُ "to contend among themselves",[203] 2– يَبَدَّلُ "to change", 3– يَعَذَّرُ "to excuse one's-self", 4– يَنَّزِعُ "to snatch, tear away", 5– يَبَسَّمُ "to smile",[204] 6– يَخَصَّمُ "to dispute", 7– يَنَضَّلُ "to struggle", 8– يَلَطَّمُ "to collide, clash" and 9– يَنَظَّرُ "to expect".[205] The assimilation is only possibly carried out in them by changing the [infixed] *t* into the consonant of the 2nd radical, because of the feebleness of the request of the [infixed] consonant that comes after [the radical]. By some grammarians this assimilation is not carried out in the perfect [of such verbs], so that it [sc. the perfect] is not mixed up with the perfect of [Form II of the *maṣdar*] تَفْعِيل [i.e. فَعَّلَ], because according to them the vowel of the [infixed] *t* [of Form VIII افْتَعَلَ] is shifted to the consonant preceding it, and the prosthetic alif is elided [resulting in فَعَلَ, e.g. خَصَّمَ from Form VIII اخْتَصَمَ]. By others, it [sc. the assimilation] is carried out by giving the 1st radical the kasra, e.g. خِصَّمَ [underlyingly اخْتَصَمَ] "to quarrell, argue", because according to them the reason of vowelling the 1st radical with the kasra [in خِصَّمَ] is to avoid the cluster **[Fol. 21 a]** of two vowelless consonants [i.e. خْصَّمَ as they elide both the vowelled infixed *t* of اخْتَصَمَ without shifting its vowel to the 1st radical, and the prefixed hamza]. By others, it occurs with the prosthetic alif, i.e. اخْصَّمَ on account of the sukūn of [the ḫ of] the base form [sc. اخْتَصَمَ]. It is possible in its imperfect to vowel the 1st radical with the kasra

وفتحها كما في الماضي نحو يَخَصَّمُ وفي فاعله ضُمَّ الفاء للإتباع مع فتحها وكسرها قيل نحو مُخُصَّمونَ. ويجيء مصدره خِصَّاماً بكسر الخاء لالتقاء الساكنين أو لنقل كسرة التاء الى الخاء ويجيء خَصَّاماً بفتح الخاء إن اعتبرتَ حركة الصاد المدغم فيها ويجيء اخَصَّاماً اعتباراً لسكون الأصل. وتدغم تاء تَفَعَّلَ وتَفاعَلَ فيما بعدها باجتلاب الهمزة كما مرَّ في باب الإفتعال نحو اطَّهَّرَ أصله تَطَهَّرَ واثَّاقَلَ أصله تَثاقَلَ ولا يُدغم في نحو اسْتَطْعَمَ لسكون الطاء تحقيقاً وفي نحو اسْتَدانَ لأنَّ أصله اسْتَدْيَنَ بسكون الدّال تقديراً ولكن يجوز حذف تائه في بعض المواضع نحو اسْطاعَ يَسْطيعُ كما مرَّ في ظلْتَ وإذا قلتَ أسْطاعَ بفتح الهمزة يُسْطيعُ بضمّ الياء يكون السين زائداً لأنّ أصله أطاعَ كالهاء في أهْراقَ.

Fol. 21a

١ نحو يَخَصَّمُ: – ح/ فاعله: اسم الفاعل ب ج هـ ز ط ل/ ضُمَّ: يضم ب هـ/ ٢ قيل: – د ل/ ٢–٣ بكسر... خَصّاما: l's margin ا/ ٣ بفتح الخاء: – ا ب د ح ط/ ٤ لسكون: بسكون ط/ الأصل: الأصلي ح/ وتفاعل: – ح/ بعدها: بعدهما د/ ٤–٥ باجتلاب: لاجتلاب ل/ ٥ الإفتعال: افتعل ط/ اطَّهر: اتطهر ط/ ٦ نحو: – د/ لأنَّ... الدال: l's margin ا: – د ل: أصله استدين هـ ح ط/ ٧ يجوز حذف: يحذف ح/ ٨ وإذا: فإذا ا/ بفتح الهمزة: – ح/ يسطيع... الياء: – ب د هـ ح ط ك ل/ يكون... زائدا: l's margin ا/ السين: – ح/ زائداً: زائدة هـ/ ٨–٩ لأنَّ... أطاع: l's margin ا: – ب/ ٩ أهراق: + إذ أصله أراق ك/

or with the fatḥa as in the perfect, i.e. يَخَصِّم. In the active participle, the 1st radical is vowelled by the ḍamma by analogy [with the ḍamma of the prefixed *m]* or by the fatḥa or the kasra [on the analogy of those who vowel its perfect with a fatḥa or a kasra]. Hence it is said مُخُصِّمون, مُخِصِّمون or مُخَصِّمون.(206)

Its *maṣdar* is خِصَّامٌ with the *ḫ* that is given the kasra either to avoid the cluster of two vowelless consonants or because of the transfer of the kasra of the [infixed] *t* [of اخْتِصَامٌ] to the *ḫ*. خَصَّامٌ occurs as well with the *ḫ* vowelled by the fatḥa if you take into consideration the vowel of the assimilated *ṣ*. Both اخِصَّام and اخَصَّامٌ occur as well on account of the sukūn of the base form [sc. اخْتِصَامٌ].

The [prefixed] *t* of [Form V] تَفَعَّلَ and of [Form VI] تَفَاعَلَ is assimilated to the consonant that follows it after the prefixation of the prosthetic alif as was mentioned about [the *t* of Form VIII] افْتِعَالٌ [concerning its assimilation to one of the consonants of تَدْذُرٌ سَصَضْطَظ following it], e.g. اطَّهَّرَ "to purify one's-self" underlyingly تَطَهَّرَ, and اثَّاقَلَ "to be borne down heavily" underlyingly تَثَاقَلَ.(207)

No assimilation [of the infixed *t* of Form X to the consonant following it] is carried out in اسْتَطْعَمَ "to ask for food" due to the sukūn of the *ṭ* in reality, and in اسْتَدَانَ "to take up a loan" underlyingly اسْتَدْيَنَ due the sukūn of the *d* theoretically.(208)

However the elision of the [infixed] *t* [of Form X] is possibly carried out in some cases, e.g. اسْطَاعَ يَسْطِيعُ "to be able, have power",(209) as was mentioned about ظَلْتَ "you continued all day /masc. sing.".(210) However, if you said أسْطَاعَ with the hamza vowelled by the fatḥa and يُسْطِيعُ with the *y* vowelled by the ḍamma, then the *s* is infixed, because its base form is [Form IV] أطَاعَ "to obey",(211)—[and its infixation is] similar to the infixation of the *h* in اَهْرَاقَ "to pour"—.(212)

II.3.1. COMMENTARY

The Doubled Verb

(169) For a general study of المضاعف "the doubled Verb" see Mu'addib, *Taṣrīf* 185-217, Ibn Yaʿīš, *Mulūkī* 45-47, Zanǧānī, *ʿIzzī* 6-7, ʿAbd al-Ḥamīd, *Taṣrīf* 609-613, de Sacy, 227-231, Farḥāt, *Baḥṯ* 52-57, Brockelmann, *Socins Grammatik* 39-40, Wright, 68-71, Blachère, 127-131, Fischer, *Grammatik* 111-113, Bakkūš, *Taṣrīf* 98-106, ʿAbd al-Raḥīm, *Ṣarf* 21-24. For a comparative study with other forms in some of the Semtic languages see Brockelmann, *Grundriß* 632-638, Wright, *Comparative Grammar* 227-234, Bauer, *Grammatik* 108-109. Moscati, *Grammar* 169 referring to von Soden, *Grundriß* 154-156, remarks that some of the verbs "connote a number of individual actions ("Kettendurative"), e.g. Akkadian *šll*, Syriac *bzz* "to plunder", Arabic *ʿdd* "to count", etc.".

(170) In some examples of doubled verbs, the 2nd of the doubled consonants, which is the 3rd radical, can be substituted by a *y* (for examples see Ḍabī, *Amṯāl* 84-85). This substitution is carried out for the sake of alleviation. In the example Form V تَقَضَّضَ, the 3rd radical *ḍ* is substituted by the *y*, hence تقضّض becomes تَقَضَّى (cf. Zamaḫšarī, 173, Lane, *II*, 2536-2537, Vernier, *I*, 73, my notes (182), (352)). The reason of this substitution is the heaviness of the repeated consonants, the ḍāds, in this combination. The example تَقَضِّيَ البازي is found in the verse said by ʿAǧǧāǧ, *Dīwān* 28, cited by Ǧawālīqī, *Šarḥ* 331, Zaǧǧāǧ, *Maʿānī I*, 341, Ibn Ǧinnī, *Sirr II*, 759, Mu'addib, *Taṣrīf* 438, Ḍabī, *Amṯāl* 85, Ibn al-Sikkīt, *Qalb* 58, Mufaḍḍal, *Fāḫir* 5, Tamīmī, *Musalsal* 215, Qālī, *Amālī II*, 172, Baṭalyawsī, *Iqtiḍāb* 138, 413, Ibn al-Šaǧarī, *Amālī I*, 389, Abū ʿUbaid, *Ġarīb I*, 124, Afandī, *Tanzīl* 426, Ibn Yaʿīš, *X*, 24, ʿAbd al-Tawwāb, *Taṭawwur* 40, Rāzī in Ḫalīl b. Aḥmad ... , *Ḥurūf* 155, Howell, *IV*, fasc. I, 1292:

"إذا ٱلكِرامُ ٱبْتَدَرُوا ٱلبَاعَ بَدَرْ   تَقَضِّيَ ٱلبازِي إذا ٱلبازِي كَسَرْ"

"When the generous hasten to the noble deed, he hastens with the swoop of the falcon, when the falcon contracts his wings".

Other examples pertaining to Form V that can be mentioned in which the 3rd radical is changed into a *y* (for them see Sībawaihi, *II*, 447, Roman, *Étude I*, 361) are: تَسَرَّيْتُ for تَسَرَّرْتُ "I had a concubine" in which the 2nd *r* is changed into a *y*, تَظَنَّيْتُ for تَظَنَّنْتُ "I formed an opinion" in which the 2nd *n* is changed into a *y* and تَقَصَّيْتُ for تَقَصَّصْتُ "I remembered [his words]" in which the 2nd *ṣ* is changed into a *y*. The *y* is substituted for the 3rd radical in other forms than Form V. It is substituted for the 2nd *l* in Form IV أَمْلَيْتُ for أَمْلَلْتُ "I dictated" (cf. Sībawaihi, *II*, 447, Roman, *Étude I*, 361) and for the 2nd *m* in Form VIII يأتَمِي for يأتَمُّ that occurs in the following verse said by Kuṯayyir, *Dīwān* 300 in which he is praising ʿAbd al-ʿAzīz b. Marwān. It is cited by Ibn Ǧinni, *Sirr II*, 760, Zamaḫšarī, 173, Ibn Yaʿīš, *X*, 24, *Mulūkī* 252, Ibn ʿUṣfūr, *I*, 374, *Ḍarā'ir* 228, Howell, *IV*, fasc. I, 1292:

"نَزُورُ ٱمْرَأً أمَا الإلهَ فيَتَقِي   وأمَا بفعْلِ الصالحِينَ فيأتَمِي".

"We will visit a man such that, whatever betide, God he fears, and, whatever betide, by the deed of the righteous he takes example".

This change of the 2nd consonant among the doubled consonants into a *y* is carried out as well in nominal forms, e.g. the *maṣdar* Form II تَصْدِيَة for تَصْدِدَة that occurs in the sur. 8: 35 (وَمَا كَانَ صَلَاتُهُمْ عِنْدَ ٱلْبَيْتِ إِلَّا مُكَاءً وَتَصْدِيَةً) "Their prayers at the House (of God) are nothing but whistling and clapping of hands". It is not however carried out in Form II of its verb يَصِدُّون that occurs with the doubling of the *d* in the sur. 43: 57 (إذا قَوْمُكَ مِنْهُ يَصِدُّونَ) "Thy people raise a clamour thereat (in ridicule)!". Another example of a *maṣdar* occurring with the doubling of the *d* is Form V التَّصَدِّى that is cited by Ḥassān, namely صَلَاتُهُمُ التَّصَدِّى وَالْمُكَاءُ "their prayer is the clapping with the hands, and whistling" (cf. Lane, *II*, 1670).

(171) The three common conjugations of the double verb are:

1– فَعَلَ يَفْعُلُ e.g. سَرَّ يَسُرُّ underlyingly سَرَرَ يَسْرُرُ

2– فَعَلَ يَفْعِلُ e.g. فَرَّ يَفِرُّ underlyingly فَرَرَ يَفْرِرُ.

3– فَعِلَ يَفْعَلُ e.g. عَضَّ يَعَضُّ underlyingly عَضِضَ يَعْضَضُ.

The more anomalous conjugation is 4– فَعُلَ يَفْعُلُ (cf. Wright, *II*, 68). Two well-known examples of verbs seem to be formed according to this conjugation, namely حَبَّ يَحُبُّ underlyingly حَبُبَ يَحْبُبُ and لَبَّ يَلُبُّ underlyingly لَبُبَ يَلْبُبُ, but there exist other verbs as well, namely رَمُمَ "to repair", خَفُفَ "to be light" (cf. Bakkūš, *Taṣrīf* 99) and شَرُرَ "to become evil" (cf. Lane, *I*, 494, Wright, *II*, 69). According to Ibn Ǧinnī, *Munṣif I*, 240 لَبُبْتَ فَأَنْتَ لَبِيبٌ "you became possessed by understanding, so you are a person of understanding" was said by Yūnus, and شَرُرْتُ فِي الشَّرِّ "I became evil, or acted with evil" was said by Quṭrub. The reason why it is preferred not to use the conjugation فَعُلَ يَفْعُلُ is according to Ibn Ǧinnī, *Munṣif I*, 240, to avoid the heaviness of the ḍamma on one of the doubled consonants. In the perfect of the doubled verbs, the vowel of the 2nd radical is dropped and the 2nd radical is assimilated to the 3rd: سَرَرَ becomes سَرْرَ and then سَرَّ, فَرَرَ becomes فَرْرَ and then فَرَّ, عَضِضَ becomes عَضْضَ and then عَضَّ, and حَبُبَ becomes حَبْبَ and then حَبَّ. In its imperfect, the vowel of the 2nd radical is not dropped but switched to the 1st radical, and then the 2nd radical is assimilated to the 3rd: يَسْرُرُ becomes يَسُرْرُ and then يَسُرُّ, يَفْرِرُ becomes يَفِرْرُ and then يَفِرُّ, يَعْضَضُ becomes يَعَضْضُ and then يَعَضُّ and يَحْبُبُ becomes يَحُبْبُ and then يَحُبُّ.

The paradigm of سَرَّ in the perfect, active, (of which the imperfect is يَسُرُّ with the imperfect's 2nd radical's vowel being a ḍamma), is the following:

	sing.	dual	pl.
1st	سَرَرْتُ		سَرَرْنَا
2nd masc.	سَرَرْتَ	سَرَرْتُمَا	سَرَرْتُمْ

2nd fem.	سَرَرْتِ	سَرَرْتُمَا	سَرَرْتُنَّ
3rd masc.	سَرَّ	سَرَّا	سَرُّوا
3rd fem.	سَرَّتْ	سَرَّتَا	سَرَرْنَ

Its imperfect in the indicative, active, is the following:

	sing.	dual	pl.
1st	أَسُرُّ		نَسُرُّ
2nd masc.	تَسُرُّ	تَسُرَّانِ	تَسُرُّونَ
2nd fem.	تَسُرِّينَ	تَسُرَّانِ	تَسْرُرْنَ
3rd masc.	يَسُرُّ	يَسُرَّانِ	يَسُرُّونَ
3rd fem.	تَسُرُّ	تَسُرَّانِ	يَسْرُرْنَ

Its imperfect in the subjunctive, active, is the following:

	sing.	dual	pl.
1st	أَسُرَّ		نَسُرَّ
2nd masc.	تَسُرَّ	تَسُرَّا	تَسُرُّوا
2nd fem.	تَسُرِّي	تَسُرَّا	تَسْرُرْنَ
3rd masc.	يَسُرَّ	يَسُرَّا	يَسُرُّوا
3rd fem.	تَسُرَّ	تَسُرَّا	يَسْرُرْنَ

Its imperfect in the jussive, active, is the following:

	sing.	dual	pl.
1st	أَسْرُرْ or أَسُرَّ		نَسْرُرْ or نَسُرَّ
2nd masc.	تَسْرُرْ or تَسُرَّ	تَسُرَّا	تَسُرُّوا
2nd fem.	تَسُرِّي	تَسُرَّا	تَسْرُرْنَ
3rd masc.	يَسْرُرْ or يَسُرَّ	يَسُرَّا	يَسُرُّوا
3rd fem.	تَسْرُرْ or تَسُرَّ	تَسُرَّا	يَسْرُرْنَ

b) The paradigm of فَرَّ in the perfect, active, (of which the imperfect is يَفِرُّ with the imperfect's 2nd radical's vowel being a kasra), is the following:

	sing.	dual	pl.
1st	فَرَرْتُ		فَرَرْنَا
2nd masc.	فَرَرْتَ	فَرَرْتُمَا	فَرَرْتُمْ
2nd fem.	فَرَرْتِ	فَرَرْتُمَا	فَرَرْتُنَّ
3rd masc.	فَرَّ	فَرَّا	فَرُّوا
3rd fem.	فَرَّتْ	فَرَّتَا	فَرَرْنَ

Its imperfect in the indicative, active, is the following:

	sing.	dual	pl.
1st	أَفِرُّ		نَفِرُّ
2nd masc.	تَفِرُّ	تَفِرَّانِ	تَفِرُّونَ
2nd fem.	تَفِرِّينَ	تَفِرَّانِ	تَفْرِرْنَ
3rd masc.	يَفِرُّ	يَفِرَّانِ	يَفِرُّونَ
3rd fem.	تَفِرُّ	تَفِرَّانِ	يَفْرِرْنَ

Its imperfect in the subjunctive, active, is the following:

	sing.	dual	pl.
1st	أَفِرَّ		نَفِرَّ
2nd masc.	تَفِرَّ	تَفِرَّا	تَفِرُّوا
2nd fem.	تَفِرِّي	تَفِرَّا	تَفْرِرْنَ
3rd masc.	يَفِرَّ	يَفِرَّا	يَفِرُّوا
3rd fem.	تَفِرَّ	تَفِرَّا	يَفْرِرْنَ

Its imperfect in the jussive, active, is the following:

	sing.	dual	pl.
1st	أَفْرِرْ or أَفِرَّ		نَفْرِرْ or نَفِرَّ
2nd masc.	تَفْرِرْ or تَفِرَّ	تَفِرَّا	تَفِرُّوا
2nd fem.	تَفِرِّي	تَفِرَّا	تَفْرِرْنَ
3rd masc.	يَفْرِرْ or يَفِرَّ	يَفِرَّا	يَفِرُّوا
3rd fem.	تَفْرِرْ or تَفِرَّ	تَفِرَّا	يَفْرِرْنَ

c) The paradigm of عَضَّ in the perfect, active, (of which the imperfect is يَعَضُّ with the imperfect's 2nd radical's vowel being a fatḥa), is the following:

	sing.	dual	pl.
1st	عَضِضْتُ		عَضِضْنَا
2nd masc.	عَضِضْتَ	عَضِضْتُمَا	عَضِضْتُمْ
2nd fem.	عَضِضْتِ	عَضِضْتُمَا	عَضِضْتُنَّ
3rd masc.	عَضَّ	عَضَّا	عَضُّوا
3rd fem.	عَضَّتْ	عَضَّتَا	عَضِضْنَ

Its imperfect in the indicative, active, is the following:

	sing.	dual	pl.
1st	أَعَضُّ		نَعَضُّ
2nd masc.	تَعَضُّ	تَعَضَّانِ	تَعَضُّونَ

2nd fem.	تَعَضِّينَ	تَعَضَّانِ	تَعْضَضْنَ
3rd masc.	يَعَضُّ	يَعَضَّانِ	يَعَضُّونَ
3rd fem.	تَعَضُّ	تَعَضَّانِ	يَعْضَضْنَ

Its imperfect in the subjunctive, active, is the following:

	sing.	dual	pl.
1st	أَعَضَّ		نَعَضَّ
2nd masc.	تَعَضَّ	تَعَضَّا	تَعَضُّوا
2nd fem.	تَعَضِّي	تَعَضَّا	تَعْضَضْنَ
3rd masc.	يَعَضَّ	يَعَضَّا	يَعَضُّوا
3rd fem.	تَعَضَّ	تَعَضَّا	يَعْضَضْنَ

Its imperfect in the jussive, active, is the following:

	sing.	dual	pl.
1st	أَعْضَضْ or أَعَضَّ		نَعْضَضْ or نَعَضَّ
2nd masc.	تَعْضَضْ or تَعَضَّ	تَعَضَّا	تَعَضُّوا
2nd fem.	تَعَضِّي	تَعَضَّا	تَعْضَضْنَ
3rd masc.	يَعْضَضْ or يَعَضَّ	يَعَضَّا	يَعَضُّوا
3rd fem.	تَعْضَضْ or تَعَضَّ	تَعَضَّا	يَعْضَضْنَ

(172) The assimilation can be carried out between two identical vowelled consonants. مَدَّ is underlyingly مَدَدَ with two vowelled dāls being its 2nd and 3rd radical. The reason of the assimilation of one consonant to the other is ثقل المُكَرَّر "the heaviness of the repeated consonant". مَدَّ pertains to the conjugation فَعَلَ يَفْعُلُ. Its perfect, active, is مَدَّ. Its imperfect of the indicative, active, is يَمُدُّ, of the subjuntive, active, يَمُدَّ and of the jussive, active, يَمْدُدْ. Its active participle is مَادٌّ. Its passive participle is مَمْدُودٌ. Its *maṣdar* is مَدٌّ.

b) As for the paradigm of its derived forms:

Form II: Its perfect, active is مَدَّدَ. Its imperfect is يُمَدِّدُ. Its imperative is مَدِّدْ. Its active participle is مُمَدِّدٌ. Its *maṣdar* is تَمْدِيدٌ. Its perfect, passive is مُدِّدَ. Its imperfect is يُمَدَّدُ. Its passive participle is مُمَدَّدٌ.

Form III: Its perfect, active is مَادَدَ. Its imperfect is يُمَادِدُ or يُمَادُّ. Its imperative is مَادِدْ. Its active participle is مُمَادِدٌ or مُمَادٌّ. Its *maṣdar* is مِدَادٌ, مُمَادَدَةٌ or مُمَادَّةٌ. Its perfect, passive is مُودِدَ. Its imperfect is يُمَادَدُ or يُمَادُّ. Its passive participle is مُمَادَدٌ or مُمَادٌّ.

Form IV: Its perfect, active is أَمَدَّ. Its imperfect is يُمِدُّ. Its imperative is أَمْدِدْ or أَمِدَّ. Its active participle is مُمِدٌّ. Its *maṣdar* is إِمْدَادٌ. Its perfect, passive is أُمِدَّ. Its imperfect is يُمَدُّ. Its passive participle is مُمَدٌّ.

Form V: Its perfect, active is تَمَدَّدَ. Its imperfect is يَتَمَدَّدُ. Its imperative is تَمَدَّدْ. Its active participle is مُتَمَدِّدٌ. Its *maṣdar* is تَمَدُّدٌ. Its perfect, passive is تُمُدِّدَ. Its imperfect is يُتَمَدَّدُ. Its passive participle is مُتَمَدَّدٌ.

Form VI: Its perfect, active is تَمَادَدَ or تَمَادَّ. Its imperfect is يَتَمَادَدُ or يَتَمَادُّ. Its imperative is تَمَادَدْ. Its active participle is مُتَمَادِدٌ or مُتَمَادٌّ. Its *maṣdar* is تَمَادُدٌ or تَمَادٌّ. Its perfect, passive is تُمُودِدَ. Its imperfect is يُتَمَادَدُ or يُتَمَادُّ. Its passive participle is مُتَمَادَدٌ or مُتَمَادٌّ.

As for Form VII, انْفَلَّ can be presented. Its perfect, active is انْفَلَّ. Its imperfect is يَنْفَلُّ. Its imperative is انْفَلِلْ. Its active participle is مُنْفَلٌّ. Its *maṣdar* is انْفِلَالٌ. Its perfect, passive is أُنْفُلَّ. Its imperfect is يُنْفَلُّ. Its passive participle is مُنْفَلٌّ.

Form VIII: Its perfect, active is امْتَدَّ. Its imperfect is يَمْتَدُّ. Its imperative is امْتَدِدْ or امْتَدَّ. Its active participle is مُمْتَدٌّ. Its *maṣdar* is امْتِدَادٌ. Its perfect, passive is أُمْتُدَّ. Its imperfect is يُمْتَدُّ. Its passive participle is مُمْتَدٌّ.

Form X: Its perfect, active is اسْتَمَدَّ. Its imperfect is يَسْتَمِدُّ. Its imperative is اسْتَمْدِدْ or اسْتَمِدَّ. Its active participle is مُسْتَمِدٌّ. Its *maṣdar* is اسْتِمْدَادٌ. Its perfect, passive is أُسْتُمِدَّ. Its imperfect is يُسْتَمَدُّ. Its passive participle is مُسْتَمَدٌّ.

(173) The assimilation can be carried out between two consonants which are close in the points of articulation, of which the 1st is the ultimate consonant of one word and the 2nd is the initial consonant of the second word following it (for a general study see Sībawaihi, *II,* 455 sqq., Zamaḫšarī, 191 sqq., Ibn Yaʿīš, *X,* 134 sqq., Howell, *IV,* fasc. II, 1666 sqq., Vollers, *Volkssprache* 25 sqq., Cantineau, *Études* 35 sqq., Fleisch, *Traité I,* 83 sqq., Roman, *Étude I,* 390-427, Wright, *I,* 15-16). In the reading of the sur. أَخْرَج شَّطْأَهُ (cf. Zamaḫšarī, 193) underlyingly أَخْرَجَ شَطْأَهُ, the vowelled *ǧ* which is the last consonant of the first word is assimilated to the vowelled *š* which is the 1st consonant of the second word, resulting in the doubling of the *š*. In the example قَالَت طَّائِفَةٌ underlyingly قَالَتْ طَائِفَةٌ, the vowelless *t* which is the last consonant of the first word is assimilated to the vowelled *ṭ* of the second word, resulting in the *ṭ's* doubling.

1– Another example than أَخْرَج شَّطْأَهُ that occurs with the assimilation of the *ǧ* to the *š* is أَخْرِج شَّبَثًا "expel Šabaṯ" (cf. Zamaḫšari, 193, Ibn Yaʿīš, *X,* 138, Vollers, *Volkssprache* 32).

– Another extraordinary assimilation is the one of the *ǧ* to the *t,* as what was said by al-Yazīdī concerning the reading of Abū ʿAmr of the sur. 70: 3-4 (ذِي الْمَعَارِج تَّعْرُجُ) "Lord of the Ways of Ascent. [The angels and the Spirit] ascend" (cf. Zamaḫšarī, 193, Ibn Yaʿīš, *X,* 138, Ibn ʿUṣfūr, *II,* 722, Vollers, *Volkssprache* 26).

2– Another example than قَالَت طَّائِفَةٌ that occurs with the assimilation of the *t* to the *ṭ* is the reading of the sur. 4: 81 (بَيَّت طَّائفةٌ) "a section of them meditate all night" (cf. Vollers, *Volkssprache* 32, Cantineau, *Études* 35).

The *t* can be assimilated to:

– the *ṯ*, e.g. سكت ثّامرٌ "a wealthy man was silent" (cf. Howell, *IV*, fasc. II, 1795, Cantineau, *Études* 35).

– the *ǧ*, e.g. sur. 22: 36 (وَجَبت جُّنوبُها) "When they are down on their sides (after slaughter)" (cf. Zamaḫšarī, 193, Vollers, *Volkssprache* 27).

– the *d*, e.g. انْعت دُّلامةَ "describe Dulāmata" (cf. Ibn Yaʿīš, *X*, 146, Vollers, *Volkssprache* 29).

– the *ḏ*, e.g. sur. 51: 1 (وَآلذَّاريت ذَّرْوا) "By the (Winds) that scatter broadcast", read so by Ibn al-ʿAlāʾ and Ḥamza (cf. Vollers, *Volkssprache* 29, Cantineau, *Études* 35).

– the *z*, e.g. سكت زّاجرٌ "a diviner was silent" (cf. Howell, *IV*, fasc. II, 1795, Cantineau, *Études* 35).

– the *s*, e.g. سكت سّامرٌ "a converser by night was silent" (cf. Howell, *IV*, fasc. II, 1795, Cantineau, *Études* 35).

– the *š*, e.g. عصبت شّرْباً "she obtained a drink" (cf. Ibn Yaʿīš, *X*, 139, Vollers, *Volkssprache* 31).

– the *ṣ*, e.g. سكت صّابرٌ "a patient man was silent" (cf. Howell, *IV*, fasc. II, 1795, Cantineau, *Études* 35).

– the *ḍ*, e.g. شُدت ضَّفَائرُها "her plaits were tightenend" (cf. Zamaḫšarī, 193). Vollers, *Volkssprache* 32 has شَدت ضّفَائرَها "she tightenend her plaits" instead.

– the *ẓ*, e.g. سكت ظّالمٌ "Ẓālim was silent" (cf. Howell, *IV*, fasc. II, 1795, Cantineau, *Études* 35).

b) Some interesting cases of assimilation in the readings of some surs. that can be presented are the following:

3– The *b*'s assimilation to:

– the *b* in the sur. 3: 151 (الرُّعب بِّما) "Terror [into the hearts of the Unbelievers], for that", read so by Abū ʿAmr (cf. Ibn ʿUṣfūr, *II*, 719); the sur. 2: 19 (لَذَهب بِّسَمْعِهِم) "He would take away their faculty of hearing", read so by Abū ʿAmr (cf. Zamaḫšarī, 195, Ibn Yaʿīš, *X*, 147).

– the *m* in the sur. 2: 284 (ويُعَذب مَّن يَشاءُ) "And punisheth whom He pleaseth" (cf. Zamaḫšarī, 195, Ibn Yaʿīš, *X*, 147, Vollers, *Volkssprache* 35).

4– The *ṯ's* assimilation to:

– the *ḏ* in the sur 3: 14 (وَالحَرْث ذَّلك) "And well-tilled land. Such are" (cf. Ibn ʿUṣfūr, *II*, 722).

5– The *ḥ's* assimilation to:

– the *ḥ* in the sur. 2: 235 (عُقْدَةَ آلنّكَاح حَّتّى) "The tie of marriage till" (cf. Ibn Yaʿīš, *X*, 137).

– the *ʿ* in the sur. 3: 185 (فَمَن زُحْزح عَّن آلنَّار) "Only he who is saved far from the Fire", read so by Abū ʿAmr as al-Yazīdī said about him (cf. Zamaḫšarī, 192, Ibn Yaʿīš, *X*, 136, Ibn ʿUṣfūr, *II*, 722, Vollers, *Volkssprache* 33).

6– The *d's* assimilation to:

– the *t* in the sur. 16: 91 (وَلا تَنْقُضوا الأيمان بَعْد تَّوكيدها) "And break not your oaths after ye have confirmed them", read so by Abū ʿAmr (cf. Ibn ʿUṣfūr, *II*, 723).

– the *ṣ* in the sur. 19: 29 (الْمَهْدِ صَبِيًّا) "a child in the craddle", read so by Abū ʿAmr (cf. Ibn ʿUṣfūr, *II,* 723).

– the *ḍ* in the sur. 41: 50 (مَسَّتْهُ مِنْ بَعْدِ ضَرَّاءَ) "After some adversity has touched him".

7. The *ḏ's* assimilation to:

– the *ǧ* in the sur. 33: 10 (إِذْ جَاءُوكُمْ) "Behold! they came on you" (cf. Zamaḫšarī, 193, Vollers, *Volkssprache* 27).

8– The *r's* assimilation to:

– the *r* in the sur. 7: 77 (وَعَتَوْا عَنْ أَمْرِ رَبِّهِمْ) "And insolently defied the order of their Lord" and the sur. 19: 2 (ذِكْرُ رَحْمَةِ) "(This is) a recital of the Mercy", read so by Abū ʿAmr (cf. Ibn ʿUṣfūr, *II,* 722).

– the *l* in the sur. 3: 147 (اغْفِرْ لَنَا) "Forgive us", sur. 9: 80 (اسْتَغْفِرْ لَهُمْ) "Whether thou ask for their forgiveness", the sur. 61: 12 (يَغْفِرْ لَكُمْ ذُنُوبَكُمْ) "He will forgive you your sins", all read so by Abū ʿAmr as mentioned by Abū Bakr b. Muǧāhid (cf. Ibn Yaʿīš, *X,* 143, Ibn ʿUṣfūr, *II,* 724),—However, according to Vollers, *Volkssprache* 35 the last sur. is read so by Yaʿqūb al-Ḥaḍrami—; the sur. 11: 78 (هُنَّ أَطْهَرُ لَكُمْ) "They are purer for you (if ye marry)!" and the sur. 22: 65 (سَخَّرَ لَكُمْ) "Has made subject to you (men)" (cf. Ibn Yaʿīš, *X,* 143, Vollers, *Volkssprache* 35).

9– The *s's* assimilation to:

– the *š* in the sur. 19: 4 (اشْتَعَلَ الرَّأْسُ شَيْبًا) "And the hair of my head doth glisten with grey", read so by Abū ʿAmr (cf. Ibn Yaʿīš, *X,* 139, Ibn ʿUṣfūr, *II,* 726).

10– The *š's* assimilation to:

– the *s* in the sur. 71: 16 (الشَّمْسَ سِرَاجًا) "[And made] the sun as a (Glorious) Lamp", read so by Abū ʿAmr (cf. Ibn ʿUṣfūr, *II,* 725).

11– The *ḍ's* assimilation to:

– the *š* in the sur. 24: 62 (لِبَعْضِ شَأْنِهِمْ), read so by Abū ʿAmr (cf. Zamaḫšarī, 193, Ibn ʿUṣfūr, *II,* 725, Vollers, *Volkssprache* 31).

12– The *ʿ's* assimilation to:

– the *ʿ* in the sur. 2: 255 (مَنْ ذَا الَّذِي يَشْفَعُ عِنْدَهُ) "Who is there can intercede in His presence" (cf. Zamaḫšarī, 192, Ibn Yaʿīš, *X,* 136).

13– The *ġ's* assimilation to:

– the *ġ* in the sur. 3: 85 (وَمَنْ يَبْتَغِ غَيْرَ الْإِسْلَامِ دِينًا) "If anyone desires a religion other than Islam (submission to God)" (cf. Zamaḫšarī, 192, Ibn Yaʿīš, *X,* 137).

14– The *f's* assimilation to:

– the *b* in the sur. 34: 9 (نَخْسِفْ بِهِمُ) "We could cause the earth to swallow them up", read so only by al-Kisāʾī and is considered weak (cf. Zamaḫšarī, 195, Ibn Yaʿīš, *X,* 146, Ibn ʿUṣfūr, *II,* 720, Vollers, *Volkssprache* 25).

– the *f* in the sur. 2: 213 (وَمَا اخْتَلَفَ فِيهِ) "Did not differ" (cf. Howell, *IV,* fasc. II, 1800).

15– The *q's* assimilation to:

– the *q* in the sur. 9: 99 (وَيَتَّخِذُ مَا يُنْفِقُ قُرُبَاتٍ) "And look on their payments as pious gifts bringing them nearer to God" (cf. Ibn Yaʿīš, *X,* 138); and the sur. 7: 143 (فَلَمَّا أَفَاقَ قَالَ) "When he recovered his senses he said" (cf. Zamaḫšarī, 193, Ibn Yaʿīš, *X,* 138).

– the *k* in the sur. 24: 45 (خَلَقَ كُلَّ دَابَّةٍ) "Has created every animal" (cf. Zamaḫšarī, 193, Ibn Yaʿīš, *X,* 138, Vollers, *Volkssprache* 34).

16– The *k's* assimilation to:

– the *q* in the sur. 47: 18 (إِذَا خَرَجُوا مِنْ عِنْدِكَ قَالُوا) "When they go out from thee, they say" (cf. Zamaḫšarī, 193, Ibn Yaʿīš, *X,* 138, Vollers, *Volkssprache* 34).

– the *k* in the sur. 20: 35 (إِنَّكَ كُنْتَ) "For Thou art He" (cf. Ibn Yaʿīš, *X,* 138); and sur. 20: 33 (كَيْ نُسَبِّحَكَ كَثِيراً وَنَذْكُرَكَ كَثِيراً) "That we may celebrate Thy praise without stint, and remember Thee withou stint" (cf. Zamaḫšarī, 193, Ibn Yaʿīš, *X,* 138).

17– The *l's* assimilation to:

– the *t* in the sur. 2: 170 (بَلْ نَتَّبِعُ مَا أَلْفَيْنَا) "Nay! we shall follow the ways" (cf. Ibn Yaʿīš, *X,* 142).

– the *r* in the sur. 89: 6 (كَيْفَ فَعَلَ رَبُّكَ) "How thy Lord dealt" (cf. Zamaḫšarī, 194, Ibn Yaʿīš, *X,* 143).

18– The *m's* assimilation to:

– the *b* in the sur. 4: 156 (مَرْيَمَ بُهْتَانًا) "Mary [a grave] false charge", the sur. 6: 53 (بِأَعْلَمَ بِالشَّاكِرِينَ) "[Does not God] know best those who are grateful?" and the sur. 16: 70 (لِكَيْلَا يَعْلَمَ بَعْدَ عِلْمٍ شَيْئًا) "So that they know nothing after having known (much)", read so by Abū ʿAmr (cf. Ibn Yaʿīš, *X,* 147, Ibn ʿUṣfūr, *II,* 719).

– the *m* in the sur. 1: 2-3 (الرَّحِيمِ مَالِكِ يَوْمِ الدِّينِ) "Most Merciful; Master of the Day of Judgment" (cf. Ibn Yaʿīš, *X,* 147).

19– The *n's* assimilation to:

– the *r* in the sur. 7: 167 (وَإِذْ تَأَذَّنَ رَبُّكُمْ) "Behold! thy Lord did declare" (cf. Zamaḫšarī, 194, Ibn Yaʿīš, *X,* 143).

– the *l* in the sur. 2: 133 (وَنَحْنُ لَهُ مُسْلِمُونَ) "to Him we bow (in Islam)", read so by Abū ʿAmr (cf. Ibn ʿUṣfūr, *II,* 725).

– the *y* in the sur. 3: 129 (يَغْفِرُ لِمَنْ يَشَاءُ) "He forgiveth whom He pleaseth" (cf. Ibn Yaʿīš, *X,* 147, Vollers, *Volkssprache* 36).

20– The *h's* assimilation to:

– the *l* in the sur. 29: 26 (فَآمَنَ لَهُ لُوطٌ) "But Lūṭ had faith in Him" (cf. Ibn Yaʿīš, *X,* 143).

– the *h* in the sur. 25: 43 (إِلَهَهُ هَوَاهُ) "[As taketh] for his god his own passion (or impulse)?", read so by Abū ʿAmr (cf. Ibn ʿUṣfūr, *II,* 726).

21– The *y's* assimilation to:

– the *y* in the sur. 11: 66 (وَمِنْ خِزْيِ يَوْمِئِذٍ) "And from the Ignominy of that Day", read so by Abū ʿAmr (cf. Ibn ʿUṣfūr, *II,* 725).

21– The *w*'s assimilation to:

– the *w* in اخْشَو وّاقدا (cf. Sībawaihi, *II*, 457) said instead of اخْشَوا واَقدا "Fear [2nd person of the masc. pl. of the imperative] one who sets fire!".

(174) The term ادغام "assimilation" is used according to two different forms by the Basrans and the Kufans. Form IV of the *maṣdar* ادْغام is among the terms used by the Kufans whereas Form VIII ادّغام underlyingly ادْتغام is among the terms used by the Basrans (cf. Howell, *IV*, fasc. II, 1663, Fleisch, *Traité I*, 243, Rāǧiḥī, *Farrā*ʾ 79). Dunqūz, *Šarḥ* fol. 54b ll.12-13 remarks:

"الإدْغام إفعالاً من عبارات الكوفيين والإدّغام إفْتعالاً من عبارات البصريين".

"The pattern ادْغام [with a single *d]* according to إفْعال, is among the expressions used by the Kufan grammarians whereas the pattern ادّغام [with a double *d*, underlyingly ادْتغام] according to افْتِعال is among the expressions used by the Basran grammarians".

The assimilation (for a detailed study see Sībawaihi, *II*, 443 sqq., Ibn ʿUṣfūr, *II*, 631 sqq., Zamaḫšarī, 188 sqq., Howell, *IV*, fasc. II, 1663 sqq., Roman, *Étude I*, 349 sqq.) can be carried out between both المتقاربين "two homogeneous consonants", i.e. two different consonants originating from a common point of articulation or from two close points of articulation, or between المتماثلين "two identical consonants", i.e. two consonants originating from one point of articulation (cf. Zamaḫšarī, 188). When the consonants are from different points of articulation, one of them is assimilated to the other which remains in its own point of articulation. This is what Ibn Masʿūd means with إلباث الحرف في مخرجه "the consonant remaining in its own point of articulation". The consonants that are homogeneous can either originate from one point of articulation or from two close points of articulation, or they can be akin in character (for discussions concerning the consonants' points of articulation and their characters see (188), (188 b)). The reason why the assimilation is carried out is the dislike of repeating twice the same consonant or of pronouncing two consonants that originate from the same point of articulation or from close points of articulation, or that are akin in character (cf. Fleish, *Arabe* 24, Cantineau, *Études* 199-202, Greenberg, *Morphemes* 162-181). Ibn Ǧinnī, *Ḫaṣāʾiṣ I*, 151 specifies:

"وكلّما تداني الحرفان أسرع انقلاب أحدهما إلى صاحبه".

"The more two consonants are close to each other the easier it is to change one of them into the other".

Consequently, the distance that exists between two consonants, for instance the *ḥ* and the *ṯ*, forbids the change of one into the other (cf. Ibn Sīda, *Muḫaṣṣaṣ XIII*, 274). In this context it is interesting to mention that Ibn Ǧinnī, *Ḫaṣāʾiṣ II*, 139-145 distinguishes between two sorts of assimilation (cf. Rāǧiḥī, *Farrā*ʾ 102-103):

1– الإدغام الأكبر "the big assimilation" (for discussions see Ibn Ǧinnī, *Ḫaṣāʾiṣ II*, 139), which is carried out between two identical consonants or between two different consonants originating from the same point of articulation or from two close points of articulation, or that are akin in character. It implies that one consonant is totally assimilated to the other so as to form a doubled consonant. Examples are مَدْدٌ "an extension" with two dāls written of which the 1st is vowelless and the 2nd vowelled, resulting in مدّ with the doubled *d*, مَدَدَ "to stretch" with two vowelled dāls resulting in مدَّ and many cases of Form VIII, e.g. اِسْتَمَعَ "to listen" that results in اِسَّمَعَ (cf. (192)) after the assimilation of the *t* to the *s*. As can be remarked both the *t* and the *s* originate from close points of articulation (for the consonants' points of articulation see (188)) and are similar in character in being among the voiceless consonants (for them see (188 b)).

2– الإدغام الأصغر "the little assimilation" (for discussions see Ibn Ǧinnī, *Ḫaṣāʾiṣ II,* 141 sqq.), is according to Ibn Ǧinnī carried out between two consonants that are phonetically related or between two vowels of which one of them is inclined to the other. In the case of consonants that are related, it implies that the 1st consonant is substituted for another consonant that is closer to the 2nd one in the point of articulation. This particular assimilation is also termed as إدْغامٌ جزئيٌّ "partial assimilation" because it implies an assimilation that is not completed (cf. Bakkūš, *Taṣrīf* 67 in the notes) or المُماثَلَةُ التَقدُميّةُ الجزئيّةُ "partial progressive assimilation" because the 1st consonant forces a change on the 2nd one (cf. ʿAbd al-Raḥīm, *Ṣarf* 38). Examples concerning this assimilation are some cases of verbs of Form VIII (for some examples see (374)), e.g. اِصْطَبَرَ said instead of اِصْتَبَرَ "to acquire patience" (for it see (192 c), (374)), اِضْطَرَبَ said instead of اِضْتَرَبَ "to be in a state of agitation" (for it see (195), (374)), in which the ir fixed *t* is changed into the *ṭ*, and اِزْدانَ said instead of اِزْتانَ "to be ornamented" (for it see (191)), in which the infixed *t* is changed into the *d*. The substitution of the *ṣ* for the *s* in, e.g. صوقٌ "market" for سوقٌ (for it and for other examples see (368)) is as well included by Ibn Ǧinnī, *Ḫaṣāʾiṣ II,* 143 within this category. Concerning the case of the partial assimilation that is carried out between two vowels, Ibn Ǧinnī, *Ḫaṣāʾiṣ II,* 141 takes up the امالة that implies the inclination of the fatḥa to the kasra (for it see (347)), for instance the inclination of a vowel to the vowel of a guttural consonant, e.g. رِغيفٌ said instead of رَغيفٌ "loaf of bread" (for it see (29)), in which the fatḥa of the *r* is changed into a kasra due to the influence of the kasra of the guttural *ġ,* and the fatḥa given to the imperfect's 2nd radical's vowel in verbs of the conjugation فَعَلَ يَفْعَلُ (for it see (30), (30 b)) with the 2nd or 3rd guttural consonant that is given the same vowel, e.g. سَأَلَ يَسْأَلُ "to ask" and سَبَحَ يَسْبَحُ "to swim".

(175) جارُ الله العلاّمةُ is a well-known nickname given to Zamaḫšarī because he frequently resided in the Holy city of Mekka (cf. Suyūṭī, *Buġya II,* 279, Howell, *I,* fasc. I, XVII-XVIII).

(176) المُدغم is the consonant that is to be assimilated to another and المُدغم فيه is the consonant to which it is assimilated to. In مدّ two dāls are uttered in the pronunciation: the 1st one is vowelless and the 2nd one is vowelled, namely مَدْدٌ, whereas in the writing one *d* is written with a *šadda* over it. In الرَّحمنُ the *l*– of the definite article *al*– is assimilated to the *r.* It is pronounced *"ar-Raḥmān"* with both the rā's whereas it is written الرَّحْمن with the *l* and with the *r* that carries the *šadda*. This assimilation of the *l–* of the article to the consonant following it is carried out when the *l–* is combined with one of الحروف الشمسيّة "the solar consonants", namely: the *t, ṯ, d, ḏ, r, z, s, š, ṣ, ḍ, ṭ, ẓ, l* and *n* (cf. Wright, *I*, 15, Fischer, *Grammatik* 25, Bakkūš, *Taṣrīf* 65). The alphabetical order of the consonants differs by the Arab grammarians who present them according to their phonetic factors. Zamaḫšarī, 193 distributes these consonants as follows: the *l* of the definite article, then the *ṭ, d, t, ẓ, ḏ, ṯ, ṣ, s, z, š, ḍ, n* and *r*. The *ṭ, d* and *t* are dentals, the *ẓ, ḏ* and *ṯ* are interdentals, the *ṣ, s* and *z* are sibilants, the *š* and *ḍ* are laterals and the *n, r* and *l* are liquids (cf. Ullendorff, *Article* 632 note 2, my notes (188 b)). The reason why the *l–* is assimilated to these consonants is that they all originate from between the teeth to the lower part of the palate, and thus are all close to the *l's* point of articulation (cf. Bakkūš, *Taṣrīf* 66). The remaining consonants are named الحروف القمريّة "the lunar or moon-consonants". The nomination "solar" is associated with the word شَمْسٌ "sun", which begins with one of the solar consonants and the nomination "lunar" is associated with the word قَمَرٌ which begins with one of the lunar consonants. For a discussion concerning the consonants, their characters and nominations see (188, b).

(177) مدّ is underlyingly مَدَدَ with both the dāls vowelled, which makes the assimilation necessary. The assimilation is however avoided in الإلحاقيّات "the coordinatives" or "the words that are coordinated to the patterns of other words by an augment or more" (for discussions see (41)), in spite of the fact that both identical consonants are vowelled. An example is قَرْدَدٌ (cf. Sībawaihi, *II*, 448, Ibn Ya'īš, *X*, 122) from the root قَرِدَ "it became contracted together", in which the 2nd *d* is added to the form, and no *d* is to be assimilated to the other because the word is quasi-coordinate to the measure فَعْلَلٌ (cf. Lane, *II*, 2513).

b) Triliteral roots can in Arabic be extended to become quadriliteral and even quinqueliteral through the repetition of one or two of their consonants (for a study see Fleish, *Arabe* 74-79, Yasū'ī, *Ġarā'ib* 44-49). This phenomenon does not occur through gemination. An example of a verb that became augmented is طَرْطَبَ "to be agitated, when said of the water" from طَرِبَ "to be moved by joy or sadness", of a noun قَرْقَسٌ "a little mosquito" and of adjectives قَهْقَرٌ "hard" and قَسْقَبٌ "thick" (cf. Fleish, *Arabe* 75).

I. The measures with the repetition of the 3rd consonant of the triliteral are formed according to:

1): فَعْلَلٌ, e.g. قَرْدَدٌ "difficult place, elevated", 2) فُعْلُلٌ and 3) فُعْلَلٌ, e.g. دُخْلُلٌ "intruder" and دُخْلَلٌ "intruder", 4) فُعْلَلٌ, e.g. خُفْدَدٌ "bat", 5) فُعْلَلٌ, e.g. عُنْدَدٌ "retreat", and 6) فِعْلِلٌ, e.g. رِمْدِدٌ "ashes" (cf. ibid 75-76; and compare with these forms the six forms mentioned by Howell, *I*, fasc. IV, 1796-1798 that concern the unaugmented strong quadriliteral in which no repetition of a consonant occurs in their structures, namely: 1) فَعْلَلٌ as جَعْفَرٌ "brook", 2)– فُعْلُلٌ as بُرْثُنٌ "claw", 3) فِعْلَلٌ as دِرْهَمٌ "dirham", 4) فُعْلَلٌ as جُخْدَبٌ "a sort of locust", 5) فِعْلِلٌ as زِبْرِجٌ "ornament" and 6) فِعَلٌّ as فِطَحْلٌ "time before the creation of mankind").

2): The first vowel is short, the second one lengthened فِعْلَالٌ (for it see زِلْزَالٌ (27)), e.g. شِمْلَالٌ "quick", فِعْلِيلٌ, e.g. سِكْتِيتٌ "very silent", فُعْلُولٌ, e.g. حُلْبُوبٌ "very black", and فَعْلُولَةٌ, e.g. بَيْنُونَةٌ "to be separated" (cf. Fleish, *Arabe* 76-77).

II. The form with the repetition of the 2nd and 3rd radical of the triliteral: فَعَلْعَلٌ, e.g. عَصَبْصَبٌ "very hard to bear" (cf. ibid 77).

III. The forms with the repetition of a biliteral element: فَعْلَلٌ, e.g. نَعْنَعٌ "mint", فَعْلَالٌ, e.g. خَلْخَالٌ "ring for the legs", فُعْلُلٌ, e.g. بُلْبُلٌ "nightingale", فِعْلِلٌ, e.g. مِشْمِشٌ "apricot", فُعْلُولٌ, e.g. صُرْصُورٌ "cricket", and فُعَلَاعِلٌ, e.g. ضُكَاضِكٌ "short in stature" (cf. ibid 78-79).

For a detailed presentation of some measures with the repetition in the Semitic languages see Brockelmann, *Grundriss* 520, Ahrens, *Verba* 168-175, Nöldeke, *Beiträge* 107-123.

(178) The assimilation between two identical vowelled consonants is forbidden in some examples that are formed according to special patterns, so that they do not become mixed up with other examples in which the assimilation is carried out (cf. Ibn Yaʿīš, *X,* 122-123, Sībawaihi, *II,* 445-446). صَكَكٌ "the colliding of the knees in running" is formed according to فَعَلٌ, سُرُرٌ "bedsteads" to فُعُلٌ, جُدَدٌ "the stripes that are on the back of the ass" to فُعَلٌ, and both طَلَلٌ "the remains of a dwelling or house" and مَدَدٌ "assistance" to فَعَلٌ. Concerning سُرُرٌ "bedsteads" Sībawaihi, *II,* 446 notes that some said سُرٌّ instead of it and alleviated. It can be added that the assimilation between two identical consonants is not to be carried out in the أَفْعِلْ of wonder, e.g. أَحْبِبْ بِزَيْدٍ إِلَيَّ "How dear is Zaid to me!" so that the formation would not be canceled (cf. Ibn ʿAqīl, *II,* 591, Howell, *IV,* fasc. II, 1699, Wehr, *Elativ).*

(179) The following variations (for them see Howell, *IV,* fasc. II, 1699) occur concerning the doubled verbs رَدَّ "to drive back", فَرَّ "to escape" and عَضَّ "to bite":

1– رُدَّ, فَرَّ and عَضَّ with the 1st radical vowelled by a ḍamma, kasra or fatḥa and the 2nd radical assimilated to the 3rd that is vowelled by a fatḥa. These variants pertain to the dialect of Asad and some other people.

2– رُدِّ, فِرِّ and عَضِّ with the kasra given to the 2nd radical which is assimilated to the 3rd. These variants pertain to the dialect of Kaʿb and Numair.

3– رُدُّ, فِرِّ and عَضَّ with the alliteration of the vowel of the 1st radical and the 2nd radical assimilated to the 3rd vowelled by a vowel that is made to conform with the vowel of the 1st. These variants pertain to the dialect of Kaʿb and Numair.

(180) No assimilation is carried out in some dialectal variants concerning حَيِيَ (for discussions see Sībawaihi, *II,* 430-431, Zamaḫšarī, 187, Ibn ʿAqīl, *II,* 588, Ibn Yaʿīš, *X,* 115-117, Howell, *IV,* fasc. I 1624 sqq., fasc. II, 1693 sqq., Wright, *II,* 94-95, Vernier, *I,* 342-343, de Sacy, *I,* 259-260, Nöldeke, *Geschichte* 245), which is a verb with weak 2nd and 3rd radical (for its paradigm see (376 b)), in spite of the fact that two identical vowelled weak consonants, i.e. the yāʾs, are combined in it. In some other dialectal variants however, the yāʾs can be assimilated.

The reason why some prefer not to assimilate the yā's in the perfect, i.e, حَيَ, is that they feel obliged by analogy to assimilate them in the imperfect causing the ḍamma to vowel the *y*, i.e. يَحْيُ, which is regarded as heavy. Those who assimilate in the perfect consider both yā's as two identical vowelled weak consonants in one word. They avoid however to assimilate the yā's in the imperfect, i.e. يَحْيَ, because of the implied heavy combination. This means that يَحْيَى occurs by all instead of يَحْيَ. It can be added that يَحْيَا with the *alif mamdūda* substituted for the *alif maqṣūra* occurs instead of يَحْيَى, in e.g. the sur. 8: 44 (وَيَحْيَا مَنْ حَيَ عَنْ بَيِّنَة) "And those who lived might live after a Clear Sign". As for the reason of this substitution it is to distinguish the imperfect from the proper name يَحْيَى *Yaḥyā* "John". No assimilation of the yā's is allowable as well concerning the subjunctive أَنْ يُحْيِيَ "he shall not quicken", in spite of the fact that the ḍamma does not vowel the *y* in this case. It occurs in the sur. 75: 40 (أَنْ يُحْيِيَ ٱلْمَوْتَى) "The power to give life to the death". It is also mentioned with one *y*, i.e. أَنْ يُحْيِ by Ibn Ǧinnī, *Ḫaṣā'iṣ I*, 306, and is the reading of Ṭalḥa b. Sulaimān and al-Faiḍ b. Ġazwān (cf. the notes in ibid). It can be noted that no assimilation of the yā's is carried out as well in the active participle, e.g. رَأَيْتُ مُحْيِياً "I saw a quickener". Ibn Masʿūd refers to a case in which the last *y* is dropped by some in the perfect of the 3rd person of the masc. pl., i.e. حَيُوا underlyingly حَيِيُوا. This elision of the *y* brings forth the statement that it is not necessary for the structure. Hence the resulting form is حَيُوا in which the *y* becomes then vowelled by a ḍamma, i.e. حَيُوا for the sake of the *ū* of the pl. (cf. Sībawaihi, *II*, 431, Ibn Manẓūr, *II*, 1080). حَيُوا occurs in the following verse said by an anonymous poet cited by Sībawaihi, *II*, 431, Ibn Yaʿīš, *X*, 116, Ibn Manẓūr, *II*, 1080, Howell, *IV*, fasc. I, 1630:

"وَكُنَّا حَسِبْنَاهُمْ فَوَارِسَ كَهْمَسٍ حَيُوا بَعْدَمَا مَاتُوا مِنَ ٱلدَّهْرِ أَعْصُرَا".

"And we have accounted them to be horsemen of Kahmas [a man from Tamīm celebrated for horsemanship and valour], who after they had died, lived through ages of time".

Some however prefer to assimilate both the yā's of the base form حَيِيُوا and say حَيُّوا (cf. Ibn Manẓūr, *II*, 1080). A parallel case to حَيُوا is عَيُوا which occurs in the following verse said by ʿAbīd b. al-Abraṣ in ʿAbīd, *Dīwān* 126, cited by Sībawaihi, *II*, 431, Ibn Ǧinnī, *Munṣif II*, 191, Ibn al-Sarrāǧ, *Uṣūl III*, 248, Muʾaddib, *Taṣrīf* 337, Zamaḫšarī, 187, Ibn ʿAqīl, *II*, 588 in the notes, Ibn Manẓūr, *II*, 1080, Howell, *IV*, fasc. I, 1628:

"عَيُوا بِأَمْرِهِمْ كَمَا عَيَتْ بِبَيْضَتِهَا ٱلنَّعَامَهْ".

"They boggled over their buisness, as the ostrich boggled over her egg".

Another version of this verse is said with ٱلْحَمَامَهْ instead of ٱلنَّعَامَهْ.

In Ethiopic no contraction occurs in the groundform of the triliteral in the perfect of the 3rd person of the masc. sing., e.g. ሐይወ *ḥáywa* "to live", በከየ *bakáya* "to weep". The only case of contraction is in ሀሎ *hallō* "he was" for ሀለወ *halláwa* that corresponds to Form II in Arabic (for a study see Wright, *Comparative Grammar* 255). In Syriac, a contraction occurs in the imperfect of ܚܝܐ "to live" into ܢܚܐ for ܢܚܝܐ, but this is not the case in Mandaean ניהייא (cf. ibid, 265).

(181) The elision of the *l* in ظَلْتَ underlyingly ظَلِلْتَ is mentioned in (210). ظَلِلْتُ offers a sequence of two identical consonants of which the 1st consonant is vowelled and the 2nd is vowelless, such which prevents the assimilation. The elision of one of the lāms is possible however resulting in ظَلْتَ or ظِلْتَ (cf. Sībawaihi, *II,* 446, Ibn Mālik, *La Alfīya* 222, Ibn ʿAqīl, *II,* 584, Vollers, *Volkssprache* 132, Wright, *II,* 69, Howell, *IV,* fasc. II, 1836 sqq., de Sacy, *I,* 228, and Wright, *Comparative Grammar* who takes as well up some corresponding cases in some the other Semitic languages). In the dialectal variant of the Banū ʿĀmir, the 2nd radical of ظَلِلْتُ is elided, and the fatḥa which is the vowelling of the 1st radical remains unchanged, namely ظَلْتُ, whereas in the dialect of the Ḥiǧāzīs the 2nd radical is elided after that its kasra is shifted to the 1st radical, namely ظِلْتُ (cf. ʿAbd al-Ḥamīd, *Taṣrīf* 611, Talmon, *ʿAyn* 184). Concerning the variant ظَلْتُ, Sībawaihi, *II,* 446 notes that they compared it to لَسْتُ "I am not", and concerning the variant ظِلْتُ, he writes that they elided [the *l]* in it and shifted the vowel to the 1st radical, as they said خِفْتُ "I was afraid" [underlyingly خَوِفْتُ]. The alleviated form ظَلْتَ occurs in the sur. 20: 97 (الَّذي ظَلْتَ عَلَيْهِ عاكِفاً) "Of whom thou hast become a devoted worshipper", which can be read with the form ظِلْتَ as well in the dialectal variant of the Ḥiǧāzīs (cf. Baiḍāwī, *Anwār I,* 605), and in the sur. 56: 65 (فَظَلْتُمْ تَفَكَّهُونَ) "And ye would be left in wonderment", mentioned by Ibn Ḫālawaihi, *Qirāʾāt II,* 199, which can be read with the form فَظِلْتُمْ (cf. Baiḍāwī, *Anwār II,* 309). ظِلْتُ or ظَلْتُ can occur in the following verse said by ʿUmar b. Abī Rabīʿa al-Maḫzūmi, cited by ʿAbd al-Ḥamīd, *Taṣrīf* 611 in the note:

"ظَلْتُ فيهَا ذَاتَ يَوْمَ وَاقفاً أسْأَلُ آلْمَنْزِلَ هَلْ فيه خَبَرْ؟".

"And this day I remained standing by it, asking the house if it had any news".

Both ظِلْتُ or ظَلْتُ with the elision of the *l* and مَلِلْتُ with its maintainance are combined in the following verse said by ʿUmar b. Abī Rabīʿa, cited by ʿAbd al-Ḥamīd, *Taṣrīf* 611 in the note:

"وَمَا مَلِلْتُ وَلَكِنْ زَادَ حُبُّكُمُ وَمَا ذَكَرْتُكِ إلاَّ ظَلْتُ كَالسَّدِرِ".

"I did not become weary but my love for you has increased. Whenever I think of you I become as the possessed".

(182) The base form of تَقَضَّى in تَقَضَّى البَازِي is تَقَضَّضَ in which the last *ḍ* is changed into a *y,* i.e. تَقَضَّى (for discussions see (170); it is also mentioned in (352)). It can be noted that تَقَضَّضَ is underlyingly تَقَضْضَضَ, in which the 1st vowelless *ḍ* is assimilated to the 2nd vowelled one. No assimilation of the 2nd *ḍ* to the 3rd one is possible as this would cancel the formation تَفَعَّلَ, as well as by principle the 3rd radical of the perfect becomes vowelless when the suffixed vowelled agent pronouns are suffixed to it, i.e. تَقَضَّضْتُ "/1st sing.", تَقَضَّضْتَ "/2nd masc. sing.", تَقَضَّضْتِ "/2nd fem. sing.", تَقَضَّضْنَا "/1st pl.", تَقَضَّضْتُمْ "/2nd masc. pl.", تَقَضَّضْتُنَّ "/2nd fem. pl.", etc., and by being vowelless prevents the assimilation to it, as the condition of the assimilation is that the 2nd of two identical consonants should be vowelled.

(183) The base form of the imperative قِرْنَ (for a study see Ibn Mālik, *La Alfīya* 222, Ibn ʿAqīl, *II,* 584-585, Ibn Manẓūr, *V,* 3579, Lane, *II,* 2499, Howell, *IV,* fasc. II, 1839 sqq., de Sacy, *I,* 229, Penrice, *Dictionary* 116) of the 2nd person of the fem. pl. is اِقْرِرْنَ, from the root قرر with 2nd and 3rd radical *r* (cf. Ibn Manẓūr, *V,* 3578). In it the 2nd *r* is vowelless due to the suffixation of the *-na* marker of the fem. pl., and by being so prevents the assimilation. اِقْرِرْنَ is formed according to اِضْرِبْنَ "hit! 2nd person of the fem. pl. (imperative)", which is of the conjugation فَعَلَ يَفْعِلُ. قِرْنَ occurs for the sake of alleviation with the elision of the 1st *r* of اِقْرِرْنَ after that its kasra is shifted to the *q* and its hamza of the imperative is elided. قَرْنَ is another dialectal variant, and its base form is then اِقْرَرْنَ. وَقَرْنَ instead of وَقِرْنَ in the sur. 33: 33 (وَقَرْنَ فِي بُيُوتِكُنَّ) occurs, which is the reading of Nāfiʿ and ʿĀṣim (cf. Ibn Ḥālawaihi, *Qirā'āt II,* 199, Ibn ʿAqīl, *II,* 585). The elision of the 2nd radical after shifting its vowel to the 1st radical is carried out as well in the 3rd person of the fem. pl. of the imperfect يَقْرِرْنَ formed according to يَفْعِلْنَ resulting in يَقِرْنَ.

(184) The 2nd *d* is vowelless in the imperative of the 2nd person of the masc. sing. أُمْدُدْ on account that the sukūn is a marker of the imperative in this form. The sukūn is stated by Ibn Masʿūd as عارض "accidental" here. On the one hand it is possible to consider the sukūn, which is the marker of the imperative, as accidental when adopting the Kufans' theory, who themselves regard the undeclinable imperative underlyingly as a declinable imperfect that is put in the jussive mood by the "virtual" *li–* of command (for discussions concerning this question see (48), (119), (120)). This means that أُمْدُدْ is underlyingly لِتَمْدُدْ according to the Kufans. On the other hand, the sukūn is considered as accidental if in a certain sentence أُمْدُدْ precedes a word in which the 1st consonant is vowelless, as the article *l–* with *waṣla* underlyingly *al-,* prefixed to a noun, as in this case the sukūn must be replaced by a kasra or ḍamma, which is a vowel of juncture (for discussions concerning the vowel of juncture see (270), (288), (377)), to avoid the cluster of two vowelless consonants. An example is أُمْدُدُ ٱلْيَدَ which is said instead of أُمْدُدْ ٱلْيَدَ "extend the hand". As the 2nd consonant of two identical consonants is accidentally vowelless, both the dissolution, i.e. أُمْدُدْ, and the assimilation, i.e. مُدَّ, مُدِّ and مُدُّ are possible (for them see Wright, *II,* 70). Those who dissolve are the Ḥiǧāzīs, whereas those who assimilate are the people of Tamīm (cf. Wright, *II,* 70 in the notes). Concerning the dissolution that is usual in the Ḥiǧāzī dialect, Dunqūz, *Šarḥ* fol. 57b. l.1 remarks:

"فلا يُدغم وهو لغة الحجازيين وهو الأقرب الى القياس ... نحو أُمْدُدْ بفكّ الإدغام

أمراً للمخاطب".

"No assimilation is carried out in it, which is the dialectal variant of the Ḥiǧāzīs, and it is the closest to the analogy... e.g. اُمْدُدْ with the dissolution in the imperative of the 2nd person of the masc. sing.".

Some examples referring to Tamīm's readings with the assimilation that is carried out in some verbs are تَمَسَّكُمْ said instead of تَمْسَسْكُمْ in the sur. 3: 120 (إِن تَمْسَسْكُمْ حَسَنَةٌ) "If aught that is good befalls you", يَحِلَّ instead of يَحْلِلْ in the sur. 20: 81 (وَمَن يَحْلِلْ عَلَيْهِ غَضَبِي) "And those on whom descends My Wrath" and تَمُنَّ instead of تَمْنُنْ in the sur. 74: 6 (وَلَا تَمْنُن تَسْتَكْثِرُ) "Nor expect, in giving, any increase (for thyself!)" (cf. Ṣubḥī, Fiqh 81). The Quraišīs read these examples with the dissolution (cf. ibid).

(185) It is impossible in the imperative of the 2nd person of the masc. sing. of فَرَّ to say فُرُّ with the ḍamma, because the ḍamma is disliked after the kasra of the 1st radical. It is however accepted in the imperative of the 2nd person of the masc. sing. of مَدَّ to say مُدُّ (mentioned in (184)) in which the ḍamma is given to the d on the analogy of the ḍamma of the 1st radical m. فَرَّ and فِرِّ are possible to be said with the fatḥa and the kasra of the r respectively (cf. de Sacy, I, 229, Wright, Comparative Grammar 230 who takes up as well some corresponding cases in some of the other Semitic languages), because the combination of the fatḥa following a kasra and a kasra following a kasra in them is not disliked. The assimilation is not carried out in the 2nd person of the fem. pl. of the imperative of مَدَّ which is اُمْدُدْنَ [and not مُدَّنَ] because the 2nd of two identical consonants, namely the d, is necessarily vowelless on account of the suffixation of the agent pronoun of the 2nd person that marks the fem. pl., the -na. It is this vowellessness that prevents the assimilation (cf. Daqr, Muʿǧam 354). The sukūn in اُمْدُدْنَ is stated as لازم "obligatory" and not accidental in comparison to the adventitious sukūn of اُمْدُدْ (for it see (184)).

(186) The paradigm of مَدَّ in the perfect, passive, is the following:

	sing.	dual	pl.
1st	مُدِدْتُ		مُدِدْنَا
2nd masc.	مُدِدْتَ	مُدِدْتُمَا	مُدِدْتُمْ
2nd fem.	مُدِدْتِ	مُدِدْتُمَا	مُدِدْتُنَّ
3rd masc.	مُدَّ	مُدَّا	مُدُّوا
3rd fem.	مُدَّتْ	مُدَّتَا	مُدِدْنَ

Its imperfect in the indicative, passive, is the following:

	sing.	dual	pl.
1st	أُمَدُّ		نُمَدُّ
2nd masc.	تُمَدُّ	تُمَدَّانِ	تُمَدُّونَ

2nd fem.	تُمَدِّينَ	تُمَدَّانِ	تُمْدَدْنَ
3rd masc.	يُمَدُّ	يُمَدَّانِ	يُمَدُّونَ
3rd fem.	تُمَدُّ	تُمَدَّانِ	يُمْدَدْنَ

Its imperfect in the subjunctive, passive, is the following:

	sing.	dual	pl.
1st	أُمَدَّ		نُمَدَّ
2nd masc.	تُمَدَّ	تُمَدَّا	تُمَدُّوا
2nd fem.	تُمَدَّاتُمَدِّي	تُمْدَدْنَ	
3rd masc.	يُمَدَّ	يُمَدَّا	يُمَدُّوا
3rd fem.	تُمَدَّ	تُمَدَّا	يُمْدَدْنَ

Its imperfect in the jussive, passive, is the following:

	sing.	dual	pl.
1st	أُمْدَدْ		نُمْدَدْ
2nd masc.	تُمْدَدْ	تُمَدَّا	تُمَدُّوا
2nd fem.	تُمَدِّي	تُمَدَّا	تُمْدَدْنَ
3rd masc.	يُمْدَدْ	يُمَدَّا	يُمَدُّوا
3rd fem.	تُمْدَدْ	تُمَدَّا	يُمْدَدْنَ

(187) The infixed *t* of Form VIII is either assimilated to or is assimilated by one of the fourteen consonants (for a study of the consonants' points of articulation and characters see (188)) preceding it which is the 1st radical (for a general study of this particular assimilation see Zamaḫšarī, 195-196, Wright, *II,* 66-67, Howell, *IV,* fasc. II, 1803 sqq.). These consonants are: 1– the hamza, 2– *t,* 3– *ṯ,* 4– *d,* 5– *ḏ,* 6– *z,* 7– *s,* 8– *š,* 9– *ṣ,* 10– *ḍ,* 11– *ṭ,* 12– *ẓ,* 13– *w* and 14– *y.* The verbs that are presented refer to each of these cases, and thus begin with verbs with 1st radical hamza and end up with verbs with 1st radical *y.* For a study of such forms that occur in some of the Semitic languages see Wright, *Comparative Grammar* 209-213.

b) The 1st radical hamza is assimilated to the infixed *t* of Form VIII. An example is اتَّخَذَ underlyingly اِئْتَخَذَ from أَخَذَ "to take", a verb with 1st hamza radical. The process that leads to this assimilation is not direct. اِئْتَخَذَ becomes at first اِيتَخَذَ with the substitution of the *y* for the hamza because of the influence of the kasra preceding it, then اِتْتَخَذَ with the substitution of the *t* for the *y,* and then the infixed *t* is assimilated to the *t,* so that it becomes اِتَّخَذَ. This change of the *y* which is not the underlying radical from the form اِيتَخَذَ, into the *t* resulting in اِتْتَخَذَ before that the tā'ˀs are assimilated, is considered as anomalous because the *y* is already substituted for the hamza which is the radical of the form اِئْتَخَذَ. For this reason some grammarians prefer to believe that Form VIII اِتَّخَذَ is formed from تَخِذَ and not from أَخَذَ (cf. 202). Concerning it

Dunqūz, *Šarḥ* fol. 58a ll.8-11 writes:

"وهـو أنَّ ادغام اتَّخَذَ شاذ اذا كان من الأَخْذ لأنَّ أصـله ائتَخَذَ قُلبت الهمزة ياء لـسكونها وانكسار ما قبلها ثمّ قُلبت الياء تاءً فأُدغـمت الـتاء في الـتاء على غـير القـياس لأنَّ الـياء المـبدَلَة لا تُقلـب تاء بل الـياء التي يجـوز أن تُقلب تاء قياساً إنّما هي الياء الأصليّة وهنا ليست الياء أصليّة".

> "It is so that the assimilation that is carried out in اتَّخَذَ is anomalous if it is from [the *maṣdar* with 1st hamza radical] الأَخْذُ "the taking", because its base form is ائتَخَذَ. The hamza in it is changed into a *y* [i.e. ايتَخَذَ] on account of its vowellessness and of the influence of the kasra preceding it, then the *y* is changed into a *t* [i.e. اتْتَخَذَ], and then the *t* is assimilated to the *t* [i.e. اتَّخَذَ], such which is not according to the analogy,—because the *y* which has already been changed from another consonant cannot be changed into a *t*, as it is rather so that the *y* that can be changed into a *t* according to the analogy should be a radical *y*, and the *y* is not a radical here—".

Compare with it اتَّزَرَ discussed in (200).

c) The 1st radical *t* is assimilated to the infixed *t* of Form VIII. The example is اتَّجَرَ underlyingly اتْتَجَرَ.

The infixed *t* of Form VIII is assimilated to the 1st radical *ṯ*. The example is اثَّارَ underlyingly اثْتَارَ. The 1st radical *ṯ* can possibly be assimilated to the infixed *t* of Form VIII, namely اتَّارَ with the doubled *t*. A similar case to اثَّارَ is اثَّرَدَ "to crumble" which can also be said اتَّرَدَ with the *t*.

(188) سَتَشْحَثُكَ خَصَفَةٌ comprehend the ten voiceless consonants (cf. Zamaḫšarī, 189, Howell, *IV*, fasc. II, 1725, (188 b)). Sībawaihi, *II*, 453 presents them in this order: the *h, ḥ, ḫ, k, š, s, t, ṣ, ṯ* and *f*. Ibn Masʿūd does not discuss fully the consonants and their points of articulation. This is why it can be appropriate to present them here. In his chapter باب الإدْغام "the chapter concerning the assimilation", Sībawaihi, *II*, 452 sqq. treats in the first section the subject of phonetics. He enumerates p. 453 the twenty-nine base consonants and specifies that they have sixteen points of articulation with the intention of explaining the phenomenon of assimilation in the next chapter. According to him:

1-3: The hamza, *h* and *ā* are from أقْصى الحلق "the farthest part of the throat", the ʿ and *ḥ* from أوسط الحلق "the middle of the throat" and the *ġ* and *ḫ* from أدْنى الحلق "the nearest part of the throat".

4-5: The *q* is from أقْصى اللسان وما فوقه من الحنك الأعلى "the farthest part of the tongue, and the part of the upper palate above it".

The *k* is أسْفل من موضع القاف من اللسان قليلاً وممّا يليه من الحنك الأعلى "lower than the *q* from the next parts of the tongue and palate towards the upper palate".

6– The *ǧ*, *š* and *y* are from وسط اللسان بينه وبين وسط الحنك الأعلى "the middle of the tongue, and from the middle part of the upper palate".

7– The ḍ is from بَيْنَ أَوَّلَ حافةِ اللسانِ وما يليه من الأضراسِ "the 1st part of the side of the tongue, and the molars below (on the left or right side)".

8– The l is from حافةِ اللسانِ مِن أدْناها الى منتهى طَرَفِ اللسانِ ما بينها وبين ما يليها من الحَنَكِ الأعلى وما فُوَيْقَ الضاحِكِ والنابِ والرباعيَةِ والثَنِيَةِ "between the nearest part of the side of the tongue, to the end of its tip, and the part of the upper palate next to it, a little above the premolar, canine, lateral incisor, and central incisor".

9-10-The n is from طَرَفِ اللسانِ بينه وبين ما فُوَيْقَ الثَنايا "what is between the tip of the tongue and the part (of the palate) a little above the central incisors".

The r is from مخرجِ النونِ غيرَ أنَه أدْخَلُ في ظهر اللسانِ قليلاً لانحرافه الى اللامِ "the point of articulation of the n except that it is farther in on the back of the tongue because it turns towards the point of articulation of the l".

11– The ṭ, d and t are from بين طَرَفِ اللسانِ واصولِ الثنايا "the tip of the tongue and the roots of the two upper central incisors".

12– The ṣ, z and s are from بين طَرَفِ اللسانِ وفُوَيْقِ الثنايا "the part which is between the tip of the tongue and the tops of the two upper central incisors".

13– the ẓ, ḏ and ṯ are from بين طَرَفِ اللسانِ وأطْرافِ الثنايا "the tip of the tongue and the edges of the two upper central incisors".

14– The f is from باطِنِ الشفةِ السُفْلى وأطْرافِ الثنايا العُلَى "the inside of the lower lip and the edges of the two upper central incisors".

15– The b, m and w are from بين الشَفَتَيْنِ "what is between the lips".

16– The single n is from الخَياشِيمِ "the upper part of the nose".

According to Western grammars, the ā, hamza and h are laryngals, the ḥ and ʿ are pharyngals, the ḫ and ġ are velars, the k and q are post-palatals, the š ǧ and y are pre-palatals, the t, d, ṭ, ḍ, and r are alveolars, the s, z, n, ṣ and l are dentals, the ṯ, ḏ and ẓ are interdentals and the f, b, w and m are labials (cf. Versteegh, *Language* 20).

b) As for their characters the Arabic consonants of the alphabet are divided between:

1– المهموسة "voiceless, low, soft, whispered", which are the ten consonants of سَتَشْحَثُكَ خَصْفَة (mentioned above). They are weak in the stress laid upon them so that they do not impede النفس "the breath" that therefore runs on with them.

2– المجهورة "voiced, loud, clear, sonorous" (mentioned as well by Ibn Masʿūd), which are the remaining nineteen consonant comprised in ظلُّ قَوَ رَبَضٍ إذْ غَزَا جُنْدٌ مُطيعٌ "the shade of Qaww was a shelter, when an obediant host made a raid" (cf. Howell, IV, fasc. II, 1726). They prevent the breath from running on with them. Sībawaihi, *II*, 453 presents them in this order: the ʾ, ā, ʿ, ġ, q, ǧ, y, ḍ, l, n, r, ṭ, d, z, ẓ, ḏ, b, m and w.

The two categories المهموسة and المجهورة can be compared to the categories voiceless and voiced. Some discussions have been raised concerning this comparison (see Wallin, *Laute* (1855) 1-69, (1858) 599-675, Vollers, *System* 130-154, Bravmann, *Materialien*, Gairdner, *Phoneticians* 252-275, Garbell, *Remarks* 303-337, Blanc, *Fronting* 12-16, Fleisch, *Études* 225-285, *Maġhūra* 193-210, *Traité I*, 219-222, Roman, *Étude I*, 73-86).

3– الشديدة "rigid" which are the eight consonants combined in أجَدْتَ طَبَقَكَ "you have made your dish excellent", whose current of sound is confined in their point of articulation, upon their vowellessness.

4– الرِّخْوَةُ "lax" which are the thirteen consonants: the *h, ḥ, ġ, ḫ, š, ṣ, ḍ, z, s, ẓ, ṯ, ḏ* and *f,* whose current of sound is not confined upon their vowellessness.

5– بين الشديدة والرِّخْوَة "intermediate" which are the eight consonants combined in لِمَ يَرُوعُنَ "why does he frighten us?" (cf. Fleischer, *Beiträge* 109).

6– المُطْبَقَة "covered" (cf. (192), (193)), which are the four consonants: the *ṣ, ḍ, ṭ* and *ẓ,* whose point of articulation is covered by the upper palate.

7– المُنْفَتِحَة "open" which are the consonants that are the opposite of the covered.

8– المُسْتَعْلِيَة "elevated" (cf. (192), (193)), which are the seven consonants: the four last-mentioned within المُطْبَقَة "covered" and the three with which there is no covering: the *ḫ, ġ* and *q,* which by articulating them, the tongue rises to the palate.

9– المُنْخَفِضَة "depressed" which are contrary to the elevated (cf. (192), (193)).

10– الذَّلَاقَة "liquid" which are collected in مُرْ بِنَفَلٍ "order [a distribution of] booty or spoil" (cf. Fleischer, *Beiträge* 101). They originate from the tip of the tongue and the lips.

11– المُصْمَتَة "muted" which are contrary to them, i.e. the twenty-three remaining consonants.

12– حُرُوفُ القَلْقَلَة "resonant" which are the five consonants combined in قَدْ طُبِجَ "it has been thumped", and are named so because of the loudness of their sound.

13– الصَّفِير "sibilant" which are the three consonants: the *ṣ, z* and *s* which make a whistling.

14– اللِّينَة "soft" which are the three weak consonants: the *ā, w* and *y* that are the weak consonants of softness susceptible to lengten the sound.

15– المُنْحَرِف "swerving" which is the *l,* because when one articulates it, the tongue swerves towards the interior of the palate.

16– المُكَرَّر "reiterated" which is the *r,* because when paused upon, the tongue falters on account of the reiteration in it.

17– الهاوِي "airy" which is the *ā,* of which the point of articulation expands more strongly to the air of the sound than the point of articulation of the *w* and the *y.*

18– المَهْتُوت "gabbled", which is the *t* from their saying رَجُلٌ مِهْتٌ "a man copious in speech". For a detailed study see Sībawaihi, *II,* 452 sqq., Zamaḫšarī, 188-190, *Kaššāf I,* 100 sqq., Howell, *IV,* fasc. II, 1702-1738, Troupeau, *Commentaire* 168-182. For a study of the main divergences between Sībawaihi's and Mubarrad's section dealing with phonation and the manner of articulating sounds see Danecki, *Mubarrad* 91-99. Furthermore, according to Zamaḫšarī, 190, al-Ḫalīl, the author of the *Kitāb al-ʿayn* names the ʿ, *ḥ, h, ġ* and *ḫ* for حَلْقِيَّة "guttural", the *q* and *k* for لَهَوِيَّتَان "uvular", the *ǧ, š* and *ḍ* for شَجْرِيَّة "orificial", the *ṣ, s* and *z* for أَسَلِيَّة "apical", the *ṭ, d* and *t* for نِطْعِيَّة "ante-palatal", the *ẓ, ḏ* and *ṯ* for لِثَوِيَّة "gingival", the *r, l* and *n* for ذَوْلَقِيَّة "tippy", the *w, f, b* and *m* for شَفَوِيَّة "labial", and the weak consonants of prolongation and softness for جُوف "hollow" (for a study see Zamaḫšarī, 190-191, Howell, *IV,* fasc. II, 1702-1739, Fleisch, *Traité I,* 212-213, Roman, *Étude I,* 47-274, Versteegh, *Language* 87-88).

Ibn Manẓūr, *I,* 17-20 has discussed the consonants by referring to some Arab linguists in باب ألقاب الْحُرُوف وَطَبائعها وَخواصها "the section of the consonants' nominations, their characters and particularities". For a description of these consonants by Arab modern linguists see Ḥassān, *Uṣūl* 119-121, Bakkūš, *Taṣrif* 34-45; for the solar and lunar consonants see (176); for the augments see (106); for the consonants of substitution see (312).

(189) The infixed *t* of Form VIII is assimilated to the 1st radical *d* preceding it. ادّانَ is underlyingly ادْتانَ (cf. Zamaḫšarī, 176, Ibn ʿAqīl, *II,* 582, Lane, *I,* 942-943) from دَيَنَ "to profess a religion", before that the assimilation is carried out in it. The *t* is among the voiceless consonants (for them see (188), (188 b)) and the *d* is among the voiced consonants (for them see (188 b)), which implies a distance between them both concerning their character. The voiced consonants are stronger than the voiceless consonants, which is the reason why it is the voiceless *t* that is assimilated to the voiced *d* (cf. Bakkūš, *Taṣrīf* 66), and not vice versa. Furthermore, both the *t* and the *d* are alveolars (cf. (188)), which implies a closeness of both their points of articulation. This is a reason more why the *t* is changed into the *d,* and then one *d* is assimilated to the other.

(190) The infixed *t* of Form VIII is assimilated to the *ḏ* preceding it. In اذّكَرَ, the infixed *t* of Form VIII of the base form اذْتَكَرَ is assimilated to the *ḏ* preceding it. The *t* is among the voiceless consonants and the *ḏ* is among the voiced consonants, which implies a distance between them both concerning their character. The voiced consonants are stronger than the voiceless consonants which is the reason why the voiceless *t* is assimilated to the voiced *ḏ* (cf. Bakkūš, *Taṣrīf* 66). Two other variants than اذّكر exist, namely اذْدَكَرَ with the *d* following the *ḏ* and ادّكَرَ with the doubling of the *d* (cf. Ibn Ǧinnī, *Munṣif II,* 331, Zamaḫšarī, 195, Ibn ʿAqīl, *II,* 582, de Sacy, *I,* 222, Vollers, *Volkssprache* 117-118, Vernier, *I,* 344-345, Wright, *II,* 66, Fleischer, *Beiträge II,* 306, ʿAbd al-Tawwāb, *Taṭawwur* 29). In both ادّكَرَ and اذْدَكَرَ, the process is more complicated. The *t* of the base form in اذْتَكَرَ is changed into the *d* in both of them, i.e. اذْدَكَرَ, because the *t* is among the voiceless consonants (for them see (188), (188 b)) and the *ḏ* is among the voiced consonants (for them see (188 b)), which implies a distance between them both in character. However as the *t* and the *d* are alveolars (for them see (188)), the *t* is changed into the *d,* as voiced consonants are stronger than voiceless consonants. In ادّكَرَ one *d* is assimilated to the other. In اذْدَكَرَ the dissolution is made possible as both the *d* and the *ḏ* are different consonants. It can as well be borne in mind that the *d* and the *ḏ* are among the voiced consonants, which implies a similarity in both their character. This explains why it is easy to substitute one for the other, i.e. ادّكر and اذّكر. The Form V يَذَّكَّرُ with the assimilation of the *t* to the *ḏ* occurs in the sur. 80: 3-4 (وَمَا يُدْرِيكَ لَعَلَّهُ يَزَّكَّى أَوْ يَذَّكَّرُ فَتَنْفَعَهُ ٱلذِّكْرَى) "But what could tell thee but that perchance he might grow (in spiritual understanding)? Or that he might receive admonition, and the teaching might profit him?" and the sur. 2: 269 (وَمَا يَذَّكَّرُ إِلَّا أُولُوا ٱلْأَلْبَابِ) "But none will grasp the Message but men of understanding" (mentioned also in (207)). It can be added that the sur. 54: 15 with the noun مُدَّكِر occurring in it (فَهَلْ مِنْ مُدَّكِرٍ) "Is there any that will receive admonition?" has been anomalously read (cf. Howell, *IV*, fasc. II, 1816).

(191) The infixed *t* of Form VIII is assimilated to the *z* preceding it. The base form of ازَانَ is ازْتانَ (cf. Zamaḫšarī, 176, 196, Wright, *II*, 66, Lane, *I*, 1279, my notes (174), (374)) before the assimilation. It can as well resemble اذْدَكَر underlyingly اذْتَكَر (for it see (190)) in the change of the *t* into the *d*, as the *t* in ازْتانَ can be changed into a *d* as well, namely ازْدَانَ. It is only the *d* that can be changed into the *z* resulting in ازَانَ and not vice versa resulting in ادَانَ, because in spite of the similarity of character of both these consonants in being among the voiced consonants (for them see (188 b)) which permitted the change of one into another, the *z* is among the sibilant consonants (for them see (188 b)), which are considered as stronger in the sound than the *d*. Another reason why the *z* is not changed into the *d* and then assimilated to it resulting in ادَانَ, is to avoid mixing it up with this verb (for ادَانَ see (189)). It can be noted that the form وَازَّيَنَتْ in the sur. 10: 24 (حَتَّى إِذَا أَخَذَتِ ٱلْأَرْضُ زُخْرُفَهَا وَازَّيَنَتْ) "Till the earth is clad with its golden ornaments and is decked out (in beauty)" (cf. also (207)) does not point to Form VIII, but to Form V in which the infixed *t* in وَازَّيَنَتْ underlyingly وَتَزَيَنَتْ is assimilated to the *z* after that the hamza has been imported by inception. However, at the interior of the word, as in this case after the *w* of the conjunction, the hamza is not more needed and ازَّيَنَتْ became وَازَّيَنَتْ with *waṣla*.

(192) The infixed *t* of Form VIII is assimilated to the *s* preceding it. The base form of اسَّمَعَ is اسْتَمَعَ (cf. Sībawaihi, *II*, 472, Zamaḫšarī, 196, de Sacy, *I*, 220, Wright, *II*, 66, my notes (174)) before the assimilation. Both the *t* and the *s* are similar in character in being among the voiceless consonants (for these consonants see (188), (188 b)) and originate from close points of articulation, as the *t* is from the tip of the tongue and the roots of the two upper central incisors and is an alveolar, and the *s* is from the part which is between the tip of the tongue and the tops of the two upper central incisors and is a dental (for the consonants see (188)). The *s* is among the sibilant consonants (for them see (188 b)) that are strong in the sound, which is the reason why it could not be changed into the *t* and then be assimilated to it, i.e. اتَّمَعَ. It can be noted that يَسْمَعُ has been anomalously read by some instead of يَسْتَمِعُ in the sur. 6: 25 i.e. (وَمِنْهُمْ مَنْ يَسْمَعُ إِلَيْكَ) "Of them there are some who (pretend to) listen to thee". Furthermore the form يَسَّمَّعُونَ of the sur. 37: 8 (لَا يَسَّمَّعُونَ إِلَى ٱلْمَلَإِ ٱلْأَعْلَىٰ) "(So) they should not strain their ears in the direction of the Exalted Assembly" is Form V يَتَسَمَّعُونَ underlyingly [and not Form VIII يَسْتَمِعُونَ], in which the *t* is assimilated to the *s*. Some read the sur. with Form I يَسْمَعُونَ instead for the sake of alleviation (cf. Ibn Manẓūr, *III*, 2095). Both suras are mentioned in (207).

b) The infixed *t* of Form VIII is assimilated to the *š* preceding it. The base form of اشَّبَهَ is اشْتَبَهَ before the assimilation.

c) The infixed *t* of Form VIII is assimilated to the *ṣ* preceding it. The base form of اصَّبَرَ is

اصْتَبَرَ before the assimilation. Another possibility is the substitution of the *ṭ* for the *t*, i.e. اصْطَبَرَ instead of اصْتَبَرَ (cf. Ibn Ǧinnī, *Munṣif II*, 326-328, Zamaḫšarī, 176, Wright, *II*, 67, Vernier, *I*, 345, Bohas, *Étude* 238-239, my notes (174), (374)). It can be noted that both the *ṣ* and the *t* have different characters: the *ṣ* is among المُسْتَعْلِيَةُ "the elevated consonants" and the *t* is among المُنْخَفِضَةُ "the depressed consonants", and the *t* is among الشديدة "the rigid consonants" and the *ṣ* is among الرِّخْوَةُ "the lax consonants" (for the consonants's characters see (188 b)). Both the *t* and the *ṭ* pertain however to close points of articulation as they both originate from the tip of the tongue and the roots of the two upper central incisors, and are alveolars (for the points of articulation see (188)), which is the reason why the *t* is changed into the *ṭ*, i.e. اصْطَبَرَ.

(193) The consonants of خغق ضظ صط (cf. Zamaḫšarī, 190) are known as المُسْتَعْلِيَةُ "elevated". They comprehend four consonants that are characterized as المُطْبَقَةُ "covered", namely the *ṣ*, *ṭ*, *ḍ* and *ẓ*, of which the point of articulation is covered by the upper palate, and three consonants with which there is no covering, namely the *ḫ*, *ġ* and *q*, which by articulating them, the tongue rises to the palate (for them see (188 b)). The *t* is among المُنْخَفِضَةُ "the depressed consonants" which are contrary to the elevated ones (for them see (188 b), Zamaḫšarī, 190, Howell, *IV*, fasc. II, 1729-1731).

(194) ستّ is underlyingly سُدْسٌ formed according to the pattern فُعْلٌ. Another example on this pattern is نُذْرٌ which occurs in the sur. 54: 16 (فَكَيْفَ كَانَ عَذَابِي وَنُذُرِ) "But how (terrible) was my Penalty and my Warning?". The *d* and the *s* of the base form سُدْسٌ are each substituted by the *t*, i.e. سُتْتٌ, and then one *t* is assimilated to the other (cf. Sībawaihi, *II*, 479, Ibn Ǧinnī, *Munṣif II*, 331, Zamaḫšarī, 175, 196, Ibn Manẓūr, *III*, 1973, Brockelmann, *Grundriss* 178, Talmon, *ʿAyn* 142, my notes (329), (333)). If one is to analyze the relations between the *s*, the *d* and the *t* in order to understand the process of substitution that leads to the assimilation, the *s* is among the voiceless consonants whereas the *d* is among the voiced consonants and the *s* is among the lax consonants whereas the *d* is among the rigid consonants (for the characters of the consonants see (188 b)). So in order to eliminate these differences of character betwen them, the *s* is changed into the *t* as both are akin in being among the voiceless consonants and the *d* is changed into the *t* because of the proximity of both their points of articulation as they both originate from the tip of the tongue and the roots of the two upper central incisors, and are alveolars (for the consonants' points of articulation see (188)). The change of the *d* into the *t* is carried out in spite of the difference of both their characters, as the *d* is among the voiced consonants and the *t* is among the voiceless consonants (cf. (188 b)), and then one *t* is assimilated to the other so that it became سِتٌّ. The similarity referred to by Ibn Masʿūd between اصْطَبَرَ (cf. (192 c)) and سِتٌّ concerns two consonants having different characters of which one is changed into the other because they originate from close points of articulation. In اصْطَبَرَ the *t* of the base form اصْتَبَرَ is changed into the *ṭ* in spite of both these consonants' different characters (for discussions see (192 c)), on account that both the *t* and the *ṭ* are alveolars, and in سُدْسٌ the *d* is changed into the *ṭ*, in spite of both these consonants' different characters, on account that both the *d* and the *ṭ* are alveolars as well. This substitution of the *t* for both the *d* and the *s* in سُدُسٌ is considered as rare by Sībawaihi, *II*, 341. An interesting example with سِتّ in it is presented by Lane, *I*, 1304, namely يَا سِتَّ جِهَاتِي "O thou who occupiest the six places in relation to me; or, who art above me, below me, before me, behind me; on my right, and on my left". The base form سُدُسٌ formed according to فُعُلٌ occurs anomalously in the following verse said by Manṣūr b. Misǧāḥ al-Ḍabbī, cited by Ibn Manẓūr, *III*, 1973, Howell, *I*, fasc. III, 962:

"فَطَافَ كَمَا طَافَ ٱلْمُصَدِّقُ وَسْطَهَا   يُخَيَّرُ مِنْهَا فِي ٱلْبَوَازِلِ وَٱلسُّدُسِ".

"Then he went round, as the collector of the poor-rate goes round, in their midst, being allowed to choose from them among the nine-year-old and the six-year-old [camels]".

For a comparative study of the word in some of the other Semitic languages see Cantineau, *Six* 72-73; for a bibliography concerning its etymology see Rundgren, *Bildungen* 145 note 1, for a discussion concerning the Syriac form *štā* "six" and the Hebrew form *štayim* "two", see Bravmann, *Studies* 158.

(195) The infixed *t* is assimilated to the *ḍ* preceding it. اضَّرَبَ is underlyingly اضْتَرَبَ, before the assimilation. The infixed *t* of the base form اضْتَرَبَ can as well be changed into the *ṭ*, i.e. اضْطَرَبَ (cf. Zamaḫšarī, 195, de Sacy, *I*, 222, Wright, *II*, 67, Vernier, *I*, 345, Bohas, *Étude* 238, my notes (174), (374)).

(196) The infixed *t* is assimilated to the *ṭ* preceding it. The base form of اطَّلَبَ is اطْتَلَبَ before the assimilation (cf. Zamaḫšarī, 195, Ibn Yaʿīš, *X*, 46, Wright, *II*, 67, my notes (374)). The reason of this substitution is that both the *t* and the *ṭ* originate from the tip of the tongue and the roots of the two upper central incisors (for the consonants see (188)).

(197) The infixed *t* is assimilated to the *ẓ* preceding it. The base form of اظَّلَمَ is اظْتَلَمَ. All three variants اظَّلَمَ, اطَّلَمَ and اظْطَلَمَ occur instead of the base form اظْتَلَمَ (cf. Sībawaihi, *II*, 472, Ibn Ǧinnī, *Sirr I*, 224, *de Flexione* 29, *Munṣif II*, 329, Zamaḫšarī, 195, Ibn Yaʿīš, *X*, 47, Wright, *II*, 67, Lane, *II*, 1921, Vernier, *I*, 345, Howell, *IV*, fasc. II, 1813, Vollers, *Volkssprache* 117-119). The *t* of اظْتَلَمَ is changed into the *ṭ* resulting in اظْطَلَمَ because of the proximity of both their points of articulation as they both originate from the tip of the tongue and the roots of the two upper central incisors, and are alveolars (for the consonants see (188)). Two possibilities are at hand: اظَّلَمَ that occurs with the change of the *ṭ* from اظْطَلَمَ into the *ẓ* and اطَّلَمَ with the change of the *ẓ* into the *ṭ*. This substitution of the *ṭ* for the *ẓ* and vice versa is carried out on account of both these consonants' common character in being among the emphatic consonants. Both Form I of the passive voice يُظْلَمُ and Form VIII of the active voice يَظْطَلِمُ occur in the following verse said by Zuhair b. Abī Sulmā al-Muzanī who is praising Harim b. Sinān in Zuhair, *Šiʿr* 104, cited by Sībawaihi, *II*, 472, Ibn Ǧinnī, *Sirr I*, 219, Muʾaddib, *Taṣrīf* 170, Zamaḫšarī, 195, Afandī, *Tanzīl* 520, Ibn Yaʿīš, *X*, 47, *Mulūkī* 316, 319, 320, Howell, *IV*, fasc. II, 1813:

"هُوَ ٱلْجَوَادُ ٱلَّذِي يُعْطِيكَ نَائِلَهُ   عَفْواً وَيُظْلَمُ أَحْيَاناً فَيَظْطَلِمُ"،

"He is the magnanimous, who gives you his largesse spontaneously; and is wronged at times, and than puts up with that wrong".

All the three variations فَيَظَّلِمُ, فَيَطَّلِمُ or فَيَظْطَلِمُ as being the last word of the rime are cited in different works (see for references Fischer/Braünlich, *Šawāhid* 227).

(198) The 1st radical *w* is assimilated to the infixed *t* of Form VIII. The base form of اتَّعَدَ (cf. de Sacy, *I,* 240, Wright, *II,* 80-81, Lane, *II,* 2902) is اوْتَعَدَ from وَعَدَ "to promise". The *w* in اوْتَعَدَ is substituted by the *t* resulting in اتْتَعَدَ, and then an assimilation of one *t* to the other is carried out. The substitution of the *t* for the *w* is frequent (cf. (96), (247), (330), (331)), on account that the points of articulation of the *t* and the *w* are close to each other as the *t* is formed from the tip of the tongue and the roots of the two upper central incisors, and is an alveolar, and the *w* is formed between the lips, and is a labial (for the points of articulation see (188)). If the *w* of the perfect اوْتَعَدَ is not replaced by the *t,* it would have to be replaced by the *y* because of the influence of the kasra preceding it, i.e. ايتَعَدَ would be said instead of اتَّعَدَ, which would confuse the reader by making him believe that the verb is with 1st weak *y* radical, i.e. يَعَدَ. As well as the combination of the kasras in ايتَعَدَ,–if one is to assume that the *y* is formed of two kasras and that it is preceded by a kasra –, is regarded as heavy. Furthermore, this awkward variation of the weak 1st radical that could refer erroneously to a *y* radical in the perfect, i.e. ايتَعَدَ and to a *w* radical in the imperfect يُوْتَعَدُ, is unacceptable.

(199) The 1st radical *y* is assimilated to the infixed *t* of Form VIII. The base form of اتَّسَرَ (cf. Zamaḫšarī, 175, 178, de Sacy, *I,* 240, Wright, *II,* 80-81) is ايتَسَرَ from يَسَرَ "to be easy". The *y* in ايتَسَرَ is substituted by the *t* resulting in اتْتَسَرَ, and then an assimilation of one *t* to the other is carried out. The substitution of the *t* for the *y* is frequent (cf. (187 b), (200), (332)), on account that the points of articulation of the *t* and the *y* are close to each other as the *t* is formed from the tip of the tongue and the roots of the two upper central incisors and is an alveolar and the *y* is formed from the middle of the tongue and from the middle part of the upper palate and is a pre-palatal (for the consonants' points of articulation see (188)). This substitution is carried out to avoid the succession of the kasras if ايتَسَرَ is said. In this forbidden variant the *y* is counted as two kasras and is preceded by a kasra, which is regarded as a heavy combination (compare the case of ايتَعَدَ discussed in (198)). It can be noted as well that the heaviness would be extreme in the *maṣdar* if the form ايتِسَارٌ is said instead of the correct form اتِّسَارٌ, as it would imply a heavy succession of four kasras,–the *y* being counted as two kasras –, which is unacceptable.

(200) The base Form VIII of أَكَلَ "he ate", a verb with 1st hamza radical, is ائتَكَلَ with a vowelless 1st radical hamza that is then changed into a *y,* i.e. ايتَكَلَ (cf. Zamaḫšarī, 178, Ibn ʿAqīl, *II,* 581, Lane, *I,* 72) due to the influence of the kasra preceding it, and in this case there is no change that is carried out from the *y* into the *t* that would result in اِتَّكَلَ. The *y* is considered as unnecessary in it as it replaces a hamza which is indicated by the groundform أَكَلَ, and does not refer to a verb with 1st weak radical *y*, i.e. يَكَلَ. An anomalous case occurs however that can be mentioned here, namely Form VIII اتَّزَرَ "to put on a loin-cloth" of أَزَرَ "to surround", a verb with 1st hamza radical. اتَّزَرَ is underlyingly ائْتَزَرَ with 1st radical hamza, then it became ايتَزَرَ with the *y* substituted for the hamza due to the influence of the kasra preceding it, and then اتَّزَرَ with the *y* changed into the *t* and the *t* assimilated to the infixed *t* (cf. Ibn 'Aqīl, *II*, 581; and compare with it اتَّخَذَ in (187 b), (202)).

(201) One *y* is not assimilated to the other in حَيِيَ in some dialects because the 2nd *y* is considered as unnecessary in the form,–and the condition of the assimilation is that the 2nd of two identical consonants should be existent,–as it is can be elided in the 3rd person of the masc. pl. of the perfect, e.g. حَيُوا or it can be changed into an *alif maqṣūra* in the 3rd person of the masc. sing. of the imperfect,.e.g. يَحْيَى (for discussions see (180)).

(202) Form VIII اتَّخَذَ (compare with it the case of اتَّزَرَ discussed in (200)), is underlyingly ائْتَخَذَ with a 1st radical hamza that refers to أَخَذَ "he took", a hamzated verb. ائْتَخَذَ becomes ايتَخَذَ with the substitution of the *y* for the hamza due to the influence of the kasra preceding the hamza (cf. (187 b)). The *y* in ايتَخَذَ is considered as unnecessary in the form, because it is not the verb's real radical, but the weak consonant by which the hamza is substituted. Similarly to this *y*, the *y* in ايتَكَلَ (for it see (200)) and the *y* in حَيِيَ which can be elided (see (201)) are considered as unnecessary. As mentioned in (187 b) some grammarians prefer to believe that اتَّخَذَ is formed from تَخَذَ (cf. (329)), and their theory became integrated in the language. As Ibn Manẓūr, *I*, 37 remarks:

"وَالاتِّخَاذُ: افْتِعَالٌ أَيْضًا مِنَ الأَخْذِ إِلَّا أَنَّهُ أُدْغِمَ بَعْدَ تَلْيِينِ الهَمْزَةِ وَإِبْدَالِ التَّاءِ، ثُمَّ لَمَّا كَثُرَ اسْتِعْمَالُهُ عَلَى لَفْظِ الافْتِعَالِ تَوَهَّمُوا أَنَّ التَّاءَ أَصْلِيَّةٌ فَبَنَوْا مِنْهُ فَعَلَ يَفْعَلُ. قَالُوا: تَخَذَ يَتْخَذُ".

"وَالاتِّخَاذُ: [Form VIII] افْتِعَالٌ is also from الأَخْذِ, except that an assimilation is carried out in it after that the hamza is changed into a weak consonant [i.e. ايتِخَاذٌ] and a change [of the *y*] into the *t* is carried out [i.e. اتِّخَاذٌ]. Then as it was often used on the pattern افْتِعَالٌ, they believed that the *t* is underlying, and so they formed from it فَعَلَ يَفْعَلُ, and said: "تَخَذَ يَتْخَذُ".

For a study see Zağğāğī, *Mağālis* 333, Ibn Ğinnī, *Ḫaṣā'iṣ II*, 287, Siğistānī, *Fa'altu* 140-141, Howell, *IV*, fasc. II, 1848 sqq., de Sacy, *I*, 236, Wright, *II*, 76-77, Lane, *I*, 29, Fleisch, *Traité I*, 150. It can be noted that al-Ḥasan and Ibn Mas'ūd read the sur. 18: 77 (لَوْ شِئْتَ لَتَخِذْتَ عَلَيْهِ

أجراً) "If thou hadst wished, surely thou couldst have exacted some recompense for it!" with لَتَخِذْتَ (cf. the note 4 to Ibn Ǧinnī, *Ḫaṣā ʾiṣ II,* 287). By doing so they applied the kasra instead of the fatḥa and referred to the variant تخذ instead of using the usual form لَتَخَذْتَ that refers to أخذ. According to Ibn Manẓūr, *I,* 37, Abū Manṣūr reported that this was the reading of Ibn ʿAbbās and Abū ʿAmr b. al-ʿAlāʾ. Concerning it, Suyūṭī, *Ašbāh III,* 97-98 in مجلس أبي عمرو بن العلاء مع أبي عبيدة "the session of Abū ʿAmr b. al-ʿAlāʾ with Abū ʿUbaida", remarks:

> "حدثنا أبو الحسن علي بن سليمان قال: حدثني محمد بن يزيد قال حدثنا المازني عن أبي عبيدة قال: سمعت أبا عمرو بن العلاء يقرأ: "لَتَخِذْتَ عَلَيْهِ أجْراً"، فسأله عنه فقال: هي لغة فصيحة...
>
> يقال اتَّخَذَ اتِّخاذاً، وتَخِذَ يَتْخَذُ تَخْذاً بمعنى واحد".
>
> "Abū l-Ḥasan ʿAlī b. Sulaimān told us: "Muḥammad b. Yazīd has told me, he said: al-Māzinī has reported to us from Abū ʿUbaida. He said: "I heard Abū ʿAmr b. al-ʿAlāʾ read (لَتَخِذْتَ عَلَيْهِ أجْراً) "Surely thou couldst have exacted some recompense for it!". So I asked him concerning it and he said: "It is a correct language"...
>
> Both اتَّخَذَ اتِّخاذاً and تَخِذَ يَتْخَذُ تَخْذاً are used with the same meaning".

It can be mentioned furthermore that the *t* can be substituded by the *s*, namely Form VIII اتَّخَذَ can become اسْتَخَذَ (for discussions see (329)). The more usual form occurs in the sur. 2: 116 (وَقَالُوا ٱتَّخَذَ ٱللَّهُ وَلَداً) "They say: "God hath begotten a son", the sur. 29: 41 (كَمَثَلِ ٱلْعَنْكَبُوتِ ٱتَّخَذَتْ بَيْتاً) "Is that of the Spider, who builds (to itself) a house" and the sur. 4: 125 (واتَّخَذَ ٱللَّهُ إبْرَاهِيمَ خَلِيلاً) "For God did take Abraham for a friend". Compare in Syriac ܐܬܬܚܕ and ܐܬܬܓܪ which seem to be derived from the secondary radicals تخذ and تجر "to trade", and ܐܫܬܚܕ (اسْتَخَذَ) which seem to be derived from the radical ܐܚܕ (cf. Wright, *II,* 77, *Comparative Grammar* 46, 280-281).

(203) The infixed *t* of Form VIII is assimilated to one of the nine consonants following it, which is the 2nd radical. These are: 1– the *t,* 2– *d,* 3– *ḏ,* 4– *z,* 5– *s,* 6– *ṣ,* 7– *ḍ,* 8– *ṭ* and 9– *ẓ*. The verbs that are presented refer to each of these cases and thus begin with verbs with 2nd radical *t* and end up with verbs with 2nd radical *ẓ*. This assimilation is carried out in the imperfect and rarely in the perfect, except in the case of اخْتَصَمَ resulting in خَصَّمَ (for it see (206)), the reason being to avoid mixing Form VIII of those verbs in the perfect with Form II of the same tense, as there is a tendency by some grammarians to shift the vowel of the infixed *t* to the 1st radical and to elide the prefixed hamza. Some examples, if such an assimilation is to be carried out in Form VIII which would result in a confusion with Form II, would be: اقْتَتَلَ "to contend among themselves" becoming اقَتَّلَ and then قَتَّلَ, ابْتَدَلَ "to change" becoming ابَدَّلَ and then بَدَّلَ, اعْتَذَرَ "to excuse oneself" becoming اعَذَّرَ and then عَذَّرَ, انْتَزَعَ "to snatch, tear away" becoming

انزَّع and then نزَّع, ابْتَسَم "to smile" becoming ابسَّم and then بسَّم, انْتَضَل "to struggle" becoming انضَّل and then نَضَّل, الْتَطَم "to collide, clash" becoming الطَّم and then لطَّم, and انْتَظَر "to expect" becoming انظَّر and then نظَّر.

b) The infixed *t* of Form VIII is assimilated to the *t* following it. The base form of يَقِتِّل with the 2nd radical being a *t*, is يَقْتَتِل "to contend among themselves" in which the fatḥa of the 1st *t*, which is the infixed consonant, is shifted to the 1st radical *q* and the infixed *t* is then assimilated to the 2nd radical *t*. It can be be added that both يَقَتِّل and يَقِتِّل occur (cf. Howell, *IV*, fasc. II, 1807, Zamaḫšarī, 195).

(204) The infixed *t* of Form VIII is assimilated to the *d* following it. The base form of يَبَدِّل with the 2nd radical being a *d*, is يَبْتَدِل "to change" in which the fatḥa of the infixed *t* is shifted to the 1st radical *b* and the infixed *t* is then assimilated to the 2nd radical *d*. Another example of a verb with 2nd radical *d* in which a similar assimilation is carried out is يَهَدِّي that occurs in the sur. 10: 35 (أَمَّنْ لَا يَهَدِّي) "Or he who finds not guidance (himself)". Abū ʿAmr and Nāfiʿ read it with both vowelless consonants combined, namely يَهْدِّي, which is disapproved by the majority and Abū Bakr read it with both the *y* and the *h* vowelled by a kasra, namely يِهِدِّي (cf. Howell, *IV*, fasc. II, 1807-1808).

b) The infixed *t* of Form VIII is assimilated to the *ḏ* following it. The base form of يَعَذِّر with the 2nd radical being a *ḏ*, is يَعْتَذِر "to excuse oneself" in which the fatḥa of the infixed *t* is shifted to the 1st radical ʿ and the infixed *t* is then assimilated to the 2nd radical *ḏ*.

c) The infixed *t* of Form VIII is assimilated to the *z* following it. The base form of يَنَزِّع with the 2nd radical being a *z*, is يَنْتَزِع "to snatch, tear away" in which the fatḥa of the infixed *t* is shifted to the 1st radical *n* and the infixed *t* is then assimilated to the 2nd radical *z*.

d) The infixed *t* of Form VIII is assimilated to the *s* following it. The base form of يَبَسِّم with the 2nd radical being a *s*, is يَبْتَسِم "to smile" in which the fatḥa of the infixed *t* is shifted to the 1st radical *b* and the infixed *t* is then assimilated to the 2nd radical *s*.

(205) The infixed *t* of Form VIII is assimilated to the *ṣ* following it. The base form of يَخَصِّم with the 2nd radical being a *ṣ*, is يَخْتَصِم in which the fatḥa of the infixed *t* is shifted to the 1st radical *ḫ* and the infixed *t* is then assimilated to the 2nd radical *ṣ*. يَخِصِّم as another variant occurs as well (cf. de Sacy, *I*, 223). The 3rd person of the masc. pl. يَخَصِّمُون occurs in the sur. 36: 49 (وَهُمْ يَخَصِّمُون) "While they are yet disputing among themselves!". Seven different readings concerning it are known to have been transmitted (for them see Ibn Manẓūr, *II*, 1177 in the note), namely: 1– يَخَصِّمُون, 2– يَخْتَصِمُون, 3– يَخَصِّمُون, 4– يَخِصِّمُون, 5– يِخِصِّمُون, 6– يَخِصِّمُون and 7– يَخْصِمُون. Fleisch, *Traité I*, 142 referring to Baiḍāwī, mentions that Abū Bakr read يخصّمون. Furthermore, referring to the *Taysīr* 184, he mentions that Ibn Kaṯīr, Warš and Hišām read يَخَصّمون, Qālūn and Abū ʿAmr read يَخَـصّمون with a vowel of support, i.e. *yaḫ^a ṣṣi-mūna* (for discussions see Fleisch, *Traité I,* 144, Cantineau, *Voyelle* 57), Ḥamza read يَخْصِمُون and ʿĀṣim, Ibn Ḏakwān and al-Kisāʾī read يَخِصّمون. Muʾaddib, *Taṣrīf* 166 mentions that يَخِصّمون was read so by al-Ḥasan al-Baṣrī, يَخْصِّمون was read so by al-Aʿraǧ, Abū Ǧaʿfar and Abū ʿAmr, both يَخِصّمون and يَخَصّمون were read so by Abū ʿAmr, يَخْصِمون was read so by al-Aʿmaš and both يَخِصّمون and يَخْتَصِمون were read so by other readers (see further for the different readings Ibn Muǧāhid, *Sabʿa* 541, Ibn Ḫālawaihi, *Qirāʾāt II,* 234, Makkī, *Kašf II,* 207).

b) The infixed *t* of Form VIII is assimilated to the *ḍ* following it. The base form of يَنَضّل with the 2nd radical being a *ḍ,* is يَنْتَضِل "to struggle" in which the fatḥa of the infixed *t* is shifted to the 1st radical *n* and the infixed *t* is assimilated then to the 2nd radical *ḍ.*

c) The infixed *t* of Form VIII is assimilated to the *ṭ* following it. The base form of يَلَطّم with the 2nd radical being a *ṭ,* is يَلْتَطِم "to collide, clash" in which the fatḥa of the infixed *t* is shifted to the 1st radical *l* and the infixed *t* is then assimilated to the 2nd radical *ṭ.*

d) The infixed *t* of Form VIII is assimilated to the *ẓ* following it. The base form of يَنَظّر with the 2nd radical being a *ẓ* is يَنْتَظِر "to expect" in which the fatḥa of the infixed *t* is shifted to the 1st radical *n* and the infixed *t* is then assimilated to the 2nd radical *ẓ.*

(206) Three variants exist concerning the active participle Form VIII of يَخِصّم, namely:
1– مُخُصّمٌ in which some give the ḍamma to the *ḫ* on the analogy of the ḍamma that vowels the prefix *m* which is characteristic for the active participle of Form VIII.
2– مُخَصّمٌ in which some give the *ḫ* the fatḥa on the analogy of the fatḥa of the *ḫ* of both the contracted forms of the Form VIII of the perfect اِخْتَصَم, namely خَصّم and اِخَصّم, whose *ḫ* they vowel with the fatḥa.
3– مُخِصّمٌ in which some give the *ḫ* the kasra on the analogy of the kasra of the contracted form of the perfect اِخْتَصَم, namely خِصّم whose *ḫ* they vowel with the kasra. The variant خِصّم from اِخْتَصَم is presumed to be خْصّم at first after the elision of the prefixed hamza from اِخْتَصَم and after that the infixed *t* is assimilated to the 2nd radical *ṣ*. The *ḫ* in خْصّم is given the kasra, i.e. خِصّم, to prevent the cluster of two vowelless consonants: the *ḫ* and the 1st *ṣ* of the doubled ṣāds, if خْصّم is to be said, as both the assimilated ṣāds are formed of a vowelless *ṣ* followed by a vowelled one, i.e. خْصْصَم which is forbidden. Another contracted form of the perfect with the *ḫ* given the kasra mentioned by Ibn Masʿūd, is اِخِصّم. It can be noted as well that in both these contracted forms of the perfect خِصّم and اِخِصّم, it is specifically the kasra which is given to the vowelless consonant *ḫ* of the base form اِخْتَصَم, as by principle the kasra is closest to the sukūn. Differently from Ibn Masʿūd, Muʾaddib, *Taṣrīf* 167 mentions only the last two variants

of the active participle, i.e. مُخَصِّم and مُخِصِّم. His theories are as well different concerning the choice of the specific vowel of the *ḫ*. He remarks namely that those who give the *ḫ* the fatḥa, i.e. مُخَصِّم do so to vowel it with the vowel of the infixed *t* of مُخْتَصِم, and those who vowel it with the kasra, i.e. مُخِصِّم do so because of the *ḫ's* nearness to the *ṣ* which is vowelled by the kasra.

(207) The infixed *t* of Form V and VI can be assimilated to the 1st radical of the verb (for a study see Zamaḫšarī, 196, de Sacy, *I*, 220-221, Wright, *II*, 64-65, ʿAbd al-Tawwāb, *Taṭawwur* 29) following it, when it is a: 1– *t*, 2– *ṯ*, 3– *ǧ*, 4– *d*, 5– *ḏ*, 6– *z*, 7– *s*, 8– *š*, 9– *ṣ*, 10– *ḍ*, 11– *ṭ* or 12– *ẓ*, after that it loses its vowel. The forms thus originated, take a prosthetic alif in the perfect as they begin with a doubled consonant: Form V تَفَعَّلَ becomes اِفَّعَّلَ and Form VI تَفَاعَلَ becomes اِفَّاعَلَ. The prosthetic alif is not needed in the imperfect: Form V اِفَّعَّلَ becomes يَفَّعَّلُ and Form VI اِفَّاعَلَ becomes يَفَّاعَلُ.

1– Form V اِطَّهَّرَ said instead of تَطَهَّرَ "to purify oneself" (cf. Howell, *IV*, fasc. II, 1829, Lane, *II*, 1887, Penrice, *Dictionary* 91). The prefixed *t* of تَطَهَّرَ is changed into the *ṭ*, then the *ṭ* is assimilated to the *ṭ*, i.e. طَّهَّرَ, and the prosthetic alif is prefixed to prevent that the word begins with a vowelless consonant, i.e. اِطَّهَّرَ that is with the dissolution طْطَهَّرَ with the 1st radical vowelless which is not accepted. Another example that can be added is Form V اِطَّيَّرَ said instead of تَطَيَّرَ "to see an evil omen" (cf. Howell, *IV*, fasc. II, 1829, Wright, *II*, 65). The 1st person of the masc. pl. اِطَّيَّرْنَا occurs in the sur. 27: 47 (قَالُوا اطَّيَّرْنَا بِكَ وَبِمَن مَّعَكَ) "They said: [1] omen do we augur from thee and those that are with thee".

2– Form VI اِثَّاقَلَ said instead of تَثَاقَلَ "to be borne down heavily" (cf. Howell, *IV*, fasc. II, 1829, Lane, *I*, 344, Penrice, *Dictionary* 25). The prefixed *t* of تَثَاقَلَ is changed into the *ṯ*, then the *ṯ* is assimilated to the *ṯ* and the prosthetic alif is prefixed to prevent beginning the word with a vowelless consonant, i.e. اِثَّاقَلَ instead of ثَّاقَلَ that is theoretically ثْثَاقَلَ with the 1st radical vowelless. The 2nd person of the masc. pl. اِثَّاقَلْتُمْ occurs in the sur. 9: 38 (اثَّاقَلْتُمْ إِلَى الْأَرْضِ فِي سَبِيلِ اللهِ) "In the Cause of God ye cling heavily to the earth?".

The following examples can be added with the assimilation of the prefixed *t* to the 1st radical being:

3– the *t*, e.g. Form V اِتَّرَّسَ instead of تَتَرَّسَ "shielded himself" (cf. Howell, *IV*, fasc. II, 1829).

4– the *ǧ*, e.g. اِجَّارَ instead of تَجَارَ "to compete" (cf. Howell, *IV*, fasc. II, 1829).

5– the *d*, e.g. Form VI اِدَّارَأَ instead of تَدَارَأَ "to repel" (cf. Howell, *IV*, fasc. II, 1829, Lane, *I*, 865, Penrice, *Dictionary* 47). The 2nd person of the masc. pl. فَادَّارَأْتُمْ occurs in the sur. 2: 72 (فَادَّارَأْتُمْ فِيهَا) "And fell into a dispute among yourselves as to the crime:".

6– the *ḏ*, e.g. Form VI اِذَّاكَرَ instead of تَذَاكَرَ "to be reminded" (cf. Howell, *IV*, fasc. II, 1829, Lane, *I*, 968, Penrice, *Dictionary* 52). The imperfect of the 3rd person of the masc. sing. يَذَّكَّرُ

occurs in both the sur. 80: 3-4 (وَمَا يُدْرِيكَ لَعَلَّهُ يَزَّكَّى أَوْ يَذَّكَّرُ فَتَنْفَعَهُ ٱلذِّكْرَى) "But what could tell thee but that perchance he might grow (in spiritual understanding)? Or that he might receive admonition, and the teaching might profit him?", and the sur. 2: 269 (وَمَا يَذَّكَّرُ إِلَّا أُوْلُوا ٱلْأَلْبَابِ) "But none will grasp the Message but men of understanding" (mentioned in (190)).

7– the *z*, e.g. Form V اِزَّيَّنَ instead of تَزَيَّنَ "to decorate itself" (cf. Howell, *IV*, fasc. II, 1829, Lane, *I*, 1279, Wright, *II*, 64, Penrice, *Dictionary* 64). The 3rd person of the fem. sing. وَٱزَّيَنَتْ occurs in the sur. 10: 24 (حَتَّى إِذَا أَخَذَتِ ٱلْأَرْضُ زُخْرُفَهَا وَٱزَّيَّنَتْ) "Till the earth is clad with its golden ornaments and is decked out (in beauty)" (mentioned in (191)).

8– the *s*, e.g. Form V اِسَّمَّعَ instead of تَسَمَّعَ "to listen" (cf. Howell, *IV*, fasc. II, 1829, Lane, *I*, 1427, 1428, Wright, *II*, 65, Penrice, *Dictionary* 72). The imperfect of the 3rd person of the masc. pl. يَسَّمَّعُونَ occurs in the sur. 37: 8 (لَا يَسَّمَّعُونَ إِلَى ٱلْمَلَإِ ٱلْأَعْلَى) "(So) they should not strain their ears in the direction of the Exalted Assembly" (mentioned in (192)). It can be noted that يَسْمَعُ that occurs in the sur. 6: 25 (وَمِنْهُمْ مَنْ يَسْتَمِعُ إِلَيْكَ) "Of them there are some who (pretend to) listen to thee" is Form VIII يَسْتَمِعُ (cf. (192)) and not Form V يَتَسَمَّعُ.

9– the *š*, e.g. Form VI اِشَّاجَرَ instead of تَشَاجَرَ "to be embroiled" (cf. Howell, *IV*, fasc. II, 1829).

10– the *ṣ*, e.g. Form VI اِصَّابَرَ instead of تَصَابَرَ "to bear patiently" (cf. Howell, *IV*, fasc. II, 1829, Lane, *II*, 1643).

11– the *ḍ*, e.g. Form VI اِضَّارَبَ instead of تَضَارَبَ "to fight" (cf. Howell, *IV*, fasc. II, 1829).

12– the *ẓ*, e.g. Form VI اِظَّالَمَ instead of تَظَالَمَ "to wrong" (cf. Howell, *IV*, fasc. II, 1829). For the elision of one of the tā's in verbs of Form V and VI that occur in the imperfect of the 2nd person of the fem. and the 3rd person of the masc. sing., i.e. تَتَفَعَّلُ resulting in تَفَعَّلُ and تَتَفَاعَلُ resulting in تَفَاعَلُ respectively, see (101)).

(208) There is no way of assimilating the infixed *t* of Form X اِسْتَطْعَمَ to the vowelless *ṭ* following it (cf. Zamaḫšarī, 196, Ibn Yaʿīš, *X*, 151, Howell, *IV*, fasc. II, 1821-1822), because of the sukūn of the *ṭ* تَحْقِيقاً "in reality" that prevents the assimilation, as the condition of the assimilation is that the 2nd consonant should be vowelled. It is not possible either to assimilate the infixed *t* of Form X اِسْتَدَانَ to the *d* following it in spite of the fact that it is vowelled by a fatḥa, because the *d* is meant to be vowelless, as the base form of اِسْتَدَانَ is اِسْتَدْيَنَ. This is why the vowelled *d* is considered as being vowelless تَقْدِيراً "implicitly" on account that the base form of the verb with the vowelless *d* is kept in mind and referred to.

(209) اِسْطَاعَ يَسْطِيعُ is Form X underlyingly اِسْتَطَاعَ يَسْتَطِيعُ (cf. Ibn Manẓūr, *IV*, 2721, de Sacy, *I*, 224, Vernier, *I*, 152, Howell, *IV*, fasc. I, 1174-1176, fasc. II, 1830-1831, Fleisch, *Traité I*, 150), in which the infixed *t* is elided for the purpose of alleviation. Both اِسْطَاعُوا with the infixed *t* elided and اِسْتَطَاعُوا with the *t* retained occur in the sur. 18: 97 (فَمَا ٱسْطَاعُوا أَنْ يَظْهَرُوهُ)

(وَمَا ٱسْتَطَاعُوا لَهُ نَقْبًا) "Thus were they made powerless to scale it or to dig through it". اسْطَاعُوا of this sur. is also read anomalously as اسْطّاعُوا by some (cf. Howell, *IV,* fasc. II, 1831). Lane, *II,* 1891 notes that this is the reading of Ḥamza al-Zayyāt. Also اسْتَاعَ يُسْتِيعُ occurs with the substitution of the *t* for the *ṭ* (cf. Ibn Ǧinnī, *Sirr I,* 202). نُستِيعُ with this substitution, occurs in the following verse said by Ǧirān, *Dīwān* 17. It is also cited by Ibn Ǧinnī, *Sirr I,* 202, *Ḫaṣāʾiṣ I,* 260:

"وفيكَ إذا لاقَيْتَنا عَجْرَفِيَّةٌ مِرارًا، فما نُستيعُ مَنْ يَتَعَجْرَفُ".

"And we notice in you—when you meet us—a harshness of speech which is bitter for us. And we cannot obey someone who is harsh!".

(210) The base form of ظَلْتَ is ظَلِلْتَ in which the 1st *l* is elided and its kasra is shifted to the *ẓ* (cf. (181)).

(211) The base form of أَسْطاعَ يُسْطيعُ is Form IV أطاعَ يُطيعُ in which the *s* is anomalously inserted after the prefixed hamza. The reason of the infixation of the *s* is considered by Sībawaihi, *I,* 7 to be a compensation for the departure of the vowel of the 2nd radical, as أطاعَ is underlyingly أطْوَعَ with the 2nd *w* radical, in which the fatḥa of the *w* is shifted to the *ṭ,* i.e. أطَوْعَ, and thus is considered by him as elided, and its vowelless *w* is changed into a vowelless *ā.* Ibn Ǧinnī, *Sirr I,* 199 refers to Sībawaihi by writing:

"وأما قولهم "أسْطاعَ يُسْطيعُ" فذهب سيبويه فيه الى أن أصله: أطاعَ يُطيعُ، وأن السين زيدت عوضا من سكون عين الفعل، وذلك أن أطاعَ أصله: أطْوَعَ، فنقلت فتحة الواو الى الطاء، فصار التقدير: أطَوْعَ، فانقلبت الواو ألفاً لتحركها في الأصل وانفتاح ما قبلها الآن".

"As for their saying أسْطاعَ يُسْطيعُ "to obey", Sībawaihi believed that its base form is أطاعَ يُطيعُ, and that the *s* is a compensation for the departure of the vowel of the 2nd radical of the verb, because أطاعَ is underlyingly أطْوَعَ, in which the fatḥa of the *w* is shifted to the *ṭ* so that it became by implication أطَوْعَ, and then the *w* is changed into an *ā* on the basis that it is vowelled in the base form and that the fatḥa precedes it now".

As for al-Mubarrad he rejects Sībawaihi's theory concerning the compensation for an elided vowel, as it is more, according to him, a question of vowel transfer than vowel elision. Ibn Ǧinnī, *Sirr I,* 199 referring to al-Mubarrad, writes:

"وتعقب أبو العباس – رحمه الله – هذا القول، فقال: إنما يُعوَض من الشيء إذا فُقد وذهب، فأما إذا كان موجوداً في اللفظ فلا وجه للتعويض منه، وفتحة العين التي كانت في الواو قد نُقلت إلى الطاء التي هي الفاء، ولم تعدم، وإنما نقلت، فلا وجه للعوض من شيء موجود غير مفقود".

"Abū l-ʿAbbās, may God grant him salvation, rejected this account by saying: "Somehow a compensation for a thing is carried out if it is lost or elided, but if it is still existent in the pronunciation then there is no reason to compensate for it. The fatḥa of the 2nd radical *w* [of أَطْوَعَ] is shifted to the *ṭ* which is the 1st radical [i.e. أَطَاعَ], which means that it is not elided but shifted. So there is no reason to compensate for something which is existent and not lost".

His opinion is also discussed by Ibn ʿUṣfūr, *I,* 224, Ibn Yaʿīš, *X,* 6, *Mulūkī* 207. As for al-Farrāʾ, his opinion is totally different from the one of Sībawaihi, al-Mubarrad and Ibn Masʿūd who refer all correctly to Form IV. According to him the base form of أَسْطاعَ is form VIII اِسْتَطاعَ with the infixed *t* elided and with the hamza given at first a kasra, i.e. اِسْطاعَ, and then anomalously given a fatḥa and made disjunctive, i.e. أَسْطاعَ. Ibn Ǧinnī, *Sirr I,* 200-201 refers to his theory by writing:

"وقال الفراء في هذا: "شَبَّهوا أسْطَعْتُ بأفْعَلْتُ". فهذا يدل من كلامه على أن أصلها: اسْتطعْت، فلما حُذفت التاء بقي على وزن "اِفْعَلْتُ"، ففتحت همزته وقُطعت. وهذا غير مرضي عندنا...".

"And al-Farrāʾ said concerning this: "They compared أَسْطَعْتُ with أَفْعَلْتُ. This is indicated from his [sc. Sībawaihi's] saying that its base form is اِسْتَطَعْتُ, and when the *t* was elided, it remained on the pattern اِفْعَلْتُ, then the hamza was given a fatḥa and was made disjunctive". But this [theory] is not satisfying by us [sc. Ibn Ǧinnī, and his followers]".

Thus the imperfect is then يَسْطِيعُ by al-Farrāʾ with the vowelling of the imperfect prefix with a fatḥa and not يُسْطِيعُ with a ḍamma (for his opinion cf. Ibn Ǧinnī, *Sirr I,* 200-201, Ibn Yaʿīš, *Mulūkī* 208, Ibn ʿUṣfūr, *I,* 226).

(212) The insertion of the *h* after the prefixed hamza in Form IV أَهْراقَ underlyingly أَراقَ is similar to the insertion of the *s* in أَسْطاعَ (for it see (211), Sībawaihi, *II,* 364). The insertion of both these consonants is considered as a compensation for the departure of the vowel of the 2nd radical of the verb. أَراقَ with the vowelless *ā* is underlyingly أَرْوَقَ with the 2nd radical *w* vowelled by a fatḥa that is shifted to the *r* preceding it, i.e. أَرَوْقَ, and then the vowelless *w* is changed into an *ā* due to the influence of the fatḥa preceding it. Concerning أَهْراقَ, Ibn Ǧinnī, *Sirr I,* 201 remarks:

"... أنّهم قد عَوّضوا من ذهاب حركة هذه العين... الهاء في قول من قال "أهْرَقْتُ"، فسكّن الهاء، وجمع بينها وبين الهمزة. فالهاء هنا عوض من ذهاب فتحة العين، لأنّ الأصل: أرْوَقْتُ أو أرْيَقْتُ، والواو عندي أقيس".

"...They have compensated for the loss of the vowel of this 2nd radical... with the *h* in the saying of he who says أَهْرَقْتُ "I poured", so he made the *h* vowelless and combined it with the hamza. Then the *h* here is a compensation for the departure of the fatḥa of the 2nd radical, because the base form is أَرْوَقْتُ or أَرْيَقْتُ, and according to my opinion the *w* [in أَرْوَقْتُ] is more according to the analogy".

Cf. Ibn ʿUṣfūr, *I*, 225-226. For the change of the hamza that is the inceptive consonant in the verb of Form I أَرَقْتُ "I spilled" into a *h*, i.e. هَرَقْتُ, see (98) and (343).

It can be mentioned that another example of a noun in which the *h* is inserted is أُمَّهَاتٌ (for a discussion of the word in Arabic and in some of the other Semitic languages see Nöldeke, *Beiträge* 69-72) underlyingly أُمَّاتٌ which is said to be the pl. of أُمَّهَةٌ "mothers" (cf. Ibn Ǧinnī, *de Flexione* 18). It occurs in the following verse said by Quṣayy b. Kilāb, an ancestor of the Prophet, cited by Howell, *IV*, fasc. I, 1167: [Only the last verse is cited by Ibn Manẓūr, *I*, 136].

"إِنِّي لَدَى ٱلْحَرْبِ رَخِيُّ ٱللَّبَبِ   مُعْتَزِمُ ٱلصَّوْلَةِ عَالِي ٱلنَّسَبِ
أُمَّهَتِي خِنْدِفُ وَٱلْيَاسُ أَبِي".

"Verily in battle I am easy in mind, resolute in attack, lofty in lineage: my mother is Ḫindif [the cognomen of Lailā bint Ḥulwān b. ʿImrān, the wife of al-Yās b. Muḍar] and my father is al-Yās".

Both the base and the augmented form are combined in the following verse said by an unknown poet, cited by Ibn Manẓūr, *I*, 136, Howell, *IV*, fasc. I, 1169:

"إِذَا ٱلْأُمَّهَاتُ قَبُحْنَ ٱلْوُجُوهَ   فَرَجْتَ ٱلظَّلَامَ بِأُمَّاتِكَا".

"When the mothers are ugly in faces, you dispelled the darkness with your mothers".

For some examples presented with the *h* inserted and considered as an augmentative consonant see Zamaḫšari, 171-172, Ibn Yaʿīš, *X*, 5.

II.4. Arabic Text: الباب الثالث في المهموز

* ٢١ ب ولا يُقال له صحيح لصيرورة همزته حرف علّة في التليين. وهو يجيء على ثلثة أضرب*
مهموز الفاء نحو أخَذَ والعين نحو سألَ واللام نحو قَرأَ. وحكم الهمزة
كحكم الحرف الصحيح إلاّ أنَها تُخفّف بالقلب وجعلها بين بين أي بين
مخرجها وبين مخرج الحرف الذي منه حركتها وقيل بين الهمزة وبين الحرف الذي
منه حركة ما قبلها والحذف وهو ثلاثة أقسام. الأوّل يكون إذا كانت ساكنةً ومتحرّكاً ما
قبلها تُقلب بشيء يوافق حركة ما قبلها للين عريكة الساكن واستدعاء ما قبلها نحو
رَاسٍ ولُومٍ وبِيرٍ، والثاني يكون إذا كانت مُتحرّكةً ومتحرّكاً ما قبلها ثمّ تُثبت لقوّة
عريكتها نحو سَألَ ولَؤمَ وسَئمَ إلاّ إذا كانت مفتوحة وما قبلها مكسوراً أو مضموماً فإنّها
لا تُثبت بل تُجعل واواً أو ياءً نحو مِيَرٍ وجُوَنٍ لأنّ الفتحة كالسكون في اللين فتُقلب
كما في السكون. فإن قيل لم لا تُقلب ألفاً في سألَ وهمزته مفتوحة ضعيفة قلنا فتحتها
* ٢٢ آ صارت* قويّة بفتحة ما قبلها ونحو لا هَناكِ المَرْتَعُ شاذ، والثالث يكون إذا كانت مُتحرّكةً
وساكناً ما قبلها ولكن تُليّن فيه أوّلاً للين عريكتها بمجاورة الساكن ثمّ تُحذف لاجتماع
الساكنين ثمّ أُعطي حركتها لما قبلها إذا كان ما قبلها حرفاً صحيحاً أو واواً أو ياءً
أصليّتين أو مزيدتين لمعنى نحو مَسَلَةٍ أصله مَسألَة ومَلَك أصله مَلأك من الألوكَة وهي
الرسالة والأحمَرُ يجوز فيه لَحْمَرُ لأنّ ألفَه لأجل سكون اللام وقد انعدم ويجوز فيه
الَحْمَرُ لطروِ حركة اللام وجَيَل وجَوَبَة وأبُوَيُّوبَ وآبْتَغي مْرَهُ ويجوز تحميل الحركة على

Fols. 21a-22a

٢ له: –ل/ ثلثة: ثلاثة ك ل/ ٣ والعين: العين ل/ الهمزة: المهموز ا/ ٤ الصحيح: + في احتمال الحركات ح/ أنها: + قد ب هـ ط ك ل/ ٥–٦ وقيل... قبلها: – د ط/ الحرف: حرف ا/ ٦ وهو... أقسام: –ا جـ د هـ ز حـ ط/ ٨ وبئر: + الا اذا كانت مفتوحة وما قبلها مكسورا او مضموما تجعل واوا وا ياء ا/ ٩ وسئم: وسُئل د ز ك ل/ ٩–١٠ فإنّها... بل: – ا ب جـ د هـ ز حـ ك/ ١٠ تجعل: يجعل د حـ/ ١١ فتحتها: فتحته د/ ١٢ بفتحه: بفتح ا/ ١٤ كان: كانت د/ ١٥ لمعنى: + واحد د/ أصله مسألة: – ا ب جـ د هـ حـ ط/ ملأك: ملئك جـ: ملاءك ط: + وهي ا/ ١٦ والأحمر: والحمر د/ ألفه: الألف ب جـ د ز حـ ط/ فيه: – د/

II.4. Translation: The 3rd Chapter is about the Hamzated Verb[213]

It is not named strong because its hamza can be changed into a weak consonant when it is softened. It falls into three sorts: **[Fol. 21 b]** 1– verbs with hamza as 1st radical, e.g. أخَذَ "to take", 2– verbs with hamza as 2nd radical, e.g. سأَلَ "to ask" and 3– verbs with hamza as 3rd radical, e.g. قرأ "to read".[214] The predicament of the hamza is the same as the predicament of the strong consonant, except that it [sc. the hamza] is alleviated[215] 1) by [its] change into a weak consonant, 2) by [its] change into a hamza بَيْنَ بَيْنَ "intermediary hamza", i.e. that is between its point of articulation and the point of articulation of the weak consonant [which supports it] that its vowel is connected to, and it is said between the hamza and the weak consonant from which it acquires the vowel,[216] 3) and by [its] elision. Then it [sc. the alleviation] is of three sorts: 1– The first one [sc. the change into a weak consonant] is carried out if it is vowelless and the consonant preceding it is vowelled. In this case it is changed in a manner that agrees with the vowel preceding it, because of the faint nature of the vowelless consonant and the requirement of what [sc. the vowel that] precedes it, e.g. رَاسٌ "head", لُومٌ "blame" and بِيرٌ "well, spring".[217] 2– The second one [sc. the change into an intermediary hamza] is carried out if it and the consonant preceding it are vowelled. It is however made firm afterwards because of the strength of its nature, e.g. سَأَلَ "to ask", لَؤُمَ "to be wicked" and سَئِمَ "to be weary",[218] unless it is vowelled by a fatḥa and the consonant preceding it is vowelled by a kasra or ḍamma, as it does not stay firm but is changed into a *w* or *y*, e.g. مِيَرٌ "exciting dissension among the people" and جُوَنٌ "receptabled for bottles or the like", because the fatḥa is similar to the sukūn in being faint. So it [sc. the hamza] is changed in the same manner as if it had a sukūn.[219] If it is asked why is it not changed into an *ā* in سَأَلَ "to ask", in which the hamza is vowelled by a fatḥa and is faint, we answered that its fatḥa became **[Fol. 22 a]** stable due to the [influence of the] fatḥa preceding it. As for لا هَنَاكِ المَرْتَعُ "may the pasture not be pleasant to you!", it is anomalous.[220] 3– The third one [sc. the elision] is carried out if it is vowelled and the consonant preceding it is vowelless. In this case it is made faint at first because of the faintness of its nature when it is combined with a vowelless consonant, then it is elided to avoid the cluster of two vowelless consonants, and then its vowel is shifted to the consonant preceding it if it is: 1– a strong consonant or 2– an original or an augmentative *w* or *y* that is attached for a meaning,[221] e.g. مَسَلَةٌ "a matter" underlyingly مَسْأَلَةٌ and مَلَكٌ "an angel" underlyingly مَلْأَكٌ, which is from الألوكة meaning "the message".[222] As for الأحمر "red", لَحْمَرُ can occur instead of it, because its *ʾa* [of the article] is prefixed for the sake of the vowelless *l* which is not vowelless any more. Also الحْمَرُ can occur because of the softness of the *l's* vowel.[223] جَيَلٌ "female hyena", جَوَبَةٌ "*Čawaba* (name of a water)", أبُويُوب "the father of Job" and اَبْتَغِي مَرَهُ "I seek for his matter" occur as well. It is possible to shift the vowel [of the hamza] to

حرف العلَة في هذه الأشياء لقوَتها ولطروَ الحركة عليها، وإذا كان ما قبلها حرف ليَن مزيداً نُظر فإن كان ياء أو واوا أو مدَتين أو ما يشبه المدَة كياء التصغير جُعلت مثل ما قبلها ثمَ أُدغم في الآخر لأنَ نقل الحركة الى هذه* الأشياء يُفضي الى تحميل * ٢٢ ب الضعيف فيُدغم نحو خَطيَة ومَقْرُوَة وأُفيَس. فإن قيل يُلزم تحميل الضعيف أيضاً في الإدغام وهو الياء الثانية قلنا الياء الثانية أصليَة فلا تكون ضعيفةً كياء جَيَلٍ، وإن كان ألفاً جُعل بين بين لأنَ الألف لا يتحمَل الحركة والإدغام نحو سايلٍ وقايلٍ. وإذا اجتمع همزتان في كلمة واحدة وكانت الأولى مفتوحةً والثانية ساكنةً تُقلب الثانية ألفاً نحو آخَذَ وآدَمَ إلاَ في أيمَة جُعلت همزتها ألفاً كما في آخَذَ ثمَ جُعلت ياءً لاجتماع الساكنين. وعند الكوفيَين لا تُقلب همزتها بالألف حتَى لا يلزم اجتماع الساكنين وقرىء عندهم أئمَة الكُفْرِ بالهمزتين. فإن قيل اجتماع الساكنين في حدَه جائز فلم لا يجوز في آمَة قلنا الألف في آمَة ليست بمدَةٍ فكيف يكون اجتماع الساكنين في حدَه. وإذا كانت مكسورة تُقلب ياءً نحو ايسَرْ أصله إإسَرْ. وإذا كانت مضمومة تُقلب* واواً * ٢٣ آ نحو أُوثِرَ. وأمَا كُلْ ومُرْ وخُذْ فشاذ. هذا إذا كانتا في كلمة واحدة وأمَا إذا كانتا في كلمتين تُخفَف الثانية عند الخليل نحو (فقد جاء آشراطُها) وعند أهل الحجاز تُخفَف كلتاهما وعند بعض العرب تُقحم بينهما ألف للفصل نحو آانْت كقول الشاعر آانْتِ ظَبْيَـةٌ أم أمُ سالمٍ. ولا تُخفَف الهمزة في أوَل الكلمة لقوَة المتكلَم في الإبتداء وتخفيفها بالحذف في ناسٍ أصله أُناس شاذ وكذلك إلَهٌ فحذفوا

Fols. 22a-23a

١ ولطروَ: وطروَ ل/ ٢ نظر: + الى ذلك الحرف ط/ ياء أو واوا: واوا او ياء ل/ او(2): – ل/ ٢ قبلها: + من غير نقل حركتها الى ما قبلها د/ ٤ وافيَس: واقيَس ح/ ٥ تكون: يكون ا ج د ه ز ح ط/ ضعيفة: ضعيفا ا/ ٦ يتحمَل: يحتمل ج د ح ط ل/ ٧ همزتان: الهمزتان ا ب ج د ز ح ط ك/ في... واحدة: – ا ج د/ آخذ: اجر ب/ ٨ أيمَة: أئمة ل/ كما: – ط/ آخذ: اجر ب/ ٩ همزتها: –ب د ز ح ط ل/ وقرئ: وقراء ا ب ح/ ١٠ فلم: لم د ح/ ١١ فكيف: كيف ا د ل/ وإذا: فإذا د/ ١٢ ايسر: ايتسر ك ل/ أصله إإسر: – د ل/ إإسر: إءسر ا/ تقلب: قلبت ج د: قلب ز/ كل... وخذ: خذ وكل ومر د/ هذا: وهذا ا ز ط/ ١٣ إذا كانتا: – د/ ١٥ كلتاهما: كلاهما ا د ز ح ط/ ١٦-١٥ آانْتِ... الشاعر: – ا د/ ١٧ إله : آله ل/

the weak consonant in these forms because of its [sc. the weak consonant's] soundness and because of the lightness of the vowel on it.(224) If the consonant preceding it [sc. the vowelled hamza] is an augmentative [vowelless] weak consonant, it is taken into account. If it is a *w* or *y*, one of the two glides lengthening the preceding vowel or what resembles to a glide as the diminutive *y*, it [sc. the hamza] is changed into the same [weak] consonant as the weak consonant preceding it, and then [the preceding weak consonant] is assimilated to it. As for the reason of this, it is that shifting its [sc. the hamza's] vowel to them [sc. the weak consonants] **[Fol. 22 b]** results in imposing a vowel on the weak one [sc. the infixed weak consonant of the intended pattern], which is why an assimilation must [instead] be carried out [from the preceding weak consonant to the hamza changed into a weak consonant following it], e.g. خَطِيَّةٌ "a sin", مَقْرُوَّةٌ "a writing read" and أُفَيِّسٌ "a little axe". If it is said that this would as well necessarily imply imposing a vowel on the weak one, which is the 2nd *y* [or the 2nd *w]* through the assimilation, we answered that the 2nd *y* [or *w]* is underlying [i.e. that it replaces an underlying radical which is the hamza] and is therefore not weak, as the [augmentative] *y* of جَيِّلٌ [that is sound].(225) If it [sc. the weak consonant preceding it] is an *ā*, it [sc. the hamza] is changed into a hamza *bayna bayna* because the *ā* cannot accept neither the vowel nor the assimilation, e.g. سايِلٌ "a questioner" and قايِلٌ "teller".(226) If two hamzas, of which the 1st is vowelled by a fatḥa and the 2nd is vowelless, are combined in one word, the 2nd one is changed into an *ā*, e.g. آخَذُ "the one who holds mostly against" and آدَمُ "tawny",(227) except in أَيِمَّةٌ "leaders in religion" whose hamza is changed into an *ā* as in آخَذُ, and then into a *y* to avoid the cluster of two vowelless consonants. However according to the Kufans, its hamza is not changed into an *ā* to prevent the cluster of two vowelless consonants, and it was recited by them [sur. 9: 12] (أَئِمَّةَ الكُفْرِ) "the chiefs of Unfaith" with both hamzas.(228) If it is stated that the combination of two vowelless consonants is possible at the beginning of the word,(229) then why is it not possible in آمَّةٌ, we answer that the alif in آمَّةٌ is not a [real] *madda,*(230) so how could the combination of two vowelless consonants be made possible at its initial? If it [sc. the 1st hamza] is vowelled by a kasra, it [sc. the 2nd hamza] is changed into a *y,* e.g. إِيسِرْ "capture! /2 masc. sing." underlyingly إِئْسِرْ. If it [sc. the 1st] is vowelled by a ḍamma, it [sc. the 2nd] is changed **[Fol. 23 a]** into a *w,* e.g. أُوثِرَ "he, or it was preferred /passive" [underlyingly أُؤْثِرَ]. As for كُلْ "eat!", مُرْ "order!" and خُذْ "take!", they are anomalous.(231) This is the case if they [sc. the hamzas] are both combined in one word. However, if they are combined in two words, the 2nd one is lightened by al-Ḫalīl, e.g. [sur. 47: 18] (فَقَدْ جاءَ آشْراطُها) "But already Have come some tokens", whereas both are lightened by the Ḥiǧāzis.(232) By some of the Arabs, the separating *ā* is inserted between both the hamzas, e.g. آأَنْتَ as in the saying of the poet: آأَنْتِ ظَبْيَةٌ أَمْ أُمُّ سالِمِ "Are you a female gazelle or Umm Sālim?".(233) The hamza is not lightened at the beginning of the word because it is strongly pronounced by the speaker at the beginning. As for its lightness through its elision in ناسٌ "people" underlyingly أُناسٌ, it is anomalous.(234) So is also إِلَهٌ "a god", in which they elided

الهمزة فصار لاهُ ثمَ أُدخل الألف واللام ثمَ أُدغم فصار الله وقيل أصله الإلَهُ فحُذفت الهمزة الثانية ونقلت حركتها الى اللام فصار اللاهُ ثمَ أُدغم فصار الله كما في يَرَى أصله يَرْأى فقلبت الياء ألفاً لفتحة ما قبلها ثمَ لُيَنت الهمزة فاجتمع ثلث سواكن فحُذفت الهمزة وأُعطيت حركتها الى الراء فصار يَرَى وهذا التخفيف واجب في يَرَى دون أخواتها لكثرة الاستعمال* (٢٣ ب) مع اجتماع حرف العلَة بالهمزة في الفعل الثقيل ومن ثمَ لا يجب يَنَى في يَنْأى ويَسَلُ في يَسألُ ومَرَى في مَرْأى. وتقول في إلحاق الضمائر رأى رأيَا رأوا رَأتْ رَأتا رَأيـن رَأيْتُ رَأيْتما رأيْتُم الى آخره وإعلال الياء سيجيء في باب الناقص. المستقبل يَرَى يَرَيَانِ يَرَوْنَ ترَى تَرَيَانِ يَرَيْنَ تَرَى تَرَيَانِ تَرَوْنَ تَرَيْنَ تَرَيَانِ تَرَيْنَ أرَى نَرَى وحكم يَرَوْنَ كحكم يَرَى ولكن حُذف الألف الذي في يَرَوْنَ لاجتماع الساكنين بواو الجمع وحُرِكَ الياء في يَرَيانِ لطروَ الحركة ولا تُقلب الياء ألفاً لأنها إذا قُلبت ألفاً يجتمع الساكنان ثمَ يُحذف فيلتبس بالواحد في مثل لَنْ يَرَى بيَرَى وأصل تَرَيْنَ تَرْأيِيْنَ على وزن تَفْعَلِيْنَ فحذفت الهمزة كما في يَرَى ونُقلت حركتها الى الراء فصار تَرَيِيْنَ ثمَ جُعلت الياء ألفاً لتحرُكها وفتح ما قبلها فصار تَرَايْنَ ثمَ حُذفت الألف لاجتماع الساكنين فصار تَرَيْنَ وسُوِي بينه وبين جمعه إكتفاءً بالفرق التقديريَ كما في تَرْمِينَ وسيجيء في باب الناقص. وإذا أُدخلت النون الثقيلة في الشرط* (٢٤ آ) كما في قوله

Fols. 23a-24a

١ ثمَ ادغم: –د/ فحذفت: فحذفوا د: فحذف ز/ ٢ ونقلت: فنقل ب د ز حـ ط ک/ حركتها: حركة الهمزة ا ب د ز حـ ط/ ٣ يرأى: يرءيُ ل/ لفتحة: لفتح ل/ لُيَنت: ليَن ا ب د هـ ز ل/ ثلث: ثلاث ل/ فحذفت: فحذف ب ز ط: ثمَ حذفت د: فحذفوا هـ/ ٤ وأُعطيت: واعطي ا د ط ل/ الى الراء: للراء د ل/ أخواتها: أخواته ل/ ٥ الإستعمال: استعماله ل/ الثقيل: + دون ساير الأفعال المهموز لقلَة استعماله جـ/ ٦ يسأل: يسئل د/ ٧ رَأت... رَأيْتُم: – ا ب جـ د هـ ز حـ ط/ ٨–٩ تَرَى... نَرَى: –ا/ ٩ يرى: + في سقوط الهمزة د/ ولكن: لكن د/ حُذف: حذفت ا/ ١٠ وحُرِكَ: وحركت ا/ الياء: – د/ لأنها: لأنه د/ ألفاً: – ا د/ ١١ الساكنان: ساكنان ا ب ک: الساكنين هـ: الساكن ط/ ١٢ ونقلت: ونقل حـ ل/ ونقلت... الراء: –د/ حركتها: فتحتها ا/ ١٣ لتحركها... وفتح: لفتحة ا ب د حـ/ ١٤ اكتفاء: واكتفي د/ ١٥ وسيجيء: فسيجيء ا/ الناقص: + ان شاء الله حـ/

the hamza so that it became لَاهٌ, and then the *ʾa* together with the *l* which is assimilated [to the 2nd *l]* were prefixed, and it became الله. It is said that its base form is الإِلَه whose 2nd hamza is elided and its vowel is shifted to the *l* so it became اللَاهٌ, and then an assimilation was carried out, and it became الله.(235)

So is also the case of يَرَى "he sees" whose base form is يَرْأَى, in which the [3rd radical] *y* is changed into an *ā* on account of the fatḥa preceding it, then the hamza is changed into a weak consonant [sc. an *ā:* يَرْاَى], such which entailed a cluster of three vowelless consonants [the *r,* the *ā* and the *alif maqṣūra],* so the hamza is elided and its vowel is shifted to the *r* so that it became يَرَى. This alleviation is necessary in يَرَى(236) and not in its cognates because of the frequency of its use, **[Fol. 23 b]** and because of [the heaviness of] the combination of the weak consonant and the hamza in the heavy verb.

However it is not allowed to say يَنَى for يَنْأَى "he retires", يَسَل for يَسْأَل "he asks"(237) and مَرَى for مَرْأَى "an aspect".(238)

You say by attaching the pronouns in the perfect: رَأَى "he saw", رَأَيَا "/3 masc. dual", رَأَوا "/3 masc. pl.", رَأَتْ "/3 fem. sing.", رَأَتَا "/3 fem. dual", رَأَيْنَ "/3 fem. pl.", رَأَيْتُ "/1 sing.", رَأَيْتُمَا "/2 pl. dual", رَأَيْتُم "/2 masc. pl.", etc. The unsoundness of the *y* shall be discussed in the section treating the verbs with weak 3rd radical.

In the imperfect: يَرَى "he sees", يَرَيَانِ "/3 masc. dual", يَرَوْنَ "/3 masc. pl.", تَرَى "/3 fem. sing.", تَرَيَانِ "/3 fem. dual", يَرَيْنَ "/3 fem. pl.", تَرَى "/2 masc. sing.", تَرَيَانِ "/2 dual", تَرَوْنَ "/2 masc. pl.", تَرَيْنَ "/2 fem. sing." تَرَيَانِ "/2 dual", تَرَيْنَ "/2 fem. pl.", أَرَى "/1 sing." and نَرَى "/ 1pl.".

The predicament of يَرَوْنَ is similar to the predicament of يَرَى except that the *alif [maqṣūra]* in يَرَوْنَ is elided [from يَرَىوْنَ] to avoid the cluster of two vowelless weak consonants, among them the *ū* of the pl.

The *y* in يَرَيَانِ is vowelled because of the lightness of the vowel. It is not changed into an *ā,* because if so was the case, there would be a cluster of two vowelless weak consonants [sc. the alifs: يَرَاانِ] that would necessitate its elision, such which would cause a confusion with the sing. [يَرَانِ], and so لَنْ يَرَى "they shall not see /subjunctive, dual, (defective)" [with the elision of the *y* instead of [لَنْ يَرَيَا], would be confused with [the sing.] يَرَى.

The base form of تَرَيْنَ "/2 fem. sing." is تَرْأَيِيْنَ, which is according to the pattern تَفْعَلِيْنَ. The hamza is elided [in it] as in يَرَى and its fatḥa is shifted to the *r* so it became تَرَيِيْنَ, then the *y* is changed into an *ā* because of its mobility and because of the [influence of the] fatḥa preceding it, so it became تَرَايْنَ, and then the *ā* is elided to avoid the cluster of two vowelless consonants [sc. the *ā* and the *y]* and it became تَرَيْنَ. It is made homonymous with its plural with the virtual difference being sufficient, as in تَرْمِينَ "you throw, /2 fem. sing. or pl.", which shall be discussed in the section treating the verbs with weak 3rd radical. If the energetic *n* is suffixed to it in the condition **[Fol. 24 a]** as in the words of

تعالى ﴿فإمّا تَرَينَ من البَشَرِ أحَداً﴾ حُذفت النون علامة للجزم وكسرت ياء التأنيث حتَى
يطـرد بجميع نـونات التـأكيـد كمـا في اخْشَينَ ويجـيء تمـامـه في بـاب اللـفـيف. الأمـر
على الأصـل ارءَ وعـلى الحـذف رَ رَيَـا رَوْا رَيْ رَيَـا رَيْـنَ، ولا يُجعل الياء ألفاً في رَيَـا
تبعاً لِيَرَيانِ ويجوز بهاء الوقف نحو رَهْ فحُذفت همزته كما في يَـرَى ثـمّ حُـذفت اليـاء
لأجـل السكون، وبالنون الثقيلة رَيَنَّ رَيَانِّ رَوُنَّ رَيِنَّ رَيَانِّ رَيْنَانِّ ويجيء بـاليـاء في رَيَـنَّ
لانـعـدام الـسـكون كـمـا في ارْمِـيَـنَّ ولم يُـحـذف واو الـجـمـع في رَوُنَّ لـعـدم ضـمّـة مـا
قبلـها بخـلاف أُغْـزُنَّ، وبالنـون الخـفـيفة رَيَـنْ رَوُنْ رَيِـنْ. الفـاعل راء الى آخـره ولا
تُحـذف همــزتـه لمـا يـجـيء في المفـعـول وقيــل لأنَّ مــا قبلـهـا ألــف والألــف لا
تـقـبـل الحركة ولكـن يجـوز لــك أن تجـعـل همـزتـه بين بـيـن كمـا في سـائـل وقُـسَ
على هـذا أرى يُـرِي إراءةً. المفـعـول مَـرْئـيَّ الى آخـره أصله مَرْؤي فـاُعـلَ * كمـا في * ٢٤ ب
مَـهـدِيٍّ ولا يـجـب حـذف هـمــزتـه لأنّ وجــوب حــذف الـهـمــزة في فعلــه غيـر
قـيـاس كـمـا مـرّ فـلا يـسـتـتـبـع المـفـعـول وغيـره، وحُـذفـت في مُـرَى أصلـه مُـرْأى
لـكثـوة مـسـتـتـبعـه وهــو أرَى ويُـرِي وأخـواتـهـمـا، والموضـع مَـرْأى والآلــة مِـرأى
وإذا حُـذفت الـهـمـزة في هــذه الأشـيـاء يجـوز بـالـقـيـاس عـلى نظـائـرهـا ألاَ انّـه
غيـر مـسـتـعـمـل. المجهـول رُئـيَ يُـرَى الى آخـرهمـا. المهمـوز الفـاء يجيء مـن خـمـسـة
أبواب نحـو أخَـذَ يـأخُـذُ وأدَبَ يـأدِبُ وأهَــبَ يـأهَــبُ وأرِجَ يـأرُجُ وأسَـلَ يأسُـلُ

Fols. 24a-24b

١ علامة: -ا/ ٢ بجميع: بجمع د/ نونات: النونات ا: نون د/ اخشينَ: + ونظيره اخشيين بيائين فقلبت الياء الاولى ألفا لتحركها وانفتاح ما قبلها جـ/ ويجيء: وسيجيء د ز/ ٣ على... الحذف: -د هـ ل/ رَوْا: رو ا/ ٥ رَيِنَّ... رَيْنَانِّ: اه ا/ ويجيء: فيجيء د هـ ز حـ ط ک ل/ ٦ ولم: فلم د/ يحذف: تحذف د ل/ ٧ اغزنَّ: اغزونَّ حـ/ وبالنون: وتقول بالنون حـ: وبنون ط/ وبالنون الخفيفة: وبالخفيفة ا د/ الفاعل: اسم الفاعل ب/ راء: + رائيان راؤن ط/ ٨ تحذف: تخفف د: يحذف ب هـ ز حـ ک ل/ المفعول: اسم المفعول حـ/ ٩ تجعل: يجعل د هـ ط/ همزته: -د ل/ سائل: + وقائل جـ ک/ ١٠ آرى: أرى ا/ مرئيّ: مَرايَّ هـ: مَرءى حـ ل/ الى... فاعلَ: -جـ هـ/ كما: + ذكرنا ط/ ١٢ في: + نحو د ل/ ١٣ آرى ويُرَى: أرَى يُرى ا/ مَرْأى: مرئ ا: مَرءى ل/ مِرْأى: مرءى ا ل/ ١٤ رُئيَ يُرَى: رءي يرءى ا: رُؤيَ يُرْءىُ ل/

the Allmighty [sur. 19: 26] (فَإِمَّا تَرَيِنَّ مِنَ البَشَرِ أَحَدًا) "And if thou doest see any man", the *n* is elided as a marker of the jussive and the *y* of the fem. is vowelled by a kasra so that it would be followed by the energetic *n*, as in اخْشَيِنَّ "you do surely dread! (imperative En. 1)".[239] It shall be fully discussed in the section treating the verbs that are doubly weak.

The imperative is underlyingly اِرْءِ and after elision رِ, رَيَا "/2 dual", رَوْا "/2 masc. pl.", رَيْ "/ 2 fem. sing.", رَيَا "/2 dual" and رَيْنَ "/2 fem. pl.".[240]

The *y* is not changed into an *ā* in رَيَا on the analogy of يَرَيَانِ.

It [sc. the masc. of the 2nd person of the imperative] is allowable with the *h* of the pause, e.g. رَهْ whose hamza is elided as in يَرَى, and then the *y* is elided for the sake of the sukūn.

It occurs with the energetic *n*: رَيِنَّ "/2 masc. sing. (imperative En. 1)", رَيَانِّ "/2 dual", رَوُنَّ "/ 2 masc. pl.", رَيِنَّ "/2 fem. sing.", رَيَانِّ "/2 dual" and رَيْنَانِّ "/2 fem. pl.". It occurs with the *y* in رَيِنَّ because of the absence of the sukūn [in the structure] as in ارْمِيَنَّ "throw! /2 masc. sing.". The *w* of the pl. is not elided in رَوُنَّ because the consonant preceding it is not vowelled by a ḍamma, as opposed to أَغْزُنَّ "attack! /2 masc. pl.".

It occurs with the single *n*: رَيَنْ "/2 masc. sing. (imperative En. II)", رَوُنْ "/2 masc. pl." and رَيِنْ "/ 2 fem. sing.".

The active participle is رَاءٍ etc. Its hamza is not elided when it occurs in the passive participle, and it is said because the weak consonant preceding it is an *ā*, and the *ā* does not accept the vowel. However, it is possible for you to change its hamza into a hamza *bayna bayna*, as in سَائِلٌ "questioner" [sc. سَايِلٌ]. Analogously, أَرَى يُرِي إِرَاءَةٌ [Form IV] "to show" occur.

The passive participle is مَرْئِيٌّ etc., underlyingly مَرْوِيٌّ, in which a change due to unsoundness is carried out [Fol. 24 b] as in مَهْدِيٌّ. The hamza should not be elided, because the necessity of eliding it in its verb [sc. يَرَى] is not in conformity with the analogy as was mentioned, so the passive participle and other forms [sc. the active participle, the imperative and others] did not follow it.

It is elided in مُرًى [the passive participle of Form IV] underlyingly مُرْأًى from frequency of usage of the form that it is subordinated to [i.e. the verb of Form IV in the imperfect] أَرَى يُرِي "to show" and both its cognates [sc. the imperative and the prohibition].

The noun of place is مَرْأًى and the noun of instrument is مِرْأًى. The elision of the hamza is possible in these forms on account of the analogy with their equivalents [sc. the imperfect, imperative], but it is not carried out.

The passive voice is رُئِيَ يُرَى etc.

The verbs with hamza as 1st radical fall into five conjugations, e.g. أَخَذَ يَأْخُذُ "to take", أَدَبَ يَأْدُبُ "to invite (to a party or banquet)", أَهَبَ يَأْهَبُ "to prepare", أَرِجَ يَأْرَجُ "to be flagrant" and أَسَلَ يَأْسُلُ "to sharpen".

والمهموز العين يجيء من ثلثة أبواب نحو رَأى يَرأى ويَئس يَيْأسُ ولَؤُمَ يَلْؤُمُ والمهموز
اللام يجيء من أربعة أبواب نحو هَنأ يَهْنِئُ وسَبأ يَسْبَأُ وصَدِئَ يَصْدَأُ وجَرُؤَ يَجْرُؤُ ولا
يجيء في المضاعف إلاّ مهموز الفاء نحو أنَ يَئِنُّ ولا تقع الهمزة في موضع حرف العلّة
ومن ثمَ لا يجيء في المثال إلاّ مهموز العين أو اللام* نحو وَأدَ وَوَجَأ ولا في الأجوف إلاّ * ٢٥ آ
مهموز الفاء أو اللام نحو آنَ وجاءَ ولا في الناقص إلاّ مهموز الفاء أو العين نحو أَبَى
ورَأى ولا في اللفيف المفروق إلاّ مهموز العين نحو وَأى ولا في المقرون إلاّ مهموز الفاء
نحو أوى. وتُكتب الهمزة في الأوَل على صورة الألف في كلّ الأحوال نحو أبٍ وأُمٍ وإبْلٍ
لخفَة الألف وقوَة الكاتب عند الإبتداء على وضع الحركات وفي الوسط إذا كانت ساكنة
تُكتب على وفق حركة ما قبلها نحو رَأسٍ ولُؤمٍ وبئرٍ وذئبٍ للمشاكلة وإذا كانت متحرَكة
تُكتب على وفق حركة نفسها حتّى تُعلم حركتها نحو سَألَ ولَؤمَ وسَئِمَ وإذا كانت
متحرِكة في آخر الكلمة تُكتب على وفق حركة ما قبلها لا على وفق حركة نفسها لأنَ
الحركة الطرفيَة عارضة نحو قَرَأ وطَرُؤَ وفَتِيءَ واذا كان ما قبلها ساكناً لا تُكتب على
صورة شيءٍ لطروَ حركتها وعدم حركة ما قبلها* نحو خَبْءٍ ودِفْءٍ وبُرْءٍ. * ٢٥ ب

Fols. 24b-25b

١ ثلثة: ثلاثة جـ ز ك ل/ يَيْأسُ: ييئس ا حـ ط/ ٢ يَهْنَأُ: يهناء ا/ وصدِئَ: وصدى ب حـ: وصدء د: وصدى هـ ط/ يَصْدَأُ: يصدِئُ ا ب حـ: يصدء د: يصدىَ هـ ط/ وجَرُؤَ يَجْرُؤُ: وجرء يجرء ا د هـ ط: وجزئ يجزئ حـ: وجزأ يجزء ك: وجرُأ يجرء ل/ ٣ يَئِنَ: ياءن ا: يأن د ل/ تقع: يقع ا د هـ ز حـ ط/ في: – د/ ٤ او اللام: ل: all/ ولا في: ل: وفي all/ ٥ او اللام: ل: واللام all/ ولا في(1+2): ل: وفي all/ او العين: ل: والعين all/ أبى: أرى ا ب جـ د ط/ ٦ ولا في(1+2): ل: وفي all/ المقرون: المفروق ا/ ٧ نحو... وإبل: – ب جـ د ط/ أب: أخ ل/ وإبل: وابن هـ ك/ ٨–٩ إذا... تُكتب: – ا جـ/ ٩ تكتب: – ب جـ د هـ ز/ وبئر: – ل/ وذئب: – د/ سَألَ: ساءل ا/ وسئم: وسُئل د/ ١١ ما... حركة: – ا د/ ١٢ عارضة: عارضيَة جـ د هـ ز ط/ كان: كانت ا ب هـ ط/ تكتب: يكتب د ط/ ١٢ وعدم: ولعدم د/ خَبْءٍ... وبُرْءٍ: خبئ ودُفئ وبُرْئ ب/

The verbs with hamza as 2nd radical fall into three conjugations, e.g. رَأَى يَرْأَى "to see", يَئِسَ يَيْأَسُ "to despair" and لَؤُمَ يَلْؤُمُ "to be wicked".

The verbs with hamza as 3rd radical fall into four conjugations, e.g. هَنَأَ يَهْنِئُ "to be beneficial", سَبَأَ يَسْبَأُ "to buy, collect (wine)", صَدِئَ يَصْدَأُ "to become rusty" and جَرُؤَ يَجْرُؤُ "to dare, venture".

Only the verbs with hamza as 1st radical occur as a doubled verb, e.g. أَنَّ يَئِنُّ "to groan, moan", and here the hamza does not replace the weak consonant.

Only the verbs with hamza as 2nd radical or 3rd radical occur as verbs with weak 1st radical, **[Fol. 25 a]** e.g. وَأَدَ "to bury alive (a newborn girl)" and وَجَأَ "to beat".

Only the verbs with hamza as 1st or 3rd radical occur as verbs with weak 2nd radical, e.g. آنَ "to come, to approach" and جَاءَ "to come".

Only the verbs with hamza as 1st or 2nd radical occur as verbs with weak 3rd radical, e.g. أَبَى "to refuse" and رَأَى "to see".

Only the verbs with hamza as 2nd radical occur as verbs with weak 1st and 3rd radical, e.g. وَأَى "to promise".

Only the verbs with hamza as 1st radical occur as verbs with 2nd and 3rd weak radical, e.g. أَوَى "to seek refuge".

The hamza is represented by an alif at the beginning of the word in all cases, e.g. أَبٌ "father", أُمٌّ "mother" and إِبْلٌ "camels", because of the lightness of the alif and because of the determination of the writer to vowel the initial consonant of the word.

If it is vowelless in the middle of the word, it is written according to the vowel preceding it, e.g. رَأْسٌ "head", لُؤْمٌ "baseness, meanness", بِئْرٌ "spring" and ذِئْبٌ "wolf" for the sake of similarity. If it is vowelled, it is written according to its own vowel so that it becomes revealed, e.g. سَأَلَ "to ask", لَؤُمَ "to be wicked, evil" and سَئِمَ "to be weary, tired".

If it is vowelled at the end of the word, it is written according to the vowel preceding it, and not according to its own vowel, because the vowel at the extremity of the word is accidental, e.g. قَرَأَ "to read", طَرُؤَ "to descend, to break in" and فَتِئَ "not to cease to be, to refrain". If the consonant preceding it is vowelless, it is written [unsupported] without representing anything [sc. a weak consonant], because of the weakness of its vowel and the vowellessness of the consonant preceding it, **[Fol. 25 b]** e.g. خَبْءٌ "a hidden thing", دِفْءٌ "warmth" and بُرْءٌ "recovery".(241)

II.4.1. COMMENTARY

The Hamzated Verb

(213) For a general study of المهموز "the Hamzated Verb" see Mu'addib, *Taṣrīf* 405-434, Zanǧānī, *ʿIzzī* 12-13, ʿAbd al-Ḥamīd, *Taṣrīf* 614-618, de Sacy, 232-236, 240-241, 247-248, 256-258, 260-261, Farḥāt, *Baḥṯ* 58-62, Brockelmann, *Socins Grammatik* 40-42, Wright, 72-77, Blachère, 162-164, Bakkūš, *Taṣrīf* 107-118, ʿAbd al-Raḥīm, *Ṣarf* 24-27. The verbs with 1st radical hamza fall into the following conjugations: 1– فَعَلَ يَفْعُلُ, e.g. أَخَذَ يَأْخُذُ "to take", 2– فَعَلَ يَفْعِلُ, e.g. أَتَى يَأْتِي "to come", and أَدَبَ يَأْدِبُ "to invite (to a party or banquet)", 3– فَعَلَ يَفْعَلُ, e.g. أَبَى يَأْبَى "to refuse" (for it see (32)), and أَهَبَ يَأْهَبُ "to prepare", 4– فَعِلَ يَفْعَلُ, e.g. أَرِقَ يَأْرَقُ "to find no sleep", 5– فَعُلَ يَفْعُلُ, e.g. أَرُجَ يَأْرُجُ "to be flagrant" and 6– فَعُلَ يَفْعُلُ, e.g. أَسُلَ يَأْسُلُ "to sharpen". The verb with 1st radical hamza is more numerous than the verb with 2nd radical hamza: 180 / 154 (cf. Bakkūš, *Taṣrīf* 114).

The verbs with 2nd radical hamza fall into the following conjugations: 1– فَعَلَ يَفْعَلُ, e.g. سَأَلَ يَسْأَلُ "to ask", and رَأَى يَرْأَى "to see". It can be noted that the fatḥa is given to its 2nd radical because it is a guttural consonant in the same manner as it is given to the 2nd radical of the strong verb of which the 2nd or 3rd radical is a guttural consonant (for it see (30)). 2– فَعِلَ يَفْعَلُ, e.g. يَئِسَ يَيْأَسُ "to despair" and 3– فَعُلَ يَفْعُلُ, e.g. لَؤُمَ يَلْؤُمُ "to be wicked".

The verbs with 3rd radical hamza fall into the following conjugations: 1– فَعَلَ يَفْعُلُ, e.g. سَاءَ يَسُوءُ "to become evil", 2– فَعَلَ يَفْعِلُ, e.g. جَاءَ يَجِيءُ "to come" and هَنَأَ يَهْنِئُ "to be beneficial", 3– فَعَلَ يَفْعَلُ, e.g. نَشَأَ يَنْشَأُ "to emerge" and سَبَأَ يَسْبَأُ "to buy, collect (wine)", 4– فَعِلَ يَفْعَلُ, e.g. صَدِئَ يَصْدَأُ "to become rusty" and 5– فَعُلَ يَفْعُلُ, e.g. جَرُؤَ يَجْرُؤُ "to dare, venture".

For a study of this class of verb with corresponding forms in some of the other Semitic languages see Brockelmann, *Grundriß* 589-594, Wright, *Comparative Grammar* 277-285.

(214) The paradigm of أَخَذَ, a verb with 1st radical hamza, in the perfect, active, which pertains to the conjugation فَعَلَ يَفْعُلُ is the following:

	sing.	dual	pl.
1st	أَخَذْتُ		أَخَذْنَا
2nd masc.	أَخَذْتَ	أَخَذْتُمَا	أَخَذْتُمْ
2nd fem.	أَخَذْتِ	أَخَذْتُمَا	أَخَذْتُنَّ
3rd masc.	أَخَذَ	أَخَذَا	أَخَذُوا
3rd fem.	أَخَذَتْ	أَخَذَتَا	أَخَذْنَ

Its paradigm in the imperfect of the indicative, active, is the following:

	sing.	dual	pl.
1st	آخُذُ		نَأْخُذُ
2nd masc.	تَأْخُذُ	تَأْخُذَانِ	تَأْخُذُونَ
2nd fem.	تَأْخُذِينَ	تَأْخُذَانِ	تَأْخُذْنَ
3rd masc.	يَأْخُذُ	يَأْخُذَانِ	يَأْخُذُونَ
3rd fem.	تَأْخُذُ	تَأْخُذَانِ	يَأْخُذْنَ

Its paradigm in the imperfect of the subjunctive, active, is the following:

	sing.	dual	pl.
1st	آخُذَ		نَأْخُذَ
2nd masc.	تَأْخُذَ	تَأْخُذَا	تَأْخُذُوا
2nd fem.	تَأْخُذِي	تَأْخُذَا	تَأْخُذْنَ
3rd masc.	يَأْخُذَ	يَأْخُذَا	يَأْخُذُوا
3rd fem.	تَأْخُذَ	تَأْخُذَا	يَأْخُذْنَ

Its paradigm in the imperfect of the jussive, active, is the following:

	sing.	dual	pl.
1st	آخُذْ		نَأْخُذْ
2nd masc.	تَأْخُذْ	تَأْخُذَا	تَأْخُذُوا
2nd fem.	تَأْخُذِي	تَأْخُذَا	تَأْخُذْنَ
3rd masc.	يَأْخُذْ	يَأْخُذَا	يَأْخُذُوا
3rd fem.	تَأْخُذْ	تَأْخُذَا	يَأْخُذْنَ

Its imperative is خُذْ. Its active participle is آخِذٌ. Its *maṣdar* is أَخْذٌ. Its perfect, passive is أُخِذَ. Its imperfect is يُؤْخَذُ. Its passive participle is مأخُوذٌ.

b) سَأَلَ, a verb with 2nd radical hamza, pertains to the conjugation فَعَلَ يَفْعَلُ. Its perfect, active, is سَأَلَ. Its imperfect of the indicative, active, is يَسْأَلُ, of the subjunctive, active, يَسْأَلَ and of the jussive, active, يَسْأَلْ. Its imperative is اِسْأَلْ. Its active participle is سَائِلٌ. Its *maṣdar* is سُؤَالٌ. Its perfect, passive is سُئِلَ. Its imperfect, passive, is يُسْأَلُ. Its passive participle is مَسْؤُولٌ.

An example of a verb with 2nd radical hamza that pertains to the conjugation فَعُلَ يَفْعُلُ, and thus has a *w* with hamza as its 2nd radical in the perfect, is بَؤُسَ "to be strong". Its paradigm of the groundform and derived forms is the following:

Form I: Its perfect, active is بَؤُسَ. Its imperfect is يَبْؤُسُ. Its imperative is اُبْؤُسْ. Its active participle is بَائِسٌ. Its *maṣdar* is بَأْسٌ. Its perfect, passive is بُئِسَ. Its imperfect is يُبْأَسُ. Its passive participle is مَبْؤُوسٌ.

Form II: Its perfect, active is بَأَّسَ. Its imperfect is يُبَئِّسُ. Its imperative is بَئِّسْ. Its active participle is مُبَئِّسٌ. Its *maṣdar* is تَبْئِيسٌ. Its perfect, passive is بُئِّسَ. Its imperfect is يُبَأَّسُ. Its passive participle is مُبَأَّسٌ.

Form III: Its perfect, active is بَاءَسَ. Its imperfect is يُبَائِسُ. Its imperative is بَائِسْ. Its active participle is مُبَائِسٌ. Its *maṣdar* is مُبَائَسَةٌ. Its perfect, passive is بُوئِسَ. Its imperfect is يُبَائَسُ. Its passive participle is مُبَاءَسٌ.

Form IV: Its perfect, active is أَبْأَسَ. Its imperfect is يُبْئِسُ. Its imperative is أَبْئِسْ. Its active participle is مُبْئِسٌ. Its *maṣdar* is اِبْآسٌ. Its perfect, passive is أُبْئِسَ. Its imperfect is يُبْأَسُ. Its passive participle is مُبْأَسٌ.

Form V: Its perfect, active is تَبَأَّسَ. Its imperfect is يَتَبَأَّسُ. Its imperative is تَبَأَّسْ. Its active participle is مُتَبَئِّسٌ. Its *maṣdar* is تَبَؤُّسٌ. Its perfect, passive is تُبُئِّسَ. Its imperfect is يُتَبَأَّسُ. Its passive participle is مُتَبَأَّسٌ.

Form VI: Its perfect, active is تَبَاءَسَ. Its imperfect is يَتَبَاءَسُ. Its imperative is تَبَاءَسْ. Its active participle is مُتَبَائِسٌ. Its *maṣdar* is تَبَاؤُسٌ. Its perfect, passive is تُبُوئِسَ. Its imperfect is يُتَبَائَسُ. Its passive participle is مُتَبَاءَسٌ.

Form VII: Its perfect, active is اِنْبَأَسَ. Its imperfect is يَنْبَئِسُ. Its imperative is اِنْبَئِسْ. Its active participle is مُنْبَئِسٌ. Its *maṣdar* is اِنْبِئَاسٌ. Its perfect, passive is أُنْبُئِسَ. Its imperfect is يُنْبَأَسُ. Its passive participle is مُنْبَأَسٌ.

Form VIII: Its perfect, active is اِبْتَأَسَ. Its imperfect is يَبْتَئِسُ. Its imperative is اِبْتَئِسْ. Its active participle is مُبْتَئِسٌ. Its *maṣdar* is اِبْتِئَاسٌ. Its perfect, passive is أُبْتُئِسَ. Its imperfect is يُبْتَأَسُ. Its passive participle is مُبْتَأَسٌ.

Form X: Its perfect, active is اِسْتَبْأَسَ. Its imperfect is يَسْتَبْئِسُ. Its imperative is اِسْتَبْئِسْ. Its active participle is مُسْتَبْئِسٌ. Its *maṣdar* is اِسْتِبْآسٌ. Its perfect, passive is أُسْتُبْئِسَ. Its imperfect is يُسْتَبْأَسُ. Its passive participle is مُسْتَبْأَسٌ.

c) قَرَأَ, a verb with 3rd radical hamza, pertains to the conjugation فَعَلَ يَفْعَلُ. Its perfect, active, is قَرَأَ. Its imperfect of the indicative, active, is يَقْرَأُ, of the subjunctive, active, يَقْرَأَ and of the jussive, active, يَقْرَأْ. Its imperative is اِقْرَأْ. Its active participle is قَارِئٌ. Its *maṣdar* is قِرَاءَةٌ. Its perfect, passive is قُرِئَ. Its imperfect is يُقْرَأُ. Its passive participle is مَقْرُوءٌ.

The paradigm of its derived forms is the following:

Form II: Its perfect, active is قَرَّأَ. Its imperfect is يُقَرِّئُ. Its imperative is قَرِّئْ. Its active participle is مُقَرِّئٌ. Its *maṣdar* is تَقْرِئَةٌ. Its perfect, passive is قُرِّئَ. Its imperfect is يُقَرَّأُ. Its passive participle is مُقَرَّأٌ.

Form III: Its perfect, active is قَارَأَ. Its imperfect is يُقَارِئُ. Its imperative is قَارِئْ. Its active participle is مُقَارِئٌ. Its *maṣdar* is مُقَارَأَةٌ. Its perfect, passive is قُورِئَ. Its imperfect is يُقَارَأُ. Its passive participle is مُقَارَأٌ.

Form IV: Its perfect, active is أَقْرَأَ. Its imperfect is يُقْرِئُ. Its imperative is أَقْرِئْ. Its active participle is مُقْرِئٌ. Its *maṣdar* is إِقْرَاءٌ. Its perfect, passive is أُقْرِئَ. Its imperfect is يُقْرَأُ. Its passive participle is مُقْرَأٌ.

Form V: Its perfect, active is تَقَرَّأَ. Its imperfect is يَتَقَرَّأُ. Its imperative is تَقَرَّأْ. Its active participle is مُتَقَرِّئٌ. Its *maṣdar* is تَقَرُّؤٌ. Its perfect, passive is تُقُرِّئَ. Its imperfect is يُتَقَرَّأُ. Its passive participle is مُتَقَرَّأٌ.

Form VI: Its perfect, active is تَقَارَأَ. Its imperfect is يَتَقَارَأُ. Its imperative is تَقَارَأْ. Its active participle is مُتَقَارِئٌ. Its *maṣdar* is تَقَارُؤٌ. Its perfect, passive is تُقُورِئَ. Its imperfect is يُتَقَارَأُ. Its passive participle is مُتَقَارَأٌ.

Form VII: Its perfect, active is اِنْقَرَأَ. Its imperfect is يَنْقَرِئُ. Its imperative is اِنْقَرِئْ. Its active participle is مُنْقَرِئٌ. Its *maṣdar* is اِنْقِرَاءٌ. Its perfect, passive is أُنْقُرِئَ. Its imperfect is يُنْقَرَأُ. Its passive participle is مُنْقَرَأٌ.

Form VIII: Its perfect, active is اِقْتَرَأَ. Its imperfect is يَقْتَرِئُ. Its imperative is اِقْتَرِئْ. Its active participle is مُقْتَرِئٌ. Its *maṣdar* is اِقْتِرَاءٌ. Its perfect, passive is أُقْتُرِئَ. Its imperfect is يُقْتَرَأُ. Its passive participle is مُقْتَرَأٌ.

Form X: Its perfect, active is اِسْتَقْرَأَ. Its imperfect is يَسْتَقْرِئُ. Its imperative is اِسْتَقْرِئْ. Its active participle is مُسْتَقْرِئٌ. Its *maṣdar* is اِسْتِقْرَاءٌ. Its perfect, passive is أُسْتُقْرِئَ. Its imperfect is يُسْتَقْرَأُ. Its passive participle is مُسْتَقْرَأٌ.

(215) The hamza can either be pronounced fully or be lightened (cf. Ṣubḥī, *Fiqh* 77-78, Rabin, 130-131). Its being pronounced fully makes it similar in its predicament to the strong consonant. The reason of its alleviation is that it is a hard heavy consonant, uttered from the farthest part of the throat. Its softening pertains to the dialect of Quraiš and to most of the inhabitants of al-Ḥiǧāz, whereas its pronouncing fully pertains to the dialect of Tamīm and Qais (cf. Sībawaihi, *II,* 168, Howell, *IV,* fasc. I, 812, 930). According to Abū Zaid referred to by Ibn Manẓūr, *I,* 26, the Ḥiǧāzīs, the Huḏail, and the inhabitants of Makka and Madīna do not pronounce the hamza. ʿIsā b. ʿUmar mentioned that Tamīm pronounce it fully and that the Ḥiǧāzīs do so only if they are obliged to.

(216) The hamza *bayna bayna* is termed as betwixt and between by Howell, *Grammar IV,* fasc. I, 930 sqq. (cf. Cachia, *Monitor* 12). This lightened hamza, which is preceded by a fatḥa, is a sort of mixture between the hamza and the weak consonant to which its vowel is connected to (cf. Sībawaihi, *II,* 168-169, Ibn Yaʿīš, *IX,* 107, Roman, *Étude I,* 324-326). If the hamza is over the alif and thus vowelled by a fatḥa, it is changed into the *ā,* e.g. سَالَ used instead of سَأَلَ

"he asked", if it is *ʿalā kursī l-yāʾ* and thus vowelled by the kasra, it is changed into the *y,* e.g. سَيِمَ used instead of سَئِمَ "he was weary", and if it is over the *w* and thus vowelled by the ḍamma, it is changed into the *w,* e.g. لَوُمَ for لَؤُمَ "he was base" (cf. Lane, *I,* 288). Concerning it, Ibn Ǧinnī, *Sirr I,* 48 writes:

"وأما الهمزة المخففة فهي التي تسمى همزة بَيْنَ بَيْنَ – ومعنى قول سيبويه "بَيْنَ بَيْنَ" أي هي بين الهمزة وبين الحرف الذي منه حركتها – إن كانت مفتوحة فهي بين الهمزة والألف ، وإن كانت مكسورة فهي بين الهمزة والياء ، وإن كانت مضمومة فهي بين الهمزة والواو... فالمفتوحة نحو قولك في سأل: سَالَ ، والمكسورة نحو قولك في سَئِمَ: سَيِمَ ، والمضمومة نحو قولك في لَؤُمَ: لَوُمَ".

> "As for the lightened hamza, it is the one that is termed *bayna bayna.* The meaning with Sībawaihi's saying *bayna bayna* is that it is between the hamza and the weak consonant to which its vowel is connected to. If it is vowelled by the fatḥa it is then between the hamza and the *ā,* if it is vowelled by the kasra it is then between the hamza and the *y,* and if it is vowelled by the ḍamma it is then between the hamza and the *w...* As for the one vowelled by the fatḥa it is in your saying concerning سَأَلَ "he asked": سَالَ, as for the one vowelled by the kasra it is in your saying concerning سَئِمَ "he was weary": سَيِمَ, and as for the one vowelled by the ḍamma it is in your saying concerning لَؤُمَ "he was base: لَوُمَ".

Nöldeke, *Grammatik* 5 compares the hamza *bayna bayna* with the french diphthong *oi, ie* or the Dutch *ooi, eeu,* etc. This hamza is considered as vowelless according to the Kufans whereas it is provided by a faint vowel close to the sukūn according to the Basrans (for their debate see Ibn al-Anbārī, *Inṣāf* Q. 105, 306-307).

(217) The vowelless hamza is considered as weak because of its sukūn. It is therefore subjected to the influence of the vowel preceding it, which is considered as strong, and is for that reason able to force it to be changed into a weak consonant that should be of the same nature as itself. When the vowelless alif with hamza is preceded by the kasra, it is changed into a *y,* e.g. بِيرٌ "well" for بِئْرٌ (cf. Fischer/Jastrow, *Dialekte* 39, Bohas, *Étude* 265), when it is preceded by the fatḥa it is changed into an *ā,* e.g. رَاسٌ "head" for رَأْسٌ (cf. (369), Nöldeke, *Grammatik* 6; for other examples see (216), (220)), and when it is preceded by the ḍamma it is changed into a *w,* e.g. مُومِنٌ "believer" for مُؤْمِنٌ (cf. Bohas, *Étude* 264-265), and لُومٌ used instead of لُؤْمٌ (cf. (362)). This change is said to be caused by the Arabs' eagerness that the vowel of the weak consonant paused upon should be made plain (cf. Howell, *IV,* fasc. I, 810). The same change of the hamza into an *ā* as in رَاسٌ said instead of رَأْسٌ occurs in Hebrew, as רַאְשׁ becomes first רָאשׁ *rāš* and then ראשׁ *rōš.* The Aramaic has רֵישׁ, ܪܝܫܐ for רָאשׁ and the Assyrian has *rēšu* or *rīšu* (cf. Wright, *Comparative Grammar* 45).

In ordinary cases when the vowelless hamza is not changed into a weak consonant, the vowel preceding it determines as well its shape. When it is preceded by the ḍamma it is changed into a *w* with hamza, ؤ, e.g. لُؤْمٌ "baseness", written with a *w* with hamza instead of لأْمٌ written with the hamza over the alif, and when it is preceded by the kasra it is changed into a *hamza ʿalā kursī l-yā'*, ئ, e.g. بئر "well, spring", written with a *hamza 'alā kursī l-yā'* instead of بإر written with the hamza under the alif (cf. Wright, *II*, 72).

(218) When the hamza that is vowelled by a ḍamma or by a kasra and that is preceded by a fatḥa is not alleviated by its change into a hamza *bayna bayna*, it is written over – in the case of the ؤ – or under, – in the case of the ئ -, the particular weak consonant that its vowel is connected to (for discussions see de Sacy, *I*, 95, Wright, *II*, 75). If the hamza is vowelled by a ḍamma, which in the base form is written over the alif, i.e. the أ, it is changed into a hamza over the *w*, ؤ. An example is لَؤُمَ "to be wicked" written with the hamza over the *w* instead of the base form لَأُمَ written with a hamza over the alif vowelled by a ḍamma. If the hamza is vowelled by a kasra, which in the base form is written under the alif, the إ, it is changed into a *hamza 'alā kursī l-yā'*, ئ. An example is سَئِمَ "to be weary" written with the *hamza 'alā kursī l-yā'* instead of the base form سَإِمَ written with a hamza under the alif.
Otherwise, the vowelled hamza that is preceded by a fatḥa can be softened and changed into a hamza *bayna bayna*, e.g. سَال, لَوُمَ and سَيِمَ used instead of سَأَل, لَؤُمَ, and سَئِمَ (for discussions see. (216)).

(219) The base form of مِيرٌ is مِئَرٌ and of جُوَنٌ جُؤَنٌ (cf. Sībawaihi, *II*, 169, Zamaḫšarī, 166). In both these examples the hamza of the base form is vowelled by a fatḥa and preceded by a kasra or a ḍamma respectively. The fatḥa is considered as faint and thus similar to the sukūn in that respect, which is why the hamza that is vowelled by the fatḥa is changed into a weak consonant of the nature of the vowel preceding it, in the same manner as the hamza that is vowelless does (for examples see (216), (217), (362)). Thus if this vowel is a kasra as in مِئَرٌ, it is changed into the *y* and if it is a ḍamma as in جُؤَنٌ, it is changed into the *w* (cf. Ibn Wallād, *Maqṣūr* 166). مِيرٌ is taken up by Zamaḫšarī, 173 as an example in which the *y* is substituted for the hamza (for this substitution see (217), (351)), and جُوَنٌ is taken up by ibid, 174 and by Ibn Ǧinnī, *Sirr II*, 573 as an example in which the *w* is substituted for the hamza (for this substitution see (217), (362)). جَوْنٌ exists also meaning "dark, black". Ṯa'ālibī, *Fiqh* 247 and Ibn Duraid, *Ištiqāq* 224 remark that the word can mean both white and black. For a study of the word see Howell, *IV*, fasc. I, 1319, Fischer, *Farb–* 27-36. The Aramaic has גון, ܓܘܢ meaning "colour" (cf. Nöldeke, *Neue Beiträge* 94).

(220) The hamza of هَنَأَكِ is lightened resulting in هَنَاكِ, or the *ā* is substituted for the hamza (for further examples of this substitution see (217), (369)). This alleviated form occurs in this line for the sake of metric exigency. The complete line is:

"رَاحَتْ بِمَسْلَمَةَ ٱلْبِغَالُ عَشِيَّةً فَٱرْعَىْ فَزَارَةُ لَا هَنَاكِ ٱلْمَرْتَعُ".

> "The mules have gone away with Maslama at evening. Then graze your camels, Fazāra. May the pasture not be pleasant to you!".

The verse is said by Farazdaq, *Dīwān* 508, and is cited by Sībawaihi, *II*, 175, Ibn Ǧinnī, *Ḫaṣā'iṣ*

III, 152, *Sirr II,* 666, Ibn al-Sarrāǧ, *Uṣūl III,* 469, Muʾaddib, *Taṣrīf* 530, Zamaḫšarī, 166, Ibn Yaʿīš, *IX,* 113, *Mulūkī* 229, Ibn ʿUṣfūr, *I,* 405, Afandī, *Tanzīl* 445, Howell, *IV,* fasc. I, 951. Zamaḫšarī, *Kaššāf II,* 528 cites لَا هَنَاكِ ٱلْمَرْتَعُ without presenting the whole verse when he is explaining one of both meanings of طه of the sur. 20. He writes that according to al-Ḥasan it is the imperative of الوطء "to set foot" underlyingly طأ in which the hamza is changed into a *h* or into an *ā* in the imperfect, i.e. يطا for يطأ, in the same manner as the hamza in لَا هَنَاكِ ٱلْمَرْتَعُ is substituted by the *ā,* and then it is conjugated in the imperative and the *h* in طه is added to mark the pause.

(221) The sorts of vowelless consonants, whether strong or weak, that can precede the hamza that is vowelled by a fatḥa, causing the hamza's elision and the transfer of its fatḥa to them, can be: 1– a strong consonant, e.g. the radical *s* in مَسْأَلَةٌ (see (222)), the radical *l* in مَلْأَكٌ (see (222)) and the *l* of the definite article *al–* in الأَحمر (see (223)), 2– the augmented *y,* e.g. جَيْأَلٌ (see (224)), the underlying *y,* e.g. the 3rd radical *y* in the imperfect of the 1st person of the sing. أَبْتَغِي in the example أَبْتَغِي أَمْرَهُ (224)) and the augmented *w,* e.g. جَوْأَبَةٌ (see (224)), and أَبُو in أَبُو أَيُّوبَ (see (224)).

(222) The base form of مَسَلَةٌ is مَسْأَلَةٌ "a matter" (cf. Zamaḫšarī, 166, Ibn Yaʿīš, *IX,* 109), in which the vowelled hamza is elided, and its vowel, the fatḥa, is shifted to the vowelless strong consonant, the 1st radical *s,* preceding it. The base form of مَلَكٌ is مَلْأَكٌ "angel" (cf. Ibn Ǧinnī, *Munṣif II,* 102-104, Zamaḫšarī, 166, Ibn Manẓūr, *I,* 110-111, Wright, *II,* 77, Vernier, *I,* 101-102, Fleischer, *Beiträge* 139, Lane, *I,* 81-82), in which the vowelled hamza is elided, and its vowel, the fatḥa, is shifted to the vowelless strong consonant, the 2nd radical *l,* preceding it. According to al-Kisāʾī, مَلْأَكٌ is derived from أَلَكَ "to convey" before that a transposition of consonants is carried out in it so that it became لَأَكَ, whereas according to Abū ʿUbaida it is from لَأَكَ and according to Ibn Kaisān from مَلَكَ (cf. Bohas, *Étude* 195-197). The *maṣdars* of أَلَكَ are أَلُوكٌ and أَلُوكَةٌ. The base form مَأْلَكٌ from أَلَكَ becomes by transposition of the *l* before the hamza مَلْأَكٌ (cf. Talmon, *ʿAyn* 142). It can be noted that Derenbourg printed in Sībawaihi, *II,* 209 l. 1 مَلَكٌ while the content requires مَلْأَك. Both مَأْلُكَةٌ and مَأْلَكَةٌ are said in the meaning of "message". مَأْلُكَةٌ occurs in the verse mentioned in (224). Compare in Hebrew מַלְאָךְ, but מְלָאכָה for מַלְאָכָה, the Aramaic ܡܲܠܐܵܟ݂ܵܐ and the Ethiopic መልአክ (cf. Wright, *Comparative Grammar* 44-45, Nöldeke, *Neue Beiträge* 34).

(223) لَحْمَرُ is from الَحْمَرُ, which is the alleviated form of الأَحْمَرُ (cf. Sībawaihi, *II,* 170, Ibn Ǧinnī, *Ḫaṣāʾiṣ III,* 90-92, *Munṣif I,* 69-70, Zamaḫšarī, 166-167, Ibn Yaʿīš, *IX,* 115-116, Howell, *IV,* fasc. I, 942-943, 959-963, Lane, *I,* 74, Wright, *II,* 269, Vernier, *I,* 102, Fleisch, *Traité I,* 108). The vowelled hamza of الأَحْمَرُ is elided, and its vowel, the fatḥa, is shifted to the vowelless strong consonant, the *l,* of the article ال preceding it. Then the connective hamza is elided, i.e.

لَحْمَرُ, as the reason of its prefixation in the first place is to prevent beginning the word with a vowelless *l,* and when this *l* was not more vowelless the hamza was not more needed. Another variant is اَلْحَمْرُ with the connective hamza maintained, because the fatḥa over the *l* is considered as feeble, as it is assumed that the *l* of the article is virtually vowelless and that its vowelling in the new form is accidental.

(224) The cases that are mentioned concern the transfer of the hamza's fatḥa after the hamza's elision, to the *y* or to the *w* preceding it, whether this specific weak consonant is underlying or an augment. If the weak consonant is an infix, the conditions of the hamza's elision and consequently of its fatḥa's transfer to it, is that that this weak consonant is not a weak consonant of prolongation, i.e. a weak consonant that lengthens the sound of the vowel preceding it (a glide), as the *ī* in فعيلَةٌ that lengthens the kasra preceding it, or the *ū* in مَفْعُولَةٌ that lengthens the ḍamma preceding it, or a weak consonant that is specific for the diminutive, as the *y* of أُفَيْعِلُ, because in these cases the hamza is assimilated to the weak consonant preceding it (for such cases see (225)). Hence, the alleviation of the hamza and the transfer of its fatḥa to the preceding weak consonant occur in جَيَلٌ said instead of جَيْأَلٌ "female hyena" from the root جأل (cf. Ibn Manẓūr, *I,* 529, Lane, *I,* 370) and in جَوَبَةٌ said instead of جَوْأَبَةٌ "*Ǧaw'aba* (name of a water)" from the root جأب (cf. Howell, *IV,* fasc. I, 938), in which the augmentative *y* and *w* are for co-ordination with فَيْعَلٌ and فَوْعَلَةٌ respectively.

The alleviation of the hamza is carried out as well if the vowelless weak consonant is not in the same word as the hamza. In this case the vowelled hamza, which is the initial consonant of the second word, is elided, and its vowel, the fatḥa, is shifted to the vowelless weak consonant which precedes it that is the ultimate weak consonant of the word before it (for a study see Sībawaihi, *II,* 171-172, Zamaḫšarī, 166, Howell, *IV,* fasc. I, 938 sqq., Vernier, *I,* 104). This occurs in أَبْتَغِيَ مَرَهُ said instead of أَبْتَغِي أَمْرَهُ "I seek for his matter" and in أَبُوَيُّوبَ said instead of أَبُو أَيُّوبَ "the father of Job" (cf. Howell, *IV,* fasc. I, 940). In the first example, the *y* of أَبْتَغِي is the 3rd radical of the verb بَغِيَ, and in the second example the *w* of أَبُو is the nominative's ending, as أَبٌ is the first element of a construct state. The fatḥa of the hamza that is shifted to these weak consonants in أَبْتَغِيَ مَرَهُ and أَبُوَيُّوبَ, and in the nouns mentioned above, i.e. جَيَلٌ and جَوَبَةٌ, is counted as feeble, because it belongs in the base forms to the hamza. This is the main reason why the weak consonants in these examples remain sound and are not changed into an *ā* due to the influence of the fatḥa preceding them. Some other examples that can be added with the vowelless consonant preceding the hamza being either a weak or a strong consonant are ذُوَ مْرِهِمْ for ذُو أَمْرِهِمْ "the author of their matter" (cf. Ibn Yaʿīš, *IX,* 109), قَاضُوَ بِيكَ for قَاضُو أَبِيكَ "the judges of your father" and مَنَ بُوكَ for مَنْ أَبُوكَ "who is your father" (cf. ibid, 110, Howell, *IV,* fasc. I, 940). Some alleviate the hamza in the sur. 23: 1 (قَدَ ٱفْلَحَ ٱلْمُومِنُونَ) "The Believers must (eventually) win through", read instead of قَدْ أَفْلَحَ ٱلْمُؤْمِنُونَ (cf. Ibn Yaʿīš, *IX,* 110, Nöldeke, *Neue Beitræge* 3) and in the sur. 4: 71 (إِلَى ٱلْهُدَاتِنَا) "Come to us", read instead of إِلَى ٱلْهُدَى ٱئْتِنَا

(cf. Howell, *IV,* fasc. I, 934-935). Other examples, just to mention a few, are لَوَ آنَ "if" for لَوْ أنَ and قَدَ آصْبَحَ "he has become" for قَدْ أصْبَحَ (for a study see Nöldeke, *Grammatik* 5). It can be noted that the one who says لَحْمَرُ (see (223)) with the elision of the connective hamza of the article, says as well مِنْ لَانَ with the *n* given a sukūn instead of مِنَ آلآنَ, and the one who says اَلَحْمَرُ with the connective hamza given the fatḥa says مِنَ لَانَ with the *n* vowelled by a fatḥa (cf. Ibn Yaʿīš, *IX,* 116, Howell, *IV,* fasc. I, 960). Accordingly with the elision of the connective hamza of the article, some read sur. 2: 71 as (قَالُوا لَانَ جِئْتَ بِالْحَقِّ) "They said: "Now hast thou brought the truth" (cf. Ibn Yaʿīš, *IX,* 116) instead of (قَالُوا آلآنَ جِئْتَ بِالْحَقِّ). Some also assimilate the *tanwīn* of the first word to the *l* of the article of the second word, elide as well the hamza of the second word and shift its ḍamma to the *l,* as Abū Amr did when he read عَادًا لُولَى instead of عَادًا آلأُولَى of the sur. 53: 50 (وَأَنَّهُ أَهْلَكَ عَادًا آلأُولَى) "And that it is He who destroyed the (powerful) Ancient ʿĀd (people)" (cf. Ibn Yaʿīš, *IX,* 116). Zamaḫšarī, *Kaššāf IV,* 34 notes that some even read the sur. with عَادُ لُّولَى instead. This is the reading of both Abū ʿAmr and Nāfiʿ (cf. Ibn Muǧāhid, *Sabʿa* 615 and see further Fischer, *Beiträge* 602-603). Furthermore the *n* of مِنَ is elided in juxtaposition with the article, e.g. مِلْكَذِبِ is said instead of مِنَ ٱلْكَذِبِ in the following verse said by an unknown poet, cited by Ibn Ǧinnī, *Sirr II,* 539, *Ḫaṣāʾiṣ I,* 311, *III,* 275, Ibn al-Šağarī, *Amālī I,* 97, 386, Ibn Yaʿīš, *IX,* 100, 116, Ibn Manẓūr, *I,* 110, Howell, *IV,* fasc. I, 961:

"أَبْلِغْ أَبَا دُخْتَنُوسَ مَأْلُكَةً   غَيْرَ ٱلَّذِي قَدْ يُقَالُ مِلْكَذِبِ".

"Convey to Abū Daḫtanūs a message, not that which is sometimes said, consisting of falsehood".

(225) The vowelless consonant preceding the vowelled hamza can be an augmented weak consonant, namely a *w* or a *y.* The condition of the hamza's assimilation to the infixed weak consonant is that this consonant should be a weak consonant of prolongation, i.e. a glide that lengthens the sound of the vowel preceding it, as the *ī* in فَعِيلَةٌ, e.g. خَطِيئَةٌ "a sin", that lengthens the sound of the kasra preceding it, or the *ū* in مَفْعُولَةٌ, e.g. مَقْرُوءَةٌ "a writing read", that lengthens the sound of the ḍamma preceding it, or that it is specific for the diminutive, as the *y* of أُفَيْعِلٌ, e.g. أُفَيْئِسٌ the diminutive of أَفْؤُسٌ pl. of فَأْسٌ "axe". If the infixed weak consonant is not any of these mentioned weak consonants and the hamza's vowel is a fatḥa, the hamza is elided and its fatḥa is shifted to the weak consonant preceding it (for discussions cf. (224)).The base form of خَطِيَّةٌ is خَطِيئَةٌ, of مَقْرُوَّةٌ: مَقْرُوءَةٌ, and of أُفَيَّسٌ: أُفَيْئِسٌ (cf. Sībawaihi, *II,* 171, 175, Ibn Ǧinnī, *Munṣif I,* 327-330, Ibn Yaʿīš, *IX,* 108-109, Howell, *IV,* fasc. I, 936-937, de Sacy, *I,* 370, Vernier, *I,* 102, 350). The vowel of the hamza in these examples could not be shifted to the weak consonant preceding it after the hamza's elision, – as in e.g. مَسْأَلَةٌ resulting in مَسَلَةٌ (222), in الأَحْمَرُ resulting in اَلَحْمَرُ (223) and in جَيْأَلٌ resulting in جَيَلٌ (224)) -, because the weak consonant is an infix in them. Thus خَطِيئَةٌ could not become خَطِيَةٌ, مَقْرُوءَةٌ could not become مَقْرُوَةٌ and أُفَيْئِسٌ could not become أُفَيَسٌ. This is why the hamza is at first lightened by its change into the same weak consonant as the one preceding it, and then an assimilation is carried out from the 1st weak consonant to the 2nd one. Thus خَطِيئَةٌ becomes خَطِيِيَةٌ after the change of the hamza into a *y*, and then خَطِيَّةٌ after the assimilation of the *y* to the *y*, مَقْرُوءَةٌ becomes مَقْرُووَةٌ and then مَقْرُوَّةٌ, and أُفَيْئِسٌ becomes أُفَيْيِسٌ and then أُفَيِّسٌ. The 1st *y* is the infixed weak consonant in both خَطِيئَةٌ formed according to فَعِيلَةٌ and أُفَيْئِسٌ formed according to أُفَيْعِلٌ, whereas the hamza in them is a radical, namely the 3rd radical in خَطِئَ and the 2nd radical in فَأْسٌ. According to a theory referred to by Ibn Masʿūd, infixed weak consonants are considered as weak in comparison to radicals which are considered as strong, unless if the radical is elided in the word, because in this case the existent infixed weak consonant can be considered as strong in comparison to the absent radical. It is the 2nd *y* among the doubled yā's and not the 1st one, in both خَطِيَّةٌ which resulted from خَطِيِيَةٌ and أُفَيِّسٌ which resulted from أُفَيْيِسٌ, that can carry the vowel, because it is a radical hamza in the base forms خَطِيئَةٌ and أُفَيْئِسٌ, that has been changed into a *y* in them. Furthermore, regarding its strength, the *y* in both these examples is compared to the augmentative *y* of جَيَلٌ (cf. (224)) that is infixed in order that the form is formed according to فَيْعَلٌ. It is only because the radical hamza of the base form جَيْأَلٌ is elided, that the *y* infix can be considered as strong by relation to it, in spite of the fact that the *y* is not a radical. Other examples similar to خَطِيَّةٌ are بَرِيَّةٌ "creation" underlyingly بَرِيئَةٌ and نَبِيٌّ "prophet" underlyingly نَبِيءٌ. Compare with the Arabic خَطِيئَةٌ, the Ethiopic ኀጢአት and the Aramaic ܚܛܝܬܐ (cf. Nöldeke, *Neue Beiträge* 36). It can be noted that نَبِيٌّ it is a loanword from the Hebrew, through the Aramaic, in which the hamza was already lost (cf. Nöldeke, *Geschichte* 1; for a study of the word see Wright, *Comparative Grammar* 46).

(226) If the vowelled hamza is preceded by an *ā*, which is a glide that lengthens the sound of the fatḥa preceding it, the hamza is changed into a hamza *bayna bayna* (for discussions see Sībawaihi, *II,* 171, Roman, *Étude I,* 333). The reason of this change is that the *ā* cannot take the vowel of the hamza if it is shifted to it, as well as it cannot be assimilated to another *ā* if the hamza is changed into one. Some patterns in which the *ā* is a glide, are the active participle فَاعِلٌ, e.g. سَائِلٌ "questioner" with the 2nd radical hamza vowelled by a kasra, from سَأَلَ "to ask", that results after the change into a *hamza bayna bayna* in سَايِلٌ and قَائِلٌ "teller" with the 2nd radical *w* from قَاوِلٌ changed into a hamza vowelled by a kasra, from قَوَلَ "to tell", that results after the change in قَايِلٌ, and the broken pl. of the nouns مَفَاعِلٌ, e.g. مَسَائِلٌ "questions" (cf. Sībawaihi, *II,* 171, Roman, *Étude I,* 333). An example that can be taken up in which the hamza is vowelled by a ḍamma and preceded by the *ā* of prolongation is جَزَاءٌ "a recompense" that is formed according to the pattern فَعَالٌ in the sentence presented by Sībawaihi, *II,* 171 جَزَاءُ أُمِّهِ "his mother's recompense". The hamza in it is changed into a *hamza bayna bayna* resulting in جَزَاوُأُمِّهِ (cf. Sībawaihi, *II,* 171, Roman, *Étude I,* 333).

(227) The base form of آخَذَ is أَأْخَذَ, and of آدَمُ أَأْدَمُ, which are both formed according to the pattern أَفْعَلُ (for it see Sībawaihi, *II,* 174, Ibn Ǧinnī, *Sirr II,* 579, 665, my notes (138)). When two hamzas are combined at the beginning of the word, the 1st of which is vowelled and the 2nd vowelless, the 2nd one is changed into an *ā*, i.e. أاخَذُ and أادَمُ, and then both the 1st hamza and the *ā* become a *madda*.

b) Both hamzas are not alleviated when they are in the position of the 2nd radical on the measure of فَعَّالٌ, e.g. رَأّآسٌ "a seller of heads" and سَأّآلٌ "a frequent asker" (cf. Ibn ʿAqīl, *II,* 554, Howell, *IV,* fasc. I, 963-964, de Sacy, *I,* 53). However, some grammarians accept the assimilation of the 1st one to the 2nd one, so that they become رَآسٌ and سَآلٌ (cf. Rāgihī, *Basīṭ* 165). In the vulgar dialects the alif may interchange with the *w,* e.g. رَوّاسٌ for رَأّآسٌ (cf. Wright, *Comparative Grammar* 47).

(228) The plural of إمَامٌ is أيِمَّةٌ underlyingly أأمِمَةٌ (for a study see Zamaḫšarī, 167, Ibn Manẓūr, *I,* 133, Howell, *IV,* fasc. I, 971 sqq., Lane, *I,* 91, Vernier, *I,* 101), in which the 2nd hamza is changed into a *y* for the purpose of alleviation, because the combination of two hamzas at the beginning of the word is regarded as heavy.

b) The anomalous combination of two hamzas sounded true at the beginning of the word is however permitted by the Kufans who recite the sur. 9: 12 as (فَقَاتِلُوا أئمّةَ ٱلْكُفْرِ) "Fight ye the chiefs of Unfaith", with أئمّة read instead of أيمّة (cf. Ibn Ḫālawaihi, *Qirāʾāt I,* 235). This is also the reading of al-Kisāʾī, Ḥamza and Ibn ʿĀmir (cf. Ibn Muǧāhid, *Sabʿa* 312), and it is disliked by Ibn Ǧinnī (cf. Ibn Ǧinnī, *Ḫaṣāʾiṣ III,* 143, *Sirr I,* 81). Likewise, ʿAṣim, Ḥamza, al-Kisāʾī and Ibn ʿĀmir read the sur. 67: 16 (أأمِنْتُم مَنْ فِي ٱلسَّمَاءِ) "Do ye feel secure that He Who is in Heaven", with أأمِنْتُم in which both hamzas are combined at the beginning of the word (cf. Ibn Muǧāhid, *Sabʿa* 644). Other readings with this disliked combination are those of the sur. 106: 2 (إئلافِهِمْ) "Their covenants", and of the sur. 10: 15 (إئت بِقُرآنٍ) "Bring us a Reading". Cf. Zamaḫšarī, 167, Ibn Yaʿīš, *IX,* 117, Howell, *IV,* fasc. I, 965, 977-978.
The combination of both hamzas sounded true at the interior of the word is more accepted in e.g. خَطَائِئِي "my sins" used instead of خَطَايَايَ (for discussions see Talmon, *ʿAyn* 239-240, Mokhlis, *Taṣrīf* 200-201) in the sentence اللّهُمَّ ٱغْفِرْ لِي خَطَائِئِي "O God forgive me my sins", which according to Zamaḫšarī, 167, Abū Zaid has heard from Abū l-Samḥ and his cousin Raddād. It can be noted concerning the word خطايا which is the pl. of خَطِيئَةٌ, that the Kufans believed that is on the pattern فَعَالَى, whereas the Basrans believed that it is on the pattern فَعَائِلَ (cf. Ḥassān, *Uṣūl* 153-154; for their debate see Ibn al-Anbārī, *Inṣāf* Q. 116, 338-341).

c) When two hamzas, of which the 2nd hamza is vowelled by a fatḥa, occur at the beginning of the word, the 2nd hamza can be changed into a *w* for the purpose of alleviation. This substitution is carried out in some cases of the 1st person of the sing. of the imperfect after the imperfect prefix hamza, e.g. the imperfect أألُّ from ألَّ in the sentence أَلَّتْ أسْنَانُهُ "his teeth decayed" (cf. Ibn Manẓūr, *I,* 112) that becomes أوَلُّ, and Form II أُوَمِّنُ "to make safe" from أَمَنَ "to be faithful", that becomes أُوَمِّنُ (cf. Howell, *IV,* fasc. I, 976).

(229) The cases referred to here concern the cluster of two vowelless consonants at the beginning of a word. This occurs when the interrogative hamza, the *ʾa,* is prefixed to a noun that begins with a conjunctive hamza vowelled by a fatḥa, e.g. أَأَيْمُنُ that results in آيْمُنُ in the example آيْمُنُ ٱللّٰهِ يَمِينُكَ underlyingly أَأَيْمُنُ ٱللّٰهِ يَمِينُكَ "Is the blessing of God your oath?", and in nouns to which the definite article *ʾal–* is prefixed to, as e.g. أَأَلْحَسَنُ that results in آلْحَسَنُ in the example آلْحَسَنُ عِنْدَكَ underlyingly أَأَلْحَسَنُ عِنْدَكَ "Is al-Ḥasan with you?" (cf. Howell, *IV,* fasc. I, 1003 and for other examples see (233 b)). آمَّةٌ with a *madda* is not accepted as it does not belong to this category (cf. (230), (233)). It can be added that in some other cases than the ones referred to here, the cluster of two vowelless consonants is accepted (for discussions see Howell, *IV,* fasc. I, 988 sqq., Bohas, *Étude* 309-311): 1– in a word occurring in pause, 2– in a word in which an assimilated letter is preceded by a weak consonant, e.g. خُوَيْصَّةٌ "dear particular friend" (cf. Howell, *IV,* fasc. I, 990, 994), in which both the *y* and the 1st *ṣ* among the doubled ṣāds is vowelless, 3– in uniflected nouns such as عَيْنْ "ʿayn", قَافْ "qāf", بَكْرْ "Bakr", 4– when the numerals are enumerated, e.g. اثْنَانْ "two" (cf. ibid, 1001-1002), and 5– in such an expression as لَاهَا آللّٰهِ in the oath (cf. ibid 1005-1006), in which both the final *ā* of لَاهَا and the *l* of the definite article of آللّٰه are vowelless.

(230) آمَّةٌ is considered as erroneous, and is therefore not accepted (cf. 229). It is underlyingly أَأْمِمَةٌ in which the 2nd hamza is changed into a *y* by the Basrans for the purpose of alleviation (cf. (228)), and then both mīms are assimilated. The 2nd hamza is changed into an *ā* at first, namely أَامِمَةٌ and then the *ā* is changed into a *y* resulting in أَيِمَّةٌ. The reason why the alif in آمَّةٌ is not considered as a pure *madda* is that the *madda* should be constituted of an alif that belongs to the base form, namely one that has not been changed from any other consonant, or one that is changed from the *w* or the *y,* and the alif in آمَّةٌ is the result of the assimilation of two hamzas. Dunqūz, *Šarḥ* fol. 66b ll. 8-9 remarks concerning it:

"لأنَّ المدَّة هي الألف الغير المقلوبة من شيءٍ او المقلوبة من واوٍ او ياءٍ والألف في آمَّة ليست كذلك".

"Because the *madda* is the alif which is not changed from any other consonant or the one changed from a *w* or a *y,* and the alif in آمَّةٌ is nothing of this sort".

(231) The elision of the hamza is obligatory in the imperatives خُذْ "take!" and كُلْ "eat!" (cf. Ibn Ǧinnī, *de Flexione* 33, Ibn Yaʿīš, *IX,* 115, Howell, *II-III,* 89-90, *IV,* fasc. I, 957-958, Wright, *II,* 76, *Comparative Grammar* 280, Vernier, *I,* 103, Talmon, *ʿAyn* 184), which are not to be said أُوخُذْ and أُوكُلْ. However, both مُرْ and أُومُرْ "enjoin!" can be said (cf. Ibn Yaʿīš, *IX,* 115). Even أْمُرْ occurs in the sur. 20: 132 (وَأْمُرْ أَهْلَكَ بِٱلصَّلَوٰةِ) "Enjoin prayer on thy people" and in the sur. 7: 199 (خُذِ ٱلْعَفْوَ وَأْمُرْ بِٱلْعُرْفِ) "Hold to forgiveness; Command what is right". It can be noted that a similar phenomenon with the elision of the prefixed hamza from of a verb in the imperative occurs in Syriac in ܙܠ "go", which however is אֱזַל (Ezra V. 15) in Biblic Aramaic, and אִירַיל in the Targums (cf. Wright, *Comparative Grammar* 280).

(232) For al-Ḫalīl, b. Aḥmad b. ʿAmr b. Tamīm al-Farāhīdīy (d. 175/791) see Sīrāfī, *Aḫbār* 38-40, Suyūṭī, *Buġya I,* 557-560, Qifṭī, *Inbāh I,* 341 sqq., Zubaidī, *Ṭabaqāt* 43 sqq., Darwīš, *Maʿāǧim* 13-16, Brockelmann, *GAL I,* 98, *S I,* 159-160, Sezgin, *Geschichte VIII,* 51-56, *IX,* 44-48, Talmon, *ʿAyn* 1-81. He wrote *Kitāb al-ʿArūd, Kitāb al-šawāhid, Kitāb al-nuqaṭ, Kitāb al-naġam, Kitāb al-ʿawāmil, Kitāb al-ǧumal* and *Kitāb al-iqāʿ.* He is mostly known for his *Kitāb al-ʿarūd* "the book of prosody" and his lexicon starting with the consonant ʿ, the *Kitāb al-ʿayn* "the book of the *ʿayn"*, which incited others after him to write lexicons (for an idea of its plan see the translation of its introduction by Haywood, *Lexicography* 28-37 and the remarks following it, 37-40; for the grammatical teaching, the material and its position in early grammar see Talmon, *ʿAyn* 127-287; for a study concerning the writing of dictionaries after it see Haywood, *Lexicography* 41 sqq., Wild, *ʿAyn* 58 sqq.; for a short discussion concerning the science of lexicography see Ibn Ḫaldūn, *Muqaddima III,* 325-332, translated by Rosenthal). Al-Ḫalīl is known as Sībawaihi's teacher. According to Reuschel, *Ḫalīl* 9, Sībawaihi refers to him in his *al-Kitāb* on 410 occasions, according to Troupeau, *Lexique* 228 on 608 occasions, according to Nāǧidī, *Sībawaihi* 98 on 522 occasions and according to Sīrāfī, *Aḫbār* 40 each time that he writes: "And I asked him", or "he said", without naming the sayer in support of his statements. According to Weil in his introduction to Ibn al-Anbārī, *Inṣāf* 69, al-Ḫalīl is: "der grösste Konstrukteur der einheimischen Grammatik". For discussions concerning his terminology see Versteegh, *Grammar* 16-20.

The linguistic phenomenon that is discussed here concerns the combination of two hamzas in two words, the 1st of which is the ultimate consonant of the first word and the 2nd one the initial consonant of the second one (for a study see Sībawaihi, *II,* 172-173, Zamaḫšarī, 167, Howell, *IV,* fasc. I, 983-986). According to al-Ḫalīl's and some other Arabs' usage, it is the 2nd hamza that is alleviated and not the 1st one. This occurs in the sur. 47: 18 (فقد جاء أشراطها), that he and his followers recite as فقد جاءَ آشراطُها with the hamza of أشراطها changed into a *waṣla.* The Ḥiǧāzīs however alleviate both the hamzas by eliding the 1st one and changing the 2nd one into a *waṣla,* namely فقد جا آشراطُها. Other examples that can be added of some surs. read with the elision of the 1st hamza are the sur. 32: 5 (مِن آلسَّمَاءِ إلى) "From the heavens to (the earth)" read as مِن آلسَّما إلى, the sur. 19: 7 (يا ذكرِيَاءُ إنَّا نُبشِّرُكَ) "O Zakarīya! We give thee good news" read as يا ذكريا إنَّا نُبشِّرُكَ and the sur. 46: 32 (أَوْلِياءُ أولئكَ) "(And no) protectors can he have (besides God): such men" read as أَوْلِيا أولئكَ.

(233) This part of the verse is transmitted by Ibn Masʿūd with ظَبْيَةٌ "gazelle" (for discussions concerning the gazelle motif in Arabic poetry see Bürgel, *Gazelle* 1-11) added to it, i.e. آأنْتِ ظَبْيَةٌ أمْ أمُّ سالِم instead of آأنْتِ أمْ أمُّ سالِم, to clarify the meaning. The verse is said by Ḏū l-Rumma, *Dīwān* 767, and is cited by Sībawaihi, *II,* 173, Ibn Ǧinnī, *Sirr II,* 723, *Lumaʿ* 44, *Ḫaṣāʾiṣ II,* 458, Muʾaddib, *Taṣrīf* 32, Zamaḫšarī, 14, 167, Ibn Yaʿīš, *IX,* 118-120, *Mulūkī* 308, Ḥarīrī, *Séances* 323, 324, Ibn Manẓūr, *I,* 3, Howell, *I,* fasc. I, 119, *IV,* fasc. I, 982:

"فَيَا ظَبْيَةَ آلوَعْسَاءِ بَيْنَ جُلَاجِلٍ وَبَيْنَ آلنَّقَا آأنْتِ أمْ أُمُّ سالِمِ".

"Then, O gazelle of the soft sandy ground between Ǧulāǧil and the sand-hill, is this really you or Umm Sālim?".

When reciting the verse, some Arabs prefer to separate the two vowelled hamzas in أأنْت by inserting an *ā,* i.e. آأنْت (cf. Sībawaihi, *II,* 173). Likewise, the insertion of the *ā* is noticed in آإيَاهُ "is it him?" that is used instead of أإيَاهُ in the following verse said by Ǧāmiʿ b. ʿAmr b. Murḫiya al-Kalbī, cited by Baġdādī, *Šarḥ* 349-350. According to Ibn Manẓūr, *II,* 858, it is said by a man from the Banū Kalb. It is also cited by Ibn Ǧinnī, *Sirr II,* 723, Zamaḫšarī, 167, Ibn Yaʿīš, *IX,* 118, Howell, *IV,* fasc. I, 982:

"حُزُقٌ إذَا مَا ٱلْقَوْمُ أَبْدَوْا فُكَاهَةً   تَفكَّرَ آإيَاهُ يَعْنُونَ أَمْ قِرْدا".

"[He is] short [in stature]: Whenever the people bring out a jest, he considers whether him they mean or an ape".

Ibn Manẓūr, *I,* 22 mentions this verse with أجْرَوْا "to bring about" instead of أبْدَوْا.

ʿAbd Allāh b. Abī Isḥāq, referred to by Ibn Manẓūr, *I,* 22, read as well the sur. 2: 6 (آأنْذَرْتَهُمْ) "Whether thou warn them", with the *ā* inserted between both the hamzas of أأنْذَرْتَهُمْ. So is also the sur. 12: 90 (آئنّكَ لأنْتَ يُوسُفُ) "They said: "Art thou indeed Joseph?" read by some with the *ā* inserted between both the hamza of أئنّكَ (cf. Howell, *IV,* fasc. I, 982). Other examples are found in sur. 13: 5 (آئذا) "when" and (آئنّا) "shall we indeed then be" read instead of أئذا and أئنّا by ʿAbd Allāh b. Abī Isḥāq, as told by Ibn ʿĀmir referred to by Ibn Muǧāhid, *Sabʿa* 357-358, 499-500.

b) The insertion of the interrogative hamza *-a* to the definite article *-al,* and the lengthening of the alif resulting in a *madda,* is also carried out by some (cf. (229)). It is remarked in the reading of the sur. 6: 143 (آلذَّكَرَيْنِ حَرَّمَ أمِ آلأنْثَيَيْنِ) "Hath He forbidden the two males, or the two females" and the sur. 27: 59 (ءآللّهُ خَيْرٌ أمْ مَا يُشْرِكُونَ) "(Who) is better? – God or the false gods they associate (with Him)?" (cf. Mu'addib, *Taṣrīf* 32-33).

(234) The base form of نَاسٌ is أنَاسٌ (for examples with the occurrence of both forms see Nöldeke, *Grammatik* 15-16; for discussions concerning أنَاس see Nöldeke, *Neue Beiträge* 111 note 5), in which the hamza at the beginning of the word is elided anomalously (cf. Ibn Ǧinnī, *Ḫaṣāʾiṣ III,* 151, Zamaḫšarī, *Kaššāf I,* 35-36, Ibn Manẓūr, *I,* 147, Howell, *I,* fasc. I, 174, Fleisch, *I,* 151). The base form occurs in the following verse said by D̲ū Ǧadan al-Ḥumairī, cited by Ibn Yaʿīš, *II,* 9, Ibn Manẓūr, *I,* 147, Howell, *I,* fasc. I, 174:

"إنَّ ٱلْمَنَايَا يَطَّلِعْنَ عَلَى آلأنَاسِ آلآمِنِينَا".

"Verily the fates come unawares upon the men free from fear".

Compare with أنَاس, אֱנוֹשׁ, אֱנָשׁ, Talmud and Mandaean St. emph. אנשי, אנאשיא (cf. Nöldeke, *Beiträge* 60, Brockelmann, *Grundriss* 351).

(235) For a study of the word الله, see Zaǧǧāǧī, *Maǧālis* 69-71, Ibn Manẓūr, *I,* 114-116, Nöldeke, *Grammatik* 16, Vernier, *I,* 101. For it occuring in some of the Semitic languages and for some reflexions concerning its origin see Fischer, *Mitteilungen* 445-446. The base form of

الله is الإِلَٰه in which the hamza is elided. However, according to Abū l-Haiṯam referred to by Ibn Manẓūr, *I,* 114, the base form of الإِلَٰه is وِلَاهٌ in which the *w* is changed into a hamza. A variant of this form, الوِلَٰه, is discussed by Ibn ʿUṣfūr, *I,* 43, who answers against those who pretend that it could be the base form of الإِلَٰه. The alleviated variant, لَاهٌ, occurs in the following verse said by al-Aʿšā, cited by Nöldeke, *Grammatik* 16 who, referring to Baġdādī, *Ḫizāna I,* 347, points to the fact that the verse is completely or partly a falsification:

"كَحَلْفَةٍ مِنْ أَبِي رِيَاحٍ يَسْمَعُهَا لَاهُهُ الكُبَارُ".

"As an oath from Abū Riyāḥ, which the great God has heard".

Ibn Ǧinnī, *Sirr I,* 430 and Ibn Manẓūr, *I,* 116 cite the verse with لَاهُمَ instead of لَاهُهُ. It is also recited by al-Kisāʾī as: يَسْمَعُهَا اللهُ واللهُ الكُبَارُ "which God has heard, and God is great". Farrāʾ, *Maʿānī I,* 204 has يَسْمَعُهَا اللَّهُمَ الكُبَارُ instead. Ibn Yaʿīš, *Mulūkī* 361 has يَسْمَعُهُ لَاهُهُ. الإِلَٰه occurs in the following verse said by al-Baʿīṯ b. Ḥuraiṯ, cited by Zamaḫšarī, *Kaššāf I,* 35, Howell, *I,* fasc. I, 173-174:

"مَعَاذَ ٱلإِلَٰهِ أَنْ تَكُونَ كَظَبْيَةٍ وَلَا دُمْيَةٍ وَلَا عَقِيلَةِ رَبْرَبِ".

"God forfend that in beauty she should be only like a doe-gazelle or a decorated image or a noble cow of a herd of wild cattle!".

It can be added that the form *HLH,* a variant of الله, occurs in the Liḥyānite inscriptions of the 5th century B.C. The form *Hallāh* is existent in the Ṣafa inscriptions five centuries before Islam and in a pre-Islamic Christian Arabic inscription ascribed to the 6th century found in Syria (cf. Hitti, *History* 100-101). The connection between the *h* and the hamza is of interest here, as the substitution of one for the other and vice versa is a common phenomenon (for a study of the substitution of the *h* for the hamza see (98), (220), (343); for the substitution of the hamza for the *h* see (114 b), (115 b), (325)).
Furthermore it can be mentioned that God's greatness and oneness in the creation is pointed out in the sur. 23: 91 (مَا ٱتَّخَذَ ٱللَّهُ مِن وَلَدٍ وَمَاكَانَ مَعَهُ مِنْ إِلَٰهٍ إِذاً لَذَهَبَ كُلُّ إِلَٰهٍ بِمَا خَلَقَ) "No son did God beget, nor is there any god along with Him: (if there were many gods), behold, each god would have taken away what he had created".

b) The variant اللَّهُمَّ (for discussions see Buhl, *Allāhumma* 327) with the double *m,* has given rise to some speculations. It is traditionally, and as I believe it to be, part of the suppressed proposition يَا ٱللَّهُ أُمَّنَا بِخَيْرٍ "O God, bring us good" (cf. Howell, *I,* fasc. I, 186, Penrice, *Dictionary* 8). Sībawaihi, *I,* 7, Ibn Ǧinnī, *Ḫaṣāʾiṣ I,* 265, Daqr, *Muʿǧam* 395 believe that it is a compensation for the elided vocative particle يَا. Roman, *Identité* 159 in the notes, draws a parallel between the element *umma* after ٱللَّه and the suffixed element *unna* of the energetic. Barth, *Nominalbildung* 128 likens the element *umma* with the Akkadian demonstratif *ammu.* اللَّهُمَّ has given rise to a debate between the Basrans who do not allow the combination of اللَّهُمَّ with the vocative يَا and the Kufans who allow this combination (for it see Ibn al-Anbārī, *Inṣāf* Q. 47, 151-153). It occurs without the vocative يَا in the sur. 39: 46 (قُلِ ٱللَّهُمَّ فَاطِرَ ٱلسَّمٰوَاتِ

(وَٱلْأَرْض) "Say: "O God! Creator of the heavens and the earth!". As for its anomalous combination with the vocative it occurs in the following verse said by Umayya b. Abī l-Ṣalt, as mentioned by Baġdādī, *Ḥizāna II,* 358 and the editor to Ibn ʿAqīl, *II,* 265 in the notes, and not by Abū Ḥirāš al-Huḏalī as mentioned by Howell, *I,* fasc. I, 186, Daqr, *Muʿǧam* 395. It is also cited by Ibn Ǧinnī, *Sirr I,* 419, 430, Ḥarīrī, *Šarḥ* 155, Ibn al-Anbārī, *Inṣāf* Q. 47, 151, *Asrār* 232, Ibn Yaʿīš, *II,* 16, Ibn ʿAqīl, *II,* 265, Ibn Manẓūr, *I,* 115, Baġdādī, *Ḥizāna I,* 358, al-Šartūnī, the commentator of Farḥāt, *Baḥṯ* 248, Howell, *I,* fasc. I, 186:

"إنِّي إذَا مَا حَدَثٌ أَلَمَّا   أَقُولُ يَا ٱللَّهَمَ يَا ٱللَّهُمَا".

"Verily I, whenever a calamity befalls me, say: "O God, O God [bring me good]!".

أَللَّهَ is an alleviated variant of أَللَّهُمَّ with the elision of the *m* (for discussions see Roman, *Identité* 158-159).

c) Another variant worth to be mentioned is the Goddesses's name أَللَاةَ underlyingly الإلَاةُ, *(al-ʾilātu* "Herodotus's *Alilat"* cf. Brockelmann, *Grundriss* 257), in which the hamza is also elided. *Lāt* may be the original of the Greek "Leto", the mother of Apollo the sun-god. As pointed ou by Yusuf Ali in Qurʾān 1623, it represents certainly a wave of sun-worship. It is also the name of one of the Pagan deities known in the Kaʿba and round about Mekka, the other deities being ʿUzzā that represents the planet Venus, and Manāt "allotted faith" whose origin is obscure, but which is also probably astral (cf. Hitti, *History* 98-99). It may be noted for the sake of curiosity that in Babylonian religion, *Allatu* is referred to as the stern queen of the infernal regions (cf. Frazer, *Adonis I,* 8-9), the goddess of darkness and desolation, as against Ishtar associated with the planet Venus, who was the goddess of the upper regions, of reproduction and fertility (cf. Gray, *Mythology* 25, 36). Ibn Fāris, *Maqāyīs I,* 127 and Ibn Manẓūr, *I,* 115 mention that the Arabs used to name the sun الإلَاهَةَ when they adored it. The word occurs in the following verse, which according to Ibn Manẓūr, *I,* 115, was said by Mayya bint Umm ʿUtba Ibn al-Ḥāriṯ, or according to Ibn Barrī to whom he refers to, by Bint ʿAbd al-Ḥāriṯ al-Yarbūʿī, or Nāʾiḥa ʿUtaiba b. al-Ḥāriṯ, or Umm al-Banīn bint ʿUtaiba b. al-Ḥāriṯ who is mourning over her father ʿUtaiba. It is also cited by Ibn Ǧinnī, *Sirr II,* 784, Ibn Duraid, *Ǧamhara I,* 316:

"تَرَوَّحْنا مِنَ اللَّعْبَاءِ عَصْراً   فَأَعْجَلْنَا الإلَاهَةَ أَنْ تَؤُوبَا".

"We returned to our homes from Laʿbāʾ [sc. a stony place in Ḥazm b. ʿUwāl] in the evening, so we urged the sun to return".

Ibn Fāris, *Maqāyīs I,* p 127 cites the last half of the verse with فَبَادَرْنَا "and we rushed" instead of فَأَعْجَلْنَا. A variant of the verse is recited by al-Fārisī, and is referred to by Ibn Manẓūr, *V,* 4041, Zabīdī, *Tāǧ IV,* 214:

"تَرَوَّحْنا مِنَ اللَّعْبَاءِ قَصْراً   وأَعْجَلْنا إِلاهَةَ أَنْ تَؤُوبَا".

"We went back to our homes from Laʿbāʾ [sc. a stony place in Ḥazm b. ʿUwāl] in a state of inertness, and we urged the sun to return".

الْأَلَاهَةُ also means the hot sun, as mentioned by Ibn Manẓūr, *V,* 4041.

(236) The base form of يَرَى is بَرْأَى, in which the hamza is elided for the sake of alleviation because it is preceded by a vowelless consonant (cf. Sībawaihi, *II,* 170, Wright, *II,* 93, Vernier,

I, 73-74) and its fatḥa is shifted to this consonant. However in poetry, in consideration to the metric exigency, the hamza can be retained. This is remarked in تَرْأَيَاهُ said instead of تَرَيَاهُ, that occurs in the following verse said by Surāqa b. Mirdās al-Azdī al-Bāriqī in Bāriqī, *Dīwān* 78, cited by Ibn Ǧinnī, *Sirr I,* 77, *II,* 826, *Ḫaṣā'iṣ III,* 153, *Muḥtasib I,* 128, *de Flexione* 34, Mu'addib, *Taṣrīf* 422, Ibn Ḫālawaihi, *Qirā'āt I,* 156, Ibn Ya'īš, *Mulūkī* 370, Ibn Manẓūr, *III,* 1538, Ibn 'Uṣfūr, *II,* 621, Ibn Hišām, *Muġnī I,* 277, Howell, *IV,* fasc. I, 941:

"أُرِي عَيْنَيَّ مَا لَمْ تَرْأَيَاهُ كِلَانَا عَالِمٌ بِالتُّرَّهَاتِ".

"I make mine eyes see what they have not seen: each of us is knowing in falsehoods".

The alleviation of the hamza is anomalous when it is carried out in the perfect of the 2nd person of the masc. sing., e.g. رَيْتَ that is used instead of رَأَيْتَ. It occurs in the following verse said by Ismā'īl b. Yasār, cited by Mu'addib, *Taṣrīf* 422, Zamaḫšarī, *Kaššāf IV,* 288, Ibn Manẓūr, *III,* 1538, al-Šartūnī, the commentator of Farḥāt, *Baḥṯ* 89 in the notes, Howell, *IV,* fasc. I, 955, Bustānī, *Muḥīṭ* 317, Vernier, *I,* 103:

"صَاحِ هَلْ رَيْتَ أَوْ سَمِعْتَ بِرَاعٍ رَدَّ فِي ٱلضَّرْعِ مَا قَرَى فِي ٱلْحِلَابِ".

"Comrade, have you seen or heard of a herdsman who put back into the udder what he had collected in the milking-vessel".

The hamza is elided in رَأَيْتَ after the interrogative hamza, i.e. أَرَيْتَ that is said instead of أَرَأَيْتَ. This occurred in the reading of some of the sur. 107: 1 (أريت) instead of (أرأيت) "Seest thou". Ibn Manẓūr, *III,* 1539 mentions that it is the reading of most of the Arabs, except the Ḥiǧāzīs, and that al-Kisā'ī read it with this alleviation. The alleviated form أَرَيْتَ occurs in the following verse said by Abū l-Aswad al-Du'alī, cited by Ibn Manẓūr, *III,* 1538, Howell, *IV,* fasc. I, 955:

"أَرَيْتَ آمْرَأً كُنْتُ لَمْ أَبْلُهُ أَتَانِي فَقَالَ آتَّخِذْنِي خَلِيلَا".

"Have you considered, [i.e. Tell me what so you think of] a man that I had not proven, who came to me and said "Do you take me for a friend?".

Afandī, *Tanzīl* 479 has رَأَيْتَ instead of أَرَيْتَ, which is not the alleviated form and which is without the interrogative أ.
It occurs also in the following verse said by Rakkāḍ b. Abbāq al-Dubairī, cited by Ibn Manẓūr, *III,* 1538:

"أَرَيْتَكَ إِنْ مَنَعْتَ كَلَامَ حُبَّى أَتَمْنَعُنِي عَلَى لَيْلَى آلْبُكَاءَ".

"Have you considered [i.e. Tell me], if you prevent me from speaking to Ḥubbā, shall you prevent me from weeping for Lailā?".

Another version of the same verse exists, as reported by Ibn Manẓūr, *III,* 1538, with لَيْلَى occurring instead of حُبَّى. It is cited in this manner by Howell, *IV,* fasc. I, 955. Also another is mentioned by Bustānī, *Muḥīṭ* 317 with يَحْيَى occurring instead of لَيْلَى, namely:

"أَرَيْتَكَ إِنْ مَنَعْتَ كَلَامَ يَحْيَى أَتَمْنَعُنِي عَلَى يَحْيَى آلْبُكَاءَ".

"Have you considered [i.e. Tell me], if you prevent me from speaking to John, shall you prevent me from weeping for John?".

(237) The alleviation of the hamza by eliding it in يَسْأَلُ resulting in يَسَلُ is anomalous (cf. de Sacy, *I,* 236, Wright, *II,* 77, Vernier, *I,* 74). Furthermore it can be noted that the alleviation of the hamza by changing it into an *ā* is carried out in this verb. Some examples are:

– سَالَتْ that is used instead of سَأَلَتْ in the following verse said by Ḥassān b. Ṯābit al-Anṣārī in Anṣārī, *Dīwān I,* 443, cited by Ibn Ğinnī, *Ḫaṣā ʾiṣ III,* 152, Ibn al-Sarrāğ, *Uṣūl III,* 470, Muʾaddib, *Taṣrīf* 530, Ibn Yaʿīš, *IX,* 114, *Mulūkī* 230, Afandī, *Tanzīl* 445, Howell, *IV,* fasc. I, 951, Roman, *Étude I,* 334:

"سَالَتْ هُذَيْلٌ رَسُولَ ٱللهِ فَاحِشَةً   ضَلَّتْ هُذَيْلٌ بِمَا سَلَتْ وَلَمْ تُصِبِ".

"Huḏail asked of the Apostle of God a lewd boon. Huḏail erred in what it asked, and did not right".

– سَالَتَانِي (cf. Nöldeke, *Grammatik* 6) that is used instead of سَأَلَتَانِي in the following verse said by Zaid b. ʿAmr b. Nufail al-Qurašī al-ʿAdawī, cited by Sībawaihi, *II,* 175, Ibn Fāris, *Ṣāḥibī* 176, Ibn al-Sarrāğ, *Uṣūl III,* 470, Howell, *IV,* fasc. I, 951 [it is not alleviated by Ibn Ḫālawaihi, *Qirāʾāt II,* 180]:

"سَالَتَانِي ٱلطَّلَاقَ أَنْ رَأَتَانِي   قَلَّ مَالِي قَدْ جِئْتُمَانِي بِنُكْرِ".

"They [sc. my two wives] have asked me for divorce, because they have seen me to be such that my wealth has become small. You [i.e. an enallage from the 3rd person to the 2nd] have brought to me an unseemly matter".

Afandī, *Tanzīl* 445 cites the same verse as follows:

"سالتماني الطلاق أن رأيتما   لي قليلا قد جئتماني بنكد".

"They [sc. my two wives] have asked me for divorce, because they have seen that what I possessed has become small. You [i.e. an enallage from the 3rd person to the 2nd] have brought misfortune to me!".

The alleviation of the hamza in يَسْأَلُونَ is not carried out by elision, but also by transposing the 2nd radical hamza before the 1st radical *s,* i.e. يَأْسَلُونَ. This occurs in a verse said by an unknown poet, cited by Howell, *IV,* fasc. I, 956:

"إذا قَامَ قَوْمٌ يَأْسَلُونَ مَلِيكَهُمْ   عَطَاءً فَدَهْمَاءُ ٱلَّذِي أَنَا سَائِلُهُ".

"When people arise, asking of their king a gift, then Dahmāʾ is that gift which I shall be asking for".

(238) مَرْأَى "aspect" has its hamza retained (cf. Howell, *IV,* fasc. I, 941). Other examples that can be added are مَرْآةٌ "outward appearance", and مِرْآةٌ "mirror".

(239) The imperfect of the indicative of the 2nd person of the fem. sing. of رَأَى is تَرَيْنَ and its Energetic I is تَرَيِنَّ. As for اِخْشَيِنَّ, the imperative of the 2nd person of the fem. sing. is اِخْشَيْ "fear you", and when the doubled *n* is suffixed to it, it became اِخْشَيِنَّ "you do surely dread" comparable to تَرَيِنَّ with the vowelling of the *y* of the fem. with the kasra when the doubled *n* is suffixed to it, to avoid the cluster of two vowelless consonants: the *y* and the 1st vowelless *n* of the doubled ones if it is said تَرَيْنَّ.

b) It can be remarked concerning تَرَيِنَّ of the sur. 19: 26 (فإمّا تَرَيِنَّ من البَشَرِ أحدًا) "And if thou doest see any man", that it was anomalously read by Ṭalḥa as being the imperfect of the indicative of the 2nd person of the fem. sing., i.e. تَرَيْنَ, with the substitution of the *n* of the indicative for the energetic *n* (cf. Šāḏilī, *ʿAnāṣir* 219). Its anomaly resides in the fact that the *n* of the indicative was not elided in the jussive as it should have been in this case.

c) Concerning the 2nd person of the masc. sing., it can be noted that in the dialect of the Ṭayyīs, the *y*, when being a 3rd radical, is elided after the kasra or fatḥa. It is said اخْشَنَّ يا زَيْدُ instead of اخْشَيَنَّ يا زَيْدُ "You do surely dread, O Zaid". Hence in their dialect, لَتَغْنَنَّ occurs anomalously instead of لَتَغْنَيِنَّ, (which is replaced by لَتَغْنَيِ in another version) in the following verse said by Ḥuraiṯ b. ʿAnnāb al-Nabhānī al-Ṭāʾī, cited by Zamaḫšarī, 40, Howell, *I*, fasc. I, 364, Freytag, *Hamasae* 279. It was meant to be with the single *n*, but this one was suppressed by poetic licence:

"إذا قالَ قَطْنِي قُلْتُ بِآللهِ حَلْفَةً   لَتُغْنَنَّ عَنِّي ذا إنائِكَ أَجْمَعا".

"When he says: "Enough for me [is the draugh of camel's milk], I say, [I swear] by God an oath, assuredly you shall make the contents of your vessel independent of me, [i.e. of my drinking it], all of it".

Likewise, ابْكَنَّ occurs instead of ابْكِيَنَّ in the following verse said by an unknown poet, cited by Howell, *IV*, fasc. I, 1564:

"وَآبْكَنَّ عَيْشًا تَقَضَّى بَعْدَ جِدَّتِهِ   طابَتْ أصائِلُهُ في ذَلِكَ آلْبَلَدِ".

"And do weep for a life that has passed away after its newness, whose evenings were pleasant in that country".

(240) The imperative of رَأَى is إرْءَ "/2 masc. sing., etc., by the Taim, with the prefixation of the initial hamza of the imperative, the vowelling of the hamza of the 2nd radical with a fatḥa and the elision of the 3rd weak radical. It is however رَ "see! /2 masc. sing.", رَيَا "/2 dual", رَوْا "/2 masc. pl." and رَيْنَ "/2 fem. pl." by the Ḥiǧāzīs who elide the initial hamza of the imperative together with the 2nd and 3rd radical and vowel the 1st radical with a fatḥa (cf. Ibn Ḫālawaihi, *Qirāʾāt I*, 156-157, Lane, *I*, 998).

(241) Different variants (for them see Howell, *IV*, fasc. I, 807-812) concerning الْبُطْءُ "slowness", الرِّدْءُ "the buttress" and الْخَبْءُ "a hidden thing" exist, in which the hamza is preceded by a vowelless consonant. The Ḥiǧāzīs alleviate by shifting the vowel of the hamza to the consonant preceding it, and then elide the hamza together with the shifted vowel on account of the pause, i.e. الْبُطْ, الرِّدْ and الْخَبْ. The Banū Tamīm give the 2nd radical a vowel that is similar to the vowel of the 1st radical, and then change the hamza into a weak consonant that carries the hamza, which is of the same nature of the vowel preceding it, i.e. البطُوْ and الرَدىْ in all three cases of the nominative, accusative or genitive. Some Arabs elide and do not shift the vowel of the hamza, and then change the hamza into a weak consonant that is homogeneous with its vowel, i.e. الْبُطُوْ and الرْدَوْ. Others shift the vowel of the hamza and change the 3rd radical into a weak consonant, i.e. الْبُطو and الْرَدى. The hamza is alleviated in آلْخَبْءَ which is read as الخَبَ of the sur. 27: 25 (يُخْرِجُ آلْخَبْءَ) "Who brings to light what is hidden", in دفْءٌ read as دفٌ by Nāfiʿ of the sur. 16: 5 (لَكُمْ فيهَا دفْءٌ) "From them ye derive warmth" and in رِدْءاً read as رِداً by Nāfiʿ of the sur. 28: 34 (أَرْسِلْهُ مَعِي رِدْءاً) "So send him with me as a helper" (cf. Muʾaddib, *Taṣrīf* 526-527, Ibn Muǧāhid, *Sabʿa* 494). For a discussion concerning the elision of the hamza at the end of the word in some of the other Semitic languages see Wright, *Comparative Grammar* 46.

II.5. Arabic Text: الباب الرابع في المثال

ويُقال للمعتلَ الفاء مثال لأنَ ماضيه مثل الصحيح في الصحَة وعدم الإعلال وقيل لأنَ
أمرَه مثل أمر الأجوف نحو عدْ وزنْ. وهو يجيء في خمسة أبواب ولا يجيء من فَعَل
يَفْعُلُ الاَ وَجَدَ يَجُدُ في لغة بني عامر فحُذف الواو في يَجُدُ في لغتهم لثقل الواو مع
ضمَ ما بعدها وقيل هذه لغة ضعيفة فأُتبع ليَعدُ في الحذف. وحكم الواو والياء إذا
وقعتا في أوَل الكلمة كحكم الصحيح نحو وَعَدَ ووُعِدَ ووَقَرَ ووُقِرَ ويَنَعَ ويُنِعَ ويَسَرَ
ويُسِرَ ويَمَنَ ويُمِنَ ونظائرها لقوَة المتكلَم عند الإبتداء. وقيل الإعلال قد يكون بالسكون
أو* بالقلب الى حرف العلَة أو بالحذف وثلاثها لا يُمكن امَا بالسكون فلتعذُّره * ٢٦ آ
وكذلك القلب لأنَ المقلوب به غالباً يكون بحرف العلَة وحرف العلَة لا يكون إلاَ ساكناً
وامَا بالحذف فلنقصانه من القدر الصالح في الثلاثيَ ولإتباع الثلاثيَ في الزوائد، ولا
يُعوَض بالتاء في الأوَل والآخر حتَى لا يلتبس بالمستقبل والمصدر في نفس الحروف ومن
ثمَ لا يجوز إدخال التاء في الأوَل في عدَةٍ للإلتباس ويجوز في التُكْلان لعدم الإلتباس
وعند سيبويه يجوز حذف التاء كما في قول الشاعر * وأخْلَفوكَ عدَ الأمْرِ الذي وَعَدوا
* لأنَ التعويض من الأمور الجائزة عنده وعند الفرَاء لا يجوز الحذف لأنَها عوض من

Fols. 25b-26a

١-٢ المثال... للمعتلَ: معتلَ الفاء د/ ٢ الفاء: ويقال له د/ الصحيح: الصحح حـ/ في الصحة: – ب/ في... الإعلال: – جـ/ ٣ أمر: – حـ/ الأجوف: + في الوزن حـ/ وهو: وهي ا/ وهو يجيء: ويجيء د/ ٤ فحذف: فحذفت ل/ من: في ل/ ٥ ضمَ: ضمة ا/ ٦ الصحيح: الصحح حـ/ ويَنَع ويُنِعَ: – از: ويقع ويُقعُ حـ/ ٦–٧ ويَسَرَ... ويُمِنَ: – ب جـ د هـ حـ ط/ ٧ ونظائرها: ونظائره جـ: –ز: وقسَ على هذا نظائرها ط/ ٨ وثلاثها: وثليثتها هـ: وكلَ واحد منها ل/ ٩ ساكناً: ساكنة ا ب جـ د حـ ط ل: + بعد القلب ط/ ١٠ ولإتباع: وللاتباع هـ/ ١١ الحروف: + المتكلَم ط/ ١٢ عدَة: العدة ا ب د هـ حـ/ ١٣ وعدوا: وعدو ط/ ١٤ الأمور: امور ط/ الجائزة: جايزة جـ/ عنده: عندهم جـ هـ/

II.5. Translation: The 4th Chapter is about the Verb with Weak 1st Radical(242)

The verb with weak 1st radical is named مثالٌ "assimilated, similar", because its perfect is similar to [the perfect of] the strong verb on account of its being sound and unaffected by a phonological change due to the weak consonant, and it was said because its imperative is similar to the imperative of the verb with 2nd weak radical, e.g. عِدْ "promise!" and زِنْ "decorate!" [from زَيَّنَ]. It falls into five conjugations. Only وَجَدَ يَجُدُ "to find" occurs according to فَعَلَ يَفْعُلُ which pertains to the dialectal variant of Banū ʿĀmir.(243) The *w* is elided in يَجُدُ [underlyingly يَوْجُدُ] in their dialect, because of the heaviness of the *w* followed by [a consonant vowelled by] a ḍamma, and it was stated that this dialectal variant is weak. As for لِيَعِدْ "let him promise!", it conforms with it regarding the elision [of the *w].*(244)

The predicament of the *w* and the *y* as 1st radicals is the same as the predicament of the strong consonant, e.g. وَعَدَ وُعِدَ "to promise, [active and passive]", وَقَرَ وُقِرَ "to stay, remain, [active and passive]", يَنَعَ يُنِعَ "to become ripe, [active and passive]", يَسَرَ يُسِرَ "to be or become easy, [active and passive]",(245) يَمَنَ يُمِنَ "to be lucky, fortunate [active and passive]", and their likes, because of the determination of the speaker to pronounce fully the initial consonant of the word.

It is said that the phonological change due to the unsound weak consonant can be carried out by: 1– rendering it [sc. the weak consonant] vowelless, **[Fol. 26 a]** 2– replacing it by another weak consonant or 3– eliding it. None of these methods can be carried out [when it concerns the 1st radical in Form I of the perfect]: As for giving it the sukūn because of the impossibility of doing so [i.e. beginning the word with a vowelless consonant], so is also the change into another consonant because the changed consonant is mostly into a weak consonant [sc. the *ā],* and the weak consonant can only be vowelless, and so is also the elision, because it implies that it [sc. the form] becomes less than the proper number determining a word in the groundform of the triliteral, – and the derived forms conformed to it -. Furthermore, it [sc. the elision] is not to be compensated by a prefixed or a suffixed *t,* so that it [sc. the perfect] is not mixed up with the imperfect and the *maṣdar* with the same consonants.(246) Hence, it is impossible to prefix the *t* in عِدَةٌ "a promise" for fear of confusion. However, it is possible [to prefix it] in التُّكْلَانُ "confidence", because no confusion can occur [with the imperfect].(247) According to Sībawaihī, the elision of the *t* is made possible [in عِدَ which occurs instead of عِدَةٌ], as in the saying of the poet:

" وأَخْلَفوكَ عِدَ الأَمْرِ الذي وَعَدوا".

"And they have broken to thee the promise of the matter which they promised".

– because the compensation is among the possible procedures according to him. However, according to al-Farrāʾ, it is impossible to elide it, as it is already a compensation for

المحذوف إلاَ في الإضافة لأنَ الإضافة تقوم مقامها وكذلك حكم الإقامة والإستقامة ونحوهما
ومن ثمَ حُذفت التاء في قوله تعالى ﴿وإقامُ الصَلاة﴾. وتقول في إلحاق الضمائر
* ٢٦ ب وَعَدَ وَعَدا وَعَدوا الى آخره. ويجوز في* وَعَدتَ إدغام الدال في التاء لقرب
مخرجهما. المستقبل يَعدُ يَعدانِ يَعدُونَ الى آخره أصله يَوْعدُ فحذفت الواو لأنَه يُلزم
الخروج من الكسرة التقديريَة الى الضمَة التقديريَة ومن الضمَة التقديريَة الى الكسرة
التحقيقيَة ومثل هذا ثقيل ومن ثمَ لا يجيء لغة على وزن فعُل وفُعِل إلاَ حبُكٌ ودُئلٌ،
وحُذفت أيضاً في تَعدُ للمشاكلة وحُذفت في مثل يَضَعُ لأنَ أصله يَوْضِعُ فحُذفت الواو ثمَ
جُعل يَضَعُ نظراً الى حرف الحلق ولا تُحذف في يُوعدُ لأنَ أصله يُأوْعدُ. والأمر عدْ عدا
عدوا الى آخره والفاعل واعدٌ الى آخره والمفعول مَوْعودٌ الى آخره والموضع مَوْعدٌ والآلة
ميعَدٌ فقُلبت الواو ياءً لسكونها ولكسرة ما قبلها وهم يقلبونها ياءً في الحاجز في نحو
قِنْيَةٍ وبغير الحاجز يكون أقلب.

Fols. 26a-26b

١ المحذوف: الحذف جـ د حـ ز: + وهو الواو حـ: الحروف الأصليَة هـ/ في: + حالة ط/ مقامها: مقام التاء ط/ ٢ التاء: –ا د ط/ الصلاة: الصلوة ا ب جـ د ز حـ: الصلوت ط/ الصلاة: + وايتاء الزكوة ب ز ط: + وأيتاء الزكاة ل/ ٣ وَعدَا وَعدوا: –ا د هـ ز/ وَعدتَ: وعدة د/ ٤ يَعدَانِ يَعدُونَ: –ا ب جـ د هـ ز حـ/ ٥–٦ ومن... التحقيقيَة: – جـ/ ٦ التحقيقيَة: الخالصة د: الحقيقيَة هـ ط/ ٧ وحذفت: فحذفت ب د: وحذف جـ ز ط: + الواو هـ حـ/ وحذفت... للمشاكلة: ا's margin ا/ مثل: – د ل/ يوضع: + بالكسر حـ/ فحذفت: وحذف د: فحذف ز/ ٨ حرف: حروف د ط/ تحذف: يحذف ب جـ د هـ ز حـ ط/ يُأوْعدُ: يؤعد حـ/ والأمر: الأمر ب جـ د هـ ز/ ٨–٩ عدا... عدُوا: –ا ب جـ د هـ حـ ط/ ٩ والفاعل: الفاعل د ل/ الى آخره[1+2]: –ا د ز حـ ط/ والمفعول: المفعول ل/ ١٠ فقلبت: قلبت ا/ لسكونها ولكسرة: لكسرة ب جـ د هـ ز ط ك ل/ ولكسرة... قبلها: – حـ/ يقلبونها: يقبلونها ب: تقبلونها ط/ ياء: – د هـ حـ ط/ في الحاجز: بالحاجز ا هـ ز حـ: مع الحاجز ب جـ د ط/ نحو: –ا/ ١١ الحاجز: حاجز د/ أقلب: أولى جـ: القلب ط/

the elided weak consonant [sc. the *w* in the base form وعْدٌ], except in the construct state, because the second element in the construct state occurs as a compensation for it [sc. the *tāʾ marbūṭa]*.(248)

So is also the predicament of اقامة "the act of being constant (in prayer)" and استقامة "the act of walking uprightly in the paths of religion" and both their likes [regarding the compensation with the *tāʾ marbūṭa]*. On account of that [sc. that the second element in the construct state is a compensation for the elided *tāʾ marbūṭa],* the *t* is elided in the words of the Allmighty, [sur. 21: 73] (وإقامُ الصلاة) "to establish regular prayers".(249)

You say when attaching the pronouns: وعَدَ "he promised", وعدَا "/2 masc. dual", وعَدوا "/3 masc. pl. etc.(250)

It is possible in **[Fol. 26 b]** وعَدتَ that the *d* is assimilated to the *t* because of the proximity of both their [sc. the *d's* and the *t's]* points of articulation.(251)

The imperfect is يَعِدُ "/3 masc. sing.", يَعِدان "/3 masc. dual", يَعِدُونَ "/3 masc. pl." etc. Its [sc. يَعِدُ 's] base form is يَوْعِدُ, in which the *w* is elided to avoid the inclination from the virtual kasra [sc. the *y]* to the virtual ḍamma [sc. the *w]* and from the virtual ḍamma [sc. the *w]* to the underlying kasra [of the 2nd radical], which is deemed as heavy.(252) On account of that, only حبُكٌ "paths" and دئُلٌ "a jackal" as dialectal variants occur according to the pattern فِعُلٌ and فُعِلٌ.(253)

It [sc. the *w]* is also elided in تَعِدُ "/2 fem. sing. or 3 fem. sing." for the sake of similarity [with يَعِدُ].

It is also elided in يَضَعُ "he puts" underlyingly يَوْضَعُ, in which the *w* is elided so that it became يَضَعُ on account of the guttural consonant.(254)

However, it is not elided in يُوعِدُ [Form IV], because its base form is يُأَوْعِدُ.(255)

The imperative is عِدْ "/2 masc. sing.", عِدَا "/2 dual", عِدوا "/2 masc. pl.", etc.(256) The active participle is واعِدٌ, etc, the passive participle is مَوْعودٌ, etc., the noun of place is مَوعِدٌ and the noun of instrument is ميعد, in which the *w* [of its base form مِوْعَدٌ] is changed into a *y* because of its sukūn and [the influence of] the kasra preceding it. They usually change it [sc. the *w]* into a *y* even if there is a separating consonant [between two vowelled consonants], as in قِنْيَةٌ "sheep or goats taken for oneself / not for sale, acquisition" [underlyingly قِنْوَةٌ].(257) So without any separating consonant, it [sc. the *w* of مِوْعَدٌ] is even more entitled to be changed.

II.5.1. COMMENTARY

The Verb with Weak 1st Radical

(242) For a general study of المثال "the assimilated verb" or "the verb with weak 1st radical *w* or *y*" see Muʾaddib, *Taṣrīf* 218-253, Ibn Ǧinnī, *Munṣif I,* 184-232, Ibn Yaʿīš, *Mulūkī* 48-52, Ibn ʿUṣfūr, *II,* 426-437, Zanǧānī, *ʿIzzī* 7-8, ʿAbd al-Ḥamīd, *Taṣrīf* 619-623, de Sacy, 237-240, Farḥāt, *Baḥṯ* 66-70, Brockelmann, *Socins Grammatik* 42-43, Wright, 78-81, Blachère, 133-136, Fischer, *Grammatik* 114-116, Bakkūš, *Taṣrīf* 119-133, ʿAbd al-Raḥīm, *Ṣarf* 27-29, Roman, *Étude II,* 971-981. For a comparative study with corresponding forms in some of the other Semitic languages see Brockelmann, *Grundriß* 596-605, Wright, *Comparative Grammar* 234-242, Bauer, *Grammatik* 113-114. Moscati, *Grammar* 169 who refers to von Soden, *Grundriß* 154-156, remarks that some of these verbs describe certain involuntary actions, e.g. Semitic *wld* "to give birth", Arabic *wǧd* "to find", Ethiopic *wdq* "to fall", while others "connote the aim or target of a motion, e.g. Semitic *wrd* "to go down", Ethiopic *wsd* "to lead to".

(243) The five conjugations that are referred to are: 1– فَعَلَ يَفْعِلُ, e.g. وَعَدَ يَعِدُ underlyingly يَوْعِدُ "to promise", 2– فَعِلَ يَفْعَلُ , e.g. وَجِلَ يَوْجَلُ "to be afraid", 3– فَعَلَ يَفْعَلُ , e.g. وَهَبَ يَهَبُ "to give" underlyingly يَوْهَبُ, 4– فَعُلَ يَفْعُلُ, e.g. وَجُهَ يَوْجُهُ "to be a man of distinction", 5– فَعِلَ يَفْعِلُ, e.g. وَمِقَ يَمِقُ "to love tenderly" underlyingly يَوْمِقُ. In the case of يَعِدُ, the *w* is elided because it is considered as heavy before the kasra in the base form يَوْعِدُ (for discussions see (252)). In the case of يَوْجَلُ it is retained whereas in the case of يَهَبُ it is elided to distinguish the conjugation فَعِلَ يَفْعَلُ from فَعَلَ يَفْعَلُ (cf. Bakkūš, *Taṣrīf* 125, ʿAbd al-Raḥīm, *Ṣarf* 28-29). In some rare cases of verbs of the conjugation فَعِلَ يَفْعَلُ , the *w* can as well be changed into a *y* or into an *ā*, e.g. وَجِلَ يَوْجَلُ يَيْجَلُ يَاجَلُ (cf. Wright, *II,* 79, Bakkūš, *Taṣrīf* 125). Furthermore, the anomalous example وَجَدَ يَجُدُ "to find" should have been وَجَدَ يَجِدُ according to the conjugation فَعَلَ يَفْعِلُ, and not according to فَعَلَ يَفْعُلُ. يَجُدُ is underlyingly يَوْجُدُ of which the 1st radical *w* is elided and the 2nd radical, the *ǧ,* is given the kasra. This form occurs by all tribes except the Banū ʿĀmir (cf. Ibn Manẓūr, *VI,* 4769, Zabīdī, *Tāǧ IX,* 253, 254, Bakkūš, *Taṣrīf* 123 in the notes) who vowel the *ǧ* with the ḍamma, i.e. يَجُدُ. The verb according to their dialect is found in the following verse said by Ǧarīr (cf. Fischer/Bräunlich, *Šawāhid* 211, Ǧarīr, *Dīwān* 453, Ed. M. al-Ṣāwī), in a poem in which he satirizes al-Farazdaq. It is not said by Labīd b. Rabīʿa al-ʿĀmirī, as mentioned by Ibn Manẓūr, *VI,* 4769, Zabīdī, *Tāǧ IX,* 253, 254, Howell, *II-III,* 247-248. Both Ibn Manẓūr and Zabīdī mention as well that according to Ibn al-Barrī the verse is said by Ǧarīr, but Zabīdī adds that according to Ibn ʿUdais it belongs to the dialectal variant of the Banū ʿAmir, and that the verse is by Labīd. This is stated as well by al-Farrāʾ, copied from him by al-Qazzāz in *al-Ǧāmiʿ* and cited by both al-Sīrāfī in the *Kitāb al-iqnāʿ* and by al-Liḥyāni in *al-Nawādir.* It is also cited by Ibn Ǧinnī, *Sirr II,* 596, *Munṣif I,* 187, Ibn ʿUṣfūr, *I,* 177, Ibn Yaʿīš, *Mulūkī* 49:

"لَوْ شِئْتِ قَدْ نَقَعَ ٱلْفُؤَادَ بِشَرْبَةٍ   تَدَعُ ٱلصَّوَادِيَ لَا يَجُدْنَ غَلِيلَا".

"If you had wanted, your saliva would have quenched [the thirst of] the heart with a single draught leaving the thirsty [ribs of the breast in such a state that] they would not experience heat of thirst".

(244) يَعِدُ is underlyingly يَوْعِدُ of which the 1st radical *w* is elided in the imperfect (cf. Zamaḫšarī, 178, de Sacy, *I,* 238, Vernier, *I,* 57, my notes (16)). Not all verbs with 1st radical *w* have their *w* elided in the imperfect. The Kufans believed that the elision of the *w* is carried out to distinguish the transitive, e.g. وَعَدَهُ يَعِدُهُ "promised it", وَزَنَهُ يَزِنُهُ "weighted it", from the intransitive in which the *w* is retained, e.g. وَحِلَ يَوْحَلُ "to fall into the mud", and وَجِلَ يَوْجَلُ "to fear". Their theory is however wrong as there exist verbs in the intransitive of which the *w* is elided, e.g. وَكَفَ الْبَيْتُ "the tent, or house, dripped with rain-water", imperfect يَكِفُ, and وَنَمَ الْذُبَابُ "the fly dropped excrement", imperfect يَنِمُ. For a study see Ibn Ǧinnī, *Munṣif I,* 188, Ibn al-Anbārī, *Inṣāf* Q. 112, 326-327, Howell, *IV,* fasc. I, 1418, Bohas, *Étude* 209-212.

(245) The paradigm of وَعَدَ, a verb with 1st radical *w,* that pertains to the conjugation فَعَلَ يَفْعِلُ, in the perfect, active, is the following:

	sing.	dual	pl.
1st	وَعَدْتُ	وَعَدْنَا	
2nd masc.	وَعَدْتَ	وَعَدْتُمَا	وَعَدْتُمْ
2nd fem.	وَعَدْتِ	وَعَدْتُمَا	وَعَدْتُنَّ
3rd masc.	وَعَدَ	وَعَدَا	وَعَدُوا
3rd fem.	وَعَدَتْ	وَعَدَتَا	وَعَدْنَ

Its paradigm in the imperfect of the indicative, active, is the following:

	sing.	dual	pl.
1st	أَعِدُ	نَعِدُ	
2nd masc.	تَعِدُ	تَعِدَانِ	تَعِدُونَ
2nd fem.	تَعِدِينَ	تَعِدَانِ	تَعِدْنَ
3rd masc.	يَعِدُ	يَعِدَانِ	يَعِدُونَ
3rd fem.	تَعِدُ	تَعِدَانِ	يَعِدْنَ

Its paradigm in the imperfect of the subjunctive, active, is the following:

	sing.	dual	pl.
1st	أَعِدَ		نَعِدَ
2nd masc.	تَعِدَ	تَعِدَا	تَعِدُوا
2nd fem.	تَعِدِي	تَعِدَا	تَعِدْنَ
3rd masc.	يَعِدَ	يَعِدَا	يَعِدُوا

3rd fem.	تَعِدُ	تَعِدَانِ	يَعِدْنَ

Its paradigm in the imperfect of the jussive, active, is the following:

	sing.	dual	pl.
1st	أَعِدْ		نَعِدْ
2nd masc.	تَعِدْ	تَعِدَا	تَعِدُوا
2nd fem.	تَعِدِي	تَعِدَا	تَعِدْنَ
3rd masc.	يَعِدْ	يَعِدَا	يَعِدُوا
3rd fem.	تَعِدْ	تَعِدَا	يَعِدْنَ

Its imperative is عِدْ. Its active participle is وَاعِدٌ. Its *maṣdar* is وَعْدٌ or عِدَةٌ. Its perfect, passive is وُعِدَ. Its imperfect is يُوعَدُ. Its passive participle is مَوْعُودٌ.

As for its derived Form VIII:

Form VIII: Its perfect, active is اِتَّعَدَ. Its imperfect is يَتَّعِدُ. Its imperative is اِتَّعِدْ. Its active participle is مُتَّعِدٌ. Its *maṣdar* is اِتِّعَادٌ. Its perfect, passive is أُتُّعِدَ. Its imperfect is يُتَّعَدُ. Its passive participle is مُتَّعَدٌ.

b) The paradigm of يَسَرَ "to be easy", a verb with 1st radical *y*, that pertains to the conjugation فَعَلَ يَفْعُلُ, in the groundform and in the derived Forms IV, VIII and X, is the following:

Form I: Its perfect, active is يَسَرَ. Its imperfect is يَيْسُرُ. Its imperative is اِيسُرْ. Its active participle is يَاسِرٌ. Its *maṣdar* is يُسْرٌ. Its perfect, passive is يُسِرَ. Its imperfect is يُوسَرُ. Its passive participle is مَيْسُورٌ.

Form IV: Its perfect, active is أَيْسَرَ. Its imperfect is يُوسِرُ. Its imperative is أَيْسِرْ. Its active participle is مُوسِرٌ. Its *maṣdar* is اِيسَارٌ. Its perfect, passive is أُوسِرَ. Its imperfect is يُوسَرُ. Its passive participle is مُوسَرٌ.

Form VIII: Its perfect, active is اِتَّسَرَ. Its imperfect is يَتَّسِرُ. Its imperative is اِتَّسِرْ. Its active participle is مُتَّسِرٌ. Its *maṣdar* is اِتِّسَارٌ. Its perfect, passive is أُتُّسِرَ. Its imperfect is يُتَّسَرُ. Its passive participle is مُتَّسَرٌ.

Form X: Its perfect, active is اِسْتَيْسَرَ. Its imperfect is يَسْتَيْسِرُ. Its imperative is اِسْتَيْسِرْ. Its active participle is مُسْتَيْسِرٌ. Its *maṣdar* is اِسْتِيسَارٌ. Its perfect, passive is أُسْتُوسِرَ. Its imperfect is يُسْتَيْسَرُ. Its passive participle is مُسْتَيْسَرٌ.

(246) The 1st weak radical cannot be affected by any change in the perfect of verbs. An example is وَعَدَ "he promised" in which the *w* remains sound. As remarked, the *w* cannot be made vowelless in it, i.e. وْعَدَ, as by principle, the initial consonant of a word must be vowelled.

It cannot either be changed into an *ā,* i.e. اعَد, because the *ā* is vowelless. It cannot either be elided, i.e. عَد, because the number of radicals would only be two, and Arabic verb forms should consist of three radicals. Furthermore if such a case can be admitted, this elision of the *w* cannot be compensated by a *t* at the beginning, i.e. تَعَد, as there is a risk of mixing this *t* with the prefixed *t* of the imperfect, which would mean that the perfect and the imperfect would be confused in the representation, i.e. تَعَد and تعدُ "you promise". The elision cannot either be compensated by the suffixed *t,* i.e. عَدَت, as the perfect would be confused in the representation with the *maṣdar* عدةٌ.

(247) The *t* is not prefixed in the *maṣdar* عدةٌ but suffixed as a compensation for the elided *w* of the base form وعْدٌ (for a presentation of such examples of *maṣdars* see Suyūṭī, *Muzhir II,* 158-159). If the *t* is supposingly prefixed, namely تعد, then the *maṣdar* can be mixed up with the imperfect تعدُ. The risk of confusing two forms is not implied however by تُكْلانٌ in which the *t* is prefixed as a compensation for the elided *w* of the base form وُكْلانٌ, as the ending *-ānun* specific for nouns keeps this form apart from the imperfect تَكِلُ "you commit anything into another's keeping /masc. sing., or she commits anything into another's keeping" from وكَل يكِلُ. Another theory is that the *t* replaces the *w* in it (cf. (330)).

(248) The complete verse is:

"إنَّ ٱلْخَلِيطَ أجَدُّوا ٱلْبَيْنَ فانْجَرَدُوا وَأَخْلَفُوكَ عِدَ ٱلأَمْرِ ٱلَّذي وَعَدُوا".

> "Verily the familiar friends have renewed the separation, and made off, and have broken to you the promise of the matter which they promised".

It is said by Abū Umayya al-Faḍl b. al-ʿAbbās b. ʿUtba b. Abī Lahab in Faḍl, *Šiʿr* 47, who has been contemporary with the Ḫalīfa ʿAbd al-Malik b. Marwān (r. 65-86/684-705) and his sons and successors al-Walīd (r. 86-96/705-715) and Sulaimān (r. 96-99/715-718). It is cited by Ibn Ǧinnī, *Ḫaṣāʾiṣ III,* 171, Muʾaddib, *Taṣrīf* 285, Suyūṭī, *Ašbāh III,* 248, Ibn Sīda, *Muḫaṣaṣ XIV,* 188, Ibn Manẓūr, *VI,* 4871, al-Šartūnī, the commentator of Farḥāt, *Baḥṯ* 67 in the notes, Howell, *I,* fasc. IV, 1527-1528, *IV,* fasc. I, 1423-1424. The point at issue concerns عِدَ underlyingly عِدَةٌ of which the *tāʾ marbūṭa* is elided when it occurs as a first element of the construct state عِدَ الأَمْر that is said instead of عِدَةُ الأَمْر in this specific verse. As already mentioned, the *tāʾ marbūṭa* in عِدَةٌ is a compensation for the elided *w* of the base form وعْدٌ (cf. (247)), and the elision of the *tāʾ marbūṭa* in عِدَ seems to be compensated by the second element of the construct state الأَمْر in this verse. Sībawaihi's attitude regarding the elision of the *tāʾ marbūṭa* (for other examples and discussions see Sībawaihi, *II,* 260-261) is more flexible than al-Farrāʾ's, as he can accept this elision even when the word to which the *tāʾ marbūṭa* is suffixed to is not the first element of a construct state, whereas al-Farraʾ can only accept this elision when the word is the first element of the construct state, as in عدَ الْأَمرِ of this verse, as he considers the second element, i.e. الْأَمرِ, to be a compensation for the elided *tā᾽ marbūṭa* (cf. Mu᾽addib, *Taṣrīf* 285). It can be added as well that there is a difference of opinion between al-Farrā᾽ and al-Aṣmaʿī concerning the variant عدَّة in this verse. According to al-Aṣmaʿī, عدَ should be read عدا as he considers it to be the pl. of عدَّة (cf. Ibn Ǧinnī, *Ḫaṣā᾽iṣ III,* 171-172). Another theory is as well propounded by Ḫālid b. Kulṯūm who reads it as عدى, pl. of عدْوَة in the meaning of نَاحِيَة "side, part" (cf. the notes to Ibn Ǧinnī, *Ḫaṣā᾽iṣ III,* 171), and the meaning of the verse becomes then: "and have failed to perform to thee the particulars of the matter that they promised".

For the same reason as with عدَّة, the *tā᾽ marbūṭa* is elided from غَلَبَة with غلَب used instead according to the opinion of al-Farrā᾽, in the sur. 30: 1-3 (آلم غُلِبَتِ ٱلرُّومُ فِي أَدْنَى ٱلْأَرْضِ وَهُمْ مِنْ بَعْدِ غَلَبِهِمْ سَيَغْلِبُونَ فِي بِضْعِ سِنِينَ) "The Roman Empire has been defeated – in a land close by; but they, (even) after (this) defeat of theirs, will soon be victorious", in which مِن بَعْدِ غَلَبِهِمْ is used instead of مِن بَعْدِ غَلَبَتِهِمْ (cf. Ibn Manẓūr, *V,* 3278-3279, Howell, *I,* fasc. IV, 1527). In the case of غَلَبِهِمْ, it can be noted that it is a noun to which a pronoun of the genitive is suffixed to. Furthermore, both the second noun that is the second element in the construct state and the suffixed pronoun are governed in the genitive. A case is pointed out by Zamaḫšarī, *Kaššāf I,* 401, quoted by Afandī, *Tanzīl* 369, concerning the reading of some of the sur. 2: 280 (وَإِنْ كَانَ ذُو عُسْرَةٍ فَنَظِرَةٌ إِلَى مَيْسَرَةٍ) "If the debtor is in a difficulty, grant him time till it is easy", in which مَيْسَرَة has been read with the *s* given a ḍamma or a kasra, and with the *tā᾽ marbūta* elided by some as they curiously consider it to be an element of a construct state, similar to both the cases of وَأَخْلَفُوكَ عدَ الْأَمْرِ (see above) and وإقام الصلاة (cf. (249)). Another case is pointed out by Suyūṭī, *Ašbāh III,* 248-249, which is the reading of some of the sur. 9: 46 (وَلَوْ أَرَادُوا ٱلْخُرُوجَ لَأَعَدُّوا لَهُ عُدَّهُ) "If they had intended to come out, they would certainly have made some preparation therefor", in which عُدَّه occurs with the elision of the *tā᾽ marbūta* instead of عُدَّتَهُ.

(249) The base form of the *maṣdar* of Form IV اقامة is اِقْوَام, in which the middle radical *w* that is vowelled by a fatḥa is changed into an *ā* after that its fatḥa is shifted to the *q,* so that it became إقاام. Then one of the alifs is elided to avoid the cluster of two vowelless consonants, the alifs, and the *tā᾽ marbūṭa* is suffixed to the word to compensate for this elision (cf. (279)). Likewise, the base form of the *maṣdar* of Form X استقامة is استقْوَام, in which the middle radical *w* that is vowelled by a fatḥa is changed into an *ā* after that its fatḥa is shifted to the *q,* so that it becomes استقاام. Then one of the alifs is elided to avoid the cluster of two vowelless weak consonants, and the *tā᾽ marbūṭa* is suffixed to the word to compensate for this elision. The reason of the elision of the *tā᾽ marbūṭa* in وإقامة that is said وإقام in the sur. 21: 73 (وإقام الصلاة وايتاء الزكاة) is the same as in عدَّة in وَأَخْلَفُوكَ عدَ الْأَمْرِ (cf. (248)), as الصلاة is the second element of the construct state وإقام الصلاة, and functions as a substitute that compensates for the elided *tā᾽ marbūṭa.* Cf. Sībawaihi, *II,* 260-261, Zamaḫšarī, 179, Ibn ʿAqīl, *II,* 574, de Sacy, *I,* 294, *Anthologie* in his commentary to Baiḍāwī, *Anwār al-tanzīl* 388, Howell, *I,* fasc. III, 1126, fasc. IV, 1571-1572, *IV,* fasc. I, 1424, Vernier, *I,* 164, 334.

(250) For the paradigm of وَعَدَ see (245).

(251) The assimilation of the 3rd radical *d* to the suffixed *t* (cf. Vernier, *I,* 57) in perfect verbs, e.g. وَعَدتَّ "you promised /masc. sing.", وَعَدتِّ "/2 fem. sing." and وَعَدتُّ "/1 sing." instead of وَعَدْتَ, وَعَدْتِ and وَعَدْتُ is a possibility. The reason of this assimilation is the proximity of the *t* to the *d* in the point of articulation, as they both originate from the tip of the tongue and the roots of the two upper central incissors (for the consonants see my notes (188)).

(252) For the paradim of وَعَدَ in the imperfect of the indicative, active, see (245). الكسرة التقديرية is translated as "the kasra that is virtually existent" and الضمّة التقديريّة as "the ḍamma that is virtually existent". The *w* is elided from the base form of the imperfect يَوْعِدُ resulting in يَعِدُ because of the dislike that the Arabs have for the combination of the kasra that follows the ḍamma and vice versa in one word. The prefixed *y* of the imperfect in يَوْعِدُ is considered as implying the existence of a virtual kasra because the kasra refers to the *y,* and the radical *w* implies the existence of a virtual ḍamma because the ḍamma refers to the *w,* and so both their combination together or the inclination of one to the other, is deemed as heavy. Furthermore الكسرة التحقيقيّة "the real kasra" that vowels the 2nd radical ʿ in يَوْعِدُ follows the *w* or the virtual ḍamma, which is a reason more why the *w* should be elided.

(253) The disliked combination of the ḍamma preceding the kasra is found in the noun حِبُكٌ (cf. Lane, *I,* 503) and of the kasra preceding the ḍamma in the noun دِئُلٌ (for discussions and other examples see (133)).

(254) The imperfect of وَضَعَ, namely يَوْضِعُ of which the 1st radical is a *w,* is formed according to the conjugation يَفْعِلُ with the 2nd radical vowelled with a kasra. The 2nd radical is however vowelled by a fatḥa, i.e. يَضَعُ, due to the influence of the 3rd radical ʿ which is a guttural consonant (cf. Howell, *IV,* fasc. I, 1419; for discussions concerning strong verbs with 2nd or 3rd radical as a guttural consonant see (30), (30 b)).

(255) The *w* is not elided in the imperfect Form IV يُوعِدُ underlyingly يُأَوْعِدُ with the infixed hamza in it, as its perfect is أَوْعَدَ formed according to أَفْعَلَ. The reason why the *w* is retained in يُوعِدُ is that it occurs in the base form يُأَوْعِدُ between a hamza vowelled by a fatḥa preceding it and a kasra following it, which is not considered as a heavy combination. The position of the *w* in Form IV يُوعِدُ is different from its position in Form I يَوعِدُ in which it follows a *y* and precedes a kasra resulting in a disliked combination, which is the reason of its elision there (cf. (252)).

(256) عِدْ is used in the imperative instead of اوْعِدْ or after the change of the 1st radical vowelless *w* into a *y* on account of the influence of the kasra preceding it, i.e. اِيعِدْ (cf. Wright, *II*, 78, de Sacy, *I*, 238). The elision of the 1st radical *w* in the imperative seems to be on the analogy of its elision in the imperfect تَعِدُ, as the imperative can be considered to be derived from the imperfect.

The paradigm of وَعَدَ in the imperative is thus the following:

	sing.	dual	pl.
2nd masc.	عِدْ	عِدَا	عِدُوا
2nd fem.	عِدِي	عِدَا	عِدْنَ

(257) For discussions concerning قِنْيَةٌ underlyingly قِنْوَةٌ in which the vowelled *w* is changed into a *y* see (113).

II.6. Arabic Text: الباب الخامس في الأجوف

ويُقال له أجوف لخلوّ جوفه عن الحرف الصحيح ويقال له ذو الثلثة لصيرورته على
ثلثة أحـرف في المتـكلّم نحو قُلْـتُ. وهـو يجيء مـن ثلثة أبـواب نحـو قَـالَ يَقُـولُ وبَـاعَ
* ٢٧ آ يَبِـيعُ وخَـافَ يَخَـافُ. قال بعض* الصـرفيّيـن أصـلاً شـاملاً في باب الإعلال يخـرج جميع
المسائل منه وهو قولهم إنّ الإعلال في حروف العلّة في غير الفاء يتصوّر فيه على ستّة عشر
وجهاً لأنّه يتصـوّر في حـروف العلّة أربعة أوجـه الحـركات الثلث والسكون وفي ما قبلها
كذلك فاضـرب الأربعة في الأربعة حتّى يحصل لك ستّة عشر وجهاً ثمّ اتـرك الساكنـة
التي ما فوقها ساكن لتعذُّر اجتماع الساكنين فبقي لك خمسة عشر وجهاً. الأربعة منها إذا
كان ما قبلها مفتـوحاً نحو قَوْلٍ وبَيْعٍ وخَوفَ وطَوُلَ ولا تُعلّ الاولى لأنّ حرف العلّة إذا
سُكنت جُعلت من جنس حركة ما قبلها للين عريكة الساكن واستدعاء ما قبلها نحو
ميزَانٍ أصله مِوْزَانٌ ويُوسرُ أصله يُيْسرُ إلاّ إذا انفتح ما قبلها لخفّة الفتحة والسكون.
وعـند بـعضـهـم يجوز القـلب نحـو قَـالَ ويُعـلُّ نحـو أغزَيْتُ أصـلـه أغْـزَوْتُ بـواو سـاكـن
* ٢٧ ب تبعاً ليُغْزي ويُعلُّ نحو كَيْنُونَة من الكَوْن مع سكون الواو وانفتاح ما قبلها لأنّ أصله*
كَيْوَنُونَة عند الخليل فأُدغمت فصارت كَيّنُونَةٌ كما في مَيّت أصله مَيْوتٌ ثمّ أُدغمت ثمّ
خُفّفت الياء الثانية فصارت كَيْنُونَةٌ كما خُفّفت في مَيْت وقيل أصله كُونُونَةٌ بضمّ الكاف
ثمّ فُتح حتّى لا يصير الياء واواً في نحو الصَيْرُورَة والغَيْبُوبَة والقَيْلُولَة ثمّ جُعلت الواو
ياءً تبعاً لليائيّات لكثرتها. ومن ثمّ قيل لا يجيء من الواويّات غير الكَيْنُونَة والدَيْمُومَة

Fols. 26b-27b

٢ أجوف: أجوفي ل/ الصحيح: الصحيحة ك/ الثلثة: الثلاثة جـ ز ل/ لصيرورته: لصيرورة ط/ ٣ ثلثة(1+2): ثلاثة جـ ز ك ل/ ٤ قال: وقال ل/ ٥ حروف: حرف ا/ على: – ل/ ٦ الثلث: الثلاث ب ط ك ل: الثلثة حـ هـ/ وفيما: وفي ما ل/ أيضاً: – ل/ ٧ يحصل: تحصل ط/ ٨ ما: – د ل/ منها: – د/ ٩ قول: القول جـ د ز/ تُعلَ: يعلَ ا ب جـ د حـ ط ز: تعتل هـ/ الأولى: الأوَل ا/ ١٠ سكنت: اسكنت د هـ حـ ط/ ١٢ القلب: – ا/ أغزيت: + فإنَ ل/ أصله أغزوت: – ب جـ ز ط/ أغزوت بواو: واو د/ ١٣ من الكون: – ز/ أصله: أصلها ط/ ١٤ فصارت كَيَنونة: – ب د هـ ز حـ ط ك/ كما: + خفَفت ز/ أصله... ميوت: – ب ط/ أصله... ادغمت: – د/ ميوت: مويت هـ/ ثمَ ادغمت: – هـ ط ل/ ١٥ خفَفت: – ب جـ ز/ الياء الثانية: – ا ب د هـ ز ط/ فصارت: فصار ب جـ حـ ط/ أصله: اصلها ب د ز ط/ ١٦ يصير: تصير ل/ والغيبوبة والقيلولة: والقيلولة والغيبوبة ب د حـ ل/ ١٧ قيل: – ا/

II.6. Translation: The 5th Chapter is about the Verb with Weak 2nd Radical(258)

It is named أجوفُ "hollow" because its middle is devoid of a strong consonant. It is also named ذو الثلاثة "the one with the three consonants", because it becomes formed of three consonants in the 1st person of the sing. [of the perfect], e.g. قُلْتُ "I said". It falls into three conjugations: 1- قَالَ يَقُولُ "to say", 2- بَاعَ يَبِيعُ "to sell" and 3- خَافَ يَخَافُ "to fear".(259) Some of the grammarians **[Fol. 27 a]** established some general principles concerning the subject of the weak consonants' unsoundness from which all the issues derive. They stated that the change due to the unsoundness of the weak consonants, when they are in other [positions] than as 1st [initial] radicals, can be conceived in sixteen cases: four cases can be thought of concerning the weak consonants, namely the vowelling by [one of] the three vowels and the vowellessness, and the same concerns the consonant preceding them. So multiply the four by four until you get sixteen cases, then exclude the vowelless weak consonant which is preceded by a vowelless consonant, because of the impossibility of combining two vowelless consonants, and so fifteen cases are left for you:(260) I—Four of them if it [sc. the weak consonant] is preceded by a fatḥa, e.g. 1- قَوْلٌ "a saying", 2- بَيْع "to sell", 3- خَوف "to fear" and 4- طَوْل "to become long". No change is carried out in the first [sc. قَوْلٌ] on the basis that if the weak consonant is vowelless it would have to be changed into a weak consonant of the nature of the vowel preceding it, because of the weakness of the nature of the vowelless weak consonant and the influence of the vowel preceding it [on it], e.g. مِيزَانٌ "balance" underlyingly مِوْزَانٌ, and يُوسِرُ "is well off" underlyingly يُيْسِرُ,(261) unless if the consonant preceding it is vowelled by a fatḥa [as in قَوْلٌ in which the weak consonant remains sound], because of the lightness of the fatḥa followed by the sukūn. By some of them, the change [into the *ā]* is made possible, e.g. قَالٌ "a saying". A change due to the unsoundness is carried out in أغْزَيْتُ "I attacked" underlyingly أغْزَوْتُ with a vowelless *w*, on the analogy of يُغْزِي "he attacks".(262) A change is carried out also in كَيْنُونَةٌ "being", that is from الكَوْنُ with the vowelless *w* and the consonant preceding it being vowelled by a fatḥa, because its base form **[Fol. 27 b]** is كَيْوَنُونَةٌ according to al-Ḫalīl, then an assimilation is carried out and it becomes كَيَّنُونَةٌ,–similarly to مَيِّتٌ "a dead man" underlyingly مَيْوِتٌ in which an assimilation is carried out –, and then the 2nd *y* is lightened so that it becomes كَيْنُونَةٌ as it is lightened in مَيْتٌ. It is said [by the Kufans] that its base form is كُونُونَةٌ with the *k* vowelled by a ḍamma, which is then given a fatḥa, [and with the *w* changed into the *y]* so that the *y* does not have to be changed into a *w*, formed according to [the *maṣdars* of verbs with 2nd radical *y]* e.g. الصَّيْرُورَةُ "becoming", الغَيْبُوبَةُ "unconsciousness" and القَيْلُولَةُ "sleeping at midday". So the *w* is changed [in كَونُونَةٌ with 2nd radical *w]* into a *y* on the analogy of the *maṣdars* with 2nd radical *y* because of their frequency.(263) Hence, it is said that only الكَيْنُونَةُ, الدَّيْمُومَةُ "continuation".

والسَيْدُودَة والهَيْعُوعَة. قال ابن جنَي في الثلثة الأخيرة تُسكن حروف العلَة فيها للخفَة ثمَ تُقلب ألفاً لاستدعاء الفتحة ولين عريكة الساكن إذا كنَ في فعل او في اسم على وزن فعل إذا كانت حركاتهنَ غير عارضة ولا تكون فتحة ما قبلها في حكم السكون ولا يكون في معنى الكلمة اضطراب ولا يجتمع فيه إعلالان ولا يُلزم ضمَ حروف العلَة في مضارعه ولا يُترك للدلالة على الأصل ومن ثمَ يُعلُ نحو قَالَ أصله قَوَلَ ونحو دَارٍ أصله دَوَرٌ لوجود الشرائط * المذكورة ويُعلَ مثل دِيَارٍ تبعاً لواحده ومثل قِيَامٍ تبعاً لفعله ومثل ٢٨ آ * سِيَاطٍ تبعاً لواو واحده وهي مشابهة بألف دَارٍ في كونها ميِّتة، أعني تُعل هذه الأشياء وإن لم تكن أفعالاً ولا على وزن أفعالٍ للمتابعة ولا يُعلُ نحو الْحَوَكَة والْخَوَنَة وَحَيَدَى وَصَوَرَى لخرُوجهنَ عن وزن الفعل بعلامة التأنيث وقيل حتَى يدللن على الأصل ونحو دَعَوُا الْقَوْمَ لطروَ حركته ونحو عَوِرَ واجْتَوَرَ لأنَ حركة العين والتاء في حكم السكون أي في حكم عين اِعْوَرَ وألف تَجَاوَرَ ونحو الْحَيَوَانِ حتَى يدلَ حركته على اضطراب معناه والمَوْتَان محمول عليه لأنَه نقيضه ونحو طَوَى حتَى لا يجتمع فيه إعلالان وطَوِيَا محمول عليه وإن لم يجتمع فيه إعلالان ونحو حَيِيَ حتَى لا يلزم ضمَ الياء في المضارع يعني إذا قلتَ حَايَ يجيء مستقبله يَحَايُ ونحو الْقَوَدِ والصَيَدِ حتَى يدلَ على الأصل.

Fols. 27b-28a

١ جنَي: الجني د/ الثلثة: الثلاثة جـ د ز ط ل/ فيها: أولًا ا/ ٢ في: – د/ ٣ ولا تكون: ويكون د/ تكون: يكون ا ب هـ حـ ط/ قبلها: + لا د/ السكون: الساكن ب د ط/ ٥ ونحو دار: ودار د ل/ ٦ ديار: + أصله دوار حـ/ ٧ سياط: + أصله سواط هـ/ تعلَ: يعل ا ب د هـ ز حـ ط/ ٨ تكن: يكن ا د هـ ز حـ ط/ على... أفعال: اسماء على وزن فعل د/ ٩ يدللن: يدل د/ ١٠ دَعَوْا: دعو ا جـ هـ ط: دعوى حـ/ ١١ حكم: – د/ ١٢ حتَى لا: لئلا د/ ١٤ إذا: + قلبت العين من حيي حـ/ والصَيَد: – د هـ حـ ط/

السَّيْدُودَة "predominance" and الهَيْعُوعَة "vomitting" occur as *maṣdars* with 2nd radical *w*.(264) Ibn Ǧinnī said concerning the three last ones [sc. بَيِع, خَوِف and طَوُل], that the weak consonants are made vowelless in them for the purpose of alleviation, and that they are then changed into an *ā* due to the influence of the fatḥa [preceding them], and because of the feebleness of the sukūn's nature.

Thus [the phonological change due to the unsoundness of the *w* and *y* is carried out]: 1- if they are in a verb or in a noun with a verbal pattern; 2- if their vowelling is not accidental; 3- if the fatḥa of the consonant preceding them does not have the state of the sukūn; 4- if the corresponding meaning of the word does not refer to intensive mobility; 5- if there is not in it [sc. the word] a risk of combining two phonological changes; 6- if the weak consonants do not necessarily become vowelled with a ḍamma in the imperfect; and 7- if they are not meant to give a clue to the base form.(265)

1- Thus the phonological change is carried out in قَالَ "to say" underlyingly قَوَلَ, and in دَارٌ "house" underlyingly دَوَرٌ, because of the existence of the mentioned **[Fol. 28 a]** conditions. As for the change that is carried out in دِيَارٌ "houses", it is on the analogy of its sing. [sc. دَار], in قِيَامٌ "standing" on the analogy of its verb,(266) and in سِيَاطٌ "whips" on the analogy of the *w* of its sing. [sc. سَوْطٌ], which is similar to the *ā* of دَارٌ in its being "dead".(267) I mean that the phonological change due to the unsoundess of the weak consonant is carried out in these examples even if they are not verbs or being on the verbal measure *f-ʿ-l* for the sake of analogy.

The phonological change is not carried out in الْحَوَكَةُ "the weavers", الْخَوَنَةُ "the traitors",(268) حَيَدَى "(a he-ass) shying at his own shadow because of his liveliness" and صَوَرَى "*Ṣawarā*, name of a water",(269) as they are excluded from [resemblance to] the verbal pattern due to the feminine marker [sc. respectively the *t* of the feminine and the abbreviated alif], and it is also said so that they give a clue to the base form.

2- It is not carried out either in دَعَوُا الْقَوْمَ "they called out for the people", because of the faintness of its vowel [sc. the ḍamma of the *w]*. 3- Nor in عَوِرَ "to be one-eyed" and اجْتَوَرَ "to be neighbours" on the basis that the vowel of the ʿ [of عَوِرَ] and [the vowel of] the *t* [of اجْتَوَرَ] are ruled by the sukūn, i. e. by the [sukūn of the] vowelless ʿ of اعْوَرَّ and the [sukūn of the vowelless] *ā* of تَجَاوَرَ [respectively].(270) 4- Nor in الْحَيَوَانُ "animal, much life", so that its vowelling gives notice of the mobility referred to by its corresponding meaning. الْمَوَتَانُ "much death" is formed according to it as it is its opposite in meaning.(271) 5- Nor in طَوَى "to fold" to prevent the combination of two unsound weak consonants. طَوَيَا "/dual" is formed according to it in spite of the fact that there is not a combination of two unsound weak consonants in it. 6- Nor in حَيِيَ "to live" so that it is not necessary to vowel the [2nd] *y* of the imperfect by a ḍamma, i.e. if you said حَايَ, its imperfect would be يَحَايُ.(272) 7- Nor in الْقَوَدُ "the retaliation" and in الصَّيَدُ "a disease in a camel's head", so that they give a clue to the base form.(273)

* ٢٨ ب الأربعة منها إذا كان ما قبلها مضموماً نحو مُيْسِرٍ وبُيِعَ* ويَغْزُوُ ولنْ يَدْعُوَ بجعل الياء في الاولى واوا لضمَة ما قبلها ولين عريكة الساكن فصار مُوسِرًا وفي الثانية تُسكن للخفَة ثمَ تُجعل واواً لضمَة ما قبلها ولين عريكة الساكن فصار بُوعَ وإذا جُعلت حركة ما قبل حرف العلَة من جنسه يجوز فصار حينئذ بيعَ. وتسكن في الثالثة للخفَة فصار يَغْزُو ولا تُعلَ في الرابعة لخفَة الفتحة ومن ثمَ لا يُعلَ عُيَبَةٌ ونُوَمَة. الأربعة منها إذا كان ما قبلها مكسوراً نحو مِوْزَانٍ ودَاعِوَة ورَضِيُوا وتَرْمِيينَ ففي الأولى تُجعل يَاءً كما مرَ وفي الثانية تُجعل ياءً لاستدعاء ما قبلها ولين عريكة الفتحة فصار دَاعِيَة ولا يُعلَ مثل دِوَلٍ لأنَ الأسماء التي ليست بمشتقَة من الفعل لا تُعلَ لخفَتها إلاَ إذا كان على وزن الفعل وهو ليس على وزن الفعل وفي الثلثة تُسكن الياء للخفَة ثمَ تُحذف لاجتماع الساكنين

* ٢٩ آ فصار رَضُوا والرابعة مثلها في الإعلال. الثلثة إذا كان* ما قبلها ساكناً نحو يَخْوَفُ ويَبْيِعُ ويَقْوُلُ يُعطى حركاتهنَ إلى ما قبلهنَ لضعف حروف العلَة وقوَة الحرف الصحيح ولكن تُجعل في يَخَوْفُ ألفاً لفتحة ما قبلها ولين عريكة الساكن العارض بخلاف الخَوْف فصرن يَخَافُ ويَبِيعُ ويَقُولُ. ولا يُعلَ نحو أعْيُنٍ وأدْوُرٍ حتَى لا يلتبس بالأفعال ونحو جَدْوَلٍ حتَى لا يبطل الإلحاق ونحو قَوَمَ حتَى لا يلزم الإعلال في الإعلال ونحو الرَمْيِ حتَى لا يُلزم الساكن في آخر المعرب ونحو تَقْوِيمٍ وتِبْيَانٍ ومِقْوَالٍ

Fols. 28a-29a

١ منها: –ا ب د هـ حـ ط ك/ الياء: الحرف العلَة حـ ل/ ١–٢ الياء في: – ب د هـ ز ط/ ٢ موسرا: موسر ا/ تسكن: يسكن جـ د ط/ ٣ تجعل: يجعل ب د هـ ز: جعل جـ حـ ط/ ٤ يجوز: جاز د: – جـ حـ ط/ في: – د/ ٥ تعلَ في: يعل ب د هـ ز حـ ط/ منها: – د/ ٦ وداعوة: وراعوة ب/ وترميين: وترمين ط/ ففي: وفي ا د/ الأولى تجعل: الاول يجعل د/ ٧ تجعل: يجعل د هـ ط/ ٨ تعلَ: يعل د: يعتل هـ/ الفعل: + فحينئذ يجوز الإعلال فيه ز/ ٩ الياء: –ا ب جـ د هـ ز حـ ط/ الثلثة: والثالثة د: الثلاثة هـ حـ ط ل/ قبلها: + قبل حرف العلَة ل/ ١١ حركاتهنَ: حركتهن د ط/ ١٢ الحرف: حروف د/ تجعل: يجعل جـ د هـ ز حـ: + الواو هـ/ ١٢ العارض: العارضي ب هـ/

II- Four of them if what precedes it [sc. the weak consonant] is vowelled by a ḍamma, e.g. 5- مُيْسِرٌ "prosperous", 6- بُيِعَ "was sold", **[Fol. 28 b]** 7- يَغْزُوُ "he attacks" and 8- لَنْ يَدْعُوَ "he shall not call". Hence in the first [sc. مُيْسِرٌ], by changing the *y* into a *w* due to the influence of the ḍamma preceding it and the faintness of the nature of the vowelless weak consonant, so it became مُوسِرٌ. In the second [sc. بُيِعَ], by making it [sc. the *y]* vowelless for the purpose of alleviation, and then by changing it into a *w* due to the [influence of the] ḍamma preceding it and the faintness of the nature of the vowelless weak consonant, so it became بُوعَ. If the vowel preceding the weak consonant [sc. the *y* of بُيِعَ] is changed into its kind [sc. the kasra], it became then بِيعَ, which is also a possibility. In the third [sc. يَغْزُوُ], it [sc. the *w]* is made vowelless for the purpose of alleviation, so it became يَغْزُو. No change is carried out in the fourth [sc. لَنْ يَدْعُوَ], because of the lightness of the fatḥa. On account of that [sc. the lightness of the fatḥa], no change is carried out in عُيَبَةٌ "one who reproaches much" and نُوَمَةٌ "one who sleeps much".(274) III- Four of them if what precedes it [sc. the weak consonant] is vowelled by a kasra, e.g. 9- مِوْزَانٌ "a balance", 10- دَاعِوَةٌ "the one who invites /fem.", 11- رَضِيُوا "they were pleased /masc. pl." and 12- تَرْمِيِينَ "you throw /fem. sing.". Thus in the first [sc. مِوْزَانٌ], it [sc. the *w]* is changed into a *y* as was mentioned. In the second [sc. دَاعِوَةٌ], it [sc. the *w]* is changed into a *y* due to the influence of vowel preceding it and the faintness of the nature of the fatḥa, so it became دَاعِيَةٌ. However, no change is carried out in دِوَلٌ "turns of fortune", because the change is not to be carried out in nouns which are not derived from verbs because of their lightness, unless if they are formed according to a verbal measure, which is not the case here. In the third [sc. رَضِيُوا], the *y* is made vowelless for the sake of alleviation, and it is then elided to avoid the cluster of two vowelless weak consonants, so it became رَضُوا [with the ḍamma of the *ḍ* instead of the kasra]. The change in the fourth [sc. تَرْمِيِينَ] is similar to it [sc. the one in رَضِيُوا].(275) IV- Three of them if it [sc. the weak consonant] **[Fol. 29 a]** is preceded by a vowelless consonant, e.g. 13- يَخْوَفُ "he is afraid", 14- يَبْيِعُ "he sells" and 15- يَقْوُلُ "he says". In them, the vowel [of the weak consonant] is shifted to the consonant preceding it because of the faintness of the weak consonant and the strength of the strong consonant. However, in يَخْوَفُ, it [sc. the *w]* is changed into an *ā* due to the influence of the fatḥa preceding it [after the transfer of the *w's* fatḥa in يَخْوَفُ to it] and the faintness of the nature of the accidental vowel [sc. the fatḥa], as opposed to [the original fatḥa of] الخَوْفُ "fear" [in which the *w* is sound because of the fatḥa's lightness]. Thus they became يَخَافُ, يَبِيعُ and يَقُولُ. No change is carried out in أَعْيُنٌ "eyes" and أَدْوُرٌ "houses", so that they would not be mixed up with the verbs, nor in جَدْوَلٌ "a rivulet", so that the formation [according to فَعْوَلٌ] does not become canceled.(276) Nor in قَوِّمْ "to straighten" to avoid a change due to an unsound weak consonant occurring after another change. Nor in الرَّمْيُ "the throwing" to prevent the occurrence of a vowelless consonant at the end of a declinable word. Nor in تَقْوِيمٌ "setting up", تِبْيَانٌ "demonstration",(277) مِقْوَالٌ "loquacious"

ومخْيَاطِ حتَى لا يجتمع الساكنان بتقدير الإعلال ومخْيَطٌ منقوص من المخْيَاطِ فلا يُعلَ
تبعاً له. فإن قيل لم يُعلَ الإقَامَةُ مع حصول اجتماع الساكنين إذا أُعلَت كإعلال أخواتها
قُلنا تبعاً لقَامَ فإنَه ثلاَثيَ أصيل في الإعلال. فإن قيل لم لا يُعلَ التَقْويمُ تبعاً لقَامَ وهو
ثلاثيَ أصيل في الإعلال قُلنا أبطل قوله قَوَمَ استتباع قَامَ وإن كان أصيلاً في الإعلال لقوَة
قَوَمَ* في الأُخوَة مع التَقْويمِ ولا يُصلح أقَامَ أن يكون مقويًا لقَامَ لأنَه ليس من ثلاثيَ * ٢٩ آ
أصيل ولا يعلَ مثل مَا أقْولَهُ وأغْيَلَت المَرْأةُ واسْتَحْوَذَ حتَى يدللن على الأصل. وتقول في
إلحاق الضمائر قَالَ قَالاَ قَالُوا قَالَتْ قَالَتَا قُلْنَ الى آخره وأصل قَالَ قَوَلَ فجُعلَ الواو ألفاً كما
مرَ. وأصل قُلْنَ قَوَلْنَ فقلبت الواو ألفاً كما مرَ ثمَ حُذفت لاجتماع الساكنين فصار قَلْنَ ثمَ
ضُمَ القاف حتَى يدلَ على الواو المحذوفة ولا يضمَ الفاء في خِفْنَ لأنَ الأصل في النقل
نقل حركة الواو الى ما قبلها لسهولتها ولا يُمكن هذا النقل في قُلْنَ لأنَه يُلزم فتح
المفتوحة ولا يُفرق بينه وبين جمع المؤنَث في الأمر لأنَهم لا يعتبرون الإشتراك الضمَي
ويكتفون بالفرق التقديريَ كما في بِعْنَ وهو مشترك بين المعلوم والمجهول أيضا أو وقع
من غرَة الواضع كما في الإثنين والجماعة من الأمر والماضي في تَفَعَلَ وتَفَاعَلَ وتَفَعْلَلَ. ولا
يُفرق بين فَعُلْنَ وفَعَلْنَ نحو طُلْنَ وقُلْنَ لأنَه يُعلم* من الطَوِيلِ أنَ أصل طُلْنَ طَوُلْنَ لأنَ * ٣٠ آ
الفَعِيلَ يجيء من فَعُلَ غالباً كما يُعلم الفرق بين خِفْنَ وبِعْنَ من مستقبلهما، أعني يُعلم

Fols. 29a-30a

١ يجتمع: يلزم اجتماع ز/ ٢–٣ لم... قيل: d's margin/ ٢ اعلَت: اعللت ب ح ط/ ٣ فإنَه... الإعلال: –ا ب ج ه ح ط/ ٤ كان: + قام ا: + قام ثلاثيًا ح/ أصيلا: أصلا ه/ ٥ لقام: للاقامة ط/ ٧ قالت... قُلْنَ: –ا ب ج د ز ح ط ك/ ألفاً: + لتحركها ب ط: + لتحرَكها وانفتاح ما قبلها ط/ ٧–٨ كما مرَ: –ب ج د ه ز ح ط ك ل/ ٨ حذفت: + الألف ط/ ٩ المحذوفة: + فصار قلن د/ الفاء: –ا ج د ه ز ح ط/ ١٠ الى... قبلها: –ا ط/ ولا... النقل: –ا/ النقل: –ب ج د ه ز/ فتح: فتحة ا ب د ه ز/ ١١ المفتوحة: المفتوح ا/ ١٢ مشترك: + أيضا د/ ١٣ تفعَل وتفاعل: تفاعل وتفعَل د/ ١٤ يعلم: تعلم ا/ اليائيَ: – ج د ه ز ح ك ل/

and مِخْيَاطٌ "needle", to avoid the combination of two vowelless weak consonants if the change is carried out. مِخْيَطٌ is contracted from مِخْيَاطٌ, and no change is carried out in it for the sake of the analogy with it.[278] If it is asked why a change is carried out in الإقَامَةُ "the performance" that causes in it a cluster of two vowelless weak consonants, as it is affected by a change that is similar to the one that could have been carried out in its cognates [sc. التَقْوِيمُ and others], we answer that it is in conformity with قَامَ "to stand up", a triliteral verb with weak radical that is fit to undergo a change.[279] If it is asked why is a change not carried out in [the *maṣdar* of Form II] التَقْوِيمُ on the analogy of قَامَ, a triliteral verb with weak radical that is fit to undergo a change, we answer that if it was to undergo a change on the analogy of قَامَ, a triliteral verb with weak radical that is fit to undergo a change, it would cancel [Form II] قَوَّمَ [Fol. 29 b], which is his [sc. the speaker's] saying, and which is related to التَقْوِيمُ.[280] Hence [Form IV] أَقَامَ is not fit to reinforce [the meaning of] قَامَ, because it is not a Form I triliteral verb. No change is carried out in مَا أَقْوَلَهُ "how well he speaks!",[281] أَغْيَلَتِ المَرْأَةُ "the woman suckled her child while she was pregnant" and اسْتَحْوَذَ "to overwhelm",[282] so that they give a clue to the base form. You say when attaching the pronouns: قَالَ "he said", قَالَا "/3 dual", قَالُوا "/3 masc. pl.", قَالَتْ "/3 fem. sing.", قَالَتَا "/3 dual", قُلْنَ "/3 fem. pl." etc.[283] قَالَ is underlyingly قَوَلَ, in which the *w* is changed into an *ā* as was mentioned. قُلْنَ is underlyingly قَوَلْنَ, in which the *w* is changed into an *ā* as was mentioned, then it is elided to avoid the cluster of two vowelless consonants, so it became قَلْنَ, and then the *q* is vowelled by a ḍamma to give notice of the elided *w*. However, the 1st radical is not vowelled by a ḍamma in خِفْنَ "they were afraid /fem. pl.", because the principle of shifting [a vowel] is to shift the vowel of the *w* [of the base form خَوِفْنَ] to the consonant preceding it because of its lightness. This transfer [of the *w's* vowel of the base form قَوَلْنَ] is not possible in قُلْنَ, because it would impose the fatḥa on a consonant that is already vowelled by a fatḥa [sc. the *q* of قَوَلْنَ]. No difference is made between it [sc. قُلْنَ "/3 fem pl. (perfect)]" and the [2nd person of the] fem. pl. of the imperative [sc. قُلْنَ], as they do not consider the homonymy of the ḍamma [of the 1st radical], but were contented by the virtual difference [between the base forms].[284] So is also the case of بِعْنَ "they sold, or they were sold /fem. pl.", which is common for both the active and passive voice.[285] Or it [sc. the homonymy] is due because of the inadvertency of the one who "posited" the language, as it occurred between the dual and pl. [of the 2nd person of the masc.] of the imperative and [the dual and pl. of the 3rd person of the masc.] of the perfect of [Form V] تَفَعَّلَ [sc. تَفَعَّلَا and تَفَعَّلُوا], [Form VI] تَفَاعَلَ [sc. تَفَاعَلَا and تَفَاعَلُوا], and [Form II of the quadriliteral] تَفَعْلَلَ [sc. تَفَعْلَلَا and تَفَعْلَلُوا]. No distinction is made between [the conjugations] فَعَلْنَ and فَعُلْنَ [after the phonological change], e.g. طُلْنَ "they became long /fem. pl." and قُلْنَ, as it is known [Fol. 30 a] from طَوِيلٌ "long" that طُلْنَ is underlyingly طَوُلْنَ, because فَعِيلٌ is mostly from فَعُلَ. As well as the distinction between [the conjugations of] خِفْنَ and بِعْنَ is known from both their imperfects. I mean that it is known

من يَخَافُ أنَ أصل خفْنَ خَوفْنَ لأنَ باب فَعَلَ يَفْعَلُ لا يجيء إلاَ من حروف الحلق ويُعلم من يَبيعُ ان أصل بعْنَ بَيَعْنَ لأنَ الأجوف اليائيَ لا يجيء من باب فَعَلَ يَفْعَلُ. المستقبل يَقُولُ الى آخره أصله يَقْوُلُ وإعلاله ما مرَ فحُذفت الواو في يَقُلْنَ لاجتماع الساكنين. الأمر قُلْ الى آخره أصله أُقْوُلْ فنُقلت حركة الواو الى القاف ثمَ حُذفت لاجتماع الساكنين ثمَ حُذفت الألف لعدم الإحتياج إليها. ويُحذف الواو في قُلِ الْحَقَ وإنْ لم يجتمع فيه الساكنان لأنَ الحركة فيه حصلت بالخارجيَ فتكون في حكم السكون تقديراً بخلاف قُولاَ وقُولَنَ لأنَ الحركة فيهما حصلت بالداخلين وهما ألف الفاعل ونون التأكيد وهما بمنزلة الداخليَ ومن ثمَ جعلوا معه آخر المضارع مبنيًا نحو هَلْ يَفْعَلَنَ ويُحذف* الألف في دَعَتَا وإن حصلت الحركة بألف الفاعل لأنَ التاء ليست من نفس الكلمة بخلاف اللام في قُولاَ. وتقول بنون التأكيد المشدَدة قُولَنَ قُولاَنِ قُولُنَ قُولِنَ قُولاَنِ قُلْنَانِ وبالخفيفة قُولَنْ قُولُنْ قُولِنْ. الفاعل قَائِلٌ الى آخره أصله قَاوِلٌ فقُلبت الواو ألفاً لتحركها وانفتاح ما قبلها كما في كِسَاءٍ أصله كِسَاوٌ وجُعل واوه ألفاً لوقوعه في الطرف ثمَ جُعل همزة ولا اعتبار لألف الفاعل لأنَها ليست بحاجزة حصينة فاجتمع ألفان ولا يُمكن إسقاط الأولى لأنَه يلتبس بالماضي وكذلك الثانية فحُركت الأخيرة فصارت همزة، ويجيء في البعض بالحذف نحو هَاعٍ ولاَعٍ والأصل هَائِعٌ ولاَئِعٌ ومنه قوله

* ٣٠ ب

Fols. 30a-30b

٣ الى آخره: – ا جـ/ أصله: – حـ/ وإعلاله... مرَ: – ز/ ما: – ا د/ فحذفت: فحذف حـ هـ/ ٤ قل: + قولا قولوا ط/ الى آخره: – ا/ القاف: + ثم جعل أقول هـ: فصار اقول حـ/ ٤–٥ ثمَ... الساكنين: inserted between two lines in ا / الواو: – د/ ٥ لعدم: لانعدام د ل/ ويحذف: وتحذف د/ ٦ حصلت: صارت جـ/ فتكون: فيكون جـ د هـ ز حـ ط/ ٧ بالداخلين: بداخلين ا/ ألف: + الف ا/ ٨ وهما: وهو ا ب د حـ ط/ بمنزلة: بمنزلت ط/ ٩ يفعلنَ: تفعلنَ ل/ ويحذف: وتحذف ب د ز ط ل/ حصلت: حصل ب جـ حـ ط/ ١٠ المشدَدة: – ا ب جـ د هـ حـ ط: + الثقيلة ز/ ١١ الى آخره: – ا جـ ط/ ١٢ وانفتاح: وانفتح ب هـ/ واوه: واو كساو ا: الواو د/ لوقوعه: لوقوعها ا ب د حـ ط/ ١٣ ولا اعتبار: والاعتبار حـ/ لألف: بألف ا ز: الألف ط/ فاجتمع: فاجتماع هـ/ ١٤ ألفان: الألفان ب هـ/ إسقاط: + الالف حـ/ لأنَه... بالماضي: – د/ الأخيرة: – ب د ز: اخرة هـ/ ١٥ والأصل: الأصل د/

from يَخَافُ "he is afraid" that خَفْنَ is underlyingly خَوِفْنَ as the conjugation فَعَلَ يَفْعَلُ does only comprehend verbs with guttural consonants [as 2nd or 3rd radical]. And it is known from يَبِيعُ "he sells" that بِعْنَ is underlyingly بَيَعْنَ, as the verb with 2nd *y* radical does not occur according to the conjugation فَعَلَ يَفْعُلُ. The imperfect is يَقُولُ "he says" etc., underlyingly يَقْوُلُ, in which the change due to the unsoundness of the weak consonant has been mentioned. The *w* is elided in [the base form يَقُولْنَ resulting in] يَقُلْنَ "they say /fem. pl" to avoid the cluster of two vowelless consonants [sc. the vowelless *w* and *l]*.(286) The imperative is قُلْ "say!" etc., underlyingly اُقْوُلْ in which the vowel of the *w* is shifted to the *q,* then its *w* is elided to avoid the cluster of two vowelless consonants [sc. the vowelless *w* and *l],* and then the [prosthetic] alif is elided because it is not more needed.(287) The *w* is elided in [قُلِ in] قُلِ الْحَقَّ "say the truth", in spite of the fact that two vowelless consonants [sc. the vowelless *w* and *l]* are not combined in it [sc. the base form قُولْ], on the basis that the vowel [of juncture] is given to it [sc. the *l* of قُلِ] due to an external consonant [sc. the vowelless *-l* of the definite article of the following word الْحَقَّ], which means that it is ruled by the sukūn virtually, (288) by contrast to [the maintainance of the *w* in] قُولَا "/2 dual (imperative)" and قُولَنَّ "/2 masc. sing.", in which the vowelling [of the *l]* is caused by both internal consonants [respectively], namely the *ā* of the agent pronoun and the energetic *n,* which occupy an internal position of the word. On account of that [sc. that the energetic *n* is internal], they made the last radical of the imperfect invariable [vowelled by the fatḥa] before it, e.g. هَلْ يَفْعَلَنَّ "are they doing? /2 masc. sing. (imperative En. 1)". The *ā* [that is substituted for the 2nd radical *w]* **[Fol. 30 b]** is elided in دَعَتَا "they prayed /fem., dual" [from دَعَوَتَا: دَعَاتَا], in spite of the fact that the vowel is given to it [sc. the *t]* on account of the agent pronoun *ā,* as the *t* is considered as not belonging to the same word, contrarily to the [radical] *l* in قُولَا "Say! /2 dual (imperative)".(289) You say with the energetic *n:* قُولَنَّ "/2 masc. sing. (imperative En. 1)", قُولَانِّ "/2 dual", قُولُنَّ "/2 masc. pl.", قُولِنَّ "/2 fem. sing.", قُولَانِّ "/2 dual" and قُلْنَانِّ "2 fem. pl.", and with the light one: قُولَنْ "/2 masc. sing. (imperative En. II)", قُولُنْ "/2 masc. pl." and قُولِنْ "/2 fem. sing.". The active participle is قَائِلٌ etc., underlyingly قَاوِلٌ, in which the *w* is changed into an *ā* on account that it is vowelled and because of [the influence of] the fatḥa preceding it, as in كِسَاءٌ "a wrapper" underlyingly كِسَاوٌ, in which the *w* is changed into an *ā* because of its occurrence at the extremity of the word, and then it [sc. the *ā]* is changed into a hamza. The [infixed] *ā* of the active participle [in قَاوِلٌ] is not taken into account because it is not a firm separative [between the vowelled *q* and the vowelled *w],* so two alifs [sc. the infixed *ā* of the active participle and the *w* changed into an *ā* in قَاالٌ] were combined together. It was impossible to drop the 1st one,—and so as well the 2nd one -, because it [sc. the active participle] would be mixed up with the perfect [sc. قَالَ "he said"]. So the last one was given a vowel and became a hamza [sc. s قَائِلٌ].(290) It [sc. the active participle] occurs in some [forms] with the elision [of the 2nd radical], e.g. هَاعٌ "vomitting" and لَاعٌ "suffering" underlyingly هَائِعٌ and لَائِعٌ. Among them [sc. these forms] are also the words of

تعالى وكُنْتُمْ ﴿عَلَىٰ شَفَا جُرُفٍ هَارٍ﴾ أي هَائر، ويجيء بالقلب نحو شَاك أصله شَائكٌ وحَاد
أصله وَاحدٌ ويجوز القلب في كلامهم نحو القسيَ أصله قُوُوسٌ فقُدّمَ السين فصار قُسُووٌ
* ٣١ آ مثل عَصُوٍ ثمّ جُعل قُسِيَ لوقوع الواوين في الطرف ثمّ كُسر القاف* إتباعاً لما بعدها
فقالوا قِسِيَ كما في عِصِيَ ومنه أيْنُقٌ أصله أنْوُقٌ ثمّ قُدّمَ الواو على النون فصار أوْنُقٌ ثمّ
جُعل الواو ياءً على غير القياس فصار أيْنُقٌ. المفعول مَقُولٌ أصله مَقْوُولٌ فأُعلَ كإعلال يَقُولُ
فصار مَقُوول فاجتمع الساكنان فحُذفت الواو الزائدة عند سيبويه لأنَ حذف الزائد
أولى والواو الأصلي عند الأخفش لأنَ الزائدة علامة والعلامة لا تُحذف. وقال سيبويه في
جوابه لا تُحذف العلامة إذا لم توجد علامة أُخرى وفيه توجد علامة أُخرى وهي الميم
فيكون وزنه عنده مَفُعْلٌ وعند الأخفش مَفُولٌ وكذلك مَبِيعٌ أصله مَبْيُوعٌ يعني أُعلَ
كإعلال يَبِيعُ فصار مَبُيوعٌ فاجتمع الساكنان الياء والواو فحُذفت الواو عند سيبويه
فصار مَبُيْعٌ ثمّ كُسر الباء حتّى تُسلم الياء وعند الأخفش حُذفت الياء فأُعطي الكسرة
* ٣١ ب لما قبلها كما مرّ في بِعْتَ فصار مَبِوعٌ ثمّ جُعل الواو ياءً كما في مِيزَانٍ فيكون وزنه مَفِعْلٌ *
عند سيبويه وعند الأخفش مَفِيلٌ. الموضع مَقَالٌ أصله مَقْوَلٌ فأُعلَ كما في يَخَافُ وكذلك
مَبِيعٌ أصله مَبْيِعٌ فأُعلَ كما في يَبِيعُ واكتُفي بالفرق التقديريَ بين الموضع وبين اسم
المفعول وهو مُعتبر عندهم كما في الفُلْك إذا قدّرتَ سكونه كسكون أُسْدٍ يكون
جمعاً نحو قوله تعالى ﴿حَتَّىٰٓ إِذَا كُنْتُمْ فِي ٱلْفُلْكِ وَجَرَيْنَ بِهِمْ﴾ وإذا قدّرتَ
سكونه كسكون قُرْبٍ يكون واحداً نحو قوله تعالى ﴿فِي ٱلْفُلْكِ ٱلْمَشْحُونِ﴾.

Fols. 30b-31b

٣ مثل عصوو: – د/ ثمّ[2]: + كسر السين حتى يسلم الياء فصار قسي د/ ٤ أينق: + على وزن أعفل بعد القلب ز: + على وزن افعل هـ: + على وزن افعل بعد القلب ط/ ٥ القياس: قياس ا هـ/ فصار أيْنُق: –ا جـ هـ حـ ط/ أينق: أونق ثم جعل الواو ياء على غير القياس د/ مَقُولٌ: + الى آخره د/ ٦ فصار مقوول: – ل/ فحُذفت: فحذف ا د هـ حـ/ حذف الزائد: ...الحذف للزيادة د: الحذف بالزيادة ل/ ٧ الزائدة: الزائد جـ د هـ ز ط/ ٨ تحذف: يحذف د/ وفيه توجد: فيه وتوجد ل/ وفيه... اخرى: – د/ ٩ أصله مَبْيُوع: – ا د هـ ز/ ١٠ فاجتمع والواو: – د ز/ الساكنان: ساكنان ا/ الياء والواو: – ل/ فحذفت: فحذف ب د هـ/ ١١ حذفت: حذف د/ ١٢ لما: الى ما د/ مرّ: –د/ ١٤ وبين اسم: واسم ل/ ١٦ بهم: + بريح طيّبة ب ط/

the Allmighty "and you were" [sur. 9: 109] (عَلَى شَفَا جُرُفٍ هَارٍ) "On an undermined sand-cliff", i.e. هَائِرٍ.[291] It [sc. the active participle] occurs with the transposition [of the consonants], e.g. شَاكٌ "sharp" underlyingly شَائِكٌ, and حَادٍ "one (in higher ordinals)" underlyingly وَاحِدٌ.[292] The transposition is possible in their language, e.g. القِسِيّ "bows" underlyingly قُووسٌ, in which the s is shifted backwards so that it became قُسُووٌ,—similarly to عَصُووٌ "sticks"—, then it became قُسِيّ to avoid the combination of both the wāws at the extremity [of the word], and then the q was vowelled by a kasra [Fol. 31 a] on the analogy of what followed it, so they said قِسِيّ as in عِصِيّ.[293] Among them [sc. the forms in which the transposition is carried out] is أَيْنُقٌ "she-camels" underlyingly أَنْوُقٌ, in which the w is made to precede the n so that it became أَوْنُقٌ, and then the w is changed into a y as opposed to the analogy, so it became أَيْنُقٌ.[294] The passive participle is مَقُولٌ "said" etc. underlyingly مَقْوُولٌ, in which a phonological change is carried out similar to the one in يَقُولُ "he says", so it became مَقُوولٌ, such which caused a cluster of two vowelless weak consonants [sc. the wāws], so the infixed w was elided by Sībawaihi on the basis that the elision of the augment is prior, whereas the original w [that is the 2nd radical] was elided by al-Aḫfaš on the basis that the augment is a marker, and the marker should not be elided. Sībawaihi answered him by saying that the marker should not be elided if there is no other marker [in the word], and here there is another marker, which is the m [prefix]. Hence its pattern is according to him مَفْعُلٌ and according to al-Aḫfaš مَفُولٌ. So is also the case of مَبِيعٌ "sold" underlyingly مَبْيُوعٌ, meaning that a phonological change is carried out in it similar to the one in يَبِيعُ "he sells", so it became مَبْيُوعٌ; then two vowelless weak consonants, the y and the w, became combined together, and the w was elided according to Sībawaihi, so it became مَبْيِعٌ, and then the b was vowelled by a kasra so that the y was sounded true [i.e. مَبِيعٌ]. However according to al-Aḫfaš, the y [of the radical] was elided, and the kasra was shifted to the consonant preceding it, as was mentioned about بِعْتَ "you sold", so it became مَبْوُعٌ, and then the w was changed into a y as in مِيزَانٌ "balance". So its pattern is مَفْعِلٌ [Fol. 31 b] according to Sībawaihi and مَفِيلٌ according to al-Aḫfaš.[295] The noun of place is مَقَالٌ underlyingly مَقْوَلٌ "speech", in which a phonological change is carried out similar to the one in يَخَافُ "he fears". So is also the case of مَبِيعٌ "offered for sale" underlyingly مَبْيَعٌ, in which a phonological change is carried out similar to the one in يَبِيعُ "he sells". The virtual difference [between the base forms],—and it is taken into consideration by them-, is sufficient [concerning مَبِيعٌ] to differenciate between the noun of place and the passive participle, as the case of الفُلْكُ "the ships", which is a plural if you take into account its sukūn that is similar to the sukūn [of the 2nd radical] of أَسْدٌ "lions", as in His saying the Sublime [sur. 10: 22] (حَتَّى إِذَا كُنْتُمْ فِي ٱلْفُلْكِ وَجَرَيْنَ بِهِمْ) "So that ye even board ships;—they sail with them", and it is a singular if you take into account its sukūn which is similar to the sukūn of قُرْبٌ "nearness", as in the words of the Allmighty [sur. 26: 119] (فِي ٱلْفُلْكِ ٱلْمَشْحُونِ) "In the ark filled (with all creatures)".[296]

الآلـة مـقَـالٌ أصلـه مـقْـولٌ، المـجـهـول قـيـلَ الى آخـره أصلـه قُـولَ فـأُسـكـن الـواو للخفَة فصار قُوْلَ وهـو لغـة ضعيفـة لثقـل الضمَـة مع الـواو وفي لغـة أُخـرى أُعطي كسرة الواو الى ما قبلها فصار قِوْلَ ثمَ صار الواو ياءً لكسرة ما قبلها فصار قيـلَ وفي لغة تُشتَم حتَى يُعلم أنَ أصـل ما قبلها مضمـوم وكذلك بِيعَ واخْتيرَ وانْقيدَ لَـهُ وقلْنَ وبعْنَ يعني يجوز فيـهـنَ ثلث لغات. ولا يجوز الإشمام في مثل أُقيمَ لعدم ضمَة ما قبل الياء ولا يجوز بـالـواو أيضاً لأنَ جـواز الـواو* لانضمام مـا قبل حـرف العلَـة وهـو ليس بموجود. وسوَي في مثل قُلْنَ وبعْنَ بين المعلوم والمجهول اكتفاءً بالفرق التقديريَ. وأصل يُقَالُ يُقْوَلُ فأُعلَ كإعلال يُخَافُ. * ٣٢ آ

Fols. 31b-32a

١ الآلة... مقول: l's margin: – ل/ مقال أصله: – د/ الى آخره: – ا/ فاسكن: فاسكنت د ل/ ٢ مع الواو: والواو ا/ اخرى: –ا د هـ/ ٣ الى ما: لما د هـ ط/ قول... فصار: – ط/ ٣–٤ وفي لغة: + اخرى حـ ط/ ٤ تشتَم: يشتم ب د هـ ز/ مضموم: مضمون حـ: ضم ب هـ/ له: – ا ب د هـ حـ/ ٥ ثلث: ثلاث ز ط ك ل/ لعدم: لانعدم ط: لانعدام ل/ ٥–٦ قبل الياء: قبلها د/ ٧ في: – د/ وبعن: – د/ ٨ كإعلال: مثل ب د ز ط/

The noun of instrument is مِقْوَلٌ underlyingly مِقْوَلٌ.

The passive voice is قِيلَ, etc.,(297) underlyingly قُوِلَ, in which the *w* is made vowelless for the purpose of alleviation, so it became قُوْلَ, which is a feeble dialectal variant, because the ḍamma is deemed heavy when it is combined with the *w* [following it]. In another dialectal variant the kasra of the *w* [of قُوِلَ] is shifted to the consonant preceding it, so it became قِوْلَ, and then the *w* was changed into the *y* due to [the influence of] the kasra preceding it, so it became قِيلَ. In another dialectal variant, it [sc. the kasra of the consonant preceding the *y* of قِيلَ] is given a flavour of the ḍamma, so that it is known that underlyingly the consonant preceding it is vowelled by a ḍamma [sc. قُيِلَ].

So is also the case of بِيعَ "it was sold", اخْتِيرَ "it was chosen", انْقِيدَ لَهُ "it was guided to him", قُلْنَ "were said /fem. pl." and بِعْنَ "were sold /fem. pl.", meaning that the three dialectal variants are possible to be applied concerning them.(298)

However, it is impossible to give the flavour of the ḍamma in the example أُقِيمَ "it was performed", because the consonant preceding the *y* is not vowelled by a ḍamma. It is also impossible [that it is said] with the *w* [instead of the *y]* because the *w* occurs only possibly **[Fol. 32 a]** if the consonant preceding the weak consonant is vowelled by a ḍamma, which is not the case here.(299)

The active and passive voice are made homonymous in قُلْنَ and بِعْنَ with the sufficiency of the virtual difference [between their base forms].(300)

The base form of يُقَالُ is يُقْوَلُ, in which a phonological change is carried out as in يُخَافُ [underlyingly يُخْوَفُ] "it is dreaded".

II.6.1. COMMENTARY

The Verb with Weak 2nd Radical

(258) For a general study of الأجوف "the Hollow Verb" or "the verb with 2nd radical *w* or *y*" see Mu'addib, *Taṣrīf* 254-291, Ibn Ǧinnī, *Munṣif I,* 233, *II,* 110, Ibn Ya'īš, *Mulūkī* 52-58, Ibn 'Uṣfūr, *II,* 437-518, Zanǧānī, *'Izzī* 8-9, 'Abd al-Ḥamīd, *Taṣrīf* 624-634, de Sacy, 241-247, Farḥāt, *Baḥt* 71-79, Brockelmann, *Socins Grammatik* 43-45, Wright, 81-87, Blachère, 136-146, Fischer, *Grammatik* 116-119, Bakkūš, *Taṣrīf* 134-150, 'Abd al-Raḥīm, *Ṣarf* 29-33, Roman, *Étude II,* 961-971. For a comparative study with corresponding forms in some of the other Semitic languages see Wright, *Comparative Grammar* 242-255, Bauer, *Grammatik* 110-113. Moscati, *Grammar* 169 who refers to von Soden, *Grundriß* 154-156, remarks that some of the verbs of which the 2nd radical is *w* "describe a change of condition or transition from one situation to the opposite one, e.g. Sem. *mwt* "to die", West Semitic *qwm* "to get up", while others "refer to types of motion, e.g. Akkadian *dwl* "to go to and fro", Hebrew and Ethiopic *rwṣ* "to run". As for verbs with 2nd radical *y,* some of them "describe a physiological function, e.g. Semitic *šyn* "to urinate", while others connote "a definite outcome or result, e.g. Semitic *s'ym* "to place, fix", Akkadian Arabic Ethiopic *ḫyr* "to elect".

(259) قَالَ يَقُولُ underlyingly قَوَلَ يَقْوُلُ, a verb with 2nd radical *w,* pertains to the conjugation فَعَلَ يَفْعُلُ. Its paradigm in the perfect, active, is the following:

	sing.	dual	pl.
1st	قُلْتُ		قُلْنَا
2nd masc.	قُلْتَ	قُلْتُمَا	قُلْتُمْ
2nd fem.	قُلْتِ	قُلْتُمَا	قُلْتُنَّ
3rd masc.	قَالَ	قَالَا	قَالُوا
3rd fem.	قَالَتْ	قَالَتَا	قُلْنَ

Its paradigm in the imperfect of the indicative, active, is the following:

	sing.	dual	pl.
1st	أَقُولُ		نَقُولُ
2nd masc.	تَقُولُ	تَقُولَانِ	تَقُولُونَ
2nd fem.	تَقُولِينَ	تَقُولَانِ	تَقُلْنَ
3rd masc.	يَقُولُ	يَقُولَانِ	يَقُولُونَ
3rd fem.	تَقُولُ	تَقُولَانِ	يَقُلْنَ

Its paradigm in the imperfect of the subjunctive, active, is the following:

	sing.	dual	pl.
1st	أَقُولَ		نَقُولَ
2nd masc.	تَقُولَ	تَقُولَا	تَقُولُوا

	sing.	dual	pl.
2nd fem.	تَقُولِي	تَقُولا	تَقُلْنَ
3rd masc.	يَقُولَ	يَقُولا	يَقُولُوا
3rd fem.	تَقُولَ	تَقُولا	يَقُلْنَ

Its paradigm in the imperfect of the jussive, active, is the following:

	sing.	dual	pl.
1st	أَقُلْ		نَقُلْ
2nd masc.	تَقُلْ	تَقُولا	تَقُولُوا
2nd fem.	تَقُولِي	تَقُولا	تَقُلْنَ
3rd masc.	يَقُلْ	يَقُولا	يَقُولُوا
3rd fem.	تَقُلْ	تَقُولا	يَقُلْنَ

Its imperative is قُلْ. Its active participle is قَائِلٌ. Its *maṣdar* is قَوْلٌ. Its perfect, passive is قِيلَ. Its imperfect is يُقَالُ. Its passive participle is مَقُولٌ.

The paradigm of the derived forms of this class of verb is the following:

Form II: Its perfect, active is قَوَّلَ. Its imperfect is يُقَوِّلُ. Its imperative is قَوِّلْ. Its *maṣdar* is تَقْوِيلٌ. Its perfect, passive is قُوِّلَ.

Form III: Its perfect, active is قَاوَلَ. Its imperfect is يُقَاوِلُ. Its imperative is قَاوِلْ. Its *maṣdar* is مُقَاوَلَةٌ. Its perfect, passive is قُووِلَ.

Form IV: Its perfect, active is أَقَالَ. Its imperfect is يُقِيلُ. Its imperative is أَقِلْ. Its active participle is مُقِيلٌ. Its *maṣdar* is اِقَالَةٌ. Its perfect, passive is أُقِيلَ. Its imperfect is يُقَالُ. Its passive participle is مُقَالٌ.

Form V: Its perfect, active is تَقَوَّلَ. Its imperfect is يَتَقَوَّلُ. Its imperative is تَقَوَّلْ. Its *maṣdar* is تَقَوُّلٌ. Its perfect, passive is تُقُوِّلَ.

Form VI: Its perfect, active is تَقَاوَلَ. Its imperfect is يَتَقَاوَلُ. Its imperative is تَقَاوَلْ. Its *maṣdar* is تَقَاوُلٌ. Its perfect, passive is تُقُووِلَ.

As another example of Form VII, اِنْقَامَ of قَامَ "to rise" can be mentioned. Its perfect, active is اِنْقَامَ. Its imperfect is يَنْقَامُ. Its imperative is اِنْقَمْ. Its active participle is مُنْقَامٌ. Its *maṣdar* is اِنْقِيَامٌ. Its perfect, passive is أُنْقِيمَ. Its imperfect is يُنْقَامُ. Its passive participle is مُنْقَامٌ.

Form VIII: Its perfect, active is اِقْتَالَ. Its imperfect is يَقْتَالُ. Its imperative is اِقْتَلْ. Its active participle is مُقْتَالٌ. Its *maṣdar* is اِقْتِيَالٌ. Its perfect, passive is أُقْتِيلَ. Its imperfect is يُقْتَالُ. Its passive participle is مُقْتَالٌ.

As another example of Form X, اِسْتَقَامَ can be mentioned. Its perfect, active is اِسْتَقَامَ. Its imperfect is يَسْتَقِيمُ. Its imperative is اِسْتَقِمْ. Its active participle is مُسْتَقِيمٌ. Its *maṣdar* is اِسْتِقَامَةٌ.

Its perfect, passive is أُسْتُقِيمَ. Its imperfect is يُسْتَقَامُ. Its passive participle is مُسْتَقَامٌ.

خَافَ يَخَافُ underlyingly خَوِفَ يَخْوَفُ, a verb with 2nd radical *w*, pertains to the conjugation فَعِلَ يَفْعَلُ. Its perfect, active, is خَافَ. Its imperfect of the indicative, active, is يَخَافُ, of the subjunctive, active, يَخَافَ and of the jussive, active, يَخَفْ.

b) بَاعَ يَبِيعُ underlyingly بَيَعَ يَبْيِعُ, a verb with 2nd radical *y*, pertains to the conjugation فَعَلَ يَفْعِلُ. Its perfect, active, is بَاعَ. Its imperfect of the indicative, active, is يَبِيعُ, of the subjunctive, active, يَبِيعَ and of the jussive, active, يَبِعْ. Its imperative is بِعْ. Its active participle is بَائِعٌ. Its *maṣdar* is بَيْعٌ. Its perfect, passive is بِيعَ. Its imperfect, passive, is يُبَاعُ. Its passive participle is مَبِيعٌ.

(260) *ʾIʿlāl* refers to the phonological change that is carried out in a word in which a weak consonant is counted as unsound. This unsoundness is caused by the weak consonant's vowelling or vowellessness and by the vowelling or the vowellessness of the sound consonant,–whether strong or weak –, preceding it. Among the common phonological changes that can be mentioned is that the weak consonant is made vowelless, is changed into another weak consonant or is elided (cf. Rāǧiḥī, *Basīṭ* 159, the Arabic text fol. 25b-26a). The sequence involved is that of a weak consonant preceded by a vowelled or by a vowelless sound strong or weak consonant. Hence the 1st weak radical that is not preceded by any other consonant in the perfect, e.g. the *w* in *waʿada* "to promise" cannot be made unsound (for discussions see (246)). The phonological change is however carried out when the 1st radical is preceded by a prefix, e.g. مِوْزَانٌ that becomes مِيزَانٌ "balance" (cf. (261)). Furthermore, the sequence of two vowelless weak consonants is as well excluded, as it is impossible to combine two vowelless weak consonants. A presentation comprehending fifteen sequences can be thought of:

1- The weak consonant is vowelless and preceded by a fatḥa.
2- The weak consonant is vowelled by a fatḥa and preceded by a fatḥa.
3- The weak consonant is vowelled by a kasra and preceded by a fatḥa.
4- The weak consonant is vowelled by a ḍamma and preceded by a fatḥa.
5- The weak consonant is vowelless and preceded by a ḍamma.
6- The weak consonant is vowelled by a kasra and preceded by a ḍamma.
7- The weak consonant is vowelled by a ḍamma and preceded by a ḍamma.
8- The weak consonant is vowelled by a fatḥa and preceded by a ḍamma.
9- The weak consonant is vowelless and preceded by a kasra.
10- The weak consonant is vowelled by a fatḥa and preceded by a kasra.
11- The weak consonant is vowelled by a ḍamma and preceded by a kasra.
12- The weak consonant is vowelled by a kasra and preceded by a kasra.
13- The weak consonant is vowelled by a fatḥa and preceded by a sukūn.
14- The weak consonant is vowelled by a kasra and preceded by a sukūn.
15- The weak consonant is vowelled by a ḍamma and preceded by a sukūn.

(261) The base form of مِيزَانٌ is مِوْزَانٌ (from the root وزن) in which the 1st radical *w* is changed into *y* because of its vowellessness and the influence of the kasra preceding it (cf. Ibn

Ǧinnī, *Munṣif I,* 220-221, Bohas, *Étude* 260). Its pl. is مَوَازِين with the *w* of the base form retained. It can be mentioned that the substitution of the *y* for the *w* is carried out anomalously despite of the fact that there is no kasra preceding the *w* in ٱلْمَيَاثِق said instead of ٱلْمَوَاثِق in the following verse said by ʿIyāḍ b. Durra al-Ṭāʾī, cited by Ibn Manẓūr, *VI,* 4764, Howell, *I,* fasc. III, 1198:

"حَتَّى لَا يُحَلَّ ٱلدَّهْرَ إِلَّا بِإِذْنِنَا وَلَا نَسْأَلُ ٱلْأَقْوَامَ عَقْدَ ٱلْمَيَاثِقِ".

"[Our preserve is] a preserve that is never made free, save by our leave; nor do we ask of the peoples the contracting of engagements".

يُوسِرُ is Form IV of the verb يَسَرَ with 1st *y* radical, in the imperfect of the indicative, active. For its paradigm in the groundform and derived forms see (245 b). The 1st vowelless radical *y* of the base form يُيْسِرُ is changed into a *w,* i.e. يُوسِرُ, due to the influence of the ḍamma preceding it. The vowelless *y* when preceded by a ḍamma, is changed into a glide, namely a lengthened *w* as in this mentioned example, and when preceded by a kasra into a glide, namely a lengthened *y,* e.g. اِيسِرْ for اِيْسِرْ "be well off!" (cf. Wright, *II,* 80).

(262) أَغْزَيْتُ is mentioned in (311). The verb is underlyingly a 3rd weak radical *w* verb from غَزَوَ. In Form IV, the *w* of the base form أَغْزَوْتُ "I raided" is changed into a *y:* أَغْزَيْتُ. This change is on the analogy of the one that is carried out in the imperfect يُغْزِي, which is underlyingly يُغْزِوُ in which the *w* is changed into *y* because of its occurrence at the end of the word and because it is preceded by a kasra. It can be mentioned that as a general rule, this change occurs in all the derived forms of the verb with 3rd weak radical *w* (for examples see Wright, *II,* 91). This specific change of the *w* into *y* is carried out as well when the *w* is the 3rd radical of the passive participle (مَفْعُولٌ) of a verb that has the perfect formed according to فَعِلَ with the 2nd radical being vowelled by a kasra, e.g. رَضِيَهُ "approved it" with the *y* vowelled by a fatḥa whose passive participle is مَرْضِيٌّ "approved" underlyingly مَرْضُوٌّ. However, the *w* of the passive participle remains sound if the 2nd radical of its verb is vowelled by a fatḥa, e.g. مَغْزُوٌّ "raided" from غَزَا whose 2nd radical *z* is vowelled by a fatḥa (cf. Howell, *IV,* fasc. I 1279-1280). This is why the change of the *w* into *y* in مَعْدُوًا that becomes مَعْدِيًا from عَدَى in which the 2nd radical *d* of the verb is vowelled by a fatḥa, is anomalous in the following verse said by ʿAbd Yaġūṯ b. Waqqāṣ al-Ḥāriṯī. It is cited by Ibn Ǧinnī, *Sirr II,* 691, *Munṣif I,* 118, *II,* 122, Ibn Yaʿīš, *X,* 22, 110, *Mulūkī* 480, Ibn ʿAqīl, *II,* 577, Tibrīzī, *Iḫtiyārāt* 771, Ibn Manẓūr, *IV,* 2325, 2847, Baġdādī, *Šarḥ* 400-401, *Ḫizāna I,* 316, Howell, *IV,* fasc. I, 1280, Wright, *II,* 91:

"وَقَدْ عَلِمَتْ عِرْسِي مُلَيْكَةُ أَنَّنِي أَنَا ٱللَّيْثُ مَعْدِيًا عَلَيْهِ وَعَادِيَا".

"And my wife Mulaika has known that it is I who am the lion, when assailed, and when assailing".

The example with the weak consonant kept sound, i.e. with مَعْدُوًا said instead of مَعْدِيًا, is cited by Saraqusṭī, *Afʿāl I,* 247. Another variant of the verse is read by some with مَغْزِيًا عَلَيْهِ

وَغَازِيًا "when raided, and when raiding" instead of مَعْدِيًا عَلَيْهِ وَعَادِيًا, with the anomalous change of the weak consonant that is carried out in مَغْزُوًا.

(263) كَيْنُونَةٌ is formed according to the pattern فَيْعَلُولَةٌ. The 2nd radical *w* is vowelled by a fatḥa in it and follows a vowelless *y*. The phonological change is carried out by changing the *w* into a *y* and assimilating the two yā's, i.e. كَيَّنُونَه (cf. Ibn Ǧinnī, *Munṣif II,* 10). The base form كَيَّنُونَةٌ is used mostly in poetic licence. It occurs in the following verse said by al-Nahšalī, cited by Ibn Ǧinnī, *Munṣif II,* 15, Ibn al-Anbārī, *Inṣāf* Q. 115, 334, Suyūṭī, *Ašbāh III,* 335, Ibn Manẓūr, *V,* 3926, Howell, *IV,* fasc. I, 1461:

"يَا لَيْتَ أَنَا ضَمَنَا سَفِينَهْ حَتَّى يَعُودَ ٱلْوَصْلُ كَيَّنُونَهْ".

"O would that we and the beloved were so placed that a boat held us, to the end that union might return in being!".

An alleviated form exists as well, namely كَيْنُونَةٌ (for discussions see Zaǧǧāǧī, *Maǧālis* 309-310, Ibn Ǧinnī, *Munṣif II,* 9-15, Zamaḫšarī, 179, Ibn al-Anbārī, *Inṣāf* Q. 115, 334-335, *Nuzha* 200, Ibn Yaʿīš, *X,* 68-70, Suyūṭī, *Ašbāh III,* 35, Ibn Manẓūr, *V,* 3959, Howell, *IV,* fasc. I, 1461-1464, Wright, *II,* 120, Bustānī, *Muḥīṭ* 799). It occurs with a *y* following the 1st radical, and not with a *w* in spite of the fact that it is a *maṣdar* of a verb with middle radical *w,* because it is made formed according to the *maṣdars* of verbs with 2nd radical *y* which are much more numerous (cf. Ibn Ǧinnī, *Munṣif II,* 12). The examples of *maṣdars* of verbs with 2nd radical *y* that Ibn Masʿūd takes up here to which كَيْنُونَةٌ is formed according to are: صَيْرُورَةٌ from صَارَ يَصِيرُ "to become", غَيْبُوبَةٌ from غَابَ يَغِيبُ "to be unconscious" and قَيْلُولَةٌ from قَالَ يَقِيلُ "to take a midday nap". It can be mentioned that a debate was raised concerning كَيْنُونَةٌ, the Basrans believing that it is alleviated from كَيَّنُونَةٌ, whereas the Kufans believing that it is alleviated from كَوْنُونَةٌ (for discussions see Ibn al-Anbārī, *Inṣāf* Q. 115, 334-335).

كَيْوَنُونَةٌ which became كَيَّنُونَه after the assimilation and كَيْنُونَه after the alleviation is compared to مَوْيِتٌ with the 2nd radical vowelless *w* followed by a *y* with a kasra, which became مَيِّتٌ after the assimilation of the *w* to the *y* and مَيْتٌ after the alleviation. مَيِّتٌ is lightened by the elision of the 2nd *y* so that it became مَيْتٌ, because of the combination of two yā's and a kasra which is deemed as heavy. Another example is سَيْدٌ which is lightened from سَيِّدٌ. According to the Kufans, the base form of مَيِّتٌ and سَيِّدٌ is فَعِيلٌ, i.e. مَوِيتٌ and سَوِيدٌ, whereas according to the Basrans the base form is فَيْعِلٌ, and some believed as well فَيْعَلٌ (for their debate see Ibn al-Anbārī, *Inṣāf* Q. 115, 334-338). Curiously enough, the Kufan al-Kisāʾī believed that the form سَيِّدٌ with the doubling of the *y,* underlyingly سَيْوِدٌ, is on the pattern فَيْعِلٌ, and by doing so, followed the Basrans' theory (cf. Muʾaddib, *Taṣrīf* 266). Another example that conforms to فَيْعِلٌ is قَيِّمٌ that occurs in the sur. 9: 36 (ذَٰلِكَ ٱلدِّينُ ٱلْقَيِّمُ) "That is the straight usage" and صَيِّبٌ that occurs in the sur. 2: 19 (أَوْ كَصَيِّبٍ مِنَ ٱلسَّمَاءِ) "Or (another similitude) is that of a rain-laden cloud from the sky". It can be mentioned that Yaʿqūb al-Ḥaḍramī, one of the ten readers of the Qur'ān (see for them Ḏahabī, *Qurrā'* 157), used the alleviated form مَيْتٌ to refer to what did not have any soul. His argument is the sur. 25: 49 (بَلْدَةً مَيْتًا) "A dead land". He used مَيِّتٌ with the doubling of the *y* to designate what had a soul (cf. Mu'addib, *Taṣrīf* 265-266). Vollers, *Volkssprache* 151, referring to Baiḍāwī mentions that Ibn Kaṯīr, Ibn ʿAmir, Abū ʿAmr and Abū Bakr preferred to use مَيْتٌ, whereas Nāfiʿ preferred مَيِّتٌ. Ibn Ḫālawaihi, *Qirā'āt I,* 109-110 mentions that Nāfiʿ, Ḥamza and al-Kisā'ī read مَيِّتٌ with the doubling of the *y* all through the Qur'ān, whereas the remaining readers among the seven read it with the single *y*. The alleviated form occurs in the following verse said by an unknown poet, cited by al-Šartūnī, the commentator of Farḥāt, *Baḥṯ* 257 in the notes, Bustānī, *Miṣbāḥ* in the notes 287, Bravmann, *Studies* 528, Carter, *Širbīnī* 376:

"إِنَّمَا ٱلْمَيْتُ مَنْ يَعِيشُ كَئِيباً كَاسِفاً بَالُهُ قَلِيلَ ٱلرَّجَاءِ".

"The dead man is simply he who lives grieving, wretched his plight and small of hope".

Both forms مَيْتٌ and مَيِّتٌ are combined in the following verse said by ʿAdī b. al-Raʿlā, cited by Mu'addib, *Taṣrīf* 113, 268, Ibn Ǧinnī, *Munṣif II,* 17, *III,* 62, Ibn Yaʿīš, *X,* 69, *Mulūkī* 466, Ibn Manẓūr, *VI,* 4295, Howell, *IV,* fasc. I, 1461, Bravmann, *Studies* 528:

"لَيْسَ مَنْ مَاتَ فَٱسْتَرَاحَ بِمَيْتٍ إِنَّمَا ٱلْمَيْتُ مَيِّتُ ٱلْأَحْيَاءِ".

"He that has died, and taken his rest, is not really dead: the really dead is only the dead of the living [i.e., is only he that is living, while his state is like that of the dead]".

For discussions see Ibn Ǧinnī, *Munṣif II,* 15-17, *III,* 61-62, Zamaḫšarī, 173, Ibn ʿAqīl, *II,* 566, Wright, *II,* 120, Rāǧiḥī, *Farrā'* 182-183. For discussions concerning مَيِّت with references to other Semitic languages see Nöldeke, *Neue Beiträge* 209.

(264) There exist only four words of patterns of *maṣdars* with 2nd radical *w* that occur formed according to فَيْعَلُولَةٌ, namely ٱلْكَيْنُونَةُ from كَانَ يَكُونُ "to be", ٱلدَّيْمُومَةُ from دَامَ يَدُومُ "to continue", ٱلسَّيْدُودَةُ from سَادَ يَسُودُ "to rule" and ٱلْهَيْعُوعَةُ from هَاعَ يَهُوعُ "to vomit" (cf. Ibn Manẓūr, *V,* 3959).

(265) بَيَعَ becomes after the phonological change بَاعَ, خَوِفَ becomes خَافَ and طَوُلَ becomes طَالَ (for discussions see Ibn Ǧinnī, *Munṣif I,* 247 to whom Ibn Masʿūd refers to). The reason of the change of the 2nd vowelled weak radical into an *ā* is due to the weak consonant's vowelling and to the influence of the fatḥa preceding it. There exist some conditions that permit the phonological change of the vowelled *w* or the *y* into an *ā*. Ibn Masʿūd mentions seven that he presents and discusses, Howell, *IV,* fasc. I, 1237 sqq. discusses eleven and Bohas/Guillaume/Kouloughli *Linguistic* 85-86 discuss three. One of the conditions that can be added here (for it see Howell, *IV,* fasc. I, 1249-1250) is that if the 2nd radical is a weak consonant that replaces an underlying strong consonant, it cannot be affected by any change as it is not the real radical of the word. An example is شَيَرَةٌ for شَجَرَةٌ "tree" (for it see Ibn Manẓūr, *IV,* 2197 sqq.) in which the *y* is substituted for the underlying strong consonant, the *ǧ*. The pl. variant شِيَرَات said instead of شَجَرَات occurs in the following verse said by Umm al-Huṭaim, and cited by Howell, *IV*, fasc. I, 1250, ʿAbd al-Tawwāb, *Taṭawwur* 20:

"إذَا لَمْ يَكُنْ فِيكُنَّ ظِلٌّ وَلَا جَنَى   فَأَبْعَدَكُنَّ ٱللَّهُ مِنْ شِيرَاتٍ".

"If there be not in you any shade, nor any fruit, then God curse you for trees!".

For some other examples of anomalies see ʿAbd al-Tawwāb, *Fuṣūl* 113.

(266) The change of the underlying *w* vowelled by a fatḥa into an *ā* is carried out in قَوَلَ which becomes قَالَ "to say" and in دَوَرٌ which becomes دَارٌ "house". The reason of this change is that they conform to the first condition mentioned by Ibn Masʿūd, which is that قَوَلَ is a verb and دَوَرٌ is a noun that is formed according to the verb form فَعَلَ. It can be noted as well that both weak consonants are vowelled by a fatḥa and are preceded by one.

In the broken pl. دِيَارٌ underlyingly دِوَارٌ (cf. Howell, *IV*, fasc. I, 1264), the 2nd radical *w* vowelled by a fatḥa is changed into a *y* due to the influence of the kasra preceding it. This change is on the analogy of the change that is carried out in its sing. دَوَرٌ that becomes دَارٌ "house".

b) The change of the *w* into the *y* is carried out in the *maṣdar* قِيَامٌ "standing" underlyingly قِوَامٌ in which the *w* is vowelled by a fatḥa and preceded by a kasra. This change is on the analogy of the change of the weak consonant that is carried out in its verb قَامَ "to stand" underlyingly قَوَمَ in which the *w* that is vowelled by a fatḥa and preceded by one is changed into an *ā*. Other examples than قِيَامٌ in which this specific change is carried out are انْقِيَادٌ "submissiveness" and اعْتِيَادٌ "accustoming oneself" underlyingly انْقِوَادٌ and اعْتِوَادٌ (cf. Howell, *IV*, fasc. I, 1261-1262). It can be remarked as well concerning قِيَامٌ that there exist cases in which the *ā* is lacking in it, as in the reading of Nāfiʿ and Ibn ʿĀmir of the sur. 4: 5 in which قِيَمًا occurs instead of قِيَامًا, i.e. (جَعَلَ ٱللَّهُ لَكُمْ قِيَمًا وَٱرْزُقُوهُمْ) "[To those weak of understanding make not over your property, which] God hath made a means of support for you but feed and clothe them" (cf. Howell, *IV*, fasc. I, 1263). The variant قِيَمًا occurs as well instead of قِوَامًا in the sur. 5: 100 in the reading of Ibn ʿĀmir, i.e. (جَعَلَ ٱللَّهُ ٱلْكَعْبَةَ ٱلْبَيْتَ ٱلْحَرَامَ قِيَمًا لِلنَّاسِ) "God made the Kaʿba, the Sacred House, an asylum of security for men". For discussions see Howell, *IV*, fasc. I, 1261-1263.

(267) A change of the weak consonant is carried out in سِيَاطٌ (mentioned in (379)) underlyingly سِوَاطٌ, in which the *w* is changed into a *y*, because its vowelled *w* is compared to the vowelless *w* of its sing. سَوْطٌ that is described as مَيتَة "dead", i.e. vowelless. Ibn Masʿūd who follows Zamaḫšarī, 182, compares it with the vowelless *ā* of دَارٌ "house". Being compared to a vowelless weak consonant, the vowelled *w* in سواطٌ is treated as being so, and as it is preceded by a kasra it is changed into the *y*, namely سِيَاطٌ. Other examples that can be added are حِيَاضٌ underlyingly حِوَاضٌ which is the pl. of حَوْضٌ "cistern" and رِيَاضٌ underlyingly رِوَاضٌ which is the pl. of رَوْضٌ "garden". Cf. Howell, *IV*, fasc. I, 1264-1265.

(268) حَوَكَةٌ which is the pl. of حَائِكٌ and خَوَنَةٌ which is the pl. of خَائِنٌ are anomalous (cf. Ibn Ǧinnī, *Munṣif I*, 332-334, Zamaḫšarī, 181, Ibn al-Anbārī, *Luma'* 55, Howell, *IV*, fasc. I, 1510). Both these triliterals differ from their verbs' measures حَوَكَ "to weave" and خَوَنَ "to betray" due to the *t* of the feminine form. This is the reason why the *w* vowelled by a fatḥa and preceded by one is not changed into an *ā* in them, and serves by its maintainance to give a clue to their base forms.

(269) حَيَدَى is an epithet (cf. Daqr, *Mu'ǧam* 56) on the measure فَعَلَى with the alif of the feminine form peculiar to the noun, and hence forbidding a phonological change due to unsoundness (cf. Howell, *IV*, fasc. I, 1251). Thus the *y* is sound in it. Other examples of epithets on this measure with strong 2nd radical that can be mentioned are: دَلَظَى "a man who thrusts vehemently" and وَقَرَى "a flock of sheep" (cf. Lane, *I*, 684). An example of a *maṣdar* on this measure is مَرَطَى, as in the example هو يَعْدُو المَرَطَى "he runs quickly, i.e. with this kind of running", and of a substantive بَرَدَى "a stream at Damascus" (cf. Howell, *I*, fasc. III, 1147).

صَوَرَى is a substantive with 2nd weak radical on the same measure, and is referred to as being the name of a water in Madīna (cf. Ibn Wallād, *Maqṣūr* 74). This word caused a dispute as it is considered by some, including Ibn Mas'ūd, to be on the measure of فَعَلَى with the alif of the feminine form peculiar to the noun, and hence forbidding the change of the weak consonant, whereas according to others it resembles the verb, as it could be formed according to فَعَلَا (for discussions see Howell, *IV*, fasc. I, 1248). The measure فُعْلَى exits as well. It can be noted that حِيكَى in the expression مِشْيَةٌ حِيكَى from حَاكَ في مَشْيِه "he moved his shoulders in his walk", is underlyingly حُيْكَى formed according to the pattern فُعْلَى, with the initial consonant vowelled by a ḍamma that is then changed into a kasra so that the *y* is sounded true. The same concerns ضِيزَى in the sur. 53: 22 (قِسْمَةٌ ضِيزَى) "A division most unfair!" (cf. Ibn al-Sarrāǧ, *Uṣūl III*, 267, Ibn Wallād, *Maqṣūr* 76, Daqr, *Mu'ǧam* 56) from ضَازَهُ حَقَّهُ "he defrauded him of his right", underlyingly ضُيْزَى formed according to the measure فُعْلَى. For a study see Zamaḫšarī, 183, Ibn Ya'īš, *X*, 97-98, Howell, *IV*, fasc. I, 1308-1309.

b) Some different patterns of nouns ending with the alif of the feminine form that can be presented here are: فُعْلَى as بُشْرَى "announcement of glad tidings", فَعَلَى as بَشَكَى "quick", فُعَلَى as أُدَمَى "a place", أَفْعَلَى as أَجْفَلَى "general invitation", فُعَالَى as حُبَارَى "a bustard", فَوْعَالَى as حَوْلَايَا "a place", فُعَالَى as شُقَارَى "a plant", فَعْلَلَى as جَحْجَبَى "a clan of the Anṣār", فُعَيْلَى as بُقَيْرَى "a game for boys", فعيلى as خليفى "being much engrossed with the buisness of the Ḫalīfa" (cf. (25)), فعلوتى as رحموتى "compassion", فعوللى as حبوكرى "calamity", فوعلى and فيعلى as خوزلى and خيزلى "a kind of gait", يفعلى as يهيرى "naught", مفعلى as مكورى "mean", مفعلى as مرعزى "the down under, or amid, the hair of the she-goat", فعللى as هربدى "a kind of walk, inclining to one side", فعللايا as بردرايا "a place", فعليا as ذربيا "calamity", فعليا as زكريا "Zachariah", فعلنى as عرضنى "a sidelong gait", فعلى as دفقى "a sort of place", فعنلى or فعنلى as جلندى or جلندى "a man's name", فعلى as سمهى "a falsehood", فعالى as صحارى "deserts" (see for it (315)), فعللى as هندبى "endive", فعلى as سبطرى "a swaggering gait" and افعيلى as اهجيرى "custom". Cf. Zamaḫšarī, 84-85, Ibn Yaʿīš, *V,* 107-110, Howell, *I,* fasc. III, 1146 sqq., Daqr, *Muʿǧam* 55-57.

(270) In دعوا القوم "they called for the people" (for other examples occurring with the vowel of juncture see (184), (288), (377)), the *w* of دعوا remains sound in spite of the fact that it is vowelled and preceded by a fatḥa. The reason of its soundness is that the ḍamma over it is considered as accidental as it is a vowel of juncture (for discussions concerning the vowel of juncture see Roman, *Étude II,* 747-749; for discussions concerning it being a kasra see 749-752; for it being a fatḥa see 752-755; for general discussions see Ibn al-Sarrāǧ, *Uṣūl II,* 367-371) given to it to avoid the cluster of two vowelless consonants, the vowelless underlying suffixed pronoun, i.e. the *w/ū* of the pl. of دعوا, and the vowelless *l-* following the *waṣla* of the definite article *al-* prefixed to the second word القوم. This is the reason why the ḍamma of the *w* of دعوا, which does not belong to the basic form but is supplied by an external factor, is characterized as feeble, and as by being so, cannot force the phonological change that is usually due to the unsoundness of the *w* vowelled by the ḍamma and preceded by the fatḥa, which is the change of the *wu* into an *ā*.

Compare with this example the example اخشوا واقدا "Fear [2nd person of the masc. pl. of the imperative] one who sets fire!", in which the suffixed pronoun of the 2nd person of the masc pl., the *w,* is vowelless and remains so, as there is no risk of combining two vowelless weak consonants, because the *w* that is the initial weak consonant of واقدا, in the word following it, is vowelled by the fatḥa. Sībawaihi, *II,* 457 presents اخشو واقدا (cf. (173)) with an assimilation that is carried out from the 1st *w* of the first word to the 2nd *w* of the second word (for the assimilation that is carried out in two words see (173)). It can be noted that the *alif wiqāya* of اخشوا is elided, resulting in اخشو.

Form I عور "was blind of one eye" has the meaning of Form VIII اعور, which is the reason why the fatḥa of the ʿ that precedes the vowelled *w* in عور is counted as being ruled by the sukūn of the ʿ of اعور. Hence the 2nd vowelled radical *w* of عور is not changed into an *ā* in spite of the fact that it is vowelled and preceded by a fatḥa, on the analogy of the vowelled *w* in اعور that is preceded by a sukūn, which is the reason why it is not changed into an *ā*. It is then as if the sukūn of the ʿ of اعور rules as well the vowelled *w* of عور and by doing so prevents it to be changed. Another example that can be compared to it is حَوِلَ "squinted", which has the meaning of اِحْوَلَّ, and which for the same reason as with عَوِرَ does not have its vowelled *w* changed into an *ā*. For a study see Sībawaihi, *II,* 399, Ibn Ǧinnī, *Munṣif I,* 259-260, Zamaḫšarī, 180, Ibn Yaʿīš, *Mulūkī* 219, 222-223, Howell, *IV,* fasc. I, 1241-1242, Bohas, *Étude* 250-251. It can be noted *en passant* that Wright, *Comparative Grammar* 243 was perplexed by the uncontraction in عَوِرَ and حَوِلَ, as he writes:

> "I do not know why خَوِفَ became خَافَ, and مَوِتَ, مَاتَ,whilst حَوِلَ and عَوِرَ remained uncontracted".

Form VIII اِجْتَوَرَ has the meaning of Form VI تَجَاوَرَ, which is the reason why the fatḥa of the *t* preceding the vowelled *w* in اِجْتَوَرَ is counted as being ruled by the sukūn of the vowelless *ā* preceding the vowelled *w* in تَجَاوَرَ. Hence the 2nd vowelled radical *w* of اِجْتَوَرَ is not changed into an *ā* in spite of the fact that it is vowelled and preceded by a fatḥa, on the analogy of the vowelled *w* in تَجَاوَرَ that is preceded by a vowelless *ā,* and which is not for that reason changed into an *ā.* It is then as if the sukūn of the vowelless *ā* of تَجَاوَرَ rules as well the vowelled *w* of اِجْتَوَرَ. It can be said that it is a rule that when Form VIII اِفْتَعَلَ with 2nd vowelled radical *w* preceded by a fatḥa has the meaning of Form VI تَفَاعَلَ that denotes the reciprocity, the *wa* is not changed into an *ā.* Another example is Form VIII اِزْدَوَجُوا "they intermarried" that has the meaning of Form VI تَزَاوَجُوا. The change of the vowelled weak consonant into an *ā* is necessary otherwise, e.g. اِخْتَانَ "was unfaithful" underlyingly اِخْتَوَنَ, that has the meaning of Form I خَانَ. If the 2nd radical is a *y,* the change of the vowelled weak consonant preceded by a fatḥa is necessary even if it is indicative of reciprocity, e.g. اِمْتَيَزُوا that becomes اِمْتَازُوا "they were distinct, one from another" which has the meaning of Form VI تَمَايَزُوا. For a study see Sībawaihi, *II,* 399-401, Ibn Ǧinnī, *Munṣif I,* 260-261, Zamaḫšarī, 180, Ibn Yaʿīš, *X,* 74-75, Howell, *II-III,* 275, *IV,* fasc. I, 1242-1243. For a study of such cases with references to other Semitic languages see Wright, *Comparative Grammar* 253-254.

(271) The base form of حَيَوَانٌ is حَيَيَانٌ (from حَيِيَ) in which the 2nd *y* is changed into a *w* for the purpose of alleviation, as the combination of two yāʾs is disliked (cf. Lane, *I,* 682). The 1st vowelled *y,* the *ya,* preceded by a fatḥa of the base form حَيَيَانٌ could have been changed into an *ā,* namely حَايَانٌ, or the 2nd *y* instead resulting in حَيَاانٌ with two alifs, and then حَيَانٌ with the elision of one *ā.* This change is not however carried out as it is preferred that the *y* is maintained with its vowel, so that the word corresponds in mobility to what it represents, which is a mobile animal (cf. Howell, *IV,* fasc. I, 1409). The example حَيَوَانٌ can seem strange as there is no verb to which it can refer with 2nd radical *y* and 3rd radical *w* (cf. Ibn Ǧinnī, *Munṣif II,* 285). It occurs in the sur. 29: 64 (لَهِيَ الْحَيَوَانُ) "that is Life indeed". حَيَوَانٌ is not to be confounded with the dual حَيَيَانٌ, of الحَيَا "rain" underlyingly حَيَيٌ in which the 2nd *y* is changed into an *ā* (cf. Ibn

Ǧinnī, *Munṣif II,* 286, Lane, *I,* 681). Another example that can be added is حَيْوَةٌ "Ḥaywa [sc. the name of a man]" underlyingly حَيْيَةٌ, with the *w* being a substitute for the *y* (cf. Ibn Ǧinnī, *Munṣif II,* 285).

b) مَوَتَانٌ is the opposite in meaning of حَيَوَانٌ and is therefore formed according to its pattern (for discussions see Ibn Manẓūr, *VI,* 4296, Lane, *I,* 679, 682, Howell, *IV,* fasc. I, 1244, 1409, 1465; for other examples of nouns formed according to their contraries see (151), (152)).

(272) The base form of طَوَى "to fold" is طَوَيَ in which the vowelled 3rd radical *y* that is preceded by a fatḥa is changed into an *alif maqṣūra*. The vowelled 2nd radical *w* that is preceded by a fatḥa is not changed into an *ā* resulting in طَاىَ, to prevent the occurrence of two phonological changes due to both weak consonants in it, as this would necessarily imply a cluster of two vowelless weak consonants, the *alif mamdūda* and the *alif maqṣūra*.

The dual of the 3rd person of the masc. sing. طَوَيَا "/dual" has its 3rd radical *y* sound and vowelled by a fatḥa preceding the suffix *ā* of the dual. Its 2nd radical *w* vowelled by a kasra, the *wi*, could have been changed into an *ā* due to the influence of the fatḥa preceding it resulting in طَايَا, without a cluster of two vowelless weak consonants being implied, but this is not carried out as it is preferred that the form is made analogous to طَوَى, in which the *w* is sound.

The vowelled 2nd radical *y* preceded by a fatḥa is not changed into an *ā* in the 3rd person of the masc. sing. of the perfect حَيِيَ "to live", i. e. حَايَ, so that its imperfect does not have to, by analogy with the perfect, have its 2nd vowelled radical *y* that is preceded by a fatḥa changed into an *ā* resulting in يَحَايُ, with the final *y* vowelled by a ḍamma, which is counted as a heavy combination (see for discussions (180)). For this reason the variant يَحْيَى is preferred.

(273) Both الْقَوَدُ "the retaliation" and الصَّيَدُ "a disease in a camel's head" have their weak consonants sound as they are intended to notify of the base forms (cf. Zamaḫšarī, 173, Howell, *IV,* fasc. I, 1251), i.e. the roots قود and صيد respectively. This means that the vowelled *w* preceded by a fatḥa in الْقَوَدُ is not changed into an *ā* as this would cause confusion on whether it is from the root قود "to lead" with 2nd *w* radical or the root قيد "to bind" with 2nd *y* radical. In the same manner the *y* in الصَّيَدُ is not changed into an *ā* as this would cause confusion on whether the form is from the root صود with 2nd *w* radical that is the base form of الصَّاد "the [consonant] ṣād", or the root صيد "to hunt" with 2nd *y* radical.

(274) The verb دَعَوَ "to call" that occurs in the subjunctive, namely لَنْ يَدْعُوَ has its 3rd radical *w* vowelled by a fatḥa as a marker of the subjunctive. The reason why the vowelled *w* remains sound in it in spite of the influence of the ḍamma preceding it,–which could have resulted in its vowellessness and its assimilation to the ḍamma, and thus in the lengthened *w/ū*, i.e. لَنْ يَدْعُو -, is that the fatḥa that vowels it is considered as light (for other examples see Ibn Ǧinnī, *Munṣif II,* 114). So there is no need to alleviate more by saying لَنْ يَدْعُ instead of لَنْ

يَدْعُوَ. It can be noted as well that the fatḥa, marker of the subjunctive, is given to it by an external factor which is the subjunctive operator لَنْ, and if this change were carried out, the subjunctive would be confused with the indicative (for examples of a few anomalous cases see my notes (51 b)). In line with this theory that the weak consonant vowelled by a fatḥa and preceded by a ḍamma remains sound, the *y* vowelled by a fatḥa and preceded by a ḍamma in عُيَبَةٌ and the *w* vowelled by a fatḥa and preceded by a ḍamma in نُوَمَةٌ remain sound (cf. Zamaḫšarī, 181, Ibn Yaʿīš, *X*, 82-83). The suffixed *tāʾmarbūṭa* marks intensiveness (for it see (52), (150)) in both of them.

(275) The *w* in مِوْزَان "a balance" is vowelless and preceded by a kasra, which is the reason why it is changed into a *y*, i.e. مِيزَان (cf. (260)).

The *w* in دَاعِوَةٌ "the one who invites /fem." from the verb دَعَوَ "to call" with *w* as 3rd radical, is vowelled by a fatḥa and preceded by a kasra, which is the reason why it is changed into a *y*, i.e. دَاعِيَةٌ.

The 3rd radical *y* in the base form رَضِيُوا "they were pleased /masc. pl." is vowelled by a ḍamma and preceded by a kasra. It can be noted that رَضِيَ is underlyingly رَضِوَ (for its paradigm see (303 b)) with the 3rd radical *w* changed into a *y* due to the influence of the kasra preceding it (cf. Lane, *I*, 1099). رَضِيُوا is the 3rd person of the masc. pl. of the perfect with the agent pronoun, the *ū*, suffixed to the 3rd weak radical vowelled by a ḍamma. As a rule, the 3rd weak radical is elided between the short vowel and the agent suffixed pronoun, the *ū* (cf. Wright, 80). According to Ibn Masʿūd's theory, the 3rd radical *y* vowelled by a ḍamma in رَضِيُوا is made vowelless due to the influence of the kasra preceding it and the heaviness that is implied, i.e. رَضِيْوا, and then is elided, i.e. رَضِوا, to avoid the cluster of two vowelless weak consonants, the vowelless *y* radical and the vowelless *ū* of the pl. Then the kasra of the *ḍ* preceding the *w* of the pl. is replaced by the ḍamma so that this *w* remains sound, i.e. رَضُوا (cf. further (49), (303), Daqr, *Muʿǧam* 390-391). Concerning this theory Dunqūz, *Šarḥ* fol. 80a ll. 18-19 writes:

"نحو رَضِيُوا أُسكن حرف العلّة للخفّة لثقل الضمّة على الياء ثمّ تُحذف حرف العلّة لاجتماع الساكنين ثمّ يُضمّ ما قبل واو الجمع لصيانتها عن التغير فصار رَضُوا".

"In the example رَضِيُوا "they were pleased /masc. pl.", the weak consonant [sc. the *y*] is made vowelless [i.e. رَضِيْوا] for the sake of alleviation because of the heaviness of the ḍamma on the *y*, then the weak consonant [sc. the *y*] is elided [i.e. رَضِوا] to avoid the cluster of two vowelless [weak] consonants [sc. the vowelless *y* and the vowelless suffixed *ū* of the agent in رَضِيْوا], then the consonant [sc. the *ḍ*] preceding the *ū* of the pl. is given a ḍamma to prevent any change to affect it [sc. the *ū*], so it became رَضُوا".

Furthermore concerning رَضُوا underlyingly رَضِيُوا, Ibn Ǧinnī, *Munṣif II*, 125-126 means that it is necessary to say it in this manner, as it is said in the sur. 5: 71 (فعَمُوا وَصَمُّوا) "So they became blind and deaf" [in which فعَمُوا is underlyingly فعَمِيُوا]. His theory (ibid, 126) concerning the phonological change is slightly different from Ibn Masʿūd's and Dunqūze's. According to him, the ḍamma is elided from the *y* in رَضِيُوا and transferred to the consonant preceding it, namely the *ḍ*, implying the change of the *ḍ's* kasra into the ḍamma as well, which results in the cluster of two vowelless weak consonants, the *w* and *y*, i.e. رَضُيْوا. The *y* is then elided to prevent this cluster resulting in رَضُوا. It can be mentioned furthermore for the sake of curiosity that al-Māzinī, who is referred to by Ibn Ǧinnī, *Munṣif II*, 125, reports that some Arabs say رَضْيُوا with the *ḍ* made vowelless and the *y* sound. According to Ibn Ǧinnī, ibid, 126 the *ḍ* is made vowelless by these Arabs for the sake of alleviation and the vowelled weak consonant remains sound as it is preceded by a sukūn.

The 3rd radical *y* in تَرْمِيِينَ is vowelled by the kasra and preceded by one. تَرْمِيِينَ from رَمَى "to throw", a verb with 3rd *y* radical (for its paradigms see (302)), is the 2nd person of the fem. sing. of the imperfect of the indicative with the ending, *-īna,* suffixed to the 3rd radical vowelled by a kasra. The 3rd vowelled radical *y* in تَرْمِيِينَ is made vowelless because of the heaviness of the kasra that vowels it, i.e. تَرْمِيْيِنَ, and then is elided to avoid the cluster of two vowelless weak consonants, namely the vowelless *y* radical and the vowelless suffixed pronoun *y* that marks the 2nd person of the fem. sing., so that it becomes تَرْمِينَ. Concerning this theory, Dunqūz, *Šarḥ* fol. 80b ll. 1-2 writes:

"تُسكن الياء في تَرْمِيِينَ لثقل الكسرة عليها ثم تُحذف لاجتماع الساكنين".

"The *y* in تَرْمِيِينَ "you throw /fem. sing." is made vowelless [i.e. تَرْمِيْيِنَ] because of the heaviness of the kasra that vowels it, then it is elided [i.e. تَرْمِينَ] to avoid the cluster of two [weak] vowelless consonants".

This elision of the 3rd weak radical is usual in the defective verb with the ending *-īna* of the 2nd person of the fem. sing. of the imperfect suffixed to it (cf. Wright, *II,* 89, Daqr, *Muʿǧam* 391). This phonological change that results in the elision of the 3rd weak radical is similar to the one that is carried out in رَضُوا, with the only difference that the 2nd radical in تَرْمِينَ is vowelled by the kasra and the 2nd radical in رَضُوا is vowelled by the ḍamma. It can be noted that this difference of the vowelling refers to their 3rd radical's vowel in the base forms. The 3rd radical *y* in رَضِيُوا is vowelled by the ḍamma because the agent pronoun *ū* that marks the 3rd person of the masc. pl. of the perfect is suffixed to it whereas the 3rd radical *y* in تَرْمِيِينَ is vowelled by the kasra because the ending *-īna* of the 2nd person of the fem. sing. of the imperfect is suffixed to it.

(276) No phonological change is carried out in أعْيُن "eyes" and أدْوُر "houses" (cf. Zamaḫšarī, 182), in spite of the fact that there exists in them a sequence that is constituted of a weak consonant vowelled by a ḍamma and preceded by a sukūn. The change that can be carried out in such a sequence, e.g. يَقْوُلُ "he says", is the transfer of the ḍamma of the *w* to the vowelless consonant preceding it and the lengthening of the *w* into *ū*, i.e. يَقُولُ. This change cannot be carried out in أَعْيُنٌ, by shifting the ḍamma of the *y* to the consonant preceding it, i.e. أَعُيْنٌ and then changing the vowelless *y* into an *ū* due to the influence of the ḍamma preceding it, i.e. أَعُونُ, because there would be a risk of confusing the substantive with the verb in the 1st person of the sing. of the imperfect أَعُونُ "I assist". Another possible change that can be carried out in it is that after shifting the ḍamma of the *y* to the consonant preceding it, i.e. أَعُيْنٌ, the ḍamma of the ʿ that is considered as heavy before the *y* can be changed into a kasra by consideration of the *y*, and then the *y* can be lengthened, i.e أَعِين. However, in this case as well, there would be a risk of confusing the substantive with the verb in the 1st person of the sing. of the imperfect أَعِينُ "I smite you with the evil eye". The change could not be carried out either in أَدْوُرٌ by transferring the ḍamma of the *w* to the vowelless consonant preceding it and lengthening the *w*, i.e. أَدُور, as there would be a risk of confusing the substantive with the verb in the 1st person of the sing. of the imperfect أَدُورُ "I turn".

جَدْوَلٌ is comparable to يَخْوَفُ "he is afraid" if one considers the sequence of a weak consonant vowelled by a fatḥa and preceded by a sukūn. The phonological procedure that is carried out in يَخْوَفُ is the transfer of the fatḥa of the *w* to the vowelless consonant preceding it, i.e. يَخَوْفُ and then the change of the vowelless *w* into an *ā* due to the influence of the fatḥa preceding it, i.e. يَخَافُ (cf. Bohas/Guillaume/Kouloughli, *Linguistic* 87-89). However this procedure cannot be carried out in جَدْوَلٌ that is from جَدَلَ "to make firm" because it is formed according to the measure فَعْوَلٌ (cf. Howell, *IV*, fasc. I, 1524). Therefore it is impossible to shift the *w*'s fatḥa to the vowelless consonant preceding it, i.e. جَدَوْلٌ, and then change the *w* into an *ā* due to the influence of the fatḥa preceding it, i.e. جَدَالٌ, as this would cancel the formation.

(277) The base form of قَوَّمَ before the assimilation is carried out in it, is قَوْوَمَ. The sequence of its 2nd *w* vowelled by a fatḥa and preceded by a sukūn is comparable to the sequence of the *w* in يَخْوَفُ (for the phonological change concerning it see (276)) that is vowelled by a fatḥa and preceded by a sukūn. The fatḥa in it could not be shifted to the vowelless weak consonant preceding it, i.e. قَوَوْمَ as this would lead to the change of the 1st *w* vowelled by a fatḥa and preceded by one into an *ā*, i.e. قَاوْمَ. The result would become a forbidden combination of two vowelless weak consonants, the *ā* and the *w*. This is what is meant by الإعلال في الإعلال, which refers to a phonological change that is carried out after another phonological change, which thus implies a forbidden combination of two vowelless weak consonants.

No change is carried out in الرَّمْيُ in spite of the fact that its vowelled *y* preceded by a sukūn is comparable to the *y* of يَبْيِعُ "he sells" that is preceded by a sukūn. The phonological change that is carried out in يَبْيِعُ is the transfer of the kasra of the *y* to the vowelless consonant preceding it and the lengthening of the *y,* i.e. يبيعُ. If such a phonological change were to be carried out in الرمْيُ, it would imply the transfer of its various vowels of declension, the ḍamma in the case of the nominative, the fatḥa in the case of the accusative and the kasra in the case of the genitive, to the vowelless consonant preceding it. In the case of the ḍamma, الرمْيُ would become الرمُيْ and then the *y* would have to be changed into a vowelless *w* to accord with the ḍamma preceding it, i.e. الرمُوْ. In the case of the fatḥa, الرمْيَ would become الرمَيْ and then the *y* would have to be changed into a vowelless *ā* to accord with the fatḥa preceding it, i.e. الرَما. In the case of the kasra, الرمْيِ would become الرمِيْ and the vowelless *y* would be lengthened, i.e. الرمِي. In all these three cases, this declinable noun would have to end with a vowelless weak consonant and without a marker of declension, which is the reason why it is preferred that in order to safeguard the declension, this *y* remains sound. Other cases of declinable substantives that end with a weak consonant, which can be vowelled by one the three different markers of the declension, and which is preceded by a sukūn, are ظَبْيٌ "gazelle" with the sound *y* and دَلْوٌ "bucket" with the sound *w.* The case of such substantives in which the last weak consonant remains sound differs from the cases of verbs in the imperfect, e.g. يَبْيِعُ in which a phonological change is carried out resulting in يبيعُ and the verb يَقْوُمُ that becomes يَقُومُ (for this see Bohas/Guillaume/ Kouloughli, *Linguistic* 88). The reason of the soundness cf the weak consonant in these nouns is to safeguard the marker of the declension. Had it not been for this reason, then the sequence that involves the last weak consonant in these substantives would be affected by a phonological change on the analogy of the change that affects the sequence that involves the weak consonant in the mentioned verbs' imperfects. This also seems to be the answer to the question that Bohas/Guillaume/ Kouloughli, *Linguistic* 88 ask:

> "As the imperfect of the FAʿALA verb always has the structure yaCCVC, say *yafʿulu* for example, we assume under a *qiyās* that *qawama* has *yaqwumu* for the primary form of the imperfect, and we will have seen that the passage from *yaqwumu* to *yaquwmu [yaqūmu]* has been effected by means of metathesis. But why must the sequence *Cwu* be transformed into *Cuw,* when it is commonly found in the language, for example in *dalwun* ('bucket'), and in *ẓabyun* ('gazelle')?".

The weak consonant remains sound in both the substantives تَقْوِيمٌ and تَبْيَانٌ, in spite of the fact that it is vowelled and preceded by a sukūn. The reason why no change is carried out in these substantives is on the one hand to prevent having a cluster of two vowelless consonants, and on the other, to prevent confusing these substantives with other forms. If supposingly the kasra of the *w* of تَقْوِيمٌ is shifted to the *q,* i.e. تَقِوْيمٌ, then a cluster of two vowelless weak consonants, the *w* and *y,* would result. The *w* would have to be changed into the *y* due to the influence of the kasra preceding it, i.e. تَقِيْيم, that would imply a cluster of two vowelless yāʾs, and then one *y* would have to be elided, which would result in one lengthened *y,* i.e. تَقِيم. The substantive could therefore be confused in its representation with the imperfect of Form IV تُقِيمُ "you set up". If the fatḥa of the *y* of تَبْيَانٌ is shifted to the *b,* i.e. تَبَيْانٌ, then a cluster of two vowelless weak consonants, the *y* and the *ā* would result. The *y* would have to be changed into an *ā* due to the influence of the fatḥa preceding it, i.e. تَبَاانٌ, which would result in a cluster of two vowelless weak consonants, the alifs, and then one *ā* would have to be elided, and the result would be تَبَانْ. The word could be confused in its representation with the passive voice of Form I of the 2nd person of the masc. sing. or the 3rd person of the fem. sing. of the imperfect, namely تُبَانُ "you are, or she is being made clear".

(278) مِقْوَلٌ with 2nd *w* radical, is contracted from the base form مِقْوَالٌ "loquacious, eloquent", and مِخْيَطٌ with 2nd *y* radical is contracted from the base form مِخْيَاطٌ "a needle" (for it see (57)). So their pattern مِفْعَلٌ is the contracted form of مِفْعَالٌ. The sequence in them is that of a weak consonant vowelled by a fatḥa and preceded by a sukūn which is similar to the sequence in يَخْوَفُ "he is afraid" in which a change is carried by shifting the *w*'s fatḥa to the consonant preceding it, and changing the *w* into an *ā* resulting in يَخَافُ (for discussions see (276)). However the 2nd weak radical remains sound in them both on the analogy of its soundness in both their base forms مِقْوَالٌ and مِخْيَاطٌ respectively. If by assumption a change is carried out in مِقْوَالٌ by means of shifting the fatḥa of the *w* to the consonant preceding it, i.e. مِقَوَالٌ, the result would be a cluster of two vowelless weak consonants, the *w* and the *ā*. The *w* would have to be changed into an *ā* due to the influence of the fatḥa preceding it, i.e. مِقَاالٌ, and one of the alifs would have to be elided, i.e. مِقَالٌ. If a similar change is carried out in مِخْيَاطٌ by shifting the fatḥa of the *y* to the consonant preceding it, i.e. مِخَيَاطٌ, the result would be two vowelless weak consonants, the *y* and the *ā*. The *y* would have to be changed into an *ā* because of the fatḥa preceding it, i.e. مِخَااطٌ, and one of the alifs would have to be elided, i.e. مِخَاطٌ. If this is to occur in both these cases, then the intended form مِفْعَالٌ would be canceled. It is noteworthy to mention however, that according to some grammarians a change ought to have been carried out in مِقْوَلٌ and in مِخْيَطٌ as they consider them to be on the pattern اِعْلَمْ with the imperfect prefix vowelled by a kasra which pertains to the dialectal variant the *taltala* (for more details see Howell, *IV*, fasc. I, 1522-1524; for the *taltala* see (32), (99), (100), (103)).

(279) The base form of the *maṣdar* of Form IV اِقَامَةٌ is اِقْوَامٌ with the 2nd radical *w* vowelled by a fatḥa and preceded by a sukūn. A change is carried out in it by shifting the fatḥa of the *w* to the consonant preceding it, i.e. اِقَوَامٌ, which results in the cluster of two vowelless weak consonants, the *w* and the *ā*, then the *w* is changed into an *ā* due to the influence of the fatḥa preceding it, i.e. اِقَاامٌ, which results in the cluster of two vowelless weak consonants, the *ā* and the *ā*, and then one of the alifs is elided and the *tā' marbūṭa* is suffixed to the word as a compensation for this elision, i.e. اِقَامَةٌ (cf. (249)). According to some grammarians, it is the 1st *ā* of اِقَاامٌ that is substituted for the 2nd radical *w*, which is elided whereas according to others it is the 2nd one that is the infixed *ā* of اِفْعَالٌ (cf. Ibn Yaʿīš, *VI*, 58, ʿAbd al-Raḥīm, *Ṣarf* 125). Concerning this example and its likes, Ibn Ǧinnī, *Munṣif I*, 291-292 remarks:

" قال أبو الفتح: أصل "إقامة، وإخافة، وإبانة: إقْوامةٌ، وإخْوافةٌ، وإبْيانةٌ" فأرادوا أن يُعلُوا المصدر، لاعتلال "أقام، وأبان" فنقلوا الفتحة من الواو، والياء، الى ما قبلهما، ثم قلبوهما ألفين، وبعدهما ألفُ "إفعالة"، فصار كما ترى "إقامةً، وإبانةً". فذهب أبو الحسن إلى أن المحذوفة هي الألف الأولى، وذهب الخليلُ إلى أنَّ المحذوفة هي الألف الثانية، وهي الزائدة – على ما تقدَّم من مذهبهما – ...".

"Abū l-Fatḥ [sc. Ibn Ǧinnī] said: "The base form of اقامةٌ "setting up", اخافةٌ "frightening" and ابانةٌ "explanation" are اقْوامةٌ, اخْوافةٌ and ابْيانةٌ. They intended to carry out a phonological change due to the unsoundness of the weak consonant in the *maṣdar* because of the phonological change that is carried out in [its verb] أقامَ "to set up" and أبانَ "to explain". So they shifted the fatḥa from the *w* [of اقْوامةٌ] and from the *y* [of ابْيانةٌ] to the consonant preceding them, then they changed them [sc. the *w* and the *y*] into an *ā* preceding the infixed *ā* of افْعالةٌ, so they became as you remark اقامةٌ and ابانةٌ. Abū l-Ḥasan believed that the elided *ā* is the 1st *ā*, whereas al-Ḫalīl believed that it is the 2nd one, which is the infixed one,—according to what has been presented from their theories".

The change is not carried out in the cognate of اقامةٌ, namely the *maṣdar* Form II تَقْويمٌ, that Ibn Masʿūd is referring to (cf. (277)).

The change due to the unsoundness of the 2nd weak radical in اقامةٌ is carried out on the analogy of the one that is carried out in the verb Form IV أقامَ underlyingly أقْوَمَ, in which the vowelled *w* is changed into an *ā* after that its fatḥa is shifted to the *q*. As well, the change that is carried out in أقامَ is on the analogy of the one that is carried out in Form I قَوَمَ, of which the vowelled *w* is changed into an *ā* due to the influence of the fatḥa preceding it, i.e. قَامَ. This is what Ibn Masʿūd means by stating that the change that is carried out in اقامةٌ is on the analogy of the one that is carried out in Form I of the verb قَامَ.

(280) The *maṣdar* of Form II تَقْويمٌ refers to the verb of Form II قَوَمَ, and not to the verb of Form I قَامَ. As there is no change that is carried out in قَوَمَ, there is no change that is carried out in تَقْويمٌ for the sake of the analogy with it (for both see (277)).

(281) The 2nd weak radical in the verb of wonder ما أفْعَلَهُ, e.g. ما أقْوَلَهُ "How well he speaks!" with 2nd *w* radical and ما أبْيَعَهُ "How well he sells!" with 2nd *y* radical, is not changed into an *ā* probably to avoid confusing the forms with Form IV of the verbs. It can be noted as well that no change is carried out in the أفْعَلُ of superiority, e.g. زَيْدٌ أقْوَلُ مِنْ عَمْرٍو "Zaid is a better speaker than ʿAmr" and أبْيَعُ "a better salesman" (cf. Sībawaihi, *II*, 403, Ibn Yaʿīš, *X*, 76, Howell, *IV*, fasc. I, 1485).

(282) No phonological change is carried out in أغْيَلَتْ and اسْتَحْوَذَ (cf. Sībawaihi, *II,* 400, Zamaḫšarī, 180, Ibn Yaʿīš, *X,* 76, Suyūṭī, *Muzhir I,* 137), which are considered as anomalous.

(283) For the paradigm of قالَ in the perfect, active, see (259).

(284) One form can represent two different forms, and it is only by الفرق التقديري "the virtual difference" that exists between both their base forms that it is possible in some cases to separate one from the other. As an example قُلْنَ is taken up, which is intended for both the 3rd person of the fem. pl. of the perfect "they said, fem. pl." and for the 2nd person of the fem. pl. of the imperative "Say! fem. pl.". The ḍamma of the *q* does not give a clue to the intended form, as it is known that it is the result of the phonological change due to the unsoundness of the 2nd weak radical. The Arabs were satisfied with both these tenses' base forms to distinguish them from one another. The base form of the 3rd person of the fem. pl. of the perfect is قَوَلْنَ and of the 2nd person of the fem. pl. of the imperative أُقْوُلْنَ. As for the change that is carried out in the perfect قَوَلْنَ, the 2nd vowelled radical *w* is changed into an *ā* as it is vowelled by a fatḥa and preceded by one, i.e. قَالْنَ, then the *ā* is elided to prevent the cluster of two vowelless consonants, the *ā* and the *l,* i.e. قَلْنَ, and then the *q* is vowelled by a ḍamma to give notice of the elided 2nd radical *w,* so it became قُلْنَ (cf. Bakkūš, *Taṣrīf* 136; for discussions that قُلْتَ is underlyingly قَوَلْتَ according to the conjugation فَعَلَ يَفْعُلُ, and not قَوُلْتَ according to فَعُلَ يَفْعُلُ in line with the theory of some who chose to believe so in order to justify why the ḍamma is given to the 1st radical see Ibn Ǧinnī, *Munṣif I,* 236-237, Bakkūš, *Taṣrīf* 142-143, Bohas/Guillaume/Kouloughli, *Linguistic* 73). As for the change that is carried out in the imperative أُقْوُلْنَ, the ḍamma that vowels the *w* is deemed as heavy on it and is therefore shifted to the vowelless consonant preceding it, i.e. أُقُوْلْنَ, then the *w* is elided to prevent the cluster of two vowelless consonants, the *w* and the *l,* i.e. أُقُلْنَ, and then the prefixed vowelled alif of the imperative is elided, as the reason of its prefixation originally is to prevent starting the word with a vowelless consonant, which is not the case here anymore as the 1st radical is now vowelled by a ḍamma, so it became قُلْنَ.

(285) The virtual difference between both the base forms of بِعْنَ in the active and in the passive voice (cf. (300)), is that the active voice is بَيَعْنَ with the *b* and the *y* vowelled by a fatḥa whereas the passive voice is بُيِعْنَ with the *b* vowelled by a ḍamma and the *y* with a kasra. As what concerns the change that is carried out in the base form of the active voice بَيَعْنَ, the 2nd vowelled radical *y* is changed into an *ā* as it is vowelled by a fatḥa and preceded by one, i.e. بَاعْنَ, then the *ā* is elided to prevent the cluster of two vowelless consonants, the *ā* and the ʿ i.e. بَعْنَ, then the *b* is vowelled by a kasra to give notice of the elided 2nd *y* radical, i.e. بِعْنَ. As what concerns the change that is carried out in the base form of the passive voice يُبْيَعَن, the kasra of the 2nd radical *y* is shifted to the 1st radical because of the heaviness of the kasra that vowels the *y,* i.e. يِبْيعَن, then the *y* is elided to prevent the cluster of two vowelless consonants, the *y* and the ʿ, i.e. بِعْنَ.

(286) For the paradigm of قالَ in the imperfect of the indicative, active, see (259). The change procedure that is carried out in يَقْوُلُ which results in يَقُولُ "he says", is that the ḍamma of the *w* is shifted to the vowelless consonant preceding it leading to the lengthening of the *w* (cf. Ibn Ǧinnī, *Munṣif I,* 247). According to one theory, the lengthened *w* is considered to be the result of the assimilation of the *w* to the ḍamma (cf. Bakkūš, *Taṣrīf* 136).

The base form of يَقُلْنَ is يَقْوُلْنَ, in which the ḍamma of the *w* is deemed heavy and is shifted to the vowelless consonant preceding it, i.e. يَقُوْلْنَ, resulting in the cluster of two vowelless consonants, the *w* and the *l,* which is why the *w* is elided, i.e. يَقُلْنَ. According to another theory the *w* is said to be shortened, which takes place when it is followed by a sukūn (cf. Bakkūš, *Taṣrīf* 136).

(287) The paradigm of قالَ in the imperative is the following:

	sing.	dual	pl.
2nd masc.	قُلْ	قُولاَ	قُولُوا
2nd fem.	قُولِي	قُولاَ	قُلْنَ

The base form of قُلْ "say!" is أُقْوُلْ, in which the vowel of the *w* is shifted to the vowelless consonant preceding it, i.e. أُقُوْلْ, resulting in the cluster of two vowelless consonants, the *w* and the *l,* which is why the *w* is elided, i.e. أُقُلْ. As the 1st radical *q* in أُقُلْ is vowelled, the prefixed prosthetic alif of the imperative is elided, because the reason of its prefixation in the first place is to prevent starting the word with a vowelless radical, which is not more the case here.

(288) The *w* is elided in the imperative قُلْ that is used instead of قُولْ to avoid the cluster of two vowelless consonants, the *w* and the *l.* It can be mentioned that Bravmann, *Studies* 195 believes that the short *u* best expresses the special intensity of the imperative. The general principle that is followed to avoid a cluster of two vowelless consonants that occur in two words is that the 1st vowelless consonant, which is the ultimate consonant of the first word, is vowelled by a kasra (cf. (184), (270), (377)). In the example قُلْ الْحَقَّ, the 3rd radical *l* of قُلْ, which is underlyingly vowelless as it marks the imperative, is given a kasra, i.e. قُلِ to avoid the cluster of two vowelless consonants, the *l* and the *-l* of the article *-al,* prefixed to the word occurring after it, i.e. الْحَقَّ. This vowelling of the *l* of قُلِ is due to an exterior factor and is therefore considered as accidental and not pertaining to the base form, which is why Ibn Masʿūd states that the *l* is في حكم السكون تقديرا "ruled by the sukūn virtually". For this reason, the accidental vowel due to an external consonant, is not a sufficient reason to maintain the 2nd weak radical, as the elision of this weak radical marks the imperative. It can be added concerning the vowel of juncture, that in some cases, the 1st vowelless consonant, that is the ultimate consonant of the first word, can be vowelled by a ḍamma for the purpose of alleviating the ḍamma of the consonant that precedes it or that occurs in the word following it. Examples in which the ḍamma precedes the vowel of juncture are: قُلُ آضْرِبْ "say strike! /masc. sing.", sur. 73: 2 (قُمُ آللَّيْلَ) "Stand (to prayer) by night" in the reading of some instead of قُمِ آللَّيْلَ (for a study see Howell, *IV*, fasc. I, 1024 sqq.) and the sur. 10: 101 (قُلُ آنظُرُوا) (Sībawaihi, *II*, 299). Examples in which the ḍamma occurs in the word following it are: the sur. 12: 31 (وَقَالَتُ آخْرُجْ) "And she said (to Joseph), "Come out before them", the sur. 38: 41-42 (وَعَذَابٍ ُ آرْكُضْ بِرِجْلِكَ) "And suffering!". (The command was given:) "Strike with thy foot" and the sur. 73: 3 (أوُ آنْقُصْ مِنْهُ قَلِيلًا) "Or a little less" (cf. Sībawaihi, *II*, 299, Bohas, *Étude* 97).

(289) The *ā* of دَعَتَا underlyingly دَعَوَتَا that Ibn Masʿūd refers to, is the 2nd vowelled radical *w* that is changed into an *ā* due to the influence of the fatḥa preceding it, i.e. دَعَاتَا. As for the reason of its elision, it is to avoid the cluster of two vowelless consonants, the *ā* and the *t*, as it is understood that the suffixed *t* of the feminine form of the 3rd person of the fem. sing. is underlyingly vowelless, and in this case it is only accidentally vowelled by a fatḥa for the sake of the suffixed agent of the dual, the *ā* (compare the case of رَمَتَا discussed in (54)). It should also be kept in mind that the pronoun of the 3rd person of the fem. sing. is latent, and that the suffixed *t* is not a pronoun but a marker of the feminine form. Seen from this perspective it does not belong to the same word as the suffixed pronoun of the subject, i.e. the *-tu* "/1st person sing.", the *-ta* "/2nd person masc. sing.", the *-ti* "/2nd person of the fem. sing.", etc. Thus in the same word, the marker of the feminine form is regarded as external, whereas the pronoun of the nominative that is suffixed to the verb is regarded as internal and thus belonging to the same word (see further for discussions (55), b)).

Both the 3rd radical *l* and the agent suffix of the dual, the *ā*, in قُولَا "Say! dual (imperative)", are regarded as internal and thus belonging to the same word. The fatḥa vowel that is given to the *l* is regarded as accidental, because it is given to it to prevent it from being combined as vowelless with the vowelless agent pronoun of the dual that follows it, namely the *ā*. As the radical *l* is internal and followed by the agent pronoun that is also considered as internal, the rule of the virtual sukūn that is the underlying marker of the imperative before that the agent pronoun of the dual, the *ā*, is suffixed to it, is not taken into account and hence does not cause the elision of the 2nd *w* radical. Hence قُولَا is said with the *w* maintained contrarily to its elision in قُلِ الْحَقَّ (cf. (288)) and contrarily to the elision of the 2nd weak radical changed into an *ā* in دَعَتَا discussed above. It can be added furthermore that the *w* is not elided in قُولَا resulting in قُلَا so that the verb with 2nd weak radical will not be confused with a verb with 3rd weak radical. Another reason why the 2nd radical *w* is sound when the pronoun is suffixed to the verb is that by principle the pronoun brings back the word to its base form (for this principle see (65)).

(290) The paradigm of the active participle قَائِلٌ is:

	sing.	dual	pl.
masc.	قَائِلٌ	قَائِلَانِ / قَائِلَيْنِ	قَائِلُونَ / قَائِلِينَ
fem.	قَائِلَةٌ	قَائِلَتَانِ / قَائِلَتَيْنِ	قَائِلَاتٌ / قَائِلَاتِ

Other encountered forms which are less regular are: قُوَّلٌ, قُوَّالٌ, قَالَةٌ, قُيَّلٌ for the masc. pl. (cf. Ibn Manẓūr, *V*, 3778).

The sequence in قَاوِلٌ (and بَايِعٌ) is that of a vowelled weak consonant preceded by a fatḥa, as in the examples خَوِفَ that becomes خَافَ "to fear", قَوَلَ that becomes قَالَ "he said" and بَيَعَ that becomes بَاعَ "he sold". In spite of the fact that there exists an *ā* between the vowelled *w* and the vowelled *q* in قَاوِلٌ, this *ā* is not taken into account as it is vowelless and occurs between two vowelled consonants. So the vowelled *w* is changed into an *ā* due to the influence of the fatḥa preceding it, i.e. قَاالٌ. The reason why one of the alifs is not dropped resulting in قَالٌ is to prevent that the active participle is confused with the perfect قَالَ "he said" in the representation. The 2nd *ā* in قَاالٌ is therefore changed into a hamza to prevent the combination of two vowelless alifs, i.e. قَائِلٌ. The vowelless *ā* in the base form قَاوِلٌ can also be compared to the vowelless *ā* in كِسَاوٌ that is not taken into account, in which the vowelled *w* is also changed into an *ā* due to the influence of the fatḥa preceding it, i.e. كِسَاا. Then the *ā* is changed into a hamza to prevent the cluster of two weak vowelless consonants, both the alifs, i.e. كِسَاءٌ (cf. (319). Other similar examples which may be added are سَمَاءٌ "sky" underlyingly سَمَاوٌ, and دُعَاءٌ "prayer" underlyingly دُعَاوٌ.

(291) The active participle هَاعٌ is from هَوِعَ "to vomit" in which the 2nd radical *w* is changed into an *ā*, i.e. هَاعَ. هَاعٌ is underlyingly هَاوِعٌ in which the hamza replaces the 2nd radical *w* resulting in هَائِعٌ (compare for the procedure the case of قَائِلٌ discussed in (290)). The active participle لَاعٌ is from لَوِعَ "to suffer, burn" in which the 2nd radical *w* is changed into an *ā*, i.e. لَاعَ. لَاعٌ is underlyingly لَاوِعٌ in which the hamza replaces the 2nd radical *w* resulting in لَائِعٌ. The active participle هَارٌ is from هَوِرَ "to demolish" in which the 2nd radical *w* is changed into an *ā*, i.e. هَارَ. هَارٌ is underlyingly هَاوِرٌ in which the hamza replaces the 2nd radical *w* resulting in هَائِرٌ. All these three active participles, i.e. هَاعٌ, لَاعٌ and هَارٌ occur with the elision of their 2nd weak radical, which is the hamza that replaces the *w* of their base forms, and seem to be formed according to the pattern فَالٌ and not فَاعِلٌ. Concerning هَارٍ of the sur. 9: 109 (عَلَى شَفَا جُرُفٍ هَارٍ) "On an undermined sand-cliff", it can be noted that Ibn Kaṯīr, Ḥamza and Ḥafṣ read هَارٍ anomalously with the fatḥa from ʿĀṣim, whereas the remaining readers among the seven read it هَارٍ (cf. Ibn Ḫālawaihi, *Qirāʾāt I*, 255).

(292) القلب refers to the transposition of the consonants, i.e. the transfer of a consonant to the position of another one. In شاكٍ the 2nd radical of the base form شاوِكٌ changed place with the 3rd radical and became at first شاكِوٌ formed according to the pattern فالِعٌ. As the form ends with a weak radical, it resembled the active participle of verbs with 3rd weak radical, e.g. رامٍ "one who is throwing" for the nominative and genitive underlyingly رامِيٌ for the nominative and رامِيٍ for the genitive (cf. (309)). This is why its last radical is changed on the analogy of this category of forms, so that it became شاكٍ. شاكٍ occurs in the following verse said by Ṭarīf b. Tamīm al-ʿAmbarī al-Tamīmi, cited by Sībawaihi, *II,* 419, Ibn Ǧinnī, *Munṣif II,* 53, *III,* 66, Ibn Ḫālawaihi, *Qirāʾāt I,* 255, Howell, *IV,* fasc. I, 1494:

"فَتَعَرَّفُونِي إِنَّنِي أَنَا ذَاكُمُ شَاكٍ سِلَاحِي فِي ٱلْحَوَادِثِ مُعْلَمُ".

"Then seek to know me: verily that I, this one, [am such that] sharp is my weapon in mishaps, am a bearer of the cognizance, *or* badge, *or* device, of the valiant".

It can be noted that the *y* is given to شاكٍ as a case marker when it occurs as the first element of a definite *iḍāfa,* e.g. شاكِي السِّلاحِ (cf. Nöldeke, *Neue Beiträge* 213) which is cited by Zamaḫšarī, *Kaššāf I,* 205 who refers to a verse said by Zuhair:

"لدى أسَدٍ شاكِي السِّلاحِ مُقذفٍ لهُ لِبَدٌ أظفارُهُ لم تُقَلَّمِ".

"In the presence of a lion whose weapon is sharp in mishap for having hurled down [its victims], that has a mane and claws which have not been pared".

Both Suyūṭī, *Muẓhir I,* 285 and ʿAbd al-Tawwāb, *Taṭawwur* 60 refer to the saying of Abū Ǧaʿfar al-Naḥḥās that only the procedure of the transposition of consonants, that occurs in شاكِي سِلاحِي from شائِكٌ and جُرُفٌ هارٍ from هائِرٌ (cf. (291)) is entitled to be considered as a transposition. Two other variants than شاكٍ which may be added in this context are شائِكٌ which is the usual form, that is underlyingly شاوِكٌ in which the 2nd radical *w* is changed into a hamza, and شاكٌ that is underlyingly شاوِكٌ that occurs with the elision of the 2nd radical *w* and is similar to the cases discussed in (291). شاكٌ occurs as the first element of the *iḍāfa* in شاكُ السِّلاحِ in the following verse said by Marḥab al-Yahūdīy when he met ʿAlī. It is cited by Ibn Manẓūr, *IV,* 2363:

"قَدْ عَلِمَتْ خَيْبَرُ أَنِّي مَرْحَبُ شاكُ السِّلاحِ بَطَلٌ مُجَرَّبُ".

"And Ḫabyar has known that I am Marḥab with the sharp weapon, a proven hero".

For discussions see Ibn Ǧinnī, *Munṣif II,* 52-54, Zamaḫšarī, 180, Ibn Yaʿīš, *X,* 77-78, Ibn Manẓūr, *IV,* 2362-2363, Howell, *IV,* fasc. I, 1494-1498, Fleischer, *Beiträge IV,* 253. For discussions concerning forms liable to a contraction similar to the one in شاكٍ in some of the other Semitic languages see Wright, *Comparative Grammar* 250-251.

As for حادٍ its base form is واحِدٌ in which the 1st radical *w* is shifted after the 3rd radical *d,* i.e. احِدو. As the *ā,* which is the infixed *ā* of the active participle فاعِلٌ is vowelless, it is impossible to start the word with it, which is the reason why the 2nd radical *ḥ* is shifted before it, i.e. حادْوٌ, and the kasra of the *ḥ* is shifted after the vowelless *d* and the *ḥ* is given a fatḥa, i.e. حَادِوٌ. The *w* in حَادِوٌ is then changed into a *y* on account of the influence of the kasra of the consonant preceding it, i.e. حَادِيٌ. As it resembles the active partiples of verbs with 3rd weak radical (compare the case of شَاكٍ discussed above) in its ending with a weak consonant, a similar change is carried out in it so that it becomes حَادٍ. So the pattern of حَادٍ is not فَاعِلٌ but عَالِفٌ.

Concerning it Ibn Manẓūr, *VI*, 4779 writes:

"وقالُوا: هُوَ حادِى عِشْرِيهِمْ وهُوَ ثانِى عِشْرِيهِمْ، واللَّيْلَةُ الْحادِيَةَ عَشْرَةَ واليَوْمُ الحادِى عَشَرَ، قالَ: وهذا مَقْلُوبٌ كَما قالُوا جَذَبَ وجَبَذَ، قالَ ابْنُ سِيدَهْ: وحادِى عَشَر مَقْلُوبٌ مَوْضِعُ الْفاءِ إلى اللامِ لا يُسْتَعْمَلُ إلاّ كَذلِكَ، وهُوَ فاعِلٌ نُقِل إلى عالِف، فانْقَلَبت الْواوُ الّتِي هِيَ الأَصْلُ ياءً لانْكِسارِ ما قَبْلَها. وحَكَى يَعْقُوبُ: مَعِي عَشَرَةٌ فأَحَدْهُنَّ لِيَه، أىْ صَيِّرْهُنَّ لِى أحَدَ عَشَرَ. قالَ أبُو مَنْصُورٍ: جَعَلَ قَوْلَهُ فَأَحَدْهُنَّ لِيَهْ، مِنَ الْحادِى لا مِنْ أَحَدٍ، قالَ ابْنُ سِيدَهْ: وظاهِرُ ذلِكَ يُؤْنِسُ بأَنَّ الْحادِى فاعِلٌ، قالَ: وَالْوَجْهُ إنْ كانَ هذا الْمَرْوِيُّ صَحِيحاً أنْ يَكُونَ الْفِعْلُ مَقْلُوباً مِنْ وَحَدْتُ إلى حَدَوْتُ، وذلِكَ أَنَّهُمْ لَمّا رَأوا الْحادِى فِي ظاهِرِ الأمْرِ عَلى صُورَةِ فاعِلٍ، صارَ كَأَنَّهُ جارٍ عَلَى حَدَوْتُ".

"And they said: He is حَادِي عِشْرِيهِمْ "the twenty-first among them" and ثانِى عِشْرِيهِمْ "the twenty-second among them", and اللَّيْلَةُ الْحَادِيَةَ عَشْرَةَ "the eleventh night" and اليَوْمُ الحَادِي عَشَرَ "the eleventh day". He said: "A transposition of consonants is carried out [in الْحَادِي] similar to [the one that is carried out] when they said جَذَبَ and جَبَذَ "to attract" [(cf. (14), (291)]. Ibn Sīda said: "A transposition of consonants was carried out in [حَادِي in the example] حَادِي عَشَرَ between the 1st and the 3rd radical, which can only be carried out in this manner, because it is on the pattern فَاعِلٌ in which a transposition of consonants is carried out by changing it to the pattern عَالِفٌ. Then the *w* which is the radical, is changed into the *y* on account of the kasra preceding it. Ya'qūb said: "I have ten so أَحَدْهُنَّ لِيَهْ "make them to be eleven to me", i.e. صَيِّرْهُنَّ لِى أَحَدَ عَشَرَ "make them to be eleven to me". Abū Manṣūr said: "In his saying فَأَحَدْهُنَّ لِيَهْ, it [sc. أَحَدْهُنَّ is] from الْحَادِى and not from أَحَد". Ibn Sīda said: "What is presumed of this makes one observe that الْحَادِى is the active participle". He said:"The guiding principle is that if what is told is correct, then a transposition of consonants is carried out in the verb from وَحَدْتُ to حَدَوْتُ. On account of that, when they found that الْحَادِى outwardly is formed according to the pattern فَاعِلٌ, it seemed to follow حَدَوْتُ...".

(293) A transposition of consonants is carried out in قِسِيٌّ underlyingly قُوُوسٌ which is the pl. of قَوْسٌ. قُوُوسٌ is on the pattern فُعُولٌ in which the radicals are transposed resulting in قُسُوٌّ that is formed according to فُلُوعٌ, as if it is the pl. of قَسْوٌ and not of قَوْسٌ. The wāws in قُسُوٌّ are changed into yā'ʾs, i.e. قُسِيٌّ, because they occur at the extremity of the word, which is disliked, then the ḍamma of the *s* is changed into a kasra due to the influence of the yā'ʾs, i.e. قُسِيٌّ, and then the *q* is vowelled by a kasra on the analogy of the kasra and *y* that follow it, i.e. قِسِيٌّ. The same procedure is carried out in عُصِيٌّ or عِصِيٌّ pl. of عصا. For discussions see Howell, *I,* fasc. III, 930, *IV,* fasc. I, 1583-1585, de Sacy, *I,* 108, Vernier, *I,* 340-341. Compare with قَوْسٌ the Hebrew קֶשֶׁת, the Targum קַשְׁתָּא [Ez. I, 28] the Syriac ܩܶܫܬܳܐ and the Ethiopic ቀስት (cf. Nöldeke, *Neue Beiträge* 132-133).

(294) The pl. of نَاقَةٌ is أَنْوُقٌ، then as the ḍamma is deemed heavy upon the *w,* the *w* is transposed made to precede the *n,* i.e. أَوْنُقٌ, and then the *y* is substituted for the *w,* i.e. أَيْنُقٌ (cf. Howell, *I,* fasc. III, 1074). This change of the *w* into a *y* does not follow the analogy as the *w* is vowelless and preceded by fatḥa, but it is carried out anyway for the sake of alleviation. Compare with it נקה, נקא and ינקא; for a detailed study with references to other similar forms see Nöldeke, *Neue Beiträge* 205.

(295) مَقْوُولٌ is the base form of the passive participle of the verb قَالَ underlyingly قَوَلَ with 2nd radical *w* and مَبْيُوعٌ is the base form of the verb بَاعَ "to sell" underlyingly بَيَعَ with 2nd radical *y*. In مَقْوُولٌ, the ḍamma is deemed as heavy over the *w* and is therefore shifted to the vowelless consonant preceding it, i.e. مَقُوْوْلٌ, which causes a cluster of two vowelless weak consonants, both the wāws. The question at issue here is which of the wāws is elided. According to Sībawaihi, it is the infixed *w* of مَفْعُولٌ that is elided, so the pattern is formed according to مَفُعْلٌ according to him, with the ḍamma shifted backwards from the 2nd radical as mentioned, and the 2nd radical retained. However according to al-Aḫfaš, the 2nd radical *w* is elided, so the pattern is formed according to مَفُولٌ according to him. In مَبْيُوعٌ, the ḍamma over the *y* is deemed as heavy and is therefore shifted to the vowelless consonant preceding it, i.e. مَبُيْوعٌ, which causes a cluster of two vowelless weak consonants, the *y* and the *w*. According to Sībawaihi, the infixed *w* is elided resulting in مَبُيْعٌ, and then the *b* is given a kasra, i.e. مَبِيعٌ. According to al-Aḫfaš, the 2nd radical *y* in مَبْيُوعٌ is elided, i.e. مَبُوعٌ, and then the *b* is given a kasra so that it indicates that the verb is with 2nd radical *y* and not 2nd radical *w,* so it became مَبِوعٌ. As the vowelless *w* is preceded by a kasra it is changed into a *y,* i.e مَبِيعٌ, similarly to مِيزَانٌ underlyingly مِوْزَانٌ (cf. (260)). The pattern is then formed according to مَفِعْلٌ according to Sībawaihi and to مَفِيلٌ according to al-Aḫfaš (cf. Ibn Manẓūr, *I,* 401). For a study see Zamaḫšarī, 180-181, Ibn Yaʿīš, *X,* 78-81, Zanǧānī, *ʿIzzī* 9, Howell, *IV,* fasc. I 1498-1501, Guillaume, *Aspects* 367-373.

b) The form مَفِيلٌ with 2nd radical *y* is used instead of مَفُولٌ with 2nd radical *w* in the following example, just to mention a few:

- مَشِيبٌ for مَشُوبٌ "mixed", which occurs in the following verse said by al-Sulaik b. al-

Salka al-Saʿdī in Ibn al-Salka, *Šiʿr* 45, cited by Mu'addib, *Taṣrīf* 321, Ibn Ğinnī, *Munṣif I,* 288, Ibn Yaʿīš, *X,* 78, Ibn Manẓūr, *IV,* 2424, Howell, *IV,* fasc. I, 1502:

"سَيَكْفِيكَ ضَرْبَ ٱلْقَوْمِ لَحْمٌ مُعَرَّصٌ وَمَاءٌ قُدُورٍ فِي ٱلْقِصَاعِ مَشِيبُ".

"Flesh laid out in the court to dry, and water of cooking-pots in the bowls, mixed [with seeds for seasoning and with sauces], will suffice thee for the sour milk of the people".

The Banū Tamīm make the passive participle with 2nd weak radical *y* complete formed according to مَفْعُولٌ, and say مَعْيُوبٌ "he is upbraided", مَخْيُوطٌ "sewn", مَكْيُولٌ "measured" and مَزْيُوتٌ "(food) dressed with olive oil, whereas the Ḥiğāzīs elide the infixed *w* of the passive participle and say مَعِيبٌ, مَخِيطٌ, مَكِيلٌ and مَزِيتٌ formed according to مَفِيلٌ. Some examples used in the *qur'ān* by the Ḥiğāzīs are مَشِيدٌ for مَشْيُودٌ in the sur. 22: 45 (وقَصْرٍ مَشِيدٍ) "And castles lofty and well-built", and مَهِيلٌ for مَهْيُولٌ which occurs in the sur. 73: 14 (وكَانَتِ ٱلْجِبَالُ كَثِيبًا مَهِيلًا) "And the mountains will be as a heap of sand poured out and flowing down".

Some examples found in verses of poetry are the following:

- مَعْيُونٌ which occurs instead of مَعِينٌ in the following verse said by al-ʿAbbās b. Mirdās al-Sulamī in ʿAbbās, *Dīwān* 108, cited by Ibn Ğinnī, *Ḫaṣā'iṣ I,* 261, Mu'addib, *Taṣrīf* 276, Ibn Manẓūr, *IV,* 3196, Howell, *IV,* fasc. I, 1503, Lane, *II,* 2218:

"قَدْ كَانَ قَوْمُكَ يَحْسِبُونَكَ سَيِّدًا وإخَالُ أَنَّكَ سَيِّدٌ مَعْيُونٌ".

"Your people have been accounting you to be a chief; but I fancy that you are a chief smitten by the evil eye".

- مَغْيُومٌ which occurs instead of مَغِيمٌ in the following verse said by ʿAlqama b. ʿAbāda, describing a male ostrich after having described a camel. It is cited by Ibn Ğinnī, *Ḫaṣā'iṣ I,* 261, *Munṣif I,* 286, *III,* 47, Mu'addib, *Taṣrīf* 276, Zamaḫšarī, 181, Ibn Yaʿīš, *X,* 80, *Mulūkī* 354, Howell, *IV,* fasc. I, 1503, Ahlwardt, *Divans* 112:

"حَتَّى تَذَكَّرَ بَيْضَاتٍ وَهَيَّجَهُ يَوْمَ رَذَاذٍ عَلَيْهِ ٱلدَّجْنُ مَغْيُومُ".

"Until he remembered eggs [belonging to him]; and a day of light rain, in which clouds were covering the overclouded sky, which aroused him".

- The fem. form مَطْيُوبَةٌ which occurs instead of مَطِيبَةٌ in the following verse said by a Tamīmī poet who is describing wine, cited by Ibn Ğinnī, *Ḫaṣā'iṣ I,* 261, *Munṣif I,* 286, *III,* 47, Mu'addib, *Taṣrīf* 275, Zamaḫšarī, 181, Ibn Yaʿīš, *X,* 80, *Mulūkī* 353, Ibn ʿUṣfūr, *II,* 460, Ibn Manẓūr, *IV,* 2732, Howell, *IV,* fasc. I, 1503:

"وكَأَنَّهَا تُفَّاحَةٌ مَطْيُوبَةٌ".

"And it is as though it were a scented apple".

Both the Banū Tamīm and the Ḥiğāzīs agree however upon making defective the passive participle with 2nd weak radical *w,* except for some forms that occur anomalously, e.g. لَفْظٌ مَقْوُولٌ "a word said" and ثَوْبٌ مَصْوُونٌ "a garment preserved", but the more used forms are مَقُولٌ and

مَصُونٌ (for a study see Ibn Yaʿīš, *X,* 80-81, Ibn ʿAqīl, *II,* 575-576, Suyūṭī, *Muzhir I,* 137, Howell, *IV,* fasc. I, 1505).

For general discussions see Zamaḫšarī, 181, Ibn YaʿıŻs, *X,* 78-81, Ibn ʿAqīl, *II,* 575-576, Howell, *IV,* fasc. I, 1498-1505, Fleischer, *Beiträge IV,* 254.

(296) مَبِيعٌ applies to both the noun of place and the passive participle. The virtual difference is only noticed between their base forms. The base form of the noun of place is مَبْيِعٌ formed according to مَفْعِلٌ in which the kasra is shifted to the vowelless consonant preceding it and the *y* is lengthened, and the base form of the passive participle is مَبْيُوعٌ (for the change see (295)) formed according to مَفْعُولٌ.

Differently from the form مَبِيعٌ that has two base forms for the noun of place and the passive participle respectively, the noun فُلْكٌ can apply to both the sing. or the pl. and does not have any base form that is specific for each one. By comparing its vowelless middle radical to the vowelless middle radical of أُسْدٌ "lions" (formed according to the pattern فُعْلٌ), which is the pl. of أَسَدٌ (formed according to the pattern فَعَلٌ), it is a pl., and by comparing it to the vowelless middle radical of the *maṣdar* قُرْبٌ of the verb قَرُبَ "to be near", it is a sing. Hence it occurs in the different sur. as:

- a pl. (and a fem.) in the sur. 10: 22 (إذا كُنْتُمْ فِي ٱلْفُلْكِ وَجَرَيْنَ بِهِمْ) "So that ye even board ships;—they sail with them"; in which فُلْكِي which is a dialectal variant of فلك has been used in the reading of Abū l-Dardā.

- a masc. sing. in the sur. 26: 119 (فَأَنْجَيْنَاهُ وَمَنْ مَعَهُ فِي ٱلْفُلْكِ ٱلْمَشْحُونِ) "So we delivered him and those with him in the ark filled (with all creatures)", in the sur. 16: 14 (وَتَرَى ٱلْفُلْكَ مَوَاخِرَ فِيهِ) "And thou seest the ships therein that plough the waves" and in the sur. 35: 12 (وَتَرَى ٱلْفُلْكَ فِيهِ مَوَاخِرَ) "And thou seest the ships therin that plough the waves".

- a fem., and may be either pl. or sing. in the sur 2: 164 (وَٱلْفُلْكِ ٱلَّتِي تَجْرِي فِي ٱلْبَحْرِ) "In the sailing of the ships through the Ocean".

It is said that when it is masc. sing. it is regarded as meaning the مَرْكَبُ "ark", and when it is fem. it has the meaning of the سَفِينَةٌ "ship" (cf. Ibn Manẓūr, *V,* 3465, Lane, *II,* 2443).

b) A few examples which apply to both the sing. and pl. (for a study see Ṯaʿālibī, *Fiqh* 219 and see the example cited in (152 b)) as the case of فُلْكٌ mentioned by Ibn Masʿūd and discussed above, that can be added in this context, are the following:

- the adjective جُنُبٌ "in a state of ceremonial impurity", e.g. رَجُلٌ جُنُبٌ "a man in a state of ceremonial impurity" and رِجَالٌ جُنُبٌ "men in state of ceremonial impurity", which occurs as a pl. in the sur. 5: 7 (وَإِنْ كُنْتُمْ جُنُبًا فَٱطَّهَّرُوا) "If ye are in a state of ceremonial impurity bathe your whole body".

- the substantive العَدُوُّ "the enemy/enemies", which occurs as a pl. in the sur. 26: 77 (فَإِنَّهُمْ

(عَدُوٌّ لِي إِلَّا رَبَّ ٱلْعَٰلَمِينَ) "For they are enemies to me; not so the Lord and Cherisher of the Worlds", and as a sing. in the sur. 4: 92 (فَإِنْ كَانَ مِنْ قَوْمٍ عَدُوٍّ لَكُمْ وَهُوَ مُؤْمِنٌ) "If the deceased belonged to a people at war with you, and he was a Believer".

- the substantive الضَيْفُ "the guest/ guests", which occurs as a pl. in the sur. 15: 68 (هَؤُلَاءِ ضَيْفِي فَلَا تَفْضَحُونِ) "These are my guests: disgrace me not".

c) A few examples which apply to both the masc. and fem. sing. as the case of فُلْكٌ, are the following:

- the substantive الطَاغُوتُ "the Evil One" which occurs as a masc. in the sur. 4: 60 (يُرِيدُونَ أَنْ يَتَحَاكَمُوا إِلَى ٱلطَاغُوتِ وَقَدْ أُمِرُوا أَنْ يَكْفُرُوا بِهِ) "Their (real) wish is to resort together for judgement (in their disputes) to the Evil One, though they were ordered to reject him", and as a fem. in the sur. 39: 17 (وَٱلَذِينَ ٱجْتَنَبُوا ٱلطَاغُوتَ أَنْ يَعْبُدُوهَا) "Those who eschew Evil,—and fall not into its worship" (for a study see Ṯaʿālibī, *Fiqh* 219; for other examples see (296)).

- the substantive الصَوْتُ which is a noun in the masc. that is treated as a fem., in the following verse said by Ruwaišid b. Kaṯīr al-Ṭāʾī, cited by Ṯaʿālibī, *Fiqh* 217, Ibn Manẓūr, *IV,* 2521, Lane, *II,* 1742:

"يَا أَيُّهَا الرَاكِبُ المُزْجِي مَطِيَّتَهُ   سَايِلْ بَنِي أَسَدٍ مَا هَذِهِ الصَوْتُ".

"O you, the rider urging on his beast, ask the sons of Asad what is this clamour?".

- the noun بَعْضٌ which is a masc., is sometimes treated as a fem. when it occurs as a first element of an *iḍāfa* construction and is followed by a second element in the non-human pl., e.g. قُطِعَتْ بَعْضُ أَصَابِعِهِ said instead of قُطِعَ بَعْضُ أَصَابِعِهِ "some of his fingers were cut off", in which قُطِعَتْ is put in the fem sing., and the anomalous reading of al-Ḥasan al-Baṣrī of the sur. 12: 10 (تَلْتَقِطْهُ بَعْضُ ٱلسَيَارَاتِ) read instead of (يَلْتَقِطْهُ بَعْضُ ٱلسَيَارَاتِ) "He will be picked up by some caravan of travellers", in which تَلْتَقِطْهُ is put in the fem. sing. (cf. Carter, *Širbīnī* 462). A parallel case is found in the following verse said by an anonymous poet, cited by Suyūṭī, *Šarḥ* 298, al-Šartūnī, the commentator of Farḥāt, *Baḥṯ* 277 in the notes and Carter, *Širbīnī* 462, in which the first element of an *iḍāfa* construction, the noun إِنَارَةٌ, which is fem. has a predicate in the masc., i.e. مَكْسُوفٌ instead of مَكْسُوفَةٌ:

"إِنَارَةُ ٱلْعَقْلِ مَكْسُوفٌ بِطَوْعِ ٱلْهَوَى   وَعَقْلُ عَاصِي ٱلْهَوَى يَزْدَادُ تَنْوِيرًا".

"The illumination of the mind is eclipsed by obedience to lust, but the mind of him who disobeys lust increases in enlightenment".

For discussions see Carter, *Širbīnī* 463 and for other examples see a part of my notes (22 c).

(297) قَالَ (for its paradigm see (259) becomes قِيلَ in the perfect of the passive voice. Its imperfect of the indicative of the passive is يُقَالُ, of the subjunctive يُقَالَ and of the jussive يُقَلْ.

(298) الإشمام means giving the consonant preceding the *w* or *y* a flavour of the ḍamma so that it notifies of the base form. In the cases discussed here, it is carried out if the consonant preceding the *w* or *y* is vowelled by the ḍamma in the base form of the passive voice. The three dialectal variants meant by Ibn Masʿūd concerning:

- بِيعَ underlyingly بُيِعَ in which the *y* is preceded by a ḍamma and so conforms to the condition, are: 1) بِيعَ, 2) بُوعَ, and 3) *išmām* "a flavour of the ḍamma" to the consonant preceding the *y* of the base form, i.e. بُـِيعَ (note in this last case that the *b's* ḍamma precedes the kasra).
- اخْتِيرَ underlyingly أُخْتُيِرَ are: 1) اخْتِيرَ, أُخْتُورَ, and 3) *išmām* to the consonant preceding the *y* of the base form, i.e. أُخْتُـِيرَ.
- انْقِيدَ underlyingly أُنْقُيِدَ are: 1) انْقِيدَ, 2) أُنْقُودَ and 3) *išmām* to the consonant preceding the *y* of the base form, i.e. أُنْقُـِيدَ.
- قِلْنَ underlyingly قُوِلْنَ (cf. (300)) are: 1) قِلْنَ, 2) قُلْنَ, and 3) *išmām* to the consonant preceding the *w* of the base form, i.e. قُـِلْنَ.
- بِعْنَ underlyingly بُيِعْنَ (cf. (300)) are: 1) بِعْنَ, 2) بُعْنَ and 3) *išmām* to the consonant preceding the *y* of the base form, i.e. بُـِعْنَ.

For a study see Sībawaihi, *II,* 398, Ibn Ǧinnī, *Munṣif I,* 248-255, 293-295, Barrānī, *Maṭālib* 113, Howell, *IV,* fasc. I, 1476-1484. It can be added that بُوعَ with pure ḍamma occurs in the dialect of the Banū Dubair and the Banū Faḫʿas. It occurs anomalously instead of بِيعَ in the following verse said by Ruʾba, cited by Ibn Yaʿīš, *VII,* 70, Suyūṭī, *Šarḥ* 277, Šinqīṭī, *Durar I,* 206, *II,* 222, Ǧarǧāwī, *Šarḥ* 95, Barrānī, *Maṭālib* 113, Daqr, *Muʿǧam* 389, Howell, *II-III,* 122:

"لَيْتَ وَهَلْ يَنْفَعُ شَيْئاً لَيْتُ   لَيْتَ شَبَاباً بُوعَ فَآشْتَرَيْتُ".

> "Would that—but does a 'would that' profit anything?—Would that youth were sold and that I bought".

Furthermore both قِيلَ and غِيضَ in the sur. 11: 44 (وَقِيلَ يَا أَرْضُ آبْلَعِي مَاءَكِ وَيَا سَمَاءُ أَقْلِعِي وَغِيضَ آلْمَاءُ) "Then the word went forth: 'O earth! swallow up thy water, and O sky! withhold (thy rain)!' And the water abated", were read with *išmām* by the seven readers (cf. Howell, *II-III,* 123).

(299) أُقِيمَ "to be performed" can only be said with the kasra given to the 1st radical *q,* and the two remaining states, namely the change of the *y* into a *w* and *išmām* are not allowable for it. Its base form is أُقْوِمَ, with the consonant preceding the *w* being vowelless. The condition for the two states is that the consonant preceding the *w* or *y* should be vowelled by the ḍamma. A similar example which can only be said with the kasra is أُسْتُقِيمَ "to be straightened up" underlyingly أُسْتُقْوِمَ, with the consonant before the *w* being vowelless. Cf. Howell, *IV,* fasc. I, 1484.

(300) The virtual difference between the base forms of the active and passive voice of قُلْنَ and بِعْنَ (for it see (285)) is the following: قُلْنَ in the active voice is underlyingly قَوَلْنَ with the *q* vowelled by a fatḥa formed according to فَعَلْنَ, whereas it is underlyingly قُوِلْنَ in the passive voice with the *q* vowelled by a ḍamma confomable to فُعِلْنَ. بِعْنَ in the active voice is underlyingly بَيَعْنَ with the *b* vowelled by a fatḥa, whereas it is underlyingly بُيِعْنَ in the passive voice with the *b* vowelled by a ḍamma. It may be noted that the ḍamma that vowels the *q* of قُلْنَ underlyingly قَوَلْنَ and the kasra that vowels the *b* of بِعْنَ underlyingly بَيَعْنَ in the active voice, are accidental due to the phonological change that is caused by their unsound 2nd weak radical, whereas they are underlying in their passive voice, namely قُوِلْنَ and بُيِعْنَ respectively that are formed according to the pattern فُعِلْنَ. It can be mentioned in this context that Sībawayhi did not wish to change the vowel of the 1st radical in the active and passive voice, as he seemed satisfied by the virtual difference of their base forms, whereas Ibn Mālik would rather have preferred verbs with the 1st radical vowelled by a kasra in the active voice, e.g. خِفْتُ "I was afraid", to be vowelled by a ḍamma in the passive voice, and verbs with the 1st radical vowelled by a ḍamma in the active voice, e.g. سُمْتُ "I got", to be vowelled by a kasra in the passive voice (cf. Daqr, *Muʿǧam* 389).

II.7. Arabic Text: الباب السادس في الناقص

ويُقال له ناقص لنقصانه في الآخر وذو الأربعة لأنّه يصير على أربعة أحرف في الإخبار عن نفسك نحو رَمَيْتُ وَدَعَوْتُ، ولا يجيء من باب فَعلَ يَفْعلُ. وتقول في إلحاق الضمائر رَمَى رَمَيا رموا رَمَتْ رَمَتا رَمَيْنَ الى آخره ورَمَى أصله رَمَيَ فقُلبت الياء ألفاً لتحرُكها وانفتاح ما قبلها كما مرّ في قَالَ، وأصل رَمَوا رَمَيوا فقُلبت الياء ألفاً لتحرُكها وانفتاح ما قبلها فصار رَمَاوْا فاجتمع ساكنان فحُذفت الألف فصار رَمَوْا وكذلك رَضُوا إلاّ أنّه ضُمّ الضاد فيه بعد الحذف حتّى لا يلزم الخروج من الكسرة الى الواو، وأصل رَمَتْ رَمَيَتْ فحُذفت الياء كما في رَمَوا وتُحذف الياء في رَمَتا وإن لم يجتمع فيه الساكنان لفظاً لأنّه يجتمع فيه الساكنان تقديراً وتمامه مرّ في قُولا، ولا يُعلّ في رَمَيْنَ كما مرّ في القول*. المستقبل يَرْمِي الى آخره أصله يَرْمِيُ فأُسكنت الياء لثقل الضمّة عليها ولا يُعلّ في مثل يَرْمِيانِ لأنّ حركته فتحة وهي خفيفة وأصل يَرْمُونَ يَرْمِيُونَ فأُسكنت الياء ثمّ حُذفت لاجتماع الساكنين فصار يَرْمِوْنَ ثمّ ضُمّ الميم حتّى لا يصير الواو ياء لسكونها وانكسار ما قبلها فصار يَرْمُونَ، وسُوّي بين الرجال والنساء في مثل يَعْفونَ اكتفاءً بالفرق التقديريّ والواو في النساء أصليّة والنون علامة التأنيث ومن ثمّ لا تسقط في قوله تعالى ﴿إلاّ أنْ يَعْفُونَ﴾، وأصل تَرْمِينَ تَرْمِيِينَ فأُسكنت الياء ثمّ حُذفت لاجتماع الساكنين وهو مشترك في اللفظ مع جماعة

* ٣٢ ب

Fols. 32a-32b

٢ ناقص: الناقص د/ ٣ ودعوت: – ج د ه ز ح ط ك ل/ ولا: وهو لا د ل/ يفعل: + بالكسر د/ ٤ رَمَيَا... ورَمَى: – ا/ رمت... رمين: – ب ج د ط/ ورمى: – د ح/ ٤–٥ لتحرّكها... قبلها: – ا ج د ط/ ٥ مرّ: – د ل/ قال: + وباع د/ ٦ رماوا: رموا ب: رماو د/ ساكنان: الساكنان د ز/ فحذفت: فحذف د ه ط/ ٨ وتحذف الياء: ويحذف د/ فيه: – د ل/ ٩ لفظاً: – ا د ز ح ك/ فيه: – د ل/ يعلّ: تعل ل/ ١٠ الى آخره: – ا/ فأُسكنت: فاسكن ا/ ١١ يعلّ: تعل ل/ الياء: + لثقل ضمتها الى الميم ح/ فتحة وهي: – ب ج د ه ز ط ل/ ١٢–١٣ فصار... يرمون: l's margin: – د ل/ لا: س ا/ ١٤ التقديريّ: التقدير د/ والواو: الواو ب ج د ه ز/ والنون: + ضمير ب د: + ضمير الجمع ط/ ١٥ علامة: وعلامة ب د/ تسقط: يسقط ا ب ج د ه ز ط/ ترميين: ترمين ل/ ١٦ الياء: + لإزالة توالي الكسرات د/

II.7. Translation: The 6th Chapter is about the Verb with Weak 3rd Radical(301)

It is named ناقص "defective" because of the defect of its 3rd radical, and ذو الأربعة "the one with four consonants" because it becomes formed of four consonants when you are talking about yourself [sc. in the 1st person of the sing. of the perfect], e.g. رَمَيْتُ "I threw" and دَعَوْتُ "I invited". It does not occur according to the conjugation فَعَلَ يَفْعُلُ. You say when attaching the pronouns: رَمَى "/3 masc. sing." [with the pronoun suppressed], رَمَيَا "/3 masc. dual", رَمَوْا "/3 masc. pl.", رَمَتْ "/3 fem. sing", رَمَتَا "/3 fem. dual", رَمَيْنَ "/3 fem. pl.", etc.(302) رَمَى is underlyingly رَمَيَ, in which the *y* is changed into an *ā* on account of its vowelling and of the [influence] of the fatḥa preceding it, as was mentioned about قَالَ "he said". رَمَوْا is underlyingly رَمَيُوا, in which the *y* is changed into an *ā* due to its vowelling and the [influence of the] fatḥa preceding it, so it became رَمَاوْا. Then as there resulted a cluster of two vowelless consonants, the *ā* was elided so that it became رَمَوْا. So is also the case of رَضُوا "they consented" [regarding the elision of the 3rd radical], except that the *ḍ* is vowelled by a ḍamma in it after the elision [of the *y* of رَضِيُوا], so that it is not necessary to incline from the kasra [of the *ḍ]* to the *ū* [of the suffixed pronoun].(303) رَمَتْ is underlyingly رَمَيَتْ, in which the *y* is elided as in رَمَوْا. The *y* is elided in رَمَتَا [underlyingly رَمَيَتَا] in spite of the fact that two vowelless consonants are not combined in the pronunciation, because they [sc. the suffixed *t* of the fem. which is underlyingly vowelless and the *ā* of the dual] are combined [as vowelless] virtually. Its counterpart was mentioned in قُولَا "Say! /masc. dual (imperative)" [with the 2nd radical *w* retained].(304) No change due to the unsound weak consonant is carried out in رَمَيْنَ "/3 fem. pl.", as was mentioned about القَوْلُ "the saying". **[Fol. 32 b]** The imperfect is يَرْمِي "/3 masc. sing." etc. underlyingly يَرْمِيُ, in which the *y* is made vowelless because of the heaviness of the ḍamma on it. No change is carried out in يَرْمِيَانِ "/3 masc. dual" because the vowel [of the *y]* is a fatḥa and it is light. يَرْمُونَ "/3 masc. pl." is underlyingly يَرْمِيُونَ, in which the *y* is made vowelless and is then elided to avoid the cluster of two vowelless consonants [sc. the *y* and the *w],* so it became يَرْمِونَ. Then the *m* is vowelled by a ḍamma to prevent that the *w* is changed into a *y* due to its sukūn and to the kasra preceding it, so it became يَرْمُونَ. The 3rd person of the masc. and fem. pl. are made homonymous in the example يَعْفُونَ "they remit" with the sufficiency of the virtual difference [of their base forms]. It is so that the *ū* [in يَعْفُونَ] in the fem. pl. is a [3rd] radical and the *-na* is the marker of the fem. pl. Hence, it is not dropped in the words of the Allmighty [sur. 2: 237] (إِلَّا أَنْ يعفونَ) "Unless they remit it".(305) تَرْمِينَ "/2 fem. sing." is underlyingly تَرْمِيِينَ, in which the [3rd radical] *y* is made vowelless and is then elided to avoid the cluster of two vowelless consonants. It is also homonym in the pronunciation with the 2nd person

النساء، وإذا أدخلتَ الجازم تسقط الياء علامة للجزم ومن ثمّ تسقط الياء في حالة الرفع علامةً للوقف في قوله تعالى ﴿وَٱلَّيْلِ إذا يَسْرِ﴾ وتنصب إذا أدخلتَ النواصب لخفّة النصب ولم تَنصب في مثل لَنْ يَخْشَى لأنّ الألف لا يحتمل الحركة. الأمر ارْمِ الى آخره أصله ارْمِي فحُذفت الياء علامة للجزم فصار ارْمِ. وأصل ارْمُوا ارمِيُوا فأسكنت الياء ثمّ
حُذفت لاجتماع الساكنين* . وأصل ارْمِي ارْمِيِي فأسكنت الياء الأصليّة ثمّ حُذفت لاجتماع * ٣٢ آ
الساكنين. ونقول بنون التأكيد الثقيلة ارْمِيَنّ ارْمِيانّ ارْمُنّ ارْمِنّ ارْمِيانّ ارْمِيْنانّ وبالخفيفة ارْمِيَنْ ارْمُنْ ارْمِنْ. الفاعل رامٍ الى آخره أصله راميٌ فأُسكنت الياء في حالتي الرفع والجرّ ثمّ حُذفت الياء لاجتماع الساكنين ولا تُسكن في حالة النصب لخفّة النصب. وأصل رامُونَ رامِيُونَ فأسكنت الياء ثمّ حُذفت لاجتماع الساكنين ثمّ ضُمّ الميم لاستدعاء الواو الضمّة وإذا أضفتَ التثنية الى نفسك فقلتَ رامِيايَ في حالة الرفع ورامِيَيَّ في حالتي النصب والجرّ بإدغام علامة النصب والجرّ في ياء الإضافة وإذا أضفتَ الجمع الى نفسك فقلتَ رامِيَّ في جميع الأحوال وأصله في حالة الرفع رامُويَ فأُدغم لأنّه اجتمع الحرفان من جنس واحد في العلية. المفعول مَرْمِيٌّ الى آخره أصله مَرْمُويٌ فأُدغم
كما في رامِيَّ وإذا أضفتَ التثنية* الى ياء الإضافة فقلتَ مَرْمِيايَ في حالة الرفع وفي حالتي * ٣٢ ب
النصب والجرّ مَرْمِيَيَّ بأربع ياآت. وإذا أضفتَ الجمع الى ياء الإضافة فقلت مَرْمِيَّ

Fols. 32b-33b

١ تسقط[1+2]: يسقط د/ الياء[2]: – ا د/ ٢ النواصب: الناصب ب ج د ز ح ط ك/ ٣ النصب: الناصب ب: الفتحة د: + نحو لن يغزو ولن يرمي ط/ الى آخره: – ا/ ٤ أصله: اصل ارم د/ أصله إرْمَيْ: –ا/ للجزم: للسكون ب د: + والوقف ز: للوقف ح ط/ فصار ارْمِ: – ا د ح/ ٦ الثقيلة: –ا ب ج د هـ ز ط: المشدّة ح/ ٧ الى آخره: –ا/ حالتي: حالة ا د/ ٨ الياء: –ا/ تسكن: يسكن د/ النصب: الفتحة د/ ١١ حالتي: حالة ا د هـ ح ط/ ١٢ راموي: + ورامِيَيَ في حالة النصب والجر د/ ١٢ واحد: + ثم كسر الميم لتصح الياء هـ/ الى آخره: – ا/ ١٤ وإذا: فاذا د/ ياء الإضافة: نفسك ح/ حالتي: حالة ا د/ ١٥ وإذا: فاذا د/ ياء الإضافة: نفسك ح/ الإضافة: المتكلّم ا/

of the fem. pl. If you make [any of] the apocopatives precede [يَرْمِي], the *y* is dropped as a marker of the jussive.(306) However, the *y* is dropped in the case of the indicative as a marker of the pause in the words of the Allmighty [sur. 89: 4] (واللَيلِ إذا يَسْرِ) "and by the Night when it passeth away".(307) If you made [any of] the subjunctivals precede [يَرْمِي], you give [the *y]* a fatḥa as a marker of the subjunctive because of the lightness of the fatḥa. However, you do not give the fatḥa as a marker of the subjunctive [to the *y* changed into an *alif maqṣūra]* in لَن يَخْشَى "he shall not dread", because the *alif [maqṣūra]* does not accept the vowel.(308) The imperative is ارْمِ "/2 masc. sing.", etc., that is underlyingly ارْمِي, in which the *y* is elided as a marker of the jussive, so it became ارْمِ. ارْمُوا "/2 masc. pl." is underlyingly ارميُوا, in which the *y* is made vowelless and is then elided to avoid the cluster of two vowelless consonants [the *y* and the *w]*. **[Fol. 33 a]** ارْمِي "/2 fem. sing." is underlyingly ارْمِيِي, in which the radical *y* is made vowelless and is then elided to avoid the cluster of two vowelless consonants [the *y* and the *y]*. You say with the energetic *n:* ارْمِيَنَّ "/2 masc. sing. (imperative En. 1), ارْمِيَانِّ "/2 common dual", ارْمُنَّ "/2 masc. pl.", ارْمِنَّ "/2 fem. sing.", ارْمِيَانِّ "/2 common dual" and ارْمِيْنَانِّ "/2 fem. pl.", and with the single *n:* ارْمِيَنْ "2 masc. sing. (imperative En. II)", ارْمُنْ "/2 masc. pl." and ارْمِنْ "/2 fem. sing.". The active participle is رامٍ etc., underlyingly رامِيٌ, in which the *y* is made vowelless in both the nominative and the genitive [because of the heaviness of the ḍamma and the kasra vowelling it], and is then elided to avoid the cluster of two sukūns [the *y's* sukūn and the nunation]. However, it is not made vowelless in the accusative because of the lightness of the fatḥa.(309) رامُونَ is underlyingly رامِيُونَ, in which the *y* is made vowelless [sc. رامِيْونَ] and is then elided to avoid the cluster of two vowelless consonants [the *y* and the *w]*, and then the *m* is vowelled by a ḍamma due to the *ū's* request for the ḍamma. If you suffix the dual's ending [sc. ـَانِ/nominative and ـَيْنِ/accusative and genitive] to yourself [sc. the 1st person of the sing. ـِي], you would say رامِيَايَ in the case of the nominative, and رامِيَيَّ in both the cases of the accusative and genitive by assimilating the marker of the accusative and of the genitive [of the dual: sc. the *y]* to the [suffixed pronoun] *y* of the genitive [of the 1st person of the sing.]. If you suffix the pl.'s ending [sc. ـُونَ /nominative and ـِينَ /accusative and genitive] to yourself [sc. the 1st person of the sing. *-ī]*, you would say رامِيَّ in all the cases, which is underlyingly رامُويَ in the case of the nominative, in which an assimilation is carried out due to the combination of two consonants of the same kind [sc. the *w* and the *y]* regarding their being among the weak consonants. The passive participle is مَرْمِيٌّ etc., underlyingly مَرْمُويٌ,(310) in which an assimilation [of the *w* to the *y]* is carried out as in رامِيَّ. If you suffix the dual's ending **[Fol. 33 b]** to the [suffixed pronoun] *y* of the genitive [of the 1st person of the sing.], you would say مَرْمِيَايَ in the case of the nominative and مَرْمِيَيَّ in both the cases of the accusative and genitive with four yāʾs. If you suffix the pl.'s ending to the [suffixed] *y* of the genitive, you would say مَرْمِيِّيَ

أيضاً بأربع ياآت في كلَ الأحوال. الموضع مَرْمَى الأصل فيه أن يأتي على وزن مَفْعِلٍ إلاَ أنَهم فرَوا عن توالي الكسرات. الآلة مِرْمَى المجهول رُمِيَ يُرْمَى الى آخرهما ولم يُعلَ رُمِيَ لخفَة الفتحة وأصل يُرْمَى يُرْمَيُ فقُلبت الياء ألفاً كما في رَمَى. وحكم غَزَا يَغْزُو مثل رَمَى يَرْمِي في كلَ الأحوال إلاَ أنَهم يبدلون الواو ياءً في أغْزَيْتُ تبعاً ليُغْزِيُ مع أنَ الياء من حروف الإبدال وحروفها إسْتَنْجَدَهُ يَوْمَ صالَ زُطٌ. الهمزة أُبدلت وُجوباً مطَرداً من الألف في نحو صَحْراءٍ لأنَ همزتها ألف في الأصل كألف سَكْرَى ثمَ جُعلت همزة لوقوعها طرفاً بعد ألف زائدة ومن ثمَ لا يجوز جعلها همزة في نحو صَحَارَى يعني لو كانت في

الأصل همزة لجاز صَحارِئُ بالهمزة في صورة ما كما يجوز في* خَطيئةٍ ومن الواو * ٣٤ آ

وجوباً مطَرداً في نحو أواصِلَ فراراً عن اجتماع الواوات وفي نحو قائِلٍ كما مرَ وفي نحو أدْؤُرٌ لثقل الضمَة على الواو وفي نحو كِساءٍ لوقوع الحركات المختلفة على الواو ومن الياء وجوباً مطَرداً نحو بائِعٍ كما مرَ وجوازاً مطَرداً من الواو المضمومة نحو أُجُوهٍ لثقل الضمَة على الواو ومن الواو غير المضمومة نحو إشاحٍ ونحو أحَدْ أحَدْ في الحديث ومن الياء نحو قَطَعَ اللهُ أدَيْه لثقل الحركة على الياء ومن الهاء نحو مَاءٍ أصله مَاهٌ ومن ثمَ يجيء جمعه مِياهٌ ومن الألف نحو قوله * هَيَجْتِ شَوْقَ ٱلْمُشْتَأَقْ * ونحو قراءة من قرأ ﴿ولاَ ٱلضَألِينَ﴾ بالهمزة ومن العين نحو * أُبَابُ بَحْرٍ ضَاحِكٍ زَهُوقٍ * لاتَحاد مخرجهن. السين أُبدلت من التاء نحو اسْتَخَذَ أصله اتَخَذَ عند

سيبويه لقربهما في المهموسيَة. التاء أُبدلت من الواو نحو تُخَمَة* * ٣٤ ب

أصلها وُخَمَة ونحو أُخْتٍ لقرب مخرجهما ومن الياء نحو ثِنْتَانِ أصله

Fols. 33b-34b

٢ عن: من ل/ يُرمَى... آخرهما: – ا/ الى آخرهما: – د/ ٣ يَغْزُو: يغزوا ا ز ح ل/ ٤ الأحوال: الأحكام ل/ اغزيت: غزيت ک/ ٥ وحروفها: + قولك ه د/ ٦ لأنَ همزتها: وهمزتها ب ه ز/ جعلت: + ألف التأنيث ح/ ٨ في: + نحو ل/ ٩ نحو[1]: – ا/ عن: من ل/ وفي: في ا/ وفي نحو[1]: ونحو د/ ١٠ ادؤر: + كما مرَ د/ وفي نحو: ونحو د ل/ ١١ المضمومة: المظمومة ط/ [2]: في نحو ل/ من: عن ا د/ ١٢ الضمَة: الظمة ط/ غير المضمومة: الغير المظمومة ط/ اشاح: اتشارح ب/ ونحو احَد: وأحَد د/ ١٢–١٤ ومن... مياه: – ج/ ومن... يجيء: – ب ه/ ١٤ قوله: – ا د/ هَيَجت ... المشتأق: يمتجب يشوق ب/ المشتاق ب ح ط/ قرأ: + قوله تعالى ج/ ١٥ بالهمزة: – ا ه ح ط ک/ ١٦ لاتَحاد: التحاد ز/ اتَخَذَ: اتتخذ ط/ ١٨ أصلها وخمة: – ب د ح ط ک ل/ ونحو اخت: وأخت د ل/ ثِنْتَان: سنتان ا: شنتان ه ط/ أصله– fols. 34b-35a l. 1 ثنيان: – ب ج د ط/

also with four yā's in all the cases. The noun of place is المَرْمَى, which by principle should have been formed according to the pattern مَفْعِلٌ, except that they avoided the succession of the kasras. The noun of instrument is مِرْمَى. The passive voice is رُمِيَ يُرْمَى, etc. No change due to the weak consonant [sc. the y] is carried out in رُمِيَ because of the lightness of the fatḥa [on it]. يُرْمَى is underlyingly يُرْمَيُ, in which the y is changed into an *alif [maqṣūra]* as in رَمَى. The predicament of غَزَا يَغْزُو "to attack" is the same as the predicament of رَمَى يَرْمِي in all cases, except that they substituted the y for the w in أَغْزَيْتُ "I attacked" in conformity with يُغْزَيُ "He attacks",(311) as the y is among the consonants of substitution which are: اسْتَنْجَدَهُ يَوْمَ صَالَ زُطٌّ "he asked him for succour on the day some Zuṭṭ (a race of Hindus) attacked".(312) The hamza is substituted for: 1- necessarily, the alif [of the feminine], in e.g. صَحْرَاء "desert",(313) because its hamza is the alif [of the feminine] underlyingly, which is similar to the *alif [maqṣūra]* of سَكْرَى "drunk /fem.",(314) and then it is changed into a hamza because of its occurrence at the extremity of the word after the augmentative alif. However, it is impossible to change it [sc. the alif of the feminine] into a hamza, in e.g. صَحَارَى "deserts", meaning that if it [sc. the alif of the feminine] is underlyingly a hamza, then صَحَارِئُ with the hamza retained would have somehow been possible, as it is possibly retained in **[Fol. 34 a]** e.g. خَطِيئَةٌ "sin".(315) 2- necessarily, the *w*, in e.g. أَوَاصِلُ "joining (pl.)", to avoid the combination of the wāws(316) in قَائِلٌ "saying" as was mentioned,(317) in أَدْؤُرٌ "houses" because of the heaviness of the ḍamma on the *w*(318) and in كِسَاءٌ "a wrapper" to avoid the different vowels on the *w*.(319) 3- necessarily, the *y*, in e.g. بَائِعٌ "seller", as was mentioned [concerning قَائِلٌ].(320) 4- possibly, the *w* which is vowelled by a ḍamma, in e.g. أُجُوهٌ "faces", because of the heaviness of the ḍamma on the *w*.(321) 5- the *w* which is not vowelled by a ḍamma, in e.g. اشاحٌ "baldric"(322) and in أَحِّدْ أَحِّدْ "make the sign with one, one" in the tradition.(323) 6- the *y*, in e.g. قَطَعَ اللّٰهُ أَدَيْهُ "God cut off his hands", because of the heaviness of the vowel on the *y*(324) 7- the *h*, in e.g. مَاءٌ "water" underlyingly مَاهٌ, and hence its pl. is مِيَاهٌ.(325) 8- the *ā*, as in his saying: هَيَّجْتَ شَوْقَ ٱلْمُشْتَأَقِ "You have excited the yearning of the yearner",(326) and in the reading of he who reads [sur. 1: 7] (وَلَا ٱلضَّأَلِّينَ) "Who go not astray".(327) 9- the ʿ, in e.g.: أُبَابُ بَحْرٍ ضَاحِكٍ زَهُوقٍ "Like a billow of a laughing, far-extending sea",—due to the oneness of their [sc. the hamza's, the *h's*, the *ā's* and the ʿ*s]* point of articulation—.(328)

The *s* is substituted for: 1- the *t*, in e.g. اسْتَخَذَ "to take for one's self" underlyingly اتَّخَذَ according to Sībawaihi, because of their common character in being among the surd consonants.(329)

The *t* is substituted for: 1- the *w*, in e.g. تُخَمَةٌ "a malady like cholera" underlyingly وُخَمَةٌ(330) and in أُخْتٌ "sister",(331) due to the proximity of both their points of articulation. 2- the *y*, **[Fol. 34 b]** in e.g. ثِنْتَانِ "the second to the one" underlyingly

ثنْيَانِ وأسْنَتُوا أصله أسْنَيُوا حتَى لا تقع الحركة على الياء ومن السين نحو ستّ أصله
سُدُسٌ ونحو * عَمْرَو بنَ يَربُوعٍ شرَارَ ٱلنَاتِ * ومن الصاد نحو لصْتٍ لقربهنَ في
المهموسيَة ومن الباء نحو الذَعَالت النون أُبدلت من الواو نحو صَنْعَانِيّ لقرب النون من
حروف العلَة ومن اللام نحو لَعَنَ لقربهما في المجهوريَة. الجيم أُبدلت من الياء المشدَدة
نحو أبُو عَلِجَ حتَى لا تقع الحركات المختلفة على الياء ومن غير المشدَدة حملاً على
المشدَدة نحو قوله :

"لاَهُمَّ إنْ كُنْتَ قَبِلْتَ حَجَتِجْ　　　فَلاَ يَزَالُ شَاحِجٌ يَأتِيكَ بِجْ".

الدال أُبدلت من التاء نحو فُزْدُ واجْدَمَعُوا لقرب مخرجهما. الهاء أُبدلت من الهمزة
نحو هَرَقْتُ ومن الألف نحو حَيَهَلَهْ وأنَهْ ومن الياء في هذه أمة الله لمناسبتها بحروف العلَة
في الخفاء ومن ثمَ لا تُمتنع الإمالة في مثل يَضْرِبَهَا وتُمتنع في مثل أكَلْتُ عِنَباً ومن
التاء وجوباً مطَرداً* في مثل طَلْحَهْ للفرق بينها وبين التاء التي في الفعل. الياء * ٣٥ آ
أُبدلت من الألف وجوباً مطَرداً نحو مُفَيْتِيحٍ ومن الواو وجوباً مطَرداً نحو
مِيقَاتٍ لكسرة ما قبلهما ومن الهمزة جوازاً مطرداً نحو ذِيبٍ ومن أحد حرفي
التضعيف نحو تَقَضِّيَ ٱلْبَازِي ومن النون نحو أنَاسِيّ ودِينَارٍ لقرب الياء من النون
ومن العين نحو ضَفَادِي لثقل العين وكسرة ما قبلها ومن التاء نحو إيتَصَلَتْ لأنَ أصله
واو ساكن ما قبلها مكسور ومن الباء نحو ثَعَالِي ومن السين نحو السَادِي
ومن الثاء نحو الثَالِي أصله الثالث لكسرة ما قبلهنَ. الواو أُبدلت من الألف

Fols. 34b-35a

١ ثنيان: شنيان هـ/ أصله أسْنَيُوا: –ا ب جـ د حـ ط/ تقع: يقع ا ب جـ د هـ حـ ط/ ١–٢ أصله سُدُسٌ: –ا ب د/ ٢ لصت: + أصله لصت لصّ حـ/ ٣ الباء: الياء ا/ الذَعالت: الزعالة ب ط/ ٥ تقع: يقع ا ب د هـ ز حـ ط/ الحركات: الحركة ا جـ ز/ الياء: + الضعيف حـ/ ومن: وعن د: + الياء حـ/ غير: الغير ا/ ٦ نحو قوله: –ا د هـ ز حـ ط/ ٩ لمناسبتها: لمناسبتهما ب هـ ط ل/ ١٠ تمتنع: يمتنع ا د ز حـ/ يضربها: تضربها د/ وتمتنع: ويمتنع ا جـ د/ ١١ طلحه: + في الوقف جـ ط: + وظلمة ز/ التي: – ب ل/ ١٢ ميقات: ميعاد ا/ قبلهما: قبلها ا د/ ١٤ البازي: + كما مرّ د/ ١٦ ما... مكسور: –ب د هـ ز حـ ط ك ل/ ثعالي: الثعالي ا د هـ ط/ ١٧ أصله الثالث: –هـ ز حـ ط ك ل/ لكسرة: لكثرة ا ب/ قبلهنّ: قبلها د/

ثِنْيَان, and in أَسْنَتُوا "they experienced drough or barrenness" underlyingly أَسْنَيُوا,(332) to avoid vowelling the *y*. 3- the *s*, in e.g. سِتّ "six" underlyingly سُدُسٌ,(333) and in: عَمْرُو بْنَ مَسْعُود شِرَارَ ٱلنَّات "'Amr b. Mas'ūd, the worst of men!".(334) 4- the *ṣ*, in e.g. لَصْتُ "robber",(335) because of their being among the surd consonants. 5- the *b*, in e.g. الذَّعَالِتُ "worn-out rags".(336)

The *n* is substituted for: 1- the *w*, in e.g. صَنْعَانِي "from a city in al-Yaman",(337) because of the proximity of the *n* to the weak consonants. 2- the *l*, in e.g. لَعَنَّ "perhaps",(338) because they [sc. the *n* and the *l*] are akin in being among the voiced consonants.

The *ǧ* is substituted for: 1- the doubled *y*, in e.g. أَبُو عَلِجّ "Abū 'Aliǧǧi [sc. Abū 'Alī]"(339) to avoid vowelling the doubled yā's [in أَبُو عَلِيّ]. 2- the single *y* in conformity with the doubled one as in his saying:

"لَاهُمَّ إِنْ كُنْتَ قَبِلْتَ حَجَتِجْ   فَلَا يَزَالُ شَاحِجٌ يَأْتِيكَ بِجْ".

"O God, if Thou hast accepted my pilgrimage, then a mule, shall not cease to bring me to Thee".(340)

The *d* is substituted for: 1- the *t*, in e.g. فُزْدُ "I succeeded"(341) and اجْدَمَعُوا "they gathered together",(342) because of the proximity of both their points of articulation.

The *h* is substituted for: 1- the hamza, in e.g. هَرَقْتُ "I spilled".(343) 2- the *ā*, in e.g. حَيَّهَلَهْ "come along!"(344) and أَنَهْ "I".(345) 3- the *y*, in e.g. هذه أَمَةُ الله "this is the servant of God",(346) because of its [sc. the *h's*] being akin to the weak consonants regarding the lightness. And hence, the deflection is not forbidden in يَضْرِبَهَا "to hit her", whereas it is forbidden in أَكَلْتُ عِنَبًا "I ate grapes".(347) 4- necessarily, the *t*, **[Fol. 35 a]** in e.g. طَلْحَة *Ṭalḥa* "to differenciate it from the *t* of the verb.(348)

The *y* is substituted for: 1- necessarily, the *ā*, in e.g. مُفَيْتِيح "a little key".(349) 2- necessarily, the *w*, in e.g. مِيقَاتٌ "time appointed for performance of an action", due to [the influence of] the kasra preceding them both [sc. the underlying *ā* and *w*].(350) 3- possibly, the hamza, in e.g. ذِيب "a wolf".(351) 4- one of the doubled consonants, in e.g. تَقَضَّى البَازِي "the hawk flew down swiftly".(352) 5- the *n*, in e.g. أَنَاسِي "men"(353) and دِينَارٌ "a dinār",(354) because of the proximity of the *y* to the *n*. 6- the ʿ, in e.g. ضَفَادِي "frogs", because of the heaviness of the ʿ and [the influence of] the kasra preceding it.(355) 7- the *t*, in e.g. ايتَصَلَتْ "it joined", because it [sc. the word] has underlyingly a vowelless *w* that is preceded by a consonant vowelled by a kasra.(356) 8- the *b*, in e.g. ثَعَالِي "foxes".(357) 9- the *s*, in e.g. السَّادِي "the sixth".(358) 10- the *ṯ*, in e.g. الثَّالِي "the third" underlyingly الثَّالِث,(359) due to the kasra preceding them.

The *w* is substituted for:

وجوباً مطّرداً نحو ضَوَارِبَ لقربهما في العلية واجتماع الساكنين ومن الياء وجوباً مطّرداً نحو مُوقِنٍ لضمّة ما قبلها ومن الهمزة جوازاً مطّرداً نحو لُومٍ كما مرّ. الميم أُبدلت من * ٣٥ ب الواو نحو فَمٍ لاتّحاد مخرجهما ومن اللام نحو قوله عليه السلام لَيْسَ* مِنْ أمْبِرِ آمْصِيَامُ في آمْسَفَرِ لقربهما في المجهوريّة ومن النون الساكنة نحو عَمْبَرٍ ومن المتحركة نحو * وكَفّك آلمُخَضّبِ آلْبَنَامِ * لقربهما في المجهوريّة ومن الباء نحو مَا زِلْتُ رَاتِماً لاّتّحاد مخرجهما. الصاد أُبدلت من السين نحو أصْبَغَ لقرب مخرجهما. الألف أُبدلت من أُختيها وجوباً مطّرداً نحو قَالَ وبَاعَ ومن الهمزة جوازاً مطّرداً نحو رَاسٍ كما مرّ. اللام أُبدلت من النون نحو أُصَيْلاَلٍ ومن الضاد نحو الْطَجَعَ لاتّحادهنّ في المجهوريّة. الزاء أُبدلت من السين نحو يَزْدُلُ ومن الصاد نحو قول الحاتم * هكذا فَزْدِي أنَهْ *. الطاء أُبدلت من التاء وجوباً مطّرداً في الإفْتِعالِ نحو اصْطَبَرَ وفي فَحَصْطُ لقرب مخرجهما. والموضع الذي لم يُقيّد من الصور المذكورة يكون جائزاً غير مطّرد.

Fols. 35a-35b

١ وجوبا مطّرداً(1+2): – ا ب د ه ز ط/ واجتماع: فاجتماع ب/ ٢ فم: قم ب/ عليه السلام: تعالى ط/ امبر: امير ب ح: البر ط/ ٤ امسفر: صقر ب: اسفر ط/ عمبر: عمير ب/ ومن: + النون ح/ المتحركة: للتحرّك ب/ نحو(2): + البنام ج د/ ٤–٥ وكفّك... اليئام: وكفل المحضب اليئام ب/ ٥ الباء: الياء ا/ نحو: – د/ ٦ الصاد: الضاد ط/ ٧ الهمزة: الهمزت ح/ ٨ النون: + جوازا غير مطّردا ح/ اصيلال: اصلال ه/ ٩ يزدل: + لاتحاد مخرجهما ح/ الحاتم: الخاتم ا ب ح ط/ هكذا: وهكذا ه/ أنه: – ب ه ز ط/ ١٠ الإفتعال: افتعل د ه ح ط: باب افتعل ل/ فحصط: محصط ب/

1- necessarily, the *ā,* in e.g. ضَوَارِب "striking, /pl.", because of both their common character in being among the weak consonants and to avoid the cluster of two vowelless consonants.(360) 2- necessarily, the *y,* in e.g. مُوقِن "to be certain", due to [the influence of the] ḍamma preceding it.(361) 3- possibly, the hamza, in e.g. لُوم "blame" [underlyingly لُؤْم] as was mentioned.(362)

The *m* is substituted for: 1- the *w,* in e.g. فَم "mouth",(363) because both their points of articulation are identical. 2- the *l,* as in His saying, may God grant Him salvation, لَيْسَ مِنْ أمْبِرِّ آمْصِيَامُ فِي آمْسَفَرِ "fasting in **[Fol. 35 b]** travelling is not an act of piety",(364) because of their common character in being among the voiced consonants. 3- the vowelless *n,* in e.g. عَمْبَر "a warehouse",(365) and the vowelled one as in وكَفَّكِ آلْمُخَضَّبِ آلْبَنَامِ "and of your hand dyed in (the tips of) the fingers with henna",(366) because of their common character in being among the voiced consonants. 4- the *b,* in e.g. مَا زِلْتُ رَاتِمًا "I have not ceased to be constant", because both their points of articulation are identical.(367)

The *ṣ* is substituted for: 1- the *s,* in e.g. أَصْبَغَ "to make flow in exceeding measure", because of the proximity of both their points of articulation.(368)

The *ā* is substituted for: 1- necessarily, both its sisters [sc. the *w* and the *y],* in e.g. قَالَ "to say" and بَاعَ "to sell". 2- allowably, the hamza in e.g. رَاس "a head", as was mentioned.(369)

The *l* is substituted for: 1- the *n* in e.g. أُصَيْلَال "evening".(370) 2- the *ḍ,* in e.g. الْطَجَعَ "to lay down to sleep",(371) because of their [sc. the *l's,* the *n's* and the *ḍ's]* common character in being among the voiced consonants.

The *z* is substituted for: 1- the *s,* in e.g. يَزْدُل "he loosens (his garment)".(372) 2- the *ṣ* as in e.g. the saying of al-Ḥātim هكذا فَزْدِي أَنَهْ "this is my way of bleeding, mine".(373)

The *ṭ* is substituted for: 1- necessarily, the infixed *t* of [Form VIII] الإفْتِعال, e.g. اصْطَبَرَ "to have patience",(374) and [the suffixed *t* of the nominative] in e.g. فَحَصْطُ "I scraped a hollow",(375) because of the proximity of both their points of articulation.

As for the cases in which it [sc. the substitution] does not follow the mentioned procedures, they are possibilities that do not follow the general rules.

II.7.1. COMMENTARY

The Verb with Weak 3rd Radical

(301) For a general study of الناقص "the Defective Verb" or "the verb with 3rd radical *w* or *y*" see Mu'addib, *Taṣrīf* 292-334, Ibn Ya'īš, *Mulūkī* 58-61, Ibn 'Uṣfūr, *II*, 518-560, Zanǧānī, *'Izzī* 9-11, 'Abd al-Ḥamīd, *Taṣrīf* 635-642, de Sacy, 249-256, Farḥāt, *Baḥṯ* 80-88, Brockelmann, *Socins Grammatik* 45-46, Wright, 88-91, Blachère, 146-161, Fischer, *Grammatik* 119-122, Bakkūš, *Taṣrīf* 151-163, Daqr, *Mu'ǧam* 390-391, 'Abd al-Raḥīm, *Ṣarf* 33-36, Roman, *Étude II*, 947-961. The verb with 3rd radical *y* is more frequent than the verb with 3rd radical *w:* 354 / 259 (cf. Bakkūš, *Taṣrīf* 157). For a comparative study with corresponding forms in some of the other Semitic languages see Brockelmann, *Grundriß* 618-632, Wright, *Comparative Grammar* 255-276, Bauer, *Grammatik* 109-110. For a study of the verb and noun in the Semitic languages see Diem, *Verba und Nomina* 15-60. Moscati, *Grammar* 169, referring to von Soden, *Grundriß* 154-156, remarks that some of the verbs with 3rd radical *y* are of "terminative meaning, e.g. Semitic (except Ethiopic) *bny* "to build", Hebrew Aramaic *gly* "to reveal", whereas verbs with 3rd radical *y* or *w* "describe durative actions, e.g. Ancient West Semitic *r'y* "to see", Akkadian Hebrew Aramaic *mnw* "to count".

(302) The paradigm of رَمَى underlyingly رَمَيَ, a verb with 3rd radical *y* and the 2nd radical being vowelled by a fatḥa, in the perfect, active, is the following:

	sing.	dual	pl.
1st	رَمَيْتُ		رَمَيْنَا
2nd masc.	رَمَيْتَ	رَمَيْتُمَا	رَمَيْتُمْ
2nd fem.	رَمَيْتِ	رَمَيْتُمَا	رَمَيْتُنَّ
3rd masc.	رَمَى	رَمَيَا	رَمَوْا
3rd fem.	رَمَتْ	رَمَتَا	رَمَيْنَ

Its paradigm in the imperfect of the indicative, active, is the following:

	sing.	dual	pl.
1st	أَرْمِي		نَرْمِي
2nd masc.	تَرْمِي	تَرْمِيَانِ	تَرْمُونَ
2nd fem.	تَرْمِينَ	تَرْمِيَانِ	تَرْمِينَ
3rd masc.	يَرْمِي	يَرْمِيَانِ	يَرْمُونَ
3rd fem.	تَرْمِي	تَرْمِيَانِ	يَرْمِينَ

Its paradigm in the imperfect of the subjunctive, active, is the following:

	sing.	dual	pl.
1st	أَرْمِيَ		نَرْمِيَ
2nd masc.	تَرْمِيَ	تَرْمِيَا	تَرْمُوا

2nd fem.	تَرْمِي	تَرْمِيَا	تَرْمِينَ
3rd masc.	يَرْمِي	يَرْمِيَا	يَرْمُوا
3rd fem.	تَرْمِي	تَرْمِيَا	يَرْمِينَ

Its paradigm in the imperfect of the jussive, active, is the following:

	sing.	dual	pl.
1st	أَرْمِ		نَرْمِ
2nd masc.	تَرْمِ	تَرْمِيَا	تَرْمُوا
2nd fem.	تَرْمِي	تَرْمِيَا	تَرْمِينَ
3rd masc.	يَرْمِ	يَرْمِيَا	يَرْمُوا
3rd fem.	تَرْمِ	تَرْمِيَا	يَرْمِينَ

Its imperative is اِرْمِ. Its active participle is رَامٍ. Its *maṣdar* is رَمْيٌ. Its perfect, passive is رُمِيَ. Its imperfect is يُرْمَى. Its passive participle is مَرْمِيٌّ.

b) An example of a verb with 3rd radical *w* is دَعَا underlyingly دَعَوَ "to call". Another example is نَدَا underlyingly نَدَوَ "to call". The paradigm of its groundform and derived forms is the following:

Form I: Its perfect, active is نَدَا. Its imperfect is يَنْدُو. Its imperative is أُنْدُ. Its active participle is نَادٍ. Its *maṣdar* is نَدْوٌ. Its perfect, passive is نُدِيَ. Its imperfect is يُنْدَى. Its passive participle is مَنْدُوٌّ.

Form II: Its perfect, active is نَدَّى. Its imperfect is يُنَدِّي. Its imperative is نَدِّ. Its active participle is مُنَدٍّ. Its *maṣdar* is تَنْدِيَةٌ. Its perfect, passive is نُدِّيَ. Its imperfect is يُنَدَّى. Its passive participle is مُنَدًّى.

Form III: Its perfect, active is نَادَى. Its imperfect is يُنَادِي. Its imperative is نَادِ. Its active participle is مُنَادٍ. Its *maṣdar* is نِدَاءٌ or مُنَادَاةٌ. Its perfect, passive is نُودِيَ. Its imperfect is يُنَادَى. Its passive participle is مُنَادًى.

Form IV: Its perfect, active is أَنْدَى. Its imperfect is يُنْدِي. Its imperative is أَنْدِ. Its active participle is مُنْدٍ. Its *maṣdar* is إِنْدَاءٌ. Its perfect, passive is أُنْدِيَ. Its imperfect is يُنْدَى. Its passive participle is مُنْدًى.

Form V: Its perfect, active is تَنَدَّى. Its imperfect is يَتَنَدَّى. Its imperative is تَنَدَّ. Its active participle is مُتَنَدٍّ. Its *maṣdar* is تَنَدٍّ. Its perfect, passive is تُنُدِّيَ. Its imperfect is يُتَنَدَّى. Its passive participle is مُتَنَدًّى.

Form VI: Its perfect, active is تَنَادَى. Its imperfect is يَتَنَادَى. Its imperative is تَنَادَ. Its active participle is مُتَنَادٍ. Its *maṣdar* is تَنَادٍ. Its perfect, passive is تُنُودِيَ. Its imperfect is يُتَنَادَى. Its passive participle is مُتَنَادًى.

Form VII: Its perfect, active is انَّدَى. Its imperfect is يَنَّدِي. Its imperative is انَّدِ. Its active participle is مُنَّدٍ. Its *maṣdar* is انِّدَاءٌ. Its perfect, passive is أُنُّدِيَ. Its imperfect is يُنَّدَى. Its passive participle is مُنَّدًى.

Form VIII: Its perfect, active is انْتَدَى. Its imperfect is يَنْتَدِي. Its imperative is انْتَدِ. Its active participle is مُنْتَدٍ. Its *maṣdar* is انْتِدَاءٌ. Its perfect, passive is أُنْتُدِيَ. Its imperfect is يُنْتَدَى. Its passive participle is مُنْتَدًى.

Form X: Its perfect, active is اسْتَنْدَى. Its imperfect is يَسْتَنْدِي. Its imperative is اسْتَنْدِ. Its active participle is مُسْتَنْدٍ. Its *maṣdar* is اسْتِنْدَاءٌ. Its perfect, passive is أُسْتُنْدِيَ. Its imperfect is يُسْتَنْدَى. Its passive participle is مُسْتَنْدًى.

(303) رَمَى is formed according to the conjugation فَعَلَ يَفْعِلُ. In the 3rd person of the masc. pl. of the perfect رَمَيُوا, the 3rd vowelled radical *y* preceded by a fatḥa is changed into an *ā* due to the influence of the fatḥa, i.e. رَمَاوْا, and then the *ā* is elided to avoid the cluster of two vowelless consonants, the *ā* and the *w*, resulting in رَمَوْا (cf. (49)). رَضِيَ is formed according to the conjugation فَعِلَ يَفْعَلُ. It is underlyingly رَضِوَ with the 3rd vowelled radical *w* changed into a *y* on account of the influence of the kasra preceding it (cf. Lane, *I,* 1099). This means that رَضِيُوا is underlyingly رَضِوُوا with the 3rd vowelled radical *w* changed into a *y* due to the influence of the kasra preceding it. Then as the ḍamma that vowels the *y* in رَضِيُوا is deemed as heavy, it is shifted to the *ḍ,* i.e. رَضُيْوا, which causes a cluster of two vowelless weak consonants, the *y* and *w* (cf. Ibn Ǧinnī, *Munṣif II,* 126). So the *y* is elided and it became رَضُوا (cf. further (49), (275)).

b) The paradigm of رَضِيَ, a verb with 3rd radical *y* (underlyingly *w)* and the 2nd radical being vowelled by a kasra, in the perfect, active, is the following:

	sing.	dual	pl.
1st	رَضِيتُ		رَضِينَا
2nd masc.	رَضِيتَ	رَضِيتُمَا	رَضِيتُمْ
2nd fem.	رَضِيتِ	رَضِيتُمَا	رَضِيتُنَّ
3rd masc.	رَضِيَ	رَضِيَا	رَضُوا
3rd fem.	رَضِيَتْ	رَضِيَتَا	رَضِينَ

Its paradigm of the imperfect of the indicative, active, is the following:

	sing.	dual	pl.
1st	أَرْضَى	نَرْضَى	
2nd masc.	تَرْضَى	تَرْضَيَانِ	تَرْضَوْنَ

2nd fem.	تَرْضَيْنَ	تَرْضَيَانِ	تَرْضَيْنَ
3rd masc.	يَرْضَى	يَرْضَيَانِ	يَرْضَوْنَ
3rd fem.	تَرْضَى	تَرْضَيَانِ	يَرْضَيْنَ

Its paradigm of the imperfect of the subjunctive, active, is the following:

	sing.	dual	pl.
1st	أَرْضَى	نَرْضَى	
2nd masc.	تَرْضَى	تَرْضَيَا	تَرْضَوْا
2nd fem.	تَرْضَيْ	تَرْضَيَا	تَرْضَيْنَ
3rd masc.	يَرْضَى	يَرْضَيَا	يَرْضَوْا
3rd fem.	تَرْضَى	تَرْضَيَا	يَرْضَيْنَ

Its paradigm of the imperfect of the jussive, active, is the following:

	sing.	dual	pl.
1st	أَرْضَ	نَرْضَ	
2nd masc.	تَرْضَ	تَرْضَيَا	تَرْضَوْا
2nd fem.	تَرْضَيْ	تَرْضَيَا	تَرْضَيْنَ
3rd masc.	يَرْضَ	يَرْضَيَا	يَرْضَوْا
3rd fem.	تَرْضَ	تَرْضَيَا	يَرْضَيْنَ

Its imperative is اِرْضَ. Its active participle is رَاضٍ. Its *maṣdar* is رِضًا or رِضْوَانٌ. Its perfect, passive is رُضِيَ. Its imperfect is يُرْضَى. Its passive participle is يُرْضَى.

(304) رَمَتَا is underlyingly رَمَيَتَا in which the 3rd vowelled radical *y* preceded by a fatḥa is changed into an *ā*, i.e. رَمَاتَا, and then the *ā* is elided in spite of the fact that the *t* following it is vowelled and not vowelless (for discussions see (54); compare the discussion concerning دَعَتَا underlyingly دَعَوَتَا in which the 3rd radical *w* is changed into an *ā* which is then elided, see (289)). The vowel of the *t* is considered as accidental due to the suffixation of the *ā* of the dual, and the underlying sukūn that it carries as a marker of the fem. is taken into consideration. The counterpart of رَمَتَا and دَعَتَا in which the 3rd weak radical is elided is قُولَا "say!" in which the 2nd radical *w* is retained (for discussions see (289)).

(305) يَعْفُوْنَ from عَفَا underlyingly عَفَوَ "to be obliterated", can apply to both the 3rd person of the masc. and the fem. pl. of the imperfect. The base form of the 3rd person of the fem. pl. has the *-na* marker of the fem. pl. suffixed to it and is formed according to يَفْعُلْنَ, i.e. يَعْفُوْنَ, whereas the base form of the 3rd person of the masc. pl. has the ending *-ūna* that marks the masc. pl. suffixed to it, and is formed according to يَفْعُلُونَ, i.e. يَعْفُوُونَ. It can be noted that in يَعْفُوْنَ that refers to the 3rd person of the fem. pl., the *ū* is the 3rd radical and the *-na* is the marker of the fem., whereas in يَعْفُونَ that refers to the masc. pl., the *ū* is the suffixed agent pronoun of the 3rd person of the masc. pl. on account that the 3rd radical *w* is elided from the base form يَعْفُوُون and the *-na* is the marker of the indicative. The *-na* of the indicative is dropped in the 3rd person of the masc. pl. in the case of the subjunctive, e.g. the sur. 2: 237 (وَأَن تَعْفُوا أَقْرَبُ لِلتَّقْوَى) "And the remission (of the man's half) is the nearest to righteousness", and in the case of the jussive as a marker for these moods. For a study see Ḥarīrī, *Šarḥ* 257, Zamaḫšarī, *Kaššāf I*, 374-375, Howell, *II-III*, 16-17, Daqr, *Muʿǧam* 47.

(306) As a rule the 3rd radical *y* or *w* of the verb with 3rd weak radical is elided in the jussive as a marker of this mood. The reason of this elision is that the weak 3rd radical holds the same position as the vowel of the strong verb. As the strong verb's 3rd radical loses its vowel and carries the sukūn as the marker of this mood, e.g. لَمْ يَضْرِبْ "he did not hit", the verb with weak 3rd radical loses its weak radical, e.g. لَمْ يَرْمِ (for its paradigm see (302)). Anomalous cases occur however in which the weak 3rd radical is retained (for discussions see (51)).

(307) According to Ibn Masʿūd, the *y* in يَسْرِي is elided in وَٱلَّيْلِ إِذَا يَسْرِ (cf. Ibn Ǧinnī, *Sirr II*, 519, *Munṣif II*, 74, Ibn al-Sarrāǧ, *Uṣūl II*, 389, Ibn Yaʿīš, *Mulūkī* 384, Åkesson, *Elision* 24) in spite of the fact that the verb is in the indicative, as a marker of the pause (for general discussions concerning the pause see Sībawaihi, *II*, 326-330, Zamaḫšarī, 160-163, Ibn Yaʿīš, *IX*, 66-90, Howell, *IV*, fasc. I, 772-873). Another variant is يَسْرْ (cf. Ibn Ǧinnī, *Sirr II*, 471) with the *y* elided and the sukūn given to the 2nd radical *r*. According to Zamaḫšarī, *Kaššāf IV*, 249, the *y* in يَسْرِي is elided in context in the course of the reading resulting in يَسْرِ, and that it and its kasra are elided as marking the pause. According to Ibn Muǧāhid, *Sabʿa* 683-684, Ibn ʿĀmir, ʿĀṣim, Ḥamza and al-Kisāʾī read يَسْرِ without a *y* in context, and not in pause. Ibn Katīr read it with a *y* in both context and pause. Nāfiʿ read it with a *y* in context and without a *y* in the pause. Abū ʿAmr read it يَسْرْ as a jussive in both the cases of the context and pause (cf. Ibn Ḫālawaihi, *Qirāʾāt II*, 476). Al-Farrāʾ, *Maʿānī III*, 260 prefers the reading with the elision of the *y* and with the kasra preceding it being maintained (cf. Rāǧiḥī, *Farrāʾ* 45). Similar to the reading وَٱلَّيْلِ إِذَا يَسْرِ with the 3rd radical *y* elided and the *r* given a kasra, is the reading of some of both the sur. 18: 64 (ذَلِكَ مَا كُنَّا نَبْغِ) "That was what we were seeking after" (cf. Ibn Ǧinnī, *Munṣif II*, 74, Ibn Yaʿīš, *Mulūkī* 384), in which نَبْغِ is said instead of نَبْغِي, and the sur. 13: 9 (ٱلْكَبِيرُ ٱلْمُتَعَال) "He is the Great, the most High" (cf. Ibn Ǧinnī, *Sirr II*, 519, Ibn al-Sarrāǧ, *Uṣūl II*, 376), in which ٱلْمُتَعَال is said instead of ٱلْمُتَعَالِي. Similar to the reading وَٱلَّيْلِ إِذَا يَسْرْ with the *r* vowelless in يَسْرْ, is the reading of some of the sur. 18: 64 (ذَلِكَ مَا كُنَّا نَبْغْ) "That was what we were seeking after" (cf. Ibn Ǧinnī, *Sirr II*, 471). Likewise, يَفْرِ or يَفْرْ with the elision of the *y* and the 2nd radical made vowelless in pause or being vowelled by a kasra, occurs in the verse said by Zuhair, *Dīwān* 813, cited by Sībawaihi, *II*, 316, 327, Ibn Ǧinnī, *Sirr II*, 47, 520, *Munṣif II*, 74, 232, Zamaḫšarī, 162, Ibn Yaʿīs, *IX*, 79, Šinqīṭī, *Durar II*, 233, Howell, *IV*, fasc. I, 832, Ahlwardt, *Divans* 82, Freytag, *Hamasae* 821:

"ولأنْتَ تَفْرِي مَا خَلَقْتَ وبعـ ـضُ القَوْمِ يَخْلُق ثمّ لا يَفْرْ".

"You do surely cut out what you have at first measured; while some people measure, and then do not cut out, [i.e. you fulfill the matter which you prepare yourself for while others evaluate the matter and do not set ahead with it]".

There seems to be a tendency that in many anomalous cases of verbs, mostly with 3rd radical *y,* that occur in the imperative and jussive, the vowel of the 2nd radical is made vowelless after that the 3rd weak radical is elided when a pronoun is suffixed to them (cf. Nöldeke, *Grammatik* 10, Rabin, 93 note 16, Fleisch, *Traité II,* 393). An example is وأرْنَا said instead of وأرِنا in the sur. 2: 128 (وأرِنا مَنَاسِكَنَا) "And show us our places for the celebration of (due) rites", which is read with the sukūn of the *r,* i.e. وأرْنَا by Ibn Kaṯīr and al-Sūsī (cf. Baiḍāwī, *Anwār I,* 84). Ibn Muǧāhid, *Sab'a* 170 mentions that Ibn Kaṯīr read it in this manner with the sukūn over the *r* whereas Nāfi', Ḥamza and al-Kisā'ī read it with the vowelling of the *r* by a kasra. According to Zamaḫšarī, *Kaššāf I,* 311, وأرْنَا is read with the *r* made vowelless by some in conformity with فَخْذ "thigh" from فَخِذ (cf. 109), but that this reading is disliked.

b) The 3rd weak radical is not elided in Form V تَجَلَّى in the sur. 92: 1-2 (وَاللَّيْلِ إِذَا يَغْشَى وَالنَّهَارِ إِذَا تَجَلَّى) "By the Night as it conceals (the light); by the day as it appears in glory" in the pause contrarily to its elision in وَاللَّيْلِ إِذَا يَسْرِ. An explanation can be the lightness of the *alif maqṣūra* (cf. Ibn Ya'īš, *Mulūkī* 384) contra the heaviness of the *y*. It can be noted as well that the verb that occurs after إذا is not a jussive in spite of the fact that it can, as in the example وَاللَّيْلِ إِذَا يَسْرِ mentioned above, resemble one. In very rare cases, due to metric exigency, إذا can seem to govern the verb in the jussive. This occurs in the following verse said by 'Abd al-Qais b. Ḫaffāf, cited by Daqr, *Mu'ǧam* 6, Barrānī, *Maṭālib* 97, Carter, *Širbīnī* 146, Åkesson, *Elision* 24, in which the jussive Form IV تُصِبْكَ is used instead of the indicative تُصِيبُكَ:

"استَغْنِ ما أغناك ربُّك بالغِنى وإذا تُصِبْكَ خَصاصةٌ فتجمَّلِ".

"Be satisfied with what God has provided you of wealth, and if poverty falls upon you, be patient!".

c) The suffix pronoun of the 2nd person of the fem. sing. of the agent, the *ī,* is elided in the imperative, and the sukūn is given to the last consonant in pause anomalously in a strong verb of Form V تَكَلَّمْ used instead of تَكَلَّمِي "talk!" in the following part of a verse said by 'Antara, *Dīwān* 183, cited by Sībawaihi, *II,* 329, Ibn Ǧinnī, *Sirr II,* 520, Ibn al-Sarrāǧ, *Uṣūl II,* 391, Tibrīzī, *Qaṣā'id* 264, Åkesson, *Elision* 26:

"يا دارَ عَبْلَةَ بالجِواءِ تَكَلَّمْ"

"O abode of 'Abla in al-Ǧiwā', speak!".

d) Likewise, the suffix pronoun of the 3rd person of the masc. pl. of the agent, the *ū,* is elided in the perfect, and the sukūn is given to the last consonant in pause anomalously in a strong verb of Form I صَنَعْ used instead of صَنَعُوا in the following verse said by Tamīm, *Dīwān* 168, cited by Sībawaihi, *II,* 328, Ibn Ǧinnī, *Sirr II,* 520, Zamaḫšarī, 162, Ibn Ya'īš, *IX,* 78, 79, Ibn al-Sarrāǧ, *Uṣūl II,* 390, Howell, *IV,* fasc. I, 835, Åkesson, *Elision* 26:

"لا يُبْعِدِ اللهُ أصحاباً تَرَكْتُهُمُ   لم أدْرِ بَعْدَ غَداةَ البَيْنِ ما صَنَعْ".

"May God not curse friends whom I have left, not knowing, after the morning of separation, what they have done!".

Compare with this case the elision of the *ū* and the 3rd radical given a ḍamma in كَانُ said instead of كَانُوا "they were", in the verse cited in (45):...فَلَو أنَّ آلأطِبَّا كَانُ حَوْلِي "O, if the physicians had been around me"..., and the examples following it. See further for the shortening of a long vowel in the middle and at the end of the word some cases illustrated by Wright, *IV,* 383-384.

(308) تَنصب means that you give the fatḥa as a marker of the subjunctive mood or that you govern the verb in the subjunctive mood. The two other terms that concern the verb's inflection is تَرفع which means that you give the ḍamma as a marker of the indicative mood or you govern the verb in the indicative mood, and تجزم which means that you give the sukūn as a marker of the jussive mood, or you govern the verb in the jussive mood. The base form of لَنْ يَخْشَى is لَنْ يَخْشَيَ in which the 3rd radical vowelled *y* is changed into an *alif maqṣūra* due to the influence of the fatḥa preceding it. According to Ibn Masʿūd's theory the *alif maqṣūra* is not vowelled by a fatḥa in the case of the subjunctive because it cannot take the vowel. Another theory that can be added is that the marker of the subjunctive is assumed to be upon the *alif maqṣūra* (cf. Howell, *II-III,* 14).

(309) In the active participle of verbs with 3rd radical *y,* the 3rd radical is elided and the *tanwīn* replaces the kasra of 2nd radical, e.g. رامٍ for both the nominative رامِيٌ and the genitive رامِيٍ (cf. Wright, *II,* 90, my notes (292)). The reason why the *y* is made vowelless, namely رامِي, and is then elided in both these cases, is the heaviness of both the ḍamma or the kasra vowelling it. It is not elided in the accusative, i.e. رامِياً because, as Ibn Masʿūd states, the fatḥa, by which he means the nunation with fatḥa, that vowels the *y* is light.

(3**10)** In the passive participle of verbs with 3rd radical *y,* the infixed *ū* of the مَفْعُول preceding the 3rd radical *y,* is influenced by it and changed into it, and consequently the preceding ḍamma that vowels the 2nd radical becomes a kasra (cf. Howell, *IV,* fasc. I, 1543, de Sacy, *I,* 108, Wright, *II,* 91, Vernier, *I,* 340-341). An example is مَرْمُوْيٌ that becomes مَرْمِيٌّ.

(311) In Form IV أغْزَيْتُ "I attacked", the vowelless *y* is substituted for the *w* of the base form أغْزَوْتُ on the analogy of the imperfect Form IV يُغْزِي "he attacks" underlyingly يُغْزِوُ (for discussions see (262)).

(312) The consonants comprised in the expression إسْتَنْجَدَهُ يَوْمَ صالَ زُطٌّ "he asked him for succour on the day some Zuṭṭ (a race of Hindus) attacked" that starts with the hamza and ends with the *ṭ,* are the consonants of substitution (cf. Zamaḫšarī, 172, Ibn Yaʿīš, *X,* 7-8, Ḥarīrī, *Séances* 646, Howell, *IV,* fasc. I, 1192-1193, Fleischer, *Beiträge* 112, Åkesson, *Conversion*

27). It is this passage of the *Marāḥ* that drew De Sacy's attention and incited him to refer to Ibn Mas'ūd in his *Grammaire I,* 33, as mentioned in my Introduction p. 7. Other phrases containing less consonants are combined by some grammarians: eleven as طَوِيتَ مِنْهَا أجدْ "do well (mayst thou be destroyed for it)", thirteen as استَنْجَدَهُ يَوْمَ طَالَ "he asked him for succour on a day that was long", fourteen as جَدٌ أنْصَتَ يَوْمَ زَلَ طَاه "a grandfather was silent on the day a cook slipped", and أنْصِتْ يَوْمَ جَدُ طاه زَلَ "be silent on the day the grandfather of Ṭāh [sc. a man's name] has slipped" (cf. Howell, *IV,* fasc. I, 1191-1192). According to their order in the phrase إسْتَنْجَدَهُ يَوْمَ صَالَ زُطٌ these consonants are: 1- the hamza, 2- the *s,* 3- the *t,* 4- the *n,* 5- the *ğ,* 6- the *d,* 7- the *h,* 8- the *y,* 9- the *w,* 10- the *m,* 10- the *ṣ,* 11- the *ā,* 12- the *l,* 13- the *ẓ* and the 14- *ṭ.* For a study of the substitution see Sībawaihi, *II,* 340-342, Ibn Ǧinnī, *de Flexione* 19-30, Ibn 'Uṣfūr, *I,* 319-415, Zamaḫšarī, 172-177, Ibn Ya'īš, *X,* 7-54, Howell, *IV,* fasc. I, 1182-1203. For the substitution occurring in two words following each other resulting in the assimilation of the first word's ultimate consonant to the initial consonant of the second word see my notes (173, b).

(313) The hamza in صَحْرَاءُ is substituted for the alif of the feminine form (cf. Ibn Ǧinnī, *de Flexione* 25, *Sirr I,* 83-84, Ibn 'Uṣfūr, *I,* 329-331, Zamaḫšarī, 172, Ibn Ya'īš, *X,* 9, Howell, *IV,* fasc. I, 1205). The base form is صَحْرَاى with an *alif maqṣūra* preceded by an *ā.* The reason of replacing the *alif maqṣūra* by a hamza is to prevent the cluster of two vowelless consonants, the *ā* and the *alif maqṣūra.*

(314) سَكْرَى formed according to the form فَعْلَى, is the fem. sing.of سَكْرَانُ "drunk" formed according to the epithet of the form فَعْلاَنُ. Its broken pls. can be of the form فِعَالٌ, فَعَالَى or فَعْلاَءُ. Cf. Howell, *I,* fasc. III, 1016-1017, Nöldeke, *Beiträge* 53.

(315) The broken pl. of صَحْرَاءُ "desert" is صَحَارَى (for it see (269 b)) or صَحَارٍ. The variant صَحَارِئُ with the hamza retained is not existent, which proves that the hamza does not belong to the base form (cf. Ibn Ǧinnī, *Sirr I,* 85). Contrarily to it, خَطِيئَةٌ "sin" occurs with the hamza of the 3rd radical retained, which proves that its 3rd radical is a hamza. Another possibility concerning it is خَطِيَّةٌ with the hamza changed into a *y* and then assimilated to the infixed *ī* of the pattern فَعِيلَةٌ (for this assimilation see (225); compare the pl. form suffixed to the pronoun of the genitive of the 1st person of the sing. خَطَائِئِي "my sins" with two hamzas that are combined together used instead of خَطَايَايَ discussed in (228 b)). The base form of the broken pl. of صَحَارَى is صَحَارِيُّ (cf. Ibn Ǧinnī, *Munṣif I,* 158, Nöldeke, *Beiträge* 53 in the notes, Howell, *I,* fasc. III, 9969). الصَّحَارِيَا occurs in the following verse said by al-Walīd b. Yazīd b. 'Abd al-Malik b. Marwān, cited by Ibn Ǧinnī, *Sirr I,* 86, Ibn Ya'īš, *V,* 58, *Mulūkī* 269, Ibn 'Uṣfūr, *I,* 330, Baġdādī, *Ḫizāna III,* 324, *Šarḥ* 95, Ibn al-Anbārī, *Inṣāf* Q. 118, 345, Howell, *I,* fasc. III, 996:

"لَقَدْ أغْدُو علَى أشْقَرَ   يَجْتَابُ الصَّحَارِيَا".

"Assuredly I sometimes go forth in the early morning upon a sorrel that traverses the deserts".

A noun on the same pattern as صَحْرَاءُ is عَذْرَاءُ "maiden". Its pl. is عذَارَى or عذَارِ and its base form is عَذَارِيُّ.

(316) The pl. of وَاصِلَةٌ "joining" is أواصِلُ underlyingly وَوَاصِلُ (for a study see Zamaḫšarī, 172, Ibn Yaʿīš, *X,* 10, Ibn ʿAqīl, *II,* 552, Howell, *IV,* fasc. I, 1218-1222, Fleisch, *Traité I,* 152, ʿAbd al-Tawwāb, *Taṭawwur* 41) that is formed according to the measure فَوَاعِلُ. In وَوَاصِلُ, the 1st radical *w* that is vowelled by a fatḥa is changed into a hamza to prevent the heavy combination of the wāws. Another example that can be added is the pl. أوَاقٍ underlyingly وَوَاقٍ, of the sing. وَاقِيَةٌ "preserver". ٱلأَوَاقِي occurs in the following verse said by Muhalhil Abī Lailā ʿAdī b. Rabīʿa al-Taġlibī, the brother of Kulaib b. Rabīʿa. It is cited by Ibn Ǧinnī, *Sirr II,* 800, *Munṣif I,* 218, Zamaḫšarī, 172, Ibn Yaʿīš, *X,* 10, Ibn ʿAqīl, *II,* 263, Ibn Hišām, *Šuḏūr* 42, Ibn Manẓūr, *VI,* 4901, al-Šartūnī, the commentator of Farḥāt, *Baḥṯ* 242 in the notes, Howell, *I,* fasc. I, 162, Wright, *IV,* 388:

"ضَرَبَتْ صَدْرَهَا إليَ وَقَالَتْ   يَا عَدِيًا لَقَدْ وَقَتْكَ ٱلأَوَاقِي".

"She smote her bosom marvelling at me [i.e. at mine escape], and said,
O ʿAdī, assuredly the preservers have preserved thee!".

The hamza is not substituted for the 1st radical *w* if the 2nd *w* replaces the infix *ā* of فَاعَلَ, as the passive voice of Form III وُورِيَ formed according to فُوعِلَ that has the active voice وَارَى, which occurs in the sur. 7: 20 (وُورِيَ عَنْهُمَا) "That was hidden from them". The reason of the substitution of the 2nd *w* for the *ā* of فَاعَلَ is the influence of the ḍamma preceding it.

Contrary to the substitution of the hamza for the *w* vowelled by a fatḥa at the initial of the word is the substitution of the *w* for the hamza vowelled by a fatḥa. An example is وَبَاكَ said instead of أبَاكَ "your father" in هُوَ يَضْرِبُ وَبَاكَ "he hits your father", and in وَخَاكَ for أخَاكَ "your brother" in هُوَ يَقْتُلُ وَخَاكَ "he kills your brother" (for these examples and others see Ibn Ǧinnī, *Sirr II,* 573-574). Note in this context the connexion between the *ʾa* in أرَّخَ "to date" and the *wa* in ወርኅ *warḫ* "month" in Ethiopic (cf. Wright, *Comparative Grammar* 71).

(317) قَائِلٌ is the active participle of the verb with 2nd *w* radical قَوَلَ. The hamza in قَائِلٌ is substituted for the the 2nd radical *w* (cf. Zamaḫšarī, 172, 180, Ibn Yaʿīš, *X,* 10, Ibn ʿUṣfūr, *I,* 327-329, Howell, *IV,* fasc. I, 1209-1210), i.e. قَاوِلٌ (cf. 290)). The change of the 2nd radical into a hamza is carried out to accord with its verb in which the 2nd radical is changed into an *ā*, i.e. قَالَ is underlyingly قَوَلَ. There exist opposite cases in which the 2nd radical is sound, e.g. the active participle عَاوِرٌ with the *w* as 2nd radical and عَايِنٌ with the *y* as 2nd radical. These examples accord with their verbs عَوِرَ "to be blind of one eye" and عَيِنَ "to be large in the eye" respectively, in which the 2nd radical is sound from fear of confusing them with عَارَ "rendered blind of one eye" and عَانَ "to smote with the evil eye".

(318) أَدْؤُرٌ (cf. Sībawaihi, *II,* 341, Ibn Ǧinnī, *Sirr I,* 98, *de Flexione* 25, Zamaḫšarī, 172, Ibn ʿUṣfūr, *I,* 335-336, Ibn Yaʿīš, *X,* 10-11, Howell, *IV,* fasc. I, 1224-1225) is the pl. of دَارٌ. The hamza in it is substituted for the single 2nd radical *w* vowelled by a ḍamma, i.e. أَدْوُرٌ. The reason of the change of the *w* into a hamza is the heaviness of the ḍamma on the *w*. Other examples that can be added are أَثْؤُبٌ underlyingly أَثْوُبٌ being the pl. of ثَوْبٌ "raiment" and أَنْؤُرٌ underlyingly أَنْوُرٌ being the pl. of نَارٌ "fire". أَنْؤُرٌ occurs in the following verse said by ʿUmar b. Abī Rabīʿa, *Dīwān* 88, cited by Ibn Ǧinnī, *Sirr II,* 804, Ibn Yaʿīš, *X,* 11, Howell, *IV,* fasc. I, 1224:

"فَلَمَّا فَقَدتُ الصَّوتَ مِنْهُمْ وَأُطْفِئَتْ مَصَابِيحُ شَبَّتْ بِالْعِشَاءِ وَأَنْؤُرُ".

"And when I lost the sound of them; and lamps that burned brightly at nightfall, and fires, were extinguished".

b) The hamza can be substituted for the *w* that is combined with another *w* (cf. Ibn Ǧinnī, *de Flexione* 25, *Sirr I,* 98, Ibn ʿUṣfūr, *I,* 335-336, Zamaḫšarī, 172, Ibn Yaʿīš, *X,* 10-11, Howell, *IV,* fasc. I, 1224-1225), e.g. سُؤُوقٌ underlyingly سُوُوقٌ that is the pl. of سَاقٌ "shank", and غُؤُورٌ underlyingly غُوُورٌ that is the *maṣdar* of غَارَ "to sink".

(319) The hamza of كِسَاءٌ replaces the 3rd radical *w* (cf. Ibn ʿUṣfūr, *I,* 326, Zamaḫšarī, 172, Ibn Yaʿīš, *X,* 9-10, Ibn al-Anbārī, *Maqṣūr* 48, Howell, *IV,* fasc. I, 1203-1204, Mokhlis, *Taṣrīf* 195, my notes (290)) of the base form كِسَاوٌ. The different vowels that can be given to the *w* which would cause a heaviness in the pronunciation, are those of the declension, i.e. the vowel of the nominative, the accusative or the genitive. The hamza replaces as well the 3rd radical *y* for the same reason, e.g. ظِبَاءٌ "gazelles" underlyingly ظِبَايٌ, and فَنَاءٌ "evanescence" underlyingly فَنَايٌ.

(320) بَائِعٌ is the active participle of the verb with 2nd radical *y* بَيَعَ. The hamza in it is substituted for the 2nd radical *y* (cf. Zamaḫšarī, 172, 180, Ibn Yaʿīš, *X,* 10, Ibn ʿUṣfūr, *I,* 327-329, Howell, *IV,* fasc. I, 1209-1210, Mokhlis, *Taṣrīf* 195) of the base form بَايِعٌ. In this example, the unsoundness is carried out by changing its weak 2nd radical into a hamza to accord with its verb in which the 2nd radical *y* is changed into an *ā*, i.e. بَيَعَ that becomes بَاعَ (for the change in the verb see Åkesson, *Conversion* 27).

(321) The base form of أُجُوهٌ is وُجُوهٌ (cf. Sībawaihi, *II,* 341, Ibn Ǧinnī, *de Flexione* 25, *Sirr I,* 92, Ibn ʿUṣfūr, *I,* 332, Zamaḫšarī, 172, Ibn Yaʿīš, *X,* 10-11, Howell, *IV,* fasc. I, 1224-1225), which is the pl. of وَجْهٌ "face" from وَجُهَ "to be a man of distinction", a verb with 1st radical *w*. In أُجُوهٌ underlyingly وُجُوهٌ, the hamza is substituted for the 1st radical *w* vowelled by a ḍamma.

The dislike of having the *w* vowelled by a ḍamma, which is the reason of its substitution into a hamza, is referred to as well by Sībawaihi, *II,* 391. Another example with this substitution is أقّتت for وُقّتت that occurs in the sur. 77: 11 (وإذا الرُّسُلُ أقّتت) "And when the apostles are (all) appointed a time (to collect); -". It is anomalously read with وُقّتت instead by Abū ʿAmr whereas the remaining six readers read it with أقّتت (cf. Ibn Ḫālawaihi, *Qirāʾāt II,* 428).

(322) The hamza in إشاحٌ is substituted for the 1st radical *w* (cf. Sībawaihi, *II,* 341) vowelled by a kasra of the base form وِشاحٌ. This substitution occurs in the Huḏailī dialect. Some other examples are إسادةٌ "cushion" for وِسادةٌ and إفادةٌ "embassy" for وِفادةٌ. Tamīm b. Abī Muqbil has إفادةٌ instead of وِفادةٌ in the following verse cited by Sībawaihi, *II,* 392, Ibn Ǧinnī, *Sirr I,* 102, Ibn Yaʿīš, *X,* 14, *Mulūkī* 274, Ibn Manẓūr, *VI,* 4881, Howell, *IV,* fasc. I, 1229:

"أمّا ٱلإفادةُ فاسْتَوْلَتْ رِكابُها عِنْدَ ٱلجَبابِيرِ بِالْبَأْسَاءِ والنِّعَمِ".

"As for the embassy, its cavalcades got hold sometimes of misfortune, and sometimes of favors, in the presence of the tyrants".

Saʿīd b. Ǧubair read the sur. 12: 76 (إعاءِ أخيه) "the baggage of his brother" for وِعاءِ أخيه (cf. Ibn Ǧinnī, *Sirr I,* 102, Zamaḫšarī, 172). Zamaḫšarī, 172-173 notes that al-Māzinī considered this substitition of the *w* vowelled by the kasra by the hamza, as *qiyās.* Qudāma, *Naqd* 48 discusses this substitution as a general principle. See further Ibn Yaʿīš, *X,* 14, Fleisch, *Traité I,* 135-136. Note in this context the connexion between وَصْلٌ and אָצִיל "joint" in Hebrew (cf. Wright, *Comparative Grammar* 71).

(323) It is related in a tradition that Muḥammad said to a man أحِّدْ أحِّدْ instead of وَحِّدْ وَحِّدْ (cf. Rāzī in Ḫalīl b. Aḥmad ..., *Ḥurūf* 137 in the note, Zamaḫšarī, 172, Ibn Yaʿīš, *X,* 14-15, Ibn Manẓūr, *VI,* 4782, Howell, *IV,* fasc. I, 1230, ʿAbd al-Tawwāb, *Fuṣūl* (1st edition) 108-110) with the substitution of the hamza for the *w* vowelled by a fatḥa, when he saw him making the sign with his two forefingers in reciting the creed.

(324) The hamza is substituted for the initial *y* vowelled by a fatḥa in أدَيه that occurs instead of the base form يَدَيه (cf. Ibn ʿUṣfūr, *I,* 346-347, Zamaḫšarī, 173, Ibn Yaʿīš, *X,* 15, Ibn Manẓūr, *VI,* 4951, Vernier, *I,* 346, Howell, *IV,* fasc. I, 1231). The reason of this substitution is the heaviness of the fatḥa that vowels the *y*. It can be noted that أدْيه with the *d* being vowelless instead of أدَيه is printed by Howell, *IV,* fasc. I, 1231 and commented on in *IV,* fasc. I, 111A. For a study concerning يَدٌ in some of the Semitic languages see Nöldeke, *Neue Beiträge* 113-116. ألَلٌ "a shortness of the upper teeth" is also said with this particular substitution of the hamza for the initial *y* vowelled by a fatḥa, instead of يَلَلٌ.

(325) ماهٌ "water" is from the root مَوَه "to mix", a verb with 2nd *w* radical. The *h* in it is substituted by the hamza, so that it became ماءٌ (cf. Ibn Ǧinnī, *Sirr I,* 100-101, Ibn ʿUṣfūr, *I,*

348-351, Zamaḫšarī, 173, Ibn Yaʿīš, *X,* 15-16, Howell, *IV,* fasc. I, 1232-1235; for a study of مِيَاه in the Semitic languages see Nöldeke, *Neue Beiträge*166-170). Its pl. form is مِيَاهٌ and its diminutive is مُوَيْهٌ (cf. Ibn Manẓūr, *VI,* 4302). Another pl. form is أَمْوَاهٌ in which the *h* is as well substituted by the hamza so that it became أَمْوَاءٌ. The reason of this substitution is that the points of articulation of the hamza and the *h* are identical, as they both originate from the farthest part of the throat, and are laryngals (for the consonants see (188)). أَمْوَاؤُهَا occurs in the following verse recited by Ibn Ǧinnī which he heard from Abū ʿAlī, and is cited by Ibn Ǧinnī, *Sirr I,* 100, *Munṣif II,* 151, Zamaḫšarī, 173, Ibn Yaʿīš, *X,* 15, Ibn ʿUṣfūr, *I,* 348, Ibn Manẓūr, *VI,* 4302, Baġdādī, *Šarḥ* 437, Howell, *IV,* fasc. I, 1233:

"وَبَلْدَةٍ قَالِصَةٍ أَمْوَاؤُهَا مَاصِحَةٍ رَأْدَ ٱلضُّحَى أَفْيَاؤُهَا".

"And many a land, whose waters were exhausted, and whose shades were passing away in the part of the noon when the sun was hight".

(326) The active participle Form VIII ٱلْمُشْتَئِقْ (in pause), from شَوَقَ "to desire", a verb with 2nd radical *w,* occurs anomalously instead of ٱلْمُشْتَاقْ, with the substitution of the hamza for the *ā,* so that the vowelled hamza corresponds to the 3rd radical of the foot مُسْتَفْعِلُنْ in the verse. The reason of this substitution is that the points of articulation of the hamza and the *ā* are identical, as they both originate from the farthest part of the throat, and are laryngals (for the consonants see (188)). According to Baġdādī, *Šarḥ* 175, Ibn al-Mustawfā said that the verse was recited by al-Farrāʾ to Ruʾba. Also ٱلْمُشْتَأَقْ has been transmitted instead of ٱلْمُشْتَئِقْ. The verse is cited by Ibn Ǧinnī, *Sirr I,* 91, *Ḫaṣāʾiṣ III,* 145, Zamaḫšarī, 172, Ibn Yaʿīš, *X,* 12-13, Ibn Manẓūr, *II,* 1405, *IV,* 2361, Howell, *IV,* fasc. I, 1227. It runs as follows:

"يَا دَارَ مَيَّ بِٱلدَّكَادِيكِ ٱلْبُرَقْ صَبْرًا فَقَدْ هَيَّجْتِ شَوْقَ ٱلْمُشْتَئِقْ".

"O abode of Mayya [sc. a woman's name] in the low-lying sands, sands mixed with stones and earth, give me patience, for you have excited the yearning of the yearner".

(327) The hamza in ٱلضَّأَلِّينَ of this sur. is substituted for the *ā* of the base form ٱلضَّالِّينَ. It is said that ٱلضَّأَلِّينَ has been read with this substitution by Ayyūb al-Siḫtiyānī (cf. Ibn Ǧinnī, *Sirr I,* 72, *Ḫaṣāʾiṣ III,* 147, *Muḥtasib I,* 46, Ibn Ḫālawaihi, *Qirāʾāt I,* 52, Zamaḫšarī, *Kaššāf I,* 73, Ibn Yaʿīš, *IX,* 130, Ibn ʿUṣfūr, *I,* 320). In the same manner, al-ʿAǧǧāǧ, *Dīwān* 289 (the 1st half of the verse) and 299 (the 2nd), said ٱلْعَأْلَمِ instead of ٱلْعَالَمِ with the substitution of the hamza for the *ā* in the following verse cited as well by Ibn Ǧinnī, *Sirr I,* 90, Ibn Ḫālawaihi, *Qirāʾāt II,* 153, Zamaḫšarī, 172, Howell, *IV,* fasc. I, 1227:

"يَا دَارَ سَلْمَى يَا ٱسْلَمِي ثُمَّ ٱسْلَمِي فَخِنْدِفٌ هَامَةُ هَذَا ٱلْعَأْلَمِ".

"O abode of Salmā, O hail, again hail! Then Ḫindif is the head of this world".

ابْأَضَّ occurs instead of ابْيَاضَّ with this substitution in the following verse said by Dukain, cited by Ibn Ǧinnī, *Sirr I,* 74, *Ḫaṣāʾiṣ III,* 148, *Muḥtasib I,* 320, Luġawī, *Ibdāl II,* 545, Ibn

ʿUṣfūr, *I,* 321, *Ḍarāʾir* 222, Ibn Manẓūr, *I,* 704, Howell, *IV,* fasc. I, 1226:

"وَحَلْبُهُ حَتَّى ٱبْيَأَضَ مِلْبَنُهُ".

"And his milking was until his milk-pail became white".

فَادْهَأَمَّتْ occurs instead of فَادْهَامَّتْ with this substitution in the following verse said by Kuṯayyir, *Dīwān* 323 from his elegy of ʿAbd al-ʿAzīz b. Marwān. It is cited by Ibn Ǧinnī, *Sirr I,* 74, Zamaḫšarī, *Fāʾiq I,* 462, Ibn ʿUṣfūr, *I,* 322, Baġdādī, *Šarḥ IV,* 170, Howell, *IV,* fasc. I, 1226. Ibn Ǧinnī, *Ḫaṣāʾiṣ III,* 127, 148 has فَاسْوَأَدَّتْ instead of فَادْهَأَمَّتْ:

"وَلِلْأَرْضِ أَمَّا سُودُهَا فَتَجَلَّلَتْ بَيَاضاً وَأَمَّا بِيضُهَا فَادْهَأَمَّتِ".

"And at the land when such that, as for its blacks they have clothed themselves in whiteness, and as for its whites, they have become black".

The substitution of the hamza for the *ā* occurs curiously enough in the speech of some in pause, as in the example رَأَيْتُ رَجُلأْ "I saw a man" (cf. Talmon, *ʿAyn* 217, Ibn Ǧinnī, *Munṣif I,* 150), that is said instead of رَأَيْتُ رَجُلاً, with the vowelless hamza in رَجُلأْ replacing the *ā* given the nunation that is the marker of the indefinite accusative in رجلاً.

b) Contrary to the substitution of the hamza for the *ā* is the substitution of the *ā* for the hamza. This occurs in Ibn Kaṯīr's reading of the sur. 27: 44 (وَكَشَفَتْ عَنْ سَاقَيْهَا) "And she (tucked up her skirts), uncovering her legs", with سَأْقَيْهَا read instead (cf. Ibn Ǧinnī, *Ḫaṣāʾiṣ III,* 145, Ibn Ḫālawaihi, *Qirāʾāt II,* 152), and in ʿAmr b. ʿUbaid's reading of the sur. 55: 39 (فَيَوْمَئِذٍ لَا يُسْأَلُ عَنْ ذَنْبِهِ إِنْسٌ وَلَا جَانٌّ) "On that day no question will be asked of man or Jinn as to his sin", with جَأنٌّ read instead (cf. Ibn Ḫālawaihi, *Qirāʾāt I,* 53, Ibn Manẓūr, *I,* 704, Ibn Yaʿīš, *X,* 13, Ibn ʿUṣfūr, *I,* 321).

c) The *w* is pronounced with a hamza anomalously, as if it is substituted for the *w* in الْمُؤْقِدِينَ for الْمُوقِدِينَ and مُؤْسَى for مُوسَى in the following verse said by Ǧarīr, *Dīwān* 288, who is expressing his love to both his children Mūsā and Ǧaʿda in a poem in which he is praising Hišām b. ʿAbd al-Malik. It is cited by Ibn Ǧinnī, *Sirr I,* 79, *Munṣif I,* 311, *II,* 203, *Ḫaṣāʾiṣ II,* 175, *III,* 146, 149, 219, Afandī, *Tanzīl* 365, Ibn Hišām, *Muġnī II,* 684, Ibn ʿUṣfūr, *I,* 91, *II,* 203, Howell, *IV,* fasc. I, 1230-1231, de Sacy, *Anthologie* [Baiḍāwī, *Tanzīl]* 17:

"أَحَبُّ ٱلْمُؤْقِدِينَ إِلَيَّ مُؤْسَى وَجَعْدَةُ إِذْ أَضَاءَهُمَا ٱلْوُقُودُ".

"Assuredly very dear to me are the two kindlers [of fire], Mūsā and his sister Ǧaʿda, when the blaze [of generosity] has lighted them up".

Zamaḫšarī, *Kaššāf I,* 138 has لحب المُؤقدان instead. He cites the following verse in his commentary to the sur. 2: 4 (وَمَا أُنْزِلَ مِنْ قَبْلِكَ وَبِالْآخِرَةِ هُمْ يُوقِنُونَ) "And sent before thy time, and (in their hearts) have the assurance of the Hereafter", in which يُوقِنُونَ is read as يُؤْقِنُونَ by Abū Ḥayya al-Numairī (cf. also Ibn Hišām, Muġnī *II,* 684). According to Afandī, *Tanzīl* 365, who refers to Abū ʿAlī who has heard it from al-Aḫfaš, it is known that Abū Ḥayya al-Numairī used to give a hamza to each vowelless *w* that is preceded by a consonant vowelled by ḍamma.

بالسُّؤق has been read for بالسُّوق by Ibn Kaṯīr of the sur. 38: 32 (بالسُّوقِ والأَعْنَاقِ) "Over (their) legs and their necks". Ibn Ǧinnī, *Sirr I,* 79, Makkī, *Kašf II,* 160, Ibn al-Ǧazarī, *Našr III,* 227-228 refer however to the reading of Qunbul. Zamaḫšarī, *Kaššāf III,* 374 compares the reading بالسُّؤق with مُؤسَى mentioned above.

(328) أُبَابٌ occurs instead of عُبَابٌ with the substitution of the hamza for the ʿ. The reason of this substitution is the closeness of the points of articulation of the hamza and ʿ, as the hamza originates from the farthest part of the throat and is a laryngal and the ʿ originates from the middle of the throat and is a pharyngal (for the consonants see (188)). This theory of the substitution concerning it is however criticized by Ibn Ǧinnī, *Sirr I,* 106, who does not consider the hamza to be substituted for the ʿ, but that the form is فُعَالٌ of أَبَّ "to prepare itself". His remark is also mentioned by Ibn Manẓūr, *I,* 4. أُبَابٌ occurs in the following verse cited by Ibn Ǧinnī, *Sirr I,* 106, Zamaḫšarī, 173, Ibn Yaʿīš, *X,* 15, Ibn ʿUṣfūr, *I,* 352, Baġdādī, *Šarḥ* 432, Howell, *IV,* fasc. I, 1235:

"وَمَاجَ سَاعَاتٍ مَلَا ٱلْوَدِيقِ أُبَابُ بَحْرٍ ضَاحِكٍ زَهُوقِ".

"And the deserts of intense heats were agitated at times, like a billow of a laughing, far-extending sea".

هَزُوقٍ instead of زَهُوقٍ has been transmitted by both Ibn Ǧinnī, *Sirr I,* 106 and Ibn Manẓūr, *I,* 4.

b) Compare the opposite case of the ʿ which replaces the hamza that is the initial consonant, e.g. عَنَّكَ for أَنَّكَ "that you" in the dialectal variant of Qais and Tamīm known as العَنْعَنَةُ (cf. Suyūṭī, *Muzhir I,* 133). Ibn Yaʿīš, *X,* 8, Åkesson, *Verb and Infinitive* 35 note 2, cite the following verse of Maǧnūn, *Dīwān* 207 in which عَنَّ replaces أَنَّ:

"فَعَيْنَاكِ عَيْنَاهَا وَجِيدُكِ جِيدُهَا سِوَى عَنَّ عَظْمَ ٱلسَّاقِ مِنْكِ دَقِيقُ".

"Then your two eyes are her two eyes, and your neck is her neck; but the bone of your shank is slender".

Ibn Fāris, *Ṣāḥibī* 53, Ibn Ǧinnī, *Sirr I,* 229, *Ḫaṣā'iṣ II,* 11, Ibn Yaʿīš, *Mulūkī* 216, Ibn ʿUṣfūr, *I,* 413, Ibn Manẓūr, *IV,* 3200, De Sacy, *Anthololologie* [the commentary to Baiḍāwī, *Anwār*] 42 mention the following verse said by Ḏū l-Rumma, *Dīwān* 371 in which أَعَنْ replaces أَأَنْ:

"أَعَنْ تَرَسَّمْتَ مِنْ خَرْقَاءَ مَنْزِلَةً مَاءُ الصَّبَابَةِ مِنْ عَيْنَيْكَ مَسْجُومُ".

"Are you searching for Ḫarqā's abandoned encampment? The water of fervent longing from both your eyes is shedding".

c) Other cases concerning the ʿ being substituted by or for another consonant, which can be added here are:

– The substitution of the ʿ by the *ġ* in the Tamīmī dialectal variant (cf. Ibn Manẓūr, *V,* 4049). This occurs in the following verse said by al-Farazdaq, cited by Ibn al-Anbārī, *Inṣāf* Q. 26, 98, Ibn Manẓūr, *V,* 4049, Howell, *IV,* fasc. I, 1390, *II-III,* 441-443:

"قِفَا يَا صَاحِبَيَّ بِنَا لَغَنَّا نَرَى ٱلْعَرَصَاتِ أَوْ أَثَرَ ٱلْخِيَامِ".

"Tarry, O my two companions, with us: maybe we shall see the courts, or the trace of the booths".

The ġ can be substituted by the ʿ in the dialectal variant of Daṯīna, e.g. عَنَمٌ said instead of غَنَمٌ "sheep" (cf. Jastrow, *Dialekte* 106). This particularity is found as well in the Yemenite dialect (cf. Diem, *Dialekte* 77 sq.). According to Růžička, the ġ in Arabic does not belong to the base form of the word (for his particular theories see Růžička, *Question* 176-237).

– The substitution of the vowelless ʿ when combined with the ṭ by the *n*, e.g. أنْطى for أعْطى "to give" (cf. Suyūṭī, *Muzhir I,* 133-134). This dialect is known as الإسْتِنْطاءُ and is peculiar to the dialect of Saʿd b. Bakr, Huḏail, al-Azd, Yaman, Madīna and Qais (for more details and interesting references see Rabin, 31-33, 54, 126).

– The substitution of the ʿ for the *ḥ,* e.g. عَتّى for حَتّى "until" (cf. Suyūṭī, *Muzhir I,* 133). This dialect is known as القَحْفَحَةُ and is peculiar to the dialect of Huḏail. As an example it can be said that the sur. 12: 35 (حَتّى حين) has been read by the reader of the Qurʾān Ibn Masʿūd as (عَتّى حين) (cf. Ibn Ǧinnī, *Muḥtasib I,* 343, the notes to *Sirr I,* 241, Zamaḫšarī, *Kaššāf II,* 319, Jeffery, *Materials* 49, Rabin, 84). For further discussions see Rabin, 84-86, Rundgren, *Bildungen* 29-32. The opposite case of the *ḥ* being substituted for the ʿ is also found in the dialect of Huḏail (for more details see Rabin, 85-86).

(329) In the case of اسْتَخَذَ, Form VIII اتخذ underlyingly اتْتَخَذَ (compare with it the case of ايتَخَذَ (187 b), (202)), is meant, in which the *s* is substituted for the 1st *t* (cf. Howell, *IV,* fasc. I, 1192). The passage referred to Sībawaihi, is found in Sībawaihi, *II,* 480. The reason why the *t* is changed into the *s* is because they are both among the voiceless consonants (for them see (188 b)). Two theories concerning اسْتَخَذَ are presented by Ibn Manẓūr, *I,* 37, the first one is the one meant by Ibn Masʿūd in this context. As for the second one, it advances the idea that اسْتَخَذَ is formed according to Form X اسْتَفْعَلَ from تَخَذَ يَتْخَذُ, and is presented here for the sake of curiosity. Ibn Manẓūr (ibid) notes that اتَخَذَ could have أخَذَ or تَخَذَ as a root (cf. Sībawaihi, *II,* 480, Ibn Ǧinnī, *Munṣif II,* 329, my notes (202)):

"وَحَكَى المُبَرِّدُ أنَّ بَعضَ الْعَرَبِ يَقُولُ: اسْتَخَذَ فُلانٌ أرْضاً يُريدُ اتخَذَ أرْضاً فَتُبْدِلُ مِنْ إحْدَى التَاءَيْنِ سِيناً كَما أبْدَلُوا التَاءَ مَكانَ السِينِ فِي قَوْلِهِمْ سِتٌ، ويَجُوزُ أنْ يَكُونَ أرادَ اسْتَفْعَلَ مِنْ تَخِذَ يَتْخَذُ فَحَذَفَ إحْدَى التاءَيْنِ تَخْفِيفاً، كَما قالُوا: ظَلْتُ مِنْ ظَلِلْتُ".

"Al-Mubarrad reported that some of the Arabs say: اسْتَخَذَ فُلانٌ أرْضاً "an unnamed person occupied an area", by which he intended [Form VIII] اتَخَذَ أرْضاً, in which one of both the tāʾs is substituted by the *s,* in the same manner as they substituted the *s* for the *t* in their saying ست "six" [(for it see (194), (333)]. It is also possible that they meant اسْتَفْعَلَ [Form X] of تَخِذَ يَتْخَذُ from which they elided one of both the tāʾs for the sake of alleviation, as they said: ظَلْتُ for ظَلِلْتُ "I continued all day" [(for it see (181)]".

(330) The *t* in تُخَمَةٌ "a malady like cholera" replaces the *w* of its base form وُخَمَةٌ. Some other examples in which this substitution is carried out (cf. Ibn Yaʿīš, *X,* 37-39) are: تُجَاهَ "in front of", تَيْقُورٌ "grave", تُكْلَانٌ "incapacity and reliance upon others" (for it see (247)), تُكَلَةٌ "a man incapable, committing his affair to another", تُكَأَةٌ "staff to lean upon", تُهَمَةٌ "suspicion", تَقِيَّةٌ "fear", تَقْوَى "to be cautious" (cf. Ibn Wallād, *Maqṣūr* 22), تَتْرَى "being consecutive, uninterrupted" (cf. ibid) that occurs in the sur. 23: 44 (ثُمَّ أَرْسَلْنَا رُسُلَنَا تَتْرَى) "Then sent We Our apostles in succession", تَوْلَجٌ "the covert of the wild animal, into which he enters", تُرَاثٌ "inheritance" that occurs in the sur. 89:19 (وَتَأْكُلُونَ ٱلتُّرَاثَ أَكْلًا لَمًّا) "And ye devour Inheritance—All with greed", تِلَادٌ "old property, what was born in your possession", and مُتْلِجٌ "putting inside" that occurs in the following verse said by Imruʾu l-Qais, cited by Zamaḫšarī, 175, Ibn Yaʿīš, *X,* 37-38, Howell, *IV,* fasc. I, 1343:

"رُبَّ رَامٍ مِنْ بَنِي ثُعَلٍ مُتْلِجٍ كَفَّيْهِ فِي قُتَرِهْ".

"Many a marksman of the Banū Ṯuʿal, putting his two hands inside his lurking-places!".

Ibn Manẓūr, *I,* 484 mentions the verse with مُخْرِجٍ "taking out" instead of مُتْلِجٍ. For other cases of the substitution of the *t* for the *w* see (96), (198), (247), (331).

(331) أُخْتٌ is from the root أخو, a verb with 3rd radical *w.* The base form of أُخْتٌ is formed according to the pattern فَعَلَةٌ, i.e. أَخَوَةٌ, and then it is changed into the pattern فُعْلٌ i.e. أُخْوٌ in which the 3rd radical *w* is changed into the *t,* so that it became أُخْتٌ (cf. Zamaḫšarī, 175, Ibn Yaʿīš, *X,* 39-40, Ibn Manẓūr, *I,* 326 sqq., Howell, *I,* fasc. III, 1370-1372, *IV,* fasc. I, 1347-1348, ʿAbd al-Tawwāb, *Taṭawwur* 91). The *t* does not mark the fem. in it according to Sībawaihi, as it is preceded by a vowelless consonant, whereas by others it is underlyingly the *h* of the fem. (cf. Ibn Manẓūr, *I,* 41). Another example that can be added in which the 3rd radical *w* is changed into the *t,* is بِنْتٌ "daughter" (for a discussion concerning it and ٱبْنٌ in some of the Semitic languages see Nöldeke, *Neue Beiträge* 135-139) underlyingly بَنَوَةٌ. According to the Basrans, the *t* in أُخْتٌ and بِنْتٌ does not mark the fem., but is a substitute for the 3rd radical in a state that is related to the feminine form, which is why it is preceded by a vowelless consonant, whereas according to the Kufans it is the *t* of the feminine form in pause and in context (cf. Ibn al-Anbārī, *Muḏakkar I,* 199, Rāǧiḥī, *Farrāʾ* 146). The Kufan theory seems valid as another dialectal variant of بِنْتٌ is ٱبْنَةٌ with the *tāʾ marbūṭa* that marks the fem. It occurs in the sur. 66: 12 (وَمَرْيَمَ ٱبْنَةَ عِمْرَانَ) "And Mary the daughter of ʿImrān" [which is cited as وَمَرْيَمَ ٱبْنَتَ with the *tāʾ mamdūda* by Muʾaddib, *Taṣrīf* 517] and in the following verse said by Abū l-ʿAmaiṯal, cited by Baġdādī, *Ḫizāna II,* 309, Howell, *Grammar IV,* fasc. I, 1348:

"لَقِيتُ ٱبْنَةَ السَّهْمِي زَيْنَبَ عَنْ عُفُرٍ وَنَحْنُ حَرَمٌ مُسْيَ عَاشِرَةَ ٱلْعَشْرِ
فَكَلَّمْتُهَا ثِنْتَيْنِ كَالثَّلْجِ مِنْهُمَا عَلَى ٱللَّوحِ وَٱلْأُخْرَى أَحَرُّ مِنَ ٱلْجَمْرِ".

"I met Zainab, the daughter of the Sahmī [sc. a relative noun from Sahm, a clan of Qurayš and Bahīla as well] after a period, when we were entering upon the state of pilgrimage, on the evening of the tenth of the first ten [days of *dū l-Ḥiğğa];* and I spoke to her two [words, one] of which there was like snow upon [i.e. with thirst], and the other one hotter than live coal".

هَنْتٌ "a thing" (for discussions concerning it see Nöldeke, *Neue Beiträge* 119-120, Fischer, *Miszellen* 873) is as well similar to أُخْتٌ and بِنْتٌ, regarding the substitution of the *t* for the *w,* as its pl. is هَنَوَاتٌ. هَنَوَاتٌ occurs in the following verse said by an unknown poet, cited by Ibn Ğinnī, *Sirr I,* 151, *II,* 559, *de Flexione* 28, *Munṣif III,* 139, Ibn al-Sarrāğ, *Uṣūl III,* 321, Ibn Yaʿīš, *I,* 53, *V,* 38, *VI,* 3, *X,* 40, *Mulūkī* 299, Ibn Manẓūr, *VI,* 4713, Howell, *IV,* fasc. I, 1349:

"أرى ٱبْنَ نِزَارٍ قَدْ جَفَانِي وَمَلَّنِي عَلَى هَنَوَاتٍ شَأْنُهَا مُتَتَابِعُ".

"I believe Ibn Nizār to have shunned me, and loathed me, on account of things of which the course is uninterrupted".

(332) The *t* is substituted for the *y* in ثِنْتَانِ underlyingly ثِنْيَانِ (cf. Zamaḫšarī, 175, Ibn Yaʿīš, *X,* 40, Ibn ʿUṣfūr, *I,* 388, Howell, *IV,* fasc. I, 1349-1350) with 3rd *y* radical, from the expression ثَنَيْتُ ٱلْوَاحِدَ "I was a second to the one" and in Form IV أَسْنَتُوا underlyingly أَسْنَيُوا (cf. ibid) with 3rd *y* radical. Referring to أَسْنَتُوا, Sībawaihi, *II,* 341 notes that the substitution of the *t* for the *y* as a 3rd radical is rare. According to some grammarians, أَسْنَتُوا is from سَنَةٌ, of which the 3rd radical is a *w* on account of the saying سَنَةٌ سَنْوَاءُ "a hard year", which means that they consider the *t* to be substituted for the *w* (cf. Howell, *IV,* fasc. I, 1349-1350). It can be mentioned that ثِنْتَانِ occurs in the dialectal variant of Tamīm (cf. Daqr, *Muʿğam* 2 in the notes, 338) whereas اثْنَانِ and اثْنَتَانِ occur by the Ḥiğāzīs (cf. ibid, 338).

(333) The double *t* in سِتّ is substituted for the *d* and the *s* of the base form سُدْسٌ (cf. (194), (329)).

(334) The *t* is substituted for the *s* in ٱلنَّاتُ that occurs instead of ٱلنَّاس. This particularity is known to be of the usage of the Yemenites and is called ٱلْوَتْمُ. ٱلنَّات occurs instead of ٱلنَّاس and أَكْيَات instead of أَكْيَاس (cf. Nöldeke, *Grammatik* 12) in these verses, which are believed to have been said by ʿIlbāʾ b. Arqam al-Yaškarī. They are cited by Rāzī in Ḫalīl b. Aḥmad ..., *Ḥurūf* 150, Ibn Fāris, *Ṣāḥibī* 109, Ibn al-Sikkīt, *Qalb* 42, Ṯaʿālibī, *Fiqh* 228, Ibn Ğinnī, *Sirr I,* 155, *Ḫaṣāʾiṣ II,* 53, Zamaḫšarī, 175, Ibn Yaʿīs, *X,* 36, Bakrī, *Samṭ II,* 703, Ibn ʿUṣfūr, *I,* 389, Ibn Ḫālawaihi, *Šawādd* 183, Tanūḫī, *Qawāfī* 123, Qālī, *Amālī II,* 71, Baġdādi, *Šarḥ* 469, Ibn Duraid, *Ğamhara III,* 33, Anṣārī, *Nawādir* 104, Ḥarīrī, *Séances* 646, Ibn Manẓūr, *I,* 148, Howell, *IV,* fasc. I, 1352-1353:

"يَا قَاتَلَ اللّٰهُ بَنِي ٱلسَّعْلَاتِ عَمْرَو بْنَ مَسْعُودٍ شِرَارَ ٱلنَّاتِ
غَيْرَ أَعِفَّاءَ وَلَا أَكْيَاتِ".

"O [my people] God slay the sons of she-devils, ʿAmr b. Masʿūd, the worst of men, incontinent and not sharp-witted!".

(335) The *t* in لِصْتٌ or لُصْتٌ is substituted anomalously for the 2nd *ṣ* of the doubled ṣāds of the base form لِصٌّ or لُصٌّ. لُصُوتٌ with this particular substitution occurs instead of لُصُوصٌ in the following verse, which is said either by ʿAbd al-Aswad b. ʿĀmir b. Ǧuwain al-Ṭāʾī according to Baġdādī, *Šarḥ* 475, or by ʿAbd al-Aswad al-Ṭāʾī according to Ibn Duraid, *Ǧamhara I,* 102-103, or by Abū l-Aswad al-Ṭāʾī according to Ibn Duraid, *Ǧamhara II,* 19. It is also cited by Ibn Ǧinnī, *Sirr I,* 156, *II,* 586, Zamaḫšarī, 175, Ibn Yaʿīš, *X,* 41, Ibn Manẓūr, *V,* 4031, *IV,* 3194, Howell, *IV,* fasc. I, 1353:

"فَتَرَكْنَ نَهْداً عُيَّلاً أَبْنَاؤُهَا وَبَنِى كِنَانَةَ كَاللُّصُوتِ ٱلْمُرَّدِ".

"Then they left Nahd [sc. a clan of Yemen] with its children destitute, and the Banū Kināna like insolent robbers".

(336) The *t* in ذُعَالَتٌ is substituted for the *b* of the base form ذُعَالِبٌ. It occurs in the following verse, which according to Ibn Manẓūr, *II,* 1504, 2100, is said by one of the Banū ʿAwf b. Saʿd. It is also cited by Ibn Ǧinnī, *Sirr I,* 157, Baġdādī, *Šarḥ* 472, Howell, *IV,* fasc. I, 1355:

"صَفْقَةُ ذِي ذَعَالِتٍ سَمُولِ بَيْعُ ٱمْرِئٍ لَيْسَ بِمُسْتَقِيلِ".

"The bargain of the poor needy purchaser, wearer of worn-out rags is, in irrevocability and conclusiveness, like a sale by a man that is not desirous of rescinding".

Another form is ذَعَالِيبُ which can occur instead of ذَعَالِيتُ. The base form ذَعَالِيبُ without the substitution of the *t* for the *b,* occurs in the following verse said by Ruʾba b. al-ʿAǧǧāǧ, cited by Ibn Yaʿīš, *X,* 41, Ibn Manẓūr, *II,* 1504, Howell, *IV,* fasc. I, 1355:

"مُنْسَرِحاً عَنْهُ ذَعَالِيبُ ٱلْخِرَقِ".

"With the bits of rags stripped off him [below]".

(337) The relative noun of صَنْعَاءُ "a city in al-Yaman" should have been صَنْعَاوِيٌّ, but صَنْعَانِيٌّ occurs anomalously instead with the substitution of the *n* for the *w.* So is also the case with بَهْرَاءُ "a tribe", whose relative noun should have been بَهْرَاوِيٌّ, but which is said بَهْرَانِيٌّ Both nouns are mentioned in (353). For discussions see Ibn Ǧinnī, *de Flexione* 25-26, *Munṣif I,* 158, *Sirr II,* 441, Zamaḫšarī, 175, Ibn Yaʿīš, *X,* 36, Ibn ʿUṣfūr, *I,* 395-396, Howell, *IV,* fasc. I, 1335-1336. Compare the Hebrew forms גִּילֹה from גִּילֹנִי and שִׁילֹה from שִׁילֹנִי (cf. Wright, *Comparative Grammar* 138-139).

(338) In لَعَنَّ, the *n* is substituted for the *l* of the base form لَعَلَّ "maybe" (cf. Ibn Ǧinnī, *Sirr II,* 442, Zamaḫšarī, 175, Ibn Yaʿīš, *X,* 36, Ibn ʿUṣfūr, *I,* 395, Howell, *IV,* fasc. I, 1336-1337; for the relations between the *l* and the *n* see Cantineau, *Esquisse* 134, *Consonantisme* 89). According to the Kufans the first *l* in لَعَلَّ is a radical, whereas the Basrans believed that it is an augment (for their debate see Ibn al-Anbārī, *Inṣāf* Q. 26, 96-99). The variant لَعَنَّا occurs instead of لعلّنا in the following verse said by Abū l-Naǧm, cited by Ibn Ǧinnī, *Sirr II,* 443, Luġawī, *Ibdāl II,* 297, Ibn Yaʿīš, *VIII,* 79:

"أُغْدُ لَعَنَّا فِي ٱلرِّهَانِ نُرْسِلُهْ".

"Be early in the morning; maybe we shall send him in the competition".

(339) The *ǧ* is substituted for the double *y* in علجّ that occurs instead of عليّ in the construct state أبو علجّ of the verse cited below. Also بِٱلْعَشِجّ occurs instead of بِٱلْعَشِيّ. This phenomenon pertains to the dialectal variant of Quḍāʿa, Banū Tamīm and Banū Saʿd, and is known as العَجْعَجَةُ. According to al-Ḫalīl, this variant is used by the Rabīʿa (cf. Talmon, *ʿAyn* 254). Both these words occur in the following verse said by an inhabitant of the desert, cited by Sībawaihi, *II,* 315, Ibn Fāris, *Ṣāḥibī* 55, Ibn Ǧinnī, *Sirr I,* 175, *de Flexione* 30, Ibn al-Sarrāǧ, *Uṣūl III,* 274, Luġawī, *Ibdāl I,* 257, Zamaḫšarī, 176, Ibn Yaʿīš, *X,* 50, *Mulūkī* 248, 329, 330, Ibn ʿUṣfūr, *I,* 353, Ibn Ǧinnī, *Munṣif II,* 178, Baġdādī, *Šarḥ* 212-213, Ḥamīrī, *Šams I,* 20, Ḥarīrī, *Séances* 646, Ibn Manẓūr, *I,* 527, Howell, *IV,* fasc. I, 1375-1376, Lane, *I,* 47, Vernier, *I,* 356, Freytag, *Einleitung* 81:

"خَالِي عُوَيْفٌ وَأَبُو عَلِجِّ اَلْمُطْعِمَانِ اللَّحمَ بِٱلْعَشِجِّ".

"My maternal uncle ʿUwayf and Abū ʿAliǧǧi [sc. Abū ʿAlī], they who provide meat for food at evening".

Ibn Manẓūr, *IV,* 2814 mentions the verse with خَالِي لَقِيطٌ "my maternal uncle Laqīṭ" instead of خَالِي عُوَيْفٌ.

(340) The *ǧ* is substituted for the single *y,* but less often than the double one in pause. An example is حجّتجْ for حجّتي, بجْ for بي, and وفرْتجْ for وفرْتي, that occur in these verses, whose author is Abū Zaid: Saʿīd b. Aus b. Ṯābit al-Anṣārī, the author of *al-Nawādir* (cf. the editor's notes to Ibn al-Sarrāǧ, *Uṣūl III,* 274). It is also cited by Ṯaʿlab, *Maǧālis* 117, Ibn Ǧinnī, *Sirr I,* 177, *de Flexione* 30, Zamaḫšarī, 176, Ibn Yaʿīš, *X,* 50, *Mulūkī* 329, Baġdādī, *Šarḥ* 215-216, Luġawī, *Ibdāl I,* 260, Ḫuḍarī, *Ḥāšiya II,* 229, Ibn ʿUṣfūr, *I,* 355, *Ḍarāʾir* 231, Ibn Manẓūr, *I,* 527, Howell, *IV,* fasc. I, 1376, Lane, *I,* 47, Vernier, *I,* 356-357, Freytag, *Einleitung* 81, Nöldeke, *Poesie* 41:

"لَاهُمَّ إِنْ كُنْتَ قَبِلْتَ حَجَّتِجْ فَلَا يَزَالُ شَاحِجٌ يَأْتِيكَ بِجْ
أَقْمَرُ نَهَّاتٌ يُنَزِّي وَفْرَتِجْ".

"O God, if You have accepted my pilgrimage, then a mule, white, braying, that jogs my hair extending to the lobe of the ear, shall not cease to bring me to You".

Another example that can be mentioned is سَعْدَجْ for سَعْدِي "Saʿdī" (cf. Sībawaihī, *I,* 361, Brockelmann, *Grundriss I,* 280). For references to Tigrē see Brockelmann, *Grundriss I,* 280.

b) The *ǧ* is also substituted for the *y* even when not in pause, as in أمْسَجْتُ and أمسى "to enter upon the time of evening" underlyingly أمْسَيْتُ and أمسيَ respectively, which become when substituted أمْسَجْتُ and أمسجَ (the latter with the weak consonant of unbinding becomes أمْسَجَا). They both occur in the following verse whose poet, according to one of the commentators of the verses of al-Fārisī's *Īḍāḥ*, referred to by Baġdādī, *Šarḥ* 486, is Ru'ba b. al-'Aǧǧāǧ, but who, according to al-Hindāwī's note to Ibn Ǧinnī, *Sirr I*, 177, who refers to the note of Fārisī, *Takmila* 566, is al-Qaisī. It is cited by Fārisī, *Takmila* 566, Ibn Ǧinnī, *Sirr I*, 177, *de Flexione* 30, Ibn al-Sarrāǧ, *Uṣūl III*, 275, Zamaḫšarī, 176, Ibn 'Uṣfūr, *I*, 355, *Ḍarā'ir* 232, Ibn Ya'īš, *X*, 50, *Mulūkī* 329, 331, Baġdādī, *Šarḥ* 486, Ibn Manẓūr, *VI*, 4206, Howell, *IV*, fasc. I, 1377, Freytag, *Einleitung* 81:

"حَتَّى إِذَا مَا أَمْسَجَتْ وَأَمْسَجَا".

"Until, whenever she entered, and he entered, upon the time of evening".

For the substitution occurring at the interior of the word see Brockelmann, *Grundriss I*, 139.

c) As for other cases of substitution concerning the ǧ that can be added here, it can be mentioned that some Arabs substitute it for the *k*, e.g. الجَعْبَةُ for الكَعْبَةُ "the Ka'ba" (cf. Suyūṭī, *Muzhir I*, 134). In the context of the biggest derivation (cf. (14 c), there is as well a semantic relation between both the ǧ and the *k*, e.g. جَدَّ "to strive earnestly" and كَدَّ "to work hard" (cf. Bohas, *Matrices* 152, for more examples see ibid, 144-146). Furthermore, the Banū Tamīm substitute the *q* by the sound *g* that is between the *k* and the *q*, e.g. *al-gawm* for القَوْمُ "the people" (for a study see Blanc, *Fronting* 33-34). A semantic relation exists as well between the uvular *k* and *q*, e.g. كَحَطَ "to be without (is said of the rains)" and قَحَطَ "to fail to set in (rains)" (cf. Bohas, *Matrices* 148, for more examples see ibid, 148-149).

(341) The base form of فُزْدُ is فُزْتُ "I succeeded" (cf. Zamaḫšarī, 176, 196, Ibn Ya'īš, *X*, 48, 151, Howell, *IV*, fasc. I, 1373) from فَوَزَ. The *d* in it is substituted for the *t* due to the influence of the *z*. As for the reason of this substitution, it is that the *z* is among the voiced consonants and the *t* is among the voiceless consonants, which implies a distance between them both regarding their characters (for the consonants' characters see (188 b)). So the voiceless *t* is changed into the voiced *d* due to the influence of the voiced *z*, resulting in فُزْدُ, because the *d*, similarly to the *z*, is a voiced consonant.

(342) The *d* in Form VIII اِجْدَمَعُوا is substituted for the infixed *t* of the base form اِجْتَمَعُوا (cf. Ibn Fāris, *Ṣāḥibī* 109, Ibn Ya'īš, *X*, 49, Howell, *IV*, fasc. I, 1372). The substitution is carried out as well in the active participle مُجْتَمِعٌ that becomes مُجْدَمِعٌ (cf. Talmon, *'Ayn* 142). Another example is اِجْدَزَّ "to cut" that occurs instead of اِجْتَزَّ in some dialectal variants. It is found in the following verse which is believed to have been said by Yazīd b. al-Ṭaṭrīya, but which according to Ibn al-Barrī referred to by Ibn Manẓūr, *I*, 615, has been said by Muḍarris b. Rib'ī al-Asadī. Baġdādī, *Šarḥ* 481-484 discusses also the dispute concerning the attribution, and concludes himself that he found it as having been said by Muḍarris b. Rib'ī al-Fiq'asī. It is also cited by Ibn Fāris, *Ṣāḥibī* 109, Ibn Ǧinnī, *Sirr I*, 187, *II*, 764, *Muhtasib I*, 74, Ibn Ya'īš, *X*, 49, *Mulūkī* 236, Ibn 'Uṣfūr, *I*, 357, Ibn al-Anbārī, *Qaṣā'id* 16, Ibn Manẓūr, *I*, 591, Howell, *IV*, fasc. I, 1372, Abū Ḥaidar, *Dual* 43:

"فَقُلْتُ لِصَاحِبِي لَا تَحْبِسَانَا   بِنَزْعِ أُصُولِهِ وَٱجْدِزْ شِيحاً".

"Then I said to my companion "Do not detain us from roasting the flesh by pulling it [sc. the tree] out by its roots, but cut some wormwood".

(343) The *h* in Form I هَرَقْتُ is substituted for the hamza of its base form أَرَقْتُ "I poured" (cf. Sībawaihi, *II,* 341, 364, de Sacy, *I,* 247, 224 note 1, Vernier, *I,* 152, 100, my notes (98); for the anomalous infixation of the *h* in Form IV see (98), (212)). So is also the case of هَرَحْتُ "I brought back the beast to the nightly resting-place" from أَرَحْتُ. Other examples are هِيَاكَ said instead of إِيَاكَ (cf. Ibn Yaʿīš, *X,* 42, Ibn Manẓūr, *I,* 188), which have been read by some of the sur. 1: 5 (هِيَاكَ نَعْبُدُ وَهِيَاكَ نَسْتَعِينُ) "Thee do we worship, and Thine aid we seek" said instead of (إِيَاكَ نَعْبُدُ وإِيَاكَ نَسْتَعِينُ), and هَذَا ٱلَّذِي said instead of أَذَا ٱلَّذِي in this verse recited by Abū Ḥasan. As for its author, Ibn Manẓūr, *III,* 1472 states that al-Liḥyānī recited it from al-Kisāʾī from the saying of Ǧamīl (b. Maʿmar). However, Baġdādī, *Šarḥ* 477 mentions that its sayer is unknown, and that it is likely to be of the poetry of ʿUmar b. Abī Rabīʿa al-Maḫzūmī, as in most of his poems he describes women to be falling in love with him. It is cited by Ibn Ǧinnī, *Sirr II,* 554, Zamaḫšarī, 175, Ibn Yaʿīš, *X,* 42, *Mulūkī* 305, Ibn ʿUṣfūr, *I,* 400, *Muqarrab II,* 178, Ibn Hišām, *Muġnī II,* 348, Fairūzābādī, *Qāmūs IV,* 481, Ibn Manẓūr, *VI,* 4598, Howell, *IV,* fasc. I, 1358.

"وَأَتَى صَوَاحِبَهَا فَقُلْنَ هَذَا ٱلَّذِي   مَنَحَ ٱلْمَوَدَّةَ غَيْرَنَا وَجَفَانَا".

"And he came to her [sc. his beloved's] companions; and they said "Is this he who bestowed affection on others than us, and forsook us?".

(344) حَيَّهَلْ is formed of حَيَّ and هَلْ or هَلَ, two sounds that mean urging and hastening (for a general study see Zamaḫšarī, 62-63; 156, 175, Ibn Yaʿīš, *IV,* 44-47, *IX,* 45, *X,* 43, Howell, *I,* fasc. II, 680-682, *IV,* fasc. I, 856). حَيَّهَلَهْ is the noun of the verb, which underlyingly is حَيَّ هَلَا (cf. Zamaḫšarī, 156, 175, Ibn Yaʿīš, *X,* 43), with the *h* substituted for the final vowelless *ā* in pause. The other variants are حَيَّ هَلْ with sukūn of the *l* in pause and حَيَّ هَلَ otherwise (cf. Wright, *II,* 294). حَيَّهَلَهْ and its variants belong to this category of words that has been determined by Sībawaihi, *I,* 104 as الأسماء المفردة التي كانت للفعل "nouns in the sing. pertaining to verbs, (whose action they denote)". Other examples of such words are: حَذَارِكَ "beware!", إِلَيْكَ "go away", رُوَيْدَ "carefully" and صَهْ "quiet". What is characteristic for them is that they all have an imperative or prohibitive meaning (for a study see Sībawaihi, *I,* 105-107, Versteegh, *Zaǧǧāǧī* 63). A verse said by a man of the Banū Bakr b. Waʾil, cited by Zamaḫšarī, 62, Ibn Yaʿīš, *IV,* 46, Ibn Manẓūr, *VI,* 4693, Howell, *I,* fasc. II, 682, has حَيَّهَلُهْ with the ḍamma as a vowel of declension over the *l:*

"وَهَيَّجَ ٱلْحَيَّ مِنْ دَارٍ فَظَلَّ لَهُمْ   يَوْمٌ كَثِيرٌ تَنَادِيهِ وَحَيَّهَلُهْ".

"And he [sc. the camel-driver] roused the tribe from an abode; and a day, in which the calling of one to another and "make haste" were many, was spent by them".

حَيَّهَلْ with the vowelless *l* occurs in the following verse said by Labīd b. Rabīʿa l-ʿĀmirī in

Labīd, *Dīwān* 183, cited by Mu'addib, *Taṣrīf* 171, Ibn Yaʿīš, *IV,* 45, Ibn Manẓūr, *VI,* 4693, Howell, *I,* fasc. II, 681:

"يَتَمَارَى فِي ٱلَّذِي قُلْتُ لَهُ وَلَقَدْ يَسْمَعُ قَوْلِي حَيَّهَلْ".

"He doubts about what I have said to him; and assuredly he does hear my saying 'Come along'".

هلا without the change of the *ā* into a *h* as well as used alone without حَيَّ, and indicating in this case reproach, has been said in the following verse said by al-Nābiġa al-Ǧaʿdī who is satirizing Laylā al-Aḫyalīya. It is cited by Zamaḫšarī, 63, Ibn Yaʿīš, *IV,* 47, Ibn Manẓūr, *VI,* 4695, Howell, *I,* fasc. II, 684:

"ألا أبْلغا لَيْلَى وَقُولا لَهَا هَلاَ لَقَدْ رَكِبَتْ أمْراً أغرَ مُحَجَلاَ".

"Now convey you both to Leyla [my message], and say to her: "Come up". By God, she has perpetrated a glaring, notorious matter".

(345) The *h* in أنَهْ (for it see (73 c), (373)) is substituted for the *ā* of أنَا (cf. Ibn Ǧinnī, *Sirr I,* 163, *II,* 555, *de Flexione* 22, 28, Zamaḫšarī, 175, Ibn Yaʿīš, *III,* 138, *IV,* 6, *IX,* 80-81, *X,* 43, Howell, *I,* fasc. II, 577). According to Ibn Ǧinnī referred to by Ibn Manẓūr, *I,* 160, the *h* in أنَهْ could be a substitute for the *ā* in أنَا, because it is so frequently used, or it could be suffixed to mark the vowel preceding it as in كِتَابِيَهْ "my book" and حِسَابِيَهْ "my account". Some other examples that consider this particular substitution (for further discussions see Wright, *IV,* 369-370) are هُنَهْ for هُنَا "here" and فَمَهْ for فَمَا "what (am I to do)?", which occur in the verse said by an unknown poet, cited by Ibn Ǧinnī, *Sirr I,* 163, *II,* 555, *Munṣif II,* 156, *de Flexione* 22, 28, Zamaḫšarī, 175, Ibn Yaʿīš, *III,* 138, *IV,* 6, *IX,* 80-81, *X,* 43, *Mulūkī* 312, 315, Ibn ʿUṣfūr, *I,* 400, Baġdādī, *Šarḥ* 479, Ibn Manẓūr, *VI,* 4716, Howell, *I,* fasc. II, 577:

"قَدْ وَرَدَتْ مِنْ أمْكِنَهْ مِنْ هَاهُنَا وَمِنْ هُنَهْ إنْ لَمْ أُرَوِّهَا فَمَهْ".

"They [sc. the camels] have come to water from many places, from here and from there: if I quench not their thirst, what [am I to do]?".

b) Some examples that consider the suffixation of the *h* of silence (for a study see Zamaḫšarī, 156, Ibn Yaʿīš, *IX,* 46, Howell, *II-III,* 719-725, Wright, *IV,* 372-373), which follow the *y* are هِيَهْ "she" for هِيَ as in the sur. 101: 10 (مَا هِيَهْ) "what this is", مَالِيَهْ for مَالِيَ as in the sur. 69: 28 (مَالِيَهْ) "my wealth", and سُلْطَانِيَهْ for سُلْطَانِيَ as in the sur. 69: 29 (سُلْطَانِيَهْ) "my power". Both last surs. and a discussion concerning the suffixation of the *h* of silence are reported by Zaǧǧāǧī, *Maǧālis* 188 in the session between Abū ʿAmr b. al-ʿAlā' and a man of the inhabitants of al-Madīna. In it, the man of the inhabitants of al-Madīna recited to Abū ʿAmr b. al-ʿAlā' a verse ending up with the word مُرُوَّتِيَهْ "sense of honor", in which the *h* of silence is suffixed. To this, Abū ʿAmr scolded him by saying: "What do we have to do with this weak poetry? Indeed this *h* is not suffixed to any word unless it renders it weak!". The inhabitant of al-Madīna argued against him by referring to the above-mentionned surs., and Abū ʿAmr was defeated. The *h* is also suffixed after the *w* in هُوَهْ "he" for هُوَ, that occurs in the following verse said by Ibn Ṯābit al-Anṣārī al-Ṣaḥābī, cited by Howell, *IV,* fasc. I, 854:

"إِذَا مَا تَرَعْرَعَ فِينَا ٱلْغُلَامُ   فَمَا إِنْ يُقَالُ لَهُ مَنْ هُوَهْ".

"When the lad grows up among us, it is not said of him: "Who is he?".

c) The *h* of silence is only suffixed in pause, is vowelless, and thus is rejected in context. This is why its occurrence in context and vowelled in قَلْبَاهُ said instead of قَلْبَاهْ, is found anomalous in the following verse said by Mutanabbī, *Dīwān III*, 362, cited by Ibn Ǧinnī, *Sirr II*, 562, Ibn Yaʿīš, *X*, 44, *Mulūkī* 310, Howell, *IV*, fasc. I, 1362:

"وَاحَرَّ قَلْبَاهُ مِمَّنْ قَلْبُهُ شَبِمٌ   وَمَنْ بِجِسْمِي وَحَالِي عِنْدَهُ سَقَمُ".

"Ah! the heat of my heart from [its love] for him whose heart is cold, and for whom sickness is in my body and disorder in my state!".

As well, the *h* is anomalously vowelled by a ḍamma or a kasra in مَرْحَبَاهُ said instead of مَرْحَبَاهْ, to avoid the cluster of two vowelless consonants, the *ā* and the *h*, in the following verse said by ʿUrwa b. Ḥizām al-ʿUḏrī, cited by Zamaḫšarī, 156, Ibn Yaʿīš, *IX*, 46, Howell, *II-III*, 725:

"يَا مَرْحَبَاهُ بِحِمَارِ عَفْرَا   إِذَا أَتَى قَرَيْتُهُ بِمَا شَاءَ".

"O people, welcome to the he-ass of ʿAfrāʾ! When he comes, I will entertain him with what he wants".

Also عَفْرَا has been said instead of عَفْرَاء and شَا instead of شَاء for the sake of metric exigency in this verse.

(346) The *h* in هذه is substituted for the *y* of the base form هَذِي (cf. (89)). The *h* is as well substituted for the *y* in the diminutive هُنَيَّةٌ of هَنَةٌ "things disapproved", which is said هُنَيْهَةٌ (cf. Howell, *I*, fasc. I, 18) on the basis that the 3rd radical of هَنْتٌ is biform, alike سَنَةٌ "a year" that has the diminutive سُنَيَّةٌ and that becomes after the substitution of the *h* for the *y* سُنَيْهَةٌ (cf. Howell, *I*, fasc. III, 1194-1195, Wright, *II*, 173).

(347) امالة "deflection" (for a study see Zamaḫšarī, 158-163, Ibn Yaʿīš, *IX*, 53-66, Howell, *IV*, fasc. I, 738-771, Wright, *I*, 10, Roman, *Étude I*, 460 sqq.) is carried out by taking the fatḥa towards the kasra. According to Ibn Ǧinnī, *Ḫaṣāʾiṣ II*, 141, it pertains to الإدغام الأصغر "the partial assimilation" (for it see (174)), as it implies the inclination of one vowel to another. It is not allowed to be carried out if the kasra precedes the *ā* by two vowelled consonants as in أَكَلْتُ عِنَبَا "I ate grapes", in which the kasra of the ʿ of عِنَبَا is preceeding two vowels, or by three vowels, as in قَتَلْتُ قِنَبَا "I twisted hemp", in which the kasra of the *q* of قِنَبَا is preceeding three vowels, because of the distance of the kasra from the *ā*. However, in يُرِيدُ أَنْ يَضْرِبَهَا "he wants to strike her" (cf. Zamaḫšarī, 158, Ibn Yaʿīš, *IX*, 56-57, Howell, *IV*, fasc. I, 745-746, Cantineau, *Cours* 132-136, Fleisch, *Traité I*, 215-216),—in spite of the fact that the kasra of the *r* of يَضْرِبَهَا precedes the *ā* by two vowels —, it is anomalous but allowed, because the *h* that is faint is not taken into account. There is then a certain analogy between the faintness of both the *h* and the weak consonants. It is this faintness of the weak consonants that allows the substitution of the *h* for them, e.g. the *y* in the example هذي أَمَةُ الله said instead as هذه أَمَةُ الله (cf. (89), (346)), and the *ā* in the example أنا said instead as أَنَهْ (cf. (345)).

(348) The *h* in طَلْحَهْ is substituted for the *tā' marbūṭa* of the base form طَلْحَةٌ in pause. Another example in which this substitution occurs is the name حَمْزَهْ that is said in pause instead of حَمْزَةْ. For a study see Ibn Ǧinnī, *Sirr II,* 562-563, Zamaḫšarī, 176, Ibn Yaʿīš, *X,* 45, Ibn ʿUṣfūr, *I,* 402, Howell, *IV,* fasc. I, 1364-1365, Fleisch, *Traité I,* 183-184. This substitution is carried out specifically in nouns to differenciate between the *tā' marbūṭa* that marks the fem. in them and the suffixed *tā' ṭawīla* that marks the fem. in verbs, e.g. ضَرَبَتْ "she hit". Furthermore it can be noted that the characteristic *tā' ṭawīla* suffixed in verbs cannot be substituted by the *h* in pause, i.e. ضَرَبَتْ cannot become ضَرَبَهْ, as there is then a risk of confusing this *h* with the suffixed pronoun of the accusative of the 3rd person of the masc. sing., the ـهُ "him", because in the written form without vowels both *ḍarabah* ضربه and *ḍarabahu* ضربه "he hit him" would look alike.

b) The substitution of the *tā' ṭawīla* by the *h* is possibly carried out in the anomalous verb هَيْهَاتَ that is said هَيْهَاهْ of the sur. 23: 36 which was read (هَيْهَاهْ هَيْهَاهْ) "Far, very far", by some. An example of a noun in the sing. is التَّابُوهْ that has been read as so by Ubbay and Zaid b. Ṯābit instead of ٱلتَّابُوتُ in the sur. 2: 248 (إِنَّ آيَةَ مُلْكِه أَنْ يَأْتِيَكُمُ ٱلتَّابُوتُ) "A sign of his authority is that there shall come to you the Ark of the Covenant". Ibn Yaʿīš, *X,* 45 remarked that التَّابُوهْ pertains to the dialectal variant of al-Anṣār and التَّابُوتُ to the dialectal variant of the Quraišī. Rabin, 109 and Vollers, *Volkssprache* 158 note that it is the alleged Medinean form. Rabin mentions furthermore that both the Arabic word and the Ethiopic *tābōt* come from Jewish Palestinian Aramaic *tēbhūta, tēbhōta,* which derive from Hebrew *tēbhāh* (for a discussion of the word's passage into some of the Arabic dialects see Rabin, 109-110).

c) The *h* is substituted for the *tā' ṭawīla* marker of the fem. pl. that is characteristic for nouns, in the dialectal variant of the Ṭayyīs. An example is كيف الإخوةُ والخَوَاهْ "How are the brothers and the sisters" in which والخَوَاهْ is said instead of والخَوَاتُ, and كيف البَنُونَ والبَنَاهْ "how are the sons and the daughters?" in which والبَنَاهْ is said instead of والبَنَاتُ (cf. Ibn ʿUṣfūr, *I,* 402).

d) An opposite phenomenon worth mentioning is that some of the Arabs, when pausing upon the *tā marbūṭa* change it into a *tā' ṭawīla.* This is known to be a wide-spread dialectal variant as mentioned by Ibn Yaʿīš, *IX,* 81, and is usual by the Ḥumair, e.g. عَرَبِيَتُ for عَرَبِيَّةٌ in pause as mentioned by Ibn Fāris, *Ṣāḥibī* 108. Some other examples are وٱلرَّحْمَتْ said instead of وٱلرَّحْمَةُ in the expression وَعَلَيْهِ ٱلسَّلامُ وٱلرَّحْمَتْ "And upon him be peace and mercy!" (cf. Ibn Yaʿīš, *V,* 89), and the following words that occur in these verses said by Abū l-Naǧm, cited by Ibn Ǧinnī, *Sirr I,* 163, *Ḫaṣā'iṣ I,* 304, Ibn Yaʿīš, *V,* 89, *IX,* 81, Šinqīṭī, *Durar II,* 214, 235, Širbīnī, *Šarḥ* 45, 46, Howell, *IV,* fasc. I, 845, Rāǧiḥī, *Farrā'* 142, 143, namely مَسْلَمَتْ for مَسْلَمَهْ,

بَعْدمتْ for بَعْدمهْ (in which the *ā* of the base form بَعْدما is substituted by the *h*, similartly to أنهْ for أنا "I" cf. (345)), الْغلْصمتْ for الْغلْصمهْ and أمتْ for أمهْ:

"وَٱللّهُ نَجَاكَ بِكَفِي مَسْلَمتْ   مِنْ بَعْدما وبَعْدما وبَعْدمتْ
صارتْ نُفوسُ ٱلْقوْمِ عِنْدَ ٱلْغلْصمتْ   وكادتِ ٱلْحرّةُ أنْ تُدْعى أمتْ".

"And God saved you by my hand, O Maslama, after, and after, and after that the souls of the people had reached the epiglottis, and the free-born girl was nearly being called a servant!".

This substitution can also occur in context as in نعْمتُ الله for نعْمَةُ الله "God's blessing" (cf. Brockelmann, *Socins Grammatik* 65) and in sur. 11: 73 رَحْمتُ آلله "The Grace of God" for رَحْمَةُ آلله (cf. Wrigh, *Comparative Grammar* 133). Brockelmann, *Socins Grammatik* 65 compares also this phenomenon with the Hebrew st. cstr. ־ת and absol. ־ה. Some other examples with the *tā*ʾ *ṭawīla* used instead of the *tā*ʾ*marbūṭa* are the readings of Nāfiʿ, Ibn ʿĀmir and Ḥamza of the sur. 44: 43 (إن شجرة ٱلزقّوم) "Verily the tree of Zaqqūm" that occurs as (إن شجرت ٱلزقّوم) and the sur. 66: 10 (إمرأة نوحٍ وآمرأة لوط)"The wife of Noah and the wife of Lūṭ" that occurs as (إمرأت نوحٍ وآمرأت لوط) (cf. Howell, *IV,* fasc. I, 845-846).

(349) مُفَيْتِيحٌ is the diminutive of مِفْتاحٌ, and is formed according to فُعَيْعِيلٌ. The last vowelless *y* in this example is substituted for the *ā* (cf. Ibn Ǧinnī, *de Flexione* 23, *Sirr II,* 731-732, Zamaḫšarī, 173, Ibn Yaʿīš, *X,* 21, Howell, *IV,* fasc. I, 1256, Bohas, *Étude* 259-260), as it is preceded by a kasra. The pattern فُعَيْعِيلٌ is appliable to every quinqueliteral noun, of which the 4th is an *ā, w,* or *y,* e.g. مِصْباحٌ "little lamp" (as مِفْتاحٌ): مُصَيْبِيحٌ, قَرْبُوسٌ "a pommel of a saddle": قُرَيْبِيسٌ, and قِنْدِيلٌ "little candelabrum" قُنَيْدِيلٌ. For a study see Sībawaihi, *II,* 119-120, Zamaḫšarī, 87, Howell, *I,* fasc. III, 1167, Wright, *II,* 166, Vernier, *I,* 198.

(350) The base form of مِيقاتٌ is مِوْقاتٌ from وَقْتٌ "time". Its pl. is مَواقِيتُ and its diminutive مُوَيْقِيتٌ. The 1st radical *w* in مِوْقاتٌ is substituted by the *y* on account of its vowellessness and the influence of the kasra preceding it. It can be noted that this change is not carried out in صِوانٌ "receptacle of a thing", because the *w* is vowelled in it, or in اجْلِوّاذٌ "continuance of journeying" and اعْلِوّاطٌ "clinging to the neck", because the *w* is double in them. For a study see Ibn Ǧinnī, *Sirr II,* 732-733, Zamaḫšarī, 173, 185, Ibn Yaʿīš, *X,* 21, Howell, *IV,* fasc. I, 1270-1271. Another example in which the vowelless 1st radical *w* is substituted by the *y* is مِيزانٌ "balance" underlyingly مِوْزانٌ (cf. (260)).

The 2nd radical *w* vowelled by a fatḥa is substituted by the *y* in the noun in the sing. كَيْوَنُونَةٌ "being" and then the yāʾs are assimilated together, i.e. كَيْنُونَةٌ (cf. (263)). Other examples concerning the substitution of the *w* by the *y* are the broken pl. دِوارٌ "houses" resulting in دِيارٌ (cf. (266)), the broken pl. سِواطٌ "whips" resulting in سِياطٌ (cf. (267)) and the *maṣdar* قِوامٌ "standing" resulting in قِيَامٌ (cf. (266 b)). The *w* vowelled by the kasra is changed into the *y* in مَيْوِتٌ "a dead man" and then the yā's are assimilated together, i.e. مَيِّتٌ (cf. (263)).

(351) The *y* in ذِيبٌ is substituted for the hamza of ذِئْبٌ (cf. Ibn Ǧinnī, *de Flexione* 23, *Sirr II,* 738, Zamaḫšarī, 173, Ibn Yaʿīš, *X,* 24, Ibn ʿUṣfūr, *I,* 378, Howell, *IV,* fasc. I, 12).

(352) The *y* in تَقَضِّيَ ٱلْبَازِي is substituted for the last *ḍ* in تَقَضُّض (cf. (170), (182)).

(353) أَنَاسِيُّ (cf. Ibn Yaʿīš, *X,* 27, Ibn Manẓūr, *I,* 148, Howell, *I,* fasc. III, 100, *IV,* fasc. I, 1296) is said to be the pl. of إِنْسَانٌ, and not of إِنْسِيٌّ "a human being, man". Its base form is أَنَاسِينُ in which the *y* is substituted for the *n,* in the same manner as the *n* is substituted for the *w* in صَنْعَاوِيٌّ that is said صَنْعَانِيٌّ and بَهْرَاوِيٌّ that is said بَهْرَانِيٌّ (cf. (337)). It occurs in the sur. 25: 49 (وَأَنَاسِيَّ كَثِيرًا) "And men in great number". Some of the Arabs say also أَنَاسِينُ according to the base form.

(354) The base form of دِينَارٌ is from the Persian دِنَّارٌ, or more probably from the Greek *δηνάριον*(cf. Penrice, *Dictionary* 49) on account of its pl. دَنَانِيرُ and diminutive دُنَيْنِيرٌ. The *y* in it is substituted for the *n* (cf. Ibn Ǧinnī, *de Flexione* 24, *Sirr II,* 757, Howell, *IV,* fasc. I, 1298, *I,* fasc. III, 1197, Wright, *II,* 175). It can be noted that both the *y* and the *n* are among the intermediate consonants (for the consonants' characters see (188 b)), which is why it is possible to substitute one for the other.

(355) The *y* in ضَفَادِي is substituted for the ʿ of the base form ضَفَادِعُ (cf. Nöldeke, *Grammatik* 13). The ʿ in ضَفَادِعُ is counted as heavy because it is a guttural consonant, and as the kasra preceding it is closer to the *y* than to the ʿ, it became more natural to replace the ʿ by the *y.* ضَفَادِي occurs in the saying of Ḫalaf al-Aḥmar, and is cited by Sībawaihi, *I,* 300, Ibn Wallād, *Intiṣār* 183, Ibn Ǧinnī, *Sirr II,* 762, Zamaḫšarī, 174, Ibn Yaʿīš, *X,* 28, Ibn ʿUṣfūr, *I,* 376, *Ḍarāʾir* 226, Baġdādī, *Šarḥ* 441, Ibn Manẓūr, *IV,* 2594, Šinqīṭī, *Durar II,* 213, Marzubānī, *Muwaššaḥ* 155, Howell, *IV,* fasc. I, 1296, Dieterici, *Mutanabbii* 500, Ibn Qutaiba, *Šiʿr* 102:

"وَمَنْهَلٍ لَيْسَ لَهُ حَوَازِقُ وَلِضَفَادِي جَمِّهِ نَقَانِقُ".

"And many a watering-place, which has no sides preventing any one from coming down to it, but to which every one is able to come down from all of its sides, and the frogs of whose main part have croakings!".

(356) The base form of ايتَصَلْتُ is اوْتَصَلْتُ from وَصَلَ "to join". اوْتَصَلْتُ has a vowelless *w* that is assimilated to the infixed *t* of Form VIII, i.e اتَّصَلْتُ. The 1st *t* of the doubled tā's is anomalously changed into a *y* resulting in ايتَصَلْتُ. فَايْتَصَلْتُ occurs in the following verse said by an unkown poet, in which he is describing a wild cow searching for her calf. It is cited by Ibn

Ǧinnī, *Sirr II,* 764, Ibn Yaʿīš, *X,* 26, *Mulūkī* 248, Ibn ʿUṣfūr, *I,* 378, *Ḍarāʾir* 228, Ibn Manẓūr, *VI,* 4850, Howell, *IV,* fasc. I, 1296:

"قَامَتْ بِهَا تَنْشُدُ كُلَّ ٱلْمُنْشَدِ فَٱيْتَصَلَتْ بِمِثْلِ ضَوْءِ ٱلْفَرْقَدِ".

"She stood in it [sc. the patch of ground], seeking with all inquiry, and joined [a calf] like the light of [the asterism called] *al-farqad,* [by which one guides oneself]".

(357) The *y* in ثعالي is substituted for the *b* of the base form ثعالب. الثعالي occurs instead of الثعالب and أرانيها instead of أرانبها (cf. Nöldeke, *Grammatik* 13) in the following verse which is believed to have been said by Abū Kāhil al-Yaškarī, as reported by Ibn al-Sikkīt, *Tahḏīb* 606, Ibn Duraid, *Ǧamhara II,* 13, Ibn Manẓūr, *I,* 445, *III,* 1742, *IV,* 2232, *VI,* 4789, Baġdādī, *Šarḥ* 443-446. Ibn Manẓūr, *I,* 485 and Ibn ʿUṣfūr, *Ḍarāʾir* 226 write as well that it has been said by a man from the Banū Yaškar. Baġdādī, *Šarḥ* remarks that some believed it to have been said by al-Namir b. Tawlab. This is also the opinion of Howell, *IV,* fasc. I, 1297 who refers to Abū Ḫalīl al-Namir b. Tawlab al-Yaškurī, who is describing a female eaglet, named *Ġubba,* that belongs to the Banū Yaškur. However, those who refer to Abū Kāhil al-Yaškarī, whom I also believe to be the poet, mean that the poet compares his camel to an eagle. The verse is also cited by Sībawaihi, *I,* 300, Ṯaʿlab, *Maǧālis* 190, Ibn Wallād, *Intiṣār* 183, Ibn Ǧinnī, *Sirr II,* 742, Ibn al-Sarrāǧ, *Uṣūl III,* 467, Zamaḫšarī, 174, Ibn Yaʿīš, *X,* 24, 28, *Mulūkī* 254, Ibn ʿUṣfūr, *I,* 369, *Ḍarāʾir* 226, Šinqīṭī, *Durar I,* 157, *II,* 213, Howell, *IV,* fasc. I, 1297:

"لَهَا أَشَارِيرُ مِنْ لَحْمٍ تُتَمِّرُهُ مِنَ الثَّعَالِي وَوَخْزٌ مِنْ أَرَانِيهَا".

"She [sc. the eagle] has bits of flesh that she dries, of foxes, and a little of her hares".

(358) The *y* in سادي is substituted for the *s* of سادس (cf. Nöldeke, *Grammatik* 13). It occurs in the following verse said by Imruʾu l-Qais, cited by Ibn Ǧinnī, *Sirr II,* 741, Zamaḫšarī, 174, Ibn Yaʿīš, *X,* 24, 28, *Mulūkī* 255, Ibn ʿUṣfūr, *I,* 368, *Ḍarāʾir* 226, Ibn Duraid, *Ǧamhara II,* 196, Šinqīṭī, *Durar II,* 213, Ibn Manẓūr, *III,* 1934, 1979, *V,* 3414, Howell, *IV,* fasc. I, 1297:

"إذا ما عُدَّ أَرْبَعَةٌ فِسَالٌ فَزَوْجُكِ خَامِسٌ وأَبُوكِ سَادِي".

"Whenever four mean unmanly fellows are reckoned, your husband is fifth, and your father sixth".

Ibn Manẓūr, *III,* 1979 mentions the verse with وحَمُوكِ سادي "and your father-in-law is sixth" instead of وأَبُوكِ سَادِي.

(359) The *y* in الثالي is substituted for the *ṯ* of الثالث (cf. Nöldeke, *Grammatik* 13). It occurs in these verses said by an unknown poet, cited by Rāzī in Ḫalīl b. Aḥmad ..., *Ḥurūf* 155, Ibn Ǧinnī, *Sirr II,* 764, *Munṣif II,* 178, *III,* 79, Zamaḫšarī, 174, Ibn Yaʿīš, *X,* 28, *Mulūkī* 255, Ibn ʿUṣfūr, *I,* 378, *Ḍarāʾir* 227, Baġdādī, *Šarḥ* 448, Šinqīṭī, *Durar II,* 212, Ibn Manẓūr, *I,* 497, Howell, *IV,* fasc. I, 1297-1298:

"يَفْدِيكِ يَا زُرْعَ أَبِي وَخَالِي قَدْ مَرَّ يَوْمَانِ وَهٰذَا ٱلثَّالِي
وَأَنْتَ بِٱلْهِجْرَانِ لَا تُبَالِي".

"My father and my maternal uncle shall be a ransom for you, O Zurʿa! Two days have passed and this is the third; and you do not care for the desertion".

(360) ضَوَارِبُ is the broken pl. of the active participle ضَارِبٌ. In its base form, the *ā* that marks the pl. is infixed after the infixed *ā* of the active participle ضَارِبٌ which causes a cluster of two vowelless consonants, the vowelless alifs, i.e. ضَاارِبٌ. The 1st *ā* is substituted by the *w* to prevent this cluster so that it became ضَوَارِبُ (cf. Ibn Ǧinnī, *de Flexione* 24, *Sirr II,* 581-582, Zamaḫšarī, 174, Ibn Yaʿīš, *X,* 29).

b) The regular broken pls. of the fem. (for a study see Zamaḫšarī, 79, Howell, *I,* fasc. III, 989) of the epithet فَاعِلٌ without the *tāʾ marbūṭa,* e.g. حَائِضٌ "menstruating" and طَالِقٌ "divorced", and of فَاعِلَةٌ with the *tāʾ marbūṭa,* e.g. ضَارِبَةٌ are the following:

- فَوَاعِلُ, as حَوَائِضُ, طَوَالِقُ, ضَوَارِبُ "striking", قَوَاتِلُ "killing", خَوَارِجُ "going ut" and جَوَالِسُ "sitting up".
- فُعَّلٌ as نُوَّمٌ "sleeping" and زُوَّرٌ "visiting".

(361) The base form of the active participle Form IV مُوقِنٌ is مُيْقِنٌ from أَيْقَنَ "he was certain". The vowelless 1st radical *y* of مُيْقِنٌ is substituted by the *w* on account of the influence of the ḍamma preceding it, i.e. مُوقِنٌ. A similar case is the active participle Form IV مُوسِرٌ from Form IV أَيْسَرَ "was well off", underlyingly مُيْسِرٌ in which the 1st radical vowelless *y* is also substituted by the *w* because it is preceded by a ḍamma. Cf. Sībawaihi, *II,* 342, Ibn Ǧinnī, *de Flexione* 24, *Sirr II,* 584, Zamaḫšarī, 174, Ibn Yaʿīš, *X,* 30, Howell, *IV,* fasc. I, 1301, Mokhlis, *Taṣrīf* 177. It can be noted as well that the imperfect Form IV يُوسِرُ from يَسَرَ, is underlyingly يُيْسِرُ in which the vowelless 1st radical *y* is changed into a *w* on account of the ḍamma preceding it (cf. (261)).

(362) The *w* in لُومٌ is substituted for the vowelless hamza of the base form لُؤْمٌ (cf. (217)). The reason of this substitution is the weakness of the vowelless hamza and the request of the ḍamma preceding it to be lengthened. The *w* is as well substituted for the hamza in the 1st person of the sing. of the imperfect verbs أُولُ said instead of أُأْلُ from the sentence أَلَّتْ أَسْنَانُهُ "his teeth decayed" and أُومِنُ said instead of أُؤْمِنُ "I make safe" from أَمِنَ "to be faithful" (cf. 228 c)).

(363) The base form of فَمٌ is فَوْهٌ (cf. Talmon, *ʿAyn* 236) on the measure of فَوْجٌ "crowd". Its 2nd radical is a *w* and its 3rd radical is a *h,* as it is proven by its broken pl. أَفْوَاهٌ and its diminutive فُوَيْهٌ, because they both restore the nouns to their base form (for the principle that the diminutive brings back the noun to its base form see (65)). The *h* of فَوْهٌ is elided for the purpose of alleviation and the *w* is changed into a *m,* i.e. فَمٌ (cf. Zaǧǧāǧī, *Maǧālis* 327, Ibn Ǧinnī, *Sirr I,* 413-421, Zamaḫšarī, 174, Ibn Yaʿīš, *X,* 33-34, Wright, *II,* 173, Vernier, *I,* 16-17, Bohas, *Étude* 232-235). According to Sībawaihi, *II,* 342, the substitution of the *m* for the *w* in فَمٌ is rare. Furthermore, it is mainly used when no pronoun is suffixed to it and when it is undefinite, e.g. هٰذَا فَمٌ "this is a mouth", رَأَيْتُ فَمًا "I saw a mouth" and نَظَرْتُ إِلَى فَمٍ "I watched a mouth". It was used anomalously declinable with a pronoun suffixed to it, namely فَمُهْ "his mouth" in pause, in this saying of Ru'ba b. al-ʿAǧǧāǧ, cited by Ḥarīrī, *Durra* 69, Howell, *I,* fasc. I, 24:

"كَالْحُوتِ لَا يُرْوِيهِ شَيْءٌ يَلْهَمُهْ يُصْبِحُ عَطْشَانَ وَفِي ٱلْبَحْرِ فَمُهْ".

"Like the fish, whom not a thing that he swallows satisfies, who becomes thirsty while his mouth is in the sea".

ظَمْآنَ has also been used instead of عَطْشَانَ in this verse in other works (cf. Howell, *IV,* fasc. I, 1323). In the case of when a pronoun is suffixed to it, the base form is used, e.g. نَطَقَ فُوهُ "His mouth spoke", قَبَّلَ فَاهُ "he kissed his mouth". فِيهْ occurs in the genitive in the pause in this saying which is believed to be by ʿAlī b. Abī Ṭālib. However, Ibn Wallād, *Maqṣūr* 27 and Ibn Manẓūr, *I,* 707 who refer to Ibn al-Kalbī, mention that the one who said the verse is ʿAmr b. Uḫt Ǧaḏīma al-Abraš. Ibn Manẓūr mentions as well that according to the tradition ʿAlī said this verse. It is cited by Ibn Manẓūr, *I,* 707, Saraqusṭī, *Afʿāl II,* 278, Howell, *I,* fasc. I, 24, Lane, *I,* 472:

"هٰذَا جَنَايَ وَخِيَارُهُ فِيهْ إِذْ كُلُّ جَانٍ يَدُهُ إِلَى فِيهْ".

"This is my gathering; and the best of it is in it, when every other gatherer has had his hand to his mouth".

Another form that can be added is فُمّ with the vowelling of the *f* by a ḍamma and the doubling of the *m,* which has been transmitted anomalously in the following verse that is supposed to be by Ru'ba b. al-ʿAǧǧāǧ, but which according to Ibn Manẓūr, *IV,* 2672, is either by al-ʿUmānī al-Rāǧiz, whose real name is Muḥammad b. Ḏu'aib al-Fuqaimīy, or as Ibn Ḫālawaih to whom he refers to mentions, by Ǧarīr who said it concerning Sulaimān b. ʿAbd al-Malik and ʿAbd al-ʿAzīz. It is cited by Ibn Ǧinnī, *Sirr I,* 415, *Ḫaṣā'iṣ III,* 211, Ibn Yaʿīš, *X,* 33, Ibn ʿUṣfūr, *I,* 391, Suyūṭī, *Ašbāh I,* 261, Šinqīṭī, *Durar I,* 13, Ibn Manẓūr, *V,* 3492, Howell, *IV,* fasc. I, 1322:

"يَا لَيْتَهَا قَدْ خَرَجَتْ مِن فُمِّهِ حَتَّى يَعُودَ ٱلْمُلْكُ فِي أُسْطُمِّهِ".

"O would that it [sc.a word that was to be spoken] had issued from his mouth, so that the kingdom might return to its owner, and its rightful claimant!".

For a discussion concerning the different forms of فَمٌ in the Semitic languages see Nöldeke, *Neue Beiträge* 171-178.

(364) اَمْ denotes determination in the dialect of Ṭayyī and Ḥimyar. This dialect is named الطُّمْطُمَانِيَّة (cf. Rabin, 49). Rabin, 35-37 discusses it within the chapter treating the Yemenite dialects, but points out p. 25 that some of the material belongs to the next three chapters that treat the dialects of Himyar, Azd, and Northern Yemen. اَمْ is said to replace anomalously the usual definite article *al-* by substituting the *m* for the *l.* It is also possible that it refers in some cases to a demonstrative element (for discussions see Cantineau, *Études* 51). It is usually prefixed to nouns of which the initial consonant is a moon-consonant (for discussions see Ibn

Hišām, *Muġnī I,* 49; for the moon- and solar-consonants see (176)), but in some cases, it occurs prefixed to nouns that begin with a solar-consonant, as some of the nouns of the example of this tradition and the verse cited below. Some examples occurring in the Yemenite dialect in which it is combined with the interrogative particle مَنْ and with a nunated definite noun whose initial consonant is a moon-consonant are مَنْ أمْ قائمٌ "who is the one standing?" said instead of مَن آلْقائمُ and مَنْ فِي أمْ بابٍ "who is at the door?" said instead of مَنْ فِي آلْبَابِ (cf. Bustānī, *Muḥīṭ* 15, Rabin, 36). This awkward nunation could be a nasalisation which affects a vowel that is standing in the pausal position, as the *m* used in the ʾÖmur colloquial near Palmyra, e.g *buyūtaka*[m] for *buyūtaka* "your houses" (cf. Cantineau, *Parlers* 18, Rabin, 36-37). The noun after this article could as well end with a vowel which marks that it is definite, as in the example cited by Ibn Hišām, *Muġnī I,* 49 اركَبْ امْفرس "ride the horse".

For the tradition لَيسَ مِنَ آلبِرِّ آلصِّيَامُ فِي آلسَّفَرِ "fasting in travelling is not an act of piety" cited without the substitution of the *m* for the *l,* see Wensinck, *Concordance III,* 461. It is said with the substitution, i.e. لَيسَ من آمبِرِّ آمْصِيامُ فِي آمْسَفَرِ by al-Namir b. Tawlab, and is cited by Ibn Ǧinnī, *Sirr I,* 423, Zamaḫšarī, 153, 174, Ibn Yaʿīš, *X,* 34, Kafrāwī, *Šarḥ* 11, Ibn Hišām, *Qaṭr* 114, *Muġnī I,* 48, Ibn ʿUṣfūr, *I,* 394, Ḥarīrī, *Durra* 183, Howell, *II-III,* 676, *IV,* fasc. I, 1330, de Sacy, *Anthologie* [Ḥarīrī, *Durra]* 63, Freytag, *Einleitung* 119, Rabin, 36 [who has however من instead of مِنَ], Cantineau, *Études* 51, Journal Asiatique, 4 sér. XIV, 347, Wright, *II,* 270, Carter, *Širbīnī* 22, 23, Barrānī, *Maṭālib* 104. According to Ibn Masʿūd, this substitution of the *m* for the *l* is carried out because of both these consonants' common character in being among the voiced consonants (for the consonants' characters see (188 b)).
A verse said by Buǧair b. Ġanama al-Ṭāʾī, cited by Zamaḫšarī, 153, Ibn Hišām, *Muġnī I,* 48, Suyūṭī, *Šarḥ* 58, Ibn Manẓūr, *I,* 139, Howell, *II-III,* 676, Rabin, 36 (who however, has يُعَاتِبُنِي "reproves me" for يُوَاصِلُنِي and وَآمْسَلَمَهْ for وَآمْسَلِمَهْ), has بِآمْسَهْمِ instead of بِالسَّهْمِ and وَآمْسَلِمَهْ instead of وَالسَّلِمَهْ:

"ذَاكَ خَلِيلِي وَذُو يُوَاصِلُنِي يَرْمِي وَرَائِي بِآمْسَهْمِ وَآمْسَلِمَهْ".

"That is my friend and he that unites with me, casting behind me the arrow and the stone [i.e. defending my reputation behind my back]".

The *m* of the article أم can be assimilated to the *m* of the initial of the noun following it in the dialectal variant of Daṯīna. This occurs in the saying cited by Landberg, *Études II,* 118 and quoted by Roman, *Étude I,* 200, in which يا آمَجْعلِي is probably underlyingly يا الْمجْعلِي:

"قل لعمّك عليّ يا آمَجْعلِي بر عوض"

"Say to your oncle ʿAlī, O am-Mèǧʿalī [sc. al-Mèǧʿalī], son of ʿAwaḍ".

(365) The vowelless *m* in عَمْبَرٌ is substituted for the vowelless *n* of the base form عَنْبَرٌ (cf. (68)).

(366) The *m* in بَنَامِ is substituted anomalously for the vowelled *n* of the base form بَنَانٌ (cf. Nöldeke, *Grammatik* 12). It occurs in the following verse said by ʿAǧǧāǧ, *Dīwān* 144 in the beginning of a poem in which he is praising Maslama b. ʿAbd al-Malik. It is cited by Rāzī in Ḫalīl b. Aḥmad ..., *Ḥurūf* 154, Ibn Ǧinnī, *Sirr I*, 422, Zamaḫšarī, 174-175, Ibn Yaʿīš, *X*, 33, 35, Ibn ʿUṣfūr, *I*, 392, Baġdādī, *Šarḥ* 455, Howell, *IV*, fasc. I, 1332:

"يَا هَالَ ذَاتَ ٱلْمَنْطِقِ ٱلتَّمْتَامِ   وَكَفَّكِ ٱلْمُخَضَّبِ ٱلْبَنَامِ".

"O Hāla [sc. name of a woman], possessed of the lisping speech, and of your hand dyed
in [the tips of] the fingers with henna".

(367) The *m* in رَاتَمًا is substituted for the *b* of the base form رَاتَبًا (cf. Zamaḫšarī, 175, Ibn Yaʿīš, *X*, 35). The reason of this substitution is that both these consonants' point of articulation is identical, as they both are labials (for the consonants see (188 b); for a study of the interchange of labials in Classical and pre-classical Arabic see Hämeen-Anttila, *Labials* 28-37). The *m* can be retained in the base form in e.g. رَتَمَةٌ "a thread bound on the finger to remind one of a want, or also a kind of tree". ٱلرَّتَمُ occurs in the following verse said by an unknown poet, cited by Ibn Manẓūr, *III*, 1579, Howell, *IV*, fasc. I, 1334, Lane, *I*, 1029:

"هَلْ يَنْفَعَنْكَ ٱلْيَوْمَ إِنْ هَمَتْ بِهِمْ   كَثْرَةُ مَا تُوصِي وَتَعْقَادُ ٱلرَّتَمْ".

"Shall the multiplicity of what you enjoin and the tying of the Ratam indeed profit you if she cares
for them?".

The substitution of the *m* for the *b* is carried out in بَنَاتُ مَخْرٍ that has been transmitted instead of بَنَاتُ بَخْرٍ "thin white clouds that come before the summer rising high in the sky" (cf. Rāzī in Ḫalīl b. Aḥmad ..., *Ḥurūf* 154, Howell, *IV*, fasc. I, 1332). كِبْنَاتُ ٱلْمَخْرِ has also occurred in a verse said by Ṭarafa, *Dīwān* 59, cited by Ibn Ǧinnī, *Sirr I*, 423. See furthermore the examples mentioned by Cantineau, *Cours* 29 and those collected by Ružička, *Dissimilation* that are mentioned passim in his book. Another example is نُغَمًا which occurred instead of نُغَبًا "gulp" in the following verse said probably by Ruʾba b. al-ʿAǧǧāǧ, cited by Ibn Ǧinnī, *Sirr I*, 426, Zamaḫšarī, 175, Ibn Yaʿīš, *X*, 33, 35, Ibn ʿUṣfūr, *I*, 393, Ibn Manẓūr, *VI*, 4487, Howell, *IV*, fasc. I, 1335:

"فَبَادَرَتْ شَاتَهَا عَجْلَى مُثَابِرَةً   حَتَّى ٱسْتَقَتْ دُونَ مَحْنَى جِيدِهَا نُغَمَا".

"Then she hastened to her sheep, hurrying, persevering, until she drew water enough for gulps
below the bend of her neck".

The interchange of *b* and *m* is also connected with Māzin b. Bakr (for the literature relating to him see Köfler, *Dialekte* (XLVII, 1940), 69) and with the dialectal variant of Māzin b. Rabīʿa. Ḥarīrī, *Durra* 73 reports (cf. Sīrāfī, *Aḫbār* 76, Rabin, 201):

"قَالَ أَبُو عُثْمَانَ فَلَمَّا مَثَلْتُ بَيْنَ يَدَيْهِ قَالَ مِمَّنِ ٱلرَّجُلُ قُلْتُ مِنْ بَنِى مَازِنْ قَالَ أَيِّ الْمَوَازِنِ أَمَازِنُ تَمِيمٍ أَمْ مَازِنُ قَيْسٍ أَمْ مَازِنُ رَبِيعَةَ قُلْتُ مِنْ مَازِنِ رَبِيعَةَ فَكَلَّمَنِى بِكَلَامِ قَوْمِى وَقَالَ لِي بَا ٱسْمُكَ لِأَنَّهُمْ يَقْلِبُونَ الْمِيمَ بَاءً وَالْبَاءَ مِيمًا قَالَ فَكَرِهْتُ أَنْ أُجِيبَهُ عَلَى لُغَةِ قَوْمِى لِئَلَّا أُوَاجِهَهُ بِالْمَكْرِ فَقُلْتُ بَكْرٌ يَا أَمِيرَ الْمُؤْمِنِينَ...".

"Abū ʿUṯmān [al-Māzinī] said: "Then when I appeared in front of him [sc. the Caliph al-Wāṯiq], he asked: "From where is the man?". I answered: "From the Banū Māzin". He asked: "From which of the Banū Māzins? From the Māzin of Tamīm, the Māzin of Qais or the Māzin of Rabīʿa?". I answered: “From the Māzin of Rabīʿa“. So he addressed me in the dialectal variant of my people and asked me: “بَا آسْمُكَ [instead of مَا آسْمُكَ] “What’s your name?”, because they usually change the *m* into the *b* and the *b* into the *m*. But I disliked to answer him according to the dialectal variant of my people as I did not want to say : “Makr”, so I answered: “Bakr, O Commander of the Faithful...”.

B and *m* interchange also in the cognate languages. In Ḥimyaritic בן stands for מַן “who”, and בן for מַן “from”. Compare also زَمَنٌ “time”, ዘመን, זְמַן and ܙܰܒܢܳܐ. In Assyrian, the *m* passes into an aspirated *b* or *v*, e.g. *argamānu* or *argavānu* “purple”, Hebrew אַרְגָּמָן and Aramaic אַרְגְּוָן (cf.Wright, *Comparative Grammar* 65).

(368) The *ṣ* in أَصْبَغَ is substituted for the *s* of its base form أَسْبَغَ (for a study see Zamaḫšarī, 176, Ibn Yaʿīš, *X*, 51-52, Howell, *IV*, fasc. I, 1378-1380, Fleisch, *Traité I*, 80-81). It occurs in the sur. 31: 20 (وَأَصْبَغَ عَلَيْكُمْ نِعَمَهُ) “And has made His bounties flow to you in exceeding measure”, underlyingly وَأَسْبَغَ, read with both the *s* and the *ṣ* (cf. Ibn Ǧinnī, *Sirr I*, 212). This substitution is carried out if the *s* occurs before the *ġ*. The reason of this substitution is the proximity of both the *s* and the *ṣ* as they both originate from the part which is between the tip of the tongue and the tops of the two upper central incissors (for the consonants see (188)). Both as well are akin in character in being among the sibilant consonants (for them see Ullendorff, *Article* 632, my notes (188 b)). Another example is صَالِغٌ that occurs instead of سَالِغٌ “shedding the tooth, which takes place in the sixth year”. It can be added that such a substitution is carried out as well if the *s* precedes:

- the *ḫ* as صَلَخَ instead of سَلَخَ “stripped of”.

- the *q*, as the readings of some of the sur. 54: 48 (مَسَّ صَقَرَ) “The touch of hell” instead of مَسَّ سَقَرَ; and صُوقٌ “market” said instead of سُوقٌ (cf. (174)) by the Banū l-ʿAnbar b. Tamīm (cf. Rabin, 195). According to Ibn Ǧinnī, *Ḫaṣā’iṣ II*, 142-143, this substitution of the *ṣ* for the *s* pertains to الإدغام الأصغر “the little assimilation” (for it see (174)).

- the *ṭ* as in صِرَاطٌ underlyingly سِرَاطٌ “path” (cf. Jeffery, *Muqaddimatān* 148) and مُصَيْطِرٌ underlyingly مُسَيْطِرٌ “dominating” (cf. ibid, Talmon, *ʿAyn* 343). It can be noted that Ibn Kaṯīr read السِّرَاطَ with the *s* according to its base form from the sur. 2: 6 (اِهْدِنَا ٱلصِّرَاطَ ٱلْمُسْتَقِيمَ) whereas the remaining readers among the seven read it with the *ṣ* (cf. Ibn Ḫālawaihi, *Qirā’āt I*, 49). In the context of the derivation (cf. 14 c), there is a semantic relation between the *s* and the *ṣ* (cf. Bohas, *Matrice* 150), e.g. سَرِحَ “to manifest, or give forth what is in one’s bosom” (cf. Lane, *I*, 1344) and Form II of صَرِحَ, namely صَرَّحَ “to make apparent, or manifest what is in one’s mind” (cf. ibid, *II*, 1675).

(369) The *ā* in قَالَ is substituted for the *w* of the base form قَوَلَ (cf. (266)) and the *ā* of بَاعَ is substituted for the *y* of the base form بَيَعَ (cf. Åkesson, *Conversion* 27). The *ā* of رَاسٌ is substituted for the hamza of the base form رَأْسٌ (for it see (217); and for another example, namely هَنَاكَ said instead of هَنَأَكَ, see (220)).

(370) The *l* in أُصَيْلالٌ is substituted for the *n* of the base form أُصَيْلانٌ (cf. Wright, *II,* 175). أُصَيْلالاً occurs in the following verse said by al-Nābiġa al-D̲ubyānī in D̲ubyānī, *Dīwān* 2 praising al-Nuʿmān b. al-Mund̲ir, and cited by Rāzī in Ḫalīl b. Aḥmad ..., *Ḥurūf* 153, Ibn al-Sikkīt, *Qalb* 5, Ibn Ǧinnī, *Lumaʿ* 28, Muʾaddib, *Taṣrīf* 338, Ibn al-Sarrāǧ, *Uṣūl III,* 275, Zamaḫšarī, 176, Ibn Yaʿīš, *Mulūkī* 106, 216, Ibn al-Anbārī, *Inṣāf* Q. 19, 79, Ḫuḍarī, *Ḥāšiya II,* 229, Naḥḥās, *Qaṣāʾid II,* 734, Tibrīzī, *Qaṣāʾid* 513, Ḥamīrī, *Šams I,* 20, Howell, *IV,* fasc. I, 1367, Ahlwardt, *Divans* 6:

"وَقَفْتُ فيها أُصَيْلالاً أُسائلُها عَيَّتْ جَوَاباً وَمَا بِالرَّبْعِ مِنْ أَحَدِ".

"I stopped in it a short time at evening, questioning it [about its inmates]: it was unable to answer, nor was any one in the abode".

Ibn Yaʿīš, *II,* 80 and Afandī, *Tanzīl* 379 mention the verse with أصيلانا said instead of أُصَيْلالاً. Afandī has as well أعييت instead of عَيَّتْ.

(371) The *l* in الْطَجَعَ is substituted for the *ḍ* of the base form اضْطَجَعَ. فالْطَجَعْ is found in the following verse said by Manẓūr b. Murt̲id al-Asadī, as mentioned by Baġdādī, *Šarḥ* 275-276, describing a wolf that meant to catch a gazelle. It is cited by Ibn Ǧinnī, *Sirr I,* 321, *Ḫaṣāʾiṣ I,* 63, 263, *III,* 163, Zamaḫšarī, 176, Ibn Yaʿīš, *IX,* 82, *X,* 46, *Mulūkī* 216, Ibn ʿAqīl, *II,* 548, Ibn ʿUṣfūr, *I,* 403, Suyūṭī, *Ašbāh I,* 601, Ibn Manẓūr, *IV,* 2554, Howell, *IV,* fasc. I, 848, 1368, Rāǧiḥī, *Farrāʾ* 141:

"لَمَّا رَأَى أَنْ لَا دَعَهْ وَلَا شِبَعْ مَالَ إِلَى أَرْطَاةِ حِقْفٍ فَالْطَجَعْ".

"When he [sc. the wolf] saw that there was no ease, and no glutting of his appetite [in the pursuit of the gazelle], he turned aside to an Arṭā tree of a curving tract of sand, and lay down to sleep".

All the four variations فَالْطَجَعْ, فَاطَّجَعْ, فَاضْطَجَعْ and فَاضَّجَعْ as the last word of the rime are cited in different works (cf. Fischer/Braünlich, *Šawāhid* 134).

(372) The *z* in يَزْدُلُ is substituted for the *s* of the base form يَسْدُلُ (cf. Ibn Ǧinnī, *Sirr I,* 196, Zamaḫšarī, 177, Ibn Yaʿīš, *X,* 52, Ibn Manẓūr, *III,* 2036). Another example with this substitution is بَزَقَ for بَسَقَ "to spit" (cf. Cantineau, *Cours* 56, *Études* 47). It can be mentioned that during the 6th/12th century, the people of al-Andalus and of Marocco used to say زَرْدابٌ for سَرْدابٌ "cellar" (cf. Laḫmī, *Madḫal* 439), and currently the people in Egypt and even other Arabs say زَعْتَر for سَعْتَر "wild thyme" (cf. Dasūqī, *Tahd̲īb* 66). The *ṣ* in صَقَر "hell" is substituted for the *s* of سَقَر, and in its turn, it is substituted by the *z* as it is said زَقَر in the dialect of Kalb. This substitution of the *z* for the *ṣ* is known as الزَّسْوُ (cf. also a part of (373)).

b) The *s* is as well substituted for the *z*. This occurs in many Arabic dialects. An example is سَحَفَ that is said instead of زَحَفَ "to crawl" (cf. Dāġir, *Tad̲kira* 85).

(373) The *z* in فَزْدِي is substituted for the *ṣ* of the base form فَصْدِي. This substitution is carried out when the *z* is vowelless and precedes the *d.* فَزْدِي occurs in this phrase said by Ḥatim when he had slaughtered a she-camel for a guest and he was asked: "Why did you not bleed her?", and he answered: هٰكَذَا فَزْدِي أَنَهْ "This is my way of bleeding, mine" with this particular substitution (cf. Ibn al-Sikkīt, *Qalb* 45, Luġawī, *Ibdāl II,* 126-128, Zaǧǧāǧī, *Maǧālis* 136, Zamaḫšarī, 177, Ibn Ya'īš, *X,* 52, Freytag, *Proverbia II,* 867, Howell, *IV,* fasc. I, 856, 1383). It can be mentioned that both هٰكَذَا and هٰذَا are said in this sentence. Another interesting phenomenon in his saying is the substitution of the *h* in أَنَهْ for the *ā* of the base form أَنَا that occurs in pause (cf. (73 c), (345)). Another example that can be addded with this substitution is فُزْدَ, which is used instead of فُزِدَ for فُصِدَ "a camel has been bled". As remarked in it, the *z* has been made vowelless for the sake of alleviation. It occurs in لَمْ يُحْرَمِ ٱلرِّفْدَ مَنْ فُزْدَ لَهُ "He has not been refused [help], he for whom a camel has been bled", which is cited by Ibn Ǧinnī, *Sirr I,* 50, Zamaḫšarī, 177, Ibn Ya'īš, *X,* 53, Zubaidī, *Laḥn* 194, Ibn Manẓūr, *V,* 3420, Freytag, *Hamasae* 645, *Einleitung* 291, Freytag, *Proverbia II,* 441, Abū 'Ubaid, *Amṯāl* 235, Howell, *IV,* fasc. I, 1382. Other examples are أَزْدَرْتُ said instead of أَصْدَرْتُ "I issued"; and مَزْدَرٌ said instead of مَصْدَرٌ "issue, way out", which occur in the following verse said by an unknown poet, recited by al-Ṣāġānī, cited by Ibn Ǧinnī, *Sirr I,* 196, Ibn 'Uṣfūr, 412, Zamaḫšarī, 177, Ibn Ya'īš, *X,* 52, Ibn Manẓūr, *IV,* 2413, Howell, *IV,* fasc. I, 1382:

"وَدَعْ ذَا ٱلْهَوَى قَبْلَ ٱلْقِلَى تَرْكُ ذِي ٱلْهَوَى مَتِينَ ٱلْقُوَى خَيْرٌ مِنَ ٱلصَّرْمِ مَزْدَرَا".

"And let the object of your love alone before hating [him]: the leaving of the object of love, while unimpaired in its forces, is better as an issue than rupture".

The substitution of the *z* for the *ṣ* is carried out when the *ṣ* is vowelled and in other cases than when it precedes the *d,* e.g. بَزَقَ for بَصَقَ "to spit", قَرَزَ for قَرَصَ "to pinch" and زَعَقَ for صَعَقَ "to scream" (cf. Cantineau, *Cours* 56, *Études* 47). It pertains to the dialectal variant of Kalb and is known as الزَّسْوُ (cf. (372)).

(374) The *ṭ* in Form VIII اِصْطَبَرَ is substituted for the infixed *t* of the base form اِصْتَبَرَ (192 c), (174). This substitution is necessary in Form VIII اِفْتَعَلَ if the *t* follows one of the consonants of covering (for them see (188 b), (193); for discussions see Bohas, *Étude* 237-239) that is the 1st radical, e.g. اِضْطَرَبَ "to be in a state of agitation" underlyingly اِضْتَرَبَ (cf. (195), (174)), اِطَّلَبَ "to seek" underlyingly اِطْتَلَبَ (cf. (196)), and اِظْطَلَمَ "to put with wrong" underlyingly اِظْتَلَمَ (cf. (197)). According to Ibn Ǧinnī, *Ḫaṣā'iṣ II,* 142-143, this substitution of one of the consonants of covering that is the 1st radical for the *t* pertains to الإدغام الأصغر "the little assimilation" (for it see (174)). In the context of the derivation (cf. 14 c), there is a semantic relation between the *t* and the *ṭ* (cf. Bohas, *Matrice* 149-150), e.g. تَرَّ "to become separated or cut off" (cf. Lane, *I,* 299) and طَرَّ "to cut off" (cf. ibid, *II,* 1833).

(375) The *ṭ* in فَحَصْطُ is substituted for the *t* that is the suffixed pronoun of the nominative of the 1st person of the sing. in the base form فَحَصْتُ (cf. Sībawaihi, *II,* 341, Ibn Ǧinnī, *Sirr I,* 219-

220, Zamaḫšarī, 176, Ibn Yaʿīš, *X,* 46-48, Ibn ʿUṣfūr, *I,* 360-361, Howell, *IV,* fasc. I, 1369-1370, Vernier, *I,* 356). This substitution is carried out when the pronoun of the nominative of the 1st person, the *-tu,* or of the 2nd persons, the *-ta* "/masc. sing." and the *-ti* "/fem. sing." of the perfect, is suffixed to a verb whose 3rd radical is one of the consonants of covering (for them see (188 b), (193)). Some examples are. حَفِظْطُ for حَفِظْتُ "I kept", حَفِظْطَ for حَفِظْتَ "you kept", حُصْطُ for حُصْتُ "I sealed" and حُصْطَ for حُصْتَ "you sealed". This substitution is usual in the dialect of the Banū Tamīm. The reason of it, is that both the *t* and the *ṭ* originate from the tip of the tongue and the roots of the two upper central incissors (for the consonants see (188)). Another theory than the pure phonetical one that is advanced by Ibn Ǧinnī, *Munṣif II,* 332-334, is that the suffixed *-t* of the nominative in Form I فَعَلْتُ is compared to the infixed *-t* of Form VIII افْتَعَلَ that is substituted by the *ṭ* when it follows one of the consonants of covering, because both these tāʾs are considered as being a part of the verb, differently from the suffixed pronoun of the accusative that is considered as separate from it (for the separation of the object suffix from the verb see (55)).

b) The substitution of the *ṭ* for the *d* is carried out as well and is anomalous, e.g. مَطَ said instead of مَدَ "to prolong", and ابْعَاطٌ said instead of ابْعَادٌ "removing to a distance" (cf. Howell, *IV,* fasc. I, 1369-1370).

II.8. Arabic Text: الباب السابع في اللفيف

يُقال له اللفيف للفّ حرفي العلّة فيه وهو على ضربين مفروق ومقرون. المفروق مثل وَقَى يَقِي* ٣٦ آ حكم فائهما كحكم وَعَدَ يَعِدُ وحكم لامهما كحكم رَمَى يَرْمِي وكذلك حكم أخواتهما. الأمر قِ قِيَا قُوا قِي قِيَا قِينَ وتقول بنون التأكيد قِيَنَّ قِيَانِّ قُنَّ قِنَّ قِيَانِّ قِينَانِّ وبالخفيفة قِيَنْ قُنْ قِنْ. الفاعل وَاقٍ والمفعول مَوْقِيٌّ والموضع مَوْقَى والآلة ميقى. المجهول وُقِيَ يُوقَى. المقرون نحو طَوَى يَطوي الى آخرهما وحكمهما كحكم الناقص ولا يُعلّ عينهما كما مرّ في باب الأجوف. الأمر اِطْوِ اِطْوِيَا اِطْوُوا اِطْوِي اِطْوِيَا اِطْوِينَ. وتقول بنون التأكيد اِطْوِيَنَّ اِطْوِيَانِّ اِطْوُنَّ اِطْوِنَّ اِطْوِيَانِّ اِطْوِينَانِّ وبالخفيفة اِطْوِيَنْ اِطْوُنْ اِطْوِنْ. وتقول في الأمر من رَوِيَ يَرْوَى رِيّاً اِرْوَ اِرْوَيَا اِرْوَوْا اِرْوَي اِرْوَيَا اِرْوَيْنَ، وبنون التأكيد المثقّلة من رَوِيَ يَرْوَى اِرْوَيَنَّ اِرْوَيَانِّ اِرْوَوُنَّ اِرْوَيِنَّ اِرْوَيَانِّ اِرْوَيْنَانِّ. وبالخفيفة اِرْوَيَنْ اِرْوَوُنْ اِرْوَيِنْ . وإذا أردت أن تعرف أحكام نوني التأكيد في الناقص واللفيف فانظر الى حرف العلّة إن كانت أصليّة محذوفة في الواحد تُردّ لأن حذفها كان للسكون* ٣٦ ب وهو انعدم بدخول النون وتُفتح لخفّة الفتحة نحو اِطْوِيَنَّ وأُغْزُوَنَّ واِرْوَيَنَّ كما في اِطْوِيَا وأُغْزُوَا واِرْوَيَا وإن كانت ضميراً فانظر الى ما قبلها

Fols. 35b-36b

٢ حرفي: حروف ب: حرف د ط/ وهو: فهو د/ مفروق ومقرون: مقرون ومفروق ا/ ٣ حكم: –ا/ ٤ وتقول بنون: وبنوني د/ ٥ والمفعول: المفعول ل/ والموضع: الموضع ل/ والآلة: الآلة ل/ ٦ الى آخرهما: –ا ط/ ٧ش٨ وتقول بنون: وبنون ا ج د ز/ ٩ وتقول... اِرْوَيَنَ: – ا: وتقول من روي يروي اِرْوِ د/ وبنون: وبنوني د/ ١٠ المثقّلة... يروي: – د ز ل/ ١٢ وتُفتح: ويفتح د/

II.8. Translation: The 7th Chapter is about the Verb that is doubly Weak(376)

It is named اللفيف "complicated, tangled" because of the combination of two weak consonants in it. It falls into two classes: 1-مفروق "verbs with weak 1st and 3rd radical", and 2- مقرون "verbs with weak 2nd and 3rd radicals combined". An example of a verb with weak 1st and 3rd radicals is وَقَى يقي "to guard, preserve". **[Fol. 36 a]** The predicament of both the 1st radicals [of its perfect and imperfect] is the same as the predicament of [the 1st radicals of the verb with 1st weak radical] وَعَدَ يعدُ "to promise", and the predicament of the 3rd radicals [of its perfect and imperfect] is the same as the predicament of [the 3rd radicals of the verb with 3rd weak radical] رَمَى يَرْمِي "to throw". So is also the predicament of both their cognates [i.e. the active and passive participles]. The imperative is قِ "preserve /masc. sing.", قِيَا "/2 dual", قُوا "/2 masc. pl.", قِي "/2 fem. sing.", قِيَا "/2 dual" and قِينَ "/2 fem. pl.". You say with the energetic *n:* قِيَنَّ "/2 masc. pl. (imperative En. 1)", قِيَانِّ "/2 dual", قُنَّ "/2 masc. pl.", قِنَّ "/2 fem. pl.", قِيَانِّ "/2 dual" and قِينَانِّ "/2 fem. pl.", and with the single *n:* قِيَنْ "/2 masc. sing.", قُنْ "/2 masc. pl." and قِنْ "/2 fem. sing.". The active participle is وَاقٍ, the passive participle مَوْقِيٌّ, the noun of place مَوْقًى, the noun of instrument مِيقًى and the passive voice وُقِيَ يُوقَى. An example of a verb with weak 2nd and 3rd radical is طَوَى يَطْوِي "to fold", etc. The predicament of [the 3rd radicals in] both of them [sc. its perfect and imperfect] is the same as the predicament of the verbs with weak 3rd radical. Their 2nd weak radical is kept sound as was mentioned in the chapter about the verb with weak 2nd radical.(377) The imperative is اطْوِ "/2 masc. sing.", اطْوِيَا "/2 dual", اطْوُوا "/2 masc. pl.", اطْوِي "/2 fem. sing.", اطْوِيَا "/2 dual" and اطْوِينَ "/2 fem. pl". You say with the energetic *n-:* اطْوِيَنَّ "/2 masc. sing. (imperative En. 1)", اطْوِيَانِّ "/2 dual", اطْوُنَّ "/2 masc. pl.", اطْوِنَّ "/2 fem. sing.", اطْوِيَانِّ "/2 dual" and اطْوِينَانِّ "/2 fem. pl.", and with the single *n-:* اطْوِيَنْ "/2 masc. sing., اطْوُنْ "/2 masc. pl." and اطْوِنْ "/2 fem. sing.". You say concerning the imperative of رَوِيَ يَرْوَى رِيًا "to quench one's thirst": ارْوَ "/2 masc. sing.", ارْوَيَا "/2 dual", ارْوَوْا "2 masc. pl.", ارْوَيْ "/2 fem. sing.", ارْوَيَا "/2 dual" and ارْوَيْنَ "2 fem. pl.", with the energetic *n* of رَوِيَ يَرْوَى: ارْوَيَنَّ "/2 masc. sing. (imperative En. 1)", ارْوَيَانِّ "/2 dual", ارْوَوُنَّ "/2 masc. pl.", ارْوَيِنَّ "/2 fem. sing.", ارْوَيَانِّ "/2 dual" and ارْوَيْنَانِّ "/2 fem. pl.", and with the single *n:* ارْوَيَنْ "/2 masc. sing.", ارْوَوُنْ "/2 masc. pl." and ارْوَيِنْ "/2 fem. sing.". If you want to know the predicament of the corroborative nūns in the verbs with weak 3rd radical and in the verbs that are doubly weak, take notice of the weak consonant. If it is a radical and elided in the sing. [in the imperative], it is restored, because its elision was due to the sukūn. **[Fol. 36 b]** This [cause] is not more existent when the *n* is suffixed. It [sc. the weak 3rd radical] is vowelled by a fatḥa because of the lightness of the fatḥa, as e.g. [the *y]* in اطْوِيَنَّ "/2 masc. sing.", [the *w]* in أُغْزُوَنَّ "you do surely raid!" and [the *y]* in ارْوَيَنَّ "/2 masc. sing.", similarly to اطْوِيَا "/2 dual", أُغْزُوَا "/2 dual" and ارْوَيَا "/2 dual". If it [sc. the weak consonant] is a pronoun take notice of the consonant preceding it:

إن كان مفتوحاً تُحرَك لطروَ حركتها وخفَة حركة ما قبلها نحو اِرْوَوُنَ وارْوَيِنَ كما في قوله تعالى ﴿وَلَا تَنْسَوُا ٱلْفَضْلَ بَيْنَكُمْ﴾ وإن كان غير مفتوح تُحذف لعدم الخفَة فيما قبلها نحو اطْوُنَ واطْوِنَ كما في أغْزُوُا ٱلْقَوْمَ ويا إمرأة أُغْزِي ٱلْقَوْمَ. الفاعل طاوٍ ولا يُعلَ واوه كما في طَوَى. وتقول من الرَي رَيَانٍ رَيَانَانِ رواءٌ رَيَا رَيَيَانِ رواءٌ أيضاً ولا يُجعل واوهما ياء كما في سِيَاطٍ حتَى لا يجتمع الإعلالان قلب الواو التي هي عين الفعل ياءً وقلبُ الياء التي هي لام الفعل همزة. وتقول في تثنية المؤنث في حالتي النصب والخفض رَيَيَيْنِ مثل عَطْشَيَيْنِ. وإذا أضفتَهُ في حالة النصب إلى ياء المتكلَم قلتَ رَيَيَيَ بخمس ياءات، الأولى منقلبة عن الواو* التي * ٣٧ آ
هي عين الفعل والثانية لام الفعل والثالثة منقلبة عن ألف التأنيث والرابعة علامة النصب والخامسة ياء الإضافة. المفعول مَطْوِيٌ الموضع مَطْوَى الآلة مِطْوَى المجهول طُوِيَ يُطْوَى الى آخرهما، وحكم لام هذه الأشياء كحكم لام الناقص وحكم عينهنَ كحكم عين طَوَى في التي اجتمع فيها إعلالان بتقدير إعلالها وفي التي لم يجتمع فيها إعلالان يكون حكمها أيضاً كحكم طَوَى للمتابعة نحو طَوَيَا وطَاوِيَانِ. تمَ

Fols. 36b-37a

١ تُحرَك: + على وفق حركة نفسها د/ حركة: – د/ ٢ بَيْنَكُمْ: – ه ز/ كان: كانت ا/ مفتوح: مفتوحة ا ج/ ٤ في: + الماضي نحو ح/ وتقول: + في اسم الفاعل ح/ من الرَيَ: – ا ح/ ٥ رَيَيَانِ: – ز/ يُجعل: تجعل ط/ ٦ الإعلالان: اعلالان د ه ط: + أحدهما ح/ قلب: قلبت ب: تقلب د ط: بقلب ه/ الفعل(1+2): – ا: الكلمة ه/ وقلب: وثانيهما قلب ح/ ٧ والخفض: في الخفض ه/ رَيَيَيْنِ: + بأربع يآءت ح/ ٨ في... النصب: – ب ج د ه ح ك ل/ قلت: فقلت ا ه/ رَيَيَيَ: رايت ريين ب ه/ بخمس: بخمسة ه ح/ ٩ والثانية: والثاني ا/ والثالثة: والثالث ا/ والرابعة: والرابع د/ ١٠ والخامسة: والخامس ا د/ ١١ الى آخرهما: – ا ب د ه ح ط/ لام(2): – ب ج د ه ح ط/ عين: – ا ب د ه ط/ ١٢ في: – د: + الكلمة ط/ فيها: – ب ج د ط ل/ اعلالان: الاعلال ب: الإعلالان ب ج د/ حكمها: حكمهما ب/ ١٣ أيضاً: – ه/ للمتابعة: + تمَ بعون الملك الوهاب في سنة ٩٦٦ كتبه الفقير يوسف بن عبد الله در محروسه قسطنطنيَة ب: – ج ح/ نحو... وطَاوِيَان: – ب/ وطاويان: + لو علَ ط/ تمَ: تمت وقع أنواع وقع أنواع في أواسط جمادي الأول في أواخر د: تمَت الكتاب بعون الله الملك الوهَاب وحسن التوفيق ه: تمَت الكتاب بعون الله الملك الوهاب ١٠٢٢ ح: تمَت الكتاب بعون الله الملك العلاَم قد وقع الفراغ من هذه النسخة الشريفة في آخر جمادي كتبه الفقير المذنب المحتاج الى رحمة الله تعالى مراد بن نصوح غفر الله له ولوالديه وأحسن إليهما وإليه ط : والحمد الله على التمام ل/

1- If it [sc. the weak consonant preceding the suffixed pronoun] is vowelled by a fatḥa, it [sc. the suffixed pronoun] is given a vowel because of the faintness of its own vowel and the ligthtness of the vowel preceding it, e.g. اِرْوَوُنَّ "/2 masc. pl." and اِرْوَيِنَّ "/2 fem. sing." similarly to [the suffixed pronoun that is given a vowel in تَنْسَوُا] in the words of the Allmighty [sur. 2: 237] (وَلَا تَنْسَوُا ٱلْفَضْلَ بَيْنَكُمْ) "And do not forget liberality between yourselves". 2- If it [sc. the weak consonant preceding the suffixed pronoun] is not vowelled by a fatḥa, it [sc. the suffixed pronoun] is elided because of the heaviness of the vowel preceding it, e.g. اطْوُنَّ "/2 masc. pl." [from اطْوُونَّ] and اطْوِنَّ "/2 fem. sing." [from اطْوِينَّ], as [it is elided in the pronunciation] in أُغْزُوا القَوْمَ "raid on the people! /masc. pl." and in يا إمرأة أُغْزِي القَوْمَ "O woman, raid on the people!".[378]

The active participle is طاوٍ of which the [2nd radical] w is kept sound, as [it is kept sound] in طَوَى. You say [concerning the active participle] of الرَّيُّ, رَيَّانُ "/masc. sing.", رَيَّانَانِ "masc. / dual", رِوَاءٌ "/masc. pl.", رَيَّا "/fem. sing.", رَيَّانِ "/fem. dual" and رِوَاءٌ "/fem. pl.".[379] Both their [sc. the homonym masc. and fem. pl.'s] w [of رِوَاءٌ] is not changed into a y as in سِيَاطٌ "whips",[380] to avoid that two unsound weak consonants are combined in it, [one of them being] the changed w that is the 2nd weak radical of the verb into the y, and the [other one being the] changed y that is the 3rd weak radical of the verb into the hamza. You say in the dual of the fem. in both the cases of the accusative and the genetive رَيَّيَيْنِ, as عَطْشَيَيْنِ "thirsty". If you suffix to it [sc. the dual of the fem.] in the case of the accusative the y of the 1st person of the sing. of the genitive, you would say رَيَّيَيَّ with five yā's: the 1st one being [the one] changed from the w, [Fol. 37 a] which is the 2nd radical of the verb, the 2nd one being the 3rd radical of the verb, the 3rd one being [the one] changed from the alif of feminization, the 4th one being the marker of the accusative and the 5th one being the y of the genetive.

The passive participle is مَطْوِيٌّ, the noun of place مَطْوَى, the noun of instrument مِطْوَى and the passive voice طُوِيَ يُطْوَى etc. The predicament of the 3rd radical of these forms is the same as the predicament of the 3rd radical of [the forms of] the verbs with 3rd weak radical, and the predicament of their 2nd radical is the same as the predicament of the 2nd radical of طَوَى on account that two unsound weak consonants would be combined together if a change concerning it is to be carried out. As for those [sc. the forms] in which there is no risk that two unsound weak consonants are combined together in them, their [2nd radical's] predicament is also the same as the predicament of [the 2nd radical in] طَوَى for the purpose af analogy, e.g. طَوَيَا "/3 dual" and طَاوِيَانِ "/dual, nominative (active participle)".

It [sc. the book] was completed".

II.8.1. COMMENTARY

The Verb that is doubly Weak

(376) For a general study of اللفيف "the Verb that is doubly Weak" see Ibn Ğinnī, *Munṣif II,* 187-241, Mu'addib, *Taṣrīf* 335-358, Ibn 'Uṣfūr, *II,* 562-589, Zanğānī, *'Izzī* 11-12, 'Abd al-Ḥamīd, *Taṣrīf* 643-648, de Sacy, 258-260, 261-262, Farḥāt, *Baḥṯ* 90-93, Wright, *II,* 91-96, Fischer, *Grammatik* 122, Blachère, 164-165, Roman, *Étude II,* 970-971, 981. For a presentation of some verbs in some of the Semitic languages see Moscati, *Grammar* 168. There also exists, but rarely, verbs in which all three radicals are weak, e.g. Arabic يَيَّا "to write the letter ي" and Akkadian *awū* "to speak", *ewū* "to become".

The paradigm of وَقَى "to guard", a verb with 1st radical *w* and 3rd radical *y* in the perfect, active, is the following:

	sing.	dual	pl.
1st	وَقَيْتُ		وَقَيْنَا
2nd masc.	وَقَيْتَ	وَقَيْتُمَا	وَقَيْتُمْ
2nd fem.	وَقَيْتِ	وَقَيْتُمَا	وَقَيْتُنَّ
3rd masc.	وَقَى	وَقَيَا	وَقَوْا
3rd fem.	وَقَتْ	وَقَتَا	وَقَيْنَ

Its imperfect in the indicative, active, is the following:

	sing.	dual	pl.
1st	أَقِي		نَقِي
2nd masc.	تَقِي	تَقِيَانِ	تَقُونَ
2nd fem.	تَقِينَ	تَقِيَانِ	تَقِينَ
3rd masc.	يَقِي	يَقِيَانِ	يَقُونَ
3rd fem.	تَقِي	تَقِيَانِ	يَقِينَ

Its imperfect in the jussive, active, is the following:

	sing.	dual	pl.
1st	أَقِ		نَقِ
2nd masc.	تَقِ	تَقِيَا	تَقُوا
2nd fem.	تَقِي	تَقِيَا	تَقِينَ
3rd masc.	يَقِ	يَقِيَا	يَقُوا
3rd fem.	تَقِ	تَقِيَا	يَقِينَ

Its active participle is وَاقٍ.

b) The paradigm of حَيِيَ or حَيَّ "to live" (for discussions see (180)), a verb with 2nd and 3rd radical *y* in the perfect, active, is the following:

	sing.	dual	pl.
1st	حَيِيتُ		حَيِينَا
2nd masc.	حَيِيتَ	حَيِيتُمَا	حَيِيتُمْ
2nd fem.	حَيِيتِ	حَيِيتُمَا	حَيِيتُنَّ
3rd masc.	حَيِيَ / حَيَّ	حَيِيَا / حَيَّا	حَيُوا / حَيُّوا
3rd fem.	حَيِيَتْ / حَيَّتْ	حَيِيَتَا / حَيَّتَا	حَيِينَ

Its imperfect in the indicative, active, is the following:

	sing.	dual	pl.
1st	أَحْيَا / أَحَيُّ		نَحْيَا / نَحَيُّ
2nd masc.	تَحْيَا / تَحَيُّ	تَحَيَّانِ	تَحْيَوْنَ / تَحَيُّونَ
2nd fem .	تَحْيَيْنَ / تَحَيِّينَ	تَحَيَّانِ	تَحْيَيْنَ
3rd masc.	يَحْيَا / يَحَيُّ	يَحَيَّانِ	يَحْيَوْنَ / يَحَيُّونَ
3rd fem.	تَحْيَا / تَحَيُّ	تَحَيَّانِ	يَحْيَيْنَ

Its imperfect in the jussive, active, is the following:

	sing.	dual	pl.
1st	أَحْيَ		نَحْيَ
2nd masc.	تَحْيَ	تَحَيَّا	تَحْيَوْا / تَحَيُّوا
2nd fem.	تَحْيَيْ / تَحَيِّي	تَحَيَّا	تَحْيَيْنَ
3rd masc.	يَحْيَ	يَحَيَّا	يَحْيَوْا / يَحَيُّوا
3rd fem.	تَحْيَ	تَحَيَّا	يَحْيَيْنَ

Its active participle is حَيٌّ.

(377) The soundnes of the *w* in طَوَى is discussed in (272).

(378) In ارْوَوُنَّ "/2 masc. pl. (imperative En. 1)", the suffixed pronoun of the 2nd person of the masc. pl., the *w/wu,* that marks the masc. pl. in the imperative ارْوُوا, follows a fatḥa and precedes the doubled nūns, i.e. ارْوَوُنَّ. The suffix *w* in the base form ارْوَوْا is vowelless, but it is in this case given a ḍamma to avoid the cluster of two vowelless consonants, the *w* and the first vowelless *n* of the doubled nūns, as the base form of ارْوَوُنَّ is ارْوَوْنْنَ with the dissolution. The same reasoning concerns ارْوَيِنَّ "/2 fem. sing. (imperative En. 1)", of which the suffixed pronoun of the 2nd person of the fem. sing., the *y/yi,* that in the base form is vowelless, is given the

kasra to avoid the cluster of two vowelless consonants, the *y* and the first vowelless *n* of the doubled nūns, as the base form of ارْوينّ is ارْوِيْنْنِ.
There is a similarity concerning the vowelling of these suffixed pronouns of the agent following a fatḥa and preceding a vowelless consonant, which is the first *n* of the doubled nūns, and the vowelling of the suffixed pronoun of the 2nd person of the masc. pl., the *w/wu,* in تَنْسَوُا in the sur. وَلَا تَنْسَوُا ٱلْفَضْلَ "you forget /masc. pl." (cf. Sībawaihi, *II,* 299, Bohas, *Étude* 326-327; for other examples see (184), (270), (288)), with the ḍamma. The suffixed pronoun of the 2nd person of the masc. pl., the *w/wu,* that marks the masc. pl. of the jussive in لَا تَنْسَوُا, follows the fatḥa of the *s* and precedes a noun to which the vowelless article *l–* is prefixed to, namely ٱلْفَضْلَ. The suffix *w/wu* is underlyingly vowelless, i.e. تَنْسَوْا, but is in this case given a ḍamma, which is a vowel of juncture, to avoid the cluster of two vowelless consonants, the *w* and the -*l* that comes after the *waṣla* of the article *l–* prefixed to ٱلْفَضْلَ following it. Other examples mentioned by Sībawaihi, *II,* 299 and Bohas/Guillaume, *Étude* 326-327 with the vowelling of the *w* of the pl. with a vowel of juncture that is the ḍamma, are رَمَوُا ٱبْنَكَ "they shot your son" and اخْشَوُا ٱللّٰهَ "fear God!". Sībawaihi, *II,* 299 mentions furthermore that some people vowel the *w* of تَنْسَوُا with a kasra, i.e. وَلَا تَنْسَوِا ٱلْفَضْلَ بَيْنَكُم, which is rare.

The base form of اطُنّ is اطُوُونّ in which the suffixed pronoun of the 2nd person of the masc. pl., the vowelless *w/ū,* is preceded by the ḍamma of the 2nd radical *w*. The combination of the *w* preceded by a *w* vowelled by a ḍamma is deemed as heavy, which is one of the reasons why the *ū* suffix is elided. Another reason of its elision is to prevent the cluster of two vowelless consonants, the *w/ū* and the 1st vowelless *n* of the doubled nūns. The base form of اطْوِنّ is اطْوِينّ in which the suffixed pronoun of the 2nd person of the fem. sing, the *y/ī,* is preceded by the kasra of the 2nd radical *w*. The combination of the *y* preceded by the kasra is deemed as heavy, which is one of the reasons why the *ī* suffix is elided. Another reason why this elision is carried out is to prevent the cluster of two vowelless consonants, the *y/ī* and the 1st vowelless *n* of the doubled nūns. There is a similarity between the elision of these suffixed pronouns of the agent following a ḍamma or a kasra and the elision of both the suffixed pronoun of the 2nd person of the masc. pl. of the imperative, the *ū,* following a ḍamma in the pronunciation in أغْزُوا الْقَوْمَ and the suffixed pronoun of the 2nd person of the fem. sing., the *ī,* following a kasra in the pronunciation in يا إمرأة أغزي الْقَوْمَ. In أغْزُوا الْقَوْمَ, the suffixed pronoun, the vowelless *ū,* preceded by the ḍamma, is elided in the pronunciation, i.e. *ʾuġzu l-qawma* is said and not *ʾuġzū l-qawma,* to avoid the cluster of two vowelless consonants, the *ū* and the -*l* of the definite article following the *waṣla* prefixed in الْقَوْمَ following it. The same applies to يا إمرأة أغزي الْقَوْمَ, in which the suffixed pronoun, the vowelless *ī,* preceded by the kasra is elided for the same reason in the pronunciation, i.e. *ʾuġzi l-qawma* is said and not *ʾuġzī l-qawma,* namely to avoid the cluster of two vowelless consonants, the *ī* and the -*l* of the definite article prefixed to the noun following it. This elision is only carried out in the pronunciation and not in the writing, so that no confusion between the different persons in the sing. and pl. occurs.

(379) رِوَاءٌ (cf. Zamaḫšarī, 182, Ibn Yaʿīš, *X*, 87-88, Howell, *I*, fasc. IV, 1671, *IV*, fasc. I, 1267-1268, 1529) is the pl. of رَيَّانُ underlyingly رَوْيَانُ, in which the *w* is changed into a *y*, and is then assimilated to the *y* on the pattern of فَعْلَانُ from رِيٌّ. The base form of رِوَاءٌ is رِوَايٌ, whose *y* is changed into a hamza as it occurs after an augmentative alif (cf. Ibn al-Anbārī, *Maqṣūr* 45). The change of its 2nd radical *w* is forbidden to avoid that two unsound weak consonants are combined together.

(380) For discussions concerning سِيَاط underlyingly سِوَاطٌ see (267).

III. BIBLIOGRAPHICAL REFERENCES

III.1. *Primary sources*

§ *1. Manuscripts used*

Dunqūz, *Šarḥ* = Dunqūz, *Šarḥ al-marāḥ,* 100311585, private.

Dunqūz, *Šarḥ B* = Dunqūz, *Šarḥ al-marāḥ B,* 959 A.H./1527, owned by the Department of Middle East languages at Lund University.

Ibn Masʿūd, *MS A* = Aḥmad b. ʿAlī b. Masʿūd, *Marāḥ al-arwāḥ,* 4166, 947/1540, Bibliothèque Nationale, Paris.

Ibn Masʿūd, *MS B* = Aḥmad b. ʿAlī b. Masʿūd, *Marāḥ al-arwāḥ,* 4167, 966/1559, Bibliothèque Nationale, Paris.

Ibn Masʿūd, *MS C* = Aḥmad b. ʿAlī b. Masʿūd, *Marāḥ al-arwāḥ,* 4168, 16th century A.D., Bibliothèque Nationale, Paris.

Ibn Masʿūd, *MS D* = Aḥmad b. ʿAlī b. Masʿūd, *Marāḥ al-arwāḥ,* 4169, 16th century A.D., Bibliothèque Nationale, Paris.

Ibn Masʿūd, *MS E* = Aḥmad b. ʿAlī b. Masʿūd, *Marāḥ al-arwāḥ,* 4170, 16th century A.D., Bibliothèque Nationale, Paris.

Ibn Masʿūd, *MS G* = Aḥmad b. ʿAlī b. Masʿūd, *Marāḥ al-arwāḥ,* 4172, 16th century A.D., Bibliothèque Nationale, Paris.

Ibn Masʿūd, *MS H* = Aḥmad b. ʿAlī b. Masʿūd, *Marāḥ al-arwāḥ,* 4173, 1033/1624, Bibliothèque Nationale, Paris.

Ibn Masʿūd, *MS I* = Aḥmad b. ʿAlī b. Masʿūd, *Marāḥ al-arwāḥ,* 4174, 17th century A.D., Bibliothèque Nationale, Paris.

Ibn Masʿūd, *MS J* = Aḥmad b. ʿAlī b. Masʿūd, *Marāḥ al-arwāḥ,* 4182, 18th century A.D., Bibliothèque Nationale, Paris.

Nīksārī, *Mifrāḥ* = Nīksārī, Ḥasan Pāšā b. ʿAlāʾa l-Dīn al-Aswad, the commentary *al-Mifrāḥ fī šarḥ al-marāḥ,*18th century, private.

Qīrawānī, *Mušakkil* = Al-Qīrawānī, M. b. A. T., *Mušakkil iʿrāb al-qurʾān,* Aḥmadīya manuscript, Aleppo.

Sīrāfī, *Šarḥ* = al-Sīrāfī, *Šarḥ kitāb Sībawaihi,* Part I and II, nr. 26181 and 26182, Library of Cairo University.

§ *2. Printed texts used*

Abū Ḥanīfa, *Maqṣūd* = see Ibn Masʿūd, *Print T.*

An., *Bināʾ*= Anonymous author, *al-Bināʾ,* see Ibn Masʿūd, *Print T.*

Ibn Kamāl Pāšā, *Falāḥ* = The Imām Šams al-Dīn Aḥmad b. Sulaimān known as Ibn Kamāl Pāšā, *al-Falāḥ šarḥ al-marāḥ,* printed together with, and in the margin of Dīkqūz (Dunqūz), *Šarḥ al-marāḥ,* Cairo 1309/1891, Library of Tübingen University (1B534).

Ibn Masʿūd, *Print K* = Aḥmad b. ʿAlī b. Masʿūd, *Marāḥ al-arwāḥ,* the printed text of the Printing House al-Ḫaidawīya, Bulaq, Egypt 1282/1866, Library of Cairo University.

Ibn Masʿūd, *Print L* = Aḥmad b. ʿAlī b. Masʿūd, *Marāḥ al-arwāḥ,* the printed text of the Printing house al-ʿUṯmānīya, 1304./1886, Library of Cairo University.

Ibn Masʿūd, *Print T* = Aḥmad b. ʿAlī b. Masʿūd, *Marāḥ al-arwāḥ,* the printed 1st work of the *Maǧmūʿa,* comprising after it *al-ʿIzzī* by al-Zanǧānī, *al-Maqṣūd* by Abū Ḥanīfī, and *al-Bināʾ* and *al-Amṯila* by anonymous authors, Būlāq 1841, housing at the Library of Tübingen University.

Ibn Masʿūd, *Print U* = Aḥmad b. ʿAlī b. Masʿūd, *Marāḥ al-arwāḥ,* the printed text of the printing house al-ʿĀmira, Būlāq 1268/1852, Library of Cairo University.

Ibn Masʿūd, *Print Y* = Aḥmad b. ʿAlī b. Masʿūd, *Marāḥ al-arwāḥ,* the printed text of the printing house al-ʿĀmira, Būlāq 1280/1864, Library of Cairo University.

Zanǧānī, *ʿIzzī* = see Ibn Masʿūd, *Print T.*

§ *3. Literature*

ʿAbbās, *Dīwān = Dīwān al-ʿAbbās b. Mirdās,* Ed. Y. al-Ǧabūrī, Bagdad 1968.

ʿAbd al-ʿAzīz, *Fuṣḥā* = ʿAbd al-ʿAzīz, Muḥammad Ḥasan, *al-Waḍʿ al-luġawī fī l-fuṣḥā al-muʿāṣira,* Cairo 1413/1992.

ʿAbd al-Ḥamīd, *Taṣrīf* = ʿAbd al-Ḥamīd, M. Muḥyī l-Dīn, *Takmila fī Taṣrīf al-afʿāl,* the work printed after Ibn ʿAqīl, *Šarḥ II.*

ʿAbd al-Qādir, *ʾAṯar* = ʿAbd al-Qādir, Ḥusain, *ʾAṯar al-nuḥāh fī l-baḥṯ al-balāġī,* Cairo 1970.

ʿAbd al-Raḥīm, *Ṣarf* = ʿAbd al-Raḥīm, Saʿd, *Muqaddimat fī ʿilm al-ṣarf,* Cairo s.a.

ʿAbd al-Tawwāb, *Fuṣūl* = ʿAbd al-Tawwāb, Ramaḍān, *Fuṣūl fī fiqh al-ʿarabīya,* (1st edition) 1973, (2nd edition), Cairo 1980.

ʿAbd al-Tawwāb, *Taṭawwur* = ʿAbd al-Tawwāb, Ramaḍān, *al-Taṭawwur al-luġawī, maẓāhiruhu wa-ʿilaluhu wa-qawānīnuhu,* Cairo 1404/1983.

ʿAbdat, *Abḥāṯ* = ʿAbdat, Dāwūd, *Abḥāṯ fī l-luġat al-ʿarabīya,* Beirut 1973.
Abīd, *Dīwān* = *Dīwān ʿAbīd b. al-Abraṣ,* Ed. Ḥ. Naṣṣār, Cairo 1957.
Abū l-Naǧm, *Dīwān* = *Dīwān Abī l-Naǧm al-ʿIǧlī,* Ed. ʿAlāʾa l-Dīn Āġā, Riad 1981.
Abū Rīda, *Rasāʾil* = Abū Rīda, *Rasāʾil al-Kindī l-falsafīya,* Part I, Cairo 1369/1950.
Abū ʿUbaid, *Amṯāl* = Abū ʿUbaid, al-Qāsim b. Sallām, *al-Amṯāl,* Ed ʿAbd al-Maǧīd Qaṭāmiš, Damascus 1400/1980.
Abū ʿUbaid, *Ġarīb* = Abū ʿUbaid, al-Qāsim b. Sallām, *Ġarīb al-ḥadīṯ,* Hyderabad 1964-1967.
Afandī, *Šarḥ* = Afandī, Muḥibb al-Dīn., *Šarḥ šawāhid al-kaššāf,* Bulaq 1281.
Afandī, *Tanzīl* = Afandī, Muḥibb al-Dīn, *Tanzīl al-ʾāyāt ʿalā l-šawāhid ʿan al-abyāt,* the last work in Zamaḫšarī, *Kaššāf IV.*
ʿAǧǧāǧ, *Dīwān* = Al-ʿAǧǧāǧ b. Ruʾba, *Dīwān,* Ed. ʿI. Ḥasan, Beirut 1971.
Aḫṭal, *Dīwān* = *Dīwān al-Aḫṭal,* Ed. T. Ṣāliḥānī, Beirut 1891.
Anīs, *Asrār* = Anīs, Ibrāhīm, *Min asrār al-luġa,* 2nd Edition, Cairo 1958.
Anīs, *Lahǧāt* = Anīs, Ibrāhīm, *Fī l-lahǧāt al-ʿarabīya,* 2nd Edition, Cairo 1952.
Anṣārī, *Dīwān* = *Dīwān Ḥassān b. Ṯābit,* Ed. W. ʿArafāt, Beirut 1974.
Anṣārī, *Nawādir* = Al-Anṣārī, Abū Zaid, *al-Nawādir fī l-luġa,* Ed. S. al-Šartūnī, Beirut 1894.
ʿAntara, *Dīwān* = *Dīwān ʿAntara b. Šaddād al-ʿAbsī,* Ed. M. Saʿīd Mawlawī, 1390/1970.
Astarābāḏī, *Šarḥ al-kāfiya* = Al-Astarābāḏī, Raḍī l-Dīn Muḥammad b. al-Ḥasan, *Šarḥ al- kāfiya fī l-naḥw li-Ibn al-Ḥāǧib,* Beirut s.a.
Astarābāḏī, *Šarḥ al-šāfiya* = Al-Astarābāḏī, Raḍī l-Dīn Muḥammad b. al-Ḥasan, *Šarḥ šāfiyat Ibn al-Ḥāǧib,* edited with *Šarḥ šawāhid* written by ʿAbd al-Qādir al-Baġdādī, 4 vol., Beirut 1395/1975.
Baġdādī, *Hadīya* = Al-Baġdādī, I. P., *Hadīyat al-ʿārifīn asmāʾ al-muʾallifīn wa-āṯār al-muṣannifīn,* Ed. K. R. Bilge, I. M. Kemal and A. Aktuç, Istanbul 1951-1958.
Baġdādī, *Ḫizāna* = Al-Baġdādī, ʿAbd al-Qādir b. ʿUmar, *Ḫizānat al-adab,* Vol. I-IV, Bulaq 1299.
Baġdādī, *Šarḥ* = Al-Baġdādī, ʿAbd al-Qādir b. ʿUmar, *Šarḥ šawāhid al-šāfiya,* Ed. M. al-Ḥasan, M. al-Zafzāf and M. Muḥyī l-Dīn ʿAbd al-Ḥamīd, Cairo 1358 A. H.
Baġdādī, *Tārīḫ* = Al-Baġdādī, al-Ḫaṭīb, *Tārīḫ Baġdād,* Cairo 1349/1931.
Baiḍāwī, *Anwār* = Al-Baiḍāwī, Nāṣir al-Dīn Abū Saʿīd ʿAbd Allāh, *Anwār al-tanzīl wa-asrār al-taʾwīl,* Ed. H. O. Freischer, 2 vol. Leipzig 1846, 1848.
Bakkūš, *Taṣrif* = Al-Bakkūš, Ṭ., *al-Taṣrif al-ʿarabī,* Tunis 1973.
Bakrī, *Samṭ* = Al-Bakrī, Ibn ʿUbayd, *Samṭ al-laʾālī fī šarḥ amālī l-Qālī,* Ed. ʿA. al-ʿAzīz al-Maymanī, Cairo 1936.
Bāriqī, *Dīwān* = *Dīwān Surāqa al-Bāriqī,* Ed. Ḥ. Naṣṣār, Cairo 1947.
Barrānī, *Maṭālib* = Barrānī, ʿAlī Nidā, *Asnā l-maṭālib li-hidāyat al-ṭālib, A nineteenth century grammatical commentary on shaykh ash-Shubrāwī's (d. 1758) Risāla,* Ed. J. Hämeen-Anttila, Helsinki 1989, *SO 66,* Edited by the Finnish Oriental Society.
Bašar, *Dirāsāt* = Bašar, Kamāl, *Dirāsāt fī ʿilm al-luġa,* Cairo 1973.
Baṭalyawsī, *Iqtiḍāb* = Baṭalyawsī, Abū Muḥammad, *al-Iqtiḍāb fī šarḥ adab al-kātib,* Ed. ʿA. al-Bustānī, Beirut 1901.
Bustānī, *Miṣbāḥ* = Al-Bustānī, B., *Miṣbāḥ al-ṭālib fī baḥṯ al-maṭālib, Muṭawwal fī l-ṣarf wa-l-naḥw* [a commentary on Farḥāt, *Baḥṯ]* together with *Risāla fī ʿilm al-ʿarūḍ wa-l-qawāfī* written by Nāṣīf al-Yāziǧī, Beirut 1854.
Bustānī, *Muḥīṭ* = Al-Bustānī, B., *Muḥīṭ al-muḥīṭ,* an Arabic-Arabic Dictionary, Libanon 1983.
Ḍabī, *Amṯāl* = Al-Ḍabī, Abū ʿIkrima, *al-Amṯāl,* Ed. R. ʿAbd al-Tawwāb, Damascus 1974.
Dāġir, *Taḏkira* = Dāġir, A., *Taḏkirat al-kātib,* Cairo 1923.
Ḏahabī, *Qurrāʾ* = Al-Ḏahabī, *Maʿrifat al-qurrāʾ al-kibār ʿalā l-ṭabaqāt wa-l-aʿṣār,* Ed. B. ʿA. Maʿrūf, Š. al-Arnāʾūṭ and Ṣ. M. ʿAbbās, Beirut 1984.
Daqr, *Muʿǧam* = Daqr, ʿAbd al-Ġanī, *Muʿǧam al-naḥw,* Beirut 1407 A.H. /1986.
Dār al-kutub al-miṣrīya = Dār al-kutub al-miṣrīya, *Fihris al-kutub al-ʿarabīya al-mawǧūda bi-l-dār li-ġāyati šahr September 1925,* II, Cairo 1345 A.H./1926.
Dārimī, *Radd* = Al-Dārimī, Abū Saʿīd ʿUṯmān b. Saʿīd, *Kitāb al-radd ʿalā l-ǧahmīya,* Ed. G. Vitestam, Lund and Leiden 1960.
Darwīš, *Maʿāǧim* = Darwīš, A., *al-Maʿāǧim al-ʿarabīya,* Cairo 1956.
Dasūqī, *Tahḏīb* = Al-Dasūqī, Muḥammad ʿAlī, *Tahḏīb al-alfāẓ al-ʿāmmīya,* Ed. ʿA. S. Hārūn and others, Cairo 1964-1967.
Ḏū l-Rumma, *Dīwān* = *Dīwān Ḏī l-Rumma,* Ed. ʿA. al-Quddūs Abū Ṣāliḥ, Damascus 1394/1974.
Ḏubyānī, *Dīwān* = *Dīwān al-Nābiġa al-Ḏubyānī,* Ed. Šukrī Faiṣal, Beirut 1968.
Faḍl, *Šiʿr* = *Šiʿr al-Faḍl b. al-ʿAbbās al-Lahbī,* Ed. M. ʿAbd al-Ḥusein al-Naǧm, in: *Maǧallat al-balāġa 7, 8, 9,* 1976-1977.
Fairūzābādī, *Baṣāʾir* = Fairūzābādī, *Baṣāʾir ḏawī l-tamyīz fī laṭāʾif al-kitāb al-ʿazīz,* Ed. M. al-Naǧǧār, Cairo 1383 sqq.
Fairūzābādī, *Qāmūs* = Al-Fairūzābādī, *al-Qāmūs al-muḥīṭ,* 4 vol., 1289.
Fārābī, *Šarḥ* = Fārābī, Abū Naṣr Muḥammad b. Muḥammad, *Šarḥ kitāb Arisṭūṭālīs fī l-ʿibāra,* Ed. W. Kutsch and S. Marrow, Beirut 1960.
Farazdaq, *Dīwān* = *Dīwān al-Farazdaq,* Ed. ʿA. al-Ṣāwī and M. al-Ṣāwī, Cairo 1936.

Farḥāt, *Baḥṯ* = Farḥāt, G., *Kitāb baḥṯ al-maṭālib fī ʿilm al-ʿarabīya,* with the annotations of Saʿīd al-Ḫūrī l-Šartūnī, 2nd print, Beirut 1883.

Fārisī, *Masāʾil* = Al-Fārisī, Abū ʿAlī, *al-Masāʾil al-baġdādīyāt,* Ed. Ṣ. al-Sinkāwī, Bagdad 1983.

Fārisī, *Takmila* = Al-Fārisī, Abū ʿAlī, *al-Takmila,* Ed. K. Baḥr al-Marǧān, al-Mūsil 1401/1981. Also edited by H. Š. Farhūd, al-Riyāḍ 1401 H.

Farrāʾ, *Maʿānī* = Farrāʾ, Abū Zakarīyā Yaḥyā b. Ziyād, *Maʿānī l-qurʾān,* 3 vol., Ed. M. Y. Naǧatī and M. ʿA. Naǧǧār, Cairo 1955-1972.

Frayḥa, *Tabsīṭ* = Frayḥa, A., *Tabsīṭ qawāʿid al-luġa al-ʿarabīya,* Beirut 1959.

Ǧāmī, *Naqd* = Jāmī, *Naqd al-nuṣūṣ,* Ed. W. C. Chittick, Tehran 1977.

Ǧamīl, *Dīwān* = *Dīwān Ǧamīl Buṯaina,* Ed. Ḥ. Nassār, Cairo 1967.

Ǧarǧāwī, *Šarḥ* = Ǧarǧāwī, ʿAbd al-Munʿim, *Šarḥ šawāhid Ibn ʿAqīl ʿalā alfīyat Ibn Mālik,* Cairo 1308.

Ǧarīr, *Dīwān* = Ǧarīr, *Dīwān,* Ed. N. Ṭah, Cairo 1971. Another edition is by M. al-Ṣāwī, Damascus.

Ǧawālīqī, *Šarḥ* = Al-Ǧawālīqī, *Šarḥ adab al-Kātib,* Ed. M. Ṣ. al-Rāfiʿī, Cairo 1350 A. H.

Ǧawharī, *Ṣiḥāḥ* = Al-Ǧawharī, *Tāǧ al-luġa wa-ṣiḥāḥ al-ʿarabīya,* Ed. A. ʿA. al-Ġafūr ʿAṭār, Cairo 1956.

Ǧawzīya, *Arwāḥ* = Ǧawzīya, Ibn Qayyim, *Hādī l-arwāḥ ilā bilād al-afrāḥ,* Ed. ʿIṣām al-Dīn al-Ṣabābiṭī, Cairo 1412 A.H.

Ǧawzīya, *Fawāʾid* = Al-Ǧawzīya, Ibn Qayyim, *al-Fawāʾid,* Ed. A. R. ʿArmūš, Beirut 1984.

Ǧirān, *Dīwān* = *Dīwān Ǧirān al-ʿAwd,* Cairo 1350/1931.

Ǧubūrī = Al-Ǧubūrī, ʿA., *Fihrist al-maḫṭūṭāt al-ʿarabīya fī maktabat al-awqāf al-ʿāmma fī Baġdād I-IV,* Bagdad 1393/1973-1394/1974.

Ḥadīṯī, *Nuḥāt* = Al-Ḥadīṯī, Ḫadīǧa, *Mawqif al-nuḥāt mina l-iḥtiǧāǧ bi-l-ḥadīṯ,* Irak 1986.

Ḥāfiẓ, *Dīwān* = Ḥāfiẓ, *Dīwān,* Ed. P. N. Khānlārī, 2nd edition, vol. 1, Tehran 1362/ 1983.

Ḥāǧǧi Ḫalīfa, *Kašf* = Ḥaǧǧī Ḫalīfa, Muṣṭafa b. ʿAbd Allāh, *Kašf al-ẓunūn ʿan asāmī l-kutub wa-l-funūn,* 2 vol., Istanbul, 1360/1941-1362/1943.

Ḫalīl, *ʿAyn* = al-Ḫalīl, b. Aḥmad al-Farāhīdī, *al-ʿAyn,* Ed. I. al-Sāmarrāʾī and M. al-Maḫzūmī, Bagdad 1980-1985.

Ḫalīl b. Aḥmad..., *Ḥurūf* = Ḫalīl b. Aḥmad wa-b. al-Sikkīt wa-l-Rāzī, *ṯalāṯat kutub fī l-ḥurūf,* Ed. R. ʿAbd al-Tawwāb, Cairo 1982.

Hallaq, *Ibn Taymīya* = Hallaq, W. B., *Ibn Taymīya on the Existence of God,* in: *AO 52,* Copenhagen 1991.

Ḥamīrī, *Šams* = Ḥamīrī, Našwān, *Šams al-ʿulūm wa-dawāʾ kalām al-ʿArab mina l-kulūm,* Ed. al-Qāḍī ʿAbdallāh al-Ǧirāfī, Cairo s.a.

Ḥarīrī, *Durra* = Al-Ḥarîrî, Abū Muḥammad al-Qāsim b. ʿAlī, *Durrat al-ġawwâṣ,* Ed. H. Thorbecke, Leipzig 1871.

Ḥarīrī, *Šarḥ* = Al-Ḥarīrī, Abū Muḥammad al-Qāsim b. ʿAlī, *Šarḥ mulḥat al-iʿrāb,* Ed. F. Fāris, Jordan 1412/1991.

Ḥarīrī, *Séances* = Al-Ḥarīrī, Abū Muḥammad al-Qāsim b. ʿAlī, *Les séances (Maqāmāt) de Hariri avec un commentaire choisi par S. de Sacy.* 2ème éd. par Reinaud et Derenbourg, Paris 1847-53.

Ḥasan, *Baḥṯ* = Ḥasan, ʿAbd Allāh ʿAlī Muḥammad, *al-Baḥṯ al-balāġī wa-marāḥil taṭawwurihi,* Cairo 1413/1992.

Ḥassān, *Luġa* = Ḥassān, Tammām, *al-Luġa baina l-miʿyārīya wa-l-waṣfīya,* Cairo 1985.

Ḥassān, *Uṣūl* = Ḥassān, Tammām, *al-Uṣūl,* Cairo 1982.

Ḫayyām, *Rubaiʿāt* = *Rubáiyát of Omar Khayyám,* Rendered into English Verse by Edward Fitzgerald with Drawings by E. J. Sullivan, New York s.a.

Ḥāzim al-Qarṭāǧannī, *Minhāǧ* = Ḥāzim al-Qarṭāǧannī, Abū l-Ḥasan, *Minhāǧ al-bulaġāʾ wa-sirāǧ al-ʾudabāʾ,* Ed. M. Ḥ. b. al-Ḫawǧa, Tunis 1966.

Hindāwī, *Manāhiǧ* = Hindāwī, Ḥasan, *Manāhiǧ al-ṣarfīyīn wa-maḏahibuhum fī l-qarnain al-ṯāliṯ wa-l-rābiʿ mina l-hiǧra,* Damascus 1409/1989.

Ḫuḍarī, *Ḥāšiya* = Ḫuḍarī, Muḥammad b. Muṣṭafā, *Ḥāšiya ʿalā šarḥ Ibn ʿAqīl ʿalā alfīyat Ibn Mālik,* Bulaq 1291.

Ibn al-Anbārī, *Aḍdād* = Ibn al-Anbārī, Abū Bakr Muḥammad b. al-Qāsim b. Muḥammad, *Kitabo-l-addad ... auctore Abu Bekr ibno-ʾl-Anbari,* Ed. T. Houtsma, Leyde 1881.

Ibn al-Anbārī, *Asrār* = Ibn al-Anbārī, Abū l-Barakāt, *Asrār al-ʿarabīya,* Ed. B. al-Bayṭār, Damascus 1377/1957.

Ibn al-Anbārī, *Inṣāf* = Ibn al-Anbārī, Abū l-Barakāt, *Kitāb al-inṣāf fī masāʾil al-ḫilāf bayna l-naḥwīyīn al-baṣrīyīn wa-l-kūfīyīn: Die grammatischen Schulen von Kufa und Basra,* Ed. G. Weil, Leiden 1913.

Ibn al-Anbārī, *Lumaʿ* = Ibn al-Anbārī, Abū l-Barakāt, *Lumaʿ al-adillah fī uṣūl an-naḥw,* Ed. Attia Amer, Stockholm 1963.

Ibn al-Anbārī, *Maqṣūr* = Ibn al-Anbārī, Abū l-Barakāt, *al-Maqṣūr waʾl-mamdūd,* Ed. Attia Amer, Stockholm.

Ibn al-Anbārī, *Muḏakkar* = Ibn al-Anbārī, Abū l-Barakāt, *al-Muḏakkar wa-l-muʾannaṯ,* Ed. M. ʿAbd al-Ḫāliq ʿUḍaima, al-Maǧlis al-aʿlā li-l-šuʾūn al-islāmīya, 1981.

Ibn al-Anbārī, *Nuzha* = Ibn al-Anbārī, Abū l-Barakāt, *Nuzhat al-alibbāʾ fī ṭabaqāt al-alibbāʾ,* Cairo 1294.

Ibn al-Anbārī, *Qaṣāʾid* = Ibn al-Anbārī, Abū l-Barakāt, *Šarḥ al-qaṣāʾid al-sabʿ al-ṭiwāl,* Ed. Hārūn, Cairo 1969.

Ibn ʿAqīl = Ibn ʿAqīl, Bihāʾ al-Dīn ʿAbdallāh, *Šarḥ ʿalā alfīyat Ibn Mālik,* Ed. M. Muḥyī l-Dīn ʿAbd al-Ḥamīd, 2 vol., s.a., with *Takmila fī taṣrīf al-afʿāl* printed after it by ʿAbd al-Ḥamīd, M. Muḥyī l-Dīn ʿAbd al-Ḥamīd. See ʿAbd al-Ḥamīd, *Taṣrīf.*

Ibn ʿAqīl, *Musāʿid* = Ibn ʿAqīl, Bihāʾ al-Dīn ʿAbdallāh, *al-Musāʿid ʿalā tashīl al-fawāʾid,* Ed. M. Kāmil Barakāt, Damascus 1980.

Ibn Duraid, *Ǧamhara* = Ibn Duraid, Abū Bakr Muḥammad b. al-Ḥasan, *Ǧamharat al-luġa,* Hyderabad 1344 H.

Ibn Duraid, *Ištiqāq* = Ibn Duraid, Abū Bakr Muḥammad b. al-Ḥasan, *al-Ištiqāq,* Ed. ʿA. S. M. Harūn, Cairo s.a.

Ibn Fāris, *Ḏamm* = Ibn Fāris, Aḥmad, *Ḏamm al-ḫaṭaʾ fī l-šiʿr.* See Saani, *Ibn Fāris.*

Ibn Fāris, *Maqāyīs* = Ibn Fāris, Aḥmad, *Muʿǧam maqāyīs al-luġa,* Ed. ʿA. S. Muḥammad Hārūn, 6 vol., 3rd print, Cairo 1402/1981.

Ibn Fāris, *Ṣāḥibī* = Ibn Fāris, Aḥmad, *al-Ṣāḥibī fī fiqh al-luġa wa-sunan al-ʿarab fī kalāmihā,* Ed. M. al-Chouémi, (bibliotheca Philologica; I), Beyrouth 1382/1963.

Ibn al-Ǧawzī, *Kanz* = Ibn al-Djauzī, Sibṭ, *Kanz al-mulūk fī kaifiyyat as-sulūk, The Treasure of Princes on the Fashion of Behaviour,* Ed. G. Vitestam, Lund 1970.

Ibn al-Ǧazarī, *Našr* = Ibn al-Ǧazarī, *al-Našr fī l-qirāʾāt al-ʿašr,* Ed. M. S. Muhaisan, Cairo 1397/1978.

Ibn Ǧinnī, *de Flexione* = Ibn Ǧinnîi, Abū l-Fatḥ ʿUṯmān, *de Flexione Libellvs,* Ed. G. Hoberg, Lipsiae 1885.

Ibn Ǧinnī, *Ḫaṣāʾiṣ* = Ibn Ǧinnī, Abū l-Fatḥ ʿUṯmān, *al-Ḫaṣāʾiṣ,* Ed. M. A. al-Naǧǧār, 3 vol., Cairo 1371/1952-1376/1956.

Ibn Ǧinnī, *Lumaʿ* = Ibn Ǧinnī, Abū l-Fatḥ ʿUṯmān, *Kitāb al-lumaʿ fi-n-naḥw,* Ed. H. M. Kechrida, Uppsala 1976.

Ibn Ǧinnī, *Muḥtasib* = Ibn Ǧinnī, Abū l-Fatḥ ʿUṯmān, *al-Muḥtasib fī tabyīn wuǧūh šawāḏḏ al-qirāʾāt wa-l-īḍāḥ ʿanhā,* Ed. ʿA. N. Nāṣif, ʿA. Ḥ. al-Naǧǧār, ʿA. F. Šalabī, Cairo 1966-1969.

Ibn Ǧinnī, *Munṣif* = Ibn Ǧinnī, Abū l-Fatḥ ʿUṯmān, *al-Munṣif fī šarḥ taṣrīf al-Māzinī,* Ed. I. Muṣṭafā, ʿA. Amīn, 3 vol., Cairo 1373/1954-1379/1960.

Ibn Ǧinnī, *Sirr* = Ibn Ǧinnī, Abū l-Fatḥ ʿUṯmān, *Sirr ṣināʿat al-iʿrāb,* Ed. Ḥ. Hindāwī, 2 vol., Damascus 1405/1985.

Ibn Ǧinnī, *Tafsīr* = Ibn Ǧinnī, Abū l-Fatḥ ʿUṯmān, *Tafsīr urǧūzat Abī Nuwās,* Ed. B. al-Aṯarī, Damascus 1386/1966.

Ibn Ǧinnī, *Tamām* = Ibn Ǧinnī, Abū l-Fatḥ ʿUṯmān, *al-Tamām fī tafsīr ašʿār Huḏail mimmā aġfalah Abū Saʿīd al-Sukkarī,* Ed. al-Qaysī, Maṭlūb and al-Ḥadīṯī, Bagdad 1381/1962.

Ibn Ǧinnī, *Taṯniya* = Ibn Ǧinnī, Abū l-Fatḥ ʿUṯmān, *ʿIlal al-taṯniya,* Ed. Ṣ. al-Tamīmī and R. ʿAbd al-Tawwāb, Cairo 1992.

Ibn Ḫair, *Fihrist* = *Fihrist Ibn Ḫair,* Ed. F. Qadāra and Ḫ. Ṭarġuwa, Cairo 1328/1963.

Ibn Ḫālawaihi, *Iʿrāb* = Ibn Ḫālawiya, Abū ʿAbd Allāh al-Ḥusain b. Aḥmad, *Iʿrāb ṯalāṯīn sūra mina l-Qurʾān,* Damascus s.a.

Ibn Ḫālawaihi, *Laysa* = Ibn Ḫālawaihi, Abū ʿAbd Allāh al-Ḥusain b. Aḥmad, *Laysa,* Ed. A. ʿAbd al-Ġafūr, Makka 1979.

Ibn Ḫālawaihi, *Qirāʾāt* = Ibn Ḫālawaihi, Abū ʿAbd Allāh al-Ḥusain b. Aḥmad, *Iʿrāb al-qirāʾāt al-sabʿ wa-ʿilaluhā,* Ed. ʿAbd al-Raḥmān b. Sulaimān al-ʿAtīmain, 2 vol., Cairo 1413/1992.

Ibn Ḫālawaihi, *Šawāḏḏ* = Ibn Ḫālawaihi, Abū ʿAbd Allāh al-Ḥusain b. Aḥmad, *Muḫtaṣar min šawāḏḏi l-qurʾān min kitābi l-badīʾ,* Cairo 1943.

Ibn Ḫaldūn, *Muqaddima* = Ibn Khaldūn, ʿAbd al-Raḥmān, *The muqaddimah, An Introduction to History,* Translated from the Arabic by F. Rosenthal, 3 vol., New York 1980.

Ibn Ḫallikān, *Dictionary* = Ibn Ḫallikān, Šams al-Dīn, *Bibliographical Dictionary,* English translation by de Slane, 4 vol., Paris 1843.

Ibn Ḫallikān, *Wafayāt* = Ibn Ḫallikān, Šams al-Dīn, *Kitāb wafayāt al-aʿyān,* Ed. I. ʿAbbās, Beirut s.a.

Ibn Ḥazm, *Aḫlāq* = Ibn Ḥazm al-Andalusī, *Kitāb al-aḫlāq wa-s-siyar,* ou *Risāla fī mudāwāt an-nufūs wa-tahḏīb al-ʾaxlāq wa-z-zuhd fī r-raḏaʾil,* Ed. E. Riad, Uppsala 1980.

Ibn Hišām, *Ǧāmiʿ* = Ibn Hišām, Ǧamāl al-Dīn Abū Muḥammad ʿAbdallāh b. Yūsuf, *al-Ǧāmiʿ al-ṣaġīr fī l-naḥw,* Ed. A. M. al-Harmīl, Cairo 1400 /1980.

Ibn Hišām, *Masālik* = Ibn Hišām, Ǧamāl al-Dīn Abū Muḥammad ʿAbdallāh b. Yūsuf, *Awḍaḥ al-masālik ilā alfīyat Ibn Mālik,* and with it *Kitab ʿuddat al-sālik ilā taḥqīq awḍaḥ al-masālik* by M. Muḥyī l-Dīn ʿAbd al-Ḥamīd, 3rd part, 5th edition, Beirut 1399/1979.

Ibn Hišām, *Muġnī* = Ibn Hišām, Ǧamāl al-Dīn Abū Muḥammad ʿAbdallāh b. Yūsuf, *Muġnī l-labīb ʿan kutub al-aʿārīb,* 2 vol., Ed. M. Mubārak and M. ʿA. Ḥ. Allāh, Beirut 1972.

Ibn Hišām, *Qatr* = Ibn Hišām, Ǧamāl al-Dīn Abū Muḥammad ʿAbdallāh b. Yūsuf, *Qatr al-nadā wa-ball al-ṣadā,* Ed. M. Muḥyī l-Dīn ʿAbd al-ḥamīd, 11th ed., s.a.

Ibn Hišām, *Šuḏūr* = Ibn Hišām, Ǧamāl al-Dīn Abū Muḥammad ʿAbdallāh b. Yūsuf, *Šuḏūr al-ḏahab,* Bulaq 1253.

Ibn al-ʿImād, *Šaḏarāt* = Ibn al-ʿImād al-Ḥanbalī, *Šaḏarāt al-ḏahab fī aḫbār man ḏahab,* Cairo 1350 A.H.

Ibn Maḍāʾ, *Radd* = Ibn Maḍāʾal-Qurṭubī, Abū l-ʿAbbās Aḥmad, *Kitāb al-radd ʿalā l-nuḥāt,* Ed. Š. Ḍaif, Cairo 1982.

Ibn Mālik, *Alfīya* = Ibn Mālik, Muḥammad b. ʿAbd Allāh, *La ʾAlfiyyah dʾIbnu-Malik* [pp. 1-227], suivie de (->)

Ibn Mālik, *Lāmīya* = Ibn Mālik, Muḥammad b. ʿAbd Allāh, *La Lâmiyyah* du même auteur [pp. 228-353] avec traduction et notes en français et un lexique des termes techniques par A. Goguyer, Beyrouth 1888.

Ibn Mālik, *Šawāhid* = Ibn Mālik, Muḥammad b. ʿAbd Allāh, *Šawāhid al-tawḍīḥ wa-l-taṣḥīḥ li-muškilat al-ǧāmiʿ al-ṣaḥīḥ,* Ed. F. ʿAbd al-Bāqī, Cairo 1957.

Ibn Manẓūr = Ibn Manẓūr, Ǧamāl al-Dīn, *Lisān al-ʿArab,* 6 vol., Beirut s.a.

Ibn Masʿūd, *Marāḥ I* = *Aḥmad b. ʿAlī b. Masʿūd on Arabic Morphology, Marāḥ al-arwāḥ,* Part one: *The strong Verb: Aṣ-ṣaḥīḥ,* Ed. with Translation, Commentary and Introduction by J. Åkesson, Leiden 1990.

Ibn Muǧāhid, *Sab'a* = Ibn Muǧāhid, Abū Bakr Aḥmad b. Mūsā, *al-Sab'a fī l-qirā'āt,* Ed. Š. Ḍaif, Cairo 1972.

Ibn al-Nadīm, *Fihrist* = Ibn al-Nadīm, Abū l-Faraǧ, *Kitāb al-fihrist,* Ed. G. Flügel, 1-2, Leipzig 1871-1872.

Ibn Qutaiba, *Ši'r* = Ibn Qutaiba, Abū Muḥammad 'Abd Allāh b. Muslim, *al-Ši'r wa-l-šu'arā',* Ed. A. Šākir, Cairo 1966.

Ibn al-Šaǧarī, *Amālī* = Ibn al-Šaǧarī, Diyā' al-Dīn Abū l-Sa'ādāt Hibat al-lāhi, *al-Amālī l-šaǧarīya,* 2 vol., Hyderabad 1349 H.

Ibn al-Salka, *Ši'r* = *Ši'r al-Sulaik b. al-Salka,* Ed. Ḥ. Ādam and K. Sa'īd, Bagdad 1984.

Ibn al-Sarrāǧ, *Uṣūl* = Ibn al-Sarrāǧ, Abū Bakr, *al-Uṣūl fī l-Naḥw,* Ed. 'A. Ḥ. al-Fatlī, Beirut 1408/1988.

Ibn Sīda, *Muḫaṣṣaṣ* = Ibn Sīda al-Andalusī, Abū l-Ḥasan 'Alī b. Ismā'īl, *al-Muḫaṣṣaṣ fī l-luġa,* Bulaq 1316-1321 A. H.

Ibn al-Sikkīt, *Qalb* = Ibn al-Sikkīt, Abū Yūsuf Ya'qūb b. Isḥāq, *al-Qalb wa-l-ibdāl,* (in the book *Kitāb al-kanz al-luġawī),* Ed. Hoffner, Beirut 1903.

Ibn al-Sikkīt, *Tahḏīb* = Ibn al-Sikkīt, Abū Yūsuf Ya'qūb b. Isḥāq, *Tahḏīb al-alfāẓ,* Ed. Louis Cheikho, Beirut 1895.

Ibn Sīna, *Šifā'* = Ibn Sīna (Avicenna), Abū 'Alī, *al-Šifā': Manṭiq, I. Madḫal,* Ed. al-Ab Qanawātī, Cairo 1371/1952.

Ibn Taymīya, *Ǧahd* = Ibn Taymīya, *Ǧahd al-qarīḥa fī taǧrīd al-naṣīḥa,* vol. 9, Transl. W. B. Hallaq as *Against the Greek logicians* (to be published), in: *Maǧmū' fatāwā šayḫ al-Islām Aḥmad b. Taymīya,* Ed. 'A. al-R. M. b. Qāsim, 37 vol., Rabat 1961a.

Ibn Tiġribirdī, *Nuǧūm* = Ibn Tiġribirdī, *al-Nuǧūm al-zāhira fī mulūk Miṣr wa-l-Qāhira,* Cairo 1933.

Ibn 'Uṣfūr = Ibn 'Uṣfūr al-Išbīlī, Abū l-'Abbās 'Alī b. Mu'min, *al-Mumti' fī l-taṣrīf,* Ed. F. al-Dīn Qabāwih, Aleppo 1390/1970.

Ibn 'Uṣfūr, *Ḍarā'ir* = Ibn 'Uṣfūr al-Išbīlī, Abū l-'Abbās 'Alī b. Mu'min, *Ḍarā'ir al-ši'r,* Ed. I. Muḥammad, Dār al-Andalus 1980.

Ibn 'Uṣfūr, *Muqarrab* = Ibn 'Uṣfūr al-Išbīlī, Abū l-'Abbās 'Alī b. Mu'min, *al-Muqarrab,* Ed. A. al-Ǧawārī and 'A. al-Ǧabūri, Bagdad 1391/1971.

Ibn 'Uṣfūr, *Šarḥ ǧumal* = Ibn 'Uṣfūr al-Išbīlī, Abū l-'Abbās 'Alī b. Mu'min, *Šarḥ ǧumal al-Zaǧǧāǧī,* Ed. Ṣ. Abū Ǧanāḥ, Bagdad 1980.

Ibn Wallād, *Intiṣār* = Ibn Wallād, Abū l-'Abbās Aḥmad b. Muḥammad, *Kitāb al-intiṣār aw Kitāb naqd Ibn Wallād 'alā l-Mubarrad fī raddihi 'alā Sībawaihi,* Ed. Bernards, M. See Bernards, *Traditions.*

Ibn Wallād, *Maqṣūr* = Ibn Wallād, Abū l-'Abbās Aḥmad b. Muḥammad, *Kitāb al-maqṣūr wa-l-mamdūd 'alā ḥurūf al-mu'ǧam,* Part I, Contributions towards Arabic Philology, Ed. Paul Brönnle, Leiden 1900.

Ibn Ya'īš = Ibn Ya'īš, Muwaffaq al-Dīn Abū l-Barā' Ya'īš, *Šarḥ al-mufaṣṣal,* 2 vol., Beirut s.a.

Ibn Ya'īš, *Mulūkī* = Ibn Ya'īš, Muwaffaq al-Dīn Abū l-Barā' Ya'īš, *Šarḥ al-mulūkī fī l-taṣrīf,* Ed. Faḫr al-Dīn Qabāwa, Aleppo 1393/1973.

'Īd, *Uṣūl* = 'Īd, Muḥammad Faraǧ, *Uṣūl al-naḥw al-'arabī,* Cairo 1978.

Ismā'īl, *Tadrīs* = Ismā'īl, Zakarīyā', *Ṭuruq tadrīs al-luġa al-'arabīya,* Alexandria 1991.

Kafrāwī, *Šarḥ* = al-Kafrāwī, *Šarḥ al-āǧurrūmīya,* Bulaq 1257.

Kaḥḥāla, *Mu'ǧam* = Kaḥḥāla, 'U. R, *Mu'ǧam al-mu'allifīn, tarāǧim muṣannifī l-kutub al-'arabīya,* 1-15, Damaskus 1367/1957-1381/1961.

Karmalī, *Luġāt* = Karmalī, A., *al-Luġāt wa-l-laṭaġāt,* in: *al-Mašriq 12,* 1903.

Kuṭayyir, *Dīwān* = Kuṭayyir, 'Izza, *Dīwān,* Ed. I. 'Abbās, Beirut 1391/1971.

Labīd, *Dīwān* = *Dīwān Labīd b. Abī Rabī'a,* Ed. I. 'Abbās, Kuweit 1962.

Laḫmī, *Madḫal* = Al-Laḫmī, Ibn Hišām, *al-Madḫal ilā taqwīm al-lisān wa-ta'līm al-bayān,* Ed. 'Abd al-Tawwāb.

Luġawī, *Ibdāl* = Luġawī, Abū l-Ṭīb, *al-Ibdāl,* Ed. 'I. al-Dīn al-Tanūḫī, Damascus 1380/1961.

Luġawī, *Marātib* = Luġawī, Abū l-Ṭīb, *Marātib al-naḥwīyīn al-luġawīyīn,* Ed. Abū l-Fāḍl Ibrāhīm, Cairo 1393/ 1974.

Ma'arrī, *Risāla* = Al-Ma'arrī, Abū l-'Alā', *Risālat al-malā'ika,* Ed. S. al-Ǧundī, Beirut s.a.

Madkūr, *Falsafa* = Madkūr, *Fī l-falsafa l-islāmīya,* Cairo 1947.

Maǧnūn, *Dīwān* = *Dīwān Maǧnūn Lailā,* Ed. 'Abd al-Sattār Farāǧ, Cairo s.a.

Maḫzūmī, *Madrasa* = Al-Maḫzūmī, M., *Madrasat al-Kūfa wa-manhaǧuhā fī dirāsat al-luġa wa-l-naḥw,* Bagdad 1958.

Maḫzūmī, *Naḥw* = Al-Maḫzūmī, M., *Fī l-naḥw al-'arabī,* Beirut 1986.

Makkī, *Kašf* = Makkī, b. Abī Ṭālib al-Qaisī al-Andalusī, *al-Kašf 'an wuǧūh al-qirā'āt al-sab' wa-'ilalihā wa-ḥuǧaǧihā,* Ed. M. al-Dīn Ramaḍān, Damascus 1394/1974.

Makkī, *Mušakkal* = Makkī, b. Abī Ṭālib al-Qaisī al-Andalusī, *Tafsīr Mušakkal 'i'rāb al-qur'ān,* Ed. 'A. Ḥ. al-Suyūrī, 2 vol. s.a.

Malā'ika, *Fu'ūl* = Malā'ika, J., *'A-ṣaḥīḥ 'iṭṭirād fu'ūl maṣdaran li-fa'ala l-lāzim,* in: *Journal of the Iraq Academy 29,* 1978.

Marzubānī, *Muwaššaḥ* = Al-Marzubānī, *al-Muwaššaḥ,* Ed. 'A. al-Baǧāwī, Cairo 1385/ 1965.

Mu'addib, *Taṣrīf* = Al-Mu'addib, al-Qāsim b. Muḥammad b. Sa'īd, *Daqā'iq al-taṣrīf,* Ed. A. N. al-Qaisī, Ḥ. Ṣ. al-Ḍāmin and Ḥ. Tūrāl, al-'Irāq 1407/1987.

Mubārak, *Naḥw* = Mubārak, M., *al-Naḥw al-'arabī,* Beirut, Cairo 1974.

Mubarrad, *Kāmil* = Al-Mubarrad, Abū l-ʿAbbās Muḥammad b. Yazīd, *al-Kāmil,* Ed. M. Abū l-Faḍl Ibrāhīm, 4 vol., Cairo s.a.

Mubarrad, *Muqtaḍab* = Mubarrad, Abū l-ʿAbbās Muḥammad b. Yazīd, *al-Muqtaḍab,* Ed. ʿA. Ḫ. ʿUḍayma, Beirut s.a.

Mufaḍḍal, *Fāḫir* = Mufaḍḍal b. Salma, *al-Fāḫir,* Ed. ʿA. al-ʿAlīm al-Ṭaḥāwī, Cairo 1960.

Mutanabbī, *Dīwān* = *Dīwān al-Mutanabbī bi-Šarḥ al-ʿUkbarī,* Ed. M. al-Saqā and I. al-Ibyārī and ʿA. al-Ḥafīẓ Šalbī, Cairo 1391/1971.

Nāǧidī, *Sībawaihi* = Nāǧidī, ʿAlī Faḫrī, *Sībawaihi, Imām al-nuḥāt,* Cairo 1953.

Naḥḥās, *Commentar* = Al-Naḥḥās, *Commentar zur Muʿallaqa,* Ed. E. Frenckel, Halle 1876.

Naḥḥās, *Qaṣāʾid* = Al-Naḥḥās, Abū Ǧaʿfar, *Šarḥ al-qaṣāʾid al-tisʿa al-mašhūrāt,* Ed. A. Ḫaṭṭāb, Bagdad 1973.

Nuṣaib, *Dīwān* = *Dīwān Nuṣaib,* Ed. D. Salūm, Bagdad 1967.

Qālī, *Amālī* = Al-Qālī, Abū ʿAlī, *Amālī,* Bulaq 1324.

Qālī, *Nawādir* = Al-Qālī, Abū ʿAlī, *al-Nawādir,* Cairo 1344/1926.

Qifṭī, *Inbāh* = Qifṭī, ʿAlī b. Yūsuf, *Inbāh al-ruwāh ʿalā anbāʾ al-nuḥāh,* Ed. M. Abū l- Faḍl Ibrāhīm, 3 vol., Cairo 1369/1950-1374/1955.

Qudāma, *Naqd* = Qudāma, *Naqd al-naṯr,* Ed. Ṭ. Ḥusain and ʿĀ. Ḥ. al-ʿAbbādī, Cairo 1933.

Quṭrub, *Aḍdād* = Quṭrub, Abū ʿAlī Muḥammad, *Das Kitāb al-aḍdād von Abū ʿAlī Muḥammad Quṭrub ibn al-Mustanīr,* Ed. H. Kofler, Islamica V, 1931-1932.

Rāḍī, *Naẓarīya* = Rāḍī, ʿA. al-Ḥakīm, *Naẓarīyat al-luġa fī l-naqd al-ʿarabī,* Cairo s.a.

Rāǧiḥī, *Basīṭ* = Rāǧiḥī, ʿAbdo, *al-Basīṭ fī ʿilm al-ṣarf,* Alexandria s.a.

Rāǧiḥī, *Farrāʾ* = Al-Rāǧiḥī, Šaraf al-Dīn, *Fī l-muṣṭalaḥ al-ṣarfī ʿinda l-Farrāʾ fī kitābati "Maʿānī l-qurʾān",* Alexandria 1992.

Rāǧiḥī, *Taṭbīq* = Al-Rāǧiḥī, ʿAbdo, *al-Taṭbīq al-ṣarfī,* Beirut 1975.

Riḍā, *Luġa* = Riḍā, Aḥmad, *Mawlid al-Luġa,* Ed. N. Riḍā, Beirut 1403/1983.

Ṣābiʾ, *Ġurar* = Ṣābiʾ, Abū l-Ḥusain Hilāl b. al-Muḥassin, *Ġurar al-balāġa, I-II,* Ed. Asʿad Ḏubyān, Beirut 1403/1983.

Šāḏilī, *ʿAnāṣir* = Šāḏilī, Abū l-Saʿūd Ḥusain, *Al-ʿAnāṣir al-asāsīyat li-l-markab al-fiʿlī wa-anmāṭihā min ḫilāl al-Qurʾān al-karīm, dirāsa taḥlīlīya taṭbīqīya,* Alexandria 1410/1990.

Ṣafadī, *Wāfī* = *Al-Wāfī bi-l-wafayāt,* taʾlīf Ṣ. Ḫ. Ibn A. al-Ṣafadī, Ed. H. Ritter, 1- Istanbul/ Beirut-Leipzig/Wiesbaden 1931- (reprinted: 1-4, Beirut-Wiesbaden 1962-1974).

Saraqusṭī, *Afʿāl* = Saraqusṭī, Abū ʿUṯmān Saʿīd b. Muḥammad al-Maʿāfirī, *Kitāb al-afʿāl,* 4 vol., vol. 4 in 2 parts, Ed. Ḥ. M. M. Šarf and M. M. ʿAllām, Cairo 1400/1980.

Ṣaymarī, *Tabṣira* = Al-Ṣaymarī, Abū Muḥammad Isḥāq, *al-Ṭabṣira wa-l-taḏkira,* Ed. F. ʿAlāʾ l-Dīn, Makka 1982.

Sayyid, *Kāfī* = Al-Sayyid, Ṣabrī Ibrāhīm, *al-Kāfī fī l-naḥw wa-taṭbīqātuhu,* 2 vol., Alexandria 1992-1993.

Sībawaihi = Sîbawaihi, Abū Bišr ʿAmr b. ʿUṯmān, *Le Livre de Sîbawaihi (Kitāb Sībawaihi), Traité de grammaire arabe,* Ed. H. Derenbourg, 2 vol., Paris 1881-1889. Réimpression: 1970.

Siǧistānī, *Faʿaltu* = Al-Siǧistānī, Abū Ḥātim, *Faʿaltu wa-afʿaltu,* Ed. Ḫ. I. al-ʿAṭīya, Bagdad 1979.

Šinqīṭī, *Durar* = Al-Šinqīṭī, Aḥmad b. al-Amīn, *al-Durar al-lawāmiʿ ʿalā hamʿ al-hawāmiʿ,* 2 vol., Cairo 1328/1910.

Sīrāfī, *Aḫbār* = Al-Sīrāfī, Abū Saʿīd, *Kitāb aḫbār al-naḥwīyīn al-Baṣrīyīn,* Ed. F. Krenkow, Paris-Beyrouth 1936.

Širbīnī, *Āǧurrūmīya* = See Carter, *Širbīnī.*

Širbīnī, *Šarḥ* = Al-Širbīnī, al-Ḫaṭīb, *Šarḥ šawāhid al-Qaṭr,* Cairo 1298.

Ṣubḥī, *Fiqh* = Ṣubḥī, Ṣ., *Dirāsāt fī fiqh al-luġa,* Beirut 2nd print 1989.

Ṣūlī, *Adab* = Al-Ṣūlī, *Adab al-kitāb,* Ed. M. B. al-Aṯarī, Cairo 1341 A.H.

Suyūṭī, *Ašbāh* = Al-Suyūṭī, Ǧalāl al-Dīn Abū l-Faḍl ʿAbd al-Raḥmān, *al-Ašbāh wa-l-naẓāʾir,* Ed. ʿAbd al-Ilāh Nabhān, 4 vol., Damascus 1406/1985.

Suyūṭī, *Buġya* = Al-Suyūṭī, Ǧalāl al-Dīn Abū l-Faḍl ʿAbd al-Raḥmān, *Buġyat al-wuʿāh fī ṭabaqāt al-luġawīyīn wa-l-nuḥāh,* Ed. M. A. F. Ibrāhīm, 2 vol., Cairo 1399 A.H.

Suyūṭī, *Hawāmiʿ* = Al-Suyūṭī, Ǧalāl al-Dīn Abū l-Faḍl ʿAbd al-Raḥmān, *Hamʿ al-hawāmiʿ šarḥ ǧamʿ al-ǧawāmiʿ fī ʿilm al-ʿarabīya,* Ed. M. B. al-Naʿsānī, 2 vol., Cairo 1327 A.H.

Suyūṭī, *Iqtirāḥ* = Al-Suyūṭī, Ǧalāl al-Dīn Abū l-Faḍl ʿAbd al-Raḥmān, *al-Iqtirāḥ fī uṣūl al-naḥw,* Ed. A. Q. Muḥammad, 1st Edition, Cairo 1396 A.H.

Suyūṭī, *Muzhir* = Al-Suyūṭī, Ǧalāl al-Dīn Abū l-Faḍl ʿAbd al-Raḥmān, *al-Muzhir fī ʿulūm al-luġa wa-anwāʿihā,* 2 vol., Cairo s.a.

Suyūṭī, *Šarḥ* = Al-Suyūṭī, Ǧalāl al-Dīn Abū l-Faḍl ʿAbd al-Raḥmān, *Šarḥ šawāhid al-muġnī,* Cairo 1322.

Ṯaʿālibī, *Fiqh* = Ṯaʿālibī, Abū Manṣūr, *Kitāb fiqh al-luġa wa-asrār al-ʿarabīya,* Beirut s.a.

Ṯaʿlab, *Faṣīḥ* = Ṯaʿlab, Abū l-ʿAbbās Aḥmad b. Yaḥyā, *Kitāb al-faṣīḥ,* Ed. J. Barth, Leipzig 1876.

Ṯaʿlab, *Maǧālis* = Ṯaʿlab, Abū l-ʿAbbās Aḥmad b. Yaḥyā, *Maǧālis,* Ed. ʿA. al-Salām Hārūn, 1375/1956.

Tamīm, *Dīwān* = *Dīwān Tamīm b. Abī b. Muqbil,* Ed. ʿI. Ḥasan, Damascus 1381/1962.

Tamīmī, *Musalsal* = Abū Ṭāhir al-Tamīmī, *al-Musalsal fī ġarīb luġati l-ʿArab,* Ed. M. al-Ǧawād, Cairo 1957.

Tanūḫī, *Qawāfī* = Al-Tanūḫī, *Kitāb al-qawāfī,* Ed. ʿU. al-Asʿad and M. al-Dīn Ramaḍān, Beirut 1970.

Ṭarafa, *Dīwān* = Ṭarafa, b. al-ʿAbd, *Dīwān,* Ed. D. al-Ḫaṭīb and L. al-Ṣaqāl, Damascus 1395/1975.

Tibrīzī, *Iḫtiyārāt* = Al-Tibrīzī, al-Ḫaṭīb, *Šarḥ iḫtiyārāt al-Mufaḍḍal,* Ed. Faḫr al-Dīn Qabāwa, Damascus 1391/1971.
Tibrīzī, *Qaṣā'id* = Al-Tibrīzī, al-Ḫaṭīb, *Šarḥ al-qaṣā'id al-'ašr,* Ed. M. M. 'Abd al-Ḥamīd, Cairo 1964.
'Ukbarī, *Masā'il* = Al-'Ukbarī, Abd Allāh b. al-Ḥusain, *Masā'il ḫilāfīya fī l-naḥw,* Ed. M. Ḫ. al-Ḥalawānī, Aleppo s.a.
'Umar b. Abī Rabī'a, *Dīwān* = *Dīwān 'Umar b. Abī Rabī'a,* Ed. M. Muḥyī l-Dīn 'Abd al-Ḥamīd, Cairo 1371/1952.
Yāqūt, *Mu'ǧam* = Yāqūt al-Ḥamawī, Abū 'Abd Allāh Ya'qūb, *Mu'ǧam al-udabā',* Ed. F. al-Rifā'ī, Printing House al-Ḥalabī 1355 A.H.
Yāqūt, *Tarākīb* = Yāqūt, M. Sulaimān, *al-Tarākīb ġair al-ṣaḥīḥa naḥwīyan fī l-kitāb li-Sībawaihi, dirāsa luġawīya,* Alexandria s.a.
Yasū'ī, *Ġarā'ib* = Al-Yasū'ī, R. N., *Ġarā'ib al-luġa l-'arabīya,* Beirut 1986.
Zabīdī, *Tāǧ* = Al-Zabīdī, Muḥammad b. Muḥammad Murtaḍā l-Ḥusainī, *Tāǧ al-'arūs min ǧawāhir al-qāmūs,* Ed. M. Ḥiǧāzī, Kuweit 1369/1969.
Zaǧǧāǧ, *Ma'ānī* = Zaǧǧāǧ, Abū Isḥāq, *Ma'ānī l-qur'ān wa-i'rābuh,* Ed. 'A. al-Ǧalīl Šalabī, Beirut 1973.
Zaǧǧāǧī, *Ǧumal* = Al-Zaǧǧāǧī, Abū Qāsim 'Abd al-Raḥmān, *al-Ǧumal,* Ed. B. Cheneb, Paris 1957.
Zaǧǧāǧī, *Īḍāḥ* = Al-Zaǧǧāǧī, Abū Qāsim 'Abd al-Raḥmān, *al-Īḍāḥ fī 'ilal al-naḥw,* Ed. M. al-Mubārak, Cairo 1378/1959. See also Versteegh, *Zaǧǧāǧī.*
Zaǧǧāǧī, *Maǧālis* = Al-Zaǧǧāǧī, Abū Qāsim 'Abd al-Raḥmān, *Maǧālis al-'ulamā',* Ed. 'A. S. M. Harūn, Kuwait 1962.
Zamaḫšarī = Zamaḫs'ario, Abū l-Qāsim Maḥmūd b. 'Umar, *al-Mufaṣṣal,* Ed. J. P. Broch, Christianiae 1840.
Zamaḫšarī, *Asās* = Al-Zamaḫšarī, Abū l-Qāsim Maḥmūd b. 'Umar, *Asās al-balāġa,* Beirut 1404 A.H./1984.
Zamaḫšarī, *Fā'iq* = Al-Zamaḫšarī, Abū l-Qāsim Maḥmūd b. 'Umar, *al-Fā'iq fī ġarīb al-ḥadīṯ*, Ed. A. F. Ibrāhīm, Cairo 1945-1948.
Zamaḫšarī, *Kaššāf* = Al-Zamaḫšarī, Abū l-Qāsim Maḥmūd b. 'Umar, *al-Kaššāf 'an ḥaqā'iq al-tanzīl wa-'uyūn al-aqāwīl fī wuǧūh al-ta'wīl,* together with the *Ḥāšiya* by al-Ǧurǧānī, Zain al-Dīn Abī l-Ḥasan al-Ḥusainī, *al-Inṣāf fīmā taḍammanahu al-kaššāf mina l-i'tizāl* by al-Mālikī, Ibn al-Munīr al-Iskandarī, and at the end of the work *Tanzīl al-'āyāt 'alā l-šawāhid 'an al-abyāt* by Afandī, Muḥibb al-Dīn, [see Afandī, *Tanzīl],* 4 vol., Cairo 1392 A.H./1972.
Zarkašī, *Burhān* = Al-Zarkašī, Badr al-Dīn Muḥammad b. 'Abd Allāh, *al-Burhān fī 'ulūm al-qur'ān,* Ed. M. A. F. Ibrāhīm, 1st edition, s.a.
Zaydān, *Maḫṭūṭāt II* = Zaydān, Yūsuf, *Fihris maḫṭūṭāt ǧāmi'at al-Iskandarīya, II,* 1995.
Zubaidī, *Laḥn* = Al-Zubaidī, Abū Bakr, *Laḥn al-'awāmm,* Ed. R. 'Abd al-Tawwāb, Cairo 1964.
Zubaidī, *Ṭabaqāt* = Al-Zubaidī, Abū Bakr, *Ṭabaqāt al-naḥwīyīn wa-l-luġawīyīn,* Ed. M. A. F. Ibrāhīm, Cairo 1954.
Zuhair, *Dīwān* = *Dīwān Zuhair b. Abī Salmā* ṣan'at Ṯa'lab, Cairo 1363/1944.
Zuhair, *Ši'r* = *Ši'r Zuhair b. Abī Salmā bi-šarḥ al-a'lam al-Šantamarī,* Ed. Faḫr al-Dīn Qabāwa, Aleppo 1393/1973.

III. 2. Secondary sources

Abed, *Logic* = Abed, Sh. B., *Aristotelian Logic and the Arabic Language in Alfārābī,* New York 1991.
Abū Ḥaidar, *Dual* = Abu Haidar, J., *Qifā nabki: The Dual Form of Address in Arabic Poetry in a New Light,* in: *JAL 19,* part 1, 1988.
Abu Haidar, *Reviews of Books* = Abu Haidar, F., *Reviews of Books:* Aḥmad b. 'Alī b. Mas'ūd on Arabic Morphology, *Marāḥ al-arwāḥ,* Part one: The strong Verb: Aṣ-ṣaḥīḥ, Ed. with Translation, Commentary and Introduction by J. Åkesson, Leiden 1990, in: *JRAS 2,* part 3, Cambridge 1992.
Ahlwardt, *Divans* = Ahlwardt, W., *The Divans of the six ancient Arabic poets Ennābiga, 'Antara, Tharafa, Zuhair, 'Alqama and Umruulqais,* London 1870.
Ahlwardt = Ahlwardt, W., *Verzeichniss der Arabischen Handschriften der Königlichen Bibliothek zu Berlin,* Nr. 1-10368, 1-9.10 [Indices], Berlin 1887-1899 *(Die Handschriften-Verzeichnisse der Königlichen Bibliothek zu Berlin,* 7-9. 16-22 (Nachdruck: Hildesheim 1980-1981).
Ahrens, *Verba* = Ahrens, K., *Der Stamm der schwachen Verba in den semitischen Sprachen,* in: *ZDMG 64,* 1910.
Åkesson, *Conversion* = Åkesson, J., *Conversion of the yā' into an alif in Classical Arabic* in: *ZAL 31,* Wiesbaden 1996.
Åkesson, *Elision* = Åkesson, *Anomalous elision and addition of a vowel in Classical Arabic,* in: *ZAL 36,* Wiesbaden 1999.
Åkesson, *Verb and Infinitive* = Åkesson, J., *The strong Verb and Infinitive Noun in Arabic,* in: *AO 52,* Denmark 1991.
Alee, *Wasīṭ* = Alee, Mouluvee Toorab, *Wasīṭ al-naḥw,* A treatise on the syntax of the Arabic language, Madras 1820.
Anwar, *Fathers* = Anwar, M. S., *The Legitimate Fathers of Speech Errors,* in: *SHL 28,* Ed. C. H. M. Versteegh, K. Koerner and H. -J., Niederehe, Amsterdam/Philadelphia 1983.
Arkoun, *Logocentrisme* = Arkoun, M., *Logocentrisme et vérité religieuse dans la pensée islamique d'après al-I'lām*

bi-manāqib al-Islām d'al-ʿAmirī, in: *SI 35,* 1972.
Arnaldez, *Sciences* = Arnaldez, R., *Sciences et philosophie dans la civilisation de Baġdād sous les premiers ʿAbbāsides,* in: *Ar 9,* 1962.
Aro, *Vokalisierung* = Aro, J., *Die Vokalisierung des Grundstammes im Semitischen Verbum,* Kap. VIII, *Schlussfolgerungen zur Geschichte des Verbal-systems,* in: *SO 31,* Helsinki 1964.
Atsiz = Kemalpaşa-oğlu'nun eserleri, in: Şarkiyat Mecmuası 6/1966/71-112 [Nr. 1-92]; 7/1972/83-135 [Nr. 93-209].
Azhar = *Fihris al-kutub al-mawǧūda bi-l-maktaba l-Azharīya* 1-7, Cairo 1365-82/1946-69.
Baalbaki, *Hierarchy* = Baalbaki, R., *Harmony and Hierarchy in Sıbawaihi's Grammatical Analysis,* in: *ZAL 24,* 1979.
Baalbaki, *Iʿrāb* = Baalbaki, R., *Iʿrāb and binā' from linguistic reality to grammatical theory,* in: *SHAG II,* Ed. K. Versteegh and M. G. Carter, Amsterdam/Philadelphia 1990.
Badawī, *Aristotles* = Badawī, A., *Aristotles, De Poetica,* Cahirae 1953.
Baldick, *Islam* = Baldick, J., *Mystical Islam, An Introduction to Sufism,* New York and London 1989.
Barth, *Grammatik* = Barth, J., *Zur vergleichenden semitischen Grammatik,* in: *ZDMG 48,* 1894.
Barth, *Nominalbildung* = Barth, J., *Die Nominalbildung in den semitischen Sprachen,* Leipzig 1889.
Barth, *Zur Frage der Nominalbildung* = Barth, J., *Zur Frage der Nominalbildung,* in: *ZDMG 44,* 1890.
Bauer, *Grammatik* = Bauer, H., *Mitteilungen zur semitischen Grammatik,* in: *ZDMG 66,* 1912.
Beeston, *Language* = Beeston, A. F. L., *The Arabic Language today,* London 1970.
Bernards, *Ǧarmī* = Bernards, M., *Abū ʿUmar al-Ǧarmī,* in: *SHAG II,* Ed. K. Versteegh and M. G. Carter, Amsterdam/Philadelphia 1990.
Bernards, *Traditions* = Bernards, M., *Changing Traditions, Al-Mubarrad's Refutation of Sībawaih and the Subsequent Reception of the Kitāb,* Leiden - New York - Köln 1997.
Blachère = Blachère, R., et Gaudefroy-Demombynes, M., *Grammaire de l'Arabe classique,* Paris 1952.
Blanc, *Fronting* = Blanc, H., *The Fronting of Semitic g and the qāl-gāl Dialect Split in Arabic,* in: *PICSS,* Jerusalem 1969.
Blau, *Judaeo-Arabic* = Blau, J., *The Emergence and linguistic Background of judaeo-Arabic, A study of the origins of Middle Arabic,* Oxford 1965.
Bohas, *Aspects* = Bohas, G., *Quelques aspects de l'argumentation et de l'explication chez les grammairiens arabes,* in: *Ar 28, fasc. 2-3.*
Bohas, *Étude* = Bohas, G., *Contribution à l'étude de la méthode des grammairiens arabes en morphologie et en phonologie d'après des grammairiens arabes "tardifs".* See Bohas/Guillaume, *Étude.*
Bohas, *Matrices* = Bohas, G., *Matrices, Étymons, Racines. Éléments d'une théorie lexicologique du vocabulaire arabe,* Paris 1997.
Bohas, *Structure* = Bohas, G., *Le PCO et la structure des racines,* in: *Développements récents en linguistique arabe et sémitique,* Damas 1993.
Bohas/Guillaume, *Étude* = Bohas, G., Guillaume, J.-P., *Étude des théories des grammairiens arabes,* I. Morphologie et phonologie, Damas 1984. See Bohas, *Étude* and Guillaume, *Aspects.*
Bohas/Guillaume/Kouloughli, *Linguistic* = Bohas, G., Guillaume, J.-P., Kouloughli, D.E., *The Arabic Linguistic Tradition,* London and New York 1990.
Bravmann, *Materialien* = Bravmann, M. M., *Materialien und Untersuchungen zu den phonetischen Lehren der Araber,* Göttingen 1934.
Bravmann, *Studies* = Bravmann, M. M., *Studies in Semitic Philology,* Leiden 1977.
Brill, *Manuscripts* = E.J. Brill, *Oriental Manuscripts offered for sale,* Catalogue no 555, Leiden 1986.
Brockelmann, *GAL* = Brockelmann, C. : *Geschichte der arabischen Litteratur,* I-II, 2 Aufl., Leiden 1943-49.
Brockelmann, *Grundriss* = Brockelmann, C., *Grundriss der vergleichenden Grammatik der semitischen Sprachen.* I. Band, *Laut und Formenlehre,* Berlin, 1908; II., Band, *Syntax,* ibid., 1913.
Brockelmann, *S* = Brockelmann, C., *Suppl. Band I-III,* Leiden, 1937-42.
Brockelmann, *Socins Grammatik* = Brockelmann, C., *A. Socins Arabische Grammatik,* Paradigmen, Literatur, Übungsstücke und Glossar, Siebente Durchgesehene und verbesserte Auflage, Berlin 1913.
Buhl, *Allāhumma* = Buhl, Fr., *Allāhumma,* in: *Encyclopaedie of Islām,* Ed. Houtsma, T. W. Arnold, R. Basset, R. Hartmann, Band I, Leiden/ Harrassowitz 1913.
Bürgel, *Gazelle* = Bürgel, J. C., *The Lady Gazelle and her Murderous Glances,* in: *JAL 20,* part I, 1989.
Cachia, *Monitor* = Cachia, P., *The Monitor, a Dictionary of Arabic Grammatical Terms,* Beirut 1973.
Cantarino, *Syntax* = Cantarino, V., *Syntax of Modern Arabic Prose, the Simple Sentence,* 3 vol., Oriental Series no. 4, Indiana University Press, Bloomington/London 1974.
Cantineau, *Consonantisme* = Cantineau, J., *Le consonantisme du sémitique,* in: *Semitica 4,* 1953.
Cantineau, *Cours* = Cantineau, J., *Cours de phonétique arabe,* 2 fascicules, Alger 1941.
Cantineau, *Dialecte* = Cantineau, J., *Le dialecte arabe de Palmyre,* Beyrouth 1935.
Cantineau, *Esquisse* = Cantineau, J., *Esquisse d'une phonologie de l'arabe classique,* in: *BSLP 126.*
Cantineau, *Études* = Cantineau, J., *Études de linguistique arabe,* Memorial Jean Cantineau, Paris 1960.

Cantineau, *Parlers* = Cantineau, J., *Études sur quelques Parters de nomades arabes de l'Orient,* Annales de l'Inst. d'Études Or. d'Alger, II-III, 1936-1937.

Cantineau, *Six* = Cantineau, J., *Le nom de nombre "six" dans les langues sémitiques,* in: *BEA 13,* 1943.

Cantineau, *Voyelle* = Cantineau, J., *La Voyelle de secours dans les langues sémitiques,* in: *Semitica II,* 1949.

Carter, *Origines* = Carter, M. G., *Les Origines de la grammaire arabe,* in: *REI 49,* 1972.

Carter, *Ṣarf* = Carter, M. G., *Ṣarf et Ḫilāf. Contribution à l'histoire de la grammaire arabe,* in: *Ar 20,* 1973.

Carter, *Širbīnī* = Carter, M. G., *Arab Linguistics, an introductory classical text with translation and notes,* Amsterdam 1981. See Širbīnī, *Āǧurrūmīya.*

Chouémi, *Verbe* = Chouémi, *Le Verbe dans le Coran, racines et formes,* Paris 1966.

Cohen, *Aḍdād* = Cohen, D., *Aḍdād et ambiguïté linguistique en arabe,* in: *Ar 8.*

Cohen, *Études* = Cohen, D., *Études de linguistique sémitique et arabe,* The Hague/Paris 1970.

Danecki, *Mubarrad* = Danecki, J., *The phonetical theory of Mubarrad,* in: *SHAG II,* Ed. K. Versteegh and M. G. Carter, Amsterdam/Philadelphia 1990.

Derenbourg = Derenbourg, H., *Les Manuscrits arabes de l'Escorial,* Paris 1884.

Diakonoff, *Semito-Hamitic* = Diakonoff, I. A., *Semito-Hamitic Languages, an Essay in Classification,* Moscow 1965.

Diem, *Dialekte* = Diem, W., *Skizzen jemenitischer Dialekte,* Beirut 1973.

Diem, *Fuʿāl* = Diem, W., *Die Nominalform fuʿāl im Klassischen Arabisch,* in: *ZDMG 120,* 1970.

Diem, *Verba und Nomina* = Diem, W., *Die Verba und Nomina tertiae infirmae im Semitischen,* Ein Beitrag zur Rekonstruktion des Ursemitischen und zur Entwicklung der Einzelsprachen, in: *ZDMG 127,* 1977.

Dieterici, *Mutanabbii* = Dieterici, *Mutanabbii carmina cum comm. Wâḥidii,* Berol. 1861.

Elamrani-Jamal, *Ibn ʿAdī* = Elamrani-Jamal, A., *Grammaire et logique d'après le philosophe arabe chrétien Yaḥya Ibn ʿAdī* (280-364 H/893-974), in: *Ar 29, fasc. I.*

Endress, *Proclus Arabus* = Endress, G., *Proclus Arabus. Zwanzig Abschnitte aus der Institutio Theologica in arabischer Übersetzung,* Beirut 1973.

Fischer, *Beiträge* = Fischer, A., *Zwei Beiträge zur arabischen Grammatik,* in: *ZDMG 63,* 1909.

Fischer, *Infinitive* = Fischer, A., *Das Geschlecht der Infinitive im Arabischen,* in: *ZDMG 60,* 1906.

Fischer, *Miszellen* = Fischer, A., *Miszellen,* in: *ZDMG 58,* 1904.

Fischer, *Mitteilungen* = Fischer, A., *Kleine Mitteilungen (ʾilāh),* in: *ZDMG 71.*

Fischer/Braünlich, *Šawāhid* = Fischer, A. und Bräunlich, E., *Schawāhid-Indices, Indices der Reimwörter und der Dichter der in den arabischen Schawāhid-Kommentaren und in verwandten Werken erläuterten Belegverse,* Leipzig und Wien, 1945.

Fischer, *Origin* = Fischer, J. B., *The Origin of tripartite division of speech in Semitic grammar,* in: *JQR 53,* 1962-1963, *54,* 1963-1964.

Fischer, *Farb-* = Fischer, W., *Farb- und Formbezeichnungen in der Sprache der Altarabischen Dichtung,* Wiesbaden 1965.

Fischer/Jastrow, *Dialekte* = Fischer, W. und Jastrow, O., *Handbuch der arabischen Dialekte,* Wiesbaden 1980.

Fischer, *Grammatik* = Fischer, W., *Grammatik des klassischen Arabisch,* Wiesbaden 1972.

Fleisch, *Arabe* = Fleish, H., *L'arabe classique, Esquisse d'une structure linguistique,* Beyrouth 1968.

Fleisch, *Esquisse* = Fleisch, H., *Esquisse d'un historique de la grammaire arabe,* in: *Ar 4,* 1957.

Fleisch, *Études* = Fleisch, H., *Études de phonétique arabe,* in: *Mélanges de l'Université Saint Joseph de Beyrouth 28,* 1949-1950.

Fleisch, *Iʿrāb* = Fleisch, H., *"Iʿrāb",* in: *Encyclopedia of Islam* (new edition), Leiden.

Fleisch, *Maǧhūra* = Fleisch, H., *Maǧhūra, mahmūsa,* examen critique, in: *Mélanges de l'Université Saint Joseph de Beyrouth 35,* 1958.

Fleisch, *Taṣrīf* = Fleisch, H., *Le Taṣrīf selon les grammairiens arabes,* in: *Communication au Congrès Intern. de Linguistique Sémitique et Chamito-Sémitique,* Paris 1969.

Fleisch, *Traité I* = Fleisch, H., *Traité de Philologie Arabe,* vol. I, *Préliminaires, Phonétique Morphologie Nominale,* Beyrouth 1961.

Fleisch, *Traité II* = Fleisch, H., *Traité de Philologie Arabe,* vol. II, *Pronoms, Morphologie verbale, Particules,* Beyrouth 1979.

Fleisch, *Verbes* = Fleisch, *Les verbes à allongement vocalique interne en sémitique,* (Études de grammaire comparée), Paris 1944.

Fleischer, *Beiträge* = Fleischer, H. O., *Beiträge zur arabischen Sprachkunde,* - in: *Berichte der k. sächs. Ges. d. Wiss. Philol.-hist. Cl. I,* 1863, pp. 93-176.

- " " (Fortsetzung.) Ibid., II, 1864, pp. 265-326.
- " " - " III, 1866, pp. 286-342.
- " " - " IV, 1870, pp. 227-295.
- " " - " V, 1874, pp. 71-158.
- " " - " VI, 1876, pp. 44-109.
- " " - " VII, 1878, pp. 65-146.

Flügel = Flügel, G., *Die arabischen, persischen und türkischen Handschriften der Kaiserlich - Königlichen*

Hofbibliothek zu Wien, 1-3, Wien 1865-1867.
Flügel, *Schulen* = Flügel, G., *Die grammatischen Schulen der Araber, Die Schulen von Basra und Kufa und die gemischte Schule*, Leipzig 1862.
Frazer, *Adonis* = Frazer, J. G., *Adonis, Attis and Osiris*, vol. 1, London 1914.
Freytag, *Darstellung* = Freytag, G. W., *Darstellung der Arab. Verskunst*, Bonn 1830.
Freytag, *Einleitung* = Freytag, G. W., *Einleitung in das Studium der Arab Sprache*, Bonn 1861.
Freytag, *Hamasae* = Freytag, G. W., *Hamasae* carmina c. Tebrisii scholiis, Vol. I. II, I. II. Bonnae 1828-51.
Freytag, *Proverbia* = Freytag, G. W., *Arabum Proverbia*, T. I. II. III, I. II. Bonnae 1838-43.
Fück, *ʿArabīya* = Fück, J., *ʿArabīya*, Berlin 1950.
Gairdner, *Phoneticians* = Gairdner, W. H. T., *The Arab Phoneticians on the Consonant and Vowels*, in: *The Moslem World 25*, 1945.
Garbell, *Remarks* = Garbell, I., *Remarks on the Historical Phonology of an East Mediterranean Arabic Dialect*, in: *Word 14*, 1958.
Ġazālī, *Tabernacle* = Al-Ġazālī, Abū Ḥāmid b. Muḥammad, *Le Tabernacle des lumières, Michkăt al-Anwăr*, traduction de l'arabe et introduction par Roger Deladrière, Paris 1981.
Giese, *Aḍdād* = Giese, F., *Untersuchungen über die Aḍdād auf Grund von Stellen aus altarabischen Dichtern*, Berlin 1894.
Goshen-Gottstein, *System* = Goshen-Gottstein, M. H., *The System of verbal Stems in the Classical Semitic Languages*, in: *PICSS*, Jerusalem 1969.
Gray, *Introduction* = Gray, L. H., *Introduction to Semitic Comparative Linguistics*, 1934.
Gray, *Mythology* = Gray, J., *Near Eastern Mythology*, London 1982.
Greenberg, *Morphemes* = Greenberg, J. H., *The Patterning of Root Morphemes in Semitic*, in: *Word 6*, 1950.
Grunebaum, *Islam* = Grunebaum, G. von, *L'Islam médiéval, Histoire et civilisation*, Paris 1962.
Guillaume, *Cause* = Guillaume, J.-P., *La 'cause' des grammairiens: Étude sur la notion de ʿilla dans la tradition grammaticale arabe (fin IIIè/IXè - milieu du IV/X s.)*. Thèse de 3ème Cycle, Université de Paris-III, s.a.
Guillaume, *Aspects* = Guillaume, J.-P., *Quelques aspects de la théorie morpho-phonologique d'Ibn Ǧinnī à propos des verbes à glide médian*. See Bohas/Guillaume, *Étude*.
Guillaume, *Morphonologie* = Guillaume, J-P., *Le Statut des représentations sous-jacentes en morphonologie d'après Ibn Ǧinnī*, in: *Ar 28*, fasc. 2-3, 1981.
Guillaume, *Principes* = Guillaume, G., *Principes de linguistique théorique de Gustave Guillaume*, Paris 1973.
Guillaume, *Système* = Guillaume, G., *La Langue est-elle ou n'est-elle pas un système?*, in: *Cahiers de linguistique structurale 1*, 1952.
Gully, *Semantics* = Gully, A., *Grammar and Semantics in Medieval Arabic, A study of Ibn Hisham's 'Mughni l-Labib'*, England 1995.
Gwynne, *A fortiori* = Gwynne, R., *The a fortiori argument in fiqh, naḥw and kalām*, in: *SHAG II*, Ed. K. Versteegh and M. G. Carter, Amsterdam /Philadelphia 1990.
Hafftner, *Aḍdād* = Hafftner, A. *Drei Quellenwerke über die Aḍdād mit Beiträgen von P. A. Salhani S. J. und einem spätarabischen Anhange*, [al-Aṣmaʿī, al-Siǧistānī, Ibn al-Sikkīt, al-Ṣaġānī] Beyrouth 1913.
Hämeen-Anttila, *Labials* = Hämeen-Anttila, J., *Interchange of Labials in Classical and Pre-classical Arabic*, the Middle East viewed from the North, in: *Papers from the first Nordic Conference on Middle Eastern Studies, Uppsala 26-29 january 1989*, Ed. B. Utas and K. S. Vikør, published by the Nordic Society for Middle Eastern Studies, Bergen 1992.
Haywood, *Lexicography* = Haywood, J. A., *Arabic lexicography. Its history, and its place in the general history of lexicography*, Leiden 1965.
Heer, *Existence* = Heer, N. L., *al-Ǧāmī's Treatise on Existence*, P. Morewedge, Ed. Islamic Philosophical Theology, State University of New York Press, Albany 1979.
Hitti, *History* = Hitti, Ph. K., *History of the Arabs from the earliest Times to the Present*, Tenth Edition, Great Britain 1970.
Howell = Howell, M. S., *Grammar of the Classical Arabic Language*, 4 parts in 7 vol., Allahabad 1880-1911.
Ibn al-Fāriḍ, *Poems* = Ibn al-Fāriḍ, *The Mystical Poems*, Ed. A. J. Arberry, London 1952.
Jastrow, *Dialekte* = Jastrow, O., *Die Dialekte der Arabischen Halbinsel*, in: *Handbuch der arabischen Dialekte*, bearbeitet und herausgegeben von W. Fischer und O. Jastrow, Wiesbaden 1980.
Jeffery, *Materials* = Jeffery, A., *Materials for the history of the text of the Qur'ān*, Leiden 1937.
Jeffery, *Muqaddimatān* = Jeffery, A., *Muqaddimatān fī ʿulūm al-qur'ān: Muqaddimat al-mabānī wa-Ibn ʿAṭīya*, Cairo 1954.
Knutsson, *Studies* = Knutsson, B., *Studies in the Text and Language of Three Syriac-Arabic Versions of the Book of Judicum with Special Reference to the Middle Arabic Elements*, Leiden 1974.
Köfler, *Dialekte* = Köfler, H., *Reste altarabischer Dialekte*, in: *WZKM*, Wien 1940-1942.
Kopf, *Influences* = Kopf, L., *Religious Influences on Medieval Arabic Philology*, in: *SI 5*, 1956.
Košut, *Streitfragen* = Košut, J., *Fünf Streitfragen der Baṣrenser und Kūfenser*, in: *Sitzungsberichte der phil.-hist. Cl. der kais. Ak. d. Wiss. in Wien vol. 38*, 1877.
Kronholm, *Ephrem* = Kronholm, T., *Motifs from Genesis 1-11 in the genuine Hymns of Ephrem the Syrian*, Uppsala

1978.
Kurylowicz, *Apophonie* = Kurylowicz, J., *L'Apophonie en sémitique,* Varsovie 1961.
Landberg, *Dathina* = Landberg, Comte Carlo de, *Dathina,* Leiden 1905-1913.
Landberg, *Études* = Landberg, Comte Carlo de, *Études sur les dialectes de l'Arabie de l'Arabie Méridionale,* vol. I: Ḥaḍramoût, vol. II Daṯīna, Leiden 1901-1913.
Lane = Lane, E. W., *Arabic-English Lexicon,* 8 in 2 vol, London 1863-1893. Reprint: 1984.
Larcher, *ʾAfʿala* = Larcher, P., Sur la valeur "expositive" de la forme *ʾafʿala* de l'arabe classique, in: *ZAL 31,* Wiesbaden 1996.
Lawkarī, *ḥaqq* = Lawkarī, Abū l-ʿAbbās Faḍl b. Muḥammad, *Bayān al-ḥaqq bi-ḍamān al-ṣidq: Manṭiq: I. Madḫal,* Ed. I. Dībāǧī, Tehran 1986.
Leemhuis, *Stems* = Leemhuis, F., *The D and H stems in Koranic Arabic. A comparative study of the function and meaning of the faʿʿala and ʾafʿala forms in Koranic usage,* Leiden 1977.
Leslau, *Soqotri* = Leslau, W., *Lexique Soqotri (Sudarabique Moderne) avec comparaisons et explications étymologiques,* Paris 1938.
Levi Della Vida = Levi Della Vida, Giorgio: *Elenco dei manoscritti arabi islamici della Biblioteca Vaticana,* Rome 1935-1965.
Løkkegaard, *ʾAšré hāʾīš* = Løkkegaard, F., *ʾAšré hāʾīš,* Ed. T. Kronholm and E. Riad, in: *OS 33-34, On the Dignity of Man, Oriental and Classical Studies in Honour of Frithiof Rundgren,* Stockholm 1984-1986.
Loucel, *Origine* = Loucel, H., *L'Origine du langage d'après les grammairiens arabes,* in: *Ar 11,* 1964.
Marçais, *Dialecte* = Marçais, W., *Le dialecte arabe des Ulâd Brahîm de Saïda,* Paris 1908.
Massignon, *Opera minora* = Massignon, L., *Opera minora,* Ed. Y. Moubarac, 1-3, Beirut 1963.
Massignon, *Réflexions* = Massignon, L., *Réflexions sur la structure primitive de l'analyse grammaticale en Arabe,* in: *Ar 1,* 1954.
Méhiri, *Théories* = Méhiri, ʿA., *Les Théories grammaticales d'Ibn Jinni,* Tunis 1973.
Merx, *Historia* = Merx, A., *Historia Artis Grammaticae apud Syros,* Leipzig 1889.
Merx, *Origine* = Merx, A., *L'Origine de la grammaire arabe,* in: *Bulletin de l'Institut Egyptien II,* 1891.
Mingana = *Catalogue of the Mingana Collection of Manuscripts* now in the possession of the trustees of the Woodbrooke Settlement, Selly Oak, Birmingham, 1-4, Cambridge 1933-1963.
Mokhlis, *Taṣrīf* = Mokhlis, H., *Théorie du Taṣrīf et traitement du lexique chez les grammairıens arabes,* Germany 1997.
Moscati, *Grammar* = Moscati, S., *An Introduction to the Comparative Grammar of the Semitic Languages,* Phonology and Morphology, 2nd printing, Wiesbaden 1969.
Nöldeke, *Beiträge* = Nöldeke, T., *Beiträge zur semitischen Sprachwissenschaft,* Strassburg 1904.
Nöldeke, *Geschichte* = Nöldeke, T., *Geschichte des Qorʾāns,* Göttingen 1860.
Nöldeke, *Grammatik* = Nöldeke, T., *Zur Grammatik des Classischen Arabisch im Anhang: Die Handschriftlichen ergänzungen in dem Handexemplar Theodor Nöldekes bearbeitet und mit zusätzen versehen von Anton Spitaler,* Darmstadt 1963.
Nöldeke, *Neue Beiträge* = Nöldeke, T., *Neue Beiträge zur semitischen Sprachwissenschaft,* Strassburg 1910.
Nöldeke, *Poesie* = Nöldeke, T., *Beiträge zur Kenntniss der Poesie der alten Araber,* Hannover 1864.
Omar, *Studies* = Omar, Ahmed Mokhtar, *Grammatical studies in early Muslim Egypt,* in: *SHAG II,* Ed. K. Versteegh and M. G. Carter, Amsterdam/ Philadelphia 1990.
Owens, *Foundations* = Owens, J., *The Foundations of Grammar, An Introduction to Medieval Arabic Grammatical Theory,* Amsterdam/ Philadelphia 1988.
Owens, *Theory* = Owens, J., *Early Arabic grammatical Theory, heterogeneity and standardization,* Amsterdam/ Philadelphia 1990.
Pellat, *Milieu* = Pellat, C., *Le Milieu baṣrien et la formation de Ǧāḥiẓ,* Paris 1953.
Penrice, *Dictionary* = Penrice, J., *A Dictionary and Glossary of the Koran,* London 1873. Reprint: 1971.
Peters, *Aristotle* = Peters, F. E., *Aristotle and the Arabs,* New York 1968.
Qurʾān = *The Holy Qurʾān,* Ed. A. Y. Ali, Maryland 1983.
Rabin = Rabin, C., *Ancient West-Arabian,* London 1951.
Raymundus, *Tasriphi* = Raymundus, J. Bapt., *Liber tasriphi: Taṣrīf al-ʿizzī* by Zanǧānī, ʿIzz al-Dīn Abū l-Faḍāʾil Ibrāhīm b. ʿAbd al-Wahhāb b. ʿImād al-Dīn b. Ibrāhīm, Rome 1610.
Reckendorf, *Syntax* = Reckendorf, H., *Arabische Syntax,* Heidelberg 1921.
Redslob, *Wörter* = Redslob, T., *Die arabischen Wörter mit entgegengesetzter Bedeutung,* Göttingen 1873.
Retsö, *Diathesis* = Retsö, J., *Diathesis in the Semitic languages, a comparative morphological study,* Leiden 1989.
Retsö, *Passive* = Retsö, J., *The Finite Passive Voice in Modern Arabic Dialects,* Göteborg 1983.
Retsö, *Sentences* = Retsö, J., *Subjectless sentences in Arabic dialects,* in: *OS 31-32,* 1982-1983.
Reuschel, *Ḫalīl* = Reuschel, W., *Al-Ḫalīl ibn Aḥmad, der Lehrer Sībawayhs, als Grammatiker,* Berlin 1959.
RIMA = *Revue de l'Institut des manuscrits arabes,* 1-26, Cairo 1375/1955-1401/1980.
Roman, *Étude* = Roman, A., *Étude de la phonologie et de la morphologie de la koinè arabe,* 2 vol., Publications de l'Université de Provence, Marseille 1983.
Roman, *Expression* = Roman, A., *Expression du je dans la langue arabe révélée,* in: *Bulletin d'Études Orientales*

de l'Institut français, vol. XXVII, Damas 1974.
Roman, *Identité* = Roman, A., *Les structures et les figures de l'expression en arabe de l'identité,* in: *Ar 40,* 1993.
Roman, *Origine* = Roman, A., *L'Origine et l'organisation de la langue arabe d'après le Ṣāḥibī d'Ibn Fāris,* in: *Ar 35,* 1988.
Rosenthal, *Aramaic* = Rosenthal, F., *A Grammar of Biblical Aramaic,* 4th ed., Wiesbaden 1974.
Rowton, *Permansive* = Rowton, M. B., *The Use of the Permansive in Classic Babylonian,* in: *JNES 21,* 1962.
Rundgren, *Bildungen* = Rundgren, *Über Bildungen mit š- und n-t- Demonstrativen im Semitischen,* Beiträge zur vergleichenden Grammatik der semitischen Sprachen, Uppsala 1955.
Rundgren, *Einfluß* = Rundgren, F., *Über den griechischen Einfluß auf die arabische Nationalgrammatik,* in: *Acta Societatis Linguisticae Uppsaliensis,* Nova Series 2:5, Uppsala 1976.
Rundgren, *Representation* = Rundgren, F., *Representation of Morphemic Categories in Arabic,* in: *OS 31-32,* 1982-1983.
Rŭžička, *Dissimilation* = Rŭžička, R., *Konsonantische Dissimilation,* Leipzig 1909.
Rŭžička, *Question* = Rŭžička, R., *La Question de l'existence du dans les langues sémitiques en géneral et dans la langue ugaritienne en particulier,* in: *Archiv Orientální 22,* 1954.
De Sacy = De Sacy, S., *Grammaire arabe,* 2 vol., Tunis 1904-1905.
De Sacy, *Anthologie* = De Sacy, S., *Anthologie grammaticale arabe,* Paris 1829.
Sanni, *Ibn Fāris* = Sanni, A., *A Fourth Century Contribution to Literary Theory: Ibn Fāris's Treatise on Poetic Licenses,* in: *JAL 24,* part I, 1993.
Sellheim, *Handschriften* = Sellheim, R., *Arabische Handschriften, Materialien zur Arabischen Literaturgeschichte,* Teil II, Stuttgart 1987.
Sezgin, *Geschichte* = Sezgin, F., *Geschichte des arabischen Schrifttums,* vol. VIII: *Lexikographie bis ca. 430 H.,* Leiden 1982, vol. IX: *Grammatik bis ca. 430 H.,* Leiden 1984.
De Slane = De Slane, *Catalogue des manuscrits arabes,* Bibliothèque Nationale, Paris 1883-1895.
Smyth, *Reviews of Books* = Smyth, W., *Reviews of Books:* Aḥmad b. ʿAlī b. Masʿūd on Arabic Morphology, *Marāḥ al-arwāḥ,* Part one: The strong Verb: Aṣ-ṣaḥīḥ, Ed. with Translation, Commentary and Introduction by J. Åkesson, Leiden 1990, in: *JAOS 112,* part 4, 1992.
von Soden, *Grundriß* = von Soden, W., *Grundriß der akkadischen Grammatik,* Roma 1952.
Steiner = Steiner, F., *Arabische Handschriften I,* Ed. E. Wagner, Wiesbaden 1976.
Ṭalas = Ṭalas, M. A., *al-Kaššāf ʿan maḫṭūṭāt ḫazā'in kutub al-awqāf,* Bagdad 1372/1953.
Talmon, *ʿAyn* = Talmon, R., *Arabic Grammar in its formative Age, Kitāb al-ʿAyn and its Attribution to Ḫalīl b. Aḥmad,* Leiden - New York - Køln 1997.
Talmon, *Who* = Talmon, R., *Who was the first Arab grammarian? A new approach to an old problem,* in: *ZAL/ J.A.L.,* Wiesbaden XV, 1985.
Taškent = Tashkent, *Sobranie vostočnych rukopisej Akademii Nauk Uzbekskoj SSR,* Ed. A. A. Semenov, 1-10, Taškent 1952-1975.
Testen, *Suffixes* = Testen, D., *On the Development of the Energic Suffixes,* in: *PAL V,* Ed. M. Eid and C. Holes, Amsterdam/ Philadelphia 1993.
Topkapı = Karatay, Fehmi Edhem, *Topkapı Sarayı Müzesi Kütüphanesi Arapça Yazmalar Kataloğu,* C. 1-4, Istanbul 1962-69.
Troupeau, *Commentaire* = Troupeau, G., *Le Commentaire d'al-Sīrāfī sur le chapitre du Kitāb de Sībawayhī,* in: *Ar 5,* 1958.
Troupeau, *Grammaire* = Troupeau, G., *La Grammaire à Baġdād du IXe au XIIIe siècle,* in: *Ar 9,* 1962.
Troupeau, *Grammairiens* = Troupeau, G., *À propos des grammairiens cités par Sībawayhi dans le Kitāb,* in: *Ar 8,* 1961.
Troupeau, *Lexique* = Troupeau, G., *Lexique-index du Kitāb de Sībawaihi,* Paris 1976.
Troupeau, *Logique* = Troupeau, G., *La Logique d'Ibn al-Muqaffaʿ et les origines de la grammaire arabe,* in: *Ar 28, fasc. 2-3,* 1981.
Troupeau, *Origine* = Troupeau, G., *L'Origine de la grammaire arabe à la lumière du Kitāb de Sībawaihi,* in: *Journal of the Jordan Academy of Arabic I,* 1978.
Ullendorff, *Article* = Ullendorff, E., *The definite article,* in: *Arabic and Islamic Studies in Honor of Hamilton A. R. Gibb,* Ed. G. Makdisi, Leiden 1965.
Ungnad, *Bezeichnung* = Ungnad, A., *Die Bezeichnung der Verbalstämme im Semitischen,* in: *OL 9,* 1906, coll. 45-47.
Ungnad-Matouš, *Des Akkadischen* = Ungnad, A., - Matouš, L., *Grammatik des Akkadischen,* München 1979.
Vernier = Vernier, D., *Grammaire arabe,* 2 vol., Beyrouth 1891.
Versteegh, *Education* = Versteegh, C. H. M., *Hellenistic Education and the Origin of Arabic Grammar,* Koerner 1980.
Versteegh, *Elements* = Versteegh, C. H. M., *Greek Elements in Arabic Linguistic Thinking,* Leiden 1977.
Versteegh, *Grammar* = Versteegh, C. H. M., *Arabic Grammar and Qur'ānic Exegesis in Early Islam,* Leiden 1993.
Versteegh, *Langage* = Versteegh, C. H. M., *The Arabic language,* Edinburgh 1996.

Versteegh, *Qiyās* = Versteegh, C. H. M., *The Origin of the Term "Qiyās" in Arabic Grammar,* in: *JLA 4,* 1980.

Versteegh, *Zağğāğī* = Versteegh, K., *The explanation of linguistic causes. Az-Zağğāğī's theory of grammar.* Introduction, translation, commentary, Amsterdam 1995.

Versteegh, *Zayd Ibn ʿAlī's commentary* = Versteegh, K., *Zayd Ibn ʿAlī's commentary on the Qurʾān.* See Suleiman, *Grammar.*

Volck/Kellgren, *Ibn Mālik, Lāmīya* = Volck, W., *Ibn Mâlik's Lâmîyat al afʿâl mit Badraddîn's Commentar von Kellgren,* Mémoires de l'académie impériale des sciences de St.-Petersbourg, tome VII, No 6, St. Petersburg 1864.

Vollers, *Review of Nöldeke* = Vollers, K., *Review of Nöldeke, Zur Grammatik,* in: *ZA 12,* 1897.

Vollers, *System* = Vollers, K., *The System of Arabic Sounds as based upon Sibaweih and Ibn Yaʿīsh,* in: *Transactions of the 9th International Congress of Orientalists 1,* London 1893.

Vollers, *Volkssprache* = Vollers, K., *Volkssprache und Schriftsprache im alten Arabien,* Strassburg 1906.

Wagner, *Dualis* = Wagner, E., *Die erste Person Dualis im Semitischen,* in: *ZDMG 102,* 1952.

Wallin, *Laute* = Wallin, G. A., *Über die Laute des Arabischen und ihre Bezeichnung,* in: *ZDMG 9,* 1855; *12,* 1858.

Walzer, *Translations* = Walzer, R., *New Light on the Arabic Translations of Aristotle,* in: *Oriens 6,* 1953.

Watson, *Kaškaša* = Watson, J. C. E., *Kaškaša with Reference to Modern Yemeni Dialects,* in: *ZAL 24,* 1992.

Wehr, *Elativ* = Werhr, H., *Der arabische Elativ,* Akademie der Wiss. u. d. Lit., Abhandl. der geistes- und sozialwissenschaftlichen Klasse, Mainz 1952, No. 7, Wiesbaden 1953.

Weiss, *Nationalgrammatik* = Weiss, J., *Die arabische Nationalgrammatik und die Lateiner,* in: *ZDMG 64,* 1910.

Weiss, *Speech* = Weiss, B. G., *A Theory of the Parts of Speech in Arabic,* in: *Ar 23, fasc. 1,* 1976.

Weiss, *Subject* = Weiss, B. G., *Subject and Predicate in the Thinking of Arabic Philologists,* in: *JAOS 105, fasc. 4,* 1985.

Weiss, *Waḍʿ* = Weiss, B. G., *ʿIlm al-waḍʿ: An Introductory Account of a later Muslim philological science,* in: *Ar 34,* fasc. 3, 1987.

Wensinck, *Concordance* = Wensinck, *Concordance et indices de la tradition musulmane,* organisés et commencés par A. J. Wensinck et J. P. Mensing, Leiden 1933 ff. Vol. VIII: *Indices* par W. Raven et J. J. Witkam, Brill 1988.

Wild, *ʿAyn* = Wild, S., *Das Kitāb al-ʿAin und die arabische Lexicographie,* Wiesbaden 1965.

Wright = Wright, W., *A Grammar of the Arabic Language,* Cambridge, Third Edition 1985.

Wright, *Comparative Grammar* = Wright, W., *Lectures on the Comparative Grammar of the Semitic Languages,* Cambridge 1890.

Yale = Nemoy, L., *Arabic Manuscripts in the Yale University Library New Haven,* Conn. 1956.

IV. ABBREVIATIONS

§ 1. Abbreviations of terms

A.D.	anno Domini
A.H.	anno Hegirae
e.g.	(Lat. *exempli grata)* for example
fem.	feminine
fol.	folio
i.e.	(Lat. *id est*) that is
l(l)	line(s)
masc.	masculine
MS(s)	manuscript(s)
p(p).	page(s)
pl.	plural

§ 2. Abbreviations of titles

AO	*Acta Orientalia*
Ar	*Arabica*
AUU	*Acta Universitatis Upsaliensis*
BEA	*Bulletin des Études Arabes*
BO	*Bibliotheca Orientalis*
BSLP	*Bulletin de la Société de Linguistique de Paris*
JAL	*Journal of Arabic Literature*
JAOS	*Journal of the American Oriental Society*
JLA	*Journal de linguistique arabe*
JNES	*Journal of Near Eastern Studies*
JQR	*Jewish Quarterly Review*
JRAS	*Journal of the Royal Asiatic Society*
JSS	*Journal of Semitic Studies*
OL	*Orientalistische Literaturzeitung*
Orientalia	*Orientalia. Commentarii Periodici Pontificii Instituti Biblici.* Rome
PAL I	*Perspectives on Arabic Linguistics I, Papers from the first Annual Symposium on Arabic Linguistics*
PAL V	*Perspectives on Arabic Linguistics V, Papers from the Fifth Annual Symposium on Arabic Linguistics*
PICSS	*Proceedings of the International Conference of Semitic Studies held in Jerusalem,* 19-23 July 1965
REI	*Revue des Études Islamiques*
SHAG II	*Studies in the History of Arabic Grammar II, Proceedings of the 2nd Symposium on the History of Arabic Grammar,* Nijmegen, 27 April-1 May 1987
SHL	*Studies in the History of Linguistics*
SI	*tudia Islamica*
SO	*Studia Orientalia*
WZKM	*Wiener Zeitschrift für die Kunde des Morgenlandes*
ZA	*Zeitschrift für Assyriologie*
ZAL	*Zeitschrift für arabische Linguistik*
ZDMG	*Zeitschrift der Deutschen Morgenländischen Gesellschaft*

V. INDICES

§ 1. Index of Qur'anic quotations in the *Marāḥ*

The references are to the fols. of the Paris MS A indicated under each page of the Arabic Edition.

33b-34b (1: 7)
32a-32b (2: 237)
36b-37a (2: 237)
15a-16a (7: 54)
22a-23a (9: 12)
30b-31b (9: 109)
30b-31b (10: 22)

§ 2. Index of verse quotations in the *Marāḥ*

لاَهُمَ إنْ كُنْتَ قَبِلْتَ حَجَتِجْ 34b-35a

هَوِيتُ السِمانَ فَشَيَبْنَنَني 11b-12a

هَيَجْتِ شُوقَ ٱلْمُشْتَاقِ 33b-34b

وأخْلَفوكَ عِدَ الأمْرِ الذي وَعَدوا 25b-26a

وكَفَّكِ ٱلْمُخَضَّبِ ٱلْبَنَامِ 35a-35b

أُبَابُ بَحْرٍ ضَاحِكٍ زَهُوق 33b-34b

أخوكَ أخُو مُكاشَرَةٍ وضِحْكٍ 5a-5b

عَمْرَو بْنَ مَسْعُودٍ شِرَارَ ٱلنَاتِ 34b-35a

فَمِثْلِكِ حُبْلى قد طَرَقْتُ ومُرْضِعٍ 13a-13b

لا هَنَاكِ المَرْتَعُ 21a-22a

§ 3. Index of names in the *Marāḥ*

الأخفش 7b-8b، 30b-31b

الأصمعي 14a-15a

البصريَون 2a-3a، 13a-13b

إبن جنَي 26b-27b

أهل الحجاز 22a-23a

الخليل 22a-23a، 26b-27b

(الزمخشري) جار الله العلاَمة 17b-18a

سيبويه 3a-4a، 17a-17b، 25b-26، 30b-31b، 33b-34b

طيَ 3a-4a

بنو عامر 25b-26

الفرَاء 14a-15a، 25b-26

الكوفيُون 2a-3a، 12a-13a، 22a-23a

يونس 13a-13b

§ 4. Index of examples in the *Marāḥ*

This index includes most of the significant Arabic examples used in the *Marāḥ*. The references are to the fols. indicated under each page of the Arabic Edition.

- الهمزة -

أبٌ 24b-25b

آانْت 22a-23a

آنَ 24b-25b

إبْلٌ 24b-25b

أبُويُوب 21a-22a

أبَى 24b-25b ، أبَى يَأبَى 3a-4a

أُوثَر 22a-23a

أُخْتٌ 33b-34b

أخَذَ 21a-22a ، أخَذَ يأخُذُ 24a-24b

اتَّخَذَ 18a-19a ، 20a-21a ، 33b-34b

اسْتَخَذَ 33b-34b

أدَبَ يأدبُ 24a-24b

آدَمُ 14a-15a ، 22a-23a

أرِجَ يأرُجُ 24a-24b

أُسْدٌ 30b-31b

أسَلَ يأسُلُ 24a-24b

أُصَيْلَالٌ 35a-35b

أكَلَ ايتَكَلَ 20a-21a

كُلْ 22a-23a

أكَلْتُ عنَباً 34b-35a

الألوكَةُ ، مَلَكٌ ، مَلأكٌ 21a-22a

إلَهٌ 22a-23a ، لاهٌ ، الله ، اللاهُ 23a-24a

أمَ 24b-25b

أيمَة ، أئمَة ، آمَة 22a-23a

أنا 5b-7a ، أنَهْ 34b-35a

أنتا 5a-5b ، أنْتُما 5a-5b ، 7a-7b

أُناس 22a-23a ، نات 34b-35a

ناس 22a-23a ، أنَاسيَ 34b-35a

أنَ يئِنُ 24b-25b

أهَبَ يأهَبُ 24a-24b

أوْلاهُم 15a-16a

إيَانا 7b-8b

إيَاهُ 7b-8b

- الباء -

بيرٌ 21a-22a

تَبَخْتَرُ 10b-11a

يَبدَلُ 20a-21a

يا بَاديَةُ ، يا باداةُ 7b-8b

بُرْءٌ 24b-25b

يَبسَمُ 20a-21a

بُشْرَى 3a-4a

تَتَبَاعَدُ 10b-11a

ابْتغيَ مَرَهُ 21a-22a

بَقِي يبْقَى 3a-4a

يَبْطَرَ 4a-4b

بَاعَ 35a-35b ، بَيَعَ ، بَاعَ يَبيعُ 26b-27b

يَبْيَعُ 28a-29a ، بيعَ 31b-32a

بُيعَ ، بُوعَ 28a-29a

بائعٌ 33b-34b

مَبيعٌ ، مَبْيُوعٌ 30b-31b

تبْيَانٌ 28a-29a

- التاء -

اتَجرَ 18a-19a

- الثاء -

اثَأرَ ، اتَأرَ 18a-19a

تَثاقَلَ ، اثَاقَلَ 21a

الثالث ، الثالي 34b-35a

ثِنْتَان 33b-34b ، ثِنْيَان 34b-35a

- الجيم -

جَبَانٌ 14a-15a

جَبَذَ ، جَذَبَ 2a-3a

جُدَدٌ ، جُدٌّ 17b-18a

جَدْوَلٌ 28a-29a

مِجْذَمٌ ، مِجْذَامَةٌ 15a-16a

المَجْزَرُ 16b-17a

تَجَلْبَبَ 4a-4b

اجْلَوَّذَ 4a-4b

اجْدَمَعُوا 34b-35a

جُنُبٌ 14a-15a

جَنَاح 1b-2a

جَهْوَرَ 4a-4b

جَوَبَة 21a-22a

اجْتَوَرَ ، تَجَاوَرَ 27b-28a

جَوْرَبٌ 16b-17a

تَجَوْرَبَ 4a-4b

جُوَنٌ 21a-22a

جَاءَ 24b-25b

جَيَلٌ 21a-22a

- الحاء -

حَبَّ ، يَحُبُّ ، حَبِيبٌ 17b-18a

حُبُكٌ 26a-26b

حُبْلِيَات 5a-5b

الْحَشَيْشِي 3a-4a

احْرَنْجَمَ 4a-4b

حِرْمَانٌ 3a-4a

حَسِبَ يَحْسِبُ 3a-4a

حَسَنٌ 14a-15a

احْتَقَرَ 4a-4b

حَلُوبَةٌ 15a-16a

مَحْمَدَة 3a-4a

الأحمَرُ ، لَحْمَرُ ، الَحْمَر 21a-22a

احْمَرَّ ، احْمَرَرَ 4a-4b

احْمَارَّ ، احْمَارَرَ 4a-4b

حَمِقَ ، حَمُقَ ، أَحْمَقُ 14a-15a

أَحْمَقُ من هَبَنَّقَة 15a-16a

تَحَمَّلَ ، تَحَمَّالٌ 3a-4a

اسْتَحْوَذَ 29a-30a

حَوْقَلَ 4a-4b

الحَوَكَةُ 27b-28a

أَحْوَلُ 14a-15a

حَيَهَلَهْ 34b-35a

حَيِيَ ، حَايَ ، يَحَايُ 27b-28a

حَيِيَ ، حَيُوا 17b-18a ، حَيِيَ 20a-21a

يَحَيُّ ، يَحيَى 17b-18a

الْحَيَوَانُ 27b-28a

- الخاء -

خَبْءٌ 24b-25b

اسْتَخْرَجَ 4a-4b ، مُسْتَخْرَج 16a-16b

خَرِقَ 14a-15a ، أَخْرَقُ 14a-15a

أدْؤر 33b-34b ، أدْوُرٌ 28a-29a
دمْتَ تَدُومُ 3a-4a
الدَيْمُومَةُ 26b-27b
دولٌ 28a-29a
ادَانَ 19a-20a
اسْتَدانَ 21a
دينَارٌ 34b-35a

- الذال -

ذئبٌ 24b-25b ، ذيبٌ 34b-35a
ذَبيحَةٌ 15a-16a
الذَعَالتُ 34b-35a
اذكَرَ، ادكَرَ، اذْدكَرَ 19a-20a
ذكْرَى 3a-4a
ذَهَابٌ 3a-4a
المَذْهَبُ 16b-17a

- الراء -

رَاس 35a-35b ، 21a-22a ، رَأس 24b-25b
رَأى 23a-24a ، 24b-25b ، يَرَى 23a-24a
رَأى ، يَرأى 24b-25b
رُئيَ يُرَى 24a-24b
يَرَى ، يَرْأى 23a-24a ، رَ 24a-24b
مرأى ، مَرْأى 24a-24b
مَرْئيَ ، مَرْؤي 24a-24b
مُرَى ، مُرْأى ، أرى ، يُرى 24a-24b
رُبَ 12a-13a
رَاتماً 35a-35b
مَرْجعٌ 3a-4a
رَحْمَةٌ 3a-4a ، الرَحمنُ 17b-18a
رَدَّ ، يَرُدُّ 17b-18a

خَشِنٌ 14a-15a
اخْشَينَ 24a-24b
لَنْ يَخْشَى 32b-33b
اخَصَمَ 20a-21a ، يَخَصَمُ 20a-21a ، 21a
خصَامٌ ، اخصَامٌ ، مُخَصَمونٌ ، مُخُصَمونَ 21a
خَطيَةٌ 22a-23a ، خَطيئَةٌ 33b-34b
خَنقٌ 3a-4a
خَافَ يَخَافُ ، خَوفَ 26b-27b
يَخَافُ 28a-29a ، 30a-30b ،يُخَافُ 31b-32a
يَخْوفُ ، الخَوْفُ 28a-29a
الْخَونَةُ 27b-28a
اخْتيرَ 31b-32a
مخْيَطٌ ، مخْيَاطٌ 5a-5b ، 29a-30a

- الدال -

دُئلٌ 13b-14a ، 26a-26b
دَحْرجَ ، تَدَحْرَجَ 4a-4b
مَدْخَلٌ ، دُخُولٌ 3a-4a
درَايَةٌ 3a-4a
دَعَوُا الْقَوْمَ 27b-28a
لم يَدْعُو ، لم يَدْعُوا 4b-5a
لَنْ يَدْعُوَ 28a-29a
دَعْوَى 3a-4a
دَاعوَةٌ ، دَاعيَةٌ 28a-29a
دفْءٌ 24b-25b
مُدُقَ 17a-17b
الدلَيلَي 3a-4a
دَلْوٌ ، أدلٌ ، أدْلُوٌ 5b-7a
مُدْهُنٌ 17a-17b
دَارٌ ، ديَارٌ ، دَورٌ 27b-28a

رَضُوا 4b-5a ، 28a-29a ، 32a-32b

أرْعَنُ 14a-15a

ارْعَوى 4a-4b

المَرْفِقُ 16b-17a

مَرْكَبٌ ، مَرْكُوبٌ 2a-3a

رَكَنَ يَرْكَنُ 13a-4a

رَمَى 32a-32b ، رُمِيَ يُرْمَى 33b-34b

رَمَوا 4b-5a ، 32a-32b ، رَمَتْ رَمَيَتْ 32a-32b

رَمَتَا ، رَمَاتَا 5a-5b

الْمَرْمَى 16b-17a ، مَرْمَى 33b-34b

الرَّمْيُ 28a-29a ، مَرْمَى 33b-34b

رامٍ راميٌ 32b-33b

مَرْمِيٌّ ، مَرْمُوِيَ ، مَرْمِيِيَ 32b-33b

رامِيَ 32b-33b

تَرْمِيينَ 28a-29a ، تَرْمِينَ 23a-24a ، 32a-32b

تَرَهْوَكَ 4a-4b

راحَ ، مراح 1b-2a

رَاوِيَةٌ 15a-16a

رَوِيَ 35b-36b

الرِّيَ 36b-37a

- الزاء -

يَزْدُلُ 35a-35b

زَلْزَلَ زِلْزَالٌ 3a-4a

زَهادةٌ 3a-4a

ازَانَ 19a-20a

- السين -

سألَ 21a-22a ، 24b-25b

يَسأل ، يَسَلُ 23a-24a

سايِلٌ 22a-23a

سُؤالٌ 3a-4a

مَسألَةٌ ، مَسَلَةٌ 21a-22a

سَئِمَ 24b-25b

سَبَأ يَسْبَأُ 24b-25b

ستَ ، سِدْسٌ 19a-20a ، 34b-35a

المسْجِدُ 16b-17a

السَّادِي 34b-35a

سَرَ يَسُرُّ ، سُرُرٌ ، سُرَ 17b-18a

سَرِقَةٌ 3a-4a

مُسْعُطٌ 17a-17b

مَسْعاةٌ 3a-4a

المَسْقِطُ 16b-17a

مِسْقامٌ 15a-16a

سَكْرَى 33b-34b

المَسْكِنُ 16b-17a

مِسْكِينَةٌ 15a-16a

اسْلَنْقى 4a-4b

مُسْلِماتٌ 5a-5b

سَمِرَ ، أسْمَرُ 14a-15a

اسْمَعَ 19a-20a

أسْنَيُوا ، أسْنَتُوا 34b-35a

أسْهِب ، مُسْهَبٌ 16a

السَّيْدُودَةَ 27b-28a

سِيَاطٌ 27b-28a ، 36b-37a

- الشين -

اشْبَهَ 19a-20a

شُجاعٌ 14a-15a

مَشْرَبٌ ، مَشْرُوبٌ 2a-3a

المَشْرِقُ 16b-17a

يُضْرَبُ 16a-16b ، تَضْرِبينَ 7b-8b ، 11a-11b

ضَرَبْتُموهُ ، ضَرَبْتُنَ 5b-7a ، يَضْرِبْنَ 11a-11b

لِيَضْرِبْ ، وَلْيَضْرِبْ ، فَلْيَضْرِبْ 11b-12a

ضَارِبٌ 4b-5a ، 8b-9b ، ضَارِبَةٌ 16a

تَضَارَبَ 4a-4b

مَضْروبٌ 16a-16b

ضارِبُويَ 7b-8b

اِضْرِبْ 20a-21a-19a-20a اِضْطَرَبَ 20a-21a

ضَوارِبُ 35a-35b

ضَفادي 34b-35a

- الطاء -

طَرُؤَ 24b-25b

اسْتَطْعَمَ 21a

طَلَبٌ 3a-4a ، اطَّلَبَ 20a-21a

طَلْحَهْ 34b-35a

المَطْلِعُ 16b-17a

طَلَلٌ 17b-18a

طَلٌّ 17b-18a

تَطهَّرَ ، اِطَّهَرَ 21a

طَوُلَ 26b-27b ، طَويلٌ 29a-30a

طُوَالٌ 15a-16a

طَوَى 35b-36b ، 36b-37a

أطاعَ 21a

أسْطاعَ يُسْطيع 21a

- الظاء -

ظَلْتَ 18a-19a ، 21a

اظْطَلَمَ ، اِظَّلَمَ ، اِطَّلَمَ 20a-21a

- العين -

عَجفَ ، أعْجَفُ 14a-15a

شُغْلٌ 3a-4a

أشْغَلُ من ذات النَحيَيْنِ 15a-16a

شَكْسٌ 14a-15a

شَمْلَلَ 4a-4b

تَشَيْطَنَ 4a-4b

شَائك ، شَاك 30b-31b

- الصاد -

اصْبِرَ 20a-21a

اصَبَّرَ اصْطَبَرَ 19a-20a ، اصْطَبَرَ 35a-35b

صَبورٌ 15a-16a ، صَبَّارٌ 15a-16a

أصْبَغَ 35a-35b

صَحْراء ، صَحَارَى 33b-34b

صَدِئَ يَصْدَأُ 24b-25b

صَديقَةٌ 15a-16a

انْصَرَفَ 4a-4b

صِغَرٌ 3a-4a

صَكَكٌ ، صَكٌّ 17b-18a

صُلْبٌ 14a-15a

صَنْعَانِيٌّ 34b-35a

صُهُوبَةٌ 3a-4a

صَوَرَى 27b-28a

الْصَيَدُ 27b-28a

الصَيْرُورَة 26b-27b

- الضاد -

الْطَجَعَ 35a-35b

ضُحَكَةٌ ، ضُحْكَةٌ 15a-16a

ضَرَبَ 3a-4a ، 4b-5a ضَرَبَ يَضْرِبُ 3a-4a

ضَرَبْتُ أنا وزَيْدٌ 5a-5b ، اضْرِبانْ 13a-13b

ضَرَبْتُ 5b-7a ، ضَرَبْتُ ضَرَبْتُ 2a-3a

أغْيَلَتِ المَرْأةُ 29a-30a

- الظاء -

أُفَيِسٌ 22a-23a

فَتِيء 24b-25b

فَتَحَ يَفْتَحُ 3a-4a

مِفْتاحٌ 17a-17b ، مُفَيْتِيحٌ 34b-35a

فَحَصْطُ 35a-35b

فَرَّ يَفِرُّ 17b-18a

فِرُّ 18a-19a

فِرَقٌ 14a-15a

فَرُوقَةٌ 15a-16a

المَفْرِقُ 16b-17a

فُزْدُ 34b-35a ، فَزْدِي أنَهْ 35a-35b

فِسْقٌ 3a-4a ، فِسِّيقٌ 15a-16a

فَضَلَ يَفْضُلُ 3a-4a

تَفَضَّلَ 4a-4b

فَقِيرَةٌ 15a-16a ، المفتقر 1b-2a

الفُلْكُ 30b-31b

فَمٌ 35a-35b

فَنَى يَفْنَى 3a-4a

فيه 7b-8b

- القاف -

قَبولٌ 3a-4a

قاتَلَ ، قِتالٌ ، قِيتالٌ 3a-4a

قَتْلٌ ، قَتَلَ يَقْتُلُ 3a-4a

قَتيلٌ 15a-16a

مَقْتَلُ الحُسَيْن 16b-17a

يَقَتِّلُ 20a-21a

قَرَأَ 21a-22a ، 24b-25b

الأعْجَمُ 14a-15a

فَخْذٌ 11b-12a

عَدُوَة 15a-16

يَعْذَرُ 20a-21a

عِصِيَ ، عَصُوو 30b-31b

عَضَ يَعَضُ 17b-18a

مِعْطِيرٌ 15a-16a

عَطْشانٌ 14a-15a ، عَطْشَيَيْنِ 36b-37a

أعْطاهُم 15a-16a

العَظايَةُ 5b-7a

يَعْفُونَ 32a-32b

عُلَبِطٌ ، عُلابِطٌ 5a-5b

أبُو عَلِجَ 34b-35a

عَلِمَ يَعْلَمُ 3a-4a ، يِعْلَمُ 10b-11a

عَلاَمَةٌ 15a-16a

عُمَرُ ، عَمْرٌو 12a-13a

عَنْبَرٌ ، عَمْبَرٌ 5b-7a ، عَمْبَرٌ 35a-35b

عَوِرَ ، اعْوَرَ 27b-28a

أعْيُنٌ 28a-29a

- الغين -

المَغْرِبُ 16b-17a

غَزا يَغْزُو 33b-34b

أغْزَيْتُ 33b-34b ، أغْزَوْتُ أغْزَيْتُ 26b-27b

أُغْزُوا القَوْمَ 36b-37a

غُفْرانُ 3a-4a

غَلَبَةٌ 3a-4a

يا غُلامي ، يا غُلاما 7b-8b

غُيَبَةٌ 28a-29a

الغَيْبُوبَةُ 26b-27b

قَوَمَ 28a-29a ، 29a-30a
تَقْويمٌ 28a-29a ، التَقْويمُ 29a-30a
قاوَمَ قواماً 2a-3a
اقامَةٌ 26a-26b ، الإقامَةُ 29a-30a
استقامَةٌ 26a-26b
انْقيدَ لَهُ 31b-32a

- الكاف -

كُبَّارٌ 15a-16a
كُدْرَةٌ 3a-4a
كَرُمَ يَكْرُمُ 3a-4a
أكْرَمَ 4a-4b ، أكْرِمْ ، تُؤكْرِمُ أأكْرِمُ ، 12a-13a
أُكْرِمَ 13b-14a ، مُكْرِمٌ 16a
كِساءٌ 30a-30b ، 33b-34b
كِساوٌ 30a-30b
كَلَمَ ، كَلامٌ 3a-4a
كُدْتَ تَكادُ 3a-4a
كَيْنُونَةٌ ، كُونُونَةٌ ، كَيَنُونَةٌ 26b-27b

- اللام -

لِ 11b-12a
لَؤمَ 21a-22a ، لَؤُمَ يَلْؤُمُ 24b-25b
لُؤمٌ 21a-22a ، 24b-25b
لُومٌ 35a-35b
لَبَّ يلُبُّ ، لَبيبٌ 17b-18a
لِصْتٌ 34b-35a
يَلَطَمُ 20a-21a
التَلْعابُ 3a-4a
لَعَنَ 34b-35a
لَقيطَةٌ 15a-16a
لَمْ 11a-11b

مَقْرُوَةٌ 22a-23a
قُرْبٌ 30b-31b
قَرْدَدٌ 17b-18a
القَرارُ 18a-19a
أقَرَ ، أقرَ 18a-19a
مِقْراضٌ 17a-17b
القِسيَ ، قُسِيَ 30b-31b
اقْشَعَرَ 4a-4b
تَقَضّى البازي 17b-18a ، 18a-19a
قَطَعَ 4a-4b
قَطَعَ اللهُ أدَيْه 33b-34b
اقْعَنْسَسَ 4a-4b
تَتَقَلَّدُ 10b-11a
قَلْسى ، قَلْنَسَ 4a-4b
قَلى يَقْلى 3a-4a
قِنْوَةٌ ، قِنْيَةٌ 12a-13a ، 26a-26b
القَوَدُ 27b-28a
قالَ 26b-27b ، 27b-28a ، 29a-30a ، 35a-35b
قَوَلَ 27b-28a ، 29a-30a ، قَوْلٌ قالٌ 26b-27b
قايِلٌ 22a-23a ، قائِلٌ 30a-30b ، 33b-34b
القَوْلُ 32a-32b ، مَقُولٌ ، مَقْوَلٌ 30b-31b
قُولا 32a-32b ، قيلَ 31b-32a
مِقْوَالٌ 28a-29a
مَا أقْوَلَهُ 29a-30a
قُلِ الْحَقَ 30a-30b
القَيْلُولَةُ 26b-27b
قامَ قياماً 2a-3a
قِيَامٌ 27b-28a
قُمْتُ قائماً 3a-4a

نَعَقَ 2a-3a

النَهْقُ 2a-3a

أَيْنُقٌ أَوْنُقٌ أُنُوقٌ 30b-31b

نُوَمَةٌ 28a-29a

- الهاء -

هُدَبِدٌ ، هُدابِدٌ 5a-5b

هُدًى 3a-4a

مَهْدِيَ 7b-8b ، 24a-24b

مَهْدَوِيَ 7b-8b

التَهْذارُ 3a-4a

هَرَقْتُ 34b-35a

أَهْراقَ 21a ، يُهَرِيقُ 10b-11a

هذي أَمَةُ اللهِ 7b-8b ، 34b-35a

هُما 4b-5a ، 5b-7a

هُمُوا 4b-5a

هَنأ يَهْنِئُ 24b-25b

هُنَ 7b-8b

هُوَ 5b-7a ، 7a-7b ، هُوا ، هُوُوا 7a-7b

هُوَ ، هيَ 7b-8b ، وَهْو ، فَهْوَ 11b-12a

هَويتُ السمان 11b-12a

هاعٌ ، هائعٌ 30a-30b ، الهَيْعُوعَةُ 27b-28a

- الواو -

وَأَدَ 24b-25b

وَأى 24b-25b

وَجَأَ 24b-25b

وَجَدَ يَجُدُ 25b-26a

وَجيفٌ 3a-4a

يَوْجَلُ وَجَلاً 2a-3a

المَوْجِلُ 16b-17a

لاَعٌ ، لائعٌ 30a-30b

لَيْسَ مِنْ أمْبِرَ آمْصِيَامُ فِي آمْسَفَر 35a-35b

لَيَانٌ 3a-4a

- الميم -

مَاءٌ ، مَاهٌ ، مِياهٌ 33b-34b

مَا زِلْتُ رَاتِماً 35a-35b

تُمْدَحُ 11a-11b

مَدَدَ ، مَدَدٌ ، مدَ 17b-18a ، مادَ 18a-19a

مدَ ، مَمَدَ 18a-19a

مَمْدود 18a-19a

مَرَرْتُ 4b-5a

مِلْحٌ 14a-15a

مَنوعٌ 15a-16a

مَيَتٌ ، مَيْتٌ ، مَيُوتٌ 26b-27b

المُوْتَانُ 27b-28a

مِيَرٌ 21a-22a

- النون -

المَنْبِتُ 16b-17a

نَحْنُ 5b-7a

وَجيفٌ 3a-4a

مُنْخُلٌ 17a-17b

يَنَزِعُ 20a-21a

نَزَوانٌ 3a-4a

نَسَابَةٌ 15a-16a

المَنْسِكُ 16b-17a

نَصيرٌ 15a-16a

يسْتَنْصِرُ 10b-11a

يَنضِلُ 20a-21a

يَنظِرُ 20a-21a

وَقَرَ وُقِرَ 25b-26a
وَقَرَ يَقَرُّ وَقاراً 18a-19a
وَقَى يَقِي 35b-36b
التُكْلانُ 25b-26a
أوْلاهُم 15a-16a
وَوَوْجَلُ 9b-10b

- الياء -

يا 7b-8b
يَئِسَ يَيْأَسُ 24b-25b
أدَيْه 33b-34b
يَسَرَ يُسِرَ 25b-26a
ايْسِرْ 22a-23a ، يُوسِرُ ، يُيْسِرُ 26b-27b
اتَسَرَ 20a-21a ، مُيْسِرٌ ، مُوسِرٌ 28a-29a
يافِعٌ ، أيْفَعَ 16a
مُوقِنٌ 35a-35b
يَمَنَ يُمِنَ 25b-26a
يَمِينٌ ، أيْمُنٌ 12a-13a
يَنَعَ يُنِعَ 25b-26a
أُجُوهٌ 33b-34b
وَاحِدٌ ، حَادٍ 30b-31b
أحَدْ أحَدْ 33b-34b
وُخَمَةٌ ، تُخَمَةٌ 33b-34b
وَرَنْتَل 9b-10b
مِوْزَانٌ 28a-29a ، مِيزَانٌ 26b-27b ، 30b-31b
اشَاحٌ 33b-34b
أواصِلُ 33b-34b
ايتَصَلَتْ 34b-35a
يَضَعُ يَوْضِعُ 26a-26b
وَعَدَ وُعِدَ 25b-26
وَعَدَ يَعِدُ 35b-36b
عِدَةٌ 25b-26a
وَعَدَتَ 26a-26b
اتَعَدَ ، ايتَعَدَ ، يَوْتَعِدُ 20a-21a
الْمَوْعِدُ 16b-17a ، مَوْعِدٌ 26a-26b
وُعِلٌ 13b-14a
مِيقَاتٌ 34b-35a

§ 5. Index of Qur'anic quotations in the Introduction and Commentary

Sur.	v.	par. or p.
1:	2-3	(173 b)
1:	5	(343)
1:	7	(93 c)
2:	4	(327 c)
2:	6	(233), (368)
2:	19	(173 b), (263)
2:	25	(21)
2:	31	(12 b)
2:	34	(6)
2:	35	(53)
2:	43	(105 b)
2:	71	(224)
2:	72	(207)
2	91	(93 c)
2:	93	(105 b)
2:	94	(105 b)
2:	102	(93 c)
2:	116	(202)
2:	128	(307)
2:	133	(173 b)
2:	143	(44 b)
2:	157	(38)
2:	164	(296)
2:	170	(173 b)
2:	213	(173 b)
2:	233	(51 b)
2:	235	(173 b)
2:	237	(305)
2:	248	(348 b)
2:	255	(173 b)
2:	269	(190), (207)
2:	280	(248)
2:	282	(142)
2:	284	(173 b)
3:	14	(173 b)
3:	61	(105 b)
3:	85	(173 b)
3:	110	(44 b)
3:	120	(184)
3:	129	(173 b)
3:	142	(51 f)
3:	147	(173 b)
3:	151	(173 b)
3:	156	(44 b)
3:	185	(173 b)
4:	1	(53 b)
4	5	(266 b)
4:	60	(296 c)
4	71	(105 b), (224)
4:	81	(173)
4	92	(296 b)
4:	101	(152 b)
4	125	(202)
4:	156	(173 b)
5:	3	(22 c), (105 b)
5:	7	(296 b)
5:	9	(105 b)
5:	20	(93 c)
5:	37	(44 b)
5:	71	(275)
5:	100	(266 b)
5:	119	(44 b)
6:	25	(192), (207)
6:	47	(105 b)
6:	53	(173 b)
6:	80	(125 g)
6:	91	(105 b)
6:	93	(44 b)
6:	143	(233 b)
7:	20	(316)
7:	50	(44 b)
7:	77	(173 b)
7:	143	(173 b)
7:	166	(105 b)
7:	167	(173 b)
7:	199	(231)
8:	35	(170)
8:	44	(180)
9:	12	(228 b)
9:	36	(263)
9:	38	(207)
9:	46	(248)
9:	64	(105 b)
9:	80	(173 b)
9:	83	(105 b)
9:	99	(173 b)
9:	109	(291)
9:	127	p. 10
10:	15	(228 b)
10:	22	(296)
10:	24	(191), (207)
10:	35	(204)
10:	101	(105 b), (288)
11:	41	(24 c)
11:	43	(24 g)
11:	44	(298)
11:	66	(173 b)
11:	73	(348 d)
11:	78	(173 b)
11:	103	(93 b)
11:	105	(51 e)
12:	10	(296 c)
12:	13	(93 d)
12:	31	(288)
12:	35	(328 c)
12:	53	(5)
12:	76	(322)
12:	90	(233)
13:	5	(233)
13:	9	(307)
14:	22	p. 3
15:	29	(5)
15:	29	(6)
15:	54	(125 g)
15:	58	(6)
15:	68	(296 b)

16: 1 (44 b)
16: 5 (241)
16: 14 (296)
16: 40 (105 b)
16: 70 (173 b)
16: 89 (25)
16: 91 (173 b)
17: 24 (6)
17: 64 (105 b)
17: 80 (24 d)
17: 93 (105 b)
18: 18 (46)
18: 64 (307)
18: 77 (202)
18: 97 (209)
19: 2 (173 b)
19: 4 (173 b)
19: 7 (232)
19: 23 (38)
19: 24 (82 b)
19: 26 (239 b)
19: 29 (173 b)
19: 61 (24 h)
19: 66 (38)
20: (220)
20: 33 (173 b)
20: 35 (173 b)
20: 77 (51)
20: 81 (184)
20: 97 (181)
20: 132 (231)
21: 54 (53)
21: 73 (249)
21: 98 (109)
22: 15 (110 b)
22: 25 (44 b)
22: 29 (110 b)
22: 36 (173)
22: 45 (295 b)
22: 65 (173 b)
22: 67 (163)
22: 78 (9)
23: 1 (45), (224)
23: 29 (24 c)
23: 36 (348 b)
23: 44 (330)
23: 91 (235)
23: 97 (105 b)
24: 45 (173 b)
24: 61 (105 b)
24: 62 (173 b)
25: 43 (173 b)
25: 49 (263), (353)
26: 77 (296 b)
26: 119 (296)
26: 215 (6)
26: 224 (51 e)
26: 227 (24 c)
27: 25 (241)
27: 27 (44 b)
27: 44 (327 b)
27: 47 (207)
27: 59 (233 b)
27: 69 (105 b)
28: 34 (241)
29: 26 (173 b)
29: 41 (202)
29: 64 (271)
29: 67 (24 g)
30: 1-3 (248)
30: 17 (24 e)
30: 27 (143 c)
30: 51 (44 b)
31: 11 (24 b)
31: 20 (368)
31: 34 (93 d)
32: 5 (232)
33: 10 (173 b)
33: 27 (42)
33: 33 (183)
34: 9 (173 b)
34: 19 (24 d)
35: 9 (44 b)
35: 12 (296)
36: 49 (205)
37: 8 (192), (207)
38: 32 (327 c)
38: 41-42 (288)
39: 17 (296 c)
39: 46 (235 b)
40: 60 (105 b)
41: 40 (105 b)
41: 50 (173 b)
42: 5 (97)
43: 57 (170)
44: 43 (348 d)
45: 24 (13 b)
46: 17 (92)
46: 32 (232)
47: 4 (24 e)
47: 18 (173b),(232)
51: 1 (173)
51: 55 (22 c)
53: 22 (269)
53: 31 (45)
53: 50 (224)
54: 15 (190)
54: 16 (194)
54: 48 (368)
55: 39 (327 b)
56: 2 (23 b)
56: 65 (181)
56: 74 (118)
56: 89 (5)
61: 12 (21), (173 b)
62: 10 (105 b)
64: 9 (21)
65: 11 (21)
66: 10 (348 d)
66: 12 (331)
67: 16 (228 b)
69: 4 (23 b)

69:	8	(23 b)
69:	21	(24 g)
69:	29	(345 b)
69:	28	(345 b)
70:	3-4	(173)
71:	10	(105 b)
71:	16	(173 b)
73:	2	(288)
73:	3	(288)
73:	14	(295 b)
74:	6	(184)
75:	40	(180)
77:	11	(321)
78:	28	(27)
78:	35	(27)
80:	3-4	(190), (207)
81:	1-2	(44 b)
89:	6	(173 b)
89:	19	(330)
89:	27-28	(5)
92:	1-2	(307 b)
94:	1	(51 f)
97:	5	(163)
101:	10	(345 b)
106:	2	(228 b)
107:	1	(236)

§ 6. Index of Qur'anic readers in the Introduction and Commentary

ʿAbd Allāh b. Abī Isḥāq (233)
Abū ʿAmr (92), (109), (173, b), (202), (204), (205), (224), (263), (307), (321)
Abū Bakr (204), (205), (263)
Abū l-Dardā (296)
Abū Ǧaʿfar (46), (51 f), (205)
Abū Ḥayya al-Numairī (327 c)
Al-Aʿmaš (205)
ʿAmr b. ʿUbaid (327 b)
Al-Aʿraǧ (205)
ʿĀṣim (24 b), (35), (110 b), (183), (205),
Ayyūb al-Siḫtiyānī (327)
Al-Faiḍ b. Ġazwān (180)
Ḥafṣ (291)
Ḥamza p. 2, (35), (53 b), (110 b), (173), (205), (209), (228 b), (263), (291), (307), (348 d)
Al-Ḥasan al-Baṣrī (120), (205), (202), (296 c)
Ḥassān (170)
Hišām (46), (205)
Ibn ʿAbbās (202)
Ibn al-ʿAlāʾ (see Abū ʿAmr)
Ibn ʿĀmir (35), (109), (228 b), (233), (266), (307), (348 d)
Ibn Ḏakwān (205)
Ibn Kaṯīr (109), (205), (263), (291), (307), (327 b), (327 c), (368)
Ibn Masʿūd (202), (328 c)
Ibn Muǧāhid (51 b)
Ibn Waṯṯāb (51 f)
Al-Kisāʾī (46), (110 b), (163), (173 b), (205), (228 b), (235), (236), (263),
Nāfiʿ (125 g), (183), (204), (224), (241), (263), (266), (307)
Al-Naḫfī (51 f)
Qālūn (205)
Qunbul (327 c)
Saʿīd b. Ǧubair (322)
Al-Sūsī (307)
Ṭalḥa b. Muṣarraf (45), (180), (239 b)
Ubbay (348 b)
Warš (205)
Yaʿqūb al-Ḥaḍrami (109), (173 b), (263)
Zaid b. Ṯābit (120), (348 b)

§ 7. Index of verse quotations in the Commentary

أما ٱشْتَقْتَ يا مَوْلَايَ حِينَ فَقَدْتَنِي (36)
أَمَا ٱلإفَادَةُ فاسْتَوْلَتْ رِكَابُهَا (322)
أَمَلْتُ خَيْرَكَ هَلْ تَأْتِي مَوَاعِدُهُ (25)
أَنْ تَقْرَآنِ عَلَى أَسْمَاءَ وَيْحَكُمَا (51 b)
إِنَارَةُ ٱلْعَقْلِ مَكْسُوفٌ بِطَوْعِ ٱلْهَوَى (296 c)
أَنَا سَيْفُ ٱلْعَشِيرَةِ فَٱعْرِفُونِي (73 c)
إِنَّ ٱلْخَلِيطَ أَجَدُّوا ٱلْبَيْنَ فَٱنْجَرَدُوا (248)
إِنَّ ٱلَّذِي سَمَكَ ٱلسَّمَاءَ بَنَى لَنَا (143 c)
إِنَّ ٱلْمَنَايَا يَطَّلِعْنَ عَلَى ٱلْأُنَاسِ ٱلْآمِنِينَا (234)
إِنَّ ٱلْمُوَقَّى مِثْلَ مَا وُقِّيتُ (24 c)
إِنَّ مِنَ الإِخْوَانِ إِخْوَانَ كَشْرَةٍ (60)
إِنَّمَا ٱلْمَيْتُ مَنْ يَعِيشُ كَئِيباً (263)
إِنِّي إِذَا مَا حَدَثٌ أَلَمَّا (235 b)
إِنِّي لَدَى ٱلْحَرْبِ رَخِيُّ ٱللَّبَبِ (212)
أَهَدَمُوا بَيْتَكَ لا أَبَا لَكَا (133)
بَلْ بَلَدٍ مِلْءُ الفِجَاجِ قَتَمُهْ (121)
بُنَيَّتِي سَيِّدَةَ الْبَنَاتِ (38)
تَرَوَّحْنَا مِنَ اللَّعْبَاءِ عَصْراً (235 c)
تَرَوَّحْنَا مِنَ اللَّعْبَاءِ قَصْراً (235 c)
ثَلاثَةُ أَحْبَابٍ فَحُبٌّ عَلَاقَةٌ (27)
جَاؤوا بِجَيْشٍ لَوْ قِيسَ مُعْرَسُهُمْ (133)
جَارِيَةٌ فِي دِرْعِهَا ٱلْفَضْفَاضِ (140)
حَتَّى إِذَا مَا أَمْسَجَتْ وَأَمْسَجَا (340 b)
حَتَّى تَذَكَّرَ بَيْضَاتٍ وَهَيَّجَهُ (295 b)
حَتَّى لَا يُحِلُّ ٱلدَّهْرَ إِلَّا بِإِذْنِنَا (261)
حُزُقٌّ إِذَا مَا ٱلْقَوْمُ أَبْدَوْا فُكَاهَةً (233)
خَالِي عُوَيْفٌ وَأَبُو عَلِجِ (339)
دَامَنَّ سَعْدُكَ لَوْ رَحِمْتَ مُتَيَّماً (125 e)
ذَاكَ خَلِيلِي وَذُو يُوَاصِلُنِي (364)
ذَكَرْتُ ٱبْنَ عَبَّاسٍ بِبَابِ ٱبْنِ عَامِرٍ (37)
رَاحَتْ بِمَسْلَمَةَ ٱلْبِغَالُ عَشِيَّةً (220)
رُبَّ رَامٍ مِنْ بَنِي ثُعَلٍ (330)
آذَنَتْنَا بِبَيْنِهَا أَسْمَاءُو (60 b)
إِبْعَدْ بَعِدْتَ بَيَاضاً لا بَيَاضَ لَهُ (140)
أَبْلِغْ أَبَا دُخْتَنُوسَ مَأْلُكَةً (224)
أَبِيتُ أَبْكِي وَتَبِيتِي تَدْلُكِي (51 e)
أُحَاذِرُ أَنْ تَعْلَمْ بِهَا فَتَرُدَّهَا (51 d)
أَحَبُّ ٱلْمُؤْقِدِينَ إِلَيَّ مُؤْسَى (327 c)
أَخَاكَ أَخَاكَ إِنَّ مَنْ لا أَخَا لَهُ (20 b)
إِذَ ٱلْعَجُوزُ غَضِبَتْ فَطَلِّق (51)
إِذَا ٱلْأُمَّهَاتُ قَبُحْنَ ٱلْوُجُوهَ (212)
إِذَا ٱلْكِرَامُ ٱبْتَدَرُوا ٱلْبَاعَ بَدَرْ (170)
إِذَا غَابَ عَنَّا غَابَ عَنَّا فُرَاتُنَا (29)
إِذَا قَالَ قَطْنِي قُلْتُ بِٱللّٰه حَلْفَةً (239 c)
إِذَا قَامَ قَوْمٌ يَاسَلُونَ مَلِيكَهُمْ (237)
إِذَا لَمْ يَكُنْ فِيكُنَّ ظِلٌّ وَلَا جَنًى (265)
إِذَا مَا تَرَعْرَعَ فِينَا ٱلْغُلَامُ (345 b)
إِذَا ما عُدَّ أَرْبَعَةٌ فِسَالٌ (358)
إِذَا ما غَدَوْنَا قَالَ وِلْدَانُ أَهْلِنَا (51 d)
أَرَى ٱبْنَ نِزَارٍ قَدْ جَفَانِي وَمَلَّنِي (331)
أَرَيْتَ ٱمْرَأً كُنْتُ لَمْ أَبْلُهُ (236)
أَرَيْتَ إِنْ جَاءَتْ بِهِ أُمْلُودَا (125 f)
أَرَيْتَكَ إِنْ مَنَعْتَ كَلَامَ حُبَّى (236)
أَرَيْتَكَ إِنْ مَنَعْتَ كَلَامَ يَحْيَى (236)
أُرِي عَيْنَيَّ مَا لَمَ تَرْأَيَاهُ (236)
اسْتَغْنِ ما أَغْنَاكَ رَبُّكَ بِالغِنَى (307 b)
اضْرِبَ عَنْكَ ٱلْهُمُومَ طَارِقَهَا (125 c)
أَعَنْ تَرَسَّمْتَ مِنْ خَرْقَاءَ مَنْزِلَةً (328 b)
أُغْدُ لَعَنَّا فِي ٱلرِّهَانِ نُرْسِلُهْ (338)
أُقَاتِلُ حَتَّى لا أَرَى لِي مُقَاتَلا (24 c)
أَقُولُ لَهَا وَدَمْعُ العَيْنِ جَارٍ (41)
أَلا أَبْلِغَا لَيْلَى وَقُولَا لَهَا هَلَا (344)
الْحَمْدُ لِلّٰهِ مُمْسَانَا وَمُصْبَحَنَا (24 c)
إِلَى أَنْ دَعَا دَاعِي الصَّبَاحِ فَحَيْعَلا (41)

كَأَنَّ صَوْتَ ٱلصَنْجِ فِي مُصَلْصَلَهْ (24 c)
كَحَلْقَةٍ مِنْ أَبِي رِيَاحِ (235)
كَفَى بِٱلنَّأْيِ مِنْ أَسْمَاءَ كَافِي (23)
لَا تُهِينَ ٱلْفَقِيرَ عَلَّكَ أَنْ (125 b)
لا لا أَبُوحُ بِحُبِّي بَثْنَةَ إِنَّهَا (20 d)
لَاهُمَّ إِنْ كُنْتَ قَبِلْتَ حَجَّتَجْ (340)
لا يُبْعِدِ اللّٰهُ أَصْحَاباً تَرَكْتُهُمُ (307 d)
لدى أَسَدٍ شاكي السِّلاحِ مُقذف (292)
لَقَدْ أَغْدُو عَلَى أَشْقَرَ (315)
لَقَدْ كَانَ لِي عَنْ ضَرَّتَيْنِ عَدِمْتُنِي (83)
لَقِيتُ ٱبْنَةَ السَّهْمِيِّ زَيْنَبَ عَنْ عُفُرٍ (331)
لَمْ يَتْرُكُوا لِعِظَامِهِ لَحْماً لَا لِفُؤَادِهِ مَعْقُولا (24)
لَمَّا رَأَى أَنْ لَا دَعَهْ وَلَا شِبَعْ (371)
لَهَا أَشَارِيرُ مِنْ لَحْمٍ تُتَمِّرُهُ (357)
لَوْ شِئْتِ قَدْ نَقَعَ ٱلْفُؤَادَ بِشَرْبَةٍ (243)
لو عُصِّرَ منه البانُ والمسكُ ٱنْعَصَرْ (109)
لِيَبْكِ أَبَا ٱلْخَنْسَاءِ بَغْلٌ وَبَغْلَةٌ (167)
لَيْتَ وَهَلْ يَنْفَعُ شَيْئاً لَيْتُ (298)
لَيْسَ مَنْ مَاتَ فَٱسْتَرَاحَ بِمَيْتٍ (264)
مَا أَنْتَ بِٱلْحَكَمِ ٱلتُّرْضَى حُكُومَتُهُ (115 b)
مَا أَنْسَ لَا أَنْسَاهُ آخِرَ عِيشَتِي (51)
مَتَى أَقُولُ خَلَتْ عَنْ أَهْلِهَا ٱلدَّارُ (45)
مِثْلُكِ أَوْ خَيْرٍ تَرَكْتُ رَذِيَّةً (121)
مَعَاذَ ٱلْإِلَهِ أَنْ تَكُونَ كَظَبْيَةٍ (235)
مَنْ لا يَزَالُ شَاكِراً عَلَى ٱلْمَعَهْ (115 b)
مُنْسَرِحاً عَنْهُ ذَعَالِيبُ ٱلْخِرَقِ (336)
نَزُورُ ٱمْرَأً أَمَّا الإلهَ فَيَتَّقِي (170)
نعمَ الساعُونَ في الحَيِّ الشُّطُرْ (29)
هَجَوْتَ زَبَّانَ ثُمَّ جِئْتَ مُعْتَذِراً (51)
هَذَا جَنَايَ وَخِيَارُهُ فِيهْ (363)
هَلْ تَعْرِفُ ٱلدَّارَ عَلَى تِبْرَاكَا (77 c)
هَلْ يَنْفَعَنْكَ ٱلْيَوْمَ إِنْ هَمَّتْ بِهِمْ (367)
هُوَ ٱلْجَوَادُ ٱلَّذِي يُعْطِيكَ نَائِلَهُ (197)
وَٱبْكِنَ عَيْشاً تَقَضَّى بَعْدَ جِدَّتِهِ (239 c)
وَأَبْيَضُ مِنْ مَاءِ ٱلْحَدِيدِ كَأَنَّهُ (140)
وَأَتَى صَوَاحِبُهَا فَقُلْنَ هَذَا ٱلَّذِي (343)
رَسْمِ دَارٍ وَقَفْتُ فِي طَلَلِهْ (121)
سَالَتْ هُذَيْلٌ رَسُولَ ٱللّٰهِ فَاحِشَةً (237)
سَالَتَانِي ٱلطَّلَاقَ أَنْ رَأَتَانِي (237)
سالتماني الطلاق أن رأيتما (237)
سَيَكْفِيكَ ضَرْبَ ٱلْقَوْمِ لَحْمٌ مُعَرَّضٌ (295 b)
صَاحِ هَلْ رَيْتَ أَوْ سَمِعْتَ بِرَاعٍ (236)
صَفْقَةُ ذِي ذَعَالِتٍ سَمُولِ (336)
ضَرَبَتْ صَدْرَهَا إِلَيَّ وَقَالَتْ (316)
ظَلْتُ فِيهَا ذَاتَ يَوْمٍ وَاقِفاً (181)
عَشِيَّةَ سُعْدَى لَوْ تَرَاءَتْ لِرَاهِبٍ (147)
عَيُّوا بِأَمْرِهِمْ كَمَا (180)
فَالْيَوْمَ قَرَّبْتَ تَهْجُونَا وَتَشْتُمُنَا (53)
فَإِنْ أَهْجُهُ يَضْجَرْ كَمَا ضَجْرَ بَازِلٌ (109)
فَإِنَّ ٱلْمُنَدَّى رِحْلَةٌ فَرُكُوبُ (24 c)
فَإِنَّهُ أَهْلٌ لِأَنْ يُؤْكَرَمَا (116)
فَأَيْنَ إِلَى أَيْنَ النَّجَاءُ بِبَغْلَتِي (20 c)
فَبَادَرَتْ شَاتَهَا عَجْلَى مُثَابِرَةً (367)
فَبَيْنَاهُ يَشْرِي رَحْلَهُ قَالَ قَائِلٌ: (77 b)
فَتَرَكْنَ نَهْداً عُيَّلاً أَبْنَاؤُهَا (335)
فَتُضْحِي صَرِيعاً مَا تُجِيبُ لِدَعْوَةٍ (110 c)
فَتَعَرَّفُونِي إِنَّنِي أَنَا ذَاكُمُ (292)
فَصَدَقْتُهَا وَكَذَبْتُهَا (27)
فَطَافَ كَمَا طَافَ ٱلْمُصَدِّقُ وَسْطَهَا (194)
فَعَيْنَاكِ عَيْنَاهَا وَجِيدُكِ جِيدُهَا (328 b)
فقال فريقُ القوم لمَّا نَشَدْتُهُم (114)
فَقُلْتُ لِصَاحِبِي لَا تَحْبِسَانَا (342)
فَلَا وَأَبِي لَنَأْتِيهَا جَمِيعاً (125 d)
فَلَمَّا فَقَدْتُ الصَّوْتَ مِنْهُمْ وَأُطْفِئَتْ (318)
فَيَا ظَبْيَةَ ٱلْوَعْسَاءِ بَيْنَ جُلَاجِلٍ (233)
فَيَا قَلْبُ دَعْ ذِكْرَى بُثَيْنَةَ إِنَّهَا (22 c)
قَامَتْ بِهَا تَنْشُدُ كُلَّ ٱلْمُنْشَدِ (356)
قَدْ عَلِمَتْ خَيْبَرُ أَنِّي مَرْحَبُ (292)
قَدْ كَانَ قَوْمُكَ يَحْسِبُونَكَ سَيِّدًا (295 b)
قَدْ وَرَدَتْ مِنْ أَمْكِنَه (345)
قَطَعَ عَمْرٌو سَاعِدَيْ وَهَبٍ (45)
كَالْحُوتِ لَا يُرْبِيهِ شَيْءٌ يَلْهَمُهُ (363)

وَاحَرَ قَلْبَاهُ مِمَنْ قَلْبُهُ شَبِم (c 345)
وَٱللّٰهُ نَجَاكَ بِكَفَّي مَسْلَمَتْ (d 348)
وإنَّ مِنَ الإخوانِ إخْوانَ كَشْرَةٍ (60)
وَبَلْدَةٍ قَالصَةٍ أمْوَاؤها (325)
وَتَضْحَكُ مِنّي شَيْخَةٌ عَبْشَمِيَّةٌ (51)
وَحَلْبُهُ حَتّى ٱبيَاضَ مَلْبَنُهْ (327)
وَدَعْ ذَا ٱلْهَوَى قَبْلَ ٱلْقِلَى تَرْكُ ذِي (373)
وَعَضُّ زَمَانٍ يا ٱبْنَ مَرْوَانَ لَم يَدَعْ (23)
وَعِلْمُ بَيَانِ ٱلْمَرْءِ عِنْدَ ٱلْمُجَرَّبِ (c 24)
وفيكَ إذا لاقَيْتَنَا عَجْرَفِيَّةٌ (209)
وقد عادَ عَذْبُ الماءِ بَحْراً فزادني (18)
وقد عادَ ماءُ الأرضِ بحراً فزادني (18)
وَقَدْ عَلِمَتْ عِرْسِي مُلَيْكَةُ أَنَّنِي (262)
وَقَفْتُ فيها أُصَيْلَالاً أُسائِلُها (370)
وَقَوْمٍ عَلَيَّ ذَوِي مِئْرَةٍ (152)
وَكَأَنَّهَا تُفَّاحَةٌ مَطْيُوبَةٌ (b 295)
وَكُنَّا حَسِبْنَاهُم فَوَارِسَ كَهْمَسٍ (180)
ولأَنْتَ تَفْرِي مَا خَلَقْتَ (307)
وَلُبْسُ عَبَاءَةٍ وَتَقَرَّ عَيْنِي (c 51)
وَلَقَدْ أَضَاءَ لَكَ الطَّرِيقُ وَأَنْهَجَتْ (c 22)
وَلَقَدْ أَمُرُّ عَلَى ٱللَّئِيمِ يَسُبُّنِي (c 93)
وَلِلْأَرْضِ أَمَّا سُودُهَا فَتَجَلَّلَتْ (327)
وَلَوْ أَنَّ وَاشٍ بِالْيَمَامَةِ دَارُهُ (23)
وَلَيْلٍ كَمَوْجِ الْبَحْرِ أَرْخَى سُدُولَهُ (121)
وَمَاجَ سَاعَاتٍ مَلَا ٱلْوَدِيقُ (328)
وَمَا زَالَ تَشْرَابِي ٱلْخُمُورَ وَلَذَّتِي (25)
وَمَا مَلِلْتُ وَلَكِنْ زَادَ حُبُّكُمُ (181)
وَمَنْهَلٍ لَيْسَ لَهُ حَوَازِقُ (355)
وَهَيَّجَ ٱلْحَيَّ مِنْ دَارٍ فَظَلَّ لَهُمْ (344)
وَيَوْمٍ كَأَنَّ ٱلْمُصْطَلِينَ بِحَرِّهِ (121)
يَا أَبْجَرَ بْنَ أَبْجَرَ يَا أَنْتَا (60)
يَا أَيُّهَا الرَّاكِبُ الْمُزْجِي مَطِيَّتَهُ (c 296)
يَا دَارَ سَلْمَى يَا ٱسْلَمِي ثُمَّ ٱسْلَمِي (327)
يا دار عَبْلَةَ بالجواءِ تَكَلَّمْ (c 307)
يَا دَارَ مَيَّ بِٱلدَّكَادِيكِ ٱلْبُرَقْ (326)
يَا قَاتَلَ اللّٰهُ بَنِي ٱلسِّعْلَاتِ (334)
يَا قَوْمِ قَدْ حَوْقَلْتُ أَوْ دَنَوْتُ (41)
يَا لَيْتَ أَنَا ضَمَّنَا سَفِينَهْ (263)
يا لَيْتَ شِعْرِي! آنَ ذُو عَجَّةٍ (c 73)
يَا لَيْتَهَا قَدْ خَرَجَتْ مِن فُمِّهِ (363)
يَا مَرْحَبَاهُ بِحِمَارِ عَفْرَا (c 345)
يَا مُرَ يَا ٱبْنَ وَاقِعٍ يَا أَنْتَا (60)
يا ميَّ لا غَرْوَ ولا مَلَاما (38)
يَا هَالَ ذَاتَ ٱلْمَنْطِقِ التَّمْتَامِ (366)
يَتَمَارَى فِي ٱلَّذِي قُلْتُ لَهُ (344)
يَفْدِيكَ يَا زُرْعَ أَبِي وَخَالِي (359)

§ 8. Index of poets in the Commentary

Al-ʿAbbās b. Mirdās al-Sulamī (295 b)
ʿAbd Allāh b. Rawāḥa al-Anṣārī (125 d)
ʿAbd al-Aswad b. ʿĀmir b. Ǧuwain al-Ṭāʾī (335)
ʿAbd al-Aswad al-Ṭāʾī (335)
ʿAbd al-Qais b. Ḫaffāf (307 b)
ʿAbd Yaġūṯ b. Waqqās al-Ḥāriṯī (51), (262)
ʿAbīd b. al-Abraṣ (180)
Abū l-Aswad al-Duʾalī (236)
Ăbū l-Aswad al-Ṭāʾī (335)
Abū Kāhil al-Yaškarī (357)
Abū l-Naǧm (109), (338), (348 d)
Abū l-ʿUmaiṯal (331)
Abū Umayya al-Faḍl b. al-ʿAbbās b. ʿUtba b. Abī Lahab (248)
Abū Zaid: Saʿīd b. Aus b. Ṯābit al-Anṣārī (340)
Al-Aḍbaṭ b. Quraiʿ al-Saʿdī (125 b)
ʿAdīy (73 c), (263)
Al-Aḫṭal (29), (109)
Al-Aḥwaṣ (60)
ʿAlī b. Abī Ṭālib (363)
ʿAlqama b. ʿAbada (24 c), (295 b)
ʿAmr b. Uḫt Ǧaḏīma al-Abraš (363)
ʿAntara (307 c)
Al-Aʿšā (235)
Al-Baʿīṯ b. Ḥuraiṯ (235)
Bint ʿAbd al-Ḥāriṯ al-Yarbūʿī (235 c)
Bišr b. Abī Ḫāzim (23)
Buǧair b. Ġanama al-Ṭāʾī (364)
Ḏū Ǧadan al-Ḥumairī (234)
Dukain (327)
Ḏū l-Rumma (233), (328 b)
Al-Farazdaq (23), (51), (115 b), (143 c), (167), (220), (243), (328 c)
Ǧāmiʿ b. ʿAmr b. Murḫiya al-Kalbī (233)
Ǧamīl (20 d), (22 c), (51 d), (121), (343)
Ǧarīr (243), (327 c), (363)
Ǧirān al-ʿAwd (83), (209)
Ḫalaf al-Aḥmar (355)
Al-Ḫansāʾ (163)
Ḥassān b. Ṯābit al-Anṣārī (237)
Ḥumaid b. Ḥuraiṯ b. Baḥdal al-Kalbī (73 c)
Ḥuraiṯ b. ʿAnnāb al-Nabhānī al-Ṭāʾī (239 c)
Ibn al-ʿAbbās (77 c)
Ibn Barrīy (22 c)
Ibn Ḥilliza al-Yaškūr (60 b)
Ibn Ṯābit al-Anṣārī al-Ṣaḥābī (345 b)
ʿIlbāʾ b. Arqam al-Yaškarī (334)
Imruʾu l-Qais (51 d), (60 b), (121), (330), (358)
ʿĪsā b. ʿUmar (37)
Ismāʿīl b. Yasār (236)
ʿIyāḍ b. Durra al-Ṭāʾī (261)
Kaʿb b. Mālik al-Anṣārī (133)
Kuṯayyir (170), (327)
Labīd b. Rabīʿa al-ʿĀmirī (243), (344)
Maǧnūn b. ʿĀmir (23), (328 b)
Maisūn bint Baḥdal (51 c)
Manṣūr b. Misǧāḥ al-Ḍabbī (194)
Manẓūr b. Murṯid al-Asadī (371)
Marḥab al-Yahūdīy (292)
Mayya bint Umm ʿUtba Ibn al-Ḥāriṯ (235 c)
Al-Māzinī (51), (106)
Miskīn al-Dārimī (20 b)
Muḍarris b. Ribʿī al-Asadī (342)
Muḍarris b. Ribʿī al-Fiqʿasī (342)
Muhalhil Abī Lailā ʿAdī b. Rabīʿa al-Taġlibī (316)
Al-Mutanabbī (140), (345 c)
Nahšal b. Ḥarrī (121)
Nuṣaib (18), (114)
Al-Qaisī (340 b)
Quṣayy b. Kilāb (212)
Al-Rāʿī (25), (147)
Rakkāḍ b. Abbāq al-Dubairī (236)
Ruʾba b. al-ʿAǧǧāǧ (24 c), (41), (51), (121), (125 f), (140), (170), (298), (363), (366), (367)
Ruwaišid b. Kaṯīr al-Ṭāʾī (296 c)
Al-Ṣābiʾ (36)
Sālim b. Dāra al-Ġaṭafānī (60)
Šamr b. ʿAmr al-Ḥanafī (93 c)
Al-Sulaik b. al-Salka al-Saʿdī (295 b)
Surāqa b. Mirdās al-Azdī al-Bāriqī (236)
Tamīm b. Abī Muqbil (307 d), (322)
Ṭarafa (25), (29), (125 c), (367)
Ṭarīf b. Tamīm al-ʿAmbarī al-Tamīmi (292)
ʿUdail (73 c)
ʿUǧair al-Salūlī Ǧāhilīy (77 b)
Al-ʿUmānī al-Rāǧiz (363)
ʿUmar b. Abī Rabīʿa (53), (181), (318), (343)
Umayya b. Abī al-Ṣalt (24 c), (235 b)
Umm al-Banīn bint ʿUtaiba b. al-Ḥāriṯ (235 c)
Umm al-Huṯaim (265)
ʿUmrān b. Ḥaṭṭān (110 c)
ʿUrwa b. Ḥizām al-ʿUḏrī (345 c)
Al-Walīd b. Yazīd b. ʿAbd al-Malik b. Marwān (315)
Yazīd b. al-Ṭaṯrīya (342)
Zaid b. ʿAmr b. Nufail al-Qurašī al-ʿAdawī (237)
Zuhair b. Abī Sulmā al-Muzanī (197), (292), (307)

§ 9. Index of peoples, tribes, leaders, celebrities, schools, places, languages and deities in the Introduction and Commentary

ʿAbd al-ʿAzīz (363)
ʿAbd al-ʿAzīz b. Marwān (170), (327)
ʿAbd al-Malik b. Marwān (248)
Abū l-Fatḥ p. 12
Abū Sufyān (133)
ʿĀd (224)
Adam (12 b), (53)
Adonis (235 c)
Akkadian (46 b), (73 c), (77), (139), (169), (235 b), (376)
ʿAlī b. Abī Ṭālib p. 6, (5), (27), (292), (363)
Allatu (235 c)
ʿAmr b. Masʿūd (334)
Ancient West Semitic (301)
Ancients p. 30
Al-Andalus p. 5, (372)
Al-Anṣār (269), (348 b), (348 b)
Apollo (235 c)
Arab p. 28, 33, (13), (43), (55), (63), (64), (176), (188 b)
Arabic p. 24, 28, 30, (12), (13 b), (14 c), (22), (39), (45), (46), (58), (60), (71), (73 c), (77), (89 b), (91), (93), (97), (105), (111 b), (132), (134), (136), (153), (157), (158), (169), (177 b), (180), (188 b), (212), (225), (233), (235), (242), (246), (258), (328 c), (348 b), (367), (372 b), (376)
Arabs p. 30, 33, (14 b), (32), (36), (37), (40), (42), (45), (51 f), (71), (77 d), (81 b), (82 b), (89 b), (97), (100), (118), (125 d), (133), (138), (217), (232), (233), (235 c), (236), (241), (252), (275), (284), (329), (340 c), (348 d), (353), (372)
Aramaic (39 b), (100), (217), (219), (222), (225), (231), (301), (348 b), (367)
Asad (77 d), (82 b), (100), (179)
Assyrian (217), (367)
Azd (328 c), (364)
Babylonian (235 c)
Baġdād (12)
Baghdadian p. 4, (12)
Bahīla (331)
Bahrāʾ (99)
Bakr b. Wāʾil (82 b), (109), (344)
Banū ʿAdīy (36)
Banū ʿĀmir (181), (243)
Banū l-ʿAnbar b. Tamīm (368)
Banū ʿAwf b. Saʿd (336)
Banū Dubair (298)
Banū Faḫʿas (298)
Banū l-Ḥāriṯ b. Kaʿb (81 b)
Banū Ibād (104)
Banū Kināna (335)
Banū Māzin (24 c), (367)
Banū Ṣabāḥ (51 d)
Banū Saʿd (339)
Banū Taim Allāh b. Ṯallaba (141)
Banū Ṯuʿal (330)
Banū ʿUḏra (115 b)
Banū Yaškar (357)
Banū Yaškur (357)
Basrans p. 3, 6, 24, 25, 27, 29, 30, (10), (12, b), (13, b), (14 b), (18)-(20), (21), (28), (29), (40), (43), (46 b), (48), (53, b), (60), (73 b), (77), (84 b), (91), (93), (101), (111), (114), (120)-(123), (139), (140), (174, b), (216), (228 b), (230), (235 b), (263), (331), (338)
Beduin p. 28
Biblic Aramaic (231)
Brussa p. 9, 10
Byblos (132)
Christian Arabic (235)
Classical p. 30
Constantinople p. 16
Ḍabba (51 d)
Damascus (269)
Daṯīna (5), (27), (328 c),(364)
Dūma (147)
Eastern (99)
Ethiopic (73 c), (77), (180), (222), (225), (242), (258), (293), (301), (316), (348 b)
Europe p. 5
Fāris (121)
French p. 5
German p. 5
Greek p. 28, (10 b), (63), (71), (125 d)
Guhrumīs (121)
Hadramaut (82 b)
Ḥamdān (77 d)
Harim b. Sinān (197)
Ḫarqāʾ (328 b)
Ḥarūrīs (145)
Ḥasan p. 6
Ḥazm b. ʿUwāl (235 c)
Ḫawaṭ b. Ǧubair al-Anṣarī (141)
Hebrew (5), (39), (73 c), (77), (97), (98), (100), (132), (139), (217), (222), (225), (258), (293), (301), (322), (337), (348 b, d), (367)
Herodotus (235 c)
Ḥiǧāzī (32), (38), (80 b), (89 b), (99), (113), (163), (181), (184), (215), (232), (236), (240), (241), (295 b), (332)

Ḥimyar (364)
Ḫindif (212)
Hišām b. ʿAbd al-Malik (327 c)
Huḏail (29), (51 e), (60), (215), (322), (328 c)
Ḥumair (348 d)
Al-Ḥusain p. 6
Ibn Nizār (331)
ʿImrān (331)
Ishtar (235 c)
Jesuite p. 7
Jewish Palestinian Aramaic (348 b)
Kaʿb (179)
Kaʿba (235 c), (266), (340 c)
Kahmas (180)
Kalb (233), (372)
Kināna (133), (335)
Kūfa p. 3
Kufans p. 3, 6, 27, 29, 30, (10), (12, b), (14 b), (15)-(20), (21), (28), (29), (40), (42), (46, b), (48), (53, b), (73 b), (77), (84 b), (91), (93), (101), (110 b), (111), (113), (114), (119)-(123), (136), (139), (140), (174), (184), (216), (228 b), (235 b), (244), (263), (331), (338)
Kulaib b. Rabīʿa (316)
Laʿbāʾ (235 c)
Lailā bint Ḥulwān b. ʿImrān (212)
Laylā al-Aḫyalīya (344)
Latin p. 5
Liḥyānite (235)
Lūṭ (348 d)
Madīna (27), (133), (215), (269), (328 c), (345 b)
Makka (215), (235 c)
Manāt (235 c)
Mandaean (180), (234)
Marocco (372)
Mary (331)
Maslama ((348 d), (366)
Maslama b. ʿAbd al-Malik (366)
Māzin b. Rabīʿa (367)
Medinean (348 b)
Muʿāwiya b. Abī Sufyān (51 c)
Muḥammad (323)
Al-Mutawakkil p. 6
Muʿtazilite (13 b)
Nahd (335)
Noah (348 d)
Northern Yemen (364)
Norway p. 7
Numair (179)
ʾÖmur (364)
Orient p. 7
Orientalists (14 c)
Oscar the Second p. 7
Ottoman p. 12
Pagan (235 c)
Palmyra (364)
Persian p. 34, (354)
Persian Gulf (99)
Persians p. 40
Pharaoh (51)
Proto-Semitic (72)
Qais (89 b), (99), (100), (215), (328 b, c), (367)
Qanbar p. 6
Quḍāʿa (73 c), (80 b), (99), (100), (339)
Quraiš (331)
Quraišīs (29), (184), (215), (348 b)
Rabīʿa (82 b), (99), (100), (339), (367)
Roman (248)
Rome p. 5
Saʿd b. Bakr (328 c)
Ṣafa (235)
Sahmī (331)
Ṣaḫr (163)
Al-Šāš p. 4
Sauri (5)
Semitic (5), (11), (12 b), (14 b), (14 c), (22), (35), (39 b), (42), (52), (62), (74), (91), (97), (105) (111 b), (125), (132), (134), (136), (138), (157), (177 b), (181), (185), (187), (194), (212), (213), (235), (241), (242), (258), (263), (270), (292), (301), (324), (325), (331), (363), (376)
Siḥr (82 b)
Soqotri (5)
South Arabic (5)
Ṣūfī (8)
Sulaimān (248)
Sulaimān b. ʿAbd al-Malik (363)
Sweden p. 7
Syria (235)
Syriac (5), (39 b), (73 c), (77), (169), (180), (202), (231), (293)
Taim (240)
Talmud (234)
Tamīm (14 b), (29), (60), (82 b), (89 b), (99), (100), (109), (113), (163), (180), (184), (215), (241), (295 b), (328 b, c), (332), (339), (340 c), (367), (368), (375)
Targum (231), (293)
Ṭayyīs (33), (38), (81), (239 c), (348 c), (364)
Thamūd (23 c)
Tigrē (340)
Turkish p. 6, 10, 15, 18
Ugaritic (73 c), (77), (100), (132)
ʿUkāz (141)
ʿUtaiba (235 c)
ʿUzzā (235 c)
Venus (235 c)
Al-Walīd (248)
West Semitic (258)
Western (26 b), (39, b), (99), (188)
Western Aramaic (100)

Al-Yās b. Muḍar (212)
Yazīd (51 c)
Al-Yazīdī (173)
Yemen (335), (364)
Yemenites (27), (82 b), (328 c), (334), (364)
Yusuf Ali (235 b)
Zaqqūm (348 d)

§ 10. Index of authors and titles in the Introduction and Commentary

The authors are those used in the bibliographical references and those referred to in the Introduction and Commentary. The titles are only those used in the bibliographical references, and do not include those cited in the Introduction and Commentary.

ʿAbbās (295 b)
ʿAbd Allāh b. Abī Isḥāq (3 b), (233)
ʿAbd al-ʿAzīz (53), (147), (149 b)
ʿAbd al-Ḥamīd (11), (39 b), (41), (169), (181), (213), (242), (258), (301), (376)
ʿAbd al-Mahdī [Al-Ḥanafī] p. 9
ʿAbd al-Qādir (44 b)
ʿAbd al-Qādir Rāšid [Ḫulūṣī Zādah] pp. 21-22
ʿAbd al-Raḥīm (10), (11), (29), (34), (35), (39 b), (138), (169), (174), (213), (242), (243), (258), (279), (301)
ʿAbd al-Raḥīm Ḫalīl p. 11
ʿAbd al-Raḥman al-Badawī p. 28
ʿAbd al-Raḥmān b. Ḫalīl Rūmī p. 11
ʿAbd al-Raḥmān b. Hurmuz (3 b)
ʿAbd al-Tawwāb p. 6, (14 b), (50), (170), (190), (207), (265), (292), (316), (323), (331)
ʿAbdat (39 b)
Abed p. 30, (46 b)
Abīd (180)
Abū l-ʿAbbās Aḥmad b. Yaḥyā [Ṯaʿlab], see Ṯaʿlab
Abū l-ʿAbbās [al-Baizūrīy], see al-Baizūrīy
Abū l-ʿAbbās [Muḥammad b. Yazīd Mubarrad], see Mubarrad
Abū ʿAlī [al-Fārisī], see al-Fārisī
Abū ʿAlī al-Šalawbīn p. 5
Abū ʿAmr b. ʿAlāʾ (51), (202), (345 b)
Abū l-Aswad al-Duʾalī (3 b), (133), (236)
Abū Bakr (17), (21), (38), (40)
Abū Bakr b. al-Qawṭīya [Ibn al-al-Qawṭīya] p. 6
Abū Bakr Muḥammad b. Aḥmad b. Manṣūr Ibn al-Ḫayyāṭ (40)
Abū Bakr Muḥammad b. al-Qāsim b. al-Anbārī (17), (21)
Abū Bišr Mattā b. Yūnus p. 28
Abū l-Fatḥ [Ibn Ǧinnī], see Ibn Ǧinnī
Abū Ǧaʿfar al-Naḥḥās (292)
Abū Ǧaʿfar al-Ruʾāsī p. 3, (92)
Abu Haidar, F., p. 7
Abū Ḥaidar, J., (23), (60 b), (342)
Abū l-Haiṯam (235)
Abū Ḥanīfa p. 5, (10), (22 c), (41)
Abū l-Ḥasan (38), (46 b), (74 b), (279), (343)
Abū l-Ḥasan al-Aḫfaš al-Ṣaġīr (74 b)
Abū l-Ḥasan Aḥmad p. 3
Abū l-Ḥasan ʿAlī b. al-Muẓaffar al-Nīsābūrī p. 25
Abū l-Ḥasan [al-Dabbāġ], see al-Dabbāġ
Abū l-Ḥasan Muḥammad b. Kaisān (46 b)
Abū l-Huḏail (13 b)
Abū Isḥāq [Zaǧǧāǧ], see Zaǧǧāǧ
Abū Manṣūr (202), (262)
Abū Muḍar al-Iṣbahānī p. 25
Abū Muḥammad ʿAbd Allah b. Muslim (92)
Abū l-Naǧm (109), (338), (348 d)
Abū Rīda (13 b)
Abū l-Samḥ (228 b)
Abū ʿUbaid (39 b), (170), (373)
Abū ʿUbaida (202), (222)
Abū ʿUmar al-Ǧarmī p. 3
Abū ʿUṯmān [al-Māzinī], see al-Māzinī
Abū l-Waqt p. 10
Abū Yūsuf (46)
Abū Zaid [Anṣārī], see Anṣārī
Afandī (45), (51), (152 b), (170), (197), (220), (236), (237), (248), (327 c), (370)
ʿAǧǧāǧ (24 c), (51), (140), (170), (327), (336), (340 b), (363), (366), (367)
Al-Aḫfaš [al-Awsaṭ] p. 3, (10), (50), (60), (74 b), (87), (133), (295), (327 c)
Ahlwardt p. 7, 13, (24 c), (295 b), (307), (370)
Aḥmad b. ʿAlī b. Masʿūd, see Ibn Masʿūd
Aḥmad b. ʿAlī b. Masʿūd b. ʿAbd Allāh [Ibn Saqqāʾ], see Ibn Saqqāʾ
Aḥmad b. al-Ṭayyib al-Saraḫšī p. 30
Ahrens (177 b)
Aḫṭal (29), (109)
Åkesson (29), (33), (34), (45), (51 d), (54), (60 b), (81, b), (109), (110, b), (307, b, c, d), (312), (320), (328 b), (369)
Alee (53), (125 b)
ʿAlī (5), (27), (292), (363)
ʿAlī b. al-Ḥasan al-Aḥmar [Ibn Mubārak] p. 3
ʿAlī b. ʿĪsā al-Rabaʿī p. 4
ʿAlī b. Safar p. 10
Al-Ālūsī [Muḥammad Ḥāmid] p. 10
Anīs (29), (60)
Anṣārī, [Abū Zaid], (215), (228 b), (334), (340)
Anṣārī, b. Ṯ., (237)
ʿAntara (307)

Anwar (60)
Aristotle p. 28
Arkoun (12)
Arnaldez p. 28
Aro (30 b)
Al-Aṣmaʿī p. 3, (22 c), (39 b), (41), (138), (248)
Astarābādī p. 5, 6, (3), (29), (138)
ʿAṭāʾ b. Abī l-Aswad al-Duʾalī (3 b)
Al-Aṯram p. 6
Atsiz 13
Azhar 13
Baalbaki (43), (51 d, f), (58)
Badawī (10 b)
Badr al-Dīn p. 5
Baġdādī p. 3, 4, 8, 9, 10, (10), (51, b), (60), (77 b), (233), (235, b), (262), (315), (325), (326), (327), (328), (331), (335), (336), (339), (340, b), (342), (343), (345), (355), (357), (359), (366), (371)
Baiḍāwī (35), (51 e), (181), (205), (249), (307), (327 c), (328 b)
Al-Baizūrīy [Abū l-ʿAbbās] p. 5
Bakkūš (11), (29), (34), (213), (242), (243), (258), (284), (286), (301)
Bakrī (334)
Baldick (8)
Bāriqī (236)
Barrānī (51 c), (115), (298), (307 b), (364)
Barth (14 b), (111 b), (235 b)
Bašar (3)
Baṭalyawsī (170)
Bauer (169), (242), (258), (301)
Beeston (105), (110)
Bernards p. 4, (12)
Blachère (11), (39 b), (41), (83), (89), (105), (139), (144), (150),(156), (163), (164), (169), (177 b), (242), (258), (301), (376)
Blanc (188 b), (340 c)
Blau (12), (43), (99)
Bohas p. 27, 29, 30, (3), (12), (14, c), (29), (34), (41), (43), (55), (68), (111), (116), (136), (138), (139), (157), (159), (164), (192 c), (195), (217), (222), (229), (244), (261), (265), (270), (276), (277), (284), (288), (340 c), (349), (363), (368), (374), (378)
Braünlich (197), (243), (371)
Bravmann (84 b), (188 b), (194), (263), (288)
Brill p. 5, 10
Brockelmann pp. 3-6, 8, 9-14, 25, 27, (11), (12), (14 b), (43 b), (52), (62), (82 b), (130), (138), (169),(177 b), (194), (213), (232), (234), (235 c), (242), (258), (301), (340, b), (348 d)
Buhl (235 b)
Būnī (176)
Bürgel (233)
Bustānī p. 7, (10), (14), (51 c), (90), (118), (121), (133), (140), (141), (143), (236), (263), (364)
Cachia (216)
Cantarino (44 b), (93 c, d, e), (132), (139)
Cantineau (39 b), (82 b), (173), (174), (194), (205), (338), (347), (364), (367), (372), (373)
Carter (3), (9), (10, b), (12), (20 b, c, d), (45), (51 c, e), (60), (65), (71), (73 b), (77), (78), (81), (108), (115, b), (132), (263), (296 c), (307 b), (364)
Caspari p. 25
Chouémi (35)
Cohen (14 b), (97)
Al-Dabbāġ [Abū l-Ḥasan] p. 5
Ḍabī (170)
Dāġir (372 b)
Ḏahabī (263)
Ḍaif p. 27
Danecki (188 b)
Daqr (25), (50 b), (60), (81), (83), (90), (93 c), (114), (121), (125, b), (139), (185), (235 b), (269, b), (275), (298), (300), (301), (305), (307 b), (332)
Dār al-kutub al-miṣrīya p. 7, 8, 10-14
Dārimī (13 b)
Darwīš p. 25, (232)
Dasūqī (372)
Derenbourg p. 5, 13
Diakonoff (29)
Diem (22 c), (328 c)
Dieterici (355)
Dīkqūz p. 10
Ḏū l-Rumma (328 b)
Ḏubyānī (370)
Dunqūz p. 10, 11, 22, (96), (174), (184), (187 b), (230), (275)
Al-Dunqūzī p. 5
Elamrani-Jamal p. 30
Endress p. 28
Faḍl (248)
Fairūzābādī (50 b), (343)
Fārābī (46 b)
Farazdaq (23), (51), (115 b), (143 c), (167), (220), (243), (328 c)
Farḥāt p. 7, (10), (60), (125, e), (159), (164)-(166), (169), (213), (235 b), (236), (242), (248), (258), (263), (296 c), (301), (316), (376)
Al-Fārisī [Abū ʿAlī] p. 4, 5, 6, 34, 40, (92), (110 c), (235 c), (325), (327 c), (340 b)
Al-Farrāʾ p. 3, 6, (19), (12), (27),

(44 b), (45), (46 b), (48), (50), (51), (53 b), (93 c), (107), (114), (118), (120), (130), (138), (174, b), (211), (235), (243), (248), (263), (307), (326), (331), (348 d), (371)
Fās p. 12
Fischer, A., (22 c), (197), (224), (235), (243), (331), (371)
Fischer, J. B., (10 b)
Fischer, W., (39 b), (41), (138), (139), (140), (156), (159), (164), (169), (176), (217), (219), (242), (258), (301), (376)
Fityān [al-Ḥalabī] p. 5
Fleisch p. 7, 25, 26, (3), (12), (22 c), (30 b), (32), (34), (39 b), (41), (43), (50), (52), (62), (74), (99), (116), (139), (143 b), (148), (149 b), (156), (159), (164), (165), (168), (173), (174), (188 b), (202), (205), (209), (223), (234), (307), (316), (322), (347), (348), (368)
Fleischer (23), (24 c), (188 b), (190), (222), (292), (295 b), (312)
Flügel p. 5, 13, (12), (133)
Frayḥa (23)
Frazer (235 c)
Freytag (24 c), (27), (51), (141), (143), (239 c), (307), (339), (340, b), (364), (373)
Fück p. 30
Gairdner (188 b)
Gāmī (13 b)
Ğamīl (20 d), (22 c), (51 d), (121), (343)
Garbell (188 b)
Al-Ğārburdīy p. 26
Ğarğāwī (142), (143 c), (147), (298)
Ğarīr (243), (327 c), (363)
Ğawālīqī (170)
Ğawzīya (2), (6)
Ġazālī (13 b)
Giese (14 b)
Ğirān (209)
Goguyer p. 5, (64), (114)
Goshen-Gottstein (29)
Gray (235 c)
Greenberg (174)
Grunebaum (13 b)
Ğubūrī p. 13
Guillaume p. 24, 32-37, (3), (34), (38), (43), (58), (265), (276), (277), (284), (295)
Gully (115)
Gwynne p. 32
Ḥadīṯī (120)
Hafftner (14 b)
Ḥāfiẓ (8)
Ḥāğği Ḫalīfa pp. 7-12
Al-Haiṯam b. Kulaib [al-Šāšī] p. 4
Al-Ḥalabī [Fityān] p. 5
Ḫalaf al-Aḥmar p. 3
Ḫālid b. Kulṯūm (248)
Ḫalīl b. Aḥmad p. 3, 32, (12), (41), (44 b), (50, b), (52), (60), (89), (115), (170), (232), (279), (323), (334), (339), (359), (366), (367), (370)
Hallaq (13 b)
Hämeen-Anttila (367)
Ḥamīrī (339), (370)
Al-Ḥanafī [ʿAbd al-Mahdī] p. 9
Ḥarīrī (53 b), (77 b, c), (106), (115), (121), (140), (143 b), (233), (235 b), (305), (312), (334), (339), (363), (364), (367)
Hārūn al-Rašīd (46)
Ḥasan (121)
Ḥasan b. ʿAlāʾ al-Dīn al-Aswad p. 10
Al-Ḥasan [Ibn al-Ṣabbāḥ] p. 5
Al-Ḫaššāb p. 8
Ḥassān p. 34, (3), (10), (55), (101), (112), (123), (188 b), (228 b)
Haywood p. 39, (3 b), (14), (41), (232)
Ḫayyam (8)
Ḥāzim al-Qarṭāğannī (60)
Heer (13 b)
Hindāwī p. 3, 24, 25, (3), (110 b), (120), (340 b)
Hitti (235, c)
Hoberg p. 4, 7
Howell p. 25, (20 b, c, d), (22 b, c), (23), (24, c), (25), (26), (27), (35), (38), (39 b), (41), (42), (45), (46), (51, b, c, d), (53, b), (60, b), (73, b, c), (77, b, c), (81), (83), (87), (89 b), (90)-(92), (101), (105), (106), (109), (114), (115, b), (121), (125, b, c, d, e, f), (132), (133), (136), (140), (142), (143 b, c), (147),(149), (152 b), (157), (159), (164), (167), (170), (173, b), (174), (175), (177 b), (178)-(181), (183), (187), (188, b), (190), (193), (194), (197), (202), (203 b), (204), (207)-(209), (212), (215)-(217), (219), (220), (223)-(225), (227 b), (228, b, c), (229), (231), (232), (233), (234), (235, b), (236)-(238), (239 c), (241), (243), (244), (248), (249), (254), (261)-(263), (265)-(271, b), (273), (276), (278), (281), (288), (292)-(294), (295, b), (298), (299),(305), (307, d), (308), (310), (312)-(327, c), (328, c), (329)-(332), (334)-(340, b), (341)-(348, d), (349)-(359), (360 b)-(371), (373), (375, b), (379)
Ḫuḍarī (27), (51), (340), (370)
Ḫulūṣī Zādah [ʿAbd al-Qādir Rāšid] p. 22
Ibn ʿAdī [Yaḥya] p. 30

Ibn al-Anbārī p. 3, 4, 27, 28, 30, 33, (12, b), (13), (14 c), (16), (18), (19), (20), (21), (29), (44 b), (45), (48), (51), (53, b), (58), (60), (77, b, c), (84 b), (93), (101), (109), (120)-(122), (130),(139), (140), (216), (228 b), (232), (235 b), (244), (263), (268), (315), (319), (328 c), (331), (338), (342), (370), (379)
Ibn ʿAqīl (51 b), (53, b), (81 b), (92), (114), (125, b, c), (126), (128), (130), (147), (178), (180), (181), (183), (189), (190), (200), (227 b), (235 b), (249), (262), (263), (295 b), (316), (371)
Ibn Baḫšāyiš [Yūsuf b. ʿAbd al-Malik] p. 9
Ibn al-Barrī (235 c), (243), (342)
Ibn Duraid (37), (133), (219), (235 c), (334), (335), (357), (358)
Ibn al-Fāriḍ (8)
Ibn Fāris (3 b)-(5), (14, b, c), (23, b), (24), (43), (44 b), (60), (77 c), (93 c), (235 c), (237), (328 b), (334), (339), (342), (348 d)
Ibn al-Ǧawzī (121)
Ibn al-Ǧazarī (327 c)
Ibn Ǧinnī [Abū l-Fatḥ] pp. 4-7, 24, 25, 26, 29, 34, (3, b), (12, b), (13 b), (14, c), (26 f), (29, b), (30), (34 b), (36)-(38), (41), (43), (46), (48), (51, b), (53, b), (55), (56), (58), (60, b), (62 b)-(66), (73 c), (77 b, c), (80 b), (81, b), (84 b), (89), (92), (93 c), (96), (106), (107), (109), (110 b, c), (111), (113), (114, b), (116), (121), (125 c), (130), (133), (170), (171), (174), (180), (190), (192 c), (194), (197), (202), (209), (211), (212), (216), (219), (220), (222)-(225), (227), (228 b), (231), (233), (234)-(237), (242)-(244), (248), (258), (261)-(263), (265), (268), (270), (271), (274), (275), (279), (284), (286), (292), (295 b), (298), (303), (307, c, d), (312), (313), (315), (316), (318, b), (321), (322), (325)-(329), (331), (334)-(340, b), (342), (343), (345, c), (347), (348, d), (349)-(351), (354)-(360), (361), (363), (364), (366)-(368), (370)-(372), (373)-(375), (376)
Ibn Ḥāǧib p. 5, 25, (37)
Ibn Ḫair p. 4
Ibn Ḫālawaihi (45), (53 b), (73 c), (81 b), (92), (93), (163), (181), (205), (228 b), (236), (237), (240), (263), (291), (292), (307), (321), (327, b), (334), (363), (368)
Ibn Ḫaldūn (3 b), (232)
Ibn Ḫallikān p. 25, (3 b)
Ibn al-Ḫayyāṭ (40)
Ibn Ḥazm (3 b), (5)
Ibn Hilāl p. 12
Ibn Hišām (23), (46), (51, b, d), (93 c), (114), (115, b), (121), (236), (316), (327 c), (343), (364)
Ibn al-ʿImād p. 4, 27
Ibn al-Kaisān (46 b), (76 b), (222),
Ibn al-Kalbī (363)
Ibn Kamāl Pāšā p. 10, 11, 22, (5), (22)
Ibn Maḍāʾ (83), (90)
Ibn Mālik p. 5, 6, (14), (22 b, c), (25), (26), (27), (32), (41), (51 d), (64), (94), (99), (114), (163), (165), (168) (181), (183), (300)
Ibn Manẓūr (5), (6), (14 b), (18), (22 c), (24 c), (25), (27), (33), (36), (38), (41), (44 b), (45), (51, e), (56), (60), (73, c), (77 b, c, d), (92), (93 c), (96), (106), (109), (113), (114), (121), (125 b, c), (133), (140), (147), (151), (152), (154), (163), (168), (180), (183), (188 b), (192), (194), (202), (205), (209), (212), (215), (222), (224), (228, c), (233), (234), (235, b, c), (236), (243), (248), (261)-(264), (271 b), (290), (292), (295, b), (296, c), (316), (322)-(327, b), (328, b, c), (329)-(331), (334)-(336), (339), (340, b), (342)-(345), (353), (355)-(359), (363), (364), (367), (371)-(373)
Ibn Masʿūd [Aḥmad b. ʿAlī] p. 4, 7-9, 11, 14, 15, 25-27, 29, 30, 34, (1)-(5), (7)-(10, b), (12), (13), (16), (17), (20), (21), (37), (39 b), (41), (43), (44), (45), (46), (48), (50), (51), (52), (60), (71), (72), (78), (96), (97), (99)-(101), (106), (111), (114), (115), (121), (123), (133), (134), (138), (150), (163), (174), (180), (184), (188, b), (194), (206), (211), (225), (233), (263), (265), (266), (267), (269), (275), (279), (288), (289), (296 b) (298), (307), (308), (309), (312), (329), (364)
Ibn Mubārak [ʿAlī b. al-Ḥasan al-Aḥmar] p. 3
Ibn Muǧāhid (24 c), (51 b), (110 b), (163), (205), (224), (228 b), (233), (241), (307)
Ibn al-Mustawfā (326)
Ibn al-Nadīm p. 3, (12)
Ibn al-Naḥḥās (8)
Ibn al-Qaṭṭāʿ p. 6
Ibn Qutaiba (355)
Ibn al-Ṣabbāḥ [Al-Ḥasan] p. 5
Ibn al-Šaǧarī (12 b), (51), (170), (224)
Ibn al-Ṣāʾiġ (10)
Ibn al-Salka (295 b)
Ibn Saqqāʾ [Aḥmad b. ʿAlī b. Masʿūd b. ʿAbd Allāh] p. 8

Ibn al-Sarrāğ p. 4, (53 b), (60), (77 b, c), (114), (125 g), (130), (180), (220), (237), (269), (270), (307, c, d), (331), (339), (340, b), (357), (370)
Ibn Sīda (13), (29), (292)
Ibn al-Sikkīt p. 6, (170), (334), (357), (370), (373)
Ibn Sīna (13 b)
Ibn Taymīya (13 b)
Ibn Tiġribirdī p. 4
Ibn ʿUdais (243)
Ibn ʿUṣfūr p. 5, (3), (35), (41), (51, b), (106), (170), (173), (174), (211), (212), (220), (235), (236), (242), (243), (258), (295 b), (301), (312), (313), (315), (317), (318, b),(319)-(321), (324), (325), (327, c), (328, b), (332), (334), (337)-(340, b), (342), (343), (345), (348, c), (351), (355), (356)-(359), (363), (364), (366), (367), (371), (373), (375), (376)
Ibn Wallād p. 6, (25), (133), (219), (269), (330), (355), (357), (363)
Ibn Yaʿīš p. 5, 6, 25, (3), (10), (11) (12), (22 c), (23, b), (24, c), (25), (26), (27), (41), (42), (43), (44), (45), (48), (51, b, c), (53, b), (54), (56), (57), (59), (60, b), (62), (63), (64)-(68), (73 b, c), (74, b), (77), (78), (81), (83), (84 b), (89), (91)-(93), (96), (105), (106), (109), (110 c), (120), (122), (125, b, c), (130), (132), (133), (136), (138), (140), (143 b), (144), (146), (156), (157), (159), (164), (165), (169), (170), (173, b), (177), (178), (180), (196), (197), (208), (211), (212), (216), (220), (222)-(225), (228 b), (231), (233), (234), (235, b), (236), (237), (242), (243), (258), (262), (263), (269, b), (270), (274), (279), (281), (282), (292), (295, b), (298), (301), (307, b, d), (312)-(327, b), (328, b), (330)-(332), (334)-(340, b), (341)-(345, b, c), (347), (348, b, d), (349)-(351), (353), (355)-(360), (361), (363), (364), (366)-(368), (370)-(372), (373), (375), (379)
ʿĪd p. 30
Imruʾu l-Qais (358)
ʿIsā b. ʿUmar (215)
Ismāʿīl (3 b), (6)
Jastrow (217), (328 c)
Jeffery (328 c), (368)
Al-Kaffawī [Ḥamīd] p. 5
Kafrāwī (364)
Kaḥḥāla p. 10
Karmalī (99)
Kellgren p. 5, (22 c), (25), (26), (27), (32), (41), (94), (99), (163), (165), (168)
Al-Kīlānī p. 6
Al-Kindī p. 5, 30
Al-Kisāʾī p. 3, (12), (45), (46), (80 b), (92), (110 b), (120), (130), (163), (173 b), (205), (222), (228 b), (235), (236), (263), (307), (343)
Knutsson p. 21
Köfler (99), (367)
Kopf p. 28
Košut (51)
Kouloughli p. 27, (3), (43), (265), (276) (277), (284)
Kronholm (138)
Kurylowicz (116)
Kuṯayyir (170), (327)
Labīd [b. Rabīʿa l-ʿĀmirī] (344)
Laḫmī (372)
Al-Laiṯ (44 b)
Landberg (27), (364)
Lane (12), (14, b), (16), (25), (31), (43), (62 b), (64), (106), (133), (140), (141), (151), (152), (154), (161), (168), (170), (171), (177), (183), (189), (191), (194), (197), (198), (200), (202), (207), (209), (253), (269), (271, b), (275), (295 b). (296), (296 c), (303), (339), (340), (363), (367), (368), (374)
Larcher (39 b)
Lawkarī (13 b)
Leemhuis (29), (39 b)
Leslau (5)
Levi Della Vida 13
Al-Liḥyāni (243), (343)
Løkkegaard (139)
Loucel (3 b)
Luġawī (3 b), (138), (327), (338), (339), (340), (373)
Lumsden (41)
Maʿarrī (12 b)
Madkūr p. 28
Mağnūn (23), (328 b)
Maḫzūmī (12), (46 b), (93), (114)
Al-Maidānī p. 5
Makkī (44 b), (205)
Malāʾika (22 c)
Marçais (39 b)
Al-Marğān [Kāẓim] p. 6
Marzubānī (46), (355)
Massignon (4), (10 b)
Matouš (46 b)
Al-Māzinī [Abū ʿUṯmān] p. 3, 4, 24, (41), (51), (106), (202), (275), (322), (367)
Méhiri p. 4, 6, 24, 25
Meillet p. 30
Merx (10 b)
Mingana p. 13
Mokhlis p. 29, (41), (228 b), (319),

(320), (361)
Moscati (72), (73 c), (77), (169), (242), (258), (301), (376)
Mu'addib p. 4, 5, 33, (11), (12), (22 c), (24 c, e), (29), (41), (42), (44 b), (45), (50), (51), (60), (73 c), (74 b), (77 c), (91), (92), (105, b), (106), (109), (120), (132), (163), (169), (170), (180), (197), (205), (206), (213), (220), (233), (236), (237), (241), (242), (248), (258), (263), (295 b), (301), (331), (344), (370), (376)
Mubārak (3 b), (46 b)
Mubarrad [Abū l-ʿAbbās] p. 4, (12), (22 c), (43 b), (46 b), (53), (74 b), (76 b), (82 b), (106), (121), (188 b), (211), (329)
Mufaḍḍal (170)
Muḥammad b. Aḥmad b. Kaisān (76 b)
Muḥammad b. Tamǧar al-Kirsānī p. 15
Muḥammad b. Yazīd al-Baṣrī [Mubarrad], see Mubarrad
[Muḥammad b. al-Mustanīr Abū ʿAlī] Quṭrub, see Quṭrub
Muḥammad b. Yaḥya b. Yūsuf al-Arunīqī p. 15
Muḥammad Ḥāmid [al-Ālūsī] p. 10
Muḥammad [al-Ġaznawī] p. 5
Murād b. Naṣūḥ p. 21
Muṣnafak p. 12
Muṣṭafā b. Muḥammad p. 10
Muṣṭafā b. Šaʿbān's [Surūrī] p. 11
Mutanabbī (140), (345 c), (355)
Nāǧidī (232)
Naḥḥās (121), (370)
Naṣr b. ʿAṣim (3 b)
Niksārī p. 8, 9, 22, (36), (37), (75 b)
Nöldeke (14 c), (24 d), (29), (45), (51, d, e), (133), (140), (177 b), (180), (212), (216), (217), (219), (222), (224), (225), (234), (235), (237), (263), (292)-(294), (307), (314), (315), (324), (325), (331), (334), (340), (355), (357), (358), (359), (363), (366)
Nuṣaib (18), (114)
Omar (8)
Owens p. 32, (3), (10 b), (12), (44), (47), (93)
Pellat (3 b)
Penrice (24 d), (118), (183), (207), (354)
Peters p. 28
Probster p. 6
Qālī (60), (170), (334)
Al-Qāsim [al-Šāṭibī] p. 5
Al-Qazzāz (243)
Qifṭī p. 3, 4, 25, 27, (3 b), (12), (17), (232)
Qīrawānī (12)
Qirra Sanān [Sanān al-Dīn Yūsuf] p. 12
Qudāma (322)
Quṭrub [Muḥammad b. al-Mustanīr] (14 c), (43 b), (73 c), (74 b), (92), (111), (115 b), (171)
Rabin (27), (33), (38), (51 e), (77 d), (80 b), (81 b), (82 b), (92), (99), (100), (113), (215), (307), (328 c), (348 b), (364), (367), (368)
Raddād (228 b)
Rāḍī (52), (60), (65), (93 c)
Rāǧiḥī (10), (12), (44 b), (46 b), (93 c), (114), (118), (120), (174, b), (227 b), (263), (307), (331), (348 d), (371)
Raymundus p. 5, (94), (168)
Rāzī (50, b), (52), (89), (170), (323), (334), (359), (366), (367), (370)
Reckendorf (20 b), (46), (53), (93), (121)
Redslob (14 b)
Retsö (13), (39 b), (132), (134), (138)
Reuschel (232)
Riad (3b), (5)
Riḍā (99)
RIMA p. 13
Roman p. 3, (12), (13 b), (29), (39 b), (41), (170), (173), (174), (188 b), (216), (226), (235 b), (237), (242), (258), (270), (301), (347), (364), (376)
Rosenthal (39 b), (232)
Rowton (46 b)
Al-Ru'āsī [Abū Ǧaʿfar] p. 3, (92)
Al-Rummānī p. 4, (3)
Rundgren (10 b), (12 b), (13), (93), (194), (328 c)
Růžička (328 c), (367)
Ṣābi' (36)
Al-Šabyāni [Abū ʿAmr] p. 6
De Sacy p. 7, (11), (12), (34), (41), (43), (53 b), (101), (115 b), (138), (140), (143 b), (144), (160), (169), (180), (181), (183), (185), (190), (192), (195), (198), (199), (202), (205), (207), (209), (213), (218), (225), (227 b), (237), (242), (244), (249), (256), (258), (293), (301), (310), (312), (327 c), (328 b), (343), (364), (376)
Šāḏilī (44 b), (51 d, f), (87), (93, c, d), (239 b)
Ṣafadī p. 8
Al-Šāfiʿī p. 8
Al-Saḫāwīy p. 5
Saʿīd b. Muṣṭafa al-Naʿsān p. 4
Sanān al-Dīn Yūsuf [Qirra Sanān] p. 12
Sanni (60)
Saraqusṭī p. 6, (36), (39 b), (41), (262), (363)

Al-Šartūnī p. 7, (60), (125 e), (235 b), (236), (248), (263), (296 c), (316)
Al-Šāšī [Al-Haiṯam b. Kulaib] p. 4
Al-Šāṭibī [Al-Qāsim] p. 5
Ṣaymarī (93)
Sayyid (3 b), (121)
Sellheim p. 8, 10
Sezgin p. 3, 4, 6, (10 b), (12), (17), (40), (43 b), (130), (138), (232)
Sībawaihi p. 3, 4, 24, 32, (3), (10 b), (12, b), (16), (20 b), (22 c), (24 c), (25), (29), (30), (32), (34), (36), (37), (39 b), (43), (44 b), (45), (51 c), (53, b), (56), (58), (60 b), (61), (63), (65), (68), (77 c), (80, b), (86), (89, b), (99), (101), (108)-(110), (114), (115), (125), (126), (128), (130), (131), (133), (138), (142), (143 b), (147), (151), (160), (163), (167), (168), (170), (173, b), (174), (177), (178), (180), (181), (188, b),(192), (194), (197), (211), (212), (215), (216), (219), (220), (222)-(227), (232), (233), (235 b), (236), (237), (248), (249), (270), (281), (282), (288), (292), (295), (298), (300), (307, c, d), (312), (318), (321), (322), (329), (331), (332), (339), (340), (343), (344), (349), (355), (357), (361), (363), (375), (378)
Sibīn al-Kūm p. 13
Siğistānī p. 4, (202)
Šinqīṭī (20 b, c, d), (51 c, e), (115 b), (125 f), (298), (307), (348 d), (355), (357)-(359), (363)
Sīrāfī p. 3, 4, (3, b), (46 b), (130), (133), (138), (232), (243), (367)
Sirbīnī (3), (9), (10), (12), (20 b, c, d), (45), (51 c, e), (60), (65), (71), (73 b), (77), (78), (81), (108), (115, b), (132), (263), (296 c), (307 b), (364)
De Slane p. 13, 15-18, 20
Smyth (52)
von Soden (169), (242), (258), (301)
Socins (169), (213), (242), (258), (301), (348 d)
Steiner p. 13
Ṣubḥī (14, c), (29), (41), (60), (99), (184), (215)
Ṣūlī (50)
Surūrī [Muṣṭafā b. Šaʿbān] p. 11 (343)
Suyūṭī pp. 3-8, 25-27, (3, b), (8), (10), (12), (13 b), (14, b), (17), (40), (41), (43 b, c), (46), (48), (51, b, c, d), (65), (89), (93 c), (99), (121), (125 d, f), (130), (138),(151), (152), (175), (202), (232), (247), (248), (263), (282), (292), (295 b), (296 c), (298), (328 b, c), (340 c), (363), (364), (371)
Ṯaʿālibī (3 b), (24 g, h), (41), (50 b), (121), (219), (296 b, c), (334)
Al-Taftāzānī [ʿUmar] p. 5
Tāğ al-Dīn ʿAbd al-Wahhāb p. 8, 11
Ṯaʿlab (12), (14 b), (17), (39 b), (40), (46 b), (48), (51 b), (163), (340), (357)
Ṭalas p. 13
Talmon (3 b), (12), (181), (194), (222), (228 b), (231), (232), (234), (327), (339), (342), (363), (368)
Tamīm (307 d)
Al-Tamīmī p. 6, (170)
Tanūḫī (334)
Ṭarafa (25), (29), (125 c), (367)
Taškent p. 13
Testen (125)
Tibrīzī (51), (262), (307 c), (370)
Topkapı p. 13
Troupeau p. 3, 6, 32, (10 b), (12), (188 b), (232)
ʿUkbarī (3), (12, b), (17), (19), (43 b, c), (48), (122)
Ullendorff (115), (176)
ʿUmar (25)
ʿUmar [al-Taftāzānī] p. 5
ʿUmar b. Abī Rabīʿa (53), (181), (318),
Ungnad (39 b), (46 b)
Vernier (22 c), (29), (34), (39 b), (41), (81), (86), (101), (114), (118), (125), (131), (138), (143 b), (143 c), (144), (145), (150)-(152), (153), (154), (158), (160), (162), (163), (165), (166), (168), (170), (180), (190), (192 c), (195), (197), (209), (222)-(225), (228), (231), (235), (236), (237), (244), (249), (251), (293), (310), (324), (339), (340), (343), (349), (363), (375)
Versteegh p. 3, 4, 27, 28, 30, (3 b), (10 b), (12, b), (13, b), (21), (43, b), (45), (46 b), (58), (92), (114), (188, b), (232), (344)
Vitestam p. 10, (13 b), (121)
Volck p. 5, (22 c), (25), (26), (27), (32), (41), (94), (99), (163), (165), (168)
Vollers p. 28, (35), (38), (51 e), (82 b), (109), (173, b), (181), (188 b), (190), (197), (263), (348 b)
Wagner (74)
Al-Wāḥidī p. 5
Wallin (188 b)
Walzer p. 28
Watson (82 b)
Wehr (139), (178)
Weil (12), (232)
Weiss p. 28, (10 b), (13), (14)
Wensinck (13 b), (364)

Wild (232)
Wright p. 7, 25, (11), (16), (22, b, c), (24 b), (25), (26), (29), (30 b), (31), (32), (34), (35), (37), (39 b), (40)-(42), (44), (49), (50, b), (51, d), (52), (54), (59), (64), (81), (83), (86), (91), (92), (94), (97), (101), (105), (109), (110, c), (111 b), (114), (115, b), (117), (118), (125), (132), (134)-(136), (138), (139), (143 b), (144)-(149 b), (150), (153), (156)-(160), (162)-(169), (171), (173), (176), (180), (181), (184), (185), (187), (190)-(192, c), (195)-(199), (207), (213), (217), (218), (222), (223), (225), (227), (231), (236), (237), (241)-(243), (256), (258), (261)-(263), (270), (275), (292), (301), (307), (309), (310), (316), (322), (337), (344), (345, b), (346), (347), (348 d), (349), (354), (363), (364), (370), (376)
Yaḥya [b. ʿAdī], see Ibn ʿAdī
Yaḥyā b. Yaʿmar (3 b)
Yale p. 13
Yaʿqūb (292)
Yāqūt p. 3, 4, (12), (40)
Yasūʿī (177 b)
Al-Yāziǧī p. 7
Yūnus p. 3, (65), (129), (130), (171)
Yūsuf b. ʿAbdallāh p. 16
Yūsuf b. ʿAbd-al-Malik [Ibn Baḫšāyiš], see Ibn Baḫšāyiš
Zabīdī (3), (5), (43), (138), (216), (235 c), (243)
Zaǧǧāǧ [Abū Isḥāq] p. 4, 6, 27, (39 b), (43 b), (74 b), (170)
Zaǧǧāǧī p. 27, 28, 30, (3 b), (10 b), (12, b), (17)-(19), (21), (22 c), (40), (43, b), (45), (46 b), (50), (51 c), (55), (58), (62), (74 b), (76 b), (77), (92), (108), (114), (120), (122), (202), (235), (263), (344), (345 b), (363), (373)
Zain al-Dīn Muḥammad b. al-Ḥasan al-Tabrīzī p. 5
Zamaḫšarī p. 25, 26, (10), (12), (16), (22, c), (23, b), (24, c),(25), (26), (27), (39 b), (41)-(43), (44), (45), (48), (51, e), (53, b), (54), (57), (59), (60), (64), (68), (81), (83), (84 b), (89), (91), (92), (93 c), (96), (105), (106), (114), (125, b), (130), (132), (136), (138), (141), (143, b, c), (144), (146), (156), (157), (159), (162)-(168), (170), (173, b), (175), (176), (180), (187), (188, b), (189), (190)-(192, c), (193), (194)-(197), (199), (200), (203 b), (207), (208), (212), (219), (220), (222)-(224), (228, b), (232), (233), (234), (235), (236), (239 c), (244), (248), (249), (263), (267)-(269, b), (270), (273), (274), (276), (282), (292), (295, b), (305), (307, d), (312), (313), (316)-(318, b), (319)-(327, c), (328, c), (330)-(332), (334), (335), (337)-(339), (340, b), (341), (343)-(345, b, c), (347), (348), (349)-(351), (355), (357)-(361), (363), (364), (366), (367), (368), (370)-(372), (373), (375), (379)
Zanǧānī p. 5, 6, 8, 25, 26, (11) (39, b), (159), (165), (169), (213), (242), (258), (295), (301), (376)
Zarkašī (93 b)
Zaydān p. 10, 11
Zenker p. 5
Zubaidī p. 3, 4, 27, (3, b), (12), (40), (43 b), (138), (232), (373)
Zuhair (197), (292), (307)

§ 11. Glossary and subject-index of the Commentary

The topics are selective only, and refer to the Commentary and to the English Translation by paragraph number. The numbers followed by letters refer to the sub-paragraphs in the Commentary only. These contain mostly additional material connected in some manner with the basic topics.

ʾ*A* interrogation. The insertion of the ʾ*a* to the definite article and its lengthening (229), (233 b).
Absolute *muṭlaq* (12).
Accidental *ʿāriḍ* (54), (184), (223), (288), (289), (304).
Active-participle *ism al-fāʿil* (136...). Anomalous case of an active participle of Form I of the triliteral formed on the measure of the passive participle of a verb of Form IV and of Form IV formed on the measure of the active participle of the verb of Form I (154). Anomalous case of an active participle of Form VIII whose kasra of the 2nd radical is elided (109). The active-participle being designated as *al-fiʿl al-dāʾim* "the permansive verb" by the Kufans (46 b), (136). The active participle as a substitute for the *maṣdar* (23). The *maṣdar* formed according to the measure of *fāʿila* (23 b). The active participle as a substitute for the passive participle (24 g). The passive participle as a substitute for the active participle (24 h). The resemblance and difference between the active participle and the perfect. The resemblance of the active participle to the imperfect in its reference to future time (46). Anomalous suffixation of the doubled *n* to the active participle because of its resemblance to the imperfect (125 f).
Paradigms of the active participle of the derived forms of the strong verbs of the triliteral, and Form I of the quadriliteral and its derived forms (153). Examples from paradigms of the doubled verb (172), (172 b), of verbs with 1st, 2nd or 3rd radical hamza (214, b, c), of verbs with 1st radical *w* (245), or *y* (245 b), of a verb with 2nd weak radical (290), of verbs with 2nd radical *w* (259), or *y* (259 b), of verbs with 3rd radical *y* (302) or *w* (302 b), (303 b), of a verb with 1st radical *w* and 3rd weak radical (376) and of a verb with 2nd radical *y* and 3rd weak radical (376 b).
Aḍdād "enantiosema".
Addition of:
– an *ā* between two vowelled hamzas (233).
– the *h* (212).
– the *h* of silence (345, b, c). Anomalous suffixation and vowelling in context (345 c).
– the *s* (211).
– the *s* or *š* after the pronoun of the accusative or genitive of the 2nd person of the fem. sing., the *-ki* (82 b).
Additional consonants, augments, *ḥurūf al-ziyāda*. See augments.
Adjective *ṣifa*. The anomalous vowelling of the 1st radical by a kasra when followed by the 2nd radical vowelled by a kasra in adjectives: the form *fiʿīlun* instead of *faʿīlun* (29). The form *faʿīlun* in the meaning of *fāʿilun* (146). The common gender given to the adjective of the form *faʿīlun* in the meaning of *mafʿūlun* (144). Its being taken anomalously as having the meaning of *mafʿūlun* (146). The form *faʿūlun* of intensiveness and as an assimilated adjective (147). The common gender given to the form *faʿūlun* in the meaning of *fāʿilun* (148). Anomalous case (152). Cases of adjectives compared with their contraries (151), (152). Cases of adjectives occurring for both the sing. and pl. (296 b). The forms of intensiveness *faʿʿālun, mifʿalun, mifʿālun, mifʿīlun* (149), *mifʿalun, mifʿālun, mifʿīlun* (149 b), (150). The forms *fiʿʿīlun, fuʿʿālun, faʿʿūlun, fuʿʿūlun, fuʿʿalun, fāʿūlun, faʿʿālatun, fāʿilatun, faʿʿūlatun, fuʿalatun, fuʿlatun, mifʿālatun, fāʿūlatun* (150). The common gender given to *mifʿalun, mifʿālun* and *mifʿīlun* (149 b). Anomalous separate fem. form given to *mifʿīlun* (151). The adjective of the form *faʿlā* (with final *alif maqṣūra*) (314). Regular broken pls. of the fem. of the epithet *fāʿūlun* and *fāʿilatun* (360 b). The adjective being substituted by the *maṣdar* (24 f). Adjectives formed on the pattern of the elative that do not refer to excess (143 c).
Afʿāl al-qulūb "mental verbs".
Aǧwaf "verbs with 2nd weak radical".
Alif. Alif al-aṣl "the underlying alif" (50 b).
Alif al-badal "the substituted alif" (50 b).
Alif al-ḍamīr "the alif which is the pronoun of the dual of the nominative" (50 b), (92).
Alif al-ilḥāq "the appended alif" (50 b).

Alif al-istifhām “the alif of interrogation” (50 b).

Al-alif al-mamdūda “the lenghtened alif” (50 b).

Al-alif al-maqṣūra “the alif that can be abbreviated” (50 b).

Alif al-munqaliba “the alif changed from another consonant” (50 b).

Alif al-nidāʾ “the vocative alif” (50 b).

Alif al-nudba “the alif of lamentation” (50 b).

Alif al-qaṭʿ “the disjunctive alif” (50 b), (114), (115), (116). The reason of vowelling the prefixed alif of Form IV with a fatḥa in the imperative (116).

Alif al-tafḍīl “the alif prefixed to the comparative and superlative forms” (50 b).

Alif al-taʾnīṯ “the alif of the feminine form” (269), (269 b).

Alif al-waṣl “the connective alif” (50 b), (111, b), (114), (115), (118). “The connective alif of the imperative”. Its vowelling. Different opinions according to the Basrans and the Kufans. Its anomalous vowelling (111).

Alif al-waṣl wa-l-ṣila “the alif suffixed to a final short vowel”. The alif suffixed in *antā* (60).

Alif al-wiqāya “the guarding alif”. Different opinions concerning the reason of the occurrence of the suffixed *ā* after the *ū* of the pl. of the perfect (50).

– The *ā* inserted between two hamzas (114 b), (233).

– The *ā* inserted between the *-na* marker of the fem. and the doubled *n* in the 3rd person of the fem. pl. of the Energetic I (128).

– The *ā* inserted between the *-na* marker of the fem. and the single *n* in the 2nd person of the fem. pl. of the Energetic II (129).

Anthropomorphism (45).

ʿĀriḍ “accidental”.

Aṣl “origin”, “principle”, “base”.

Aṣlī “underlying”, “underlyingly”.

Assimilated adjective *ṣifa mušabbaha* (138).

Assimilation *iddiġām*. The two measures *idġām* and *iddiġām*. Two sorts of *ʾiddiġām: ʾiddiġām ʾakbar* “total assimilation“ (174) and *ʾiddiġām ʾaṣġar* “little assimilation” (29), (30), (174), (347), (368), (374). Reasons why the assimilation is carried out (174). The assimilation that is carried out in strong verbs of Form IX and XI (40).

Assimilation of:

– the 1st radical hamza to the infixed *t* of Form VIII (187 b), (200).

– the infixed *t* of Form V and VI to the 1st radical of the verb following it, which is: the *d*, the *ḏ*, the *ǧ*, the *t* and the *ṯ*, (207), (190), the *s*, the *z* (207, (191), the *ḍ*, the *š*, the *ṣ*, the *ṭ*, and the *ẓ* (207).

– the infixed *t* of Form VIII to one of the following consonants preceding it, which is the 1st radical: the hamza (187 b), (202), the *d* (189), the *ḏ* (190), the *ḍ* (195), the *s* (192), (174), the *š* (192 b), the *ṣ* (192 c), the *t* (187 c), the *ṯ* (187 c), the *ṭ* (196), the *z* (191) and the *ẓ* (197).

– the infixed *t* of Form VIII to one of the following consonants following it, which is the 2nd radical (203): the *d* (204), the *ḏ* (204 b), the *ḍ* (205 b), the *s* (204 d), the *ṣ* (205), (206), the *t* (203 b), the *ṭ* (205 c), the *z* (204 c) and the *ẓ* (205 d).

– the 1st radical *t* to the infixed *t* of Form VIII (187 c).

– the 1st radical *ṯ* to the infixed *t* of Form VIII (187 c).

– the 1st radical *w* to the infixed *t* of Form VIII (198).

– the 1st radical *y* to the infixed *t* of Form VIII (199).

– the 2nd radical to the 3rd in the perfect and imperfect of doubled verbs (171).

– the 3rd radical *d* to the suffixed *t* in perfect verbs (251).

– the hamza changed into a weak consonant and the assimilation of both weak consonants (225), (227, b).

– the *l*– of the article to the solar consonants (176).

– the *m* of the article *-am* to the initial *m* of the noun following it (364).

– the *m* to the *n* (67).

– the *nunation* of the first word to the *l* of the article of the second word (224).

– two identical consonants (172).

– the *w* to the *t* (356).

– the *w* to the *y* (86).

– the *y* to the *y* (86), (180), (263), (350).
– the ultimate consonant of the first word to the initial consonant of the second word (173)-(173 b):
– the ultimate ʿ to the initial ʿ (173 b).
– the ultimate *b* to the initial *b, m* (173 b).
– the ultimate *d* to the initial *ḍ, ṣ, t* (173 b).
– the ultimate *ḏ* to the initial *ǧ* (173 b).
– the ultimate *ḍ* to the initial *š* (173 b).
– the ultimate *f* to the initial *b, f* (173 b).
– the ultimate *ǧ* to the initial *š, t* (173).
– the ultimate *ġ* to the initial *ġ* (173 b).
– the ultimate *h* to the initial *h, l* (173 b).
– the ultimate *ḥ* to the initial ʿ, *ḥ* (173 b).
– the ultimate *k* to the initial *k, q* (173 b).
– the ultimate *l* to the initial *r, t* (173 b).
– the ultimate *m* to the initial *b, m* (173 b).
– the ultimate *n* to the initial *l, r, y* (173 b).
– the ultimate *q* to the initial *k, q* (173 b).
– the ultimate *r* to the initial *l, r* (173 b).
– the ultimate *s* to the initial *š* (173 b).
– the ultimate *š* to the initial *s* (173 b).
– the ultimate *t* to the initial *d, ḏ, ḍ, ǧ, s, š, ṣ, ṯ, ṭ, z, ẓ* (173).
– the ultimate *ṯ* to the initial *ḏ* (173 b).
– the ultimate *w* to the initial *w* (173 b).
– the ultimate *y* to the initial *y* (173 b).

Augments, additional consonants, *ḥurūf al-ziyāda* (39 b), (41), (69), (106), (177, b), (212), (221), (225), (338), (379).

Badal "substitution".

Base, underlying *aṣl* (3), (19), (36), (38), (39 b), (40), (44), (54), (57), (65), (67)-(70), (74 b), (75 b), (78), (79), (89), (111), (113), (116), (125), (180), (182), (183), (187 b), (188), (190), (191), (192, b, c), (194)-(200), (203 b)-(206), (208), (210)-(212), (218), (219), (222), (224), (225), (227), (230), (234)-(236), (243), (247)-(249), (252), (255), (261)-(263), (268), (271)-(273), (275), (277)-(279), (284)-(292), (295), (296), (298)-(300), (305), (308), (311), (313), (315), (319)-(322), (324), (327), (328 c), (330), (331), (333), (335), (336), (338), (341)-(343), (346), (348, d), (350), (353)-(357), (360)-(363), (365)-(372), (373)-(375), (376), (378), (379).

Bināʾ "invariability".

Cluster of two vowelless consonants *iltiqāʾ al-sākinain* (36), (43 b), (54), (59), (69), (125 b), (129), (130), (184), (206), (229), (239), (241), (249), (270), (272), (275), (277), (278), (279), (284)-(289), (295), (303), (307), (313), (345 c), (360), (378). General principle when two vowelless consonants are combined in two words (270), (288), (377).

Common gender:
– the adjective of the form *faʿīlun* in the meaning of *mafʿūlun* (144).
– the form *faʿūlun* in the meaning of *fāʿilun* (148).
– the adjectives *mifʿalun, mifʿālun* and *mifʿīlun* (149 b).

Compensation *taʿwīḍ*. Compensation of:
– the elided 1st weak radical of the *maṣdar* by the *tāʾ marbūṭa* (16), (247), (248), and by the prefixed *t* (247).
– the elided 1st weak radical of the *maṣdar* by the suffixed *t* (247).
– the unsound 2nd weak radical or the infixed *ā* by the *tāʾ marbūṭa* (249), (279).
– the elided *tāʾ marbūṭa* in a word that is the first element of an *iḍāfa* construction by the word being its second element (248).
– the departure of the vowel of the 2nd radical by the infixed *s* (211) or the infixed *h* (212).
– the elided vocative particle *yā* by the ending *-mma* in *allāhumma* (235 b).

Conjugation, morphology, phonology, *taṣrīf* (3).

Conjunction. The vowelled *h* of the independent pronouns of the 3rd person of the singular *huwa* and *hiya* and the vowelled *l*– of command given a sukūn after some conjunctions (110). The question according to the Kufans and Basrans on whether the conjunction that precedes *rubba* or the theoretical elided *rubba* governs the noun in the genitive or not (121). The emphasis of a preposition in the case of a noun coupled by a conjunction to a pronoun in the genitive suffixed to a preposition. The acceptance of such a coupling without emphasizing the preposition by the Kufans and by others. An anomalous case (53 b).

Consonants, letters, *ḥurūf*. The consonants, their points of articulation, their characters and nominations (188, b):
additional consonants, augments *ḥurūf al-ziyāda*. See augments.
airy consonant *al-ḥarf al-hāwī* (188 b).
alveolar consonants (188), (194).
ante-palatal consonants *al-ḥurūf al-niṭʿīya* (188 b).
apical consonants *al-ḥurūf al-asalīya* (188 b).
covered consonants *al-ḥurūf al-muṭbaqa* (188 b), (193), (374), (375).
dental consonants (52), (176), (188).
depressed consonants *al-ḥurūf al-munḫafiḍa* (188 b), (192 c), (193).
elevated consonants *al-ḥurūf al-mustaʿliya* (188 b), (192 c), (193).
emphatic consonants (197).
gabbled consonant *al-ḥarf al-mahtūt* (188 b).
gingival consonants *al-ḥurūf al-liṯawīya* (188 b).
guttural consonants *al-ḥurūf al-ḥalqīya* (29), (30), (31), (32), (174), (188 b), (254), (355).
interdental consonants (176), (188).
intermediate consonants *al-ḥurūf bayna l-šadīda wa-l-raḫwa* (188 b), (354).
labial consonants *al-ḥurūf al-šafawīya* (188, b), (367).
laryngal consonants (188), (325), (326).
lateral consonants (176).
lax consonants *al-ḥurūf al-raḫwa* (188 b), (192 c), (194).
liquid consonants *ḥurūf al-ḏalāqa* (188 b), (176).
lunar, or moon-consonants *al-ḥurūf al-qamarīya* (176). Definite nouns occurring anomalously nunated whose initial consonants are moon-consonants (364).
muted consonants *al-ḥurūf al-muṣmata* (188 b).
open consonants *al-ḥurūf al-munfatiḥa* (188 b).
orificial consonants *al-ḥurūf al-šağarīya* (188 b).
pharyngal consonants (188), (328).
post-palatals (188).
pre-palatals (188).
reiterated consonant *al-ḥarf al-mukarrar* (188 b).
resonant consonants *ḥurūf al-qalqala* (188 b).
rigid consonants *al-ḥurūf al-šadīda* (188 b), (192 c), (194).
sibilant consonants *ḥurūf al-ṣafīr* (188 b), (176), (368).
soft consonants *al-ḥurūf al-layyina* (188 b).
solar, or sun-consonants *al-ḥurūf al-šamsīya* (176), (364).
consonants of substitution *ḥurūf al-badal* (312).
swerving consonant *al-ḥarf al-munḥarif* (188 b).
tippy consonants *al-ḥurūf al-ḏawlaqīya* (188 b).
two uvular consonants *al-ḥarfāni al-lahawīyatāni* (188 b), (340 c).
velar consonants (188).
voiced consonants *al-ḥurūf al-mağhūra* (188 b)-(190), (191), (194), (341), (364).
voiceless consonants *al-ḥurūf al-mahmūsa* (174), (188, b)-(190), (192), (194), (329), (341).
weak consonants *ḥurūf al-ʿilla*. See weak consonants.
weak consonants of prolongation, glides, *al-ḥurūf al-layyina*. See glides.
weak consonants of prolongation and softness, hollow weak consonants, glides, *al-ḥurūf al-ğūf*. See glides.

Context (82 b), (89 b), (331), (307), (345 c), (348 d).

Coordinated to another pattern by the addition of an augment or more to its root *mulḥaq*, definition, forms coordinated to: Form I of the quadriliteral *faʿlala*, Form II of the quadriliteral *tafaʿlala*, Form

III of the quadriliteral *ʾifʿanlala* and Form IV of the quadriliteral *ʾifʿalalla* (41). Coordinatives *ilḥāqīyāt* (177).

Corroborative *n* (125), (126), (130), (131). Reason of vowelling the doubled *n* with a kasra (126 b). Elision of the single *n* when a vowelless consonant occurs after it (125 b). Its anomalous elision (125 c). Elision of the doubled *n* (125 d). Anomalous suffixation of the doubled *n* in the perfect (125 e). Anomalous suffixation of the doubled *n* to the active participle (125 f). Alleviation of the doubled *n* and its replacement by a single one (125 g). Anomalous suffixation of the single *n* on the analogy of the doubled one (130).

Declension *iʿrāb* (3), (43). Definitions (43). The reasons of the declension or undeclinability of the three parts of speech. The Basrans' opinions concerning the declension and undeclinability (43). The Basrans' and the Kufans' opinions concerning the undeclinability of the verbs (123), the declension of the imperfect (122) and the undeclinability or declension of the imperative (44), (48), (119), (120), (123), (184). The reasons why the marker of declension occurs specially at the end of the word and not at its beginning or middle (43 b). A discussion concerning which is underlying the declension or the undeclinability (43 c).

Definite article *al-taʿrīf*. Different opinions concerning its structure (115). Assimilation of the *l* of the article *al–* to the solar consonants (176). *Am–* (364). Other categories of *al–* than being the definite article. *Al–* prefixed to the noun, to the perfect, to the imperfect and to the adverb (115 b). The insertion of the interrogative *ʾa* to the definite article and its lengthening (229), (233 b). Definite noun occurring with the nunation (364). Elision of the *n* of the preposition *min* in juxtaposition with the article (224).

Deflection *imāla* (347), (174).

Demonstrative pronoun of the fem. sing. *hāḏihi* underlyingly *hāḏī*. Substitution of the *h* for the *y* in it (89). Its different dialectal variants (89 b).

Derivation *ištiqāq* (3). Three sorts of derivation: little, big and biggest (14), the big derivation (14 b), the biggest derivation (14 c), (340 c), (368), (374).

Derivative *firʿ* (12), (13 b), (43 c). The *maṣdar's* or the verb's derivatives (10).

Dialectal variants. The *ʿağʿağa* (339), *ʿanʿana* (328 b), *al-istinṭāʾ* (328 c), *kaskasah, kaškašah* (82 b), *šinšinna* (82 b), *qaḥfaḥa* (328 c), *rasw* (372), (373), *taltala* (32), (99), (103), (278), *ṭumṭumānīya* (364), *watm* (334).

Dissolution (178), (180), (181), (184), (185), (190), (208).

Doubled verb *muḍāʿaf* (169...). Its four conjugations. The assimilation that is carried out in its perfect and imperfect (171). Paradigms of doubled verbs of Form I in which the imperfect's 2nd radical's vowel is: a ḍamma (171), (172), a kasra (171 b), a fatḥa (171 c). Paradigm of a verb in the derived forms (172 b). The assimilation of the 2nd radical to the 3rd in the perfect and imperfect (171). The change of the 2nd of the doubled consonants, which is the 3rd radical, into a *y* (170), (182), (352). Elision of one of its radicals (181), (183), (210). Anomalous cases of verbs (179).

Dual. Change of the ending of the dual of the accusative and genitive *-ayni* into *-āna, -ānu* or *-āni* (81 b), (92). The *ā* of the dual that occurs anomalously (81 b). The reasons why the *ā* is chosen for the dual (92). The reasons why the *n* of the dual is vowelled by a kasra (92). Anomalous vowellings (81 b), (92).

Elative *ism al-tafḍīl* (139...). The elative formed according to the pattern specific for colors (140), the passive participle (141), the pattern of the derived Form IV of a verb (142), the pattern specific for defects (143), formed from a substantive and the passive voice of a verb (143 b). Words formed according to the pattern of the elative without referring to excess (143 c). The elative of verbs with 2nd weak radical (281).

Elision *ḥaḏf*. Elision of:
- the connective alif of the article (223), (224).
- the *ā* (266 b), (278), (289), (303), (304).
- the *ā* in the quadriliteral forms *fuʿālilun* and *faʿālilun* resulting in *fuʿalilun* and *faʿalilun* (56).
- the *ā* in the instrumental form *mifʿāl* resulting in *mifʿal* (57), (278).
- the ḍamma of the 2nd radical in nouns of Form I: *faʿlun* for *faʿulun* (109).
- one of the doubled consonants (181), (183), (210).
- the fatḥa of the 2nd radical in nouns of Form I: *faʿlun* for *faʿalun* (109).
- the fatḥa in verbs of Form I: *faʿla* used instead of *faʿala* and in a verb of Form VII (45).

– the hamza (19), (114), (221), (222), (223), (224), (231), (232), (234), (235), (235 c), (236), (237), (240), (241), (291), (292).
– the prefixed vowelled hamza of the imperative in doubled verbs (183), (184), (185) and in verbs with 2nd weak radical (284), (287).
– one of the hamzas in a verb with 1st radical hamza in the 1st person of the sing. of the imperfect (19).
– the prefixed hamza of the imperative (231), (240).
– the prefixed hamza of Form VIII of the perfect (206).
– the *ī* suffixed pronoun of the agent of the 2nd person of the fem. sing. in the imperfect and imperative and the sukūn given to the last consonant in pause (307 c). Its elision in the Energetic (126).
– the *ī* suffixed pronoun of the agent of the 2nd person of the fem. sing. in the imperative of a verb with 3rd weak radical in the pronunciation (378).
– the kasra of the 2nd radical in nouns of Form I: *faʿlun* for *faʿilun* (109) and in an active participle of Form VIII (109).
– the kasra of the 2nd radical in verbs of Form I of the active voice: *faʿla* for *faʿila* (109), the kasra of the 2nd radical and its transfer to the 1st radical: *fiʿla* for *faʿila* (29), the kasra of the 2nd radical in verbs of Form I of the passive voice (109).
– the *li–* of the imperative (110 c).
– the vowel of the *li–* of the imperative (110, b).
– one marker of the fem. (58).
– the 2nd weak radical changed into a hamza in 2nd weak radical active participles (292).
– the 3rd radical *h* (363).
– the indicative *n* in the 2nd person of the fem. sing. (51 e).
– the indicative *n* before the doubled *n* in the 3 person of the masc. dual of the Energetic (127).
– the single *n* (125 b), (125 c).
– the doubled *n* (125 d).
– the doubled *n* and its replacement by a single one (125 g).
– the infix *n* in a noun (56).
– the *n* of the preposition *min* in juxtaposition with the article (224).
– *rubba* (121).
– the *tāʾ marbūṭa* in words being the first term of an *iḍāfa* construction and in other cases (248), (249).
– the infixed *t* marking the reflexivity or the prefixed *t* of the imperfect in verbs of Form V and VI in the 2nd person of the fem. and the 3rd person of the masc. sing. of the imperfect (101).
– the infixed *t* in a verb of Form VIII (211).
– the infixed *t* in a verb of Form X (209).
– the *ū* suffix pronoun of the agent of the 3rd person of the masc. pl. of the perfect, and the sukūn given to the last consonant in pause (307 d). Its elision in the Energetic (126). Its elision in the perfect (45), (307 d).
– the *ū* suffix pronoun of the agent of the 3rd person of the masc. pl. of the imperative of the Energetic I in a verb with 2nd and 3rd weak radical (378), and of a verb with 3rd weak radical in the imperative in the pronunciation (378).
– the unsound 2nd weak radical (36), (38), (249), (279), (284), (285), (286), (287), (288), (289), (291), (292), (295).
– the unsound 2nd weak radical or the infixed *ā* (249), (279).
– the vowel of the indicative (51 e).
– the vowel of the 2nd radical in doubled verbs in the perfect (171).
– the *wa* of *huwa* (77 b).
– the *w* as the 1st radical in the perfect of a verb with 1st radical *w* (246).
– the *w* as the 1st radical in the imperfect of a verb with 1st radical *w* (16), (19), (244), (252), (254), and in the *maṣdar* (16), (247), (248).
– the 2nd weak radical or the infixed *w* in passive participles of verbs with 2nd weak radical (295).
– the 2nd weak radical changed into a hamza in active participles of verbs with 2nd weak radical (291), (292).
– the 3rd radical *w* in a verb with 3rd radical *w* (305).
– the 3rd weak radical in participles of verbs with 3rd weak radical (295), (309), and in the jussive (306).

– the *ya* of *hiya* (77 c).
– the 3rd radical *y* in participles of verbs with 3rd radical *y* (23), (295), (309).
– the 3rd radical *y* in verbs with 3rd radical *y* (33), (49), (51 e), (54), (180), (201), (239 c), (240), (275), (292), (303), (304), (307).
– the 3rd radical *y* after the kasra or fatḥa before the doubled *n* in the 2nd person of the masc. sing. of the Energetic I (239 c).
Emphasizing, the emphasized *mu'akkad,* the emphasizer *mu'akkid* (17), (20), (20 b). The emphasis that occurs with nouns (20 b), verbs (20 c), particles (20 d). The emphasis of the suffixed pronoun of the nominative when an independent agent is coupled to it. An anomalous case. The Kufans' acceptance of this connection without the necessity of emphasizing the pronoun (53). The emphasis of a preposition in the case of a noun coupled by a conjunction to a pronoun in the genitive suffixed to a preposition. The acceptance of such a coupling without emphasizing the preposition by the Kufans and by others. An anomalous case (53 b).
Enantiosema *aḍdād* (14 c).
Fi'l dā'im "permansive verb".
Fir' "derivative".
Ǧazm "jussive".
Glides, weak consonants of prolongation, *al-ḥurūf al-layyina, al-ḥurūf al-ǧūf* (188 b), (224), (225), (226), (261).
Grammar *naḥw.* The first grammarians to write about it (3 b).
Ḫabar "predicate".
Ḥadaṯ "accident".
Ḥaḏf "elision".
Hamza. Its alleviation (98), (114), (116), (118), (215), (216), (217), (218), (219), (220), (221), (222), (223), (224), (225), (226), (227), (228), (231), (232), (234), (235), (236), (237), (241). Reason why it is alleviated (215). Its sounding true (116), (215), (227 b), (228 b), (231), (236), (238). The hamza *bayna bayna* (216), (218), (226). Combination of two hamzas in two words (232). The substitution of the hamza for: the *ā* (326), (327), the alif of the feminine form (313), the *w* (50 b), (235), (290), (291), (292), (316), (317), (318, b), (319), (321), (322), (323), (327 c), or written as a *w* with a hamza (218), (327 c) and the *y* (228 b), (319), (320), (324), (379).
Hamzated verbs *mahmūz.* Its conjugations (213...). Paradigms of verbs with 1st (214), 2nd (214 b) or 3rd radical hamza (214 c).
Heaviness *ṯiqal:*
– the ḍamma is heavier than the fatḥa or the kasra (34 b).
– the combination of the ḍamma preceding the kasra and the kasra preceding the ḍamma is heavy (133), (252), (253).
– the heaviness of the combination of both the wāws (78).
– the heaviness of the combination of the two tā's: the *t* prefix of the imperfect and the *t* infix marker of the reflexivity in Form V and VI in the 2nd person of the fem. and the 3rd person of the masc. sing. of the imperfect (101).
– the intransitive is heavier than the transitive (34 b).
– the kasra is considered as heavy in relation to the light fatḥa (75 b).
– the pl. is considered as heavy in relation to the dual (92).
– verbs are considered to be heavier than nouns (58).
– the vowel is heavier than the sukūn (92).
– the heavy *ū* is chosen for the rarely used masc. pl. and the light *ā* for the frequently used dual in nouns (92).
Ḫiffa "lightness".
Homonymy *ištirāk.* Homonymy of:
– both the noun of place and the passive participle of a verb with 2nd weak radical (296).
– both the suffixed pronouns of the nominative of the fem. and masc. of the duals of the 3rd person: the *ā* (72).
– the 3rd person of the fem. pl. of the perfect and the 2nd person of the fem. pl. of the imperative of a verb (284).

– the 3rd person of the fem. and the 3rd person of the masc. pl. of a verb (305).
– a few verbs designating both the active and passive voice (285), (300).

Ḫumāsī "quinqueliteral".

Ḥurūf "consonants, letters":
al-ḥurūf al-asalīya "the apical consonants".
ḥurūf al-badal "the consonants of substitution".
al-ḥurūf bayna l-šadīda wa-l-raḫwa "the intermediate consonants".
ḥurūf al-ḏalāqa "the liquid consonants".
al-ḥurūf al-ḏawlaqīya "the tippy consonants".
al-ḥurūf al-ğūf "weak consonants of prolongation and softness, hollow weak consonants, glides".
al-ḥurūf al-ḥalqīya "the guttural consonants".
al-ḥarf al-hāwī "the airy consonant".
al-ḥarfāni al-lahawīyatāni "the two uvular consonants".
al-ḥurūf al-layyina "the glides of prolongation", "soft consonants", "glides".
al-ḥurūf al-liṯawīya "the gingival consonants".
al-ḥurūf al-mağhūra "the voiced consonants".
al-ḥurūf al-mahmūsa "the voiceless consonants".
al-ḥarf al-mahtūt "the gabbled consonant".
al-ḥarf al-mukarrar "the reiterated consonant".
al-ḥurūf al-munḫafiḍa "the depressed consonants".
al-ḥarf al-munḥarif "the swerving consonant".
al-ḥurūf al-mustaʿliya "the elevated consonants".
al-ḥurūf al-muṭbaqa "covered consonants".
al-ḥurūf al-niṭʿīya "the ante-palatal consonants".
ḥurūf al-qalqala "the resonant consonants".
al-ḥurūf al-qamarīya "the lunar, or moon-consonants".
al-ḥurūf al-raḫwa "the lax consonants".
al-ḥurūf al-šadīda "the rigid consonants".
al-ḥurūf al-šafawīya "the labial consonants".
ḥurūf al-ṣafīr "the sibilant consonants".
al-ḥurūf al-šağarīya "the orificial consonants".
al-ḥurūf al-šamsīya "the solar, or sun-consonants".
ḥurūf al-ziyāda "the additional consonants, the augments".

Iḏ and *iḏā* (44 b). *Iḏā* that seems to govern the verb in the jussive (307 b).

Iddiġām "assimilation". *ʾIddiġām ʾakbar* "total assimilation" and *ʾiddiġām ʾaṣġar* "partial assimilation".

Iʿlāl "unsoundness of the weak consonant".

Ilḥāqīyāt "coordinatives".

Iltiqāʾ al-sākinain "cluster of two vowelless consonants".

Imāla "deflection".

Imperative *amr.* (Its paradigm (105). Twenty-three meanings in the Qurʾān (105 b). The Kufans' opinion that it is declinable (48), (119), (120), (123), (184), and that of the Basrans that it is undeclinable (48), (123). The reason why the imperative is undeclinable (45), (48). Reasons why the connective hamza of the imperative is given a kasra. Its anomalous vowelling (111). The reason why the prefixed hamza of Form IV is given a fatḥa (116). The imperative being substituted by the *maṣdar* (24 e). Elision of the *ī* being the suffixed pronoun of the nominative of the 2nd person of the fem. sing. in the imperative, and the last consonant being made vowelless. Cases of verbs with 3rd radical *y,* in which the short vowel of the 2nd radical is made vowelless after the elision of the 3rd weak consonant (307). Paradigms of strong verbs, Energ. I and II (125). Paradigm of a verb with 1st radical *w* (256). Paradigm of a verb with 2nd radical *w* (287).

Imperfect *muḍāriʿ.* Its two sorts (91). Its prefixes (94), (96), (97), (104), the infix (88), the infixes and suffixes (92). The opinions of the Kufans and Basrans concerning its declension (122), (123). The reasons why it is declinable (46), (47), (93). Cases concerning the active participle (93, b) and the passive participle occurring instead of the imperfect (93 b). The resemblance of the active participle to the imperfect in its reference to future time (46). The imperfect's occurrence instead of the perfect

(93 c). The imperfect's occurrence as indicating present time (93 d). The imperfect denoting the future (93, e). The debate between the Basrans and Kufans concerning the reasons of vowelling the imperfect's final radical with a ḍamma (93). The reason why the *y* is chosen as an infix in the ending *-īna* suffixed to the imperfect of the 2nd person of the fem. sing. (88), (89). An opinion stating that the *ī* is not a pronoun but a marker of the fem. (87). Its elision in the Energetic (126). The reasons why the *ū* is chosen to mark the masc. pl. (92). Its elision in the Energetic (126). The reasons why the *n* of the 2nd person of the fem. sing. and 2nd and 3rd persons of the pl. of the imperfect of the indicative is vowelled by a fatḥa. The reasons why the *n* of the 2nd person and 3rd persons of the dual of the imperfect of the indicative is given a kasra (92).

Paradigms of the imperfect of a strong verb of Form I in the indicative, subjunctive and jussive (92). Paradigms of strong verbs, Energ. I and II (125). Paradigms of doubled verbs of Form I whose imperfect's 2nd radical is vowelled by a ḍamma (171), (172), kasra (171 b) and fatḥa (171 c). Paradigms of verbs with 1st, 2nd or 3rd radical hamza (214, b, c). Paradigms of verbs with 1st radical *w* (245), or *y* (245 b). Paradigms of verbs with 2nd radical *w* (259), or *y* (259 b). Paradigms of verbs with 3rd radical *y* (302) or *w* (302 b), (303 b). Paradigm of a verb with 1st radical *w* and with 3rd weak radical (376) and of a verb with 2nd radical *y* and with 3rd weak radical (376 b).

Importance of morphology (3), (4).

Indicative *raf*ʿ. Its use instead of the jussive (51), (239 b) and the subjunctive (51 b). Its being replaced by the jussive (51 e). The reasons why the *n* of the 2nd person of the fem. sing. and 2nd and 3rd persons of the pl. of the imperfect of the indicative is vowelled by a fatḥa. The reasons why the *n* of the 2nd person and 3rd persons of the dual of the imperfect of the indicative is given a kasra (92).

Paradigm of the imperfect of the indicative of a strong verb of Form I (92). Paradigms of doubled verbs of Form I whose imperfect's 2nd radical's vowel is a ḍamma (171), (172), kasra (171 b) and fatḥa (171 c). Paradigms of verbs with 1st, 2nd or 3rd radical hamza (214, b, c). Paradigms of verbs with 1st radical *w* (245), or *y* (245 b). Paradigms of verbs with 2nd radical *w* (259), or *y* (259 b). Paradigms of verbs with 3rd radical *y* (302) or *w* (302 b), (303 b). Paradigm of a verb with 1st radical *w* and 3rd weak radical (376) and of a verb with 2nd *y* and 3rd weak radical (376 b).

Inflection *iʿrāb* (3).

Intransitive *lāzim* (22 c), (34 b). The intransitive is heavier than the transitive (34 b).

Invariability *binā*ʾ. Definitions. The Basrans' opinions concerning the declension and the undeclinability (43). A discussion concerning which is underlying the declension or the invariability (43 c). The reasons why the imperfect is declinable (47), the perfect is undeclinable (44), and the imperative is undeclinable (45), (48).

Iʿrāb "declension", "inflection" (3), (43).

*Išbā*ʿ "saturation".

Ism "noun":

ism al-āla "noun of instrument".

ism al-fāʿil "active participle".

ism al-ǧins "generic noun".

ism al-mafʿūl "passive participle".

ism al-makān "noun of place".

ism al-tafḍīl "elative".

ism al-waḥda "noun of individuality".

ism al-zamān "noun of time".

Išmām "flavour of the ḍamma". Its condition (298). Cases in which it is forbidden (299).

Ištiqāq "derivation".

Ištirāk "homonymy".

Juncture *waṣl* (184), (270), (288), (378).

Jussive *al-ǧazm*. The reason why the sukūn is chosen to mark it (92). The jussive mood in the verbs corresponding to the genitive case in the nouns (108). Its being replaced by the indicative (51), (239 b). Its occurrence after the subjunctival *an* (51 d). Its replacing the indicative (51 e). Cases in which the jussive is not taken into consideration (51), (51 f). Cases of verbs with 3rd radical *y*, in which the short vowel of the 2nd radical is made vowelless after the elision of 3rd weak radical (307). *Iḏā* seeming to govern the verb in the jussive (307 b).

Paradigm of a strong verb of Form I in the imperfect of the jussive, active (92). Paradigm of doubled verbs of Form I whose imperfect's 2nd radical's vowel is a ḍamma (171), (172), kasra (171 b) and fatḥa in the active voice (171 c). Paradigm of a doubled verb of Form I whose imperfect's 2nd radical's vowel is a ḍamma in the passive voice (186). Paradigms of verbs with 1st, 2nd or 3rd radical hamza (214, b, c). Paradigms of verbs with 1st radical *w* (245), or *y* (245 b). Paradigms of verbs with 2nd radical *w* (259), or *y* (259 b). Paradigms of verbs with 3rd radical *y* (302) or *w* (302 b), (303 b). Paradigm of a verb with 1st radical *w* and 3rd weak radical (376) and of a verb with 2nd *y* and 3rd weak radical (376 b).

Lafīf "verbs with 1st and 3rd weak radicals, and verbs with 2nd and 3rd weak radical".

Lāzim "intransitive", "obligatory".

La– "the assertative particle" (114).

Letters *ḥurūf*. See consonants.

Li– imperative *lām al-amr* (107), (110). The sukūn given to the *li*– of command after some conjunctions (110). Its being anomalously given the sukūn after *ṯumma* (110 b). Its anomalous elision (110 c).

Lightness *ḫiffa*.
- The light *ā* is chosen for the frequently used dual and the heavy *ū* for the rarely used masc. pl. in nouns (92).
- The fatḥa is considered as light in relation to the heavy kasra (75 b).
- The fatḥa and kasra are lighter than the heavy ḍamma (34 b).
- Nouns are considered to be lighter than verbs (58), (59).
- The sukūn is lighter than the vowel (92).
- The transitive is lighter than the intransitive (34 b).

Mağhūl "passive voice".

Mahmūz "hamzated verb".

Maṣdar "verbal noun".

Mental verbs *af'āl al qulūb*. Combination of both the pronouns of the nominative and of the accusative of the same person in them (83).

Metathesis (14 b).

M as an infix or suffix in a pronoun or noun (62). Anomalous cases in which the *m* can be prefixed or infixed to the verbs (62 b).

Miṯāl "verbs with weak 1st radical".

Morpheme (3).

Morphology *ṣarf, taṣrīf*. A generative system (3). Importance of morphology (3), (4).

Mu'akkad "emphasized", *mu'akkid* "emphasizer".

Mubtada' "topic".

Muḍā'af "doubled verb".

Mulḥaq "coordinated to another pattern by the addition of an augment or more to its root".

Muta'addī "transitive".

Muṭlaq "absolute".

N. Corroborative *n* (125), (126), (130), (131). Doubled and single nūns. Paradigms (125). Reason of vowelling the doubled *n* with a kasra (126 b). Elision of the single *n* when a vowelless consonant occurs after it (125 b). Its anomalous elision (125 c). Elision of the doubled *n* (125 d). Anomalous suffixation of the doubled *n* to the perfect (125 e) and to the active participle (125 f). Alleviation of the doubled *n* and its replacement by a single one (125 g). Anomalous suffixation of the single *n* on the analogy of the doubled one (130).
The reasons why a kasra is chosen for the *n* of the dual. Its anomalous vowellings. The reasons why the *n* of the 2nd person of the fem. sing. and the 2nd and 3rd persons of the pl. of the imperfect of the indicative is vowelled by a fatḥa. The reasons why the *n* of the 2nd person and 3rd persons of the dual of the imperfect of the indicative is given a kasra (92). Anomalous elision of the 3rd radical *y* preceding the energetic *n* in the 2nd person of the masc. sing. (239 c).

Nāqis "verbs with 3rd weak radical".

Naql "transfer", "shift".

Naṣb "subjunctive".

Nidā' "vocative".

Noun *ism*. The debate between the Basrans and the Kufans concerning the etymological derivation of *al-ism:* the Basrans regarding the noun as logicians whereas the Kufans regarding it as philologists (12

b). The noun's superiority in relation to the verb according to the Basrans (12 b), (13, b). The resemblance of the noun to the imperfect (47), (92), (93), (126 f). Nouns are considered to be lighter than verbs (58), (59). The reasons why the *ā* is chosen for the dual (92) and the *ū* for the sound masc. pl. (92). Nouns being treated as masc. and fem. (22 c), (296 c). Cases concerning a noun that occurs for the masc., fem., sing. and pl. (296). Cases of nouns that occur for both the sing. and the pl. (152 b), (296, b). Nouns formed according to their contraries (151), (152), (271 b). Patterns of nouns ending with the alif of the feminine form (269, b). Examples of nouns with a -*y* prefix (97). Examples of nouns in which the disliked combination of the ḍamma preceding the kasra and the kasra preceding the ḍamma occurs (133). A noun in the nominative occurring instead of the accusative (23). Anomalous elision of the kasra or ḍamma of the 2nd radical in nouns of Form I (109). The separate gender given to the form *faʿīl* in the meaning of *mafʿūl* (145). Nouns in the sing. pertaining to verbs (whose action they denote) (344).

Noun of individuality *ism al-waḥda* (52).

Noun of instrument *ism al-āla* (164...). The patterns *mifʿalun, mifʿalatun* and *mifʿālun* (167). The patterns *mufʿulun, mufʿulatun* and *mifʿulatun* (168).

Noun of kind *ism al-ḥāla* (166).

Noun of place *ism al-makān* (159...). Examples of nouns of place on the measure *mafʿilun* (163). Noun of place of the verb with 1st radical *w* (160). Noun of place of the verb with 3rd radical *y* (162).

Noun of time *ism al-zamān* (159...). The form of the passive participle of what exceeds three consonants occurring as the form of the noun of time (24 d).

Nouns that express the doing of an action once *ism al-marra* (165).

Obligatory *lāzim.* The sukūn in the 2nd person of the fem. pl. of the imperative of the doubled verb is stated as obligatory (185).

Oneness *tawḥīd.* the Basrans' concept of the *maṣdar's* oneness contra the verb's plurality (12). Comments concerning the concepts of oneness and independency contra plurality and dependency referring to the fields of philosophy and theology (13 b).

Origin *aṣl* (12), (13 b), (43 c).

Passive-participle *ism al-mafʿūl* (157...). The passive participle as a substitute for the *maṣdar* (24). The *maṣdar* as a substitute for the passive participle (24 b). The *maṣdar* of the derived forms of the triliteral occcurring on the pattern of the passive participle (24 c). The form of the passive participle of what exceeds three consonants occurring as the form of the noun of time and as a *maṣdar* (24 d). The active participle as a substitute for the passive participle (24 g). The passive participle as a substitute for the active participle (24 h). The passive participle occurring instead of the imperfect (93 b). The Kufans' argument that the *maṣdar* is formed according to the passive participle contra the Basrans argument that it is formed according to the noun of place (18). The forms *mafuʿlun* and *mafūlun* of the passive participle of verbs with 2nd radical *w* or *y* (295). The form *mafīlun* used instead of *mafūlun* and *mafyūlun* (295 b).

Paradigms of the passive participle of the derived forms of strong verbs of the triliteral, and Form I of the quadriliteral and its derived forms (158). Examples from the paradigms of doubled verbs (172), (172 b), of verbs with 1st, 2nd or 3rd radical hamza (214, b, c), of verbs with 1st radical *w* or *y* (245), (245 b) of verbs with 2nd radical *w* (259), or *y* (259 b), and of verbs with 3rd radical *y* (302) or *w* (302 b), (303 b).

Passive voice *al-maǧhūl* (132...). The reason why the ḍamma is chosen to vowel the 1st radical of the form *fuʿila* (132). *Fuʿla* said instead of *fuʿila* (109). Homonymy of a few verbs designating both the active and passive voice (285), (300). The elative formed from the passive voice of a verb (143 b). Paradigm of a strong verb of Form I in the perfect and imperfect (132). Paradigms of the derived forms II-X of the strong verb in the perfect and imperfect of the indicative (134). Examples from the paradigms of doubled verbs (172), (172 b), (186), of verbs with 1st, 2nd or 3rd radical hamza (214, b, c), of verbs with 1st radical *w* or *y* (245), (245 b), of verbs with 2nd radical *w* (259), or *y* (259 b), of a verb with 2nd radical *w* (297), of verbs with 2nd weak radical (298), of verbs with 3rd radical *y* (302) or *w* (302 b), (303 b), of a verb with 1st radical *w* and 3rd radical weak (376) and of a verb with 2nd radical *y* and 3rd radical weak (376 b).

Pause *waqf* (48), (82 b), (89 b), (220), (229), (241), (326), (307, b, c, d), (327), (331), (340 b), (344), (345 c), (348 d), (363), (373). Addition of the *h* of silence (345) after the *y* and the *w* (345 b). Its anomalous vowelling in some cases (345 c). Substitution of the *ǧ* for the single *y* (340), the *tāʾ ṭawīla* for the *tāʾ marbūṭa* (348 d) and the *h* for the *ā* in pause (345, (348 d). Elision of the *ī*, suffix pronoun of the agent of the 2nd person of the fem. sing., in the imperative, and the sukūn given to the last consonant (307 c). Elision of the *ū*, suffix pronoun of the agent of the 3rd person of the masc. pl., of the perfect, and the sukūn given to the last consonant (307 d) or the ḍamma (45). Cases of verbs occurring with the elision of the 3rd radical *y* and the kasra or sukūn given to the last consonant (307).

Perfect *māḍī*. Its three sorts (42). The reasons why the perfect is undeclinable (44), (46). The reason why the perfect's marker of invariability is the fatḥa (45). Cases of the elision of the suffixed *ū* of the 3rd person of the masc. pl. in the perfect (45), (307 d). The occurrence of the perfect instead of the imperfect, and thus its resemblance to it (42), (44 b). The ressemblance and the difference existing between the active participle and the perfect (46). The perfect being substituted by the imperfect (93 c). A verb designating both the 3rd person of the fem. pl. of the perfect and the 2nd person of the fem. pl. of the imperative (284). Anomalous suffixation of the doubled *n* in the perfect (125 e).

Paradigm of a strong verb of Form I in the perfect active (42). Paradigms of the derived forms of the strong verb of the triliteral in the perfect and imperfect (39 b). The quadriliteral and its derived forms (41). Paradigms of doubled verbs of Form I whose imperfect's 2nd radicals' vowel is a ḍamma (171), (172), kasra (171 b) and fatḥa (171 c). Paradigms of verbs with 1st, 2nd or 3rd radical hamza (214, b, c). Paradigms of verbs with 1st radical *w* or *y* (245, b). Paradigms of verbs with 2nd radical *w* (259), or *y* (259 b). Paradigms of verbs with 3rd radical *y* (302) or *w* (302 b), (303 b). Paradigm of a verb with 1st radical *w* and 3rd radical weak (376) and of a verb with 2nd radical *y* and 3rd radical weak (376 b).

Permansive verb *al-fiʿl al-dāʾim* (46), (46 b), (93), (136).

Phonology, morphology, conjugation, *taṣrīf* (3).

Plural. The reason why the *n* of the sound masc. pl. is vowelled by a fatḥa. The reasons why the *ū* is chosen to mark the sound masc. pl. in nouns and in verbs in the 2nd and 3rd persons of the masc. pl. of the imperfect of the indicative (92).

Predicate *ḫabar* (12 b), (13), (44), (58).

Principle *aṣl*.

- The dimininutive (65), (363), the pronouns (65), the dual (65), (289) and the broken pl. (363) bring back the word to its base form.
- The marker should not be elided (101).
- Two markers of the fem. can be combined together in the light noun (58), 59).
- Two markers of the fem. cannot be combined together in the heavy verb (58), (97).
- A declinable marker should not be combined with an undeclinable one (127).
- The *-na* agent pronoun of the 3rd person of the fem. pl. should not be combined with the doubled *n* (128).
- Verbs are undeclinable (122). The Basrans' and the Kufans' opinions (123).
- Four vowelled consonants cannot follow each other in one word (55). Cases in which this occurs (55), (56).
- A vowelless consonant cannot begin a word (43 b), (102), (111), (207), (284).
- A vowelless consonant is not a sufficient separative between two vowelled ones (112), (113), (290).
- Two vowelless consonants cannot be combined. See cluster of two vowelless consonants. General principle when two vowelless consonants are combined in two words (270), (288), (378).
- Two tāʾs of the fem. cannot be combined together (58), (88), (97).
- The *w* at the end of the word cannot be preceded by a ḍamma in nouns (63), (64).

Pronouns.

- The independent pronouns of the nominative. Paradigm (76).

The independent pronoun of the nominative of the 1st person of the sing. *anā* (73), (345), (373). Its dialectal variants (73 c). The debate between the Basrans and the Kufans concerning its structure (73 b). The reason why one form is sufficient for it (73).

The independent pronoun of the nominative of the 2nd person of the masc. sing. with the suffixed *ā*, *antā*. The structure of this pronoun without the suffixed *ā*, i.e. *anta* (60).

The reason why the *m* is infixed in the independent pronoun of the nominative of the dual *antumā* (60). The reason why the dual exists for the 2nd persons (73). The base forms of *antumā* and *antum*

(79). The reasons why the *t* in *anta* is given a fatḥa, the *t* in *anti* is given a kasra and the *t* in *antumā* is given a ḍamma (76 b).
The *h* of the independent pronouns of the 3rd person of the singular *huwa* and *hiya* given a sukūn after both the conjunctions (110). Different opinions concerning the structure of *huwa* and *hiya* by the Kufans and Basrans (77). Anomalous elision of the *wa* of *huwa* (77 b) and the *ya* of *hiya* (77 c). Some anomalies concerning their structures (77 d).
Theories concerning *humā* and *hum* (78).
The reason why no dual is chosen for the independent pronoun of the nominative of the 1st person of the pl. *naḥnu* (74). The reason of the vowelling of its 2nd *n* with the ḍamma (74 b).
– The suffixed pronouns of the nominative of the perfect. Paradigm (75). The suffixed pronoun of the nominative is considered by the Arab philologists as one with its verb differently from the pronoun of the accusative (55). The reason why the suffix agent pronoun of the 1st person of the sing., the *-tu,* is chosen for the perfect (70). Substitution of the *ṭ* for the *t* in the suffix agent pronouns *-tu, -ta* and *-ti* (375). The reasons why the suffixed *t* is given a fatḥa to mark the 2nd person of the masc. sing., a kasra to mark the 2nd person of the fem. sing. and why the infixed *t* is given a ḍamma to mark the dual (75 b). The homonymy of both the suffixed pronouns of the nominative of the duals of the fem. and of the masc. of the 3rd persons, the *ā* (72). The reason why the *n* in the suffixed pronoun of the nominative of the 2nd person of the fem. pl., *-tunna,* is doubled (67), (69). The emphasis of the suffixed pronoun of the nominative when it is coupled to another agent. An anomalous case. The Kufans' acceptance of this connection without the necessity of emphasizing the antecedent (53). Latency of the suffixed pronoun of the nominative (90).
The reason why the *y* is chosen as an infix in the ending *-īna* suffixed to the imperfect of the 2nd person of the fem. sing. (88), (89). Its elision in the Energetic (126). The reasons why the *ā* is chosen as a suffix for the dual (92). The reasons why the *ā* of the agent marking the dual of the imperfect Energ. I and II is not elided (126). The cases when the *ū* is maintained or elided in the suffixed pronoun of the nominative of the 2nd person of the masc. pl., *-tumū,* of the perfect (65). The reasons why the *ū* is chosen to mark the masc. pl. in the imperfect of the indicative (92). Its elision in the Energetic (126).
– The separate pronouns of the accusative. Paradigm (84). The opinions of the Kufans and Basrans concerning their structures (84 b).
– The suffixed pronouns of the accusative. Paradigm (82). The combination of both the suffixed pronouns of the nominative and of the accusative of the same person in the mental verbs (83).
– The suffixed pronouns of the genitive. Paradigm (85). The change of the suffixed pronoun of the genitive of the 1st person of the sing., the *ī,* when attached to a noun following the vocative *yā,* into an *ā* (81).
The vowelling of the suffixed pronoun of the genitive of the 3rd person of the masc. sing., *hu* or *hi* (80). Some anomalies (80 b).
The emphasis of a preposition to which a pronoun of the genitive is suffixed to when coupled to another noun in the genitive with a preposition by the Basrans. The acceptance of such a coupling without emphasizing the preposition by the Kufans and others. An anomalous case (53 b).
Qalb "transposition".
Quadriliteral *rubāʿī.* The derived measures of the triliteral that are formed according to Form I of the quadriliteral *faʿlala,* to Form II of the quadriliteral *tafaʿlala,* to Form III of the quadriliteral *ʾifʿanlala* and to Form IV of the quadriliteral *ʾifʿalalla* (41). Triliteral roots which can be extended to become quadriliteral (177 b) through the repetition of one or two of their consonants (27), (177 b). The elision of the *ā* in the forms *fuʿālilun* and *faʿālilun* resulting in *fuʿalilun* and *faʿalilun* (56).
Quinqueliteral *ḫumāsī.* Triliteral roots which can be extended to become quinqueliteral through the repetition of one or two of their consonants (177 b).
Rafʿ "indicative".
Repetition. Some measures with the repetition of one or two consonants (27), (177 b).
Rubāʿī "quadriliteral".
Rubba. Its occurrence and its elision. The question according to the Kufans and Basrans on whether it is the conjunction that precedes *rubba* or the theoretical elided *rubba* that puts the noun in the genitive (121).
Ṣaḥīḥ "strong verb".

Ṣarf "morphology".
Saturation *išbāʿ* (60), (60 b).
Shift *naql.* See transfer.
Ṣifa "adjective".
Ṣifa mušabbaha "assimilated adjective".
Soundness of the weak consonant. Cases in which no change of the weak consonant is carried out (19), (224), (268), (269), (270), (272), (273), (274), (276), (277), (278), (279), (280), (281), (282), (289), (317), (350), (377).
Strength.
– The ḍamma is the strongest among the vowels (74), (132).
– The infixed weak consonant is considered as strong in relation to the elided radical (225).
– The passive voice reveals strength by referring to both the agent and the object (132).
– The pl. is stronger than the dual (92).
– The radical is considered as strong in relation to the augment (225).
– The separate pronoun of the 1st person of the pl., *naḥnu,* reveals strength as it comprehends two meanings, the one of the dual and the one of the pl. (74).
Strong verb *ṣaḥīḥ* (11...). The conjugations: *faʿala yafʿilu* (29), concerning a verb with 1st weak and 3rd guttural radical (254), *faʿala yafʿulu* (29), *faʿila yafʿalu,* the anomalies *fiʿila* and *fiʿla* (29), *faʿala yafʿalu* when the 2nd or 3rd radical is a guttural consonant (30), (174), some anomalies (30 b), *faʿula yafʿalu* (36), *faʿula yafʿulu* (34), *faʿila yafʿilu* (35) and *faʿila yafʿulu* (38). Anomalous forms of verbs (29), (30 b), (31), (32), (33), (35), (36), (37), (38). The reasons why *faʿila* becomes *yafʿalu* and *faʿala* becomes *yafʿilu* in the imperfect (29 b). *Faʿula yafʿulu* (34). The reason why *faʿula* has its 2nd radical vowelled by a ḍamma (34 b). *Faʿila yafʿulu* (37). *Tifʿalu* (the dialectal variant: the *taltala)* (32), (99), (103), *yifʿalu* (32), (100).
A presentation of the order of the derived forms of the triliteral in Arabic grammars (39). Presentation of the order of the derived forms of the triliteral verb with their numbering according to Western grammars, their paradigms in both the perfect and the imperfect, and their meanings (39 b). Assimilation carried out in verbs of Form IX and XI (40).
A presentation of the quadriliteral and its derived forms with their numbering and their meanings (41). Quadriliterals formed from the patterns of triliterals that are coordinated to other forms of quadriliterals by the addition of an augment or more to their roots *mulḥaq.*(41), definition, measures coordinated to the groundform of the quadriliteral *faʿlala,* measures coordinated to Form II of the quadriliteral *tafaʿlala,* to Form III of the quadriliteral *ʾifʿanlala* and to Form IV of the quadriliteral *ʾifʿalalla* (41).
Examples of verbs of four consonants being a combination of syllables in well-known expressions (41).
Subjunctive *naṣb.* The reason why the fatḥa has been chosen to mark it (92). Its being replaced by the indicative (51 b). Its occurrence after the suppressed subjunctival *an* (51 c). Its replacing the jussive (51 f).
Paradigm of a strong verb of Form I in the imperfect of the subjunctive, active (92), of doubled verbs of Form I whose imperfect's 2nd radicals' vowel is a ḍamma (171), (172), kasra (171 b) and fatḥa (171 c), of a doubled verb of Form I whose imperfect's 2nd radical's vowel is a ḍamma in the passive voice (186), of verbs with 1st, 2nd or 3rd radical hamza (214, b, c), of verbs with 1st radical *w* or *y* (245), (245 b), of verbs with 2nd radical *w* (259), or *y* (259 b), and of verbs with 3rd radical *y* (302) or *w* (302 b), (303 b).
Substitution *badal.*
1) Substitution of forms:
– the active participle for the *maṣdar* (23).
– the imperfect for the perfect (93 c).
– the indicative for the jussive (51), (239 b).
– the indicative for the subjunctive (51 b).
– the jussive for the indicative (51 e).
– the *maṣdar* for the adjective (24 f).
– the *maṣdar* for the imperative (24 e).
– the *maṣdar* for the passive participle (24 b).

– the passive participle for the *maṣdar* (24).
– the perfect for the imperfect (42), (44 b).
– the subjunctive for the jussive (51 f).
2) Substitution of consonants and vowels:
– the *ā* for the *alif maqṣūra* (180).
– the *ā* for the hamza (50 b), (217), (218), (220), (237), (327 b), (369).
– the *ā* for the *w* (36), (38), (50 b), (211), (265), (266), (270), (276), (278), (279), (284), (369).
– the *ā* for the *y* (33), (50 b), (54), (81, b), (265), (270), (271), (285), (303), (304), (369).
– the *alif maqṣūra* for the *y* (272), (308).
– the ʿ for the *ḥ* (328 c).
– the ʿ for the hamza (328 b).
– the ʿ for the *ġ* (328 c).
– the *b* for the *m* (367).
– the *d* for the *t* (207), (341), (342).
– the *ḏ* for the *t* (207).
– the *ḍ* for the *t* (207).
– the ḍamma for the suffixed pronoun of the nominative of the masc. pl., the *ū*, (45).
– the *g* for the *q* (340 c).
– the *ġ* for the ʿ (328 c).
– the *ǧ* for the *k* (340 c).
– the *ǧ* for the double *y* (339).
– the *ǧ* for the single *y* in pause (340) and in context (340 b).
– the *h* for the *ā* (344), (345), (347), (348 d), (373).
– the *h* for the hamza (98), (220), (235), (343).
– the *h* for the *tāʾ marbūṭa* (348), for the *tāʾ ṭawīla* (348 b) and for the *t* of the fem. pl. (348 c).
– the *h* for the *y* (89), (346), (347).
– the hamza for the *ā* (326), (327).
– the hamza for the alif of the feminine form (313).
– the hamza for the ʿ (328).
– the hamza for the *h* (114 b), (115 b), (235), (325).
– the hamza for the *w* (50 b), (235), (290), (291), (292), (316), (317), (318, b), (319), (321), (322), (323), (327 c), or written as a *w* with a hamza (218), (327 c).
– the hamza for the initial *w* vowelled by a ḍamma (321), by a kasra (322), by a fatḥa followed by an augmentative *w* (316), for the single *w* (323), for the middle *w* vowelled by a ḍamma (318) and for the *w* coupled with another *w* (318 b).
– the hamza for the *y* (228 b), (319), (320), (324), (379).
– the hamza for the initial *y* (324).
– the hamza for the *y* in the active participle of a verb with 2nd radical *y* (320).
– the *hamza ʿalā kursī l-yāʾ* for the hamza (217), (218), (241).
– the *l* for the *ḍ* (371).
– the *l* for the *n* (370).
– the *m* for the *b* (367).
– the *m* for the *l* (364).
– the *m* for the vowelless *n* (68), (365) and for the vowelled *n* (366).
– the *m* for the *w* (78), (363).
– the *madda* for both hamzas (227, b), (229), (233 b).
– the *n* for the vowelless ʿ (328 c).
– the *n* for the *l* (338).
– the *n* for the *w* (337), (353).
– the single *n* for the doubled *n* (125 g).
– the *n* of the indicative for the energetic *n* (239 b).
– the *s* for the *t* (202, (207), (329).
– the *s* for the *z* (372 b).
– the *ṣ* for the *s* (368), (372), (174).
– the *ṣ* for the *t* (207)

– the *š* for the *k* (82 b).
– the *š* for the *t* (207).
– the *t* for the *b* (336).
– the *t* for the *d* (194), (333).
– the *t* for the *s* (52), (194), (329), (333), (334).
– the *t* for the *ṣ* (335).
– the *t* for the *ṭ* (209).
– the *t* for the *w* (52), (96), (198), (247), (330), (331).
– the *t* for the *y* (187 b), (199), (200), (332).
– the *t* for the 3rd radical *w* (331).
– the *tāʾ marbūṭa* for the elided *w* (16).
– the *tāʾ ṭawīla* for the *tāʾ marbūṭa* (348 d).
– the *ṯ* for the *t* (207).
– the *ṭ* for the *d* (375 b).
– the *ṭ* for the *t* (174), (192 c), (194), (195), (196), (197), (207), (374), for the *t* being the suffixed pronoun of the nominative of the 1st and 2nd persons of the sing. (375).
– the *ṭ* for the *ẓ* (197).
– the *w* for the augmented *ā* (360).
– the *w* for the hamza (217), (218), (219), (226), (227 b), (228 c), (362).
– the *w* for the *y* (261), (271), (303), (361).
– the *w* with hamza for the hamza (217).
– The *waṣla* for the hamza (232).
– the *y* for: the *ʿ* (355), the *ā* (59), (230), (349), the *b* (357), the *ḍ* (170), (182), (352), the *d* (170), the *ǧ* (265), the hamza (66), (187 b), (200), (202), (217), (218), (219), (225), (226), (228), (315), (351), the *l* (170), the *m* (170), the *n* (170), (353), (354), the *r* (170), the *s* (358), the *ṣ* (170), the *t* (356), the *ṯ* (359) and the *w* (113), (257), (260), (262), (263), (266, b), (267), (275), (293), (294), (295, b), (310), (311), (350), (379), (380).
– the *z* for the *s* (372).
– the *z* for the *ṣ* (372), (373).
– the *z* for the *t* (207).
– the *ẓ* for the *t* (207).
– the *ẓ* for the *ṭ* (197).
Syntax *naḥw*. The aim and usefulness of grammar. Love of the Arabic language (3 b).
T. The *tāʾ marbūṭa* and *ṭawīla* (52).
Al-tāʾ li-l-taḫṣīṣ "the *t* of particularization" (52).
Al-tāʾ li-taʾkīd al-mubālaġa "the *t* meant to strenghten the idea of intensiveness" (52), (150), (274).
Augmented *t* (52).
Substituted *t:* the *t* for the *b* (336), the *t* for the *d* (194), (333), the *t* for the *s* (52), (194), (329), (333), (334), the *t* for the *ṣ* (335), the *t* for the *ṭ* (209), the *t* for the *w* (96), (198), (247), (330), (331), the *t* for the *y* (187 b), (199), (200), (332), the *t* for the 3rd radical *w* (331), the *tāʾ marbūṭa* for the elided *w* (16), the *tāʾ ṭawīla* for the *tāʾ marbūṭa* (348 d).
Al-taʿrīf "definite article".
Taṣrīf "conjugation", "morphology", "phonology".
Tawḥīd "oneness".
Taʿwīḍ "compensation".
Terms. Basrans and Kufans (46 b), (136), (174).
Ṯiqal "heaviness".
Title *Marāḥ al-arwāḥ* (5). Its importance (8).
Topic *mubtadaʾ* (12 b), (13), (44), (58).
Transfer, shift *naql* (14 b), (36), (74 b), (92), (181), (183), (203)-(205, b, c, d), (210)-(212), (221)-(226), (236), (241), (249), (275)-(279), (284)-(287), (292), (295), (296), (303). Transfer of:
– the vowel of the hamza to the consonant preceding it in one word (221)-(224), (241), and in two words (224).
– the vowel of a weak consonant to the consonant preceding it (36), (211), (212), (249), (275)-(279), (284)-(287), (295), (296), (303).

– the vowel of the 2nd radical to the 1st radical in the imperfect of the doubled verb (171).
– the vowel of the 2nd radical, which is the 1st consonant among the doubled consonants, to the 1st radical after the 2nd radical's elision in the perfect of the doubled verb (181), (210), in the imperative of the 2nd person of the fem. pl. and in the 3rd person of the fem. pl. of the imperfect (183).
– the vowel of the infixed *t* of Form VIII to the 1st radical (203, b), (204, b, c, d), (205, b, c, d).
– the vowel of the *n* of *naḥnu* to the *ḥ* preceding it (74 b).
Transitive *muta'addī* (22 c). The transitive is lighter than the intransitive (34 b).
Transposition *qalb* (14 b), (222), (237), (292), (293), (294).
Tripartite division: noun, verb and particle (10 b), (63). The reasons of their declension or undeclinability (43).
Unsoundness of the weak consonant *i'lāl* (15), (16), (19), the different sequences (260).
1) Change of:
– the *ā* into the hamza (290).
– the augmented *ā* into a *w* (360).
– the *ā* into the *y* (349).
– the *w* into the *ā* (16), (36), (38), (40), (243), (249), (266), (270), (276), (278), (279), (284), (289).
– the *w* into the hamza (290), (291), (292).
– the *w* into the *y* (16), (113), (257), (243), (260), (262), (263), (266 b), (267), (275), (292), (293), (294), (295 b), (303), (350), (379).
– the *y* into the *ā* (270), (285), (303).
– the *y* into the *alif maqṣūra* (180), (201), (272).
– the *y* into the hamza (319), (379).
– the *y* into the *w* (261), (271), (361).
2) Elision of:
– the *w* as the 1st radical in the perfect of a verb with 1st radical *w* (246).
– the *w* as the 1st radical in the imperfect of a verb with 1st radical *w* (16), (19), (244), (252), (254), and in the *maṣdar* (16), (247), (248).
– the unsound 2nd weak radical (36), (38), (249), (279), (284), (285), (286), (287), (288), (289), (291), (292), (295).
– the unsound 2nd weak radical or the infixed *ā* (249), (279).
– the 2nd weak radical or the infixed *w* in passive participles of verbs with 2nd weak radical (295).
– the 2nd weak radical changed into a hamza in active participles of verbs with 2nd weak radical (291), (292).
– the 3rd radical *w* in a verb with 3rd radical *w* (305).
– the 3rd weak radical in participles of verbs with 3rd weak radical (295), (309), and in the jussive (306).
– the 3rd radical *y* in participles of verbs with 3rd radical *y* (23), (295), (309).
– the 3rd radical *y* in verbs with 3rd radical *y* (33), (49), (51 e), (54), (180), (201), (239 c), (240), (275), (292), (303), (304), (307).
– the 3rd radical *y* after the kasra or fatḥa before the doubled *n* in the 2nd person of the masc. sing. of the Energetic I (239 c).
Relative noun or adjective *ism al-nisba* (156).
Underlying, underlyingly, base *aṣlī* (16), (19), (48), (49), (50 b), (54), (56), (58), (65), (77), (88), (96), (97), (98), (109), (114), (119), (121), (127), (149 b), (161), (169), (171)– (174), (177), (180), (181), (182), (184), (187 b, c), (189), (191), (192), (194), (195), (200), (202), (209), (211), (212), (220), (221), (224), (226), (228), (229), (230), (235 c), (243), (244), (248), (255), (257), (259, b), (262), (263), (265)-(267), (269), (270), (271), (275), (279), (284), (288)-(293), (295), (298), (299), (300), (302)-(305), (311), (316)-(319), (321), (329), (331), (332), (340 b), (344), (350), (361), (364), (368), (374), (378), (379), (380).
Verb *fi'l* (28), (29). Verbs being considered to be heavier than nouns (58). The debate concerning the verb which is considered as the origin of the derivation according to the Kufans, and the *maṣdar* which is considered as the origin of derivation according to the Basrans (12)-(21): The verb's dependency on its agent in the sentence contra the independence of the *maṣdar* as a noun (12 b), (13), (58). The Basrans' concept of the verb's plurality contra the *maṣdar's* oneness (12). Some comments about some terms referring to the fields of philosophy and theology (13 b). The Kufans' argument

pertaining to the field of morphology that stresses upon the idea of the dependence of the *maṣdar* on the verb, regarding the unsoundness or the soundness of the weak consonant in its structure (15), (16). The Basrans' argumentation against this opinion (19). The Kufans' argument referring to the field of syntax: the verb is the regent and governs the *maṣdar* in the accusative and the *maṣdar* is emphasized by the verb (17). The Basrans' and the Kufans' opinions concerning the undeclinability of the verbs (123), the declension of the imperfect (122) and the undeclinability or the declension of the imperative (48), (119), (120), (123), (184).
Anomalous elision of the kasra of the 2nd radical in verbs of Form I (109). Anomalous elision of the fatḥa in a verb of Form I and in a verb of Form VII (45). The 2nd radical made vowelless in the perfect together with the 1st radical given a kasra (29). The anomalies *fiʿila* and *fiʿla* (29).

Verbal noun *maṣdar*. Its definitions (12, b). Its derivatives (10). The debate concerning the *maṣdar* being the origin of derivation according to the Basrans and the verb being the origin of the derivation according to the Kufans. See for it Verb. The Kufans' argument that the *maṣdar* is formed according to the passive participle contra the Basrans argument that it is formed according to the noun of place (18). The Basrans' argumentation that the *maṣdar* is regarded as a noun of place (21).
The *maṣdar* being substituted by the active participle (23). The *maṣdar* formed according to the measure of *fāʿila* (23 b). The *maṣdar* being substituted by the passive participle (24). The passive participle being substituted by the *maṣdar* (24 b). The *maṣdar* as a substitute for the imperative (24 e). The *maṣdar* as a substitute for the adjective (24 f).
The *maṣdar's* patterns of the groundform of the triliteral (22). Other forms including other classes than the strong verb (22 b). The patterns' indications (22 c). The *maṣdar* of the derived forms of the triliteral occurring on the pattern of the passive participle (24 c). The form of the passive participle of what exceeds three consonants occurring as the form of the *maṣdar* (24 d). Some forms that express intensification: *tafʿālun* and *fiʿʿīlay* (25). The analogy of the *maṣdars'* measures of the derived forms of the triliteral and quadriliteral with their verbs' measures (26). Well-known derived forms of the *maṣdar* of the strong triliteral verb with their numbering. Well-known forms of the *maṣdar* of the groundform and derived forms of the quadriliteral with their numbering (26 c). Forms of the *maṣdar* of the derived forms of the triliteral and quadriliteral which are not analogous with their verbs: *fiʿʿālun, fiʿālun* and *fiʿālun* (27). Examples from the paradigms of doubled verbs (172), (172 b), of verbs with 1st, 2nd or 3rd radical hamza (214, b, c), of verbs with weak 1st radical in the groundfrom and derived forms (245), (245 b), of verbs with 2nd radical *w* (264), of verbs with 3rd radical *w* (259), or *y* (259 b) and of verbs with 3rd weak radical *y* (302) or *w* (302 b), (303 b).

Verbs with weak 1st radical *miṯāl* (242...). The different conjugations. The conjugation *faʿala yafʿulu* (243). Paradigms of verbs with 1st radical *w* or *y* (245), (245 b). Paradigm of a verb with 1st radical *w* in the imperative (256). The elision of the *w* in the imperfect of a verb with 1st radical *w* (16), (244), (252) and in the *maṣdar* (16), (247), (248). Its elision in the imperative (256). Its maintainance in different forms (16), (244), (246), (255). The reason of its maintainance or its elision in the imperfect according to the Kufans and to the Basrans (244). Noun of place of the verb with 1st radical *w* (160).

Verbs with 2nd weak radical *aǧwaf* (258...). Paradigms of verbs with 2nd radical *w* (259), or *y* (259 b). Paradigm of a verb with 2nd radical *w* in the imperative (287) and in the passive voice (297). Paradigm of the active participle with 2nd weak radical (290). Some active participles with the anomalous elision of the 2nd weak radical changed into a hamza (291), some with the transposition of the consonants (292), and some with the change of the hamza into a weak consonant (226). Form I *faʿila* that has the meaning of *ifʿalla* and Form VIII *iftaʿala* that has the meaning of Form VI *tafāʿala* in verbs with 2nd radical *w* (270). The forms *mafuʿlun* and *mafūlun* of the passive participle of verbs with 2nd radical *w* or *y* (295). The form *mafīlun* used instead of *mafūlun* and *mafyūlun* (295 b). Passive participle and noun of place with 2nd radical *y* (296).

Verbs with 3rd weak radical *nāqis* (301...). Paradigms of a verb with 3rd radical *y* (302) or *w* (302 b), (303 b). The elision of the 3rd radical (33), (49), (54), (239 c), (275), (292), (303). Cases of verbs occurring with the elision of the 3rd radical *y*, and the kasra or sukūn given to the last consonant in the pause (307). A case in which the 3rd radical is retained in pause (307 b). Cases in which the jussive is not taken into consideration (51), (51 f). The vowelling of the 3rd radical *y* when it precedes the energetic *n* in the 2nd person of the fem. sing. (239). Its elision by some in the 2nd person of the masc. sing. (239 c). Active participle of a verb with 3rd radical *y* (309), passive participle (310), noun of place (162). An anomalous case concerning a verb of Form IX (40).

Verbs with weak 1st and 3rd radical and verbs with 2nd weak and 3rd radical *lafīf* (376...). Paradigm of a verb with 1st radical *w* and 3rd weak radical (376) and of a verb with 2nd radical *y* and 3rd weak radical (376 b). Discussions concerning an example (180). The vowelling of the suffixed pronoun of the 2nd person of the masc. pl. and the 2nd person of the fem. sing. of the imperative of the Energetic 1 before the doubled nūns (378).

Vocative *nidā*ʾ. When the vocative *yā* precedes a noun to which the suffix pronoun of the genitive of the 1st person of the sing., the *ī*, is attached to, different dialectal variants are allowable. Change of the suffixed *ī* into an *ā* when preceded by a kasra, and of the underlying *ya* into an *ā* when preceded by a kasra (81).

Compensation of the doubled *m* of *allāhumma* for the elided vocative particle (235 b).

Waqf "pause".

Waṣl "juncture".

Weak consonant(s) *ḥurūf al-ʿilla* (15), (16), (19), (36), (40), (45), (70), (92), (111), (112), (180), (188 b), (202), (216)-(219), (224), (225), (229), (241), (260), (262), (265), (266 b), (267), (269), (270), (274)-(279), (290), (292), (303), (340 b), (347), (379).

Weakness.

– The fatḥa is considered as the weakest among the three vowels (45).

– The *h* is considered as too weak to hinder the deflection (347).

– The infixed consonant is considered as weak in relation to the radical (225).

– The elided radical is considered as weak in relation to the infixed consonant (225).

– The perfect is considered as weak as its action is completed and done with (45).

– The sukūn between two vowelled consonants is considered as too weak to hinder the influence of the vowel preceding it on the vowel following it (112), (113), (290).

Printed in the United States
By Bookmasters